American Journal of International Law

VOLUME 82
1988

Published by

American Society of International Law

AMERICAN JOURNAL OF INTERNATIONAL LAW

VOLUME 82 CONTENTS 1988

[No. 1, January 1988, pp. 1–238; No. 2, April 1988, pp. 239–441; No. 3, July 1988, pp. 443–703; No. 4, October 1988, pp. 705–952.]

PAGE

The 1871 London Declaration, Rebus sic Stantibus and a Primitivist View of the Law of Nations *David J. Bederman* 1
Threats of Force *Romana Sadurska* 239
Terrorism on the High Seas: The Achille Lauro, Piracy and the IMO Convention on Maritime Safety *Malvina Halberstam* 269
Jan Mayen in Perspective *Elliot L. Richardson* 443
Which Law Applies to the Afghan Conflict? *W. Michael Reisman & James Silk* 459
Advancing the Freedom of Religion or Belief Through the UN Declaration on the Elimination of Religious Intolerance and Discrimination *Donna J. Sullivan* 487
International Discovery after Aerospatiale: The Quest for an Analytical Framework *David J. Gerber* 521
Legitimacy in the International System *Thomas M. Franck* 705
Self-Executing Treaties *Jordan J. Paust* 760

Agora

McDougal-Lasswell Redux
The McDougal-Lasswell Proposal to Build a World Public Order *Gray L. Dorsey* 41
The Dorsey Comment: A Modest Retrogression *Myres S. McDougal* 51

Is the ASIL Policy on Divestment in Violation of International Law?
The Action Violates International Law and Policy *George N. Barrie* 311
The Action Does Not Violate International Law *Paul C. Szasz* 314

The U.S. Decision Not to Ratify Protocol I to the Geneva Conventions on the Protection of War Victims (Cont'd)
The Rationale for the United States Decision *Abraham D. Sofaer* 784

Editorial Comments

Understanding the Act of State Doctrine's Effect *Frederic L. Kirgis, Jr.* 58
The Alien Tort Statute and the Founding of the Constitution *Anthony D'Amato* 62

Taking Treaties Seriously — *Thomas M. Franck* 67
Improving the Image of the United States in International Human Rights — *Louis B. Sohn* 319

Notes and Comments

Lump Sum Aggreements: Their Continuing Contribution to the Law of International Claims — *Richard B. Lillich & Burns H. Weston* 69
The Meaning of "People" in the African Charter on Human and Peoples' Rights — *Richard N. Kiwanuka* 80
Professor William W. Bishop, Jr. (1906–1987):
A Tribute — *Eric Stein* 321
Personal Recollections — *Elizabeth S. Bishop* 323
Alien Tort Claims, Sovereign Immunity and International Law in U.S. Courts — *Frederic L. Kirgis, Jr.* 323
Further Thoughts on the Chambers Procedure of the International Court of Justice — *Shigeru Oda* 556
Waldemar A. Solf (1913–1987) — *Harry H. Almond, Jr.* 562
The Francis Deák Prize 565
Perestroika and International Law — *John Quigley* 788

Correspondence 102, 331, 564, 797
Contemporary Practice of the United States Relating to International Law — *Marian Nash Leich* 103, 336, 566, 803
Judicial Decisions — *Monroe Leigh* 126, 351, 580
International Decisions — *Peter D. Trooboff* 816

Current Developments

The Thirty-ninth Session of the International Law Commission — *Stephen C. McCaffrey* 144
The ABM Treaty Interpretation Resolution 151
Statement by Expert Panel: Deep Seabed Mining and the 1982 Convention on the Law of the Sea 363
Triennial Elections of Five Members of the International Court of Justice 369
Inter-American Commission on Human Rights Finds United States in Violation — *Donald T. Fox* 601
Second Session of the UN Committee on Economic, Social and Cultural Rights — *Philip Alston & Bruno Simma* 603

Book Reviews and Notes — *Edited by Detlev Vagts* 166, 370, 616, 841
Books Received 233, 436, 696, 919
International Legal Materials. Contents, Vol. XXVI, Nos. 5–6 (1987); Vol. XXVII, Nos. 1–4 (1988) 237, 439, 702, 924
Table of Cases 926
Index 928

LIFE MEMBERS OF THE AMERICAN SOCIETY OF INTERNATIONAL LAW 1987–1988

Gerald Aksen
Stanley Anderson
Masahiko Asada
Calvin A. Behle
Richard S. S. Bright
John C. Brooks
Ian Brownlie
John Carey
Chin-Yung Chao
Stephen S. F. Chen
Max Chopnick
J. G. Clarke
H. Alberta Colclaser
Carter K. Combe
Rebecca J. Cook
Jorge Antonio De Marzi
Dermott J. Devine
John E. Donnelly
Peter D. Ehrenhaft
Robert Eikel
Richard J. Erickson
Eleanor H. Finch
Richard I. Fine
Roger D. Fisher
Stefan Forch
Carl Mason Franklin
Gaudencio Garcia
Moti Lal Govila
Robert T. Greig
Joseph P. Griffin
Richard Kennedy Guelff
Judith R. Hall
Robert D. Hayton
Dan F. Henderson
Robert E. Herzstein
Gary N. Horlick
Christopher C. Joyner
William S. Kenney
Yoshito Kita
Elizabeth Lay
Monroe Leigh
Frankie Fook-lu Leung
Cynthia C. Lichtenstein
Mrs. Brunson MacChesney
Myres Smith McDougal
Samuel Pyeatt Menefee
John M. Metzger
Clifford L. Michel
James A. R. Nafziger
Andre W. G. Newburg
J. D. Nyhart
Hisashi Owada
Mauricio Perez-Badell
Hernán Pérez Loose
Ellis L. Phillips
Jane M. Picker
Robert J. Radway
Charles S. Rhyne
Elliot L. Richardson
Alfred P. Rubin
Mark Sandstrom
Tetsuo Sato
Oscar Schachter
Cabot Sedgwick
Yukio Shimada
William I. Shore
Anne Patricia Simons
Dwight J. Simpson
Owen Meredith Smaw
Earl A. Snyder
Jane Sommerich
John H. Spencer
Henry J. Steiner
Edward P. Torrey
Tullio Treves
J. W. van der Zanden
L. W. Wadsworth
Edith Brown Weiss
Elmer E. Welty
Ulrich Woelker
C. U. Zachrisson
Peaches Zaphiriou

SUPPORTING AND CONTRIBUTING MEMBERS OF THE AMERICAN SOCIETY OF INTERNATIONAL LAW 1987–1988

SUPPORTING

Mitchell Brock
Charles N. Brower
Alexander D. Calhoun
William Gilbert Carter
Anthony A. D'Amato
Robert MacCrate
William B. Matteson
Covey T. Oliver
George M. Pavia
Walter S. Surrey
Peter W. Thornton
Peter D. Trooboff
Jack G. Wasserman
Basil S. Yanakakis

CONTRIBUTING

Richard L. Abbott
Richard B. M. Abrams
Richard C. Allison
Manuel R. Angulo
Steven Wright Baker
J. Truman Bidwell
Roman A. Bninski
John Arthur Boyd
George W. Brandt
Aron Broches
David Carliner
C. J. Chen
Donald E. Claudy
Philip F. Cohen
John P. Corrigan
Samuel S. Cross
Michael Danaher
John L. A. De Passalaqua
George C. Denney
James M. Denny
Edward A. Dragon
Malcolm T. Dungan
Richard A. Eastman
Aly H. Elghatit
F. Javier Fabregat
Philip A. Faix, Jr.
Stanley F. Farrar
Benjamin B. Ferencz
John Basil Gantt
David G. Gill
Michael A. Gleim
Joseph Gold
L. F. E. Goldie
Thomas R. Graham
Ernest A. Gross
James V. Hackney
Herbert J. Hansell
Joel B. Harris
Thomas E. Haven
H. Healy
Cecil Hunt
Oliver T. Johnson
Joseph S. Kaplan
Charles J. Keever
Lee A. Kimball
Paul L. Laskin
James Leitner
Robert T. Lemon, II
Edwin Deane Leonard
Jacques L. Leroy
David M. Levitan
George N. Lindsay
Carlos A. Lopez-Guevara
G. Lorinczi
Ralph M. McDowell
A. F. Maulsby
Gerald D. Morgan
Frank E. Nattier
Franz M. Oppenheimer
Guillermo F. Peroni
Jose Martins Pinheiro Neto
Willis L. M. Reese
A. R. Richstein
Bruce L. Rockwood
James F. Sams
J. P. Schwebel
Charles M. Spofford
Samuel A. Stern
Isaac N. P. Stokes
Robert M. Thomas, Jr.
Robert B. von Mehren
Paul C. Warnke
John Stowell Williams
F. L. Wiswall
Richard Young

American Journal of International Law

January 1988
Vol. 82 No. 1

Published by
American Society of International Law

PATRONS OF THE SOCIETY

ARTHUR H. DEAN (deceased)
HERMAN PHLEGER (deceased)
GENEVIEVE E. TILLAR (deceased)
W. ROBERT MORGAN
BRUNSON MACCHESNEY (deceased)
ALONA E. EVANS (deceased)
JOHN N. HAZARD
JOHN R. STEVENSON
ARTHUR R. ALBRECHT
ALWYN V. FREEMAN (deceased)
EDWARD DUMBAULD
KEITH HIGHET
STEPHEN M. SCHWEBEL
WILLIAM D. ROGERS
SEYMOUR J. RUBIN
JOHN LAWRENCE HARGROVE
FRANK A. BAUMAN
RICHARD W. EDWARDS, JR.
ALMESHAL HUSSAM

In Memoriam

DR. JAMES BROWN SCOTT
HENRY C. MORRIS
ARTHUR K. KUHN
ALEXANDER FREEMAN
STANLEY P. SMITH

PATRONAGE, GIFTS AND BEQUESTS

Upon donation to the Society of $5,000 or more by gift or bequest, any member of the Society or individual eligible for membership may be elected a Patron of the Society. Upon donation of at least $5,000 in the name of a deceased person, such person may be elected a Patron posthumously.

Gifts and bequests may be made in the name of the American Society of International Law, Washington, D.C. Such contributions are deductible from federal returns for income, estate and gift tax purposes. The Society is incorporated by Act of Congress approved September 20, 1950 (64 Stat. 869).

MANLEY O. HUDSON MEDAL

The American Society of International Law bestows from time to time without regard to nationality a gold medal to commemorate the life work of Manley O. Hudson. Such awards are made for preeminent scholarship and achievement in international law and in the promotion of the establishment and maintenance of international relations on the basis of law and justice. Medals have been awarded to Manley O. Hudson (1956), Lord McNair (1959), Philip C. Jessup (1964), Charles De Visscher (1966), Paul Guggenheim (1970), Myres S. McDougal (1976), Eduardo Jiménez de Aréchaga (1978), Richard Reeve Baxter (1981), Oscar Schachter (1981), Hardy Cross Dillard (1982), Suzanne Bastid (1984), Marjorie M. Whiteman (1985) and Leo Gross (1986).

The AMERICAN JOURNAL OF INTERNATIONAL LAW (ISSN 0002-9300) is published quarterly, in January, April, July and October, and is supplied to all members of the American Society of International Law. Annual subscription rate to nonmembers is $50.00, plus $4.00 postage outside U.S.A.

EDITORIAL OFFICE:
NEW YORK UNIVERSITY SCHOOL OF LAW
40 WASHINGTON SQUARE SOUTH
NEW YORK, N.Y. 10012

BUSINESS OFFICE:
2223 MASSACHUSETTS AVENUE, N.W.
WASHINGTON, D.C. 20008-2864

Second-class postage paid at Washington, D.C. and at additional mailing office. POSTMASTER: If undeliverable, send notice on Form 3579 to the American Journal of International Law, 2223 Massachusetts Ave., N.W., Washington, D.C. 20008-2864.

Printed by Lancaster Press, Lancaster, Pa. 17603

AMERICAN JOURNAL OF INTERNATIONAL LAW

VOL. 82 | January 1988 | NO. 1

CONTENTS

PAGE

The 1871 London Declaration, Rebus sic Stantibus and a Primitivist View of the Law of Nations *David J. Bederman* 1

Agora: McDougal-Lasswell Redux
The McDougal-Lasswell Proposal to Build a World Public Order *Gray L. Dorsey* 41
The Dorsey Comment: A Modest Retrogression *Myres S. McDougal* 51

Editorial Comments
Understanding the Act of State Doctrine's Effect *Frederic L. Kirgis, Jr.* 58
The Alien Tort Statute and the Founding of the Constitution *Anthony D'Amato* 62
Taking Treaties Seriously *Thomas M. Franck* 67

Notes and Comments
Lump Sum Agreements: Their Continuing Contribution to the Law of International Claims *Richard B. Lillich & Burns H. Weston* 69
The Meaning of "People" in the African Charter on Human and Peoples' Rights *Richard N. Kiwanuka* 80
Correspondence 102

Contemporary Practice of the United States Relating to International Law *Marian Nash Leich* 103

Judicial Decisions *Monroe Leigh* 126

Current Developments
The Thirty-ninth Session of the International Law Commission *Stephen C. McCaffrey* 144
The ABM Treaty Interpretation Resolution 151

Book Reviews and Notes *Edited by Detlev Vagts*
Falk, Richard. *Reviving the World Court* (Leo Gross) 166
Bernhardt, Rudolf (ed.). *Encyclopedia of Public International Law. Instalment 8* (Domingo E. Acevedo) 175
Peterson, M. J. *The General Assembly in World Politics* (Richard N. Swift) 178
International Law and the Grotian Heritage: A Commemorative Colloquium (Milner S. Ball) 183
Merrills, J. G. *International Dispute Settlement* (Richard B. Bilder) 184
Fritzemeyer, Wolfgang. *Die Intervention vor dem Internationalen Gerichtshof* (Julia B. Kokott) 186

James, Alan. *Sovereign Statehood: The Basis of International Society* (Harold K. Jacobson) 188
Breitenmoser, Stephan. *Der Schutz der Privatsphäre gemäß Art. 8 EMRK* (Jochen A. Frowein) 189
Borgese, Elisabeth Mann. *The Future of the Oceans: A Report to the Club of Rome* (David A. Colson) 191
Pontecorvo, Giulio (ed.). *The New Order of the Oceans: The Advent of a Managed Environment* (David A. Colson) 191
Smith, Robert W. *Exclusive Economic Zone Claims: An Analysis and Primary Documents* (Bernard H. Oxman) 193
Richardson, Jacques G. (ed.). *Managing the Ocean: Resources, Research, Law* (Gordon B. Baldwin) 196
Flinterman, Cees, Barbara Kwiatkowska and Johan G. Lammers (eds.). *Transboundary Air Pollution: International Legal Aspects of the Co-operation of States* (Edith Brown Weiss) 197
Schmandt, Jurgen, and Hilliard Roderick (eds.). *Acid Rain and Friendly Neighbors: The Policy Dispute between Canada and the United States* (Tracy Dobson) 200
Damaška, Mirjan R. *The Faces of Justice and State Authority* (Mathias Reimann) 203
Maxeiner, James. *Policy and Methods in German and American Antitrust Law* (Barry E. Hawk) 208
Baptista, Luiz O., and Pascal Durand-Barthez. *Les Associations d'Entreprises (Joint Ventures) dans le commerce international* (Wallace R. Baker) 214
Wulff, Otto. *Entwicklungshilfe zwischen Völkerrechtsordnung und Weltwirtschaftssystem* (Dietrich Kappeler) 220
Riddle, Dorothy I. *Service-Led Growth: The Role of the Service Sector in World Development* (David B. Yoffie) 224
Bourne, C. B. (ed.). *The Canadian Yearbook of International Law. Volume XXIII, 1985* (Forest L. Grieves) 225
Soviet Year-Book of International Law, 1985 (John N. Hazard) 227
Meissner, Boris. *Aussenpolitik und Völkerrecht der Sowjetunion* (William E. Butler) 229
Briefer Notices: Naff and Matson (eds.), 230; Fitzmaurice, 231; Francescakis, 231.
Collected Essays: *German Yearbook of International Law. Vol. 28, 1985, 231; Israel Yearbook on Human Rights. Vol. 16, 1986, 232; The Italian Yearbook of International Law. Vol. VI, 1985, 232; Netherlands Yearbook of International Law. Vol. XVII, 1986, 232; The Palestine Yearbook of International Law. Vol. II, 1985, 232; South African Yearbook of International Law. Vol. 11, 1985–1986, 232.*
Books Received 233
International Legal Materials. Contents, Vol. XXVI, No. 5 (September 1987) and No. 6 (November 1987) 237

The American Journal of International Law

The views expressed in the articles, editorial comments, book reviews and notes, and other contributions which appear in AJIL are those of the individual authors and are not to be taken as representing the views of the Board of Editors or the American Society of International Law.

Manuscripts in triplicate may be sent to the Editor in Chief of AJIL, Professor Thomas M. Franck, New York University School of Law, New York, N.Y. 10012. All footnotes should be typed double space at the end of the manuscript. Please do not make multiple submissions to other journals. Persons making submissions are invited to indicate whether their manuscript is available on an IBM-PC diskette. AJIL uses WordPerfect 4.2. Subscriptions, orders for back numbers, correspondence with reference to AJIL and books for review should be sent to the AMERICAN JOURNAL OF INTERNATIONAL LAW (ISSN 0002-9300), 2223 Massachusetts Avenue, N.W., Washington, D.C. 20008-2864.

The American Society of International Law

The American Society of International Law was organized in 1906 "to foster the study of international law and to promote the establishment and maintenance of international relations on the basis of law and justice."

Society membership is open to all persons of whatever nationality and profession who are interested in its objectives. Dues are: regular, $70; special category, $30 for persons *not* resident in a member country of the Organisation for Economic Co-operation and Development; intermediate, $30; student, $20. Membership application form is printed at the back of each issue of AJIL.

THE 1871 LONDON DECLARATION, REBUS SIC STANTIBUS AND A PRIMITIVIST VIEW OF THE LAW OF NATIONS

*By David J. Bederman**

International law is the most rarefied of social sciences. Even so, it has scarcely any sense of its intellectual history. International law is finely articulated, oblique in its analysis, and respectful of its position as an arbiter of national competition and conflict. But aside from the casual citation to an ancient arbitration or the consultation of a famous publicist for an essential principle, little credence has been given to its historical development as either a collection of doctrines or a learned study. This article offers both an intellectual history of an international law doctrine and a *tour d'horizon* of the nature of discourse in our discipline.

These two exercises are intimately connected. It makes little sense to discuss international law theory without reference to a particular set of doctrines, rules that arguably govern the behavior of states. Likewise, international law doctrines are empty unless informed by some conception of how they evolved, what they mean and the ideas of those scholars that have thought about them before us. The methodology used in this article is therefore unabashedly historical.

That is why the concept "law of nations" pervades these pages. We need to recognize that international law is inherently a modern invention. The very term was the creation of that most Enlightened of men, Jeremy Bentham,[1] and did not really gain currency until this century. In the course of its development, international law has managed to lay its own intellectual snares, dig formidable doctrinal pitfalls and rig theoretical trapdoors. It is wonderfully complex. It seems, by comparison, that the law of nations is easily reducible to a multivolume treatise, now gathering dust in our law libraries.

As used in this article, the term "primitivist" captures one response to this antihistorical attitude toward international law. Primitivists are our discipline's metaphysicians. They view international law's first principle, sovereignty, through a doctrinal prism that combines rules of state behavior

* M.Sc., University of London, 1984; J.D., University of Virginia, 1987. Research for this article was undertaken at the Hague Academy of International Law, with the generous financial assistance of the American Bar Association Section of International Law and Practice (Baxter Scholarship), as well as that of the Center for Law and National Security, University of Virginia School of Law.

[1] *See* J. BENTHAM, AN INTRODUCTION TO THE PRINCIPLES AND MORALS OF LEGISLATION 296 (Burns & Hart eds. 1970) (2d ed. 1823). For an excellent review of Bentham's contributions, see Janis, *Jeremy Bentham and the Fashioning of "International Law,"* 78 AJIL 405 (1984).

derived from both natural and positive sources. They see law and morality as equally binding on states. Quite simply, a primitivist considers the nation-state as the enduring and essential element of global order, as the only proven instrument for managing violence and relations among the largest human communities.

The "primitive" in "primitivism" is not, therefore, intended as a pejorative description of the "law of nations." Quite the contrary: primitivism describes the sense of honesty and forthrightness, confidence and respect for order inherent in the former law of nations. The primitivist knows that the process of rule making between nations is a contest, a struggle for law. Blood need not be spilled. In fact, states can truly coexist and cooperate with each other, provided that the fundamental premise of sovereignty is not betrayed. The primitivist world vision is therefore not Hobbesian, even though competition is required when norms are developed and enforced between entities that are supreme within their own sphere, but also seek to conduct themselves on an equal basis with other supreme states.

The primitivist view of the law of nations is illustrated in this article in relation to an enduring problem in the history and theory of our discipline: the tension between the doctrines of *pacta sunt servanda* and *rebus sic stantibus.* The vehicle for surveying this complex problem, so reflective of the other traps international law has created for itself, is a combination of diplomatic and intellectual history. The diplomatic history principally narrated here is of the London Conference of 1871. A pivotal episode in the 19th century's ongoing melodrama of the Eastern Question, the conference produced two truly memorable pronouncements.

The first was a comment by Baron Brunnow, Russia's representative at the negotiations. "In our time," he said, "treaties rarely live to a great age."[2] As shall be seen, the remark was laden with heavy, and perhaps unintended, irony. But Brunnow was also commenting on the passing of a diplomatic order, one that emphasized stability and balance, certainty and trust; in short, all that was associated with the principle of pacta sunt servanda. The duty to observe treaties in good faith stood at the center of international law's doctrinal universe. The events leading up to the London Conference revealed, however, a contrary principle: that treaties cease to bind nations when there has been a fundamental change in circumstances. This is the doctrine of rebus sic stantibus.

Pacta sunt servanda and rebus sic stantibus express different visions of international law. One is harmonious, predictable and stable; the other is dynamic, dangerous and uncertain. Why should we expect treaties to be performed in good faith? What compels states, endowed with overweening sovereignty, to fulfill their obligations? What fundamental national interests must necessarily take precedence over international responsibilities? How can the notion that fundamental changes in circumstances can terminate treaties be reconciled with the promise of good faith made by countries when signing? Can international law countenance this apparent contradic-

[2] Letter from Baron Brunnow, *reprinted in* 72 GR. BRIT. PARL. PAPERS 13 (1871–72) [hereinafter 72 PARL. PAPERS].

tion between rebus sic stantibus and pacta sunt servanda? One can legitimately ask which rhetoric manages to strengthen the international legal order.

This question was asked at the London Conference. The answer was a brief declaration, the second remarkable product of the negotiations. The protocol read in its entirety: "[I]t is an essential principle of the Law of Nations that no Power can liberate itself from the engagements of a Treaty, nor modify the stipulations thereof, unless with the consent of the Contracting Parties by means of an amicable arrangement."[3] This, then, is the text. All else is context, whether one is using the literary critic's tools of *oeuvre* and univocality or the international lawyer's methods of *travaux préparatoires* and custom.

The elaborate and widely divergent interpretations of the London Declaration prompted a historian to say that "[o]ne would despair if one attached too great importance to the disparate constructions that international doctrine has given . . . to the developments which occurred in 1870–1871."[4] This article surveys this scholarship in depth and concludes that the meaning of the London Declaration has changed, just as the underlying doctrine of rebus sic stantibus has, itself, moved in and out of fashion. For the remainder of the 19th century, publicists tried to moderate and soften the brazen use of the doctrine as an instrument of high state policy. Peaceful change, the watchword of interwar international jurisprudence, dictated the peculiar gloss given to rebus sic stantibus during that time, a view largely accepted by postwar modern scholars. Today we are left with a doctrine often explained (almost apologetically) as an oddity, a mutt in international law's kennel of theories.

The traditional critique of rebus sic stantibus is made by those who see pacta sunt servanda as the discipline's first principle. Advocates of the new critical jurisprudence have opened an altogether novel avenue of attack: rebus sic stantibus is not international law at all. It is just poorly disguised power politics. The critics make a strong contention that no interpretation of the London Declaration, or of the rebus sic stantibus doctrine itself, can successfully resolve the essential paradox of sovereignty in international law. Nations, they conclude, cannot be both supreme and equal. Any doctrine or declaration, therefore, that seemingly permits both, by allowing states to agree that there can be no unilateral modification of treaty obligations, in reality only indicates the internal contradictions of international law.

This critical line of argument accords with Jan Verzijl's warning about the evolution of discourse in this area:

> A new evaluation of [rebus sic stantibus's] intrinsic merits as a legal principle and of its value as a rule of positive law would seem, therefore, not only, not to be a waste of time, but almost to be a necessary duty for anyone conscious of his obligation to contribute to the mainte-

[3] The London Declaration, Jan. 17, 1871, 18 Martens Nouveau Recueil 278 (1873), *reprinted in* 3 T. Hertslet, Map of Europe by Treaty 1901 (1890). The declaration was signed by Great Britain, Austria, France, Italy, Russia, Turkey and North Germany (later the German Confederation).

[4] 6 J. Verzijl, International Law in Historical Perspective 358 (1973).

nance of the essential bases of that law and of his responsibility not to allow their erosion by inadmissible and destructive theories.[5]

The critical jurists have correctly identified the essential contradiction in the doctrine, but we have known it all along. In recognizing this paradox, international legal scholars need not despair. We can more than countenance the contradiction; we can embrace it. A primitivist approach provides one satisfactory response to the problems of legal obligation and sovereignty. It also has the virtue of avoiding the fictions and rationalizations often used by other traditional schools in their attempt to discard rebus sic stantibus, while salvaging the remainder of international law theory. Primitivist argument can repel the critical attack on the traditional rhetoric of the functionalists and realists. All the primitivist demands for this saving act is recognition of the historical place of the nation-state system at the center of a constructive struggle for law.

I. THE STRAITS QUESTION AND THE TYRANNY OF TREATIES

The 19th century was a time of prodigious diplomatic activity in Europe, all of it predicated on the rule of law and the development of international legal precepts. During this period, respect for treaties produced a diplomatic environment that was remarkably stable and consistent, even while the political machinations of the powers involved were often volatile.

What has become the public international legal regime of today was first developed, practiced and exercised in the 19th century. The major diplomatic questions of the day often revolved around the interpretation of treaties and agreements, and these instruments were regarded as the fundamental basis of interstate relations. The interests of states often changed during this time, depending on the correlation of forces in the European balance of power.[6] Nevertheless, the rule of law, as nascent and minimal as it was, was scrupulously observed. The dependence on treaties in the regulation of states' relations seemed to satisfy all the parties involved. It injected a sense of rationality and regularity into European diplomacy after the disruptions of the French Revolution and the Napoleonic period.[7] Implicit in the negotiation and application of treaties was the idea of contracts between equals; hence, state sovereignty and independence were constantly and forcefully asserted and maintained. Finally, this order inherently promoted a balance of power system in Europe, which required a sense of collegiality among all of the great powers for its maintenance.

[5] *Id.* at 344.

[6] For an excellent theoretical description and general history of the dynamics of the "Concert of Europe," see E. GULICK, EUROPE'S CLASSICAL BALANCE OF POWER (1955).

[7] The best history of the concluding phases of the Napoleonic period and the resultant creation of the Congress system is H. NICOLSON, THE CONGRESS OF VIENNA (1946). For another view, see H. KISSINGER, A WORLD RESTORED (1977 ed.) *See also* Protocol of Aix-la-Chapelle, Nov. 15, 1818, Art. 1, 69 Parry's TS 365, 4 Martens Nouveau Recueil 554 (in which Austria, France, Britain, Prussia and Russia pledged "never to depart . . . from the principles of intimate union which has hitherto presided over all of their common relations and interests").

This diplomatic order, established in 1815, showed severe signs of strain by 1870. The relatively flexible maintenance of the balance of power began to break down in the wake of the Crimean War and later events, which resulted in the entrenchment of animosities and coalitions between states on the European landscape. State security and sovereignty were not to be taken for granted. Nations began to assume "high" policies that were not subject to negotiation, compromise or regulation by treaty. International relations ceased to be fluid, and in the process ironically became less predictable. The challenge to the sanctity of agreements and the uncertainty over the collective nature of treaties demanded that states explore more oblique, and more ominous, ways to conduct their international relations. What was before a tyranny of treaties, a regime of binding international obligations, became a system of state desire, which transcended the rational and predictable and entered the domain of vengeance, greed and paranoia.

Among the eddies contributing to this diplomatic maelstrom was the Straits Question. This dispute involved those nations which opposed Russian expansion into the Mediterranean through the strategic outlets of the straits.[8] The Dardanelles and the Bosporus were dominated by the Ottoman Empire, whose disintegration was the major issue of the Eastern Question in the 19th century. It was a highly charged and emotional matter. The disposition of the straits came to the fore only when the powers saw that Russia needed to be contained, and that if they failed, Russian aggression would topple the balance.

Every treaty that arbitrated the regime of the straits was concluded after a round of Russian diplomatic or military attempts to secure tacit or effective control of the region. The successive treaties of Kuchuk-Kainardji,[9] Istanbul,[10] and Unkiar-Skelessi[11] gradually eroded the "ancient rule" of the

[8] *See generally* M. ANDERSEN, THE EASTERN QUESTION: 1774–1923 (1966); P. GRAVES, THE QUESTION OF THE STRAITS (1931); P. MOSELY, RUSSIAN DIPLOMACY AND THE OPENING OF THE EASTERN QUESTION IN 1838 AND 1839 (1934); J. SHOTWELL & F. DEÁK, TURKEY AT THE STRAITS: A SHORT HISTORY (1941).

[9] The Treaty of Kuchuk-Kainardji, July 21, 1774, Russia–Ottoman Empire, 45 Parry's TS 349, 2 Martens Nouveau Recueil 286, ended the 6-year war between the two states. Before 1774, there had been no Eastern Question since no non-Turkish vessels plied the Black Sea. It was the private domain of the sultan: a closed sea (*mare clausum*). The growing influence of Russia and its occupation of the Crimea changed this situation. This Treaty granted Russia the right to have merchant vessels on the Black Sea. *See* M. ANDERSEN, *supra* note 8, at xi–27.

[10] Mutual Defense Treaty, Sept. 21, 1805, Russia–Ottoman Empire, 58 Parry's TS 215, *reprinted in* 1 J. HUREWITZ, DIPLOMACY IN THE NEAR AND MIDDLE EAST: A DOCUMENTARY RECORD: 1535–1914, at 72 (1956). The terms of this Treaty, never ratified, are still shrouded in mystery, even though it has been cited conclusively by later authorities. In dispute is whether Article VII gave Russia the right to transit the straits with warships. Thanks to accusations that the Russian scholar and imperial archivist, Sergei Goriainov, falsified this evidence, and the generally conflicting texts that exist, it will never be known whether the Turks granted this extraordinary privilege, a right they jealously guarded in the decades after 1805. Hurewitz, *Russia and the Turkish Straits,* 14 WORLD POL. 605 (1961–62).

[11] Defensive Alliance, July 8, 1833, Russia–Ottoman Empire, 84 Parry's TS 1, 11 Martens Nouveau Recueil 655, *reprinted in* 1 J. HUREWITZ, *supra* note 10, at 106. Russia had found an opportunity to reassert its influence over the Porte when the Ottoman regime was threatened

Ottoman Empire that no foreign warship could transit the straits when the Porte was at peace. This rule vested all sovereignty in the sultan and, in its original articulation, was a sound policy for a great empire that could hold its own against any attacker. In the face of Russian expansionism, however, it was an invitation to disaster.[12]

The 1840 London Conference on the Pacification of the Levant[13] and the Straits Convention[14] of the following year established the legal regime of the straits until 1871. The new system required that the ancient Ottoman rule be codified as a principle of public international law, and thus recognized that the sultan was formally surrendering his right to open the straits at his discretion during peacetime.[15] The 1841 Convention also set forth the promise of the great powers "to respect this determination of the Sultan,

---

by the insurgent Mehmet Ali of Egypt in 1833. This treaty was the price Turkey had to pay for Russian aid at that time. *See* M. ANDERSEN, *supra* note 8, at 84–87.

A "separate and secret" clause annexed to the treaty provided that the Porte would "confine its action in favour of the Imperial Court of Russia to closing the strait of the Dardanelles, that is to say, not allowing any foreign vessels to enter therein under any pretext whatsoever." Defensive Alliance, *supra,* Annex, Art. 1. Interpretations of this provision have varied. One scholar suggested that it acted as "a draw-bridge which the Sultan was obliged to raise at the bidding of the Tsar." C. PHILLIPSON & N. BUXTON, THE QUESTION OF THE BOSPHOROUS AND DARDANELLES (1917) (citing Goriainov; *see supra* note 10). *But cf.* P. MOSELY, *supra* note 8, at 11, 23 (quoting the Russian foreign minister, Count Nesselrode, as suggesting that the treaty only reaffirmed the ancient rule).

These arguments notwithstanding, the accord was limited in duration to 8 years.

[12] Moreover, the ancient Ottoman rule was "particularly offensive to Russia, whose Black Sea fleets would be confined" to that sea. "On the other hand, the Ottoman rule also offered Russia a certain protection by preventing foreign warships entering the Black Sea through the Straits to attack her there. As long as Russia had no major interest in the Mediterranean this latter consideration prevailed." 2 E. BUEL, INTERNATIONAL STRAITS: A TREATISE ON INTERNATIONAL LAW 276–77 (1947).

[13] A second crisis in 1839–1840, precipitated by Mehmet Ali's near overthrow of the sultan, resulted in western intervention on behalf of the Turks. In this way, Britain, Austria and Prussia circumvented what would have been another show of force by Russia on the sultan's behalf, complicated further by France's strong and intransigent support for Mehmet Ali. *See* M. ANDERSEN, *supra* note 8, at 88–109. The London Convention, July 15, 1840, 90 Parry's TS 285, 1 Martens Nouveau Recueil 156, defused a crisis that was far more serious than that of 1833 (*see supra* note 11) owing to the very real possibility of great-power intervention on both sides.

[14] July 13, 1841, 92 Parry's TS 7, 2 Martens Nouveau Recueil 128, *reprinted in* 1 J. HUREWITZ, *supra* note 10, at 123 (signed by Britain, Russia, Austria, Turkey, Prussia and France).

[15] J. SHOTWELL & F. DEÁK, *supra* note 8, at 37; C. PHILLIPSON & N. BUXTON, *supra* note 11, at 77. In 1840–1841 Russia suffered an even greater defeat than France, against which (as supporter of Mehmet Ali and Egypt) the treaties were directed. "Russian warships were closed in the Black Sea, the Straits were placed under the surveillance of European powers and limits were imposed upon the rights of Turkey itself since the latter was no longer free to open the Straits to the warships of any power whatsoever." ITALIAN LIBRARY OF INFORMATION, THE REGIME OF THE STRAITS (1941) (available in English at Princeton University Library). The Straits Convention also saw the end of this round of aggression against Turkey by Russia and its contentment with a status quo that prevented enemy forces from threatening it in the Black Sea.

and to conform themselves to the principle above declared."[16] This was a collective and mutual guarantee among the great powers: violation of the regime would represent a challenge not only to the Porte but also to the European balance. It was the first international instrument that directly incorporated a collective organization preserving a legal regime. To be sure, it was embryonic in conception. It also was based on an unstable diplomatic equilibrium that would persist only as long as Russia forsook its ambitions against Turkey.[17]

The Crimean War was the first major breach of the European peace after 1815, and it was a desultory and strikingly inconclusive conflict. Great Britain and France fought Russia to preserve a balance of power that Austria and Prussia were taking only a limited role in maintaining.[18] The Treaty of Paris of 1856 ended the war and sealed the Russian defeat not only by reasserting the prevailing straits regime but also by entirely demilitarizing the Black Sea.[19] This legal regime was to be preserved by the vigilance of those powers that sought to contain Russia. Great Britain, France and Austria accordingly agreed that any infraction of the Paris Treaty would be a *casus belli,* and they placed their military and naval forces at the Porte's disposal to protect the independence and integrity of the Ottoman Empire.[20] A wartime coalition thus was transformed and crystallized into a peacetime alliance. By this Tripartite Covenant, the competition among the great powers in Europe shed the aspect of a passive balancing of power.

What was remarkable in European diplomacy from the late 18th to the mid-19th centuries was how law and politics were neatly separated as relative impulses of state behavior. The rule of law was synonymous with the operation of international conferences and the sense that all disputes could be adjusted peaceably. Peace treaties, in particular, were respected in an almost metaphorical way: they embodied the Concert of Europe. After a

[16] *See* Straits Convention, *supra* note 14, Art. 1.

[17] Indeed, between 1841 and 1856, Russia was the chief guarantor of the regime. The tsarist Government vociferously protested the least indication that either the letter or the spirit of the 1841 Convention had been violated. St. Petersburg even challenged France's dispatch of two warships into the Bosporous (with Ottoman permission) in 1847 to escort home a fleet of grain vessels attempting to avert a famine in Provence. Russia demanded and secured a statement that this incident would not be used as a precedent for allowing transit of warships through the straits. C. PHILLIPSON & N. BUXTON, *supra* note 11, at 151–52.

[18] *See* M. ANDERSEN, *supra* note 8, at 114–39.

[19] Peace Treaty, Mar. 30, 1856, Arts. 11, 13 and 14, 114 Parry's TS 409, 15 Martens Nouveau Recueil 770. The imposed demilitarization was a form of international servitude and occupied the gray area between obligations and territorial rights. "The particular treaty provisions . . . belong in the category of territorial rights whose violation did not involve any act of transgression on the territorial possessions of other states." A. DAVID, THE STRATEGY OF TREATY TERMINATION 27 (1975). Andersen described the demilitarization of the Black Sea as "extremely harsh and unprecedented. Not until the even more stringent restrictions imposed on Germany in 1919 was a state to be forced to submit to so obvious and flagrant a limitation on its military freedom of action." M. ANDERSEN, *supra* note 8, at 144. This analogy to the Versailles peace settlement is instructive and will be discussed further below.

[20] Tripartite Covenant, Apr. 15, 1856, Great Britain–France–Austria, 114 Parry's TS 497, 15 Martens Nouveau Recueil 790.

conflict, peace was negotiated and the result necessarily captured the balance. Enforcing a treaty was just a matter of pretending that the balance had not been materially altered in the interim.

Seen in this way, the idea that a fundamental change of circumstances could terminate a treaty would have been considered bizarre by the statesmen of the time. Circumstances could never change fundamentally. The outbreak of a general war was considered the only meaningful test of the validity of the current international order. Any answers to the Eastern Question only came after war.

Rebus sic stantibus would not have been pronounced a legal theory worthy of serious consideration by contemporary international publicists. In fact, they did not recognize it as a legal doctrine at all. It was a creature of political theory, with its origins in the statecraft of Cicero,[21] the theology of St. Thomas Aquinas[22] and the reaction to Machiavelli's first expression of realpolitik.[23] In civil law the doctrine of changed circumstances remained vibrant and reached its zenith in the 18th and 19th centuries, precisely when it was found to be suspect in the international arena.[24]

Municipal law and the law of nations operated independently in this respect. As a matter of state practice, rebus sic stantibus was rarely invoked before 1870 and there was no cogent sense of its application.[25] The crisis of 1870 introduced rebus sic stantibus as both a legal doctrine and a diplomatic rationale. It could bring about political change without war or, if grossly abused, itself cause conflict.

II. The Crisis of 1870

Russia's Renunciation

The powers had won a convincing victory over Russia in 1856, and in so doing they discarded a "series of treaties by which Russia had gradually

[21] See 3 Cicero, De officiis *29, where it is noted that a ransom need not be paid to a pirate since he is *hostis humani generis* (enemy of all mankind). Implicit in this advice is the recognition of a change in circumstance, that is, no longer being in the captivity of the marauder.

[22] 1 T. Aquinas, Summa theologica 80–84 (English Dominican trans. 1935) (noting that a man's promise may be excused "if circumstances have changed with regard to persons and the business at hand").

[23] *See* N. Machiavelli, The Prince 98 (Marriot ed. 1960) (1513) (A "wise lord" ought not to keep faith when "the reasons which caused him to pledge it exist no longer"). *But cf.* 2 J. Textor, Synopsis juris gentium (Bate trans. 1916) (1680) (assertion that treaties need not be observed if new political situations arise is false and made only by "pseudo-politicians whispering into the ears of Princes").

[24] See A. Vamvoukos, Termination of Treaties in International Law 5–15 (1985), who notes that Spinoza was the first to imply that rebus sic stantibus had a different character when applied to relations between individuals rather than to those between nations. *Id.* at 13; *see also* B. Spinoza, Tractus theologico-politicus 139 (Wernham trans. 1958) (1st ed. 1670). Rebus sic stantibus came to be regarded in this period as an implicit clause in agreements, intended by the parties to permit freedom of action with a change of circumstances. A. Vamvoukos, *supra,* at 10–15. Hence the full name of the doctrine, *clausula rebus sic stantibus.*

[25] A. Vamvoukos, *supra* note 24, at 61–67, cites only five major episodes prior to the incident described in the next section. Ten other minor events could also have involved an invocation of rebus sic stantibus as a ground for terminating a treaty. *Id.* at 121–22 nn.1–10.

acquired a special right of interference in the affairs of Turkey."[26] Russia was relegated to an isolated position in the European order, which bred discontent on its part.[27] The Treaty of Paris had been designed to limit future Russian aggression. Because the Treaty did not reincorporate Russia into the European balance of power, the tsarist Government was unable to help curb Napoleon III's and, later, Bismarck's aggressions.[28] So it was that "the programme of Paris . . . , in its turn, [was] arrested by Russia's impatience with the merely coordinate position assigned to her in the councils of Europe."[29]

By 1870, the guarantees of security offered by the Paris Treaty could not compensate for its disadvantages to Russia. Its inability to muster a real deterrent against British naval displays in the Black Sea and its uncertainty over Turkish capabilities and intentions contributed to Russia's insecurity. Furthermore, there had been numerous violations of the straits regime between 1856 and 1870.[30]

On October 27, 1870, Tsar Alexander II told his ministers of the plan to denounce the Black Sea clauses of the Paris Treaty.[31] On November 9, two diplomatic notes written by the Russian foreign minister, Prince Gorchakov, were conveyed to Lord Granville, Britain's foreign minister.[32] Although the two notes are necessarily considered together, they give unequal weight to the two grounds Russia invoked in terminating these treaty provisions: material breach and rebus sic stantibus.[33]

A major premise of both arguments was the original rationale for the neutralization of the Black Sea. Prince Gorchakov stated it in these terms in his first circular:

[26] T. HOLLAND, A LECTURE ON THE TREATY RELATIONS OF RUSSIA AND TURKEY FROM 1774 TO 1853, at 1 (1877); *see also* F. VALI, THE TURKISH STRAITS AND NATO 24 (1972).

[27] Russia was approached on a number of occasions by states desiring its support, e.g., in 1858 when Austria sought diplomatic aid against France, and in 1867 when Austria was again trying to fend off a Prussian invasion. C. PHILLIPSON & N. BUXTON, *supra* note 11, at 101–02. Each time Russia refused to be embroiled in the dispute.

[28] *See* M. ANDERSEN, *supra* note 8, at 149–72.

[29] T. HOLLAND, *supra* note 26, at 30.

[30] With the exception of light war vessels granted transit permission (*firmans*) for legation service and the Danubian patrol (*see* Paris Treaty, *supra* note 19, Art. 19), nine foreign warships passed through the straits during this period, including one British, one Austrian, one Prussian, one Russian and three American vessels. *See* C. PHILLIPSON & N. BUXTON, *supra* note 11, at 119. Cf. BRIT. PARL. REP., *reprinted in* 3 T. HERTSLET, *supra* note 3, at 1895, which observed that one British ship illegally transited in 1862; one American in 1866; two American, two Austrian, one French and one Russian in 1868; and one Prussian in 1869. "It appears also that in 7 other instances, questions had arisen with regard to the passage of Foreign Ships of War through the Straits, but that in no case had a violation of the Treaty been shown to have taken place." *Id.*

[31] *See* M. ANDERSEN, *supra* note 8, at 172.

[32] *See* 3 T. HERTSLET, *supra* note 3, at 1892–93. The diplomatic notes were channeled through Russia's ambassador to London, Baron Brunnow. Copies were then dispatched to all other signatories of the Paris Peace Treaty. The first note was dated Oct. 31, 1870 (new style); the second, Nov. 1, 1870 (new style).

[33] *See* Haraszti, *Treaties and the Fundamental Change of Circumstances,* 146 RECUEIL DES COURS 1, 16–17 (1975 III).

> By laying down this principle the signatory Powers intended to remove any possibility of a conflict between the Powers bordering on the Black Sea, or between them and the Maritime Powers [namely, France and Britain]. It was intended to increase the number of the Territories which have been accorded the benefit of Neutrality by the unanimous consent of Europe, and thus protect Russia herself from all danger of attack.[34]

The minister went on to say that "15 years' experience has proved that this principle, on which the safety of the whole extent of the Russian Frontiers in this direction exclusively depends, is no more than a theory."[35]

The recitation of treaty breaches[36] was supplemented by a description of the circumstances that had changed since 1856. Foremost among these was the consolidation of a new Roumanian state out of the former Principalities of Moldavia and Wallachia, resulting in an additional riparian power on the Black Sea that could menace Russian security.[37] The Russian Government also cited the recent introduction of ironclad vessels as a disturbing new element in the naval balance.[38]

The Russian foreign minister explained that the Treaty of Paris had not

> escaped the modifications to which most European transactions have been exposed, and in the face of which it would be difficult to maintain that the written Law, founded upon the respect for Treaties as the basis of Public Right and regulating the relations between States, retains the moral validity which it may have possessed at other times.[39]

Here was tacit, but confused, recognition of the dynamic nature of international relations and the need for treaties to be flexibly interpreted. Nevertheless, the tsar declared that "[t]reaties, violated in several of their essential and general clauses, should [not] remain binding *in other clauses* directly affecting the interests of his Empire."[40] Because the straits regime was being violated, Russia argued, the neutralization of the Black Sea should end. Gorchakov was thus proposing selective treaty observance. Although other Russian interests might have been compromised by the creation of Roumania and the change in the European balance, the Government intended to abrogate only the related provisions on demilitarization of the Black Sea.

Russia's use of rebus sic stantibus was fully intended as a challenge to the existing balance of power, and not necessarily directed toward a particular legal regime. In this respect, the second circular was written as a diplomatic palliative. It invoked the notion of a fundamental change of circumstances

[34] *See* 3 T. HERTSLET, *supra* note 3, at 1892.

[35] *Id.*

[36] *See supra* note 30.

[37] As a practical matter, Roumania had no navy and could hardly have threatened Russia. *See* Haraszti, *supra* note 33, at 17. Prince Gorchakov admitted this point when he said, in the second circular, that "the consequences which may ensue to a Great Country from the creation of a small quasi Independent State" were largely irrelevant. *See* 3 T. HERTSLET, *supra* note 3, at 1896.

[38] 3 T. HERTSLET, *supra* note 3, at 1894.

[39] *Id.* at 1893.

[40] *Id.* at 1894 (emphasis added).

but cloaked it in the guise of needed reforms for the international order.[41] Gorchakov was careful, however, to state that Russia still deemed itself bound by the remaining provisions of the Treaty, including the then prevailing straits regime. The Russians thus attempted to retain all the protection the Treaty had to offer in preventing foreign incursions into the Black Sea, while keeping their own naval forces at liberty to threaten Turkey. Almost as an aside in the first note, the Russian foreign minister assured the powers that "His Imperial Majesty has no wish to revive the Eastern Question."[42]

The Russians had picked the perfect moment to repudiate the Black Sea clauses: the height of the Franco-Prussian War of 1870. The debacle at the battle of Sedan, clearly signaling a new epoch in European history, gave Russia its opportunity. Napoleon III was in captivity and the French were incapacitated. Prussia had pledged support for the Russian plan.[43] Austria had more than once ascribed little importance to the neutralization of the Black Sea.[44] Italy had internal problems of its own. Only England would oppose the Russian fait accompli, and even then Prince Gorchakov figured that "the British government might fight for the neutrality of Egypt; it would not fight for the neutrality of the Black Sea."[45] Russia wagered that if there was any opposition by the great powers to its provocative action, it would be expressed with "pen and ink" rather than warships and troops.

The Diplomatic and Legal Crisis

If the Russians had expected universal recognition or tacit approval of their breach of international custom, they were disappointed. The diplomatic crisis they triggered was intensified by the Porte's response.[46] On November 15, the Russian envoy, Ignatiev, delivered a letter to Turkey, which was received by Foreign Minister Ali with the words, "You bring us

[41] Gorchakov noted that the British had previously acquiesced in alterations to other aspects of the Paris Treaty regime. *Id.* at 1896.

[42] *Id.* at 1895. The Russians could also claim as another special circumstance warranting treaty termination that the Russian Empire was now at peace with the other powers. *See Protocols of the 1871 London Conference, reprinted in* 18 Martens Nouveau Recueil 273, 276 [hereinafter *Conference Protocols*], and 61 BRIT. & FOREIGN ST. PAPERS 1193 (1870–71); *see also* Haraszti, *supra* note 33, at 17. The Russian claim was rather disingenuous, since the Paris Treaty had actually ended the hostilities. If taken literally, Russia might have been implying that since the Treaty was unequal and unilaterally imposed, it could be abrogated. *See also* Gorchakov's dispatch to Vienna, Nov. 22, 1870, 60 STAATSARCHIV, No. 4236, at 130–31 (Austrian Foreign Papers), *quoted in* C. HILL, THE DOCTRINE OF REBUS SIC STANTIBUS IN INTERNATIONAL LAW 48 (1934) ("Europe today is no longer that which signed the treaty of 1856" and "the political conditions in which this transaction was concluded have been radically changed").

[43] *See* M. ANDERSEN, *supra* note 8, at 172.

[44] *See* W. MOSSE, THE RISE AND FALL OF THE CRIMEAN SYSTEM 161 (1963).

[45] *See* P. GRAVES, *supra* note 8, at 122.

[46] The Russian foreign minister had decided to forward the circular letters, *supra* note 32, to Constantinople only after they had been received by the other powers. The Porte thus learned about this development from the English ambassador to Turkey.

war."[47] In communications between St. Petersburg and Constantinople, the Russians tried first to placate the Turks by suggesting a bilateral treaty, an idea that would have short-circuited the international conference that would inevitably be proposed.

The Turks were perturbed by Russia's diplomatic coup. Musurus Pasha, the Ottoman ambassador to London, said that "Turkey would never submit to these pretensions" and was prepared, itself, to renounce all of the Treaty of Paris, notwithstanding the consequences.[48] The Turks regarded the Black Sea clauses as the linchpin of the Paris Treaty. Without them, there was little of substance to guarantee Turkish security in the Treaty. Turkey's belligerent attitude, however, was not shared by Austria, Prussia and Italy, which advised the Porte to take no action against Russia without the other signatories of the Paris Treaty. Nevertheless, these states did oppose Russia's unilateral denunciation of the Black Sea clauses.[49]

It was not until December 1870 that the rhetoric in the communications of Russia, Britain and Turkey took on an edge of ill-disguised hostility and the mood of impending conflict. Meanwhile, the British response to the Russian circulars was framed in the steady language of Lord Granville; it was delivered to St. Petersburg on November 20.[50] Primarily a legal document, it did not really speak to the substantive aspects of Russia's claim that the Paris Treaty had been materially violated.[51]

Granville first challenged Gorchakov's argument that a breach of one aspect of a treaty could result in the termination of the whole instrument. The British foreign secretary turned next to Russia's purported unilateral modification of the Treaty. If Russia, instead of declaring the Black Sea provisions void, had petitioned the powers for relief, "Her Majesty's government would not have refused to examine the question in concert with the co-signataries to the Treaty."[52] This was hardly a promise that Britain would have acceded to Russia's request. It was only a rhetorical flourish, a plea that another nation "play by the rules" of international intercourse.

The balance of Lord Granville's criticism of the Russian action reads as a reaffirmation of the sanctity of international contracts:

> Yet it is quite evident that the effect of [unilateral termination], and of any proceeding which, with or without avowal, is founded upon it, is to bring the entire authority and efficacy of Treaties under the discretionary control of each one of the Powers who may have signed them: the result of which would be the entire destruction of Treaties in their

[47] B. Jelavich, The Ottoman Empire, the Great Powers, and the Straits Question, 1870–1887, at 29 (1973).

[48] *Id.* at 28.

[49] *See* 72 Parl. Papers, *supra* note 2, at 52–53 (for Austrian and Prussian position). Italy believed that the 1856 treaties (including the Tripartite Covenant) had outlived their usefulness. *Id.*

[50] *See* 3 T. Hertslet, *supra* note 3, at 1898–1900.

[51] Lord Granville noted that this question was "wholly independent of the reasonableness or unreasonableness, on its own merits, of the desire of Russia to be released from the observation of the stipulations of the Treaty of 1856 respecting the Black Sea." *Id.* at 1898–99.

[52] *Id.* at 1900.

> essence. For whereas their whole object is to bind Powers to one another, and for this purpose each one of the parties surrenders a portion of its free agency, by the doctrine and proceeding now in question, one of the parties in its separate and individual capacity brings back the entire subject into its own control, and remains bound only to itself.[53]

This statement is evocative of the famous principle that a "man should not be the judge of his own cause."[54] The British were articulating a basic principle of municipal law and transferring it to the realm of international law.[55]

If the Russians were impressed by the analytical precision of the British arguments, they gave no indication of it. Instead, Gorchakov began circulating communications of an extraordinarily inflammatory nature. One letter to Granville asserted that the tsar's decision was irrevocable, and that the Ottomans had better accept it or they "would be exposed to the most serious of dangers."[56] Gorchakov further said that the Christian populations of the Ottoman Empire, "whose past tranquility was greatly to be attributed to the influence of Russia," would rise in arms against the sultan "on the first misunderstanding between the two governments."[57] This suggestion was poorly received in London and, no doubt, contributed to the threat of war. That the potential for conflict was lessened at all was in large part attributable to Bismarck's diplomacy.[58]

The holding of an international conference was the only way that the signatories of the Tripartite Covenant of 1856 could forestall the action against Russia, as stipulated by that agreement.[59] Indeed, the chief contributing factor to the war scare in the British Parliament was the understanding that the Covenant mandated military action by the British, French and Austrians to preserve the Paris Treaty.[60] Yet these powers no longer felt themselves bound to preserve the Paris regime. It was an artificial agreement, created to perpetuate a balance of power that was really untenable in 1856 and utterly irrelevant by 1871. With France's defeat and Austria's lack

[53] *Id.* at 1899.

[54] The doctrine is known as *nemo debet esse judex in propria causa. See* CODE J. 3.5.

[55] This is arguably one of the first explicit incorporations of "the general principles of law recognized by civilized nations." *See* Statute of the International Court of Justice, 59 Stat. 1055 (1945), TS No. 993, Art. 38, para. 1(c). The idea that nations may not be judges of their own causes seems to be a sine qua non in international law. Nevertheless, this assertion will be critically reviewed in section IV *infra.*

[56] *See* W. MOSSE, *supra* note 44, at 166. [57] *Id.*

[58] While Bismarck had encouraged the Russian action, he realized in late November that it could touch off a second Crimean War and thus leave in question Prussia's victories in France. *See* M. ANDERSEN, *supra* note 8, at 172. Bismarck enthusiastically received Lord Granville's envoy, Odo Russell, in Paris and discussed the prospects for an international conference to review the situation. The only condition for Britain's support for such a meeting was that "it in no way be prejudiced by any previous assumption as to the result of its deliberations." E. SATOW, INTERNATIONAL CONGRESSES 27–28 (1920). After some haggling, London was made the site of the conference and it was decided that it would be conducted at the ambassadorial level. *See* 3 T. HERTSLET, *supra* note 3, at 1900.

[59] *See supra* note 20 and accompanying text.

[60] *See* 72 PARL. PAPERS, *supra* note 2, at 6.

of interest in the matter, it fell to Britain to invoke the provisions of the Tripartite Covenant.

Lord Granville and Prime Minister Gladstone refused to do so, even as they reminded the Russians about the sanctity of treaties. The British then engaged in some creative interpretations of their rights and obligations under the Covenant. They suggested that since the Russian Government had only stated its *intention* to repudiate the Black Sea clauses, it would be improper for one of the signatories alone to determine the reaction of the other parties. Postponement of a decision was called for.

Gladstone later produced an even more artful excuse for avoiding British obligations under the Tripartite Covenant:

> [S]tringent as it is in its terms, it does not appear to me to have much force as a covenant at present, when Turkey declares her own incapacity to fight except with (virtually) our money. Guarantees as such seem to me to presuppose the capacity of any guaranteed State to fight for herself; and then to supply a further auxiliary defence. At least I think it must be so the case where nothing is expressed to give a different construction to the guarantee.[61]

This was a wholly perverse invocation of the notion of incapacity or impossibility as a ground for treaty termination. It was not a question of Britain's inability to defend the Porte but, rather, of denying protection to a beneficiary of a treaty provision because it lacked the ability to defend itself.

These rationalizations aside, Britain's policy in this matter was best described by Granville when he wrote Gladstone, on December 10, 1870, that "what sticks in my gizzard is the Tripartite Treaty. How very foolish of us it was to have contracted it. But there it is, with obligations as binding as were ever contracted."[62] Here is an unequivocal rejection of the policy that necessitated the Crimean War and would have required another armed intervention on behalf of Turkey. The system of alliances and balances that the Paris Treaty had crystallized was now totally dissolved.

It is ironic that both Russia and Great Britain pursued policies that placed the effectiveness of treaties in real doubt. Russia was just more blatant, more forthright and honest in renouncing what it perceived to be an intolerable international servitude. The attempt by Britain to finesse its way out of the guaranty for the Paris regime, when juxtaposed with its criticism of Russia's unilateral action, gave evidence of either confusion about the nature of international law or, more likely, hypocrisy in the service of state policy. At any rate, both of these actions meant that there could be no stability in international relations if it was impossible to count on the fulfillment of solemn obligations.[63] Treaties became only "scraps of paper," to be torn up when more important issues seemed to be involved.

[61] Letter of Dec. 12, 1870, *reprinted in* B. JELAVICH, *supra* note 47, at 35.

[62] Letter of Dec. 10, 1870, *reprinted in* B. JELAVICH, *supra* note 47, at 36.

[63] *See* J. SHOTWELL & F. DEÁK, *supra* note 8, at 48.

The London Conference and Convention

Notwithstanding the bluster and saber rattling of the great powers, the threat of a general war had clearly been defused before the London Conference opened on January 17, 1871. Britain's unwillingness to invoke the Tripartite Covenant, Austria's vacillations,[64] France's defeat and removal from the ranks of the great powers, and Turkey's serious policy dilemma[65]—all were indications of an international order very different from that of 1856. The unification of Germany and Italy created two new power centers in Europe. Contemporary statesmen were undoubtedly shocked by Prussia's decisive defeat of France. The Russian denunciation of the Black Sea clauses must have seemed to be a rather insignificant sideshow compared to the drama played out at Sedan and Paris.

The London Conference resolved no great political questions since none were advanced on its agenda. In this respect, this negotiation was primarily a legal exercise. It involved both the diplomatic adjustment of the legal regime of the straits and the consideration of a principal tenet of the international legal order, the sanctity of treaties. Too often, the London Declaration is seen by lawyers as the only product of the negotiation, as if the actual resolution of the crisis were merely incidental to the great powers' affirmation or denunciation of the rebus sic stantibus doctrine.

This was not so. The declaration was adopted almost as an afterthought at the opening session of the conference, a ritualistic affair where the diplomats devoted more time to thanking their hosts than to considering legal concepts.[66] Also at this meeting, Baron Brunnow presented the reasons for Russia's demand for an adjustment to the Paris Treaty.[67] Turkey's ambassador, Musurus Pasha, responded at the next meeting,[68] and insisted on the reinstitution of the "ancient rule" for the straits.[69]

[64] The instructions that Vienna-Budapest gave to the ambassador in London, Apponyi, were characteristically equivocal: "[We] shall be ready to follow England wherever she wishes to go [in resolving this matter]." *See* B. JELAVICH, *supra* note 47, at 36–37. *Cf.* text accompanying note 44 *supra* (for contrary instructions).

[65] The Ottomans were in a perilous diplomatic position. Their two chief guarantors against Russian incursions had been neutralized: France by military defeat and Britain by its manifest unwillingness to offer support. B. JELAVICH, *supra* note 47, at 6, 42. The Porte was confronted with a horrible dilemma. It could attempt to maintain the balance of power in the Near East created by the Paris Treaty and face the possibility of a war with Russia; or it could forsake the Paris regime, which had given the Turks 15 years of relative peace and tranquility, and seek an alliance with Russia and so recreate the conditions of Unkiar-Skelessi (*see supra* note 11).

[66] *See Conference Protocols, supra* note 42, at 273–78 (Jan. 17, 1871).

[67] *Id.* at 275–76. Baron Brunnow explained the circumstances under which the 1856 Treaty had been concluded and how these had changed, and that these circumstances and facts "ont déterminé les Puissances signataires à donner leur adhésion à différentes modifications qui ont contribué à altérer, en partie, la lettre des stipulations primitives." *Id.* at 275. *See also supra* notes 34–40 and accompanying text.

[68] *Id.* at 278–82 (Jan. 24, 1871).

[69] This would mean that the Porte would "be freed from any international engagement relative to [the straits] and [that it would reserve] the right to open them or to close them to warships of other powers as its interests and security demand." *See* Foreign Minister Ali's

In response to this proposal, the British formulated a new straits regime that would allow

> His Imperial Majesty the Sultan, in virtue of the right of sovereignty which he exercises over the Straits, . . . the right in time of peace to open them by way of temporary exception in the sole case where the interest of the security of his empire leads him to recognize the necessity of the presence of ships of war of non-riverian powers.[70]

This oblique proposal essentially provided that the straits would always be closed to Russian warships, but that in time of need "non-riverian" ships could transit them. The proposal was strikingly punitive and gave Russia's enemies substantial advantages.

Moreover, it placed Turkey in a completely untenable position. The British proposal, in fact, limited the rights of the sultan, took from him the means of acting in accordance with the needs of his empire, and unduly provoked Russia.[71] At the conference's third meeting, Musurus criticized the British wording since it was not made clear what "non-riverian" referred to. If it meant the straits themselves, Russia but not Turkey would be allowed transit rights. If it referred to the Black Sea, not only Turkey, but also Russia and Roumania could not seek passage.[72] Musurus suggested that "non-riverian states" be changed to "friendly powers."[73] The Turk's approach was astute: he realized that any straits regime that so blatantly discriminated against Russia would be renounced by that nation within a few years.

Curiously, Russia gave no support to the Turkish counterproposal.[74] As a consequence, between February 3 and the next substantive meeting on March 13, a compromise was sought between the British and Ottoman proposals. One came from an unexpected quarter, the Italian delegate, Cordona. His proposal was elegant in its ambiguity. The sultan would be able to open the straits "in time of peace to vessels of friendly and allied Powers, in case the Sublime Porte would judge it necessary in order to

---

instructions to Musurus, *reprinted in* B. JELAVICH, *supra* note 47, at 44. Under the 1841 Straits Convention, the Ottoman Empire had been barred from opening the straits altogether. *See supra* notes 15–16 and accompanying text.

[70] *See* 61 BRIT. & FOREIGN ST. PAPERS 1199 (1870–71); *Conference Protocols, supra* note 42, at 284 (Feb. 3, 1871) (trans. by author).

[71] *See* B. JELAVICH, *supra* note 47, at 49.

[72] *Conference Protocols, supra* note 42, at 285 (Feb. 3, 1871).

[73] *Id.* at 284.

[74] Brunnow was undoubtedly receiving contradictory instructions from Gorchakov. He had been told not to demand any concession that would compromise the goal of getting recognition for the remilitarization of the Black Sea. *See* B. JELAVICH, *supra* note 47, at 53, 55. Some historians have criticized Brunnow for his poor handling of this situation. *See* C. PHILLIPSON & N. BUXTON, *supra* note 11, at 7. This is probably unjustified. Brunnow was sensitive only to the problem of not appearing to undercut Turkish power. He undoubtedly knew that Musurus was right: Russia would have quickly renounced the clause if the British proposal prevailed. Russia, in fact, did just that when it entirely rejected the Paris Treaty regime and attacked the Turks in 1876. *See infra* note 79.

secure the stipulations of the Treaty of Paris."[75] This provision satisfied all of the powers[76] and was incorporated into the Treaty adopted by the conference.[77]

The new legal regime for the straits was even more unmanageable than the one of 1841. The signatories of the London Treaty disagreed on the definition of warships, peacetime and "friendly and allied Powers," and on what would constitute a safeguard to the execution of the Treaty of 1856.[78] But the major question was whether the 1871 convention required the approval of the other signatories for the sultan to give transit permission.[79] Ultimately, the 1871 Treaty did not change the legal regime of the straits at all. It merely averted a crisis and gave Turkey 6 more years of rest before the next episode of the Eastern Question.

III. An Intellectual History of the London Declaration

Contemporary Opinion

Although the negotiation of the London Treaty is well documented, the process by which the London Declaration[80] was concluded remains relatively obscure. The received wisdom is that it was signed at the insistence of Lord Granville as a necessary preliminary measure before the substantive negotiations on the Straits Question could proceed.[81] The declaration thus served as a neat piece of diplomatic misdirection: reinforcing Britain's plea that the outcome of the London Conference not be prejudged,[82] while granting Russia all that it desired. This criticism was most witheringly applied by members of Parliament who opposed the Government's manner of conducting the negotiations. The protocol containing the declaration was variously referred to as a "sham,"[83] a "pompous piece of unmeaning solemnity"[84] and a "worthless document."[85]

[75] *Conference Protocols*, *supra* note 42, at 298 (Mar. 13, 1871); 72 Parl. Papers, *supra* note 2, at 4.

[76] For the Ottoman Empire, this proposal not only reaffirmed the right of the sultan to open the straits at his discretion, but it also invoked the spirit of the Paris Treaty and so guaranteed Turkish independence. Britain and Austria were pleased since they assumed that Russian ships would be enjoined from passage, as that could never be compatible with the purposes of the Paris Treaty. Russia, of course, held exactly the opposite opinion.

[77] Treaty of London, Mar. 13, 1871, Art. 2, 143 Parry's TS 99, 18 Martens Nouveau Recueil 303, 3 T. Hertslet, *supra* note 3, at 1919.

[78] *See* B. Jelavich, *supra* note 47, at 86.

[79] *See* E. Buel, *supra* note 12, at 283; C. Phillipson & N. Buxton, *supra* note 11, at 162–63. This dispute nearly precipitated a war when British warships entered the straits to preserve Ottoman independence at the height of the Russo-Turkish War of 1876–1878. *Id.* at 154–55.

[80] *See supra* note 3.

[81] *See, e.g.*, B. Sinha, Unilateral Denunciation of Treaty Because of Prior Violations by Other Party 80 (1966); W. Hall, International Law 300 (1880) (implying that the declaration was an attempt by Granville to dislodge Russia from its position renouncing the neutralization of the Black Sea).

[82] *See supra* note 58.

[83] 205 Parl. Deb. (3d ser.) 900 (1871) (remarks by Sir Charles Dilke).

[84] *Id.* at 917 (remarks by Mr. Somerset Beaumont).

[85] *Id.* at 954 (remarks by Sir Robert Peel, quoting Sir Charles Dilke).

This characterization of the proceedings emptied the declaration of all legal meaning. Not surprisingly, it is the most persistent interpretive view in this intellectual history. But it is also revisionist. This version implies that Russia was the unambiguous victor in the diplomatic exchange and that all it gave in return was a paltry promise to observe treaties in good faith. While the straits regime agreed to at London may have operated later to Russia's benefit, it was not so intended at the time.[86]

The theory that the London Declaration was a sham also stumbles on the assertion that it was a fait accompli perpetrated by Lord Granville and adopted without opposition from any of the other parties at the conference. In fact, there were 13 versions of the declaration.[87] The one originally advanced by Britain was one of the mildest in tone.[88] By contrast, the proposal first submitted by Austria's ambassador, Count Apponyi, declared that termination or modification of a treaty was entirely barred unless application was made to all of the parties and their consent secured.[89] This formulation combined both a substantive rule and a definitive procedural plan for the termination of a treaty provision. While supported by Italy,[90] this wording was objected to by Russia.[91] Apponyi prepared a second draft that closely paralleled a British proposal, and these together dictated the form of the agreed-upon declaration.[92]

[86] *See supra* notes 74–79 and accompanying text.

[87] 206 PARL. DEB. (3d ser.) 794 (1871) (remarks by Lord Granville, who also said that "[t]his very delay . . . shows that it was our desire to make [the declaration] complete, and I am not sure that it was not worded even a little more strongly than on abstract grounds we might be entitled to expect"; *id.*).

[88] 205 PARL. DEB. (3d ser.) 900 (1871) (remarks by Sir Charles Dilke).

[89] The Austrian draft read: the assembled plenipotentiaries "sont d'accord pour reconnaître comme un principe essentiel du droit des gens, qu'aucune puissance ne peut se délier ou se dégager des engagements d'un traité, ou en modifier les stipulations, sans en avoir préalablement communiqué et adressé la demande aux autres parties contractantes, et avoir obtenu leur assentiment." Letter from Apponyi to Count Beust, Austrian foreign minister, Dec. 31, 1870, *quoted in* B. POURITCH, DE LA CLAUSE «REBUS SIC STANTIBUS» EN DROIT INTERNATIONAL PUBLIC 103 (1918). This strong draft again indicates the inherent contradictions in Austria-Hungary's position, since it was ostensibly supporting both Russia and Britain in the negotiations. *See also* 72 PARL. PAPERS, *supra* note 2, at 52–53 (letter from Apponyi to Granville saying that the 1856 Treaty was too severe); G. HARASZTI, SOME FUNDAMENTAL PROBLEMS OF THE LAW OF TREATIES 334 & n.20 (1973) (quoting Count Beust as accepting the idea that the progress of time could bring into question the operation of treaties); and *supra* notes 44 and 64. The Austrian draft, at any rate, seemed to articulate a rule of unanimous consent for treaty changes.

[90] *See* 72 PARL. PAPERS, *supra* note 2, at 42–43 (quoting the Italian reply to the Gorchakov circular as saying that "a previous concert is the necessary condition of any change that it may seem advisable to introduce" in a treaty regime).

[91] Letter from Russia to Austria, Nov. 22, 1870, in which Gorchakov confirmed that no treaty concluded in common could be modified except by common consent, but that "such transaction does not preserve its obligatory value for all except as long as its essential bases and its conditions have been equally observed and maintained." *See* C. HILL, *supra* note 42, at 50 n.16. From that statement, one can wonder whether Russia was really sincere in entering negotiations without prejudging their outcome. *See supra* note 82 and accompanying text.

[92] *See* B. POURITCH, *supra* note 89, at 104 (draft contained in Apponyi's letters to Beust of Jan. 5 & 12, 1871). For the final draft of the declaration, see text at note 3 *supra*.

If Britain, Prussia, Russia, Austria, Turkey and Italy had reached some understanding about what the declaration meant, they evidently failed to inform the French delegate when he arrived on March 31, 1871.[93] Having been told earlier that the document was a "mere formal matter,"[94] the Duke of Broglie made two curious remarks before signing the declaration on France's behalf. The first was that he welcomed the occasion to support a "salutary rule of European society—that is, not to bring about any essential change in international relations without the examination and consent of all the Great Powers."[95] An echo of the fading strains of the Concert of Europe,[96] this interpretation clearly saw the declaration in terms of the European balance of power and as an instrument of political, not legal, principles.[97] But then the French delegate remarked that he saw no reason to modify the Treaty of Paris and that no real change of circumstances had arisen.[98] One can legitimately wonder if Broglie saw this diplomatic exercise as a sham or was applying his construction of the declaration to the situation at hand.

Broglie's confusion may be excused in light of other contemporary opinion about the question to be dealt with by the declaration. Two of the greatest political thinkers of the time, John Stuart Mill and Chancellor Bismarck, likewise ran astray on this issue. Both would have agreed with Rylands's statement in Parliament that "treaties, . . . like pie-crust, . . . were made to be broken."[99] Mill's interpretation, issued in the wake of the Gorchakov circular, was expressed in these terms:

> If a lawless act . . . has been committed in the present instance, it does not entitle those who imposed the conditions to consider the lawlessness only, and to dismiss the more important consideration, whether, even if it was wrong to throw off the obligation, it would not be still more wrong to persist in enforcing it. If, though not fit to be perpetual, [the Treaty of Paris] has been imposed in perpetuity, the question when it becomes right to throw it off is but a question of time. No time being fixed, Russia fixed her own time, and naturally chose the most convenient.[100]

There was also a prescriptive element in Mill's writing. He suggested that nations should abstain from imposing unreasonable conditions that cannot possibly be kept and that treaties should be limited in duration.[101]

[93] *See Conference Protocols, supra* note 42, at 296 (Mar. 13, 1871). The French minister had been delayed owing to the last phases of the war with Prussia.

[94] *See* 205 PARL. DEB. (3d ser.) 899 (1871) (remarks by Sir Charles Dilke).

[95] *See Conference Protocols, supra* note 42, at 296–97 (Mar. 13, 1871) (trans. by author).

[96] *See supra* notes 6 and 7 and accompanying text.

[97] *See* E. HOYT, THE UNANIMITY RULE IN THE REVISION OF TREATIES: A RE-EXAMINATION 7 (1959). Like the Apponyi draft, *supra* note 89, the French interpretation required unanimous consent to change a treaty regime.

[98] *See Conference Protocols, supra* note 42, at 297 (Mar. 13, 1871).

[99] *See* 205 PARL. DEB. (3d ser.) 922, 927 (1871) (speech by Mr. Rylands).

[100] Mill, *Treaty Obligations,* 8 FORTNIGHTLY REV. (n.s.) 715 (1870), *excerpted in* 5 J. B. MOORE, DIGEST OF INTERNATIONAL LAW 339–40 (1906).

[101] 5 J. B. MOORE, *supra* note 100, at 339.

Although not phrased in international legal terms, Mill's concerns foreshadowed a second broad strand of interpretation for the London Declaration. He offered a way to discriminate both morally and legally between those international obligations susceptible of enforcement and those that were not. This view informed later protests not only that "unequal" treaties should not be observed, as a matter of international morality, but also that conventions containing servitudes should likewise be subject to the mandate of "peaceful change," an essential ingredient of the international legal order.

By contrast, Bismarck's statements in the state correspondence and before the Bundesrat in November 1870 reveal a darker side to the diplomatic exercise over the straits. He said that invocation of a change in circumstances as a ground for treaty termination was in the exclusive domain of the great powers, an attribute of their primary role in maintaining the balance of power in Europe.[102] By regarding remilitarization of the Black Sea as a question of diplomacy, and not one of international law, Bismarck expressed a notion of pure realpolitik.[103] Rebus sic stantibus became merely a surrogate for the expression of higher state policy. While Broglie suggested that the London Declaration was a useful legal fiction, the German chancellor would have considered it simply irrelevant, or worse, an untoward restriction on sovereignty.

Publicists' Writings before the Great War

Commentary on the London Declaration by international law scholars before World War I reflected only the perspectives of Parliament, Broglie and the Iron Chancellor. In short, the document was given little credence as an instrument articulating international legal norms. These publicists were evidently troubled by the declaration as a statement of law, so simple and self-evident were its terms.

William Hall could write in 1880 that the principle embodied in the declaration was "indisputable," although "in a declaration of the kind made it would have been impossible to enounce it with those qualifications which have been seen to be necessary in practice."[104] Hall's point is one that would often be repeated in the literature: if the declaration purported to be an absolute prohibition on unilateral termination or modification of treaties, it could not be accepted at face value. Yet Hall also made the corollary obser-

[102] *See* Haraszti, *supra* note 33, at 19 n.7. *See also* C. HILL, *supra* note 42, at 50 & n.15 (quoting Bismarck as saying that Germany would judge the dispute merely by the canons of good faith).

[103] *See* 2 O. BISMARCK, REFLECTIONS AND REMINISCENCES 270 (London 1898) ("No great nation will ever be induced to sacrifice its existence on the altar of fidelity to contract when it is compelled to choose between the two"), *quoted in* 5 J. B. MOORE, *supra* note 100, at 340. *See also* F. SMITH, INTERNATIONAL LAW 10 (4th ed. 1911) ("A most damaging blow was struck by one of the greatest European statesmen of the nineteenth century, and international law will not soon recover from the cynical contempt with which Prince Bismarck . . . was never tired of bespattering it").

[104] W. HALL, INTERNATIONAL LAW 300 (1880).

vation that if the declaration did not really mean this, then the "force of its assertion may have been impaired by the fact that Russia, as the reward of submission to law, was given what she had affected to take. But the concessions made were dictated by political considerations, with which international law has nothing to do."[105] This conclusion was often cited by contemporary writers as the definitive statement on the status of the declaration in international law.[106]

The distinction Hall relied on was between law and politics. Other writers saw the London Conference, instead, as a sort of passion play. A. C. Boyd, writing as editor of Henry Wheaton's treatise, branded Russia's action as "utterly subversive of all international morality"; and he lamented that if the other powers acquiesced in it, "all public faith was at an end."[107] His most biting criticism was reserved for the declaration itself:

> It is melancholy to think that the most civilised Powers of the world should have considered it necessary to put forward such a declaration . . . . It shows that international law, however much talked of and appealed to, has not yet acquired that moral force by which alone the welfare of nations in their mutual intercourse can be secured.[108]

T. J. Lawrence later wrote that the London protocol was declaratory, but "not declaratory of International Law."[109] He asserted that repudiation of a treaty was a "question of morality rather than of law" and that, indeed, these questions transcended law altogether.[110]

These doubts about the adequacy of international law were even better expressed by James Lorimer in *The Institutes of the Law of Nations.* His critique of the declaration was based on its underlying premise that unanimity is desirable in the conclusion and abrogation of treaties. Lorimer argued that the unanimity rule reflected the absolute independence of states. However, this application of sovereignty "amounts to a total repudiation of international responsibility: it is a denial of the existence both of international rights and international duties, and, as a necessary consequence, of the possibility of international law, either public or private."[111]

[105] *Id.*

[106] *See, e.g.*, F. SMITH, *supra* note 103, at 10 ("the Declaration is sometimes cited as a success for the authority of international law: it is to be hoped that its principles will not be exposed to many such Pyrrhic victories"); T. J. LAWRENCE, PRINCIPLES OF INTERNATIONAL LAW 328 (4th ed. 1911) ("a little consideration will show that [the declaration] is as untenable as the lax view that would allow any party to a treaty to violate it on the slightest pretext"); L. Renault, Question d'Orient 27 (unpub., Cours de doctorat, Paris, 1913–14) (describing the London Conference as a "diplomatic comedy"). Westlake made substantially these same points in 1904, but also referred to the Paris Treaty's provision concerning neutralization of the Black Sea as perpetuating an obsolescent regime. *See* 1 J. WESTLAKE, INTERNATIONAL LAW 285–86 (1904).

[107] H. WHEATON, ELEMENTS OF INTERNATIONAL LAW 96a (Boyd ed. 1880).

[108] *Id.* at 96b.

[109] T. J. LAWRENCE, THE PRINCIPLES OF INTERNATIONAL LAW 98 (3d rev. ed. 1909).

[110] T. J. LAWRENCE, *supra* note 106, at 327–28.

[111] 1 J. LORIMER, THE INSTITUTES OF THE LAW OF NATIONS 47 (1883). *See also* T. J. LAWRENCE, *supra* note 106, at 328 ("International Law certainly does not give a right of veto on political progress to any reactionary member of the family of nations . . .").

Admittedly, Lorimer's preferred system was based on a naive municipal law model of statutory authority.[112] But his insight produced the first interpretation of the London Declaration that emphasized its role as a procedural guide.[113] More importantly, Lorimer's assessment of international law, emphasizing as it does the tension between the sovereignty and equality of states, sounds the same warning as the work of modern critical legal scholars.

Interwar Perspectives

World War I was the decisive moment in reshaping thinking about the role of law in international politics. Not surprisingly, this intellectual reappraisal by legal scholars quickly turned to issues of managing state sovereignty in a world that depended on predictability and cooperation to secure the peace. This line of inquiry, in turn, led to critical assessments of the nature and force of international obligations as expressions of a stable world order. While the conduct of the Versailles Peace Conference itself was reminiscent of the earlier Concert system,[114] it still signified a renunciation of the atavistic fashion of international relations that prevailed before the Great War. A social Darwinistic vision of competing states was replaced by communitarian notions of cooperation and consensus.

Integral to reconciling international obligations with ensuring a peaceful order was the League of Nations Covenant.[115] Article 19 provided that "[t]he Assembly may from time to time advise the reconsideration by Members of the League of treaties which have become inapplicable, and the consideration of international conditions whose continuance might endanger the peace of the world."[116] This clause was the basis of the League's mandate for peaceful change, a concept that embraced more than the re-

[112] *See* C. Murphy, The Search for World Order 154 (1985).

[113] 1 J. Lorimer, *supra* note 111, at 48 ("If Russia committed an error then, it was the formal error which Lord Granville alleges against her . . .").

[114] *See supra* notes 6 and 7 and accompanying text.

[115] League of Nations Covenant art. 19. *Cf.* Preamble ("The High Contracting Parties, in order to promote international cooperation and to achieve international peace and security . . . by the maintenance of justice and a scrupulous respect for all treaty obligations in the dealings of organized peoples with one another, agree to this Covenant").

[116] *Id.*, art. 19. The French version of this article is slightly different since it raises the possibility that both treaties and international situations may be subject to "nouvel examen," or reconsideration. The provision was subsequently interpreted so that the advice to reconsider treaties

> can only be given . . . when the state of affairs existing at the moment of their conclusion has subsequently undergone, either materially or morally, such radical changes that their application has ceased to be reasonably possible, or in cases of the existence of international conditions whose continuance might endanger the peace of the world.

Report of the Committee of Jurists, 2 League of Nations O.J. 466 (1921) (offered as advice to the League Assembly when Bolivia invoked the clause against Chile). The jurists clearly envisioned consideration of the doctrine of rebus sic stantibus whenever Article 19 was invoked. The emphasis on both "material" and "moral" grounds for treaty termination is also significant.

consideration of whether treaties should be permanent or not.[117] But on that issue, Article 19 clearly established a legalistic, and critical, tenor for commentary on the London Declaration by interwar publicists.

One of the first scholars writing after the war could therefore announce that the London Declaration offered too rigorous and absolute a principle for the law of nations.[118] Pouritch did not, however, confine himself to pointing out the impossibility of enforcing a doctrine that prohibited the modification of treaties, save with the permission of all the parties.[119] He concluded that the whole posture of the powers at the London Conference raised suspicions about the outcome and that the declaration was pure hypocrisy.[120]

With the causes of the last war firmly placed in the minds of those writing after Versailles, any codification of the principle that treaties should be observed would seem laughable and naive. If Pouritch was more oblique in his invective, Ronald Roxburgh's edition of Oppenheim's treatise, published just after the signing of the Peace Treaty, was direct in its criticism. The renunciation of the 1878 Treaty of Berlin by the Austro-Hungarian Empire,[121] and its subsequent annexation of Bosnia and Herzegovina, was unquestionably a critical juncture in the events leading to the general war. "Thus the standard value of the declaration . . . has become doubtful again," Roxburgh wrote, "and must remain doubtful until an independent international court is created with jurisdiction to set aside a treaty obligation which has become too oppressive."[122]

What is presumed here, of course, is that the protocol signed at London was previously declaratory of international law, and that its force waxed or waned with the vicissitudes of state practice.[123] Not only did this presump-

[117] For more on Article 19 of the Covenant, see L. WOOLF, REVISION OF TREATIES AND CHANGES IN INTERNATIONAL LAW (1934); H. HU, TREATY REVISION UNDER ARTICLE 19 OF THE COVENANT (1931); W. SCHNEIDER, DIE VÖLKERRECHTLICHE CLAUSULA REBUS SIC STANTIBUS UND ARTICLE 19 DER VÖLKERBUNDSSATZUNG (1931); M. RADOÏKOVITCH, LA RÉVISION DES TRAITÉS ET LE PACTE DE LA SOCIÉTÉ DES NATIONS 135 (1930) ("the obligation to remain faithful to treaties has its limits"); Fischer Williams, *The Permanence of Treaties,* 22 AJIL 89, 99–102 (1928); A. GOELLNER, L'ARTICLE 19 DU PACTE DE LA SOCIÉTÉ DES NATIONS 10 (1925) (the rule of pacta sunt servanda is tempered and conciliated by the doctrine of rebus sic stantibus); Z. ALINSKI, LES POSSIBILITÉS DE LA RÉVISION DES TRAITÉS D'APRÈS LE PACTE DE LA SOCIÉTÉ DES NATIONS (1924) (all volumes available at the Hague Academy of International Law Library).

[118] *See* B. POURITCH, *supra* note 89, at 80.

[119] *Id.* at 80–81 ("La Conférence a proclamé le principe de l'impossibilité d'une dénonciation unilatérale, un principe contradictoire et incompatible avec ses travaux postérieurs, car, en réalité, elle a reconnu la règle *rebus sic stantibus* et ne s'est occupée que d'en organiser la procédure").

[120] *Id.* at 106.

[121] Ironically, the 1878 Berlin Conference was convened when the straits regime created at London in 1871 disintegrated into the Russo-Turkish War. *See supra* note 79.

[122] 1 L. OPPENHEIM, INTERNATIONAL LAW 693 (R. Roxburgh 3d ed. 1920).

[123] One reason for this was states' insistence on imposing servitudes on other nations. Oppenheim's treatise suggested that these clauses (of which the demilitarization of the Black Sea was certainly one) should also be subject to the rebus sic stantibus doctrine. *Id.* at 371. For a

tion evade the question whether the declaration really reflected custom; it was also a criticism of Covenant Article 19. If states were incapable of upholding the London Declaration's rule, then surely a provision that gave a collection of state representatives (the League Assembly) the right to render international obligations inapplicable was curious indeed. Roxburgh, and others,[124] instead suggested that a judicial tribunal should rule on these matters.

American publicists in the 1920s, by contrast, were reacting to the rejection of the League Covenant by the Senate and tended to discount entirely efforts to establish a normative basis for the alteration of treaty regimes. Charles Fenwick followed both Lawrence and Hall in their characterizations of the declaration[125] but added that nations have a primary right of self-preservation and that the rebus sic stantibus doctrine was intended to promote that right.[126]

Other theorists were simply devious in their interpretations of the London Declaration. L. H. Woolsey, for example, set it up as a sort of straw man. He characterized the declaration as "so-called precedent" for the unilateral termination of treaties.[127] But he then reconsidered, took note of the negotiating history and concluded that all the declaration meant was "that a treaty cannot be annulled by one of the parties without the consent of the other in circumstances which involve no change in the fundamental conditions on which the treaty is based and which show no violation of the treaty by the other party."[128] This obviously skirted the critical issue presented by the London Declaration: whether, even with a change of circumstances, unilateral modification of a treaty is permitted. Woolsey was the first to imply that the declaration, by its very terms, *confirmed,* rather than denied, the use of the rebus sic stantibus ground.

This insight was a major contribution to the parallel, and more immediate, debate on the termination of unequal treaties in international law. Figuring prominently in a cause célèbre before the Permanent Court of International Justice,[129] the problem of unequal treaties was also relevant to defeated Germany and the small neighbors or overseas dependencies of the

---

contemporary treatment of the problem, see S.S. Wimbledon (Fr./Italy/Japan/UK v. Ger.), 1923 PCIJ (ser. A) No. 1 (Judgment of June 28) (legal status of the Kiel Canal under Versailles Treaty).

[124] *See* 1 L. OPPENHEIM, *supra* note 122, at 693; Fischer Williams, *supra* note 117, at 102.

[125] C. FENWICK, INTERNATIONAL LAW 347 (1924).

[126] *Id.* at 345.

[127] Woolsey, *The Unilateral Termination of Treaties,* 20 AJIL 346, 349 (1926).

[128] *Id. See also* 1 P. COBBETT, CASES ON INTERNATIONAL LAW 339–40 (F. Grey 5th ed. 1931) (substantially repeats this passage and adds that this "rule may probably be regarded as the primary rule from which the law of nations on this subject starts").

[129] See Denunciation of the Treaty of November 2nd, 1865, between China and Belgium (Belg. v. China), 1927 PCIJ (ser. A) No. 8 (Order of Jan. 8), where Belgium sought relief from China's announced denunciation of an 1865 peace treaty containing "unequal" extraterritorial provisions. This case was ultimately settled by agreement. It was also the first case of nonappearance before the World Court when China refused to agree to the Court's jurisdiction.

great powers. When termination was looked at from this perspective, international law publicists inevitably focused on the futility of enforcing onerous servitudes imposed by victors over the vanquished. Russia's exclusion from the Black Sea came to be equated with the "spheres of influence" in China and the demilitarization of the Rhineland.[130]

This criticism of regimes that purported to be "perfect and perpetual peaces"[131] could have easily merged with notions of peaceful change, as expressed in the League Covenant. But it did not. Instead, those who wrote between the wars about the problem of unequal treaties generally rejected recourse to an international tribunal, the legal mechanism favored by those who advocated peaceful change.[132] Moreover, the latter publicists were openly contemptuous of the idea that revisions to an onerous peace treaty could be negotiated by those states that had originally imposed it. Such changes, mused the authors of one historical text, even if "undertaken without a war, would have to be bought dearly."[133]

A unique perspective on this issue was offered by John Fischer Williams, Britain's legal representative to the commission enforcing German war reparations. There was a certain irony in his characterizing the neutralization of the Black Sea as appropriate for the application of rebus sic stantibus to overturn an international servitude,[134] while failing to mention the comparable provisions of the Treaty of Versailles on the Rhine and Saar territories.[135] Fischer Williams had only the advantage of hindsight; his sole basis for distinguishing a regime eligible for modification was whether it was vital enough to command support.[136] This reasoning not only was tautological, but also ignored the "struggle" for law in international relations, a process that required nations to engage in unilateral acts to achieve their ends.

Fischer Williams's interpretation of the London Declaration followed his tunnel vision. He suggested that the "legal principle of *rebus sic stantibus* is

[130] Putney, *The Termination of Unequal Treaties,* 21 ASIL PROC. 87, 89 (1927).

[131] G. BUTLER & S. MACCOBY, THE DEVELOPMENT OF INTERNATIONAL LAW 523 (1928).

[132] Putney, *supra* note 130, at 90 (characterizing termination of unequal treaties as neither "a matter of strict legal right" nor one that "can be settled by arbitration or before any world court or The Hague. It is still a question of diplomacy, and, to a large extent, a question of force, as to what a country is able to secure"). The chief proponent of the principle that an international tribunal should rule on claims of rebus sic stantibus was the influential Harvard Research on International Law. *See* Harvard Draft on the Law of Treaties, Art. 28, para. (a), *reprinted in* 29 AJIL Supp. 1096 (1935) [hereinafter Harvard Draft].

[133] G. BUTLER & S. MACCOBY, *supra* note 131, at 524. *See also* P. WILD, JR., SANCTIONS AND TREATY ENFORCEMENT 13 and 16 (1934); H. KRABBE, THE MODERN IDEA OF THE STATE 265–67 (Sabine & Shepard trans. 1930) (rejecting the possibility of negotiated modifications to treaties when "support for a decision between right and wrong" is based on the "unstable foundations of an unorganized legal community").

[134] Fischer Williams, *supra* note 117, at 95.

[135] *See* Treaty of Peace between the Allied and Associated Powers and Germany, June 28, 1919, Arts. 42–50, 1919 Gr. Brit. TS No. 4 (Cmd. 153), 225 Parry's TS 188 [hereinafter Versailles Treaty] (Article 44 provided that "[i]n case Germany violates [the demilitarization of the Rhine] she shall be regarded as committing a hostile act against the powers signatory of the present Treaty and as calculated to disturb the peace of the world").

[136] Fischer Williams, *supra* note 117, at 98 ("In such conditions the Black Sea clauses might be said to be nothing but reminders of a system that was dying or dead").

not affected by the doctrine of the London Conference of 1871; that doctrine remains intact."[137] Rebus sic stantibus, according to this theory, operated of its own force to invalidate a dead or obsolete treaty. "It is not that one party has a right to break an existing tie, but that the tie itself is already broken."[138] Fischer Williams could not, however, answer the objection that if nations were not themselves to invoke the rebus sic stantibus doctrine (and so remain true to the London Declaration), what authority should do so?[139]

This was the last station on this intellectual track. It returns us, not surprisingly, to Article 19 of the Covenant and its defects. Together, Fischer Williams and Woolsey defined the interwar paradox of peaceful change. Woolsey, perhaps unintentionally or even disingenuously, had only half reconciled the conflict between the declaration and the rebus sic stantibus doctrine. Fischer Williams contributed the realization that for this reconciliation to take place, a state had either to deny the "struggle for law" or to surrender its power to challenge a burdensome regime to a supranational authority.

The London Declaration nonetheless received substantial homage during this period. It was repeated verbatim in the first convention on the law of treaties[140] and in the League Council's denunciation of Hitler's remilitarization of the Rhineland in 1935.[141] It was also cited by the World Court in an opinion refusing to apply rebus sic stantibus.[142] This recognition spurred the development of a new interpretive school. It emphasized that the declaration was not inconsistent with the rebus sic stantibus doctrine and that it dictated only the *manner* of modifying the terms of a treaty. The reconciliation offered here was that the declaration spoke only to procedural issues, namely, the propriety of unilateral termination.[143] This view, signifying a third major strand of thought about the declaration, was quickly accepted among writers of international law treatises.[144]

137 *Id.* at 91.

138 *Id.* at 91–92.

139 *Id.* at 102–03; note 124 *supra* and accompanying text.

140 Havana Convention on Treaties, Feb. 20, 1928, Art. 10, Pan-Am. L. & T.S. No. 34, *reprinted in* 4 M. HUDSON, INTERNATIONAL LEGISLATION 2378 (1931) ("No State can relieve itself of the obligations of a treaty or modify its stipulations except by the agreement, secured through peaceful means, of the other contracting parties"). *See also* Harvard Draft, *supra* note 132, at 984.

141 16 LEAGUE OF NATIONS O.J. 546–52, 569–71 (1935) (resolution of Apr. 18, 1935) ("it is an essential principle of the law of nations that no Power can liberate itself from the engagements of a treaty nor modify the stipulations thereof unless with the consent of the contracting parties"; *id.* at 551).

142 See Free Zones of Upper Savoy and the District of Gex (Fr. v. Switz.), 1929 PCIJ (ser. A) No. 22, at 29–30 (Order of Aug. 19) (Negulesco, J., sep. op.), where it was argued that the London Declaration recognized the rebus sic stantibus doctrine but refused a right of unilateral termination. *See also* Oscar Chinn Case (UK v. Belg.), 1934 PCIJ (ser. A/B) No. 63, at 134 (Judgment of Dec. 12) (van Eysinga, sep. op.) (repeating London Declaration in interpreting the 1885 Act of Berlin).

143 See *supra* note 113 and accompanying text, for Lorimer's hint at this theory.

144 *See, e.g.*, T. HUANG, THE DOCTRINE OF REBUS SIC STANTIBUS IN INTERNATIONAL LAW 60 (1935) (available at the Hague Academy of International Law Library); Harvard Draft,

Seemingly ignored was John Stuart Mill's challenge to create a legal ground for reconciling perpetual treaties with peaceful change. It was taken up by only one scholar in this period. Using the common law of contracts as the essential premise of his analysis, Harold Tobin suggested that the London Declaration established a rule prohibiting unilateral termination only for those treaties which dealt with political (rather than technical) matters and which contained stipulations of different rights and duties for the parties.[145] Agreement constituted the necessary consideration to make the treaty binding.[146] Tobin also made the critical distinction between a rule that prevented unilateral denunciation of a treaty, and one that required unanimous consent for change. The London Declaration, he supposed, was evidence only of the first proposition.[147]

This interpretation, although supported by Tobin only with spurious historical evidence,[148] constituted the most lawyerly reading of the declaration. Those publicists that propounded the procedural nuances of the declaration were just finding a convenient shortcut to resolve the paradox presented by the provenance of the London negotiation. As the 1930s wore to a close, however, the cynicism that had prevailed in the writings of international lawyers after the Great War reappeared. The London Declaration did not escape the wrath of those who witnessed Japan's invasion of China, Germany's renunciation of Versailles and Locarno, and that most insidious of moments in contemporary international relations, the appeasement at Munich. One American wrote in 1939, with perfect justness, that the London Declaration could be ignored since states "refuse to recognize themselves as moral persons, or as bound by treaty," and that "the occasion of this very proclamation makes almost a comedy of the principle it enunciates as essential to international law."[149]

Between the wars, therefore, the three most vital interpretations of the London Declaration were fully explicated. The declaration was certainly at times seen as a sham, and more often as expressive of Bismarck's vision of realpolitik than of Broglie's useful legal fiction. The League Covenant's challenge of managing peaceful change produced, in an ironic fashion, a paradox that allowed no reconciliation of unequal treaties or burdensome servitudes with the declaration's express terms. The only way to make this intellectual transit was to characterize the declaration as a mere procedural prescription. But this notion failed to make the necessary distinction be-

---

supra note 132, at 1124; J. HATSCHEK, AN OUTLINE OF INTERNATIONAL LAW 171 (C. Manning trans. 1930); 1 D. ANZILOTTI, COURS DE DROIT INTERNATIONAL 458–59 (G. Gidel trans. 1929).

145 *See* H. TOBIN, THE TERMINATION OF MULTIPARTITE TREATIES 194 (1933).

146 *Id.* at 204.

147 *Id.* at 221.

148 Tobin noted that the negotiators at London proceeded to modify the 1856 Paris Treaty without the approval of some minor states that had signed the earlier document. *Id.* at 220. The author apparently forgot that Italy was the successor state to the previous Kingdom of Sardinia, and that the North German Confederation had succeeded Prussia. Therefore, all the parties to the Paris Treaty participated in the London negotiations.

149 Rodgers, *Future International Laws of War,* 33 AJIL 441, 444 (1939).

tween a rule of unanimity and a bar on unilateral action. And without this distinction, the paradox of peaceful change was never resolved.

Modern Views

Postwar theorists have added little to this interpretive landscape, except for new rhetorical plantings. Peaceful change, for example, was transformed by the United Nations Charter into the more neutral, and less controversial, idea of the "peaceful adjustment" of disputes.[150] The London Declaration, consequently, was pressed into service as evidence of this very abstract duty of states.[151] Under the circumstances, few writers had to resort to criticism of the declaration as a legal sham or diplomatic pretense since it had ceased to be cited as support for a relevant rule of international relations.[152]

If the declaration was neutralized in the process of being co-opted as a "general principle of law,"[153] it was also given virtually no recognition in the codification of the law of treaties.[154] This was so despite the fact that the 1969 Vienna Convention on the Law of Treaties[155] partially answered John Stuart Mill's call for a legal ground to distinguish those treaties that could be renounced under the rebus sic stantibus doctrine.[156]

Only the procedural nuances of the declaration were subject to further inquiry after the Second World War. One group of scholars rather self-

[150] *See* UN CHARTER art. 14.

[151] *See* A. ROSS, A TEXTBOOK OF INTERNATIONAL LAW 221–22 (1947); *cf.* J. BRIERLY, LAW OF NATIONS 207–08 (2d ed. 1936) (noting that Covenant Article 19 was an improvement on the declaration).

[152] *But see* Poch de Caviedes, *De la Clause «rebus sic stantibus» à la clause de révision dans les conventions internationales,* 118 RECUEIL DES COURS 105, 181 (1966 II) (who makes this argument). Another way that scholars reconciled rebus sic stantibus with pacta sunt servanda was to claim that both were positive-law doctrines and that the former could be legally narrowed in definition. *See* Kunz, *The Meaning and Range of the Norm Pacta Sunt Servanda,* 39 AJIL 180, 190 (1945). This approach was hinted at in the Harvard Draft, *supra* note 132, at 991–92.

[153] Arguably the weakest of the primary sources of international law. ICJ Statute, *supra* note 55, Art. 38, para. 1(c). *See also* B. CHENG, GENERAL PRINCIPLES OF LAW APPLIED BY INTERNATIONAL COURTS AND TRIBUNALS 113, 118–19 (1953) (arguing that rebus sic stantibus is only applicable in cases where a treaty is interpreted beyond the bounds of what the parties had originally intended).

[154] The declaration was not mentioned once in what was the most comprehensive analysis of the law concerning the termination of treaties, conducted by the Institute of International Law. *See* 49 ANNUAIRE DE L'INSTITUT DE DROIT INTERNATIONAL 1–297 (1961).

[155] *See* Vienna Convention on the Law of Treaties, *opened for signature* May 23, 1969, Art. 62, UNTS Regis. No. 18,232, UN Doc. A/CONF.39/27 (1969), *reprinted in* 8 ILM 679 (1969) [hereinafter Vienna Convention]. For a summary of the negotiating history of Article 62, see S. ROSENNE, THE LAW OF TREATIES 324–27 (1970).

[156] The Vienna Convention provides that rebus sic stantibus cannot be invoked as a ground for termination unless the change in circumstances complained of (1) was an essential basis of consent by the parties (a condition suggested by Tobin, *supra* note 146); (2) was not foreseen at the time of negotiation; (3) radically transforms the obligations of the parties (likewise a concern of Tobin, *supra* note 145); (4) was not a result of breach by the complaining state; and (5) does not affect the establishment of a boundary. Vienna Convention, *supra* note 155, Art. 62.

consciously followed Tobin's lead in identifying the dangers of interpreting the declaration to mean that all parties had to agree to the revision of a treaty.[157] One of these writers, like Tobin, premised his criticism on a misreading of the declaration and its negotiating history.[158]

Another scholar, Haraszti, also failed to explain why the declaration should be regarded merely as a ban on unilateral action.[159] But his is still the most honest rendering of a "limited" reading since he admitted that while "the conference emphasized the need of an amicable agreement, it was silent on the question what should happen if there was no chance for such an agreement."[160] Emphasis on that part of the declaration requiring amicable agreement is a peculiarly modern, post-Charter development.[161] Haraszti's ideas, which mirrored a socialist view of international law, are preferable to the often naive confidence of Western writers in the Charter principle of "peaceful settlement of disputes."[162] The latest interpretive vision of the declaration likewise questions this optimism.

IV. The Postmodern Critical Attack and a Primitivist Response

Interpretations of the London Declaration written after the United Nations Charter essentially repeated the interwar scholarship, with special emphasis on solving the paradox of pacta sunt servanda and rebus sic stantibus with procedural geometry. The duty to observe international obligations became a duty to negotiate in good faith. The affirmative mandate of "peaceful change," of modifying obsolescent or dangerous duties, was transformed into the modest and more realistic notion that states should behave properly in their international relations. The United Nations Charter became that most "perfect of peaces." Since aggression was outlawed, it was assumed that all change would be peaceful. This retreat from principle undoubtedly gave rise to the critical jurisprudence in international law.

[157] *See* E. Hoyt, *supra* note 97, at 7; B. Sinha, *supra* note 81, at 79–81.

[158] B. Sinha, *supra* note 81, at 81 (where the declaration is interpreted as applicable only to a situation where there is a material breach of treaty terms).

[159] *See* G. Haraszti, *supra* note 89, at 336–37. This argument is substantially repeated in Haraszti, *supra* note 33, at 16–19.

[160] G. Haraszti, *supra* note 89, at 337.

[161] Cf. E. Kaufmann, Das Wesen des Völkerrechts und die Clausula rebus sic stantibus (1911), where the most extreme version of the rebus sic stantibus doctrine was expressed. Kaufmann rejected the idea that an amicable overture is required before unilateral termination. *Id.* at 221.

[162] *See* van Bogaert, *Le Sens de la clause «rebus sic stantibus» dans le droit des gens actual,* 70 Revue Générale de Droit International Public 49, 59 (1966) (an isolated modern instance where the declaration was fully endorsed). Jan Verzijl's answer to Haraszti's inquiry, about what the declaration did *not* resolve, is also indicative of Western optimism. He suggested that questions of the application of rebus sic stantibus should be referred to an "impartial tribunal on the basis of the law in force." *See* 6 J. Verzijl, *supra* note 4, at 359. *See also supra* notes 132–33 and accompanying text.

While the literature produced by the critical legal studies movement is now burgeoning,[163] those members of the school who have focused on international law have only offered sparse commentary. But what has been produced readily defines the contours of the critical attack on international law, both as a set of doctrines and as a discipline.[164] The risks in simplifying the critical jurisprudence are great since it is extraordinarily dependent on philosophical and literary tools of interpretation for its vitality and cogency.[165] The critical attack on international law is as much doctrinal (noting the fallacies in essential principles) as it is structural (attacking the manner of discourse in the discipline).

Critical jurists have identified three contradictions in the conception of international law. They are progressively more concrete. The first is structural, the apparent lack of connectedness and relevance among the theory, doctrine and practice of international law.[166] The second contradiction is rhetorical. It stems from the observation that international law discourse suffers from binary arguments of a transformational character.[167] The critics suggest that something must be wrong if every argument based on international law principles can be "flipped" to express the opposite normative or prescriptive opinion.

What is wrong, of course, is the substance of the third, and final, doctrinal paradox. This contradiction causes the other two and is the insight of the critical jurisprudence that merits response here.[168] It is none other than the

[163] *See, e.g.*, THE POLITICS OF LAW (D. Kairys ed. 1982); Peller, *The Metaphysics of American Law*, 73 CAL. L. REV. 1151 (1985); Duncan Kennedy, *The Structure of Blackstone's Commentaries*, 28 BUFFALO L. REV. 205 (1979).

[164] The best exponent of this school is David Kennedy. His views in *Theses about International Law Discourse*, 23 GER. Y.B. INT'L L. 353 (1980) [hereinafter Kennedy, *Theses*], form the essential basis for this author's characterization of the critical international law jurisprudence. See also his latest contribution, *The Sources of International Law*, 2 AM. U.J. INT'L L. & POL'Y 1 (1987) [hereinafter Kennedy, *Sources*]. For other critical approaches to international law, see A. CARTY, THE DECAY OF INTERNATIONAL LAW? A REAPPRAISAL OF THE LIMITS OF LEGAL IMAGINATION IN INTERNATIONAL AFFAIRS (1986) (with significant doctrinal reservations); J. Boyle, *Ideals and Things: International Legal Scholarship and the Prison-house of Language*, 26 HARV. INT'L L.J. 327 (1985); Note, *Applying the Critical Jurisprudence of International Law to the Case Concerning Military and Paramilitary Activities in and against Nicaragua*, 71 VA. L. REV. 1183 (1985) [hereinafter Virginia Note].

[165] *See, e.g.*, R. DEGEORGE & F. DEGEORGE, THE STRUCTURALISTS: FROM MARX TO LEVI-STRAUSS (1972): Gabel, *Intention and Structure in Contractual Conditions: Outline of a Method for Critical Legal Theory*, 61 MINN. L. REV. 601 (1977).

[166] *See* Kennedy, *Theses, supra* note 164, at 359–60.

[167] *Id.* at 364–67. "Binary argument" means that the responses to an inquiry reduce to two (apparently) mutually incompatible ideas. *Id.* "Transformation" means that an idea can stand for its opposite when viewed at either a more abstract or a more concrete level. It also means that the contradictory ideas can themselves cease to be in conflict. For examples of transformation, see Virginia Note, *supra* note 164, at 1188–90.

[168] Ignoring the other two contradictions opens the analysis below to the criticism that it, too, suffers from the defect of binary/transformative argument. Without undertaking a full rhetorical assessment of this phenomenon, one can still say that it applies to *all* modes of intellectual discourse, not just law. Skillful rhetoricians, which the critical jurists certainly are, can always "flip" an argument. *See also* Kratochwil, *Is International Law "Proper" Law?*, 69 ARCHIV FÜR RECHTS- UND SOZIAL PHILOSOPHIE 13 (1983).

collision between sovereign authority and sovereign equality: all nations are supreme within their own spheres but stand together as equals.[169] Autonomy conflicts with cooperation, independence with interdependence, separation with sharing. Obviously, this observation is not novel, and those that advance it do not pretend it is.[170]

It is also no accident that this criticism finds its doctrinal fulfillment in the paradox of pacta sunt servanda and rebus sic stantibus. Yet, strangely enough, the critical scholars have yet to use this as the centerpiece of any attack on an international legal order that countenances both the solemnity of obligation and the necessity of change. That this has gone unnoticed in their literature[171] is particularly surprising, given the critical imperative to deconstruct a positivist basis for international law norms.[172]

[169] *See* Kennedy, *Theses, supra* note 164, at 368–72. The critics' terminology for this tension in sovereignty has shifted. In a more recent article, Kennedy referred to it as the paradox of "normative autonomy" and "normative authority." Kennedy, *Sources, supra* note 164, at 23.

[170] This is implicit in David Kennedy's article, *Primitive Legal Scholarship,* 27 HARV. INT'L L.J. 1, 7–10 (1986).

[171] *But see* Kennedy, *Theses, supra* note 164, at 373 n.23, where he observes that

> reciprocity will not tell a state whether it prefers a world in which states respect treaties or in which they do not. . . . Either strictness or mercy may be reciprocal. At this point one is returned to a decision to follow or break the treaty. . . . [T]reaty breaking is associated with national autonomy, and following [a treaty] with international solidarity. But the reverse may as well be true. To release a state from a harsh treaty may be an expression of merciful community solidarity, while to hold a state to such a treaty may be an expression of national autonomy.

Kennedy emphasizes here the notion of "reciprocity" in state relations, and leaves unaddressed the paradox of rebus sic stantibus.

Kennedy does, however, treat this issue in a later article. *See* Kennedy, *Sources, supra* note 164, at 57–70. His emphasis there is on characterizing rebus sic stantibus as containing elements of both "hard" and "soft" rhetorics for discourse on sources of international law. Kennedy is particularly interested in what he identifies as the two faces of the rebus sic stantibus doctrine: one consensual (the *clausula* impliedly inserted in all international agreements), and the other premised on justice (relieving the hardship imposed by obligations). *Id.* at 57–61. Nevertheless, in his treatment of rebus sic stantibus, Kennedy does not really attack what are arguably the inherent contradictions between it and the principle of pacta sunt servanda.

This problem was discussed earlier in one piece of proto-critical literature. *See* 2 A. OSTROWER, LANGUAGE, LAW, AND DIPLOMACY 794–98 (1965) (noting that the "peaceful" in "peaceful change" was a misnomer because of the rebus sic stantibus doctrine).

Anthony Carty (*supra* note 164) deals directly with the London Declaration and the problem of rebus sic stantibus in international law theory. But one can legitimately wonder if he is a member of the critical school. His methodology approximates the critical rhetoric, but he concludes that international relations are in a "state of nature," and that international law remains natural law, a result that associates him with the realist branch of the discipline. *See infra* note 190.

[172] The critical jurists apparently accept the supremacy of positive over natural law. *See* Virginia Note, *supra* note 164, at 1190. But then Kennedy contends that positive law is an empty vessel. *See* his *Theses, supra* note 164, at 383–84. Treaties, of course, are the ultimate source of positive law in international relations. *See* ICJ Statute, *supra* note 55, Art. 38, para. 1(a).

The critics' view of the hierarchy of sources in international law is fully explicated in Kennedy, *Sources, supra* note 164, at 17–20, where he notes that

> some hierarchy seems to need to be established in order to develop an internally coherent and sufficiently independent scheme of authority. Otherwise, the scheme might produce

Sketching the critical interpretation of the rebus sic stantibus doctrine and, by implication, the London Declaration begins with this imperative. The intellectual history of the declaration reveals a tension between those positivists who view law as "separate and critical" of state behavior and those who see it as "grounded in and fused with" international custom.[173] The first group sees the rule of law as actually ordering state behavior. They believe that the demands of nationhood inevitably require states to respect rules of conduct. Let us call them functionalists. The second school of thought cannot allow the state to separate its practice from its principles. The only true content to international law, realists would argue, is state practice.

Each of these theories, however, carries a fatal defect. If law is separate from the life of the nation-state system, then the problem of "normative source" arises: "it is impossible either to determine the applicability of a given legal norm to a factual situation or to distinguish a permissive legal rule from a mere gap in the legal system."[174] Thus, the critic rebuts functionalism by asking, "How do we know that a rule of international law reflects a norm of state behavior?" The emphasis here is on the "how"; consequently, the critics call this problem "normative source." The critic questions the sources of international law and suggests that they cannot produce rules that can be applied to actual state behavior or, even worse, that when they are applied, they can be dismissed as "optional," as not really being rules at all.

If the critics spend most of their energies attacking functionalist theory, it is because realist thought seems to succumb so quickly. Viewing law as in identity with state behavior simply deprives rules of what the critics call "normative legitimacy." Here the line of inquiry is neatly switched. The critic can ask, "Why should we believe this norm of state behavior is really a rule of international law?" This question demands an answer framed in terms of right and sanction, of "legitimacy." The realist cannot answer since any departure "from a currently recognized norm . . . may . . . indicate a shifting consensus toward a new behavioral norm."[175] Because of this fluidity, realists have no principled way to answer the critics' question. They might as well, and often do, respond that "rules are rules."

> equally authoritative norms among which one would then be obliged to choose on the basis of their content. . . .
>
> The sense that hierarchy needs explaining, like the sense that the abstract boundaries of enumerated sources need elaboration, reveals the shared sense that sources discourse is meant to delimit abstractly and authoritatively the norms which bind states in such a way that they might remain free to establish and disagree about the content of these norms as their interests or a natural order might dictate.

Id. at 18–20 (citations omitted).

[173] *See* Kennedy, *Theses, supra* note 164, at 383.

[174] *See* Virginia Note, *supra* note 164, at 1191. The critics call this an "objective" view of positive international law.

[175] *Id.* This is the "subjective" position for positive international law.

The events leading to the negotiations at London captured both realist and functionalist tendencies. Russia's selective renunciation of the peace of 1856 was a challenge to the established diplomatic order.[176] It represented a departure from the norms of state behavior, an episode in the ongoing "struggle for law." Alternatively, the denunciation of the Black Sea clauses could have indicated a shifting consensus to a new order that rejected international servitudes and accepted changes in circumstances as an important element in the equation to preserve peace. The great powers' response to Russia's unilateral action also reflected uncertainty about the legitimacy and sensibility of the old international regime.[177] But the lesson of the London Conference was that the diplomatic order could quickly right itself. The new straits regime adopted at London created a new order, albeit temporarily.[178] The declaration could have enunciated either the old rule of the Concert system or a new regime for interstate relations.

This last inquiry has been treated, with varying degrees of sensitivity, by the scholars who have written about the declaration and its underlying doctrinal significance. Observers who considered the declaration a sham, most notably the Frenchman Broglie and Chancellor Bismarck,[179] must have believed that international law had no identity beyond that conferred on it by the nation-state system. Bismarck's conception was, once again, pure realpolitik. The state was supreme; it could not be judged, nor would it judge.[180] Broglie had anticipated the arguments of Hall and Lorimer in the generation before the Great War.[181] They, like the critics of today, wanted to place their confidence in international law but could not. In their time there were too few legal norms; today there are too many.[182]

In contrast, those that followed the admonition of John Stuart Mill and sought a legal or moral basis to distinguish "worthy" from "unworthy" treaties were doing nothing more than searching for international law norms separate and distinct from state practice. This typically functionalist project had two faces. The first was developed by those who had witnessed the origins of World War I and knew that the nation-state system was atavistic. It could not manage change peaceably. The London Declaration, as a result, was misguidedly cited as favoring an objective rule of rebus sic

[176] *See supra* notes 26–45 and accompanying text. *See also* A. CARTY, *supra* note 164, at 72–73.

[177] Great Britain, Austria and France could have triggered the provisions of the Tripartite Covenant, *supra* note 20. *See generally supra* notes 46–63 and accompanying text. *See also* A. DAVID, *supra* note 19, at 28 ("The Declaration of London also marked the beginning of a new era in which legitimacy and controlling power concerning the termination of international agreements became divorced from one another").

[178] *See supra* notes 64–77 and accompanying text.

[179] *See supra* notes 93–103 and accompanying text.

[180] *See supra* note 102. This also describes the primitivist position; see below.

[181] *See supra* notes 104–13 and accompanying text.

[182] *See* Dinstein, *International Law as a Primitive Legal System,* 19 N.Y.U. J. INT'L L. & POL. 1, 7–8 (1986) (for the observation that international law norms have proliferated in recent years); Boyle, *supra* note 164, at 339. The susceptibility of international law to novel, and destructive, norms was also noted by Jan Verzijl, text at note 5 *supra.*

stantibus.[183] But far from assisting in the process of peaceful change, the rebus sic stantibus doctrine was used to deny unilateral actions of states by requiring recourse to some supranational authority or tribunal. This attempt to make international law independent of the nation-state system completely failed to prevent the next general war.[184] Functionalism was unworkable in the interwar period not for lack of organization or will but, rather, because of a defect in conception. Peaceful change, the centerpiece of this "perpetual peace," had plainly failed as a theory. It was later emptied of all meaning.

The second aspect of the functionalist project to reconcile rebus sic stantibus with pacta sunt servanda met with happier results. Initiated by Tobin,[185] and completed in the Vienna Convention,[186] a legal ground was found to permit the operation of changed circumstances on treaties. But a critic will argue that any attempt to codify treaty law in this way would be objectionable to both realists and functionalists. It is untenable in precisely the same way that the procedural interpretations of the London Declaration during the interwar period were misleading and contradictory.[187] Modern critical scholars, therefore, are now contributing to a debate that was seemingly adjourned 50 years ago.

Indeed, the parallelism between the critics' argument and the Williams-Tobin dialogue is apparent. Both start with the major premise that the declaration can stand for a rule proscribing unilateral modification of treaties *and* for a rule requiring unanimous consent. The interwar publicists wrote that something was wrong if both of these interpretations could be espoused. Although they identified this paradox, they failed to reconcile it. Some leaned toward a functionalist solution, that a supranational authority would decide proposed treaty revisions, while others leaned toward the realist view that rebus sic stantibus had to be granted full doctrinal force.

The critics contend that these answers are all wrong. Both functionalist and realist theories of this essential element of positive law run afoul of their individual contradictions. How can the functionalist goal, of law liberated from state behavior, be achieved if the positive law of treaties demands that all parties to a convention agree to its termination or modification? One nation can always be the spoiler if there is a rule of unanimous consent. Earlier writers, including Lorimer and Lawrence, warned about this veto phenomenon and the critics have taken up their concerns. The interwar experience with aggressive totalitarian regimes only confirmed that nations seeking to upset the rule of law could exploit the "normative source" problem. The postwar response, of a sanctioned great-power veto in the United

[183] *See supra* notes 127–28 and 134–39 and accompanying text.

[184] One commentator said that as a result of these interpretations of the London Declaration, "[t]he rules were perceived as static, while flexibility, adjustment, and change were regarded as political questions. Not only did they not take notice of the problems of peaceful change in the relevant social framework, but they also totally ignored the dynamic aspect of conflict situations . . . ." A. David, *supra* note 19, at 28–29.

[185] *See supra* notes 145–47 and accompanying text.

[186] *See supra* notes 155–56 and accompanying text.

[187] *See supra* notes 143 and 144 and accompanying text.

Nations Security Council, represented only an admission of the problem by functionalists, not a solution.

Even when the declaration is more modestly interpreted as a ban on unilateral modification of treaties, it is wholly inconsistent with the realist position. How can that ideal, of law in identity with state practice, be countenanced if the will of one nation is denied? When one nation seeks treaty revision and is refused by its negotiating partners, we have the problem of normative legitimacy. Who grants the right to seek or deny change in the international order? In theory, it should not matter whether the change being sought is progressive or reactionary, important or trivial. Nevertheless, these are critical factors for the realist. The negotiating history of the London Treaty in 1871 demonstrates the application of these factors and the formation of a paradigmatically realist resolution to a crisis over treaty revision. But the new straits regime did not solve the Eastern Question at all. It invited, and incurred, diplomatic disaster.

The critical jurists can therefore suggest that neither the realist nor the functionalist condition can be fulfilled. And, they might add, if neither positivist ambition can be achieved with the most positive of sources of international law (actual agreements between states), the balance of international law (which is premised on "custom" and "general principles") cannot be seriously entertained.

That outline of the critical jurisprudence on the London Declaration includes its contribution to both the doctrinal confusion surrounding rebus sic stantibus and the peculiar scholarly debate it sparked. Defining the character of a response begins by identifying the unstated assumptions of the critics' conclusion that the essential contradiction in international law is sovereignty. Two illusions are apparent. The first is that there is just one axial opposition in international law discourse.[188] The second is that the struggle for law in the nation-state system is entirely adversarial.[189]

Identification with these two proposed fallacies of the critical jurisprudence results in a particular theoretical division of the discipline.[190] Both

[188] Onuf, *Do Rules Say What They Do? From Ordinary Language to International Law,* 26 Harv. Int'l L.J. 385, 392 (1986) ("A number of opposed, very general principles structure international legal discourse and not all of them derive from the opposition of sovereignty and cooperation").

[189] *Id.*

[190] Here is a schematic representation of these oppositions:

		Sovereignty is the only relevant issue: *agree*	*disagree*
Nations can cooperate	*agree*	PRIMITIVIST	FUNCTIONALIST
	disagree	CRITIC	REALIST

The critical view has been explicated above. The functionalist and realist schools, of course, enjoy the greatest currency today and the scholarly debate has proceeded on the assumption that sovereignty can be overcome in international relations. The functionalist and realist disagree strongly, however, over whether this is a desirable development.

functionalists and realists disagree with the critics' proposition that sovereignty is the sole organizing principle among nations. Even the most extreme debate between these schools' surrogates, antilegalism and world peace through law, assumes that there are other such organizing principles. The functionalist believes that human necessity can overcome the parochialism of states. The realist knows that only power matters. A response to the critical jurisprudence that accepts the first illusion (that only sovereignty matters) but rejects the second (that nations can never cooperate) may rightly be called "primitivist."

This designation signals a return to the study of metaphysics in the law of nations, particularly those first principles which make no distinction between legal and moral authority.[191] This study, a retrospective on classical "individualistic" international law,[192] reveals a doctrinal universe that is quite a bit more cogent and congenial than that viewed by the critical legal studies movement. Sovereignty may indeed be the enduring paradox of the nation-state system, but it need not impair the development of legal norms.

The primitivist accepts the state as the controlling instrument in relations among the largest human aggregations. It has earned this status not only because of an extraordinary legal fiction,[193] but also through recognition by its ostensible competitor, international organizations.[194] In addition, the nation-state is mandated by the highest sanction that people respect. This "higher mandate" can be defined in a variety of ways. It can be sociobiological: the human need to form into meaningful relationships and communities for protection, love and support. It may also be divine. In the parable of the Tower of Babel, after all, the verdict of the Lord remade the City of

[191] The best description of the style and doctrinal views of the primitive international legal scholars (those writing before 1648) is by David Kennedy, *supra* note 170, at 5–10. "Primitivist," as used in this article, means an approach to the first principles of international law that emphasizes the unity of natural and positive sources in law and morality. In a later article, Kennedy noted that publicists writing before 1648 tended not to "establish a hierarchy among sources, but suggested that norms from each [category] might, depending upon their content, overrule those of another." Kennedy, *Sources, supra* note 164, at 90. This observation applies to how primitivists view not only the sources of international law, but also its doctrinal contents. This approach produces, in turn, "source discourse," which Kennedy disparagingly describes as "simply catalogu[ing] norms which comport[] with sovereign will." *Id.*

[192] M. SHAW, INTERNATIONAL LAW 17–25 (2d ed. 1986). The relevance of this sort of review has been consistently questioned. In E. YAMBRUSIC, TREATY INTERPRETATION (1987), no less than ten fundamental changes have been noted between today's world order and that of the Peace of Westphalia. *Id.* at 2. But one can question whether some of these are real changes. Seventeenth-century international relations were, like today's, polycentric, profuse and ideologically divergent (with the impact of the Enlightenment), featuring different levels of "human development" (a comparison of British and Russian cultures should suffice) and limitations on sovereignty.

[193] Dinstein, *supra* note 182, at 25 (for a discussion of the use of this legal fiction in international law).

[194] *See* UN CHARTER, Preamble ("We the Peoples of the United Nations"); LEAGUE OF NATIONS COVENANT, Preamble (recognizing that observance of treaty obligations is essential to "the dealings of organized peoples with one another").

God into the nations of men.[195] This "cult of sovereignty,"[196] far from being a "mockery" of the "deepest aspirations of humanity,"[197] is seen by the primitivist as the most successful way to manage violence.[198]

The primitivist further believes that international law is incapable of distinguishing between positive and natural sources for its doctrines. This is illustrated by the "problem" of rebus sic stantibus and pacta sunt servanda. While the critical scholar would argue that the paradox they present reflects the essential contradictions in international law, the primitivist does not see it as an issue at all. In contending that pacta sunt servanda is a natural-law principle par excellence,[199] the critics actually seek to discredit it in comparison with the more virile and robust positive-law basis for rebus sic stantibus. This, as noted above,[200] is an essential part of the critical jurisprudential mission.

Though a first principle of "classical" international law, pacta sunt servanda is not natural law. The duty to execute international obligations in good faith necessitates a positive-law source for the norm to be enforced.[201] Moreover, although this positive-law norm is "an original, unique, and juridically undemonstrable hypothesis,"[202] the realization that states must *consent* in order to be bound does not need elaborate proof.[203]

[195] *Genesis* 11:1–9.

[196] Paul Ramsey, one of the leading Christian ethicists, discusses this phenomenon. See his book of essays, THE JUST WAR 9, 178–79 (1968). Although Ramsey's endorsement of the nation-state system is qualified by the notion of justness (both in war and in peace), this does not detract from his view that the state is the institution that must be controlled so that individual aggression can be channeled. *Id.* at 419, 499.

[197] C. JENKS, LAW IN THE WORLD COMMUNITY 32, 34 (1967).

[198] One example unifies primitivist and modern visions of state supremacy: they agree that the state is the only human authority that can wage war. *See* 2 T. AQUINAS, SUMMA THEOLOGICA 578 (O. Sullivan rev. ed. 1952) ("just war" demands state action); UN CHARTER, Preamble, arts. 1, 2 (nations are charged with preventing aggressive wars contrary to the Charter). *See also* Mushkat, *Who Can Wage War? An Examination of an Old / New Question,* 2 AM. U.J. INT'L L. & POL'Y 97, 98–101, 104–07 (1987).

[199] *See* Kennedy, *Sources, supra* note 164, at 42–43; Boyle, *supra* note 164, at 337. This is not a new idea. *See* Harvard Draft, *supra* note 132, at 989 (citing Paradier-Fodéré and Redslob).

[200] *See supra* note 172 and accompanying text.

[201] *See, e.g.,* 1 D. ANZILOTTI, *supra* note 144, at 42–44.

[202] Kelsen, *Les Rapports de Système entre le droit interne et le droit international public,* 14 RECUEIL DES COURS 227, 302 (1926 IV).

[203] This assertion has two faces. "Auto-limitation" means that treaties are only binding because states wish to be bound. This is analogous to free-will theories in municipal contract law. *See* Harvard Draft, *supra* note 132, at 987, 988; A. CARTY, *supra* note 164, at 71–72 (relying on Vattel for this affirmation of pacta sunt servanda); notes 21–25 *supra* and accompanying text.

The second face of this assertion bears on the issue of interpretation of agreements. Some scholars suggest that "[w]hen a treaty imposes obligations but does not provide any authoritative means for interpreting them, it is understood that the parties to the treaty will have the power to interpret their obligations for themselves." J. ELKIND, NON-APPEARANCE BEFORE THE INTERNATIONAL COURT OF JUSTICE 118 (1984). This is a much milder proposition than the primitivist would assert. This exception does not even reach the issue of termination of treaty obligations. For more on this "auto-interpretation" theory, see Watson, *Autointerpreta-*

The rebus sic stantibus doctrine has similarly defied this natural/positive-law typology. It began as a political theory.[204] The rule changed to a positive-law notion based first on the implicit *clausula* attached to all agreements,[205] and then on the rubric of peaceful change.[206] This last transformation was particularly significant. "Peaceful change" envisioned a positive-law mechanism (the action of the League Assembly) to deny a positive-law right (the sanctity of treaties). Peace was placed as the supreme goal. The rule of law, arguably the first principle of positive law, was rejected to that extent. Today, the rebus sic stantibus doctrine allows states the freedom, within substantial definitional limits,[207] to alter or cancel treaty obligations.

Throughout its doctrinal life, rebus sic stantibus has been offered as both a vehicle for, and a brake on, change in the international order. The intellectual history of the London Declaration indicates the persistence of both tendencies. Whenever the doctrine was later invoked in state practice,[208] the pattern of démarche, denunciation and negotiation seen at London in 1871 was repeated. The doctrine could mask aggression, redress inequality, heighten international tensions or serve justice. The critics' fundamental contradiction of sovereignty has not led, in this paradigmatic case, to the inevitable ruin of international life.

Even though the rebus sic stantibus doctrine is not susceptible to the deconstruction the critics suggest, it is reminiscent of one absurdity in international law theory. This is the general principle, seemingly entrenched in the law of nations, that a state may not be a judge of its own cause.[209] Were this a mere rule of procedure for international tribunals, the primitivist writer might argue that the supremacy of the state is not compromised by an agreement to arbitrate. But the principle has been applied to substantive situations, many of which involve the settlement of disputes arising from rights and duties created by treaties.[210]

---

tion, Competence, and the Continuing Validity of Article 2(7) of the Charter, 71 AJIL 60 (1977); H. LAUTERPACHT, THE FUNCTION OF LAW IN THE INTERNATIONAL COMMUNITY 3 (1933).

[204] *See supra* notes 21–23 and accompanying text.

[205] *See supra* note 24.

[206] *See supra* notes 115–48 and accompanying text.

[207] *See* Vienna Convention, *supra* note 155, Art. 62.

[208] *See* A. VAMVOUKOS, *supra* note 24, at 72–127.

[209] *See* B. CHENG, *supra* note 153, at 279–89; 1 J. B. SCOTT, ACTS AND DOCUMENTS, SECOND INTERNATIONAL PEACE CONFERENCE 367 (1907) ("It is a universally accepted doctrine that no one can be a judge in his own cause and all systems of law adopt it"). *See also supra* notes 54 and 55 and accompanying text.

[210] *See* UN CHARTER art. 27, para. 3 (compelling Security Council members party to a dispute to abstain in certain instances); South-West Africa—Voting Procedure, 1955 ICJ REP. 67, 90, 98–99 (Advisory Opinion of June 7) (Lauterpacht, J., sep. op.) (suggesting that it was a principle of wide general application, not confined to strictly judicial proceedings); Article 3, paragraph 2 of the Treaty of Lausanne (Frontier between Turkey and Iraq), 1925 PCIJ (ser. B) No. 12, at 32 (Advisory Opinion of Nov. 21) (ruling that states in the League Council should abstain from voting in disputes between themselves); B. CHENG, *supra* note 153, at 279 n.4

Nemo debet esse judex in propria causa has permeated international law discourse, which is inevitable since it implicates the self-judgment of states, and rebus sic stantibus is the ultimate form of self-judgment. Pacta sunt servanda is not the real counterbalance of rebus sic stantibus. The two can truly be reconciled by definitionally narrowing either the one or the other to the extent that all contradiction is removed, as is doctrinally the case today. But the notion of non-self-judgment cannot be trivialized in this fashion; and, as a consequence, it is potentially destructive of international order. It fundamentally contradicts the primitivist credo that states are supreme within their spheres and that their capacity for self-judgment cannot be usurped or delegated.

Non-self-judgment also constituted the unspoken and underlying assumption of the entire debate on the London Declaration. Lord Granville, it may be recalled,[211] summoned only this one legal ground for his critique of Prince Gorchakov's circular. Arguments admitting the existence of rebus sic stantibus, but denying its factual or doctrinal applicability to Russia's denunciation, were subordinated to the categorical assertion that a state may not judge its own continued participation in a treaty regime in the face of new circumstances. Perhaps the simple diction of the London Declaration had more meaning than its diplomatic context alone conveyed. The rhetorical emphasis is on freedom of action: a state may not "*liberate* itself from the *engagements* of a Treaty, nor modify the *stipulations* thereof."[212]

Lord Granville's hand is evident here,[213] for the construction of the passage was intended to constrain that capacity of sovereignty for self-judgment. It was the last strain of the Concert of Europe, the finale of the former law of nations. Baron Brunnow's ironic aside on the permanence of treaties set the tenor for the new international legal order. To those jurists and publicists that contributed to the intellectual history charted in this article, people who actually experienced Sarajevo and Munich, Versailles and Yalta, London in 1871 must have seemed a moment of apparent, but deceptive, sanity. No wonder they resented it. No wonder that, as a diplomatic exercise, the London Declaration was destined to be irrelevant.

Nevertheless, as an episode in legal imagination in international affairs,[214] it was perhaps unsurpassed in richness and texture, influence and importance. It was a moment that has since troubled the functionalists in their attempts to reconcile the "science" of international law with the reality of state practice. The declaration has likewise upset the realists' vision of power politics, for it was an apparent renunciation of that which the nation-state

---

(citing three arbitrations, involving state termination of commercial contracts, where the non-self-judgment principle was applied).

211 *See supra* notes 53–55 and accompanying text.

212 London Declaration, *supra* note 3 (emphasis added).

213 *Cf. supra* notes 87–92 and accompanying text.

214 This phrase is borrowed from A. CARTY, *supra* note 164, at 1–2, 131. *See also* David Kennedy, Book Review, 81 AJIL 451 (1987) (for another opinion of Carty's contribution).

valued most. Far from confusing the critical jurists, this process of thought has apparently conformed with their prophecy of the intellectual bankruptcy of international law.

Only the primitivists applaud. Only they unconditionally accept the durability of the nation-state system. State authority could not have been willed away by the delegates at London in 1871; nor can it today be discredited by those who seek answers to the essential character of interstate relations outside the orbit of sovereignty. The state's position in the universe of international law is still pre-Copernican. It continues to revolve around itself. And so it is no surprise that the "science" of international law has little advanced since its first principles were "discovered" some three and a half centuries ago. We may have abandoned the rhetoric of the law of nations but, like the physical realities of gravity and motion, we cannot escape it.

AGORA: MCDOUGAL-LASSWELL REDUX

THE MCDOUGAL-LASSWELL PROPOSAL TO BUILD A WORLD PUBLIC ORDER

The January 1959 issue of this *Journal* carried the famous proposal by Myres S. McDougal and Harold D. Lasswell to build a world public order based on human dignity that would save the world from nuclear Armageddon and protect democratic values.[1] The authors expressed the belief that the democratic countries were responding ineffectively to Marxist-Leninist expansionism because they appealed to international law rules and principles that were asserted or assumed to be universal but, in fact, did not have universal effectiveness. Two dangers existed, therefore: the universal triumph of totalitarianism or nuclear war between blocs led by the United States and the Soviet Union. The proposed world public order would make it possible to escape this horrendous dilemma.

The authors defined all their terms, so they must be understood as terms of art. In ordinary language, a "public order" is an effective, peaceful, law-governed society.[2] A society based on "human dignity" is posited to be one that is egalitarian and democratic.[3] *If* all the people on earth could be brought into such a society, the world would be safe from totalitarianism and nuclear Armageddon. Therefore, this Comment will address two questions: (1) Is the McDougal-Lasswell proposal a feasible plan for achieving a universal, egalitarian-democratic society? (2) Is there any alternative way to avoid the universal triumph of totalitarianism and nuclear Armageddon?

FEASIBILITY OF THE MCDOUGAL-LASSWELL PROPOSAL

In traditional international law, the aspirations of individuals for justice, peace and security are served by a system in which territorially identified nation-states are internally and externally sovereign, but are subject to the

[1] McDougal & Lasswell, *The Identification and Appraisal of Diverse Systems of Public Order*, 53 AJIL 1, 4–5 (1959), *reprinted in* M. S. MCDOUGAL & ASSOCIATES, STUDIES IN WORLD PUBLIC ORDER 3 (1960), *and in* M. S. MCDOUGAL & W. M. REISMAN, INTERNATIONAL LAW ESSAYS 15 (1981) [hereinafter cited to AJIL version].

Professor McDougal has written a response to this Comment, which appears below. My replies to his observations have been incorporated in these footnotes.

[2] *Id.* at 8, 10. "Public order" is "the basic features of the social process in a community," which, in turn, are defined as the prevailing distribution of goal values, the preferred distribution pattern, the process of moving from one to the other, and implementing institutions, all of which are protected by the legal order. A legal order consists of decisions that are authoritative and controlling, together with institutions and sanctions.

[3] *Id.* at 11. "The essential meaning of human dignity as we understand it can be succinctly stated: it refers to a social process in which values are widely and not narrowly shared, and in which private choice, rather than coercion, is emphasized as the predominant modality of power."

limiting norms of international law. The failure of traditional international law to attain universal effectiveness and the increasingly effective drive toward universality by the totalitarian regimes, led by the Soviet Union, have created the present dangers that McDougal and Lasswell seek to avoid.

McDougal and Lasswell attempt to bypass the internal and external sovereignty of nation-states by defining a "world social process" in which individuals participate directly.[4] They acknowledge that there is not a world society (public order), but they say that the world "community" is characterized by "interaction," which is a matter of "going and coming, of buying and selling, of looking and listening; and more."[5] They assert:

> The participants in the world social process are acting individually in their own behalf and in concert with others with whom they share symbols of common identity and ways of life of varying degrees of elaboration. Whether acting through one channel or the other the fundamental goal stays ever the same, the maximization of values within the limits of capability.[6]

The assertion that individuals participate directly in the world social process has the most profound significance. Implicit in this assertion is rejection of the basic proposition of the Universal Declaration of Human Rights that "[a]ll human beings are . . . endowed with reason and conscience . . . ."[7] This is the central tradition of Western civilization. If human beings are deemed to be rational and moral in nature, it follows that they organize and govern the cooperative actions of society in accordance with shared beliefs, which give rise to a shared set of meanings in terms of which they understand and respond to events, and to shared values, purposes and principles. This means that a cultural community is necessary to the formation of a human society.[8]

In a culture-dependent society, members can anticipate the actions of others because they know in accordance with shared meanings, desire in accordance with shared values, intend in accordance with shared purposes,

[4] Lasswell and associates claim to *observe* this process "wholly apart from their 'definitions.' " McDougal, *The Dorsey Comment: A Modest Retrogression*, *infra* at p. 51, 52 [hereinafter McDougal]. But raw observational data are formulated in conceptions. Their conceptions flow from the assumption that human actions are influenced only by consciousness of the internal and external aspects of other actions. *See* my note 11 *infra*. Voluntary cooperation in any society can occur only among those who are able to understand each other because they use the same set of meanings for interpreting observed events. Lasswell and associates' assertion that there is no cultural link between observations and actions is itself a premise about human nature that could become a belief and generate a set of meanings and other components of a culture. Indeed, that is exactly what Lasswell and associates have been trying to foster. *See* my text at pp. 47-50 *infra*.

[5] McDougal & Lasswell, *supra* note 1, at 7, 11.

[6] *Id.* at 7.

[7] Art. 1, GA Res. 217 (III) (Dec. 10, 1948).

[8] Professor McDougal incorrectly attributes to me the view that cultures cannot transcend the boundaries of nation-states. McDougal, *infra* at pp. 51–52. It is my position that many states can be based on versions of the same culture, as in Western Europe, but that no society and legal system can come into being except on the basis of some culture.

and guide and limit their actions in accordance with shared principles. Such a society is characterized by a network of rights and obligations. Realization of rights depends upon faithful performance of obligations. Obligations are enforced if need be, and conflicts of interest are resolved on the basis of an objective determination of the common good. To use another set of meanings without fully disclosing to others the differences and their significance is to fail to communicate in good faith. To take the benefit of rights and refuse to fulfill obligations is to fail to act in good faith.

A member of a culture-dependent society cannot participate, in good faith, in a world social process in any way that is inconsistent with the member's obligations to fellow members of the society. In the United States, for example, failing to give "true faith and allegiance" to the United States is a serious offense; it is treason if it involves giving aid and comfort to enemies.

It is precisely the general obligation of allegiance to territorially identified national societies that is implicitly denied by McDougal and Lasswell when they assert that participants in the world social process act on their own behalf, either individually or in concert with others—instead of the national society acting in the world social process on behalf of its members.[9] This denial is incident to their attempt to build a world society (world public order) without building a universal culture of shared beliefs, meanings, values, purposes and principles. McDougal and Lasswell base this attempt on a comprehensive model of the world social process worked out earlier by Lasswell in collaboration with Abraham Kaplan.[10] According to Lasswell and Kaplan, human beings are actors and they are conscious only of the internal and external aspects of acts.[11]

Persons seek to realize values through their own acts and the coordinated acts of groups. A *value* is a preferred event. Any statement expressing desire for realization of a value is a *demand*. *Expectation* refers to the preferred or described occurrence of an event. If one is indifferent to the occurrence, the expectation statement is descriptive; if one has a feeling about the occurrence (desiring it or dreading it), the expectation is *sentimentalized*. *Symbols* refer to the subjective factors in a social (or political) event. An *operation* is

[9] *See* text at note 5 *supra*.

[10] During World War II Lasswell was Director of War Communications Research in the Library of Congress. A political scientist, he had been "occupied with the theory of propaganda for many years." Lasswell had been seeking to achieve an analysis that would provide the empirical significance needed for devising effective strategy and tactics of propaganda and intelligence. He sought the help of Abraham Kaplan, a specialist in the philosophy of language and scientific methodology. The analysis was finished by the end of 1945. Kaplan joined the Philosophy Department of the University of California at Los Angeles; Lasswell became a professor at Yale Law School. The analysis was published in 1950. H. LASSWELL & A. KAPLAN, POWER AND SOCIETY, at v–vi (1950).

[11] *Id.* at 10–13. "A *person* is an actor characterized as to personality." "The *personality* is the totality of the personality traits pertaining to an actor." "A *personality trait* is a kind of act characteristic of a self." "The self . . . is the set of . . . roles which the ego adopts . . . [in all the groups of persons about whose opinion that person cares]." "An *ego* is an actor using symbols." "A symbol is whatever has meaning or significance in any sense."

the nonsymbol event in an act. (Marking a ballot and dropping it in the ballot box is the nonsymbol event in the act of voting.) The act in its significance (voting) is a *practice*, instead of an *operation*. A *response* is an act, or pattern of acts, characterized in relation to factors that explain or may explain its occurrence. A response is *externalized* if it brings about changes in the environment (by which is meant events, other than the act itself, within which the act is included). An *internalized* response is a factor in the *predisposition* of a person towards future acts.[12]

The cooperation that is characteristic of society begins, according to Lasswell and Kaplan, with identification. "*Identification* is the process by which a symbol user symbolizes his ego as a member of some aggregate or group of egos . . . ."[13] An *aggregate* consists of persons making the same demand, or having the same expectations, identifications or sentiments. A *group* is an organized aggregate. *Organization* is a pattern of solidarity and cooperation. *Solidarity* is the integration of diversified perspectives. *Cooperation* is the integration of diversified operations. A *perspective* is a pattern of identifications, demands and expectations.[14]

The foregoing definitions by Lasswell and Kaplan must be kept in mind when reading the statement of the "world social process" in the 1959 McDougal-Lasswell proposal:

> A value is a preferred event; and if we were to begin to list all the specific items of food and drink, of dress, of housing, and of other enjoyments, we should quickly recognize the unwieldiness of the task. Hence for the purpose of comparing individuals and peoples with one another we find it expedient to employ a brief list of categories where there is place for health, safety and comfort (well-being), for affection, respect, skill, enlightenment, rectitude, wealth and power. Human beings the world over devote their lives to the incessant shaping and sharing of values, activities which they accomplish by making use of patterns of varying degrees of distinctiveness.
>
> Each identifiable "practice" is a pattern of subjectivities (perspectives) and of operations. The practices which are relatively specialized to the shaping and sharing of value we identify as an "institution."

[12] *Id.* at 3–28.

[13] *Id.* at 11–12.

[14] *Id.* at 18–31. It will be seen that I have scrupulously used the meanings of Lasswell and associates in stating their proposal, so that I could criticize what they actually propose, rather than what they would appear to be proposing if I were to use the meanings flowing from my own set of meanings in interpreting their words. Professor McDougal, however, applies the meanings of Lasswell and associates to my words and therefore misunderstands some of my statements. For instance, of my reference to the rational nature of human beings, McDougal says that for me persons are "entirely selfish, enjoying no conception of common interest." McDougal, *infra* at p. 56. But it is I who assert that obligation to existing political societies makes individual participation in a world social process treasonable if contrary to the national interest. *See* my text, *supra* at p. 43. It is Lasswell and associates who make "good faith" meaningless and "loyalty" a sentimental identification or demand. *See* my text, *infra* at p. 46. With respect to culture, Professor McDougal says that I leave it "highly mystical," but he supports this by reference to an article in which *Lasswell* found culture to be mystical, and ignores my explanations in my Comment and my book (to which he refers). McDougal, *infra* at p. 55.

> Hence we recognize institutions of government, specialized to the shaping and sharing of power; economic institutions, which focus upon the production, distribution and consumption of wealth; religious and ethical institutions, specialized to the grounding and specification of responsible conduct; mass media and other institutions of enlightenment; schools of arts, trades and professions, and associated institutions of skill; pervasive patterns of social class, which are basic institutions of respect; the institutions of family and friendship (affection); and of health, comfort and safety (well-being). These institutions, organized and unorganized, utilize the resources of nature in greater or less degree in the shaping and sharing of preferred outcomes of the social process.[15]

How do individuals and groups achieve values? Values being sought are goal values, preferred events. Values already achieved are base values. Persons acting individually or in groups use base values to effect outcomes that will maximize their goal values. All base values (e.g., wealth, power, respect) can be used to achieve a desired outcome with respect to any goal value. In the world power process, individuals use whatever base values they have at their disposal to achieve desired power. Base values are made instrumental to desired outcomes by "strategies," which are "classified according to the degree to which they rely upon symbols or material resources." Diplomacy depends primarily upon symbols; military strategy employs weapons. Every strategy employs inducements and deprivations, and proceeds in isolation or coalition.[16] Inclusive groups of sufficient scope are characterized by a public order, which is protected by a legal order.[17]

The McDougal-Lasswell proposal is a plan to induce individuals in the currently existing diverse systems of public order to use all base values at their disposal to achieve and preserve the value distribution pattern of the proposed world public order. Since it is assumed that individuals enter into a public order system solely for the purpose of maximizing their goal values, all that is needed is to show a sufficient number of persons in diverse systems of public order that their goal values will be truly maximized by supporting the world public order.

Therefore, saving the world from nuclear Armageddon and universal totalitarianism becomes a task for scholars. The scholars, particularly scholars of international law, must "disclose to as many as possible of the effective leaders, and constituencies of leaders, throughout the globe the compatibility between their aspirations and the policies that expedite peaceful co-operation on behalf of a public order of human dignity."[18] The scholars are to perform two indispensable functions: "the function of providing intelligence and of making recommendations to all who have the will and capability of decision."[19] This is goal clarification on a global scale.

McDougal and Lasswell assume that the key decision makers to whom the savior-scholars would impart intelligence and make recommendations

[15] McDougal & Lasswell, *supra* note 1, at 7.
[16] *Id.* at 8.
[17] *Id.* at 10.
[18] *Id.* at 29.
[19] *Id.* at 28.

would be free to shift all the base values at their disposal from support of a national public order to support of the recommended world public order. They make this assumption because in the Lasswell-Kaplan world social process, achieving the cooperation of a society (public order) does not involve obligations with respect to understanding or actions. "Belief" is not a shared premise of understanding, but a predisposition to act. "Faith" is a sentimentalized expectation (and therefore can be neither "good" nor "bad"). "Loyalty" is a sentimentalized identification or demand.[20] Each Lasswell-Kaplan acting/aware human being pursues maximization of his/her values. The benefits of division of labor are obtained by integrating the subjective and external aspects of acts. Such a society, if it could be achieved, would not be culture-dependent. Shared beliefs, meanings, values, purposes and principles would be irrelevant, if not impossible. Cooperation would rest upon coincidence of goals. The absence of an obligation of allegiance would leave key decision makers free to shift support to the recommended world public order.

In the Lasswell-Kaplan social process, the absence of shared beliefs, meanings, values, purposes and principles also makes it impossible to discuss such a shift of support in terms of truth or morality, or to distinguish between good faith persuasion and manipulation or deception. Lasswell-Kaplan acting/aware human beings are equal in that each has a set of goal values that he/she is seeking to maximize, and each is unable to reason with others and to reach agreements about the world they live in, the purpose of life, what is to be desired and what shunned, the causes of events, and a just distribution of rights and obligations in a cooperative effort to survive and prosper. However, each can determine the share of goal values he/she wants, observe the present distribution of goal values, observe factors that affect the distribution of goal values, anticipate the effect upon value distribution of new events such as scientific inventions, and plan strategy and tactics to accomplish the desired goal value distribution as rapidly and efficiently as possible.[21]

In the social process of Lasswell-Kaplan persons, actor *A* is trying to maximize *A*'s goal values by imparting to all other actors the intelligence gained by *A* through empirical investigation, and by recommending to them that they act in ways that will maximize *A*'s goal values. *A* is making a manipulative use of intelligence. This is why Lasswell and McDougal call their jurisprudence "configurative." Lasswell and Kaplan defined a "configurative approach" as one that adopts the manipulative and the contemplative approach.[22] Lasswell said that his collaboration with McDougal began when Lasswell "was in search of colleagues in various fields of knowledge who perceived the importance of a configurative approach and who

[20] H. LASSWELL & A. KAPLAN, *supra* note 10, at 21 n.7, 24.

[21] McDougal & Lasswell, *supra* note 1, at 11–15. These are the steps that the authors specify for the scholars who undertake to clarify the values of the key decision makers that are targeted to shift their base values to the support of the proposed world public order.

[22] H. LASSWELL & A. KAPLAN, *supra* note 10, at xiii.

were willing to develop the implications of a comprehensive working model of the social process."[23]

The manipulation involved in the configurative approach to the world social process would be relatively benign if the persons who are caused to shift their base values from a national public order to the proposed world public order share the goal values of the manipulators. McDougal and Lasswell assume that the key decision makers whose support the savior-scholars would cause to be shifted will share the goal of an egalitarian-democratic distribution of values, which they assert to be the essential meaning of human dignity. They say, "We postulate this goal, deliberately leaving everyone free to justify it in terms of his preferred theological or philosophical tradition."[24] On the question whether key decision makers in the diverse systems of public order do share the postulated goal, the authors say: "Fortunately, advantage may be taken of the fact that the major systems of public order are in many fundamental respects rhetorically unified. All systems proclaim the dignity of the human individual and the ideal of a worldwide public order in which this ideal is authoritatively pursued and effectively approximated."[25]

Granting, *arguendo*, the truth of the assertion, a unity that is only rhetorical is not a strong basis for attracting the support of key decision makers in national public orders—especially when it is realized that national societies would not willingly be deprived of the base values sought to be shifted to the world society. And the national societies would have a valid claim upon those base values. Individuals form societies to get the benefit of cooperation; the base values at the disposal of an individual result from the functioning of the society, not from the independent efforts of the individual. The difficulties arising out of an attempt to put the values created by one society at the service of another society are objective; they cannot be evaporated by rhetoric. Furthermore, the targets of the McDougal-Lasswell plan are key decision makers precisely because they are the beneficiaries of unequal distribution of values in their national systems. Why would they be attracted to a world society in which values were more equally distributed?

McDougal and Lasswell further assert that "[t]he modern world is a cauldron of aspiration for a better life on the part of millions of human beings hitherto devoid of any expectation of receiving serious consideration."[26] Doubtless this is true, but the proposed world society cannot be built by the have-nots of the national societies, who have few base values to bring with them. It seems likely, therefore, that those who would be attracted to a McDougal-Lasswell world society (public order) of egalitarian-democratic human dignity would not bring the base values to make it viable, and those who control the needed base values would not be so attracted.

Furthermore, the proposed world society (public order) of egalitarian-democratic human dignity, does not, in fact, avoid dependence upon a

[23] Lasswell, *Introduction*, in W. M. REISMAN & B. WESTON, TOWARD WORLD ORDER AND HUMAN DIGNITY, at xiii, xvi (1976).

[24] McDougal & Lasswell, *supra* note 1, at 11.

[25] *Id.* at 5.

[26] *Id.* at 6.

culture. The evidence for this conclusion begins with an inadvertent admission against interest by Lasswell and Kaplan. Their core definition of the entities that participate in the world social process, namely, an acting organism that is aware of the internal and external aspects of acts, is not the statement of a scientific fact—like gravity. It is a nonempirical premise about human nature, an idea. When such an idea seeps into the consciousness of enough persons over a sufficient period of time to become, for them, a part of the reality they must reckon with, like it or not, it becomes a belief.[27]

Such an idea/belief is capable of generating a set of meanings that believers use to understand and respond to events. The delineation of the meanings implied by the Lasswell-Kaplan premise is precisely the task undertaken by them in their analysis of the world social process.[28] Lasswell and Kaplan anticipated that a set of shared values would be used to guide and justify social relations established under conditions understood in terms of the meanings they proposed. They said:

> From a manipulative standpoint, the social sciences are better designated as *policy sciences*—their function is to provide intelligence pertinent to the integration of values realized by and embodied in interpersonal relations. We conceive of political science as one of the policy sciences—that which studies influence and power as instruments of such integration. The problem of social policy is that of creating conditions under which power can and does act integratively in relation to the major values of society as a whole.[29]

The configurative approach combines the study of empirical propositions of political science (the contemplative aspect) with the value judgments of political doctrine (the manipulative aspect). Political science, as a policy science, studies the present distribution of power, but it also studies how to change that distribution so that it accords with the distribution preferred by the investigator.

> The functions of the scientist overlap and interact with those of the policy maker. . . .
>
> . . . Our own values are those of the citizen of a society that aspires toward freedom. Hence we have given special attention to the formulation of conditions favorable to the establishment and continuance of a free society.[30]

In the 1959 proposal, McDougal and Lasswell established the set of purposes by postulating a goal of egalitarian-democratic human dignity. All who adhere to the nonempirical premise[31] and adopt the set of meanings are

[27] J. ORTEGA Y GASSET, CONCORD AND LIBERTY 18–19 (1946).

[28] *See* H. LASSWELL & A. KAPLAN, *supra* note 10.

[29] *Id.* at xii.

[30] *Id.* at xiii.

[31] Professor McDougal denies that this postulation is metaphysical or transempirical because a "designative reference" is made "to the interactions of individual human beings." McDougal,

expected to join in pursuit of the purpose, which is defined in terms of values.

There followed, from McDougal and various associates, sometimes including Lasswell, a spate of massive volumes,[32] and a flood of articles, book reviews, speeches and comments,[33] that put forward principles and rules for every issue of international law. Julius Stone pointed out that in none of these studies did McDougal and associates make the comprehensive empirical investigation that they specify for the scholars who are charged with building the world public order.[34] This is understandable. McDougal and associates were not, in fact, engaged in building the world public order—they were engaged in building a world culture of egalitarian-democratic human dignity, whose adherents would then build the world public order. All the components of a culture are there: the nonempirical premise that is to be adhered to as a belief, the set of meanings, the purpose and the values to be shared, the implicated principles and rules. In their teaching, at Yale Law School, McDougal and Lasswell recruited promising young scholars into the culture of human dignity in their famous seminar, "Law, Science and Policy."[35]

To the extent that McDougal and Lasswell proposed building a world public order (society) that would not be culture-dependent, it must be concluded that the proposal is not feasible.[36] The conclusive proof is the fact

---

infra at p. 54. But whether a proposition is empirical is determined by whether it is derived from, or based on, empirical data, not whether it is expected to be applied to empirically knowable events. On McDougal's version of empirical, the word of God from the mouth of an evangelistic preacher would be empirical because the members of the flock are expected to abide by it in their interactions.

[32] M. S. McDougal & Associates, Studies in World Public Order, 1058 pp. (1960); M. S. McDougal & F. Feliciano, Law and Minimum World Order, 872 pp. (1961); M. S. McDougal & W. Burke, The Public Order of the Oceans, 1226 pp. (1962); M. S. McDougal, H. Lasswell & I. Vlasic, Law and Public Order in Space, 1147 pp. (1963); M. S. McDougal & H. Lasswell, The Interpretation of Agreements and World Public Order, 410 pp. (1967); M. S. McDougal, H. Lasswell & L. Chen, Human Rights and World Public Order, 1016 pp. (1980); M. S. McDougal & W. M. Reisman, International Law in Contemporary Perspective: The Order of the World Community, 1548 pp. (1981).

[33] *See Bibliography*, in W. M. Reisman & B. Weston, *supra* note 23, at 579.

[34] J. Stone, Visions of World Order 29 (1984).

[35] *See* Lasswell, *supra* note 23.

[36] Professor McDougal asserts that I find "the promotion of the values of human dignity on a transnational scale" to be "as dangerous to peace as the promotion of totalitarianism." McDougal, *infra* at pp. 55–56. I suppose this is intended to be scathing; but it is close to the mark. Worldwide victory by totalitarianism would cause immeasurable suffering. But promotion on a transnational scale of a *postulated* "human dignity" that everyone is free to define according to the shared, operational meaning of human dignity in each of the world's cultures will only undermine the effective power of national societies, and it can never generate sufficient *voluntary* cooperation to bring into being a nontotalitarian world society. The acting/aware human beings of Lasswell and associates are free to shift their support from national societies to a world society of postulated human dignity; but they would do so only if convinced they could get more of what they want, and they would remain free to shift their support back to a national society, or to a world society of a different type, whenever self-interest would be served. I do not wish to face a choice between worldwide tyranny and worldwide anarchy.

that they themselves turned to the effort to build, through policy science, a world culture of egalitarian-democratic human dignity as the basis for building the world public order.

An Alternative Way to Avoid Totalitarianism and Nuclear Armageddon

In their statement that all of the major systems of public order are rhetorically unified, McDougal and Lasswell say, "All systems proclaim the dignity of the human individual and the ideal of a worldwide public order in which this ideal is authoritatively pursued and effectively approximated."[37] This statement implicitly acknowledges that the diverse systems have different operative meanings of "dignity" and of "human individual." These meanings are a part of the differing cultures. To the extent that McDougal and Lasswell proposed a new culture of egalitarian-democratic human dignity that would be embodied in a worldwide public order, they have complicated the problem, instead of solving it. They have added one more culture candidate for universal adherence and universal social implementation.

If the struggle for universality between culture-dependent social systems cannot be resolved by building a social system that is not culture-dependent, it is time to question the assumption that one culture and one social system should, or inevitably will, become universal. The assumption is reinforced by the desire for the same sort of effective law enforcement in the world arena that is achieved within national societies, and by the fear of nuclear disaster if the present struggle between culture-dependent social systems continues.

Surely, it is time to recognize that the greatest danger arises from the claim of each of the competing cultures to universal validity. This claim to universal validity fueled the cultural imperialism of the European nation-states and the United States, which, by military conquest and economic pressure, brought all other peoples under colonialism, or the threat of it. The claim of universal validity for the culture of Marxism-Leninism fuels the new cultural imperialism of the "socialist bloc" states,[38] which conquer by international revolution. Why should the world be condemned to a future in which these two cultures (and perhaps the new culture of egalitarian-democratic human dignity) contend for universality, and all peoples not actively engaged in the contention have no alternative but to accept the direction and control of the winner, or share in the apathy of stalemate or the holocaust of nuclear destruction?

As long as the assumption of cultural universality is held, cultural differences divide the peoples of the earth, because it must be determined which will prevail and dominate. As soon as the assumption of cultural universality is relinquished, cultural differences are seen as welcome diversity. The

[37] McDougal & Lasswell, *supra* note 1, at 5.

[38] This author has called these states "party-states." G. Dorsey, Beyond the United Nations 7–17 (1986).

Jewish people preserved a distinctive culture throughout two thousand years of diaspora, and those Jews who wish to do so can now participate in building and preserving a society based on that culture. There is continuing validity in the traditional Indian culture, in Islamic culture, in Buddhist culture, in traditional Chinese culture, in sub-Sahara African culture. Surely, diversity will increase as new potentialities of life and nature are discovered by science and made possible by technology.[39]

The alternative way to avoid the universal triumph of totalitarianism and nuclear Armageddon is to pursue the more modest goal of clusters of national societies based upon a variety of cultures. This goal follows from acceptance of cultural diversity, instead of cultural universality, as the basis of international law. Every culture grasps some part, but not the whole, of the rich and complex meaning of existence. It should be the basic principle of international law that persons who share fundamental beliefs about the world and human nature have the right to organize and govern their activities in accordance with the social implications of those beliefs; but they do not have the right to impose the beliefs or the social system upon others. In a world characterized by clusters of national societies based on a variety of cultures, peace and security would depend upon an international law of cultural tolerance and negotiated agreements based on mutual advantage.

GRAY L. DORSEY*

THE DORSEY COMMENT: A MODEST RETROGRESSION

It seems to me, with all respect, that the Comment by Professor Dorsey exhibits a minimum understanding both of the contemporary world and of the theory and intellectual procedures recommended by Harold Lasswell and his associates for inquiry about the role of international law in that world. Certainly Professor Dorsey and Lasswell and associates observe very different worlds, have very different conceptions of international law, and recommend very different methods of inquiry. It is not clear that Professor Dorsey is constrained by empirical observation and modern scientific methods of inquiry.

For Professor Dorsey, as developed in this Comment and in his book,[1] there is no global community of humankind in the sense of an interdetermination and interdependence in the shaping and sharing of values. All he can observe is an aggregation of nation-states, each characterized by a unique, impermeable "culture" that stops short at national boundaries. "The nation-state system," he explains, "is a cultural system." "This

[39] This paragraph is quoted from my book, *id.* at 83–84.

* Charles Nagel Professor of Jurisprudence and International Law, School of Law, Washington University at St. Louis; President (1975–1979), International Association for Philosophy of Law and Social Philosophy.

[1] G. DORSEY, BEYOND THE UNITED NATIONS: CHANGING DISCOURSE IN INTERNATIONAL POLITICS AND LAW (1986) [hereinafter Book].

means," he adds, "that the members have much the same beliefs about the world, human nature, what is worth having, how to know, who can know, and have much the same values and purposes."[2] He nowhere explains why beliefs, natures, values and purposes cannot transcend the inherited, and continuously changing, boundaries of nation-states. According to Dorsey, the individual human being and his many associations other than the nation-state cannot act directly in world social process; the nation-state must act for them.[3] It would be treason for the individual to act, since in violation of "obligation" to the nation-state.[4] For some incredible reason, for individuals to act directly in world social process would be to reject "the basic proposition of the Universal Declaration of Human Rights that '[a]ll human beings are . . . endowed with reason and conscience . . . .' "[5] It seems that rational human beings can only organize in exclusive communities with people who think and talk exactly as they do; hence, people "endowed with reason" must opt for tribal and smaller units and cannot participate in a transnational social process. While he offers no map of a comprehensive, global process of effective power, Professor Dorsey does repeatedly insist that the bases of effective power are to be found in assets irretrievably locked within the boundaries of nation-states and that it is futile to try to change the situation.[6] The conception of international law projected by Professor Dorsey is that of the positivist paradigm: a body of rules that regulates the interactions of, expresses the "sovereignty" of, nation-states, without applying directly to the activities of individual human beings and their various associations. In his book he states concisely: "International Law . . . is the body of rules for distributing among states the authority to govern human activities."[7] A contrasting conception of transnational expectations and decisions about authority and control, relating to the activities of all participants in a global community process, would be dangerously conducive of a destructive universality.

Lasswell and associates, both in the article under attack by Professor Dorsey and numerous other monographs and books,[8] have observed, and sought to map, a very different world. They can observe that there is in fact, wholly apart from their "definitions," a comprehensive earth-space community of the whole of humankind, transcending all national boundaries, in the sense of interdetermination and interdependence in the shaping and sharing of all values, even that of survival.[9] The participants in this most comprehensive community process they observe to be, not merely nation-states,

[2] Book at 31.

[3] We are tempted to ask: Did anyone ever see a "nation-state" "coming and going" or "buying and selling" or "looking and listening"? Dorsey, *The McDougal-Lasswell Proposal to Build a World Public Order*, *supra* at p. 41, 42 [hereinafter Comment].

[4] *Id.* at 43.

[5] *Id.* at 42.

[6] *Id.* at 47.

[7] Book at 4.

[8] The citations offered by Professor Dorsey are ample.

[9] Expansion and documentation of the description offered in this paragraph may be found in M. S. McDougal & W. M. Reisman, International Law Essays (1981), and M. S. McDougal, H. Lasswell & L. Chen, Human Rights and World Public Order (1980).

but the individual human beings who create nation-states and all their other groupings and associations, such as international governmental organizations, political parties, pressure groups and private associations specialized to all demanded values. They discern also, as a most important component within the comprehensive community process, an ongoing process of effective power, equally global in reach, in which decisions are in fact taken and enforced by severe deprivations or high indulgences, irrespective of the wishes of particular participants.[10] The bases of power at the disposal of participants in this process of effective power, they note, are not restricted to physical resources hermetically sealed within nation-states; resources are important only as potential values, and in a world in which individuals and goods are in constant movement, reciprocities and retaliations with respect to all values become bases of power. In addition, as science and technology advance on a global scale, enlightenment and skill, as well as conceptions of rectitude and responsibility, become of increasing significance.

Many of the decisions taken in the larger process of effective power, Lasswell and his associates further observe, are taken, not by sheer naked power or from convenience, but rather from perspectives of authority: these decisions are made by participants who are expected to make them, in accordance with policy criteria expected by community members, in established structures of authority, with enough bases in power to secure consequential control, and by prescribed procedures. Upon close examination, this flow of authoritative decision within the larger, global community can be seen, as within lesser communities, to be composed of two distinct, though interrelated, kinds of decisions: "constitutive" decisions, which establish and maintain the most comprehensive process of authoritative decision, and "public order" decisions, made within the constitutive process, in regulation of the larger community's different value processes. The constitutive decisions are those that establish who the authoritative decision makers are, what fundamental policies they are to apply to what problems, the arenas of their interaction, the bases of power at their disposal, the procedures that they may employ, and the various activities or functions by which law is made and applied. The public order decisions are those that determine how resources are allocated and employed, how wealth is produced and distributed, how human rights are promoted and protected, how enlightenment is encouraged or blighted, how health is fostered or neglected, and so on. The conception of international law recommended by Lasswell and his associates makes reference to the totality of this flow of authoritative decision, both constitutive and public order, within the global community: international law is most realistically regarded, after the model of the American Legal Realists with respect to the law of any community, as that comprehensive process of authoritative decision by which the members

[10] Extended description of the global process of effective power is offered by McDougal, Reisman & Willard, *The World Process of Effective Power: The Global War System*, in POWER AND POLICY IN QUEST OF LAW: ESSAYS IN HONOR OF EUGENE VICTOR ROSTOW 353 (M. S. McDougal & W. M. Reisman eds. 1985).

of the larger community of humankind seek to clarify and secure their common interests in the shaping and sharing of all values. The inherited body of rules, described as international law in the positivist frame, with its abundant complementarities, ambiguities and incompletions, has meaning only insofar as it refers to past decision or to the guidance, not command, of future decision.

For detailed inquiry about the role of law (the making of decisions and their consequences) in the larger global community of humankind, Lasswell and associates recommend both a comprehensive, careful mapping of that process, including its components in effective power and authoritative decision, and the employment of a number of distinct, though interrelated, intellectual procedures.[11] They recognize that the making or recommending of decisions, rational by the criteria of common interest, requires that the decision maker or scholar be able to formulate problems in terms of the values at stake, both for the immediate parties and for the various communities of which they are members, and to explore the largest possible context of such problems for identifying and testing options in decision in terms of their value consequences for the different parties and communities. Hence, for the mapping of community processes, both comprehensive and lesser, they proffer theory for description in terms both of component value processes (power, respect, enlightenment, wealth, well-being, skill, affection, rectitude) and of institutional practices specialized to each value (participation, perspectives, situations, base values, strategies, outcomes), which can be made as comprehensive and as precise as any particular problem may require.[12] From such description, it may be seen that the notion of impermeable national cultures is a delusion: different people may pursue the same values, achieve the same value consequences, by many different institutional practices.

For guidance in making or recommending particular decisions, Lasswell and associates recommend the explicit postulation, rather than derivation or assumption, of a fundamental community commitment to the historic values of human dignity, as contemporaneously expressed in the emerging global bill of human rights (the Universal Declaration of Human Rights, the many ancillary conventions and decisions) and many national constitutions and decisions.[13] It should require no elaboration that there is nothing metaphysical or transempirical in the postulation of a community commitment in terms that make a designative reference to the interactions of individual human beings in the shaping and sharing of particular values.[14] The more

[11] These recommendations are stated in some detail in the article attacked by Professor Dorsey. *See also* the citations referred to *supra* note 8.

[12] The relevant global processes are described in these terms in great detail in M. S. McDougal, H. Lasswell & L. Chen, *supra* note 9.

[13] In chapter 4 of McDougal, Lasswell, and Chen, *id.*, we document that this postulation is rapidly becoming customary international law. In later chapters of the book, we illustrate how the postulated policies may be, and are being, applied to a variety of particular problems.

[14] In his Comment, *supra* at p. 48, Professor Dorsey refers to our postulated goal of "egalitarian-democratic human dignity" as having a "nonempirical premise." A postulation that

specific intellectual procedures recommended by Lasswell and associates as manifestly relevant, even indispensable, to the making or recommending of decisions rational by the criteria of common interest may briefly be recapitulated.

First, the clarification of goal. A provisional relation of postulated community commitments and authoritative prescriptions to particular problems in projection of possible outcomes in decision. Such possible outcomes are provisional since they require testing by the other relevant intellectual procedures.

Second, description of trend. The examination of past trends in decision upon problems raising comparable policies for whatever wisdom they may yield about options in decision and the value consequences of different options. Note may be taken not only of immediate consequences but of aggregate consequences through time.

Third, analysis of conditioning factors. An exploration of the environmental and predispositional factors affecting past decisions upon comparable problems and of the constraints that such factors have imposed upon the choice of options.

Fourth, projection of future developments. The projection of value goals, trends and conditions into the future, considering how probable changes in conditions may affect both options in decision and the value consequences of different options in decision.

Fifth, invention and consideration of policy alternatives. The identifying and the making of a culminating commitment that best expresses the common interests in postulated values of the parties to a problem and of the communities of which they are members. For some problems in some contexts it may be necessary to reorganize the framework of interaction between the parties, in a reformulation of the problem, in order to achieve an appropriate integration of all interests.

Professor Dorsey offers no systematic statement of descriptive theory or intellectual procedures. The key concept in the structure of his argument is that of "culture," which is left highly mystical.[15] All we can learn is that it has many national forms, sometimes has "nonempirical" premises that seep into consciousness, and is very difficult, if not impossible, to change. He makes no explicit postulation of a community commitment to goal values and derides the suggestion that "an egalitarian-democratic distribution of values" is an "essential meaning" of human dignity.[16] The promotion of the values of human dignity on a transnational scale he finds as dangerous to

makes a designative reference to interactions between human beings in the shaping and sharing of values is scarcely nonempirical.

[15] Lasswell indicates some of the difficulties in describing culture, and the interrelations of culture and personality, in *Person, Personality, Group, Culture*, 2 PSYCHIATRY 523 (1939). Professor Dorsey is confronted with especial difficulties because of the miraculous powers he attributes to culture. His conception bears some resemblance to the community "geist" of the historical jurists of the previous century.

[16] Comment at 47.

peace as the promotion of totalitarianism.[17] He indicates no particular intellectual procedures as especially relevant to inquiry about law in his world and mocks the specific tasks Lasswell and associates recommend as relevant, if not indispensable, to rational decision and recommendation in the common interest.[18] He suggests that the social sciences seek to be empirical but have limited predictive capabilities "because human actions are not determined by nature but by culture."[19] He finds difficulty in that "the currently dominant method of thought about human associations is concerned with empirical evidence of causal relations between antecedent and consequent events of human behavior" and in that questions of "right or wrong" are determined by "their practical consequences."[20] He suggests a preference for the methods of the Middle Ages when questions of right and wrong were determined "by moral philosophy, which reasoned deductively from assumed truths about the world and human nature."[21] He asserts that "if the cultural basis of human action is not understood and respected, attempts to control human events beneficially, can be disastrous"[22] and insists that the "failure to recognize the cultural basis of human action and association produces its most dangerous illusions in peace activism."[23] It is most unhappy that Professor Dorsey gives us so few clues about how to recognize this all-important "cultural basis." Possibly, as Justice Stewart said of pornography, we can only know it when we see it.

It may be noted that the dangers dichotomized by Professor Dorsey at the beginning of his Comment, as between the triumph of totalitarianism and nuclear war, do not exhaust the possibilities. There is the further possibility of a continuing inadequate international legal system in which expectations of violence and anxiety remain high, crippling all productive activities and leaving the vast numbers of people already under totalitarian rule permanently denied opportunity for lives of human dignity. In his proposal that we "pursue the more modest goal of clusters of national societies based upon a variety of cultures"[24] and forgo the transnational promotion of the values of human dignity, Professor Dorsey would appear to opt for this third alternative. For many observers such a choice can represent only an anachronistic, defeatist nostalgia. It is a last cry, in a rapidly changing world, for national exclusivism and tribalism. People of different nations and cultures are, so it appears to be thought, unalterably different. The growth of heterogeneous systems with some degree of homogeneity is an illusion. The United States, for example, does not exist. Rational people, endowed with reason, are entirely selfish, enjoying no conception of common interest. They are unable to see that collaborative arrangements may be productive and enhance the values and security of both themselves and others. Such a perception is evidently alien to Professor Dorsey's conception of rational, reason-endowed people. His people do indeed operate in the Middle Ages.

[17] *Id.* at 50.
[18] *Id.* at 46.
[19] Book at 92.
[20] *Id.* at 89.
[21] *Id.*
[22] *Id.* at 93.
[23] *Id.* at 96.
[24] Comment at 51.

They build walls around the little pieces of the planet they think they control and dig moats beyond the walls. They are oblivious to the extraordinary interchange of values in the contemporary world and the inescapable interdeterminations and interdependences so created with respect to all values, including security. Each, within his own little nation-state, cultivates his own culture and resource environment while excluding all others from any of the values that he thinks he alone has created. The question is not whether this individual triumphs over totalitarianism. He must himself become increasingly totalitarian as he maintains a garrison state to protect what he regards as his. The relevant question is whether he can survive in a clump of clusters half-slave and half-free.

In the very article under attack by Professor Dorsey, Lasswell and I pointed out that the spokesmen of the totalitarian powers have the most to gain by the approach recommended by him. We wrote:

> Strange as it may seem at first glance, the most convincing interpretation is that the existing imperfections of the system can be used by them [the spokesmen of the totalitarian powers] to help prevent further advances toward a world order with genuine measures of security. For it is in the name of such allegedly universal doctrines of international law as sovereignty, domestic jurisdiction, non-intervention, independence and equality—all of which appear to fortify claims to freedom from external obligation—that the case is made to resist the institutional reconstructions which are indispensable to security.[25]

We added: "It is high time that the community of scholars abandon a conception of their rôle in history whose principal effect is to condemn them to inaccuracy and futility."[26]

MYRES S. MCDOUGAL*

[25] McDougal & Lasswell, *The Identification and Appraisal of Diverse Systems of Public Order*, 53 AJIL 1, 4 (1959).

[26] *Id.* at 28.

* Of the Board of Editors.

EDITORIAL COMMENTS

UNDERSTANDING THE ACT OF STATE DOCTRINE'S EFFECT

A few years after the *Sabbatino* case[1] was decided, Louis Henkin demonstrated that the act of state doctrine is a federal choice-of-law rule.[2] He showed that the effect of declining to apply it in any given case is simply to remove it as the controlling choice-of-law rule. In the absence of a statutory directive, the court would then use its normal choice-of-law approach to select the governing law. It might look to international law principles, but only insofar as they are incorporated into federal statutory or common law in the United States, and only if the choice-of-law process selects U.S. law. On the other hand, if the act of state doctrine is applied, its effect is either to choose the foreign law and preempt any escape device, or—essentially the same thing—to preclude the application of United States regulatory law (such as U.S. antitrust law) to conduct that stems from a foreign governmental act.

Judges have not universally recognized Professor Henkin's insights.[3] More than 20 years after *Sabbatino* was decided, courts in the United States continue to misunderstand the effect of applying—or of deciding not to apply—the act of state doctrine. Even the U.S. Court of Appeals for the Second Circuit, which hears a disproportionate number of act of state cases, has not always worked deftly with the doctrine. Surprisingly, too, the Department of State's Office of the Legal Adviser still displays an uncertain grasp of the doctrine's effect. This state of affairs was illustrated again in *Chemical Bank II*.[4]

Chemical Bank II arose out of the expropriation of Cuban Electric Co., a Florida corporation that was headquartered and doing its business in Cuba. The expropriation was one of a series directed against U.S. business interests in Cuba. Cuban Electric had outstanding debts to three New York banks, which the Cuban Government did not pay. Either it assumed Cuban Electric's debts and then refused to pay the American creditors, or it as-

[1] Banco Nacional de Cuba v. Sabbatino, 376 U.S. 398 (1964).

[2] *See* Henkin, *Act of State Today: Recollections in Tranquility*, 6 COLUM. J. TRANSNAT'L L. 175 (1967). As Chief Reporter of the revised *Restatement of Foreign Relations Law*, Professor Henkin has continued to view the act of state doctrine, in most cases, as "a special rule of conflict of laws." RESTATEMENT OF FOREIGN RELATIONS LAW OF THE UNITED STATES (REVISED) [hereinafter RESTATEMENT (REVISED)] §469 Reporters' Note 1 (Tent. Draft No. 7, 1986).

[3] Nor have commentators, though they normally pay some deference to him. For a recent critique of the doctrine's choice-of-law explanation, see Chow, *Rethinking the Act of State Doctrine: An Analysis in Terms of Jurisdiction to Prescribe*, 62 WASH. L. REV. 397, 431–35 (1987). Professor Chow gives only passing reference to the essential point that the doctrine is a federal choice-of-law rule, superseding state choice of law even in diversity cases. *Id.* at 434–35 n.251. His preferred rationale, however, is based on principles of legislative jurisdiction and turns out to be basically a choice-of-law approach. *Id.* at 447–74.

[4] Banco Nacional de Cuba v. Chemical Bank N.Y. Trust Co., 822 F.2d 230 (2d Cir. 1987). *Chemical Bank I* was an earlier appeal in the same case, 658 F.2d 903 (2d Cir. 1981).

sumed only those debts the company owed to non-Americans. The three New York banks also held deposits from some private Cuban banks that were later nationalized. Banco Nacional, as the successor to the private Cuban banks, sued the New York banks to recover the deposits. The New York banks filed setoff counterclaims based on the amounts Cuban Electric had owed them. They claimed, and the court agreed, that the counterclaims were properly asserted against Banco Nacional, since it was the agent or alter ego of the Cuban Government.

Banco Nacional relied on the act of state doctrine in defense to the counterclaims. The Second Circuit's panel treated this not as a choice-of-law issue, but as a question of justiciability. So did the State Department's Legal Adviser, in a Bernstein letter to the court.[5] In a similar case, another panel of the Second Circuit, having one member in common with the panel on *Chemical Bank II*, had done the same thing.[6]

In both cases, the facts were found indistinguishable from those in the *Citibank* case.[7] In *Citibank* the Supreme Court held the act of state doctrine inapplicable, even though it could not muster a majority opinion to explain why. Each of these cases involved a Bernstein letter, a counterclaim limited to a setoff and no showing that examination of the Cuban Government's acts would interfere with U.S. foreign relations. The absence of any of these factors probably would have led to the opposite result.[8]

[5] A Bernstein letter is a letter from the Department of State saying that judicial examination of the foreign government's act in the case at hand would not hamper the conduct of U.S. foreign relations. *See* Bernstein v. N.V. Nederlandsche-Amerikaansche Stoomvaart-Maatschappij, 210 F.2d 375 (2d Cir. 1954). The letter in *Chemical Bank II* disclaimed any interest in having the act of state doctrine applied to the counterclaims, concluding that "the Department of State does not perceive foreign relations difficulties that should bar adjudication of these cases on the merits." The letter also said that the situation "does not compel us to call upon the court to abstain from its normal duty to adjudicate cases properly before it." *Chemical Bank II*, 822 F.2d at 236.

[6] Banco Nacional de Cuba v. Chase Manhattan Bank, 658 F.2d 875 (2d Cir. 1981). The common member was the author of both opinions.

[7] First Nat'l City Bank v. Banco Nacional de Cuba, 406 U.S. 759 (1972).

[8] A majority of the Justices in *Citibank* rejected the Bernstein letter as a controlling factor, and an even greater majority declined to treat the limited counterclaim as significant. As for the third factor, everyone concedes that the act of state doctrine applies if examination of the foreign government's act, done within its own territory, would demonstrably impede the conduct of foreign relations.

Another possible way around the act of state doctrine might have been to characterize Cuba's repudiation or nonassumption of debts owed to U.S. interests as "private" or "commercial." *Cf.* Alfred Dunhill of London, Inc. v. Republic of Cuba, 425 U.S. 682 (1976). Quite properly, the court in *Chemical Bank II* did not take this route. Cuba clearly made a political decision not to pay U.S. creditors.

It could also have been argued that Cuba had taken property (the claims of the creditors) situated outside Cuba, if the claims had their situs in New York. It is generally thought that the act of state doctrine does not apply to takings of property outside the acting state's territory. *See* RESTATEMENT (REVISED), *supra* note 2, §469 Reporters' Note 4 (Tent. Draft No. 7, 1986). In fact, though, Cuba did everything it needed to do within its own territory and effectively blocked the creditors' claims. That should satisfy the territorial requirement, regardless of where the debts had their technical "situs."

Another panel of the Second Circuit demonstrated a far superior grasp of the act of state doctrine's effect in the *Lamborn* case.[9] The doctrine was interposed as a defense to a setoff counterclaim based on a Cuban expropriation, but there was no Bernstein letter. The panel applied the act of state doctrine, treating it as a matter of federal substantive law to be applied on the merits of the case. In effect, though not in so many words, the court used the doctrine to choose Cuban law on the counterclaim.[10] The Cuban expropriation was "nonjusticiable" only in the very limited sense that an act having the effect of law in Cuba was held not subject to judicial reexamination using some other body of law.

Once the court in *Chemical Bank II* had worked its way around the act of state doctrine, it jumped to the conclusion that international law supplied the rule of decision for the counterclaims. It did not stop to examine applicable choice-of-law rules in the forum. Nor did it ask whether federal law in the United States incorporates rules of international law governing the conduct of foreign governments at home. Clearly, it was not applying international law as an international tribunal would. In fact, in purporting to apply international law to the Cuban governmental conduct, it applied a distinctly American brand of international law.

This last point—the likelihood that American judges would apply a parochial version of international law to judge foreign acts of state—may have been at the root of the Supreme Court's unwillingness in *Sabbatino* to engraft an international law exception onto the act of state doctrine.[11] In *Chemical Bank II*, the Second Circuit's panel fulfilled that prophecy by looking almost entirely to United States sources for its holding that a state's discriminatory conduct, nullifying the claims of foreign creditors, violates international law.[12]

It is probable that an international tribunal would have reached the same result, despite the paucity of international authority finding a violation solely on the basis of discrimination against foreign nationals.[13] Thus, the

[9] Empresa Cubana Exportadora, Inc. v. Lamborn & Co., 652 F.2d 231, 238–39 (2d Cir. 1981).

[10] *Cf.* Ricaud v. American Metal Co., 246 U.S. 304, 309 (1918) (in an act of state case, the action of the foreign government "must be accepted by our courts as a rule for their decision").

[11] *See* 376 U.S. at 433 (where the Supreme Court majority revealed a certain skepticism regarding lower courts' ability in future cases to handle less clear violations of international law than occurred in *Sabbatino* itself).

[12] The court relied heavily on the *Restatement (Second)* and the *Restatement of Foreign Relations Law (Revised)*. Both *Restatements* disclaim a parochial point of view, saying that they represent "the opinion of The American Law Institute as to the rules that an international tribunal would apply if charged with deciding a controversy in accordance with international law." RESTATEMENT (REVISED), *supra* note 2, *Introduction* (Tent. Draft No. 5, 1984) (quoting RESTATEMENT (SECOND)). But as anyone who attended the ALI debates on the revised *Restatement* knows, the Institute's opinion is shaped by the views and interests of its (American) members.

The court in *Chemical Bank II* cited only two non-American sources: a British scholar (B. A. Wortley) and a 1931 arbitral award by the Mexican-U.S. General Claims Commission. The point in the arbitral award on which the court relied was actually a quotation from an American textbook, 1 J. SUTHERLAND, LAW OF DAMAGES 126 (4th ed. 1916). *See* Dickson Car Wheel Co. v. United Mexican States, 4 R. Int'l Arb. Awards 669, 681 (1931).

[13] Recent arbitral awards that have considered assertions of discriminatory taking or breach of contract have found additional grounds for holding the governmental acts unlawful, or have

point is not that the American court reached the wrong conclusion, but that in reaching its conclusion it applied an Americanized version of international law to the acts of a foreign government, without recognizing that it had engaged in a choice-of-law process or that its application of the chosen law was parochial.

When an American court applies U.S. law to the foreign acts of a foreign government, and when that U.S. law has a strong regulatory character, a jurisdiction-to-prescribe issue is presented. This, too, the panel in *Chemical Bank II* failed to perceive. As in transnational antitrust cases, the court is fashioning a remedy for conduct abroad by a non-U.S. national that is not countenanced by U.S. standards. When the conduct is by a foreign government rather than by a private cartel, the issue is all the more sensitive.[14]

As it did on the issue of discrimination, the panel in *Chemical Bank II* may well have stumbled its way to a justifiable result on this point. This is primarily because—as noted above—its conclusion on discrimination probably would have been reached also by an international tribunal. The legitimacy of a foreign government's complaint about the reach of U.S. prescriptive jurisdiction is diluted, though not entirely eliminated, if the rule prescribed is no more stringent than one an international tribunal would prescribe. Arguably, the panel's result might also be supported by the rationale of objective territoriality often used in international antitrust cases, since the effects of the Cuban action were foreseeably felt by the banks in the United States. This rationale, though, has its own parochial credentials.[15]

Not only should U.S. courts, in applying or declining to apply the act of state doctrine, reach justifiable results; they should know how they got there and they should take a justifiable route to get there. The panel in *Chemical Bank II* was lucky; it reached a justifiable conclusion without betraying much awareness of how to go about it. Other courts may not be so lucky in close cases.[16]

FREDERIC L. KIRGIS, JR.

---

failed to find that there actually was discrimination against foreign nationals. *See* BP Exploration Co. (Libya) Ltd. v. Libyan Arab Republic, 53 ILR 297, 329 (1979); Libyan American Oil Co. v. Libyan Arab Republic, 20 ILM 1 (1981); Kuwait v. American Independent Oil Co., 21 ILM 976 (1982); American International Group, Inc. v. Iran, 4 IRAN-U.S. CLAIMS TRIBUNAL REP. 96 (1983), 23 ILM 1 (1984); Liberian Eastern Timber Corp. v. Liberia, 26 ILM 647 (1987). *Cf.* Schachter, *International Law in Theory and Practice*, 178 RECUEIL DES COURS 9, 314–21 (1982 V).

Of course, the Cuban discrimination in *Chemical Bank II* was in the form of an uncompensated deprivation of rights. Thus, the court did not have to rely solely on discrimination to find an international law violation, but it did so nevertheless.

[14] This point is more fully developed in Kirgis, *Act of State Exceptions and Choice of Law*, 44 U. COLO. L. REV. 173, 182–85 (1972), and *Addendum*, *id.* at 379, 380–85 (1973). *Cf.* Chow, *supra* note 3, at 447–74.

[15] *See* RESTATEMENT (REVISED), *supra* note 2, §402 comment *d* and Reporters' Note 2 (Tent. Draft No. 6, 1985).

[16] The approach outlined in this Comment should be applied even in a case involving the Second Hickenlooper Amendment. The amendment, 22 U.S.C. §2370(e)(2) (1982), contains its own choice of (U.S.) law but should be interpreted to apply only when a claim of title or other right to property stems from a violation of "true" international law—not just of standards asserted by the United States Government. *See* Kirgis, *supra* note 14, at 181–82, 185–86.

THE ALIEN TORT STATUTE AND THE FOUNDING OF THE CONSTITUTION

At this time of celebration of the bicentennial anniversary of the Constitution, students of international law might have a special interest in reexamining the allegedly obscure origin of the Alien Tort Statute for the light it throws on how the new nation worked out a role for international law in foreign relations. The Alien Tort Statute, part of the Judiciary Act of 1789, originally provided that "the district court . . . shall also have cognizance, concurrent with the courts of the several States, or the circuit courts, as the case may be, of all causes where an alien sues for a tort only in violation of the law of nations or a treaty of the United States."[1] In referring to that statute in a 1975 case, Judge Friendly said it was "a kind of legal Lohengrin; . . . no one seems to know whence it came."[2] It is true that no capsule summary of legislative history can be found explaining the origin of the Alien Tort Statute, but that is far from saying that the Founding Fathers let it slip in inadvertently.

It is not my purpose here to give a detailed legislative history of the Alien Tort Statute, but rather to recount in general terms what my investigation of that history has revealed. Inasmuch as invocation of the statute is becoming more frequent in human rights litigation in American courts,[3] there is no doubt that scholarly analyses of the legislative history will be forthcoming in the near future to complement an important recent study of the subject by Professor William Casto.[4]

In examining the record it should be recalled that the delegates at the Constitutional Convention assumed that if a particular issue "on the table" did not get into the Constitution, it would not necessarily be abandoned. Rather, the Founding Fathers negotiated a wide range of issues that we might characterize as belonging to the "organic laws" of the new nation. Some of these organic laws were so basic that they would find their way eventually into the draft of the Constitution proper. Others, somewhat less important, would be enacted by the First Congress as part of the structural statutory law of the new nation. The Founding Fathers were thus able to negotiate both *whether* a particular principle would govern the nation and *where* that principle would be located. The Committee on Style had a signifi-

[1] Judiciary Act of 1789, ch. 20, §9, 1 Stat. 73, 77 (1789) (currently, with minor changes, 28 U.S.C. §1350 (1982)).

[2] ITT v. Vencap, Ltd., 519 F.2d 1001, 1015 (2d Cir. 1975).

[3] *See* T. FRANCK & M. GLENNON, FOREIGN RELATIONS AND NATIONAL SECURITY LAW 136 (1987). An important decision applying the Alien Tort Statute, though not on a human rights issue, was handed down after this editorial was drafted. *See* Amerada Hess Shipping Corp. v. Argentine Republic, 830 F.2d 421 (2d Cir. 1987), *reprinted in* 26 ILM 1375 (1987), *summarized infra* at p. 126.

[4] Casto, *The Federal Courts' Protective Jurisdiction over Torts Committed in Violation of the Law of Nations*, 18 CONN. L. REV. 467 (1986). My basic disagreement with Professor Casto lies in his characterization of the Alien Tort Statute as jurisdictional only, and not providing a statutory cause of action. *Id.* at 479. My position to the contrary is suggested in D'Amato, *Judge Bork's Concept of the Law of Nations Is Seriously Mistaken*, 79 AJIL 92, 100–04 (1985).

cant role in this process, successfully arguing that the Constitution should not be an overly lengthy document.[5]

The Founding Fathers showed flexibility and comprehensiveness in including the term "law of nations" both in the new Constitution and in the organic legislation of 1789. The general idea was that crimes against the law of nations needed to be put into the Constitution proper so as to allow Congress to preempt any state legislation to the contrary, whereas jurisdiction over torts against the law of nations—where there was no preemptive need—was inserted into the organic legislation. Thus, Congress was given the power in section 8 of Article I of the Constitution to "define and punish Piracies and Felonies committed on the high Seas, and Offenses against the Law of Nations."[6] On the other hand, torts in violation of the law of nations were relegated to the First Judiciary Act. Here it was clearly recognized that it was not as important to preempt state initiatives, for as long as an alien could *choose* to sue in a federal court, there was no harm done if *concurrent* jurisdiction over the same tort was available in state court. Hence the original language of the Alien Tort Statute, above quoted.

Why did the Founding Fathers believe it important to have the Alien Tort Statute be part of the nation's organic legislation? While there were many specific incidents whose remedy the Framers may have had in mind—as ably recounted by Professor Casto[7]—the overriding purpose was to maintain a rigorous neutrality in the face of the warring European powers. The United States was still weak militarily, compared to England, France and Spain. Many years would be needed before the new nation could stand firm against any aggressive threat from abroad. During the formative years of buildup, it was imperative that no excuse, no *casus belli*, be given to a foreign power.

It is somewhat difficult today for us to appreciate the mind-set of the Framers in regard to this overriding question of national security, because we tend to think that wars in that era were launched for reasons of national aggrandizement and conquest. We also think that the situation is entirely different today in the nuclear and television age. The fear of nuclear war has put a damper on any enthusiasm for wars of national aggrandizement, and television has vividly portrayed situations involving abuse of our nationals or our interests abroad. The major foreign-policy turning points of both the Carter and the Reagan administrations involved American hostages taken by, or at the behest of, Iran. As the plight of these hostages appeared on nightly television, we thought that our national outrage over and concern about individual persons must be a hallmark of heightened

[5] The United States, therefore, ended up with a brief Constitution and a lengthy set of organic laws. Some countries (e.g., France) have just the organic legislation, which operates in the aggregate as a Constitution, while others (e.g., South Korea) have a very lengthy Constitution that contains all of the "organic" legislation.

[6] Interestingly, the Framers meant by "define" not our current usage, which suggests the idea of "inventing," but rather the old, broader usage, which emphasized the idea of "articulating" or "recognizing." *See* United States v. Smith, 18 U.S. (5 Wheat.) 153, 160–62 (1820) ("piracy" is sufficiently defined under the law of nations as to need no further definition by Congress).

[7] Casto, *supra* note 4.

sensitivity in our era to human rights and of the empathic power of the media.

The fact is that two or three centuries ago, the plight of individual citizens in foreign countries, and not territorial ambitions, was the major excuse for war. The masses of people then were pretty much like the masses today; they reacted far more to stories of maltreatment of their fellow citizens, even when the stories were largely through word of mouth and rudimentary pamphlets, than they did to the plottings of kings and princes for national expansion. The public was quite cynical about the latter; the pursuit of conquest usually meant privation, the possible disastrous loss of the war, or even in victory the enhancement of the kings and princes with no discernible benefits to the people. As a general matter, kings and princes had a hard time raising armies, because armies in those days were voluntary organizations. The best way to raise an army was to whip up public sentiment against a foreign country, and public sentiment was most easily aroused when stories could be spread of insults to ambassadors abroad or denials of justice to fellow citizens traveling abroad. An insult to the nation's honor that could be felt in sympathy by every citizen was much more effective in mobilizing the troops than were appeals for conquest.[8]

The most influential international law writer of the time, Emmerich de Vattel, referred specifically to "denial of justice" to aliens abroad as a justification for wars of reprisal launched by the alien's home nation.[9] Accordingly, Alexander Hamilton wrote in *The Federalist*:

> As the denial or perversion of justice by the sentences of courts, as well as in any other manner, is with reason classed among the just causes of war, it will follow that the federal judiciary ought to have cognizance of all causes in which the citizens of other countries are concerned.[10]

One way the Constitution reflected this concern was by providing in Article III for the extension of judicial power to cases and controversies "between a State, or the Citizens thereof, and foreign States, Citizens or Subjects" (the "Diversity Clause"). To make sure that tort claims based on violations of the law of nations were cognizable in federal courts, regardless

[8] I even suspect that a major factor in the victory of the colonies over Great Britain was the fact that King George lacked specific stories to tell of colonists' maltreatment of British officials, and hence had to rely on less visceral appeals based on the loss of tax revenue from the colonies. As a result, Britain did not commit the resources to the American Revolution that it could have committed had there been a more persuasive national excuse for mobilizing armies and transporting them across the Atlantic. If I am correct in this assessment, then the revolution was won largely because American leaders in those days accurately perceived the need to couch their demands for independence in terms of political usurpation, while successfully avoiding and for the most part prohibiting what today would be called "terrorism" against British officials or British subjects.

[9] 3 E. DE VATTEL, THE LAW OF NATIONS, bk. II, ch. XVIII, §350, at 230–31 (Carnegie ed. trans. Fenwick 1916) (1758 ed.). The Supreme Court continues to use Vattel as the authoritative source of what the "law of nations" meant to the Founding Fathers. *See* United States Steel Corp. v. Multistate Tax Comm'n, 434 U.S. 452 (1978).

[10] THE FEDERALIST NO. 80, at 517 (A. Hamilton) (Sesquicentennial Ed. E. M. Earle introd.).

of jurisdictional amount (there was originally a $500 limitation in diversity cases), the Alien Tort Statute was designated to be part of the First Judiciary Act by the negotiators at the Constitutional Convention. Insofar as the Alien Tort Statute derives its power from the Diversity Clause, it allows an alien plaintiff to sue American citizens. But it is also possible under the statute for an alien plaintiff to sue an alien defendant (if the case involves other sufficient jurisdictional contacts with the United States). This power derives from the second way that the Constitution reflected Hamilton's concern—by the "Arising Under" clause of Article III, which extends federal judicial power to all cases "arising under [the] Constitution, the Laws of the United States, and Treaties made . . . under their Authority."[11]

It is not difficult to read between the lines of Alexander Hamilton's statement. He was obviously afraid of what state courts might do in cases involving foreigners. State courts assuredly had jurisdiction, if they wanted it, over cases concerning the citizens of other countries, and could have dealt (as they can deal today) with torts against international law. But state courts in 1787 were notoriously biased against foreigners.[12] The result in state court could be the occasion of the very thing Hamilton feared most—the denial of justice to an alien. Hence, federal courts, with judges more insulated against state passions and more aware of the importance of maintaining neutrality for the new nation, were given direct jurisdictional authorization over cases brought by aliens alleging torts in violation of the law of nations.

Thus, the Alien Tort Statute was an important part of a national security interest in 1789. Acutely recognizing that denials of justice could provide a major excuse for a European power to launch a full-scale attack on our nation, the Founding Fathers made sure that any such provocation could be nipped in the bud by the impartial processes of federal courts. From today's vantage point, we can only say that their idea succeeded admirably. The reason the Alien Tort Statute is comparatively obscure today is that it worked.

A final question that can be raised is why the Framers did not simply divest all courts, federal and state, of jurisdiction over these potentially

[11] So far as I am aware, this specific argument—that the Alien Tort Statute allows suits between alien parties because of the "Arising Under" clause—has not yet been made in an American court. However, it would seem to follow from the Supreme Court's reasoning in Verlinden B.V. v. Central Bank of Nigeria, 461 U.S. 480, 491–97 (1983) ("Arising Under" clause validates an action by an alien against a foreign nation under the Foreign Sovereign Immunities Act), coupled with The Paquete Habana, 175 U.S. 677, 700 (1900) ("International law is part of our law . . .").

[12] Indeed, the very jurisdictional limitation of $500 operated to drive contract claims of British subjects against American citizens that were for less than $500 into state courts. The $500 limitation thus represented a compromise between the supporters of the national Government who wanted, at least in the larger cases, to ensure the implementation of the Definitive Treaty of Peace concluding the Revolutionary War ("Creditors on either Side shall meet with no lawful Impediment to the Recovery of the full value in Sterling Money of all bona fide Debts heretofore contracted") and the state-minded delegates who wanted to force British creditors into hostile state courts. Definitive Treaty of Peace, Sept. 3, 1783, United States–Great Britain, 8 Stat. 80, TS No. 104; *see* Casto, *supra* note 4, at 507–08.

war-inciting cases involving foreigners, and instead settle the cases politically in the executive branch of the national Government. Indeed, in suggesting that the Alien Tort Statute raises problems of constitutionality in regard to separation of powers, Judge Bork has indicated his strong preference for executive resolution of cases having foreign–policy implications.[13] Under the Reagan administration in particular, we have seen a thrust toward the political resolution of conflicts involving foreign interests and away from their judicial resolution—in the areas of extradition, extraterritorial application of U.S. law, act of state and sovereign immunity regarding denial of human rights. Why is it that the Founding Fathers did not opt for political instead of judicial control over such matters?

A little-known historical incident may illuminate this question. In 1794 a French fleet descended upon the British colony of Sierra Leone on the African coast. Led by an American slave trader who had a grudge against the colony, the French ransacked and plundered it for 2 weeks.[14] The British ambassador protested to the Government of the United States about the conduct of the American slaver and several other American citizens who had accompanied him in the attack. If the United States attempted to pay reparations to Great Britain, France surely would have been angered and might have been provoked into military hostilities against the United States. On the other hand, if the United States failed to do anything, Great Britain would have regarded the failure as a denial of justice. Fortunately, the Founding Fathers had foreseen this very dilemma a half-dozen years earlier when they enacted the Alien Tort Statute. Accordingly, the United States Government turned the matter over to Attorney General Bradford, who wrote a legal opinion addressed to the British minister plenipotentiary. The Attorney General explained:

> [T]here can be no doubt that the company [the Sierra Leone company] or individuals who have been injured by these acts of hostility have a remedy by a *civil* suit in the courts of the United States; jurisdiction being expressly given to these courts in all cases where an alien sues for a tort only, in violation of the laws of nations, or a treaty of the United States; . . . such a suit may be maintained by evidence taken at a distance, on a commission issued for that purpose . . . .[15]

Here, then, was the remedy. By providing for an impartial system of federal courts that had jurisdiction over such controversies, the new Government could shun political entanglements and no-win situations. The "law of nations" would serve as an impartial standard, acceptable to all nations, and torts committed by American citizens in violation of that law would be redressed through its application by federal courts. The fact that there is no further record of the incident (at least as far as I have been able to find) is a

[13] Tel-Oren v. Libyan Arab Republic, 726 F.2d 774 (D.C. Cir. 1984), *cert. denied*, 440 U.S. 1003 (1985). Given Judge Bork's reputation for insisting on the original intent of the Framers, it is rather interesting to find him saying in this case that the Framers did not understand separation of powers.

[14] For details of the incident, see C. FYFE, A HISTORY OF SIERRA LEONE 59–61 (1962).

[15] 1 Op. Att'y Gen. 57, 59 (1795).

good indication that Great Britain was satisfied with the Attorney General's opinion.

The imperative security interests that animated Alexander Hamilton and Attorney General Bradford are fortunately not as scary today. The military power of the United States today is such that insults and denials of justice to foreign nations will not jeopardize our existence. Nevertheless, the perception that we will deal fairly and impartially with cases having foreign implications, and not make political bargaining chips out of them, is still significant in terms of our national ideals, which include a free economic market, basic political freedoms for all people and willingness to submit to the rule of law.

ANTHONY D'AMATO

TAKING TREATIES SERIOUSLY

Treaties are the bones and sinew of the global body politic, making it possible for states to move from talk through compromise to solemn commitment. They are also its moral fiber, the evidence that governments and people have pledged their "full faith and credit" to one another.

This makes it all the more disturbing that the United States seems increasingly content to be perceived by other nations as indifferent to its most solemn treaty obligations. By refusing to pay our agreed assessed share of the United Nations budget, we have violated Article 17(2) of the UN Charter, the preeminent global treaty. By closing the Palestine Liberation Organization's observer mission to the United Nations, we will be violating the spirit and the consistent practice, if not the literal letter, of Article 4, section 11(5) of the Headquarters Agreement that we signed and ratified as a concomitant of establishing the United Nations in New York. That provision obliges the host country to impose no "impediments to transit to or from the headquarters district of . . . persons invited to the headquarters district by the United Nations." Successive U.S. administrations have read this as guaranteeing a right of establishment sufficient to allow the accessing delegation to function effectively. Our own Secretary of State has deplored such actual or potential violations, to no notable effect on Congress.

True, Article 1, section 8 of the Constitution of the United States, by assigning the "power of the purse" to the legislative branch, has mandated a sharing of all subject matter responsibility, even for the conduct of foreign relations. But the Constitution, in Article 2, section 2, has also established an orderly procedure by which Congress—through the Senate's advice and consent power—participates in pledging America's word to other nations. It is both morally and politically reprehensible for Congress to tell the world that America's word is no longer to be trusted.

Here we are, blaming the Russians for alleged violations of the ABM Treaty while displaying cavalier indifference to our own gross violations of treaties that the rest of the world takes seriously. Here we are, insisting on keeping a U.S. base in Cuba (yes, Cuba!) because it is ours by virtue of an 85-year-old treaty. And here we are, negotiating a new free-trade partnership with Canada and mutual arms reduction with the Soviet Union, by *treaty*, all the while undermining the credibility of our commitment.

True, nations other than the United States have violated solemn agreements. But this has never been a cost-free or victimless offense. Violator nations simply stop being trusted. They thus lose the ability to enter into effective obligations, becoming like an irresponsible person whose credit cards have been canceled. That is why all states at least *say* they subscribe to the view that, by customary law or by operation of Article 26 of the Vienna Convention on the Law of Treaties, *pacta sunt servanda* unless lawfully terminated or rendered inoperable. And it explains why the occasional violators, when charged with violations, always try to assert their innocence. The U.S. Congress, by contrast, heedlessly mandates actions that its own Government admits are in flagrant breach of treaty obligations.

One need but peruse the current issue of the U.S. *Treaties in Force* to see that we are party to thousands of treaties and agreements establishing civilized rules of travel, trade, diplomacy, arms control, the environment, antiterrorism, health, military base management and myriad other subjects of profound practical concern to Americans. A nation that deliberately sets out to debase its treaty-worthiness, quite simply, is in danger of becoming a global street person: self-destructive and heedless of its own best interests.

THOMAS M. FRANCK

NOTES AND COMMENTS

Lump Sum Agreements: Their Continuing Contribution to the Law of International Claims

Since there exists no international judicial system to adjudicate international claims in the ordinary course of events,[1] individuals and business enterprises with grievances against a foreign country have looked, both jointly and severally, either to the "espousal" of their claims by their government—a discretionary act guaranteeing no ultimate redress—or, assuming their government has been able to negotiate a *compromis* with the foreign country involved, to the adjudication of their claims by an ad hoc international tribunal, almost always one without funds from which to pay awards once rendered. However, the volume and complexity of the claims spawned by World War II, the arrival of Marxist governments in Eastern Europe and elsewhere, and the emergence of an economically restless Third World have rendered the espousal process increasingly less effective; and efforts to establish ad hoc international tribunals have been almost uniformly unproductive during the past four decades (the Algerian Accords establishing the Iran–United States Claims Tribunal[2] being the rare exception that proves the general proposition).

Since World War II, therefore, the United States, the United Kingdom, France and numerous other countries have attempted to resolve the international claims of their nationals primarily by another means, namely, by negotiating lump sum settlement agreements under which the respondent state pays a fixed—sometimes called an "*en bloc*" or "global"—sum to the claimant state, and the latter, generally through a national claims commission established pursuant to domestic legislation (such as the United States Foreign Claims Settlement Commission,[3] the British Foreign Compensation

[1] The Nottebohm Case (Liechtenstein v. Guat.), Second Phase, 1955 ICJ Rep. 4 (Judgment of Apr. 6), and Barcelona Traction, Light & Power Co., Ltd. (Belg. v. Spain) (New Application), 1970 ICJ Rep. 4 (Judgment of Feb. 5), stand out as rare postwar examples of resort to the International Court of Justice for the adjudication of international claims. The United States recently instituted proceedings against Italy in the *Raytheon* case, which will be decided by a five-judge Chamber of the Court. *See* Elettronica Sicula S.p.A. (ELSI), Constitution of Chamber, 1987 ICJ Rep. 3 (Order of Mar. 2).

[2] Declaration of the Government of the Democratic and Popular Republic of Algeria Concerning the Settlement of Claims by the Government of the United States of America and the Government of the Islamic Republic of Iran, *reprinted in* 75 AJIL 422 (1981), 20 ILM 230 (1981). *See generally* The Iran–United States Claims Tribunal 1981–1983 (R. Lillich ed. 1984).

[3] For relevant discussion, see R. Lillich, International Claims: Their Adjudication by National Commissions (1962).

Commission[4] and the French *commissions de répartitions*[5]), adjudicates the separate claims and allocates a share of the fund to each successful claimant. While use of lump sum agreements dates back to the commencement of the modern law of international claims (the Jay Treaty of 1794[6]), in the last 40 years this procedural device has become, without doubt, the paramount vehicle for settling international claims.

A dozen years ago, as part of a series of studies of the postwar lump sum settlement–national claims commission process,[7] we completed a two-volume treatise describing and evaluating the substantive norms and procedural techniques found in 139 lump sum agreements concluded between the end of World War II and 1975;[8] currently, we are at work on a supplementary volume, examining 29 additional lump sum agreements made public, and for the most part concluded, in the period since 1975.[9] Remarkably, despite a division in the global community arguably greater than ever before and despite the "extralegal" influences that tailor specific agreements to the particular needs of the contracting states, a preliminary assessment of the norms emerging from these 29 lump sum agreements reveals little variation (albeit occasionally some progressive development) from the norms emanating from the 139 similar agreements surveyed previously—which, in turn, were in many instances identical to the norms established before heavy reliance on the lump sum settlement–national claims commissions device.

This Note revisits the jurisprudential significance of this finding, which, if confirmed upon further analysis, lends additional support to our earlier thesis that lump sum agreements have been and are likely to remain an important source of international law, in general, and of the contemporary law of international claims and state responsibility, in particular. The jurisprudential issue has been the subject of intense debate ever since 1970, when the International Court of Justice in the *Barcelona Traction* case[10] gave lump sum settlements short shrift in just 16 lines, despite the fact that

[4] For relevant discussion, see R. LILLICH, INTERNATIONAL CLAIMS: POSTWAR BRITISH PRACTICE (1967).

[5] For relevant discussion, see B. WESTON, INTERNATIONAL CLAIMS: POSTWAR FRENCH PRACTICE (1971).

[6] Agreement with Great Britain, Nov. 19, 1794, 8 Stat. 116, TS No. 105. When one of the three international claims commissions established under the Jay Treaty broke down, Great Britain and the United States negotiated the first modern lump sum agreement. Agreement with Great Britain, Jan. 8, 1802, 8 Stat. 196, TS No. 108.

[7] *See* R. LILLICH, *supra* note 3; R. LILLICH & G. CHRISTENSON, INTERNATIONAL CLAIMS: THEIR PREPARATION AND PRESENTATION (1962); R. LILLICH, *supra* note 4; and B. WESTON, *supra* note 5. *See also* INTERNATIONAL CLAIMS: CONTEMPORARY EUROPEAN PRACTICE (R. Lillich & B. Weston eds. 1982).

[8] *See* R. LILLICH & B. WESTON, INTERNATIONAL CLAIMS: THEIR SETTLEMENT BY LUMP SUM AGREEMENTS (2 vols. 1975).

[9] These lump sum agreements are listed in the appendix to this Note. The authors would welcome copies of, or citations to, others they may have overlooked.

[10] 1970 ICJ REP. at 40. *See* Lillich, *The Rigidity of Barcelona*, 65 AJIL 522 (1971). *See also* Round Table, *Toward More Adequate Diplomatic Protection of Private Claims: "Aris Gloves," "Barcelona Traction," and Beyond*, 65 ASIL PROC. 333 (1971).

such settlements, with no diminution in their use anticipated, already numbered over a hundred at the time. Far from reflecting (much less creating) international law, the Court declared, lump sum agreements were *sui generis*, prescribing no more than a *lex specialis*; therefore, having no legal effect beyond the unique circumstances giving rise to them, lump sum agreements were not to be dignified as "sources" of general international law.

In our 1975 treatise, we devoted nearly an entire chapter to demonstrating that the International Court of Justice was incorrect in its approach to these agreements, unfortunately not to the satisfaction of all courts and commentators.[11] We concluded:

> first, that lump sum agreements fall squarely within the ambit of subparagraphs 1(a) and (b) of Article 38 of the Statute of the International Court of Justice; second, that as "sources" of "international custom" they can and must be treated in the same manner as any other international prescription; third, that this treatment should be both contextual and policy-oriented in character; and, finally, that as a result of such treatment (but only after such treatment) they can be accorded binding, analogical, or no effect whatsoever. Continued adherence to a theory that would deny the validity of these conclusions by relegating the whole phenomenon of lump sum agreement-making to an inferior status within the pantheon of international [legal] prescription is . . . to deny a growing edge of international law. Worse, it is to misconceive the nature of law and legal process.[12]

We continue to believe that the above statement properly specifies how, as a jurisprudential matter, lump sum agreements should be treated, *Barcelona Traction* notwithstanding.

Since the above statement was written, however, certain developments have taken place that oblige us to acknowledge that, as an empirical matter, lump sum agreements have yet to be accorded the full jurisprudential significance that we believe should attach to them. For instance, the United States Court of Appeals for the Second Circuit, in its much cited opinion in *Banco Nacional de Cuba v. Chase Manhattan Bank*,[13] rejected the argument, advanced by Cuba's counsel,[14] that lump sum agreements had contributed to the development of a partial compensation rule. In urging that Chase Manhattan had no right to more than partial (50 percent) compensation because past negotiated settlements had resulted in payment no greater than 40–60 percent of the value of the claims, Banco Nacional, according to

[11] *See infra* text accompanying notes 13–33.

[12] 1 R. LILLICH & B. WESTON, *supra* note 8, at 43.

[13] 658 F.2d 875 (2d Cir. 1981). *See* Note, *International Law: An "Appropriate" Compensation Standard for Nationalized Property:* Banco Nacional de Cuba v. Chase Manhattan Bank, 66 MINN. L. REV. 931 (1982).

[14] *See* Rabinowitz, *The Impact of the Cuban Nationalizations on Compensation and Valuation Standards*, in 4 THE VALUATION OF NATIONALIZED PROPERTY IN INTERNATIONAL LAW 133, 143–44 (R. Lillich ed. & contrib. 1987) [hereinafter VALUATION]. The first of the undersigned was called by Cuba as an expert witness on negotiated settlements and lump sum agreements. *Id.* at 143 n.38.

Circuit Judge Amalya Kearse, was confusing adjudication with compromise. Wrote Judge Kearse:

> Partial compensation inheres in the process of negotiation and compromise; we should no more look to the outcome of such a process to determine the rights and duties of the parties in expropriation matters than we would look to the results of settlements in ordinary tort or contract cases to determine the rules of damages to be applied. Were we to adopt the view pressed by Banco Nacional, either there would be no incentive for an expropriating state to negotiate a settlement, or, more likely, the prospect of a partial compensation award in a court would lead to the negotiation of a settlement at an even lower level. Carrying the process to its logical conclusion, the courts would then be asked to take into account these lower settlements in making the next adjudicated awards.[15]

"We are concerned with the parties' rights and duties," Judge Kearse concluded, "and we do not believe that international law as to compensation is merely descriptive of their conciliatory actions."[16]

International arbitral tribunals, too, have weighed the jurisprudential importance of lump sum agreements and reached somewhat the same conclusion.[17] For example, assessing the present state of customary international law on the question of compensation for nationalized property, the Iran–United States Claims Tribunal, in *Sedco, Inc. v. National Iranian Oil Co. and Iran*,[18] found much state practice of questionable evidentiary value. The Tribunal pointedly referred to lump sum agreements between states and to compensation settlements negotiated between states and foreign companies. Both types of agreement, the Tribunal observed, are too inspired by "non-judicial" considerations to be of much value as evidence of custom accepted as law.[19] The U.S. arbitrator, Charles N. Brower, in a separate opinion, agreed with "the reservations expressed in the Interlocutory Award in regard to lump sum settlement agreements between States."[20] He further observed "that where juridical concerns are more involved, as when the disputes are capable of being referred to enforceable arbitration, then settlements more closely approximate full compensation."[21]

Other U.S. arbitrators, in separate opinions to the Tribunal's awards, also have discussed and downplayed the juridical impact of lump sum agree-

[15] 658 F.2d at 892.

[16] *Id.*

[17] *Cf., e.g.*, In the Matter of an Arbitration Between the Government of the State of Kuwait and the American Independent Oil Co. (AMINOIL), 21 ILM 976, 1036–37 (1982).

[18] Case No. 129, [Interlocutory Award No.] ITL 59-129-3 (Mar. 27, 1986) (Chamber 3), *reprinted in* 25 ILM 629 (1986).

[19] *Id.*, 25 ILM at 633 (citing *Barcelona Traction*, *supra* note 1, and *AMINOIL*, *supra* note 17).

[20] 25 ILM at 641–42 (Brower, Arb., sep. op.). In a footnote he reiterated that "such settlements are suspect as guides to the substance of customary international law." *Id.* at 642 n.11.

[21] *Id.* at 642 (citing Seidl-Hohenveldern, *Austrian Practice on Lump Sum Compensation by Treaty*, 70 AJIL 763, 766–67 (1976), who made this point in connection with the Austrian-Italian Agreement of July 17, 1971, 1973 BUNDESGESETZBLATT NO. 635, *reprinted in* 1 R. LILLICH & B. WESTON, *supra* note 8, at 319).

ments. Thus, Howard M. Holtzmann, in *INA Corp. v. Iran*,[22] was critical of what he considered to be one scholar's[23] "almost exclusive reliance" on lump sum settlements in deriving contemporary state practice because, he said, such settlements "are not motivated by *opinio juris*, but rather are generally products of the particular prevailing social, economic, and political constraints bearing on the parties."[24] Similarly, but more categorically, in his separate opinion in *American International Group, Inc. v. Iran*,[25] Richard M. Mosk stated that

> [p]ost World War II settlement practice has not modified international custom regarding promptness of compensation. Such settlements do not reflect legal determinations, but rather are negotiated resolutions of claims that obligations were breached. Each settlement agreement should be deemed *sui generis*. *See Barcelona Traction Case*, 1970 I.C.J. 3, 40 (Judgment of 5 February).[26]

Arbitrator Mosk added: "Certainly the lengthy negotiation process leading to lump sum settlements has no bearing on the appropriate time for the payment of compensation."[27]

Finally, scholarly opinion, much of which ignores the continued flow of lump sum agreements, is mixed on the weight to be accorded to them.[28] Two commentators writing from diametrically opposed positions recently have found common ground in discounting the impact of such settlements upon the customary international law governing compensation for nationalized property. Thus, Brice Clagett, a champion of the Hull ("prompt, adequate and effective") rule, argues that lump sum agreements "do not constitute legal precedents either impairing or creating exceptions to the traditional rule of customary international law requiring payment of going-concern value."[29] He continues:

> An international settlement for less than full value . . . no more proves a change in the international-law rule regarding compensation than a domestic settlement of a domestic dispute for less than full value proves a change in the compensation rules of the municipal legal system. In any dispute, regardless of its domestic or international character, financial or other considerations peculiar to the dispute may prompt the parties involved to enter into accommodations before

[22] 8 IRAN-U.S. CLAIMS TRIBUNAL REP. [hereinafter IRAN-U.S. C.T.R.] 373 (1985 I).

[23] *See* Schachter, *Compensation for Expropriation*, 78 AJIL 121, 126 (1984).

[24] 8 IRAN-U.S. C.T.R. at 399 (citing and quoting *Barcelona Traction, supra* note 1, *AMINOIL, supra* note 17, and *Chase Manhattan Bank, supra* note 13).

[25] 4 IRAN-U.S. C.T.R. 96 (1983 III).

[26] *Id.* at 116 n.1 (Mosk, Arb., concurring).

[27] *Id.*

[28] Thus, the reporters of the American Law Institute's new *Restatement* find their juridical impact "ambiguous." RESTATEMENT OF FOREIGN RELATIONS LAW OF THE UNITED STATES (REVISED) §712 Reporters' Note 1, at 131 (Tent. Draft No. 7, 1986) [hereinafter RESTATEMENT (REVISED)].

[29] Clagett, *Just Compensation in International Law: The Issues Before the Iran-United States Claims Tribunal*, in 4 VALUATION, *supra* note 14, at 31, 78 (later citing *Barcelona Traction, supra* note 1, and *Chase Manhattan Bank, supra* note 13).

judgment for reasons wholly extraneous to their legal rights or obligations.

In international disputes, moreover, political or economic considerations may sometimes force a party or a nation to accept a settlement for less than full value despite the legal merits of its claim, particularly if no adequate international forum exists in which the legal dispute involved may be adjudicated or arbitrated. Recognizing this fact, the United States has declared that "[a]cceptance by U.S. nationals of less than fair market value [as compensation for the expropriation of their property or contractual interests] does not constitute acceptance of any other standard by the U.S. Government." Applying the same rationale, the International Court of Justice has explicitly declared in another context that lump sum settlements are "*sui generis*," "specific agreements . . . reached to meet specific situations," and hence not supportive of a new international legal norm or an emerging *opinio juris*.[30]

At the other extreme is M. Sornarajah, an advocate of the view that compensation for nationalized property is a matter exclusively within the jurisdiction of the nationalizing state.[31] Noting that lump sum agreements involve not only "a rejection of the requirement of full compensation" but also "a rejection of the claim that assessment of compensation is a matter conclusively for the national tribunals," he asserts that "it would be too optimistic to regard them as having given rise to any rule of law,"[32] or at least one binding upon the developing states. His explanation of this apparent non sequitur is as follows:

> If the lump sum agreements do indeed constitute custom, then whatever principles that are drawn from them are not binding on the newly independent States which were emerging from colonialism around the period these agreements were being concluded. Since the Afro-Asian and Latin American States were asserting the principle of self-determination and permanent sovereignty over natural resources quite consistently during the formation of the customary practices contained in the lump sum agreements, they could argue that these customary practices are not binding upon them as they were "persistent objectors". Though the idea of a rule as to compensation being drawn from the lump sum agreements is attractive as the rule would be based on actual compromise settlements, yet such a rule may fail to secure universal

[30] *Id.* at 78–79 (citing *Barcelona Traction, supra* note 1, and *Chase Manhattan Bank, supra* note 13).

[31] Article 2(2)(c) of the Charter of Economic Rights and Duties of States, GA Res. 3281, 29 UN GAOR Supp. (No. 31) at 50, UN Doc. A/9631 (1975), unconditionally endorsed by Sornarajah, purports to "codify" this view. For a comprehensive, contextual critique of the issue in general and Article 2(2)(c) in specific, see Weston, *The New International Economic Order and the Deprivation of Foreign Proprietary Wealth: Some Reflections upon the Contemporary International Law Debate*, in INTERNATIONAL LAW OF STATE RESPONSIBILITY FOR INJURIES TO ALIENS 89 (R. Lillich ed. & contrib. 1983) [hereinafter Weston in STATE RESPONSIBILITY], a revised version of *The Charter of Economic Rights and Duties of States and the Deprivation of Foreign-Owned Wealth*, 75 AJIL 437 (1981).

[32] M. SORNARAJAH, THE PURSUIT OF NATIONALIZED PROPERTY 215 (1986).

> acceptance because it predated the claims made by the developing nations and does not take into account their particular interests. Hence, while the lump sum agreements constitute practice which involves the rejection of both full compensation and the exclusive competence of the national tribunals to assess compensation, one may have to reluctantly concede that the International Court of Justice may have been correct in characterizing them as *lex specialis*. They indicate a possible way in which nationalization disputes may be settled. But they give rise to no rule of international law.[33]

Sornarajah's dismissal of lump sum agreements rests upon reasoning not unlike that advanced by Samy Friedman over three decades ago,[34] namely, that international law contains no rule requiring a state to compensate foreigners when it nationalizes their property, and that lump sum agreements providing for compensation are not sources of state practice that help to create such a rule, even one based upon partial compensation. This reasoning was faulty when first advanced, wrong when we wrote our treatise,[35] and even more in error today, when yet another 29 lump sum agreements have been made that further underpin the compensation principle. Authorities such as Judge Eduardo Jiménez de Aréchaga,[36] Subrata Roy Chowdhury[37] and F. V. García-Amador[38]—all jurists from developing

[33] *Id.* at 216–17.

[34] S. FRIEDMAN, EXPROPRIATION IN INTERNATIONAL LAW 221 (1953). *Cf.* Knapp, *Comment*, 48 INT'L L. ASS'N REP. 177 (1958).

[35] *See* 1 R. LILLICH & B. WESTON, *supra* note 8, at 248–49.

[36] In Jiménez de Aréchaga's view, lump sum agreements demonstrate "that the legal foundation of the payment of compensation in the event of nationalization must be looked for in certain legal principles different from the classical doctrine." Jiménez de Aréchaga, *International Law in the Past Third of a Century*, 159 RECUEIL DES COURS 1, 299 (1978 I).

[37] According to Chowdhury:

> An empirical survey shows that a large number of agreements of the lump sum type were concluded which did not follow the Hull rule . . . .
>
> . . . [A]lthough the forms of the lump sum agreements in the postwar period vary considerably, the general trend seems to establish that none of the three components of the Hull rule, i.e. promptness, adequacy and effectiveness, was followed by and large in postwar state practice. On the contrary, the trend indicates the adoption of partial and negotiated compensation arrangements, depending upon the circumstances of each case.

Chowdhury, *Permanent Sovereignty and Its Impact on Stabilization Clauses, Standards of Compensation and Patterns of Development Co-operation*, in PERMANENT SOVEREIGNTY OVER NATURAL RESOURCES IN INTERNATIONAL LAW: PRINCIPLE AND PRACTICE 42, 59–60 (K. Hossain & S. R. Chowdhury eds. 1984).

[38] Professor García-Amador has stated the following:

> [L]ump sum agreements, far from envisaging "just" or "adequate" compensation, provided for "partial" negotiated indemnification, the amount of which varied appreciably depending on the circumstances. In the case of lump sum agreements, there is no absolute uniformity with regard to the rule followed in valuing the property and determining the amount of compensation, which is understandable in view of the diversity of the situations giving rise to this type of international settlement.

García-Amador, *The Proposed New International Economic Order: A New Approach to the Law Governing Nationalization and Compensation*, 12 LAW. AM. 1, 46–47 (1980) (footnote omitted).

states and all, moreover, writing in the decade after the Charter of Economic Rights and Duties of States[39]—have acknowledged this principle and found support for it in lump sum agreement practice.[40]

Two writers in particular have addressed at some length the weight to be accorded lump sum agreements, and without the preconceptions of Clagett or Sornarajah. Rudolf Dolzer, after noting both the International Court of Justice's dictum in *Barcelona Traction* and the views we expressed in our treatise, reaches the following, more balanced assessment:

> Certainly, lump sum agreements tend to have an "exceptional character" inasmuch as they relate to a variety of damages that occurred during war or warlike situations, and they also reflect the specifically political factors that characterize the necessity of resuming diplomatic and political ties under certain conditions; the precise formula reached in any such agreement thus has no particular value for the determination of customary law. On the other hand, an empirical survey easily demonstrates that a large number of agreements of the lump sum type have been concluded; *the International Court of Justice has not explained why such a large mass of state practice should not reveal, in a general way, any opinion prevailing in state practice. Much therefore speaks in favor of recognizing, for the purposes of customary law, not specific elements in specific treaties, but the general trend emerging from what seems to be common to such agreements.* A survey of lump sum agreements from this perspective yields two basic conclusions: that the Hull rule has not been observed in practice, and that the Calvo Doctrine (as applied to property rights) explains this practice even less than the Hull rule.[41]

Similarly, Vratislav Pechota, in a comment on the United States–Czechoslovak Agreement of 1981,[42] rejects the polarized views of Clagett and Sornarajah holding lump sum agreements to be juridically impotent. "It has been maintained," he observes,

[39] *See* note 31 *supra*.

[40] Indeed, to the extent that they suggest that the conclusion of many inadequate lump sum agreements has helped to establish a partial compensation norm, they obviously regard them as not only principle-reinforcing, but also norm-creating. For our views, rejecting a partial compensation rule but nevertheless recognizing that the impact of lump sum agreements upon the amount-of-compensation issue cannot be dismissed out of hand, see 1 R. LILLICH & B. WESTON, *supra* note 8, at 247–56. Our views obviously conflict with the ones held by both Clagett and Sornarajah. *Cf. id.* at 259:

> Regardless of one's leanings in the oft-heated debate over whether international law requires "prompt, adequate and effective" compensation or no compensation at all upon the major deprivation of foreign-owned wealth, few will find complete satisfaction in [our views]. The reason is that lump sum settlement practice has undeniably compromised the polar policy preferences advanced in this connection.

[41] Dolzer, *New Foundations of the Law of Expropriation of Alien Property*, 75 AJIL 553, 559–60 (1981) (emphasis added) (footnotes omitted).

[42] Pechota, *The 1981 U.S.-Czechoslovak Claims Settlement Agreement: An Epilogue to Postwar Nationalization and Expropriation Disputes*, 76 AJIL 639 (1982). The treaty in question is the Agreement on the Settlement of Certain Outstanding Claims and Financial Issues, Jan. 29, 1982, Czechoslovakia–United States, *reprinted in* 21 ILM 371 (1982).

> that the global settlements following the postwar nationalizations in the East European countries are "negotiated compromises and as such do not constitute a departure from the traditional international law principle";[43] yet, while they have created no new law common to the West and the East, their prevalence in the settlement practice cannot fail to undermine each side's case concerning the content of relevant international rules. Several scores of such global settlements have been reached through negotiation and compromise; *it would surely be wrong to dismiss them as diplomatic decisions that are addressed to private pecuniary claims and have no legal effect beyond the unique circumstances giving rise to them.* In the absence of other precedents, it is difficult to see how international customary law could preserve the classical doctrine of responsibility for nationalization predicated on the existence of an unlawful act, or, on the other hand, how it could create a universal norm recognizing the right of the nationalizing state to determine unilaterally the conditions under which property is taken from foreigners and whether or not compensation should be paid. Common sense and justice require a reappraisal of the doctrines unsustained by practice, so as to enable international law to play its proper role in facilitating rationality in decisions.[44]

Both Dolzer and Pechota thus endorse our views that lump sum agreements are important sources of the law of international claims in general, and, more specifically, that such settlements, together with investment treaties, arbitral awards and other relevant expressions of community expectation, support "the proposition that the principle of compensation as an international regulatory norm is yet alive even if under attack."[45] The controversy now, as when we first addressed the question, really focuses not upon the *principle*, but upon the *amount*, of compensation; and this question, in turn, raises the important issue of precisely what constitutes "just" compensation,[46] as well as the technical questions concerning the valuation standards to be used in determining it.[47] Here, the lump sum settlement–national claims commission device has made a real contribution towards a new consensus on compensation.[48] For example, although considerable ad-

[43] Stevenson, Comment, 54 ASIL PROC. 111, 112 (1960).

[44] Pechota, *supra* note 42, at 642–43 (emphasis added).

[45] Weston in STATE RESPONSIBILITY, *supra* note 31, at 106. As Judge Baxter, writing about lump sum agreements nearly two decades ago, remarked, "If *some* compensation is always paid, this may furnish proof that compensation must be paid in some degree and that nationalization without compensation is unlawful." Baxter, *Treaties and Custom*, 129 RECUEIL DES COURS 25, 87 (1970 I).

[46] The adjective "just," long preferred by us for its relatively value-free connotations, is now found in §712(1) of the American Law Institute's new *Restatement*. For some thoughts on the elements constituting just compensation, see RESTATEMENT (REVISED), *supra* note 28, §712 comment *d*, at 122–23. *See also* Lillich, *The Valuation of Nationalized Property in International Law: Toward a Consensus or More "Rich Chaos"?*, in 3 VALUATION, *supra* note 14, at 183, 195–204 (R. Lillich ed. & contrib. 1975).

[47] *See generally* 1–4 VALUATION, *supra* note 14 (R. Lillich ed. & contrib. 1972, 1973, 1975 & 1987).

[48] *See* 1 R. LILLICH & B. WESTON, *supra* note 8, at 247–56.

ditional data gathering will be required before any definitive conclusion can be reached, it now appears that the less lump sum settlements involve wartime or immediate postwar deprivations, the more compensation they provide.[49] In other words, a preliminary assessment of the additional 29 lump sum agreements now in hand suggests that such settlements continue to have a useful impact upon the compensation question, although one not always appreciated by courts and commentators.

One final point needs making, and it is one that cannot be overstressed. All the dissents from, or reservations to, the norm-creating impact of lump sum agreements that have been made by courts and commentators since *Barcelona Traction* pertain *exclusively* to matters of compensation (and, to a lesser extent, valuation). With respect to the other norms, standards or rules found in them—for instance, the continuous nationality requirement, the eligibility of direct or indirect stockholder claims, the rules of attribution and whether certain claims, e.g., "creeping expropriation" claims, are compensable—lump sum agreements never have been the object of criticism. Indeed, as to these norms, they are widely and frequently relied upon as relevant sources of international law, even by the Iran–United States Claims Tribunal.[50] Moreover, whatever the response of courts and commentators to lump sum agreements, the response of governments has been to continue to use them extensively as precedent for further such settlements. However much some international lawyers may wish the contrary, lump sum agreements, unlike the Cheshire cat, stubbornly refuse to fade away. Since they definitely are here to stay, a fact attested to by the appendix that follows, it is high time that the international community fully acknowledge their continuing contribution to the law of international claims.

RICHARD B. LILLICH & BURNS H. WESTON*

APPENDIX

CHRONOLOGICAL LIST OF AGREEMENTS

1. Denmark-Norway Agreement of Apr. 28, 1969, 736 UNTS 427.
2. Denmark-Hungary Agreement of Mar. 18, 1971, 797 UNTS 364.

[49] Thus, Pechota predicted that the U.S.-Czech Agreement of 1981 would generate more than 100% of certified U.S. claims, plus some interest, an "unprecedented" amount. Pechota, *supra* note 42, at 640. Although it seems that the actual figure is closer to 71%, FOREIGN CLAIMS SETTLEMENT COMMISSION OF THE UNITED STATES, 1985 ANN. REP. 43, it still represents a considerable improvement in the amount obtained compared to the record of recovery until 1975.

[50] Although the Tribunal has not invoked lump sum agreements directly, it has made use of them indirectly through resort to the jurisprudence of the Foreign Claims Settlement Commission of the United States, which adjudicates claims following the conclusion of U.S. lump sum agreements, the model for many of the provisions of the Claims Settlement Agreement. *See, e.g.*, International Schools Services, Inc. v. National Iranian Copper Industries Co., 5 IRAN-U.S. C.T.R. 338, 346 n.1 (1984 I).

* Of the Board of Editors. Research for this Note was made possible by a grant from the Exxon Education Fund to the Procedural Aspects of International Law Institute.

3. Switzerland-Hungary Agreement of Mar. 26, 1973, 964 UNTS 1973, 1974 RECUEIL OFFICIEL DES LOIS ET ORDONNANCES DE LA CONFÉDÉRATION SUISSE [RO] 1056, 1974 SAMMLUNG DER EIDGENÖSSISCHEN GESETZE [AS] 1506.
4. Canada-Czechoslovakia Agreement of Apr. 18, 1973, 1973 Can. TS No. 24.
5. Belgium–Federal Republic of Germany, Dec. 5, 1973, 954 UNTS 470.
6. United States–Peru Agreement of Feb. 19, 1974, 1 UST 227, TIAS No. 7792.
7. Federal Republic of Germany–Greece Agreement of June 13, 1974, 1975 BUNDESGESETZBLATT FÜR DIE REPUBLIK DEUTSCHLAND, TEIL 1 [BGB1] II 1085, 994 UNTS 165.
8. Austria-Czechoslovakia Agreement of Dec. 19, 1974, 1975 BUNDESGESETZBLATT FÜR DIE REPUBLIK ÖSTERREICH [BGB1] No. 152, 995 UNTS 325.
9. Federal Republic of Germany–Poland Agreement of Oct. 9, 1975, 1976 BGB1.II 393, 1016 UNTS 241.
10. Great Britain–Romania Agreement of Jan. 12, 1976, 1976 Gr. Brit. TS No. 9 (Cmd. 6376).
11. Poland–Great Britain Agreement of Mar. 30, 1976, 1976 Gr. Brit. TS No. 49 (Cmd. 6520), 1029 UNTS 87.
12. United States–Egypt Agreement of May 1, 1976, 4 UST 4214, TIAS No. 8446.
13. Switzerland-Morocco Agreement of June 6, 1978, 1978 BUNDESBLATT [BB] 1.II 729, 1981 RO 144, 1981 AS 145.
14. Great Britain–Cuba Agreement of Oct. 18, 1978, 1979 Gr. Brit. TS No. 20 (Cmd. 7452).
15. United States–People's Republic of China Agreement of May 11, 1979, 2 UST 1957, TIAS No. 9306.
16. Austria-Yugoslavia Agreement of Mar. 19, 1980, 1980 BGB1 No. 3037.
17. Switzerland-Zaire Agreement of Oct. 8, 1980, 1981 BB1.I 181, 1984 RO 170, 1984 AS 170.
18. Canada-Cuba Agreement of Nov. 7, 1980, 1981 Can. TS No. 18.
19. Canada–People's Republic of China Agreement of Aug. 20, 1981, 1981 Can. TS No. 21.
20. Great Britain–Czechoslovakia Agreement of Jan. 29, 1982, 1982 Gr. Brit. TS No. 21 (Cmd. 8557).
21. United States–Czechoslovakia Agreement of Jan. 29, 1982, 21 ILM 371 (1982).
22. Canada-Bulgaria Agreement of June 14, 1982, 1982 Can. TS No. 14.
23. Great Britain–Mauritius Agreement of July 7, 1982, 1983 Gr. Brit. TS No. 6 (Cmd. 8785).

24. Great Britain–Vanuatu Agreement of Mar. 13, 1984, 1984 Gr. Brit. TS No. 55 (Cmd. 9293).
25. Finland–German Democratic Republic Agreement of Oct. 3, 1984, 1984 SUOMEN ASETUSKOKOELMA No. 65.
26. United States–Ethiopia Agreement of Dec. 19, 1985, 25 ILM 56 (1986).
27. Great Britain–Union of Soviet Socialist Republics Agreement of July 15, 1986, 1986 Gr. Brit. TS No. 65 (Cmd. 30).
28. Sweden–German Democratic Republic Agreement of Oct. 24, 1986, 1987 SVERIGES ÖVERENSKOMMELSER MED FRÄMMANDE MAKTER No. 4.
29. Great Britain–People's Republic of China Agreement of June 5, 1987, 1987 Gr. Brit. TS No. 37 (Cmd. 198).

THE MEANING OF "PEOPLE" IN THE AFRICAN CHARTER ON HUMAN AND PEOPLES' RIGHTS

INTRODUCTION

The African Charter on Human and Peoples' Rights,[1] also known as the Banjul Charter on Human and Peoples' Rights,[2] was adopted by the 18th Assembly of Heads of State and Government of the Organization of African Unity (OAU), held in Nairobi in June 1981. Contrary to some expecta-

[1] OAU Doc. CAB/LEG/67/3/Rev.5 (1981), *reprinted in* 21 ILM 59 (1982), 27 REV. INT'L COMM'N JURISTS 76 (1981) [hereinafter Banjul Charter]. For views on general aspects of the Charter, see COMMISSION TO STUDY THE ORGANIZATION OF PEACE, REGIONAL PROTECTION OF HUMAN RIGHTS IN AFRICA (1980); O. C. EZE, HUMAN RIGHTS IN AFRICA: SOME SELECTED PROBLEMS (1984); N. S. REMBE, AFRICA AND REGIONAL PROTECTION OF HUMAN RIGHTS (1985); HUMAN RIGHTS AND DEVELOPMENT IN AFRICA (C. E. Welch & R. I. Meltzer eds., 1984); Kannyo, *The Banjul Charter on Human and Peoples' Rights: Genesis and Political Background,* in Welch & Meltzer (eds.), *supra,* at 128; D'Sa, *Human and Peoples' Rights: Distinctive Features of the African Charter,* 29 J. AFR. L. 72 (1985); Gittleman, *The African Charter on Human and Peoples' Rights: A Legal Analysis,* 22 VA. J. INT'L L. 667 (1982); Mumba, *Prospects for Regional Protection of Human Rights in Africa,* HOLDSWORTH L. REV. 101 (1982); Okere, *The Protection of Human Rights in Africa and the African Charter on Human and Peoples' Rights: Comparative Analysis with the European and American Systems,* 6 HUM. RTS. Q. 141 (1984); Turack, *The African Charter on Human and Peoples' Rights: Some Preliminary Thoughts,* 17 AKRON L. REV. 365 (1984); Umozurike, *The African Charter on Human and Peoples' Rights,* 77 AJIL 103 (1983). *See also* I. Diaite, La Notion de peuple de l'application de la Charte africaine des droits de l'homme et des peuples (paper presented at the Symposium International sur les Droits de l'Homme et des Peuples, Dakar, Oct. 25–30, 1982).

[2] Actually, this was the title finally agreed upon in honor of the drafting history of the Charter and to avoid confusing it with the 1963 Charter of the Organization of African Unity. However, the original title continues in use, even within OAU circles. *See* Gittleman, *supra* note 1, at 667. In this paper, the shorthand form Banjul Charter will be used.

tions,[3] the Charter stayed in limbo for only 5 years.[4] It entered into force on October 21, 1986, after the deposit of the 26th instrument of ratification, the number required by its Article 63(3). By April 16, 1987, there were 33 states parties to the Charter,[5] which makes it the largest regional human rights system in existence.[6]

The Banjul Charter departs, in very significant ways, from contemporary multilateral human rights instruments. One of these is the dynamic entrenchment of the concept of "peoples" into international human rights theory—a concept, however, that had long enjoyed some currency in international law.[7] As early as 1790, the decree of the French Constituent Assembly referred to both the rights of man and the rights of peoples.[8] More recently, the term has been liberally invoked "in a number of international instruments on human rights, and General Assembly resolutions, more particularly those dealing with self-determination and permanent sovereignty over natural resources."[9] For example, the Charter of the United Nations was adopted in the name of "We the Peoples" and it recognized, in Article 1(2), the principle of "self-determination of peoples." Common Article 1 of the 1966 International Human Rights Covenants deals with the right of peoples to self-determination. Furthermore, and specifically, in July 1976, a group of eminent individuals meeting in Algiers proposed to the world the Universal Declaration on the Rights of Peoples (Algiers Declaration),[10] in which a number of peoples' rights were elaborated.

[3] *See, e.g.*, Gittleman, *The African Commission on Human and Peoples' Rights: Prospects and Procedures*, in GUIDE TO INTERNATIONAL HUMAN RIGHTS PRACTICE 153, 160 (H. Hannum ed. 1984); Ojo & Sesay, *The O.A.U. and Human Rights: Prospects for the 1980s and Beyond*, 8 HUM. RTS. Q. 89, 101 (1986).

[4] By contrast, the International Human Rights Covenants of 1966 (International Covenant on Civil and Political Rights, and International Covenant on Economic, Social and Cultural Rights, annexed to GA Res. 2200 (XXI) (Dec. 19, 1966)) took 10 years to enter into force; the European Convention for the Protection of Human Rights and Fundamental Freedoms of 1950 took 3 years; and the American Convention on Human Rights of 1969 took 10 years.

[5] Information furnished by Adwoa Coleman-Tommy, an OAU legal officer, in a letter to the present writer dated Apr. 16, 1987.

[6] The European Convention has 21 parties, while the American system covers 19 states.

[7] *See, e.g.*, Virally, *Panorama du droit international contemporain: Cours général de droit international public*, 183 RECUEIL DES COURS 9, 57 (1983 V).

[8] Brownlie, *The Rights of Peoples in Modern International Law*, 9 BULL. AUSTL. SOC'Y LEGAL PHIL. [hereinafter BULL. AUSTL. SOC'Y] 104, 107 (1985).

[9] N. S. REMBE, *supra* note 1, at 122. *See, e.g.*, common Art. 1 of the 1966 Human Rights Covenants, *supra* note 4; GA Res. 1514 (XV) (Dec. 14, 1960); GA Res. 1803 (XVII) (Dec. 14, 1962); GA Res. 2625 (XXV) (Oct. 24, 1970).

[10] For the text, see IODC BULL., September 1976, at 47 [International Documentation Center]; R. FALK, HUMAN RIGHTS AND STATE SOVEREIGNTY 225 (1981). For discussion of the declaration, see POUR UN DROIT DES PEUPLES: ESSAIS SUR LA DÉCLARATION D'ALGER (A. Cassese & F. Jouve eds., 1981); Rigaux, *The Algiers Declaration of the Rights of Peoples*, in UN LAW/FUNDAMENTAL RIGHTS: TWO TOPICS IN INTERNATIONAL LAW 211 (A. Cassese ed. 1979); Falk, *The Algiers Declaration of the Rights of People and the Struggle for Human Rights*, in R. FALK, *supra*, at 185.

In spite of this concern for peoples and peoples' rights, the term "people" has not been authoritatively defined in any of the instruments that employ it. Moreover, it is not used to convey identical meanings in all these instruments. The intention of this paper, therefore, is to attempt to work out the meaning of the term "people" as used in the Banjul Charter, which the architects deliberately left undefined "so as not to end up in difficult discussion."[11] It will be argued that its meaning is not consistent in the Charter, as it is always determined by the context of the particular rights referred to. However, before the various meanings of the term are discussed, it might be helpful briefly to reflect upon the philosophy underlying the concept of "people" and the relationship between peoples' and human rights in the Banjul Charter.

PHILOSOPHY OF THE CONCEPT

Peoples' rights in the Banjul Charter are the embodiment of the African conception and philosophy of a person in society. In Africa, a person is not regarded as "an isolated and abstract individual, but an integral member of a group animated by a spirit of solidarity."[12] This point was stressed in the OAU rapporteur's report:

> Noting that in Africa, Man is part and parcel of the group, some delegations concluded that individual rights could be explained and justified only by the rights of the community. Consequently, they wished that the Draft Charter made room for the Peoples' Rights and adopt[ed] a more balanced approach to economic, social and cultural rights on the one hand and political and civil rights on the other.[13]

This attitude stands in stark contrast to the atomistic view of the western world, which regards individuals as locked in a constant struggle against society for the redemption of their rights.[14] Paragraph 4 of the Preamble to

[11] Rapporteur's Report, OAU Doc. CM/1149 (XXXVII), Ann. 1, at 4, para. 13 (1981), *quoted in* N. S. REMBE, *supra* note 1, at 112. This is not the only instance where an international instrument intentionally eschews defining a crucial term. For example, the International Law Commission during its work on the draft Declaration on the Rights and Duties of States declined to define what a state was. The Commission did not believe that any useful purpose would be served by such a definition and preferred to allow the word to be interpreted according to international practice. *See* 1949 Y.B. INT'L L. COMM'N 289; Lachs, *Development and General Trends of International Law in Our Time,* 169 RECUEIL DES COURS 2, 29 (1980 IV).

[12] Okere, *supra* note 1, at 148.

[13] Rapporteur's Report, *supra* note 11, at 3, para. 10, *quoted in* N. S. REMBE, *supra* note 1, at 121.

[14] *See* M'Baye, *Human Rights in Africa,* in THE INTERNATIONAL DIMENSIONS OF HUMAN RIGHTS 584 (K. Vasak ed. 1982), who states:

> The European conception of human rights, that is to say, a set of principles whose essential purpose is to be invoked by the individual against the group with which he is in conflict, is not met in traditional Africa. In Africa, the individual, completely taken over by the archetype of the totem, the common ancestor or the protective genius, merges into the group.

Id. at 588–89.

the Charter emphasizes the need to preserve the African perspective.[15] It requires the parties to take "*into consideration* the virtues of their historical tradition and the values of African civilization which should inspire and characterize their reflection on the concept of human and peoples' rights."[16]

There is yet another way of looking at the concept of "peoples." This is the one that inspired the Algiers Declaration.[17] "People" could be used in contradistinction to their state. This view, by separating the people from their state, does for collectivities what civil liberties do for individuals. It seeks to reserve a certain amount of political and economic space for peoples qua peoples. This space, or peoples' sovereignty, becomes critical where the interests of the people and those of the state diverge. Richard Falk, one of the principal proponents of the Algiers Declaration, explained this view as follows:

> Given [the] combination of domestic and international factors, it becomes clear that governments cannot be entrusted with the role of serving as the guardian of fundamental human rights. In this regard, the whole tradition of international law is to some extent regressive in the current era. Even the United Nations is an organization of states in which the interests of peoples are misleadingly assumed to be legitimately represented by governments. To the extent that the Third World is pledged to solidarity in its efforts to promote a new international economic order, it represents a coalition of capitalist and socialist governing structures. As such it seeks a *geographical redistribution* of wealth, power, and prestige. . . . As such, it is only a partial response to the structural base of domination, and must be supplemented from more populist and socialist perspectives. . . . A first step is for people to insist upon their own legitimacy as a source of rights, even as against the state.[18]

In my view, this perspective is as important as the first one. However, I do not think it was seriously contemplated by Africa's leaders when they

[15] *Cf.* Howard, *Is There an African Concept of Human Rights?*, in FOREIGN POLICY AND HUMAN RIGHTS II (R. J. Vincent ed. 1985); University of Toronto Development Studies Programme, Working Paper No. A:8 (1983).

[16] *See* Banjul Charter, *supra* note 1. The traditionalist approach must be submitted to rigid scrutiny, as many traditions are either of questionable relevance and utility or plainly oppressive (especially to women). The words of A. M. Babu, a leading African socialist activist, are worth noting:

> The politics and ideology of the past were the concentrated expression of their economics, the economics of the past, and have no relevance to the economics of the present or the economics of the future. . . .
>
> If those early forms of social organization also contained elements of democracy, it was the democracy of that particular time, totally unfitted to the democratic practice of man in the present epoch. To say that an African can learn democracy simply by looking backward to see how our great-grandparents behaved is not only meaningless but downright reactionary.

A. M. BABU, AFRICAN SOCIALISM OR SOCIALIST AFRICA? 58 (1981).

[17] *See supra* note 10.

[18] Falk, *supra* note 10, at 189–90 (emphasis in original).

adopted the Charter. The substantive provisions of the Banjul Charter and the OAU Charter, as well as OAU practice generally, indicate considerable deference to sovereignty and other state rights.

Human Rights vs. Peoples' Rights

The full title of the Banjul Charter raises the controversial question of the difference and relationship between (individual) human rights and (collective) peoples' rights. The relationship between the two must clearly be appreciated to avoid compromising either. In this connection, Roland Rich's three-premise approach could be a particularly helpful starting point:

> (1) The individual remains the primary subject of international human rights law.
>
> (2) International human rights law recognises the existence of groups.
>
> (3) The enjoyment of individual human rights requires certain human rights to devolve directly upon groups.[19]

The first is now generally accepted and does not require detailed examination. The individual is the cardinal subject of international human rights law. The second premise is rapidly becoming a well-settled principle, as international human rights law has already extended recognition to groups of persons as such. These include minorities, colonized peoples and indigenous populations.[20] It is the third that requires a closer look, for it is the raison d'être of collective rights.

Karel Vasak referred to collective rights, similar to those covered in the Banjul Charter, as belonging to the third generation of human rights and termed them "solidarity rights." According to him, rights under this umbrella

> seek to infuse the human dimension into areas where it has all too often been missing, having been left to the State or States. . . . [T]hey are new in that they may both be *invoked against* the State and *demanded* of it; but above all . . . they can be realized only through the concerted efforts of all the actors on the social scene: the individual, the State, public and private bodies and the international community.[21]

Here we can detect elements of peoples' sovereignty, not only in the political, but in the economic sphere as well. In addition, and perhaps more

[19] Rich, *The Right to Development: A Right of Peoples?*, 9 Bull. Austl. Soc'y 120, 123 (1985).

[20] *Id.* at 124.

[21] K. Vasak, For the Third Generation of Human Rights: The Rights of Solidarity, paras. 9–10 (Inaugural Lecture, 10th Study Session of the International Institute of Human Rights, Strasbourg, July 1979, mimeo.), *quoted in* Marks, *infra,* at 441. For critical appraisals of the notion of a third generation of human rights, see Alston, *A Third Generation of Solidarity Rights: Progressive Development or Obfuscation of International Human Rights Law?*, 29 Neth. Int'l L. Rev. 307 (1982); Marks, *Emerging Human Rights: A New Generation for the 1980s?*, 33 Rutgers L. Rev. 435 (1981).

importantly, Vasak emphasized the need for concerted action in the effort to deliver certain rights—hence the solidarity tag.

The basic question, however, remains: are collective rights human rights or not? Part of the problem lies in the terminology itself. This is evident, for example, in the following comment:

> Can human rights, as opposed to obligations, be vested in States? . . . [T]here is no precedent in international law for the vesting of human rights in States. Human rights are vested in the individual. Certain collective rights derive from those individual rights, especially from the right to freedom of association. But does that mean that these rights extend to States or Governments?[22]

On the surface, it appears logical to state that a human right can only be enjoyed by a human being. Louis Sohn perhaps would respond to this observation by reminding us that because collective rights are always ultimately destined for individuals, they are *ipso facto* human rights:

> One of the main characteristics of humanity is that human beings are social creatures. Consequently, most individuals belong to various units, groups, and communities; they are simultaneously members of such units as a family, religious community, social club, trade union, professional association, racial group, people, nation, and state. It is not surprising, therefore, that international law not only recognizes inalienable rights of individuals, but also recognizes certain collective rights that are exercised jointly by individuals grouped into larger communities, including peoples and nations. These rights are still human rights; the effective exercise of collective rights is a precondition to the exercise of other rights, political or economic or both. If a community is not free, most of its members are also deprived of many important rights.[23]

The drafters of the 1966 International Human Rights Covenants adopted a similar position. That was why they included the collective right to self-determination in the Covenants and gave it pride of place. This strong endorsement, however, did not convince detractors of collective rights. Therefore, I suggest that collective rights be regarded as *sui generis.* They are not individual, but collective; they belong to groups, communities or peoples. When the group secures the rights in question, then the benefits redound to its individual constituents and are distributed as individual human rights. This concept can be illustrated by taking Professor Sohn's example of the club further: In an interclub tennis tournament, only clubs have the right to participate even though individuals actually play the game. Members as skilled as Navratilova or Lendl would not have an automatic right to play in tournaments. Contestants are entered by their clubs in accordance with the internal arrangements of those clubs. The individual's right to play can only be expressed in and through the club. This right is

[22] Taperrel, *Comment,* 9 BULL. AUSTL. SOC'Y 160 (1985). *Cf.* Crawford, *infra* note 69.

[23] Sohn, *The New International Law: Protection of the Rights of Individuals Rather Than States,* 32 AM. U.L. REV. 1, 48 (1982). *See also* Gros Espiell, *Self-Determination and Jus Cogens,* in A. Cassese (ed.), *supra* note 10, at 167–73.

actualized, first, by protecting the club's rights in the wider setting; and then by the individual's rights in the club. International collective and individual rights are no different.

Consequently, the Banjul Charter, by separating peoples' from human rights, does not obfuscate but progressively develops international human rights law. It shows, in clear terms, that there is a conceptual difference between collective (peoples') rights and individual (human) rights.

Furthermore, the Charter approaches the two categories in a balanced manner; it does not give the impression of favoring one category over the other. The fact that individual rights are not as well secured as one would have wished is due not to a preference for collective rights but to the political realities of the continent and the OAU. Governments were not yet ready in 1981 to have their affairs completely opened to international scrutiny. Moreover, a close examination of the Charter reveals that, in most of the cases, peoples' rights (as opposed to state rights) do not fare much better than individual rights. However, in its own way, the Banjul Charter at least theoretically recognizes that all classes of rights (political, economic, individual and collective) are equal and synergetic. This result is a far cry from the position maintained by Eugene Kamenka on the place of the "new" collective rights:

> The point is to recognise any claim made for this third-generation of rights as valid only in so far as it extends, rather than destroys, first generation rights—i.e. the autonomy of individuals and their civil and political liberties. To say this is to insist that second and third generation rights are to be read through, understood in terms of, first generation rights.[24]

This interpretation, without any doubt, would have the effect of dragging the human rights debate back over mountains already conquered and bridges already crossed;[25] it represents a distinct philosophical and ideological choice. In this regard, the Banjul Charter sought to consolidate the gains made in the interpretation and rationalization of international human rights.

The Meaning of "People"

The definition of "people" has primarily been approached in the context of the right to self-determination, where it has been used to indicate an ethnic community or a community that identifies itself as such because of common interests. Yoram Dinstein, writing with Middle Eastern problems in mind, identified subjective and objective qualities of the term:

> The objective element is that there has to exist an ethnic group linked by common history. . . .

[24] Kamenka, *Human Rights, Peoples' Rights,* 9 Bull. Austl. Soc'y 148, 158 (1985).

[25] *See, e.g.,* Final Act of the International Conference on Human Rights (Proclamation of Tehran), May 13, 1968, UN Doc. A/CONF.32/41 (1968); GA Res. 32/130 (Dec. 16, 1977); Jhabvala, *On Human Rights in the Socio-Economic Context,* 31 Neth. Int'l L. Rev. 149 (1984); Sohn, *supra* note 22, at 62–64.

> . . . It is not enough to have an ethnic link in the sense of past genealogy and history. It is essential to have a present ethos or state of mind. A people is both entitled and required to identify itself as such.[26]

Ian Brownlie expanded on that definition but laid more emphasis on identity:

> No doubt there has been continuing doubt over the definition of what is a "people" for the purpose of applying the principle of self-determination. Nonetheless, the principle appears to have a core of reasonable certainty. This core consists in the right of a community which has a distinct character to have this character reflected in the institutions of government under which it lives. The concept of distinct character depends on a number of criteria which may appear in combination. Race (or nationality) is one of the more important of the relevant criteria, but the concept of race can only be expressed scientifically in terms of more specific features, in which matters of culture, language, religion and group psychology predominate. The physical indicia of race and nationality may evidence the cultural distinctiveness of a group but they certainly do not inevitably condition it. Indeed, if the purely ethnic criteria are applied exclusively many long existing national identities would be negated on academic grounds as, for example, the United States.[27]

In a report written for the United Nations, Aureliu Cristescu offered a limited definition of the term "people" for the purposes of the right to self-determination. He preceded it by explaining that the United Nations had proceeded cautiously, albeit firmly, in the struggle against colonialism and that it would not be possible to produce a definition covering all possible situations. From the specific situations already witnessed, he believed the following elements had emerged:

> (a) The term "people" denotes a social entity possessing a clear identity and its own characteristics;
>
> (b) It implies a relationship with a territory, even if the people in question has been wrongfully expelled from it and artificially replaced by another population;
>
> (c) A people should not be confused with ethnic, religious or linguistic minorities, whose existence and rights are recognized in article 27 of the International Covenant on Civil and Political Rights.[28]

Among these three writers, the main attributes of peoplehood are presented, namely, commonality of interests, group identity, distinctiveness

[26] Dinstein, *Collective Human Rights of Peoples and Minorities,* 25 INT'L & COMP. L.Q. 102, 104 (1976).

[27] Brownlie, *supra* note 8, at 107–08.

[28] A. CRISTESCU, THE RIGHT TO SELF-DETERMINATION, HISTORICAL AND CURRENT DEVELOPMENT ON THE BASIS OF UNITED NATIONS INSTRUMENTS, para. 279, UN Doc. E/CN.4/Sub.2/404/Rev.1, UN Sales No. E.80.XIV.3 (1981); Ermacora, *The Protection of Minorities Before the United Nations,* 182 RECUEIL DES COURS 247, 327 (1983 IV).

and a territorial link. It is clear, therefore, that "people" could refer to a group of persons within a specific geographical entity (e.g., the Alur of Uganda or the Amandebele of Zimbabwe) as well as to all the persons within that entity (e.g., Ugandans or Zimbabweans). Both these references are common, but that does not make their use unambiguous. Cristescu's exclusion of minorities depended on certain assumptions that, as we shall soon see, are no longer tenable.

A. *"People" as Possessors of the Right to Political Self-Determination*

Under Article 20 of the Banjul Charter, the right to self-determination is guaranteed to all peoples.[29] However, paragraph 2 of Article 20 singles out colonized and oppressed peoples as the possessors of that right. This is the least problematic of the uses of "people." Under current international law, as evidenced, for example, by the practice of the United Nations,[30] the

[29] Article 20 of the Charter, *supra* note 1, reads as follows:

> 1. All peoples shall have the right to existence. They shall have the unquestionable and inalienable right to self-determination. They shall freely determine their political status and shall pursue their economic and social development according to the policy they have freely chosen.
>
> 2. Colonized or oppressed peoples shall have the right to free themselves from the bonds of domination by resorting to any means recognized by the international community.
>
> 3. All peoples shall have the right to the assistance of the States parties to the present Charter in their liberation struggle against foreign domination, be it political, economic or cultural.

[30] The Declaration on Principles of International Law Concerning Friendly Relations and Co-operation among States in Accordance with the Charter of the United Nations, GA Res. 2625 (XXV), *supra* note 9, when dealing with the principle of equal rights and self-determination of peoples, provides, inter alia:

> Nothing . . . shall be construed as authorizing or encouraging any action which would dismember or impair, totally or in part, the territorial integrity or political unity of sovereign and independent States conducting themselves in compliance with the principle of equal rights and self-determination of peoples as described above and thus possessed of a government representing the whole people belonging to the territory without distinction as to race, creed or colour.

See further para. 6, Declaration on the Granting of Independence to Colonial Countries and Peoples, GA Res. 1514 (XV), *supra* note 9. The UN Secretary-General, commenting on the Biafran crisis, stated: "So, as far as the question of secession of a particular section of a Member State is concerned, . . . [a]s an international organization, the United Nations has never accepted . . . and I do not believe it will ever accept the principle of secession of a part of its Member State." UN MONTHLY CHRON., February 1970, at 36. On UN law and practice, see generally M. POMERANCE, SELF-DETERMINATION IN LAW AND PRACTICE: THE NEW DOCTRINE IN THE UNITED NATIONS (1982); Emerson, *Self-Determination,* 65 AJIL 459, 464 (1971); A. CRISTESCU, *supra* note 28; Swan, *Self-Determination and the United Nations Charter,* 22 INDIAN J. INT'L L. 264 (1982); A. RIGO-SUREDA, THE EVOLUTION OF THE RIGHT TO SELF-DETERMINATION: A STUDY OF UNITED NATIONS PRACTICE (1973).

Organization of African Unity[31] and individual states,[32] political self-determination is generally equated with freedom from colonial-type rule. It does not extend to insistence by one sector of the population of an independent (or majority-ruled) state on its own form of self-determination, culminating, perhaps, in secession.[33]

Following this line of reasoning, Eisuke Suzuki suggested that, in reality, there are only three remaining opportunities for the exercise of this right in Africa: the dismantling of minority rule in South Africa, the achievement of independence for Namibia and the resolution of the problem of the Western Sahara.[34] International law has chosen to deny such groups as the Eritreans the right (privilege?) of designating their struggle as one for the attainment of the right to self-determination. That may be so, but even in the clear-cut cases there remain a few problems. Would the Amazulu, Amaxhosa, Basotho or other peoples of South Africa, for example, be entitled to pursue their own (genuine) independence from the Pretoria regime? By this, I do not mean the type of pseudo-independence that the apartheid Bantustan policy is all about,[35] but rather sovereign independence to the

[31] *See generally* Ijalaye, *Was "Biafra" at any Time a State in International Law?*, 65 AJIL 551 (1971); Nayar, *Self-Determination Beyond the Colonial Context: Biafra in Retrospect*, 10 TEX. INT'L L.J. 321 (1975); Akinyemi, *The Organization of African Unity and the Concept of Non-Interference in Internal Affairs of Member-States*, 46 BRIT. Y.B. INT'L L. 393 (1972–73); Ginther, *Re-defining International Law from the Point of View of Decolonisation and Development of African Regionalism*, 26 J. AFR. L. 49 (1982); Kamanu, *Secession and Self-Determination in Africa: An O.A.U. Dilemma*, 12 J. MOD. AFR. STUD. 355 (1974); Blay, *Changing African Perspectives on the Right to Self-Determination in the Wake of the Banjul Charter on Human and Peoples' Rights*, 29 J. AFR. L. 147, 149–55 (1985); OAU CHARTER arts. 2(1)(a) and (c), and 3(2), (3) and (5); OAU Res. AHG/16/1 (1964).

OAU Resolution AHG/16/1 (1964) provides, inter alia, that the Assembly of Heads of State and Government "declares that all Member States pledge themselves to respect the frontiers existing on the achievement of national independence." *See* 1st Ordinary Session of the Assembly of Heads of State and Government, July 17–21, 1964, *reprinted in* I. BROWNLIE, BASIC DOCUMENTS ON AFRICAN AFFAIRS 360–61 (1971).

[32] *See, e.g.*, ANGOLA CONST. art. 4: "The People's Republic of Angola shall be a unitary and indivisible State whose inviolable and inalienable territory shall be that defined by the present geographical limits of Angola, and any attempt at separatism or the dismembering of its territory shall be vigorously combated." *See further* SENEGAL CONST. art. 2; GABON CONST. art. 4; EGYPT CONST. art. 3; MALI CONST. art. 2; and Art. 1, Djibouti Const. Law No. 1 (LR/77–001, 1977). For these and other constitutions cited *infra*, see CONSTITUTIONS OF THE COUNTRIES OF THE WORLD (A. Blaustein & G. Flanz eds.).

[33] *Cf.* Nanda, *Self-Determination in International Law: The Tragic Tale of Two Cities—Islamabad (West Pakistan) and Dacca (East Pakistan)*, 66 AJIL 321 (1972). *See further* Nayar, *Self-Determination: The Bangladesh Experience*, 7 HUM. RTS. J. 231 (1974); Turp, *Le Droit de sécéssion en droit international public*, 20 CAN. Y.B. INT'L L. 24 (1982).

[34] Suzuki, *Self-Determination and World Public Order: Community Response to Territorial Separation*, 16 VA. J. INT'L L. 779 (1976). *See and compare generally* Amankwah, *Self-Determination in the Spanish Sahara: A Credibility Gap in the United Nations' Practice and Procedure in the Decolonisation Process*, 14 COMP. & INT'L L.J. SOUTHERN AFR. 34 (1981). An overview of the Eritrean problem is given in Medhin, *Eritrea: Background to Revolution*, 28 MONTHLY REV. 29 (1976).

[35] For a fuller discussion of this issue, see Richardson, *Self-Determination, International Law and the South African Bantustan Policy*, 17 COLUM. J. TRANSNAT'L L. 185 (1978); Swan, *Self-Determination Pretoria Style: The Case of Transkei*, 3 WHITTIER L. REV. 475 (1981); Norman, *The*

exclusion of all other peoples. Would such independence be a permissible exercise of the right under paragraph 2 of Article 20 of the Banjul Charter, entitling the people concerned to the assistance mentioned in paragraph 3 of that article? I think not. The analogy of the ban on secession from independent countries would apply here with equal force. That people would be seceding from a future state. International law already treats the right to self-determination as tied to a specific geographically defined territory. Further subdivisions would not be consistent with that position. Moreover, a people wishing to go its separate way, as, say, in South Africa, would have to renounce the authority of the liberation movement representing it. In our example, this would be the African National Congress or the Pan Africanist Congress, both of which are recognized by the OAU. That organization would be most unlikely to support any such secessionist aspirations.

From the foregoing, we can conclude that the first meaning of "people" is all the different communities (peoples), in fact, all persons within the boundaries of a country or geographical entity that has yet to achieve independence or majority rule. Once independence (or majority rule) is achieved, no further independence is permissible. The rights of the different peoples would thereafter be protected as minority rights.

Before leaving this point, I should observe that the rule against secession as an exercise of the right to self-determination is only a general one. Although it is backed by a solid body of UN, OAU and state practice, it can still admit a few exceptions. The independence of Bangladesh was one. Ved Nanda, in a definitive article on the subject,[36] demonstrated the existence of a set of circumstances that combined to lend a cloak of legitimacy to what would otherwise have been impermissible in international law. These were the physical separation of East from West Pakistan and the total domination of the former by the latter; the nature of their ethnic and cultural differences; the disparity in their economic growth to the disadvantage of East Pakistan; the electoral mandate to secede; the brutal suppression of dissent in East Pakistan; and the viability of both regions as separate entities.[37] The fact that the United Nations was presented with a fait accompli was also significant.

Although many of the secessionist claims in various parts of Africa have been characterized by some of the elements of the Bengali struggle, few have come close to matching it. For example: The secessionist activities in Katanga and Biafra were roundly condemned by the United Nations and the OAU as threats to sovereignty and territorial integrity. The situation in southern Sudan has not attracted much international legal concern. The

---

Transkei: South Africa's Illegitimate Child, 12 NEW ENG. L. REV. 585 (1977). *Cf.* Dekieffer & Hartquist, *Transkei: A Legitimate Birth,* 13 NEW ENG. L. REV. 428 (1978); Booysen, *The South African Homelands and Their Capacity to Conclude Treaties,* 8 S. AFR. Y.B. INT'L L. 58 (1982).

[36] *See* Nanda, *supra* note 33; *see also* Nanda, *Self-Determination under International Law: Validity of Claims to Secede,* 13 CASE W. RES. J. INT'L L. 257 (1981); Chen, *Self-Determination: An Important Dimension of the Demand for Freedom,* 75 ASIL PROC. 88 (1981).

[37] Nanda, *supra* note 33, at 328.

conflict in Eritrea has practically been shoved into a closet despite Eritrea's illegal absorption into the Ethiopian Empire in 1962.[38] Finally, the unilateral declaration of independence by the Saharan Arab Democratic Republic (SADR), as well as its subsequent admission into the OAU in 1982, was not an exercise in secession. Moroccan and Mauritanian claims to the territory of Western Sahara had been rejected by the International Court of Justice.[39] Subsequently, Morocco attempted to annex the territory by settling civilians there,[40] which implied that the Spanish were simply being replaced by Moroccans. The ensuing struggle for independence was akin to one against colonial rule. The fact that it did not fit the usual pattern of colonialism is not technically relevant.[41] The admission of the SADR into the OAU was a tribute more to the intense political and diplomatic activity of POLISARIO than to a legal principle. Moreover, the OAU Secretary General was faced with a 27-19 vote in favor of admission and therefore had no choice in the matter. The SADR, however, subsequently withdrew from the OAU.[42] Some of the interesting conclusions that can be drawn from the whole exercise are that the organization does not always have to seek compromises that do not address the real issues; that African unity can survive a crisis of that magnitude; and that maybe it could survive a successful assertion of self-determination by way of secession.

B. *"Peoples" as the Different Minorities*

The problems of minority protection were of prime concern to the League of Nations. Indeed, the modern international human rights edifice owes much of its character to the minority regimes set up in the aftermath of the Great War. This concern for minorities was inherited by the United Nations.[43] However, the problems facing the United Nations are far more

[38] The lack of serious involvement has been attributed by Malcolm Shaw, inter alia, to "the important status enjoyed in Africa by Ethiopia, at least prior to the revolution, Soviet and Cuban involvement and the complicating Arab dimension, coupled with the anti-secessionist stance adopted by the vast majority of African States." Shaw, *Dispute-Settlement in Africa,* 37 Y.B. WORLD AFF. 149, 158 (1983).

[39] Western Sahara, 1975 ICJ REP. 12, 67 (Advisory Opinion of Oct. 16); Shaw, *The Western Sahara Case,* 49 BRIT. Y.B. INT'L L. 118 (1978).

[40] Franck, *The Stealing of the Sahara,* 70 AJIL 694 (1976); Shaw, *supra* note 38, at 160.

[41] *Cf.* Blay, *supra* note 31, at 156–57. [42] *Id.* at 157.

[43] *Cf.* Suter, *Address,* in HUMAN RIGHTS FOR ABORIGINAL PEOPLE IN THE 1980S, at 37 (G. Nettheim ed. 1983):

> The League of Nations paid particular attention to the protection of minorities. It set standards which we are only now beginning to equal, such as the right of individuals to petition an international body regarding the alleged violation of their rights by their government. This concern arose partly from the belief that aggrieved minority populations are a potential cause of international unrest. . . . The UN was given the same task but it decided not to deal quite so much specifically with minorities as sueh but to improve the general economic and social well-being of all people. This neatly side-stepped the fact that almost all nations have problems with minority populations and avoided head-on collisions between the UN bodies and governments which are sensitive about minority questions.

Id.

extensive than those of the League, as the modern Organization must operate in an expanded context with a proliferation of members and minorities. One of these problems was to work out an acceptable definition of who constituted a minority. Several definitions were essayed with varying degrees of success.[44] The most satisfactory and acceptable was the one proffered by Francesco Capotorti in a report commissioned by the UN Sub-Commission on Prevention of Discrimination and Protection of Minorities. He suggested that a

> [m]inority is a group numerically inferior to the rest of the population of a State, in a non-dominant position whose members—being nationals of the State—possess ethnic, religious or linguistic characteristics differing from those of the rest of the population and show, if only implicitly, a sense of solidarity, directed towards preserving their culture, traditions, religion or language.[45]

The pertinent question, for present purposes, is whether or not a minority, thus defined, can be referred to as a "people" entitled to enjoy the peoples' rights contained in the Banjul Charter. If we do not confine ourselves within the straitjacket of assuming that peoplehood and the right to self-determination automatically lead to independent statehood, it is not difficult to appreciate that, indeed, a minority can fulfill all the requirements of a "people." As Felix Ermacora correctly argued:

> Unless the United Nations has not developed clear-cut ideas about the holder of the right to self-determination my opinion is that minorities also can be considered holders of the right to self-determination. Minorities must be considered as people. They must live also in a territory or they must have been living in a territory which is now occupied; they must have cultural or religious characteristics; they must be politically organized so that they can be represented; and they must be capable of an economic independence. It does not depend on governments as to how they are describing an entity as a people; it depends on objective and subjective criteria of a group. It depends also on the self-consciousness of identity. I think therefore, that national and racial, perhaps also religious, minorities could be considered peoples in the sense of an autonomous concept of the United Nations instruments. For them self-determination is inalienable.[46]

[44] Ermacora, *supra* note 28, at 268–81.

[45] F. Capotorti, Study on the Rights of Persons Belonging to Ethnic, Religious and Linguistic Minorities, UN Doc. E/CN.4/Sub.2/384/Rev.1, UN Sales No. E.78.XIV.1 (1979), *quoted in* Ermacora, *supra* note 28, at 276. Jules Deschênes, in a recent seminal paper, proposed the following definition of "minority":

> A group of citizens of a State, constituting a numerical minority and in a non-dominant position in that State, endowed with ethnic, religious or linguistic characteristics which differ from those of the majority of the population, having a sense of solidarity with one another, motivated, if only implicitly, by a collective will to survive and whose aim is to achieve equality with the majority in fact or in law.

Deschênes, Promotion, Protection and Restoration of Human Rights at the National, Regional and International Levels: Prevention of Discrimination and Protection of Minorities, UN Doc. E/CN.4/Sub.2/1985/31, para. 181, at 30.

[46] Ermacora, *supra* note 28, at 327.

It must be emphasized that total independence is not the exclusive form in which the right to self-determination is realizable.[47] What is important is that the rights of the group and its members receive recognition and protection.

Since secession is generally impermissible in current international law, all references to political self-determination, in relation to independent states, should mean respect for minority rights.[48] By the injunction of Article 19 that "[n]othing shall justify the domination of a people by another," the Banjul Charter proscribes external and internal forms of colonialism.[49] Minorities are entitled not to lose their identity and interests in the aggregation of the whole. Professor Sohn's views on common Article 1 of the 1966 International Covenants apply here with equal force. He wrote:

> The Covenants clearly endorse not only the right of external self-determination, but also the right of internal self-determination: the right of a people to establish its own political institutions, to develop its own economic resources, and to direct its own social and cultural evolution. . . . A people should be free both from interference by other peoples or states and from deprivation of its right to self-determination by a tyrant or dictator.[50]

In this connection, Ermacora[51] was undoubtedly justified in his criticism of Héctor Gros Espiell's assertion that contemporary international law does not recognize the right of minorities to self-determination.[52] Ermacora pointed out that "[i]t is not sufficient to state 'it is peoples as such that are

[47] *Id.* at 298–303. *See also* GA Res. 1514 (XV), *supra* note 30. For comments on a treaty option (like New Zealand's Waitangi Treaty of 1840) in the search for solutions to problems facing Aborigines in Australia, see WE CALL FOR A TREATY (J. Wright ed. 1985); "IT'S COMING YET . . . ": AN ABORIGINAL TREATY WITHIN AUSTRALIA BETWEEN AUSTRALIANS (S. Harris ed. 1979). *See generally* Barsh, *Indigenous Peoples: An Emerging Object of International Law,* 80 AJIL 369 (1986).

[48] Pierre Carignan made the following observations:

> Minority rights are a case where collective rights are given a sub-collectivity with no legal personality. In this case, rights are given individuals within the minority. They are, however, not given them *ut singuli,* but only as members of the collectivity. In this sense, we can characterize minority rights simply as being "more collective than individual": individuals are advantaged but only as individual members of the collectivity. Another aspect also makes minority rights distinct: no longer are all members of the collectivity active subjects of the right. For this reason, at one and the same time, while one member's rights may be respected another's may be denied.

Carignan, Address, in Report of the First Seminar on Human Rights Organized by the Human Rights Research and Education Centre, University of Ottawa, at 2 (1985). *See further* Rechetov, *Minority Rights in Contemporary International Law,* 31 REVUE HELLÉNIQUE DE DROIT INTERNATIONAL 154 (1978); Popovski, *Les Droits des minorités ethniques,* 26 QUESTIONS ACTUELLES DU SOCIALISME 62 (1976).

[49] *See generally* Sornarajah, *Internal Colonialism and Humanitarian Intervention,* 11 GA. J. INT'L & COMP. L. 45 (1981); Cassese, *Political Self-Determination—Old Concepts and New Developments,* in A. Cassese (ed.), *supra* note 10, at 137.

[50] Sohn, *supra* note 23, at 50.

[51] Ermacora, *supra* note 28, at 328.

[52] H. GROS ESPIELL, THE RIGHT TO SELF-DETERMINATION: IMPLEMENTATION OF UNITED NATIONS RESOLUTIONS, para. 56, UN Doc. E/CN.4/Sub.2/405/Rev.1, UN Sales No. E.79.XIV.5 (1980).

entitled to the right of self-determination' without analysing the conceptional relationship between 'minority' as a man-made conception and 'people' as an archetypic concept."[53] Plainly, if the term "people" is understood in context, and the right to self-determination unrestrictively interpreted, it is not difficult to apply the latter to minorities. Professor Gros Espiell's interpretation was an extension of earlier attempts, within the United Nations, "to confine the right of self-determination to the peoples of the non-self-governing territories, which belong to colonial empires that are the objects of specific obligations under article 1(3) of both Covenants as well as under articles 73 and 76 of the U.N. Charter."[54] The assumption was also made that emergence into a sovereign nation is the logical conclusion of pursuing the right to self-determination.

The right to existence in Article 20 addresses the problem of genocide—perhaps the single worst threat to minorities. In other cases involving self-determination, a people within a state should be sufficiently protected by respect for both its minority rights (e.g., language, culture, religion) and the human rights of its members. That this protection may break down and that minorities everywhere, especially in the Third World, are constantly in fear of repression are actualities that cannot be assured an unequivocal collective solution by international law. Such violations are regarded as violations of individual and minority rights and treated accordingly. The International Covenant on Civil and Political Rights of 1966 adopted a similar approach. In addition to individual rights and liberties, it made room for the protection of minority rights in Article 27.[55]

In light of the problem of pluralism, some of the newer African constitutions have recognized that the best guarantee of harmony and national unity is a serious commitment to minority rights. Article 3 of the 1979 Constitution of Benin (formerly Dahomey) is a good example of this trend:

> The Popular Republic of Benin is a unified multi-national state. All nationalities are equal in rights and duties. Consolidating and developing their union is a sacred duty of the State, which shall assure to each one a full development in unity through a just policy toward nationalities and an inter-regional balance.

[53] Ermacora, *supra* note 28, at 328.

[54] Sohn, *supra* note 23, at 49.

[55] Article 27 of the Covenant, *supra* note 4, states: "In those States in which ethnic, religious or linguistic minorities exist, persons belonging to such minorities shall not be denied the right, in community with the other members of their group, to enjoy their own culture, to profess and practise their own religion, or to use their own language." *See further* Provisions of International Instruments Relevant to the Problem of Persons Belonging to National, Ethnic, Religious or Linguistic Minorities, Note by the Secretary-General, UN Doc. E/CN.4/Sub.2/L.735 (1980); Tomuschat, *Protection of Minorities under Article 27 of the International Covenant on Civil and Political Rights,* in VÖLKERRECHT ALS RECHTSORDNUNG—INTERNATIONALE GERICHTSBARKEIT—MENSCHENRECHTE: FESTSCHRIFT FÜR HERMANN MOSLER 949 (1983); de Montigny, *L'O.N.U. et la protection internationale de minorités depuis 1945,* 13 REVUE JURIDIQUE THÉMIS 389 (1978); Capotorti, *The Protection of Minorities under Multilateral Agreements on Human Rights,* 2 ITALIAN Y.B. INT'L L. 3 (1976); Szabo, *Les Minorités et les droits de l'homme,* 23 ACTA JURIDICA 1 (1981); Kelly, *National Minorities in International Law,* 31 DENVER J. INT'L L. 253 (1973); Smith, *Ethnic Identity and World Order,* 12 J. INT'L STUD. 149 (1983).

All acts of regionalism shall be rigorously prohibited.

All nationalities shall be free to use their spoken and written language and to develop their own culture.

The State shall actively aid those nationalities living in undeveloped areas to attain the economic and cultural level of the country as a whole.[56]

Where minority and individual rights are respected, there will not be many motives for secession. The concept of "people," in this sense, is designed to achieve that objective.

C. "People" as the State (Economic Self-Determination)

Rights falling under the category of economic self-determination are set forth in Articles 21 and 22. These articles vest the rights concerning the exploitation and disposal of natural resources in peoples and states.[57] The problems addressed by the right to self-determination in the economic sense are determined by internal and external factors. This is the justification for vesting the right in both the people and the state. The Westphalian international order of the current epoch requires peoples to act through states when dealing with other peoples, states and entities. In the field of development, the state is an inevitable intermediary. This arises from the fact that

> *underdevelopment is a structural phenomenon linked to a given mode of international economic relations, and to a certain international division of labour.* Indeed, underdevelopment is the *direct result* of this division. Even

[56] *See also* Art. 9, Djibouti Const. Law No. 2 (LR/77-002, 1977).

[57] These two articles provide as follows:

Article 21

1. All peoples shall freely dispose of their wealth and natural resources. The right shall be exercised in the exclusive interest of the people. In no case shall a people be deprived of it.

2. In case of spoliation the dispossessed people shall have the right to the lawful recovery of its property as well as to an adequate compensation.

. . . .

4. States Parties to the present Charter shall individually and collectively exercise the right to free disposal of their wealth and natural resources with a view to strengthening African unity and solidarity.

5. States Parties to the present Charter shall undertake to eliminate all forms of foreign economic exploitation particularly that practised by international monopolies so as to enable their peoples to fully benefit from the advantages derived from their natural resources.

Article 22

1. All peoples shall have the right to their economic, social and cultural development with due regard to their freedom and identity and in the equal enjoyment of the common heritage of mankind.

2. States shall have the duty, individually or collectively, to ensure the exercise of the right to development.

> under the best conceivable government, in a country of outstanding wealth and resources, this international division of labour will indubitably, through the machinery of the international order, act like a leech, draining the country of its life-blood.[58]

These circumstances render it imperative to equate "peoples" with the state where the right to development is concerned. An entity less than the state cannot effectively contest the right to development in the international arena. The argument posited by Judge Bedjaoui against an individualistic extrapolation of the right to development would also apply to groups of people: "the individual's pursuit of the right to development vis-à-vis his State can only weaken the State and would occur at the very time when the State needs to be strengthened if it is to neutralize the negative effects of the international factors which counteract its collective development."[59]

The internal laws of many African countries give the state control over the major means of development, especially over the exploitation of natural resources. For example, Article 4 of the 1977 Constitution of the Democratic Republic of São Tomé and Principé provides in part:

> 1. In the economic realm, the State shall have as its objective the destruction of the colonial economic structure and the abolition of unjust privileges established in favor of foreign nations or individuals, the abolition of the underdeveloped state of the nation, and the creation of conditions suitable for elevating the standard of living of the workers and the general well-being of the entire population.
>
> 2. The land and the natural resources of the soil and subsoil, in territorial waters and on the continental shelf of the islands, shall be the property of the State, which shall determine the conditions of their improvement and their use.[60]

Some other constitutions vest natural resources in the people, as opposed to the state or government.[61] These include the Constitutions of Benin,[62] the Congo[63] and Egypt.[64] In practice, however, there is very little difference between the two approaches as natural resources are usually managed by the state through the government of the day. Whether the people benefit or not depends on the propensities of that government.

The "state-centric" character of the Banjul Charter reflects the position adopted by the proponents of the "New International Economic Order" (NIEO). For example, the Charter of Economic Rights and Duties of States of 1974 deals with state rights, which is why the right to permanent sover-

[58] Bedjaoui, *The Right to Development and the Jus Cogens,* LESOTHO L.J., No. 2, 1986, at 93, 98 (emphasis in original).

[59] *Id.* at 99.

[60] *See also* LIBERIA CONST. art. 22(b); ANGOLA CONST. art. 11; and SUDAN CONST. art. 37.

[61] *See, e.g.,* NIGERIA CONST. art. 40(3).

[62] Article 19 provides, in pertinent part: "State property is the property of the People as a whole. . . . Mineral resources, waters and forests, uncultivated lands and other natural resources that the law declares to be State property shall be the property of the People as a whole." BENIN CONST. art. 19.

[63] CONGO CONST. art. 30.

[64] EGYPT CONST. art. 24.

eignty over natural resources was vested in states.[65] The United Nations, however, had already created a precedent for the vesting of economic rights in states. General Assembly Resolution 1803 (XVII) of 1962 recognized the right of peoples and nations to permanent sovereignty over natural resources.[66]

As was mentioned above, the alternative of letting peoples contest the right to development directly in the international economic arena is not viable. However, equating states with "peoples" assumes that the interests of the people are adequately represented by their state—a rarity in most developing countries, as we all know. In consequence, equating peoples and states further strengthens the state and subjects the rights of the people to the whims of whoever controls the political process. This was the major valid criticism of the NIEO[67] and one of the reasons it has not been a success. For example, according to Shadrack Gutto:

> [P]rovisions such as those requiring transnational corporations to exchange industrial and trade information are absurd and unworkable; the same applies to the principles that attack concession gained by coercion. The latter principle is worthless in most third world countries where the leaderships are dependent on these same foreign interests for their social and political survival. It should be recognized that foreign investors are *inherently part and parcel of the political economies within which they operate.* To say that they should not "intervene" in the internal affairs of the countries they operate in is absurd and demonstrates the nature of legal thinking that fails to recognize the integrated nature of foreign capital. Provisions on the duty of states to regulate the activities of transnational corporations are also only relevant if one assumes a political leadership whose social interests and ideology stands in contradiction to those of such foreign institutions.[68]

In sum, the apparently progressive introduction of the concept of "peoples" into the Banjul Charter could actually turn out to be counterproductive in some respects, that is, where the rights and interests of the people are not respected by the state. In such situations, peoples' rights might initially be treated as state rights[69] and then degenerate into sectarian, class, government, regime and clique rights. In the extreme, they could become certain individuals' rights. This ultimate perversion has already come to pass in many African countries, such as Zaire,[70] where the incum-

[65] Art. 2, GA Res. 3281 (XXIX) (Dec. 12, 1974). *See also* Art. 4(e), Declaration on the Establishment of a New International Economic Order, GA Res. 3201 (S-VI) (May 1, 1974).

[66] Rich, *supra* note 19, at 125.

[67] Falk, *supra* note 10, at 189–90.

[68] Gutto, *Responsibility and Accountability of States, Transnational Corporations and Individuals in the Field of Human Rights to Social Development: A Critique,* in THIRD WORLD LEGAL STUDIES ASSOCIATION, HUMAN RIGHTS AND DEVELOPMENT 175, 180–81 (1984) (emphasis in original).

[69] *See generally* Crawford, *The Rights of Peoples: "Peoples" or "Governments"?,* 9 BULL. AUSTL. SOC'Y 136 (1985).

[70] *See, e.g.,* G. GRAN, DEVELOPMENT BY PEOPLE 137–38 (1983); G. GRAN, ZAIRE: THE POLITICAL ECONOMY OF UNDERDEVELOPMENT (1979).

bents have unfettered control over the disposal of natural resources and state wealth. In situations of despotic misrule, one of the first casualties is usually the economy, as the governors embark on orgies of personal enrichment. The outrageous exploits of such dictators as Amin, Bokassa and Nguema are legendary.[71] Indeed, politics in Africa, and the developing world generally, sometimes seems like a business venture.[72]

The intention of this third sense of "peoples" is not to take the ownership of natural resources away from the people; it is to give control to the country, so as to enable it effectively to protect and administer those resources for and on behalf of the people. Antonio Cassese, commenting on Article 1(2) of the Covenants, insisted on the need for popular sovereignty even in the economic arena:

> Article 1(2) . . . is not merely a reaffirmation of the right of every state over its own natural resources; it clearly provides that the right over natural wealth belongs to *peoples.* This has two distinct consequences. For dependent peoples, the right implies that the governing authority is under the duty to use the economic resources of the territory in the interest of the dependent people. In a sovereign state, the government must utilize the natural resources so as to benefit the whole people. The right of the people over natural resources, and the corresponding duty of the government, are but a consequence, in economic matters, of the people's right to (internal) self-determination in the political field. Just as the people of every sovereign state have a permanent right to choose their own form of government . . . , so the people are entitled to insist that the natural resources of the nation be exploited in the interest of the people.[73]

[71] An observer for the International Commission of Jurists at the trial of Macías Nguema recorded:

> The funds of the State had become totally confused with those of Macías. . . . Macías, as Head of State, took the national treasury to his palace of Nzeng Ayong . . . in the country near the border with Gabon. He administered the funds of the State from his house and sometimes from Bata—for he had not ventured into the capital for five years—without consulting either the bank or the ministry concerned.

A. ARTUCIO, THE TRIAL OF MACÍAS IN EQUATORIAL GUINEA: THE STORY OF A DICTATORSHIP 15 (International Commission of Jurists/International University Exchange Fund, 1979).

[72] *See, e.g.,* A. TÉVOÉDJRÈ, HUMAN RIGHTS AND DEMOCRACY IN AFRICA 13 (UN Univ. Annual Lecture Series, No. 2, 1985):

> In essence, politics in African countries became a very lucrative business, driving the ruling classes to hold on to power and opponents to strive by every possible means, including unconstitutional ones, to come into office. In the process, the voice of the people at the grass-roots level in the decision-making machinery of many African countries (the very essence of democracy) got drowned in a flood of political party quibbling, biases, and favours for party activists and adherents. In the final analysis, the misallocation of resources deprived some sections of the community of essential development, as distribution on considerations other than those of economic viability or feasibility became the yardstick of resource allocation.

[73] Cassese, *The Self-Determination of Peoples,* in THE INTERNATIONAL BILL OF HUMAN RIGHTS: THE COVENANT ON CIVIL AND POLITICAL RIGHTS 92, 103 (L. Henkin ed. 1981).

There is no necessary contradiction between the third meaning noted above, which equates "people" with the state, as long as the state acts for the benefit of all the people, and Professor Cassese's view, which underlines the need for democracy in the economic realm. This third meaning refers to the external application of the right to economic self-determination. The state would control the commanding heights of the economy so as to minimize leakage and benefit the people, that is, all the peoples. Under present circumstances, however, to achieve this goal, it is imperative that the state be controlled by the people—in the democratic sense. This is the message of the Algiers Declaration. It deals seriously with the relationship between peoples and their state[74] in a way the Banjul Charter does not. This omission needs urgent correction; otherwise, the whole basis of peoples' rights in the economic sense will hang in doubt.

D. "People" as All Persons Within a State

The corporate status of the state works very well, provided one is dealing with external matters and entities. Its misuse and abuse internally leads to the problems alluded to in the previous section. Because of the inherent nature of states and governments, at this point in time, a distinction must be drawn (internally, that is) between the people and their state. This distinction, although not well demarcated in the Banjul Charter, is important to recognize. The meaning of "people" it conveys is close to that discussed in section *A* above, the difference being that the state in question is independent or majority ruled. It is through this meaning that one can easily appreciate the duties of states toward their people, duties provided for in the Banjul Charter.[75]

Furthermore, "people" in this sense amounts to the aggregate of the different peoples in the sense noted in section *B*, referring to minorities. As such, the people have collective rights *against* their state. One of these is the uninterrupted enjoyment of the right to self-determination, which should protect the people against oppression and exploitation. To quote from another of Professor Cassese's numerous contributions on the subject:

> It should be added—with the force and clarity that can be found in the Algiers Declaration—that when the rights and fundamental freedoms of members of a people are systematically denied this means that that people's right of self-determination is also infringed. From this point of

[74] *See* Arts. 7 and 28 of the Universal Declaration on the Rights of Peoples, *supra* note 10, which read, respectively, as follows:

> Every People has the right to have a democratic government representing all the citizens without distinction as to race, sex, belief or color, and capable of ensuring effective respect for the human rights and fundamental freedoms of all.
>
> Any People whose fundamental rights are seriously disregarded has the right to enforce them, especially by political or trade union struggle and even, in the last resort, by the use of force.

[75] *See, e.g.*, Arts. 18, 25 and 26 of the Banjul Charter, *supra* note 1.

> view "internal" political self-determination is, therefore, the *synthesis and the summa of human rights.* Thus, "internal" political self-determination does not generically mean "self-government" but rather (a) the right to choose freely a government, exercising all the freedoms which make the choice possible (freedom of speech, of association, etc.) and (b) the right that the government, once chosen, continues to enjoy the consensus of the people and is neither oppressive nor authoritarian.[76]

The Banjul Charter provides for a set of individual rights and liberties, which should complement and reinforce the rights of peoples. However, the timorous approach to the protection of individual rights (or, indeed, any rights claimable against a state party) does not offer much hope for this meaning of peoples to be significantly asserted.

Provided the Commission is allowed to function effectively, it could redeem some of the ground apparently conceded to states and governments. It will be in the interest of all African countries and their peoples for popular democracy to be given a chance. The lofty ideals of the peoples' rights in the Banjul Charter—such as peace and development—depend, in large measure, on respect for individual rights.[77] Peoples' rights cannot be a substitute for individual human rights.

Conclusion

My intention has been to identify the meaning(s) of the term "people" as used in the African Charter on Human and Peoples' Rights. We have seen that the concept was adopted as a way of preserving the African conception of man and society. It was also resorted to as a legal tool in the struggle against external forms of political, social and economic domination. The Charter does not even pretend to extend the meaning of "people" to embrace popular sovereignty, such as, perhaps, in the manner of Corazon Aquino's Filipino revolution of January 1986. This omission raises problems of consistency, and thus makes more than one definition of "people" necessary to fit the different references to "people" and "peoples" in the Charter. In this paper, we have worked out four definitions:

(*A*) all persons within the geographical limits of an entity yet to achieve political independence or majority rule;

(*B*) all groups of people with certain common characteristics who live within the geographical limits of an entity referred to in (*A*), or in

[76] Cassese, *supra* note 49, at 154–55 (emphasis in original).

[77] Babu observes in this regard:

> Saddled with a kind of leadership which relies on commandism in place of rational persuasion, a large part of Africa is indeed not yet free. Which convincingly explains why the people do not respond effectively to the leaders' calls for more efforts in "nation-building," which simply means sacrifices and more voluntary efforts in place of the proper material incentives. . . . To invoke duty from a people without rights is to make democracy stand on its head. In the modern world, the people's rights are prior to their duties, and the reversal of this order equals tyranny.

A. M. Babu, *supra* note 16, at 172. *See further* Cassese, *supra* note 73, at 92.

an entity that has attained independence or majority rule (i.e., minorities under any political system);

(*C*) the state and the people as synonymous (however, this is only an external meaning of "people"); and

(*D*) all persons within a state.

There are instances in the Charter where "people" refers to more than one of the four meanings; for example, in relation to the rights to development (Article 22), peace (Article 23) and a clean environment (Article 24).

If four interpretations sounds like too many, it merely points up the confusion about, and ambivalence of the subject. The different interpretations also correspond to the various scenarios in which peoples' rights could be asserted.[78] These various factors indicate the enormity of the task facing the African Commission on Human and Peoples' Rights, which was constituted during the 1987 OAU Assembly of Heads of State and Government. In the course of its work, it will have to decide, sooner or later, whether to strengthen governments or peoples. Its inclination will definitely depend on the "extent [to which] the members of the African Commission turn out to be representatives of peoples, as distinct from representatives of governments."[79] Their perception of the role of the Commission and of human and peoples' rights within the global framework will also play a vital part.

As a final general comment, it should be pointed out that the concept of "peoples" should be an enabling tool. It should empower the people to do something about their future; to take charge of their destiny and control their affairs. The only way they can do so in today's world is if the dichotomy between them and their state is minimized. If it endures, there is little hope of realizing any of the peoples' rights in the Charter. In other words, the Banjul Charter must move closer to the Algiers Declaration in its use of "people."

RICHARD N. KIWANUKA*

[78] For a typology and discussion of the different ways that the right to self-determination could be claimed, see R. C. A. White, *Self-Determination: Time for a Reassessment?*, 28 NETH. INT'L L. REV. 147 (1981).

[79] Crawford, *supra* note 69, at 136.

* Senior Tutor in Law, University of Western Australia, Perth. I am indebted to Associate Professor Francis Auburn of the Law School, University of Western Australia, for valuable comments on an earlier draft.

CORRESPONDENCE

The *American Journal of International Law* welcomes short communications from its readers. It reserves the right to determine which letters should be published and to edit any letters printed. Letters should conform to the same format requirements as other manuscripts.

TO THE EDITOR IN CHIEF:

June 8, 1987

I was surprised to see that Professor Michael J. Glennon (81 AJIL 116, 128–29 (1987)) believes that the Hague Court may refuse to accept a new U.S. declaration under Article 36, paragraph 2 of the Court's Statute, on the ground that the U.S. Government is continuing (if that is the case) to defy the Court's Judgment in the *Nicaragua* case.

As the competence to verify states' declarations was not entrusted to the Court, it may neither accept nor refuse such instruments outside the framework of cases brought before it. By adopting the Court's compulsory jurisdiction, states incur obligations in relation to every other state that has made a similar declaration. At the most, those other states might react unfavorably to an American declaration by limiting the scope *ratione personae* of their declarations, e.g., by a reservation excluding from the jurisdiction of the Court disputes with states that are not in compliance with its decisions. Nevertheless, the validity of such reservations may be seriously doubted.

As for the general idea of Professor Glennon's Comment, I would have considered it reasonable to urge the Court to make use of the Connally reservation (along the lines proposed by Judge Lauterpacht in the fifties) if the United States had not explicitly waived invoking it at the jurisdictional stage of the case—at first, provisionally (see the U.S. Counter-Memorial of 1984, at p. 9), and later, by not referring to it. The only way the Court could have raised the question *proprio motu* would have been to invoke its "inherent jurisdiction" and to dismiss the case for lack of jurisdiction. However, the Court would have been placed in a somewhat awkward position, not—as Professor Glennon suggested—because of the *Tehran* case (where the Court's jurisdiction was *not* based on the U.S. Declaration of 1946), but because of the *Interhandel* case (where the Court did not deal with the U.S. objection based on the Connally reservation but, instead, declared the Swiss Application inadmissible).

Finally, as far as the term "deniers of international law" is concerned, it is noteworthy that the origin is to be traced back to German doctrine at the turn of the 19th century. That label—die Leugner des Völkerrechts—was attributed to writers who denied that international norms were something more than moral prescripts.

JANUSZ STAŃCZYK*

* Institute of State and Law, Polish Academy of Sciences.

CONTEMPORARY PRACTICE OF THE UNITED STATES RELATING TO INTERNATIONAL LAW

MARIAN NASH LEICH*

The material in this section is arranged according to the system employed in the annual *Digest of United States Practice in International Law,* published by the Department of State.

INTERNATIONAL ORGANIZATIONS

(U.S. *Digest,* Ch. 2, §4.C)

Observer Delegation—Palestine Liberation Organization

By a letter dated September 15, 1987, Ambassador James E. Nolan, Director of the Office of Foreign Missions of the Department of State, notified the Palestine Information Office that the Department of State had designated it as a "foreign mission" within the meaning of section 202(a)(4) of the Foreign Missions Act, 22 U.S.C. §4302(a)(4), and that, pursuant to that designation, the Department had determined that the office was required to cease operating as a foreign mission representing the Palestine Liberation Organization. An enclosed Determination and Designation of Benefits, signed by Deputy Secretary of State John C. Whitehead also on September 15, 1987, required the Palestine Information Office to comply within 30 days.[1] The major portion of the latter text follows:

> Pursuant to the authority of the President of the United States to conduct foreign affairs under Article II of the United States Constitution, including his authority to receive ambassadors, and the authority vested in me by the Foreign Missions Act, 22 U.S.C. §§4301–4314 (hereinafter referred to as "the Act"), I hereby determine that it is reasonably necessary to protect the interests of the United States to require that the Palestine Information Office cease operation as a mission representing the Palestine Liberation Organization.
>
> The Palestine Information Office is being required to cease operation as a mission representing the PLO because of U.S. concern over terrorism committed and supported by individuals and organizations affiliated with the PLO, and as an expression of our overall policy condemning terrorism. The organizations and individuals associated with the PLO who support terrorism include, among others, Abu Al-Abbas, recently retained as a member of the PLO Executive Com-

* Office of the Legal Adviser, Department of State.

[1] Subsequently, in response to a letter dated Sept. 25, 1987, from the Director of the Palestine Information Office (PIO), Hasan Abdel Rahman, to Deputy Secretary Whitehead, and following an approach to the Department of State by the American Civil Liberties Union, representing the PIO and its director, the Department extended the time limit for complying with its original closure order to Dec. 1, 1987. *See* letter, Ambassador Nolan to Mr. Rahman, Oct. 13, 1987, Dept. of State File No. P87 0140-0806, in response to *id.,* No. P87 0140-0807.

mittee, who was responsible for the Achille Lauro hijacking, which included the murder of an American citizen, Leon Klinghoffer. At the Palestine National Congress meeting in April, 1987, other groups which have been responsible for terrorist acts in recent years against many peoples, including Palestinians, were reunited with the PLO. The United States supports the legitimate rights of the Palestinian people. It acknowledges and respects the right of the Palestinian people to achieve their legitimate rights through a process of peaceful negotiations designed to achieve a resolution of the Arab-Israeli conflict and the Palestinian issue. It is important that Palestinian representatives participate in all stages of that process. However, the U.S. believes that acts of terrorism, committed purportedly on behalf of the Palestinian people by some groups and individuals associated with the PLO and others, have done grievous damage to the achievement of legitimate Palestinian rights which are broadly supported by individuals and states opposed to terrorism, but which support instead the peaceful settlement of disputes. Terrorism by this minority of Palestinians and their supporters has been a serious obstacle to the realization of a peaceful settlement of the Arab-Israeli conflict, and an accommodation between Israelis and Palestinians.

In order to achieve the objective of terminating operation of the Palestine Information Office as a foreign mission, I hereby also determine that it is reasonably necessary to protect the interests of the United States to require that the Palestine Information Office divest itself of all real property which it currently occupies or in which it has a real property interest (through ownership, lease or otherwise) in the United States, pursuant to 22 U.S.C. §4305(b)(3). I also hereby determine that it is reasonably necessary to protect the interests of the United States to require that the Palestine Information Office and its employees and agents acting on its behalf acquire and dispose of real property (by purchase, lease, exchange, construction or otherwise) from or through the Office of Foreign Missions under such terms and conditions as may be established by the Director of the Office of Foreign Missions, pursuant to 22 U.S.C. §4304(b). In addition, and for the same purpose, under the authority of section 4304(b)(2) to protect the interests of the United States, I hereby designate as benefits for the purposes of the Act the acquisition from any person or entity subject to the jurisdiction of the United States or use in the United States by the Palestine Information Office and its agents or employees acting on its behalf of the following services and goods:

Services

(1) public utilities and services, including telephone and telegraph, mail, public transportation and sanitation services; and

(2) personal services of individuals engaged within the United States for whatever purpose, whether on a temporary or regular basis. Such personal services include:

(a) services relating to public relations, information, publishing, printing, advertising, distribution of literature, or mailing;

(b) plumbing, electrical, construction, maintenance, engineering, architectural or related services;

(c) packing, shipping, cartage and related services, including provision of packing materials; and
(d) financial services.

Goods

(1) motor vehicles;
(2) construction equipment and materials;
(3) equipment and materials for the maintenance of the mission, including typewriters, telephones, xerox machines and related materials;
(4) computers and automated data processing equipment; and
(5) furnishings for offices.

I hereby determine that it is reasonably necessary to protect the interests of the United States to require that the Palestine Information Office and its agents or employees acting on its behalf discontinue use and dispose of all benefits defined in the Act and this Determination and Designation of Benefits which it currently owns or uses. I also hereby require that the Palestine Information Office and its employees and agents acting on its behalf acquire and dispose of all benefits defined in the Act or this Determination and Designation of Benefits from or through the Office of Foreign Missions under such terms and conditions as the Director of the Office of Foreign Missions may specify. 22 U.S.C. §4304(b).

. . . .

It shall be unlawful for any person subject to the jurisdiction of the United States directly to supply, or contract to supply, the aforementioned benefits to the Palestine Information Office, or to any agent or employee thereof acting on its behalf, other than in accordance with section 4311(a) of the Act, this determination and any subsequent determination.[2]

An underlying Designation of Palestine Information Office as a Foreign Mission, also signed by Deputy Secretary Whitehead on September 15, 1987, and enclosed with the notification, read:

Pursuant to the authority vested in me by the Foreign Missions Act, 22 U.S.C. §§4301–4314 (hereinafter referred to as "the Act"), I hereby designate the Palestine Information Office ("PIO") as a "foreign mission" within the meaning of section 202(a)(4) of the Act (22 U.S.C. §4302(a)(4)), in that the Palestine Information Office is a foreign mission as defined by that section.

Designation of the Palestine Information Office as a foreign mission is based on the following:

—it is an entity.
—it is substantially owned and/or effectively controlled by the PLO.
—the PIO conducts its functions on behalf of an organization which has received privileges and immunities under US law. The PLO is accorded certain privileges and immunities by virtue of its status as an

[2] Dept. of State File No. P87 0123-1609, 52 Fed. Reg. 37,035–36 (1987).

observer to the United Nations. Further, the PLO clearly engages in "some aspect of the conduct of international affairs," as evidenced by, for example, its membership in the League of Arab States and its status at the United Nations.

—it is involved in "other activities." The PIO registration statement under the Foreign Agents Registration Act indicates that the PIO engages in political activity and political propaganda on behalf of the PLO.[3]

Diplomatic Privileges and Immunities

(U.S. *Digest,* Ch. 4, §1)

Crimes by Foreign Mission Personnel: Corrective Measures

By a circular note to the Chiefs of Mission at Washington, dated September 21, 1987, the Chief of Protocol of the Department of State, Ambassador Selwa Roosevelt, called to their attention the serious concern of the United States Government at alleged criminal activity by certain members of diplomatic missions or members of their families. The note pointed out that bills recently introduced in both the Senate and the House of Representatives[1] evidenced the fact that Congress shared this concern, and it summarized the measures, consistent with international law, that the Department of State takes in cases involving serious criminal conduct.

The major portion of the note follows:

> The Department of State wishes to reiterate to the missions that criminal violations will not be tolerated by the United States Government or the community at large. In this regard, the Department of State refers to its circular note of March 21, 1984.[2] While the Department will continue to take necessary action as required by international law to preserve the immunity of persons involved in allegedly criminal behavior, the Department wishes to summarize here the corrective measures consistent with international law that are taken in cases involving serious criminal conduct, in particular crimes of violence, recurrent offenses of a less serious nature, or other egregious abuses of immunity.
>
> As a matter of policy, the Department requests a waiver of immunity by the sending state so that all allegations may be adjudicated fully. In the absence of a waiver of immunity the United States Government normally requires that the alleged offender depart the country. In certain cases, however, the Department retains discretion to require the departure of the alleged offender even though a waiver of immunity may have been granted.
>
> The missions are advised further that when such cases involve dependents, the Department may require the removal of the principal

[3] Dept. of State File No. P87 0123-1613, 52 Fed. Reg. 37,035 (1987).

[1] S. 1437 and H.R. 3036, 100th Cong., 1st Sess. (1987).

[2] *See* 78 AJIL 656 (1984).

from whom privileges and immunities are derived and the members of his or her family when the sending government declines to waive immunity or the Department determines that such action otherwise is necessary or appropriate.

In all cases involving injury to persons or damage to property, the Department pursues vigorously the interests of the aggrieved parties in obtaining prompt restitution by individual offenders or by their governments.

Moreover, in order to ensure a complete record in each case, or to lay the basis for possible prosecution in appropriate cases, the Department has notified law enforcement officials throughout the United States to prepare cases carefully and completely and properly document each incident at the time of an alleged crime so that charges against offenders may be pursued as far as possible in the U.S. judicial system.

The Department wishes to remind the missions that in any case involving criminal activity no ban exists on the arrest and prosecution of a person formerly entitled to privileges and immunities who returns to the United States, unless it can be proved that the crime related to the exercise of official functions. The Department recognizes that the threat of prosecution may serve, as a practical matter, to prevent individuals who commit crimes while in privileged status from returning to the United States. To ensure that such individuals do not return without appropriate review by United States authorities, henceforth the Department will require that the sending government forward the passport of the alleged offender (and of family members in appropriate cases) to the Department before he or she departs the United States so that the visa may be revoked and the form I–94 returned to the Immigration and Naturalization Service. Should the alleged offender leave the United States before the visa is cancelled, the Department may not accept a replacement on the mission staff of the offender (or of his or her principal in the case of a crime committed by a dependent), until the visa is revoked.[3]

On August 5, 1987, Ambassador Roosevelt submitted the views of the Department of State on S. 1437, "a bill to make certain members of foreign diplomatic missions and consular posts in the United States subject to the criminal jurisdiction of the United States with respect to crimes of violence." She explained that the Department could not support the proposed legislation because it would be detrimental to U.S. interests abroad and would place the United States in violation of its international obligations. Portions of Ambassador Roosevelt's testimony follow:

Concern for U.S. Interests Abroad

. . . .

. . . The bill would eliminate immunity for crimes of violence, defined as "the use, attempted use or threatened use of physical force against the person or property of another." This is a large category of

[3] Dept. of State File No. P87 0126-0965.

crimes. Other countries might respond by eliminating immunity even more broadly.

Similarly, the terms "reckless driving," "drug trafficking," and "driving under the influence of alcohol or drugs" might be interpreted broadly by other countries. In addition, even if another country eliminated immunity for precisely the same crimes that the bill would cover, Americans still would face unequal treatment. Those serving in countries with similar legislation could be arrested, detained, and questioned until the matter was fully adjudicated. In the United States, persons might be free on bail pending trial, but in another country, they might be held for months.

. . . .

The language of the proposed legislation covers only members of the administrative and technical staff and the service staff of diplomatic missions and consular employees. Persons not affected would be diplomatic agents, members of their families, and family members of the administrative and technical staffs of embassies.

. . . .

The members of the administrative and technical staff of an embassy must have full criminal immunity in order to perform their jobs effectively. These personnel perform tasks fundamental to the operation of the embassy. Many of them, including communicators who transmit encoded messages and secretaries who type the missions' classified documents, engage in very sensitive work. They and their families could be subjected to the same pressures that diplomats face. We cannot take great comfort in the full immunity of the ambassador, of the FBI legal attache, of a military attache, or of the personnel of other agencies engaged throughout the world in such sensitive work as fighting terrorism and drugs, if we know that those who do their clerical work and transmit their classified material back to Washington could be interrogated and jailed by hostile receiving-state authorities.

The Need for Immunity

If the intent of the bill is also to reduce the immunity of family members of diplomats and family members of the administrative and technical staff—as we have been led to believe informally—we cannot support the proposal.

Under the Vienna Convention on Diplomatic Relations, members of the family of a diplomatic agent have full criminal immunity, as do members of the administrative and technical staff of a mission and their families. Lower level members of embassy staffs have criminal immunity for their official acts. . . .

We believe complete immunity from criminal jurisdiction assured to diplomats is fundamental to diplomatic relations. Diplomats could not perform their duties if they faced criminal liability under local law for normal performance of their jobs or if they could be harassed by the receiving state bringing false charges. Moreover, the diplomat's own immunity would be meaningless if his family residing with him did not have the same immunities. The threat of actions against family members could be used to intimidate the diplomat.

. . . .

So far I have only addressed the effect of the bill on our personnel at embassies. But the bill would also affect some personnel at consulates. Although the proposed legislation would not affect consular officers, it would affect consular employees, who perform in consulates the same functions that administrative and technical staff perform in embassies. The immunity from jurisdiction accorded to consular officers and consular employees by the Vienna Convention on Consular Relations . . . is much more limited than the regime which applies to diplomats. Consular immunity applies only to acts performed in the exercise of consular functions, i.e., to "official acts." When a case is brought, the court determines whether the acts were performed in the exercise of consular functions. Family members have no official acts and have no immunity. Thus, consular officers are now subject to jurisdiction with respect to most "crimes of violence," as, indeed, are consular employees. While consular officers and employees may raise their functional immunity as a defense in connection with a speeding charge or accident, this itself is not a bar to judicial action. The courts would determine whether or not such a defense would apply.

Thus, even with respect to the more limited immunity accorded consular employees, the bill would place the United States in violation of the Vienna convention and would put U.S. personnel at risk of reciprocal measures. . . .

At this point, I should point out that there are countries with which the United States has concluded treaties extending broader immunities for consular personnel. The United States has entered into such agreements with the Soviet Union, the People's Republic of China (P.R.C.), Bulgaria, the German Democratic Republic (G.D.R.), Hungary, Poland, and Romania. A similar agreement also exists with the Philippines. (Bulgaria, the G.D.R., and Romania have no consular posts in the United States.) Thus, our consular employees in such countries as the U.S.S.R. and the P.R.C. have full criminal immunity, and we are obligated to provide the same immunities to consular employees of those countries. The proposed legislation, therefore, would violate these bilateral agreements in addition to violating the Vienna conventions.

Recent Steps

While the Department of State cannot support the proposed legislation, which would call into question the entire framework of diplomatic immunity, we have taken a variety of steps to curtail abuses of diplomatic immunity that are wholly consistent with international law.

Incidentally, it may be of interest to the committee that the British Foreign Office instituted a full review of the Vienna convention in the aftermath of the fatal shooting of a policewoman by a gunman in the Libyan Embassy and the attempted abduction of a Nigerian exile. The British concluded that it would be wrong to amend the Vienna convention as the solution to the abuse of diplomatic immunity but, instead, implemented a firmer policy in the application of the convention.

. . . .

Barring Reentry. Some years ago, I initiated a system to bar the reentry into the United States of serious offenders entitled to criminal immunity at the time of expulsion. . . .

We have found, however, that the system was not perfect and that, in at least three cases, the persons expelled reentered the United States. To prevent any other such occurrence, we will ensure that the diplomatic visa is canceled before an alleged offender leaves the country. Should the person leave before this is done, we will inform the mission concerned that the principal alien cannot be replaced until the visa has been canceled.

Police Guidance. In March, the Department published updated and more comprehensive written guidance for law enforcement officers on the handling of incidents involving foreign diplomatic and consular personnel. It has been distributed nationwide.[4] . . . [W]e have pointed out the necessity for careful and complete police work at the time of the incident in order to lay the basis for possible future prosecution when immunity ceases to exist. In other words, we urge that charges be pursued as far as possible in our judicial system. After the offender leaves the United States, the existence of an outstanding arrest warrant may be entered into the records of the immigration authorities. The existence of the warrant and the knowledge that the Federal Government will assist in serving the warrant would deter an offender from attempting to return to the United States.

. . . .

Parental Responsibility. In particularly egregious cases involving juvenile offenders, I have had the entire family expelled from the United States. This policy ensures that parents will be fully accountable for the acts of their children.

Traffic Offenses. In September 1985, the Department's Office of Foreign Missions instituted a program to monitor traffic violations and increase the observance of traffic laws and regulations. Under the program, the Department assesses points for all traffic violations using the American Association of Motor Vehicle Administrators' standardized point system. . . . Up to this time, 15 drivers' licenses have been permanently suspended. We do not permit a member of the diplomatic community who has operated a motor vehicle under the influence of alcohol to operate a motor vehicle in the United States again. The program has had a salutary effect on the driving habits of privileged personnel.

Firearms. In May 1986, we reissued a circular [note] on the subject of firearms, pointing out that failure to comply with local laws and regulations pertaining to firearms will subject the offender to expulsion.[5]

Identification Documents. Recently, the Office of Protocol began issuing newly designed identification documents to all embassy personnel entitled to any degree of immunity. The cards identify the individual, state the type of immunity which he has, and provide phone numbers to call 24 hours a day if a law enforcement official has questions. In cases where immunity is limited, the cards state that the bearer is not

[4] DEPT. OF STATE, PUB. NO. 9533, GUIDANCE FOR LAW ENFORCEMENT OFFICERS (1987).

[5] For the circular note to the Chiefs of Mission at Washington, May 21, 1986, regarding the possession and carrying of firearms by foreign diplomatic or consular personnel, see Dept. of State File No. P86 0069-0831.

immune from arrest. Similar cards will be issued to consular officers and employees next year.

Definition of "Members of the Family." The Vienna convention requires the parties to extend privileges and immunities to family members forming part of the household but does not define family members. In May 1986, we informed the missions that we would set age limits beyond which the Department no longer would extend privileges and immunities to dependent children. The cutoff age is 21, unless the child is a full-time student, in which case the age limitation is 23. This step has reduced the number of persons entitled to privileges and immunities.

We are continually reviewing means to reduce the numbers of persons entitled to immunity. For example, we are not obligated by the Vienna convention to extend full immunity to aliens "permanently resident in the United States." Accordingly, we propose to terminate privileges and immunities for locally hired members of embassy staffs who have resided in the United States for 10 years or more.[6]

CONSULAR OFFICERS AND CONSULATES

(U.S. *Digest,* Ch. 4, §2)

Moratorium on Honorary Consular Posts

A circular note from the Secretary of State to the Chiefs of Mission at Washington, dated September 25, 1987, informed them of the establishment of a 1-year moratorium, commencing October 5, 1987, on the opening of all new honorary consular posts in the United States and its territories.

In an earlier circular note, dated February 27, 1985, the Department of State had set out new guidelines that it would thenceforth apply when considering requests for consent to the establishment of consular posts,

[6] DEPT. ST. BULL., No. 2127, October 1987, at 29; DEPT. OF STATE, CURRENT POLICY NO. 993, DIPLOMATIC IMMUNITY AND U.S. INTERESTS (1987).

In addition to diplomats and administrative and technical staff of embassies and their families, criminal immunity in the United States is extended to diplomats at the Organization of American States and members of missions to the United Nations, as well as a small number of persons at the World Bank and International Monetary Fund.

On Oct. 8, 1987, the Senate agreed to a floor amendment to the Foreign Relations Authorization Act, Fiscal Year 1988, S. 1394, proposing the Diplomatic Immunity Abuse Prevention Act. That Act would have required the Secretary of State, inter alia, to request that sending states waive the diplomatic immunity of individuals believed to have committed serious criminal offenses (particularly crimes of violence), in order to permit their prosecution. *See* 133 CONG. REC. S13,795–97 (daily ed. Oct. 8, 1987).

The Senate/House committee of conference deleted the proposed Act and substituted a requirement for the Secretary of State to (1) study the feasibility of increasing the minimum liability insurance coverage required of members of foreign missions and their families, and (2) report within 90 days on various other issues that the proposed Act would have addressed. The substitute provision became §137 of the Foreign Relations Authorization Act, Fiscal Years 1988 and 1989, approved as Pub. L. No. 100-204, Dec. 22, 1987. *See* H.R. REP. NO. 475, 100th Cong., 1st Sess. 123–25 (1987).

recognition of consular officers and continuation of consular posts in existence at that time, particularly those headed by honorary consular officers.[1]

The 1-year moratorium would be limited, however, to honorary consular establishments. It would not apply to requests for consent to the opening of new consular posts headed by career officers, or to changing existing posts from career to honorary status, or to maintaining existing honorary consular posts, provided these had not been closed for more than 1 year. During the 1-year moratorium, the Department would also consider, within the existing ceiling, requests to open honorary consular offices to replace offices being closed in other cities. Pending requests for agreement to the opening of honorary consular offices would be reviewed in accordance with existing criteria, as set forth in the note of February 27, 1985.

The circular note of September 25, 1987 continued:

> The Department has noted that notwithstanding the Secretary's circular note of February 27, 1985, there continues to be an increase in the number of requests for the establishment of consular posts headed by honorary consular officers. A review of the Department's records indicates that numerous countries maintain large numbers of consular offices in the United States and its territories. During the one-year moratorium the Department of State will conduct a detailed review of consular representation in the United States and will contact on a case-by-case basis the embassies of those governments with large numbers of honorary consular offices to discuss possible adjustments. The Department believes that it would be helpful also if the Chiefs of Mission could review their current consular organizations in this country and consider closing or consolidating establishments. The Chiefs of Mission also are requested to review personally all requests to maintain honorary consulates in order to ensure that there continues to be a need for consular services at each location.
>
> The Department of State anticipates that a general reduction in the number of honorary consular posts in the United States will assist it, over the long term, to fulfill its obligations to protect consular premises when necessary while also ensuring that consular services are provided to the greatest degree possible.[2]

Judicial Assistance

(U.S. *Digest,* Ch. 6, §6)

United States–United Kingdom Treaty (Concerning the Cayman Islands)

On August 4, 1987, President Reagan transmitted to the Senate for advice and consent to ratification the Treaty between the United States of America and the United Kingdom of Great Britain and Northern Ireland Concerning the Cayman Islands Relating to Mutual Legal Assistance in Criminal Matters, with protocol, signed at Grand Cayman on July 3, 1986,[1]

[1] *See* 79 AJIL 1051 (1985).
[2] Dept. of State File No. P87 0126-0968.
[1] S. Treaty Doc. 8, 100th Cong., 1st Sess. (1987).

together with related notes exchanged at London the same day. The Treaty follows upon an earlier agreement by an exchange of letters at London on July 26, 1984,[2] under which Cayman Island authorities undertook to provide U.S. authorities with access to documentary information in the Cayman Islands relating to narcotics trafficking, for use in proceedings, including grand jury proceedings, in the United States.

The 1986 Treaty, representing a "major breakthrough in United States efforts to enlist the cooperation of Caribbean 'bank secrecy' jurisdictions in the investigation and prosecution of transborder crime," contains provisions similar to those in other mutual legal assistance treaties (MLATs) in force with Italy, the Netherlands, Switzerland and Turkey,[3] as well as some innovations.

In a report to the President, dated July 23, 1987, Secretary of State George P. Shultz discussed its provisions, in part as follows:

> The treaty will not require implementing legislation, and will utilize existing authority of the Federal courts, particularly 28 U.S.C. 1782.
>
> Article 1 provides for assistance in all matters involving "the investigation, prosecution, and suppression of criminal offenses". The treaty thereby permits mutual assistance at the investigative stage (such as grand jury proceedings), as well as after formal charges have been filed. It also provides for assistance in civil and administrative proceedings relating to narcotics trafficking. The treaty provides solely for government-to-government mutual assistance, and thus is not intended to create rights in private persons either to gather evidence or secure other assistance or to suppress or exclude in civil or criminal proceedings evidence obtained under the treaty.
>
> Article 2 provides for a Central Authority in each State who is responsible for transmitting, receiving and handling requests under the treaty on behalf of Federal and State agencies, courts and other authorities in that State. The Central Authorities are, respectively, the Attorney General of the United States and the Cayman Mutual Legal

[2] Agreement between the United States and the United Kingdom Concerning the Cayman Islands and Narcotics Activities, July 16, 1984, *reprinted in* 24 ILM 1110 (1985) (entered into force Aug. 29, 1984, extended for a 6-month period Nov. 26, 1986, and for a further 6-month period May 29, 1987).

[3] *See* Treaty between the United States and Italy on Mutual Assistance in Criminal Matters, with memorandum of understanding, Nov. 9, 1982 (entered into force Nov. 13, 1985); Treaty between the United States and the Netherlands on Mutual Assistance in Criminal Matters, with exchange of notes, June 12, 1981, TIAS No. 10734 (entered into force Sept. 15, 1983); Treaty between the United States and Switzerland on Mutual Assistance in Criminal Matters, with related notes, May 25, 1973, 27 UST 2019, TIAS No. 8302 (entered into force Jan. 23, 1977); and Treaty between the United States and Turkey on Extradition and Mutual Assistance in Criminal Matters, June 7, 1979, 32 UST 3111, TIAS No. 9891 (entered into force Jan. 1, 1981).

The United States has also signed a Mutual Legal Assistance Treaty with the Republic of Colombia, Aug. 20, 1980, and a Convention on Mutual Assistance in Criminal Matters with the Kingdom of Morocco, Oct. 17, 1983. Although the Senate has voted advice and consent to ratification of both and President Reagan has signed the U.S. instruments of ratification, they have not yet entered into force.

Assistance Authority, which under Cayman Islands law is constituted by their Chief Justice, acting alone in an administrative capacity.

Article 3 permits the denial of assistance with respect to classes of cases, including most notably, offenses not punishable by more than one year of imprisonment and matters relating directly or indirectly to the regulation of taxes. The bar to assistance in tax matters is subject to exceptions for narcotics trafficking, covered by Article 19(3)(c), and tax fraud (e.g., fraudulent promotion of tax shelters and certain offenses in connection with illegally obtained income) for which assistance may be requested under Articles 19(3)(d) and (e) as discussed below. Other bases for denying requests include when the request[:] fails to conform to the treaty (e.g., does not set forth the required information); relates to political or military crimes not constituting offenses under ordinary criminal law; does not establish "reasonable ground", i.e., a precise, rational explanation, for believing both that the specified offense has been committed and that the requested information is in the territory of the Requested Party; or where execution of the request would be contrary to the Requested Party's "public interest", a phrase which the Parties intend to construe narrowly. Instead of denying a request, the Requested Party may make execution subject to the Requesting Party's acceptance of appropriate conditions.

Article 4 provides that written requests in an agreed-to standard format must necessarily include specific information and should also include certain other information "to the extent necessary and possible".

Article 5 obligates the Parties promptly to undertake diligent efforts to execute a request, by, *inter alia,* arranging without cost to the Requesting Party for any necessary administrative or judicial action, including the issuance by its courts of subpoenas, search warrants, or other orders. This provision for reciprocal legal representation should be a significant advance in international legal cooperation since the cost of retaining counsel abroad to present and process letters rogatory has sometimes been quite high. In the United States, it is anticipated that most requests will be transmitted to federal investigators, prosecutors, or judicial authorities for execution, and, that when compulsory process is required, the Department of Justice would ask a federal court to issue the necessary process under 28 U.S.C. 1782 and the treaty. This article also provides, *inter alia,* for requests to be executed strictly in accordance with the law of the Requested Party. It is stipulated, however, that the method of execution specified in a request should be followed if possible, since those methods may be designed by the Requesting Party to ensure the admissibility of the evidence collected at trial in its country or to enhance the utility of the evidence for specific purposes (e.g., to improve the scientific accuracy of forensic tests). Provision is also made for postponing or making execution subject to conditions where execution would otherwise interfere with an ongoing investigation or legal proceeding in the Requested Party, and for informing the Requested Party of the outcome of execution or of the reasons for denial.

Article 6 provides that the Requesting Party shall reimburse the Requested Party for only those costs specified; otherwise the latter assumes the expenses incurred in executing a request. The costs specified include travel expenses for witnesses agreeing to appear voluntarily in the Requesting Party, which are provided in order to ensure for Caymans witnesses treatment similar to that accorded a person subpoenaed within the United States, and other extraordinary fees which the Requesting Party is typically asked to pay. The only additional cost to the Requesting Party which has not been included in other U.S. mutual legal assistance treaties (MLATs) is the reasonable costs of providing to the Requesting Party's Central Authority documents or records specified in the request, e.g., costs similar to those incurred when subpoenas are issued in the U.S. for comparable evidence, including bank or business records. This provision neither obligates nor prevents the Requesting Party from providing additional funds for witnesses who may be somehow involved in the investigation where it wishes to assist the individual with the costs of legal representation.

Article 7 restricts the use of any information or evidence obtained under the treaty to investigations, prosecution or suppression of criminal offenses stated in the request, absent prior consent of the Requested Party to other uses. Such other uses include inquiries, examinations, audits, efforts to identify targets, or use in any prosecutions or proceedings other than that for which assistance was granted. Unlike other MLATs which impose conditions of confidentiality only when necessary, this treaty provides that all information or evidence furnished under the treaty shall be treated as confidential except when disclosure is necessary for purposes of prosecution of an offense described in the request. Unlike some U.S. MLATs, this treaty imposes certain restrictions on additional uses of such information or evidence even after the information or evidence has been made public in a proceeding forming part of a prosecution.

Article 8 provides that the Requested Party may compel the taking of testimony or production of documents for the Requesting Party by means (e.g., subpoenas) available under, and in accordance with, the Requested Party's laws. The Requested Party shall notify the Requesting Party of any claim of immunity, incapacity or privilege asserted pursuant to the Requesting Party's law by an individual giving evidence, in order that the Requesting Party may determine its applicability. The article also makes provision to enable interested parties to be present during the taking of evidence and for authentication of unofficial documentary evidence in a form which complies with United States law.

Article 9 ensures that pursuant to a request, the Requested Party shall provide copies of its publicly available government records and may, in its discretion, provide any record or information in the possession of its government departments or agencies but not publicly available to the same extent and under the same conditions as such records or information would be made available to its own law enforcement and judicial authorities. The form and procedures specified for authenticating official records satisfy the requirements of United States law (Rule 902(3) of the Federal Rules of Evidence).

Article 10 provides that the Requested Party shall invite, but not compel, witnesses located in its territory to appear in the Requesting State.

The Requesting State shall pay the expenses of such voluntary appearance in accordance with Article 4(3)(g). The article also ensures such witness' "safe conduct" while the witness is present in the Requesting State. This phrase encompasses immunity from service of civil process, detention or any restriction of personal liberty with regard to acts or convictions which preceded the witness' departure from the Requested State while the witness is present in the Requesting State and for up to ten days after presence in the Requesting State is no longer required.

Article 11 authorizes the transfer of a person in custody of either Party to the other for purposes of providing testimony or where such person's presence is needed, subject to the consent of such person and the relevant Party or Parties. Authority is also provided to keep such person in custody unless release is authorized by the Sending State.

Article 12 is a standard MLAT provision which requires the Requested Party to take all necessary steps to locate or identify persons (e.g., witnesses, potential defendants, or experts) who are believed to be in its territory and are needed in connection with the investigation, prosecution and suppression of a criminal offense in the Requesting Party.

Article 13 obligates the Requested Party to arrange for the service of any document (e.g., summons, complaints or other legal documents) relating to a request for assistance, but leaves it to that Party's discretion to serve a subpoena or other process requiring the attendance of a person before any authority or tribunal in the Requesting Party. The Requesting Party must transmit a document inviting the appearance of a person in the Requesting Party a reasonable time before the scheduled appearance.

Article 14 provides that a request involving the search, seizure and delivery of an article shall be carried out if the Requesting Party provides justification for such action under the laws of the Requested State. In the United States, a Caymans request would have to be supported by showing that probable cause for the search exists, and in the Caymans, the United States request would have to demonstrate compliance with the Caymans corresponding evidentiary standard. . . .

Article 15 provides for the return of documents or articles furnished in executing a request as soon as possible, absent a waiver of this requirement by the Requested Party. . . .

Article 16 stipulates that a Party may notify the other of proceeds of a criminal offense believed to be in the territory of the other Party, in order that the Parties shall, to the extent permitted by their law, assist each other in proceedings regarding forfeiture or restitution of proceeds of an offense, or the collection of fines imposed as a sentence for an offense. It is contemplated that proceeds, which would include money, vessels or other valuables used in perpetrating the crime or acquired as a result of the crime, may be seized in aid of prosecution, or be subject to a temporary restraining order to assist in a civil action for return of the assets, or to some comparable action. The provision for assistance in forfeiture proceedings expressly authorizes assistance in an area in which countries do not necessarily otherwise assist each other—in execution of their penal laws. It is also consistent with a recently enacted U.S. legislative provision which applies, to the extent provided by treaty, to permit equitable sharing of forfeited property with a foreign government in order to reflect that government's contribution in narcotics investigations leading to seizure or forfeiture.

Article 17 provides that this treaty does not preclude either Party from utilizing other relevant international agreements or arrangements (e.g., Interpol), which may offer means of securing assistance or cooperation. Unless such other agreement or arrangement specifically applies, however, a Party must seek assistance under the treaty for cases falling within its coverage. The third paragraph addresses a particular Caymans and British concern for respecting Caymans bank secrecy laws by providing that unilateral compulsory measures (e.g., grand jury and trial subpoenas) for the production of documents in the territory of the other Party not be enforced in the first instance. The last paragraph relieves a Party from the obligation not to use such measures (subject to certain timing conditions), where either denial of a request or an unreasonable delay in execution of a request may be jeopardizing the successful completion of an investigation, prosecution or other proceeding. The article does not, however, cover administrative summonses of agencies such as the Internal Revenue Service or the Securities and Exchange Commission, so long as the matter being investigated does not constitute a criminal offense under the treaty. Neither does it preclude issuance of a subpoena or material witness warrant for any persons temporarily in the United States, even though the disclosure of information protected by Caymans secrecy laws may be required.

Article 18 encourages the parties to consult periodically to maximize use made of the treaty and specifically to apprise each other of the status and disposition of proceedings using evidence obtained under the treaty. The article also permits the Central Authorities to solicit the assistance of their diplomatic and political authorities to resolve difficulties arising in the course of implementing the treaty provisions.

Article 19 sets forth certain necessary definitions. The first two paragraphs distinguish between "the Contracting Parties"—the United States and the United Kingdom—and "the Parties"—the United States and the Cayman Islands. This reflects the Caymans status as a dependent territory of the United Kingdom which must undertake international obligations on behalf of the Caymans. The third paragraph defines "criminal offense" as including any conduct punishable by more than one year's imprisonment in both Parties, or racketeering, drug trafficking, failing to report transfers of illegally acquired money, fraud in connection with tax shelters, tax evasion or other offenses involving income obtained in illegal activities, failing to report transfers of illegally acquired funds, insider securities practices (including insider trading), violations of the Foreign Corrupt Practices Act or participation in any of these crimes. The treaty also permits the Parties to add other offenses to this list by exchange of diplomatic notes.

. . . .

The Protocol provides that the terms of the treaty may be made applicable, in whole or in part, to certain other British dependencies in the Caribbean by exchange of notes between the United States and the

United Kingdom. This will permit the other jurisdictions, as they become ready, to enter a treaty relationship with the United States for mutual legal assistance, but will avoid the need for the United States and the United Kingdom to conclude separate treaties with respect to each dependency.[4]

Marine Environment

(U.S. *Digest,* Ch. 7, §9)

Prohibition Against Dumping of Plastics and Other Garbage

On November 5, 1987, the Senate by a vote of 93-0 (with 7 senators absent and not voting) gave its advice and consent to Annex V, Regulations for the Prevention of Pollution by Garbage from Ships, an Optional Annex to the 1978 Protocol Relating to the International Convention for the Prevention of Pollution from Ships, 1973 (MARPOL 73/78),[1] subject to an understanding.

A report on Annex V by Secretary of State George P. Shultz, dated January 21, 1987, accompanied the President's letter of transmittal to the Senate of February 9, 1987. The Secretary's report stated, in major part:

> Annex V and the other Optional Annexes, III and IV which deal with pollution from packaged harmful substances and sewage, were transmitted only for the information of the Senate when the original MARPOL Convention was transmitted to the Senate on March 22, 1977 for its advice and consent to ratification. Optional Annexes III and IV are still the subject of ongoing review[,] and Senate advice and consent to them is not now being sought. The MARPOL Protocol entered into force for the United States on October 2, 1983.
>
> Annex V establishes international regulations for prohibiting or otherwise restricting discharges into the oceans of all types of garbage generated during the normal operation of ships. Annex V will not completely solve the pollution threat of garbage disposal into the oceans[,] but I believe that it is a critical first step in dealing with this international problem. Effective implementation of it would make a significant contribution to reducing the amount of vessel-generated plastic garbage and other debris which are currently entering the marine environment, seriously endangering a variety of marine life, including birds, marine mammals, turtles and seals. United States ratification would demonstrate to the world the United States' resolve to protect that environment, giving due consideration to the joint efforts of the international community in the International Maritime Organization and other fora.
>
> A major purpose of Annex V is to prohibit (subject to limited exceptions) the disposal into the sea of all plastics, including but not

[4] S. Treaty Doc. 8, *supra* note 1, at V–X.

[1] International Convention for the Prevention of Pollution from Ships, *done* Nov. 2, 1973, *reprinted in* 12 ILM 1319 (1973), and Protocol, *done* Feb. 17, 1978, *reprinted in* 17 ILM 546 (1978).

limited to synthetic ropes, synthetic fishing nets and plastic garbage bags. Disposal into the sea of other garbage must be made as far as practicable from the nearest land but in any case is prohibited (subject to limited exceptions) if the vessel's distance from the nearest land is less than 25 nautical miles for dunnage, lining and packing materials which will float, and 12 nautical miles for food wastes and all other garbage including paper products, rags, glass, metal, bottles, crockery and similar refuse. Reception facilities capable of accepting garbage from vessels will be required at ports and terminals. We expect the private sector will be capable of providing the additional reception facilities required by this Annex.

As compared to mandatory Annexes I and II on pollution by oil and noxious liquid substances in bulk to which the United States is bound and which have been construed to apply only to seagoing vessels, Annex V will apply to all ships operating in the marine environment.

As with all other MARPOL 73/78 regulations in force for them, States bound by Annex V will be required to apply Annex V regulations to all ships, including those of non-party States, using their ports or otherwise under their jurisdiction.

Annex V will enter into force 12 months after the date on which not less than 15 States, the combined fleets of which constitute not less than 50 percent of the gross tonnage of the world's merchant shipping, have become parties to it. Annex V has not yet entered into force, having been ratified by 27 States representing only approximately 45% of the world's shipping tonnage. . . .

This Annex has been under active study by the United States and other nations in an effort to make its provisions more meaningful and enforceable. The International Maritime Organization's Marine Environment Protection Committee (MEPC) at its 23rd session, July 7–11, 1986 agreed to a United States-proposed technical amendment to Annex V. This amendment—deletion of the words "or synthetic material incidental to the repair of such nets" from regulation 6(c)—would clarify and strengthen the prohibition on disposal of non-repairable sections of synthetic fishing nets, a problem which is contributing to an increase in the mortality of several marine species. The MEPC also agreed with the United States' proposal that this amendment should be circulated with a view to formal adoption in accordance with Article 16 (tacit amendment procedure) of MARPOL 73/78, after entry into force of Annex V so as not to require States that have already ratified the Annex to reratify it. This amendment procedure was established to achieve more effective and rapid implementation of technical amendments to MARPOL 73/78 Annexes.

The United States Coast Guard has prepared an environmental assessment indicating that United States ratification of Annex V would not have a significant adverse impact on the environment and would indeed be environmentally beneficial. The environmental assessment will be transmitted separately to the Senate Committee on Foreign Relations. Annex V will require implementing legislation which is being prepared.

Annex V has the support of the United States Coast Guard, National Oceanic and Atmospheric Administration, the Marine Mammal Com-

> mission and all other interested agencies of the Executive Branch as well as environmental organizations and a substantial majority of the maritime industry. Although there has been some opposition within the maritime industry, I do not believe it will cause a problem in the ratification process.[2]

During the Senate floor debate on Annex V, Senator Lloyd Bentsen and several other senators, concerned to obtain extra protection for the Gulf of Mexico as a "special area" under Regulation 5 of the annex, sponsored an amendment to the committee-approved resolution of ratification that made the Senate's advice and consent to ratification subject to the following understanding:

> (1) The United States Government shall make every reasonable effort to have the Gulf of Mexico designated a "special area" governed by the terms of Regulation 5 of Annex 5 to the Protocol Relating To The International Convention For The Prevention Of Pollution From Ships, 1973 (MARPOL 73/78).
>
> (2) The President shall include this understanding incorporated by the Senate in the Resolution of Ratification in the instrument of Ratification to be deposited with the Secretary-General of the International Maritime Organization.[3]

On October 13, 1987, the House of Representatives passed H.R. 940, the Plastic Pollution Research and Control Act of 1987, one purpose of which was to implement the provisions of Annex V.[4]

ENVIRONMENTAL AFFAIRS

(U.S. *Digest,* Ch. 11, §1)

Protection of the Ozone Layer

On September 16, 1987, at the conclusion of a United Nations Environment Programme-sponsored conference at Montreal, the United States signed a Protocol to the Convention for the Protection of the Ozone Layer.[1] The Montreal Protocol on Substances That Deplete the Ozone Layer provides for reduction of emissions worldwide of certain specified substances that can "significantly deplete or otherwise modify the ozone layer in a

[2] S. TREATY DOC. NO. 3, 100th Cong., 1st Sess., at v–vi (1987). *See also* S. EXEC. REP. NO. 8, 100th Cong., 1st Sess. (1987).

Testifying in support of Annex V at a committee hearing on July 31, 1987, Senator John H. Chafee noted that the Soviet Union had recently become the 28th nation to ratify it and that, if the Senate approved the resolution of advice and consent, nations representing more than 50% of the world's shipping tonnage would have ratified Annex V, which would give it the force of international law. *Id.* at 8.

[3] 133 CONG. REC. S15,846 (daily ed. Nov. 5, 1987).

[4] *Id.* at H8564–76 (daily ed. Oct. 13, 1987).

[1] Convention for the Protection of the Ozone Layer, *done* Mar. 22, 1985, S. TREATY DOC. NO. 9, 99th Cong., 1st Sess. (1985). *See* 80 AJIL 157 (1986). The Senate voted its advice and consent to ratification on July 24, 1986. 132 CONG. REC. S9615–18 (daily ed. July 24, 1986).

manner . . . likely to result in adverse effects on human health and the environment," including potential climatic effects.

Article 2 of the Montreal Protocol, "Control Measures," sets out a series of core undertakings that will apply according to a specific timetable to both consumption and production of such substances, with 1986 being used as the base year. Annex A to the Protocol identifies the controlled substances by their chemical formulas, categorizing them either under Group I, consisting of five chlorofluorocarbons, or Group II, consisting of three halons. (Some undertakings under the Protocol differ as between the two groups.) Annex A also specifies for each substance an ozone-depleting potential and notes that the potentials are "estimates based on existing knowledge and will be reviewed and revised periodically."

Under paragraph 1 of Article 2, each party is required to ensure that for the 12-month period beginning on the first day of the seventh month following entry into force of the Protocol, and in each 12-month period thereafter, its calculated level of consumption of the substances in Group I of Annex A (chlorofluorocarbons) does not exceed its 1986 calculated level of consumption. (For purposes of Article 2 and Article 5, "Special Situation of Developing Countries," calculated levels of production, imports and exports, and consumption are determined in accordance with Article 3.) By the end of the same period, each party producing one or more of these substances must ensure that its calculated level of such production does not exceed its 1986 calculated production level, except that such level may have increased by no more than 10 percent, based on the 1986 level. Such increases are permitted only to satisfy the basic domestic needs of parties operating under Article 5 and for the purposes of "industrial rationalization," defined in Article 1 as the transfer of all or a portion of one party's calculated level of production to another party "for the purpose of achieving economic efficiencies or responding to anticipated shortfalls in supply because of plant closures."

Paragraph 2 of Article 2 sets out consumption and production reductions with respect to Group II substances (halons), which are frozen at 1986 levels with no further reductions being called for. The freeze is likewise subject to a 10 percent permissible increase as to production. The reduction is to begin on the first day of the 37th month following entry into force of the Protocol. Mechanisms for implementing measures under paragraph 2 are to be decided by the parties at their first meeting following the first scientific review.

Paragraph 3 of Article 2 imposes a limitation on both consumption and production of Group I substances for the period July 1, 1993–June 30, 1994, and in each 12-month period thereafter, of 80 percent of 1986 calculated levels. A 10 percent increase in production is also permitted to satisfy the basic domestic needs of parties operating under Article 5 and for purposes of industrial rationalization between parties.

Paragraph 4 of Article 2 further reduces consumption and production levels of Group I substances, for the period July 1, 1998–June 30, 1999, and in each 12-month period thereafter, to 50 percent of their 1986 calculated levels. The production increase permitted to satisfy the basic domestic needs of parties operating under Article 5 and for purposes of industrial rationalization between parties is raised, however, up to 15 percent of the 1986 calculated level of production. The provisions of paragraph 4 apply unless the parties decide otherwise at a meeting, by a two-thirds majority of parties present and voting, representing at least two-thirds of the total calculated consumption level of these substances of the parties; this decision is to be considered and made in the light of assessments referred to in Article 6 of the Protocol (which provides for the quadrennial assessment and review of control measures, beginning in 1990).

Paragraph 5 permits a party whose 1986 calculated level of production of Group I substances was less than 25 kilotons to transfer to or receive from another party production in excess of the limits set out in paragraphs 1, 2 and 3 of Article 2, provided that the total combined calculated levels of production of the concerned parties does not exceed the production limits set out in Article 2.

Paragraph 6 of Article 2 is in the nature of a grandfather clause. Any party that is not operating under Article 5 and has facilities for the production of controlled substances (i.e., any of the substances listed in Annex A) that were under construction, or contracted for, prior to September 16, 1987 (the date the Montreal Protocol was opened for signature), and were provided for in national legislation prior to January 1, 1987, may add the production from such facilities to its 1986 production of such substances to determine its 1986 calculated production level, provided (1) that such facilities are completed by December 31, 1990; and (2) that such production does not raise the party's annual calculated *consumption* level of the controlled substances above 0.5 kilograms per capita. (This provision was included because of the Soviets' concern that plants already provided for in their 1986–1990 national plan would be rendered obsolete.)

Under paragraph 7, any transfer of production pursuant to paragraph 5 or any addition of production pursuant to paragraph 6 must be notified to the secretariat of the 1985 Vienna Convention for the Protection of the Ozone Layer. (Until the 1985 Vienna Convention enters into force, the United Nations Environment Programme is to act as temporary secretariat for that Convention.)

Paragraph 8 of Article 2 relates to parties that are member states of a regional economic integration organization (REIO) as defined in Article 1(6) of the 1985 Vienna Convention. Such parties may agree that they shall jointly fulfill their Article 2 obligations, provided that their total combined calculated *consumption* level does not exceed the levels required under Article 2. All such member states as well as the REIO concerned must be parties to the Protocol and must notify the secretariat of the manner in which they plan to implement such joint fulfillment.

Paragraph 9 of Article 2 sets out procedures under which the parties may decide, on the basis of assessments made pursuant to Article 6, whether adjustments to the ozone-depleting potentials specified in Annex A should be made and, if so, what they should be, and whether further adjustments and reductions of production or consumption of the controlled substances from 1986 levels should be undertaken, and, if so, what their scope, amount and timing should be. If the parties cannot achieve agreement by consensus, such decisions "as a last resort" must be adopted by a two-thirds majority vote of the parties present and voting, representing at least 50 percent of the parties' total consumption of the controlled substances.

Under paragraph 10, the parties may similarly decide, on the basis of such assessments and under the amendment procedure of the 1985 Vienna Convention, whether any substances, and if so, which, should be added to, or removed from, any annex to the Montreal Protocol, as well as the mechanism, scope and timing of the control measures that should apply to them.

Paragraph 11 permits the parties, notwithstanding the provisions of Article 2, to take more stringent measures than those it requires.

Article 3 sets out the procedures for calculating control levels for purposes of Articles 2 and 5 of the Protocol. Production control levels are determined by multiplying a party's annual production of each controlled substance by its ozone-depleting potential specified in Annex A. Import and export control levels are determined in the same way. Calculated levels of consumption are determined by adding calculated levels of production and imports, and subtracting exports, all as so determined. However, beginning on January 1, 1993, no export of controlled substances to nonparties shall be subtracted in calculating an exporting party's consumption level.

Article 4 of the Protocol complements the undertakings stipulated in Article 2 by imposing trade restrictions between parties and states not party to the Protocol. Within 1 year of entry into force of the Protocol, each party must ban the import of *controlled substances* from any nonparty state. Beginning on January 1, 1993, no party operating under paragraph 1 of Article 5 of the Protocol (i.e., a developing country) may export any controlled substance to any nonparty state. Within 3 years of entry into force of the Protocol, and following the procedures set out in Article 10 of the 1985 Vienna Convention (governing adoption and amendment of annexes), the Montreal parties are required to elaborate in an annex a list of *products containing controlled substances.* Thereafter, parties not objecting to the annex will have 1 year after it becomes effective in which to ban the import of such products from any state not party to the Montreal Protocol.

Under paragraph 4 of Article 4, the parties to the Protocol must determine, within 5 years of its entry into force, the feasibility of banning or restricting from states not party thereto the import of *products produced with, although not containing, controlled substances.* If such feasibility is determined, the parties, following the procedures in Article 10 of the 1985 Vienna Convention, must elaborate a list of such products in an annex. Parties not objecting to this annex will have 1 year after it becomes effective in which to ban or restrict the import of such products from any state not party to the Montreal Protocol.

Under other provisions of Article 4, the parties must discourage the export to any state not party to the Protocol of technology for producing and for utilizing controlled substances, and must refrain from providing new subsidies, aid, credits, guarantees or insurance programs for the export to nonparty states of products, equipment, plants or technology that would facilitate the production of controlled substances. These prohibitions do not apply, however, to products, equipment, plants or technology that improve the containment, recovery, recycling or destruction of controlled substances, or that promote the development of alternative substances, or that otherwise contribute to the reduction of emissions of controlled substances.

Article 4 does, however, permit the import of controlled substances, of products containing controlled substances and of products produced with, but not containing, controlled substances from a state not party to the Protocol, if the parties determine, by a meeting, that the nonparty state is in full compliance with Articles 2 and 4 of the Protocol, and if that state has submitted data to that effect as specified in Article 7, "Reporting of Data."

Article 5, "Special Situation of Developing Countries," provides a limited grace period for any party that is a developing country with an annual calculated level of consumption of the controlled substances of less than 0.3 kilograms per capita on the date of entry into force of the Protocol for it, or any time thereafter within 10 years of the Protocol's entry into force. In order to meet its basic domestic needs, such a developing-country party may delay compliance with the control measures set out in Article 2, paragraphs 1–4, by 10 years after that specified therein, but must not exceed an annual calculated consumption level of 0.3 kilograms per capita. Any such party may use either the average of its annual calculated consumption level for the period 1995–1997, or a calculated consumption level of 0.3 kilograms per capita, whichever is lower, as the basis for complying with the required control measures.

Under other provisions of Article 5, the parties undertake to facilitate access to environmentally safe alternative substances and technologies for developing-country parties, as well as to facilitate provision of financial assistance to them in this regard.

Article 8 of the Protocol, "Non-Compliance," requires the parties at their first meeting to consider and approve "procedures and institutional mechanisms" for determining noncompliance with Protocol provisions and for "treatment of Parties found to be in non-compliance."

Further provisions cover "Research, Development, Public Awareness and Exchange of Information" (Article 9); "Technical Assistance" (in general) (Article 10); "Meetings of the Parties" (Article 11); "Secretariat" (Article 12); "Financial Provisions" (Article 13); "Relationship of This Protocol to the [1985 Vienna] Convention" (Article 14); and "Signature" (Article 15).

Under Article 16, "Entry into Force," the Protocol shall enter into force on January 1, 1989, provided that at least 11 instruments of ratification, acceptance, approval or accession have been deposited by states or regional economic integration organizations representing at least two-thirds of 1986 estimated global consumption of the controlled substances, and provided that the provisions of paragraph 1 of Article 17 of the 1985 Vienna Convention (i.e., that govern its entry into force) have been fulfilled. If the conditions for entry into force of the Montreal Protocol have not been fulfilled by January 1, 1989, it is to enter into force on the 90th day following the date on which they have been fulfilled. An instrument deposited by a regional economic integration organization shall not be counted as additional to those deposited by its member states.

Article 17, "Parties Joining After Entry into Force," requires any such party, subject to Article 5, to "fulfil forthwith the sum of the obligations under Article 2, as well as under Article 4, that apply at that date" to states and regional economic integration organizations that became parties upon the Protocol's entry into force.

Article 18, "Reservations," prohibits reservations to the Protocol.

Article 19, "Withdrawal," applies the withdrawal provisions of Article 19 of the 1985 Vienna Convention to the Montreal Protocol, except with respect to developing-country parties. Any such party may withdraw from the Protocol by giving written notification to the depositary (the United Nations Secretary-General) at any time after 4 years of assuming the obligations set out in Article 2, paragraphs 1–4. Such withdrawal will take effect upon the expiration of 1 year after the date of its receipt by the depositary, or on such later date as the notification of withdrawal may specify.[2]

[2] For the text of the Montreal Protocol, see S. TREATY DOC. NO. 10, 100th Cong., 1st Sess. (1987); 26 ILM 1550 (1987).

JUDICIAL DECISIONS

MONROE LEIGH

Federal jurisdiction—Foreign Sovereign Immunities Act—destruction of neutral shipping by belligerent during war—Alien Tort Claims Act provides federal jurisdiction over foreign sovereign for tortious violations of international law

AMERADA HESS SHIPPING CORP. v. ARGENTINE REPUBLIC. 830 F.2d 421. U.S. Court of Appeals, 2d Cir., September 11, 1987.

Appellants, Liberian corporations United Carriers (United) and Amerada Hess Shipping (Amerada), owners and charterers respectively of the vessel *Hercules,* appealed from the dismissal of their complaint against Argentina for the destruction of the *Hercules* during the Falkland Islands war. Despite warnings that the *Hercules*—a neutral vessel—would be traversing the South Atlantic, Argentine military aircraft allegedly bombed the *Hercules* in international waters nearly 500 miles from the Falkland Islands. After it was determined that an undetonated bomb could not safely be removed or disarmed, the *Hercules* was scuttled. Appellants first attempted to bring a claim in Argentina for the destruction of the *Hercules* but were unable to engage Argentine lawyers owing to "the politically charged nature of the claim and knowledge" that the Argentine Government opposed the claim.[1] Appellants then filed a lawsuit in the United States District Court for the Southern District of New York, which held that, notwithstanding the provisions of the Alien Tort Claims Act (28 U.S.C. §1350 (1982)) (ATCA), Argentina enjoyed sovereign immunity under the provisions of the Foreign Sovereign Immunities Act (28 U.S.C. §§1330, 1602–1611 (1982)) (FSIA) for its alleged destruction of the *Hercules.*[2] On appeal, a divided three-judge panel of the United States Court of Appeals for the Second Circuit (per Feinberg, J.) reversed, remanded, and *held:* the Alien Tort Claims Act provides, and the FSIA does not preclude, federal subject matter jurisdiction over suits sounding in tort by aliens against foreign sovereigns for violations of international law.[3]

The court first analyzed Argentina's actions under international law. The court examined "treaties, case law and treatises" and concluded that international law proscribes "attacking a neutral ship in international waters, without proper cause for suspicion or investigation." The court also observed that "[w]here the attacker has refused to compensate the neutral, such action is analogous to piracy, one of the earliest recognized violations of international law."[4] The court next turned to the "jurisdictional ramifications" of this finding of a violation of international law.

[1] Amerada Hess Shipping Corp. v. Argentine Republic, 638 F.Supp. 73, 74 (S.D.N.Y. 1986) (quoting appellants' Verified Complaint).

[2] *Id.* at 75–76.

[3] 830 F.2d 421, *reh'g denied* (2d Cir. Nov. 18, 1987).

[4] *Id.* at 424. *See also* note 14 *infra.*

The court began by analyzing the ATCA in some detail. The court first quoted the plain words of the statute: "The district courts shall have original jurisdiction of any civil action by an alien for a tort only, committed in violation of the law of nations or a treaty of the United States."[5] Observing that the statute "means what it says," the court concluded that "[i]f an alien brings a suit, for a tort only, that sufficiently alleges a violation of the law of nations, then the district court has jurisdiction" over the matter.[6] In response to Argentina's argument that the ATCA does not provide jurisdiction over foreign sovereigns, the court first observed that "it may be—at least as to loss of a vessel under the circumstances alleged here—that absolute sovereign immunity did not govern when the Alien Tort [Claims Act] was enacted."[7] However, the court found no need to decide that issue because it determined that the ATCA must be interpreted in light of international law as it exists today.

The court noted that the "modern view" is that "sovereigns are not immune from suit for their violations of international law."[8] The court argued that "[i]f sovereign acts were immunized today from scrutiny under international law, the exception would nearly swallow the rule." The court therefore concluded that "[s]ince the sinking of a neutral vessel on the high seas without justification violates a substantive principle of international law, no matter who does the sinking, there is no immunity under international law in this case." Thus, the court held that since Argentina had violated international law and was not immune under international law for this violation, appellants had stated a cause of action cognizable under the ATCA.[9]

The court next rejected Argentina's argument that the FSIA provides the "exclusive basis for obtaining jurisdiction over foreign sovereigns" even if the ATCA would otherwise provide jurisdiction. Noting the rule of statutory construction directing courts to construe domestic statutes consistently with international law where possible, and having already found that international law would deny Argentina immunity, the court observed that it would construe the FSIA also to deny immunity in the instant case unless it found a clear congressional intent to the contrary.[10]

The court first addressed the "apparently comprehensive language" of Second Circuit and Supreme Court precedents, and of the legislative history indicating that the FSIA is the exclusive means of obtaining jurisdiction

[5] 830 F.2d at 424–25 (quoting 28 U.S.C. §1350 (1982)).

[6] *Id.* at 425.

[7] *Id.* The court cited as support for this proposition a case where the Supreme Court held that " 'the prize property which [the vessel] brings into our ports is liable to the jurisdiction of our Courts,' notwithstanding any claim of sovereign immunity." *Id.* (quoting The Santissima Trinidad, 20 U.S. (7 Wheat.) 283, 354 (1822)).

[8] *Id.* (relying on Paust, *Federal Jurisdiction over Extraterritorial Acts of Terrorism and Nonimmunity for Foreign Violators of International Law under the FSIA and the Act of State Doctrine,* 23 VA. J. INT'L L. 191, 221–32 (1983); Bazyler, *Litigating the International Law of Human Rights: A "How To" Approach,* 7 WHITTIER L. REV. 713, 733–34 (1985)).

[9] *Id.* at 426.

[10] *Id.*

over foreign sovereigns. Acknowledging that this "authority accurately states the general rule," the court nevertheless determined that because "Congress was not focusing on violations of international law when it enacted the FSIA . . . we do not believe these pronouncements were intended to cover all violations of international law in general and actions under the Alien Tort [Claims Act] in particular."[11] Moreover, according to the court, none of the goals of Congress in enacting the FSIA suggests that Congress intended to eliminate jurisdiction under the ATCA. Therefore, because "[i]nternational law violations are simply not discussed in the statute or the legislative history outside of the commercial context," the court concluded that international law violations were not the "focus" of the apparently comprehensive language in Supreme Court and Second Circuit precedents and the FSIA's legislative history.[12]

In addition, the court concluded that construing the FSIA to bar appellants' claim "would actually frustrate Congress' purpose." That purpose, according to the court, was to ensure judicial resolution of immunity issues on the " 'basis of a statutory regime which *incorporates standards recognized under international law.*' "[13] Thus, since Congress wished the courts to apply the "international law of sovereign immunity" in these cases—and since that law would deny Argentina immunity—the court held that "a grant of immunity here would fly in the face of [Congress's] central premise."[14] The court therefore concluded that nothing in the FSIA preempted the jurisdictional grant of the ATCA.[15]

Judge Kearse dissented from the panel's decision, arguing that the FSIA is the "exclusive framework within which the courts of the United States [are] . . . to rule on foreign states' claims of sovereign immunity."[16] Judge Kearse objected particularly to the majority's characterization of the ATCA as a statute that grants federal courts subject matter jurisdiction. She noted that though international law is a part of U.S. common law, "federal court subject-matter jurisdiction is not a matter of common law" and therefore cannot derive from international law, but rather must derive from a specific congressional grant.[17] Even assuming that Congress "intended to allow fed-

[11] *Id.*

[12] *Id.* at 427.

[13] *Id.* (quoting H.R. REP. NO. 1487, 94th Cong., 2d Sess. 6613 (1976), *reprinted in* 1976 U.S. CODE CONG. & ADMIN. NEWS 6604) (emphasis by court)).

[14] *Id.*

[15] The court briefly examined whether the assertion of personal jurisdiction over Argentina satisfied constitutional standards and found that it did because Argentina's actions were "sufficiently related to the United States for Argentina to have been on notice that it might be sued here." *Id.* at 428.

The court also speculated that Argentina's actions in bombing the *Hercules* might have amounted to piracy. *Id.* at 424. This seems clearly incorrect, however, in light of the requirement that a piratical act be "committed for private ends." Art. 101(a), Convention on the Law of the Sea, *opened for signature* Dec. 10, 1982, *reprinted in* UNITED NATIONS, THE LAW OF THE SEA: UNITED NATIONS CONVENTION ON THE LAW OF THE SEA, UN Sales No. E.83.V.5 (1983).

[16] 830 F.2d at 430 (Kearse, J., dissenting).

[17] *Id.* at 429. Judge Kearse's reasoning echoes somewhat that of the district court. The district court, in rejecting appellants' argument that the ATCA provided jurisdiction, also

eral subject-matter jurisdiction to ebb and flow with the vicissitudes of 'evolving standards of international law,' " Judge Kearse argued, it was improper for the court to "disregard the clearly restrictive provisions of the [FSIA] . . . , which were 'intended to preempt any other State or Federal law (excluding applicable international agreements) for according immunity to foreign sovereigns.' "[18] Judge Kearse concluded, therefore, that since the FSIA, by its terms, sets forth no exception denying immunity in the instant case, she would affirm the district court's decision.

This decision sets a new precedent in interpretation of the FSIA and a most important one. The Second Circuit's decision to allow a suit otherwise precluded by the FSIA to proceed on the basis of ATCA jurisdiction is clearly at odds with other—albeit inferior—federal court decisions addressing this issue. Indeed, one court has declared that "to hold that the Alien Tort Claims Act gives a cause of action and subject matter jurisdiction where the FSIA forbids it would make a nullity of the Foreign Sovereign Immunities Act."[19] Moreover, as the Second Circuit itself acknowledges, its decision is inconsistent with the language of Supreme Court opinions and the FSIA's legislative history. It is understood that Argentina will seek a Supreme Court review of the Second Circuit's decision, which does not comport with the intent of those who drafted the FSIA.

Foreign Sovereign Immunities Act—commercial activity exception applicable to government-issued bonds—statute not retroactive for tsarist bonds

CARL MARKS & CO. v. UNION OF SOVIET SOCIALIST REPUBLICS. 665 F.Supp. 323.
U.S. District Court, S.D.N.Y., July 31, 1987.

Plaintiffs, holders of debt instruments issued by the Imperial Russian Government in 1916, filed a class action suit against the USSR under the Foreign Sovereign Immunities Act (28 U.S.C. §§1330, 1602–1611 (1982)) (FSIA or the Act) to enforce the obligation to pay principal and interest on the bonds. Defendant responded with a diplomatic note to the Department of State asserting that it enjoyed absolute sovereign immunity and would not appear in a U.S. court. At the court's direction, plaintiffs, who had previously served defendant under 28 U.S.C. §1608(a), served an additional notice on the United States Attorney for the Southern District of New

---

noted that the federal courts "are courts of limited jurisdiction." *Amerada*, 638 F.Supp. at 76. The district court also observed that "[p]erhaps Congress could empower federal courts to hear cases such as this," but found itself "constrained by Congress's failure to do so." *Id.*

[18] 830 F.2d at 430 (Kearse, J., dissenting) (quoting H.R. REP. NO. 1487, *supra* note 13, 1976 U.S. CODE CONG. & ADMIN. NEWS at 6610).

[19] *In re* Korean Air Lines Disaster of September 1, 1983, Misc. No. 83-0345, slip op. at 11 (D.D.C. Sept. 1, 1985). *See also* Siderman v. Republic of Argentina, No. CV 82-1772-RMT (MCx), slip op. at 3 (C.D. Cal. Mar. 9, 1985) (ATCA "does not provide an exemption to foreign sovereign immunity").

York and the Soviet Ambassador at the Soviet Embassy in Washington, D.C. When defendant failed to appear in response to this additional notice, the court ordered the entry of a default against the USSR, and thereafter entered a final judgment of default against it. On defendant's motion to vacate the default and dismiss the complaint, the U.S. District Court for the Southern District of New York (per Brieant, J.) granted the motion to vacate, dismissed the complaint as void for want of jurisdiction, and *held* that the Foreign Sovereign Immunities Act did not apply retroactively to claims accruing before 1952.

In support of its motion to vacate, defendant argued that the court had lacked subject matter jurisdiction under the FSIA to order a judgment against it in the first instance and, therefore, that the default judgment should be vacated as void for want of jurisdiction. Plaintiffs argued that the court had jurisdiction under the FSIA in this case on two bases. First, they argued, the issuance of bonds fell within the "commercial activity" exception of the FSIA.[1] Second, they asserted that the statute could be applied retroactively. The court accepted plaintiffs' first argument, concluding that under the plain language of the statute and under its legislative history,[2] the issuance of bonds constituted a commercial activity upon which a foreign sovereign could ordinarily be sued in the United States.

In arguing that the FSIA should be given retroactive effect to control the claims in this case, plaintiffs maintained that the FSIA plainly states that it is applicable to all actions against a foreign state without limitation as to time; that retrospective application would not deprive the Soviet Union of any antecedent rights because absolute sovereign immunity had never been a matter of right but was merely grounded in comity; that the FSIA was a remedial statute, doing no more than providing a mechanism for enforcing independently existing rights; and finally, that a number of courts had applied the FSIA in cases involving transactions that had occurred before its effective date.[3] Defendant conceded that the FSIA could apply to claims arising prior to its effective date[4] but maintained that the Act could not reach back any further than 1952, the point at which the United States formally announced that it would adopt a restrictive theory of sovereign immunity,[5] thereby confining immunity to suits involving the public acts of a foreign sovereign.

[1] 28 U.S.C. §1605(a)(2) (no jurisdictional immunity if action of the foreign state is "based upon a commercial activity carried on in the United States by the foreign state . . . or upon an act outside the territory of the United States in connection with a commercial activity of the foreign state elsewhere and that act causes a direct effect in the United States").

[2] H.R. REP. NO. 1487, 94th Cong., 2d Sess. 14 (1976), *reprinted in* 1976 U.S. CODE CONG. & AD. NEWS 6604, 6613 (characterizing commercial acts within the meaning of the FSIA as "those which private persons might normally perform" and noting, "Moreover, both a sale of bonds to the public and a direct loan from a U.S. commercial bank to a foreign government are activities which are of a commercial nature and should be treated like other similar commercial transactions"). H.R. REP. NO. 1487 at 10.

[3] 665 F.Supp. 323, 336. [4] *Id.* at 347.

[5] Letter of Jack B. Tate, Acting Legal Adviser, Department of State, to Acting Attorney General Philip B. Perlman, May 19, 1952, *reprinted in* 26 DEPT. ST. BULL. 984–85 (1952).

The court rejected plaintiffs' arguments as to retroactivity. Both the plain language and the legislative history of the statute indicated that its effect was to be only prospective. The court found support for this conclusion in the fact that the FSIA provided for a 90-day grace period between its passage and its effective date,[6] and in the fact that the jurisdictional section of the Act provided that the district courts "shall have" jurisdiction over the cases specified in the statute.[7] The court also rejected plaintiffs' characterization of sovereign immunity as no more than "a matter of grace and comity on the part of the United States, and not a restriction imposed by the Constitution,"[8] observing that all rights grounded in the "natural law of international relations" are enforceable only by appeal to grace and comity. Since the U.S. courts had recognized the principle of absolute sovereign immunity as late as 1926,[9] the court had "no hesitation in holding that a foreign sovereign's pre-1926 settled expectation that it was absolutely immune from suit in the United States courts rises to the level of an antecedent right."[10] Moreover, the court reviewed the experience of the USSR in litigation in U.S. courts over the Litvinov Assignment and its repudiation of foreign debts and concluded that the Soviet Union had a justified expectation of absolute sovereign immunity from suit in U.S. courts arising from repudiation of foreign debts prior to the issuance of the Tate letter, and that this expectation was properly regarded as an antecedent right. Thus, the court concluded that the FSIA is not merely a remedial statute that can be applied retroactively.

Finally, the court rejected plaintiffs' argument that prior cases had applied the FSIA to situations where the operative events had allegedly occurred before 1952. The court determined that the cases cited by plaintiffs[11] were unpersuasive because each involved situations where the claims in question had actually accrued after 1952. The *Schmidt* case involved notes on which Poland had defaulted in 1939 because of the outbreak of World War II. The court noted that Poland had listed the Polish Treasury notes at issue as state debts in 1946, which extended the limitations period until 1952, and that a Polish plenipotentiary had corresponded with a U.S. Assistant Secretary of State expressing Poland's intention to negotiate directly with American bondholders, which, if it were an acknowledgment, would have extended the limitations period to 1966. In *Von Dardel,* an action

[6] 665 F.Supp. at 336 (citing Jackson v. People's Republic of China, 596 F.Supp. 386, 388 (N.D. Ala.), *aff'd,* 794 F.2d 1490 (11th Cir. 1984), *cert. denied,* 107 S.Ct. 1371 (1987)).

[7] 28 U.S.C. §1330(a) (1982).

[8] Plaintiffs relied on this statement from Verlinden B.V. v. Central Bank of Nigeria, 461 U.S. 480, 486 (1983). *See* 665 F.Supp. at 337.

[9] *See* Berizzi Bros. Co. v. S.S. Pesaro, 271 U.S. 562, 572 (1926) (extending immunity in an in rem action to a merchant ship owned and controlled by the Italian Government).

[10] 665 F.Supp. at 338.

[11] Schmidt v. Polish People's Republic, 579 F.Supp. 23 (S.D.N.Y.), *aff'd,* 742 F.2d 67 (2d Cir. 1984); Von Dardel v. Union of Soviet Socialist Republics, 623 F.Supp. 246 (D.D.C. 1985); and Asociacion de Reclamantes v. United Mexican States, 561 F.Supp. 1190 (D.D.C. 1983), *aff'd,* 735 F.2d 1517 (D.C. Cir. 1984), *cert. denied,* 470 U.S. 1051 (1985).

against the Soviet Union for the seizure and detention of the Swedish diplomat Raoul Wallenberg, the court characterized the alleged wrongful conduct as an "ongoing tort," which preserved the claim indefinitely. Finally, in *Reclamantes,* the Mexican Government had assumed the obligation to compensate its own nationals for claims that they had been deprived of property in Texas at the time the Republic of Texas had been incorporated into the United States, and it had consistently acknowledged its obligation to pay plaintiffs' claims up to the point when the case was filed in 1982.

Relying on two cases where the courts "rejected a contention that the FSIA is applicable retroactively to commercial transactions that occurred in the early part of the century,"[12] the court held that it would be inequitable to divest the foreign sovereign of the absolute immunity enjoyed prior to 1952.[13] It remains to be seen whether other courts will follow the recent trend of limiting the retroactive effect of the FSIA to those claims which matured after the formal adoption of restrictive sovereign immunity by the United States.

United Kingdom Case Note

Export controls—extraterritorial effect of U.S. economic sanctions against Libya—failure of London branch bank to pay demands

Libyan Arab Foreign Bank v. Bankers Trust Co. 1986 L. Nos. 1567, 4048.

High Court of Justice, Queen's Bench Division, Commercial Court, London, September 2, 1987.

Plaintiff, Libyan Arab Foreign Bank (Libyan Bank), a Libyan corporation wholly owned by the Central Bank of Libya, filed a lawsuit in London against Bankers Trust Co., a New York corporation, after defendant refused to pay sums out of the plaintiff's dollar account held at the London branch of Bankers Trust to the plaintiff. On January 8, 1986, Bankers Trust had failed to make a requested 2:00 P.M. transfer to its London branch on behalf of the Libyan Bank. At about 4:10 P.M. that same day, the Secretary of the Treasury informed Bankers Trust that the President had just signed an executive order prohibiting payments by U.S. persons, including foreign branch banks, to Libyan entities.[1] Subsequently, the Libyan Bank made several demands for payments, clearly stating that it would accept payment by any recognized means, including in the sterling equivalent. Bankers

[12] 665 F.Supp. at 348 (relying on Slade v. United States of Mexico, 617 F.Supp. 351 (D.D.C. 1985), *aff'd mem.,* 790 F.2d 183 (D.C. Cir. 1986), *cert. denied,* 107 S.Ct. 1360 (1987); and Jackson v. People's Republic of China, 596 F.Supp. 386 (N.D. Ala. 1984), *aff'd,* 794 F.2d 1490 (11th Cir. 1986), *cert. denied,* 107 S.Ct. 1371 (1987)).

[13] *Id.* at 349.

[1] Exec. Order No. 12,544 (Jan. 8, 1986), 51 Fed. Reg. 1235 (1986). The day before, the President had issued an executive order prohibiting trade between the United States and Libya. Exec. Order No. 12,543, *id.* at 875.

Trust did not comply with any of these demands on the ground that it would be unlawful under the President's executive order for it to do so. Actions were commenced on the basis of noncompliance with each of the demands, raising a number of claims.[2] After reviewing the relationship between the parties, the proper law of the contract, the effect of supervening illegality in a jurisdiction where acts are to be performed and the nature of a bank's obligations related specifically to the various forms of transfer and payment that were demanded, the High Court of Justice in London (per Staughton, J.) rejected defendant's arguments and *held:* that in the circumstances of the case and pursuant to the relationship between the parties, Bankers Trust had an obligation to comply with a demand for payment in cash in London from the London account and hence was liable in damages for the sum in question.

Turning first to the relationship between the parties, the court observed that the Libyan Bank held two dollar-denominated accounts with Bankers Trust: a current or demand account at Bankers Trust's New York branch and a call, or interest-bearing, account at the London branch. The accounts were operated by Bankers Trust on a "managed account" system. At the time of the relevant events,[3] this system worked as follows. A "peg" balance of $500,000 was maintained in New York. At 2:00 P.M. each day, the balance on the New York account was reviewed. Any balance exceeding $500,000 was transferred to the interest-bearing account in London. If the balance was less than $500,000, a transfer from London to New York took place to restore the peg balance. The only entries on the London account were credits from or debits to the New York account. The nature of the arrangement led the court to conclude that it was "a term of [the] arrange-

[2] Six related claims were made altogether. The first two claims are discussed in the text. The third claim concerned the nonexecution of payment instructions on January 8. This claim failed for two reasons. First, the court held that Bankers Trust was entitled to delay executing the instructions because there was no obligation to execute them by a particular time. Second, Libyan Bank had produced no evidence of any loss suffered as a result of the failure to execute the payments. The fourth claim alleged that the information disclosed to the Federal Reserve Bank on January 7 and 8 about the status of the account amounted to a breach of the duty of confidence owed to Libyan Bank. This claim also failed because any such breach of confidence caused the Libyan Bank no loss. Furthermore, the court reached a "tentative conclusion" (a final conclusion was not necessary in view of the finding of no loss) that there may be a public interest exception to the banker's duty of confidence that applied in this case. The fifth claim alleged frustration of the contract between Libyan Bank and Bankers Trust as an alternative to the first two claims, seeking return of the same sums, i.e., the balance of sums paid in the past to Bankers Trust by Libyan Bank, under the Law Reform (Frustrated Contracts) Act 1943. This claim would have failed (had it been necessary to decide it) for two reasons. First, Bankers Trust's obligations had not been frustrated—merely suspended. Second, the Act only directs sums to be returned that were paid "in pursuance of" a contract. There was no obligation on Libyan Bank to deposit sums with Bankers Trust. The sixth claim is discussed in note 3 *infra.*

[3] The operation of the system changed in April 1984. The result of this change was a significant reduction in interest payable to Libyan Bank, which did not become aware of the change until the latter part of 1985. The sixth claim (which was successful) arose from these events but is unrelated to the freeze and is not discussed further here.

ment that all the Libyan Bank's transactions should pass through New York."[4]

Turning to the question of the proper law of the contract, the court accepted the "general rule" that "the contract between a bank and its customer is governed by the law of the place where the account is kept, in the absence of agreement to the contrary."[5] In the present case, the London account was "kept" in London,[6] despite the fact that all transactions had to pass through New York. Moreover, "the rights and obligations of the parties in respect of the *London* account were governed by English law."[7]

As to the issue of supervening illegality, the court first set out the general principles involved: "Performance of a contract is excused if (i) it has become illegal by the proper law of the contract, or (ii) it necessarily involves doing an act which is unlawful by the law of the place where the act has to be done."[8] In reviewing the relevant precedents, the court drew a distinction between acts that performance *necessarily involves* and acts that one party takes to *equip* itself for performance. Performance is not excused in the latter case, but is in the former instance because of the illegality in the place where the act is to be performed. The court also noted that

> [a]n English contract should and will be held invalid on account of illegality if the real object and intention of the parties necessitates them joining in an endeavour to perform in a foreign and friendly country some act which is illegal by the law of such country notwithstanding that there may be, in a certain event, alternative modes or places of performing which permit the contract to be performed legally.[9]

In this case, however, there was no suggestion or evidence that it was the real object and intention of the Libyan Bank that any illegal act should be performed in New York.

The difficulty in the case was ascertaining when performance "necessarily involves" doing an illegal act in another country. This required a discussion of the nature of Bankers Trust's obligations and of the methods of payment and transfer consistent with those obligations, as well as consideration of the extent to which acts in New York were involved. The court noted that the basic contractual obligations of a bank include several implied terms, including "(a) the promise of the bank to repay is to repay at the branch of the bank where the account is kept, and (b) the bank is not to be called upon to pay until payment is demanded at the branch at which the account is kept."[10] Thus, to succeed, Libyan Bank had to "allege a demand made

[4] 1986 L. Nos. 1567, 4048, slip op. at 9. [5] *Id.* at 22.

[6] *Id.* at 23.

[7] *Id.* at 26 (emphasis added). The court concluded that the contractual arrangement was probably governed in part by English law and in part by New York law. Accepting that this was unusual, the court noted that there was authority for severable parts of a contract to be governed by separate proper laws, and also that branches of a bank may be treated as entities separate from their head offices for some purposes. *Id.*

[8] *Id.* at 19.

[9] *Id.* at 21 (quoting Foster v. Driscoll, [1921] 1 K.B. 470, 521).

[10] *Id.* at 27 (quoting Richardson v. Richardson, 1927 P. 228, 232).

which Bankers Trust were obliged to comply with."[11] It was therefore necessary to consider what demands the Libyan Bank was entitled to make and whether Bankers Trust was obliged to comply with them.

After reviewing the possible forms and means of payment and transfer, the court noted that all these means of transfer were irrelevant, so long as the managed-account arrangements subsisted because, as noted above, it was a term of that arrangement that the London account be used only to transfer a credit to New York. However, the court held that the Libyan Bank was entitled to terminate, and had in fact terminated, the managed-account relationship. This meant that Bankers Trust was obliged to make transfers from the London account on the instruction of Libyan Bank, provided no infringement of U.S. law *in* the United States was involved.

Bankers Trust argued that its obligations should be limited by an implied term to the effect that a transfer of funds from the London account would be effected through a U.S. clearing system.[12] The term was said to be implied from the relevant international market usage and the course of dealing between the parties. The court rejected this argument, relying on the evidence of Libyan Bank's expert, which was inconsistent with the Eurodollar market usage alleged. Furthermore, the actual course of dealing did not, on the evidence, support the argument.[13] The court also rejected an argument by Bankers Trust that Eurodollar deposits cannot be withdrawn in cash.

Considering these points, the court returned to the possible forms of transfer and determined in each case "whether it was a form of transfer which Libyan Bank were entitled to demand, whether it ha[d] in fact been demanded, and whether it would necessarily involve any action in New York."[14] There were only two forms of payment that satisfied all these criteria: payment in cash in dollars and payment in cash in sterling. With regard to payment in cash generally, the court stated that "every obligation in monetary terms is to be fulfilled, either by the delivery of cash, or by some other operation which the creditor demands and which the debtor is either obliged to, or is content to, perform."[15] The court quoted with approval a statement from the report of Libyan Bank's expert that "[a]s to the demand for payment in cash, I regard this simply as the assertion of a customer's inalienable right."[16] It had apparently been accepted by Bankers Trust's counsel in argument that there would be no breach of New York law involved if Bankers Trust obtained from New York a sufficient quantity of dollar bills and dispatched it to its London office. Such an act by Bankers

[11] *Id.* at 28.

[12] CHIPS and Fedwire are the two U.S. electronic clearing systems. *Id.* at 40.

[13] Under earlier arrangements, the London account had been used as a current account. The court looked at transactions from this earlier period to determine the "course of dealing." *Id.* at 40–42.

[14] *Id.* at 46.

[15] *Id.* at 51.

[16] *Id.* at 50. The court accepted the principle but preferred the word "fundamental" to "inalienable." *Id.* at 51.

Trust would be to equip itself for performance and would not necessarily involve performance.

These findings having been made, Bankers Trust's liability on the primary claim followed almost inexorably. The court found that even if it had not held that payment should have been made in cash in dollars, it would have held that payment should have been made in sterling. The court reviewed the authorities and concluded that in discharging its liabilities, a foreign currency debtor is entitled to choose between foreign currency and sterling; if one route is blocked, the debtor is obliged to perform in the other. Thus, Bankers Trust had breached its legal obligations and the court entered a judgment of $292 million in favor of Libyan Bank. Bankers Trust did not argue before the court, but instead reserved the right to argue before the House of Lords, that payment in London would expose it to sanctions under U.S. law. Therefore, this opinion did not address that argument.

This is a significant judicial opinion, but perhaps of even greater importance is the U.S. Government's response to it. On October 9, 1987, the Office of Foreign Assets Control of the Department of the Treasury issued a license to Bankers Trust permitting it to pay the judgment of $292 million in this case to Libyan Bank. Two reasons probably explain the decision to grant Bankers Trust a license at this time. First, because interest on judgments in Great Britain accumulates at a 15 percent rate (about $25 million per annum on this judgment), if permission to comply was to be granted to Bankers Trust at all, it was better to grant permission sooner rather than later. Second, a British appellate court might have upheld the lower court's ruling on broader grounds, which would add significant scope and precedential weight to an already adverse finding. Whatever the reason for the decision to grant the license, it represents an important concession by the United States on the extraterritorial effect of U.S. economic sanctions.

Decisions of the Iran–United States Claims Tribunal

Arbitration—termination of long-term petroleum products agreement—applicable law for internationalized contracts—lost profits as a compensable element of damage

Mobil Oil Iran Inc. v. Islamic Republic of Iran. AWD 311-74/76/81/150-3.
Iran–United States Claims Tribunal, The Hague, July 14, 1987.

Claimants, the American members of an international group of major Western oil companies collectively called the "Consortium," brought individual claims in the aggregate amount of over $1 billion against the Government of Iran and the National Iranian Oil Co. (NIOC).[1] Claimants sought to

[1] Of the 11 cases originally filed, 7 were subsequently settled and resulted in Awards on Agreed Terms (Charter Iran Petroleum Co., Sohio-Iran, American Independent Oil Co., Iran

recover damages for respondents' breach and wrongful termination of the 1973 Sale and Purchase Agreement (SPA or 1973 agreement) for long-term supply and purchase of petroleum products or, in the alternative, for expropriation of their rights under the 1973 agreement. In a partial award on jurisdiction, liability and compensable elements of damages, Chamber Three of the Iran–United States Claims Tribunal[2] found that certain communications in March 1979 constituted an agreement to terminate the 1973 agreement and *held,* inter alia: that "Respondents [were] liable to the Claimants for the losses which the Claimants legitimately could have expected to recover pursuant to successful negotiation of an agreement settling all the issues relating to the termination of the [1973 agreement]."[3]

The 1973 agreement entitled the Consortium members to lift until 1993 all crude oil produced from a defined area in Iran, less the amount needed for Iran's internal requirements and less a stated amount for export for Iran's own account. The 1973 agreement governed all aspects of this relationship, including the transfer of assets to NIOC in liquidation of a 1954 agreement, pricing formulas, requirements for the oil companies to make capital advances and provide technical services, refining obligations and the sale of natural gas liquid products.

The Tribunal found that many of the main provisions of the 1973 agreement were changed, either unilaterally (notwithstanding its provision prohibiting changes without the mutual consent of the parties) or by tacit agreement. Despite repeated efforts beginning in 1976 to negotiate a new arrangement, no such arrangement had been reached when on March 10, 1979, NIOC sent the Consortium a letter stating that the 1973 agreement "proved to be inoperative soon after the Effective Date due to the fact that the [Consortium] failed to comply with certain essential provisions of the Agreement." The letter specified the basis on which NIOC was prepared to structure its future relationship with the oil companies. On March 23, 1979, the companies replied that while they were reserving their rights, they

---

Chevron Oil Co., Transocean Gulf Oil Co., Getty Iran Inc., and Texaco Iran Ltd.). The four remaining claimants were Mobil Oil Iran Inc., San Jacinto Eastern Corp., Arco Iran, Inc. and Exxon Corp. The Chamber consolidated the hearings of the claims of the oil companies because they all arose out of the same contract.

[2] For background information on the Iran–United States Claims Tribunal, see 77 AJIL 642 (1983). These cases, like many others, were "bifurcated" for the purpose of consideration by the Chamber. In Phase 1 the Chamber undertook to consider three issues: jurisdiction, liability and elements of damages. In Phase 2 the Tribunal will consider quantification of damages and counterclaims by Iran.

[3] AWD 311-74/76/81/150-3, slip op., para. 175. The Chamber found that claimants were entitled to compensation for capital advances by them that were to be treated as prepayments for future oil deliveries; assets transferred to NIOC in 1973 in liquidation of a 1954 agreement (known as the 1954 "Consortium Agreement"); and the taking of certain crude oil and natural gas liquid products that claimants were prevented from lifting. The Chamber rejected claimants' claim for losses on refining operations at Abadan based on alleged breaches of the 1973 agreement's cost provisions, but it invited claimants to resubmit the claim under a different legal theory.

desired to enter into negotiations with NIOC for the purpose of settling all outstanding claims under the 1973 agreement. Negotiations commenced, but they had not been concluded when the hostages crisis arose in November 1979 and resulted in their dissolution.

The Chamber first decided that it had jurisdiction over the claims. Among others, the Chamber rejected respondents' argument that the rights and obligations under the 1973 agreement were joint and several and could not be asserted by the Consortium members individually. The Chamber did not read the 1973 agreement to prevent a company from acting on its own behalf. Affirming prior Tribunal decisions, it also held that for purposes of its own jurisdiction, it was sufficient that a cause of action of a U.S. claimant against Iran or an Iranian Government–controlled entity existed on January 19, 1981, irrespective of whether a claim had been filed with a court, and that the establishment in 1980 by Iran of a special commission with exclusive jurisdiction over claims arising out of the nullification of petroleum agreements did not affect the Tribunal's jurisdiction.[4]

The Chamber next addressed whether respondents were liable for the claims. With respect to certain investments and advances made by the companies pursuant to the 1973 agreement and certain existing stocks of petroleum and gas products, the Chamber found respondents liable and ruled that the only remaining issue was quantification of the amounts owed. To determine respondents' liability, the Chamber examined issues of applicable law, repudiation of the 1973 agreement and expropriation.

On applicable law, the Chamber found that general principles of commercial and international law were applicable to all substantive issues[5]

> [i]n view of the international character of the [1973 agreement], concluded between a State, a State agency [i.e., NIOC] and a number of major foreign companies, of the magnitude of the interests involved, of the complex set of rights and obligations which it established, and of the link created between this Agreement and the sharing of oil industry benefits throughout the Persian Gulf Countries.[6]

In rejecting respondents' argument that the 1973 agreement was to be governed by Iranian law, the Chamber specifically noted that "the usual choice of law clause, which can be found in many international contracts and refers to the interpretation *and* implementation of the contract, was studi-

[4] *See* Amoco Iran Oil Co. v. Iran, ITL 12-55-2 (Dec. 30, 1982), 1 IRAN-U.S. CLAIMS TRIBUNAL REP. [hereinafter IRAN-U.S. C.T.R.] 493 (1981–82); Philips Petroleum Co., Iran v. Iran, ITL 11-39-2 (Dec. 30, 1982), *id.* at 487.

[5] *See* Libyan American Oil Co. v. Government of the Libyan Arab Republic (Apr. 12, 1977) (Mahmassani, Arb.), 20 ILM 1 (1981); Kuwait and American Independent Oil Co. (Mar. 24, 1982) (Reuter, Sultan & Fitzmaurice, Arbs.), 21 ILM 976 (1982); Texas Overseas Petroleum Co./California Asiatic Oil Co. v. Government of the Libyan Arab Republic (Jan. 19, 1977) (Dupuy, Arb.), 17 ILM 3 (1978).

[6] Slip op., para. 81.

ously avoided, and . . . reference is made to Iranian law solely for interpretation of the Agreement."[7]

The Chamber next addressed claimants' argument that NIOC's letter of March 10, 1979 constituted a repudiation of the 1973 agreement. According to respondents, there was no repudiation because the 1973 agreement was rendered inoperative long before 1979 as a result of breach by the oil companies of its essential terms. In the alternative, the respondents urged the Chamber to find that the 1973 agreement was terminated by *force majeure.* While the Chamber agreed that "a number of [the 1973 agreement's] most important provisions were replaced by *ad hoc* agreements, or even *de facto* ones, often reluctantly and only implicitly accepted by one party or the other,"[8] it refused to find that the 1973 agreement had been frustrated before March 1979. With respect to respondents' *force majeure* argument, the Chamber found that the situation prevailing in Iran after the revolution resulted in the suspension of the 1973 agreement but had not yet ripened into effecting its termination. The Chamber supported its finding by noting that by March 10, 1979, a new Iranian Government had been formed and oil exports had resumed, albeit in smaller quantities.[9]

Notwithstanding these findings, the Chamber did not find that Iran and NIOC had breached the agreement in March 1979; rather, it considered NIOC's March 10 letter as "the first expression of . . . a new policy in relation to the Agreement" which was "radically different from that of the previous Government in the oil industry,"[10] and claimants' response of March 23 as acceptance of an offer to terminate.[11] This mutual agreement to terminate, the Chamber concluded, did not relieve respondents of their obligation to compensate claimants for their rights under the 1973 agreement because "a reconciliation of interest was to take place between [the parties]"[12] as a specific condition of the termination. Because the hostages crisis frustrated the ensuing negotiations to resolve the outstanding claims, the Chamber decided that it would determine in a second stage of the arbitration "what the parties could legitimately have expected from negotiations conducted in good faith on the basis of the March 1979 agreement."[13]

As guidelines for the second stage, the Chamber noted that in order to assess these "legitimate expectations," it would consider (1) "the duties and obligations of both parties under the [1973 agreement] and all related

[7] *Id.*, para. 78. Article 29 of the 1973 agreement provided that the "Agreement shall be interpreted in accordance with the laws of Iran." *Id.*, para. 59.

[8] *Id.*, para. 111.

[9] This decision is consistent with other Tribunal awards on the effect of the *force majeure* conditions prevailing in Iran. *See, e.g.*, Sylvania Technical Systems, Inc. v. Iran, AWD 180-64-1 (June 27, 1985) (Chamber 1); Starrett Housing Corp. v. Iran, ITL 32-24-1 (Dec. 19, 1983), 4 IRAN-U.S. C.T.R. 122 (1983 III).

[10] Slip op., para. 119.

[11] *Id.*, para. 122. As a consequence of this finding, the Chamber found that no expropriation had occurred. *Id.*, para. 130.

[12] *Id.*, para. 126.

[13] *Id.*, para. 161.

agreements and arrangements," as these agreements have evolved over time; (2) "[e]ach Party's record in performing the Agreement"; and (3) "all circumstances affecting the exercise of such rights and the performance of such obligations, as they could be observed or foreseen at the time of the March 1979 agreement."[14] Accordingly, the Chamber determined that claimants were entitled to damages for their investments and advances, as well as for the withheld natural gas liquid and crude oil products. Finally, the Chamber reserved its decision "whether and to what extent the Claimants could legitimately expect to recover lost profits as a result of the premature discontinuance of the [1973] Agreement" until after it was briefed further on this matter.[15] The quantification of damages also will be decided in the second stage of this arbitration.

In his concurring opinion, American Arbitrator Charles N. Brower agreed that the award should be governed by international law and that the oil companies should be permitted to make further submissions with regard to their alleged losses at the Abadan refinery, a claim the Chamber had not allowed under the theory originally advanced by the claimants. Brower disagreed, however, with the Chamber's characterization of the exchange of letters as the claimants' voluntary decision to terminate the 1973 agreement; he argued that this characterization was based on the unrealistic assumption that the claimants would have released their rights without a legal quid pro quo.[16]

This decision is consistent with a long line of awards by Chamber Three on most issues, including its findings with respect to jurisdiction, applicable law, *force majeure* and the right to lost profits. Indeed, despite its finding of a mutual agreement to terminate, the Chamber recognized in principle that claimants are entitled to lost profits.

State responsibility for injuries to aliens—wrongful expulsion—attribution of responsibility to successor government for actions by supporters of revolution

SHORT v. ISLAMIC REPUBLIC OF IRAN. AWD 312-11135-3.
Iran–United States Claims Tribunal, The Hague, July 14, 1987.

Claimant, U.S. citizen Alfred Short, filed a claim against the Islamic Republic of Iran, respondent, alleging that respondent had wrongfully expelled him from Iran. The United States also filed a "Request for an Interlocutory Award" on behalf of approximately 1,500 U.S. claimants who left Iran during the period from October 1978 through February 1979, asking the Tribunal to hold the Government of Iran liable for the collective wrongful expulsion of all of these Americans. Respondent challenged the Tribunal's jurisdiction over this claim, contended that claimant had de-

[14] *Id.*

[15] *Id.*, para. 175.

[16] Brower likened such a characterization to supposing "that a condemned man who spurns the ritual proffer of a blindfold when marched before the firing squad thereby consents to his execution." Concurring Opinion of Arbitrator Brower, para. 2.

parted from Iran voluntarily on the instruction of his employer, and argued that the causes of the U.S. nationals' departure from Iran cannot be attributed to the Government of Iran. A divided Chamber Three of the Tribunal dismissed the claim, *holding* that: (1) it had jurisdiction over the claim; (2) it would be contrary to the jurisdictional function of the Tribunal to make a generalization beyond the facts in the case before the Tribunal; and (3) international responsibility of a state for wrongful expulsion can be engaged only where the circumstances or events causing the departure of the alien are attributable to agents—not mere supporters—of a successful revolutionary movement. At the same time, Chamber Three refused the U.S. request for an interlocutory award.

The Chamber first noted that it had jurisdiction over the claim, despite respondent's arguments that (1) the expulsion allegation was tortious in nature and thus fell outside the jurisdiction of the Tribunal, and (2) the alleged expulsion resulted from "popular movements in the course of the Islamic Revolution of Iran" and therefore was excluded from the Tribunal's jurisdiction pursuant to Article 2(1) of the Claims Settlement Declaration. The Chamber observed that the fact that an allegation "may be characterized as a tortious act or conduct, is of no effect upon the Tribunal's jurisdiction."[1] The Chamber also noted that only claims arising from injuries as a result of popular movements during the revolution that were *not* an act of the Government of Iran were excluded from the Tribunal's jurisdiction. Therefore, because claimant alleged that the actions that caused his expulsion were attributable to the Government of Iran, the claim was properly before the Tribunal.

As to the U.S. Government's request for an interlocutory award on behalf of all Americans who fled from Iran from October 1978 to February 1979, the Chamber noted that because it was "able to decide all issues in this Case in this Award,"[2] the request for an interlocutory award was moot. The Chamber also made the following observation:

> In any event, although the Award in this Case might provide useful guidance to parties dealing with other cases presenting similar issues, the allegations made in each claim have to be evaluated individually in taking into account the circumstances particular to the case. No generalization, therefore, can be made on the basis of the facts appertaining to a specific case, and it would be contrary to the jurisdictional function of the Tribunal to make such a generalization. It is up to the parties in similar cases to draw from the present Award the conclusions that they consider to be valuable for their own case.[3]

Turning to the merits of the claim, the Chamber noted that, in light of the relevant principles of state responsibility, the issue to be decided was whether "the facts invoked by the Claimant as having caused his departure from Iran are attributable to Iran, either directly, or indirectly as a result of

[1] AWD 312-11135-3, slip op., paras. 9, 11.
[2] *Id.*, para. 27.
[3] *Id.*

its deliberate policies, or whether they reveal a lack of due diligence in meeting Iran's international duties towards the Claimant."[4] The Chamber determined that the claimant's departure from Iran could not be attributed to Iran for two reasons.

First, the Chamber considered whether the acts of supporters of a revolution can be attributed to the government following the success of the revolution. The Chamber recognized that where a revolution leads to the establishment of a new government, the state is held responsible for the acts of the overthrown government insofar as the latter maintained control of the situation. In addition, the successor government is responsible for the acts imputable to the revolutionary movement that established it, even if those acts occurred prior to its establishment, as a consequence of the continuity existing between the new organization of the state and the organization of the revolutionary movement. However, the Chamber noted that this case was different because the claimant departed at a time when the predecessor government was unable to control events but the revolutionary movement had not yet been able to establish control over any part of Iranian territory. Moreover, the claimant was unable to identify the actions of any *agent* of the revolutionary movement that had compelled him to leave Iran. Concluding that the acts of "supporters" of a revolution cannot be attributable to the government following the success of the revolution just as the acts of supporters of an existing government are not attributable to the government, the Chamber refused to examine the effects of actions by supporters of the revolutionary movement.

Second, the Chamber considered whether the actions of the agents of the revolution were sufficient to cause claimant's expulsion from Iran. The Chamber noted that although declarations by Ayatollah Khomeini were antiforeign and anti-American, they were of a "general nature and did not specify that Americans should be expelled *en masse*."[5] The Chamber referred to the International Court of Justice's decision in the *Hostages* case,[6] where the Court refused to find that the students' actions in taking over the U.S. Embassy were authorized by general anti-American declarations by government officials. Similarly, in this case, the Chamber concluded that the general anti-American declarations did not amount to authorizing the revolutionaries to act in such a way as to force the claimant to leave Iran. Therefore, since the claimant's departure from Iran could not be imputed to the wrongful conduct of Iran, the Chamber dismissed the claim.

In a separate, dissenting opinion, American Arbitrator Charles N. Brower noted, "It is inherent in a constructive mass expulsion that the acts effectuating it will be, in a high degree, general, unspecific, unfocused and indirect."[7] Moreover, Brower contended that

[4] *Id.*, para. 29. [5] *Id.*, para. 35.

[6] United States Diplomatic and Consular Staff in Tehran (U.S. v. Iran), 1980 ICJ REP. 3, 29 (Judgment of May 24).

[7] Dissenting Opinion of Arbitrator Brower, slip op. at 12.

> even if the accumulated acts to which the Claimant (and others) fell victim cannot be traced directly to the Ayatollah's pronouncements, his total failure in that context to act in any way to quell the expulsive fervor of his adherents as it arose and peaked over a period of months should permit attribution to him of responsibility for the consequences.[8]

Finally, Brower challenged the majority's conclusion that international law does not attribute to the successor government the acts of unorganized or loosely organized adherents of the successful revolution.

This is the first Tribunal decision to address the expulsion claims of U.S. citizens. The United States had hoped to establish a favorable decision that would govern the hundreds of pending claims for wrongful expulsion. Instead, this decision indicates that each expulsion claimant will be required to present specific evidence of the particular actions by agents of the revolution that caused him or her to leave Iran. Two subsequent Tribunal awards addressing similar expulsion claims will be discussed in the April issue of the *Journal*.[9]

CURRENT DEVELOPMENTS REGARDING JUDICIAL DECISIONS REPORTED IN THE JOURNAL, 1987

Chaser Shipping Corp. v. United States, 649 F.Supp. 736, 81 AJIL 419; *aff'd mem.,* 819 F.2d 1129, *cert. denied,* N.Y. Times, Jan. 12, 1988, at A20, col. 4 (U.S. Jan. 11, 1988).

Coalition to Preserve Integrity of American Trademarks v. United States, 790 F.2d 903, 81 AJIL 217; *cert. granted sub nom. K Mart Corp. v. Cartier, Inc.,* 107 S.Ct. 642.

Jackson v. People's Republic of China, 794 F.2d 1490, 81 AJIL 214; *rehearing en banc denied,* 801 F.2d 404, *cert. denied,* 107 S.Ct. 1371.

Republic of the Philippines v. Marcos, 806 F.2d 344, 81 AJIL 417; *cert. denied,* 107 S.Ct. 2178.

West v. Multibanco Comermex, S.A., 807 F.2d 820, 81 AJIL 660; *cert. denied,* 107 S.Ct. 2483; *reh'g denied,* 56 U.S.L.W. 3115.

[8] *Id.* at 13.

[9] Rankin v. Islamic Republic of Iran, AWD 326-10913-2 (Nov. 3, 1987); Yeager v. Islamic Republic of Iran, AWD 324-10199-1 (Nov. 2, 1987).

CURRENT DEVELOPMENTS

The Thirty-ninth Session of the International Law Commission

The International Law Commission of the United Nations held its 39th session from May 4 to July 17, 1987, under the Chairmanship of the present author. The Commission adopted five articles on the Draft Code of Offences against the Peace and Security of Mankind and six articles on the law of the non-navigational uses of international watercourses. The two other topics discussed at the 39th session were international liability for injurious consequences arising out of acts not prohibited by international law and relations between states and international organizations (second part of the topic). The remaining three substantive items on the Commission's agenda —jurisdictional immunities of states and their property, the status of the diplomatic courier and the diplomatic bag not accompanied by diplomatic courier, and state responsibility—were not considered at this session.[1]

At its 1986 session, the Commission adopted on first reading its drafts on jurisdictional immunities and the diplomatic courier and bag. Those drafts have been sent to governments for their comments and will be given a second reading beginning at the Commission's 1988 session or as soon thereafter as comments have been received from a sufficient number and variety of governments. Because the special rapporteur for state responsibility was not reelected to the Commission in last year's quinquennial elections, the Commission had no report on that topic before it for discussion. In addition, the rapporteur for jurisdictional immunities, Ambassador Sompong Sucharitkul, did not stand for reelection to the Commission in 1986. New special rapporteurs were therefore appointed for both state responsibility and jurisdictional immunities, Professor Gaetano Arangio-Ruiz for the former, and Ambassador Motoo Ogiso for the latter.

Draft Code of Offences against the Peace and Security of Mankind

The five articles adopted by the Commission form a portion of the introductory or "general part" of the code. As currently envisaged by the special rapporteur, Minister Doudou Thiam, the code will consist of a general part, containing principles applicable to the entire code, and a "special part," containing sections on crimes against peace, war crimes and crimes against humanity. Whether the draft will also contain a proposed statute of an international criminal court is not yet settled. The Commission had referred this question to the General Assembly in 1983 but has not yet received an answer.

[1] *See* Report of the International Law Commission on the work of its thirty-ninth session, 42 UN GAOR Supp. (No. 10), UN Doc. A/42/10 (1987) [hereinafter Report].

The five articles adopted at the 39th session, which are part of Chapter 1: Introduction, provide as follows:

PART I *Definition and Characterization*

Article 1

Definition

The crimes [under international law] defined in this draft Code constitute crimes against the peace and security of mankind.

Article 2

Characterization

The characterization of an act or omission as a crime against the peace and security of mankind is independent of internal law. The fact that an act or omission is or is not punishable under internal law does not affect this characterization.

PART II *General principles*

Article 3

Responsibility and punishment

1. Any individual who commits a crime against the peace and security of mankind is responsible for such crime irrespective of any motives invoked by the accused that are not covered by the definition of the offence and is liable to punishment therefor.

2. Prosecution of an individual for a crime against the peace and security of mankind does not relieve a State of any responsibility under international law for an act or omission attributable to it.

Article 5

Non-applicability of statutory limitations

No statutory limitation shall apply to crimes against the peace and security of mankind.

Article 6

Judicial guarantees

Any individual charged with a crime against the peace and security of mankind shall be entitled without discrimination to the minimum guarantees due to all human beings with regard to the law and the facts. In particular:

1. He shall have the right to be presumed innocent until proved guilty;

2. He shall have the right:

(a) In the determination of any charge against him, to have a fair and public hearing by a competent, independent and impartial tribunal duly established by law or by treaty;
(b) To be informed promptly and in detail in a language which he understands of the nature and cause of the charge against him;

(c) To have adequate time and facilities for the preparation of his defence and to communicate with counsel of his own choosing;
(d) To be tried without undue delay;
(e) To be tried in his presence, and to defend himself in person or through legal assistance of his own choosing; to be informed, if he does not have legal assistance, of this right; and to have legal assistance assigned to him and without payment by him in any such case if he does not have sufficient means to pay for it;
(f) To examine, or have examined, the witnesses against him and to obtain the attendance and examination of witnesses on his behalf under the same conditions as witnesses against him;
(g) To have the free assistance of an interpreter if he cannot understand or speak the language used in court;
(h) Not to be compelled to testify against himself or to confess guilt.[2]

Several points should be made with regard to Article 1. While it is entitled "*Definition,*" the article obviously does not define what amounts to an offense or crime against the peace and security of mankind. The Commission rather opted for the approach followed in the 1954 version of the draft code, namely, definition by enumeration. Second, as is evident from this text of Article 1, the Commission decided to recommend that the word "offences" in the English title of the draft be changed to "crimes" to reflect the extremely serious nature of the acts and practices involved. Third and finally, a point of considerable controversy was whether to include the words "under international law," which appear in brackets. Some members supported inclusion, pointing to the fact that these words appeared in Article 1 of the 1954 version and arguing that the very nature of the crimes in question made them crimes under international law. Other members feared that this language might give the impression that the code dealt with, or at least had implications for, crimes committed by states. They also noted that the phrase raised the question whether the crimes dealt with in the code might be covered by rules of general international law, independently of the code.

Article 2 was inspired by Principle II of the "Principles of International Law recognized in the Charter of the Nürnberg Tribunal, and in the Judgment of the Tribunal," adopted by the Commission in 1950. Principle II provides: "The fact that internal law does not impose a penalty for an act which constitutes a crime under international law does not relieve the person who committed the act from responsibility under international law."[3] Thus, the purpose of the article is to prevent invocation of rules of internal law as a defense to an otherwise valid prosecution under the code. That is, characterization of an act under internal law cannot be invoked against the characterization of the same act under the code.

Paragraph 1 of Article 3 states the important principle that the subjects of the code are individuals, not states. Paragraph 2 of that article recognizes

[2] *Id.* at 22, 24, 25, 28 and 29–30.

[3] *Id.* at 24. *See also* the Commission's 1950 report, [1950] 2 Y.B. INT'L L. COMM'N 364, 374, UN Doc. A/CN.4/SER.A/1950/Add.1.

that the act for which an individual is responsible under the code may also be attributable to a state, and provides that prosecution of the individual would not relieve the state of responsibility. Paragraph 1 also prevents the accused from invoking any motive as an excuse or justification unless such defenses are provided for in the definition of the crime itself.

The special rapporteur had proposed an Article 4, entitled "*Aut Dedere Aut Punire.*" As its title implies, the article dealt with the duty to try or extradite an individual accused of having committed a crime against the peace and security of mankind. The Commission decided to defer action on this article until a later stage of its work on the project, since it implicates questions of enforcement of the code.

Article 5 is self-explanatory. Article 6 sets forth the procedural guarantees to be accorded an individual accused of having committed a crime under the code. It is modeled closely on Article 14 of the International Covenant on Civil and Political Rights and, indeed, in large part reproduces that article.

Non-navigational Uses of International Watercourses

The Commission had adopted six articles on watercourses at its 1980 session under the special rapporteurship of Professor (now Judge) Stephen Schwebel, but the articles were reopened when Judge Schwebel's successor, Minister (now Judge) Jens Evensen, proposed certain modifications of them in 1983 and 1984. Because of the priority assigned to other topics, as well as yet another change in rapporteurship (upon Minister Evensen's election to the ICJ), the Commission was unable to make further progress on watercourses until this year. The articles adopted at the 39th session, however, lay a firm foundation for future work on this subject.

An important decision taken by the Commission, which enabled it to proceed without becoming entangled in doctrinal disputes, was to defer defining "international watercourses" for the time being. As those who have followed the Commission's work on this topic will be aware, the articles adopted in 1980 were based upon the "system" concept—an outgrowth of the river basin approach rejected earlier as being too closely tied to uses of land territory. By deferring the question of the definition and scope of the topic (set forth in Article 1), the Commission has left to one side determination of whether to continue to base its work on the system approach. (Nevertheless, the debates in the Commission suggest that the system concept is as controversial in the newly constituted Commission as it ever was.) The Commission will continue its work on the basis of the provisional working hypothesis that was accepted in 1980, and will place the term "system" in brackets wherever it appears in the text of an article.

The other major departure from the 1980 articles is the decision not to employ the controversial concept of an international watercourse as a "shared natural resource." Many members of the Commission and representatives in the Sixth (Legal) Committee of the General Assembly were uncomfortable with applying the concept to international watercourses because of its uncertain legal implications in that context. It appears that the

Commission will generally follow the approach to this problem proposed by the current special rapporteur (the present author), which would give effect to the main principles underlying the concept of a shared natural resource —equitable utilization and the duty to cooperate—without using the expression itself in the text of an article.

Articles 2–5, which together with the deferred Article 1 will constitute Part I: Introduction, as adopted at the 39th session provide:

Article 2

Scope of the present articles

1. The present articles apply to uses of international watercourse[s] [systems] and of their waters for purposes other than navigation and to measures of conservation related to the uses of those watercourse[s] [systems] and their waters.

2. The use of international watercourse[s] [systems] for navigation is not within the scope of the present articles except in so far as other uses affect navigation or are affected by navigation.

Article 3

Watercourse States

For the purposes of the present articles, a watercourse State is a State in whose territory part of an international watercourse [system] is situated.

Article 4

[Watercourse] [System] agreements

1. Watercourse States may enter into one or more agreements which apply and adjust the provisions of the present articles to the characteristics and uses of a particular international watercourse [system] or part thereof. Such agreements shall, for the purposes of the present articles, be called [watercourse] [system] agreements.

2. Where a [watercourse] [system] agreement is concluded between two or more watercourse States, it shall define the waters to which it applies. Such an agreement may be entered into with respect to an entire international watercourse [system] or with respect to any part thereof or a particular project, programme or use, provided that the agreement does not adversely affect, to an appreciable extent, the use by one or more other watercourse States of the waters of the international watercourse [system].

3. Where a watercourse State considers that adjustment or application of the provisions of the present articles is required because of the characteristics and uses of a particular international watercourse [system], watercourse States shall consult with a view to negotiating in good faith for the purpose of concluding a [watercourse] [system] agreement or agreements.

Article 5

Parties to [watercourse] [system] agreements

1. Every watercourse State is entitled to participate in the negotiation of and to become a party to any [watercourse] [system] agreement that applies to the entire international watercourse [system], as well as to participate in any relevant consultations.

2. A watercourse State whose use of an international watercourse [system] may be affected to an appreciable extent by the implementation of a proposed [watercourse] [system] agreement that applies only to a part of the watercourse [system] or to a particular project, programme or use is entitled to participate in consultations on, and in the negotiation of, such an agreement, to the extent that its use is thereby affected, and to become a party thereto.[4]

Articles 6 and 7, in Part II: General Principles, were also adopted at the 39th session and read as follows:

Article 6

Equitable and reasonable utilization and participation

1. Watercourse States shall in their respective territories utilize an international watercourse [system] in an equitable and reasonable manner. In particular, an international watercourse [system] shall be used and developed by watercourse States with a view to attaining optimum utilization thereof and benefits therefrom consistent with adequate protection of the international watercourse [system].

2. Watercourse States shall participate in the use, development and protection of an international watercourse [system] in an equitable and reasonable manner. Such participation includes both the right to utilize the international watercourse [system] as provided in paragraph 1 of this article and the duty to co-operate in the protection and development thereof, as provided in article . . . .

Article 7

Factors relevant to equitable and reasonable utilization

1. Utilization of an international watercourse [system] in an equitable and reasonable manner within the meaning of article 6 requires taking into account all relevant factors and circumstances, including:

(a) geographic, hydrographic, hydrological, climatic and other factors of a natural character;

(b) the social and economic needs of the watercourse States concerned;

(c) the effects of the use or uses of an international watercourse [system] in one watercourse State on other watercourse States;

(d) existing and potential uses of the international watercourse [system];

[4] Report, *supra* note 1, at 54, 56, 57 and 66.

(e) conservation, protection, development and economy of use of the water resources of the international watercourse [system] and the costs of measures taken to that effect;

(f) the availability of alternatives, of corresponding value, to a particular planned or existing use.

2. In the application of article 6 or paragraph 1 of the present article watercourse States concerned shall, when the need arises, enter into consultations in a spirit of co-operation.[5]

Articles 2 through 5 follow closely Articles 1 to 4 as adopted in 1980. Aside from the fact that the term "system" appears in brackets, the major differences are that paragraph 3 of Article 4 requires only consultation rather than negotiation, and paragraph 2 of Article 5 entitles the state in question to become a party to the watercourse agreement rather than entitling it only to participate in the negotiation of such an agreement. Articles 6 and 7 are new. Article 6 states the fundamental principle of equitable utilization, which is a cornerstone of the entire draft. It also introduces the concept of equitable participation—which emphasizes the importance of active involvement and cooperation by states in the use, management and development of international watercourses. Article 7 sets forth a list of factors to be used in determining what amounts to an equitable and reasonable utilization of an international watercourse. The Commission found it necessary to avoid using the word "determining" in the text of the article because, in the view of some members, that word implied that the decision would be made not by states but by a third-party dispute resolution body. While the factors set forth in Article 7 could be used by an arbitral or other tribunal in resolving a concrete dispute, the article contemplates that, in the first instance at least, states will make the "determination" that their utilizations are equitable and reasonable.

International Liability for Injurious Consequences Arising out of Acts not Prohibited by International Law

The Commission held a general, but extensive, discussion of international liability on the basis of the third report of the special rapporteur, Ambassador Julio Barboza. The report contained six draft articles for the Commission's consideration. The articles were of an introductory character and were submitted principally for discussion purposes; they will be reformulated in the special rapporteur's next report on the basis of the discussion in the Commission this year.

The debate highlighted the fact that, while the Commission has been working on this topic since 1980,[6] the project is still at an embryonic stage of development. There remains no clear understanding within the Commission of the kinds of activities to which the draft would apply, nor is there agreement on the fundamental question whether the applicable standard of

[5] *Id.* at 69–70 and 82.

[6] While the Commission included the topic in its program of work in 1978, the first report of the original special rapporteur, Professor Robert Q. Quentin-Baxter, was not discussed until 1980.

liability is strict (objective) or based on fault. There is even disagreement within the Commission over whether the purpose of the draft is to provide for prevention or compensation. These areas of uncertainty will doubtless be clarified as the Commission focuses on concrete proposals of the special rapporteur and adopts the first draft articles on the topic.

Relations Between States and International Organizations (Second Part of the Topic)

The Commission has not given this topic high priority since work commenced on it in 1976, and its development is therefore still in the formative stages. Because of the absence of three topics from the active agenda this year, however, the Commission was able to devote more time than usual to international organizations. The Commission had completed work on the first part of the topic in 1971. That set of draft articles formed the basis of the 1975 Vienna Convention on the Representation of States in their Relations with International Organizations of a Universal Character.[7] The second part of the topic, currently before the Commission, deals with the status, privileges and immunities of international organizations, their officials, experts and other persons engaged in their activities who are not representatives of states.

At the 1987 session, the Commission focused its discussion principally upon the third report of the special rapporteur, Ambassador Leonardo Díaz-González. That report contained a proposed outline of the subject matter to be covered by the draft articles. The outline was a comprehensive one and sparked a debate as to whether the draft should attempt to set forth general principles and rules covering the entire field or whether it should be confined to filling gaps in existing instruments. Also discussed was whether the draft should be addressed to regional international organizations or should be confined to international organizations of a universal character. Some members expressed concern that the draft might call into question certain principles already embodied in international agreements—particularly if the rules of the draft eventually found their way into a convention. The special rapporteur nonetheless concluded that he would proceed to present draft articles to the Commission on the basis of the outline contained in his third report.

STEPHEN C. MCCAFFREY*

THE ABM TREATY INTERPRETATION RESOLUTION

On September 22, 1987, the Committee on Foreign Relations of the U.S. Senate filed its report on *The ABM Treaty Interpretation Resolution.*[1] This followed publication of the 828-page volume of joint hearings before the

[7] *Done* Mar. 14, 1975, UN Doc. A/CONF.67/16 (1975), *reprinted in* 1975 UN JURID. Y.B. 87, UN Sales No. E.77.V.3.

* Member, United Nations International Law Commission; Professor of Law, University of the Pacific, McGeorge School of Law.

[1] S. REP. NO. 164, 100th Cong., 1st Sess. (1987). *See* 133 CONG. REC. S12,498 (daily ed. Sept. 22, 1987).

Committees on Foreign Relations and on the Judiciary, *The ABM Treaty and the Constitution.*[2] The resolution on interpreting the Treaty, S. Res. 167,[3] was reported favorably by a vote of 11-8 (with minority views). It reaffirmed the propriety of the "narrow interpretation" of the ABM Treaty.

The following excerpts from the Foreign Relations Committee's report include a portion of the additional views of Senators Helms, Pressler and Trible.

> The committee is aware of *no* instance in which a treaty was reasonably supposed by the Senate, when it consented to ratification, to mean one thing, and it was argued later by the Executive to mean something altogether different. Even, however, if such a precedent could be adduced, the Committee recalls its comments in 1978 in reporting out the Panama Canal Treaties: "The Constitution is not amended by violation; express prohibitions and requirements, such as those contained in the . . . Treaty Clause, are not expunged through non-observance."
>
> . . .
>
> Custom, to the extent that it is pertinent, demonstrates a longstanding practice of the Executive to ratify the treaty—and only the treaty—that has received the advice and consent of the Senate. In the above-cited report, the Committee stated that "customary constitutional law in this country requires that the President give effect to treaty conditions imposed by the Senate." Those conditions may be explicit, as they are when formally reduced to express reservations, understandings, or other statements; or they may be implicit, as they were in the case of the ABM Treaty, where their content is to be gleaned from statements by Senators and by administration officials in which the Senators present acquiesced.
>
> It bears heavy emphasis that the *form* of the Senate's understanding of a treaty's meaning is constitutionally irrelevant, for it is substance that controls. As Professor Louis Henkin, Chief Reporter of the *Revised Restatement,* testified before the Committee:
>
>> The President can only make a treaty that means what the Senate understood the treaty to mean when the Senate gave its consent. That is indisputable when the Senate has made its understanding plain in the form of a proposed reservation or an explicit understanding.
>>
>> The same principle governs when the Senate's understanding of a treaty provision is not expressed in a formal resolution, but is apparent from the Senate's deliberations leading to its expression of consent.
>>
>> The Senate's understanding of the treaty to which it consents is binding on the President. He can make the treaty only as so under-

[2] *The ABM Treaty and the Constitution: Joint Hearings Before the Senate Comms. on Foreign Relations and on the Judiciary,* 100th Cong., 1st Sess. (1987).

[3] S. Res. 167, 100th Cong., 1st Sess. (1987). A section-by-section analysis of the Treaty begins on p. 37 of the report, S. Rep. No. 164, *supra* note 1.

> stood. He cannot make the treaty and insist that it means something else.

Professor Henkin directly addressed the question whether the Senate is required to "formalize" its understanding of a treaty's meaning, as proponents of the Reagan Revision have asserted. He said:

> I do not think the formality of a reservation or understanding by the Senate is a constitutional requirement. The Constitution says nothing of the kind. I think what the Constitution clearly implies is that it is what the Senate understands the treaty to mean—that that is what the treaty means for purposes of its consent.
>
> . . .
>
> Custom also illuminates other matters, such as the weight to be accorded the so-called "negotiating record." The Committee uses this term with some hesitation, for three reasons:

—First, "negotiating record" is normally a term of art used to describe an *agreed* negotiating record. Since it is only the joint intent of the parties that has significance under international law, notes unilaterally compiled by one party cannot control a treaty's meaning. Accordingly, in the strict sense, no genuine "negotiating record" was consolidated and agreed to at the time the ABM Treaty was ratified; nor therefore will one ever exist. Rather, the "record" referred to today is an assemblage of internal U.S. Government documents put together only recently—through an office-to-office survey conducted by personnel working for the State Department Legal Adviser, Mr. Abraham Sofaer. The committee notes that the Soviet Union could as validly assert the significance of its own "negotiating record," which may or may not exist but which the United States has not yet seen.

—Second, there is no guarantee that the Legal Adviser's staff was able to find all the pieces of the U.S. "record" they have patched together. Indeed, Mr. Sofaer has candidly described the process, telling the House Foreign Affairs Committee in 1985 that he and his staff "obtained from various sources everything that we could find that might be relevant to the issue of future systems and components." Yet all must realize what Mr. Sofaer has acknowledged: that this disjointed assembly process might well have produced a fragmentary product—a collage, really, that represents something less than the total picture of what actually transpired during the ABM Treaty negotiations. If Mr. Sofaer is to assert the preeminence of this assemblage in the interpretation of the ABM Treaty, he must logically be prepared to accept that the solemn obligations of the United States under the ABM Treaty must be altered each and every time a new document is recovered casting a different nuance of meaning on the collage.

—Third, even if—as seems unlikely—every piece of that "record" were recovered, there is no reason to believe that the American negotiators chose to reduce to writing all relevant materials bearing on the question now at issue. Of the nine key ABM Treaty negotiators on the U.S. side, eight today affirm that the traditional interpretation has always been valid; and the ninth—Ambassador Nitze, currently a Reagan adviser—also did so until the Reagan Revision was propagated in October 1985.

Thus, it seems highly likely that, had those officials believed in 1972 that the current issue would ever arise, they would have produced memoranda—which would now be a part of the "negotiating record"—affirming what is now called the traditional interpretation. Indeed, if members of the American negotiating team had believed that their instructions, responses, and various and sundry musings would someday be viewed as dispositive concerning the ABM Treaty's meaning, would they not have taken more care in assembling a single, complete and cohesive record?[4]

. . . .

The Senate Foreign Relations Committee can only lament the decisionmaking process by which the Administration has attempted its radical revision of the ABM Treaty. That process cannot be surmised from a snapshot of any point in the chronology, for a frozen moment would suggest a policy process that is merely irregular. Greater truth emerges from reviewing the series of misstatements followed by repudiations superseded by disavowals—every step informed by one maxim: interpret now, justify later. The full picture is of a policy process not merely unusual, but so substandard as to breach the requirement of international law that a treaty be interpreted in good faith.

The Reagan Administration's first formal legal statement attempting to justify its unprecedented treaty "reinterpretation" emanated from the Legal Adviser in October 1985, when Mr. Sofaer issued a memorandum concluding that such radical action was justified by a review of the Treaty's "negotiating record."

Mr. Sofaer made this claim having consulted no member of the 1972 negotiating delegation—with the lone exception of his colleague, Ambassador Nitze. Nor did Mr. Sofaer even have before him the full "negotiating record" his novel theory of treaty interpretation required. Indeed, as recently as March this year, he freely acknowledged that there were still "many memos—and they are continuing to turn up, Senator, out of the boxes that are arriving in my office from various storage facilities . . ." Thus did Mr. Sofaer summarize his truly astounding theory that a treaty's meaning may always, at any time, be subject to alteration by the chance discovery of a document, internal to the government of either party to a treaty, pertaining to its negotiating history.

Nonetheless, beginning in October 1985, Mr. Sofaer had no hesitation in assuring all who would listen that if only they could review the secret record, they too would agree that the Reagan Revision was justified. He so testified to key congressional committees that month. He so lectured the American Society of International Law in April 1986. And he so instructed readers of the Harvard Law Review in an article published June 1986. "Trust me," was his plea.

Mr. Sofaer offered assurance that not only did the "negotiating record" support his new reading of the Treaty, but that the ratification

[4] S. REP. NO. 164, *supra* note 1, at 48–50.

record did as well. This latter assurance, however, Mr. Sofaer repudiated—for a while, at least. Confronted with evidence that his account of the ratification record was a distortion, Mr. Sofaer admitted in a letter to Senator Nunn in March 1987 that he "did not provide a complete portrayal of the ratification proceedings with respect to this issue." He wrote further that he "did not review this material personally," and shortly thereafter informed Senator Levin that the problem was attributable to "young lawyers" in his office.

This was the state of affairs when the Foreign Relations and Judiciary Committees undertook joint hearings earlier this year. Though Mr. Sofaer was obviously a key witness, he resisted the Committees' invitation to appear, claiming to be in the midst of another thorough "study" of the ratification record and about to undertake a separate "study"—apparently for the first time—of "subsequent practice" under the Treaty. His thinking on the desirability of testifying apparently clarified by the prospective issuance of a subpoena, Mr. Sofaer appeared on March 26.

Given his ongoing "study" of the ratification record, the Committees might have expected Mr. Sofaer to display on March 26 a tentativeness concerning the propriety of the "reinterpretation." It would, after all, hardly be intellectually honest to engage in the study of a matter—the ratification record—which had no bearing on the ABM Treaty's meaning. Purportedly, the Legal Adviser was engaged in a serious review of one critical element on which his ultimate conclusions would depend.

Consequently, the Committee requested that Mr. Sofaer confine his testimony to what could be addressed without further study: basic constitutional principles surrounding the making and interpretation of treaties. To the Committees' surprise, therefore, Mr. Sofaer had not the slightest hestitation in affirming the Administration's "reinterpretation" once again and reiterating his unqualified endorsement of its legality. Evidently, contrary to what the Committee had earlier been led to believe, the "study" on which Mr. Sofaer was then embarked would have no effect on the Administration's view of the Treaty.

The Committees should probably not have been surprised. For it has become increasingly clear that the Administration has relied on Mr. Sofaer's "studies" not to determine what is legally valid but to justify aims already decided on. Mr. Richard Perle, the Assistant Secretary of Defense who led the Pentagon's effort to rewrite the Treaty, testified to the Committee that he had not once read the Legal Adviser's original analysis. From all the Committee can determine, Mr. Perle's driving curiosity concerning the legality of the "reinterpretation" set the standard for the Administration.

The measure of Mr. Sofaer's judicial instinct was illustrated when he represented to the Committees that Senator Nunn had joined him in finding the text of the ABM Treaty "ambiguous." This was a wholly false claim, given that Senator Nunn had just commenced a series of widely publicized speeches detailing the lack of evidence supporting the Administration's interpretation of the Treaty. Informed of Mr. Sofaer's testimony, Senator Nunn immediately wrote to the Committees that Mr. Sofaer "misrepresents my conclusions on the subject."

Senator Nunn underscored that he had gone to "some lengths in my speech, including repeating a key sentence, to present my conclusions in a manner which would preclude anyone from misconstruing" the conclusions. Obviously, Mr. Sofaer was undeterred.

As to the ratification record, Mr. Sofaer's original contentions—set forth in October 1985 and temporarily repudiated in his March 1987 testimony—were soon reinstated in a May 1987 statement announcing that his new "study," now completed, showed that the ratification record permits the "reinterpretation."

The process that has produced such "studies" was related to the Committees by one of the participants, Mr. William Sims, an attorney in the Legal Adviser's office from August 1985 to January 1986. A junior lawyer who in his own words had "limited experience in international law," Mr. Sims was assigned to help Mr. Sofaer analyze the "reinterpretation" issue. Yet Sims found himself denied access to a crucially relevant DOD memorandum critical of the "reinterpretation," and soon became aware that U.S. Government experts known to be unfriendly to the "reinterpretation" effort were being systematically ignored. "Their views were not solicited," Mr. Sims testified. "There was no full interagency deliberation." "[L]oyalty has been escalated to such a high level that objectivity seems to have been lost." As a consequence, "the procedure was flawed, resulting in conclusions that were inaccurate."

Mr. Sims resigned from Mr. Sofaer's office in protest to enter private practice, but not before concluding that any balanced analysis of the text of the Treaty, the negotiating record, and its subsequent interpretation would "provide a document . . . that is compelling in its support of the narrow interpretation."

. . . .

The United States Government needs such public servants—persons willing to place duty over ambition in defending the integrity of the law. Nowhere is this more true [than] in the law of foreign relations, where the discipline of judicial review is often unavailable. Here, Congress and the State Department share a special responsibility for heightened care in respecting applicable international and constitutional standards. Frequently, there will be no judicial backstop if they err.

The Legal Adviser stands alone among lawyers within our Federal Government. He is the first guardian, and often the last, of the United States Government's commitment to the rule of law in two different legal systems—constitutional and international. His title is unique among the chief lawyers for Federal Departments and Agencies. He is not called "general counsel" because he is, in effect, not only general counsel to the Department of State, but also the prime counselor to the entire Government, including the President, on legal matters involving international affairs and diplomacy. His title is shared with colleagues in the foreign offices of other nations; together, they represent the principal expositors of the law of nations for their governments and the world.

The Legal Adviser is thus charged with American compliance with—and American efforts to enforce—the most momentous elements of

of the modern state system. He highlights the importance to the development of the concept of the writings of Jean Bodin and Thomas Hobbes.

James describes sovereignty as "constitutional independence," which means "that a state's constitution is not part of a larger constitutional arrangement" (p. 25). According to James, this formal, legal criterion can easily be ascertained from the practice of states. Sovereign states, in his view, inevitably possess territory, people and government. The type and effectiveness of the government is irrelevant to the possession of sovereignty, as is the absolute or relative strength of the state. The only issue is whether or not the state is constitutionally apart, not contained within a broader constitutional scheme. A territory that meets this criterion is eligible to participate regularly and fully in international relations. States exercise this capacity for participation to varying extents and with differential effectiveness. The internal corollary of "constitutional independence" is supremacy.

In James's view, sovereignty is "a legal, absolute, and unitary condition" (p. 39). It is legal because constitutional independence is a matter of law. It is absolute because sovereignty is either present or absent. It is unitary because sovereignty cannot be possessed simultaneously by a state and its component entities.

Defining the concept, explicating the definition and showing how it is applied in international relations occupy about one-third of the book. Most of the remaining two-thirds is devoted to dealing with what the author describes as quandaries and quarrels. In these sections James argues against definitions of sovereignty or statements about the concept by various commentators, scholars and officials. For instance, there is an analysis of how participation in international organizations or conditions of interdependence or dependence do not diminish sovereignty as he has defined it. Although his arguments are virtually always cogent and convincing, they sometimes make tedious reading.

The monograph is almost exclusively based on British and U.S. sources, and the former tend to receive slightly greater attention. It is primarily a political science or international relations treatise. It contains very few references to legal issues or cases. Those who are primarily interested in legal matters will nevertheless find it useful because of its extensive analysis of writings about and practices concerning sovereignty.

HAROLD K. JACOBSON
Board of Editors

Der Schutz der Privatsphäre gemäß Art. 8 EMRK. By Stephan Breitenmoser. Basel and Frankfurt am Main: Helbing & Lichtenhahn, 1986. Pp. 399. Sw.F.65.

This is a most useful book for anybody who wants to inform himself about the case law of the European Commission and Court of Human Rights on Article 8 of the Convention. Offering critical comments as he goes along, the author examines the different guarantees contained in Article 8 and describes the jurisprudence of the Convention organs. After some general discussion, there are sections that deal with private life (pp. 84*ff.*), sexual life (pp. 88 *ff.*), problems of marriage and family life (pp. 102 *ff.*), corporal integrity (pp. 132*ff.*) and private life in prison (pp. 213*ff.*). Protection of the domicile (pp. 252–303) and of correspondence (pp. 304–99) form the two other main chapters. For each topic, we are given a detailed description of the evolving jurisprudence of the European Commission and Court of Human Rights.

If the reviewer, who has to admit his possible bias as a member of the European Commission of Human Rights, does not find the book fully satisfying, this may be mainly due to the difficulties faced by the author. Given such an abundant and wide-ranging case law, it is, perhaps, nearly impossible to deduce the real trends. It may be that the author sometimes took as a static situation what is in fact an evolving system of guarantees. The task was probably made even more difficult by the existence of the two organs, Commission and Court, which do not always speak with the same tongue, the Court intervening in relatively few cases, though, of course, with the full authority to render a final judgment. Sometimes one has the feeling that the author could have grasped the evolution more clearly had he tried to group the cases according to which ones contain important findings concerning Article 8, and which present rather summary dicta.

The reviewer would suggest, for instance, that the discussion beginning on page 120 should have included the important *Hendriks* case. Beginning on page 112, the author seems to base his criticism of the Commission on case law that has been clearly overruled. Today the Commission considers deportation of one family member as always interfering with the rights under Article 8(1), even if the other family members may follow. Only under Article 8(2) can it be considered whether it would be easy for the whole family to take up residence abroad. It is certainly an overinterpretation to deduce from the decisions that homosexuals may marry one another (p. 101). In fact, the Commission has rejected a similar case. The author could not yet take into account the Court's important (and to this reviewer very disappointing) judgment in the *Rees* case, which denied a transsexual —one of the very tragic personalities, according to medical opinion—the right to human identity in accordance with his appearance (pp. 137 *ff.*). In the area of secret surveillance, the case of *Leander,* recently decided by the Court, is of great importance.

As already stated, the book is a very useful source of information. However, it does not go far enough to allow Article 8, one of the key provisions in the European Convention protecting human dignity, to be fully evaluated. Nevertheless, many specific suggestions made by the author should certainly be considered by the Convention organs. Since one hopes that will be done, the lack of an index and a table of cases is to be regretted.

JOCHEN A. FROWEIN
Heidelberg

The Future of the Oceans: A Report to the Club of Rome. By Elisabeth Mann Borgese. Montreal: Harvest House, 1986. Pp. xvi, 144. Index. $9.95, paper.

The New Order of the Oceans: The Advent of a Managed Environment. Edited by Giulio Pontecorvo. New York: Columbia University Press, 1986. Pp. xv, 277. Index. $30.

Here are two books on oceans policy and the law of the sea by two prominent and experienced writers in this field. Each extols the work of the Third UN Conference on the Law of the Sea. Each develops the idea that the 1982 LOS Convention, negotiated at the conference, is but a halfway house on the way to a yet unseen new ocean regime. Each in its own way views with consternation U.S. oceans policy in the 1980s. From these common themes, the works diverge in their style, content and vision of the future.

Elisabeth Mann Borgese's book is much more than a reiteration of the recent themes of ocean law and policy discussions. It is a book of vision, and a challenge to traditional thinking. She sees the oceans as a laboratory within which mankind can pursue new economic, political and social institutions. She celebrates the common heritage of mankind. She glories in the success of the third conference, not because it created a perfect system, but, as she says, because it set forth principles upon which to build a new system of economic and social relationships.

Borgese organizes *The Future of the Oceans* into six chapters. Chapter 1, "Ocean Sciences," is a short summary of recent scientific discoveries. The author concentrates on the global and interdisciplinary nature of scientific cooperation. She questions the use of science for purposes of national aggrandizement.

Chapter 2, "The Marine Revolution," is about the new ocean technologies and the economic uses of the sea. It focuses on aquaculture, energy and the mining of deep seabed metals.

In chapter 3, "The Economics of the Common Heritage," Borgese becomes more controversial. She calls the oceans "a great laboratory for establishing a new order" (p. 44). She renews her call for an ocean development tax. She suggests that the pattern for mining the deep seabeds set forth by the Third Law of the Sea Conference should set an example for the future. And she sees the development of the exclusive economic zone not as an expression of nationalism, but as a transition from a laissez-faire ocean economic system to one of integrated economic ocean management on a multinational basis that transcends national boundaries.

In chapter 4, "Constitution for the Oceans: Systems-Maintaining" and chapter 5, "Constitutions for the Oceans: Systems-Transforming," Borgese reviews the text of the 1982 Convention. Chapter 4 is a discussion, more or less, of traditional law of the sea issues in traditional legal and policy terms. In this summary, one finds a useful and succinct overview that comes as a bit of a surprise in the wake of chapter 3's controversial, if not to say radical, economic discussion. Chapter 5 reviews the new institutions to be established pursuant to the 1982 Convention. This chapter abounds with confidence and optimism that these institutions, while admittedly imperfect, nonetheless set the stage for the promotion of the "common heritage" as foreseen by the author.

The book concludes with a sixth chapter entitled the "Philosophy of the Common Heritage." In this chapter Borgese discusses the ideological and philosophical setting for the emerging new economic order as she sees it.

Borgese's book is stimulating, to say the least. This reviewer cannot help but say that if the conference did what Borgese said it did, and has the implications she says it has, it is no wonder that the Reagan administration (or perhaps any other administration that might have been elected in the United States in 1980) saw fit to question the continuing U.S. participation in the negotiations. Furthermore, it is none too clear how she sees the transition from an ocean that is now full of national claims, to one that is governed by the principles she espouses. The provocative thoughts in this volume will raise the hackles of some. No matter what one's outlook may be, however, one's thinking will be challenged. This is an eminently readable book.

The New Order of the Oceans, edited by Giulio Pontecorvo, stands in contrast to Borgese's book in many respects. It is a series of papers by eight authors. One of the most notable differences is the orientation in the Pontecorvo work toward the more immediate future, and toward the role of nation-states in ocean issues. At the same time, there is an underlying theme, at least in Pontecorvo's own writing in this volume, that corresponds with Borgese's. That is, they share the view that the regime of the oceans articulated in the 1982 Convention is a way station between "the freedom of the sea" and some new ocean system that is not yet understood.

In the first chapter, Pontecorvo develops this idea. He notes that human perceptions of the oceans change. He recalls how quickly such changes come about. He suggests that the initial idealism associated with the "common heritage" was undermined during the conference as the economic realities of geographic advantage were realized. In chapter 2, Pontecorvo addresses the redistribution of income and wealth that occurred in the restructuring of the law of the sea—which, of course, benefited the coastal states that were blessed with fisheries and hydrocarbons off their coasts.

In chapter 3, Professor Oscar Schachter refines the thought that the law of the sea is far from static, even those provisions designed to stabilize maritime claims that are found in the 1982 Convention. He stresses that while the Convention imposes standards and determines conduct, it remains to be transformed by practice and interpretation.

Chapter 4, by David Ross, is devoted to ocean science. Ross puts a gloss on one of the more unfortunate parts of the 1982 Convention. As he says, "[T]he LOS treaty problems facing marine scientists may be even more complex than the research they are trying to perform" (p. 83). The Convention promotes rigid, yet unpredictable, bureaucratic structures in which the marine scientific community must work at the international level. Nonetheless, Ross indicates that these negative aspects of the Convention may be overcome by cooperation between marine scientists and coastal states anxious to exploit their marine potential.

In chapter 5, Marne Dubs provides an overview of the myth and reality of deep seabed mining. For anyone who wants to know what went wrong and where we are heading in relation to deep seabed mining, this reviewer highly recommends this chapter.

Chapters 6, 7 and 8 give us a different perspective. Written by Frank Njenga of Kenya, Andrés Aguilar Mawdsley of Venezuela and Hasjim Djalal of Indonesia, these chapters provide the reader with African, Latin American and Asian viewpoints on the law of the sea from three of the most influential conference participants. It is useful to be reminded, as we are in these chapters, that the exclusive economic zone was an African proposal; and that the Latin Americans, despite their internal differences, maintained a common front during the conference so as to attain many objectives. Hasjim Djalal recounts the disappointment felt in the ASEAN countries when the United States decided not to sign the Convention.

In chapter 9, Ambassador Thomas Clingan gives an overview of U.S. policy and strategies during the nearly 10 years of conference negotiations. Clingan is one of the few U.S. negotiators who labored from the beginning to the end of the conference. He is therefore well suited to provide a balanced and objective report of the U.S. position, its objectives and the changing evaluation of interests that went into the position as events unfolded.

In the final chapter, Professor Jonathan Charney writes of the unfinished business of the conference. By unfinished business he means, essentially, issues not addressed such as Antarctica; issues dealt with ambiguously such as maritime boundaries; issues of customary law; and issues of an institutional nature such as dispute settlement, participation by international organizations and the role of political entities other than nation-states. Charney's chapter is mostly a listing; nevertheless, it raises an intriguing set of questions. He posits that in the light of political and economic realities, the 1982 Convention's life is likely to be in the 20–24-year range. It is interesting to contemplate whether by that time we will be taking up Charney's unfinished business, or heading toward the new ocean constitution foreseen by Borgese.

DAVID A. COLSON
U.S. Department of State

Exclusive Economic Zone Claims: An Analysis and Primary Documents. By Robert W. Smith. Dordrecht, Boston, Lancaster: Martinus Nijhoff Publishers, 1986. Pp. xiv, 501. Index. Dfl.350; $166.50; £112.25.

The question whether international law now includes an institution called the 200-mile exclusive economic zone is no longer open to serious debate. The critical question is the legal content of the zone as it affects many different uses of the sea. On the level of customary law, the resolution of that question entails inquiry into state practice. On the level of conventional law, the question also may involve an inquiry into the interpretive practice of the parties or, more broadly, of the many states that assert or maintain a general policy of respecting the provisions of the 1982 Convention on the Law of the Sea regarding matters such as the exclusive economic zone. For those interested in this question, this new book is an exceedingly valuable addition to their library.

Over three-quarters of the book sets forth the primary national laws and instruments of 73 countries regarding the exclusive economic zone. In so doing, it documents the rapid absorption into state practice of a legal institution, affecting one-third of the oceans, that did not exist, as such, prior to the commencement of the Third UN Conference on the Law of the Sea. If only as a convenient reference tool, this compilation would in itself justify the substantial cost of the volume for many users. Other compendiums are more difficult to use and may not be as up-to-date. Indeed, one hopes means will be found to keep this work current.

The book contains much more than primary sources to commend it. The fold-out map of 200-mile maritime claims as of May 1985, carefully distinguishing claims of territorial seas, exclusive economic zones and fishing zones, is an extraordinary piece of work. It makes clear to any student of the subject that the future of global navigation and communication may now be more dependent on the substance of the regime within 200 miles than on the geographic limits of coastal state jurisdiction. The caution of coastal states in extending the economic zone regime into the waters of semi-enclosed seas in some regions such as the Mediterranean, Aegean, Black and Red Seas and the Persian Gulf is vividly contrasted with the aggressive assertion of that regime in the Caribbean Sea and in South and East Asia.

The first 60 pages are filled with useful analysis. The two annexes and three graphs indicating the number of different types of claims made in different years illustrate the intimate relationship between the Law of the Sea Conference and the actual behavior (or at least claims) of states. Indeed, the author points out that a number of discrepancies between national legislation and the 1982 Convention are due to the fact that the laws enacted during the negotiations were based on earlier negotiating drafts of the Convention. One is left to ponder how state practice might have developed if the chairmen of the conference committees charged with issues of coastal state jurisdiction had been less willing to rely primarily on tentative results of informal negotiations for their successive negotiating texts.

One of the most fascinating parts of the analysis involves a discussion of claims that have been retracted as a result of the Convention, in particular by the explicit substitution of 12-mile territorial seas and 200-mile economic zones for territorial sea claims that previously extended up to 200 miles. While the number is small, this is the first evidence in this century of a reversal of the trend toward ever broader assertions of coastal state jurisdiction as a matter of both geographic and substantive limits. In this respect, the Convention may have achieved what protests, threats, economic retaliation and occasional military confrontations failed to achieve.

The seven tables provide useful analytical summaries of coastal state claims. Perhaps the most intriguing is the table that compares exclusive economic zone claims with the provisions of the 1982 Convention in seven substantive categories. As one examines the data and related texts, one may ponder again whether the cost of denying the Convention nearly universal ratification is too high.

To appreciate the utility of a tabulation that courageously eschews the ubiquitous "maybe" of legal analysis, one need not agree with every one of the summary conclusions conveyed in tabular or graphic form, or for that matter in the textual analysis. Intricate legal issues are involved in determining the nature and content of a particular claim. The reader is free to consult the primary sources in the same volume.

This reviewer, for example, has consistently disagreed with the tendency to regard Argentina's 200-mile claim as a territorial sea. To be sure, that is what the Argentine law calls it. What matters, however, is that the Argentine law (as the author notes) expressly respects freedom of navigation and overflight in the zone. This would seem to bring the claim closer to an exclusive economic zone and to respect for the requirements of international law than the nomenclature might suggest. While according a different meaning to a widely used term of art is not the most desirable form of draftsmanship, Argentina is free to give the zone any name it pleases for internal purposes.[1]

It is this kind of difficulty that the author has attempted, with substantial success, to resolve through analysis, footnotes and, of course, the incorporation of primary sources. One must bear in mind that the nature of the task—a documentation and brief analysis of national economic zone claims—necessarily limits its scope. If one does not bear in mind these limitations, one might be (unintentionally) misled.

For example, Canada's assertion of pollution jurisdiction beyond the territorial sea is absent from various compilations, presumably because the claim was not characterized as an exclusive economic zone, although it undoubtedly influenced the content of the economic zone regime at the conference. The exclusion from the relevant compilation of West Germany's mindless extension of the territorial sea is presumably based either on the claim's very limited application to a specific area or on the charitable assumption that the claim can be justified by an imaginative application of special rules regarding roadsteads. To solve all problems of this sort would be to expand the endeavor into a multivolume analysis of all types of coastal state claims.

The author and publisher should be congratulated for annexing texts from both part V (Exclusive Economic Zone) and part VII (High Seas) of the

[1] Article 310 of the Law of the Sea Convention, on declarations and statements made with a view to harmonizing national law with the Convention, in effect confirms this. One of its purposes was to facilitate ratification by states that had used nomenclature in earlier national laws that has been superseded by new terminology in the Convention such as "exclusive economic zone" and "archipelagic waters."

Convention. They provide a convenient and appropriate frame of reference for comparing coastal state claims, and properly reflect the fact that much of the high seas regime is incorporated by reference into the economic zone regime. Still, the precise scope of coastal state jurisdiction with respect to at least two matters (regulation of pollution and marine scientific research) emerges from other parts of the Convention. Because the Convention defines the continental shelf in terms of an alternative 200-mile limit, various provisions regarding the continental shelf, for example, with respect to drilling, living resources, and cables and pipelines, are also relevant. The provisions regarding compulsory settlement of disputes are fundamental aspects of the balance struck on navigation and pollution, whose omission from national policy and legislation is significant in any comparison with the Convention.[2] Again, bearing in mind limitations of space, scope and cost, "second best" may in fact be the best choice.

The leading maritime powers of any given time have usually assumed much of the burden of ensuring that the world's ships have access to adequate hydrographic charts and other information pertaining to navigation. In this century, those employed by the Office of the Geographer of the U.S. Department of State have worked diligently to extend that custom to include information regarding the political geography of the sea, reflected both in government and personal publications. As a result, we have all benefited from their knowledge, skill and access to information. In this new book, Robert Smith ably contributes to a worthy tradition established by his predecessors that one hopes will be continued as he assumes different responsibilities.

BERNARD H. OXMAN
Board of Editors

Managing the Ocean: Resources, Research, Law. Edited by Jacques G. Richardson. Mt. Airy, Md.: Lomond Publications, Inc., 1985. Pp. xv, 407. Index. $28.95.

This book's large subject and optimistic theme suggesting that the oceans can really be managed contains 35 essays by authors from 17 countries and three international organizations. Only two of the authors are from the United States; three are from the Soviet Union. Most of the essays were previously published in less widely distributed UNESCO publications but now are made available in this third volume in a series of UNESCO-sponsored works edited by Jacques G. Richardson, former editor of the UNESCO journal, *Impact of Science on Society.*

Each essay is a plainly stated review of a particular subject, event or problem, without footnotes, and followed by an occasional reference or end note. One is a collage of cartoons illustrating the creation, life and fate of a sand dune. Another reviews the contribution of satellites to mapping the

[2] *See Statement by Expert Panel: U.S. Policy on the Settlement of Disputes in the Law of the Sea,* 81 AJIL 438 (1987).

oceans. The value and drama of submarine archaeology in Alexandria, Egypt, is explained. Indeed, there is something about every significant field of inquiry in oceanography and marine science. These essays review and explain the latest advances in science and technology and are well written and nicely illustrated. Occasionally a value judgment intrudes. For example, Dr. Frank Barnaby, in a review of naval power, concludes that "superpower naval activity is the greatest threat to world security" (p. 370).

The ill-starred law of the sea conferences are reviewed somewhat incompletely by René-Jean Dupuy of France, and by M. C. W. Pinto of Sri Lanka. They both conclude that the failure to achieve agreement is tragic. Given the lofty goals of UNESCO, and the interests of Third World scientists and other scholars supported by it, these social science essays are understandably biased in favor of maximizing an international ocean regime.

Professor Dupuy's essay on the impact on the law of the sea discussions of theories on a new international economic order highlights the legal theme in the volume. He correctly notes that the discussions beginning in 1974 must be considered in the light of the discussions that same year that led to the Charter of Economic Rights and Duties of States. The motivations that lead many nations to support proposals that rich countries contribute to poor countries are clear. It is by no means certain, however, that contributions by rich countries (which harbor poor as well as rich inhabitants) to poor countries (which harbor wealthy people as well) necessarily make a better world. The case for the provisions on redistribution of wealth in the Law of the Sea Convention is not convincingly argued.

Without discernible misgivings, each author supports proposals in the Law of the Sea Convention that are objected to by the United States. Surely, in a volume purporting to cover all significant matters of ocean management, there is room for explaining key disputes, and why some nations, including the United States, do not invariably see a "duty to cooperate" (see essay by María Eduarda Gonçalves, p. 242). Is a mandatory transfer of advanced technology to those lacking the skills to use this technology lawful, or wise (p. 275)? Answers to these issues are clear to the authors, but an intelligent reader may not be so easily persuaded.

This volume is readable and interesting. Insofar as political judgments are concerned, the reader should recognize and understand the premises of the writers.

GORDON B. BALDWIN
University of Wisconsin–Madison Law School

Transboundary Air Pollution: International Legal Aspects of the Co-operation of States. Edited by Cees Flinterman, Barbara Kwiatkowska and Johan G. Lammers. Dordrecht, Boston, Lancaster: Martinus Nijhoff, 1986. Pp. xviii, 372. Indexes. Dfl.199; $91.50; £65.95.

The traditional conception of international environmental problems is that they arise from pollutants spilling over the border of one country into another. Most of our experience has been in trying to control transfrontier pollution. Today, acid deposition and toxic pollution from longer range atmospheric transport are major problems facing countries. Increasingly, however, transboundary air pollution is only a small part of the serious environmental problems we face today such as tropical deforestation, loss of biological diversity, degradation from hazardous and nuclear waste disposal, and climatic change induced by greenhouse gases. These problems in substantial part challenge the traditional transfrontier framework. In addressing these, as well as the important air pollution problems, it is useful to have clearly before us a review and critique of the agreements and regimes that we have already established to control transboundary air pollution. This book is intended to provide that.

Transboundary Air Pollution is a collection of essays focused on the international agreements, bi- or multilateral regimes, and private international law remedies for controlling transboundary air pollution, particularly acid rain. The book addresses these issues by regions: North America, Western Europe, Central and Eastern Europe, Africa and the developing world. There are also two chapters devoted to the global problem of controlling emissions of chlorofluorocarbons to protect the ozone layer. The collection will be of interest to all specialists in international environmental law. Its high price may make it less accessible to others.

The collection is unusual in that it begins with a technical explanation of the causes of transboundary air pollution, written by Alcamo, a researcher at the International Institute for Applied Systems Analysis in Vienna, and Runca, an engineer in Verona. In their presentation, the authors use graphs, simple diagrams and a chemical reaction formula, which may tempt some readers to skip the chapter. This would be a mistake. The authors provide a clear and useful explanation of the technical dimensions of transboundary air pollution, which is relevant to controlling it. This is followed by a chapter by Gündling, which provides technical legal analysis of the provisions of the Convention on Long Range Transboundary Air Pollution of the Economic Commission of Europe.

The next three chapters explore transboundary air pollution in the North American context. In chapters 3 and 4, Murphy and Handl analyze prior and existing legal arrangements for controlling air pollution between Canada and the United States. While Murphy is relatively sanguine about their potential for addressing present problems, Handl argues that a new "comprehensive air quality agreement" is "indispensable" and that in the long term we will have to establish new institutional arrangements to address the problems (p. 64). Both pieces are well researched and carefully crafted. It would have been useful, however, to explore the potential role of the International Joint Commission in controlling air pollution, especially acid deposition. The recent findings that airborne transport of toxic pollutants, including PCBs and other banned pollutants, constitutes one of the major pollution problems facing the Great Lakes,[1] and maybe other border areas,

[1] U.S. National Research Council, Royal Society of Canada, The Great Lakes Water Quality Agreement: An Evolving Instrument for Ecosystem Management (1985).

raise issues that may need to be addressed by agreements and institutions whose jurisdiction extends beyond air quality control.

In chapter 5, Applegate and Bath, a civil engineer and a political scientist, provide a fascinating and refreshingly frank account of the difficulties encountered in controlling air pollution in the El Paso and Ciudad Juárez airshed. As Kiss comments in the last chapter, they demonstrate how international borders can become convenient excuses for inaction, a phenomenon not confined to the Mexican/U.S. border.

The next five chapters examine efforts to control transboundary air pollution in Western Europe. Bothe supplies an overview of national and international regulatory instruments, while Ercman gives us a good record of the activities of the Council of Europe and the European Economic Community. Broms lays out a technical explanation of the provisions of the Nordic Convention on the Environment; Phillips provides an excellent inquiry into the implementation of the Nordic Convention. Phillips questions whether the Convention has had a significant impact, and suggests ways to improve implementation of its objectives. These include granting the right to individuals and environmental organizations to sue polluters to prevent future harm and to receive compensation (p. 165). In chapter 10, Bunge sets forth an informative review of bilateral efforts between France and West Germany to control border pollution.

A review of efforts in the socialist countries of Europe to control transboundary air pollution appears in chapters 11 and 12. Vukas writes from the Yugoslav perspective, while Sommers writes from the Polish. Sommers's review of the activities of the Council of Mutual Economic Assistance in the environmental area and the bilateral Polish agreements for controlling air pollution is informative.

In chapter 13, Okidi examines the issues from the perspective of the developing countries. He argues that environmental conservation and economic development must proceed together and he reviews the initiatives under way to implement this. His outline of initiatives in Africa is especially useful.

In the first of the two chapters on the global problem of depletion of the high-level ozone layer, Williams analyzes the efforts to regulate chlorofluorocarbons on the basis of available scientific evidence and foresees a trend toward deregulation; recent developments cast doubt upon this interpretation. In the second chapter on the subject, Rummel-Buska sets forth the history of the negotiations for the Convention on the Protection of the Ozone Layer and a technical analysis of its provisions.

In chapter 16, Rest considers questions of responsibility and liability for transboundary air pollution. He provides a careful, if inconclusive, review of international law relevant to liability for environmental injury, and a useful examination of domestic judicial decisions within Western Europe on compensation under private law in cases of transfrontier pollution.

The last two chapters, by Vukas and Kiss, contain concluding observations on the theme. Kiss's chapter is essential reading for the book, for it attempts to integrate the disparate chapters into a cohesive framework. It could usefully be treated as an introductory essay to the volume.

The book is noteworthy for containing under one cover a review of regional and bilateral efforts to control transboundary air pollution on several continents as well as information otherwise difficult to locate. As with any multiauthored volume, some chapters are much better and more useful than others. The several that explore in detail how agreements are actually implemented are especially significant contributions to the literature and should be read by anyone interested in the practice of international law or international relations generally.

EDITH BROWN WEISS
Georgetown University Law Center

Acid Rain and Friendly Neighbors: The Policy Dispute between Canada and the United States. Edited by Jurgen Schmandt and Hilliard Roderick. Durham: Duke University Press, 1985. Pp. 332. Index. $45.

We are faced with dead and dying lakes, fish and forests; reduced agricultural yields; and the destruction of priceless works of art. Still unknown are the long-term effects on human health and on microorganisms essential to continuation of the earth's life cycle; the synergistic effects of airborne chemical compounds; the specific sources of the pollution; the ability of soils and bodies of water to absorb acid rain deposition without permanent damage; and the most appropriate methods and costs of control. It is difficult to induce political action in the face of uncertainty about the scientific and economic impact of pollution and the regional nature of the damage. Moreover, interest group pressure is powerful, and our political systems are not geared to facilitating binational problem solving or to allocating the costs of control equitably and cutting political ties to other, unrelated, issues. A substantial commitment to new research and monitoring is needed, together with an immediate strengthening of controls while work is under way to develop and test longer term solutions.

Schmandt, a public-policy specialist, Roderick, a physicist, and a team of 15 graduate students present a masterful analysis of the policy problems raised by acid rain in the United States and Canada. While it is detailed, the discussion is clean, objective, understandable and compelling. Weaving substantive and institutional factors into their analysis, the authors skillfully portray the controversy's multifaceted nature. They show an obvious command of the numerous components of the acid rain controversy. They deftly describe the interplay of science and policy, singling out a pressing problem in this area: the many important unanswered scientific questions that make those in a position to act reluctant to adopt proposed solutions. Acknowledging the significant gap in critical information, the authors nevertheless are persuasive in urging that policymakers in the United States and Canada not delay in adopting much more stringent control measures for SO_2 and NO_x, the precursors to acid rain.

Many obstacles stand in the path of the imposition of further controls. A multitude of governments and agencies in the two countries are involved. The book contains both an excellent overview and a more detailed picture of the incredible complexities involved in this aspect of the issue, including past and present cooperative efforts. Many governments have a stake in the resolution of this problem, yet it is clear that an ecosystem approach, which would largely ignore political boundaries, is essential.

Also stalling abatement action is our current inability to trace acid rain to its source. The industries accused of creating acid rain argue against costly control measures because a causal relationship between their operations and acid rain has not been established. At present, policymakers must confront the difficult task of considering industry controls based only on circumstantial evidence of contribution. The authors make it clear, however, that scientists will soon develop tracing methods.

Scientific uncertainty regarding the effects of acid rain sets up another major barrier in the road to political action, according to the authors. Unlike other environmental problems, acid rain has not been definitively linked to damage to human health, although such a link is suspected. Effects on human health were the driving force behind the relatively speedy action taken by the U.S. Congress in response to air and water pollution. Establishment of a similar link for acid rain would hasten political action.

When legislation on air and water pollution was initiated and enacted in the United States, a strong national consensus existed in favor of decisive and immediate action. Such a consensus, which would help to create a situation of much lower political risk for elected officials, has not emerged regarding acid rain. Canada is engaged in a massive and effective lobbying effort in the United States to raise acid rain consciousness. Realizing the crucial role of U.S. policy, given the origin of Canada's acid rain damage, Canadians are working hard to influence U.S. policymakers and the general public.

Much research remains to be funded and conducted on this relatively new problem. Without unequivocal research data, elected policymakers are reluctant to make decisions that will anger powerful special interests when the need for action may not be appreciated by their other constituents. In addition to exercising raw political power, opponents of control have persuasively argued that the costs of control exceed the uncertain benefits to be gained.

The intransigence of the Reagan administration on the acid rain issue is a recurrent theme of the book. The authors do not judge, but they point out the unwillingness of President Reagan and others in his administration (except William Ruckelshaus) to acknowledge the problem. As a result, the United States has not taken any significant action to solve it, except to sponsor more research. The fact that the United States is primarily an exporter of acid rain strongly influences Reagan's policy position. A comparatively small amount of acid rain comes from Canada to the northeastern United States—the bulk of it moves from south to north (and from west to east). The Reagan administration is not inclined to impose huge costs on

U.S. industry to solve what it sees as primarily Canada's problem, and Canadian efforts to seek solutions cooperatively have repeatedly been rebuffed.

One chapter addresses the advantages and disadvantages of making acid rain policy through the Canadian court system. Limitations include judges' tendencies to have nationalistic mind-sets, the difficulty of enforcing judgments across international boundaries and the lack of enforceable international law. Also problematic are Canada's standing rules, which, unlike those in the United States, preclude virtually all foreign participation save that of attorneys general in some cases. Archaic Canadian class action statutes render a theoretically sound approach useless. As always, the costs of litigation are high, discouraging many from pursuing legitimate claims. Another major obstacle is the total lack of federal environmental protection authority in Canada, which results in a fragmented, localized, hence inadequate approach to problem solving.

On the positive side, successful tort cases may create pressure for reform. The publicity surrounding such cases can be effective in causing the public and, as a result, policymakers, to assign higher priority to this emerging environmental issue. The U.S. court system and regulatory agencies are much more receptive to this kind of litigation and intervention, but the limitations mentioned above, as well as the costs of litigation, remain, in many cases, insurmountable obstacles.

In spite of these difficulties, the authors express some optimism about the ability of the United States and Canada to work together to find and implement solutions to the acid rain problem. Increasingly, they agree on the ends to be achieved though much disagreement remains on the appropriate means to be used. Realistic about the obstacles discussed above, they cite successful past and present joint efforts in other areas of endeavor.

Despite the many unanswered scientific questions, a growing number of scientists are convinced that acid rain, if unabated, may bring about irreversible and therefore extremely grave environmental consequences. For this reason, the authors urge that policymakers must hasten to impose much more stringent controls. It is a dynamic problem that requires a dynamic solution—one that changes as new facts and control methods are discovered.

Acid Rain and Friendly Neighbors is useful not only because of the particular issue discussed but also because it helps to establish an analysis of and a process for solving other serious environmental problems. It raises issues common to many of these problems: the inability of policymakers to engage in long-term planning and the fact that political borders block problem solving. If the United States and Canada succeed in effectively controlling acid rain, their efforts will provide a model on which policymakers worldwide may build in searching for solutions to the increasing number of problems that ignore political boundaries.

TRACY DOBSON
Michigan State University

The Faces of Justice and State Authority: A Comparative Approach to the Legal Process. By Mirjan R. Damaška. New Haven and London: Yale University Press, 1986. Pp. xi, 247. Index. $26.

The title of this book is directly reminiscent of Sybille Bedford's *The Faces of Justice,* which, since its appearance in 1961, has become a classic of comparative law.[1] The similarity, however, is deceptive. While both books are about legal procedure, they approach the topic from opposite directions. Bedford's book, as its subtitle makes clear, is "a traveller's report" from the courtrooms of Europe, an impressionistic portrayal of criminal procedure for a general audience. Mirjan Damaška's treatise, in contrast, is a sophisticated attempt to build a theoretical framework for comparative studies of the legal process.

Traditionally, comparativists have viewed forms of legal process as characterized by a fundamental dichotomy between continental (civil law) procedure as inquisitorial, or dominated by judges, and Anglo-American (common law) procedure as adversarial, or run by the parties. Of course, this is a dangerously overgeneralized picture. Comparative scholarship has increasingly distinguished different kinds of procedure (e.g., criminal and civil), its phases and its forms in individual countries. As a result, a more refined and accurate picture has gradually emerged. Nevertheless, comparativists continue to work within the parameters of the inquisitorial/adversarial dichotomy.

The study by Damaška is the result of dissatisfaction with this traditional mold, which, in his view, fails to capture much of the essence of procedural forms (pp. 3–6). As an alternative, he presents a set of more complex categories based on attitudes towards state authority and on concepts of government (pp. 8–12). Despite its division into six chapters, the book consists of three substantive parts. In the first and second, Damaška develops two allegedly independent pairs of theoretical procedural models (chs. I and II, and III–V). In the third part, he combines them and applies them to various examples (ch. VI).

The first pair of models juxtaposes two structures of state authority that express two "ideals of officialdom" (p. 16). The "Hierarchical Ideal" is essentially a version of the classical model of bureaucracy. Professionalization of officials and long terms of office lead to specialization and routinization, which generate emotional disengagement and institutional thinking. Decisions are seen as acts of institutions rather than of people, who remain mostly anonymous. The organization in tall pyramids of authority entails a division of labor under which lower officials deal with, and shield their superiors from, the factual details, while the higher echelons decide the broad questions. The pronounced hierarchy promotes a strong sense of uniformity and order. This, in turn, fosters a preference for technical standards of decision making, a "logical legalism" (p. 23) that values logical

[1] Damaška borrowed the title to express his admiration for Bedford's book (p. xi).

consistency more highly than individual justice (pp. 18–23). These general characteristics of the "Hierarchical Ideal" lead to particular procedural features. For example, the stratification of authority suggests division of the adjudication process into a series of stages, invites regular superior review and thus de-emphasizes a concentrated trial event. The resulting piecemeal adjudication is held together by an all-important file that incorporates the proceedings and travels up the hierarchy with the case (pp. 47–56).

The alternative model, the "Coordinate Ideal," is dominated by lay people who serve short terms of office and therefore make decisions in a personal, rather than institutional, fashion. Lacking pronounced stratification of authority, this model is pervaded by a spirit of equality, not subordination. Thus, power spheres are overlapping and blurry around the edges. This rather loosely organized body of lay officials prefers nontechnical standards of justice that reflect general community norms. The resulting lower degree of order and consistency of decisions is accepted since coordinate officials, who lack the routine and detachment of their hierarchical brethren, stay closer to the messy detail of the facts of life and thus have a greater tolerance for disorder. Individual justice is more important than logical consistency (pp. 23–28). As a consequence of a single decision-making level, the legal process before coordinate officials is concentrated in the trial event. The trial decision is presumed to be final and reversals at a higher level are the exception. Thus, there is no need for an extensive file. Instead, the proceedings, including the evidence, tend to be oral (pp. 57–66).

Damaška's second set of models builds on the dichotomy between two notions of the state. The "reactive state" embraces a laissez-faire philosophy and does not endorse a specific substantive notion of the good life. Its judiciary is a neutral arbiter of the conflicts within society. It de-emphasizes substantive norms and tends to enforce the contestants' (real or hypothetical) bargains. The thrust of state-made law is procedural. Providing only a forum and the rules for dispute resolution, the reactive state recognizes the parties' autonomy and gives them broad control over the legal process. The resulting "conflict solving type of proceeding" (p. 97) has the character of a contest between two formally coequal disputants before the state official as the neutral decision maker (pp. 73–80; 97–147).

In contrast, the "activist state" seeks to implement specific substantive values. The judicial process is just one among many ways of pursuing this goal. Disputes between members of society trigger the legal process, but their resolution is merely incidental to the primary goal of promoting official policy. Since they manifest this policy, substantive norms are of central importance, while procedural rules are adjective only. The adjudicator, charged with the implementation of official values and thus not truly neutral, dominates the proceedings, in which the parties are essentially objects who are acted upon in, rather than exercising control over, the process. Thus, the process has the character of an inquest (pp. 80–88; 147–80).

Damaška develops the ramifications of these theoretical models with much more finesse than a short summary can reflect. He views the two sets of variables as independent. Any concept of authority can be coupled with any goal of the state (pp. 13, 182), producing varying degrees of harmony or tension between them. In the final chapter, Damaška explores the implications of the four possible combinations. For each constellation he gives historical examples such as the criminal process under the ancien régime for the hierarchical/activist combination (pp. 186–89), and classical Anglo-American civil procedure for the coordinate/reactive type (pp. 219–22). Thus emerges a historically illustrated, two-dimensional view of procedure that surpasses the traditional adversarial/inquisitorial dichotomy in theoretical sophistication and complexity.

The theoretical sophistication and complexity demand concentrated study and limit the audience to the professionally interested. Also, for an American reader, the continental character of the discourse impedes access. The book is the product of a mind trained in civil-law thinking and displays the concomitant vices and virtues. The search for a general theory makes the discourse often abstract and conceptual. Form sometimes takes the lead while substance has to follow. Rigorous organizational patterns[2] and formal completeness of discussion are maintained at the cost of occasional redundancy.

Beyond that, two stylistic idiosyncrasies create more hardship for the reader. First, the text is rife with words and maxims in foreign languages (predominantly Latin), mostly without translation. Most are superfluous for those familiar with their meaning (and with the languages used) and confusing for others. Second, the author indulges in metaphors drawn from all sorts of nonlegal contexts. While many are of delightful felicity, their sheer mass is distracting.[3]

In evaluating the book, its achievement in its own terms must be distinguished from judgment about its general approach. The latter is, of course, not new. While Max Weber receives only scant credit,[4] Damaška clearly builds largely on his foundations.[5] Accordingly, Damaška's fundamental premise is that the shape of legal processes is best (though, of course, not exclusively) explained as the result of sociopolitical factors, particularly attitudes toward official power. This premise is obviously debatable. As an alternative to a focus on sociopolitical determinants outside of the legal system itself, explanations can be sought within it. For example, the differ-

[2] Witness the well-structured and detailed table of contents (pp. vii–x).

[3] Could it be that they indicate the desire of a continental emigrant, operating in the still somewhat alien American culture, to build himself a more familiar intellectual environment out of elements from his European heritage? At least from the perspective of one in a similar situation, such a desire would be completely understandable.

[4] Weber's "ideal types" are mentioned only in passing (p. 9).

[5] This is true not only for the concept of "pure types" itself, but also for the idea of designing these "pure types" along the lines of structures of authority. *See* M. WEBER, ECONOMY AND SOCIETY 212–301 (G. Roth & C. Wittich eds. 1978). Even the dual typology with two independent sets of variables that can be combined into four constellations is borrowed from Weber. *See* MAX WEBER ON LAW IN ECONOMY AND SOCIETY xlii–lii (M. Rheinstein & E. Shils trans. 1954); *see also* A. KRONMAN, MAX WEBER 76 (1983). This diminishes the originality of Damaška's approach, but, of course, not necessarily its promise.

ences between procedural forms can be linked to the different fate of the jury in various systems, or to the varying influence of Roman law and of the canonical process, or to unequal concentrations of judicial power. To be sure, these internal factors are connected with sociopolitical ones, and no serious comparativist would deny the combined influence of both. But the emphasis primarily on one or the other approach determines one's perspective and thrust of research. While the respective merit of these approaches is a formidable issue well beyond the scope of this review, the reader should be aware that Damaška's emphasis on sociopolitical factors represents one choice where another might have been made.

Even those readers who accept Damaška's basic approach will close the book with ambivalent reactions, probably not quite sure how to sort them out. Indeed, evaluation of the book even on its own terms is difficult because these terms themselves are ambiguous. Damaška's models have a dual character. On the one hand, they are proffered as an attempt to reduce the "stupendous diversity" of the procedural world "to a manageable set of patterns" (p. 3). Like the chemical elements in the periodic table (p. 241), they do not exist in purity in the real world (which consists of amalgams). But the way in which they categorize the world is the result of quasi-scientific observation of real phenomena. In that sense, they are presented as a *descriptive picture* of the procedural universe, albeit in idealized form. On the other hand, Damaška warns that his "archetypes" are "a design detached from historical contingency" (p. 12). In this second dimension he presents them as *analytical tools* that should, again like the system of chemical elements, "assist us in tracing similarities and differences in component parts" (p. 3). As a result of this hybrid character, the book constantly mingles descriptive with analytical elements.

The dual nature of this discourse requires that the book's achievement be evaluated in two, internally connected, dimensions. In the first, Damaška's essay is an attempt to describe procedural phenomena as expressions of particular notions of state authority or state purpose. Throughout Damaška pursues sophisticated and logically consistent arguments in an attempt to persuade the reader that these notions lie at the heart of the types of procedure. Hence, he assumes that such notions provide adequate *explanations* for the phenomena.[6] His case is well worth arguing. To one familiar with continental and Anglo-American notions of legal process, his models have considerable intuitive appeal. Yet their success as explanations of procedural forms is limited because they do not reach much beyond this intuitive level. Their true explanatory power must ultimately be measured through empirical verification. In this respect, however, the evidence is weak. Damaška presents relatively few data from a range spanning 20 cen-

[6] Certainly, Damaška must not be misunderstood as claiming that individual procedural features owe their very existence to these concepts. But his fundamental hypothesis is that these features appear in certain typical groups (approaching his ideals to varying degrees) *because* they all stem from, or are at least compatible with, the same underlying notion of state authority or state purpose.

turies, half a dozen countries and a variety of procedural forms. These data are so sparse and eclectic, and so carefully selected from a huge, all-encompassing pool, that their support for Damaška's assumptions has little significance. They are not proof for his theory, but mere illustrations of it. Thus, there is a multitude of reservations to most explanations and examples, many of which Damaška himself frankly recognizes. While no general model is free from these problems, in Damaška's case the qualifications are so numerous and wide ranging that they often threaten to dismantle the rule. For example, it is hard to find *any* modern legal system that is closer to the "coordinate" than to the "hierarchical ideal," since even in the common law orbit, hierarchical structures, perhaps simply inherent in modern government, are ubiquitous and probably dominant. As a result, Damaška's explanation for the different forms of procedure is not proven superior to alternative theories such as the prevalence of divergent notions of truth in various societies. In sum, as explanations of procedural types, his models are plausible, but he does not conclusively make the case that concepts of state authority and state purpose are of overriding importance.

However, providing such an explanation is not the only, and perhaps not even the main, ambition of the book. In its other dimension its models purport to present a fresh set of tools for the comparative analysis of legal processes. Now the data perform an entirely different function, one in which they have much more force. They are no longer (weak) empirical support for the veracity of the explanations of procedural forms, but vivid evidence of the models' functional utility: the discussion of procedural realities provides examples for the insights these tools can generate. In this regard, Damaška's achievement is impressive. Here the book fulfills its ambitious promise to lead the reader beyond the conventional perspectives. While the framework does not always lead to radically new groupings, and the basic dichotomy between continental and Anglo-American procedure is reaffirmed in many respects, Damaška presents a much richer view of this dichotomy: the classical features of the continental style are regarded as a quite harmonious coalescence of hierarchical and activist notions, while their Anglo-American counterparts are characterized as an interaction of coordinate and reactive elements. But Damaška's framework goes beyond a more sophisticated view of old groupings. He uses its greater complexity and breadth to demonstrate that the traditional adversarial/inquisitorial dichotomy ought to be abandoned in favor of much more differentiated categories, which often cut across the borders between the civil and common law cultures. Furthermore, his models allow one to capture important procedural aspects that have escaped the traditional typology altogether. For example, many crucial features of Soviet procedure, like the power of officials to initiate litigation even against the aggrieved party's will, or to bring nonparties into the lawsuit as representatives of social interests, make sense only if one considers the impact of an activist concept of the state on the shape of the legal process (pp. 194–98). Here, as well as in many other instances, the book sheds new light on old facts and helps to transform knowledge into understanding.

As an overall result, the reviewer's mixed reaction to the book is a reflection of its limited success in explaining procedural forms, on the one hand, and of its achievement in introducing a fresh set of analytical tools on the other. Of course, while it can be highly desirable to combine explanatory aspects with the development of analytical tools, the book would gain clarity if the line between the two were more clearly drawn, and the evidence for the veracity of the former and the utility of the latter more distinctly earmarked.

However, the limitations of the book as an explanation of the forces behind procedural forms, as well as its methodological ambiguity, are hardly manifestations of intellectual limitations on the part of the author. They were perhaps inevitable, given the ambitiousness of the project. In some respects, the author demands more from his approach than it can yield. Semiconscious of the danger, he fights it by keeping his focus narrow and his goals restricted through a multitude of careful curtailments and caveats. But he does not resist the temptation to combine the construction of a promising analytical framework with an effort also to explain the origin of the procedural species, and he thereby demands more of his models than they can give. Indeed, perhaps such an effort cannot be wholly successful because the shape of legal processes is the result of too many ingredients, at least some of which lie on an emotional and subconscious level, accessible to intuitive understanding, but—in the end—not explainable by any single theory.

Despite these reservations, the book is highly valuable. In comparative law, fresh perspectives are a rare breed. This already makes Damaška's essay an important intellectual enrichment of its field. Beyond his own achievement, however, Damaška also wants to provide new impulses for more refined thinking about comparative procedure. Whether others will be receptive remains to be seen.

MATHIAS REIMANN
University of Michigan Law School

Policy and Methods in German and American Antitrust Law: A Comparative Study. By James Maxeiner. New York, Westport and London: Praeger Publishers, 1986. Pp. xiii, 174. Index. $37.50.

James Maxeiner has written a perceptive and provocative book comparing the enforcement of German and U.S. antitrust laws. The book adopts a nontraditional comparative law approach in that it does not provide a detailed description of the German and U.S. antitrust substantive rules.[1] Rather, it examines the relationship between "legal method" and antitrust law enforcement, with emphasis on the different ways in which the German

[1] For descriptions of the German antitrust laws, see D. HOFFMANN & S. SCHAUB, THE GERMAN COMPETITION LAW (1983); R. MUELLER, M. HEIDENHAIN & H. SCHNEIDER, GERMAN ANTITRUST LAW (3d ed. 1984); B5 WORLD LAW OF COMPETITION: FEDERAL REPUBLIC OF GERMANY, pt. 9 (J. von Kalinowski ed. 1985).

and U.S. legal systems treat antitrust policy issues. Thus, Maxeiner's volume should interest not only the antitrust bar but also a broader audience concerned with the comparative function of legal systems generally.

Maxeiner starts with the well-founded observation that there is far greater debate today about U.S. antitrust law and policy than about German antitrust law and policy. German antitrust law, which borrowed many of its policy premises and substantive principles from the United States in the 1950s, is one of the two most comprehensively enforced antitrust regimes outside the United States.[2] German antitrust law, however, has generated far less controversy than U.S. antitrust law and enforcement, particularly the latter's asserted uncertainty and expensive application resulting from open-ended statutory norms and decentralization of enforcement. Maxeiner states that this lack of certainty and difficulty of application fail to meet the minimum standards required by the "Rule of Law."

Maxeiner's thesis is that many of these inadequacies arise from deficiencies in legal method and not from flawed substantive rules. He supports this thesis by comparing enforcement of German and U.S. antitrust laws. Maxeiner groups the most important differences in legal methods into four categories: (1) U.S. antitrust law is applied primarily through the courts in determining rights and duties of individual parties, while German antitrust law is applied primarily through administrative bodies; (2) the German statutes set forth far more detailed substantive rules than U.S. statutes, which rely more on judicial interpretation to provide specific norms; (3) German antitrust law is applied through subsumption of a particular fact situation under a given norm by an active decision maker, while U.S. antitrust law is applied ordinarily to resolve a particular dispute by a passive decision maker with the identification and formulation of issues controlled by the adversaries and their lawyers; and (4) enforcement of German antitrust law is centralized in specialized decision makers, while U.S. antitrust law enforcement relies on autonomous and nonspecialized decision makers. Through greater specificity of statutory rules and greater reliance on specialized administrative enforcement, German antitrust law attempts to allocate policy judgments to administrators, while U.S. antitrust law tends to treat policy decisions as matters for resolution by courts in particular cases involving adjudication of the rights and duties of individual parties.

These four differences in legal method mean that U.S. courts are less constrained than German decision makers (either courts or administrators) in making those policy judgments essential to the application of antitrust laws. Maxeiner argues that *stare decisis* and other common law constraints on U.S. courts function poorly or not at all. Decisions are frequently fact-specific and thus not directly subject to the narrow rules developed by precedent. In the German system, more specific and detailed statutory rules are the principal means of limiting decision making and policymaking. Moreover, the German allocation of jurisdiction and remedies among adminis-

[2] The other is the competition law of the European Communities. *See* 2 B. HAWK, UNITED STATES, COMMON MARKET AND INTERNATIONAL ANTITRUST, chs. 7–13 (2d ed. 1985).

trative and judicial authorities further limits policymaking. This is particularly true with respect to the separation in German antitrust law of claims for retrospective relief (like damages) and claims for prospective relief (like injunctions). Similarly, German antitrust law is said to tailor remedies more narrowly and carefully to substantive rules, unlike U.S. antitrust law, which tends to provide a broad array of possible legal and equitable remedies.

The relative lack of constraint on U.S. decision makers is said to increase uncertainty and costs, as well as give too much policymaking power to the courts. This situation is exacerbated by the fact that private parties, and not the administrative authorities or specialized courts, are chiefly responsible for antitrust enforcement. This results from both the antitrust policy decision favoring private enforcement and the nature of the common law adversary system. Finally, Maxeiner argues that certainty and predictability are enhanced under the German antitrust system because German enforcers are largely centralized, coordinate and collegiate. Centralization of enforcement in a single antitrust agency (the Bundeskartellamt) and reliance on specialized tribunals contrast strongly with the highly decentralized and nonspecialized U.S. system.

Maxeiner concludes that the common law private adversary system and the American overreliance on judicial decision making constitute a serious mismatch between the legal methods employed and the antitrust policy decisions required. He regrets that a wide recognition of this mismatch is apt to trigger suggestions not to change the legal system but rather to ask less of it, i.e., fewer antitrust laws or more relaxed enforcement. Maxeiner recognizes, however, that substantial changes in the underlying U.S. legal system are unlikely and he concludes with the more practical observation that comparison of the German and U.S. experiences suggests limitations on resort to judge-made antitrust law.

Maxeiner is correct that U.S. antitrust law has generated more controversy than its German counterpart. But that controversy has centered more on disagreement about substantive rules than on the uncertainty and expense of U.S. antitrust enforcement.[3] United States antitrust enforcement has been marked by a radical shift in judicial and scholarly attitudes during the last two decades. When German antitrust law was born in the late 1950s, U.S. antitrust law was in its most expansionary period. This resulted from the convergence of a predominant economic theory that was highly distrustful of large firms and concentrated markets. Strong inferences of anticompetitive behavior and performance were drawn from high market concentration and significant barriers to entry were generally presumed to exist. Production and other efficiencies were either disregarded or even affirmatively relied on to invalidate business arrangements such as mergers.[4] Political or social antitrust goals favored deconcentration of markets, freedom of opportunity for individual traders and freedom of con-

[3] Of course, disagreement about substantive rules can result not only from differences in policy analysis but also from concerns about the predictability and costs associated with the rules. *See, e.g.*, Easterbrook, *The Limits of Antitrust,* 63 TEX. L. REV. 1 (1984).

[4] *See* FTC v. Procter & Gamble Co. (Clorox), 386 U.S. 568 (1967).

sumer choice. This convergence implied broad per se prohibitions and strict scrutiny of business practices including vertical restraints and conglomerate mergers. This inhospitality toward business arrangements came under increasing criticism in the 1970s. The principal academic critics were the Chicago School.[5] In 1981 the Justice Department embraced the Chicago School's approach with the accession of William Baxter to the head of the Antitrust Division.[6] That school makes allocative efficiency the exclusive antitrust policy objective. Its adherents are skeptical of claims that more than merely transitory market power exists. They reject political objectives such as protection of small traders and deconcentration. This implies antitrust enforcement that is limited to traditional cartel behavior and large horizontal mergers that raise risks of collusion. Other economic theorists in the 1970s began to accord more recognition to business efficiencies—reduction of transaction costs and avoidance of "free riding." The same period has seen significant parallel shifts in case law such as the reversal of the *Schwinn* per se rule on vertical nonprice restrictions.[7] The courts have said that they were giving predominant, if not exclusive, weight to economic values as opposed to social and political ones. Lower courts have been increasingly tolerant of vertical restraints,[8] cooperation among competitors[9] and mergers.[10]

In sum, the controversy about the proper scope of the U.S. antitrust laws results from shifts in economic theories and political goals rather than from criticisms of antitrust legal method as that term is used by Maxeiner. For example, commentators adhering to the more traditional antitrust school[11] or who call for a more dynamic economic theory emphasizing strategic behavior[12] do not rest their criticism of the recently relaxed substantive antitrust rules on flaws in legal method.

The history of U.S. antitrust law in the last 20 years suggests that the common law system of open-ended antitrust statutes with loose rein given to the courts to interpret those statutes perhaps provides a significant advantage vis-à-vis the more tightly cabined German system. The former permits courts and enforcement authorities to adapt antitrust law to developments

[5] *See* R. BORK, THE ANTITRUST PARADOX (1978); and R. POSNER, ANTITRUST LAW (1976).

[6] The Federal Trade Commission also embraced the same approach at about the same period with the appointment of James Miller as Chairman.

[7] Continental T.V. v. GTE Sylvania, 433 U.S. 36 (1977) (overruling United States v. Arnold, Schwinn & Co., 388 U.S. 365 (1967)).

[8] *See, e.g.*, Westman Comm'n Co. v. Hobart Int'l, 796 F.2d 1216 (10th Cir. 1986); Valley Liquors v. Renfield Importers, 678 F.2d 742 (7th Cir. 1982).

[9] *See, e.g.*, Rothery Storage & Van Co. v. Atlas Van Lines, 792 F.2d 210 (D.C. Cir. 1986).

[10] *See, e.g.*, United States v. Siemens Corp., 621 F.2d 499 (2d Cir. 1980) (conglomerate merger); Stroh Brewing Co. v. Malmgren, 1982-1 TRADE CAS. (CCH) ¶64,670 (W.D. Wis. 1982) (horizontal merger); United States v. Black & Decker Mfg. Co., 430 F.Supp. 729 (D. Mass. 1976) (conglomerate merger).

[11] For example, see Fox, *The Modernization of Antitrust*, 66 CORNELL L. REV. 1140 (1981).

[12] *See, e.g.*, Williamson, *Antitrust Enforcement: Where It's Been, Where It's Going*, 27 ST. LOUIS U.L.J. 289 (1983). For a discussion of the possible effect of U.S. antitrust law developments on the law of the European Communities, see Hawk, *The American (Antitrust) Revolution: Lessons for the EEC?*, EUR. COMP. L. REV. (forthcoming).

in economic theory. Although economics lacks the precision of the natural sciences, there is a substantial body of economics relevant to antitrust law that has a sufficient empirical basis to constitute a reasonably objective set of analytical rules. Changes in these rules resulting from advances in theoretical analysis or empirical data should continue to inform application of the antitrust laws. If they do not, antitrust enforcement risks being based on outmoded economics. The U.S. "legal method" permitted the courts to reverse course when developments in economic theory suggested that non-price vertical restraints could enhance efficiencies and thus should not be subject to a per se ban. New developments in economic theory may themselves require, and properly so, new antitrust rules. For example, the static bias of the Chicago School may underestimate the dynamics of many market practices, particularly strategic behavior like nonprice predation. The necessary price of this flexibility is uncertainty, but it is a price worth paying, given the evolving state of economics.

To argue in favor of judicial flexibility as necessary to ensure that antitrust law remains anchored in the shifting sands of economic theory is not to argue in favor of judicial carte blanche. Changing antitrust law to reflect advances in economic theory is far more modest than changing antitrust law to reflect changes in the content of the underlying economic, social and political policy objectives. A shift from a per se ban on territorial restrictions to a rule of reason out of recognition of the economic benefits of such restrictions is entirely appropriate and desirable. The court acts consistently with the legislative purpose, for it can safely be assumed that Congress intended courts to take into account evolutions in economic theory as long as the basic legislative goal of free and open competition is not undermined.[13] It is an entirely different matter for a judicial or enforcement agency to decide to exclude sociopolitical values from section 7[14] merger analysis and to limit policy considerations to risks of unilateral or concerted exercise of market power to raise prices (which appears to be present Justice Department policy). It is far less clear whether Congress intended that the political and essentially legislative decision whether and what kind of non-economic values underlie the antitrust laws should be delegated to the courts. There is no need to grant courts flexibility to add and subtract social and political values to reflect perceived changes in political theory or in community acceptance of those values.

Moreover, economics is not a natural science and developments in economic theory do not provide courts with entirely objective principles and rules. Arguments couched in economic theory may contain political values. The Chicago School's promotion of allocative efficiency and "consumer welfare" in the strict sense as the exclusive antitrust standard is ultimately a political judgment and cannot be justified on the basis of empirically verifi-

[13] For example, even if the entire body of economic theory ultimately rejected competition and free markets, courts would remain constrained to follow the fundamental legislative goal of competition expressed in the antitrust laws.

[14] 15 U.S.C. §18 (1982).

able or value-free developments in economic theory. This cautions a critical examination of proposals to alter existing antitrust rules because of developments in economic theory.

In sum, the U.S. antitrust regime is more flexible than the German. This flexibility has the significant advantage of permitting courts and enforcement agencies more easily to fine tune antitrust rules to reflect evolutions in economic theory. German antitrust enforcement remains more firmly wedded to economic premises and analyses, many of which were developed several decades ago and have been rejected in the United States as no longer valid. The other side of the coin is the risk that U.S. courts and enforcement agencies will take on the essentially legislative task of changing the antitrust rules to reflect differences in political and social values. For example, elimination of the protection of small traders is highly unlikely, if not impossible, in the German system; in the United States, that policy objective has been largely eliminated without any legislative change.

Of course, there has been and continues to be criticism about the uncertainty, excessive costs and litigation delays associated with enforcement of U.S. antitrust law. In 1979, a national commission set up to study the antitrust laws focused on a number of procedural and institutional deficiencies.[15] The recent symposium issue of the *Georgetown Law Journal* examined private antitrust actions in some depth.[16] Uncertainties in the rules have been particularly marked during the last 10 years of transition from the traditional economic and political antitrust policy objectives to the prevailing ones. For example, the movement away from per se rules to the rule of reason has reduced predictability in the near term. Courts and commentators are responding by attempting to formulate more predictable and less costly truncated rules of reason.[17] Private antitrust enforcement has also been criticized as inhibiting competitive conduct, and legislation to limit treble damages to price fixing and hard-core cartel behavior has been introduced by the Reagan administration.[18]

This debate about deficiencies in antitrust procedures and enforcement mechanisms is secondary to the main U.S. antitrust debate about economic, political and social policy objectives. Perhaps because of this more fundamental debate, proposals to reduce the uncertainty and costs associated with U.S. antitrust enforcement rarely go so far as Maxeiner's criticisms. As he recognizes, there is no reason to expect that the United States will adopt the German system. The American tradition and concern for decentralization

[15] *See* REPORT OF THE NATIONAL COMMISSION FOR THE REVIEW OF ANTITRUST LAWS AND PROCEDURES (1979).

[16] 74 GEO. L.J. 999 (1986).

[17] As to court decisions, see Ball Memorial Hosp. v. Mutual Hosp. Ins., 784 F.2d 1325 (7th Cir. 1986); United States v. Realty Multi-List, 629 F.2d 1351 (5th Cir. 1980). As to commentators, see 7 P. AREEDA, ANTITRUST LAW 361 (1986); and Easterbrook, *supra* note 3. The Solicitor General advocated adoption of a "structured rule of reason" in National Collegiate Athletic Ass'n v. Board of Regents of the University of Oklahoma, 468 U.S. 85 (1984).

[18] *See* Antitrust Remedies Improvements Act of 1987, *reprinted in* ANTITRUST & TRADE REG. REP. (BNA), No. 52, at 350 (Feb. 19, 1987).

of enforcement and the continued importance given private enforcers militate strongly against adoption of the centralized German system. Indeed, the congressional[19] and state[20] criticism of the present enforcement policies of the Justice Department makes centralization even less likely.

This is not at all to conclude that little useful can be learned from the German system. Many aspects of it are extremely attractive and could be readily introduced into U.S. antitrust usage with no loss of the desirable flexibility. Although specialized tribunals may remain unacceptable in the United States, greater judicial control in antitrust actions is certainly essential. The absence of jury trials in the German system at the minimum suggests rethinking of the use of juries in complex antitrust litigation. Perhaps most importantly, the German tailoring of remedies to fit particular offenses and the separation of the culpability issue from other antitrust issues are particularly attractive tools to reduce the uncertainty and costs now associated with U.S. antitrust litigation. These aspects also suggest that U.S. courts should pay greater attention to the formulation of *ex ante* antitrust rules.

Maxeiner's volume reflects much thought and work. It also evidences considerable familiarity with German antitrust enforcement and German legal method generally. The volume constitutes a real contribution to both comparative literature and antitrust law.

BARRY E. HAWK
Fordham Law School

Les Associations d'Entreprises (Joint Ventures) dans le commerce international. By Luiz O. Baptista and Pascal Durand-Barthez. Paris: FEDUCI—Librairie Générale de Droit et de Jurisprudence, 1986. Pp. iv, 285. Index. F.300.

"Associations of Enterprises" is both practical and theoretical in its effort to define the international joint venture—a creature of international commercial law. It analyzes the origin of the elements of the joint venture in U.S. law, distinguishes it from the U.S. partnership, notes the difficulty of defining an international joint venture, discusses French entities or contracts that most closely resemble joint ventures and touches on the joint venture laws of a number of Eastern countries. The term "joint venture" is used throughout the book because it is the most commonly used name.[1]

[19] For example, Congress effectively blocked the Justice Department from attacking the per se ban on resale price maintenance before the Supreme Court in the *Monsanto* litigation.

[20] For example, the National Association of Attorneys General issued its own set of Vertical Restraints Guidelines in reaction to those issued by the Justice Department. *See* NAAG, VERTICAL RESTRAINTS GUIDELINES (1985), *reprinted in* ANTITRUST & TRADE REG. REP. (BNA), No. 49, at 996 (Dec. 5, 1986).

[1] There are several other books in French on the same general subject as "Associations of Enterprises": e.g., B. MERCADAL & P. JANIN, LES CONTRATS DE COOPÉRATION INTER-EN-

The international character of the book is a reflection of the nationalities of the authors. Professor Luiz O. Baptista, a scholar and member of the São Paulo Bar, received his doctor of laws in Paris where he presented a thesis on "Joint Ventures in International Relations," which served as basic research for this book. Pascal Durand-Barthez is the head of the legal department in a large French company with significant international business.

The value of the book for the French-speaking lawyer and businessman lies in the fact that it will give him a better understanding of an international joint venture, which is a product of American law, French experience and a Scottish name. The authors also explain the concept of fiduciary duties between joint venturers, which is not an easy task in French since the trust is not a part of the *romano-germanique* legal system. They believe this concept can be usefully transposed from U.S. partnership law to international joint ventures, presumably by inserting the fiduciary obligations into a section of the joint venture agreement relating to duties of the parties.

Common law lawyers who read French should find the book informative. They can learn about the problems posed by translating the joint venture idea into French law, including the difficulties of adapting the various French companies for use in an equity joint venture. Many rules relating to French company law cannot be changed by agreement of the shareholders, unlike the more flexible U.S. rules. Voting agreements between shareholders are of uncertain validity. In addition, there is a good description of each of the forms of French companies that resemble a joint venture.

In the first part of their book, Baptista and Durand-Barthez, after exploring the history of joint ventures, make an effort to define international joint ventures. Then they classify them on the basis of the type of businesses that use them and the different types of entities that participate in them. In trying to formulate a definition, the authors in this section of the book employ a method that is analytical and theoretical.

Professor Lesguillons, in his two-page preface, which provides an excellent summary, states that the results of the authors' efforts to define an international joint venture are disappointing. This is also the authors' view. However, the effort was not a waste of time. The attempt to find a definition is instructive to the reader. The difficulties of definition arise from the fact that international joint ventures in reality take a number of different forms representing various business situations, some of which resemble one an-

---

TREPRISES (1st ed. 1974), does not refer to the term "joint venture" except to say it is a competitor in international business language with "coopération inter-entreprise" (p. 3). This book is primarily focused on France, although it does have sections on international arbitration, international contracts and choice of laws.

M. DUBISSON, LES GROUPEMENTS D'ENTREPRISES POUR LES MARCHÉS INTERNATIONAUX (1979), and P. FRANCESCHINI & L. PELISSIER, DROIT ET PRATIQUE DES UNIONS ET GROUPEMENTS D'ENTREPRISES (1981), are oriented more toward the construction industry.

Baptista and Durand-Barthez's book, which focuses primarily on developing countries, is by far the most international in scope, although the Dubisson book has a section on the Belgian, English, Swiss and German law on temporary associations and partnerships.

other. They utilize parts of different countries' legal systems and create their own law as set forth in the terms of the contracts that make them up. For example, a joint venture may include a company constituted in a developed, developing or non-market economy state. Since the international joint venture is really a variety of different types of legal creations, it would be surprising if one definition were satisfactory.

The second chapter is called "Typologies des Joint Ventures" and the approach here is not unlike classifications in zoology. Distinctions are made by listing the different types of businesses where joint ventures are commonly used. The examples given are (1) petroleum, where the joint ventures were initially between U.S. oil companies, but later extended to situations where the host country or an entity owned by it became a party; and (2) mining ventures, syndicates of banks, construction consortiums (which are not usually equity joint ventures), research or joint manufacturing, and investment joint ventures for foreign investors, primarily in developing countries.

The authors then go through a different classifying exercise based on the nature of the parties to the joint venture. The parties can be (1) nations with an agreement in the form of a treaty; (2) nations and private entities where, the authors note, inequality may result if the nation attempts to retain and utilize its sovereign powers; and (3) private persons or entities.

The third section lists the characteristics of contracts that have been referred to as *accords de coopération* (cooperation agreements) and concludes that most are joint ventures. Agreements between groups of enterprises are also discussed, as well as Dubisson's definition of a *groupement.* This section (p. 44) reiterates the definition of an international joint venture, i.e.,

> an association of contractual nature, where resources and risks are shared, the parties have a right to participate on an equal basis in the management, with a limited purpose and duration. . . . [The authors also add] that the division of profits (which may or may not involve a company organization) is also an element that practitioners associate with a joint venture.[2]

Part 2 of the book, "Organization and Functioning of Joint Ventures," starts off on a more practical note. Section 1 discusses the nature and contents of a typical basic agreement and states that the basic agreement is

[2] In *Host Country Regulation of Joint Ventures and Foreign Investment* (p. 110), Jesuald W. Salacuse defines an international joint venture as "essentially an economic or financial relationship which may be cast into a variety of legal forms, depending upon the law of the host country in question." AMERICAN BAR ASSOCIATION, JOINT VENTURING ABROAD: A CASE STUDY (1985).

Other attempts at definition have been made in the context of EEC antitrust law. *See* CCH Explanation of Art. 85(3) of the Treaty of Rome, 2 Common Mkt. Rep. (CCH) ¶2061.13, at 1673-2, where a "joint venture is generally described as an enterprise subject to joint control by two or more companies that are economically independent of each other." 2 H. SMIT & P. HERZOG, THE LAW OF THE EUROPEAN ECONOMIC COMMUNITY, at 3-199 (1986), offer the following: "Every collaborative effort on some aspect of the production and marketing process may be termed a joint venture."

sometimes only a preliminary agreement that more or less disappears once a joint venture company is constituted and the other (satellite) agreements begin to function.

Here the authors speak of the importance of the "whereas clauses" in recording the intention of the parties. They continue by saying that there can be contradictions between the principle of majority rule in company law and the equality (*paritaire*) principle "that generally dominates the joint venture" (p. 51). The authors previously stated: "We have underlined in several places the equality [*parité*] of the contracting parties of the joint venture" (p. 41).

If it is true that the equality principle often prevails in joint ventures, this reviewer would have liked to have had more discussion and explanation. This reviewer believes that equality may be an important element in many joint ventures, particularly those in developing countries where there are deeply engrained suspicions of foreign economic domination. In some countries, Hungary, for example, foreign investors are not allowed to own a majority interest. In China, equality is a basic principle in joint venture law in the sense that, philosophically at least, neither party should have an unfair advantage over the other, i.e., there should be "mutual benefit." However, the law does permit foreigners to own a majority interest. Some international professional partnerships have equality as a basic principle, but others do not. Therefore, this reviewer is not convinced that "parity" or equality is necessarily a fundamental principle of international or national joint ventures. Since a joint venture is a contract, there is no reason why unequal arrangements cannot be made if the contributions, expenses and performance of one party are greater than the other's. On the other hand, the treatment of others as equals as a rule of conduct is undoubtedly a sound policy that facilitates cooperation.

Subsequent sections deal with majority control by one participant and 50:50 joint ventures, which are said to be more troublesome in that decision making can be blocked unless some special mechanism is provided. Such devices are discussed in a later section entitled "Conflict Resolution."

The problems posed by controlling a joint venture are outlined, including the use of voting trusts, management agreements, holding companies or other legal mechanisms customary in the countries concerned. Other problems mentioned are those which arise in trying to adapt articles of incorporation and bylaws (*statuts*) to incorporate joint venture agreements. Contracts superimposed on a joint venture corporation often are of doubtful validity in jurisdictions that prohibit voting agreements. Nevertheless, they are common. Where they are of questionable legality, the authors caution that they be used only if extralegal considerations provide guarantees that the contracts' provisions will be respected. The authors add that industrial property agreements not only provide methods of enforcing quality requirements relating to products, but also provide indirect methods of control.

Joint venture contracts require substantial investments and have a long life; thus, questions relating to duration are most important (pp. 65–69). Provisions in joint ventures may provide for judicial adjustment of contracts in the event of unforeseen circumstances that threaten the basic equilibrium of the contract and render performance excessively onerous for one of the parties. The authors cite provisions in a number of countries' laws that allow for this possibility.

In the chapter on satellite agreements, the important problems of termination, choice of law and dispute resolution are discussed. The authors suggest that it may be desirable to have arbitrators apply equitable principles (*amiable composition*) to the basic agreement, while satellite agreements may more appropriately be subjected to a national law.

The next section discusses the various forms of the operating companies available for use in a joint venture. It is stated that the majority of joint ventures are corporate. The choice to incorporate, according to the authors, is dictated by the desire to secure limited liability and to have a better defined and commonly recognized form through which joint venture activities can be carried on, despite the fact that the form chosen is often too rigid to embody the underlying agreements of the parties.

The different French companies that are possible candidates for a joint venture operating company are discussed, together with their advantages and disadvantages. The list includes the *société en nom collectif* (partnership), the *société en commandite* (limited partnership), the S.A.R.L. (limited liability company), the S.A. (corporation), the G.I.E. (Groupement d'Intérêt Economique) and the cooperative. Other forms that do not constitute legal entities are inventoried, such as a *société de fait* (a company in fact) or *société en participation* (a hidden partnership). United States closed corporations and U.S. partnerships are mentioned as well.

The following section deals with satellite agreements annexed to the basic agreement, such as those specifying how personnel will be made available, financing agreements and industrial property agreements. A different definition of "joint venture" is attempted in this section in terms of form, i.e., a basic agreement plus satellite agreements. It is suggested that the basic agreement is the legal cause (*cause juridique*) of all the agreements and the joint venture itself is a system of contracts.

The problems that arise when a national government is a joint venture partner, its prerogatives and control over the joint venture, conflict resolution and the special problems that arise when dealing with a non-market economy state are discussed. A final chapter focuses on control by a host government through authorization of the investment in a joint venture, technology transfers and tax and competition policy.

The conclusion, which is not set apart in a separate section (perhaps due to a printing error), appears in the last two pages of section IV, "The Control of the State of the International Joint Venture." The authors conclude that their definition appears valid, provided the concept of profit divided among the parties is understood broadly, i.e., as almost any form of economic advantage. If this definition is accepted, the international joint venture need not show a profit throughout its life so long as it procures different economic benefits such as "access to a new technology, penetration of a new market, tax advantages or simply as high dividends as possible" for the original joint venture parties (p. 182).

The authors close with the question whether legislative definition of the joint venture would be helpful. They note that the French Groupement d'Intérêt Economique (G.I.E.) was, to a certain extent, an attempt to do so that was only relatively successful. They conclude that, given the great diversity of situations in which joint ventures are used and the need for flexibility, legislative intervention in France would not be helpful. A number of non–market economy countries have reached the opposite conclusion in enacting specific legislation relating to joint ventures. Hungary (pp. 139–40), Romania (pp. 140–41), China (pp. 144–45) and, in January 1987, Russia have issued a decree; others have laws on foreign investment that permit joint ventures, i.e., Yugoslavia (pp. 19, 38, 142), Poland, Bulgaria and Russia (p. 142). On the other hand, the authors think the French legislature should change French rules prohibiting voting agreements between shareholders in a joint venture context.

After reading this book, one is impressed with the interest and importance of the subject. The creation of international joint ventures for cross-border investment that work in the three major legal systems, i.e., the Anglo-Saxon, *romano-germanique* and non–market economy systems, is a breathtaking feat for any legal institution. The importance of the subject has been noted in another recent book in the United States, which states that the developed countries' quest for untapped markets, combined with the developing nations' desires for new technology and foreign investments, makes the international joint venture a favored and necessary medium for doing business abroad.[3]

Some recent figures also reflect the existence of substantial numbers of joint ventures.[4] As to the future development of this institution, the authors in their foreword state "that only the slow harmonization of the internal law by international treaties will provide the security of real legal norms."

"Associations of Enterprises" suggests additional subjects for research. It would be instructive to have more statistics on how many international joint ventures exist, when they were constituted, how they have worked, what

[3] *See* David N. Goldsweig's foreword in JOINT VENTURING ABROAD: A CASE STUDY, *supra* note 2. This book provides a hypothetical case, form agreements and articles on various aspects of joint ventures.

W. FRIEDMANN & G. KALMANOFF, JOINT INTERNATIONAL BUSINESS VENTURES (1961), concluded that joint ventures were increasing in number and constituted an important postwar expression of changing relationships between industrially developed and less-developed countries.

[4] POLITIQUE DE LA CONCURRENCE ET LES ENTREPRISES COMMUNES 13 (1986), published by the OECD, gives us an idea of the importance of the international joint venture in the EEC. Increasing concentrations of industry are occurring not only through acquisitions but also through agreements between independent companies, which, if highly integrated, are often like partial mergers.

In 1974, 49% of all mergers and acquisitions taking place in the EEC were in the form of joint venturelike arrangements (*entreprises communes*). The percentage dropped to 26 in 1982–1983. However, in 1982 and 1983, the number of international joint ventures with third countries equaled intracommunity joint ventures and in 1983–1984, their number exceeded the latter. Likewise, two-thirds of Switzerland's joint ventures were between Swiss and foreign companies.

problems have arisen and how and why they have failed.[5] Are joint ventures particularly suited to economic cooperation with developing countries? Is majority control usually retained by the developing country?

Although the joint venture is more complicated to operate than a wholly owned subsidiary in terms of management and relations with joint venture partners, it can be used as a vehicle for improving a company's competitive position in developed countries[6] and it is often the only alternative available for working in developing countries and non–market economy countries. It provides a framework for entities in these latter countries where no party need be exploited and each can find its best interest in receiving the latest technology and training for personnel, developing industrial, commercial and financial skills, or generally being a more active participant in international business. In all these ways, the international joint venture can play an increasing role in fostering economic cooperation and development.

WALLACE R. BAKER
Of the Illinois Bar

Entwicklungshilfe zwischen Völkerrechtsordnung und Weltwirtschaftssystem. By Otto Wulff. Baden-Baden: Nomos Verlagsgesellschaft, 1986. Pp. 300.

To what extent can law promote development? To what extent is development law tributary to economic facts and evolutions? To what extent can and do political and ideological conceptions affect the law and economics of development? These are some of the questions the author attempts to deal

---

According to ICC statistics for 1986, 14% of the cases in arbitration related to joint ventures, which indicates considerable interest in this form of doing business and also illustrates that serious conflicts arise. These statistics are found on page 3 of a speech by Stephen R. Bond, Secretary General of the I.C.C. Court of Arbitration, Paris, "Arbitration of Construction Disputes under Auspices of the International Chamber of Commerce," given before the Second Annual Construction Litigation Superconference, April 8–9, 1987.

[5] *See* Reynolds, *The "Pinched Shoe" Effect of International Joint Ventures,* COLUM. J. WORLD BUS., Summer 1984, at 23. The conclusion of this study is that three-fourths of the 52 Indian-U.S. joint ventures studied survived profitably for 10 years or more. Nevertheless, even though the initial aims of the partners were reasonably congruent, as time passed, the changing locus of power led to a divergence in objectives. In almost every instance, this divergence tended to reduce the value of the joint venture as an instrument of the aims of the American partner. Thus, although most of the American firms continued their Indian ventures, they found the "fit" less comfortable than at the outset and this "pinched shoe" effect eventually dissolved the partnership for some of them.

In the worst situation in case of a breakup, a company, by entering into a joint venture and contributing technology, may have merely created a powerful competitor with lower labor costs.

[6] *Business International* will soon publish a major research report on competitive alliances, i.e., joint ventures and other forms of collaboration, recounting the experiences of over 40 European, U.S. and Japanese firms. BI/IDEAS IN ACTION, June 8, 1987, reports on a 50:50 joint venture between Italy's Montedison and the U.S.'s Hercules, combining complementary strengths, i.e., leading technology (Montedison) and a global distribution network (Hercules).

with in this book. The first chapter examines the general foundations of development policies. It provides some definitions and lists the main worldwide institutions involved: ECOSOC, UNCTAD, GATT, UNIDO, the Bretton Woods institutions and a number of UN specialized agencies. The author indicates the scope of cooperation between the EEC and regional institutions in the developing world and outlines the principal motivating factors behind development cooperation. He provides an overview of what was achieved in general terms up to the end of 1983. The second chapter deals with the legal aspects of development cooperation. No legal causality is found between colonialism and present-day economic conditions in the Third World that would justify a claim to compensation (pp. 44–46). Nor does the author find it possible to construe a legal obligation for development aid on the grounds of worldwide solidarity or on the basis of the UN Charter (pp. 46–49).

The third chapter considers the principal issues of the North-South dialogue. As regards the debt problem, the author notes that Third World countries generally admit the legally binding nature of loan agreements and look for economic and political arguments to ease their burden. He rejects the political arguments and is against the cancellation of debts (pp. 51–55). On trade, the author notes that basically beneficial measures such as the General System of Preferences[1] are partly undone by restrictive practices that do not fall under GATT regulations, such as rules of origin and quality control. As a result, only countries on the threshold of industrialization benefit from the GSP (pp. 58–67).

With respect to raw materials, which provide the bulk of the exports of poorer developing countries, the author blames the collapse of commodity prices on the oil crisis and notes the ineffectiveness of traditional commodity agreements and the limited success of the EEC Stabex scheme.[2] He also deplores the failure of the Common Fund agreement to come into force (pp. 68–74).[3] This is followed by a spirited defense of investment protection agreements and Western investment policies in general (pp. 74–79). As for the recent codification of the law of the sea by the 1982 UN Convention, it is seen as unduly favoring the principal coastal states by greatly extending the area of their jurisdiction; as giving too much power to the flag states in the matter of shipping regulations and environmental protection (or the

[1] Adopted within the framework of UNCTAD in October 1970 and put into effect by the EEC in July 1971 and by most other OECD countries in January 1972. It falls within the ambit of chapter IV of GATT and was accordingly given a waiver from the general most-favored-nation clause. Its purpose is to give free access to developed markets for specific products from developing countries.

[2] Stabilization fund for exports of agricultural commodities from ACP countries (*see* note 5 *infra*) to the EEC, introduced by the first Lomé Convention in 1975. The second Lomé Convention introduced a similar scheme for certain minerals, known as Sysmin.

[3] Agreement on a Common Fund for Commodities adopted under the auspices of UNCTAD in 1980. It has not become effective owing to the failure of the main providers of capital, including the United States, to ratify it.

lack of it), thus preventing any effective international regulation of those issues; and as having set up a totally unrealistic regime for the exploitation of the Area.[4] The author fully supports those Western countries that have refused to sign the Convention (pp. 79–88). As for transfer of technology, the author thinks that it must be linked to investment protection. He opposes the easy and cheap transfer of new technologies, which in his view are to be protected in the interest of general world development (pp. 88–92).

The first half of the fourth chapter considers regional developments in the Third World. The author notes the lack of success of South-South cooperation in general, which he partly blames on the attitude of OPEC countries and that of more developed LDCs, which tend to behave in much the same way as their industrialized counterparts (pp. 94–97). This is followed by short surveys of regional cooperation in Latin America (pp. 97–99) and in the Southeast Asia/Pacific area (pp. 99–101). In both instances, in spite of a few minor achievements, the author mainly sees failure to reach the goals set. There is nothing on regional cooperation in Africa. In the second part of the chapter, the author once more turns to legal considerations. He examines the attitude toward international law of the Non-Aligned Movement, which he sees as oscillating between wholesale condemnation of the traditional international legal order as protecting only the interests of the industrialized countries, and attempts to use this same legal order with a view to codifying the postulated "New International Economic Order" (pp. 102–06). This is followed by short reviews of the Islamic and socialist approaches to international law (pp. 106–09; 109–15), neither of which is seen as having provided any significant new contribution to the international legal order.

The fifth chapter considers whether the European approach to development cooperation represents an alternative to worldwide approaches. It begins with an excellent survey of legal arrangements concluded between the EEC and various parts of the developing world (ACP countries,[5] Mediterranean countries and ASEAN[6] in particular) on pages 117–19. This is followed by an economic analysis of the various relationships, which closely accords with the official views prevalent in the Federal Republic of Germany (pp. 120–36). The lack of impact of cooperation with very poor countries is blamed on their poverty itself, which, the author believes, makes it difficult to produce a lasting effect on their economies. He finds the main achieve-

[4] This term designates the seabed and ocean floor beyond the jurisdiction of states, i.e., outside the limits of their continental shelves. The regime provides for the setting up of an Enterprise, which is to exploit parts of the Area, while granting concessions to states for the exploitation of the remainder. The terms of the concessions include the obligation of making the technologies used available to the Enterprise so that it can use them for its own activities. It is mainly this provision that several Western countries find objectionable.

[5] Sixty-six African, Caribbean and Pacific countries that, for the purpose of negotiating with the EEC, form a single group.

[6] Association of South-East Asian Nations grouping the Philippines, Indonesia, Malaysia, Singapore and Thailand.

ment of the Lomé[7] process to be the promotion of investments in the ACP countries.

In his conclusions (pp. 137–46), the author credits the developing countries with realizing the importance of legal instruments in the promotion of development cooperation, while blaming them for wanting to reject many of the general rules of international law.[8] The consensual nature of the international legal order makes it difficult for one group of countries to impose its views on others. Third World countries thus tend to resort to declarations of principles whose content is rejected at least in part by the very countries to whom they are addressed. On the economic side, the author firmly endorses the official views of his country and the United States. He pleads for better coordination with a view to promoting development policies that will follow a free enterprise approach, and he expresses satisfaction with the renunciation of socialist policies by several developing countries. He fully agrees with the World Bank that stress should be laid on agriculture and labor-intensive industries, on financial orthodoxy and discipline so that external debts can be paid, and on a realistic appraisal of development policies. In a last return to legal considerations, the author wonders whether international law as we know it today still has a common conceptual foundation.

The second half of the volume is made up of excerpts from official documents such as treaties, declarations by organs of international institutions and policy guidelines, as well as statistical data on various aspects of development cooperation. Annex 8 provides a list of some regional economic institutions in the Third World, which is rather outdated with respect to Africa.[9]

Dr. Wulff's book is a good and reasonably brief presentation of current views on international development cooperation as held particularly by official circles of the Federal Republic of Germany and the United States. This is tempered by a very sympathetic approach to the plight of the developing countries, in particular as regards the contradiction between the stated objectives of freer trade proclaimed by Western countries and the restrictive measures they constantly take to protect their industries against competition from the Third World. Those diplomats of the Third World involved in economic negotiations with the West who know German should make this book compulsory reading before sitting down at the negotiating table, or even prior to drawing up their negotiating brief.

DIETRICH KAPPELER
University of Nairobi

[7] Lomé, the capital of Togo, where the EEC-ACP conventions were signed in 1975, 1979 and 1984.

[8] Many Western politicians and scholars level this accusation against both socialist countries and countries of the Third World. In fact, the only major principle contested by these countries is that of the sanctity of private property of foreigners.

[9] There is no mention of the Southern African Development Coordination Council (SADCC), the Preferential Trade Area for Eastern and Southern Africa (PTA) and the Communauté Economique des Etats d'Afrique Centrale (CEEAC). As for OCAM, which is listed, it was dissolved in 1985.

Service-Led Growth: The Role of the Service Sector in World Development. By Dorothy I. Riddle. New York: Praeger Publishers, 1986. Pp. xiv, 289. Index. $37.95.

Ever since Daniel Bell published his controversial *The Coming of the Post Industrial Society* in 1973, there has been a vigorous debate in the academic literature about the relative importance of manufacturing versus services in an economy. On one side of the debate are those who argue that manufacturing is critical: without the production of goods, the argument goes, no economy can remain strong and vibrant. As Stephen Cohen and John Zysman wrote in their recent study, *Manufacturing Matters,* "There is no such thing as a post-industrial economy. . . . The wealth and power of the United States depends upon maintaining mastery and control of production."[1]

On the other side of the debate is a growing list of scholars to which we must add Dorothy Riddle, as revealed by the book under review. In the tradition of Bell and more recently Ronald Shelp,[2] Riddle has written a rather conventional book about the expanding role of the service sector and services' essential role in economic growth.

The first third is a lengthy review of the literature on services. The author explores the variety of ways that services have been defined as well as different theories about the impact of services on the economy. Part of the problem with studying the service sector, as Riddle correctly notes, is that everyone has a different definition. As a result, the data on services tend to be incompatible across time, across countries and especially across academic studies. Unlike manufacturing, for which everyone has a definition and can usually agree on standards of measurement, services are often treated as a residual. After proposing a definition, Riddle proceeds to examine the so-called myths of the service sector: the myth of the low value of services; the myth of low productivity of services; and the myth of de-industrialization. Her claim is that services have been systematically misunderstood and undervalued. "It is the service sector," she asserts, "not the manufacturing sector, which is indispensable" (p. 104).

Part 2 examines various trends related to services in global markets, followed by part 3, which looks at prescriptions for governments and firms. Of particular interest are the chapters on trade in services—one of the top priorities for the next round of the General Agreement on Tariffs and Trade. In her fifth chapter, Riddle focuses on conceptualizing the trade-in-services issue, while in the ninth, she focuses on policy recommendations. As she suggests, conceptualizing trade in services is even more difficult than providing definitions for domestic services. Part of the confusion lies in the accounting system, which includes interest on bank loans and repatriated

[1] *Quoted in* Cohen & Zysman, *Why Manufacturing Matters: The Myth of the Post-Industrial Economy,* CAL. MGMT. REV., No. 3, Spring 1987, at 23.

[2] R. SHELP, BEYOND INDUSTRIALIZATION: ASCENDANCY OF THE GLOBAL SERVICE ECONOMY (1981).

earnings of multinationals as traded services; and part of the confusion is a function of trying to separate the "location" of the service from its "ownership." It is not immediately evident, for instance, whether one should look at where the service is being performed (e.g., in the United States for a French client versus the service being performed in France) or focus on the owner of the service (e.g., an American firm purchasing French services versus an American firm in France purchasing services from the U.S. headquarters). Nor is it immediately evident whether services should be treated as trade or investment. There is a presumption that services should be treated like goods, but it is not clear whether the operation of an American accounting office in France with French nationals is any more of a trade issue than the operation by General Motors of a factory in Germany.

While this book does not resolve these difficult questions, it does a creditable job of surveying many of the conceptual and mythological issues. The primary weakness of the book is that it fails to make an original contribution to the literature. Like so much of the debate on services versus manufacturing, the author relies on aggregate, ad hoc statistics to prove that services are critical. Most of the numbers used illustrate the size and growth of the service sector; occasionally, the author performs a correlation. However, the evidence marshaled in support of the book's theme of the critical role of services in the world economy is not conclusive. One cannot conclude, one way or the other, from the data presented that services are the essential link in economic growth. Similarly, conceptual work on trade in services is essential if the GATT is going to make progress during the next round of negotiations. However, this book does little more than review existing approaches to the negotiations.

To advance the debate about services versus manufacturing, and to reach a better understanding of the international dimensions of services, a careful examination of the linkages between industrial production and services at the micro-, industry level, rather than the macrolevel, would probably constitute a better research vehicle. If this study had provided us with more detailed empirical research, we might have learned more about how services and the industrial economy interact.

DAVID B. YOFFIE
Harvard Business School

The Canadian Yearbook of International Law. Volume XXIII, 1985. Edited by C. B. Bourne. Vancouver: University of British Columbia Press, 1986. Pp. 498. Index. $38.50.

Perhaps the increasing significance of sea law and issues of maritime jurisdiction is evident in the fact that four of the six articles in the latest *Yearbook* treat such questions. Nevertheless, one of the remaining two articles is likely to be the most provocative in that its author, L. C. Green, expresses the frustrations of many students of international law in wondering *Is There a Universal International Law Today?*

In tracing the roots of international law, Green finds that early conceptions of *jus gentium* or *jus inter gentes* reflected a notion of universal application. A review of selected classical writers (e.g., Vitoria, Suárez, Pufendorf, Wolff) shows support for the universality principle, but also an acknowledgment (e.g., Grotius, Gentili) of regional diversity. However, a study of modern trends in law and politics suggests that particularization is now the dominant theme. States, or groups of states, tend to articulate interests in an area of activity or in a geographical region that are vital to themselves, to the detriment of universal participation. Issues that come before the United Nations or form part of the flow of modern world politics readily reveal the divisions; they involve such matters as religious diversity, differing economic systems, Third World concerns, the Monroe and Brezhnev Doctrines, Canadian Arctic claims, the jurisdiction of the International Court of Justice, human rights, ideology and the law of the sea.

The author offers the following observation: "Even if we are prepared to accept that there was in the past a universal international law, there is little hope that we will ever see its existence again" (p. 32). He predicts an increase in regional and political groupings and advises: "Perhaps the wisest approach is to accept this fact and abandon the pretence that consensus in the United Nations or adoption of conventions that stand little chance of general, let alone universal, ratification is the route towards establishment of an international rule of law" (*id.*). The future of international law is seen as hinging on *intra*regional respect for regional norms and potential *inter*regional "ad hoc international law" reflecting agreement in specific areas.

The other "nonmaritime" article, by Sharon A. Williams, examines Canada's Criminal Law Amendment Act of 1985. This massive act (212 sections and 5 annexes) covers a wide range of domestic offenses, but the author focuses on provisions relating to international criminal law, particularly hostage taking and offenses against nuclear material. She reminds us that antiterrorist conventions gain in effectiveness as the number of adhering states grows and safe havens for terrorists disappear. Canada's action in the Criminal Law Amendment Act to combat terrorism is seen by her as a "fine example" for other states. Particular attention should be paid to *aut dedere, aut judicare* provisions in multilateral antiterrorist conventions, which require states (such as Canada) to prosecute alleged offenders in custody if for some reason they cannot be extradited.

The remaining four articles treat maritime questions. In an article that would have been strengthened by the inclusion of maps and diagrams, Geoffrey Marston examines the *Strait of Georgia Reference* decided by the Supreme Court of Canada in May 1984. The disputes concerned title to the seabed and subsoil of the Strait of Juan de Fuca, the Strait of Georgia, Johnstone Strait and Queen Charlotte Strait, and were referred to the Court by British Columbia.

Francis Rigaldies discusses the status of the Gulf of St. Lawrence in international law in an article that includes a number of helpful maps. The author traces the Canadian claims to the gulf as "internal waters," which are based upon straight baselines drawn across the Straits of Belle Isle (45 miles) and Cabot (54 miles). He believes that Canada's historic claims to the area are very strong and that a "clear and unequivocal" proclamation of Canadian sovereignty is not needed now for two reasons: there is no reason to provoke an unnecessary confrontation with the United States, and Canada already exercises enough jurisdiction over the area to protect its interests.

L. L. Herman probes the "modern concept of the off-lying archipelago in international law," arguing that the 1982 Law of the Sea Convention contains many unclear definitions, including those of such terms as archipelagoes, islands, atolls, reefs, rocks and low-tide elevations. Recent decisions (the *Gulf of Maine* and *Libya / Malta Continental Shelf* cases) suggest that states will now be more interested in maximizing jurisdictional claims by the careful selection of base points. Previously unimportant geographical features will now come under close scrutiny.

The final article, by M. L. Jewett, is the second installment of a study begun in the previous *Yearbook.* The focus is a dispute between Newfoundland and Canada concerning claims to the continental shelf, in particular, the status of the continental shelf in 1949, the date of union of Newfoundland with Canada. An extensive review of general practice and UK practice shows that no legal regime of the continental shelf had become customary international law before 1949. Therefore, Newfoundland could not have acquired any rights to exploit the continental shelf before 1949 and any such rights must rest with the Canadian federal Government.

Although the foregoing commentary has focused on the articles in the *Yearbook,* the notes and comments section always offers lively discussion of prominent international legal questions, and the current selection is no exception. The section on current Canadian practice and cases in international law is worth the reader's time, as is the selection of book reviews.

FOREST L. GRIEVES
University of Montana

Soviet Year-Book of International Law, 1985. Moscow: Publishing House "Nauka," 1986. Pp. 360. 4 rubles, 60 kopeks.

Debate still stirs over whether there are three international laws or only one universal one, if a reader may take positions set forth in the 1985 Soviet *Year-Book* as representative. I. P. Blishchenko of the Foreign Ministry calls for more research on socialist international law as if it were one of three systems (socialist, capitalist and developing world). I. I. Lukashuk rises at the annual meeting to rebuke him, insisting on the validity of G. I. Tunkin's position that there is only one universal law created through the "coordination of wills" of the member states of the three groups. A. P. Movchan of the United Nations Committee on Human Rights, writing the leading paper in the *Year-Book,* also upholds the Tunkin view, but evidently the revered senior scholar has not yet convinced all of his colleagues.

Perhaps Blishchenko was only saying that the practice of socialist states within a universal international law needs to be studied in greater depth than it has been to date, but Lukashuk did not interpret him to mean as much. To Westerners, the argument over whether a new independent system of law has been brought into being by socialist practice or whether socialist states provide only a school of interpretation within a universal law seems pedantic, but, as the debate in the *Year-Book* indicates, the issue is still alive. Blishchenko proves that Tunkin's position is still challenged by a younger generation that seems to need to reassert the doctrinaire position of the 1930s, that socialism has brought about qualitative change in the corpus of international law as evidenced by the practice of socialist states.

The *Year-Book* is by no means limited to scholastic argument. Much of the material is practical, especially in the field of private international law, to which the *Year-Books* are now devoting more space. V. Yu. Odintsova argues that since the USSR has joined the Universal (Geneva) Copyright Convention, there is reason to amend its civil law fundamentals to exclude some provisions—notably, those that permit the use in cinema, radio and television programs of copyrighted works without consent of the author, although with payment of royalties. Also, she would eliminate permission to use without payment articles in the public press that have "no current informational character."

B. S. Smirnov is practical when he attacks the European Community's antidumping law as discriminatory against socialist products. O. Z. Yusis defends Soviet interests in a thorough review of judicial decisions of Western states that refuse to acknowledge Soviet nationalization decrees in the Baltic Republics because the United States and some others refuse to recognize their incorporation into the USSR. In his view, this position is unfounded, for the republics are indubitably republics of the USSR.

On the 10th anniversary of the Final Act of Helsinki, A. I. Stepanov and V. A. Kozhevnikov reaffirm the Soviet interest in preserving the inviolability of European frontiers, which they find confirmed in the Act. They make no mention, however, of the human rights "basket" in the Act to which Western eyes are turned and without which Western statesmen would not have signed the Act.

A. V. Chernichenko reaffirms the long-held Soviet position that Article 2(7) of the UN Charter is of paramount importance. He analyzes arguments that a distinction must be drawn between "interference" and "intervention" in the domestic jurisdiction of states. He agrees that the Security Council can vote to "intervene" when it finds a threat to peace. He doubts that a resolution of the General Assembly calling for action can be supported as legal "intervention" even if it is based on recognition that fascism is a threat to peace or that environmental protection is a global problem, as some scholars argue. He has no doubt that Article 2(7) is violated when a General Assembly resolution flows from "clearly biased discussion, instigated by political consideration," especially when member states seek to enforce the resolution by force or threat of force. In short, he would classify as illegal "interference" enforcement action that has not passed the test of the veto.

R. V. Dekanosov insists that waters must now be divided into three categories: territorial, continental shelf and economic zone, in that different international law norms apply to each. He notes that while fishing and freedom of navigation are permitted in the economic zone, foreign exploitation of the resources of the continental shelf is forbidden. He does not consider a fourth zone now claimed by some states; they argue that even on the high seas ships may be boarded and fines levied if fish that spawn in a coastal state's rivers have been caught. Soviet law now provides for this conservation measure.

As in the past, the *Year-Book* includes valuable tables in the form of chronicles of Soviet and Eastern European legislation on matters of international concern, including adherence to multilateral conventions. Summaries are provided of Soviet decrees on the economic zone, protection of the environment on the Arctic Sea coast, interlibrary loans across state frontiers, the entry and transit of foreigners, the issuance to foreigners of residence permits and the new regime for direct relationships between Soviet enterprises and foreign firms.

Fortunately for non-Russian readers, English translations have lengthened over the years, but the shorter "scientific reports" are still printed only in Russian. Often they are helpful to foreigners, and they might well be summarized also.

JOHN N. HAZARD
Board of Editors

Aussenpolitik und Völkerrecht der Sowjetunion. By Boris Meissner. Cologne: Verlag Wissenschaft und Politik, 1987. Pp. 358.

Professor Meissner, a major figure in postwar West German studies of Soviet and East European law, was honored in 1985 by a monumental *Festschrift*[1] arranged by colleagues and former students. With the help of Hans Heinrich Mahnke, who contributes an appreciative foreword that avoids replicating the *Festschrift* tribute, Meissner has assembled 16 of his articles and essays, all previously published in sundry places between 1960 and 1985, on Soviet foreign policy and Soviet approaches to international legal doctrine and practice. Ordered thematically into two sections, the volume treats, respectively, Soviet theories of foreign policy and international legal doctrine, and Soviet practice of international law and foreign policy.

In American terms a jurist, political scientist and diplomat with a strong bent for Sovietology, a combination well represented in the activities of the Institut für Ostrecht der Universität Köln, which he directed for decades, Meissner approached these topics from a broad perspective and his articles meld nicely without being unduly outdated by the passage of events. In part 1 the essays examine the relationship between Soviet theories of foreign policy and international law, the trends in Western and Soviet international legal doctrines, the elements of continuity between imperial and postrevolutionary Russian international legal science (here, perhaps understandably, given his German Baltic background, he gives much greater due to the

[1] *See* SOWJETSYSTEM UND OSTRECHT 886 (G. Brunner, T. Schweisfurth, A. Uschakow & K. Westen eds. 1985).

European roots of Russian doctrine than the present reviewer would), and Soviet concepts of peaceful coexistence, socialist international law, sovereignty and self-determination.

Soviet foreign policy and state practice he rightly sees as reflecting a combination of constant and variable factors from the pre- and post-1917 periods. He gives much attention to Soviet alliance policy since the mid-1950s in part 2 and to key "frontier" issues, including Afghanistan and, above all, relations with the German Democratic Republic. Given his generational and geopolitical roots, it is not surprising that Far Eastern and Arctic concerns figure slightly in Meissner's perception of the key postwar issues.

The essays have been beautifully reset, apparently without changes—the opportunity to rectify a few infelicities not having been seized. It is to Meissner and his associates that we also owe two splendid bibliographies on Soviet public and private international law,[2] a contribution overlooked by Mahnke in his foreword. International lawyers will welcome this collection of Meissner's thoughtful reflections, and some may be inspired enough to consult collateral volumes containing his evaluations of Soviet domestic affairs and social structure.

WILLIAM E. BUTLER
University of London

BRIEFER NOTICES

Water in the Middle East: Conflict or Cooperation? Edited by Thomas Naff and Ruth C. Matson. (Boulder and London: Westview Press, 1984. Published in cooperation with the Middle East Research Institute, University of Pennsylvania. Pp. xvii, 236. $25.) The product of a pilot research project of the Middle East Research Institute of the University of Pennsylvania, this book underscores the importance of water as "an impetus toward cooperation."

A team of researchers studied the history, hydrology and technical aspects of several river systems—the Jordan, the Litani, the Euphrates, the Orontes and the Nile—and has highlighted their common problems. These relate primarily to both water quantity and water quality. Even though these problems are well-known, the researchers note a persistent tendency in the Middle East to produce energy-intensive and high-consumptive agricultural schemes. These policies are driven by the pressures of population growth and further exacerbate the situation.

The researchers emphasize the need to link the resolution of the Middle East conflict between Israel and the Arab countries, especially the Jordan water problem, to the Palestinian problem. They aptly conclude: "As water shortages appear and increase, there will be more requests for U.S. assistance, especially from Israel. Anticipatory planning of that assistance to pro-

[2] B. MEISSNER, SOWJETUNION UND VÖLKERRECHT 1917 BIS 1962 (1963), reviewed at 58 AJIL 537 (1964); and B. MEISSNER, SOWJETUNION UND VÖLKERRECHT 1962–1973 (1977).

mote cooperation and avoid last-minute bail-outs seems a wise, if rare, course."

VED P. NANDA
University of Denver

The Law and Procedure of the International Court of Justice. Vols. I and II. By Gerald Fitzmaurice. (Cambridge: Grotius Publications Limited, 1986. Pp. xli, 860. Index. $152.) These two volumes usefully gather together the distinguished writings of the late Sir Gerald Fitzmaurice, Legal Adviser of the British Foreign Office, and later a judge of the International Court of Justice and then of the European Court of Justice.

La Pensée des autres en droit international privé. Comptes Rendus bibliographiques (1946–1984) réunis en hommage à leur auteur. By Phocion Francescakis. (Thessaloniki: Aristotelian University of Thessaloniki, 1985. Pp. xlviii, 497. Indexes. Distributed in France by Dalloz. F.335.) This volume assembles the book reviews written by a major figure in international law who made for himself a distinguished career as an editor and a teacher in France.

COLLECTED ESSAYS

With this issue, the *Journal* inaugurates a practice of presenting simply the tables of contents of certain volumes that do not lend themselves readily to unified reviews because they consist of loosely linked contributions by different authors. Yearbooks and *Festschriften* are the principal varieties of such work. It is believed that publication of such tables of contents serves a useful end, particularly in respect of those yearbooks that are published in English but because they are published abroad are not caught by the *Index of Legal Periodicals* and similar guides to the literature.

German Yearbook of International Law. Volume 28, 1985. Edited by Jost Delbrück, Wilhelm A. Kewenig and Rüdiger Wolfrum. (Berlin: Duncker & Humblot, 1986. Pp. 555. DM 212.)

Alfred de Zayas, Jakob Th. Möller & Torkel Opsahl, *Application of the International Covenant on Civil and Political Rights under the Optional Protocol by the Human Rights Committee;* César Sepúlveda, *The Inter-American Commission on Human Rights of the Organization of American States;* Martin Bullinger, *Freedom of Expression and Information;* Albert Bleckmann, *The Subjective Right in Public International Law;* Håkon Eriksen, *The Legal Status of the Sami in Norway;* Wilhelm Wengler, *New Australian Constitution Case Law on Race Discrimination* (in German with English summary); Jost Delbrück & Klaus Dicke, *The Christian Peace Ethic and the Doctrine of Just War from the Point of View of International Law;* Trutz Rendtorff, *Christian Ethics and the Doctrine of Just War;* Elmar Rauch, *Military Uses of the Oceans;* L. F. E. Goldie, *Special Problems Concerning Deep Seabed Mining in the Event of Non-Participation in UNCLOS;* Uwe Jenisch, *Sovereign Rights in the Arctic;* Hubertus Welsch, *The London Dumping Convention and Sub-Seabed Disposal of Radioactive Waste;* Mark M. Boguslavsky, *Technology Transfer and International Law;* Tobias Stoll, *Proprietary Protection of Computer Software in National and International Perspective;* Wolfgang Seiffert, *Völkerrechtliche Aspekte der Verlängerung des Warschauer Paktes* (with English summary).

Israel Yearbook on Human Rights. Volume 16, 1986. (Published under the auspices of the Faculty of Law, Tel Aviv University. Pp. 340.)

Yoram Dinstein, *The Interaction of International Law and Justice;* Fania Domb, *Human Rights through Peace Treaties;* L. C. Green, *Institutional Protection of Human Rights;* Ruth Lapidoth, *The Right of Return in International Law, with Special Reference to the Palestinian Refugees;* Natan Lerner, *The U.N. Convention on Torture;* P. J. van Krieken, *Torture or Asylum;* Leo Gross, *Draft Code of Offences Against the Peace and Security of Mankind;* Daphna Shraga, *Human Rights in Emergency Situations under the European Convention on Human Rights;* Herman Schwartz, *Current Movements in American Constitutional Law;* Norman L. Cantor, *On Clear and Present Danger, Clear Probability, and Free Speech Standards in Israel;* Smadar Ottolenghi, *Deprivation of the Right of Certain Residents in Israel to Elect their Local Government Authorities;* Dan Shnit, *The Foetus as a Legal Person under Israeli Law.*

The Italian Yearbook of International Law. Volume VI, 1985. (Milan: Dott. A. Giuffrè Editore, 1986. Pp. xii, 467. Index. $70. Distributed by Oceana Publications, Inc.)

Luigi Condorelli & Zidane Mériboute, *Some Remarks on the State of International Law Concerning Military Activities in Outer Space;* Natalino Ronzitti, *Demilitarization and Neutralization in the Mediterranean;* Enzo Cannizzaro, *The Legal Nature of NATO's 1979 "Dual-Track" Decision and the Installation of Missile Bases in Europe;* Mauro Politi, *Safeguards Against Nuclear Proliferation;* Antonio Filippo Panzera, *Some Considerations on the Review of the 1977 Environmental Modification Techniques (ENMOD) Convention;* Luigi Migliorino, *Declarations and Reservations to the 1971 Seabed Treaty;* Ennio Triggiani, *Some Thoughts on Most-Favoured-Nation Treatment.*

Netherlands Yearbook of International Law. Volume XVII, 1986. (Published jointly with the Netherlands International Law Review and under the auspices of the Interuniversity Institute for International Law, T.M.C. Asser Instituut, The Hague, 1986. Pp. 400. Index. Dfl.125; $45.)

V. D. Degan, *Internal waters;* A. Ch. Kiss & D. Shelton, *Systems analysis of international Law;* I. F. Dekker & H. H. G. Post, *The Gulf War from the point of view of international law.*

The Palestine Yearbook of International Law. Volume II, 1985. (Nicosia: Al-Shaybani Society of International Law Ltd., 1985. Pp. 236. $30.)

Sabri Jiryis, *Settlers' Law;* Lea Tsemel, *Double Standard Justice in Israel.*

South African Yearbook of International Law. Volume 11, 1985–1986. (Pretoria: VerLoren van Themaat Centre for International Law, University of South Africa. Pp. 301. Index. R25; $20.)

Gina Dashman, *United States Corporate Disinvestment from South Africa;* George N. Barrie, *International Law and Economic Coercion—A Legal Assessment;* Désirée Sauermann, *The Regulation of Multinational Corporations and Third World Countries;* Colleen H. Hall, *Prisoners' Rights in International Law;* H. A. Strydom, *A Transcendental View of Some Aspects of International Law and Society;* Gerhard Erasmus, *Mandates, Military Service and Multiple Choice;* C. J. Botha, *Anticipatory Self-Defence and Reprisals Re-examined. South African Attacks on ANC Bases in Neighbouring States.*

BOOKS RECEIVED*

International Law—General

Gray, Christine D. *Judicial Remedies in International Law.* Oxford: Clarendon Press; New York: Oxford University Press, 1987. Pp. xix, 250. Index. $57.

Green, N. A. Maryan. *International Law* (3d ed.). London: Pitman Publishing, 1987. Pp. xlviii, 333. Index.

Ott, David H. *Public International Law in the Modern World.* London: Pitman Publishing, 1987. Pp. xxi, 390. Index. £14.95.

Wegen, Gerhard. *Vergleich und Klagerücknahme im internationalen Prozeß.* Berlin: Duncker & Humblot, 1987. Pp. 484. DM 188.

International Economic Law & Relations

Arndt, Sven W., and Lawrence Bouton. *Competitiveness: The United States in World Trade.* Washington: American Enterprise Institute for Public Policy Research, 1987. Pp. 120. $16, cloth; $7.95, paper. Distributed by University Press of America, Inc.

de Vries, Margaret Garritsen. *Balance of Payments Adjustment, 1945 to 1986: The IMF Experience.* Washington: International Monetary Fund, 1987. Pp. xi, 336. Index. $14.50.

Doxey, Margaret P. *International Sanctions in Contemporary Perspective.* New York: St. Martin's Press, 1987. Pp. xi, 175. Index. $37.50.

Goodman, Louis W. *Small Nations, Giant Firms.* New York and London: Holmes & Meier, 1987. Pp. xiii, 181. Index. $39.50, cloth; $19.75, paper.

Johnston, Charles R., Jr. (comp./ed.). *Law & Practice of United States Regulation of International Trade.* New York, London, Rome: Oceana Publications, Inc., 1987. $175.

Lange, Dieter, and Gary Born (eds.). *The Extraterritorial Application of National Laws.* Paris and New York: ICC Publishing S.A.; Deventer: Kluwer Law and Taxation Publishers, 1987. Pp. x, 57. Dfl.50; £16.95; $24.

Lovett, William A. *World Trade Rivalry: Trade Equity and Competing Industrial Policies.* Lexington and Toronto: D.C. Heath and Company, 1987. Pp. xxxv, 260. Index. $35.

Schmitthoff, Clive M., with assistance from John Adams. *Schmitthoff's Export Trade: The Law and Practice of International Trade* (8th ed.). London: Stevens & Sons, 1986. Pp. lix, 689. Index.

Seidl-Hohenveldern, Ignaz. *Corporations in and Under International Law.* Cambridge: Grotius Publications Limited, 1987. Pp. xviii, 138. Index. £25; $45.

Law of the Sea & Maritime Law

Adede, A. O. *The System for Settlement of Disputes under the United Nations Convention on the Law of the Sea: A Drafting History and a Commentary.* Dordrecht, Boston, Lancaster: Martinus Nijhoff Publishers, 1987. Pp. xv, 285. Dfl.165; $67.50; £45.50.

Attard, David Joseph. *The Exclusive Economic Zone in International Law.* Oxford: Clarendon Press; New York: Oxford University Press, 1987. Pp. lxiv, 350. Index. $78.

Churchill, R. R. *EEC Fisheries Law.* Dordrecht, Boston, Lancaster: Martinus Nijhoff Publishers, 1987. Pp. xxviii, 299. Index. Dfl.165; $80; £50.95.

Mahmoudi, Said. *The Law of Deep Sea-Bed Mining: A Study of the Progressive Development of International Law Concerning the Management of the Polymetallic Nodules of the Deep Sea-Bed.* Stockholm: Almqvist & Wiksell International, 1987. Pp. 362. Index. SEK 525.

Wiktor, Christian L., and Leslie A. Foster. *Marine Affairs Bibliography. A Comprehensive Index to Marine Law and Policy Literature Cumulation: 1980–1985.* Dordrecht, Boston, Lancaster: Martinus Nijhoff Publishers, 1987. Pp. xv, 685. Indexes. Dfl.375; $189; £127.50.

* Mention here neither assures nor precludes later review.

Human Rights

Boyle, Francis Anthony. *Defending Civil Resistance Under International Law.* Dobbs Ferry: Transnational Publishers, Inc., 1987. Pp. xxii, 378. Index. $45.50.

Empell, Hans-Michael. *Die Kompetenzen des UN-Menschenrechtsausschusses im Staatenberichtsverfahren (Art. 40 des Internationalen Paktes über bürgerliche und politische Rechte).* Frankfurt am Main, Bern, New York: Peter Lang, 1987. Pp. viii, 294. Sw.F.65.

Foster, Don, with Dennis Davis & Diane Sandler. *Detention & Torture in South Africa: Psychological, legal & historical studies.* New York: St. Martin's Press, 1987. Pp. vi, 250. Index. $29.95.

Halberstam, Malvina, and Elizabeth F. Defeis. *Women's Legal Rights: International Covenants an Alternative to ERA?* Dobbs Ferry: Transnational Publishers, Inc., 1987. Pp. xii, 208. Index. $35.

Robbers, Gerhard. *Sicherheit als Menschenrecht: Aspekte der Geschichte, Begründung und Wirkung einer Grundrechtsfunktion.* Baden-Baden: Nomos Verlagsgesellschaft, 1987. Pp. 292. Indexes. DM 70.

Rodley, Nigel S. *The Treatment of Prisoners Under International Law.* Paris: UNESCO; Oxford: Clarendon Press; New York: Oxford University Press, 1987. Pp. xxii, 374. Index. $74, cloth; $28.50, paper.

Stover, Eric. *The Open Secret: Torture and the Medical Profession in Chile.* Washington: Committee on Scientific Freedom and Responsibility, American Association for the Advancement of Science, 1987. Pp. vi, 82.

Tomasevski, Katarina (ed.). *The Right to Food: Guide through Applicable International Law.* Dordrecht, Boston, Lancaster: Martinus Nijhoff Publishers, 1987. Pp. xix, 387. Index. Dfl.165; $75.50; £56.75.

Environment & Natural Resources

Ross, Lester, and Mitchell A. Silk. *Environmental Law and Policy in the People's Republic of China.* New York, Westport and London: Quorum Books, 1987. Pp. xvi, 449. Index. $75.

Triggs, Gillian D. (ed.). *The Antarctic Treaty regime: Law, Environment and Resources.* Cambridge and New York: Cambridge University Press, 1987. Pp. xxi, 237. $54.50.

International Organizations

Damrosch, Lori Fisler (ed.). *The International Court of Justice at a Crossroads.* Published under the auspices of the American Society of International Law. Dobbs Ferry: Transnational Publishers, Inc., 1987. Pp. xxviii, 511. Index. $67.50.

Sinclair, Ian. *The International Law Commission.* Cambridge: Grotius Publications Limited, 1987. Pp. viii, 177. Index. £28; $49.

European Community Law

Ballarino, Tito. *Lineamenti di diritto comunitario* (2d ed.). Padua: CEDAM, 1987. Pp. xxi, 343. Indexes. L. 25.000.

Burrows, F. *Free Movement in European Community Law.* New York: Oxford University Press, 1987. Pp. xxxvi, 346. Index. $69.

Jacobs, F. G. (ed.). *Yearbook of European Law 1985.* Volume 5. New York: Oxford University Press, 1986. Pp. xiii, 475. Index. $82.

Pliakos, Asteris. *Les Droits de la défense et le droit communautaire de la concurrence.* Brussels: Etablissements Emile Bruylant, 1987. Pp. xiii, 469. Index. BF 2,811.

Rudden, Bernard, and Derrick Wyatt (eds.). *Basic Community Laws* (2d ed.). New York: Oxford University Press, 1986. Pp. xvi, 407. $45, cloth; $17.95, paper.

Private International Law

Sykes, Edward I., and Michael C. Pryles. *Australian Private International Law* (2d ed.). Sydney: The Law Book Company Limited, 1987. Pp. lxxxix, 772. Index. $69.50.

International Labor Law

International Labour Law Reports. Volume 5. Dordrecht, Boston, Lancaster: Martinus Nijhoff Publishers, 1987. Pp. xxxix, 403. Dfl.225; $110.50; £76.50.

Immigration & Refugees

Fourlanos, Gerassimos. *Sovereignty and the Ingress of Aliens: With Special Focus on Family Unity and Refugee Law.* Stockholm: Almqvist & Wiksell International, 1986. Pp. xiv, 186. SEK 190.

Legomsky, Stephen H. *Immigration and the Judiciary: Law and Politics in Britain and America.* Oxford: Clarendon Press; New York: Oxford University Press, 1987. Pp. xxxix, 345. $68.

State Responsibility

Spinedi, Marina, and Bruno Simma (eds.). *United Nations Codification of State Responsibility.* New York, London, Rome: Oceana Publications, Inc., 1987. Pp. xi, 418. Index. $75.

Taishoff, Marika Natasha. *State Responsibility and the Direct Broadcast Satellite.* London and New York: Frances Pinter (Publishers), 1987. Pp. xii, 203. Index. $29. Distributed by Columbia University Press.

U.S. Law & Foreign Relations

Dorman, William A., and Mansour Farhang. *The U.S. Press and Iran: Foreign Policy and the Journalism of Deference.* Berkeley, Los Angeles, London: University of California Press, 1987. Pp. x, 272. Index. $29.95.

Gregor, A. James, and Virgilio Aganon. *The Philippine Bases: U.S. Security at Risk.* Washington: Ethics and Public Policy Center, 1987. Pp. xiv, 132. Index. $17.50, cloth; $7.95, paper. Distributed by University Press of America, Inc.

Lowe, James Trapier. *Our Colonial Heritage: Diplomatic and Military.* Lanham, New York, London: University Press of America, 1987. Pp. x, 326. Index. $32.50, cloth; $19.75, paper.

Marshall, Burke (ed.). *A Workable Government? The Constitution After 200 Years.* New York and London: W. W. Norton & Company, 1987. Pp. x, 262. Index. $19.95, cloth; $9.95, paper.

Reams, Bernard D., Jr., and Stuart D. Yoak. *The Constitution of the United States: A Guide and Bibliography to Current Scholarly Research.* Dobbs Ferry: Oceana Publications, Inc., 1987. Pp. xvii, 545. Indexes. $65.

Sheleff, Leon Shaskolsky. *Ultimate Penalties: Capital Punishment, Life Imprisonment, Physical Torture.* Columbus: The Ohio State University Press, 1987. Pp. xi, 492. Indexes. $27.50.

Siegan, Bernard H. *The Supreme Court's Constitution: An Inquiry Into Judicial Review and Its Impact on Society.* New Brunswick and Oxford: Transaction Books, 1987. Pp. xi, 215. Indexes. $29.95, cloth; $14.95, paper.

Arms Control & Disarmament

Calvo-Goller, Notburga K., and Michel A. Calvo. *The SALT Agreements: Content—Application—Verification.* Dordrecht, Boston, Lancaster: Martinus Nijhoff Publishers, 1987. Pp. xxvi, 428. Index. Dfl.135; $66.50; £46.50.

Garthoff, Raymond L. *Policy Versus the Law: The Reinterpretation of the ABM Treaty.* Washington: The Brookings Institution, 1987. Pp. x, 117. $8.95.

McMillan, Stuart. *Neither Confirm Nor Deny: The Nuclear Ships Dispute between New Zealand and the United States.* New York, Westport, London: Praeger, 1987. Pp. viii, 177. Index. $37.95.

Pogany, Istvan (ed.). *Nuclear Weapons and International Law.* New York: St. Martin's Press, 1987. Pp. xiii, 253. Index. $35.

Stützle, Walther, Bhupendra Jasani and Regina Cowen (eds.). *The ABM Treaty: To Defend or Not to Defend?* Published under the auspices of the Stockholm International Peace Research Institute. Oxford and New York: Oxford University Press, 1987. Pp. x, 219. Index. £8.95.

Weeramantry, C. G. *Nuclear Weapons and Scientific Responsibility.* Wolfeboro, N.H.: Longwood Academic, 1987. Pp. vi, 188. $25.

Development

World Development Report 1987. Published for The World Bank. New York: Oxford University Press, 1987. Pp. xii, 285. $26, cloth; $12.95, paper.

International Relations & Politics

Binnendijk, Hans, with Peggy Nalle and Diane Bendahmane (eds.). *Authoritarian Regimes in Transition.* Washington: Foreign Service Institute, U.S. Department of State, 1987. Pp. xxvi, 336.

Burlet, Jacques de. *Traité de l'état civil. Volume II: Les relations internationales.* Brussels: Maison F. Larcier, S.A., 1987. Pp. 243. Index. BF 1,975.

Prescott, J. R. V. *Political Frontiers and Boundaries.* London and Boston: Allen & Unwin, 1987. Pp. xv, 315. Index. $39.95.

Starke, Linda (ed.). *State of the World 1987.* New York and London: W. W. Norton & Company, 1987. Pp. xvii, 268. Index. $18.95, cloth; $9.95, paper.

Regional & Foreign Law & Politics

Ansay, Tuğrul, and Don Wallace, Jr. (eds.). *Introduction to Turkish Law* (3d ed.). Deventer: Kluwer Law and Taxation Publishers, 1987. Pp. xiv, 279. Index. Dfl.94; £29; $46.

Bell, J. Bowyer. *The Gun in Politics: An Analysis of Irish Political Conflict, 1916–1986.* New Brunswick and Oxford: Transaction Books, 1987. Pp. x, 371. Index. $24.95.

Chiu, Hungdah, Y. C. Jao and Yuan-li Wu (eds.). *The Future of Hong Kong: Toward 1997 and Beyond.* New York, Westport, London: Quorum Books, 1987. Pp. vi, 262. Index. $45.

Ioffe, Olimpiad S., and Peter B. Maggs. *The Soviet Economic System: A Legal Analysis.* Boulder and London: Westview Press, 1987. Pp. ix, 326. Index. $45.

Jacobini, H. B. *Romanian Public Law: Some Leading Internal Aspects.* Boulder: East European Monographs, 1987. Pp. ix, 182. Index. $25. Distributed by Columbia University Press.

Sethi, S. Prakash (ed.). *The South African Quagmire: In Search of a Peaceful Path to Democratic Pluralism.* Cambridge, Mass.: Ballinger Publishing Company, 1987. Pp. xvi, 444. $29.95.

Taggart, Michael (ed.). *Judicial Review of Administrative Action in the 1980s: Problems and Prospects.* Auckland: Oxford University Press, in association with the Legal Research Foundation Inc., 1986. Pp. xx, 208. Index. $42.50.

Thoolen, Hans (ed.). *Indonesia and the Rule of Law: Twenty Years of 'New Order' Government.* A study prepared by the International Commission of Jurists and the Netherlands Institute of Human Rights (SIM). London: Frances Pinter (Publishers), 1987. Pp. xii, 208. $30. Distributed by Columbia University Press.

Wiarda, Howard J., and Mark Falcoff, with Ernest Evans and Jiri and Virginia Valenta. *The Communist Challenge in the Caribbean and Central America.* Washington: American Enterprise Institute for Public Policy Research, 1987. Pp. xiv, 249. Index. $24.75, cloth; $11.50, paper. Distributed by University Press of America, Inc.

Miscellaneous

Staudt, Ronald W., and Bernard J. Farber (eds.). *The Dow Jones–Irwin Handbook of Microcomputer Applications in Law.* Homewood, Ill.: Dow Jones–Irwin, 1987. Published under the auspices of the American Bar Association. Pp. xviii, 278. Index. Demonstration diskette included. $120.

INTERNATIONAL LEGAL MATERIALS*

CONTENTS

VOL. XXVI, NO. 5 (September 1987)

PAGE

TREATIES AND AGREEMENTS

Bahrain–Kuwait–Qatar–Saudi Arabia–United Arab Emirates: *Charter Establishing Gulf Cooperation Council,* Including Rules of Procedure and Unified Economic Agreement 1131

Costa Rica–El Salvador–Guatemala–Honduras–Nicaragua: Agreement on *Procedure for Establishing Firm and Lasting Peace in Central America* 1164

India–Sri Lanka: Agreement to Establish *Peace and Normalcy in Sri Lanka* 1175

Syrian Arab Republic–Syrian Petroleum Co.–Pecten Ash Sham Company–Syria Shell Petroleum Development B.V.–Deminex Petroleum Syria GMBH: Contract for the *Exploration, Development and Production of Petroleum* 1186

United Nations: Convention on *Conditions for Registration of Ships* 1229

JUDICIAL AND SIMILAR PROCEEDINGS

Belgium: Commercial Court (Namur) Decision in Shareholders *v.* Compagnie de Saint-Gobain (*Extraterritorial Effects of French Nationalization Law*) 1251

International Court of Justice: Advisory Opinion on Application for Review of Judgment No. 333 of the U.N. Administrative Tribunal (*Yakimetz Case*) 1264

United Nations Secretary-General: Ruling on *Rainbow Warrior Affair* between France and New Zealand 1346

United States: Court of Appeals for the Second Circuit Decision in Amerada Hess Shipping Corporation and United Carriers, Inc. *v.* Argentine Republic (*Jurisdiction over Claim that Foreign Sovereign Violated International Law; Alien Tort Statute; Foreign Sovereign Immunities Act*) 1374

LEGISLATION AND REGULATIONS

France: Laws concerning the *Privatization of Nationalized Enterprises* 1388

OTHER DOCUMENTS

United States: Securities and Exchange Commission *No-Action Letters concerning the French Privatization Program* 1408

FEATURE DOCUMENTS

Iran-Iraq War and Navigation in the Gulf 1422

The Incident of the *U.S.S. Stark* 1423

Statements 1423

Letters to Congress 1425

Map Pinpointing Incident 1426

U.S.-Iraqi Exchange of Notes on Liability and Compensation 1427

The *U.S. Plan to Protect Kuwaiti Ships in the Gulf by Putting Them under U.S. Flags* 1429

Statements 1429

Map Indicating Silkworm Missile Sites 1432

Secretary of Defense Report (Weinberger Report) 1433

Senator Nunn's Response to Weinberger Report 1464

* ILM subscription, $100; concessionary rate to ASIL members, $50. Address orders to ILM, 2223 Massachusetts Ave., NW, Wash., D.C. 20008. Outside U.S., please add $5.50.

The *United Nations Security Council Resolution Calling for an Immediate Cease-fire* . 1479
Security Council Resolution 598 (1987) 1479
Iranian Response to Resolution 1481
Iraqi Response to Resolution 1485

RECENT ACTIONS REGARDING TREATIES TO WHICH THE UNITED STATES IS A PARTY 1488
RECENT ACTIONS REGARDING TREATIES TO WHICH THE UNITED STATES IS NOT A PARTY 1490
NOTICE OF OTHER RECENT DOCUMENTS (not reproduced) 1491

VOL. XXVI, NO. 6 (November 1987)

Cumulative Table of Contents for Volume XXVI i

TREATIES AND AGREEMENTS
African Petroleum Producing Countries: Agreement Establishing the *African Petroleum Producers' Association* 1493
Belgium–Canada–Italy–Netherlands–Union of Soviet Socialist Republics: Agreement on the *Resolution of Practical Problems with respect to Deep Seabed Mining Areas*, and Exchange of Notes between the United States and the Parties to the Agreement 1502
United Nations
Vienna Convention for the *Protection of the Ozone Layer* 1516
Montreal Protocol on *Substances that Deplete the Ozone Layer* 1541

JUDICIAL AND SIMILAR PROCEEDINGS
Iran–United States Claims Tribunal:
Iran *v.* United States Case concerning the *Balance Remaining in the Fund Held by the Federal Reserve Bank of New York pursuant to the Algiers Accords*
Interlocutory Award 1562
Partial Award with Concurring Opinion 1581
Iran *v.* United States Case concerning *Interpretation of Algiers Declarations with respect to Whether U.S. is Obligated to Satisfy Promptly any Award Rendered in Favor of Iran against U.S. Nationals*—Decision 1592
United Kingdom: High Court of Justice (Queen's Bench Division, Commercial Court) Judgment in Libyan Arab Foreign Bank *v.* Bankers Trust Company (*Extraterritoriality of U.S. Order to Freeze Libyan Assets; Banking Procedures for Clearing Eurodollar Accounts; Status of Accounts Held in London*) 1600

OTHER DOCUMENTS
United Nations
International Conference on Drug Abuse and Illicit Trafficking: Decisions of the Conference
Comprehensive *Multidisciplinary Outline of Future Activities in Drug Abuse Control* 1637
Declaration of the International Conference on Drug Abuse and Illicit Trafficking 1722
Preparatory Commission for the International Sea-Bed Authority and for the International Tribunal for the Law of the Sea:
Statement of *Understanding for Proceeding with Deep Sea-Bed Mining Applications* 1725
Decision of the General Committee on the *Application of India as a Pioneer Investor* 1728

RECENT ACTIONS REGARDING TREATIES TO WHICH THE UNITED STATES IS A PARTY 1736
RECENT ACTIONS REGARDING TREATIES TO WHICH THE UNITED STATES IS NOT A PARTY 1742
NOTICE OF OTHER RECENT DOCUMENTS (not reproduced) 1743
INDEX TO VOLUME XXVI 1745

ANNUAL PATRON, SUPPORTING, AND CONTRIBUTING MEMBERS OF THE AMERICAN SOCIETY OF INTERNATIONAL LAW 1987–1988

ANNUAL PATRON

Eli Whitney Debevoise

SUPPORTING

Mitchell Brock
Charles N. Brower
Alexander D. Calhoun
William Gilbert Carter
Anthony A. D'Amato
Robert MacCrate
William B. Matteson
Covey T. Oliver
George M. Pavia
Walter S. Surrey
Peter W. Thornton
Peter D. Trooboff
Jack G. Wasserman
Basil S. Yanakakis

CONTRIBUTING

Richard L. Abbott
Richard B. M. Abrams
Richard C. Allison
Manuel R. Angulo
Steven Wright Baker
Gordon L. Becker
J. Truman Bidwell
Roman A. Bninski
John Arthur Boyd
George W. Brandt
Aron Broches
Richard P. Brown
David Carliner
C. J. Chen
Donald E. Claudy
Philip F. Cohen
John P. Corrigan
Samuel S. Cross
Michael Danaher
John L. A. De Passalaqua
George C. Denney
James M. Denny
Edward A. Dragon
Malcolm T. Dungan
Richard A. Eastman
Aly H. Elghatit
F. Javier Fabregat
Philip A. Faix, Jr.
Stanley F. Farrar
Benjamin B. Ferencz
John Basil Gantt
David G. Gill
Michael A. Gleim
Joseph Gold
L. F. E. Goldie
Thomas R. Graham
Ernest A. Gross
James V. Hackney
Herbert J. Hansell
Joel B. Harris
Thomas E. Haven
H. Healy
Cecil Hunt
Oliver T. Johnson
Joseph S. Kaplan
Charles J. Keever
Lee A. Kimball
Paul L. Laskin

James Leitner
Robert T. Lemon, II
Edwin Deane Leonard
Jacques L. Leroy
David M. Levitan
George N. Lindsay
Carlos A. Lopez-Guevara
G. Lorinczi
Ralph M. McDowell
A. F. Maulsby
Gerald D. Morgan
Frank E. Nattier
Franz M. Oppenheimer
Guillermo F. Peroni
Jose Martins Pinheiro Neto
Willis L. M. Reese
A. R. Richstein
Bruce L. Rockwood
James F. Sams
J. P. Schwebel
Charles M. Spofford
Samuel A. Stern
Isaac N. P. Stokes
Robert M. Thomas, Jr.
Sigmund Timberg
Robert B. von Mehren
Paul C. Warnke
John Stowell Williams
F. L. Wiswall
Richard Young

LIFE MEMBERS OF THE AMERICAN SOCIETY OF INTERNATIONAL LAW 1987–1988

Gerald Aksen
Stanley Anderson
Masahiko Asada
Calvin A. Behle
Richard S. S. Bright
John C. Brooks
Ian Brownlie
John Carey
Chin-Yung Chao
Stephen S. F. Chen
Max Chopnick
J. G. Clarke
H. Alberta Colclaser
Carter K. Combe
Rebecca J. Cook
Jorge Antonio De Marzi
Dermott J. Devine
John E. Donnelly
Peter D. Ehrenhaft
Robert Eikel
Richard J. Erickson
Eleanor H. Finch
Richard I. Fine
Roger D. Fisher
Carl Mason Franklin
Gaudencio Garcia
Moti Lal Govila
Robert T. Greig
Joseph P. Griffin
Richard Kennedy Guelff
Judith R. Hall
Robert D. Hayton
Dan F. Henderson
Robert E. Herzstein
Gary N. Horlick
Christopher C. Joyner
William S. Kenney
Yoshito Kita
Elizabeth Lay
Monroe Leigh
Frankie Fook-lu Leung
Cynthia C. Lichtenstein
Mrs. Brunson MacChesney
Myres Smith McDougal
Samuel Pyeatt Menefee
John M. Metzger
Clifford L. Michel
James A. R. Nafziger
Andre W. G. Newburg
Hisashi Owada
Mauricio Perez-Badell
Hernán Pérez Loose
Ellis L. Phillips
Jane M. Picker
Robert J. Radway
Charles S. Rhyne
Elliot L. Richardson
Alfred P. Rubin
Mark Sandstrom
Tetsuo Sato
Oscar Schachter
Cabot Sedgwick
Yukio Shimada
William I. Shore
Anne Patricia Simons
Dwight J. Simpson
Owen Meredith Smaw
Earl A. Snyder
Jane Sommerich
John H. Spencer
Henry J. Steiner
Edward P. Torrey
Tullio Treves
J. W. Van Der Zanden
L. W. Wadsworth
Edith Brown Weiss
Elmer E. Welty
Ulrich Woelker
C. U. Zachrisson
Peaches Zaphiriou

Vol. 13, No. 9 September 1987

INTERNATIONAL LAW & TRADE PERSPECTIVE

THE CONGRESS

Foreign Relations Authorization Act 2
The ABM Treaty Interpretation Resolution . . . 6
H.R. 3 Trade Subconferences 7

THE COURTS

The "In" Porters, S.A. v. Hanes Printables, Inc. . . 7
Baglab Limited v. Johnson Matthey Bankers Limited . . 9
Zernicek v. Brown & Root, Inc. 10

THE LEGAL PERIODICALS

Active Defense: State Military Response to International Terrorism 11
Settlement of the Question of Hong Kong 11
Terrorism, Insurgency and Geopolitics: The Errors of U.S. Foreign Policy 12
The Response of the "Escape Clause" of the GATT and Section 201 of the Tariff and Trade Act of 1974 to the Needs of Developing Countries 12
The Future of International Commercial Arbitration: A Single Transnational Institution? 13
The Future of Multilateralism and Efforts to Combat International Terrorism 13
Input Dumping and Upstream Subsidies: Trade Loopholes Which Need Closing 14
Civil Remedies for Uncivil Wrongs: Combating Terrorism Through Transnational Public Law Litigation . . . 14
Private International Law in the People's Republic of China: Principles and Procedures 15
Topic Issue - Intervention 15
New Student International Law Journal 17
Contents of Journals Received 17

NOTABLES

Treaty Interpretation - Theory and Reality 20
Antidumping and Countervailing Duties and the GATT: An Evaluation and a Proposal for a Unified Remedy for Unfair International Trade 20
Annotation - Right to Asylum Notice 20

P.O. Box 27495
Washington, D.C. 20038

AMERICAN SOCIETY OF INTERNATIONAL LAW
2223 MASSACHUSETTS AVENUE, N.W., WASHINGTON, D.C. 20008-2864, (202) 265-4313
Be sure to check membership type on reverse side.

Name (please print) ______________________

Mailing Address ______________________

Street, P.O. Box, etc. ______________________

City, State, Zip ______________________

Country ______________ Phone ______________

Member, U.S. Bar?______ State:______ Year______

School, Firm or Other Affiliation:______________________
(name & address)
____

Please start my membership January 1, ________. Membership is on a calendar year basis, and includes the *Journal* and the *Newsletter.* Check below for special rate on *Proceedings* or *International Legal Materials.*

☐ *Proceedings of the Annual Meeting,* at $15.
☐ *International Legal Materials.* Subscription at special member rate of $50 (plus $5.50 for mailing outside U.S.A.) for six issues per year.

VERIFICATION OF STUDENT STATUS. I hereby certify that the above applicant is regularly registered in

School:______________________ Completion year:__________

Signed______________________Title______________________Date__________

$__________ **Amount Enclosed** (U.S. Dollars) Signature______________________

AMERICAN SOCIETY OF INTERNATIONAL LAW
2223 MASSACHUSETTS AVENUE, N.W., WASHINGTON, D.C. 20008-2864, (202) 265-4313
Be sure to check membership type on reverse side.

Name (please print) ______________________

Mailing Address ______________________

Street, P.O. Box, etc. ______________________

City, State, Zip ______________________

Country ______________ Phone ______________

Member, U.S. Bar?______ State:______ Year______

School, Firm or Other Affiliation:______________________
(name & address)
____

Please start my membership January 1, ________. Membership is on a calendar year basis, and includes the *Journal* and the *Newsletter.* Check below for special rate on *Proceedings* or *International Legal Materials.*

☐ *Proceedings of the Annual Meeting,* at $15.
☐ *International Legal Materials.* Subscription at special member rate of $50 (plus $5.50 for mailing outside U.S.A.) for six issues per year.

VERIFICATION OF STUDENT STATUS. I hereby certify that the above applicant is regularly registered in

School:______________________ Completion year:__________

Signed______________________Title______________________Date__________

$__________ **Amount Enclosed** (U.S. Dollars) Signature______________________

AMERICAN SOCIETY OF INTERNATIONAL LAW
2223 MASSACHUSETTS AVENUE, N.W., WASHINGTON, D.C. 20008-2864, (202) 265-4313
Be sure to check membership type on reverse side.

Name (please print) ______________________

Mailing Address ______________________

Street, P.O. Box, etc. ______________________

City, State, Zip ______________________

Country ______________ Phone ______________

Member, U.S. Bar?______ State:______ Year______

School, Firm or Other Affiliation:______________________
(name & address)
____

Please start my membership January 1, ________. Membership is on a calendar year basis, and includes the *Journal* and the *Newsletter.* Check below for special rate on *Proceedings* or *International Legal Materials.*

☐ *Proceedings of the Annual Meeting,* at $15.
☐ *International Legal Materials.* Subscription at special member rate of $50 (plus $5.50 for mailing outside U.S.A.) for six issues per year.

VERIFICATION OF STUDENT STATUS. I hereby certify that the above applicant is regularly registered in

School:______________________ Completion year:__________

Signed______________________Title______________________Date__________

$__________ **Amount Enclosed** (U.S. Dollars) Signature

Membership Status *(Check one)**

☐ **Regular Membership:**
$70 a year. Persons, regardless of nationality or profession, resident in a member country of the OECD (see below).

☐ **Special Membership:**
$30 a year. Persons *not* resident in a member country of the OECD (see below).

☐ **Intermediate Membership:**
$30 a year. Persons who are under 30 years of age at the time of application for membership may be Intermediate Members for the first three consecutive years of membership.
Date of Birth ______________________

☐ **Student Membership:**
$20 a year, and certification of student status (see form on reverse).

The member countries of the OECD are Australia, Austria, Belgium, Canada, Denmark, Federal Republic of Germany, Finland, France, Greece, Iceland, Ireland, Italy, Japan, Luxembourg, Netherlands, New Zealand, Norway, Portugal, Spain, Sweden, Switzerland, Turkey, United Kingdom, United States.

☐ **Contributing Membership:**
$100 a year.

☐ **Supporting Membership:**
$200 a year.

☐ **Annual Patron:**
$500 a year. Any individual or organization eligible for membership may become an Annual Patron for a contribution of at least $500.

☐ **Retired Membership:**
$25 a year. Persons who are age 70 and older, and retired.

☐ **Corporate Membership:**
$1,500 a year. Any corporation, partnership, association, or other organization acceptable to the Executive Council is eligible for Corporate Membership.

☐ **Life Membership:**
$1,000 payment.

☐ **Patron:**
One-time contribution of $5,000.

*Includes $30 allocation for *The American Journal of International Law*

Membership Status *(Check one)**

☐ **Regular Membership:**
$70 a year. Persons, regardless of nationality or profession, resident in a member country of the OECD (see below).

☐ **Special Membership:**
$30 a year. Persons *not* resident in a member country of the OECD (see below).

☐ **Intermediate Membership:**
$30 a year. Persons who are under 30 years of age at the time of application for membership may be Intermediate Members for the first three consecutive years of membership.
Date of Birth ______________________

☐ **Student Membership:**
$20 a year, and certification of student status (see form on reverse).

The member countries of the OECD are Australia, Austria, Belgium, Canada, Denmark, Federal Republic of Germany, Finland, France, Greece, Iceland, Ireland, Italy, Japan, Luxembourg, Netherlands, New Zealand, Norway, Portugal, Spain, Sweden, Switzerland, Turkey, United Kingdom, United States.

☐ **Contributing Membership:**
$100 a year.

☐ **Supporting Membership:**
$200 a year.

☐ **Annual Patron:**
$500 a year. Any individual or organization eligible for membership may become an Annual Patron for a contribution of at least $500.

☐ **Retired Membership:**
$25 a year. Persons who are age 70 and older, and retired.

☐ **Corporate Membership:**
$1,500 a year. Any corporation, partnership, association, or other organization acceptable to the Executive Council is eligible for Corporate Membership.

☐ **Life Membership:**
$1,000 payment.

☐ **Patron:**
One-time contribution of $5,000.

*Includes $30 allocation for *The American Journal of International Law*

Membership Status *(Check one)**

☐ **Regular Membership:**
$70 a year. Persons, regardless of nationality or profession, resident in a member country of the OECD (see below).

☐ **Special Membership:**
$30 a year. Persons *not* resident in a member country of the OECD (see below).

☐ **Intermediate Membership:**
$30 a year. Persons who are under 30 years of age at the time of application for membership may be Intermediate Members for the first three consecutive years of membership.
Date of Birth ______________________

☐ **Student Membership:**
$20 a year, and certification of student status (see form on reverse).

The member countries of the OECD are Australia, Austria, Belgium, Canada, Denmark, Federal Republic of Germany, Finland, France, Greece, Iceland, Ireland, Italy, Japan, Luxembourg, Netherlands, New Zealand, Norway, Portugal, Spain, Sweden, Switzerland, Turkey, United Kingdom, United States.

☐ **Contributing Membership:**
$100 a year.

☐ **Supporting Membership:**
$200 a year.

☐ **Annual Patron:**
$500 a year. Any individual or organization eligible for membership may become an Annual Patron for a contribution of at least $500.

☐ **Retired Membership:**
$25 a year. Persons who are age 70 and older, and retired.

☐ **Corporate Membership:**
$1,500 a year. Any corporation, partnership, association, or other organization acceptable to the Executive Council is eligible for Corporate Membership.

☐ **Life Membership:**
$1,000 payment.

☐ **Patron:**
One-time contribution of $5,000.

*Includes $30 allocation for *The American Journal of International*

American Journal of International Law

April 1988
Vol. 82 No. 2

Published by
American Society of International Law

PATRONS OF THE SOCIETY

PATRONAGE, GIFTS AND BEQUESTS

Upon donation to the Society of $5,000 or more by gift or bequest, any member of the Society or individual eligible for membership may be elected a Patron of the Society. Upon donation of at least $5,000 in the name of a deceased person, such person may be elected a Patron posthumously.

Gifts and bequests may be made in the name of the American Society of International Law, Washington, D.C. Such contributions are deductible from federal returns for income, estate and gift tax purposes. The Society is incorporated by Act of Congress approved September 20, 1950 (64 Stat. 869).

MANLEY O. HUDSON MEDAL

The American Society of International Law bestows from time to time without regard to nationality a gold medal to commemorate the life work of Manley O. Hudson. Such awards are made for preeminent scholarship and achievement in international law and in the promotion of the establishment and maintenance of international relations on the basis of law and justice. Medals have been awarded to Manley O. Hudson (1956), Lord McNair (1959), Philip C. Jessup (1964), Charles De Visscher (1966), Paul Guggenheim (1970), Myres S. McDougal (1976), Eduardo Jiménez de Aréchaga (1978), Richard Reeve Baxter (1981), Oscar Schachter (1981), Hardy Cross Dillard (1982), Suzanne Bastid (1984), Marjorie M. Whiteman (1985) and Leo Gross (1986).

The AMERICAN JOURNAL OF INTERNATIONAL LAW (ISSN 0002-9300) is published quarterly, in January, April, July and October, and is supplied to all members of the American Society of International Law. Annual subscription rate to nonmembers is $50.00, plus $4.00 postage outside U.S.A.

EDITORIAL OFFICE:
NEW YORK UNIVERSITY SCHOOL OF LAW
40 WASHINGTON SQUARE SOUTH
NEW YORK, N.Y. 10012

BUSINESS OFFICE:
2223 MASSACHUSETTS AVENUE, N.W.
WASHINGTON, D.C. 20008-2864

Second-class postage paid at Washington, D.C. and at additional mailing office. POSTMASTER: If undeliverable, send notice on Form 3579 to the American Journal of International Law, 2223 Massachusetts Ave., N.W., Washington, D.C. 20008-2864.

Printed by Lancaster Press, Lancaster, Pa. 17603

AMERICAN JOURNAL OF INTERNATIONAL LAW

VOL. 82 April 1988 NO. 2

CONTENTS

		PAGE
Threats of Force	*Romana Sadurska*	239
Terrorism on the High Seas: The Achille Lauro, Piracy and the IMO Convention on Maritime Safety	*Malvina Halberstam*	269
Agora: Is the ASIL Policy on Divestment in Violation of International Law? Further Observations		
The Action Violates International Law and Policy	*George N. Barrie*	311
The Action Does Not Violate International Law	*Paul C. Szasz*	314
Editorial Comment		
Improving the Image of the United States in International Human Rights	*Louis B. Sohn*	319
Notes and Comments		
Professor William W. Bishop, Jr. (1906–1987):		
A Tribute	*Eric Stein*	321
Personal Recollections	*Elizabeth S. Bishop*	323
Alien Tort Claims, Sovereign Immunity and International Law in U.S. Courts	*Frederic L. Kirgis, Jr.*	323
Correspondence		331
Contemporary Practice of the United States Relating to International Law	*Marian Nash Leich*	336
Judicial Decisions	*Monroe Leigh*	351
Current Developments		
Statement by Expert Panel: Deep Seabed Mining and the 1982 Convention on the Law of the Sea		363
Triennial Elections of Five Members of the International Court of Justice		369
Book Reviews and Notes	*Edited by Detlev Vagts*	
D'Amato, Anthony. *International Law: Process and Prospect* (Frederic L. Kirgis, Jr.)		370
Recueil des Cours de l'Académie de Droit International de La Haye, 1985. 4 vols. (Thomas Carothers)		374
Malekian, Farhad. *The System of International Law: Formation, Treaties, Responsibility* (Harold G. Maier)		381
Nguyen Quoc Dinh (Patrick Daillier and Alain Pellet eds.). *Droit International Public* (3d ed.) (Elisabeth Zoller)		384
Carreau, Dominique. *Droit International* (Elisabeth Zoller)		385
Rosenne, Shabtai. *Breach of Treaty* (Herbert W. Briggs)		387

Sondaal, Henricus Hermanus Maria. *De Nederlandse Verdragspraktijk* (Theo van Boven) 389
Dugard, John. *Recognition and the United Nations* (M. J. Peterson) 391
Schwebel, Stephen M. *International Arbitration: Three Salient Problems* (Herbert W. Briggs) 394
Entin, M. L. *Mezhdunarodnye sudebnye uchrezhdenya* (Richard Szawlowski) 396
Henrikson, Alan K. (ed.). *Negotiating World Order: The Artisanship and Architecture of Global Diplomacy* (Lawrence S. Finkelstein) 399
Rebagliati, Orlando Rubén. *La Plataforma Continental y su límite exterior* (David D. Caron) 403
Hossain, Kamal, and Subrata Roy Chowdhury (eds.). *Permanent Sovereignty Over Natural Resources in International Law: Principle and Practice* (Thomas W. Wälde) 405
Boutard-Labarde, Marie-Chantal. *Nationalisations Imposées—Nationalisations Négociées* (Rudolf Dolzer) 409
Dowty, Alan. *Closed Borders: The Contemporary Assault on Freedom of Movement* (Peter H. Schuck) 411
Bassiouni, M. Cherif (ed.). *New Horizons in International Criminal Law* (William Sumner Kenney) 413
Swinarski, Christophe. *Studies and essays on international humanitarian law and Red Cross principles in honour of Jean Pictet* (Alfred-Maurice de Zayas) 416
Dashwood, Alan, Richard Hacon and Robin White. *A Guide to the Civil Jurisdiction and Judgments Convention* (David G. Litt) 419
Josephson, Harold (ed.). *Biographical Dictionary of Modern Peace Leaders* (F. M. Carroll) 419
Uschakow, Alexander, and Dietrich Frenzke. *Der Warschauer Pakt und seine bilateralen Bündnisverträge: Analyse und Texte* (Kazimierz Grzybowski) 420
McWhinney, Edward. *Supreme Courts and Judicial Law-Making: Constitutional Tribunals and Constitutional Review* (Mauro Cappelletti) 421
Seward, Bernard L., Jr. (ed.). *Technology Control, Competition and National Security: Conflict and Consensus* (Kenneth W. Abbott) 425
Lebiecki, Andrzej E. *Załatwianie Międzynarodowych Sporów Gospodarczych* (Jay G. Polach) 428
Szász, Iván. *The CMEA Uniform Law for International Sales* (2d rev. ed.) (John O. Honnold) 429
Khadduri, Majid. *The Islamic Conception of Justice* (Joseph L. Brand) 431
McCreary, Don R. *Japanese-U.S. Business Negotiations: A Cross-Cultural Study* (Walter L. Ames) 433
Briefer Notices: Remacha, 435; Castel, de Mestral and Graham, 436.
Books Received 436
International Legal Materials. Contents, Vol. XXVII, No. 1 (January 1988) and No. 2 (March 1988) 439

The American Journal of International Law

The views expressed in the articles, editorial comments, book reviews and notes, and other contributions which appear in AJIL are those of the individual authors and are not to be taken as representing the views of the Board of Editors or the American Society of International Law.

Manuscripts in triplicate may be sent to the Editor in Chief of AJIL, Professor Thomas M. Franck, New York University School of Law, New York, N.Y. 10012. All footnotes should be typed double space at the end of the manuscript. Please do not make multiple submissions to other journals. Persons making submissions are invited to indicate whether their manuscript is available on an IBM-PC diskette. AJIL uses WordPerfect 4.2. Subscriptions, orders for back numbers, correspondence with reference to AJIL and books for review should be sent to the AMERICAN JOURNAL OF INTERNATIONAL LAW (ISSN 0002-9300), 2223 Massachusetts Avenue, N.W., Washington, D.C. 20008-2864.

The American Society of International Law

The American Society of International Law was organized in 1906 "to foster the study of international law and to promote the establishment and maintenance of international relations on the basis of law and justice."

Society membership is open to all persons of whatever nationality and profession who are interested in its objectives. Dues are: regular, $70; special category, $30 for persons *not* resident in a member country of the Organisation for Economic Co-operation and Development; intermediate, $30; student, $20. Membership application form is printed at the back of each issue of AJIL.

* (1906–1987). † (1898–1987).
‡ (1903–1987).

THREATS OF FORCE

*By Romana Sadurska**

International agreements apparently treat an unauthorized threat of force and the actual use of force as equally grave, yet distinct, wrongs.[1] If, however, formal legal appraisals of specific situations are taken as indicators of existing practice, it seems that the threat of force has no separate significance, as it were, beyond the use of force:[2] either it precedes actual violence and therefore is eclipsed in legal appraisals by the latter,[3] or it is not followed by the use of force and thus ceases to demand prompt legal consideration. Such an attitude toward the question of threat implicitly acknowledges that threats of force are a ubiquitous element of international relations and that they may not be detrimental, indeed may even be beneficial, to the preserva-

* Lecturer, Faculty of Law, University of Sydney. I gratefully acknowledge useful comments and criticism of Christine Chinkin, James Crawford, Paul Finn, David Mason and Wojciech Sadurski.

[1] Article 2(4) of the United Nations Charter provides: "All members shall refrain in their international relations from the threat *or* use of force against the territorial integrity or political independence of any state, or in any other manner inconsistent with the Purposes of the United Nations" (emphasis added). *See also* UN CHARTER art. 39. The Declaration on Principles of International Law Concerning Friendly Relations and Co-operation among States in Accordance with the Charter of the United Nations, GA Res. 2625 (XXV) (Oct. 24, 1970), *reprinted in* 65 AJIL 246 (1971), proclaims that every state has "a duty to refrain" from a threat or use of force (against the territorial integrity or political independence, etc.) and characterizes them as "a violation of international law." The Declaration on the Inadmissibility of Intervention in the Domestic Affairs of States and the Protection of Their Independence and Sovereignty, GA Res. 2131 (XX) (Dec. 12, 1965), *reprinted in* 60 AJIL 663 (1966), provides: "No state has the right to intervene . . . in the internal or external affairs of any other state. Consequently, armed intervention and all other forms of interference or attempted threats . . . are condemned." *See also* Art. 2, Agreement Governing Activities of States on the Moon and Other Celestial Bodies, GA Res. 34/68 (Dec. 5, 1979), *reprinted in* 18 ILM 1434 (1979) (entered into force July 11, 1984); and Art. 2, Draft Code of Offences Against the Peace and Security of Mankind, [1984] 1 Y.B. INT'L L. COMM'N 4, UN Doc. E/CN.4/SER.A/1984.

[2] Commenting on Article 2(4), Schachter observes: "Curiously, it has not been invoked much as an explicit prohibition of such implied threats." Schachter, *The Right of States to Use Armed Force,* 82 MICH. L. REV. 1620, 1625 (1984). Hopple, Rossa & Wilkenfeld, *Threat and Foreign Policy: The Overt Behavior of States in Conflict,* in 5 SAGE INT'L Y.B. FOREIGN POL'Y STUD., THREATS, WEAPONS AND FOREIGN POLICY 19 (P. McGovan & C. W. Kegley, Jr., eds. 1980), state: "Aside from the work of Charles McClelland, few researchers have attempted to analyze the idea of threat as either a theoretical concept or an empirical phenomenon." *See also id.* at 39–40 nn.2–3.

[3] E.g., in Military and Paramilitary Activities in and against Nicaragua (Nicar. v. U.S.), Merits, 1986 ICJ REP. 14 (Judgment of June 27) [hereinafter Nicaragua v. U.S.], Nicaragua claimed that the United States "in breach of its obligations under general and customary international law, has used . . . the threat of force against Nicaragua" (*id.* at 19). But the Court concentrated on the actual use of force or acts that, in its interpretation, amounted to the use of force.

tion of international order. On the other hand, the attitude of apparent tolerance of threats of force ignores that they produce consequences whether or not they are followed by resort to force and for this reason need to be scrutinized more closely and their lawfulness evaluated. This situation reflects a dissonance between the absolutist aspiration of the international principle prohibiting the threat of force and the complex, often ambiguous and rather pragmatic code applied in international practice.

In this paper, I first describe the phenomenon of threat of force and the functions of threats of force in the international community. Next, I discuss the legal status of the threat of force in international law. I argue that in practice international actors, contrary to the official language of international agreements (which equate in this respect the use and the threat of force), recognize a separate set of criteria of lawfulness for the threat of force. This test is less stringent than the one for the use of force and includes consideration of security, the remedial nature of the threat, its rationality and economy, and its consequences. This practical attitude toward the threat of force stems from the preoccupation of international law with international peace and security above all. Moreover, I suggest that states tend to condemn an illicit threat less explicitly and effectively than an illegal use of force, despite the fact that the threat may result in a comparable violation of international law.

I. Phenomenology of Threat

In a recent paper, Oscar Schachter made these observations about the difficulties of ascertaining situations of threat:

> What is meant by a "threat of force" has received rather less consideration. Clearly, a threat to use military action to coerce a state to make concessions is forbidden. But in many situations the deployment of military forces has unstated aims and its effect is equivocal. The preponderance of military strength in some states and their political relations with potential target states may justifiably lead to an inference of a threat of force against the political independence of the target state.[4]

Although Schachter's comment is limited to the interpretation of Article 2(4) of the United Nations Charter,[5] it reflects some of the analytical problems relating to the threat of force in other contexts, for instance, aggression or political intervention. These problems have some bearing on under-

[4] Schachter, *supra* note 2, at 1625.

[5] Schachter concludes that Article 2(4) has a sufficiently determinate content to provide restraints on the use of armed force, and therefore the interpretive questions concerning the meaning of "threat of force" are "peripheral" to his interest. He admits, nonetheless, that "in some situations" they "are of importance . . . and they indicate that the precise scope of the article requires further definition." *Id.* As Stone, *De Victoribus Victis: The International Law Commission and Imposed Treaties of Peace*, 8 VA. J. INT'L L. 356, 372 (1968), observes: "It would surely be a massive inadvertence to many sharp and complex legal controversies surrounding article 2(4) . . . to suggest that the exact scope of article 2(4) itself . . . is in any sense 'clear-cut.' "

standing the functions of threats and appraising their lawfulness. The more important analytical difficulties are the range and often equivocal character of behavior and situations that may amount to a threat of force, the difficulties in proving a threat, the subjective character of perceptions of threat, the ambiguity in the apparent tolerance for certain forms of threat or for certain threateners, and the uncertainty inherent in establishing a causal link between a threat and the subsequent behavior of the target. Hence, it seems useful to precede discussion of the legal status of the threat of force in international law with a description of its anatomy, unobstructed by any normative judgments.

The Concept of Threat

A threat is an act that is designed to create a psychological condition in the target of apprehension, anxiety and eventually fear, which will erode the target's resistance to change or will pressure it toward preserving the status quo.[6] In this sense, the threat of force constitutes a form of coercion because it aims at the deliberate and drastic restriction or suppression by one actor of the choices of another.[7] The application of economic instead of military pressure should make no difference in characterizing the behavior as threatening, even though it may be legal under international law.[8] Also, the lack

[6] In social practice, this method of influencing human behavior is much more frequently employed than actual physical coercion. McDougal, Reisman & Willard, *The World Process of Effective Power: The Global War System,* in POWER AND POLICY IN QUEST OF LAW 353, 376 (M. S. McDougal & W. M. Reisman eds. 1985), observe: "much of the strategic use of bases in the world effective power process involves prepositioning and communication rather than actual use."

[7] As Friedrich A. Hayek put it:

> By "coercion" we mean such control of the environment or circumstances or a person by another that, in order to avoid greater evil, he is forced to act not according to a coherent plan of his own but to serve the ends of another. Except in the sense of choosing the lesser evil in the situation forced on him by another, he is unable either to use his own intelligence or knowledge or to follow his own aims and beliefs.

F. HAYEK, THE CONSTITUTION OF LIBERTY 20–21 (1960).

[8] Several authors argue that economic coercion applied *ad extremis* is capable of destruction of values comparable to the effect of the employment of military force. M. S. MCDOUGAL & F. FELICIANO, LAW AND MINIMUM WORLD PUBLIC ORDER 30–32 (1961); Higgins, *The Legal Limits to the Use of Force by Sovereign States: United Nations Practice,* 37 BRIT. Y.B. INT'L L. 269, 276–77 (1961); D. BOWETT, SELF-DEFENCE IN INTERNATIONAL LAW 24 (1958). The common law courts more and more often accept the doctrine of economic duress under which the threat goes not to the person, but to his or her economic interests. *Cf.* E. A. FARNSWORTH, CONTRACTS 259 (1982); R. GOFF & G. JONES, THE LAW OF RESTITUTION 222–39 (1986). By contrast, the International Court of Justice interprets the notion of force narrowly. Recently, Nicaragua claimed that the actions of an economic nature taken by the United States caused its economy a loss of $36 million per annum. Nicaragua v. U.S., 1986 ICJ REP. at 69. The ICJ not only did not consider this issue in the context of Article 2(4), but also did not even find such actions to be a breach of the customary law principle of nonintervention. *Id.* at 126. But some dicta suggest that the Court's position is ambiguous: "The element of coercion, which defines, and indeed forms the very essence of prohibited intervention, is *particularly obvious* in the case of intervention which uses force . . . ." *Id.* at 108 (emphasis added).

of armed resistance in response[9] should be irrelevant to establishing the existence of threat, except, perhaps, for the highly unlikely situation where a government is so fainthearted as to yield to an obviously implausible threat. The relevant feature of threat as a form of coercion is not so much the kind of force applied, but rather the purpose and outcome of the threat: a genuine reduction in the range of choices otherwise available to states.

International law is not concerned, of course, with all forms of coercion or, in particular, with all forms of threats.[10] Traditionally, it purports to regulate the use and the threat of armed force.[11] Although Article 2(4) of the Charter does not specify the type of coercion it forbids, most writers assume that it refers to the physical use of armed force alone.[12]

In the international arena, a threat of force is a message, explicit or implicit,[13] formulated by a decision maker and directed to the target audience, indicating that force will be used if a rule or demand is not complied with.[14] This message may be expressed in many forms. First, it can be clearly articulated—orally or in a document or communiqué—by stating the claim and indicating the potential consequences of failure to comply. For instance, the British note of August 2, 1946 concluded with the threat that if Alba-

[9] In the discussions in the General Assembly's Sixth Committee in 1952, the Soviet delegate held that the German occupation of Czechoslovakia and Austria in 1938 following a threat of force constituted aggression. 6 UN GAOR C.6 (288th mtg.) at 213, UN Doc. A/C.6/SR.288 (1952). The British delegate, citing the same cases, expressed the opinion that the aggressor might achieve his purpose just as certainly by subverting from within the will to resist of the country attacked as by the use of physical force from outside. 6 UN GAOR C.6 (281st mtg.) at 166, UN Doc. A/C.6/SR.281 (1952).

[10] *See* "The Foundation of International Actors' Approach to the Threat" *infra.*

[11] If one accepts a functional approach to the interpretation of the term "force," "armed force" not only means the military, naval or air forces of a state, but also may include its militia, security and police forces, as well as armed bands, subversives, insurgents and guerrilla groups supported by this state and operating against another state. I. BROWNLIE, INTERNATIONAL LAW AND THE USE OF FORCE BY STATES 361 (1963).

[12] L. GOODRICH, E. HAMBRO & A. SIMONS, CHARTER OF THE UNITED NATIONS: COMMENTARY AND DOCUMENTS 48 (3d rev. ed. 1969). Also a recent colloquy on interpretation of Article 2(4), *Restraints on the Unilateral Use of Force,* 10 YALE J. INT'L L. 261 (1985), including papers by Falk, Gordon, Reisman, Rostow and Schachter. This conclusion, although not contradicted by the *travaux préparatoires* of the Charter, cannot be said to be clearly confirmed by them. The Brazilian proposal to include the words "and from the threat or use of economic measures" was rejected by 26-2 votes. It is not clear, however, why the amendment was rejected. Possibly, the delegates agreed with the representative of Belgium that, given the phrase "or in any other manner," the change was superfluous. Docs. 784, I/1/27; 123, I/1/5; 215, I/1/10, 6 UN CIO Docs. 334–35, 559, 609 (1945). *See also* Paust & Blaustein, *The Arab Oil Weapon—A Threat to International Peace,* 68 AJIL 410, 416–17 (1974) (arguing in favor of a broad interpretation of "force" in Article 2(4)); Farer, *Political and Economic Coercion in Contemporary International Law,* 79 AJIL 405 (1985) (arguing against it).

[13] "The best example of . . . 'concealed threat' was the first Sputnik of October 1957: this great scientific achievement would have been nothing more if the implication that for the first time the USSR could destroy American cities had not been evident." Farrands, *The Regional Use of Force,* in THE USE OF FORCE IN INTERNATIONAL RELATIONS 70, 84–85 (F. Northedge ed. 1974).

[14] I. BROWNLIE, *supra* note 11, at 364, defines a threat as consisting "in an express or implied promise by a government of a resort to force conditional on non-acceptance of certain demands of that government."

nian coastal guards in the future attempted to prevent passage through the Corfu Channel and opened fire on British warships, the fire would be returned.[15]

Second, an explicit, though more general, threat can be included in a defensive alliance treaty (the Warsaw Pact, NATO, SEATO) or a bilateral agreement on military assistance in the event of aggression against one of the parties, or even in a domestic statute.[16]

Third, a threat can also consist in a series of communications whose sequence forms the actual message. In March 1939, the German Government requested that Poland agree to the unification of the Free City of Gdańsk (Danzig) with the Third Reich. The Polish Government refused to comply and, instead, entered into an agreement with the United Kingdom providing for mutual assistance in case of aggression. On April 28, 1939, Germany renounced the Agreement on Non-Aggression with Poland of January 26, 1934,[17] which made the threat of war implicit and imminent.

Fourth, a threat can be deduced from certain positive actions (for instance, moving army units into proximity with the target audience,[18] engaging in military maneuvers,[19] increasing a military budget, or deploying certain weapons[20]) and even from the threatener's failure to take such actions. The U.S. decision to abstain on a Security Council resolution condemning the Israeli air raid on the PLO headquarters in Tunisia on October 1, 1985[21] could be construed as a threat that the United States would respond in a similar fashion to future terrorist attacks, both against the perpetrators and against countries harboring them. This interpretation seemed particularly credible when the message of abstention was read in the context of other U.S. communications, especially Secretary of State George Shultz's exposition of antiterrorist doctrine: "We will need the flexibility to respond to terrorist attacks in a variety of ways, at times and places of our own choosing."[22]

Fifth, the threat may be indirect, i.e., addressed to a proxy target audience, though in fact aimed at reaching the main adversary. Following the flight of the United States U–2 reconnaissance plane over Soviet territory on May 1, 1960, Premier Khrushchev stated:

[15] Corfu Channel case (UK v. Alb.), 1949 ICJ REP. 4, 27 (Judgment of Apr. 9).

[16] Article 36 of the Soviet Law on the State Boundary, VEDOMOSTI SSR, NO. 48, 1982, item 891, *reprinted in English in* 22 ILM 1055 (1983) (entered into force Mar. 1, 1983), provides for the use of weapons against, inter alia, an "intrusion on the territory of the USSR." *See also* text accompanying note 83 *infra.*

[17] THE BRITISH WAR BLUE BOOK, MISC. NO. 9, DOCUMENTS CONCERNING GERMAN-POLISH RELATIONS AND THE OUTBREAK OF HOSTILITIES BETWEEN GREAT BRITAIN AND GERMANY ON SEPTEMBER 3, 1939, at 22–28, 37–40 (1939).

[18] *See* Wright, *Gunboat Diplomacy Updated for the 1980's, Washington Increases Use of Overseas Military Maneuvers,* N.Y. Times, Mar. 13, 1983, §4, at 4, cols. 3, 4, 5.

[19] Ratner, *The Gulf of Sidra Incident of 1981: A Study of the Lawfulness of Peacetime Aerial Engagements,* 10 YALE J. INT'L L. 59, 64–67 (1984).

[20] The deployment of Soviet missiles in Cuba was perceived by the United States as a threat justifying the naval blockade of the island.

[21] N.Y. Times, Oct. 6, 1985, §1, at 22, col. 5.

[22] *Id.*, Oct. 26, 1984, at A12, col. 4. The air raid on Tripoli in 1986 confirmed this interpretation.

> [I]f such flights are repeated, we shall take appropriate countermeasures.
>
> . . . Those countries that have bases on their territories should note most carefully the following: if they allow others to fly from their bases to our territory we shall hit at those bases.
>
> . . . Those who lease your territory, operate against us from your territory. Their lands are far from us while your land is near. . . . Let them draw the appropriate conclusions.[23]

Similar threatening messages (these examples are far from exhaustive) almost never appear in isolation or as discrete events. They are usually preceded and followed by a stream of other communications in which the actors may be, by turns, a threatener and a target audience mutually influencing one another.[24] Although for the purposes of legal appraisal a single particularly important and dangerous message is usually selected, coercion is not a sporadic incident of organized life but an ongoing process precariously balanced between maintenance and destruction of social processes and values.

The threatener normally employs several complementary strategies of pressure simultaneously.[25] A threat of military action may be accompanied by economic sanctions, inflammatory propaganda and deliberate manipulation of the media. Besides the target itself, the latter measures are likely to be aimed at three different audiences: the people of the other country; the threatener's immediate community, whose support is sought; and a larger international community that the threatener may wish to convince of the legitimacy of the claim, as a preliminary step in the favorable appraisal of the lawfulness of the threat itself.[26]

Whether a message or, more realistically, the flow of threatening messages creates psychological pressure and, in fact, induces the behavior desired by the threatener depends on the addressee's perception of it. Only communications that arouse the anticipation of severe deprivation or destruction of values in the target audience and, hence, trigger a reaction of stress that leads to accommodating or adaptive behavior as the only reasonable alternative can be regarded as a threat.[27] This type of psychological

[23] 5 M. Whiteman, Digest of International Law 714–15 (1965).

[24] Consider the threatening postures of the United States and Iran in the Persian Gulf during the second half of 1987.

[25] *Cf.* Christol & Davis, *Maritime Quarantine: The Naval Interdiction of Offensive Weapons and Associated Matériel to Cuba, 1962,* 57 AJIL 525, 529–30 (1963). See generally, on the strategies of enforcement, Reisman, *Sanctions and Enforcement, reprinted in* M. S. McDougal & W. M. Reisman, International Law Essays 428 (1981).

[26] The Soviet threat of invasion of Poland in 1980 and 1981 (*see* text accompanying notes 96–103 *infra*) was reinforced by a Soviet media campaign accusing Solidarity of terrorism and alleging that the events in Poland constituted a fundamental threat to postwar European borders and Soviet strategic interests.

[27] Hopple, Rossa & Wilkenfeld, *supra* note 2, at 44. McDougal, Reisman & Willard, *supra* note 6, at 378, list the following potential responses to threat: (1) flight and its variants, accommodation and self-subordination; (2) approach and confrontation; (3) encirclement; and (4) penetration.

reaction can also be caused by a warning, i.e., a message whose content can be substantially similar to that of a threat. The difference between a warning and a threat, however, is important and consists in the function and attitude of the communicator.[28] The threatener holds itself out as both willing and able to occasion the loss of values to the target if the latter does not comply with the former's demand; while the warner merely puts the audience on notice to behave with proper caution so as to avoid damage or injury.

In some situations, the threatener's message operates as a warning toward one audience (*A*) *and* as a threat toward the other (*B*). What distinguishes them is not the causal relation (the threatener may, in fact, cause the loss to *A*), but rather the intent to inflict the injury on *B* if the demand is not complied with. Certain general threats operate in this way as both a warning to *A* and a threat to *B*. The threatener may not want to point out the target and, consequently, the threat is formulated in general terms. Nevertheless, circumstances may make clear who is being threatened and who is merely being put on notice to behave with proper caution to avoid injury or damage. In such situations, the threatener does not intend to penalize *A* but sends a warning that *A* is acting at its own peril.[29] Such general threats are usually unopposed by the international community because the countries that are unlikely to be affected perceive them as warnings rather than threats.

The threat is effective when the target perceives it as being so grave as to leave no reasonable option but compliance.[30] This perception, in turn, depends on the target's rational or irrational belief system:[31] on the relative importance of threatened values to the target audience[32] and on the credibility of the threat in the target's eyes.[33]

International law plays a certain role in the assessment of the credibility of a threat. At the very least, it performs a predictive function. Rules of international law reflect shared expectations of international actors, especially about the legitimate policy, the appropriate decision makers and the proper means of sustaining prescribed behavior.[34] Law therefore has value as a

[28] I owe the clarification of this point to Paul Finn.

[29] Consider, e.g., a Swedish threat to sink foreign submarines. *See infra* text accompanying notes 82–86.

[30] The perception of "reasonableness," of course, is conditioned by personal factors. A threat can be effective, even though there exists a reasonable alternative. A threatened person may be cowardly, or paranoid, or opportunistic, or simply ignorant. Admittedly, in foreign-policy matters responses to threats are more rationally calculated because of the often collective character of decision making. This rationality should not, however, be overestimated. Its limits are explored in I. Janis, Victims of Groupthink 2–135 (1972); I. Janis & L. Mann, Decision Making: A Psychological Analysis of Conflict, Choice, and Commitment (1977).

[31] Although a threat may be grounded in the objective reality, it is always interpreted by the target in terms of its own biases, values and interests.

[32] Hopple, Rossa & Wilkenfeld, *supra* note 2, at 32, observe: "An individual who ranks a given value higher is more likely to be sensitized to perceive threats in that area."

[33] A threat may fail despite its objective credibility if the target does not recognize it as such. Consider Stalin's perception of the Barbarossa Plan.

[34] McDougal & Reisman, *The Prescribing Function in the World Constitutive Process: How International Law Is Made*, *reprinted in* M. S. McDougal & W. M. Reisman, *supra* note 25, at 355.

predictor of possible or probable reactions of the international community to the conduct of the actors (both the threatener and the target audience) and, as such, can be a useful guide to rational behavior. At best, international law can form a network of restraining influences on the conduct of both parties that will eliminate violence as a method of resolving the problem. More realistically perhaps, law constitutes one of the elements (not necessarily the most powerful[35]) in the complex calculus of risks and benefits faced by the threatener and the target.

Functions of the Threat of Force

Threats perform three basic functions in the international community. First, a threat of force may be meant to operate as notice of the likelihood of a sanction to support a norm or demand enunciated by the threatener. The use of the word "sanction" in this context does not prejudge the question of lawfulness of the threat. It is banal to recall that many rules of social behavior are backed by sanctions, even though not all of them are law.[36] Thus, a threat in international relations may be either a delict or a licit sanction, depending on the appraisal of its lawfulness.

Second, a threat of force may be used to speed up resolution of a dispute by nonforcible measures. In some circumstances, delaying settlement of a dispute may work in favor of one of the parties. Hence, the party, for instance, may reject diplomatic negotiations or arbitration, or may refuse to abide by a resolution of the Security Council purporting to resolve the dispute. In such a situation, a threat of force may be the only effective way to induce the party to cooperate in the peaceful resolution of the dispute or conflict.

Third, the threat of force plays the role of a ritualized substitute for violence.[37] Since coercion and aggression are inescapable parts of life, international actors seek to render them less dangerous. Actions that can injure the adversary tend to be removed to the end of several sequences of conflict.[38] The aggressive drive is satisfied by the adoption of deterrent pos-

[35] McGinley, *Ordering a Savage Society: A Study of International Disputes and a Proposal for Achieving Their Peaceful Resolution*, 25 HARV. INT'L L.J. 43, 59–60 (1984), states: "Even the most sacred principles of international law are of no consequence . . . when vital national interests—the power and authority of the elite—are involved."

[36] In a family, rules of obedience to parents are reinforced by a system of sanctions and so are the rules established by a band of thugs offering paid "protection" to their victims. Certain social sanctions may, in fact, be illicit by the standards of state-made law. Cruel corporal punishment, even if meant to support an unobjectionable rule, can qualify as child abuse, while "protection" is punishable as extortion.

[37] It is instructive for our purpose to consider the function of ritualization in controlling intraspecific aggression among animals. *See* Lorenz, *Ritualized Fighting*, in AGGRESSION, HOSTILITY AND VIOLENCE: NATURE OR NURTURE? 44 (T. Maple & D. Matheson eds. 1973). Lorenz observes: "intraspecific aggression is, in Man, just as much a spontaneous instinctive drive as in most other higher vertebrates." *Id.* Storr, *Possible Substitutes for War*, *id.* at 306, 309, adds: "The idea that we can get rid of aggression seems to me to be nonsense."

[38] In the Cuban missile crisis, the choice of a naval blockade "had the advantage of being a low-level action that would serve as a non-humiliating warning and would still 'maintain the options' . . . permitting a gradual, controlled escalation later on, if necessary." I. JANIS, *supra* note 30, at 144.

tures, displays of might and threatening communications. The idea of nuclear deterrence, i.e., preserving the peace among the superpowers and their allies through the assurance of mutual destruction, is a prime example of this function of the threat. Similarly, military and economic alliances that project power and the determination to use it may dissuade a potential adversary from taking an action detrimental to their interests.

Many states need to demonstrate their resolution to defend their policies by force, and these displays of might are often as much for domestic as for international consumption. If they manage sufficiently to impress the adversary, they may achieve the desired effect without the need for force. The continuation of the Falklands conflict long after the de facto cessation of hostilities illustrates this point. Both the United Kingdom and Argentina have been engaged in a stream of minor nonviolent incidents, involving mainly Argentine fishing boats and British helicopters, within the 150-mile zone established by the British around the Falkland Islands. For Argentina it has been a way of saying to the world and its domestic public that the struggle for the Malvinas is not over; for the British, that it is over and that they are firmly in control.[39] Argentina has asserted its claims to sovereignty over the islands by challenging British jurisdiction but without resorting to arms, and the United Kingdom has consolidated its control by assuming a convincingly threatening posture.[40]

The substitution of threats for violence is only possible if the actors, first, properly interpret the adversary's communications and, second, accept the most fundamental rule of this ritual: restrain themselves from overstepping the line between verbal conflict and armed hostilities. Both requirements are difficult. The former, because threatening messages may be ambiguous enough to be misread and because the line between the threat of force and limited use of force is fluid.[41] The latter, because the conflict threshold usually is implicit only, and in many disputes it may change in different stages of the crisis.

Thus, the threat of force, far from precipitating fighting, may be an effective mechanism for dissuading international actors from using violence. This outcome, however, can be achieved only if the threatening messages are properly interpreted and the adversaries exercise sufficient self-restraint to observe the conflict threshold. Needless to say, this is a precarious game.[42]

[39] See the correspondence from the British and Argentine representatives to the President of the Security Council in the Supplements for 1982 and 1983 of the *Official Records.*

[40] The United Kingdom made a considerable financial effort to improve its military capabilities in the South Atlantic, including the building of a military airfield and connected radar and communication facilities. 38 UN SCOR Supp. (July–Sept. 1983) at 59–60, UN Doc. S/15938, and (Oct.–Nov. 1983) at 85, UN Doc. S/16135 (1983) (letters dated Aug. 25 and Nov. 9, 1983, from the British representative to the President of the Security Council). *Cf.* The Times (London), Oct. 8, 1983, at 5.

[41] Consider the dynamics of midair interception of an aircraft: when two fighters force an aircraft to land, after firing warning shots, is it still a threat of force or is it already a limited use of force?

[42] According to Lorenz: "[A]bnormally high intensity of ritualized activity causes true aggression in Freud's sense, that is to say a recrudescence of the phylogenetically older, unritual-

II. Legal Status of the Threat of Force

The Foundation of International Actors' Approach to the Threat

On rare occasions when the threat of force is noticed as a discrete phenomenon distinguishable from the use of force, the assumption held most commonly is that its legality is predicated upon the legality of the use of force under the same circumstances. The International Court of Justice spoke about the two in one breath when it found Article 2(4) of the Charter to be declaratory of customary international law.[43] If the Court's conclusion seems somewhat dubious with respect to the use of force,[44] it is even more so where a threat is concerned. The only pre-Charter prohibition of the use of force referred to actual war and not to the threat of it.[45] It is possible, of course, that the Charter has generated a new rule of international customary law.[46] But to find out whether it has, the Court would have to look at the practice and *opinio juris* of the states that are not parties to the Charter. In these matters, however, as Judge Jennings pointed out,

> there are obvious difficulties about extracting even a scintilla of relevant "practice" . . . from the behaviour of those few States which are not parties to the Charter; and the behaviour of all the rest, and the *opinio juris* which it might otherwise evidence, is surely explained by their being bound by the Charter itself.[47]

---

ized behavior patterns. In other words, ritualized redirection suddenly breaks down and the partners proceed to fight with a fury never otherwise observed in goose combat." Lorenz, *supra* note 37, at 53.

[43] Nicaragua v. U.S., 1986 ICJ REP. at 99–105. Both the United States and Nicaragua claimed that Article 2(4) expressed customary and general international law. *Id.* at 99. *See also* I. BROWNLIE, *supra* note 11, at 112; Gordon, *Article 2(4) in Historical Context,* 10 YALE J. INT'L L. 271, 274, 275 (1985).

[44] Nicaragua v. U.S., 1986 ICJ REP. at 531 (Jennings, J., dissenting).

[45] Parties to the 1928 Kellogg-Briand Pact (Treaty for the Renunciation of War as an Instrument of National Policy, *reprinted in* 4 M. O. HUDSON, INTERNATIONAL LEGISLATION 2522, 2524–25 (1931)) declared that "they condemn recourse to war for the solution of international controversies, and renounce it as an instrument of national policy in their relations with one another." Waldock, *General Course on Public International Law,* 106 RECUEIL DES COURS 1, 231 (1962 II), holds that "[t]he illegality of recourse to . . . armed intervention not amounting to war was not established beyond all doubt by the law of the League, or by the Nuremberg and Tokyo Trials. That was brought about by the law of the Charter . . . ." Although Brownlie presents the most comprehensive argument in support of the thesis that "[b]y 1939 a norm of illegality [of the use of force for selfish purposes] had appeared as a part of customary law" (I. BROWNLIE, *supra* note 11, at 424), he admits reluctantly that "a reader may feel justified in doubting the validity of a customary rule which derives from the practice of a period in which lawlessness seemed to be rife" (*id.* at 425).

[46] A treaty can generate a rule that, "while only conventional or contractual in its origin, has since passed into the general *corpus* of international law, and is now accepted as such by the *opinio juris,* so as to have become binding even for countries which have never, and do not, become parties to the Convention." North Sea Continental Shelf (FRG/Den.; FRG/Neth.), 1969 ICJ REP. 3, 41 (Judgment of Feb. 20).

[47] Nicaragua v. U.S., 1986 ICJ REP. at 531 (Jennings, J., dissenting).

Even if the Court were able to establish that the practice of nonmember states conforms with the prohibitions on the threat of force, it would probably be impossible to demonstrate that they behave so as a matter of customary law rather than by virtue of Article 2(6) of the Charter.[48] It provides that "[t]he Organization shall ensure that States which are not Members of the United Nations act in accordance with these Principles so far as may be necessary for the maintenance of international peace and security." Hence, it seems unnecessary for all practical purposes and theoretically dubious to characterize the prohibition of the threat of force as a rule of customary international law.

At first sight, it seems reasonable to say that when a threat is made in circumstances where resort to force would be unlawful, the threat itself is also unlawful. Ian Brownlie states: "If the promise is to resort to force in conditions in which no justification for the use of force exists, the threat itself is illegal."[49] This view corresponds with our legal intuitions inherited from the municipal legal order. In domestic law, respect for the individual's autonomy of choice forms a philosophical rationale for the prohibition of duress, undue influence and criminal threat. Personal freedom is considered such an important social value that the organized community is concerned about the limitation of liberty itself by an action of a fellow citizen. The form of coercion that fetters individual freedom is only of secondary importance in this context. What counts is that the individual's liberty is curtailed by an act performed outside the authorized system of enforcement.

In the international legal order, the view that the threat and use of force should be treated equally, at least as far as legal rhetoric goes, can be sustained if we accept the premise that the ultimate value protected by international law is the freedom of states from external pressure. Certainly, international law is concerned with the political independence of states;[50] and when this value is at stake, an effective threat of force can reasonably be analogized to the actual employment of force: they both exert pressure that makes the target state behave in a way it otherwise would not have chosen. However, the preoccupation of international law with the political independence of states is not inspired by the concern of individualist liberalism with the freedom of political elites, but rather by the need for peace and order among nations. If, indeed, the international legal system deserves the epithet "primitive,"[51] then it is more Hobbesian than Lockean.

The Charter makes this premise explicit. The opening words of the Preamble express the determination of "the Peoples of the United Nations . . .

[48] *Id.* at 531.

[49] I. BROWNLIE, *supra* note 11, at 364, 431. Schachter, *supra* note 2, at 1625, observes: "the applicability [to threats of force] of article 2(4) in principle can hardly be denied."

[50] *Cf.* UN CHARTER art. 2(4); GA Res. 2131 (XX), *supra* note 1; Nicaragua v. U.S., 1986 ICJ REP. at 131: "Every State possesses a fundamental right to choose and implement its own political, economic and social systems."

[51] *See* Dinstein, *International Law as a Primitive Legal System*, 19 N.Y.U. J. INT'L L. & POL. 1 (1986).

to save succeeding generations from the scourge of war," and Article 1(1) states as the first among the purposes of the Organization, "to maintain international peace and security." This purpose is of such importance that the Charter declares preservation of peace and security an obligation *erga omnes* authorizing member states to ensure that the rest of the international community acts in accordance with this goal.[52] None of the other purposes of the Charter expressed in Article 1 attains the same legal status. Respect for the political independence of states is not even included among these purposes. It is a principle that should be observed to further the purposes of the Organization, but it is not a purpose in itself.[53]

The Charter prohibits the use of force in violation of the political independence and territorial integrity of a state *because* it may lead to international instability, breach of the peace and/or massive abuses of human rights. But if that is the rationale of Article 2(4), then there is no justification for the claim that the use of force and the threat of force should be treated equally. Typically, an effective threat of force can violate the political independence of a state, but even an effective threat will not have the same destructive consequences as the use of force. (As a matter of fact, in specific cases, an effective threat may be an economical guarantee against open violence.)[54] Therefore, there is no reason to assume that the threat will *always* be unlawful if in the same circumstances the resort to force would be illicit. Consider, for instance, a nuclear strike in response to a conventional armed attack. Although prima facie it could well qualify as self-defense under Article 51 of the Charter, it is likely to fail the test of proportionality[55] and ultimately be appraised as unlawful. Does it follow that the threat to use nuclear arms is also unlawful? Minimum nuclear deterrence, insofar as it discourages aggression against some targets, is perceived by many international actors as compatible with the purposes of the United Nations. In their view, the legal appraisal of the threat should be similar to the verdict on the use of force only if they produce comparable *results*.

It seems that as long as the threat of force does not jeopardize peace or lead to massive violations of human rights, international actors demonstrate varying degrees of approval or more or less reluctant tolerance for unilateral threats. Although "the line between 'self-help' and a narrower doctrine of 'self-defence' has not in all cases been the subject of agreement between either states or jurists,"[56] it can be said with some confidence that the threat of force is most often situated on the self-help side of this line. But if, as

[52] Art. 2(6).

[53] Article 2 states: "The Organization and its Members, in pursuit of the purposes stated in Article 1, shall act in accordance with the following Principles . . . ."

[54] But, as James Crawford pointed out to me, an environment in which threats of force are regularly used is likely to be very unstable. *Cf.* note 42 *supra.*

[55] Cf. the diplomatic correspondence ensuing from the *Caroline* incident. 2 J. MOORE, DIGEST OF INTERNATIONAL LAW 412 (1906); 29 BRIT. & FOREIGN ST. PAPERS 1138 (1840–41) (self-defense may involve "nothing unreasonable or excessive"; "the act, justified by the necessity of self-defence, must be limited by that necessity and kept clearly within it").

[56] I. BROWNLIE, *supra* note 11, at 282.

many authorities believe, self-help involving threats of force is illicit, how can the approval or tolerance for the threat of force be explained? The shortest answer rests on the very fact that international law, like any other kind of law, is intimately linked with coercion: denying this does not change the reality itself.

The threat or use of force can be a manifestation of what Bertrand Russell called "naked power"—a compulsion pure and simple, unsupported by an authority recognized by a relevant legal community.[57] But the threat of force can also be a necessary ingredient that transforms an authoritative rule of behavior into law by signaling the existence of a power that is able, or at least genuinely attempting, to control the compliance of the target with the norm.[58] From Hobbes[59] to Kelsen,[60] legal writers have emphasized that sanction is an indispensable element of law; sanctionless law is a contradiction in terms.[61]

The drafters of the Charter obviously shared this view, subject to certain exceptions. The Charter does not prohibit coercion as such but attempts to centralize its application. It created a unique system that was meant to break radically with the past by offering the member states collective security in exchange for the abdication of their customary prerogative of resort to force other than in self-defense.[62] The scheme was as much the result of abhorrence of war as it was an expression of the hope that the concert of Allies would last beyond the victory over the Axis.[63] However, by the end of the 1940s, the consensus between the superpowers, upon which the effective operation of the collective security mechanism was predicated, deteriorated into the Cold War and arms race. Ever since, the Security Council has been unable to function in accordance with the original design. Sporadic revivals of the superpowers' interest in cooperation have been too ephemeral to bring the collective security system to life. The hope for a centralized enforcement machinery vanished.[64] This created a dissonance between the

[57] B. RUSSELL, POWER: A NEW SOCIAL ANALYSIS 57 (1957).

[58] G. HOMANS, THE HUMAN GROUP 282 (1951), writing about social control, observes: "no custom is self-sustaining. . . . A regularity of behavior persists, similar events recur in similar circumstances, only because departure from regularity is met by resistance. Nor is the resistance mere inertia."

[59] T. HOBBES, LEVIATHAN, ch. 17, at 223 (Penguin ed. 1981), warned that "Covenants, without the Sword, are but Words, and of no strength to secure a man at all."

[60] H. KELSEN, GENERAL THEORY OF LAW AND STATE 29 (1961), states: "a rule is a legal rule because it provides for a sanction."

[61] According to J. AUSTIN, THE PROVINCE OF JURISPRUDENCE DETERMINED 127 (1965), international law is not positive law because there is lacking a determinate sovereign that the nations habitually obey and because the international system of rules is supported only by moral sanctions.

[62] UN CHARTER, ch. VII.

[63] Coll points out that "[t]he world was to be managed by the great powers, which would use their preponderance of force to keep the peace and punish future aggressors." Coll, *The Limits of Global Consciousness and Legal Absolutism: Protecting International Law from Some of its Best Friends,* 27 HARV. INT'L L.J. 599, 608 (1986).

[64] Franck, *Who Killed Article 2(4)?*, 64 AJIL 809, 810 (1970); J. MURPHY, THE UNITED NATIONS AND THE CONTROL OF INTERNATIONAL VIOLENCE 21 (1983). Bowett, *Reprisals*

absolutist aspirations expressed in Article 2(4) and the reality of international law, which relies on a balanced mechanism of threats, economic and political pressure and limited violence[65] to resolve conflicts, preserve the status quo and introduce social change. Often agreements that appear to be the fruit of "a spirit of cooperation" represent no more than unwilling submission to vigorous pressure. Even in situations where compliance with rules seems to result from expectations of reciprocity, it is possible that an implicit threat of severe deprivations attendant upon nonperformance (deprivations resulting from the decreased activity of the threatener or from its retaliatory measures) constitutes the main motivation to follow the rule, while the absence of threat contributes to the decline of restraints on unlawful behavior.[66]

How much unilaterally applied coercion the international community is prepared to tolerate is not clear. Practice does not seem sufficiently unambiguous to make unfailingly intelligible distinctions among genuine approval of acts of self-help, reluctant acquiescence in them and resigned recognition of a fait accompli. Commentators vary in their assessments of the present state of the law pertaining to armed coercion: from interpretations of Articles 2(4) and 51 as allowing strictly limited exceptions only,[67] to

---

Involving Recourse to Armed Force, 66 AJIL 1, 2 (1972), writes: "It cannot be doubted that a total outlawry of armed reprisals, such as the drafters of the Charter intended, presupposed a degree of community cohesiveness and, with it, a capacity for collective action to suppress any resort to unlawful force which has simply not been achieved."

[65] Although limited violence is more common in international relations than full-fledged war, some writers argue that the latter cannot be excluded as a mechanism for enforcing international law. An act of legitimate self-defense "may amount to or may result in war." P. JESSUP, A MODERN LAW OF NATIONS 163 (1968). H. KELSEN, PRINCIPLES OF INTERNATIONAL LAW 23–29 (1952), argued that international law authorizes two types of sanctions: reprisals and war. Despite the fact that war had been outlawed by the Kellogg-Briand Pact, Kelsen thought that the prohibition concerned only a war of aggression and not a war in response to aggression. *Id.* at 26–27.

[66] L. HENKIN, HOW NATIONS BEHAVE 97 (1979), observes that gross violations of international law occur much less frequently than transgressions in small matters because states anticipate that the response will be proportionate and try to avoid serious consequences. *Cf.* H. LASSWELL, POWER AND PERSONALITY 181 (1948), who noted:

> When anthropologist Hallowell visited the Salteaux people, he was struck by their politeness and friendliness in dealing with one another and with him. Gradually he learned that this had a potent sanction in the expectation that the other fellow might secretly have more magical power than you had.
>
> Law is socialized retaliation.

[67] I. BROWNLIE, *supra* note 11, at 431–32, accepts the lawfulness of actions in the following circumstances: in individual or collective self-defense (excluding anticipatory self-defense); when authorized by a competent international organ; where a treaty confers a right to intervene; to terminate acts of trespass; and when arising from natural catastrophe. Schachter, *supra* note 2, at 1620, sees the following as lawful: self-defense against an armed attack (including anticipatory self-defense); armed assistance (if requested) to another state subject to an unlawful attack; and intervention to protect the state's own nationals in a foreign country who are in imminent peril (I. BROWNLIE, *supra* note 11, at 433, considers the legality of humanitarian intervention to be "doubtful").

suggestions of a "partial revival of a type of unilateral *jus ad bellum*."[68] Some writers conclude with resignation that if the present trend continues, "we shall achieve a position in which, while reprisals remain illegal *de jure*, they become accepted *de facto*."[69]

Policy arguments against the individual use of armed force are powerful. The destructive potential of modern technologies of warfare makes any use of armed force, except for the most obvious instances of self-defense, suspect a priori. However, when lesser forms of coercion are considered, the policy against individually applied force loses some of its persuasiveness. With respect to economic coercion, there seems to be a slowly growing consensus that "a state's use of economic power to influence another state is prima facie legitimate or, even if arguably illegitimate, not the sort of delinquency the target state is entitled to regard as 'aggression.' "[70] The arbitral tribunal in the United States–France aviation dispute found that the U.S. threat of retaliatory economic action was lawful. "If a situation arises which, in one State's view, results in the violation of an international obligation by another State, the first State is entitled, within the limits set by the general rules of international law pertaining to the use of armed force, to affirm its rights through 'counter-measures.' "[71] This approach to economic pressure reflects the recognition that the international legal order would be effectively subverted if it were denied resort to all forms of coercion. Indeed, some argue that, if effectively and prudently used, economic coercion could

[68] Reisman, *Criteria for the Lawful Use of Force in International Law*, 10 YALE J. INT'L L. 279, 281 (1985), identifies the following circumstances in which "one finds varying support for unilateral uses of force":

> self-defense, which has been construed quite broadly; self-determination and decolonization; humanitarian intervention; intervention by the military instrument to replace an elite in another state; uses of the military instrument within spheres of influence and critical defense zones; treaty-sanctioned interventions within the territory of another state; use of the military instrument for the gathering of evidence in international proceedings; use of the military instrument to enforce international judgments; and counter-measures such as reprisals and retorsions.

Reisman cautions, however, that these categories "are not determinative." Any action must be measured by the criteria of the "maintenance of the minimum order" and "enhancement of the ongoing right of peoples to determine their own political destinies." *Id.* at 282. Coll, *supra* note 63, at 613, interprets Article 2(4) as involving no more than "a good faith commitment to abstain from *clear aggression* that involves a disproportionate use of force and violates other principles of the Charter" (emphasis in original). Interpretation of the concept of "clear aggression" should be guided by "the principles of prudence and the just war tradition." *Id.* at 613–14.

[69] Bowett, *supra* note 64, at 10–11.

[70] Farer, *supra* note 12, at 411. A contrary view was taken by J. STONE, CONFLICT THROUGH CONSENSUS: UNITED NATIONS APPROACHES TO AGGRESSION (1977). Paust and Blaustein, *supra* note 12, at 410, argue that economic coercion may amount to aggression. The resolution on the Definition of Aggression, GA Res. 3314 (XXIX) (Dec. 14, 1974), *reprinted in* 69 AJIL 480 (1975), does not include economic aggression (Article 1 defines aggression as "the use of armed force"). The effectiveness of the Arab oil embargo probably changed the developing countries' assessment of the lawfulness of economic coercion.

[71] Case Concerning the Air Services Agreement of 27 March 1946 (U.S. v. Fr.), 18 R. Int'l Arb. Awards 417, 443 (1978), 54 ILR 304, 337 (1979).

decrease the level of violence in the international community while enhancing compliance with the law.[72]

Illustrations of the Problem

Before discussing the criteria that states seem to adopt while appraising the lawfulness or illegality of threats of force, I consider the following incidents.[73] They are selected from a large number of events as illustrations of various criteria applied to the legal assessment of threats of force. As different as these incidents are, they reveal nonetheless that, despite the sweeping prohibition of the threat of force by Article 2(4), international actors seem more than reluctant to condemn all threats of force falling short of self-defense. They devote a good deal of time to the continuous mutual monitoring of threatening messages and to their interpretation. Judging from the reactions, only some of these threats are considered to be delictual and even those which are looked upon as illicit do not meet with the same kind of disapproval as the use of force under the same circumstances.

The Cuban Quarantine. In 1962 the Soviet Union began to construct medium-range ballistic missile sites in Cuba and to deliver weaponry to the island.[74] The United States apparently perceived this action as a strategic threat and asked the Soviet Union to terminate the military build-up and to withdraw all the missiles from Cuba. In his broadcast to the nation on October 22, 1962, President Kennedy denounced the Soviet action as a "deliberately provocative and unjustified change in the *status quo*" and declared, "Should these offensive military preparations continue, . . . fur-

[72] The reluctance of the ICJ to consider economic coercion as illicit might be due to such considerations. *Cf. supra* note 8. Seidl-Hohenveldern, *The United Nations and Economic Coercion,* 18 REVUE BELGE DE DROIT INTERNATIONAL 9, 14 (1985), argues:

> Larger States often consider even the prohibition of the use of armed force hardly compatible with their interests. . . . If [they] would [be] deprived even of their means of economic retaliation, or see their use submitted to severe restrictions, I would be afraid that they would then brush aside as unrealistic any rule attempting to restrict their freedom of action and would resort even to armed force in defence of their rights.

Cf. Wallensteen, *Economic Sanctions: Ten Modern Cases and Three Important Lessons,* in DILEMMAS OF ECONOMIC COERCION: SANCTIONS IN WORLD POLITICS 87, 127 (M. Nincic & P. Wallensteen eds. 1983), who says: "effective economic sanctions, in some situations, reduce the incentive for military action." But Deese, *The Vulnerability of Modern Nations: Economic Diplomacy in East-West Relations, id.* at 155, 169, points out that economic coercion, if not carefully planned and executed, may precipitate the use of armed force.

[73] Reisman, *International Incidents: Introduction to a New Genre in the Study of International Law,* 10 YALE J. INT'L L. 1, 12–13 (1984), defines "incident" as an "overt conflict between two or more actors in the international system" that is resolved in "some non-judicial fashion." The incident, in contrast to "practice," "takes a single critical event as a prism through which the reactions of elites to particular behavior may be examined and assessed as an indication of their views of law."

[74] According to Donelan and Grieve, "The latter full United States estimate was that 42 MRBMs and 24–32 IRBMs (Intermediate Range Ballistic Missiles) arrived in Cuba or were on their way." M. DONELAN & M. GRIEVE, INTERNATIONAL DISPUTES: CASE HISTORIES 1945–1970, at 234 n.4 (1973).

ther action will be justified."[75] When the U.S. request failed, President Kennedy ordered on October 23 that the delivery of offensive weapons and military equipment to Cuba be interdicted. The United States threatened that all vessels proceeding to Cuba would be subject to visit and search and that those carrying military equipment would be ordered to change their destination. Refusal to comply was to be met with force.[76] Although on October 23 the Soviet Union formally rejected the U.S. note announcing the blockade, the 20 Soviet ships nearest to the blockade line stopped or altered course.[77] Both the United States and the Soviet Union immediately convened the Security Council and introduced draft resolutions—the United States calling for withdrawal of missiles under United Nations observation,[78] the Soviet Union condemning the blockade and proposing tripartite negotiations among the two main protagonists and Cuba.[79] Not surprisingly, the Security Council failed to adopt any resolution and the dispute was finally resolved in bilateral negotiations: the missiles were withdrawn and the United States terminated the blockade.

The Organization of American States (OAS) and the overwhelming majority of United States allies in the North Atlantic Treaty Organization (NATO) expressed univocal support for the U.S. action.[80] The action of the Soviet Union met with the approval of its allies within the Eastern bloc, but outside the Soviet zone of influence the only expression of mild support was a draft resolution cosponsored in the Security Council by Ghana and the United Arab Republic requesting that the Secretary-General confer with the parties, which were meanwhile to refrain from aggravating the situation.[81]

Foreign Submarines in Swedish Waters. On March 3, 1983, the Swedish Government adopted an Ordinance Containing Instructions for the Armed Forces in Times of Peace and in State of Neutrality.[82] It provides that a foreign submarine found submerged in internal waters shall be forced to surface and be taken to an anchorage for further action, while a foreign submarine found within 12 miles of Swedish territorial waters shall be turned away from the territory. If necessary, in either situation armed force may be used without prior warning.[83] Simultaneously, the navy's share of military spending was increased to provide for the development of im-

[75] 47 DEP'T ST. BULL. 715, 716, 718 (1962); L. SOHN, CASES ON THE UNITED NATIONS 993 (1973).

[76] Proclamation No. 3504, Interdiction of the Delivery of Offensive Weapons to Cuba, 27 Fed. Reg. 10,401 (1962), *reprinted in* 57 AJIL 512 (1963) [hereinafter Proclamation].

[77] M. DONELAN & M. GRIEVE, *supra* note 74, at 236.

[78] L. SOHN, *supra* note 75, at 1006. [79] *Id.* at 1010.

[80] The United Kingdom and Canada had some reservations, but "public opinion of these countries was won by the publication of the aerial photographic evidence of the Soviet missile sites." M. DONELAN & M. GRIEVE, *supra* note 74, at 235.

[81] L. SOHN, *supra* note 75, at 1013.

[82] SUBMARINE DEFENSE COMMISSION, COUNTERING THE SUBMARINE THREAT, APP. 2, at 81 (S.O.U. No. 13, 1983) [hereinafter REPORT].

[83] Sec. 15, Ordinance Containing Instructions for the Armed Forces in Times of Peace and in State of Neutrality, *id.* at 82.

proved surveillance systems and the deployment of new incident depth charges and antisubmarine torpedoes.[84]

By passing this legislation, Sweden responded to a series of intrusions into its waters by foreign submarines. The most dramatic chapter in this history began on October 1, 1982, when a foreign submarine was spotted in Harsfjarden, near the top-secret Musko naval base.[85] What followed was the largest military operation involving both the navy and other armed forces ever conducted during peacetime in Sweden. Depth charges and mine detonations, however, failed to force the intruders to the surface and no evidence of wreckage was found.[86]

The widely publicized threat to sink foreign submarines in peacetime was approved by some states and tolerated by others.[87] No state protested or expressed any concerns about the new Swedish policy, and the international media reported the incident in terms generally sympathetic to the Swedish Government's action.[88]

An Appraisal Based on Article 2(4). Assuming, for the moment, that the threat of force shares its legal status with the use of force, and that the use of force is governed by the Charter, the threat must be considered as prohibited by Article 2(4) unless it is employed in self-defense authorized under Article 51.

In both incidents sketched earlier, the actors resorted to the threat of force in circumstances that probably could not justify defensive measures under Article 51 of the Charter. That article affirms "the inherent right of individual or collective self-defense if an armed attack occurs against a Member State of the United Nations." In neither of these incidents did the threateners claim that an armed attack had taken place, or that the actions of the target states amounted to one.[89] Yet the international community generally approved of their conduct.

Even assuming that the customary right of anticipatory self-defense was not eliminated by Article 51,[90] it is quite doubtful that any of these actions would pass the customary test of lawfulness as defined in the diplomatic correspondence resulting from the *Caroline* incident. In the classic formulation of Secretary of State Daniel Webster, a preventive military action is

[84] REPORT, note 82 *supra,* at 83, 90.

[85] *Id.* at 104–05; Sadurska, *Foreign Submarines in Swedish Waters: The Erosion of an International Norm,* 10 YALE J. INT'L L. 34, 37–38 (1984).

[86] The Submarine Defense Commission alleged, however, that the submarines belonged to the Soviet Union. REPORT, note 82 *supra,* at 41.

[87] Including the Soviet Union, which has a similar domestic statute. *See* note 16 *supra.*

[88] Sadurska, note 85 *supra,* at 51–52.

[89] *Cf.* A. CHAYES, THE CUBAN MISSILE CRISIS 23 (1974).

[90] D. BOWETT, *supra* note 8, at 188–89; M. S. MCDOUGAL & F. FELICIANO, *supra* note 8, at 232–41; Fitzmaurice, *The General Principles of International Law Considered from the Standpoint of the Rule of Law,* 92 RECUEIL DES COURS 1, 171 (1957 II) (supporting the lawfulness of anticipatory self-defense). I. BROWNLIE, *supra* note 11, at 275–79; P. JESSUP, *supra* note 65, at 166–67; L. HENKIN, *supra* note 66, at 141–44 (rejecting the right of anticipatory self-defense).

lawful if "the necessity of self-defence [is] instant, overwhelming, and leaving no choice of means, and no moment for deliberation."[91]

In the Cuban quarantine incident, at first at least, the perceptions of threat varied among the members of the Executive Committee of the National Security Council. Secretary of Defense Robert McNamara is said to have argued that the missiles on Cuba made little strategic difference, and McGeorge Bundy urged a traditional diplomatic approach.[92] Reportedly, the members of the committee tacitly recognized that no firm conclusion could be drawn as to why the Soviet Union had set up missiles in Cuba. They examined "a wide variety of plausible explanations, including the nonsinister possibility that the Russians were merely trying to increase their bargaining power for negotiating the withdrawal of American missile sites near the Soviet Union."[93] In view of the Bay of Pigs affair and public demands for the invasion of Cuba by many American politicians during 1962, it is also likely that missiles were requested by Cuba as a deterrent rather than an offensive measure.[94] The members of the committee were probably aware of this possibility. If such doubts indeed existed, the necessity of anticipatory self-defense cannot be considered as "overwhelming" and "leaving no choice of means."

In the Swedish incident, any claim of anticipatory self-defense would also be difficult to sustain. Apparently, no sign of hostile intent on the part of an intruding submarine is necessary to justify a forcible action—its mere presence is sufficient. The ordinance simply provides that "[a] foreign submarine . . . found submerged . . . shall be forced to surface."[95] It is doubtful that the mere presence of a submerged submarine creates a danger that justifies any anticipatory self-defense.

If the Charter standard of lawfulness of a threat of force in self-defense, even so broadly interpreted as to include anticipatory measures, were the only criterion employed by international appraisers, the general approval of the threats made by the United States and Sweden would be difficult to explain. In fact, the legality of the conduct of both threateners was predicated on a different set of criteria that are discussed later in this paper. They may be highlighted by a contrasting illustration—an incident in which the threat of force was probably recognized as illegal. However, the form of

[91] 29 BRIT. & FOREIGN ST. PAPERS, *supra* note 55, at 1138; 2 J. MOORE, *supra* note 55, at 412. The debate in the Security Council following Israel's attack on a nuclear reactor in Iraq indicates that many states consider Webster's formula to be an accurate statement of the existing customary rule. The action of Israel was judged unlawful for failing to meet this standard of behavior. 36 UN SCOR (2285–88th mtgs.), UN Docs. S/PV. 2285–88 (1981).

[92] I. JANIS, *supra* note 30, at 150; M. DONELAN & M. GRIEVE, *supra* note 74, at 234.

[93] I. JANIS, *supra* note 30, at 159.

[94] Wright, *The Cuban Quarantine,* 57 AJIL 546, 549–50 (1963). But McDougal, *The Soviet-Cuban Quarantine and Self-Defense,* 57 AJIL 597 (1963), argues that the blockade was justified anticipatory self-defense.

[95] *See* text accompanying note 83 *supra.*

disapproval of the threatener's behavior indicates that, contrary to the appearances created by the language of Article 2(4), the threat of force is in actuality treated as a lesser international wrong, even if its consequences are comparable to the lasting effects of the use of force.

The Imposition of Martial Law in Poland. On August 31, 1980, Solidarity, the first independent trade union in the Soviet bloc, was created; on December 13, 1981, Polish authorities introduced martial law, putting an end to the peaceful revolution in Poland. In between these two dates, Poles lived under the threat of Soviet invasion.

The Soviet Union twice undertook preparations for military intervention in Poland, reaching a state of readiness in December 1980[96] and in March 1981.[97] In addition to the regular army, in November 1980 and in February 1981 reservists in the western republics of the Soviet Union were mobilized. East Germany closed the districts bordering on Poland to foreign military attachés and the U.S. Department of State announced that several Warsaw Pact countries had put their armed forces on alert.[98] "The Soviets were surveying invasion routes, had set up an elaborate communications system throughout Poland [and] were conducting intensive photo reconnaissance flights out of Czechoslovakia and East Germany . . . ."[99] On December 8, 1980, four Soviet divisions entered Polish territory. The Western military attachés in Poland interpreted these movements as a likely attempt at "creeping invasion" by the gradual introduction of troops.[100] Even after the Warsaw Pact Organization met in Moscow on December 5, 1980, and apparently gave the Polish elite an ultimatum to solve the crisis internally or face intervention by the Pact forces, troops were held in readiness along the Polish border until late that month. The second mobilization in the western republics of the Soviet Union was coupled with military exercises by the Warsaw Pact armies within and around the Polish borders.[101] Although the maneuvers were terminated on April 7, 1981, the Soviet Union reportedly

[96] The Soviet command planned the invasion by 1 East German, 2 Czechoslovak and 15 Soviet divisions for December 8, 1980. Kuklinski, *Wojna z narodem widziana od środka* (The war against the nation as seen from within), KULTURA, No. 4/475, 1987, at 22. Colonel Kuklinski was the chief of strategic planning and defense in the Polish General Staff and played a key role in the preparation of martial law while secretly reporting to the United States on the military plans.

[97] *See* text accompanying notes 101–02 *infra.*

[98] N.Y. Times, Nov. 27, 1980, at A11, col. 1; J. CARTER, KEEPING FAITH: MEMOIRS OF A PRESIDENT 584 (1982).

[99] J. CARTER, *supra* note 98, at 584.

[100] N. ASCHERSON, THE POLISH AUGUST 216 (1981). Similar actions involving 32 combat helicopters and 47 military aircraft in total took place on Apr. 3 and 8, 1981. Kuklinski, *supra* note 96, at 35.

[101] N.Y. Times, Mar. 19, 1981, at A3, col. 1; *id.*, Mar. 27, 1981, at A11, cols. 1–6; *id.*, Apr. 8, 1981, at A8, col. 1. According to Kuklinski, *supra* note 96, at 31, 150,000 soldiers participated in the maneuvers, including 30,000 on Polish territory. The evidence presented by Kuklinski suggests that the maneuvers were conceived so as to be easily transformable into an invasion. *Id.* at 31–35.

never withdrew the command system it had installed to supervise an invasion.[102]

The interests of the Polish political elite responsible for the introduction of martial law coincided with those of the Soviet Union, but their motives did not overlap exactly. General Jaruzelski wanted to spare the country Soviet intervention, occupation and deportations.[103] Martial law was perceived by the elite, and the overwhelming majority of the people, as a lesser evil.

In response to the introduction of martial law, President Reagan announced on December 29, 1981 a list of sanctions against Poland and the Soviet Union.[104] The Soviet package included the suspension of Aeroflot services and of current negotiations for, or the operation of, a few agreements of lesser importance. Three more significant measures included the postponement of negotiations for a new long-term grain agreement[105] and an embargo on the export to the Soviet Union of high-technology and oil and gas equipment. The national security implications of high-technology exports and the Soviet construction of a pipeline from Siberia to Western Europe were for some time a major preoccupation of the U.S. administration.[106] In this situation, it is not unreasonable to suggest that the introduction of martial law created a convenient pretext to frustrate a Soviet project perceived by the United States as endangering Western security.[107] The United States invited the allies to adopt similar measures, but Western Europe declined,[108] limiting its appraisal of the Soviet behavior to mild admonitions without making any reference to the Charter provisions that govern the threat of force.[109] It suffices to contrast this response with the widespread condemnation in the United Nations of the Soviet invasion of Czechoslovakia[110] to appreciate that the threat of force, even when it violates the political independence and self-determination of a people, meets

[102] *Id.* at 37–38.

[103] According to Kuklinski, the news about the Soviet plans to intervene in November 1980 shocked General Jaruzelski and his staff. *Id.* at 23. They were clearly aware that "[i]f they don't strike first, the Red Army together with the other armies of the Warsaw Pact will do the job for them." *Id.* at 25.

[104] *See* Contemporary Practice of the United States, 76 AJIL 379, 382–84 (1982).

[105] This did not prevent the United States from selling 100,000 tons of grain to the Soviet Union after only 2 months of interruption of deliveries. Rousseau, *Chronique des faits internationaux,* 85 REVUE GÉNÉRALE DE DROIT INTERNATIONAL PUBLIC 543, 610 n.98 (1982).

[106] DeSouza, *The Soviet Gas Pipeline Incident: Extension of Collective Security Responsibilities to Peacetime Commercial Trade,* 10 YALE J. INT'L L. 96, 99–100 (1984).

[107] Sanctions against the Soviet Union were lifted on Nov. 13, 1982. N.Y. Times, Nov. 14, 1982, §1, at 1, col. 6.

[108] Although the Commission of the European Economic Community took decisions reducing by half imports of manufactured goods from the Soviet Union, EEC member states effectively eroded the prohibition by claiming exceptions. Rousseau, *supra* note 105, at 610.

[109] Cf. the declaration adopted by the member states of the EEC on Jan. 4, 1982, *quoted in id.* at 609.

[110] During the general debate in the General Assembly, 76 speakers representing all geographic areas strongly criticized the Soviet action. "Of the eight speakers who defended the

with a different reaction than the use of force under similar circumstances.[111]

The Emerging Criteria for the Legal Appraisal of Threats

The perception of threats as a prudent and economical sanction does not square comfortably with the standard picture of international law. The purpose of this section is to bring into relief some trends that apppear to form a pattern of shared expectations about the acceptability of this function of threats of force.

Considerations of Security. In the Cuban missile crisis, the United States relied on Articles 6 and 8 of the Inter-American Treaty of Reciprocal Assistance and Article 52 of the UN Charter as the legal bases of its conduct.[112] Resort to these provisions was justified by the claim, ostensibly supported by the resolution of October 23, 1962 of the OAS Council,[113] that the security of the entire hemisphere was jeopardized by the events taking place in Cuba. In the words of President Kennedy, the quarantine was specifically designed "to ensure that the Government of Cuba cannot continue to receive from the Sino-Soviet powers military material and related supplies which may threaten the peace and security of the Continent."[114] By adopting a threatening posture, the United States communicated to the world its commitment to maintaining the status quo in the zone considered vital to its security.[115]

International actors responded to this stance with varying degrees of support or tolerance. This reaction may be explained by the fact that a legitimate concern for security may be caused by situations that cannot justify even anticipatory self-defense. Since, in our volatile world, subjective perceptions of security dangers can lead to acts that jeopardize peace, states may be inclined to consider as licit those threats which help to restore an upset equilibrium in the international order.

Other states have also voiced claims backed by threats of force to control certain areas outside their territorial domain if deemed vital to their security.[116] In July 1982, after the cessation of hostilities, the United Kingdom

---

Soviet action, only one was from outside the Soviet bloc." *Summary of Developments During 23d Session of the U.N. General Assembly,* Contemporary Practice of the United States, 63 AJIL 569, 569 (1969).

[111] Note that the invasion of Czechoslovakia did not involve many casualties, which makes the comparison, and contrast, with the Polish situation so much more telling.

[112] Proclamation, note 76 *supra,* 57 AJIL at 512. Meeker, *Defensive Quarantine and the Law,* 57 AJIL 515, 523 (1963).

[113] 47 U.S. DEP'T ST. BULL. 723 (1962).

[114] Proclamation, note 76 *supra,* 57 AJIL at 512. *See also* Dep't of State, Memorandum: Legal Basis for the Quarantine of Cuba, *reprinted in* A. CHAYES, note 89 *supra,* at 143.

[115] *Cf.* text accompanying note 75 *supra.*

[116] E.g., no state ever challenged the validity of the air defense identification zone (ADIZ) established by Australia. Pyman & Morris, *Australia and International Air Law,* in INTERNATIONAL LAW IN AUSTRALIA 456, 460–61 (K. Ryan ed. 1984). Under domestic regulations pertaining to an ADIZ, interception procedures include implicit and explicit threats of force.

notified Argentina that, "to minimize the risk of misunderstandings or inadvertent clashes," it was establishing a 150-nautical-mile zone around the Falklands. It asked the Argentine Government "to ensure that their warships and military aircraft do not enter the zone . . . where they would pose a potential threat to our forces." Argentine civil aircraft and shipping were also excluded and requested to stay clear of other British dependencies in the South Atlantic.[117] Despite Argentine protests[118] and the apparent incongruence of the British policy with the freedom of the high seas, the "protection zone" did not evoke international concern outside Latin America.[119] The British action in all likelihood was considered a prudent measure conforming with the Vattelian recommendation that "a State which has received an injury has the right to provide for its future security by depriving the offender of the means of doing harm."[120]

International silence in response to the threat by Sweden to sink foreign submarines found submerged in its territorial waters can be partially explained by the lack of direct interest in the matter of the overwhelming majority of states. For them, it was only a warning to behave with caution. The real target of the threat was the Soviet Union, and possibly the United States. International tolerance probably stemmed also from the recognition that the measures adopted by Sweden were dictated by the need to maintain the credibility of its policy of neutrality, which forms the cornerstone of Sweden's security. To allow Swedish territorial and internal waters to be transformed into a training ground for the superpowers' submarines would have compromised this policy, which, within its territory, Sweden was entitled to enforce.

Not every perception of threat, however, is taken as sufficient to justify a concern for security. The international community seems to examine the reasonableness of the perceptions of threat. In the Cuban crisis, the United Kingdom and Canada believed for a while that the United States had an idée fixe about Cuba; hence, they had been reluctant to support the trade embargo, designed to isolate the country economically and diplomatically, well

---

Procedures for Aircraft Operating in an ADIZ, Aeronautical Information Pub. RAC/OPS–0–101 (Sept. 4, 1980). The ICAO Council adopted an "attachment" ("Interception of Aircraft," applicable Nov. 26, 1981) to Annex 2 ("Rules of the Air") of the Chicago Convention recommending that states refrain from the use of weapons in all cases of interception of civil aircraft; *reprinted in* 22 ILM 1185 (1983).

[117] 37 UN SCOR Supp. (July–Sept. 1982) at 21, UN Doc. S/15307 (1982) (letter dated July 22, 1982 from the representative of the United Kingdom to the President of the Security Council claiming the measure was taken in accordance with Article 51).

[118] Argentina considered the British action a military threat and called for negotiations, "within the framework of the United Nations and in accordance with the relevant resolutions," on the final settlement of the dispute. *Id.* at 24, UN Doc. S/15313 (1982) (letter dated July 26, 1982 from the Argentine representative to the President of the Security Council).

[119] The Western alliance probably appreciates the strategic value of the Falklands in countering the Soviet threat in the South Atlantic, particularly as the importance of access to Antarctica is growing.

[120] 3 E. DE VATTEL, THE LAW OF NATIONS, bk. III, ch. III, §45, at 250 (Carnegie trans. 1916) (1758).

before the first indications of the installation of missiles on the island. Only the evidence of the Soviet involvement made them drop their reservations.[121]

By contrast, the situation in Poland could hardly be interpreted as a threat to Soviet security. The Solidarity movement was peaceful, nonviolent and concerned with internal affairs. Its leadership and the Catholic Church were well aware that they had nothing to win in a confrontation with the Soviet Union and almost certainly everything to lose in the event of armed intervention.[122] Their attitude reflected an ingrained understanding among the Poles that geopolitical reality makes some accommodation with the Soviet Union the sine qua non of the territorial integrity of the country. The Soviet claim that the events in Poland jeopardized the security of the Eastern bloc[123] could not be considered reasonable, which probably contributed to the appraisal of the Soviet threat as illicit.

Moreover, the international community appears not to endorse the claims that security concerns justify the suppression of internal self-determination of the states within the zone. In the Cuban missile incident, the threatening posture was adopted by the United States to deter changes within the zone to the benefit of the rival without, however, imposing any political changes in Cuba; but in the Polish crisis, the Soviet Union effectively prevented the overwhelming majority of Poles from exercising their right of political self-determination.[124] The international community did not seem to accept such an action as legitimate.

Vindication of a Denied Right. International actors seem to tolerate a threat of force for the vindication of a denied right, provided the right is well established in customary international law or in an agreement.[125] Although

[121] M. DONELAN & M. GRIEVE, *supra* note 74, at 235.

[122] On Dec. 10, 1980, the episcopate issued a communiqué warning: "None may act in such a manner as to drive our fatherland into danger of losing freedom or its existence as a sovereign state." *Quoted in* N. ASCHERSON, *supra* note 100, at 222.

[123] *See, e.g.*, letter from the Central Committtee of the CPSU to the Central Committee of the PCP, June 5, 1981: "[W]e, like the other fraternal parties, are disturbed by the fact that the offensive by antisocialist forces in Poland threatens the interests of our entire commonwealth, its cohesion, its integrity and the security of its borders . . . ." N.Y. Times, June 11, 1981, at A8, col. 4.

[124] The Reagan administration does not seem to find repugnant the idea of intervention into internal affairs of a country in order to induce its government to install democracy. Nicaragua v. U.S., 1986 ICJ REP. at 383 (Schwebel, J., dissenting). But the International Court of Justice did not endorse this policy. "[N]o such general right of intervention, in support of an opposition within another State, exists in contemporary international law." Nicaragua v. U.S., 1986 ICJ REP. at 109.

[125] 2 L. OPPENHEIM, INTERNATIONAL LAW 154 (7th ed. 1948), states that Article 2(4) does not exclude "the use of force in fulfilment of the obligations to give effect to the Charter." Fitzmaurice, *supra* note 90, at 171–72. J. STONE, AGGRESSION AND WORLD ORDER 100–01 (1958), expresses the view that states may use force to vindicate a right. The *travaux préparatoires* imply that the framers intended to prevent any loopholes from being included in the prohibition in Article 2(4). Doc. 784, I/1/27, 6 UNCIO Docs. 334–35 (1945); Doc. 885, I/1/34, *id.* at 400. This aspiration is consonant with the original design of the collective security system. J. STONE, OF LAW AND NATIONS 5, 8 (1974), however, argues that the use of force to accomplish some just end is permissible under Article 2(3) of the Charter.

this is not a sufficient condition of lawfulness, it remains its necessary and preliminary test. The decision of the International Court of Justice in the *Corfu Channel* case may be interpreted as confirming the point. On May 15, 1946, two British cruisers were fired at by an Albanian battery while passing through the North Corfu Channel. This incident led to a dispute in which the United Kingdom contended that the Corfu Channel was an international strait through which passage must not be hindered or prohibited by a coastal state in times of peace. The Albanian Government asserted that foreign warships had no right to pass through Albanian territorial waters located within the channel without prior notification to and permission from the Albanian authorities. Diplomatic negotiations between the two Governments culminated in the British note of August 1946 threatening the use of force.[126] This message was backed by the dispatch of a squadron of four British warships through the channel on October 22, 1946. The aim of the mission was not merely to carry out passage for the purpose of navigation, but also to test Albania's attitude. The passage was clearly understood by the Albanian coast guards as a threat of force.[127] In the case submitted to the International Court of Justice, one of the issues was whether the passage of the British warships on October 22 constituted a violation of the sovereignty of Albania. The Court held that

> the legality of this measure taken by the Government of the United Kingdom cannot be disputed, provided that it was carried out in a manner consistent with the requirements of international law. The "mission" was designed to affirm a right which had been unjustly denied. . . .
>
> . . . .
>
> . . . [T]he Court has arrived at the conclusion that the United Kingdom did not violate the sovereignty of Albania by reason of the acts of the British Navy in Albanian waters on October 22nd, 1946.[128]

Thus, the Court affirmed that the threat of force applied as a measure of enforcement of a right that had been unlawfully denied (in this case, the right of innocent passage through an international waterway in peacetime) was licit.[129]

Oscar Schachter argues against the view that force may lawfully be used to vindicate or secure a legal right, on the ground that "to accept it would

[126] 1949 ICJ REP. at 27.

[127] The Albanian Government alleged that the British ships "were manoeuvring and sailing in diamond combat formation with soldiers on board; the position of the guns was not consistent with innocent passage; the vessels passed with crews at action stations." *Id.* at 30. The Court refuted the allegations of noninnocent passage but admitted that the purpose of the British action was "to demonstrate such a force that she [Albania] would abstain from firing again on passing ships." *Id.* at 31.

[128] *Id.* at 30–32.

[129] For criticism of the "unfortunate implications" of this point of the Court's decision, see I. BROWNLIE, *supra* note 11, at 283–89. The arbitral tribunal in the U.S.-France aviation dispute found that the threat of economic action to retaliate for the violation of an international obligation was lawful. *See* text accompanying note 71 *supra.*

deprive article 2(4) of much of its intended effect."[130] To support this opinion, he quotes the *Corfu Channel* decision in which, according to his interpretation, the Court "squarely answered this argument by rejecting the British claim that it used naval force for minesweeping in order to vindicate its legal right. The court noted that notwithstanding its aim, the British action was a derogation of Albanian territorial sovereignty."[131] Such a reading of the *Corfu Channel* decision tends to gloss over the ambivalence of the Court's attitude and the ambiguity of the Judgment. In fact, the United Kingdom was held liable for violating Albanian territorial sovereignty by its mine-sweeping operations on November 12 and 13, 1946, carried out in Albanian waters. The purpose of this exercise was not to "vindicate legal rights," as Professor Schachter assumes, but to secure evidence that Albania was responsible for the explosion of mines on October 22, 1946.[132] But the conduct of the United Kingdom on October 22, when the British warships asserted the legal right of innocent passage of navies through international waterways, was held lawful *despite* a full demonstration of the threat of force by the British. Hence, in the *Corfu Channel* decision, the Court found that a military operation of mine sweeping in violation of the territorial sovereignty of a state is illegal and constitutes an international delict, but a threat of force to secure an illegally denied right of innocent passage in times of peace is a legitimate sanction employed by an authorized enforcer. Note that the sanction has a strictly limited remedial purpose, rather than a retributive aim, and does not result in prolonged violation of the territorial integrity of the offending state or its political independence.[133] There is no logical reason to believe that this principle should be restricted solely to the right of innocent passage.

In the Swedish incident, one of the important considerations that made the international community abstain from expressing any condemnation of Sweden's readiness to sink foreign submarines in peacetime could have

[130] Schachter, *supra* note 2, at 1626. [131] *Id.*

[132] Even this part of the ruling is not free of ambivalence. The Court made no reference to the Charter provisions on the use of force. By admitting the evidence (mines) that the United Kingdom had obtained in an illegal way, the Court allowed the violator to enjoy the benefits of the lawless act and de facto recognized that some instances of the use of force even in violation of territorial sovereignty may be tolerated. *Cf.* Reisman & Freedman, *The Plaintiff's Dilemma: Illegally Obtained Evidence and Admissibility in International Adjudication,* 76 AJIL 737, 746–48 (1982). Consider also the response of the ICJ to the failed hostages rescue operation in the Iranian desert. The Court declined to say that it was either morally or legally impermissible and made no reference to Article 2(4). Instead, it awarded reparations to the United States without deducting any amount to compensate Iran for the violation of its territorial sovereignty. United States Diplomatic and Consular Staff in Tehran (U.S. v. Iran), 1980 ICJ REP. 3, 43–44 (Judgment of May 24).

[133] One of the arguments legitimizing humanitarian intervention is that it does not purport to affect political independence and that the breach of a state's territorial integrity is only temporary. Waldock, *supra* note 45, at 240. By this standard, Israel's Entebbe operation was lawful, while the U.S. intervention in Grenada attracted overwhelming condemnation by the United Nations, including the Western allies. GA Res. 38/7 (Nov. 3, 1983).

been the recognition that Sweden was exercising a right to control access to its territory by the submarines. Both Article 14(6) of the Convention on the Territorial Sea and the Contiguous Zone[134] and Article 20 of the United Nations Convention on the Law of the Sea[135] require submarines passing through territorial waters to navigate on the surface and to show their flag. These provisions reflect coastal states' understandable apprehension about the use of their territories by foreign navies. Assuming, as many states do, that there exists in international law a corresponding right of the coastal states to be free from undetected submarine passage, Sweden's threat of force against unauthorized vessels might be seen as a vindication of this right.

Prudence and Economy. The international community seems to approve, or at least tolerate, the actions of a threatener that proceeds with prudence, carefully balancing individual and community values, and strives to achieve the results in the most economical way, by rationally relating means to aims.[136]

The Cuban quarantine was planned so as to leave several options open and allow for the gradual intensification of pressure on the Soviet Union. The interception and search of vessels was to be carried out "within a reasonable distance of Cuba, of prohibited or restricted zones and of prescribed routes."[137] Force was to be used only

> in case of failure or refusal to comply with directions, or with regulations or directives of the Secretary of Defense issued hereunder, after reasonable efforts have been made to communicate them to the vessel or craft, or in case of self-defense. In any case, force shall be used only to the extent necessary.[138]

The only ship to be boarded, which was subsequently allowed to proceed, was a Panamanian-owned cargo vessel under charter to the Soviet Union; a Soviet oil tanker was cleared after visual checking from alongside.[139] Other ships heading for Cuba changed course of their own accord.

All of these circumstances suggest that the United States endeavored to build pressure incrementally, avoiding at the beginning any direct clash with the Soviet Union, so as to prevent, if possible, an overt military confrontation.

The development by Sweden of "incident weapons" designed to create numerous scattered punctures in a submarine's hull that are not big enough

[134] Apr. 29, 1958, 15 UST 1606, TIAS No. 5639, 516 UNTS 205.

[135] UN Doc. A/CONF.62/122, *opened for signature* Dec. 10, 1982, *reprinted in* UNITED NATIONS, THE LAW OF THE SEA: UNITED NATIONS CONVENTION ON THE LAW OF THE SEA, UN Sales No. E.83.V.5 (1983).

[136] Bowett, *supra* note 64, at 11, observes: "it may be that the more relevant distinction today is not between self-defense and reprisals but between reprisals which are likely to be condemned and those which, because they satisfy some concept of 'reasonableness,' are not."

[137] Proclamation, note 76 *supra,* 57 AJIL at 513.

[138] *Id.*

[139] M. DONELAN & M. GRIEVE, note 74 *supra,* at 236.

to sink the submarine immediately, but are sufficient to force it to the surface without causing the death of the crew (although that depends on how quickly the damaged vessel is able to surface), probably helped win international tolerance for the Swedish policy. Measured against the security risk posed by the submarine violations and particularly the need to maintain the credibility of the policy of neutrality, the potential danger to intruding submarines seemed relatively limited. Since, at the same time, efforts at preventing incursions by nonforcible methods proved ineffective, the "incident weapons" appeared to represent a rational response.[140]

By contrast, the massive display of military force by the Soviet Union within and around Polish borders to counter an unarmed, nonviolent social movement was probably judged by international actors as excessive and as dangerously increasing tension in that part of the world.

Consequences of the Threat. A threat may be carefully calculated and meet, under a certain set of circumstances, all the criteria of prudence and economy. It may aim at enforcing an illegally denied right without causing any prolonged violation of the territorial sovereignty, or fettering the political independence, of the target. It may be justified by the need for security. Yet it may fail to gain the approval of the international community. For ultimately, international law is less concerned with the intentions of the threatener than with the outcomes of its behavior. Imagine, for a moment, that a NATO submarine on a surveillance mission of the Warsaw Pact's naval maneuvers in the Baltic, or a marine research submarine, inadvertently wanders off course into Swedish territorial waters where it is damaged by the "incident weapons" and sunk as a result. The prudential calculus would lose much of its power in the face of the fact that Sweden was not a target of any hostile act and that innocent lives were lost.

In the final account, the threatener is judged by the consequences of the threatening action. The ultimate question is: have the benefits for the overall security and welfare of the community balanced the harm resulting from the conduct of the threatener? In a world full of tensions and sadly lacking in mutual trust, actions that further peace and stability deserve legal blessing.

III. Conclusions

This paper began with the observation that formal legal appraisals of threats to use force are conspicuously rare in the international arena. Several explanations seem possible. First, state elites demonstrate a relatively high degree of tolerance for the operation of naked-power mechanisms in international relations. They recognize that the threat of force is a ubiquitous "fact of life," that irrespective of official disapproval of violence, at least some conflicts among international actors will continue to be settled by force; consequently, they reserve their condemnations for more dramatic

[140] Sadurska, *supra* note 85, at 50.

displays of unauthorized coercion. Second, international actors realize that skillfully managed threats can ritualize aggression. They can provide an outlet for the human propensity to violence and effectively defuse it. Third, some general threats are perceived by an overwhelming majority of states merely as warnings, the real threat being directed to a specific, individual target audience. Fourth, in some situations, particularly when the threat does not lead to the actual employment of armed force, it may be difficult to prove coercive intent, or a causal link between the threat and an injury. Fifth, the threat of force may result in speeding up the peaceful resolution of disputes, by putting pressure on a party that refuses to settle because delay works in its favor. Sixth, the international actors may perceive a threat of force as a legitimate sanction applied by an individual enforcer. They acknowledge that in a system lacking centralized enforcement, the control necessary for sustaining the authority of prescription must on occasions be exercised unilaterally. Consequently, the conclusion that "the applicability of article 2(4) . . . [to situations involving a threat of force] can hardly be denied"[141] is correct only with respect to some incidents.

An occasional transgression of a rule does not obliterate it, provided the norm is reasserted as valid by the relevant legal community.[142] Hence, the fact that some unlawful threats of force remain unpunished does not amount to their acceptance, provided the international community invokes the prohibition of such threats, even if it is unwilling to take any stronger action. In reality, international actors often express their condemnation of threats in words rather than deeds. However meager the effects of such declarations in some situations, it is simplistic to assume that words spoken in the international arena carry no weight unless supported by a plausible economic sanction or military threat. A verbal condemnation can hurt its target, particularly when ideology and prestige are the values at stake.[143] On the other hand, when states abstain from resorting even to a verbal condemnation, there is some justification for skepticism about the support they are lending to the rule abused by the threatener. The boundary between international law and politics becomes blurred when *opinio juris* of states is not expressed properly and promptly.

[141] Schachter, *supra* note 2, at 1625. Schachter goes on to say: "A blatant and direct threat of force, used to compel another state to yield territory or make substantial political concessions (not required by law), would have to be seen as illegal under article 2(4) . . . ." *Id.*

[142] *Cf.* H. KELSEN, PURE THEORY OF LAW 88, 212–13 (1970); Reisman, *Looking, Staring and Glaring: Microlegal Systems and Public Order,* 12 DEN. J. INT'L L. & POL'Y 165, 174 (1983).

[143] Schachter observes on the General Assembly resolution criticizing the Soviet invasion of Afghanistan and its effect on the attitudes of Islamic countries and some Western European Communist parties:

> One could not say that the resolution itself determined the attitude of these bodies, but the fact that it was used widely to underline and record the condemnation is evidence of its effect. At the very least, it was viewed as a political setback for the USSR with a potentially long-term negative effect on its claim as champion of national sovereignty.

Id. at 1622.

It may happen that the immediate effect of the threat confirms the prudence and rationality of the decision to make it and the threatener is acquitted in the court of the international community. It is understandable, of course, that international actors make an appraisal of a single, particularly dramatic or dangerous event rather than withhold their verdict until all the repercussions of the act can be assessed. But the formation of normative expectations is a dynamic process in which the lawfulness of any particular behavior may be reevaluated in the light of its lasting consequences and changing circumstances. Hence, the conclusions derived from the study of incidents are often tentative. Nonetheless, they bring into dramatic relief the fact that the legality of a threat of force cannot be judged solely by reference to Article 2(4). This prescription expresses venerable aspirations. Yet support for them should not lead to the abdication of realism. In international law praiseworthy, but absolutist, standards do not necessarily make good performers.

TERRORISM ON THE HIGH SEAS: THE ACHILLE LAURO, PIRACY AND THE IMO CONVENTION ON MARITIME SAFETY

*By Malvina Halberstam**

INTRODUCTION

On October 7, 1985, the *Achille Lauro,* an Italian-flag cruise ship, was seized while sailing from Alexandria to Port Said.[1] The hijackers, members of the Palestine Liberation Front (PLF), a faction of the Palestine Liberation Organization (PLO),[2] had boarded the ship in Genoa, posing as tourists. They held the ship's crew and passengers hostage, and threatened to kill the passengers[3] unless Israel released 50 Palestinian prisoners.[4] They also threatened to blow up the ship if a rescue mission was attempted.[5] When their demands had not been met by the following afternoon, the hijackers shot Leon Klinghoffer, a Jew of U.S. nationality who was partly paralyzed and in a wheelchair, and threw his body and wheelchair overboard.[6] The

Editorial Note: The Convention for the Suppression of Unlawful Acts Against the Safety of Maritime Navigation was adopted on March 10, 1988 at a Diplomatic Conference in Rome and was signed by 23 states, including the United States, on that date. This article went to press before the Diplomatic Conference began and the discussion is based on the draft Convention agreed upon by the *Ad Hoc* Preparatory Committee. Although there were no major changes in the draft Convention, some additions and deletions were made, which will be noted in a subsequent issue.

* Professor of Law, Benjamin N. Cardozo School of Law, Yeshiva University. Much of the material for this article was gathered while the author served as Counselor on International Law, U.S. Department of State, Office of the Legal Adviser, and headed the U.S. delegation to meetings at which various drafts of the IMO Convention were considered. The views expressed are the author's and do not necessarily represent the position of the United States Government. The author wishes to express her appreciation to Jacki Knapman, Cardozo '90, Jodi Peikoff, Cardozo '89, and Babette Sommer, Cardozo '89, for their assistance in the preparation of this article.

[1] It was not clear from the newspaper reports whether the initial seizure was on the high seas or within the territorial waters of Egypt. *Compare* N.Y. Times, Oct. 8, 1985, at A1, col. 6, *with id.,* Oct. 13, 1985, §1, at 22, col. 6. However, there is no doubt that the ship was on the high seas while being held by the hijackers.

[2] For a discussion of the relationship between the PLO and the PLF and a suggestion that the initial raid was endorsed by the PLO, which officially denied involvement, see McGinley, *The Achille Lauro Affair—Implications for International Law,* 52 TENN. L. REV. 691, 699 (1985). *See also* N.Y. Times, Oct. 17, 1985, at A12, col. 2; TIME, Oct. 28, 1985, at 32–33.

[3] The hijackers segregated the Americans and Jews on board and threatened to kill them if their demands were not met. *See* N.Y. Times, Oct. 13, 1985, §1, at 24, col. 5.

[4] N.Y. Times, Oct. 10, 1985, at A11, col. 1; *id.,* Oct. 8, 1985, at A1, col. 6; Documents Concerning the *Achille Lauro* Affair, 24 ILM 1509, 1556 (1985). Among those whose release from prison in Israel was demanded was Samar al-Qantari who had murdered a 5-year-old girl in Nahariya by dashing her head against a rock. N.Y. Times, Oct. 9, 1985, at A18, col. 6.

[5] N.Y. Times, Oct. 8, 1985, at A1, col. 6.

[6] Smith, *The Voyage of the* Achille Lauro, TIME, Oct. 21, 1985, at 30–31.

United States characterized the seizure as piracy,[7] a position that has been supported by some commentators and opposed by others.[8]

Part I of this article examines the customary international law on piracy and the piracy provisions of the 1958 Geneva Convention on the High Seas and the 1982 United Nations Convention on the Law of the Sea to determine whether acts such as the seizure of the *Achille Lauro* constitute piracy under customary international law and/or under these Conventions.

The seizure of the *Achille Lauro* also provided the impetus for the drafting of a convention on maritime terrorism.[9] In November 1986, the International Maritime Organization (IMO) established an *Ad Hoc* Preparatory Committee, open to all states, to consider a Convention for the Suppression of Unlawful Acts Against the Safety of Maritime Navigation, based on a draft submitted by Austria, Egypt and Italy. The committee agreed upon a draft Convention at a meeting in Rome in May 1987. A diplomatic conference, at which the Convention is to be adopted, is scheduled for March 1988.

Part II of this article focuses on the Convention for the Suppression of Unlawful Acts Against the Safety of Maritime Navigation. It summarizes the key provisions and analyzes the arguments for and against those that

[7] The seizure was characterized as piracy by the President, 24 ILM at 1515; N.Y. Times, Oct. 12, 1985, at A6, cols. 1–6; and by the Legal Adviser, *id.*, Dec. 30, 1985, at A1, col. 5; and the Justice Department obtained arrest warrants charging the hijackers with hostage taking, conspiracy and "piracy on the high seas," 24 ILM at 1554–57.

[8] *Compare* Gooding, *Fighting Terrorism in the 1980's: The Interception of the* Achille Lauro *Hijackers,* 12 YALE J. INT'L L. 158, 159 (1987) ("While it may be contended that the taking of the *Achille Lauro* is not included within [the 1958 Geneva Convention on the High Seas] definition [of piracy] because there was no second vessel involved or because the hijackers did not act for 'private ends,' customary international law and the history of the enforcement of the norm against piracy indicate that such a position is unfounded"), and McGinley, *supra* note 2, at 700 ("Thus it is evident that the seizure of the *Achille Lauro* was piracy *jure gentium*"), *with* Note, *Towards a New Definition of Piracy: The* Achille Lauro *Incident,* 26 VA. J. INT'L L. 723, 748 (1986) ("The Palestinians' actions, however, do not qualify as piracy under international law . . . ").

[9] Although there are several conventions dealing with specific aspects of terrorism, such as hijacking of airplanes (Hague Convention on Suppression of Unlawful Seizure of Aircraft, Dec. 16, 1970, 22 UST 1641, TIAS No. 7192, 860 UNTS 105), sabotage of airplanes (Convention for the Suppression of Unlawful Acts Against the Safety of Civil Aviation, Sept. 23, 1971, 24 UST 564, TIAS No. 7570) [hereinafter Montreal Convention], hostage taking (Convention Against the Taking of Hostages, Dec. 17, 1979, *reprinted in* 18 ILM 1456 (1979)), and assault on internationally protected persons (Convention on the Prevention and Punishment of Crimes Against Internationally Protected Persons, Including Diplomatic Agents, Dec. 14, 1973, 28 UST 1975, TIAS No. 8532), there is at present no convention on maritime terrorism.

There is no generally accepted definition of terrorism, the meaning of which is, of course, very controversial, and no attempt to define it will be made here. The *Restatement (Third) of U.S. Foreign Relations Law* notes that though there "has been wide condemnation of terrorism," international agreements to define and punish it have not yet been widely ratified because of inability to agree on its definition. RESTATEMENT (THIRD) OF FOREIGN RELATIONS LAW OF THE UNITED STATES §404 comment *a* (1988) [hereinafter RESTATEMENT (THIRD)]. For a discussion of various attempts to define terrorism, see Levitt, *Is Terrorism Worth Defining?*, 13 OHIO N.U.L. REV. 97 (1986).

have been or are likely to be controversial. Some of these were specifically reserved for resolution by the Diplomatic Conference; others, though agreed upon by the Preparatory Committee, may nevertheless be reconsidered by the Diplomatic Conference.

While the Convention will be an important step in the development of the international law against terrorism, it will not completely supersede the customary international law or the provisions on piracy under the Geneva and UN Conventions. First, the Convention will, of course, only apply among states that ratify it.[10] Second, there are matters dealt with by customary law and/or by the Geneva and UN Conventions not addressed by this

[10] The question arises whether the Convention, *infra* note 11, applies to an offender who is a national of a state that has not ratified the Convention but is found in the jurisdiction of a state party, and, if so, whether such application is consistent with generally recognized principles of international law. Article 3, defining the offenses, states, "any person commits an offence . . ." (*see* "Defining the Offenses" in pt. II *infra*). Article 10 provides that a state party "in the territory of which the offender or alleged offender is found shall, . . . if it does not extradite him, be obliged, *without exception whatsoever and whether or not the offence was committed in its territory,*" to submit the case to its authorities. Similar provisions are contained in the conventions dealing with airplane sabotage and hijacking, hostage taking and attacks on internationally protected persons. *See infra* note 101.

At least one commentator questions the theoretical justification for the application of a convention proscribing terrorism, or a particular aspect of terrorism, to nationals of a state that has not ratified it. *See* Paust, *Extradition of the* Achille Lauro *Hostage-Takers: Navigating the Hazards,* 20 VAND. J. TRANSNAT'L L. 235, 254 (1987) ("Universal jurisdiction under the Hostages Convention . . . is highly suspect with regard to defendants who are not nationals of a signatory to the Hostages Convention"). Since terrorist acts are often committed by nationals of states that encourage or condone terrorism, limiting the application of antiterrorist treaties to nationals of state parties would significantly undermine their effectiveness. It would mean that the community of states is essentially helpless to take legal measures against terrorists who are nationals of states that do not ratify the conventions.

A fairly strong argument can be made for applying the conventions to a national of a nonparty if the offense occurred in the territory of a state party. Clearly, the state in whose territory the act occurred (and for ships, the flag state) has jurisdiction under international law. There is no question that a state can regulate conduct in its territory, making certain conduct criminal and providing for the apprehension, trial and punishment of those who engage in it. There is no reason why such a state cannot enter into a treaty with other states—just as the state of nationality of the offender can—authorizing those states to apprehend, try and punish the offender. This would, of course, not resolve the problem of a terrorist act committed by a national of a state that is not a party to the convention in the territory of a state that is not a party.

The simplest argument for applying the conventions in the latter situation is that terrorism is subject to universal jurisdiction under existing customary international law. Alternatively, one might argue that once the respective conventions are ratified by a large number of states, as is true of the airplane hijacking and sabotage conventions (*see infra* text at note 128), they create customary international law. *See* RESTATEMENT (THIRD), *supra* note 9, §§404, 423. *See also* Paust, *supra,* at 250 (who holds that terrorism involves a violation of fundamental human rights recognized by customary international law). As for the Convention for the Suppression of Unlawful Acts Against the Safety of Maritime Navigation, if one takes the position that terrorist acts on the high seas constitute piracy, there is no problem, as universal jurisdiction is generally accepted.

Finally, even if one questions whether a customary rule of law subjecting terrorism to universal jurisdiction has emerged, it seems fairly clear that the underlying conduct involved in most acts of terrorism, e.g., hijacking, hostage taking, attacks on diplomats, is generally considered an offense under the laws of most states and by the international community. If so, the

Convention.[10a] Matters not regulated by this Convention continue to be governed by the rules and principles of general international law, as the Convention makes clear in the Preamble.[11] Thus, the application of the customary law on piracy and of the Geneva and UN provisions on piracy to terrorist acts on the high seas continues to be of practical as well as scholarly significance.

I. Piracy

Customary International Law

Although piracy is the oldest and perhaps only crime over which universal jurisdiction was generally recognized under customary international law,[12] there was no authoritative definition of piracy under customary law.[13] It was not settled, for example, whether *animus furandi,* an intent to rob, was a necessary element, whether acts by insurgents seeking to overthrow their government should be exempt, as were acts by state vessels and by recog-

---

state in which the offender is found is not applying its laws to criminalize conduct by a non-national that was not otherwise criminal, but is only applying its laws on jurisdiction to a non-national found in its territory. It is arguable that by coming into the state, the perpetrator is subjecting himself to that state's jurisdiction, even if it would not have jurisdiction without his presence. Presence has long been a basis for jurisdiction in civil matters. *See, e.g.,* Pennoyer v. Neff, 95 U.S. 714 (1877). The question has not come up in criminal matters because a state generally will not apply the penal laws of another state, but it would not be unreasonable to make it a basis of jurisdiction in such matters, where holding the offender criminally responsible for the act comports with fundamental fairness, particularly if there is no other forum with a stronger claim to jurisdiction willing and able to try him.

[10a] For example, the Convention does not address who may free a ship being held by terrorists. Under customary law, any state may seize a pirate ship; under the Geneva Convention, states having an opportunity to do so may have an obligation to act against a pirate ship. *See* notes 59–60 *infra* and accompanying text. Therefore, whether a ship under the control of terrorists constitutes a pirate ship may be of great practical significance. For the position that a ship seized by terrorists and converted by them to their own use may constitute a pirate ship under customary law, see note 67 *infra* and accompanying text.

[11] The Preamble states: "AFFIRMING FURTHER that matters not regulated by this Convention continue to be governed by the rules and principles of general international law . . . ." *See* Draft Convention for the Suppression of Unlawful Acts Against the Safety of Maritime Navigation, IMO Doc. PCUA 2/5, Ann. 1, at 2 (June 2, 1987) [hereinafter Convention].

[12] "[P]iracy by the law of nations, in its jurisdictional aspects, is *sui generis.*" S.S. Lotus, 1927 PCIJ (ser. A) No. 10 (Sept. 7), 2 M. HUDSON, WORLD COURT REPORTS 20, 70 (Moore, J., dissenting). The Draft Convention on Jurisdiction with Respect to Crime, prepared by the Harvard Research in International Law, 29 AJIL Supp. 435 (1935), provided for two categories of universal jurisdiction. However, only jurisdiction over piracy was absolute, or unconditional. Universal jurisdiction for other offenses depended on specified conditions, e.g., that the crime was "committed in a place not subject to the authority of any State." *Id.* at 440–41.

[13] The discussion in this section deals with the customary law of piracy as it had developed prior to the adoption of the Geneva Convention on the High Seas. Although the customary law of piracy was not superseded by the Convention since not all states ratified it and it may not cover all aspects of piracy, with respect to those issues addressed by the Geneva Convention, its adoption focused attention on its provisions and substantially stopped the further development of customary law. *See, e.g.,* the discussion of the *Santa María* seizure *infra.* Although the seizure occurred before the Geneva Convention came into effect (but after it was adopted), several of the commentators discussed it with respect to the provisions of the Convention.

nized belligerents, and whether the act had to be by one ship against another or could be on the same ship. Brierly stated: "There is no authoritative definition of international piracy, but it is of the essence of a piratical act to be an act of violence, committed at sea or at any rate closely connected with the sea, by persons not acting under proper authority."[14]

Courts in the United States and Britain and a number of prominent publicists took the position that any unauthorized act of violence committed on the high seas is piracy. Thus, Oppenheim's *International Law*, edited by Sir Hersch Lauterpacht, stated:

> Piracy, in its original and strict meaning, is every unauthorised act of violence committed by a private vessel on the open sea against another vessel with intent to plunder (*animo furandi*). The majority of writers confine piracy to such acts, which indeed are the normal cases of piracy. But there are cases possible which are not covered by this narrow definition, and yet they are treated in practice as though they were cases of piracy. Thus, if the members of the crew revolt and convert the ship, and the goods thereon, to their own use, they are considered to be pirates, although they have not committed an act of violence against another ship. Again, if unauthorised acts of violence, such as murder of persons on board the attacked vessel, or destruction of goods thereon, are committed on the open sea without intent to plunder, such acts are in practice considered to be piratical. Therefore several writers, correctly, it is believed, oppose the usual definition of piracy as an act of violence committed by a private vessel against another with intent to plunder. However, no unanimity exists among them concerning a fit definition of piracy, and the matter is therefore very controversial. If a definition is desired which really covers all such acts as are in practice treated as piratical, piracy must be defined as *every unauthorised act of violence against persons or goods committed on the open sea either by a private vessel against another vessel or by the mutinous crew or passengers against their own vessel.*[15]

In a landmark English decision, *In re Piracy Jure Gentium*, the court endorsed as the "nearest to accuracy" Kenny's definition "where he says piracy is *any armed violence at sea which is not a lawful act of war*."[16]

Although piracy was frequently defined as "robbery at sea,"[17] both U.S. and English courts have held that actual robbery is not an essential element. More than a century ago, Justice Story wrote:

> A pirate is deemed, and properly deemed, *hostis humani generis*. But why is he so deemed? Because he commits hostilities upon the subjects

[14] J. BRIERLY, THE LAW OF NATIONS 154 (1928), *quoted in* Harvard Research in International Law, Comment to the Draft Convention on Piracy, 26 AJIL Supp. 749, 750 (1932) [hereinafter Harvard Research, Piracy]. For the text of the draft Convention, see *id.* at 743. The Comment includes a comprehensive review of, and extensive quotations from, various authorities.

[15] 1 L. OPPENHEIM, INTERNATIONAL LAW 608–09 (Lauterpacht 8th ed. 1955) (footnotes omitted) (emphasis in original). For a review and discussion of the definitions suggested by various publicists, see Harvard Research, Piracy, *supra* note 14, at 749–51, 769–80.

[16] *In re* Piracy Jure Gentium, 1934 App. Cas. 586, 598, *reprinted in* 3 BRIT. INT'L L. CASES 836, 842 (1965) (emphasis added).

[17] *See infra* text accompanying note 28.

> and property of any or all nations, without any regard to right or duty, or any pretence of public authority. *If he willfully sinks or destroys an innocent merchant ship, without any other object than to gratify his lawless appetite for mischief, it is just as much a piratical aggression, in the sense of the law of nations, and of the act of Congress, as if he did it solely and exclusively for the sake of plunder, lucri causa.* The law looks to it as an act of hostility, and being committed by a vessel not commissioned and engaged in lawful warfare, it treats it as the act of a pirate . . . .[18]

More recently, Viscount Sankey stated:

> When it is sought to be contended, as it was in this case, that armed men sailing the seas on board a vessel, without any commission from any state, could attack and kill everybody on board another vessel, sailing under a national flag, without committing the crime of piracy unless they stole, say, an article worth six-pence, their Lordships are almost tempted to say that a little common sense is a valuable quality in the interpretation of international law.[19]

One of the more controversial areas under customary law concerned the treatment of insurgents who had not achieved the status of recognized belligerents. In *The Ambrose Light,* a U.S. court, refusing to exempt insurgents, reasoned:

> [T]he liability of the vessel to seizure, as piratical, turns wholly upon the question whether the insurgents had or had not obtained any previous recognition of belligerent rights, either from their own government or from the political or executive department of any other nation; and that, in the absence of recognition by any government whatever, the tribunals of other nations must hold such expeditions as this to be technically piratical. . . . Wheaton defines piracy as "the offense of depredating on the high seas without being authorized by any sovereign state, or with commissions from different sovereigns at war with each other." Rebels who have never obtained recognition from any other power are clearly not a sovereign state in the eye of international law, and their vessels sent out to commit violence on the high seas are therefore piratical within this definition.

The court concluded that such insurgents who

> send out vessels of war are, in legal contemplation, merely combinations of private persons engaged in unlawful depredations on the high seas; that they are civilly and criminally responsible in the tribunals for all their acts of violence; that in blockading ports which all nations are entitled to enter, they attack the rights of all mankind, and menace with destruction the lives and property of all who resist their unlawful acts; that such acts are therefore piratical, and entitle the ships and tribunals of every nation whose interests are attacked or menaced, to suppress, at their discretion, such unauthorized warfare by the seizure and confiscation of the vessels engaged in it.[20]

[18] United States v. Brig Malek Adhel, 43 U.S. (2 How.) 210, 232 (1844) (emphasis added).

[19] *In re* Piracy Jure Gentium, 3 BRIT. INT'L L. CASES at 840.

[20] United States v. The Ambrose Light, 25 Fed. 408, 412–13 (S.D.N.Y. 1885) (citations omitted). Compare the following language in The Magellan Pirates, 164 Eng. Rep. 47, 48 (1853):

Hall, on the other hand, argued that it was improper to treat insurgents fighting for political independence as pirates. Attacking the state's ships at sea was one of the ways they might gain such independence; the essence of piracy was that it was for private, as contrasted with public, ends; and insurgents attempting to overthrow their government were not a threat to all nations (*hostis humani generis*), as their attacks were limited to ships of the state from which they were seeking independence. He said:

> Most acts which become piratical through being done without due authority are acts of war when done under the authority of a state, and, as societies to which belligerent rights have been granted have equal rights with permanently established states for the purposes of war, it need scarcely be said that all acts authorized by them are done under due authority. . . . It is impossible to pretend that acts which are done for the purpose of setting up a legal state of things, and which may in fact have already succeeded in setting it up, are piratical for want of an external recognition of their validity, when the grant of that recognition is properly dependent in the main upon the existence of such a condition of affairs as can only be produced by the very acts in question. It would be absurd to require a claimant to justify his claim by doing acts for which he may be hanged. Besides, though the absence of the competent authority is the test of piracy, its essence consists in the pursuit of private as contrasted with public ends. Primarily the pirate is a man who satisfies his personal greed or his personal vengeance by robbery or murder in places beyond the jurisdiction of a state. The man who acts with a public object may do like acts to a certain extent, but his moral attitude is different, and the acts themselves will be kept within well-marked bounds. *He is not only not the enemy of the human race, but he is the enemy solely of a particular state.*[21]

Most of those who took the position that insurgents fighting for independence should be exempt from the laws of piracy stressed that the exemption applied only if the acts were directed solely against a particular state and nationals and vessels of all other states were unharmed. Hyde, for example, stated that the "United States has at various times expressed reluctance to treat as piratical the operating of insurgent vessels engaged in furthering a public end, *and when directed solely against persons and property associated with governments sought to be overthrown.*"[22] He cited as support a

---

> It is true that where the subjects of one country may rebel against the ruling power, and commit divers acts of violence with regard to that ruling power, that other nations may not think fit to consider them as acts of piracy. . . . I think it does not follow that, because persons who are rebels or insurgents may commit against the ruling power of their own country acts of violence, they may not be, as well as insurgents and rebels, pirates also; pirates for other acts committed towards other persons. It does not follow that rebels or insurgents may not commit piratical acts against the subjects of other states, especially if such acts were in no degree connected with the insurrection or rebellion.

For a discussion of these and other cases on point, see Johnson, *Piracy in Modern International Law,* 43 GROTIUS SOC'Y TRANSACTIONS 63, 76–81 (1957).

[21] 3 F. WHARTON, INTERNATIONAL LAW DIGEST 471–72 (2d ed. 1887) (quoting W. HALL, INTERNATIONAL LAW 233–34 (1st ed. 1884) (emphasis added)).

[22] C. HYDE, INTERNATIONAL LAW CHIEFLY AS INTERPRETED AND APPLIED BY THE UNITED STATES 774 (2d ed. 1945) (emphasis added).

memorandum from the Solicitor of the Department of State that gave as the test for determining whether a vessel is piratical "whether it confines itself to depredations against its own country or commits depredations against vessels of other countries."[23]

Thus, while there was no authoritative definition of piracy, it may fairly be concluded that under the prevailing view of piracy in customary international law, terrorist acts such as the seizure of the *Achille Lauro* and the murder of one of its passengers would not have been exempt. Even those publicists who urged, and those states that accepted, an exemption for insurgents extended it only to insurgents whose acts were directed against a particular state.

Provisions on Piracy under the Geneva and UN Conventions

Attacks with a Political Purpose: "For Private Ends." Both the 1958 Geneva Convention on the High Seas (Geneva Convention),[24] to which the United States is a party, and the 1982 United Nations Convention on the Law of the Sea (UN Convention),[25] to which the United States is not a party, have provisions on piracy. Article 15 of the former and Article 101 of the latter provide:

> Piracy consists of any of the following acts:
>
> (a) any illegal acts of violence, detention, or any act of depredation, committed for private ends by the crew or the passengers of a private ship or a private aircraft, and directed:
>
> (i) on the high seas, against another ship or aircraft, or against persons or property on board such ship or aircraft;

[23] *Id.* at 775. The full opinion is reprinted in 2 G. HACKWORTH, DIGEST OF INTERNATIONAL LAW 697 (1941). The memorandum specifically rejected the position of *The Ambrose Light,* that the laws of piracy apply to acts by all insurgents who have not achieved the status of recognized belligerents. Wharton's position was similar to that of Hyde and the State Department: "Armed cruisers, which, though claiming to be commissioned by insurgents, prey on merchant vessels of all nationalities, indiscriminately, are to be regarded as pirates." *See* 3 F. WHARTON, *supra* note 21, at 457. In The Magellan Pirates, 164 Eng. Rep. 47 (1853), Lushington took the position that the same persons may be considered both insurgents and pirates, depending on whom they attack. *See supra* note 20.

[24] Apr. 29, 1958, 13 UST 2312, TIAS No. 5200, 450 UNTS 82. The Convention did not enter into force until Sept. 30, 1962.

[25] UN Doc. A/CONF.62/122, *opened for signature* Dec. 10, 1982, *reprinted in* UNITED NATIONS, THE LAW OF THE SEA: UNITED NATIONS CONVENTION ON THE LAW OF THE SEA, UN Sales No. E.83.V.5 (1983). The Convention has not yet been ratified by a sufficient number of states to bring it into force. President Reagan announced on July 9, 1982, that the United States would not sign this Convention because of major problems in its seabed-mining provisions. 1982 PUB. PAPERS: RONALD REAGAN 911–12. President Reagan's Ocean Policy Statement of Mar. 10, 1983 recognized that "the convention also contains provisions with respect to traditional uses of the oceans which generally confirm existing maritime law and practice and fairly balance the interests of all states," and declared that "the United States is prepared to accept and act in accordance with the balance of interests relating to traditional uses of the oceans—such as navigation." 1983 *id.* at 378–79.

(ii) against a ship, aircraft, persons or property in a place outside the jurisdiction of any State;

(b) any act of voluntary participation in the operation of a ship or of an aircraft with knowledge of facts making it a pirate ship or aircraft;

(c) any act of inciting or of intentionally facilitating an act described in subparagraph (a) or (b) of this article.

J. P. A. François, the special rapporteur for the International Law Commission, which drafted the Geneva Convention, stated that in preparing the articles on piracy, he had relied heavily on the Draft Convention on Piracy prepared by the Harvard Research in International Law and the Comment to the Draft (Comment) by Professor Bingham, the reporter.[26] Article 3 of the Harvard draft provides in part:

> Piracy is any of the following acts, committed in a place not within the territorial jurisdiction of any state:
>
> 1. Any act of violence or of depredation committed with intent to rob, rape, wound, enslave, imprison or kill a person or with intent to steal or destroy property, for private ends without bona fide purpose of asserting a claim of right, provided that the act is connected with an attack on or from the sea or in or from the air.[27]

The term "for private ends" is not defined in the Geneva Convention on the High Seas or in the Harvard Draft Convention on Piracy, nor can its meaning be determined unequivocally in either of these documents. It is arguable, however, on the basis of the *travaux préparatoires,* that "for private ends" was used in the Harvard draft to exclude acts by unrecognized insurgents who limited their attacks to the state from which they were seeking independence, and was used in the Geneva Convention for that purpose and also to exclude attacks by state ships, and that neither the Harvard draft nor the Geneva Convention was intended to exclude all attacks that were animated by a political motive.

It is clear that "for private ends" was not used either in the Harvard draft or in the Geneva Convention to limit piracy to acts done with an intent to rob (*animus furandi*), notwithstanding the body of opinion that such intent was a necessary element of piracy. Professsor Bingham stated in the Comment:

> Acts done with other purposes than robbery also are put under the common jurisdiction, although the typical piracy is usually defined as robbery on the high seas; for there is no good reason why one who does an act with intent to kill, wound, rape, enslave or imprison, or to steal or maliciously destroy property, which would be piracy if done to rob, should not be subjected to more probable retribution through the

[26] Summary Records of the Seventh Session, [1955] 1 Y.B. INT'L L. COMM'N 19, 25, UN Doc. A/CN.4/SER.A/1955; Report of the International Law Commission to the General Assembly, 2 UN GAOR Supp. (No. 9), UN Doc. A/3159 (1956), *reprinted in* [1956] 2 Y.B. INT'L L. COMM'N 253, 282, UN Doc. A/CN.4/SER.A/1956/Add.l. For citation to the Harvard Draft Convention on Piracy and Comment, see *supra* note 14.

[27] Harvard Research, Piracy, *supra* note 14, at 768–69.

> common jurisdiction of all states, instead of to a lesser chance of apprehension and punishment by a single state (or one of two or three states) which may not have the present force, or opportunity or interest to serve the cause of security and order in the locality.[28]

In presenting his draft to the International Law Commission, the rapporteur listed as one of the principles on which it was based "that *animus furandi* did not have to be present."[29] He supported his position by quoting the Comment to the Harvard draft and the writings of several publicists. The Commission explicitly adopted the rapporteur's position in its report to the General Assembly.[30]

What remains unclear is whether the "for private ends" proviso was intended to exclude all acts done for political purposes or only acts committed by unrecognized insurgents that would be lawful if committed by recognized belligerents. The Comment to the Harvard draft states:

> It may be thought advisable to exclude from the common jurisdiction certain doubtful phases of traditional piracy which can now be left satisfactorily to the ordinary jurisdiction of a state, or of two or three states, stimulated to action on occasion by diplomatic pressure . . . . *Therefore the draft convention excludes from its definition of piracy all cases of wrongful attacks on persons or property for political ends, whether they are made on behalf of states, or of recognized belligerent organizations, or of unrecognized revolutionary bands.*[31]

Specifically with reference to the "private ends" requirement, the Comment observes:

> Although states at times have claimed the right to treat as pirates unrecognized insurgents against a foreign government who have pretended to exercise belligerent rights on the sea against neutral commerce, or privateers whose commissions violated the announced policy of the captor, and although there is authority for subjecting some cases of these types to the common jurisdiction of all states, it seems best to confine the common jurisdiction to offenders acting for private ends only. There is authority for the view that this accords with the law of nations.[32]

The Comment then refers to Article 16,[33] where it states:

> This Article covers *inter alia* the troublesome matter of illegal forcible acts for political ends against foreign commerce, committed on the high sea by unrecognized organizations. For instance a revolutionary

[28] *Id.* at 786. *See also id.* at 790, *quoted in* [1955] 1 Y.B. INT'L L. COMM'N at 70; M. S. MCDOUGAL & W. BURKE, THE PUBLIC ORDER OF THE OCEANS 810 (1962).

[29] [1955] 1 Y.B. INT'L L. COMM'N at 41.

[30] "The intention to rob (*animus furandi*) is not required. Acts of piracy may be prompted by feelings of hatred or revenge, and not merely by the desire for gain." [1956] 2 Y.B. INT'L L. COMM'N at 282. *See also* M. S. MCDOUGAL & W. BURKE, *supra* note 28, at 811.

[31] Harvard Research, Piracy, *supra* note 14, at 786 (emphasis added).

[32] *Id.* at 798.

[33] Article 16 provides: "The provisions of this convention do not diminish a state's right under international law to take measures for the protection of its nationals, its ships and its commerce against interference on or over the high sea, when such measures are not based upon jurisdiction over piracy." *Id.* at 857.

> organization uses an armed ship to establish a blockade against foreign commerce, or to stop and search foreign ships for contraband, or to seize necessary supplies from foreign ships. These acts are illegal under international law, *at least if the revolutionary organization has not been recognized as a belligerent by the offended state,* and in some cases the offended state has proceeded to capture or destroy the offending ship.[34]

It appears from this language that the Harvard draft sought to exclude from the definition of piracy acts that were illegal because the revolutionary organization had not been recognized as a belligerent, but would have been legal if it had been so recognized. Further, the Comment notes that "some writers assert that such illegal attacks on foreign commerce by unrecognized revolutionaries are piracies in the international law sense; and there is even judicial authority to this effect." It concludes, however, that "the better view [is] that these are not cases falling under the common jurisdiction of all states as piracy."[35] But, as noted above, and as the quotations in the Comment confirm,[36] the proponents of the position that acts by insurgents should not constitute piracy—the position that the Comment to the Harvard draft accepts as the "better view"—took that position only with respect to insurgents whose acts were directed solely against the state whose government they sought to overthrow, not those who attacked ships of all nations indiscriminately. The Comment also explains that Article 16

> leaves unaffected the right of an offended state to seize and punish the offenders in accordance with the precedents cited (and, of course, this may, at the option of the prosecuting state, include conviction and punishment for piracy under its municipal law); but it does not concede jurisdiction on the ground of piracy in the international sense to *states not offended or threatened.*[37]

Again, the reference to "states not offended or threatened" suggests that the drafters contemplated situations in which the threat or injury was directed against a particular state, not against all states. Similarly, it is arguable that the "for private ends" provision in Article 3, to which Article 16 was the counterpart, was intended to exclude only acts directed against a particular state.[38]

The International Law Commission devoted considerable discussion to the "for private ends" proviso. After quoting from the Comment to the Harvard Draft Convention on Piracy the language reproduced in part above,[39] the rapporteur stated that "following the Harvard precedent, he had defined as piracy acts of violence or depredation committed for private

[34] *Id.* (emphasis added).

[35] *Id.*

[36] *See id.* at 857–61 (quoting the Report of the Sub-Committee of the League of Nations Committee of Experts for the Progressive Codification of International Law; C. HYDE, *supra* note 22, §233 (1st ed. 1922); W. HALL, *supra* note 21, at 314–15 (8th ed. 1924); and others).

[37] *Id.* at 857 (emphasis added).

[38] Otherwise, the category of cases excluded from universal jurisdiction by the "for private ends" language of Article 3 would be greater than the category of cases for which jurisdiction by the injured state was recognized under Article 16, a result that could clearly not have been intended.

[39] *See supra* text accompanying note 32.

ends, thus leaving outside the scope of the definition all wrongful acts perpetrated for a political purpose."[40] He continued:

> Although States at times have claimed the right to treat as pirates unrecognized insurgents against a foreign government *who have pretended to exercise belligerent rights on the sea against neutral commerce,* or privateers whose commissions violated the announced policy of the captor, and although there is authority for subjecting some cases of these types to the common jurisdiction of all States, it seems best to confine the common jurisdiction to offenders acting for private ends only.[41]

He, too, was apparently interpreting "for private ends" to exclude from the application of the laws of piracy acts by "unrecognized insurgents" exercising belligerent rights without having achieved belligerent status.

The discussion thereafter focused on whether acts by state vessels can constitute piracy. The report went on to quote Oppenheim: "Private vessels only can commit piracy. A man-of-war or other public ship, so long as she remains such, is never a pirate . . . ."[42] Responding to a complaint by Poland that China's seizure of its ships constituted piracy, the rapporteur is summarized as having said that "[n]o warship . . . could be described as a pirate ship in the international sense of the word."

> The principle of common jurisdiction, according to which a pirate was treated with universal public enmity, could only exist where the political element was lacking and where the ship concerned was not the public property of a State.
>
> . . . *All that was made clear by the words "for private ends",* as used in article 23, and the Polish memorandum was in fact a challenge to that element of his definition of piracy. *He would insist on those words being retained.*[43]

Jaroslav Zourek argued in response that "[m]any authorities, including L. Oppenheim, held that state-owned vessels could also be guilty of piracy, and that notion had been further substantiated by the 1937 Nyon Arrangement."[44] Zourek was referring to an agreement concluded by nine states[45] at Nyon during the Spanish Civil War, when unidentified submarines were attacking ships in the Mediterranean. Declaring that the attacks on ships not belonging to either of the conflicting parties should be treated as "acts of piracy," the agreement provided for collective measures "against piratical acts by submarines." A supplementary agreement extended the Nyon Arrangement to attacks by surface vessels and aircraft.[46]

Responding to Zourek, Sir Gerald Fitzmaurice stressed that, since no state had admitted ownership of the submarines in question, it was reasonable to assume that they were acting "for private ends." Fitzmaurice concluded that "[i]f he was right in arguing that the Nyon Arrangement had been based on that fact, the Special Rapporteur's point that piracy was

[40] [1955] 1 Y.B. INT'L L. COMM'N at 40.

[41] *Id.* at 41.

[42] *Id.*

[43] *Id.* (emphasis added).

[44] *Id.* at 43.

[45] Great Britain, Bulgaria, Egypt, France, Greece, Romania, Turkey, the Union of Soviet Socialist Republics and Yugoslavia.

[46] *See* 2 G. HACKWORTH, *supra* note 23, at 693.

essentially a crime committed by private individuals not in the performance of a public or authorized duty was reinforced."[47] At a subsequent meeting, he repeated that "*the real basis of the agreement reached at Nyon was the assumption that the acts had been unauthorized because no government would admit responsibility;* otherwise the normal representations would have been made."[48]

Clearly, the submarines were acting for "political" or "public ends," not for "private ends" as these terms are commonly understood. Fitzmaurice, however, was equating "public" with "authorized," and acts committed for "private ends" with acts that were not authorized and for which no government was willing to assume responsibility. He interpreted the "for private ends" proviso as referring to acts that had not been authorized by a government; as such, they were subject to the laws of war and should therefore not be subject to the laws of piracy.

Nevertheless, Fitzmaurice recognized that the term "for private ends" did not convey the idea clearly, since it "did not immediately convey that an act committed by a vessel of war on the authority of its government did not constitute piracy in the ordinary sense of the term as understood in international law, though it might be an act of aggression."[49] When the Commission thereafter defeated, by 11 to 2, a Soviet motion to delete "for private ends," it did so to reject the suggestion by Communist bloc states that the laws of piracy should apply to state vessels. This was made plain by Mr. Hsu, who, speaking immediately before the vote was taken,

> observed that a government, whether recognized or not by other States, continued to exist. He feared that if State A did not recognize State B, State B would retaliate by not recognizing State A and if each treated the vessels of the other as pirates the peace of the world would be gravely endangered.[50]

Similarly, the rapporteur "urged the Commission to reflect most carefully on the consequence of allowing seizure of a warship by a State on suspicion that it had committed acts of piracy. Such a step carried far more serious implications than in the case of seizure of merchantmen."[51] It was never suggested by anyone that the "for private ends" language would exempt terrorist acts.[52]

[47] [1955] 1 Y.B. INT'L L. COMM'N at 43–44.

[48] *Id.* at 56 (emphasis added).

[49] *Id.* These statements are all the more noteworthy since François, in rejecting the Polish complaint, and Fitzmaurice, in rejecting the suggestion that the Nyon Arrangement indicated an extension of the laws of piracy to state vessels, could have relied on the private vessel requirement rather than on the "private ends" proviso, as they did. *See supra* text accompanying notes 43 and 47–48. In a paper discussing the Commission's draft, D. H. N. Johnson stated, "It is arguable that it would be better to emphasize the lack of due authority as the essence of piracy, rather than, as does the International Law Commission, the fact that piracy is a crime committed for 'private ends.' " Johnson, *supra* note 20, at 77 n.21. He does not, however, consider the two tests coextensive. *Id.*

[50] [1955] 1 Y.B. INT'L L. COMM'N at 57. [51] *Id.*

[52] Zourek even stated that "the Commission had accepted the thesis that an insurgent vessel committing acts of piracy against a third State was a pirate," though Yuen-li Liang, Secretary to the Commission, said "he had no recollection of such a decision." *Id.* at 56.

The "for private ends" proviso may be interpreted as excluding from the laws of piracy not only insurgents who direct their acts solely against the state whose government they seek to overthrow, but also all those whose acts have no personal motive, whether monetary or otherwise. This interpretation is consistent with the statements in the Comments to the Harvard draft and to the Geneva Convention that the desire for personal gain is not essential. The Harvard Comment quoted the statement by Hyde that

> as piracy does not necessarily involve the taking of property, the absence of an intent to steal is not necessarily decisive of the character of what takes place. According to Dana, "the motive may be gratuitous malice, or the purpose may be to destroy, in private revenge for real or supposed injuries done by persons or classes of persons, or by a particular national authority."[53]

Even if the proviso were so interpreted, it would not necessarily exempt the acts of the hijackers of the *Achille Lauro.* Although the hijackers were allegedly members of a terrorist organization whose avowed aim is to destroy Israel, they seized an Italian ship that had just left Egypt on its way to Israel, and killed a U.S. national, a crippled Jewish man who clearly could not have offered any resistance. The motive may well have been "gratuitous malice," or "private revenge for real or supposed injuries done by persons or classes of persons" (Jews) or by a particular "national authority" (Israel). Claims that the hijackers had intended to use the ship to attack Israel and only seized it, took the passengers hostage and killed Klinghoffer when they were discovered and their purpose frustrated, support rather than negate the position that their acts were piratical. Under this scenario, there was no political purpose at the time they killed Klinghoffer, assuming there had been one at the outset.

While the particular facts of the *Achille Lauro* incident may bring the hijackers within the definition of piracy even under this interpretation of the "private ends" provision, piracy so defined might not apply to terrorist acts in different circumstances.[54] Moreover, while the interpretation is possible, it is more likely that the intention was to exclude unrecognized insurgents acting against a foreign government and ships acting under public authority, as indicated by the Comments to the Harvard draft and the discussion by the International Law Commission quoted above.[55] Further, the rationale for exempting insurgents from the laws of piracy does not apply to random seizures of vessels and attacks on their passengers. Exclusion cannot be justified on the ground that, in the words of Hall, "it is by the

[53] Harvard Research, Piracy, *supra* note 14, at 806.

[54] Though one might take the position that the deliberate, indiscriminate murder of civilians regardless of the identity, status or nationality of the victim is always "gratuitous malice," as no political purpose can be served thereby; certainly not the destruction of the government the insurgents seek to overthrow, or recognition as belligerents, the justification urged by Hall for exempting insurgents from the laws of piracy. *See* quote in text accompanying note 21 *supra.*

[55] Significantly, the rapporteur for the International Law Commission quoted these passages concerning insurgents but did not quote the Hyde passage, text accompanying note 53 *supra. See supra* text accompanying notes 39–41.

performance of such acts that independence is established and its existence proved."[56] Nor can it be said of the terrorist, as Hall said of the insurgent whose exemption he advocated, that "his moral attitude is different, and the acts themselves will be kept within well-marked bounds. He is not only not the enemy of the human race, but he is the enemy solely of a particular state."[57]

One commentator suggested that the reason for the "private ends" proviso in the Geneva Convention, which he interpreted as a departure from customary law and a narrowing of the definition of piracy (rather than an incorporation of that law and resolution of the unsettled question concerning insurgents in favor of exclusion, as suggested by the present writer), was to impose a *duty* on states to take measures against piracy. He said, "States might have been reluctant to accept a rule which might create liability in numerous situations."[58]

Article 14 of the Geneva Convention provides: "All States shall cooperate to the fullest possible extent in the repression of piracy . . . ." The commentary to the International Law Commission's draft Article 38, which became Article 14 of the Geneva Convention, states: "Any State having an opportunity of taking measures against piracy, and neglecting to do so, would be failing in a duty laid upon it by international law."[59] Johnson interpreted this to mean that a state that failed to discharge the duty is liable for "the payment of reparation to other States whose shipping was molested by the pirates in question."[60]

It might be argued that if and to the extent that the "private ends" language is interpreted as narrowing the definition of piracy under customary international law, that narrowing only applies insofar as the Convention imposes a duty on states to exercise jurisdiction but does not preclude the exercise of jurisdiction in other situations to the extent permitted by customary international law. This result, however, does not appear to have been the intent of the authors of the Harvard draft or of the International Law Commission. The Harvard Comment makes clear that the purpose was to establish uniform rules: "The theme of this draft convention is the definition of this extraordinary basis of jurisdiction and the specification of the conditions and limitations pertaining to the exercise of jurisdiction on this

[56] *See* W. HALL, *quoted in* text accompanying note 21 *supra*.

[57] *Id.* at 234.

[58] Crockett, *Toward a Revision of the International Law of Piracy*, 26 DE PAUL L. REV. 78, 97 (1976).

[59] [1956] 2 Y.B. INT'L L. COMM'N at 282. The Harvard draft, *supra* note 14, similarly provided, "The parties to this Convention agree to make every expedient use of their powers to prevent piracy, separately and in co-operation." Art. 18. However, the Comment specifically rejected any implication that this might impose a duty on states to act. The introduction states, "the draft convention does not assert a definite duty of signatories to seize or prosecute all pirates. It imposes on them by Article 18 only a general discretionary obligation to discourage piracy by exercising their rights of prevention and punishment as far as is expedient." Harvard Research, Piracy, *supra* note 14, at 760.

[60] Johnson, *supra* note 20, at 65.

ground."[61] And the Comment to the piracy provisions of the Geneva Convention states:

> The questions arising in connexion with acts committed by warships in the service of rival Governments engaged in civil war are too complex to make it seem necessary for the safeguarding of order and security on the high seas that all States should have a general right, let alone an obligation, to repress as piracy acts perpetrated by the warships of the parties in question.[62]

This assertion seems to indicate that the article was intended to limit the right, as well as the obligation, to act. It also indicates, as stated earlier, that the Commission's primary concern was to exclude from the laws of piracy ships of belligerents engaged in hostilities.

It was mentioned above that the UN Convention on the Law of the Sea reiterated the piracy provisions of the Geneva Convention. I have found no recorded discussion of these provisions at any of the conferences preceding the adoption of the Convention and several of the participants have assured me that there was no such discussion. Although commentators on the subject urged that the definition of piracy be modified to make clear that terrorist acts on the high seas were piratical,[63] the importance and controversial nature of other matters apparently precluded consideration of piracy.

Attacks Against Another Ship. The question whether an act on board a ship, such as the murder of one passenger or crew member by another passenger or crew member, or the seizure of the ship by members of the crew, constitutes piracy was not settled under customary international law. The consensus, however, seemed to be that it depended on whether it was appropriate in the circumstances of the particular case to hold the flag state responsible for the acts. If the vessel retained its national character and remained subject to the authority of the flag state, it was not a pirate ship and only that state had jurisdiction. Where the ship did not submit to the authority of any state and no state could be held responsible for its acts, it became subject to the jurisdiction of all states.[64] Thus, Hall stated:

> Piracy includes acts differing much from each other in kind and in moral value; but one thing they all have in common: they are done under conditions which render it impossible or unfair to hold any state responsible for their commission. A pirate either belongs to no state or organised political society, or by the nature of his act he has shown his intention and his power to reject the authority of that to which he is properly subject. . . . If a commissioned vessel of war indulges in illegal acts, recourse can be had to its government for redress; if a sailor commits a murder on board a vessel the authority of the state to which it belongs is not displaced, and its laws are able to assert themselves; but

[61] Harvard Research, Piracy, *supra* note 14, at 768.

[62] [1956] 2 Y.B. INT'L L. COMM'N at 282.

[63] *See* B. DUBNER, THE LAW OF INTERNATIONAL SEA PIRACY 50–51, 54–55, 59 (1980); Crockett, *supra* note 58.

[64] See generally authorities quoted in Harvard Research, Piracy, *supra* note 14, at 809–20.

> if a body of men of uncertain origin seize upon a vessel and scour the ocean for plunder, no one nation has more right of control over them, or more responsibility for their doings, than another, and if the crew of a ship takes possession of it after confining or murdering the captain, legitimate authority has disappeared for the moment, and it is uncertain for how long it may be kept out.[65]

The Convention's requirement that the act be committed by the crew or passengers of one ship "against another ship" was apparently intended to codify this customary law. In presenting this element of the definition of piracy to the International Law Commission, Rapporteur François quoted the Harvard Comment:

> Some definitions of piracy are broad enough to include robberies and other acts of violence or depredation committed on board a merchant ship on the high sea by a passenger or a member of the crew who is not in control of the ship. Mutiny on the high seas has sometimes been included. The great weight of professional opinion, however, does not sanction an extension of the common jurisdiction of all States to cover such offences committed entirely on board a ship which by international law is under the exclusive jurisdiction of a State whose flag it flies. Even though a mutiny succeeds, the common jurisdiction would not attach. *It should attach, however, if the successful mutineers then set out to devote the ship to the accomplishment of further acts of violence or depredation* (of the sort specified in Article 3, 1) on the high sea or in foreign territory.[66]

After quoting what he termed the dissenting view of Lawrence, the rapporteur invoked Oppenheim, who, he said, "summed up better the consensus of legal opinion on that issue," as follows:

> [A] simple act of violence on the part of crew or passengers does not constitute in itself the crime of piracy, not at least as far as international law is concerned. If, for instance, the crew were to murder the master on account of his cruelty, and afterwards carried on the voyage, they would be murderers, but not pirates. *They are pirates only when the revolt is directed, not merely against the master, but also against the vessel, for the purpose of converting her and her goods to their own use.*[67]

[65] W. HALL, *supra* note 36, at 310–11, *quoted in id.* at 817–18. *See also id.* at 819 (quoting Wheaton: "But, if such a vessel passes into the control of the robbers or murderers on board, and the lawful authority is in fact displaced, and she becomes an outlaw, any nation may seize the vessel and try the criminals"; H. WHEATON, ELEMENTS OF INTERNATIONAL LAW, note by Dana to §124 (8th ed. Dana 1866)).

[66] [1955] 1 Y.B. INT'L L. COMM'N at 42–43 (quoting Harvard Research, Piracy, *supra* note 14, at 809–10 (emphasis added)).

[67] *Id.* at 42 (emphasis added). The Commentary to Article 39 states: "(vi) Acts committed on board a ship by the crew or passengers and directed against the ship itself, or against persons or property on the ship, cannot be regarded as acts of piracy." It goes on to state, however: "*The view adopted by the Commission in regard to point (vi) tallies with the opinion of most writers.* Even where the purpose of the mutineers is to seize the ship, their acts do not constitute acts of piracy." [1956] 2 Y.B. INT'L L. COMM'N at 282 (emphasis added). As the passages quoted in the text indicate, the rapporteur made clear that in his view the consensus was best summed up by Oppenheim, i.e., that the seizure does constitute piracy where it is directed not only against the

The Santa María *Incident*

The *Santa María,* a Portuguese cruise ship, was seized by Captain Galvão, a well-known political opponent of the Salazar Government, and a number of persons who had either boarded in the guise of passengers or were members of the original crew.[68] One crew member was killed and eight others were wounded in the process. Galvão declared the seizure to be "the first step aimed at overthrowing the Dictator Salazar of Portugal."[69] In a broadcast to the outside world, he said that he had captured the *Santa María* "in the name of the Independent Junta of Liberation led by General Humberto Delgado, the legally elected President of the Portuguese Republic who has been fraudulently deprived of his rights by the Salazar Administration."[70]

Portugal asked U.S., Dutch and British vessels to search for and capture the vessel "in accordance with the well defined terms of international law governing piracy and insurrection on board ship."[71] The *Santa María* was eventually sighted in international waters by British and U.S. naval vessels and boarded by the commander of a U.S. destroyer. Galvão agreed to surrender the ship, provided he received assurances that he would be treated as an insurgent.[72] After the ship was securely anchored in Brazil, the State Department announced that the United States "had acted under the international laws against piracy."[73]

Commentators disagreed on whether the seizure constituted piracy. Fenwick, apparently applying customary international law, took the position that it was piracy. He wrote:

> [Galvão] said he was an insurgent, . . . that he was taking the first step in a revolt against the dictator . . . . Well, international law does recognize the status of insurgents.
>
> . . . But here third states have . . . [required] something equivalent to a "status of insurgency"; and even then the alleged insurgents might not seize the property of the third state or inflict injury upon its nationals. . . .

---

master but also against the vessel for the purpose of converting her and her goods to the perpetrators' use. This, of course, was exactly the case of those who seized the *Achille Lauro.* After taking the ship, the hijackers killed one of the passengers, held the others hostage and apparently planned to use the ship to attack Israel.

[68] The facts are summarized in B. DUBNER, *supra* note 63, at 148–49; and N. JOYNER, AERIAL HIJACKING AS AN INTERNATIONAL CRIME 109–11 (1974).

[69] Green, *The* Santa Maria: *Rebels or Pirates,* 37 BRIT. Y.B. INT'L L. 496 (1961).

[70] N. JOYNER, *supra* note 68, at 109.

[71] *Id.* at 110 (quoting KEESING'S CONTEMPORARY ARCHIVES, Feb. 24–Mar. 4, 1961, at 17,951).

[72] *Id.* at 111.

[73] *Id.* Galvão was given political asylum by Brazil. *Id.* Joyner states that "had Great Britain and the United States not been sympathetic towards the revolution which Galvao and his followers proposed, [they] would have delivered [the *Santa María*] directly to the Portuguese government in Lisbon." *Id.* n.119.

> . . . The law of insurgency applies to armed conflicts between the group in rebellion and the government against which it is rebelling; *it cannot justify attacks upon civilian lives and property.*[74]

Whiteman took the position that the seizure was not piracy under the Geneva Convention, though she apparently viewed it as being for "private ends," notwithstanding its political motive. After reciting the facts, including Galvão's opposition to Salazar and his support for Delgado, she concluded: "Since the ship was taken over by certain of its own passengers (apparently for private ends), and not by another ship, as at first reported, it was considered that for this, if for no other reason, article 15 of the 1958 Convention was inapplicable."[75]

Green argued that the seizure did not constitute piracy under customary law "since it was in no way directed against any non-Portuguese interest." It would not constitute piracy under the Geneva Convention because it did not satisfy the requirement that "the illegal act must be directed 'against another ship' " and because "the treatment of the ship once she had been seized, together with the statements made by Captain Galvão and General Delgado, made it perfectly clear that this seizure was not made 'for private ends.' "[76]

Franck, while noting that it was "not clear just what 'public' objective the rebels hoped to achieve," was willing to assume that it was for public, rather than private, ends and was therefore not piratical, but he used the case to argue the absurdity of the "two ship" requirement.[77]

The seizure of the *Santa María* differed from that of the *Achille Lauro* in several important respects. The ship was Portuguese and was seized by a well-known opponent of the existing Government of Portugal. He gave repeated assurances that he did not want to harm any interests or nationals of other countries. The seizure was carried out by insurgents fighting for political independence whose acts were directed against the government they sought to overthrow. It therefore arguably met the conditions for exemption of insurgents under customary international law.[78] Those who seized the *Achille Lauro,* on the other hand, did not limit their target to a particular state. They seized an Italian ship, deliberately killed a U.S. national, and held hostage and threatened persons of diverse nationalities—clearly not satisfying the conditions for exemption of insurgents under customary law. Both incidents, however, involved the seizure and endangered the lives of nationals of third states.

* * * *

The customary law of piracy can perhaps be best understood as an attempt to balance the need for universal jurisdiction against the reluctance of

[74] Fenwick, *"Piracy" in the Caribbean,* 55 AJIL 426, 426–27 (1961) (emphasis added).
[75] 4 M. Whiteman, Digest of International Law 666 (1965).
[76] Green, *supra* note 69, at 503.
[77] Franck, *"To Define and Punish Piracies"—The Lesson of the Santa Maria: A Comment,* 36 N.Y.U. L. Rev. 839, 840 (1961).
[78] *See supra* notes 20–22 and accompanying text.

states to permit encroachment on their exclusive jurisdiction. States accepted universal jurisdiction over piracy because pirates (1) attacked the ships of all states indiscriminately and were thus a threat to all states, and (2) were not subject to the authority of any state, and therefore no state could be held responsible for their acts. This both created the practical need and provided the theoretical justification for the exercise of universal jurisdiction. Universal jurisdiction was justified theoretically on the ground that pirates are *hostis humani generis,* the enemies of all mankind; it was necessary pragmatically because no state could be held responsible for their acts under international law.[79] Where the actor was not potentially a threat to all states or the act was done under the authority of a state, universal jurisdiction was denied. Thus, acts by state vessels, by recognized belligerents or by those on board a ship that continued to accept the authority of the flag state were not piratical.

Insurgents who had not achieved the status of recognized belligerents presented a problem. However, to the extent that they confined their attacks to the ships and property of a particular state, they were not *hostis humani generis.* Some publicists urged,[80] and some states, including the United States,[81] agreed, that such insurgents should also be exempt from the laws of piracy.[82] Insurgents who did not confine their attacks to ships and property of the government they sought to overthrow (and to measures to prevent neutral ships from assisting such governments) were considered pirates.[83]

The Comment makes clear that the purpose of the piracy provisions in the Harvard Draft Convention on Piracy was to provide for universal jurisdiction over acts that were potentially a threat to all states and to exclude from such jurisdiction acts that were directed against a single state. It states:

> *[N]o such offence which by its nature raises an apprehension on the part of all states concerning the safety of their nationals or their property or commerce should be left outside the scope of the salutary common jurisdiction* . . . .
>
> Nevertheless, the opposition to bringing under the common jurisdiction offences against the interests of a single state, and the insistence on some international factual element in the definition of piracy, are strong enough to make it expedient to exclude from the definition of piracy offences which involve only ships and territory under the ordinary jurisdiction of one state and which are not incidents of an enterprise with purposes of wider scope. . . . *In all these cases of piracy, then, there is an element which engages the interest of the international community, and this should satisfy at once the theoretical and the practical insistence on a factual offence against international interests.*[84]

[79] *See* Hall's arguments, *supra* at text accompanying notes 21 and 65, and Sir Gerald Fitzmaurice's explanation of the Nyon Agreement, *supra* at text accompanying notes 47–49.

[80] *See supra* text accompanying note 21.

[81] *See supra* text accompanying notes 22–23.

[82] Organized insurgents have been recognized as having belligerent rights and limited governmental rights in other contexts as well. *See* L. HENKIN, R. PUGH, O. SCHACHTER & H. SMIT, INTERNATIONAL LAW: CASES AND MATERIALS 190–91 (2d ed. 1987).

[83] *See supra* note 23.

[84] Harvard Research, Piracy, *supra* note 14, at 807–08 (emphasis added).

A strong argument can be made for the application of the customary law of piracy to terrorist acts on the high seas. Both the theoretical justification and the pragmatic necessity for universal jurisdiction apply to such acts. Terrorists today, like pirates of old, are a threat to all states and no state is willing to assume responsibility for their acts. Since they do not confine their attacks to the vessels of a particular state, but attack vessels and nationals of many states indiscriminately, they are *hostis humani generis* in the truest sense. Since no state has accepted responsibility for their acts, there is no state against which claims for redress can be made.

In the past, pirates used one ship to attack another and the motive was material gain. Today, terrorists such as the hijackers of the *Achille Lauro* seize a ship, threaten its passengers and kill them without regard to the flag it flies or the nationality of the victims. That they do so by boarding the ship disguised as crew or passengers, rather than by attacking it from another ship, or that they are motivated by hate, revenge or a desire to call attention to a political cause rather than by a desire for material gain, does not affect the two essential elements that have justified assertion of universal jurisdiction in the past: that they are a threat to all states, and that no state can be held responsible for their acts.

While there was no authoritative definition of piracy under customary international law, there is substantial support in the writings of scholars that such acts would constitute piracy under customary international law. Thus, Oppenheim concludes: "There is substance in the view that, by continuous usage, the notion of piracy has been extended from its original meaning of predatory acts committed on the high seas by private persons and that *it now covers generally ruthless acts of lawlessness on the high seas by whomsoever committed.*"[85]

Moreover, customary international law is not static; it is constantly evolving. "International law has not become a crystallized code . . . but is a living and expanding branch of the law."[86] This evolution is exemplified by the customary law of piracy itself. At one stage, piracy was defined as robbery on the high seas and material gain was a necessary element; at a later stage, *animus furandi* was no longer required. Just as Viscount Sankey and Justice Story held that actual robbery was not an essential element of piracy,[87] so a judge today might reasonably conclude that the laws of piracy should apply to terrorist attacks even though the motive was something other than personal gain.[88] The exemption for insurgents would not exclude present-day terrorists, since it applied only to insurgents who confined their attacks to a particular state.

[85] 1 L. OPPENHEIM, *supra* note 15, at 613–14 (emphasis added); *see also supra* note 15 and accompanying text.

[86] *In re* Piracy Jure Gentium, 3 BRIT. INT'L L. CASES at 839.

[87] *See supra* notes 18–19 and accompanying text.

[88] The suggestion was made by Sir Hersch Lauterpacht some time ago. He said:

> As the notion of piracy *jure gentium* has never been rigidly confined to one type of unlawful action and as the kind of lawlessness with which it was in the beginning predominantly connected is now becoming a historical survival, it would not seem improper to describe and treat as piratical such acts of violence on the high seas which by their

It is also arguable that the definitions of piracy in the Geneva Convention on the High Seas and the UN Convention on the Law of the Sea were not intended to exclude indiscriminate attacks by terrorists. Both Conventions define piracy as an act committed "for private ends" by "one ship against another." Although "for private ends" can certainly be interpreted as excluding any acts that have a political purpose and there is language in the *travaux préparatoires* contrasting "private ends" with "political ends," it appears fairly clear that the term "political ends" was used to refer to acts by a "revolutionary organization that had not been recognized as a belligerent by the offended state."[89] Thus, one may reasonably take the position, based on an analysis of the *travaux préparatoires,* that "for private ends" was only intended to exclude acts by insurgents who had not yet achieved the status of belligerents (but whose acts would be lawful if done by belligerents),[90] and acts by state vessels that had been authorized by a state and for which that state assumed responsibility.[91]

The two-ship requirement is more problematic. On its face, the provision clearly excludes acts perpetrated by "passengers" on the same ship. Nevertheless, it is arguable that at least in the Harvard Draft Convention on Piracy, the language was intended to exclude from universal jurisdiction criminal acts by one passenger or crew member against another, or mutiny against the captain, where the ship continued to accept the authority of the flag state, and not to exclude an attack directed "against the vessel, for the purpose of converting her . . . to [the attackers'] own use."[92] Certainly, there is no indication in the Comment to the Harvard draft, in the statement by the rapporteur for the International Law Commission or in the report by the Commission to the General Assembly that the authors either of the Harvard draft or of the Geneva Convention ever considered, let alone decided, that terrorist acts at sea not limited to a specific state whose government the attackers were seeking to overthrow should be exempt from the universal jurisdiction applicable to piracy.[93]

However, even if the piracy provisions of the Geneva and UN Conventions were not intended to exempt indiscriminate attacks on the high seas from universal jurisdiction, the definition of piracy in these Conventions

---

ruthlessness and disregard of the sanctity of human life invite exemplary punishment and suppression.

H. Lauterpacht, Recognition in International Law 307–08 (1948).

[89] *See supra* text accompanying note 34.

[90] *See supra* text accompanying notes 31–41.

[91] *See supra* text accompanying notes 42–49.

[92] *See supra* text accompanying note 67.

[93] There is no reference to terrorist acts in the Harvard Draft Convention on Piracy or in the voluminous Comment to it. The Comment to the Draft Convention on Jurisdiction with Respect to Crime, *supra* note 12, which was published three years later, in 1935, following the Marseilles assassinations in 1934, cites a resolution by the Council of the League of Nations that referred to "terrorist activity with a political purpose" and to "crimes committed with a political and terrorist purpose." 29 AJIL Supp. at 554. *See also infra* text accompanying note 163.

lends itself to that interpretation. An interpretation of those provisions as encompassing such acts requires resort to the *travaux préparatoires.*[94] Moreover, the *travaux préparatoires* are not unequivocal.[95] As the comments on the seizures of the *Santa María* and the *Achille Lauro* demonstrate, there is considerable difference of opinion among scholars over whether the seizure of a ship on the high seas for a "political cause" constitutes piracy under the Geneva Convention.[96] Thus, even if one finds sufficient historical and/or teleological justification for concluding that the piracy provisions of the Geneva and UN Conventions are applicable to maritime terrorism, it would be preferable to adopt a convention dealing with maritime terrorism specifically, as has been done with airplane hijacking and sabotage, hostage taking and attacks on diplomats, the other terrorist acts that have begun to plague the international community.

II. THE DRAFT CONVENTION FOR THE SUPPRESSION OF UNLAWFUL ACTS AGAINST THE SAFETY OF MARITIME NAVIGATION

Following the seizure of the *Achille Lauro,* Italy, on the initiative of Professor Ferrari Bravo, its Legal Adviser, joined by Austria and Egypt, proposed a convention against maritime terrorism. A draft, modeled on existing conventions, particularly the Hague and Montreal Conventions against airplane hijacking and sabotage, and the Hostage Convention,[97] was submitted to the IMO. At its meeting in November 1986, the Council agreed unanimously that the matter was appropriate for consideration by the IMO and that it required urgent attention.[98] To avoid the possible delays that might result from its submission to the overburdened Legal Committee, which would normally have considered the Convention, the Council de-

[94] Whether resort to the *travaux préparatoires* is appropriate is also debatable. Under Article 31 of the Vienna Convention, "A treaty shall be interpreted in good faith in accordance with the ordinary meaning to be given to the terms of the treaty in their context and in the light of its object and purpose." The article permits a "special meaning" to be given to a term "if it is established that the parties so intended." Article 32, "Supplementary means of interpretation," provides:

> Recourse may be had to supplementary means of interpretation, including the preparatory work of the treaty and the circumstances of its conclusion, in order to confirm the meaning resulting from the application of article 31, or to determine the meaning when the interpretation according to article 31:
>
> (a) leaves the meaning ambiguous or obscure; or
> (b) leads to a result which is manifestly absurd or unreasonable.

Vienna Convention on the Law of Treaties, *opened for signature* May 23, 1969, UNTS Regis. No. 18,232, UN Doc. A/CONF.39/27 (1969). While it is arguable that the meaning of "for private ends" is "ambiguous or obscure," it would be difficult to make that argument with respect to the two-ship requirement (though it may perhaps be argued that it leads to a result that is manifestly absurd or unreasonable). *See* Franck, *supra* note 77.

[95] *See supra* text accompanying notes 40–41.

[96] *See supra* text accompanying notes 8, 68–78.

[97] For these three Conventions, see *supra* note 9.

[98] *See* IMO Doc. C 57/25 (Oct. 1, 1986).

cided to establish an *Ad Hoc* Preparatory Committee open to all states, with "the mandate to prepare, on a priority basis, a Draft Convention for the Suppression of Unlawful Acts Against the Safety of Maritime Navigation," using the draft submitted by Austria, Egypt and Italy as a basis.[99]

The Preparatory Committee met for a week in March 1987 in London, and for a week in May 1987 in Rome, to consider the proposed Convention. At the conclusion of the Rome meeting, the committee agreed on a draft Convention, though several important issues, considered to be of a political nature, were left for resolution by a diplomatic conference, to be held in Rome in March 1988, at which the Convention was to be adopted.

Although it is entitled Convention for the Suppression of Unlawful Acts Against the Safety of Maritime Navigation, its operative provisions deal not so much with the suppression of such acts, as with the apprehension, conviction and punishment of those who commit them. Only one provision addresses the problem of prevention or suppression directly. Article 13 requires states to cooperate in the prevention of offenses by:

> (a) taking all practicable measures to prevent preparation in their respective territories for the commission of those offences within or outside their territories;
>
> (b) exchanging information in accordance with their national law, and co-ordinating administrative and other measures as appropriate to prevent the commission of offences set forth in article 3.[100]

The heart of this Convention, as of the other antiterrorist conventions, is the "extradite or prosecute" requirement—the obligation of each state party to the Convention in which an alleged offender is found either to extradite the offender to one of the states that has jurisdiction under the Convention or to submit the case to its authorities for prosecution.[101] The Convention further provides that "the offences set forth [in the Convention] shall be treated, for the purposes of extradition between States Parties, as if they had been committed not only in the place in which they occurred

[99] *See* IMO Doc. C 57/WP.1, para. 25(a)(2) (Nov. 12, 1986). The explanatory note by the cosponsors stated that while there are three conventions dealing with the safety of air navigation, "the safety of maritime navigation is not covered by any similar instrument." IMO Doc. C 57/25, Annex, at 2 (Oct. 1, 1986).

[100] Convention, *supra* note 11, Art. 13(1)(a) and (b).

[101] *Id.*, Art. 10(1), which reads:

> The State Party in the territory of which the offender or the alleged offender is found shall, in cases to which article 7 applies, if it does not extradite him, be obliged, without exception whatsoever and whether or not the offence was committed in its territory, to submit the case without delay to its competent authorities for the purpose of prosecution, through proceedings in accordance with the laws of that State. Those authorities shall take their decision in the same manner as in the case of any ordinary offence of a grave nature under the law of that State.

There are identical or substantially similar provisions in the Hague Convention (Art. 7), the Montreal Convention (Art. 7), the Hostage Convention (Art. 8) and the Internationally Protected Persons Convention (Art. 7), all *supra* note 9.

but also in a place within the jurisdiction of the State Party requesting extradition."[102]

The following summary and analysis of the main provisions of the Convention notes in particular the problems that arose in the course of the negotiations, the manner in which they were resolved and the issues that were reserved for resolution by the Diplomatic Conference.

Defining the Offenses

Article 3 provides:

> 1. Any person commits an offence if that person unlawfully and intentionally:
>
> (a) by force or threat thereof or any other form of intimidation seizes or exercises control over a ship; or
> (b) performs an act of violence against a person on board a ship if that act is likely to endanger the safe navigation of the ship; or
> (c) destroys a ship or causes damage to a ship or to its cargo which is likely to endanger the safe navigation of the ship; or
> (d) places or causes to be placed on a ship, by any means whatsoever, a device or substance which is likely to destroy that ship, or cause damage to that ship or its cargo which endangers or is likely to endanger the safe navigation of the ship; or
> (e) destroys or seriously damages maritime navigational facilities or seriously interferes with their operation, if any such act is likely to endanger the safe navigation of ships; or
> (f) communicates information which he knows to be false, thereby endangering the safe navigation of ships; or
> (g) injures or kills any person, in connection with the commission or the attempted commission of any of the offences set forth in subparagraphs (a) to (f).
>
> 2. Any person also commits an offence if that person:
>
> (a) attempts to commit any of the offences set forth in paragraph 1 if that attempt is likely to endanger the safe navigation of the ship; or
> (b) abets the commission of any such offence perpetrated by any person or is otherwise an accomplice of a person who commits such an offence; or
> (c) threatens to commit any of the offences set forth in paragraph 1, subparagraphs (b) and (c), if that threat is likely to endanger the safe navigation of the ship.

An early version of the draft did not include a provision (now paragraph 1(g)) making it an offense to injure or kill someone in connection with the commission or the attempted commission of the offense. Although such a provision was included in the draft submitted to the IMO by the cosponsors, several states urged its deletion or modification when the draft was considered by the Preparatory Committee.[103] Their comments were of three

[102] Convention, *supra* note 11, Art. 11(4).

[103] *See Ad Hoc* Preparatory Committee on the Suppression of Unlawful Acts Against the Safety of Maritime Navigation, Report of the First Session, IMO Doc. PCUA 1/4, para. 30 (Mar. 16, 1987).

types: that the provision should be deleted entirely; that injuring or killing a person should be an aggravating circumstance but not a separate crime; and that the language originally used—"during the commission" of the offense —might be interpreted to apply to a murder that was not connected with the terrorist attack. Those states that took the first two positions argued that the Convention was intended to suppress acts against the safety of maritime navigation, and that the killing of a passenger on a seized ship that did not endanger maritime navigation should not be included, while one that caused such endangerment would already be covered under paragraph 1(b). Other states, however, maintained that since the deliberate killing of a person on board a ship by the terrorists who seized it is a distinct crime, it should be a separate offense, not merely an aggravating circumstance.

The provision was retained in the draft Convention adopted by the Preparatory Committee, with some drafting modifications designed to avoid its being interpreted as applicable to murders that were committed during a terrorist attack but unconnected with it. While making murder a separate offense was not one of the questions left for resolution by the Diplomatic Conference, it may be raised again when the Convention is considered at the Diplomatic Conference.

Except for the Convention on Internationally Protected Persons, none of the antiterrorist Conventions make it an offense to injure or kill a person. For example, the Hague Convention makes it an offense for terrorists to seize an airplane, but not to kill a passenger after the seizure, as happened in the TWA hijacking in 1985; and the Hostage Convention makes it an offense to seize or detain and threaten to kill or injure a person, but not to murder the person seized. The failure to include murder as a separate offense is a major gap in the other antiterrorist conventions that should not be repeated in this Convention.

First, as several states argued, the deliberate killing of one or more persons aboard a ship by terrorists who seize it is a heinous act that should be a separate offense, not merely an aggravating circumstance. Second, the failure to include this provision in the Convention would make it difficult to prosecute the offenders for such a killing. While it would presumably be an offense under the law of the flag state even if not included as a separate offense under the Convention, the flag state would not be entitled to extradition of the offender for murder under the Convention. The extradite or prosecute provision of the Convention applies to "offenses" under the Convention. The inclusion of murder as an aggravating circumstance, rather than as an "offense," would therefore not provide a basis for extradition for murder. Furthermore, if the offender were extradited to the flag state for other offenses under the Convention, that state would not have jurisdiction to try him for the murder, since under the laws of extradition a state may generally not try a person for any offenses other than those for which he was extradited.[104]

[104] *See, e.g.*, 1 J. B. MOORE, TREATISE ON EXTRADITION AND INTERSTATE RENDITION 217 (1891) ("Among writers on international law there is almost uniform concurrence in the

While the argument that the killing of a passenger after the ship has been seized does not endanger maritime safety and therefore should not be an offense has superficial logic, the reason for protecting the safety of maritime navigation *is* to protect those who use it. The impetus for this Convention was the seizure of the *Achille Lauro* and the deliberate murder of a crippled, wheelchair-bound passenger by the perpetrators. It riveted the attention of the world and shocked and outraged people everywhere.[105] Both the UN General Assembly and the Security Council passed resolutions condemning terrorism,[106] and the General Assembly invited the IMO "to study the problem of terrorism aboard or against ships with a view to making recommendations on appropriate measures."[107] It would be ironic, indeed, if the Convention that was drafted in response to that resolution and the act that triggered it did not make that murder an offense.

Jurisdiction

States Obligated or Authorized to Establish Jurisdiction. The draft Convention establishes two types of jurisdiction: obligatory and discretionary. Article 7 provides that each state party "shall take such measures as may be necessary to establish its jurisdiction" when the offense is committed "(a) against or on board a ship flying the flag of the State at the time the offence is committed; or (b) in the territory of that State, or inside the outer or lateral limits of its territorial sea; or (c) by a national of that State." It further provides that a state party "may also establish its jurisdiction" over any such offense when:

> (a) it is committed by a stateless person whose habitual residence is in that State;
> (b) during its commission a national of that State is seized, threatened, injured or killed;
> (c) it is committed in an attempt to compel that State to do or abstain from doing any act; or
> (d) the demise-charterer in possession of the ship concerned in the offence [is a national of that State and] has its principal place of business in that State.[108]

Thus, the draft Convention provides that the state of nationality of the offender, the flag state and, when the offense is committed in the territory

---

opinion that a person surrendered for one offence should not be tried for another until he shall have been replaced within the jurisdiction of the surrendering state or had an opportunity to return thereto"); 6 M. WHITEMAN, DIGEST OF INTERNATIONAL LAW 728 (1968).

[105] The seizure of the *Achille Lauro* and murder of Klinghoffer were reported extensively, including front-page stories in the *New York Times* for seven consecutive days and cover stories in both *Newsweek* and *Time* magazines.

[106] GA Res. 40/61 (Dec. 9, 1985); SC Res. 579 (XXXX) (Dec. 18, 1985); *reprinted in* 80 AJIL 435 and 437, respectively (1986).

[107] GA Res. 40/61, *supra* note 106, para. 13.

[108] Convention, *supra* note 11, Art. 7(1) and (2). The brackets are in the draft Convention. The precise scope of this provision was left open by the Preparatory Committee. *See infra* note 160.

or territorial sea of a state, the latter state are required to establish jurisdiction. The state of habitual residence of a stateless person, the state of nationality of the victim, the state whose conduct the terrorists seek to affect by the attack (hereinafter target state) and the state (of nationality or principal place of business) of a demise charterer in possession of the ship may establish jurisdiction. Even though jurisdiction under each of the latter categories is permissive, not obligatory, there was some opposition to each of these provisions, with particularly strong opposition to jurisdiction by the state of nationality of the victim and by the target state. Nevertheless, indicative votes called for by the chairman showed overwhelming support—32 in favor, 4 against and 3 abstentions—for jurisdiction by the state of nationality of the victim[109] and substantial, though lesser, support—16 in favor, 8 against and 14 abstentions—for jurisdiction by the target state.[110] As a result, both were included in the draft adopted by the Preparatory Committee.

The states that objected to jurisdiction by the state of nationality of the victim and/or by the state whose conduct the terrorists seek to compel took the position (1) that nationality and territoriality are the generally accepted bases of jurisdiction and should not be expanded, and (2) that jurisdiction based on nationality of the victim may vest jurisdiction in a number of states and may result in conflicts of jurisdiction. It was also argued that a provision for target state jurisdiction is unnecessary, as that state will be the flag state or the state whose nationals are seized and threatened. Other states, however, stressed the strong interests of these states and argued that since the purpose of the Convention is to ensure that certain acts will not go unpunished, it is more important to eliminate the possibility of "negative jurisdiction," i.e., that no state will prosecute the offenders, than to eliminate the possibility of conflicts of jurisdiction.

Textbooks on international law generally list five bases of jurisdiction: nationality, territoriality, passive personality, the protective principle and universality.[111] The most widely accepted bases of jurisdiction under inter-

[109] *See* IMO Doc. PCUA 2/5, at 18, para. 89 (June 2, 1987).

[110] *Id.*, para. 94.

[111] The Comment to the Draft Convention on Jurisdiction with Respect to Crime, *supra* note 12, states:

> An analysis of modern national codes of penal law and penal procedure, checked against the conclusions of reliable writers and the resolutions of international conferences or learned societies, and supplemented by some exploration of the jurisprudence of national courts, discloses five general principles on which a more or less extensive penal jurisdiction is claimed by States at the present time. These five general principles are: first, the territorial principle, determining jurisdiction by reference to the place where the offence is committed; second, the nationality principle, determining jurisdiction by reference to the nationality or national character of the person committing the offence; third, the protective principle, determining jurisdiction by reference to the national interest injured by the offence; fourth, the universality principle, determining jurisdiction by reference to the custody of the person committing the offence; and fifth, the passive personality principle, determining jurisdiction by reference to the nationality or national character of the person injured by the offence.

29 AJIL Supp. at 445.

national law are nationality and territoriality, and with respect to ships, the flag state.[112] However, if jurisdiction is limited to the state of nationality of the offender and to the flag state in case of terrorist attacks on the high seas, a serious gap may result. The state of nationality of the offender may not wish to prosecute—indeed, it may applaud the act rather than condemn it—and the flag state, for economic or political reasons, may not be in a position to prosecute, particularly if it is a small state that serves as a flag of convenience.

Nor is the problem eliminated by the extradite or prosecute provision in Article 10. Although that article requires any state party in whose territory the offender is found, if it does not extradite him, to submit the case to its competent authorities for prosecution "without any exception whatsoever and whether or not the offence was committed in its territory," some states apparently interpret it to mean that the state in which the offender is found has an obligation to prosecute only if a request for extradition is received.[113] In addition, some states have indicated that under their domestic law they *cannot* prosecute without a request for extradition. Thus, if jurisdiction is limited to the state of nationality and to the flag state, and these states do not request extradition, the offender may escape punishment, even if found in a state that would like to see him brought to justice.

While jurisdiction based on the nationality of the victim, the so-called passive personality principle, is not as widely accepted as jurisdiction on grounds of nationality or territoriality, some states do assert jurisdiction on that basis. For example, French law provides that an alien who commits a crime outside the territory of the Republic may be prosecuted and judged pursuant to French law, when the victim is of French nationality.[114] And the United States has recently enacted legislation establishing extraterritorial jurisdiction over terrorist acts abroad against U.S. nationals.[115] Jurisdiction based on nationality of the victim is also provided for by other multilateral conventions.[116]

[112] *See* UN Convention on the Law of the Sea, *supra* note 25, Arts. 91 and 92; Geneva Convention on the High Seas, *supra* note 24, Arts. 5 and 6. Flag state jurisdiction has been viewed as an application of the territoriality principle, as an application of the nationality principle and as *sui generis. See* RESTATEMENT (THIRD), *supra* note 9, §402 Reporters' Note 4.

[113] This interpretation appears to be inconsistent with the legislative history. Proposals so to provide were made and rejected in the course of the negotiations both on the Hostage Convention and on the Internationally Protected Persons Convention. A commentator states, "[T]his legislative history leaves no doubt that the obligation to submit to competent authorities is in no way dependent on a request for extradition." Rosenstock, *International Convention Against the Taking of Hostages: Another Community Step Against Terrorism,* 9 DEN. J. INT'L L. & POL'Y 169, 181 (1980).

[114] Law No. 75-624, July 11, 1975, J.O. July 13, 1975, *cited in* 102 JOURNAL DU DROIT INTERNATIONAL 962 (1975), *quoted in* L. HENKIN, R. PUGH, O. SCHACHTER & H. SMIT, INTERNATIONAL LAW: CASES AND MATERIALS 53 (1980). The Comment to the Draft Convention on Jurisdiction with Respect to Crime, *supra* note 12, lists some 28 states that provide for penal jurisdiction based on nationality of the victim. 29 AJIL Supp. at 578–79.

[115] *See* Omnibus Diplomatic Security and Antiterrorism Act of 1986, §1202, Pub. L. No. 99-399, 100 Stat. 895, 896 (1986) (18 U.S.C.A. §2331 (Supp. 1987)).

[116] *See* Hostage Convention, *supra* note 9, Art. 5(d); Convention Against Torture and Other Cruel and Inhuman or Degrading Treatment or Punishment, GA Res. 39/46, Art. 5(1)(c)

In commenting on the passive personality principle, the *Restatement (Third) of Foreign Relations Law of the United States* (hereinafter *Restatement (Third)*) states: "The principle has not been generally accepted for ordinary torts or crimes, but it is increasingly accepted as applied to terrorist and other organized attacks on a state's nationals by reason of their nationality, or to assassination of a state's diplomatic representatives or other officials."[117]

These provisions can also be justified under the "protective principle," which has long been accepted as a basis of jurisdiction under international law.[118] Traditionally, the protective principle has been applied to permit a state to prosecute non-nationals for such acts as swearing falsely to the state's consul or counterfeiting the state's money. However, the rationale of the protective principle, that a state has a concern and a right to prosecute those who threaten its governmental functions, regardless of the nationality of the offender and regardless of where the act was committed, applies equally to terrorist acts committed in an attempt to coerce the will of a state or when its nationals are targeted for terrorist attack simply because they are its nationals.

The Comment to the Draft Convention on Jurisdiction with Respect to Crime, prepared by the Harvard Research in International Law, states:

> There is justification for the enactment of penal legislation based upon the protective principle in the inadequacy of most national legislation punishing offences committed within the territory against the security, integrity and independence of foreign States. So long as the State within whose territory such offences are committed fails to take adequate measures, *competence must be conceded to the State whose fundamental interests are threatened.*[119]

It notes that some states provide, under this principle, "for the punishment of anyone who, by unauthorized hostile acts, exposes the State to a declaration of war *or its citizens to reprisals.*"[120]

The *Restatement (Third)* provides that, under international law, a state may exercise jurisdiction to prescribe and apply its law with respect to "certain conduct outside its territory by persons not its nationals that is directed against the security of the state or against a limited class of other state

---

(Dec. 17, 1984). *See also* Convention for the Prevention and Punishment of Crimes Against Internationally Protected Persons, Including Diplomatic Agents, *supra* note 9, Art. 3(1)(c) ("when the crime is committed against an internationally protected person . . . who enjoys his status as such by virtue of functions which he exercises on behalf of that State"); Convention on Offenses and Certain Other Acts Committed on Board Aircraft, Sept. 14, 1969, 20 UST 2941, TIAS No. 6768, 704 UNTS 219, Art. 4(b).

[117] RESTATEMENT (THIRD), *supra* note 9, §402 comment *g*.

[118] The Comment to the Draft Convention on Jurisdiction with Respect to Crime, *supra* note 12, states that "[i]n addition to the evidence of almost universal approval of the protective principle" in municipal legislation, it "has also been supported by various resolutions of international organizations, by conferences on penal law, and to a limited extent in treaties." 29 AJIL Supp. at 551.

[119] *Id.* at 552 (emphasis added).

[120] *Id.* (emphasis added).

interests."[121] A comment indicates that this subsection restates the "protective principle of jurisdiction."[122]

Finally, jurisdiction over terrorist acts may also be justified under the universality principle. Unlike the other bases of jurisdiction, which depend on the existence of a link between the state asserting jurisdiction and either the offense, the offender or the victim, the universality principle permits all states to assert jurisdiction with respect to certain offenses—offenses that because of their nature are of concern to all states. Piracy has long been an example of such an offense, as discussed earlier. It seems indubitable that today terrorist attacks should be in this category.[123] In the last few decades, there have been hundreds of terrorist attacks in and against the citizens of various states, of differing political persuasions, in which innocent men, women and children have been brutally murdered. Such attacks are no less—and perhaps are more—of a threat to states today than was piracy centuries ago.

The Draft Convention on Jurisdiction with Respect to Crime includes under the universality principle jurisdiction by a state with respect to "any crime committed outside its territory by an alien," if the crime was committed "to the injury of the State asserting jurisdiction or of one of its nationals" in a place not subject to the authority of any state.[124] The drafters

[121] RESTATEMENT (THIRD), *supra* note 9, §402(3).

[122] *Id.* §402 comment *f.*

[123] In discussing the universality principle, the *Restatement (Third)* states that, under this principle, a state "has jurisdiction to define and prescribe punishment for certain offenses recognized by the community of nations as of universal concern," *id.* §404, even though it has "no links of territory . . . or of nationality with the offender (or even the victim)," *id.* comment *a.* In this category, the *Restatement* includes "piracy, slave trade, attacks on or hijacking of aircraft, genocide, war crimes, and perhaps certain acts of terrorism," *id.* §404.

[124] Art. 10(c), 29 AJIL Supp. at 440–41. The provisions for jurisdiction based on universality under the draft Convention are:

ARTICLE 9. UNIVERSALITY—PIRACY

A State has jurisdiction with respect to any crime committed outside its territory by an alien which constitutes piracy by international law.

ARTICLE 10. UNIVERSALITY—OTHER CRIMES

A State has jurisdiction with respect to any crime committed outside its territory by an alien, other than the crimes mentioned in Articles 6, 7, 8 and 9, as follows:

(a) When committed in a place not subject to its authority but subject to the authority of another State, if the act or omission which constitutes the crime is also an offence by the law of the place where it was committed, if surrender of the alien for prosecution has been offered to such other State or States and the offer remains unaccepted, and if prosecution is not barred by lapse of time under the law of the place where the crime was committed. The penalty imposed shall in no case be more severe than the penalty prescribed for the same act or omission by the law of the place where the crime was committed.

(b) When committed in a place not subject to the authority of any State, if the act or omission which constitutes the crime is also an offence by the law of a State of which the alien is a national, if surrender of the alien for prosecution has been offered to the State or States of which he is a national and the offer remains unaccepted, and if prosecution is not barred by lapse of time under the law of a State of which the alien is a national. The penalty imposed shall in no case be more severe than the penalty prescribed for the same act or omission by the law of a State of which the alien is a national.

stressed that even jurists who otherwise rejected the passive personality principle supported this assertion of jurisdiction. Thus, the Comment quotes with approval the following statement by Wharton:

> If an American citizen is murdered or plundered abroad, it is the duty of his country to exact redress and retribution. . . . *If the crime is committed* in a barbarous or semi-barbarous land, *where a demand for extradition is not recognized, and where justice is not inflicted in accordance with civilized jurisprudence, then we have the right to execute justice ourselves,* by seizing the offenders and trying them according to our laws, in all cases in which these laws embody crimes against men, irrespective of local limitations. Ignorance of law would, indeed, avail as a defense as to offences not *mala in se.* But as to offences *mala in se,* wherever the rights of a citizen are assailed, then it is the prerogative of his state to require redress.[125]

Further, in support of including this application of the universality principle, even though it would be "rarely invoked," the Comment notes that "there will be occasions where either it must be invoked or the offender permitted to go unpunished."[126] Unfortunately, with respect to terrorist acts the offender may be permitted to go unpunished even if the act is not committed in "a place not subject to the authority of any state."

One delegation indicated that it might propose that the extradite or prosecute requirement apply only with respect to requests by states that assert jurisdiction under the mandatory provisions and that it not apply to requests by states that assert jurisdiction under the optional provisions. Such a proposal, if adopted, would effectively vitiate the provisions for optional jurisdiction, for these provisions would then not impose an obligation on a state in which the offender is found to extradite or prosecute and would not confer a right to extradition on a state with optional jurisdiction. It is difficult to discern any purpose that would be served by the provisions specifying the optional bases of jurisdiction if the extradite or prosecute requirement does not apply with respect to them. While they establish that a state may exercise jurisdiction in the circumstances specified, it is doubtful that a provision in the Convention is necessary to do that. Even if it were, paragraph 4 provides that the Convention "does not exclude any criminal jurisdiction exercised in accordance with national law."[127]

All of the existing antiterrorist conventions have in fact gone beyond the nationality and territoriality bases of jurisdiction. Each convention not only authorizes but also requires the state in which the offender is found to

---

(c) When committed in a place not subject to the authority of any State, if the crime was committed to the injury of the State assuming jurisdiction, or of one of its nationals, or of a corporation or juristic person having its national character.

(d) When committed in a place not subject to the authority of any State and the alien is not a national of any State.

Id.

[125] 29 AJIL Supp. at 590 (emphasis added). [126] *Id.* at 573–74.

[127] Convention, *supra* note 11, Art. 7(4).

submit the case to its authorities for prosecution if it does not extradite him, notwithstanding that the offense was not committed in its territory or by its national. Some of these conventions have been widely ratified. For example, the Hague Convention has been ratified by 130 states, and the Montreal Convention by 131 states.[128] Thus, the international community clearly does not consider it inappropriate for a state without national or territorial links to try a person for a terrorist act. If a state that has no contacts with the offense or the offender other than the offender's presence may try him criminally for the offense, there can be no objection to trial by a state that has substantial interests, such as the state of nationality of the victim or the target state. The question, then, is whether other states should have an obligation to extradite to a state that asserts jurisdiction on one of these grounds. If the state of nationality of the offender or the flag state requests extradition, the state in which the offender is found has the option of extraditing him to one of those states. Furthermore, the state in which the offender is found always has the option of submitting the case to its own authorities for prosecution. Therefore, the only instance in which a state would be bound under the Convention to extradite to the state of nationality of the victim or to the target state is if it is unwilling to submit the case to its authorities for prosecution and no other state has requested extradition. That is, the state in which the offender is found would only be obligated to extradite to the state of nationality of the victim or to the target state if there is no other state willing to prosecute. Surely, it is preferable to have the offender tried by the state of nationality of the victim or by the target state than to have him escape prosecution altogether.

It has also been argued that it is unnecessary to have a separate provision for target state jurisdiction as that state will generally also be the flag state or the state of nationality of the victim. While that may be true in most instances, it is not always so. The *Achille Lauro* flew an Italian flag and the person killed was a U.S. national, but the demand was for Israel to release prisoners.[129] Similarly, U.S. citizens were taken hostage in Lebanon and the demand was for Kuwait to release prisoners.[130]

Finally, those who oppose target state jurisdiction argued that it was inappropriate since the offenses defined by the Convention were against persons, not states. "According to these delegations, there must be strict concordance between the cases of jurisdiction and the offences in question."[131] This argument is not supported by logic or policy. Jurisdiction is always by the state. Sometimes it is based on acts directed against the state; at others, on acts by or against individuals that have a link with the state. Taken to its logical conclusion, this argument would preclude jurisdiction based on the nationality of the offender as well. There, too, "strict con-

[128] U.S. DEP'T OF STATE, 1987 TREATIES IN FORCE.

[129] *See supra* note 4 and accompanying text.

[130] *See* Jacobsen, *A Comment,* 8 WHITTIER L. REV. 763, 764 (1986) ("The demand for my father's release, along with that of the other American Hostages, was simple: Release of seventeen prisoners held . . . in Kuwait, in exchange for the Americans").

[131] IMO Doc. PCUA 2/5, at 18, para. 93 (June 2, 1987).

cordance between the cases of jurisdiction and the offences in question is lacking." Nor are there compelling policy reasons to require strict concordance between the offenses and jurisdiction. Such concordance usually establishes a state's interest. However, as indicated above, when terrorists seek to affect the conduct of a particular state, as for example by threatening to destroy a ship they have seized unless that state releases certain prisoners, that state clearly has an interest. Its foreign relations may be seriously affected, whether it decides to succumb to the terrorist demands or not. Moreover, if the concern is truly lack of concordance, rather than opposition to jurisdiction on this basis, the problem can easily be remedied by the inclusion of a provision to the effect that "it shall be an offence to commit any of the offences set forth in article 7(1) in order to compel a state to do or abstain from doing an act."

Provisions for jurisdiction by the state of nationality of the victim and by the target state are particularly important from the U.S. perspective. The United States is unlikely to be the state of nationality of the offender and not very likely to be the flag state, but has already been and will unfortunately probably continue to be the state of nationality of the victim and one of the states whose conduct terrorists seek to affect by their attacks.[132] That is probably also true of other Western states and has already proved to be true of one Arab state.[133]

Priority Among States Having Jurisdiction. Although some states urged that the Convention provide an order of priority among states having jurisdiction, and particularly that the flag state be given priority, such proposals were strongly opposed by most states and were rejected. The draft Convention, however, does provide:

> A State Party which receives more than one request for extradition from States which have established jurisdiction in accordance with article 7 and which decides not to prosecute shall, in selecting the State to which the offender or the alleged offender is to be extradited, pay due regard to the interests and responsibilities of the State Party whose flag the ship was flying at the time of the commission of the offence.[134]

Some states objected to this provision as well, arguing that it was unnecessary, would create an undesirable precedent and would infringe on the sovereign discretion of each state. Others, however, noted that the provision did not establish a right to priority by the flag state and urged inclusion of this provision as a compromise.

While this provision clearly does not require the state in which the offender is found to give priority to the flag state, it creates unnecessary ambiguity. What does it mean for a state to "pay due regard to the interests and responsibilities" of the flag state? If all it means is that the state in which

[132] *See* N.Y. Times, Nov. 26, 1985, at A1, col. 5 ("U.S. persons and interests abroad have been the foremost target for terrorists"); Levitt, *Combatting Terrorism Under International Law,* 18 TOLEDO L. REV. 133, 134 (1986).

[133] Kuwait. *See supra* note 130 and accompanying text.

[134] Convention, *supra* note 11, Art. 11(5).

the offender is found should consider the interests of the flag state, that requirement is already present, as the flag state is one of the states entitled to request extradition, and this provision is therefore not necessary. If the provision means more than that, it is not clear what.

Application of the Convention

The draft Convention is fairly broad in scope both in its definition of "ship" and in its delineation of when the Convention applies. It defines a "ship" as "a vessel of any type whatsoever not permanently attached to the sea-bed, including dynamically supported craft, submersibles, or any other floating craft."[135] It provides that the Convention shall apply "if the ship is navigating in waters beyond the outer or lateral limits of the territorial sea of the flag State or its schedule includes navigation in those waters."[136] Moreover, even when the ship is not so navigating, the draft Convention provides that "it shall nevertheless apply," with the exception of certain articles, if the offender is found in a state other than the flag state.[137] These provisions are the result of extensive discussions and negotiations; earlier drafts were substantially narrower. For example, the draft initially submitted to the IMO by the cosponsors limited the offenses to acts committed on board or against a ship "in service."[138]

The "in service" language was based on the "in flight" language of the Hague and Montreal Conventions[139] dealing with aircraft hijacking and sabotage, respectively. However, application of the "in service" limitation to ships presented both substantive and definitional problems.[140] Is a ship

[135] *Id.*, Art. 1. A Protocol to the Convention incorporates or parallels its provisions with respect to offenses committed "on board or against fixed platforms located on the continental shelf." IMO Doc. PCUA 2/5, Ann. 2, Art. 1 (June 2, 1987).

[136] Convention, *supra* note 11, Art. 4(1). [137] *Id.*, Art. 4(2).

[138] *See* IMO Doc. C 57/25, Annex, Art. 2 (Oct. 1, 1986). Paragraph 1 states:

> 1. Any person commits an offence if that person unlawfully and intentionally:
>
> a) by force or threat thereof, or by any other form of intimidation, seizes a ship *in service* or exercises control of it; or
>
> b) performs or threatens an act of violence against a person on board a ship *in service* if that act or threat is likely to endanger the safety of navigation; or
>
> c) destroys a ship *in service* or causes damage to such ship or to its cargo which renders the ship incapable of operation or which is likely to endanger its safe operation; or
>
> d) places or causes to be placed on a ship *in service* by any means whatsoever, a device or substance which is likely to destroy that ship, to cause damage to the ship or its cargo which renders the ship incapable of operation or which is likely to endanger its safe operation; or
>
> e) injures or kills any person during the commission of any of the offences defined in this article.

Id. (emphasis added).

[139] *See* Hague Convention, *supra* note 9, Arts. 1, 3; Montreal Convention, *supra* note 9, Arts. 1, 2.

[140] The draft initially submitted to the IMO Council by the cosponsors stated that a "ship is considered 'in service' from the beginning of the prepassage preparation of the ship by port personnel or by the crew for a specific passage until the completion of disembarkation or unloading." IMO Doc. C 57/25, Annex, Art. 1 (Oct. 1, 1986). The English (but apparently not

from which all passengers and crew have disembarked that is being cleaned and readied for the next trip "in service"? What about a ship temporarily in port because it is undergoing repairs? A cruise ship whose next voyage has not yet been set? A number of delegations criticized the "in service" limitation as ambiguous, difficult to apply and unnecessarily restrictive. While some delegations urged its retention, others considered such a limitation undesirable as a matter of policy and took the position that the Convention should apply unless the ship was completely withdrawn from navigation. After lengthy discussion of various definitions of "in service," the Preparatory Committee decided to omit the "in service" limitation altogether. The draft Convention adopted by the committee does provide that the Convention shall not apply to a ship "which has been withdrawn from navigation or laid up."[141]

Similarly, earlier drafts did not apply the Convention to all offenses committed on the high seas. For example, an early draft circulated by the cosponsors provided that the Convention would apply "if the place of departure or the place of arrival of the ship . . . lie[s] outside the territory of the flag state." The reason for this formulation was that some states initially opposed application of the Convention to offenses committed against or on board ships navigating between two ports of the flag state, even if a short part of the route involved navigation on the high seas. However, the proposed formulation would also have excluded application of the Convention to offenses where a major part of the route was on the high seas, e.g., a ship going from Marseilles to St. Maarten. Suggestions were made for various other formulations, including one under which application would have depended on the ratio of distance navigated on the high seas to distance navigated in territorial waters. Here, too, the difficulties of articulating a formulation that would exclude voyages involving brief passage on the high seas but include those involving substantial navigation on the high seas, and the view of various states that there was no reason to exclude even the former, resulted in the elimination of this limitation and the adoption of the provision quoted above.[142] Under this formulation, the Convention will apply not only to offenses committed on the high seas, but also to those committed in territorial waters if the ship is scheduled to navigate on the high seas. Further, a state may declare at the time of ratification that the Convention shall apply to ships navigating in straits used for international navigation in cases not covered by Article 4(1).[143] Conversely, it may also declare "that it shall not apply the Convention where the ship is navigating in internal waters and its schedule does not include navigation beyond the outer or lateral limits of the territorial sea."[144]

---

the French) provided that a ship is also considered in service when temporarily in port for repairs.

[141] Convention, *supra* note 11, Art. 2(1)(b). [142] *See supra* text accompanying note 136.

[143] Convention, *supra* note 11, Art. 5(2).

[144] *Id.*, Art. 5(1). This provision was intended to permit states to exempt foreign flag ships navigating exclusively in the internal waters of another state.

Other Provisions

Article 8 obligates a state in whose territory the offender is present to "take him into custody or take other measures to ensure his presence for such time as is necessary to enable any criminal or extradition proceedings to be instituted"; "to immediately notify" those states that have jurisdiction under Article 7(1) and, "if it considers it advisable," any other interested state; and immediately to make a preliminary inquiry into the facts. A person against whom such measures have been taken has the right to communicate "without delay" with a representative of his state of nationality, or if he is a stateless person, the state of which he is a habitual resident, and to be visited by a representative of that state.[145] Any person against whom proceedings are being carried out in connection with any of the offenses defined by the Convention "shall be guaranteed fair treatment at all stages of the proceedings, including enjoyment of all the rights and guarantees provided for such proceedings by the law of the State in the territory of which he is present."[146]

Article 12 obligates states to offer one another "the greatest measure of assistance in connection with criminal proceedings . . . , including the supply of the evidence at their disposal necessary for the proceedings." In addition, Article 14 provides that any state having reason to believe that an offense will be committed must furnish any relevant information in its possession to those states that would have jurisdiction under Article 7. These provisions are either taken verbatim or are substantially similar to provisions in the Hague, Montreal and Hostage Conventions.

Other articles provide that the Convention "shall not apply to a warship or a ship owned or operated by a State when being used as a naval auxiliary or for customs or police purposes";[147] that nothing in the Convention "shall affect the immunities of warships and other Government ships operated for non-commercial purposes";[148] that each state "shall make the offences set forth in article 3 punishable by appropriate penalties which take into account the grave nature of those offences";[149] that this Convention "does not exclude any criminal jurisdiction exercised in accordance with national law";[150] and that nothing in this Convention "shall be construed as affecting in any way the existing rules of international law pertaining to the competence of states to exercise investigative or enforcement jurisdiction on board ships not flying their flag."[151]

Questions Referred to the Diplomatic Conference

Several controversial issues were considered to be of a "political nature" and were left open for resolution by the Diplomatic Conference.

Person Acting on Behalf of a Government. A proposal was introduced by Kuwait to insert the words "whether acting on his own initiative or on

[145] *Id.*, Art. 8(3).

[146] *Id.*, Art. 10(2).

[147] *Id.*, Art. 2(1)(a).

[148] *Id.*, Art. 2(2).

[149] *Id.*, Art. 6.

[150] *Id.*, Art. 7(4).

[151] *Id.*, Art. 9.

behalf of a government" following "any person" in the chapeau of Article 1, so that it would read, "Any person, *whether acting on his own initiative or on behalf of a government,* commits an offence if that person unlawfully and intentionally" commits the proscribed acts.[152] The purpose of the proposal was to make the Convention applicable to persons who commit an offense acting on behalf of a government. The Kuwaiti delegation emphasized that its proposal did not affect state responsibility and was concerned only with personal responsibility.[153]

While some delegations agreed that the Convention should apply regardless of whether the offender was acting in his own capacity or on behalf of a government, most expressed the view that the Convention already so provided by the words "any person." Some also expressed concern that inclusion of this language might create problems of interpretation with respect to other antiterrorist conventions that do not use this language. Others expressed the fear that inclusion of an express provision might make the Convention less acceptable to some states. Since the delegations remained divided over an express provision, it was agreed that this presented a political question that should be referred to the Diplomatic Conference.[154]

Offenses by Governments. The most significant question referred to the Diplomatic Conference involves a proposal by Saudi Arabia: at the first session of the Preparatory Committee in London, and again at the second session in Rome, Saudi Arabia submitted additions to the Preamble and the substantive provisions that would make the Convention applicable not only to persons but also to governments.[155] This proposal is different from the Kuwaiti proposal, discussed above. The Kuwaiti proposal would make clear that a person who engages in the proscribed conduct is not relieved of responsibility therefor because he is acting on behalf of a government. Under the Saudi proposal, the Convention would impose responsibility for the offense on the state itself.

For example, under the Saudi proposal, the chapeau of what is now Article 3, defining the offenses, would be amended to read, "Any *ordinary person or government* commits an offence . . . ." With respect to individuals who engage in the proscribed conduct, the Convention makes provision for their prosecution or extradition. These provisions have no application to states; a state cannot be prosecuted or extradited. Another article in the Saudi proposal provides that the "State whose naval forces . . . committed any of the offences shall" inform the Secretary-General of the "measures taken to put an immediate end to such offence."[156] The use of force by states is governed by an elaborate and complex body of international law, developed over many centuries and modified by the UN Charter. Whether a state's use of force is lawful or not is—and should be—determined by the application of this body of law.

[152] IMO Doc. PCUA 2/4 (May 8, 1987).
[153] *See* IMO Doc. PCUA 2/5, at 12, para. 65 (June 2, 1987).
[154] *Id.* at 13, para. 68.
[155] *See* IMO Doc. PCUA 1/3/3 (Feb. 26, 1987).
[156] *Id.*, Art. 12.

AGORA: IS THE ASIL POLICY ON DIVESTMENT IN VIOLATION OF INTERNATIONAL LAW? FURTHER OBSERVATIONS

The Action Violates International Law and Policy

It was with great surprise and some disappointment that I took note in the July 1987 issue of the *American Journal of International Law* of the decision by the American Society of International Law to divest its investment portfolio of stocks in all corporations with direct investments in South Africa. Despite the sentiments that may have motivated this decision, many of which are reflected in the Note of Henry J. Richardson III,[1] there were no doubt many arguments voiced to the contrary at the meeting of the Society when the matter was discussed.

As a South African academic involved in the teaching of international law and an avid reader of this *Journal*, I feel it a duty to state certain consequences and realities of this type of economic sanction—realities that mitigate most strongly against the continuation of economic sanctions against this country. The consequences were all predicted in great detail at the outset of the sanctions campaign and have all come to fruition.

(1) The pressure on American companies to withdraw their investments from South Africa has seriously undermined whatever influence these companies had in South Africa and has undermined the examples they tried to set.

(2) Sanctions and disinvestment have resulted in making poor blacks even poorer.

(3) Assets relinquished by disinvesting American corporations have been snapped up at bargain basement prices by local and foreign entrepreneurs.

(4) A patriotic closing of the ranks has taken place; the resultant swing towards the right has had as a consequence replacement of the liberal Progressive Federal Party by the ultra-right-wing Conservative Party as the official parliamentary opposition.

(5) Whatever influence the United States may have had has waned dramatically, as the man in the street has turned his face away from Washington; this goes for whites as well as blacks.

(6) Increasing unemployment due to disinvestment has taken place; this has affected blacks more than whites.

(7) The effect on the South African economy as a whole has been negligible. At present, the economy is resilient and is in an upward phase. South Africa is one of the few countries in Africa—if not the

[1] Richardson, *Divestment of the Stock Portfolio of the Society*, 81 AJIL 744 (1987).

only one—that is steadily paying its debts. The latest meeting of the International Monetary Fund bears this out.

(8) The so-called front-line states—the states on South Africa's borders—have increased their trade with South Africa dramatically despite being the most vociferous in calling for sanctions.

In September, for example, the Government of Zimbabwe bought one-third of the shares in Delta Corporation, a South African–controlled group that is Zimbabwe's biggest trading conglomeration.

These are but a few examples. To quote Chief Mangosuthu Buthelezi, political head of South Africa's five-and-a-half million Zulus: "You do not rid a house of a snake by burning down the house." As succinctly put by the editor of the South African news magazine *Inside South Africa* in October 1987, "Those who advocated the policy of economic sanctions and disinvestment against South Africa have created a mess which has obstructed the removal of apartheid instead of assisting it."

As one who earns his daily bread by teaching international law, I have great problems not only with the *effectiveness* of international economic coercion in persuading a recalcitrant state to toe the line, but also with the *legality* in international law of such coercion.

I have no problem with the permissibility in international law of applying economic coercion when used in the exercise of the right of *self-defense* or as a legitimate *reprisal*. On these two aspects, contemporary international law is clear. In South Africa's case, however, economic coercion is being applied in circumstances where neither self-defense *nor* reprisals are applicable. This forces me to conclude that the economic coercion (divestment and disinvestment) being applied does not fall within the realm of legitimacy.

Two General Assembly resolutions have expressly prohibited the use of economic coercion. The Declaration on the Inadmissibility of Intervention in the Domestic Affairs of States and the Protection of Their Independence and Sovereignty expressly declares in paragraph 2: "No State may use or encourage the use of economic, political or any other type of measures to coerce another State in order to obtain from it the subordination of the exercise of its sovereign rights . . . ."[2] The Declaration on Principles of International Law concerning Friendly Relations and Co-operation among States in Accordance with the Charter of the United Nations resolves the same in almost identical language.[3]

These two declarations of 1965 and 1970 are reinforced by the fourth paragraph of the 1973 resolution on Permanent Sovereignty over Natural Resources, which emphasizes "the duty of all States to refrain in their international relations from . . . economic or any other form of coercion aimed against the territorial integrity of any State and the exercise of its national jurisdiction."[4]

[2] GA Res. 2131, 20 UN GAOR Supp. (No. 14) at 11, UN Doc. A/6014 (1965).
[3] GA Res. 2625, 25 UN GAOR Supp. (No. 28) at 121, UN Doc. A/8028 (1970).
[4] GA Res. 3171, 28 UN GAOR Supp. (No. 30) at 3, UN Doc. A/9030 (1973).

According to Christopher C. Joyner, who has conducted extensive research into this aspect, "General Assembly resolutions have repeatedly stressed the illegality of boycotts and censured economically coercive actions."[5] Hartmut Brosche deduces from paragraph 2 of the Declaration on the Inadmissibility of Intervention[6] (which is reproduced in the Declaration on Friendly Relations, as mentioned above) and from Article 2(3) and chapter VI of the United Nations Charter that

> it is quite clear that embargoes, boycotts, blockades, reprisals, or other kinds of economic and political pressure do not constitute procedures of pacific settlement. They are not peaceful means and not appropriate for the solution of disputes. The use or imposition of such measures would constitute a violation of the obligation to settle international disputes by peaceful means.
>
> . . . Due to these facts it becomes evident that the use of any kind of pressure is contrary to the principle of peaceful settlement of disputes.[7]

Rosalyn Higgins goes so far as to maintain that "[t]here is a certain body of opinion which regards a very high degree of economic coercion as tantamount to the use of force."[8] I admit that this "body of opinion" may go too far, but, as concluded by Tom Farer,[9] the fact that economic coercion cannot be brought under the prohibition of the "use of force" under Article 2(4) of the UN Charter does not mean that economic coercion is not a violation of international law on other grounds.

As I understand the position, modern authority states that when a state intentionally uses its extraterritorial policies as cudgels for the attainment of foreign policy goals or to register international protest, or when it attempts to coerce the sovereign will of another government, these policies are considered interventionist. Such action is seen to be premeditated dictatorial interference in the affairs of another state.[10] Modern authority declares that, unless justified by self-defense or securing redress, an economic boycott violates well-established principles of international law and is a direct and unjustifiable interference in the affairs of a nonconsenting target state.

The authorities are clear that a fundamental norm of international law is the sovereign right of a state to independence in conducting both its domestic and its foreign policies. As Joyner declares:

[5] Joyner, *The Transnational Boycott as Economic Coercion in International Law: Policy, Place, and Practice*, 17 VAND. J. INT'L L. 205, 251 (1984).

[6] *See* note 2 *supra*.

[7] Brosche, *The Arab Oil Embargo and United States Pressure Against Chile: Economic and Political Coercion and the Charter of the United Nations*, 7 CASE W. RES. J. INT'L L. 3, 32 (1974).

[8] R. HIGGINS, THE DEVELOPMENT OF INTERNATIONAL LAW THROUGH THE POLITICAL ORGANS OF THE UNITED NATIONS 176 (1963).

[9] Farer, *Political and Economic Coercion in Contemporary International Law*, 79 AJIL 405 (1985).

[10] J. BRIERLY, THE LAW OF NATIONS 402 (6th ed. 1963); 1 L. OPPENHEIM, INTERNATIONAL LAW: A TREATISE 305 (H. Lauterpacht 8th ed. 1955); 5 M. WHITEMAN, DIGEST OF INTERNATIONAL LAW 452 (1965); Fenwick, *Intervention: Individual and Collective*, 39 AJIL 645 (1945); Burke, *The Legal Regulation of Minor International Coercion: A Framework for Inquiry*, in ESSAYS ON INTERVENTION 87 (R. Stanger ed. 1964); Joyner, *supra* note 5, at 205, 230.

> If the national policies of one state unduly or dictatorially contravene another state's external affairs, such an intervention may be deemed illegal. A state's external independence . . . is as important as its internal independence. Resort to a boycott, therefore, may constitute an undue or excessive interference into both the internal and external affairs of the target state . . . .[11]

When the essence of economic coercion becomes intentional compulsion, its legality is susceptible to legal criticism. Economic coercion that seeks as its paramount purpose to influence certain behavior exceeds the parameters of legality. If such coercion does not fall within the ambit of either *self-defense* or *legitimate* redress, it is illegal economic intervention and should be construed as such.

Economic coercion that intentionally interferes with the trading patterns of a state that has committed *no offense* against the instigating government(s) is illegal in international law. Economic coercion is circumscribed by the rule that it may be employed only as a sanction in support of self-defense or redress for an international wrong. Ann Thomas and A. J. Thomas state that coercive activity of an economic nature cannot be used to force the will of another state "unless [it] is used in the exercise of the right of self-defense or reprisal."[12] Farer agrees when he declares that economic coercion is excused only if it is an act of self-defense or reprisal.[13]

This interpretation of the legitimate use of economic coercion as being confined to the exercise of the right of self-defense or genuine reprisal is widely held by eminent authorities on international law.[14]

GEORGE N. BARRIE*

THE ACTION DOES NOT VIOLATE INTERNATIONAL LAW

I am pleased to have been given an opportunity to respond to Professor Barrie's arguments that the decision of the Executive Council of the Society to divest its portfolio of stocks in all corporations with investments in South Africa was both substantively misguided and legally improper.

[11] Joyner, *supra* note 5, at 233.

[12] A. THOMAS & A. J. THOMAS, JR., THE CONCEPT OF AGGRESSION IN INTERNATIONAL LAW 90–91 (1972), *quoted in* Farer, *supra* note 9, at 411.

[13] Farer, *supra* note 9, at 411.

[14] *See* Muir, *The Boycott in International Law*, 9 J. INT'L L. & ECON. 187 (1974); Bowett, *International Law and Coercion*, 16 VA. J. INT'L L. 245 (1976); Nawaz, *Limits of Self-Defence: Legitimacy of Use of Force against Economic Strangulation?*, 16 INDIAN J. INT'L L. 252 (1976); Rubenfeld, *Legal and Tax Implications of Participation in International Boycotts*, 32 TAX L. REV. 613 (1977); Parry, *Defining Economic Coercion in International Law*, 12 TEX. INT'L L.J. 1 (1977); Blum, *Economic Boycotts in International Law*, *id.* at 5; Lillich, *The Status of Economic Coercion in International Law: United Nations Norms*, *id.* at 17; Paust & Blaustein, *The Arab Oil Weapon—A Threat to International Peace*, 68 AJIL 410 (1974); Shihata, *Destination Embargo of Arab Oil: Its Legality Under International Law*, in ECONOMIC COERCION AND THE NEW INTERNATIONAL ECONOMIC ORDER 153 (R. Lillich ed. 1976); Buchheit, *The Use of Non-Violent Coercion*, in *id.* at 39; Bilder, *Comments on the Legality of the Arab Oil Boycott*, 12 TEX. INT'L L.J. 41 (1977).

* Professor of International Law, Rand Afrikaans University, Johannesburg.

Let me say immediately that I do not propose to address the policy issues at all. These were more than adequately covered by Professor Richardson's Note,[1] which very fairly summarized the arguments, pro and con, that were raised in the Executive Council. I will simply say that all the negative factors advanced by Professor Barrie were indeed considered by the Council, whose members individually weighed these to arrive, by a close vote, at the decision indicated.

More significant for jurists is the challenge against the legal propriety of the Society's decision, on the ground that divestment was designed as a coercive act, which would have been permissible only as an act of "self-defense" or "legitimate reprisal."

Liminally, let me point out that, under the circumstances, this challenge is misconceived, for the principle of the illegitimacy, under modern international law, of economic coercion—which Professor Barrie documents thoroughly and convincingly—evidently applies only to the actions of states. This appears clearly from the quoted excerpts of the two General Assembly resolutions he principally relies on: the Declaration on the Inadmissibility of Intervention in Domestic Affairs[2] and Permanent Sovereignty over Natural Resources.[3] Nothing suggests that these strictures against economic coercion were meant to apply to the actions of individuals or corporations, much less learned societies. These entities of domestic law remain free, as a matter of international law,[4] to deal or not to deal with foreign entities or even with states as their self-interest or conscience dictates; the only possible prohibitions on such entities that might be derived from international law might apply to actions that would promote slavery, genocide, apartheid or certain types of discrimination by race, gender or religion.

Thus, there can be no question that the Society, in taking its own divestment decision, in parallel but not in concert with other similar bodies, did not in any way violate the letter or the spirit of any international legal principle.

Having thus deflected, as it were on a procedural ground, the actual thrust of Professor Barrie's charge, I will venture to examine the more interesting question whether that charge would have been valid if addressed to the action of a state; for example, to the anti–South Africa boycott

[1] Richardson, *Divestment of the Stock Portfolio of the Society*, 81 AJIL 744 (1987).

[2] Declaration on the Inadmissibility of Intervention in the Domestic Affairs of States and the Protection of Their Independence and Sovereignty, para. 2, GA Res. 2131 (XX) (Dec. 21, 1965).

[3] Permanent Sovereignty over Natural Resources, para. 6, GA Res. 3171 (XXVIII) (Dec. 17, 1973). See also, to the same effect, the Declaration on the Prohibition of Military, Political or Economic Coercion in the Conclusion of Treaties, para. 1, *annexed to* Final Act of the United Nations Conference on the Law of Treaties, UN Doc. A/CONF.39/26 (1969), *reprinted in* UNITED NATIONS CONFERENCE ON THE LAW OF TREATIES, OFFICIAL RECORDS, DOCUMENTS OF THE CONFERENCE 285, UN Doc. A/CONF.39/11/Add.2 (1971).

[4] Domestic law may, of course, prohibit or penalize participation by nationals in international boycotts. *See, e.g.*, Foreign Boycotts, in the Export Administration Act, 50 U.S.C. App. §2407 (1982), and International Boycott Determinations, in the Internal Revenue Code, 26 U.S.C. §999 (1982).

legislation recently enacted by the U.S. Congress over a presidential veto.[5] Such legislation, of course, is explicitly designed to coerce the South African Government into abandoning important domestic practices, i.e., those that implement apartheid.

As hinted above, I am ready to concede, and even to assert, that modern international law normally prohibits states from exercising economic coercion against others for political ends, clearly if these are selfish, but even if they might be considered laudable.[6] Indeed, I am somewhat doubtful about Professor Barrie's repeated assertion that in addition to self-defense, "legitimate reprisal" might justify economically coercive acts—just as I consider that self-defense in strict accordance with Article 51 of the UN Charter, but not reprisal or retorsion, is the sole legitimate exception to the Article 2(4) prohibition against the threat or use of force by states, other than a collective enforcement action organized pursuant to or in accordance with the Charter.

However, just as the Charter explicitly restricts the use of military force when exerted by states acting individually, but allows—indeed commands—it by Articles 25 and 42 when the world community is directed by the Security Council to act collectively, so the general prohibition against individual economic coercion is lifted when the world community acts collectively under the leadership of a competent UN organ.

An obvious argument that is likely to be interposed at this point is that the Security Council is the only organ competent to mobilize (under Article 41 of the Charter) the economic force of member states to act in a coercive mode, and that the Council has thus far refused to do so against South Africa (by reason of the vetoes cast by several permanent members). But the International Court of Justice has indicated, most pertinently in its *Certain Expenses* opinion,[7] that although the Security Council has a primary role in countering threats to international peace and security and in mobilizing the force of member states, it does not have an exclusive role in doing so. In particular, the General Assembly, which under Charter Articles 10 and 11 may make recommendations to UN members on any question or matter within the scope of the Charter, may use that power to induce the world community to take collective coercive action.

This is not to say that the General Assembly has precisely the same powers in this field as the Security Council. While the latter's decisions are binding on UN members under Charter Article 25, those of the Assembly remain recommendations and need not be complied with. But, *if* complied with,

[5] Chapter 60 (Anti-Apartheid Program) of the U.S. Code Title on Foreign Relations and Intercourse, 22 U.S.C.A. §5001 (West Supp. 1987). *See, in particular, id.* §§5051–5073.

[6] *See* Szasz, *The International Legal Aspects of the Human Rights Program of the United States*, 12 CORNELL INT'L L.J. 161 (1979) (in particular, Part I: U.S. Human Rights Policy and International Economic Assistance).

[7] Certain Expenses of the United Nations (Article 17, paragraph 2, of the Charter), 1962 ICJ REP. 151, 162–65 (Advisory Opinion of July 20). *See also* Military and Paramilitary Activities in and against Nicaragua (Nicar. v. U.S.), Jurisdiction and Admissibility, 1984 ICJ REP. 392, 434–35, para. 95 (Judgment of Nov. 26).

then the recommendation surely absolves those states of any implicit restraints against individual coercive economic action, since those restraints (just like those in Charter Article 2(4)) are designed to proscribe the use of national power for selfish or even for worthy but idiosyncratic purposes, but not to preclude collective action to further the ends of the world community.[8]

In fact, the General Assembly has repeatedly called on states, pending the adoption of mandatory sanctions by the Security Council, to take appropriate measures to isolate South Africa totally, in response both to the continued implementation of its policy of apartheid and the ancillary repressive measures necessitated by that policy,[9] and to its failure to relinquish its continued illegal occupation of Namibia[10]—practices that have also embroiled South Africa in continuous military and paramilitary conflicts with most of its neighbors.

These motives, incidentally, serve to answer a possible objection to the General Assembly's having called for the imposition of sanctions, i.e., that the issues in relation to which these recommendations were made are not within the competence either of the Assembly or of the Organization because they lie solely within the domestic jurisdiction of South Africa.[11] With respect to Namibia and also the conflicts with neighbors, this argument evidently cannot be made at all. But even with respect to apartheid and the related security excesses, it is too late in the day to argue that massive human rights violations are essentially within the domestic jurisdiction of the state concerned and thus outside the competence of the international community. Certainly, the experience of the Second World War, which informed the negotiation of the Charter, has taught us that human rights must be a universal concern from which the world community turns away at its peril.[12] That lesson has indeed been learned and is being applied increasingly, albeit still rather unevenly and perhaps sometimes unfairly. While the concerns of the United Nations over the current implementation of human rights largely started with questions raised in respect of South Africa,[13] they now extend to the practices of more and more states.[14] The fact that this one

[8] Also, while compliance by a state with a directive of the Security Council under Charter Article 41 would presumably relieve that state, by reason of Articles 25 and 103, of its obligation to comply with any contrary treaty provisions (e.g., under a treaty of friendship and commerce), compliance with a recommendation of the General Assembly may not have such an absolving effect.

[9] *See, e.g.*, para. 7, GA Res. 41/35B (Nov. 10, 1986).

[10] *See, e.g.*, para. 72, GA Res. 41/39A (Nov. 20, 1986).

[11] *See* UN CHARTER art. 2(7).

[12] *See, in particular, id.*, arts. 1(3) and 55(c).

[13] *See, e.g.*, GA Res. 44 (I) (Dec. 8, 1946) (Treatment of Indians in the Union of South Africa); 141 (II) (Nov. 1, 1947) (Question of South West Africa); 616A and B (VII) (Dec. 5, 1952) (The question of race conflict in South Africa resulting from the policies of *apartheid* of the Government of the Union of South Africa).

[14] *See, e.g.*, GA Res. 41/95 (South Africa), 41/156 (Guatemala), 41/157 (El Salvador), 41/158 (Afghanistan), 41/159 (Iran), and 41/161 (Chile) (all adopted on Dec. 4, 1986 at the 41st session).

country has so long and so frequently found itself in the dock suggests that its violations are both persistent and serious, and that the international community is quite likely justified in moving gradually towards stricter and more generally applied measures against a system that continues to flout generally perceived standards of humanity.

Perhaps Professor Barrie will object to much of the above on the ground that it relies not on the "hard" law of treaty obligations but on the "soft" law of declarations and other resolutions of international organs and on the teachings of publicists based on such decisions.[15] But should he deny the validity of all this emerging law—i.e., both that of human rights and that justifying collective action mandated by competent international organs—he would cut off the limb to which he has attached himself, for the asserted prohibition against economic coercion rests on precisely the same type of declarations and resolutions. As maintained above, these constitute good law, but so do the other principles on which the above arguments rely.

PAUL C. SZASZ*

[15] The term "soft law" apparently was originated by Judge R. R. Baxter in *International Law in "Her Infinite Variety,"* 29 INT'L & COMP. L.Q. 549, 550 (1980). See also the brief analysis and critique of the concept by Professor Prosper Weil in *Towards Relative Normativity in International Law?*, 77 AJIL 413, 414–15 n.7 (1983).

* Deputy to the Legal Counsel and Director, General Legal Division, Office of Legal Affairs, United Nations. The views expressed herein are, however, solely those of the author.

EDITORIAL COMMENT

Improving the Image of the United States in International Human Rights

On December 10, 1987, La Vicaría de la Solidaridad (Vicariate of Solidarity) of Chile was awarded the Carter-Menil Human Rights Prize, in recognition of its pioneering efforts to provide legal assistance to political prisoners and economic and social help to their families. On that occasion, former President Jimmy Carter made a wide-ranging address on the state of human rights today, in which he described the accomplishments of the last 40 years, noting in particular the treaties and agreements through which human rights were made matters of international concern and ceased to be subject to the exclusive jurisdiction of states. He pointed out, however, that international measures of supervision have not kept up with the new legislative efforts, in part because the United States has refused to ratify the instruments that established the institutions necessary to promote human rights. By failing to participate in these common endeavors, the United States has weakened the very international institutions that have become the strongest defenders of human rights. It has also made it easier for violators of these rights to deny the United States authority to complain about their infractions, since the United States itself has not accepted the obligations that it asks them to honor.

President Carter considered it essential that the United States prove to the world that its commitment to human rights is "clear, consistent, indisputable, and unequivocal," and that it is ready to protect them not only abroad but also at home. The United States can prove this commitment, for instance, by establishing a permanent human rights review body in the Department of State and creating the office of "an Advocate General whose duty it would be to report to Congress any apparent violations by our government of international law."

This idea is clearly a practicable one. It does not require the ratification of an international agreement, nor would it submit the United States to interference by any external authority. It would only establish a domestic procedure that could authoritatively certify that the United States complies with those customary rules of international human rights law which the Congress of the United States has accepted in numerous legislative pronouncements and has followed up by actually making violation of these rules the subject of economic sanctions against several states.

President Carter's suggestion should be promptly followed by Congress, acting either on a proposal by the Administration or on its own initiative. Taking into account the successful experience of several Scandinavian and other governments, such an Advocate General might be given the following duties: (1) to report to Congress on any violations by any United States official of generally accepted rules of the international law of human rights; (2) to submit to Congress opinions on the conformity of any proposed legislation with these rules; (3) to present amicus curiae briefs in cases before federal and state courts that involve issues of international human rights law; and (4) to investigate all cases in which an individual claims to have been the victim of a violation of that law by the United States, and present to Congress an annual report on these investigations.

Many other states have accepted the jurisdiction of the United Nations Human Rights Committee to investigate such claims. The United States should find it possible to appoint at least an independent federal official who would have the authority to investigate them. An act of this kind may help to restore some of the prestige the United States has lost by refusing to ratify generally accepted human rights treaties.

LOUIS B. SOHN

NOTES AND COMMENTS

Professor William W. Bishop, Jr. (1906–1987)

A Tribute

Professor William W. Bishop, Jr., died on December 29, 1987, in Ann Arbor, Michigan. He was struck down by a heart attack after feeding the birds in the snowy garden of his home. He loved nature and all its beings and his last act on this earth conjures up the tranquil picture of Saint Francis. On the day before his death, he worked in his Law School office on a revision of his casebook. A life full of meaning and a merciful death.

This *Journal* and the American Society of International Law owe a great debt to Professor Bishop. A member of the Society since 1933, he was its Vice-President, and Honorary President. He held the arduous task of editor in chief of the *American Journal of International Law* for a total of 10 years. He was fiercely loyal to the Society and to the *Journal* and made them a focus of his professional life.

Professor Bishop received two degrees from the University of Michigan and studied also at Harvard and Columbia Universities. He was assistant legal adviser in the United States Department of State from 1939 to 1947 and in this capacity he joined the United States Delegation to the Council of Ministers and the Paris Peace Conference in 1946. He joined the University of Michigan Law Faculty in 1948, and from 1966 served as the Edwin D. Dickinson University Professor of Law until his retirement from regular teaching in 1976. He was a member of the Permanent Court of Arbitration from 1975 to 1981.

Renowned as he was for his scholarship, perhaps the greatest contribution of Professor Bishop was in legal education. His international law casebook, which first appeared in 1953, was over the years the most widely used text on the subject in American law schools. By providing a consistent historical perspective and the traditional systematic presentation, the book aimed at preserving in this country a patrimony of knowledge necessary for the continuation of the worldwide dialogue among international lawyers. At the same time, the text included a wealth of material on the application of international law in American courts, foreshadowing the dramatic increase of international and foreign law cases in domestic courts. The successive editions brought into law school classrooms for the first time the newly developing areas, ranging from space law to the institutional experimentations in Europe and human rights.

Professor Bishop was a star teacher. His courses in international law and conflict of laws, as well as his seminars on treaties and the law of the sea, were among the most popular offerings in the extensive Michigan program. Students were his first priority and he gave them most of his time and energy. He even allowed his much prized membership in the Institut de Droit International to lapse because its meetings coincided with the teaching term at Michigan. He built a worldwide group of devoted alumni with whom he kept in regular contact.

Professor Bishop's scholarly writings, appearing in major part in this *Journal,* ranged widely over the entire field of international law, from the law of the sea, jurisdiction and immunities, to the status of treaties in international and American law. They were surveyed most competently by his friend and "substitute editor in chief," the late Professor Brunson MacChesney.[1] I wish to highlight here only the two sets of lectures he gave at the Hague Academy of International Law: the *General Course of Public International Law,*[2] a classic, undiminished by the lapse of time, and *Reservations to Treaties,* [3] a masterly treatment of an important aspect of the law of treaties. In a number of his writings, the author foreshadowed solutions that were later realized. Alas, some of his eminently sensible views on the law of the sea were not followed.

The opening address that Professor Bishop delivered at the 75th Anniversary Convocation commemorating the founding of the American Society of International Law may be seen as his ultimate view of the state of his discipline.[4] It is firmly grounded in the positivist doctrine: "We have now," he said, "basically the same system of customary law and treaties that existed back when the American Society of International Law was founded in 1906." Yet there follows a most effective account of the dramatic changes, highlighting the incongruity and shortcomings of the system and, in fact, actual changes in the system itself, such as the novel sources and newly emerging "person" in international law, the individual and his basic rights. Symptoms of, and trends toward, systemic reform are clearly identified, even though, to paraphrase Oscar Schachter, Professor Bishop did not believe "in the power of exhortation divorced from socio-historical conditions" as a way for "a transition to a warless world." One is impressed by Professor Bishop's principled stand on the use of force issue, his emphasis on the indispensable acceptance of third-party dispute settlement procedures and the need for changes in the "older law" on state responsibility for injury to aliens.

Professor Bishop was a modest, private and uniquely selfless person of great integrity. There were three types of happenings he never missed: the University of Michigan fall football games, the concert series and the meetings of the American Society of International Law. He was active in the Boy Scouts of America throughout his life.

After the death of his wife, Mary S. Bishop, also a member of the Society, he lived alone, in close contact with his daughter, Dr. Elizabeth S. Bishop of East Lansing, Michigan. His colleagues and friends throughout the world will miss him.

ERIC STEIN*

[1] 74 MICH. L. REV. 856 (1976).
[2] 115 RECUEIL DES COURS 147 (1965 II).
[3] 103 RECUEIL DES COURS 245 (1961 II).
[4] *International Law, 1906–1981,* 75 ASIL PROC. 1, 22 (1981).
* Of the Board of Editors.

Personal Recollections

My father's interest in international law dated, at least, from the time he took Professor Reeves's course in the subject while an undergraduate at the University of Michigan in 1928. Following his retirement from the Law School, he taught that same course to undergraduate political science students in 1980 and 1981. He said that some of them wondered about a professor who was teaching a course over 50 years after taking it! Nevertheless, the course was popular and the students enjoyed the enthusiasm with which he approached each class. My father taught almost every year after his mandatory retirement from the Law School in 1976; his last teaching was a seminar on treaties and the law of the sea in the winter of 1986. Since that time he had been working on the revision of his casebook—a task he did not finish.

He came to Ann Arbor in 1915, as a boy of 9, when his father was appointed Librarian of the University of Michigan. The university was always the center of his life and, despite a number of years spent on the East Coast, he always considered Ann Arbor to be his home. My early memories include the university football games, hikes and picnics in the university arboretum, and foreign students coming to our home to visit and discuss international law. My parents had met while both were lawyers in the Department of State in Washington, D.C., during World War II. My mother, Mary S. Bishop, shared his interest in international law and his love of the outdoors and travel. I have many happy memories of the months we spent living in Rome in 1957–1958 and again in 1965, and of trips through France, Holland, England and Scandinavia. My father enjoyed seeking out Roman ruins and picnic sites by the sea, climbing mountains, and seeing old friends, and he had a special liking for the paintings of Raphael and Rembrandt. Last summer he completed his goal of eventually visiting all 50 states; we spent a glorious month together in Alaska, the last one, seeing glaciers and plentiful wildlife.

As I hear now from many of his former students and colleagues, scattered throughout the world, I am learning more of his devotion to teaching. He really loved to teach, whether it was leading bird hikes and stargazing with his Boy Scouts, helping me with algebra and Latin, or explaining the fine points of a treaty to a law student. As many know, his office at the Law School was piled high with books and papers, but he could lay his hands on the appropriate ones at once! He savored life, and I rejoice in the fact that he was able to be active and involved to the very end.

Elizabeth S. Bishop*

Alien Tort Claims, Sovereign Immunity and International Law in U.S. Courts

A neutral merchant vessel, carrying no contraband, is attacked and damaged on the high seas by Argentine aircraft during the Falklands/Malvinas

* East Lansing, Michigan.

war, in violation of customary international law. Although the vessel is owned by a Liberian company and is registered in Liberia, its ultimate ownership is American and it is engaged in U.S. maritime commerce. As a practical matter, diplomatic remedies are unavailable, and the pursuit of a remedy within the attacking state's judicial system appears to be futile. When presented with the opportunity to provide a remedy, an American court—understandably—will be sorely tempted to do so. In *Amerada Hess Shipping Corp. v. Argentine Republic*,[1] a panel of the U.S. Court of Appeals for the Second Circuit yielded to the temptation.

In *Amerada Hess*, the court assumed the facts to be as set forth above.[2] The court found the aerial attack to be in violation of customary international law. Although it did not discuss this point with much erudition, its conclusion was correct on the assumed facts.[3]

The plaintiffs asserted federal jurisdiction under the Alien Tort Claims Act.[4] It gives federal courts jurisdiction over "any civil action by an alien for a tort only, committed in violation of the law of nations or a treaty of the United States." The American-controlled Liberian corporate plaintiffs were aliens, and they were the alleged victims of a tort committed in violation of the law of nations. That is all the court had to find to satisfy the federal subject-matter jurisdictional requirements of the Alien Tort Claims Act.[5] Instead, the court went on to discuss sovereign immunity as an aspect of federal jurisdiction under that Act. This led it astray.

"The modern view," according to the court, "is that sovereigns are not immune from suit for their violations of international law."[6] The court

[1] 830 F.2d 421 (2d Cir. 1987), *reprinted in* 26 ILM 1375 (1987), *petition for cert. filed*, 56 U.S.L.W. 3592 (U.S. Mar. 1, 1988) (No. 87-1372).

[2] The case came up after the district court had granted the defendant's motion to dismiss for lack of jurisdiction. Thus, the court of appeals accepted the plaintiffs' allegations as true. The stated facts are essentially as reported at the time of the alleged attack. *See* N.Y. Times, June 9, 1982, at A23, col. 1.

[3] *See* UN CHARTER art. 2(4); Convention on the High Seas, Apr. 29, 1958, Arts. 2, 6, 450 UNTS 82, 13 UST 2312, TIAS No. 5200; Convention on the Law of the Sea, *opened for signature* Dec. 10, 1982, Arts. 87, 92, UN Doc. A/CONF.62/122, *reprinted in* UNITED NATIONS, THE LAW OF THE SEA: UNITED NATIONS CONVENTION ON THE LAW OF THE SEA, UN Sales No. E.83.V.5 (1983), and 21 ILM 1261 (1982). *See also* note 19 *infra*. The court relied on Articles 22 and 23 of the Convention on the High Seas.

[4] 28 U.S.C. §1350 (1982).

[5] It would not necessarily be all the court would have to find in order to establish the constitutionality of the Alien Tort Claims Act, as applied to these facts. *Amerada Hess* probably would be within the federal judicial power (Article III of the Constitution) only if it were a case "arising under . . . the Laws of the United States, and Treaties made, or which shall be made, under their Authority." (No attempt was made, apparently, to bring it within the admiralty and maritime jurisdiction.) For international customary or treaty law to be within the quoted language, it would have to be self-executing or embodied in a federal statute. Specific human rights norms—such as the norm against torture—should be held self-executing, but it is less clear that the norms involved in *Amerada Hess* would be (or that they are somehow incorporated by reference in §1350). The court in *Amerada Hess* did not address the constitutional issue.

[6] 830 F.2d at 425, *reprinted in* 26 ILM at 1380. For this, the court relied on Paust, *Federal Jurisdiction over Extraterritorial Acts of Terrorism and Nonimmunity for Foreign Violators of International Law Under the FSIA and the Act of State Doctrine*, 23 VA. J. INT'L L. 191, 221–32 (1983); Bazyler, *Litigating the International Law of Human Rights: A "How to" Approach*, 7 WHITTIER L. REV. 713, 733–34 (1985).

discussed this view in terms that failed to differentiate between (1) "immunity" from international responsibility, which of course does not exist when a state violates international law, and (2) immunity from the jurisdiction of the domestic courts of other states. Nothing it said demonstrated the absence of the latter type of immunity, at least in modern times.[7]

Still dealing with the Alien Tort Claims Act, the court then confused the sovereign immunity defense with an argument made by the Nuremberg defendants. The Nuremberg argument, which the court in *Amerada Hess* identified as a sovereign immunity defense, was that governmental officials, acting for the state, are protected from personal responsibility under international law. The international tribunal at Nuremberg rejected that argument in the case of crimes against international law.[8] It has nothing to do with the immunity or nonimmunity of the Argentine Government in a civil action in a domestic court of another nation. The question is not simply whether Argentina violated international law, but whether a domestic court outside Argentina has the authority to summon the Argentine Government to appear and answer for its conduct.

The court might have been spared entry into these thickets if the Foreign Sovereign Immunities Act (FSIA)[9] had not juxtaposed sovereign immunity with federal jurisdiction. The two are analytically distinct, but the FSIA requires a plaintiff relying on its jurisdictional section[10]—a separate jurisdictional grant from that in the Alien Tort Claims Act—to get past a defendant's claim of sovereign immunity at the jurisdictional stage. The court in *Amerada Hess* did not rely on the FSIA for its subject matter jurisdiction. Nevertheless, since the defendant raised the sovereign immunity issue, the court might have thought that, as it is relevant to subject matter jurisdiction under the FSIA, it would be relevant even under the Alien Tort Claims Act.

Having mistakenly discussed sovereign immunity in the context of the Alien Tort Claims Act, the court next turned to the FSIA itself. Somehow, the majority of the panel became convinced that the focus of the FSIA is limited to commercial situations,[11] leaving the immunity *vel non* of noncommercial sovereign acts to some other body of law (i.e., the Alien Tort Claims

[7] Some commentators have argued that, historically, sovereign immunity did not apply to a foreign sovereign accused of committing acts in violation of international law. *See* A. D'AMATO, INTERNATIONAL LAW: PROCESS AND PROSPECT 201–04 (1987); Paust, *supra* note 6, at 238–41. The commentators and the court in *Amerada Hess* have cited The Santissima Trinidad, 20 U.S. (7 Wheat.) 283 (1822), for this proposition. That case involved a claim against goods unlawfully taken as prize by a foreign public vessel, but not in the possession of the foreign sovereign. Instead, the goods were in the possession of a private bailee. The Schooner Exchange v. M'Faddon, 11 U.S. (7 Cranch) 116 (1812), applied sovereign immunity to preclude private libelants from asserting that a public vessel in the possession of the French navy had been taken from them in violation of international law. Thus, sovereign immunity seems firmly established historically, even in cases involving an alleged violation of international law.

[8] Judgment of the International Military Tribunal at Nuremberg, Oct. 1, 1946, 41 AJIL 172, 220–21 (1947) [hereinafter Nuremberg Judgment].

[9] 28 U.S.C. §§1330, 1602–1611 (1982).

[10] 28 U.S.C. §1330.

[11] The majority did recognize one exception, in §1605(a)(5) (torts causing harm in the United States). That exception, of course, did not apply to the facts in the case.

Act, if an alien alleges a violation of international tort law). According to the majority, "Congress was not focusing on violations of international law when it enacted the FSIA."[12] Thus, Argentina's noncommercial, unlawful attack on the Liberian vessel would not be covered by the FSIA.

This is clearly incorrect. Section 1604 of the FSIA says that, subject to certain international agreements, "a foreign state shall be immune from the jurisdiction of the courts of the United States and of the States except as provided in sections 1605 to 1607 of this chapter." Those exceptions deal primarily, but not exclusively, with commercial matters. One of them, not mentioned by the majority of the panel, deals expressly with expropriations in violation of international law.[13] Thus, Congress did focus on international law violations, and permitted an exception from immunity for certain ones—not including attacks on neutral vessels. The residual immunity of section 1604 would apply. Its subordination to certain international agreements relates to agreements delineating immunities in domestic courts, not to agreements rendering unlawful such conduct as the bombing of a merchant vessel on the high seas.

The court compounded its error on sovereign immunity by suggesting that international law would *preclude* immunity in this situation. It then said, "Since Congress did not express a clear intent to contradict the immunity rules of international law,"[14] the FSIA would not "preempt" the Alien Tort Claims Act. International law probably requires immunity, rather than precluding it, in this situation, in the absence of a waiver by the sovereign defendant. This conclusion is indicated by state practice, as reflected in the work of the International Law Commission on the jurisdictional immunities of states and their property.[15] The Commission's draft articles immunize public acts, without distinguishing acts that violate international law from those that do not.

As much as one might wish that sovereign immunity were precluded in domestic courts for foreign governments' acts in violation of international norms of civilized behavior, it simply is not so as a matter of international or statutory law. The wish may even be misguided as a matter of policy. Federal judges in the United States typically are not experts in international law.[16] Nor are their law clerks. When they deal with international law

[12] 830 F.2d at 426, *reprinted in* 26 ILM at 1381. Judge Kearse entered a forceful dissent on this point.

[13] 28 U.S.C. §1605(a)(3). Although expropriations usually are of property used for commercial purposes, the acts of expropriation are not commercial acts.

[14] 830 F.2d at 427, *reprinted in* 26 ILM at 1382–83.

[15] *See especially* Report of the International Law Commission on the work of its thirty-second session, UN Doc. A/35/10 (1980), *reprinted in* [1980] 2 Y.B. INT'L L. COMM'N, pt. 2 at 1, 137–57, UN Doc. A/CN.4/SER.A/1980/Add.1. In its commentary to draft Article 6 on jurisdictional immunities, the Commission reviewed state practice and concluded that, "in the general practice of States as evidence of customary law, there is little doubt that a general rule of State immunity has been firmly established as a norm of customary international law." *Id.* at 149. The Commission has recognized a number of exceptions, but they do not encompass the *Amerada Hess* situation.

[16] It is increasingly evident that federal judges should be given training in basic international law, and in the relationship between international and domestic law. To the extent that the

questions, they are dealing with an unfamiliar system shaped by unfamiliar sources and mechanisms. They bring to the task their legal training and the assimilation of values prevalent in a militarily powerful, politically stable capitalist nation. They are not always presented with international law violations as clear as the one alleged in *Amerada Hess*. It is far from certain that they will make fully supportable, nonparochial judgments on international law issues that will determine whether or not a foreign sovereign is subject to their assertion of adjudicative power.[17]

The court's wishful thinking in *Amerada Hess* extended even to its assertion of personal jurisdiction over Argentina. Finding the constitutional requirements for personal jurisdiction satisfied, the court said:

> We note at the outset that certain universal offenses, like piracy and genocide are offenses against the law of nations wherever they occur. . . . The allegations here probably fall within this class of offense. Since, under international law, a state may punish these offenses even when they occur outside the state's territory, it has been argued that such occurrences always have sufficient "effects" within the United States to satisfy due process.[18]

It is debatable whether an attack on a merchant vessel in wartime should be equated with genocide or piracy. Perhaps so, since it could be a war crime.[19] But the real problem here is the confusion between jurisdiction to prescribe and jurisdiction to adjudicate. To say that certain offenses are "universal" is to say that any nation may prescribe rules prohibiting them and may enforce those rules if it catches the offenders. It says nothing about jurisdiction to adjudicate the matter when the alleged offender is not otherwise before the domestic court or subject to its process.[20]

The court did say that it need not decide the "universal jurisdiction" question in this case; hence, its declaration on the matter was dictum. One hopes it will not be taken at face value.

The court went on to decide that Argentina's actions, as alleged, were sufficiently related to the United States to permit suit in the U.S. District Court. The Second Circuit panel pointed to these factors:

---

judiciary acquires expertise in international law, the strength of the argument in the text diminishes.

[17] This objection loses some force when the violation of international law is clear, as it seems to have been in *Amerada Hess*. But judges in domestic courts are not well equipped to distinguish clear violations from unclear ones. This is true in the sovereign immunity context, as it is in the act of state context. *Cf.* Banco Nacional de Cuba v. Sabbatino, 376 U.S. 398, 433–35 (1964). Even in the *Amerada Hess* situation, the court relied on the wrong provisions of the Convention on the High Seas. *See* note 3 *supra*.

[18] 830 F.2d at 428, *reprinted in* 16 ILM at 1383 (citing Paust, *Draft Brief Concerning Claims to Sovereign Immunity and Human Rights: Nonimmunity for Violations of International Law Under the FSIA*, 8 HOUSTON J. INT'L L. 49, 69–70 (1985)).

[19] *See* Nuremberg Judgment, *supra* note 8, at 304; COMMENTARY ON THE ADDITIONAL PROTOCOLS OF 8 JUNE 1977 TO THE GENEVA CONVENTIONS OF 12 AUGUST 1949, at 607 (Y. Sandoz, Ch. Swinarski & B. Zimmermann eds. 1987).

[20] For the distinction between jurisdiction to prescribe and jurisdiction to adjudicate, see RESTATEMENT (THIRD) OF FOREIGN RELATIONS LAW OF THE UNITED STATES §401 (1988) [hereinafter RESTATEMENT (THIRD)]. *See also id.*, ch. 2, Introductory Note.

- the United States notified Argentina that the vessel would be passing through the South Atlantic on neutral business;
- the vessel was plying the United States domestic trade;
- Argentina was aware of the U.S. interest in protecting the freedom of the high seas;
- Argentina has benefited from the freedom of the seas;
- Argentina has the means to defend a suit in the United States;
- if the United States were to decline to exercise personal jurisdiction, substantive policies of international law would be undermined; and
- fairness weighs in favor of exercising jurisdiction, since the plaintiffs were unable even to obtain a hearing on their grievance in Argentina.

These factors, even in the aggregate, would not seem to satisfy the minimum contacts test.[21] Argentina's act had no connection with the United States, nor did the harm occur there. To use the words of the United States Supreme Court, it could not be said that "the defendant's conduct and connection with the forum State are such that he should reasonably anticipate being haled into court there."[22] Moreover, though the plaintiffs were U.S.-controlled, they were not U.S. nationals and their vessel was not registered in the United States. Instead, they chose Liberian nationality and registration, presumably to avoid the burdens of U.S. law. This diminishes the interest of the United States in providing a forum.[23]

Even if the normal Supreme Court standard for personal jurisdiction were met, it would not necessarily follow that there is jurisdiction to adjudicate in a case such as this. Transnational sensitivities are directly involved when the defendant is not only foreign, but a foreign government. Circumspection in extending the judicial long arm seems highly appropriate.[24]

It might be argued that the activities of the Argentine Embassy in the United States supply a sufficient governmental presence to render the Argentine Government (though not the embassy or its staff) amenable to a lawsuit arising out of its political activities elsewhere. But even if this argument is tenable, it does not get around the sovereign immunity defense.

The problem in *Amerada Hess* is not simply that the court made new law on sovereign immunity or on any of the jurisdictional matters, but that it did so by blurring distinctions that enable decision makers to identify relevant

[21] *See* International Shoe Co. v. Washington, 326 U.S. 310 (1945).

[22] World-Wide Volkswagen Corp. v. Woodson, 444 U.S. 286, 297 (1980).

[23] *Cf.* Asahi Metal Industry Co. v. Superior Court, 107 S.Ct. 1026, 1034 (1987).

[24] *See* Born, *Reflections on Judicial Jurisdiction in International Cases*, 17 GA. J. INT'L & COMP. L. 1, 28–44 (1987) (arguing for heightened scrutiny of jurisdictional claims in international cases, even when the defendant is not the sovereign). *Cf.* RESTATEMENT (THIRD), *supra* note 20, §421 (which says that the exercise of jurisdiction to adjudicate must be "reasonable," without distinguishing between the requirements of constitutional law and of international law).

policies underlying the rules in question. Moreover, it did so by misconstruing a statutory rule of immunity embodied in the FSIA. One simply cannot usefully think about "immunity" (or nonimmunity) from international responsibility in the same terms as one thinks about immunity from the jurisdiction of courts of another state. One cannot usefully think about sovereign immunity without recognizing, as the background to the exceptions set forth by the FSIA, that it accepts the basic international rule of immunity for political acts. One cannot usefully think about jurisdiction to prescribe in the same terms as jurisdiction to adjudicate. And one cannot fruitfully think about jurisdiction to adjudicate, at least in the United States, without thinking about such things as minimum contacts with U.S. territory and the degree of U.S. interest in providing a forum.

To criticize the court's reasoning and result in *Amerada Hess* is not necessarily to criticize the well-known *Filartiga* case,[25] also decided under the Alien Tort Claims Act. *Filartiga* involved a claim of torture, made against a Paraguayan police official. The Paraguayan Government was not joined as a defendant. Consequently, the significant issues did not concern sovereign immunity. Nevertheless, *Filartiga* did involve issues related to sovereign conduct, and the court did not acquit itself altogether satisfactorily in that connection.

In *Filartiga*, the court showed convincingly that customary international law prohibits torture. That is not the same, however, as showing that an individual who commits torture is personally responsible under customary international law.[26] A persuasive argument to this effect can be made if the perpetrator or instigator is a public official acting under color of state authority, and if the act otherwise fits within the accepted definition of torture[27]—despite the fact that the relevant international instruments focus on the duties of states rather than individuals. The reason is the same as in the case of war crimes: the acts not only are committed by individuals who abuse official positions of power, but also are universally condemned on humanitarian grounds. Unfortunately, the court in *Filartiga* made only the most fleeting reference to individual responsibility for torture under international law.[28]

The court in *Filartiga* thus reached a justifiable result,[29] but it missed an excellent opportunity to provide the full justification. This reminder of

[25] Filartiga v. Pena-Irala, 630 F.2d 876 (2d Cir. 1980).

[26] *See* D'Zurilla, *Individual Responsibility for Torture Under International Law*, 56 TULANE L. REV. 186 (1981).

[27] For a current definition, see Convention Against Torture and Other Cruel, Inhuman or Degrading Treatment or Punishment, Art. 1, GA Res. 39/46 (Dec. 10, 1984). A similar definition appears in the Declaration on the Protection of All Persons from Being Subjected to Torture and Other Cruel, Inhuman or Degrading Treatment or Punishment, GA Res. 3452 (XXX) (Dec. 9, 1975). Neither the Convention nor the declaration expressly provides that an individual violates international law by committing torture.

[28] 630 F.2d at 890. *Cf.* Carmichael v. United Technologies Corp., 835 F.2d 109, 113–14 (5th Cir. 1988).

[29] Notwithstanding Judge Bork's individual opinion to the contrary in Tel-Oren v. Libyan Arab Republic, 726 F.2d 774, 798–823 (D.C. Cir. 1984), *cert. denied,* 470 U.S. 1003 (1985).

the difficulties of federal judges in dealing with subtle or complex international law questions does not mean that they can or should avoid all international law issues. As long as they are circumspect in exerting their power directly over foreign governments (a circumspection dictated by the FSIA, but not observed in *Amerada Hess*) and are diffident about questioning the official acts of recognized foreign governments taken within their own territories (the province of the act of state doctrine, but not at issue in *Amerada Hess*),[30] they have a role to play in the development of international law.

The role is particularly useful in civil cases involving any of a rather short list of egregious and universally condemned human rights violations, so long as sovereign immunity, limits on jurisdiction to adjudicate and the act of state doctrine do not stand in the way. Regrettably, they will stand in the way in many cases. But not in all. The violations include those set forth in section 702 of the new *Restatement*.[31] They could also include the most widely condemned, clearly defined examples of terrorism, such as hostage taking,[32] as well as clearly defined war crimes.[33] The international norms prohibiting these human rights violations, whether in treaty or customary form, are intended to protect individuals and are sufficiently clear, precise and obligatory to be self-executing in civil actions brought in U.S. courts. The risk of judicial error on substantive international law issues in such cases is not as great as it is in cases involving hazier or more controversial norms.[34]

FREDERIC L. KIRGIS, JR.*

[30] It arguably was at issue in *Filartiga*, but the court managed to finesse the point. 630 F.2d at 889–90. *See also* Forti v. Suarez-Mason, 672 F.Supp. 1531, 1544–47 (N.D. Cal. 1987).

[31] The list consists of genocide; slavery or slave trade; murder or causing the disappearance of individuals; torture or other cruel, inhuman or degrading treatment or punishment; prolonged arbitrary detention; systematic racial discrimination; and consistent patterns of gross violations of internationally recognized human rights. *See* RESTATEMENT (THIRD), *supra* note 20, §702. The section deals with violations committed as a matter of state policy; it does not address individual responsibility. Nevertheless, each of the listed offenses should entail individual responsibility under international law if the individual is acting under color of state authority.

For a case following the lead of *Filartiga* by applying the Alien Tort Claims Act to prolonged arbitrary detention by military personnel under the command of the defendant, a former general in Argentina, see Forti v. Suarez-Mason, 672 F.Supp. 1531 (N.D. Cal. 1987).

[32] *See* GA Res. 40/61 (Dec. 9, 1985) (referring to acts of terrorism as criminal); SC Res. 579 (Dec. 18, 1985) (referring to the taking of hostages and abductions as offenses of grave concern to the international community); both *reprinted in* 80 AJIL 435 (1986).

[33] *See* Geneva Convention Relative to the Protection of Civilian Persons in Time of War, Aug. 12, 1949, Art. 147, 75 UNTS 287, 6 UST 3516, TIAS No. 3365; Protocol I Additional to the Geneva Conventions of 12 August 1949, and Relating to the Protection of Victims of International Armed Conflicts, June 10, 1977, Arts. 11, 85(3), UN Doc. A/32/144, Ann. 1, *reprinted in* 16 ILM 1391 (1977).

[34] *Cf.* Banco Nacional de Cuba v. Sabbatino, 376 U.S. 398, 428 (1964).

* Of the Board of Editors.

CORRESPONDENCE

TO THE EDITOR IN CHIEF:

As the regular reviewer of this *Journal* for the *Annuaire français de droit international*, I am much concerned over an increasingly noticeable and disturbing trend: American authors quote and cite less and less French doctrine. The reverse is not as markedly true, although French lawyers could certainly benefit from greater awareness of American international legal writings.

An empirical comparison I have made between the *Journal* (vol. 80, 1,095 pp.) and the *Annuaire* (1986, 1,255 pp.) shows that out of a total of 2,880 footnotes in the former, only 41 (i.e., 1.4 percent) cite references in French, while 209 footnotes—out of a total of 2,874—(i.e., 7.3 percent) refer to texts written in English in the *Annuaire*;[1] and there is absolutely no doubt that some major books in French were overlooked in the articles published by the *Journal* in 1986.

The French figures are surely not very satisfactory, but the American ones are really deplorable. What can the reasons be for this American ignorance (or arrogance)?

One explanation might be that French writings in international law are not worthy of attention, but, if this be the case, it would apply to other languages as well, to which American lawyers pay even less attention, only 22 footnotes (i.e., 0.76 percent) citing works in all other languages in the 1986 AJIL.

A second explanation could relate to acquisitions. In a recent book review devoted to a book in Slovenian, Professor Peter B. Maggs wrote:

> The footnote citations and bibliography reflect the current crisis in the distribution of international legal materials, a crisis caused by the combination of high book and journal prices and the need to conserve foreign exchange for debt service. Cutbacks in book purchasing and library subscriptions inevitably have a negative effect on the quality of scholarship not only in Yugoslavia, but in the numerous other countries with balance-of-payments problems.[2]

I am aware that the United States is facing balance-of-payments problems, but I do not think the situation is that bad!

Moreover, the existence of French writings cannot be said to be ignored. To the *Journal*'s credit, the Book Reviews section makes a reasonable effort to present international law books written in French (11 reviews out of 128 in 1986, compared to 19 publications in English, out of 81, reviewed in the "*bibliographie critique*" of the *Annuaire*); and the tone of the reviews is generally favorable.

[1] The comparison is even more impressive if it deals only with the articles, excluding Notes and Comments and other features: 112 notes—out of 600—refer to English texts in the *Annuaire* (18.7%), whereas 29—out of 1,370—refer to French texts in the *Journal* (2.1%).

[2] Maggs, Book Review, 80 AJIL 403, 403–04 (1986) (reviewing DANILO TÜRK, NAČELO NEINTERVENCIJE V MEDNARODNIH ODNOSIH IN V MEDNARODNEM PRAVU (1984)).

The most convincing explanation therefore seems to be, quite simply, that our American colleagues do not read French. But, as the same seems to be true for Spanish, German, Italian, Japanese and Russian, they certainly deprive themselves of the indispensable comparative dimension, and this also raises a more general and difficult "cultural" problem. "Self-confinement"[3] might be the way empires collapse. . .

ALAIN PELLET*

TO THE EDITOR IN CHIEF:

October 23, 1987

On March 7, 1986, the Panel on the Law of Ocean Uses, under the Chairmanship of Louis Henkin, adopted a statement on U.S. Policy on the Settlement of Disputes in the Law of the Sea (*reprinted in* 81 AJIL 438 (1987)). The statement proposes the reciprocal acceptance by the United States, in its relations with other states, of "the obligation to submit to third-party arbitration or adjudication, disputes regarding the interpretation and application of the rules affecting navigation, overflight and pollution, as set forth in the [1982 UN] Convention" on the Law of the Sea (*id.* at 439). Although 2 years were devoted to formulating the statement,[1] it seems to express no more than a rather general vision of a possibly beneficial course for U.S. oceans policy and to ignore the difficulties inherent in implementation of the complex dispute settlement scheme established under the Convention.[2]

For the sake of completeness, however, it should be noted that members of the Panel, in particular Louis B. Sohn, Horace B. Robertson and Bernard H. Oxman, have referred generally to these obstacles in studies published elsewhere.[3] In 1984 Sohn and Kristen Gustafson suggested that the United States file a supplementary declaration with the International Court of Justice accepting the Court's jurisdiction with respect to the principles and rules of customary international law codified in the Convention, except

[3] The French word "*nombrilisme*" would probably be more appropriate, but I do not find any convenient English translation. A literal rendering would be "navelism."

* Agrégé des Facultés de droit, Professeur à l'Université de Paris Nord et à l'Institut d'Etudes Politiques de Paris.

[1] *See* the 1984 *Exchange between Expert Panel and Reagan Administration Officials on Non-Seabed-Mining Provisions of LOS Treaty,* 79 AJIL 151 (1985).

[2] UN Doc. A/CONF.62/122, *opened for signature* Dec. 10, 1982, *reprinted in* UNITED NATIONS, THE LAW OF THE SEA: UNITED NATIONS CONVENTION ON THE LAW OF THE SEA, UN Sales No. E.83.V.5 (1983), and 1 UNITED NATIONS CONVENTION ON THE LAW OF THE SEA 1982, A COMMENTARY 206 (M. Nordquist ed. 1985). For the status of the Convention, see LAW OF THE SEA BULL., Special Issue No. 1, March 1987 (UN Office for Ocean Affairs and the Law of the Sea).

[3] *See, e.g.,* Sohn, *Peaceful Settlement of Disputes in Ocean Conflicts: Does UNCLOS III Point the Way?*, 46 LAW & CONTEMP. PROBS. 195 (1983); Sohn, *Dispute Settlement,* in THE UNITED STATES WITHOUT THE LAW OF THE SEA TREATY 126 (L. Juda ed. 1983); Robertson, *Navigation in the Exclusive Economic Zone,* 24 VA. J. INT'L L. 865, 913 (1984); Oxman, Dispute Settlement with and among Non-Parties to the Law of the Sea Convention: Navigation and Pollution (20th Annual Conference of the Law of the Sea Institute (LSI), Miami, July 24, 1986).

those dealing with deep seabed mining (governed by part XI).[4] This alternative was not included in the Panel's 1986 statement or in what, to my knowledge, is the only major assessment of its considered effect by a Panel member, a paper presented by Oxman at the Law of the Sea Institute in July 1986. While endorsing the idea proposed in the statement, Oxman stressed what was missing from it, namely, that "[t]he most difficult obstacle to this approach is convincing other states to agree."[5]

Although the anticipated difficulty of persuading other states to go along should not serve as a deterrent, efforts to this effect should be preceded by a careful examination of both the undoubted pros and the numerous cons of the proposed action. The usefulness of linking the dispute settlement obligation to substantive navigational and environmental rights and duties of states as established in the Convention should not be permitted to obscure the obstacles attendant upon linking procedural questions with substantive problems pertaining to the rights and duties of states under international law in general, and the law of the sea in particular. Such obstacles were clearly evidenced during the *travaux préparatoires* of the 1969 Vienna Convention on the Law of Treaties in the context of the procedure to be followed with respect to invalidity, termination, withdrawal from or suspension of the operation of a treaty (part V). Shabtai Rosenne has shown that the International Law Commission rejected the view (strongly urged upon it by two of its special rapporteurs, Sir Gerald Fitzmaurice and Sir Hersch Lauterpacht) that the good faith of a party claiming grounds for invoking the invalidity or termination of a treaty should be tested by that party's willingness to submit the claim to impartial binding settlement.[6] As a result, if there are objections to such claims, the Vienna Convention obliges states merely to "seek a solution through the means indicated in Article 33 of the Charter of the United Nations"—a provision of the Convention whose viability has not yet been tested.[7] Moreover, the same obligation is contained in the 1986 Convention on the Law of Treaties Between States and International Organizations or Between International Organizations; Special Rapporteur Reuter referred to it as "the minimum that could be done and the maximum that could be envisaged."[8]

The compulsory dispute settlement scheme established in part XV of the 1982 Law of the Sea Convention is characterized by numerous limitations and exceptions; in fact, the only categories of dispute specifically subjected to it are those related to *jus communicationis* and pollution. This limited scope of part XV is the result of careful accommodation of the conflicting positions of the maximalists and the minimalists on the general question of compulsory impartial settlement going beyond the formulation of Article 33 of the Charter.[9] The legislative history of this delicate compromise does

[4] L. B. SOHN & K. GUSTAFSON, THE LAW OF THE SEA IN A NUTSHELL 246 (1984).

[5] Oxman, *supra* note 3, at 14.

[6] Rosenne, *The Settlement of Treaty Disputes under the Vienna Convention of 1969*, 31 ZEITSCHRIFT FÜR AUSLÄNDISCHES ÖFFENTLICHES RECHT UND VÖLKERRECHT [ZAÖRV] 1, 2–4 (1971).

[7] Art. 65, para. 3 of the Convention, *opened for signature* May 23, 1969, UNTS Regis. No. 18,232, UN Doc. A/CONF.39/27, *reprinted in* 63 AJIL 875 (1969), 8 ILM 679 (1969).

[8] [1982] 1 Y.B. INT'L L. COMM'N 153, UN Doc. A/CN.4/SER.A/1982. *See* Art. 65, para. 3 of the Convention, *done* Mar. 21, 1986, UN Doc. A/CONF.129/15, *reprinted in* 25 ILM 543 (1986).

[9] *Cf., e.g.*, Oda, *Some Reflections on the Dispute Settlement Clauses in the UN Convention on the Law of the Sea*, in ESSAYS IN INTERNATIONAL LAW IN HONOUR OF JUDGE MANFRED LACHS 646 (J.

not seem to justify any assumption about the readiness of other states (especially maritime powers and states granting flags of convenience) to commit themselves in advance to compulsory arbitration or adjudication of navigational and environmental disputes without becoming parties to the Convention. This is all the more reason to believe that states' reluctance to accede to the Convention may be due not only to objections regarding part XI, but also to misgivings about the compulsory settlement of disputes provided for by part XV.[10] It also seems worth mentioning that Soviet writers expressly maintain that the lack of recourse to compulsory procedures (and accordingly, the impossibility of defending shipping interests in the 200-mile zones), so long as the Convention has not entered into force, is an important reason for the prompt ratification of the Convention.[11]

In addition, one of the main incentives for states to accept compulsory dispute settlement under the Convention was its limitation to disputes related to the interpretation or application of the Convention itself.[12] Implementation of the Panel's proposal outside the Convention would thus entail recourse by the court or tribunal to the norms of customary (and not conventional) law, as partly embodied or crystallized in the Convention, a written law not yet in force.[13] Another obstacle related to the substance of part XV is posed by the flexibility with respect to the choice of a competent forum and the multiplicity of forums that evolved from the Montreux Compromise.[14] In particular, notwithstanding the advance preparation in this regard, the International Tribunal for the Law of the Sea will only be established when the Convention enters into force; consequently, until then and as long as the United States remains a nonparty, its options as to the competent forums will (presumably) be reduced in most cases to the ICJ and arbitration.[15] Furthermore, for those states which are reluctant to accept, or even clearly preclude, jurisdiction of the ICJ, arbitration will arguably be the only possible "choice" in the period preceding the establishment of the Tribunal.

A whole set of more specific problems may also be encountered in the implementation of the expert Panel's submission; for instance, those relating to the controversial "incidental" jurisdiction governed by Article 290, which stipulates the binding (and not simply advisory as with the ICJ) char-

---

Makarczyk ed. 1985); Rosenne, *The Settlement of Disputes in the New Law of the Sea*, IRANIAN REV. INT'L REL., Nos. 11–12, 1978, at 401.

[10] Shabtai Rosenne made this point in a conversation I had with him in February 1987.

[11] *See, e.g.*, A. Kolodkin, V. Andrianov & V. Kisilev, The Legal Implications of Participation or Non-Participation in the UNCLOS, and G. G. Shinkaretskaya, Legal Order in the World Ocean and Peaceful Settlement of International Disputes (papers presented at the 15th *Pacem in Maribus* Convocation, Malta, Sept. 7–11, 1987). *Cf.* the discussion at the 1984 LSI workshop, in CONSENSUS AND CONFRONTATION: THE UNITED STATES AND THE LAW OF THE SEA CONVENTION 496–503 (J. Van Dyke ed. 1985).

[12] *See* Art. 293, para. 1. *Cf.* Jaenicke, *Dispute Settlement under the Convention on the Law of the Sea*, 43 ZAÖRV 814, 816 (1983).

[13] *Cf.* Sohn, *Unratified Treaties as a Source of Customary International Law*, in REALISM IN LAW-MAKING: ESSAYS IN HONOUR OF WILLEM RIPHAGEN 231 (A. Bos & H. Siblesz eds. 1986).

[14] *Cf.* Rosenne, *UNCLOS III—The Montreux (Riphagen) Compromise*, in *id.* at 169, 170.

[15] *Cf.* Finlay, Letter to the Editor in Chief, 81 AJIL 927 (1987).

acter of provisional measures.[16] In particular, the fact that the Convention grants a clear *privilège de juridiction* in this respect to the Law of the Sea Tribunal necessitates consideration of how the provisional measures are to be applied before the Tribunal is established and the United States becomes a party to the Convention. Other matters deserving further in-depth inquiry include the lack of a time limit for the exhaustion by states of noncompulsory procedures of dispute settlement; the protection of states provided for in Article 294 against unjustified legal proceedings instituted in abuse of legal process, or those which are not prima facie well founded;[17] and the requirement of prior exhaustion of local remedies established in Article 295.[18] Moreover, although it is often assumed and is repeated in the Panel's statement that the Tribunal might play an important role at least in settling disputes related to the prompt release of detained vessels, the detailed arguments made by Judge Shigeru Oda against this assumption deserve careful consideration.[19]

The foregoing remarks are by no means intended to imply that the expert Panel's proposal in the main amounts to no more than an interesting theory invented with a view to accommodating the U.S. position as a nonsignatory.[20] Instead, I have tried to express certain reasons for doubt, which, in their complexity, seem to require further examination.

BARBARA KWIATKOWSKA*

[16] *Cf.* A. O. ADEDE, THE SYSTEM FOR SETTLEMENT OF DISPUTES UNDER THE UNITED NATIONS CONVENTION ON THE LAW OF THE SEA 65, 140–42 (1987); Rosenne, *supra* note 9, at 424; Ranjeva, *Le Règlement des différends*, in TRAITÉ DU NOUVEAU DROIT DE LA MER 1105, 1147–50 (R. J. Dupuy & D. Vignes eds. 1985).

[17] On obstacles related to preliminary proceedings, see Rosenne, *Settlement of Fisheries Disputes in the Exclusive Economic Zone*, 73 AJIL 89, 101 (1979).

[18] For detailed examination of controversy over application of this requirement (especially with regard to transboundary pollution), see, e.g., Goldie, *Concepts of Strict and Absolute Liability and the Ranking of Liability in Terms of Relative Exposure to Risk*, 16 NETH. Y.B. INT'L L. 175, 218–19 (1985); J. G. LAMMERS, POLLUTION OF INTERNATIONAL WATERCOURSES 618–24 (1984).

[19] *See* Art. 292 of the Convention. *Cf.* Oda, *Fisheries under the United Nations Convention on the Law of the Sea*, 77 AJIL 739, 747–49 (1983); and Oda, *supra* note 9, at 649–51.

[20] This attitude was evident in an oral comment by Ambassador Hasjim Djalal of Indonesia on Oxman's paper, *supra* note 3. See also the rather careful reaction of David Colson of the U.S. Department of State to Oxman's comment, in CONSENSUS AND CONFRONTATION, *supra* note 11, at 512–13 and 521. Note also, however, the statement of the U.S. Panel on the Law of Ocean Uses dated Sept. 25, 1987, *Deep Seabed Mining and the 1982 Convention on the Law of the Sea*, *reprinted infra* at p. 364, which emphasizes the benefits of adherence to the Convention to be gained by the United States (and its limited economic and security interests in deep seabed mining in the foreseeable future).

* Associate Director, Netherlands Institute for the Law of the Sea, Faculty of Law, University of Utrecht.

CONTEMPORARY PRACTICE OF THE UNITED STATES RELATING TO INTERNATIONAL LAW

Marian Nash Leich*

The material in this section is arranged according to the system employed in the annual *Digest of United States Practice in International Law,* published by the Department of State.

Renunciation of Nationality

(U.S. *Digest,* Ch. 3, §1)

Involuntary Return (Deportation) to United States

By a circular telegram dated December 12, 1987, the Department of State informed all United States diplomatic and consular posts of a change in its policy with respect to the involuntary return to the United States of U.S. nationals who might renounce U.S. nationality without first possessing another or without having been accepted for permanent residence by another country and who would thereby become stateless.

The Department announced that if such persons were to renounce their U.S. citizenship on or after December 11, 1987, and were ordered by a foreign country to be deported, they would, in general, be readmitted to the United States, in a parole status authorized by the Immigration and Naturalization Service under section 212(d)(5) of the Immigration and Nationality Act (8 U.S.C. §1182(d)(5) (1982)). The United States would still retain the option of refusing to accept a particular renunciant, if it were concluded that to do so would adversely affect significant United States interests.

The Department's message continued:

> 3. The Department wishes to emphasize that the new policy does not affect the right of AMCITS [American citizens] to renounce their nationality. Rather it relates solely to the continuing international responsibility that the United States may have with respect to its former nationals.
>
> 4. In adopting the foregoing policy, the Department recognized that humanitarian concerns dictate that it be applied prospectively only (i.e., we will not, except in extraordinary cases where the national interest clearly warrants such action, support the involuntary return of renunciants who established themselves abroad or became stateless before December 11, 1987). Renunciants will be presumed to fall within the scope of the new policy unless they can present to the consular officer satisfactory evidence that they had established adequate contacts in the foreign state prior to December 11, 1987. In cases of doubt, the Department will make the final decision about

* Office of the Legal Adviser, Department of State.

whether to accept the renunciant for return to the United States after examining the evidence and coordinating with the Immigration and Naturalization Service.

5. The Department has adopted this change in policy on a world-wide basis for two principal reasons: because the previous policy of generally refusing repatriation of stateless renunciants had generated acrimony and long-term irritants in our relations with other countries and because there would be serious adverse implications for the United States if other countries were to adopt the former U.S. policy.[1]

EXTRADITION

(U.S. *Digest*, Ch. 3, §5)

United States–Canada Agreement: Protocol of Amendment, 1988

On January 11, 1988, Secretary of State George P. Shultz and Canadian Secretary of State for External Affairs Joe Clark signed a Protocol Amending the Treaty on Extradition between the United States of America and Canada.[1] The two Secretaries also exchanged letters that addressed problems related to the transborder abduction of persons to the United States by civilian agents of bail-bonding companies, an offense that the two Governments recognize as extraditable under the Treaty.

By deleting the schedule of extraditable offenses formerly annexed to the Treaty and by providing, instead (in replacement Article 2 to the Treaty), that an offense is extraditable if punishable in both countries by more than 1 year's imprisonment, the 1988 Protocol greatly expands the class of extraditable offenses. In addition, replacement Article 2 provides that an offense is extraditable, notwithstanding:

(i) that conduct such as interstate transportation or use of the mails or of other facilities affecting interstate or foreign commerce, required for the purpose of establishing jurisdiction, forms part of the offense in the United States, or

(ii) that it relates to taxation or revenue or is one of a purely fiscal character.

The "dual criminality" provision of the Protocol ensures, also, that the offense of parental kidnapping is extraditable, where a noncustodial parent criminally abducts his or her child and flees across the United States–Canadian border.[2]

[1] Circular telegram, State 386507.
The posts were given instructions for ensuring that prospective renunciants understood that their renunciation of U.S. nationality might not prevent their involuntary return to the United States.

[1] Dec. 3, 1971, 27 UST 983, TIAS No. 8237, *as amended* by exchange of notes June 28 and July 9, 1974.

[2] *See* 18 U.S.C. §1073 (1982) and Parental Kidnaping Prevention Act of 1980, Pub. L. No. 96-611, §10(a), 94 Stat. 3566, 3573 (1980).

Under Article III of the Protocol, in cases where the offense for which extradition is sought was committed outside the territory of the requesting state, the requested state is authorized to grant extradition in its discretion, even if its own laws do not provide for jurisdiction over such an offense committed in similar circumstances.

Article IV of the Protocol replaces the restrictions upon the applicability of the political offense exception (contained in Article 4(1)(iii) of the 1971 Treaty) that were formerly set out in Article 4(2) of the Treaty, as amended by the exchange of notes in 1974.[3] Article 4(2), as replaced by the 1988 Protocol, obliges the parties not to apply the political offense exception in cases involving certain violent crimes, typically committed by terrorists, and reads:

> (2) For the purpose of this Treaty, the following offenses shall be deemed not to be offenses within subparagraph (iii) of paragraph 1 of this Article:
>
> (i) An offense for which each Contracting Party has the obligation pursuant to a multilateral international agreement to extradite the person sought or to submit the case to its competent authorities for the purpose of prosecution;
> (ii) Murder, manslaughter or other culpable homicide, malicious wounding or inflicting grievous bodily harm;
> (iii) An offense involving kidnapping, abduction, or any form of unlawful detention, including taking a hostage;
> (iv) An offense involving the placing or use of explosives, incendiaries or destructive devices or substances capable of endangering life or of causing grievous bodily harm or substantial property damage; and
> (v) An attempt or conspiracy to commit, or counselling the commission of, any of the foregoing offenses, or aiding or abetting a person who commits or attempts to commit such offenses.

Article VI of the Protocol replaces Article 11(3) of the Treaty, increasing from 45 to 60 days the time during which a person may be detained under an application for provisional arrest, pending a request for extradition.

Article VII of the Protocol amends the Treaty by adding Article 17 *bis*, which provides for consultation between the executive authorities of the requested and the requesting states, if both contracting parties have jurisdiction to prosecute the person for the offense for which extradition is sought. New Article 17 *bis* requires that the requested state, in deciding whether to extradite the person or to submit the case to its own authorities for prosecution, must consider "all relevant factors." These include, but are not limited to: "(i) the place where the act was committed or intended to be committed or the injury occurred or was intended to occur; (ii) the respective interests of the Contracting Parties; (iii) the nationality of the victim or the intended victim; and (iv) the availability and location of the evidence."

Article VIII of the Protocol provides that, notwithstanding Article 18(2) of the Treaty, the Protocol is to apply in all cases where the request for

[3] *See supra* note 1.

extradition is made after its entry into force, regardless of whether the offense was committed before or after that date.[4]

The substantive texts of the letters exchanged between Secretary of State Shultz and Secretary of State for External Affairs Clark follow:

(Secretary Shultz to Secretary Clark)

I refer to the Protocol Amending the Treaty on Extradition between the United States and Canada we signed today and have the honor to address to you the following.

The United States and Canada recognize that the transborder abduction of persons found in Canada to the United States of America by civilian agents of bail bonding companies, so-called "bounty hunters", is an extraditable offense under the United States–Canada Extradition Treaty.

Where a person has been charged with or convicted of such an offense in Canada and is found within the jurisdiction of the United States, the United States agrees, upon request, to commence extradition proceedings against such a person pursuant to the Treaty in order that the person may be returned to Canada.

The United States will use its best efforts to honor Canadian requests for testimony, information, or other assistance pertaining to such abductions.

Canada and the United States agree to cooperate to deter such transborder abductions. To assist in achieving that purpose, the United States will continue to exert its best efforts to inform those engaged in business as bail bondsmen or bounty hunters and other interested parties of the positions set forth in this exchange of letters.

Canada and the United States agree to consult promptly concerning any case of transborder abduction involving bounty hunters which might arise in the future. The purpose of such consultations shall be to address matters relating to any such case, including any request by the Government of Canada for the return of the person so abducted. In the event of return, the Governments agree to co-operate to have the abducted person escorted to Canada and taken into custody at the border, pursuant to a request for provisional arrest, pending the outcome of extradition proceedings. For the purpose of these consultations, the principal law enforcement contact for the United States will be the Director of the Office of International Affairs of the Criminal Division of the Department of Justice.

I have the honor to propose that this letter and your reply constitute an understanding between our two Governments which is not intended to create or otherwise alter legal obligations for either Government nor to create or otherwise alter any rights or privileges for private parties.

(Secretary Clark to Secretary Shultz)

I have the honour to acknowledge receipt of your letter of today's date concerning transborder abduction of persons found in Canada to

[4] Dept. of State Files L/T.

> the United States of America by civilian agents of bail bonding companies, so-called "bounty hunters". I accept your proposal that your letter and this reply constitute an Understanding between our two Governments which is not intended to create or otherwise alter legal obligations for either Government nor to create or otherwise alter any rights or privileges for private parties.[5]

International Maritime Law

(U.S. *Digest,* Ch. 7, §12)

Icebreaker Voyages in Arctic—U.S.-Canadian Agreement

On January 11, 1988, Secretary of State George P. Shultz and Canadian Secretary of State for External Affairs Joe Clark signed an agreement at Ottawa that sets forth the terms under which the two Governments will cooperate in increasing their knowledge of the Arctic marine environment through research conducted during icebreaker voyages and in facilitating safe, effective icebreaker navigation off their Arctic coasts.

The agreement recognizes the particular interests and responsibilities of the two countries as neighboring states in the Arctic and the desirability of cooperation in order to advance their shared interests in Arctic development and security. It also affirms that navigation and resource development in the Arctic must not adversely affect the region's unique environment and the well-being of its inhabitants.

The two Governments undertake to facilitate navigation by their icebreakers in their respective Arctic waters and to develop cooperative procedures for this purpose. The two Governments agree to take advantage of their icebreaker navigation to develop and share research information, "in accordance with generally accepted principles of international law," in order to advance their understanding of the area's marine environment. The United States Government pledges that "all navigation by U.S. icebreakers within waters claimed by Canada to be internal will be undertaken with the consent of the Government of Canada." Paragraph 4 of the agreement provides: "Nothing in this agreement of cooperative endeavour between Arctic neighbors and friends nor any practice thereunder affects the respective positions of the Governments of the United States and of Canada on the Law of the Sea in this or other maritime areas or their respective positions regarding third parties."

The agreement entered into force upon signature, and may be terminated at any time by 3 months' written notice given by one Government to the other.[1]

The agreement had its origin in the public controversy in Canada in 1985, caused by the transit of the Northwest Passage by the U.S. Coast Guard icebreaker *Polar Sea.* The controversy led to a claim by the Canadian Government, publicly announced on September 10, 1985, that the waters in question were internal Canadian waters, subject to full Canadian sover-

[5] *Id.*

[1] Dept. of State Files L/T.

eignty. The Canadian Government drew straight lines around the outer perimeter of its Arctic islands to establish this claim, which the United States does not recognize as having any basis under international law. The two Governments subsequently discussed some type of pragmatic arrangement for enhanced cooperation in Arctic waters, as between good neighbors and friends. These discussions were given new impetus at the 1987 summit meeting in Ottawa, where President Reagan and Prime Minister Mulroney agreed to find a solution.[2]

ARMS CONTROL AND DISARMAMENT
(U.S. *Digest,* Ch. 14, §7)

Treaty Between United States and USSR

On January 25, 1988, President Reagan transmitted to the Senate for advice and consent to ratification the Treaty Between the United States of America and the Union of Soviet Socialist Republics on the Elimination of Their Intermediate-Range and Shorter-Range Missiles, signed on December 8, 1987 at Washington, on the occasion of the state visit of Mikhail Gorbachev, General Secretary of the Central Committee of the Communist Party of the Soviet Union.

In his letter of transmittal the President described the Treaty as "an unprecedented arms control agreement in several respects," marking the first time that the two nations had agreed "to eliminate, throughout the world, an entire class of their missile systems." Significantly, he pointed out, the eliminations would be achieved "from markedly asymmetrical starting points that favored the Soviet Union."

Under the Treaty both parties are obligated to eliminate all of their intermediate-range and shorter-range, ground-launched ballistic and cruise missiles, their launchers, and specified support structures and support equipment. Shorter-range missiles (those with a range capability between 500 and 1,000 kilometers) are to be eliminated within 18 months after entry into force of the Treaty. Intermediate-range missiles (those with a range capability between 1,000 and 5,500 kilometers) are to be eliminated—in two phases—within 3 years after entry into force of the Treaty. The Treaty provides for comprehensive on-site inspections to aid in verifying compliance, including the continuous monitoring of certain facilities. The parties will continue the exchange of detailed information (begun prior to signature of the Treaty) to facilitate such verification, and, in addition, will cooperate in enhancing verification by national means.

The Treaty consists of four documents that set out the basic obligations of the two parties and the means of their implementation: (1) the Treaty articles, (2) the Memorandum of Understanding (MOU) on Data, (3) the Protocol on Elimination, and (4) the Protocol on Inspection.[1]

[2] For President Reagan's address before a joint session of the Canadian Parliament, Apr. 6, 1987, see 23 WEEKLY COMP. PRES. DOC. 353, 357 (Apr. 13, 1987); DEPT. ST. BULL., No. 2123, June 1987, at 3, 7.

[1] For a description of the components of the Treaty, see Secretary Shultz's report, *infra.*

President Reagan's letter of transmittal states, in regard to on-site inspections:

> The Treaty provides that on-site inspections are permitted at specified locations in the United States and the Soviet Union as well as in the Basing Countries in Western and Eastern Europe [the United Kingdom, Belgium, the Netherlands, the Federal Republic of Germany, Italy, the German Democratic Republic and Czechoslovakia] where U.S. or Soviet missiles, launchers, and related support structures and support equipment subject to the Treaty are or have been located. The different types of "short-notice" on-site inspections for which the Treaty provides are designed to contribute to our ability to verify Soviet compliance, while protecting all U.S. and Allied nuclear and conventional forces not subject to the Treaty as well as other sensitive intelligence and defense facilities.
>
> In addition to "short-notice" on-site inspections, the Treaty provides for other types of on-site inspections, including the continuous presence of U.S. inspectors at the Soviet facility at Votkinsk, at which SS–25 and SS–20 missiles have been assembled, and a continuous Soviet presence at the identified facility at Hercules Plant #1 located at Magna, Utah, at which stages of Pershing II missiles formerly were produced.[2]

Finally, the President transmitted to the Senate for its information the Agreement Among the United States of America and the Kingdom of Belgium, the Federal Republic of Germany, the Republic of Italy, the Kingdom of the Netherlands and the United Kingdom of Great Britain and Northern Ireland Regarding Inspections Relating to the Treaty Between the United States of America and the Union of Soviet Socialist Republics on the Elimination of Their Intermediate-Range and Shorter-Range Missiles (the Basing Country Agreement), which was signed at Brussels on December 11, 1987. The Basing Country Agreement confirms that the five Allied Basing Countries will permit the inspections called for in the Treaty.

The President transmitted for the Senate's information, as well, notes exchanged between the United States and the German Democratic Republic and Czechoslovakia, on December 23, 1987 and January 5, 1988, respectively, in which each country agreed to the conduct of inspections under the Treaty within its territory by the United States. The Soviet Union was to exchange identical notes with the five Allied Basing Countries.

The President's letter to the Senate was accompanied by a report on the Treaty from Secretary of State George P. Shultz, dated January 20, 1988, the major portion of which follows:

Introduction

> . . . .
>
> The Treaty is the fruit of many years' labor and of this Administration's firm policy regarding the Soviet deployment of SS–20s threatening our Allies in Europe and Asia. It was negotiated in Geneva and at ministerial meetings in Washington, Moscow, and Geneva. In addition to the U.S. Arms Control and Disarmament Agency and the Depart-

[2] S. TREATY DOC. 11, 100th Cong., 2d Sess., at IV (1988).

ment of State, representatives of the Joint Chiefs of Staff, the Central Intelligence Agency, the Secretary of Defense, and the Defense Intelligence Agency all played important roles in its development.

Throughout the negotiating process, we consulted extensively with our NATO and Asian allies, particularly the Western European Basing Countries in which missile systems, support structures, or other equipment subject to the Treaty are located: Belgium, the Federal Republic of Germany, Italy, The Netherlands, and the United Kingdom. Contemporaneously with the negotiation of the Treaty, the United States negotiated the Basing Country Agreement with these countries, providing for their approval and assistance in the implementation of the Treaty's inspection provisions. We also regularly advised Congress, in Washington and during the Congressional Observer Group's meetings in Geneva, on the progress of the negotiations and on the objectives of the United States in negotiating the Treaty.

Background Information

The Treaty had its genesis in the Soviet deployment of SS–20 intermediate-range missiles beginning in 1977. The SS–20 is an accurate, three-warhead, ground-mobile ballistic missile, whose deployment by the Soviet Union increased an already existing imbalance in favor of Soviet theater nuclear forces. These Soviet deployments not only directly threatened our NATO and Asian Allies, they also raised questions about the ability of the United States and its Allies to deter a Soviet attack on Western Europe. In December 1979, after thorough consultations among the Allies, NATO reached what became known as the "dual-track" decision. On the one hand, NATO would proceed to deploy a limited number of U.S. Pershing II missiles and ground-launched cruise missiles in Western Europe to maintain its deterrent capability. On the other hand, the United States would pursue arms control negotiations with the Soviet Union with a view to establishing a balance in intermediate-range nuclear missile forces at a lower and equal level.

Under this Administration, the "dual-track" decision was reaffirmed, and on November 18, 1981, the United States proposed the "zero option" to the Soviet Union. Pursuant to this proposal, the United States would have cancelled its planned deployments to Europe of Pershing II missiles and cruise missiles if the Soviet Union would have agreed to eliminate all of its intermediate-range nuclear missiles.

Today, more than six years later, the U.S. "zero option" proposal constitutes the basis of the Treaty. The six years of negotiations, however, did not produce this result easily. For example, while the United States emphasized for years its preference for the "zero option," the Soviets at first insisted on retaining a residual force of intermediate-range missiles and on counting the independent British and French nuclear deterrents as though they were forces of the United States. The United States rejected that position. Moreover, the Soviets walked out of the negotiations in November 1983 when the United States began deployments of intermediate-range missiles in Europe. It was not until January 1985 that the Soviets agreed to return to the negotiations. They did not agree to the "zero option" until July 1987.

Soviet shorter-range missiles—the SS–12 and SS–23—can fulfill many of the same military missions as the Soviet intermediate-range missiles. Therefore, from the outset, the United States insisted upon concurrent constraints on shorter-range missiles in order to enhance the effectiveness of limits on intermediate-range missiles. In the Summer of 1987, after the Soviets proposed the elimination of shorter-range systems in Europe, the United States proposed that the shorter-range systems of both sides be eliminated on a global basis. In response to the U.S. proposal, the Soviets accepted the "zero option" for shorter-range missiles as well.

For much of the negotiations, the Soviet Union argued that the Treaty should focus only on missile systems located in Europe and that missiles located outside of Europe should be exempt from the Treaty or subject to less stringent restrictions. The United States, however, insisted on a "global" approach in view of the mobility and transportability of the Soviet missile systems. The Soviets eventually agreed to this approach.

During the last months of the negotiations, the Soviet Union insisted that U.S. warheads associated with the Pershing IA missiles belonging to the Federal Republic of Germany be included in the Treaty. The United States had insisted from the beginning of the negotiations that systems belonging to third countries would not be part of, or be affected by, the Treaty. On August 26, 1987, the Federal Republic of Germany announced that it would dismantle its Pershing IA missiles when the United States and the Soviet Union had eliminated all of their intermediate-range and shorter-range missiles pursuant to the Treaty. This unilateral decision by the Federal Republic is completely separate from the Treaty. This decision represents a policy of the Federal Republic of Germany that is not legally binding upon the Parties to the Treaty. Following the Federal Republic's unilateral decision, the United States and the Soviet Union agreed that they will eliminate their intermediate-range missiles by 15 days prior to the end of the three-year elimination period specified by the Treaty. At that point, the conditions established by the Federal Republic will have been met, and the existing program of cooperation will have therefore ceased. The U.S. reentry vehicles now associated with the Federal Republic's Pershing IA missiles will then be withdrawn and returned to U.S. territory. The United States will eliminate them in accordance with the Protocol on Elimination. The Treaty and its associated documents will not affect existing programs of cooperation.

The Treaty: Its Structure and Content

The Treaty obligates the United States and the Soviet Union to eliminate all of their intermediate-range and shorter-range ground-launched, weapon-delivery, ballistic and cruise missiles, their launchers, and specified support structures and support equipment. The Treaty requires periodic data exchanges and gives each Party the right to carry out verification measures, including on-site inspections.

The Treaty consists of four documents, which set forth the basic obligations and the means of implementing those obligations. These are:

The Treaty Articles, which obligate the Parties to eliminate all of their intermediate-range and shorter-range missile systems within three years and 18 months, respectively; not to possess such missile systems after elimination; not to produce or flight-test such missiles in the future; and to carry out provisions to facilitate effective verification of the terms of the Treaty;

The Memorandum of Understanding (MOU) on Data, which contains the data, including site diagrams and photographs that are integral parts of the MOU, exchanged between the Parties prior to the signing of the Treaty regarding the locations, numbers, and characteristics of each Party's intermediate-range and shorter-range missile systems as of November 1, 1987;

The Protocol on Elimination, which sets forth the detailed procedures for eliminating missiles, launchers, support structures, and support equipment subject to the Treaty; and

The Protocol on Inspection, which sets forth the detailed procedures for conducting on-site inspections, including "short-notice" inspections, "baseline" inspections, "close-out" inspections, "elimination" inspections, and continuous portal monitoring.

Reduction Obligations

The Treaty provides that each Party must eliminate all of its intermediate-range and shorter-range missile systems. Intermediate-range missiles have a range capability between 1000 and 5500 kilometers; shorter-range missiles have a range capability between 500 and 1000 kilometers.

The existing types of intermediate-range and shorter-range missiles are listed in Article III of the Treaty. For the United States, these are the Pershing II intermediate-range ballistic missile, the BGM–109G intermediate-range cruise missile, and the Pershing IA shorter-range ballistic missile. For the Soviet Union, the existing types of missiles are the SS–20 intermediate-range ballistic missile, the SS–5 intermediate-range ballistic missile, the SS–4 intermediate-range ballistic missile, the SS–12 shorter-range ballistic missile, and the SS–23 shorter-range ballistic missile. All intermediate-range missile systems must be eliminated within three years after entry into force of the Treaty. All shorter-range missile systems must be eliminated within 18 months. For ground-launched ballistic and cruise missiles not listed in Article III as "existing types," range capability is determined in accordance with criteria set forth in paragraph 4 of Article VII of the Treaty.

Upon entry into force of the Treaty, neither Party may produce or flight-test any intermediate-range or shorter-range missiles or produce any stages of such missiles or launchers of such missiles. The Parties are prohibited from conducting any launches of shorter-range missiles. During the first six months following entry into force of the Treaty, however, each Party may launch up to 100 intermediate-range missiles for the purpose of destroying them. Once all intermediate-range and shorter-range missile systems have been eliminated, neither Party may thereafter possess any intermediate-range or shorter-range missile systems.

Also, the Treaty takes account of the fact that the first stage of the Soviet SS–25 intercontinental ballistic missile, which is not subject to the Treaty, is outwardly similar to the first stage of the SS–20 intermediate-range ballistic missile, which is subject to the Treaty. The Parties are permitted to produce a ground-launched ballistic missile (GLBM), having a range such that it is not subject to the Treaty, that uses one stage, and only one stage, outwardly similar to, but not interchangeable with, a stage of an existing type of intermediate-range ground-launched ballistic missile that is subject to the Treaty. However, to strengthen the ban on missile production, the Parties are prohibited from producing any other stage that is similar to, but not interchangeable with, a stage of any existing type of intermediate-range ground-launched ballistic missile. In order to help verify compliance with this provision, the United States has the right to establish a portal monitoring system, including resident inspectors, to monitor continuously the portal of each facility at which SS–25 and SS–20 missiles have been assembled. Currently there is one such facility at Votkinsk. For its part, the Soviet Union has the right to establish a continuous portal monitoring system at a former U.S. intermediate-range GLBM production facility at Magna, Utah.

Verification Obligations

The scope and intrusiveness of verification called for in this Treaty are unprecedented in the history of arms control agreements between the United States and the Soviet Union. Verification obligations fall under five basic categories:

—locational restrictions
—elimination requirements
—national technical means of verification
—data exchanges
—on-site inspections.

Locational Restrictions

In order to facilitate verification, the Treaty imposes a number of restrictions on activities relating to intermediate-range and shorter-range missile systems during the elimination periods. For example, pending elimination:

—All intermediate-range missiles and their launchers must be located in deployment areas or at support facilities, such as storage or repair facilities, or be in notified transit between them. All such areas and facilities must be named and their locations described. An intermediate-range missile or launcher located elsewhere (and not in a notified transit) would thus be in violation of the Treaty.

—Within 90 days after the Treaty enters into force, all deployed shorter-range missiles, as well as deployed and non-deployed launchers of such missiles, must be moved to elimination facilities. The remaining non-deployed shorter-range missiles must be moved to elimination facilities within one year. Until their removal to elimination facilities, shorter-range missiles and their launchers must be located at missile operating bases, be located at missile support facilities, or be in transit.

—Transit of intermediate-range and shorter-range missiles between permitted locations must be completed within 25 days and, following the completion of transit, information regarding the transit must be provided within 48 hours.

Elimination Requirements

Article X of the Treaty sets forth the basic requirements regarding the elimination of specific items and facilities and obligates the Parties to carry out the required elimination activities in accordance with the specific procedures set forth in the Treaty and the Protocols on Elimination and Inspection. The locations at which elimination takes place are specified in the MOU or in subsequent updated data. The Protocol on Elimination sets forth detailed procedures for the elimination of missiles, launchers, launch canisters, shelters, missile transporter vehicles, missile erectors, launch stands, propellant tanks, and training items, as appropriate, for each Party. Techniques such as burning, demolition, crushing, and flattening are specified for eliminating transportable items at designated elimination facilities. Techniques for eliminating fixed structures *in situ* are specified, including dismantlement, excavation, and demolition. Provisions governing elimination of missiles through launch, static display, and loss or accidental destruction are also included.

National Technical Means of Verification

The Treaty recognizes the utility of national technical means of verification, such as reconnaissance satellites, and each Party agrees not to interfere with such means of verification. With a view to enhancing the utility of national technical means, concealment measures are strictly limited. Furthermore, the Soviet Union is required, up to six times a year during the period of elimination, to open on short notice the roofs of SS–25 garages in order to help U.S. national technical means ensure that SS–20s are not deployed at SS–25 strategic missile bases that are not subject to on-site inspections.

Data Exchanges

The Treaty requires detailed exchanges of data and notifications. Each Party is required to notify the other each time a missile or launcher is moved and of any change in the data base originally set forth in the MOU. Each Party must advise the other of the scheduled date of elimination activities, the movement of items that are to be eliminated from the areas specified in the MOU to elimination facilities, and the completion of elimination activities. Such notifications are required to be made through the Nuclear Risk Reduction Centers established pursuant to the Agreement Between the United States and the Soviet Union on the Establishment of Nuclear Risk Reduction Centers of September 15, 1987. The notifications are designed to provide a continuously updated data base, which will serve as a baseline against which other observations can be measured.

On-site Inspections

The Treaty provides for a wide variety of on-site inspections. The scope of the inspection measures is unprecedented in the history of arms control agreements. The on-site inspections to be carried out include:

—"baseline" inspections, between 30 and 90 days after entry into force of the Treaty, to help verify the initial update of data contained in the categories set forth in the MOU;

—"close-out" inspections to verify the elimination of specified facilities;

—"elimination" inspections to observe actual elimination of missiles, launchers, and support equipment at elimination facilities;

—"elimination" inspections to confirm the completion of the process of elimination with respect to items lost or accidentally destroyed or placed on static display and with respect to training equipment;

—"short-notice" inspections of certain declared and formerly declared facilities, during the three-year elimination period and for a ten-year period thereafter, to aid in verifying that all Treaty-prohibited activity has ceased; and

—"continuous portal monitoring" by the United States at the designated portal and perimeter of the facility at Votkinsk, at which SS–25 and SS–20 missiles have been assembled, to ensure that stages of the SS–20 are not covertly manufactured as stages of the SS–25 ICBM. The Soviet Union may install continuous portal monitoring at the designated portal and perimeter of the Hercules Plant #1 located in Magna, Utah, at which stages of Pershing II missiles formerly were produced. If, at any time after the initial two years of the Treaty, assembly of SS–25s ceases at Votkinsk, continuous portal monitoring would continue for another 12 months and then cease along with the monitoring of the plant at Magna, Utah. The United States could reestablish continuous portal monitoring if the Soviets resumed SS–25 missile assembly at Votkinsk or anywhere else.

The specific procedures for the conduct of these inspections, including provisions governing access for on-site inspections and the infrastructure for a continuous portal monitoring system, are set forth in the Protocol on Inspection.

Inspectors and their supporting aircrews will be designated by each Party in advance by means of lists submitted to the other Party. Specific grounds on which a Party may object to a particular individual are set forth. The Annex to the Protocol on Inspection specifies the privileges and immunities to be accorded inspectors and aircrew members during the inspection process, including immunity from criminal prosecution and inviolability of their person.

The Protocol on Inspection designates certain "points of entry" for each country in which missile systems subject to the Treaty are located. A Party intending to carry out an inspection must notify the other Party, through the Nuclear Risk Reduction Centers, not less than a specified number of hours before the inspection team will reach the point of entry. Within a specified time after arrival at the point of entry, the Inspecting Party must indicate the specific site to be inspected. An inspection team must depart the point of entry for the inspection site within a specified number of hours from its arrival at the point of entry. The Inspected Party must provide transport for the inspection team from the point of entry to the inspection site. In the case of "baseline," "close-out," and "short-notice" inspections, the Inspected Party must ensure that the inspection team arrives at the site within nine hours of its specification of the inspection site.

In general, one hour after notification of a specific inspection site has been provided, the Inspected Party may not remove any Treaty-limited item from that site prior to inspection. Except for continuous portal monitoring and "elimination" inspections, the period of time an inspection team may remain at an inspection site for a given inspection is 24 hours, with one eight hour extension if agreed to by the Inspected Party. There is a limit on the number of inspections that may be conducted simultaneously. Inspection procedures vary depending upon the specific type of inspection involved.

Ratification

The Treaty will enter into force when the constitutional procedures for ratification of the United States and the Soviet Union have been satisfied and the instruments of ratification have been exchanged. The MOU, the Protocol on Elimination, and the Protocol on Inspection are integral parts of the Treaty and upon exchange of the instruments of ratification will enter into force as part of the Treaty. The U.S.-GDR and U.S.-Czechoslovak Notes, which are included herewith for the information of the Senate, will also enter into force simultaneously with the Treaty. The Basing Country Agreement will do so as well, following completion of the constitutional procedures of each of the Parties to it and notification thereof to all other Parties.

Amendments

Amendments to the Treaty are subject to the same ratification procedures as the Treaty itself. However, some of the provisions and procedures contained in the Protocols on Elimination and Inspection are highly detailed and technical. It is recognized that it may be necessary to adjust some of them to take into account unforeseen situations. Accordingly, the Protocols provide that the Parties may, in the Special Verification Commission established by the Treaty, agree upon measures necessary to improve the viability and effectiveness of the Protocols. The Protocols provide that such measures, which would be technical in nature and would not affect the Parties' basic obligations, would not be considered to be amendments and thus would not require ratification.

Non-Conflicting Obligations

The Parties commit themselves not to assume any international obligation or undertaking that would conflict with the provisions of the Treaty. This provision will not in any way affect existing or future patterns of defense cooperation with U.S. Allies in other areas, including strategic forces, short-range nuclear forces (with a range capability below 500 kilometers), or conventional forces.

Duration and Withdrawal

The Treaty is of unlimited duration. As an exercise of its national sovereignty, a Party may withdraw following six months' notice to the other Party if it determines that extraordinary events related to the subject matter of the Treaty have jeopardized its supreme interests.

The Basing Country Agreement

The Basing Country Agreement is a necessary complement to the Treaty. The Treaty and the Protocol on Inspection provide for on-site inspection to verify compliance with the provisions of the Treaty not only in U.S. and Soviet territory, but also in the countries in which U.S. and Soviet missile systems are located. Many of the items that the United States must eliminate are within the territory of our Western European Allies. By means of the Basing Country Agreement, the five Allied Basing Countries, on whose territory U.S. systems subject to the Treaty are located, consent to inspections at facilities subject to the Treaty within their territory by Soviet inspectors conducted in accordance with the Treaty and its Protocols. This formal consent on the part of the Allied Basing Countries provides the legal basis for the United States to make its commitment to the Soviet Union that Soviet inspections can be carried out on the territory of the Allied Basing Countries.

Exchanges of Notes

Each Basing Country is exchanging diplomatic Notes with the Party that will conduct inspections within its territory. The Notes record the acknowledgement of each Basing Country and the Inspecting Party that the Basing Country has agreed to inspections within its territory conducted in accordance with the terms of the Treaty, including the Protocol on Inspection, and that the Inspecting Party has obligated itself to comply with the terms of the Treaty and to respect the laws and regulations of the Basing Country during the inspections. The Notes state that they do not in any way affect the reciprocal obligations between the United States and the Soviet Union under the Treaty. The countries that base U.S. systems subject to the Treaty are Belgium, the Federal Republic of Germany, Italy, The Netherlands, and the United Kingdom; the Basing Countries for Soviet systems are the German Democratic Republic and Czechoslovakia.

Inspections of SS–4 Silos

In addition to the Treaty documents discussed above, the United States and the Soviet Union agreed to an exchange of letters between Ambassadors Glitman and Obukhov, dated December 7, 1987, relating to the U.S. inspections of silo launchers for Soviet SS–4 intermediate-range ballistic missiles. This agreement gives the United States the right to conduct a total of up to six on-site inspections of former silo launchers of SS–4 missiles. Organizational matters relating to such inspections will be arranged through the Special Verification Commission, which was established by the Treaty.[3]

[3] *Id.* at VII–XVI. The Secretary's report to President Reagan was accompanied by an article-by-article analysis of the Treaty articles, the Memorandum of Understanding, the Protocol on Elimination and the Protocol on Inspection. The latter contains an Annex on Privileges and Immunities of Inspectors and Aircrew Members. The report was also accompanied by an article-by-article analysis of the Basing Country Agreement signed at Brussels on Dec. 11, 1987. That Agreement, as well, contains a corresponding Annex on Privileges and Immunities of Inspectors and Aircrew Members.

The Agreement on the Establishment of Nuclear Risk Reduction Centers, mentioned at p. 347 *supra,* provides for the establishment of a Nuclear Risk Reduction Center in each capital for communication at the government-to-government level by direct satellite links. The communications capability of each Center has been described as "very similar to—but separate from—the modernized Direct Communications Link ("Hot Line"), which is reserved for heads of government." For the Agreement and its two Protocols, see DEPT. ST. BULL., No. 2128, November 1987, at 34, *reprinted in* 27 ILM 78 (1988). *See further* 78 AJIL 891 (1984).

JUDICIAL DECISIONS

MONROE LEIGH

Federal jurisdiction—act of state doctrine precludes federal court jurisdiction over antitrust challenge to actions of foreign sovereign instrumentality taken pursuant to laws of foreign sovereign

O.N.E. SHIPPING LTD. v. FLOTA MERCANTE GRANCOLOMBIANA, S.A. 830 F.2d 449.

U.S. Court of Appeals, 2d Cir., October 1, 1987.

Appellant, a Bermudan shipping corporation engaged in the transport of liquid bulk cargo (LBC) from U.S. gulf ports to Central and South American countries, appealed from the dismissal of its antitrust action against Flota Mercante Grancolombiana, S.A., a Colombian government instrumentality, and other shipping companies. Appellant alleged that appellee had entered into charter agreements with other, non-Colombian shippers, which illegally excluded appellant from competing in the business of shipping LBC from the United States to Colombia in violation of the Sherman Antitrust Act (15 U.S.C. §§1, 2 (1982)). Appellee had entered into these arrangements pursuant to Colombian cargo reservation laws mandating that only Colombian-owned or Colombian-chartered vessels ship LBC to Colombia; Colombian government officials approved the chartering agreements. The district court applied a comity balancing test and dismissed the complaint on the ground that the interests of Colombia in protecting its shipping industry outweighed those of the United States in enforcing its antitrust laws. Upon the appellant's motion for reconsideration, the district court sanctioned appellant under Rule 11 of the Federal Rules of Civil Procedure.[1] On appeal, a divided three-judge panel of the United States Court of Appeals for the Second Circuit (per Pollack, J.) affirmed the dismissal of the antitrust claim, reversed the imposition of Rule 11 sanctions and *held* that the act of state doctrine precludes consideration of an antitrust action against a government instrumentality for its actions taken pursuant to a foreign sovereign protectionist law.

The court characterized the appellant's suit as a direct challenge to Colombia's cargo reservation laws and to the legality of appellee's space-chartering agreements pursuant thereto. The court found that Colombia's cargo reservation laws—which require that the first 50 percent of all licensed shipments to Colombia be carried by Colombian vessels or vessels chartered by a Colombian company—serve several legitimate purposes, including the development of a strong Colombian merchant marine and economy. The court also noted that the Government of Colombia (GOC) had repeatedly

[1] 830 F.2d 449, 450.

informed the United States Department of State of "its strong support for the cargo reservation laws and the chartering agreements thereunder."[2]

Given these facts, the court approved the district court's conclusion that since the GOC had an ownership interest in appellee, and a "strong interest in its protectionist legislation . . . there would be probable adverse effects upon [U.S.] foreign relations" were it to assert jurisdiction.[3] Though asserting that Congress had enacted the Foreign Trade Antitrust Improvements Act of 1982[4] (the Act) "[i]n an effort to provide a single standard to determine whether American antitrust laws apply to a given extraterritorial transaction," the court concluded that Congress had "left it to the courts" to decide this issue.[5] In making that decision, the court turned first to the act of state doctrine as its rule of decision.

Noting that the act of state doctrine is "designed primarily to avoid judicial inquiry" into the acts, policies and motivations of foreign governments, the court first observed that the doctrine may be applied regardless of whether the foreign government is named as a party or its actions are merely challenged in the pleadings.[6] Next, the court impliedly rejected the approach of the lower court, which "engaged in the broader analysis of the possible adverse effects upon foreign relations" using a balancing-of-interests test. Rather, a court should first undertake a "preliminary assessment" of the likely impact on international relations of judicial consideration of the sovereign's acts. For purposes of that assessment, the court's determination may be informed but not dictated by the position of the executive.[7]

Applying these rules, the court first concluded that appellant's allegation would require that the district court examine and "pass judgment on" the acts and motivations of the GOC. Moreover, since the "causal chain" between appellant's injury and appellee's alleged conduct could not be established absent an inquiry into the motives of the GOC, the court held that the antitrust claims had to be dismissed. In addition, the court asserted that inasmuch as the conduct of the defendants had been "compelled" by the GOC, they were entitled to assert the defense of "foreign government compulsion."[8] Finally, the court found support for its holding in Congress's provision of an alternate dispute resolution procedure before the Federal Maritime Commission. Since this alternative remedy had been pursued by appellant, the court concluded that "courts should avoid the unnecessary irritant of a private antitrust action."[9]

Judge Cardamone dissented from the panel's decision, arguing that neither the Foreign Trade Antitrust Improvements Act nor traditional notions of comity mandated a dismissal of appellant's suit. Judge Cardamone first argued that the provisions of the Act excluding export commerce from the antitrust laws did not apply because the case at bar involved import commerce: "U.S. corporations import from foreign flag lines the service of

[2] *Id.* at 451.

[3] *Id.*

[4] Pub. L. No. 97-290, 96 Stat. 1246 (codified at 15 U.S.C. §6a (1982)).

[5] 830 F.2d at 451–52.

[6] *Id.* at 452.

[7] *Id.*

[8] *Id.* at 453.

[9] *Id.* at 454.

shipping their goods from the United States to Colombia."[10] Moreover, even if the commerce could be considered to be "export commerce," Judge Cardamone argued, the antitrust laws would still be applicable given that commerce's effect on a person doing business in the United States, i.e., appellant. In light of these factors, and given consistent federal court jurisdiction over shipping disputes, Judge Cardamone concluded that it is "obvious that Congress did not aim to deprive federal courts of jurisdiction over suits like the instant one."[11]

Judge Cardamone agreed with the majority that Congress left to the courts "how to employ notions of international comity in extraterritorial antitrust cases."[12] He argued, however, that in light of "controlling" Supreme Court precedent, the panel had given too much weight to the interest of the GOC in its cargo reservation laws. According to Judge Cardamone, both *United States v. Sisal Sales Corp.*[13] and *Continental Ore Co. v. Union Carbide & Carbon Corp.*[14] established that the mere fact that anticompetitive conduct is aided by foreign protectionist legislation does not "oust federal courts from jurisdiction on comity grounds."[15] After applying the holdings of these cases to the facts at hand, Judge Cardamone concluded that "[appellee] and its associates' actions brought about unlawful consequences in the United States for which they should be answerable in federal court."[16]

The most significant aspect of this decision is the majority's rejection of the balancing test employed by the lower court. Instead, the court suggests that if a lawsuit directly implicates a foreign government's motives or actions, jurisdiction should not be exercised no matter what the strength of U.S. interests in pursuing the suit.

Decisions of the Iran–United States Claims Tribunal

State responsibility toward foreign nationals—expulsion—liability of state for actions of revolutionaries—relevance of intent of person expelled during revolution

YEAGER v. ISLAMIC REPUBLIC OF IRAN. AWD 324-10199-1.
Iran–United States Claims Tribunal, The Hague, November 2, 1987.

RANKIN v. ISLAMIC REPUBLIC OF IRAN. AWD 326-10913-2.
Iran–United States Claims Tribunal, The Hague, November 3, 1987.

Claimants in these two cases were among over 1,500 United States nationals to bring claims before the Iran–United States Claims Tribunal alleg-

[10] *Id.* at 455.

[11] *Id.* at 456.

[12] *Id.* at 457.

[13] 274 U.S. 268 (1927).

[14] 370 U.S. 690 (1962).

[15] 830 F.2d at 457. The majority asserted that these cases were inapposite because "both related to alleged conspiracies entered into in the United States by United States citizens which sought to monopolize trade in the United States." *Id.* at 453 n.4. In contrast, the instant action involved agreements entered into by foreign parties, which were approved by the GOC and related to Colombian commerce. *Id.*

[16] *Id.* at 458.

ing wrongful expulsion from Iran at the time of the Islamic Revolution.[1] The opinion by Chamber One in *Yeager* and that of Chamber Two in *Rankin,* together with an earlier expulsion decision issued by Chamber Three,[2] complete the Tribunal's initial exposition of the expulsion issue.

In the first expulsion claim addressed by Chamber One, Kenneth P. Yeager, a U.S. national employed by Bell Helicopter International Co. (BHI) in Iran, claimed $134,147 from Iran as damages for his alleged wrongful expulsion. Chamber One of the Tribunal *held* Iran liable for unlawful expulsion, awarding Yeager $13,966 in damages.[3]

Yeager claimed that, beginning in October 1978, he and all other Americans in Iran were the target of a *de facto* expulsion from Iran by means of a campaign of violence and intimidation instigated by the Ayatollah Khomeini and other leaders of the Islamic Revolution. After the Ayatollah Khomeini returned to Iran on February 1, 1979, Yeager allegedly was directly threatened with violence by neighbors and others, and began to sell his belongings at low prices. On February 13, 1979, immediately after the success of the revolution, armed Revolutionary Guards[4] came to Yeager's apartment, gave him and his wife 30 minutes to pack their belongings, and took them by car to the Tehran Hilton Hotel where other BHI employees were assembled. They were kept there under guard until February 17, when they and other BHI employees and families were bused to the airport. At the airport, Revolutionary Guards seized $1,466 in cash from Yeager and his wife. They were put on a plane and flown to Germany. Soon thereafter, Iran canceled BHI's contracts in Iran, and BHI later terminated Yeager's employment contract.[5]

Iran asserted that Yeager left Iran voluntarily, and it denied any responsibility for the claimed expulsion or the related damages. Iran argued that the Revolutionary Guards were independent of the Government and that their conduct was not attributable to the Government. In any case, Iran argued that the Revolutionary Guards' actions were intended only to protect and assist Yeager in his voluntary departure.[6]

The Tribunal declined to rule on Yeager's claim that the anti-Americanism allegedly incited by the leaders of the revolution brought about a *de facto* expulsion. Instead, Chamber One found the actions of the Revolutionary Guards to constitute a *de jure* expulsion. Although the Revolutionary

[1] These two cases were assigned to Chambers One and Two with the intention that rulings in these cases, together with one other expulsion case assigned to Chamber Three (*infra* note 2), would provide guidance as "representative cases" for the other claims alleging expulsion. *See* Separate Opinion of Judge Brower with Respect to Orders in Cases 10159 et al. (June 4, 1986), *reprinted in* IRANIAN ASSETS LITIGATION REP., June 13, 1986, at 12,403.

[2] Short v. Islamic Republic of Iran, AWD 312-11135-3 (July 14, 1987) (Chamber 3), *summarized in* 82 AJIL 140 (1988).

[3] AWD 324-10199-1, slip op., paras. 50, 74 [hereinafter Yeager].

[4] The Revolutionary Guards or "Revolutionary Komitehs" served as a *de facto* security force loyal to the Ayatollah Khomeini during the revolution. Soon after the victory of the revolution, they were officially incorporated into the Government. *Id.*, paras. 39–40.

[5] *Id.*, paras. 8–14.

[6] *Id.*, paras. 19–23.

Guards were at the time not an official organ of the Iranian state, the Tribunal held that their actions were attributable to Iran under the principle that a state is responsible for the acts of private persons "if it is established that those persons were in fact acting on behalf of the State."[7] The Tribunal determined that the Revolutionary Guards were exercising governmental authority with the knowledge and acquiescence of the revolutionary Government, which made Iran liable for their acts.[8]

Turning to the lawfulness of the expulsion, Chamber One found that this expulsion went beyond a state's broad discretion to expel foreigners, since giving Yeager only 30 minutes to prepare for departure violated the state's duty to give a foreigner adequate time to wind up his affairs.[9] Thus, the Tribunal found Iran liable for the value of Yeager's goods left behind, although it valued them at only $12,500, discounting the claimed amount of $28,660 by a deemed 33 percent depreciation, deducting imputed shipping costs and disallowing recovery for goods allegedly sold at sacrifice prices immediately prior to the expulsion.[10] The Tribunal also awarded Yeager the cash seized from him by Revolutionary Guards at the airport, on the ground that the seizure was within the guards' function as customs or security officers. It disallowed, however, a claim for $284 in cash allegedly extorted from Yeager by an Iran Air official in January 1979 in order to allow Yeager's daughter to board a plane, on the ground that the extortion, as an illegal act outside the function of that official, was not imputable to Iran.[11] The Tribunal also denied the claim for lost salary, holding that since Yeager's employment contract with BHI was terminable by BHI for force reductions, Yeager's loss of salary was not caused by his expulsion but by the termination by Iran of its contracts with BHI. It thus held that Yeager "would have lost his job and the benefits associated therewith anyway, even if he had not been expelled," and denied recovery.[12]

Jack Rankin, the claimant in the second of the two cases, *Rankin v. Islamic Republic of Iran,* was also a U.S. national employed by BHI in Iran who was evacuated under guard on February 17, 1979, together with other BHI

[7] *Id.*, para. 42 (citing Draft Articles on State Responsibility adopted by the International Law Commission on first reading, Art. 8(a), [1980] 2 Y.B. INT'L L. COMM'N, pt. 2 at 30–34, UN Doc. A/CN.4/SER.A/1980/Add.l).

[8] *Id.*, paras. 42–48. Since Yeager's arrest occurred after the declaration of the new revolutionary Government, the Tribunal was not called upon to consider a state's responsibility for acts committed by a successful revolutionary movement before it obtained power.

[9] *Id.*, paras. 49–50. The Tribunal did not consider whether the expulsion was a violation of the Treaty of Amity, Economic Relations, and Consular Rights between the United States and Iran, Aug. 15, 1955, 284 UNTS 93, TIAS No. 3853, 8 UST 899 [hereinafter Treaty of Amity]. *Cf. infra* note 15, Chamber Two's discussion of Iran's liability under the Treaty of Amity.

[10] Yeager, slip op., paras. 17, 55–59.

[11] *Id.*, paras. 61–67.

[12] *Id.*, para. 60. The Tribunal declined to rule on a final claim for funds frozen in Yeager's account with Bank Mellat, a Government-controlled bank. The Tribunal declared that the legality of Bank Mellat's refusal to release the funds depends on the validity under international law of certain postrevolutionary exchange control regulations but, for unstated reasons, it deferred resolution of that issue until a later stage. *Id.*, paras. 70–71.

staff. On February 12 of that year, in response to the disorder and anti-American sentiment in Tehran that accompanied the success of the revolution, Rankin and his wife had packed a few belongings and driven to the Hilton Hotel in Tehran, where terminated BHI employees had gathered prior to leaving Iran, although Rankin's employment had not been terminated. Soon thereafter, the hotel was occupied by armed Revolutionary Guards who confined all BHI employees to their rooms for 5 days, after which they, together with other BHI employees (like the claimant in *Yeager*) who had forcibly been brought to the hotel, were bused to the airport and evacuated. Rankin claimed that conditions in Iran in early 1979, in particular the anti-Americanism fomented and exploited by the leaders of the revolution, amounted to *de facto* expulsion. He sought $81,648 from Iran as the value of personal property left behind and his terminated employment contract.[13] Chamber Two of the Tribunal unanimously denied Rankin's claim for losses arising from his alleged expulsion, *holding* that his departure was not attributable to Iran.[14]

In analyzing the claim, Chamber Two identified two stages in the development of the anti-American policy evident in the Islamic Revolution. The Tribunal determined that prior to the return of the Ayatollah Khomeini to Iran on February 1, 1979, the leaders of the revolution had adopted no general policy of expulsion of foreigners.[15] The Tribunal found that after February 1, the leaders of the revolution and, subsequently, the successor Government, adopted a general policy "to reduce, if not to eliminate, the influence of foreigners and to reduce drastically and promptly the numbers of foreigners in Iran, which caused the departure of most Americans."[16] This policy was crystallized in the present case on February 12 (the same day Rankin went to the Hilton Hotel) when Dr. Ibrahim Yazdi, a leader of the revolution and Deputy Prime Minister of the Provisional Revolutionary Government, allegedly informed the general manager of BHI that all BHI contracts were terminated and all BHI employees must leave,[17] events that in fact took place. According to the Tribunal, however, the existence of this general policy of expelling Americans was not sufficient to establish Iran's liability to Rankin, as it is necessary in each case to determine whether Iran's expulsion policy, rather than "the general turmoil and disorder" accompanying the revolution, was the actual cause of an individual claimant's departure.[18] The Tribunal found the record in the present case to be ambiguous

[13] AWD 326-10913-2, slip op., paras. 3–10 [hereinafter Rankin]. BHI terminated Rankin's employment contract after he left Iran. *Id.*, para. 10.

[14] *Id.*, para. 39.

[15] Nevertheless, the Tribunal concluded that anti-American statements made during that time by the revolutionary leaders were inconsistent with the requirements of customary international law as well as the Treaty of Amity, *supra* note 9, and stated that Iran would be liable for any damages to U.S. property interests "caused by these [anti-American] pronouncements, and . . . not just the result of the general unrest and mass demonstrations of the revolutionary period." Rankin, slip op., para. 30(c).

[16] *Id.*, paras. 28, 30(d).

[17] *Id.*, para. 28.

[18] *Id.*, para. 30(e).

in this regard; it was unclear whether Rankin had intended to leave Iran permanently at the time he joined other BHI employees at the Hilton Hotel, or whether he had intended to remain in Iran and was forced out solely by the Revolutionary Guards. The Tribunal thus held that Rankin had failed to prove that he left because of the Government's expulsion policy rather than because of general difficulties of life in Iran during the revolution, and denied the claim.[19]

The three representative expulsion cases decided by the Tribunal involve claimants who left Iran under different circumstances. The claimant in Chamber Three's expulsion case, *Short v. Islamic Republic of Iran*,[20] had departed from Iran on February 8, 1979, several days before the official proclamation of the new revolutionary Government. Chamber Three decided that there was no *de facto* expulsion because the claimant alleged no particular expulsion acts specifically directed at him by identifiable agents of the new Government.[21] In *Yeager*, on the other hand, Chamber One had little difficulty in finding that the Revolutionary Guards' armed arrest, detention and forced evacuation of Yeager constituted a *de jure* expulsion. The facts of the *Rankin* case occupy a middle ground between *Short* and *Yeager*. Although Rankin was not taken from his home by armed Revolutionary Guards, as was Yeager, he was detained by Revolutionary Guards and was in fact evacuated together with Yeager.

Chamber Two's finding that *Rankin* is nevertheless more similar to *Short* than to *Yeager* is open to serious question. In light of its recognition that by, at the latest, February 12, 1979,[22] Iran had adopted an official governmental policy to expel all Americans—and explicitly all BHI employees—remaining in Iran, Chamber Two's opinion fails to justify its emphasis on an expelled claimant's subjective state of mind at the time of departure. It should make no legal difference that someone Iran wrongfully expelled was considering leaving voluntarily. Moreover, even if intent is a relevant issue, Chamber Two put the burden of proving intent on the wrong party. Given the Tribunal's finding that on the relevant date Iran had an express policy of expelling Americans, the Tribunal should not have required Rankin to prove that he intended to stay in Iran. In any case, once Rankin was in the hotel, his state of mind became irrelevant, as he was confined by Revolutionary Guards, unable to change his mind if he wanted to, and ultimately sent out of Iran in the same evacuation as Yeager, who another Chamber found *was* expelled.[23]

[19] *Id.*, paras. 38–39.

[20] AWD 312-11135-3, *supra* note 2.

[21] The Tribunal's refusal to adapt traditional concepts to meet the new circumstances of the Iranian Revolution drew a sharp dissent in *Short* from the American arbitrator, Charles N. Brower. *Id.*

[22] The Chamber found the adoption of the policy to have occurred sometime between the return of the Ayatollah (Feb. 1) and the proclamation of the Islamic state (Feb. 12).

[23] Chamber One at no time considered whether Yeager had intended to remain indefinitely in Iran, focusing only on his treatment by the Revolutionary Guards, which was, after they were in the hotel, apparently identical for Yeager and Rankin. *See id.*, paras. 35–38.

Expropriation—standard of compensation under international law—lost profits as an element of damages—rejection of "discounted cash flow" method of valuation

AMOCO INTERNATIONAL FINANCE CORP. v. ISLAMIC REPUBLIC OF IRAN. AWD 310-56-3.
Iran–United States Claims Tribunal, The Hague, July 24, 1987.

Amoco International Finance Corp., a United States company, brought a claim before the Iran–United States Claims Tribunal seeking the value of its 50 percent interest in Kharg Island Chemical Co. Ltd. (Khemco), an Iranian corporation that the claimant alleged had been expropriated by Iran. Chamber Three of the Tribunal found that the claimant's interest in Khemco was lawfully expropriated by Iran and *held* that Iran is therefore bound to pay the claimant one-half of the full "going concern value" of the company. The Tribunal did not make an award of damages at this stage, however, as it declined to rely exclusively on either party's proposed methods of calculating compensation, and scheduled further briefing. Arbitrator Brower filed an extensive opinion concurring in the basic result of the award, while taking issue with much of its analysis and many of its conclusions; Arbitrator Ansari concurred in part and dissented in part, but without opinion.

Khemco, a 50:50 joint venture established in 1967 by Amoco International, S.A., a Swiss subsidiary of the claimant,[1] and the National Petrochemical Company of Iran (NPC) owned and operated a natural-gas processing plant on Kharg Island in the Persian Gulf. In 1979 the Iranian Government announced that it intended to buy out all foreign shares in petrochemical plants. Negotiations followed for the sale of Amoco International's interest in Khemco, but no sale was concluded. Rather, in July 1979, over Amoco International's objection, the Government took control of Khemco's operations and sales. Subsequently, on December 24, 1980, the Government issued a decree declaring "null and void" the agreement by which Khemco was established, effectively formalizing the expropriation of Amoco International's interest in Khemco.

Iran did not vigorously deny that the result of its actions was the expropriation of the claimant's interest in Khemco.[2] Therefore, the key issues the Tribunal focused on were (1) the lawfulness of the expropriation, (2) the appropriate standard of compensation, and (3) the method of calculation of the compensation.

[1] Since under the Tribunal's jurisdictional grant only United States nationals may make claims before it, the claimant brought the claim of its Swiss subsidiary under Article VII, paragraph 2 of the Declaration of the Democratic and Popular Republic of Algeria Concerning the Settlement of Claims by the Government of the United States of America and the Islamic Republic of Iran (Jan. 19, 1981), *reprinted in* 75 AJIL 422, 424–25, which permits U.S. nationals to bring claims owned by their non-U.S. subsidiaries.

[2] Iran urged the Tribunal to find that the joint venture agreement was terminated by *force majeure* prior to Iran's decree annulling the agreement, and therefore to hold that by the time of expropriation the contract was of no value. Iran conceded, however, that if the contract was not terminated by reason by *force majeure*, it was expropriated by the decree.

The claimant asserted that Iran effectively expropriated Khemco in July 1979, when the Government took actual control over Khemco's operations,[3] and that the expropriation was unlawful as a violation of the Treaty of Amity and Economic Relations[4] as well as of customary international law, because it infringed Iranian law, included no provision for compensation and was in breach of contract. The Tribunal disagreed, however. First, while the Tribunal accepted that in July 1979 Iran "practically depriv[ed] Amoco of its rights in the management of Khemco,"[5] it held that the actual expropriation occurred only in December 1980, when the Government formally annulled the claimant's rights in Khemco.[6] Since it deemed the nationalization to have occurred in December 1980 pursuant to a government decree authorized by apparently valid legislation, the Tribunal rejected the claimant's contention that the expropriation was without Iranian legislative authority.[7] Similarly, while it recognized that no compensation was paid, it found that a claims procedure contained in the authorizing legislation[8] provided sufficiently "adequate provision" for compensation.[9] Finally, it dismissed the claimant's argument that the agreement between Amoco International and NPC establishing Khemco contained a "stabilization clause" that bound the Government of Iran not to breach or expropriate the contract. The Tribunal found that NPC, while a governmental entity, was not the Government, and thus its contractual obligations did not bind Iran. In any case, it determined that the contract contained no clause obliging the Government not to breach or expropriate the contract.[10] On this basis, the Tribunal held that the expropriation was lawful.[11]

The Tribunal next addressed the standard of compensation appropriate for a lawful expropriation. The claimant argued that it made no practical difference in this case whether the expropriation was lawful or unlawful

[3] The claimant alleged alternatively that if Khemco was not expropriated by Iran in July 1979, then NPC certainly breached its joint venture agreement with Amoco International by which Khemco was owned and operated. The Tribunal found that NPC was not liable for breach because, in excluding Amoco International from management and profits, NPC had "acted as an instrument of the Iranian Government." AWD 310-56-3, slip op., para. 174. The Tribunal concluded that therefore the alleged breach must be considered not as a separate cause of action but as part of the expropriation claim. *Id.*, para. 177.

[4] Treaty of Amity, Economic Relations, and Consular Rights, U.S.-Iran, Aug. 15, 1955, 284 UNTS 93, TIAS No. 3853, 8 UST 899.

[5] Slip op., para. 181.

[6] *Id.*, para. 132. Nevertheless, the Tribunal determined that in order to recognize the reality of the claimant's situation as of July 31, 1979, that date would be used as the date of valuation of Khemco for purposes of determining compensation. *Id.*, para. 181.

[7] *Id.*, para. 132. The contract was nullified pursuant to the Single Article Act Concerning the Nationalization of the Oil Industry of Iran, promulgated in January 1980 by Iran's Revolutionary Council.

[8] The Single Article Act pursuant to which the decree of annulment was made provides that "claims arising from conclusion and execution of [annulled] agreements shall be settled by the decision of ['a special commission appointed by the Minister of Oil']."

[9] Slip op., para. 137.

[10] *Id.*, para. 173.

[11] The Tribunal rejected as factually unsubstantiated contentions that the nationalization was discriminatorily aimed at only American interests, and that it was not for a public purpose. *Id.*

since in either case Iran is bound by the Treaty of Amity and by customary international law to pay the "full equivalent" of the property taken, and the claimant sought no more than the full equivalent. The Tribunal, however, found, with reference to the *Chorzów Factory* case decided in 1928 by the Permanent Court of International Justice,[12] that "a clear distinction must be made between lawful and unlawful expropriations, since the rules applicable to the compensation to be paid by the expropriating State differ according to the legal characterization of the taking."[13] The Tribunal identified in *Chorzów Factory* the following dichotomy: if an expropriation is unlawful, the compensation awarded must " 'wipe out all the consequences of the illegal act and reestablish the situation which would, in all probability, have existed if this act had not been committed' " (i.e., *restitutio in integrum,* restitution in kind or its monetary equivalent). In case of a lawful taking, the standard is payment of the full "value of the undertaking at the moment of dispossession, *i.e.,* 'the just price of what was expropriated.' "[14] While these standards may appear equivalent, the Tribunal interpreted them to mean that in a lawful expropriation compensation is the "going concern value," including tangible assets, contractual rights and "future prospects," but *excluding* lost profits. A payment of compensation including lost profits is reserved only to wrongful expropriations.[15] Applying this standard to the present case, the Tribunal found the claimant entitled to its share of the full going concern value of Khemco as of the valuation date, determined without specific recognition of future profits.[16]

Turning to the proper method of valuation, the Tribunal rejected both parties' recommended methods as inadequate alone to produce an accurate measure of the required "going concern value." The respondents had proposed that Khemco be valued with reference to its net book value. The Tribunal found that resort to net book value would omit from valuation intangibles such as contractual rights, good will and commercial prospects.[17] On the other hand, the Tribunal also rejected the claimant's suggestion that it use the "discounted cash flow" method (DCF) to establish the value of the company. The claimant urged that application of the DCF method, which is used widely in the business and financial world, would accurately indicate Khemco's value on the chosen date by estimating the likely future earnings of the company as of the valuation date and discounting those earnings to recognize reasonably foreseeable risks involved in the enterprise. The Tribunal, however, flatly rejected the DCF method as a means of determining the compensation for a lawful expropriation; it held that since the DCF

[12] Factory at Chorzów (Ger. v. Pol.), 1928 PCIJ (ser. A) No. 17 (Judgment of Sept. 13).

[13] Slip op., para. 192.

[14] *Id.,* para. 196 (quoting 1928 PCIJ (ser. A) No. 17, at 47).

The Tribunal also held that the Treaty of Amity would govern the standard of compensation only of a lawful expropriation, since "[a] nationalization in breach of the Treaty . . . would render applicable the rules relating to State responsibility, which are to be found not in the Treaty but in customary law." *Id.,* para. 189.

[15] *Id.,* paras. 201–04.

[16] *Id.,* paras. 263–64.

[17] *Id.,* para. 255.

method, in the claimant's words, was intended to "place the foreign investor in as good an economic position as he was before the expropriation," it was calculated to result in *restitutio in integrum,*[18] which the Tribunal had earlier decreed was the correct standard of compensation only for unlawful expropriations. The Tribunal also found the DCF method to be inappropriate because it is based not on an examination of the value of the various expropriated assets of a company, but rather solely on analysis of its lost earnings,[19] again an analysis reserved, in the Tribunal's view, only to unlawful expropriations. The Tribunal moreover found the DCF method too speculative and uncertain to be useful in valuation by an international tribunal.[20]

Having rejected the valuation methods suggested by the parties, the Tribunal made no determination concerning the level of compensation due the claimant. Rather, it asked the parties to submit additional information on the tangible and intangible assets of Khemco, its commercial prospects and liabilities, and the "legitimate expectations" of its owners, and to express their views on the most appropriate method—apart from those already rejected—for this information to be used to calculate the going concern value of the company.[21] The Tribunal's final award will be issued after receipt of this further briefing.

The *Amoco* award confirms the line of Tribunal cases finding that under both the Treaty of Amity and customary international law the appropriate minimum standard of compensation for expropriation is the "full value" or "full equivalent" of the expropriated enterprise.[22] Nevertheless, the award may be questioned on several points. For instance, it is unique among Tribunal awards in its emphasis on the distinction between lawful and unlawful expropriations, a distinction no previous award has considered at all significant.[23] Additionally, no prior award has rejected lost profits as an element of

[18] *Id.*, para. 227.

[19] *Id.*, para. 229.

[20] *Id.*, para. 230.

[21] *Id.*, para. 267.

[22] SEDCO, Inc. v. National Iranian Oil Co., ITL 59-129-3 (Mar. 27, 1986) (Chamber 3), *reprinted in* 25 ILM 629 (1986), *summarized in* 80 AJIL 969 (1986); Tippetts, Abbett, McCarthy, Stratton v. TAMS-AFFA Consulting Engineers of Iran, AWD 141-7-2 (June 29, 1984) (Chamber 2), *reprinted in* 6 IRAN-U.S. CLAIMS TRIBUNAL REP. [hereinafter IRAN-U.S. C.T.R.] 219 (1984 II); American International Group, Inc. v. Islamic Republic of Iran, AWD 93-2-3 (Dec. 19, 1983) (Chamber 3), *reprinted in* 4 IRAN-U.S. C.T.R. 96 (1983 III).

[23] *See, e.g.*, Starrett Housing Corp. v. Islamic Republic of Iran, AWD 314-24-1 (Aug. 14, 1987) (Chamber 1) (no distinction made as to lawfulness of the expropriation); *see id.*, Concurring Opinion of Arbitrator Holtzmann, slip op. at 6; SEDCO, Inc. v. National Iranian Oil Co., *supra* note 22, slip op. at 13 (full value to be awarded "regardless of whether or not the expropriation was otherwise lawful").

The award can also be faulted for its reasons for finding this particular taking to have been lawful. The holding of lawfulness depended heavily upon the Tribunal's finding that the expropriation was supported by Iranian legislative authority and that adequate provision for "just compensation" had been made at the time of taking. Since the legislation and the claims procedure appeared many months after the Government had exercised actual and exclusive control over Khemco's operations and sales, the Tribunal had to ignore its own precedents that such control, when unequivocal and unrevoked, amounts to expropriation. *See* SEDCO, Inc. v. National Iranian Oil Co., ITL 55-129-3 (Oct. 28, 1985) (Chamber 3), *reprinted in* 9 IRAN-U.S. C.T.R. 248, 274–75 (1985 II) (expropriation occurs when actual *de facto* control is exercised full value, or has found lost profits to be a component of compensation only where the taking was unlawful.[24] Finally, the rejection of the DCF method of valuation by international tribunals on the basis of a novel and highly specialized interpretation of the *Chorzów Factory* case is inconsistent with valuation theories used in sophisticated commercial transactions today.

Whether this award will be followed as an accurate exposition of the present state of the international legal principles governing compensation for expropriation remains to be seen. At least one subsequent Tribunal case, however, has declined to follow some of the *Amoco* principles. In *Starrett Housing,*[25] Chamber One made no distinction based on the lawfulness of the expropriation there at issue, and its substantial award of the "full value" of the expropriated enterprise included compensation for lost profits. Moreover, in determining the fair market value of the enterprise, Chamber One wholeheartedly adopted the DCF method,[26] implicitly challenging the *Amoco* award's rejection of that method.

---

over entity, not when later formalized); *accord* Foremost Tehran, Inc. v. Islamic Republic of Iran, ITL 1-220-37/231-1 (Apr. 11, 1986) (Chamber 1), slip op. at 22; Phelps Dodge Corp. v. Islamic Republic of Iran, AWD 217-99-2 (Mar. 19, 1986) (Chamber 2), slip op. at 12–14. Further, as pointed out in Arbitrator Brower's concurring opinion, the claims procedure did not in fact offer much hope of just compensation, as all settlements reached pursuant to it were based on net book value, a standard the award rejects as below the requirements of international law. *See* AWD 310-56-3, Concurring Opinion of Arbitrator Brower, slip op., para. 8.

[24] *See, e.g., American International Group, Inc., supra* note 22, 4 IRAN-U.S. C.T.R. at 109–10 (expropriation lawful; lost profits awarded); Payne v. Islamic Republic of Iran, AWD 245-335-2 (Aug. 8, 1986) (Chamber 2) (expropriation not found unlawful; lost profits awarded).

[25] *Starrett Housing Corp., supra* note 23.

[26] *Id.*, slip op., para. 279.

CURRENT DEVELOPMENTS

Statement by Expert Panel: Deep Seabed Mining and the 1982 Convention on the Law of the Sea

It is time for all nations to try again to achieve agreement on the legal regime that should govern mining in the deep seabed. Such an agreement would bring general adherence to the 1982 Convention and achieve a universal Law of the Sea.

The 1982 Convention on the Law of the Sea represented the culmination of fifteen years of negotiation to achieve a general, comprehensive agreement on the law of the sea. In 1982, however, President Reagan announced that the United States would not adhere to the Convention because it could not accept elements of the regime for mining the seabed beyond national jurisdiction.

The draft regime for the deep seabed was negotiated on the assumption and the expectation that deep seabed mining would become a commercial reality well before the end of the century. Intervening developments and new studies now indicate that deep seabed mining will not be economically feasible until well into the twenty-first century, if at all. During the decades ahead, then, mining in the deep seabed will be possible only for a few governments that might decide to pursue such mining (though it be uneconomical), with heavy government subsidies, for political reasons.

The delayed prospects for the economic development of deep seabed minerals warrant re-examination by all states of the mining regime proposed in the 1982 Convention, and present new opportunities for reaching general agreement on the Law of the Sea.

We recommend that all nations:

1) re-evaluate their requirements for a satisfactory mining regime in light of the changed industrial and economic circumstances, and

2) support measures that would remove the obstacle posed by the deep seabed mining issue to widespread entry into force of a comprehensive Law of the Sea Convention.

The Deep Seabed Provisions of the 1982 Convention and U.S. Objections

Part XI of the 1982 Convention sets forth principles which it was universally agreed should apply to "The Area." There was agreement that the Area would be open to use by all. Agreement was reached on the legal status of the Area and its resources, as well as of the superjacent waters and air space. States must use the Area exclusively for peaceful purposes, and are obliged to protect the marine environment and to respect other activities at sea. There was agreement on compulsory and binding dispute settlement procedures. There was also general agreement that the exploration and exploitation of deep seabed mineral resources must provide opportunities for private as well as state-owned firms, and for meaningful participation by Third World states.

Other provisions in Part XI, however, were concluded after difficult negotiations, and some of these later proved to be unacceptable to the United States. When President Reagan announced that the United States would not sign the Convention, he indicated the following reasons:

> 1) The powers and functions of the Authority, and the composition, procedures, and voting arrangements of the Assembly and the Council, create a decision-making process that would not give the United States (and other technologically advanced states) a voice that fairly reflects and protects their interests.
>
> 2) The Convention sharply limits the number of initial mining operations and authorizes limitations on the extraction of minerals from the deep seabed, so as not to compete with states that produce such minerals in their territory. The United States objects to "protectionism" in principle, and these and other provisions, together with inadequacies of the decision-making process would deter development of deep seabed minerals, including possible future extraction of minerals other than manganese nodules. The result would be less-than-assured access for qualified deep seabed miners.
>
> 3) The Convention requires the transfer of technology to the Authority and to developing states. The United States objects to provisions requiring mandatory transfer of technology owned by private persons.
>
> 4) The Convention provides for the sharing of financial and other economic benefits with "national liberation" movements.
>
> 5) The Convention contains provisions for amendment, allowing modification of the deep seabed mining regime without the approval of the United States.

Changed Circumstances

The most controversial provisions of Part XI were based on assumptions or predictions that have proven to be mistaken in important respects.

> 1) Projected demand for deep seabed minerals
>
> It was predicted that demand for minerals derived from polymetallic nodules would continue to increase steadily at previous rates; some believed that, at an early date, the production of manganese nodules from the deep seabed would be competitive with the increasingly expensive extraction of the same minerals from depleted and/or less accessible land-based resources.
>
> *Those predictions have proven to be mistaken. Altered market conditions, discoveries of additional land-based sources, and the improved efficiency of land-based mining, will result in a long postponement (if not abandonment) of, and slower projected rates of growth for, commercial deep seabed mining operations.*
>
> 2) Technological developments
>
> Several provisions, notably the limits on the number and size of the first group of mine sites and on allowable production tonnages, were

based on assumptions regarding the technological capabilities of the 1970's.

Those technologies have already changed and further change is certain. When —and if—commercial deep seabed mining in fact takes place, the limits specified in the Convention may prove starkly anachronistic.

In the 1970's, many assumed that technologies relevant to deep seabed mining were novel, precious to the industries and countries involved, and unavailable to others.

"Know-how" is still closely held, but the basic component technologies that make up mining systems are now well known and available on the open market.

3) New seabed minerals

Discoveries in the late 1970's and early 1980's of polymetallic sulfide and cobalt/manganese crust deposits have sparked interest in the possibility of commercial development of seabed minerals other than polymetallic nodules.

Significance of changed circumstances for the Convention regime

The failure of those assumptions and predictions has affected the Convention regime in the following important ways:

1) It has postponed the time when a full-scale International Seabed Authority could become self-supporting from revenues produced by seabed minerals development; it has postponed the time when the pioneer investors identified in Resolution II of the Law of the Sea Conference would undertake extensive training and exploration intended to enable the Enterprise to carry out mining activities in pace with states and other entities.

These changed prospects suggest that the operations of the Authority and of the Enterprise, as well as the training and exploration requirements, should be tailored to take account of projected levels of seabed mining activities and the resulting income to the Authority.

2) The number and size of initial mining operations, and provisions authorizing production ceilings, were based on technology that is becoming outdated. In particular, the sustained reduced rate of growth in demand for nickel (the trigger in the formula for limiting production) means that the predicted economic consequences of deep seabed mining are likely to be different from those which the formula addressed.

The changed prospects of seabed mining call for re-examination of production limitations or at least of the formula used.

3) The U.N. Conference on the Law of the Sea negotiated provisions mandating the transfer of technology on the assumption that the technology might not be readily available on the open market. That assumption may no longer be valid.

The Convention provisions on transfer of technology need to be reconsidered.

4) It will be some time before deep sea deposits of minerals other than manganese nodules become commercially attractive, and it is

likely that deposits within national jurisdiction will be developed first. But a number of provisions in the 1982 Convention are specific to manganese nodules and would need to be adapted to the development of other minerals.

An effective regime for seabed mining should clearly distinguish provisions applicable to all seabed minerals and provisions specific to particular minerals.

International Developments

As of September, 1987, there have been 34 of the 60 ratifications required to bring the 1982 Convention into force. Many states have refrained from ratifying the Convention pending clarification of its future.

The Preparatory Commission, called for by the Conference on the Law of the Sea, has been meeting to negotiate rules and regulations necessary to establish and implement a functioning deep seabed regime. These negotiations have become somewhat bogged down in details, losing sight of the objective of producing a viable mining regime; to date, the participants have postponed controversial issues of decision-making procedures and criteria.

Lack of progress is due in large part to the lack of urgency resulting from the changed market conditions for seabed minerals, as well as to uncertainty about support for the Convention. Even if the Preparatory Commission completes its plan of work, its product may never be implemented successfully unless there is accommodation to new economic and commercial realities and widespread participation in the regime.

International developments outside the framework of the 1982 Convention also reflect political and legal uncertainties. The United States and a few other developed states are of the view that, in the absence of general agreement on a new regime, deep seabed mining is a lawful exercise of the freedom of the high seas, open to all nations. Most states of the world have taken the position that deep seabed mining is lawful only pursuant to an agreed international regime.

The United States has joined with France, Belgium, the Federal Republic of Germany, Italy, Japan, the Netherlands, and the United Kingdom to conclude a Provisional Understanding on Deep Seabed Matters. The United States Government considers the Provisional Understanding to be a significant step towards developing an acceptable alternative to the mining regime set forth in the 1982 Law of the Sea Convention. The other seven parties to the Provisional Understanding take the view that the Understanding is compatible with the documents adopted by the Law of the Sea Conference. They have participated in the work of the Preparatory Commission and have sought to achieve some clarification (or modification) of the Convention regime through the Preparatory Commission. Their aim in joining the Provisional Understanding is to preserve the option of an alternative mining regime in the event that the outcome of the Preparatory Commission discussions is not satisfactory. This situation could result in two competing legal regimes for deep seabed mining, creating legal and political uncertainties that would deter deep seabed mining by any entity, whether a state, an international organization, or a private corporation.

United States Interests

The changed circumstances make clear that, for the foreseeable future, the United States has limited economic and security interests in deep seabed mining. But the United States shares the compelling interests of all states in achieving universal agreement on a comprehensive law of the sea, which requires agreement also on a regime for the deep seabed.

The position of the United States on the 1982 Convention reflected early studies which suggested that access to deep seabed polymetallic nodules was highly desirable for the national security of the United States. That interest now appears to have been exaggerated. Economic conditions and the availability of substitutes have depressed demand for deep seabed minerals. Cheaper land-based sources for some nodule minerals have been identified. Moreover, deep seabed sites are highly vulnerable to disruption. Also, if two or three other states should proceed with deep seabed mining for political reasons, with heavy governmental subsidy, the United States would not suffer: the minerals and the technology would be available to the United States on the world market (and other governments would be bearing the burden of the subsidies).

The United States, then, has no compelling need to pursue deep seabed mining at an early date. On the other hand, the United States has immediate as well as long term interest in the non–deep seabed parts of the Law of the Sea Convention and in obtaining adherence to them by all states. [This panel has addressed these interests in our statement, "United States Policy on the Law of the Sea," 79 American Journal of International Law 151 (1985).] Conflict and uncertainty as to the deep seabed mining regime cloud other activities on the high seas that are of major interest to the United States. Conflict and uncertainty as to deep seabed mining have also raised difficult issues with Third World countries and allies.

The two-ringed international negotiations—in the Preparatory Commission, and among parties to the Provisional Understanding—promise no resolution that is in the interest of the United States. To some extent the other parties to the Provisional Understanding have interests that parallel those of the United States at the Preparatory Commission, but their interests do not fully coincide with those of the United States; nor can other states exert the bargaining power that the United States has in international negotiations. Negotiations in the Preparatory Commission may be concluded without satisfactorily accommodating the interests of the United States and of most other parties to the Provisional Understanding. If two competing legal regimes were to emerge, the development of deep seabed resources of interest to the United States would likely be deterred. Alternatively, the Preparatory Commission might achieve agreement on a limited set of amendments that would prove satisfactory to some Western developed states, but not to the United States. United States nationals might then seek sponsorship from parties to the Convention; their participation might compel the United States to join the Convention even if substantial change in its provisions had not been made.

Whether or not a new agreement emerges from the Preparatory Commission, a United States–supported deep seabed mining regime outside of the Convention might well prove unworkable. If so, not only would the United States objectives in the deep seabed be frustrated, but its greater interests in other aspects of the law of the sea would suffer.

Conclusion

Agreement on the regime for the deep seabed is indispensable to agreement and bringing into force an effective, comprehensive Convention on the Law of the Sea. Changed circumstances affecting deep seabed mining give the United States and all nations of the world the opportunity to reconsider their positions on the deep seabed regime and its relationship to the other benefits of the Law of the Sea Convention. There is little doubt that non–deep seabed interests of all nations are predominant and that the deep seabed regime has placed unnecessary obstacles to the full realization of those interests.

Reconsideration should take into account the changed circumstances of deep seabed mining, its limited economic importance for the foreseeable future, and the continuing economic, industrial, political, and legal problems posed by the regime for the deep seabed contained in the Convention. Reconsideration should include an exploration of what the Preparatory Commission could accomplish within its mandate. Reconsideration might also contemplate other international procedures, or agreed fora, including the possibility of bringing the Convention into effect and the use by contracting parties of the provisions for amending the Convention (including reopening negotiations on the regime for the deep seabed at the Review Conference (Article 155)).

We believe that the international community should seek to negotiate an agreed regime that:

1) clarifies institutional and procedural details in the deep seabed mining regime and identifies specific criteria to serve as a basis for decision-making,

2) eliminates detailed provisions that are or will soon be outdated, and

3) defers consideration of detailed implementing regulations on matters that are subject to economic and industrial developments until there is real interest in beginning deep seabed mining.

This alternative is reasonable and practical. Objections may come from some states committed to the alleged gains obtained in the detailed regime, but those gains are ephemeral if they cannot be put into practice. Other objections may come from members of the mining industry who prefer the certainty of any regime—since certainty permits planning—to the uncertainty of future negotiations; but certainty purchased at the price of a system that is out of date before it is implemented would have little value.

New understanding of the limited importance of deep seabed mining at this time makes it possible for nations to re-evaluate their positions and take the necessary steps to reconcile the existing international differences. The interests of all nations would be served best by removing the obstacles posed by the deep seabed mining regime to widespread adherence to the Law of the Sea Convention. Only widespread adherence to the Convention will help all states realize the important benefits of the Convention.

PANEL ON THE LAW OF OCEAN USES*

TRIENNIAL ELECTIONS OF FIVE MEMBERS OF THE INTERNATIONAL COURT OF JUSTICE

On November 11, 1987, the United Nations General Assembly and Security Council reelected Judges Ago (Italy), Schwebel (United States), Bedjaoui (Algeria) and Tarassov (USSR) as Members of the International Court of Justice. On the same day, M. Shahabuddeen (Guyana) was elected to be a Member of the Court; his term will begin on February 6, 1988.

Judge Shahabuddeen was born on October 7, 1931. He qualified for his Bachelor of Laws (London) in 1953 and was called to the bar (Middle Temple, London) in February 1954. His subsequent degrees include a Master of Laws in 1958, a Bachelor of Science (honors) in economics in 1959, a Doctor of Philosophy in 1970 and a Doctor of Laws in 1986 (all at London).

Judge Shahabuddeen served his country as Solicitor General from 1962 to 1973 (with the rank of Justice of Appeal from 1971). He has been Attorney General since 1973 (ranking immediately after the Head of the Judiciary), Minister of Justice since 1978, Acting Foreign Minister from time to time since April 1980, Vice President since 1983, Deputy Prime Minister from 1984 to 1985, and First Deputy Prime Minister since August 1985. In addition, he has represented Guyana at numerous international and regional conferences.

In 1969 Judge Shahabuddeen attended the Hague Academy of International Law; he has served his Government as Chief Legal Adviser on all major international questions since 1973.[1]

* This statement, subtitled "A Statement by the Panel on the Law of Ocean Uses," was adopted on September 25, 1987. The following members of the Panel participated: Jonathan I. Charney, Thomas A. Clingan, Jr., John Lawrence Hargrove, Louis Henkin, Jon L. Jacobson, M. Casey Jarman, Terry L. Leitzell, Edward Miles, J. Daniel Nyhart, Bernard H. Oxman, Giulio Pontecorvo, Horace B. Robertson, Jr., and Louis B. Sohn. The Panel on the Law of Ocean Uses is an independent group of specialists in oceans law and policy sponsored by the Council on Ocean Law.

[1] This report is based on ICJ Communiqué No. 87/29 and its Annex, Nov. 13, 1987.

BOOK REVIEWS AND NOTES

EDITED BY DETLEV VAGTS

International Law: Process and Prospect. By Anthony D'Amato. Dobbs Ferry: Transnational Publishers, Inc., 1987. Pp. vi, 250. Index. $45.50.

This is not a book for an international law neophyte.[1] It is a collection of sophisticated, often challenging, essays by one of the most original thinkers in the field. Most of the essays have been previously published, although Professor D'Amato has revised them—some considerably more than others—for this book.[2]

Two principal themes run through the essays. The first emerges from D'Amato's thesis that, juridically, a state is defined by its interests and (especially) by its entitlements (pp. 90–94). D'Amato argues that retaliatory deprivation of entitlements is the primary, and the only universal, mechanism for the enforcement of international law. This argument does not refer to collective enforcement measures by international organizations acting under authorizations set forth in their constituent instruments.[3] Instead, it refers to unilateral enforcement measures, including the use of armed force when an offending state's challenge to individual or collective values is particularly serious. More about this later.

The second principal theme is that modern international law is no longer constricted by the traditional concept that states, alone, are the subjects and objects of the system. His focus here is on human rights and the means of enforcing them. Again, D'Amato goes beyond traditional limits, offering the idea that nationals of a state that violates their fundamental human rights may be considered as "internationals" of any other state that wishes to protect them (p. 106). The protection may occur in the latter state's domestic courts (unfettered, he suggests, by notions of sovereign immunity). In extreme cases, at the level of genocide, slavery and widespread torture, he regards armed unilateral intervention as lawful (p. 226). Here the two principal themes coalesce.

D'Amato frequently eschews conventional thinking, which presents an inviting target to a reviewer. It is not difficult to pose counterarguments to

[1] Except the postscript, which outlines prospects for careers in international law. It seems out of place in this book.

[2] References to the previously published versions are at page iv of the book under review. Some of the republished work is a bit dated, e.g., chapter 8 on territorial apartheid in Namibia. Even that chapter, though, is useful for assessing the Bantustan policy in South Africa itself.

[3] UN CHARTER ch. VII is only one such authorization. Article 19 of the Charter (loss of General Assembly vote for excessive arrears in payment of dues) is another. The constituent instruments of many specialized agencies contain provisions authorizing collective deprivations of entitlements for specified departures from the organizations' norms. Unlike the sanctions in chapter VII of the Charter, these sanctions generally are uninhibited by a veto power.

most of the points he makes. This reviewer is not above the temptation to indulge in that to some extent. But let it be said first that original thinking in international law or any other field is at a premium, and should be applauded whenever the thoughts are incisive and carefully formulated. D'Amato's essays qualify.

A fundamental objection to D'Amato's stress on the legitimacy of unilateral enforcement is that it necessarily promotes auto-interpretation by the enforcing state of conduct—or even of future conduct—by actors in another state. Sometimes the unlawfulness of the conduct is clear, as in Iran's detention of U.S. hostages. But this certainly is not always the case. Auto-interpretation obviously magnifies the risk of error or of deliberate mischaracterization of a less-than-clear situation, and therefore magnifies the risk that enforcement measures will exacerbate the situation.[4] Collective interpretation is fallible too, and is not always feasible, but at least it opens the door to arguments not necessarily tainted by the self-interest of the enforcing state.

D'Amato is led to normative approval of Israel's 1981 attack on the Iraqi nuclear reactor, though he would couple his stamp of legality with a duty to compensate Iraq (pp. 83–87).[5] He would not do this under the banner of Israeli self-defense, but rather by treating Israel as the protector and enforcer of community interests in removing a potential source of nuclear weapons from the hands of an unstable regime when collective mechanisms (such as inspections by the International Atomic Energy Agency) are inadequate (pp. 79–83). Israel, indeed, may have performed a community service, but if the service is characterized as unilateral enforcement of community values without any deference to the collective mechanism the community has set up, the precedent is troublesome. A self-defense characterization, though not wholly satisfactory, might engender a more manageable precedent.

Dealing with human rights, D'Amato attacks what is increasingly a straw man when he knocks down the notion that whatever a government does to its own nationals is its own business (p. 105). There is more than enough positive international law to rebut that notion.[6] The problem for D'Amato is that the positive law does not easily open a path to the remedies he finds potentially the most effective: enforcement in the domestic courts of any

[4] *Cf.* Stein, *Collective Enforcement of International Obligations,* 47 ZEITSCHRIFT FÜR AUSLÄNDISCHES ÖFFENTLICHES RECHT UND VÖLKERRECHT 56, 65–66 (1987). *See also* Zemanek, *The Unilateral Enforcement of International Obligations, id.* at 32, 38–39 (setting forth the widely shared view that the use of armed force in reprisal is unlawful).

[5] He acknowledges that international law has not yet gone this far (pp. 83–84).

[6] *See, e.g.,* American Convention on Human Rights, Nov. 22, 1969, *reprinted in* ORGANIZATION OF AMERICAN STATES, HANDBOOK OF EXISTING RULES PERTAINING TO HUMAN RIGHTS IN THE INTER-AMERICAN SYSTEM, OEA/Ser.L/V/II.60, Doc. 28, at 29 (1983); [European] Convention for the Protection of Human Rights and Fundamental Freedoms, Nov. 4, 1950, 213 UNTS 221; Convention on the Prevention and Punishment of the Crime of Genocide, Dec. 9, 1948, 78 UNTS 277; INTERNATIONAL LABOUR ORGANISATION CONST. arts. 24–26, Apr. 20, 1948, 15 UNTS 35.

state that can bring the violator or the violator's property within its grasp, and unilateral enforcement by armed force in extreme cases.

D'Amato's first remedy faces at least three legal hurdles, even if we assume that the violator or the violator's property is within the court's clutches. The first is sovereign immunity, if the defendant is the foreign state or its instrumentality.[7] Even under the restrictive theory of sovereign immunity, most governmental deprivations of civil or political rights should be immune from challenge in domestic courts of other states, as public acts.[8] D'Amato relies on the old case of *The Santissima Trinidad*[9] for the proposition that "Justice Story [for the Court] found no defense of sovereign immunity to be applicable when the foreign state itself was alleged to have violated international law" (p. 203). But the case merely involved a claim for restitution of goods unlawfully taken as prize by an Argentine public vessel. No claim was made directly against the foreign sovereign or its public vessel. The goods had been taken ashore and were in the possession of a bailee—not a situation to which sovereign immunity would normally apply, whether or not there had been a violation of international law in the chain of circumstances leading to the claim.[10]

The second hurdle is easier to negotiate. What authority gives the United States jurisdiction to prescribe rules prohibiting egregious human rights violations by foreign governments against their own nationals in their own territories? The universality principle, answers D'Amato, drawing an analogy to jurisdiction to prescribe rules against piracy (p. 107). Despite the obvious distinctions between piracy on the high seas and the acts of a government at home against its own nationals, he is probably right so long as the violation is of a kind universally condemned.

The third hurdle stems from Circuit Judge Bork's individual opinion in *Tel-Oren v. Libyan Arab Republic.*[11] D'Amato devotes 15 pages (pp. 204–19)

[7] Sovereign immunity is not a problem if the defendant is a functionary of the foreign state, as in Filartiga v. Pena-Irala, 630 F.2d 876 (2d Cir. 1980), but enforcement of a judgment in such a case is likely to be a significant problem.

[8] The decision of the Second Circuit in Amerada Hess Shipping Corp. v. Argentine Republic, 830 F.2d 421 (2d Cir. 1987), 26 ILM 1375 (1987), *petition for cert. filed,* 56 U.S.L.W. 3592 (U.S. Mar. 1, 1988) (No. 87-1372), offers D'Amato some comfort. Sovereign immunity was denied to the Argentine Government in a civil action arising out of its bombing of a neutral merchant vessel on the high seas during the Falkland Islands hostilities. The court relied on the Alien Tort Statute, 28 U.S.C. §1350, brushing aside the Foreign Sovereign Immunities Act, 28 U.S.C. §§1330, 1602–1611, as irrelevant to noncommercial claims of violation of international law. This is not the place to analyze *Amerada Hess.* Suffice it to say that the majority's reasoning in that case is faulty. Elsewhere in this issue I have tried to explain why. *See* p. 323 *supra.*

[9] 20 U.S. (7 Wheat.) 283 (1822).

[10] In the leading sovereign immunity case of the same era, The Schooner Exchange v. M'Faddon, 11 U.S. (7 Cranch) 116 (1812), the claim was directly against a naval vessel flying the French flag. The libelants asserted that the vessel had been forcibly taken from them at sea by order of Napoleon—an assertion of a taking in violation of international law. D'Amato says (p. 202) that nothing in the case showed a French violation of international law, but the libelants were not allowed to make that showing because the vessel was in the possession of the foreign sovereign and therefore had immunity.

[11] 726 F.2d 774, 798–823 (D.C. Cir. 1984), *cert. denied,* 470 U.S. 1003 (1985).

to it, rightly criticizing Bork for his view that nearly all customary and treaty rules are non-self-executing. Bork's view could lead to the exclusion of individuals as claimants in domestic courts under nearly all rules of international law. As D'Amato points out, this possibility is distressing. One hopes that courts henceforth will agree with D'Amato and not with Bork: the most significant provisions in the Covenant on Civil and Political Rights do generate self-executing norms even for nonparties.[12] They are specific enough to be enforced, they call for no affirmative governmental implementation and they are intended to benefit individuals.

Of course, for the Covenant to supply norms for nonparties, decision makers must recognize that treaties may generate custom. Several years ago, D'Amato cogently made this argument;[13] he devotes most of chapter 6 in the present book to a rebuttal of Michael Akehurst's objections to his argument.[14] D'Amato reasserts "that generalizable provisions in treaties (especially multilateral treaties) ipso facto generate customary rules" (p. 145). If by this he means that (1) they ipso facto represent relevant state practice, and (2) such state practice could, without more, create custom (as in the case of generalizable provisions in widely subscribed-to multilateral treaties or in a consistent string of bilateral treaties), he is surely correct.[15] That this is what he does mean is clearer from his earlier book than from the present one.[16]

Much more could be said about D'Amato's interesting and provocative book. One more point will have to suffice. In an appendix to chapter 5 and in chapter 10, D'Amato places his own interpretation on several recent uses of armed force—the aborted U.S. incursion into Iran to rescue the hostages, the Iraqi invasion of Iran and U.S. military activities involving Grenada and Nicaragua. He argues that the sophisticated observer should look beyond what the U.S. and Iraqi Governments said their goals were, and discern what they really were doing. In that light, he views these incidents as state practice supporting or developing a customary rule permitting the use of force to redress particularly serious human rights violations. The trouble with this interpretation is that the lawmaking process of assertion and acqui-

[12] On "self-executing custom," see Henkin, *International Law as Law in the United States,* 82 MICH. L. REV. 1555 (1984); Kirgis, *Federal Statutes, Executive Orders and "Self-Executing Custom,"* 81 AJIL 371 (1987).

[13] A. D'AMATO, THE CONCEPT OF CUSTOM IN INTERNATIONAL LAW 103–66 (1971).

[14] *See* Akehurst, *Custom as a Source of International Law,* 47 BRIT. Y.B. INT'L L. 1 (1974–75).

[15] The International Court has recognized the concept of "instant custom" (though not in these words), stemming from some multilateral treaties. North Sea Continental Shelf Cases (FRG/Den.; FRG/Neth.), 1969 ICJ REP. 3, 42, para. 73 (Judgment of Feb. 20). See also the cases treating the exclusive economic zone, as articulated in the UN Convention on the Law of the Sea, as custom: Case Concerning the Continental Shelf (Tunisia/Libyan Arab Jamahiriya), 1982 ICJ REP. 18, 74 (Judgment of Feb. 24); Delimitation of the Maritime Boundary in the Gulf of Maine Area (Can. v. U.S.), 1984 ICJ REP. 246, 294 (Judgment of Oct. 12); Military and Paramilitary Activities in and against Nicaragua (Nicar. v. U.S.), Merits, 1986 ICJ REP. 14, 111 (Judgment of June 27).

[16] *See* A. D'AMATO, *supra* note 13, at 104, 117–18, 121, 160, 266, 272. But see *id.* at 162–64, where he seems to go further and to suggest that generalizable provisions in treaties necessarily establish instant custom.

escence depends on reactions to what is being asserted, or at least to what decision makers outside the acting state perceive is being asserted. If the acting government asserts one thing but secretly intends another, it is untenable to treat international acquiescence as anything other than acquiescence in what was being asserted—unless the actor's ulterior motive is readily apparent. One should be careful about identifying and characterizing the unspoken motives of governments.

Anyone with a background in international law could hardly read this book without being stimulated to rethink some of the traditional concepts. One need not always agree with D'Amato to recognize the importance of his challenge to comfortable channels of thought.

FREDERIC L. KIRGIS, JR.
Board of Editors

Recueil des Cours de l'Académie de Droit International de La Haye, 1985. Vols. I, II, III and IV. (Vols. 190, 191, 192 and 193 of the collection.) Dordrecht, Boston, Lancaster: Martinus Nijhoff Publishers, 1986. Vol. I: pp. 400; vol. II: pp. 413; vol. III: pp. 475; vol. IV: pp. 403. Dfl.155; $62.50; £42.95.

The 1985 *General Course on Private International Law* at the Hague Academy was given by Professor Friedrich Juenger (University of California at Davis). Juenger's course consists of a historical review and exhaustive critique of the orthodoxies of multilateralism ("[a] choice from among the potentially applicable local rules of decision premised on ascertaining their personal and territorial reach" (p. 168)) and unilateralism ("[t]he interposition of choice-of-law rules" (*id.*)) in conflicts of law, as well as an energetic argument in favor of a substantive law approach ("[t]he creation of multistate rules of decision" (*id.*)). He begins the historical overview by touching on Greek and Roman law just long enough to draw conclusions that prefigure the ultimate conclusions of his overall study: he asserts that the need for choice-of-law rules was obviated by the existence of substantive law unity in Greece and by supranational laws in Rome. He then locates the origin of modern conflicts rules in the "preposterous" (p. 140) reasoning of certain glossators of 12th-century Upper Italy who, he says, incorrectly read into Justinian's *Code* the proposition that multistate problems should be solved by choosing among competing local laws rather than by creating a special *jus gentium.* Tracing the development of conflicts rules from that early point to the 20th century, he chronicles the separate, but related, fortunes of multilateralism and unilateralism in numerous European countries and the United States.

Juenger assembles a litany of shortcomings of the multilateralist and unilateralist doctrines and argues that these shortcomings are not simply wrinkles at the edges of basically sound theories but fundamental deficiencies. His many criticisms of multilateralism and unilateralism include the following: that the process of localizing a legal relationship to determine on a principled basis the seat of the relationship or the scope of a law is artificial and illusory; that choosing the applicable law by conflicts principles rather than looking to the substantive result frequently leads to bad decisions; that courts have great difficulty ascertaining foreign laws and policies necessary in the choice-of-law process; that both multilateralism and unilateralism reflect an outmoded preoccupation with state sovereignty; and that both doctrines, marked by "esoteric vocabulary and warped conceptual instrumentarium" (p. 293), are overly complex and confusing.

Juenger explores "the American conflicts revolution" (p. 207), the new approaches to conflicts law that have emerged in the United States in the past 50 years and have "swept the classical doctrine out of the courts and the classrooms" (p. 227)—such as the proper law approach, interest analysis and the functional approach. He is clearly sympathetic to these approaches, particularly because they question the primacy of decisional uniformity, but his ultimate judgment of them is surprisingly negative. He argues that they reflect no genuinely new ideas, that they are only new blends of old ingredients in conflicts law. Further, they do not consistently lead courts to achieve just results, but instead function "as giant escape devices that free courts from the constraints of rules and permit them to reach whatever results they prefer" (p. 251).

With his extensive critical analysis of existing doctrines and practices carefully laid out, Juenger devotes the remainder of the course to explicit advocacy of the solution that he has been implicitly presenting all along—the abandonment of the multilateral and unilateral doctrines and the wholesale adoption of a substantive law approach. On his account, when faced with a conflicts situation, judges should compare the merits of the competing laws and apply those that give the "best" results. If judges focus on the merits of competing laws rather than on conflicts rules, better justice will result. And contrary to expectations, a substantive law approach will produce decisional uniformity. As judges directly address the merits of competing laws in their decision making and opinion writing, a *jus commune* will evolve, derived from domestic sources, but supranational in purpose. Furthermore, the substantive law approach will make for happier judges. They will not have to face arcane conflicts rules or delve into the policies behind foreign laws. Foreign laws will be presented as models for their consideration, not as rigid precepts. Judges will enjoy their new-found creative freedom, "for it is surely easier to make good law than to mimic a hypothetical foreign court's modes of reasoning" (p. 287).

Juenger's position has the heady appeal that often attends the advocacy of replacing troublesome, overworked procedural models with a unified, result-selective approach. But his account leaves significant questions unanswered. To start with, his contention that judges will stop favoring local laws over foreign laws is unconvincing—the pattern of preference for the *lex fori* is well established and the evidence he marshals for its progressive extinction is unimpressive. More broadly, his contention that a *jus commune* will evolve when judges directly address the merits of competing laws lacks credibility. Why should the differences between cultures and societies that have led to differing laws simply disappear because judges rather than legislatures are made responsible for lawmaking? Further, it seems unlikely that most, or even many, states will be quick to turn their courts into explicit lawmaking forums, even if only for multistate legal situations. Again, the evidence he cites (public law in some civil law systems) seems insufficient support for the broader proposition.

Readers will undoubtedly diverge widely in their assessment of Juenger's arguments for the adoption of a result-selective approach. But all will enjoy his impressive command of the literature and his sharp analytical skills.

The course by Professor Jacques Foyer (University of Paris) on *Problèmes de conflits de lois en matière de filiation* provides an informative review of contemporary developments in the field of filiation law, as well as an indication of some of the problems an emergent substantive law approach poses in what might be considered a well-suited test case for such a method: a limited, relatively homogeneous geographical domain (Western Europe) and an area of law in which there is a growing consensus on basic values (protection of the interest of the child). Foyer reports that result-selective methods have been replacing the multilateral method in West European filiation law since the 1930s, with that transition linked to broader changes in societal conceptions of marriage and family. He examines at length the major new result-selective conflicts methods, including the passing of laws that explicitly permit choice of most favorable laws, the construction of hierarchical sets of specific conflicts rules, the diversification of applicable conflicts rules, and others.

These new methods are used by different nations for the pursuit of a common value (protecting the child's interest), yet Foyer finds that they tend to lead to the application of the *lex fori* over competing foreign laws. That is to say, nations agree on a common value but tend to find their own law the best expression of it. Foyer also discovers that the pursuit of a common value has led to a proliferation of both competing national rules of filiation and conflicts methods, with the consequent risk of increased disputes. Foyer's course demonstrates the difficulty a substantive law approach can have both in overcoming the tendency for courts to apply the *lex fori* rather than competing foreign rules and in unifying the divergent laws generated in support of apparently common values.

The lectures by Leonel Pereznieto Castro (Autonomous National University of Mexico) entitled *La tradition territorialiste en droit international privé dans les pays d'Amérique latine* add an interesting perspective to the two courses discussed above. They cover an area of conflicts law in which neither the multilateral method nor the substantive law approach is prominent. With little exception, Pereznieto Castro asserts, the territorial or unilateral method dominates Latin American conflicts law. He anchors his comparative analysis in the postulate that territorialism is a basic element of human nature and he briefly delves into ethnological, sociological and anthropological studies that make that point. Although he draws only a very schematic link between the general argument that territoriality is a basic human instinct and specific analyses of territoriality in conflicts law, his attempt to root his legal study in a theory of human nature is an interesting variation on the relatively predictable debate over competing methods in conflicts law.

Pereznieto Castro locates the specific origins of the strong territorialist tradition in Latin American conflicts law in two sources—the strict territorialism of the Spanish legal tradition inherited by much of Latin America and the fact that the formative period of the different Latin American legal systems was a time when concern over state sovereignty generally was a dominant motif of Latin American politics and culture. In extensive analyses of Argentine, Chilean and Mexican law, Pereznieto Castro highlights three basic variations of the Latin American method: a liberal version (Argentina) in which some provision is made for the application of foreign laws; an absolute version (Mexico) in which almost no such provision is made; and a middle version (Chile). He also details the dominant use of the territorial method in inter-American law conventions of both the 19th and the 20th centuries. He notes that there is a growing tendency in both domestic Latin American laws and inter-American conventions for more "international" (p. 380) solutions to be found to conflicts problems.

Pereznieto Castro makes few, if any, judgments as to the merits of the territorialist method and takes no more of an advocacy stance than an understated inclination to look with favor at the movement away from strict territorialism. His aim is to explicate the past and present place of territorialism in Latin American law, and this he does quite well.

Two other courses dealt with private international law, *Le droit international privé des Communautés européennes* by Professor Giorgio Badiali (University of Perugia, Italy) and *Conflicts of Laws in International Transport Law* by Professor Oleg Nikolaevich Sadikov (Moscow). After some reflections on the differences between the legal system of the European Communities and the domestic legal systems of member states, Badiali focuses on the choice-of-law process used by the European Communities when questions arise in which the Communities have an interest, but which are not covered by Community law itself. He refers to this process as "the private international law of the European communities" (p. 37) but distinguishes it from conventional private international law—it does not involve choosing between the application of foreign law and the *lex fori,* but rather choosing which member state's law should apply given the absence of applicable Community law. Following an elaborate theoretical analysis of the choice process, Badiali considers some specific situations where it arises in the fields of contract, corporate and family law.

Sadikov's short, but thorough, course on international transport law reviews the diverse approaches national courts take in conflicts cases involving international carriage by land, sea and air. Sadikov finds a pervasive non-uniformity of conflicts rules in all areas except that of carriage by rail. He recommends the development of international treaties as a means of harmonizing conflicts rules and cites as positive examples the conventions governing international rail transport.

One course, the lectures by Professor Joe Verhoeven (Catholic University of Louvain) on *Relations internationales de droit privé en l'absence de reconnais-*

sance d'un Etat, d'un gouvernement ou d'une situation, addressed a public international law topic through an analysis combining public and private international law. After a brief introduction reviewing some basic aspects of recognition doctrine in public international law, Verhoeven examines at length the effect that nonrecognition of a state or government has on the decision making of national courts. He considers two types of cases: those in which national courts apply rules of public international law—concerning, for example, the obligatory force of treaties, diplomatic privileges and immunities, or the laws of war—to situations involving a nonrecognized state or government; and private international law cases in which national courts apply or consider applying the law of a nonrecognized state or government. He finds that—with the exception of U.S. practice, which is "dominated by the concern of the judiciary not to go against the directions given by the State Department in international relations" (p. 177)—nonrecognition is without consequence for the national judge applying public international law or choosing which state law to apply. For Verhoeven, this finding weighs heavily as an argument in favor of the declaratory theory.

Two of the courses explore the application of comparative law methods to international law. The course by Professor William Butler (University College, London), entitled *Comparative Approaches to International Law,* surveys the general applicability of the comparative method to international law, while that given by Professor Antonio Cassese (University of Florence), *Modern Constitutions and International Law,* applies the comparative method to a specific topic—the treatment of international law in modern constitutions.

Butler asserts that the traditional separation between comparative law and international law is weakening and that the comparative method is being increasingly applied to international law. He lauds this tendency and implores international lawyers to use not only the comparative method but also the substantive knowledge, insight and experience—the "lore" (p. 71) of comparative law—in their work. To stimulate this tendency, he proffers a host of topics in international law that he believes could benefit from the application of the comparative method. These topics include the history of international law, international institutions, international adjudication, subsystems of international law and the relation of municipal law to international law. For each topic, Butler does not actually undertake any comparative analysis; rather, he limits himself to showing how the comparative method could best be applied, what the most interesting points of focus would be and what the rewards of such analysis might be. He also discusses the application of substantive knowledge in comparative law to international law and sets out some preliminary thoughts on how insights gained from comparative studies of socialist legal systems, Islamic law and Chinese law could be applied to the analysis of international law.

Butler's course demonstrates well the value to be gained when a highly cosmopolitan legal scholar brings his knowledge to bear on the question of expanding traditional methodologies in international law. In the space of his relatively brief course, he generates enough provocative and promising lines of inquiry to keep a good number of international law scholars productively occupied for some time.

Cassese's course stands as a good example of the sort of study Butler is propounding. Cassese examines the treatment accorded to international law in modern national constitutions. His inquiry is structured on four principal questions: whether most national constitutions defer to international customary law, whether they defer to international treaties, what provisions they make for national participation in international organizations that have the power to restrict sovereignty and whether they prohibit war. He performs rigorous textual analyses on relevant provisions of dozens of constitutions, shedding light on the many nuances of language that states have developed to mitigate and qualify what priorities they do grant to international law. He gives some emphasis to the constitutions of Western European countries but draws on a very wide range of countries.

Cassese's basic finding is straightforward: most states do not accord primacy to international law in their national constitutions. This finding is most pronounced with respect to Third World countries. In fact, he discovers that some Third World countries have even recently repealed constitutional provisions according primacy to international law. Cassese cautions that his generally negative finding does not mean that most states systematically disregard international law. Analysis of the language of constitutional provisions inevitably is only a starting point for analysis of the practice of states in this domain. With that significant limitation recognized—and Cassese himself acknowledges it openly—his study constitutes a commendable example of the value of thorough comparative work.

One of the most basic, yet also difficult, questions faced by scholars and practitioners of public international law is determining what state practice is with respect to any given area of customary law. In his course, *Méthodes de recherche de la coutume internationale dans la pratique des Etats,* Professor Luigi Ferrari Bravo (University of Rome) addresses this subject in a useful manner. By examining the many different manifestations or forms of state practice relevant to customary international law, Ferrari Bravo develops what he calls a phenomenology of contemporary state practice.

Ferrari Bravo looks first at the bilateral practice of states, studying the many forms of such practice, including diplomatic correspondence, "diplomacy by mass media" (declarations or interviews by government officials given to the press, radio or television) (p. 266), instructions or guidance papers used by government officials, bilateral declarations by states, publications or speeches by government legal advisers, legislative acts, administrative acts and domestic jurisprudence. He then reviews the forms of multilateral practice, including those pertaining to both international conferences, such as governmental preparation papers and position papers, and international organizations, such as statements by spokespersons and resolutions made by the organizations. Each of these many bilateral and multilateral forms is analyzed with regard to questions such as how it developed, the particular ways it is used and the weight it should have in evaluations of the formation or modification of customary norms.

Although Ferrari Bravo engages in little explicit theorizing, his course as a whole advocates a particular view of customary international law, a view that can be summarized as follows: The contemporary period is a time of great change in international relations, and it is imperative that international law evolve in parallel fashion. As international relations become more varied and complex, the forms of state practice relevant to customary international law become more varied and complex as well. International legal scholars must broaden their analyses of state practice so as to generate definitions and rules that reflect the rapidly changing forms of practice. In particular, more attention must be given to the many forms of practice arising from the multilateral domain.

One can take issue with Ferrari Bravo on numerous specific points, such as where lines should be drawn in the analysis of the many potential forms of state practice, but his basic message about the need for an updated approach to state practice is of undeniable validity and importance. Ferrari Bravo's distinguished background as a scholar-practitioner is well reflected in his successful attempt to analyze the question of state practice in a way that is both of immediate use to practitioners and of considerable interest to scholars.

Why states should hold some forms of killing in war to be illegal, but others legal, has never received a single, well-settled answer. This troubling question arises throughout *Arms, Armaments and International Law,* the lectures given by Professor Frits Kalshoven (University of Leiden) on the laws of war limiting the use of certain weapons. In his review of the early lawmaking activity in the field, Kalshoven analyzes the 1868 Declaration of St. Petersburg[1] and then quotes extensively from a speech given the same year by a Major G. V. Fosbery of H.M. Bengal Staff Corps who, doubting the philosophical validity of attempts to draw legal distinctions among methods of killing in war, asked, "Are any of the deaths to which the greater number of the killed in war are put, strictly speaking, humane? or, if they are not, what is this humanity of which so much is made?" (p. 210). After tracing the line of lawmaking in this area through the Hague Peace Conferences of 1899 and 1907 and the League of Nations Disarmament Conference of 1932–1934, Kalshoven devotes a good deal of attention to the renewed activity that arose in the 1970s to limit the use of certain conventional weapons in war. Such efforts were sparked, he contends, by the Vietnam War—not so much because of anything exceptional in the types of weapons actually used in that conflict, but because of the intense media coverage of the war. After a detailed review of the preparatory conferences sponsored by the International Red Cross and the Swiss Government, Kalshoven studies the 1979–1980 UN conference on restricting certain conventional

[1] Declaration Renouncing the Use, in Time of War, of Explosive Projectiles Under 400 Grammes Weight, *signed at* St. Petersburg, Dec. 11, 1868.

weapons[2] and the 1980 convention that resulted from that conference. He also considers recent lawmaking efforts related to both disarmament and limitations on the use of weapons of mass destruction.

Kalshoven concludes his course with an appraisal of the lawmaking efforts he has surveyed. The appraisal is unfortunately brief and formalistic. This is an area of public international law in which, no matter how skillful the explication given—and Kalshoven's is skillful indeed—an absence of attempts to relate the structures and content of the law to the actual practice of states tempts the reader to question the significance of the law itself. Kalshoven's closing recommendation that we focus on "the patient continuation of the law-making process" (p. 325) lacks force without there having been some attempt to evaluate the actual effectiveness of the law in this field.

A short course entitled *International Personality* was given by Professor David Feldman (Kazan State University, USSR). Feldman introduces the subject with a consideration of the theoretical foundations of the concept of international personality, and then focuses on three particular aspects. First, he takes up the problem of defining the term "state." He examines numerous definitions and is highly critical of those that do not stress sovereignty as an essential attribute of states. Second, he studies the classification of states by different criteria. The distinction between federations and confederations is given special attention, with reference to the status of the Soviet republics. Third, he takes up the subject of recognition, highlighting the many complexities and ambiguities of that difficult topic. Feldman's course is a highly theoretical exposition, based on an interesting range of sources, with emphasis on the Soviet perspective.

Finally, Sadruddin Aga Khan (United Nations) lectured on *Les bases éthiques pour le droit et la société: Perspectives de la Commission indépendante sur les questions humanitaires internationales,* reviewing the broader moral concerns at issue in modern international law, and Professor Andrej Kopff (Jagiellonian University, Kraków) analyzed the subject, object and limits of copyright law in *The Influence of Technical Progress on Development of Creativity and the Law of Intellectual Property.*

THOMAS CAROTHERS
Of the New York Bar

The System of International Law: Formation, Treaties, Responsibility. By Farhad Malekian. Uppsala, 1987. Pp. xii, 232. Index.

As its title suggests, this book deals with international legal theory, the law of treaties and state responsibility. The author's purpose is "to give an elementary understanding of these essential fields to those who have some

[2] United Nations Conference on Prohibitions or Restrictions of Use of Certain Conventional Weapons Which May Be Deemed to Be Excessively Injurious or to Have Indiscriminate Effects.

interest in international law" (general remarks, unnumbered page). He accomplishes this, but with the clear bias, often specifically articulated, of a Third World international lawyer who distrusts a system that he views as having primarily Western origins.

The book is divided into three parts, each of which corresponds to one of the three subtitular topics. It also has a bibliography, an appendix (the text of the Vienna Convention on the Law of Treaties) and a detailed table of contents. The three parts read as if they were composed as independent papers. End notes appear after each part, a format that makes referring to them difficult. This failing is in some measure compensated for by the table of contents and the arrangement of each part into decimally numbered sections and subsections. The placement of the notes is nonetheless annoying when one seeks to identify the supporting material. More annoying is the occasional omission of any source at all after some statements whose truth is far from self-evident.

Part I, entitled "Formation of the International Legal System," deals in 76 pages with the history, nature, sources and enforcement of international law, and concludes with discussions of international law in national legislatures and of the socialist theory of international law with emphasis on the views of the Soviet Union. Part II, considerably shorter, treats the nature, formation, function, enforcement and interpretation of treaties, with their effect on third parties and with their amendment and termination.

Part III, shorter still, discusses the theory and types of state responsibility, state acts that may lead to such responsibility and the substantive violations that may determine responsibility. It also includes "A Draft Proposal on the International Criminal Responsibility of States," reproduced from an earlier work by the author (pp. 151–52).

A recurring theme of this book is that because international law, especially customary international law, has its origins in the West, it cannot accurately be said to bind non-Western states as well.

> Customary international law requires the achievement of a consensus in the interplay between social and economic circumstances. . . . Contemporary international law in its present western form has not been able to achieve a consensus. States of the world cannot therefore share in the values of a system in which they have never consented to participate in [*sic*]. In this respect, the validity of customary international law can only be measured if (a) common consent, (b) modification, (c) adaption, and above all, (d) participation of all states small and large is achieved [pp. 35–36].

On this same basis, the author attacks the use of general principles of law as evidence of international consent to be bound by their content because "there does not exist a common principle recognized by all nations" (p. 39).

He also challenges the practice of generalizing from decisions of the International Court of Justice beyond the cases actually decided. He writes: "The judges are not trusted because of the privacy of their cultural, material, inter-ideological, [and] political [modalities], and above all the effective penetration of economic modalities . . . ." Emphasizing a purely positivist view of international adjudication, he continues, "It is neither pragmatic nor legal to accept that the International Court of Justice can lay down a source of international law without a certain common consent of states" (p. 40).

Surprisingly, in the light of these comments, he takes the position that resolutions of the UN General Assembly may bind even those who do not vote for them. "It is the intention of the participants which is of high importance to the validity of the resolution. Where the majorities [*sic*] intention is to be bound to a resolution, it should be obligatory for all" (*id.*). He concludes that newly emergent nations need not recognize earlier law created without their consent.

> In fact, contemporary nations of the world should act on the basis of their own volition. In particular this is evident when we speak of the new born states. These states ethnically cannot build their international relations upon sources which are the product of a bygone time. According to the needs of the international community, it is not necessary to interweave all international relations with remnants of past relations [p. 51].

The text lacks a certain coherence. The author adopts a point of view also held by other scholars from Third World countries. Unfortunately, his analysis fails to state clearly the opposing points of view and to criticize their philosophical and jurisprudential bases in order to make his case.

At one point he seems to adopt a traditional (and pragmatic) view of the nature of law in a consensual system. He writes:

> Rules of international law should not be measured upon their sanctional power but they should be considered according to the consent of states. Common consent appears to be the main reason for obedience to the rules of international law. States are assumed to be bound by generally accepted rules. In fact, it is a matter of reciprocal interest for states to obey the accepted rules. Obedience to the system of international law is the perpetual need of predictability of states' conduct [p. 56].

Three pages later, however, he takes a different tack: "[T]he basic reason for the legal weakness of the system of international law is due to the fact that in the interpretation of the rules of international law, states use their ideologies rather than the common legal principles" (p. 59). Apparent contradictions of this kind abound and raise serious doubts about the author's ability to follow the chain of his own logic to appropriate supportable conclusions. In fairness, it must be said that some of the difficulties in communication may be attributable to difficulties with English syntax. A good English-language proofreader or editor would have improved the text considerably.

This book is principally useful as an illustration of a Third World view of the international legal system, conditioned in large part not by jurisprudential considerations but by cultural and historical differences. The international legal system that the author describes resembles the one with which Western scholars are familiar, but the heavy overlay of cultural bias, sometimes without clear identification, makes the book's value for the general reader and for scholars, or as an auxiliary teaching tool, difficult to assess. It does provide some useful insight into a "nontraditionalist" view of international law while accepting traditional generalizations about the origins and nature of the international legal system. There is no real effort, however, to reconcile this inconsistency or to point out with any degree of clarity both the intersections and the divergences between the conflicting views.

HAROLD G. MAIER
Board of Editors

Droit International Public (3d ed.). By Nguyen Quoc Dinh. Revised and updated by Patrick Daillier and Alain Pellet. Paris: Librairie Générale de Droit et de Jurisprudence, 1987. Pp. 1189. Indexes. F.290.

Droit International Public by Daillier and Pellet recasts, rather than merely updates, the treatise published in 1975 by the late Professor Nguyen Quoc Dinh. Whereas Nguyen Quoc Dinh followed by and large the teaching and writings of Georges Scelle,[1] Daillier and Pellet have brushed aside the objectivist approach "for having too often led to the refashioning of international reality in accordance with theoretical postulates" (p. 100, para. 58). Their "fundamental choice" is to adhere to "a necessary observation of reality in both its diversity and heterogeneity" (*id.*). Despite this "noncommittal" approach to international law, the fact remains that their analysis inclines toward indulgence and sympathy for the Third World's legal discourse.

The first part of the book (pp. 101–363) addresses the international lawmaking process, which the authors view as being either conventional or nonconventional. Among nonconventional sources of international law, Daillier and Pellet consider customary law to be a "spontaneous" lawmaking process (p. 291) like general principles of law and equity (pp. 316, 322). Resolutions of international organizations pertain in their view to a "voluntary" lawmaking process (pp. 328, 335). It may be doubted whether the so-called voluntary lawmaking process is limited to resolutions of international organizations. On the other hand, the dichotomy between "spontaneous" and "voluntary" lawmaking processes is hardly convincing insofar as the two adjectives refer to two separate and distinctive features of the channels through which international norms come into being.

In the second part of the book (pp. 365–642), Daillier and Pellet examine the subjects of international law under two headings: states and other entities. The analysis of states' sovereignty and territorial jurisdiction is in line with the classical continental approach, which ignores the U.S. *Restatement*'s threefold division: jurisdiction to prescribe, jurisdiction to adjudicate and jurisdiction to enforce. It is worth noting that the comments on state sovereignty are supplemented by references to "economic sovereignty" (pp.

[1] NGUYEN QUOC DINH, DROIT INTERNATIONAL PUBLIC 112, para. 74 (1st ed. 1975).

425–28, para. 310), which, in practical terms, comes into play in favor of Third World countries alone.

As far as the international status of individuals and corporations is concerned, Daillier and Pellet strongly support the "wisdom" of the U.S. Supreme Court in the 1964 *Sabbatino* case (p. 618) but reproach some international tribunals for having ruled excessively in favor of corporate interests in certain international oil disputes (p. 626). The authors unfortunately do not substantiate their claim.

The third part of the book, which covers "international relationships" (pp. 643–1075), deals with various topics among which two in particular may be singled out. First, with respect to the use of force between states (pp. 808–25), Daillier and Pellet seemingly take the view that armed force is lawful when used to give effect to the right of colonial peoples to self-determination (pp. 819–20). They also consider the lawfulness of humanitarian intervention to be an "unsettled issue" (p. 823) and seemingly approve the acceptance by the World Court, in the *Nicaragua* case,[2] of the legitimacy of humanitarian intervention only when limited to the purposes hallowed in the practice of the Red Cross (p. 824). Second, in discussing the regulation of international economic relations (pp. 879–951), the authors have provided what may be regarded as an introduction to the field. They analyze the "New International Economic Order" quite extensively (pp. 893–911) but touch lightly upon the GATT multilateral trade system (pp. 933–35). Their main concern seems to be with the North-South dialogue and the economic difficulties of Third World countries.

In conclusion, *Droit International Public* is a well-informed manual of international law. Each chapter contains substantive bibliographic references and the book is supplemented with a detailed index, a table of texts and documents, and a table of cases. On the whole, it is a useful and richly documented source of information, particularly on the Third World's positions on international legal issues.

ELISABETH ZOLLER
Rutgers School of Law–Camden

Droit International. By Dominique Carreau. Paris: Pedone, 1986. Pp. vi, 616. Index.

Droit International by Carreau is an innovative approach to the international legal system. Unlike traditional manuals and treatises, *Droit International* discards the usual classifications and headings of international law such as sources of law, subjects of law and state jurisdiction. Carreau reorganizes the international legal system under four new headings: "The Supremacy of International Law" (pp. 39–92), "The International Lawmaking Process" (pp. 93–298), "The Application of International Norms" (pp.

[2] Military and Paramilitary Activities in and against Nicaragua (Nicar. v. U.S.), Merits, 1986 ICJ REP. 14, 125, para. 243 (Judgment of June 27).

299–485) and "The Review Process of the Application of International Law" (pp. 487–596). The reason for this reorganization (p. 37) is to be found in the concern of the author to expose his students to the legal framework of the international system before addressing the applicable substantive rules, since, depending on the law school curriculum, the latter may be studied further in specialized courses.

Carreau operates on the premise that international law can no longer be defined as the branch of law that regulates relations between states. He follows Jessup's well-known approach and defines international law as "all law that regulates actions or events that transcend national frontiers" (p. 32, para. 68). This "transnational law" approach enables him to address topics that used to be given little consideration such as "agreements entered into by, or between, nonstate entities" (pp. 156–79), with interesting insights on state and international contracts, and "nonbinding international agreements" (pp. 180–94), which the author aptly describes as "perfectible treaties" (*traités à parfaire*). His portrayal of unilateral acts by states and by international organizations as written norms of international law (*normes écrites,* p. 195) is more controversial. Carreau endorses the view that international organizations are endowed with an external normative authority, and he goes so far as to write: "This external normative authority of international organizations is carried out through acts that are *imprecisely* phrased 'resolutions,' 'recommendations,' 'regulations,' etc. . . ." (p. 220, para. 602, emphasis added). The alleged imprecision notwithstanding, resolutions and recommendations have never meant statutes. Likewise, Carreau's analysis of customary law is disputable. He follows René-Jean Dupuy who coined the popular phrase in French *coutume sauvage* ("wild" as opposed to "tame" customary law or *coutume sage*), and views customary law as "the only possible source of international law together with general principles of law" (p. 261, para. 712) in certain new spheres of international financial and economic relations.

With respect to the application of international law in municipal law, Carreau's book is useful for its clear and well-informed presentation of international law as applied by French courts (pp. 469–85). Although French law does not subscribe to the political question doctrine, an old, established tradition in French courts is to refrain from interpreting treaties whenever judicial construction involves "questions of public international law." In such cases French courts call upon the French Foreign Office for "authoritative" interpretation. Carreau's criticism and analysis of this practice leads to the suggestion that French courts, by a different route, reach results that are indeed very similar to those attained by their American counterparts.

As far as the use of force among states is concerned, Carreau makes suggestive comments in regard to forceful intervention (pp. 502–05). His view is that "it is possible to envision extreme situations where forceful intervention is not unlawful" (p. 503, para. 1320). He mentions in particular "systematic violations of *jus cogens* norms" (*id.*). His thesis, which is actually shared by several other international scholars, offers an additional confirmation that the closed system of the UN Charter as enshrined in Articles 2(4) and 51 is not accepted as the only possible law on the subject.

The last chapter of the book (pp. 584–96) ought to be of particular interest to American readers. It deals mainly with the act of state doctrine and its equivalent in continental legal systems. Carreau expresses the view that national courts are entitled to enforce universally accepted international rules in opposition to foreign acts of state. Nevertheless, he warns against the possibility of parochialism in that regard.

On the whole, *Droit International* is a challenging and well-articulated manual of international law that deserves to be recognized as an interesting addition to French international pedagogy. Last, but by no means least, it is a useful reminder of the impossibility of disassociating teaching from scholarship.

ELISABETH ZOLLER
Rutgers School of Law–Camden

Breach of Treaty. By Shabtai Rosenne. Cambridge: Grotius Publications Limited, 1985. Pp. xii, 142. Index. $27; £15.

This volume is an expanded version of the Hersch Lauterpacht Memorial Lectures delivered at the University of Cambridge in March 1985 by Ambassador Rosenne. His purpose was to review the impact on one another of the codification of the law of treaties embodied in the 1969 Vienna Convention on the Law of Treaties and the codification of the law of state responsibility currently being formulated by the International Law Commission.

The antecedents of both codifications are examined with the notation that, curiously, the outstanding Harvard Research Draft on the Law of Treaties of 1935 contained no clear provision on "breach," nor did the terms "breach" and "violation" appear in the indexes of Lauterpacht's *Collected Papers*. Rosenne himself concludes these lectures with the pessimistic observation that, despite a large amount of case law, "there is no generally accepted definition of what is meant by 'breach of a treaty' " (p. 123).

Of course, Article 60 of the Vienna Convention defines a material breach of a treaty as a repudiation of the treaty or a violation of an essential provision. It also provides that breach of a treaty does not itself terminate a treaty or justify any unilateral termination of the treaty.

Rosenne, however, dislikes the term "breach," calls it an "awkward word" and insistently characterizes it as "pejorative." Indeed, he finds that on the conceptual level, the Vienna Convention procedure exhibits a "fundamental weakness" in its "over-emphasis on a legal approach not really compatible with general diplomatic experience or the diplomatic temperament" (p. 36). This penchant for diplomatic rather than judicial settlement, which recurs throughout the lectures, may appear surprising from the author of the most constantly used guide to *The Law and Practice of the International Court* (1965).

To the reviewer, the lectures are flawed by the very exaggerated distinction Rosenne insistently makes between "the law of the treaty-instrument" and "the law of the treaty-obligation." This distinction Rosenne traces to a so-called decision by the 1950 membership of the International Law Commission, which reads, "A majority of the Commission favoured the explanation of the term 'treaty' as a 'formal instrument' rather than as an 'agreement recorded in writing'" (p. 3). In fact, this conclusion resulted from a debate over whether a treaty was the agreement concluded or the instrument in which the agreement was recorded (an obvious aid in interpreting the agreement). No distinction between the treaty-instrument and the treaty-obligation appears to have arisen. Moreover, a reexamination by this reviewer of the proceedings of the International Law Commission and of the Vienna Conference (Committee of the Whole, Plenary Sessions, Amendments) reveals no consideration or discussion of the distinction here made by Rosenne. On this point, Article 2, paragraph 1(a) of the Vienna Convention adopts the International Law Commission's definition of a treaty as an international agreement embodied in an instrument or related instruments, a definition that fails to support Rosenne's distinction.

It is therefore startling to find that Articles 38 and 43 of the Vienna Convention—which provide that a rule embodied in a treaty may also be binding as a rule of customary international law (as the International Court of Justice has just held in *Nicaragua v. United States*)—are alleged by Rosenne to have been "inserted with the express purpose of connecting the instrument with the obligation or, if you like, of separating the law of the instrument from the law of the obligation" (p. 4). Similarly, Rosenne finds that Article 45—on loss of a ground for terminating a treaty because of inconsistent conduct (the *allegans* rule)—applies the "estoppel" principle only to the law of the treaty-instrument and not to the obligation set forth in the instrument (p. 7).

It appears that in purporting to distinguish the law of the treaty-instrument from the law of the treaty-obligation, Rosenne is really distinguishing the law of treaties from the law of state responsibility (e.g., for breach of a treaty); but doctrinal compartmentalization into systems, "subsystems" and "sub-subsystems" (pp. 93, 103) goes beyond what is needed for an understanding of the applicable international law.

Almost half of the book examines the concept of "breach of treaty" in the law of state responsibility, with critical attention to the International Law Commission's not yet completed draft. Here again the author's pessimism leads him to conclude that

> it may be a disservice to international law in general, and to the stability and the integrity of treaty relationships in particular, to attempt to give greater precision both to the concept of breach of a treaty, and to the methods of redressing the undesirable consequences of a duly established breach [p. 124].

One may hope that Rosenne's pessimism about "the anarchical state of present-day international law" will not prevent him from preparing for us a completely updated revision of his magisterial treatise on the International Court of Justice.

HERBERT W. BRIGGS
Board of Editors

De Nederlandse Verdragspraktijk. By Henricus Hermanus Maria Sondaal. The Hague: T.M.C. Asser Instituut, 1986. Pp. xv, 381. Indexes. English summary.

This study of the treaty practice of the Kingdom of the Netherlands was presented as a doctoral dissertation at the University of Leiden. The author is an official of the Netherlands Ministry of Foreign Affairs. For more than 16 years, Sondaal was a staff member of the Treaties Department of the Ministry, including 6 years as head of that department. With many years of practical experience and immediate access to all relevant source materials, Sondaal was eminently qualified to make an in-depth study of Dutch treaty practice. However, writing a scholarly book in connection with one's own career experiences is not without risks. There is unquestionably the advantage and the benefit of a great deal of inside information and practical familiarity with the subject matter. On the other hand, the author may be inclined, as a result of close association with certain policies and practices, to take a priori positions. This reviewer could not escape the impression that the book reflects a strong identification with the role and interests of the Treaties Department.

Sondaal states in the introduction that it is difficult to gain a clear and coherent picture of Dutch treaty practice from references scattered through treaty publications and parliamentary documents and records. The main thrust of the study was to make such a presentation on the basis of critical analysis and to make certain suggestions for improvement.

The book is divided into 11 chapters. Chapter 1 deals with the definition of a treaty from the point of view of both international and constitutional law. Chapter 2 describes the structure of a treaty, as viewed from the standpoint of international law. Chapter 3 is devoted to the power to make treaties, and chapter 4 presents the Dutch practice regarding the negotiating process, adoption and authentication of treaties. Chapter 5 examines the application of treaties to third states. Chapter 6 deals extensively, on the basis of constitutional provisions and practice, with the respective roles of the Council of Ministers, the Council of State and Parliament in the process of concluding a treaty. Chapter 7 treats a number of issues concerning the rule of parliamentary approval, in particular, to what extent this rule is applicable in cases of provisional application of a treaty, its denunciation, suspension, extension, modification or amendment. Chapter 8 sets out the special constitutional relationships with respect to treaty making of the three constituent parts of the Kingdom of the Netherlands, i.e., the Netherlands, the Netherlands Antilles and Aruba. Chapters 9 and 10 deal respectively with the publication of treaties and with depositaries and registration. The final chapter contains a few general conclusions.

It is obvious that for a study of this nature the Vienna Convention on the Law of Treaties provides an important frame of reference. Of particular interest are Sondaal's observations regarding Article 18 of the Vienna Convention, which spells out the obligation of signatory states and states parties not to defeat the object and purpose of a treaty prior to its entry into force. In this connection, he discusses the Provisional Understanding Regarding Deep Seabed Matters and the attached Memorandum of Implementation, which deal with authorization for the exploitation of the hard mineral resources of the seabed and were signed on August 3, 1984, by several industrialized nations, including the Netherlands. In parliamentary debates it was argued that the Netherlands, having already signed the UN Convention on the Law of the Sea, would defeat the object and purpose of the latter treaty if it became a party to the Provisional Understanding. In this matter, Sondaal disassociates himself from the official governmental position by expressing his "serious doubts" whether Article 1 of the Provisional Understanding is compatible with the seabed regime under the Convention. Sondaal stresses quite rightly the importance of Article 18 of the Vienna Convention inasmuch as this provision goes beyond serving the (reciprocal) interests of states and intends to take due account of the collective interests of the international community in such matters as the law of the sea, the nonproliferation of nuclear weapons, and human rights and fundamental freedoms.

While it is true that treaty practice usually does not constitute the most dynamic part of international law and international relations, some treaty issues may pose highly controversial and political questions. This was particularly the case with regard to the agreement laid down in an exchange of letters of November 4, 1985, between the Kingdom of the Netherlands and the United States concerning the stationing on Netherlands territory of U.S. Air Force ground-launched cruise missiles. The Netherlands Government had indicated that it would seek the approval of Parliament before the agreement would become binding, in accordance with Article 91 of the Netherlands Constitution. One of the constitutional and political issues at stake was whether the agreement was in conflict with the Netherlands Constitution and would need approval by at least two-thirds of the votes on the basis of Article 91, paragraph 3. The practical implications resulted from the political reality that although the Government could count on a simple majority in Parliament, more than one-third of the members of Parliament were radically opposed to deployment of the missiles. It appears that this contentious matter has now lost some of its edge because of the progress made in the nuclear arms negotiations between the two superpowers. The matter did, of course, raise questions of treaty law, but the more important legal and moral aspects related to sovereignty, international cooperation and armed conflicts. Sondaal prudently confined himself to discussing some questions of treaty law, inter alia, by rightly rejecting the claim of some that the agreement was invalid as a result of the manifest violation of fundamental provisions of Netherlands constitutional law (Article 46 of the Vienna Convention).

It is not surprising that Sondaal defends repeatedly and tirelessly the primacy of the Minister for Foreign Affairs in the conclusion of treaties. Foreign affairs is no longer the exclusive domain of the head of state and the Foreign Minister. Growing international cooperation at intergovernmental levels and in the supranational context of the European Communities has an impact on many fields of public welfare and public order and unavoidably leads to the progressive involvement in international affairs of other cabinet ministers. Moreover, the present Dutch Prime Minister reserves a larger role in international affairs to himself than did his predecessors who, in accordance with Dutch constitutional traditions, exercised more self-restraint in this domain. Sondaal sees in these developments potential sources of friction. With great insistence, as if it were an *oratio pro domo,* he pleads for maintaining the primary responsibility of the Minister for Foreign Affairs in the handling of treaty matters. As Sondaal argues, the Foreign Minister's staff is equipped with the necessary skill and expertise and constitutes a guarantee of a consistent and coherent policy with regard to treaty law and practice. It is also the Minister for Foreign Affairs and his staff who are in the best position to strike the right balance between the international and national interests that play a role in the conclusion of treaties. Sondaal's plea is convincing. It is also this reviewer's opinion that the conclusion of treaties, with its many formal and substantive intricacies, is, *par excellence,* the domain of competence and responsibility of the Minister for Foreign Affairs. But it is obvious that this competence and this responsibility do not release the Foreign Minister from the obligation to consult, cooperate and coordinate with all other authorities who have a direct interest in the treaty-making process.

Sondaal has succeeded in his endeavor to present Dutch treaty practice in a clear and coherent manner. The book is written in Dutch and is therefore only accessible to Dutch readers. In view of the special focus on Dutch treaty practice, its translation into a more accessible language is not a matter of course. However, Sondaal's study contains sufficient elements of interest to a broader international readership. The author might therefore consider preparing a briefer version of his book in English, going well beyond the too succinct English summary included in his dissertation. It would also be of value to have treaty experts from various nations prepare a collective volume on comparative treaty practice. The study by Sondaal prompts one to think in that direction.

THEO VAN BOVEN
University of Limburg, Netherlands

Recognition and the United Nations. By John Dugard. Cambridge: Grotius Publications Limited, 1987. Pp. xiv, 192. Index. £27; $48.

This published version of the 1986 Hersch Lauterpacht Memorial Lectures at Cambridge University offers a new look at the law on recognition of states. The author contends that legal scholars and national leaders alike misunderstand the current state of that law because they ignore the way in which "collective practice within the United Nations has materially altered the traditional law of recognition premised on unilateral decision-making by States" (p. ix).

The basic argument is straightforward, though difficult to follow because an important element is not introduced until chapter 4 (pp. 45–51). In more logical order, Dugard argues as follows. Recognition of statehood has two components, acknowledgment of an entity's legal status and establishment of formal diplomatic relations or other official bilateral contacts with it. While states retain unilateral discretion in the latter, authority to acknowledge or deny legal status is now concentrated in the UN General Assembly and Security Council. The authority of the United Nations to acknowledge status stems from the fact that only states may become members, and membership is acquired when a positive recommendation from the Security Council is affirmed by a two-thirds majority of the General Assembly. Since even members voting against an approved application must accept the applicant as a fellow member, they must perforce accept its statehood.

The United Nations also has authority to deny status as a state because members are obliged to follow all General Assembly and Security Council recommendations against acknowledging statehood. Dugard supports this second claim partly by interpreting the Charter, but mainly by appeal to the notion of *jus cogens.* Entities that owe their existence to a use of force by one state against another, originate in interference with the exercise of the right of self-determination or practice systematic racism have violated fundamental norms of international law, and consequently must be denied recognition as states. Thus, when a UN political organ recommends nonrecognition of such an entity, it is simply reminding states of their already existing obligations.

Both claims are plausible and attractive at first glance, particularly for acknowledgment of status as a state. Comembership in the United Nations does require all old members to treat the newly admitted member as an equal for purposes of organization-related activity. To the extent that the rights and duties of UN membership overlap with the traditional rights and duties of states, admission does carry the same legal implications as recognition of statehood. The argument deals less well with instances when the new entity decides against seeking UN membership. Where its claim to statehood has been recognized for some time, as in the case of Switzerland, nonmembership will not pose any problems. However, where a newly emerged entity opts to remain outside the United Nations, difficulties might arise if Dugard's argument were reversed into a presumption that failure to seek UN membership means that an entity is uncertain about its own claim to statehood. On the nonrecognition side, the UN political organs have coordinated certain collective denials of statehood more vigorously than would have been possible otherwise. In addition, the notion that certain entities are so flawed that they should be denied status is attractive to those seeking normative bases for world order other than rule by the strong.

As formulated here, however, the argument suffers from several serious weaknesses. These fall under three headings: overestimating the independent influence of UN organs; assuming that there is broad support for the whole notion of *jus cogens;* and assuming that there is general agreement that the particular rules cited are already accepted as "fundamental norms."

Whether one accepts Dugard's argument depends most heavily on whether one accepts his assumption that the UN political organs function as independent actors. It is at least equally, and to this reviewer's mind more, plausible to regard them as places where states publicly express previously developed agreements or disagreements. Dugard implicitly admits this interpretation in chapter 3 where he traces changes in UN admission practices. He might have taken the thought further had he looked more at cases where the members failed to arrive at a consensus, such as Biafra and Bangladesh (mentioned briefly) or Eastern Timor and Western Sahara (not analyzed in the text). As it stands, most of the analysis focuses on cases where the members came to broad agreement. This focus has the unfortunate effect of making the UN bodies look more influential than they actually are.

The use of *jus cogens* in developing rules for denying statehood to entities that meet the traditional requirements of defined territory, permanent population, government and ability to enter into relations with other states builds nicely on interwar efforts to develop doctrines of collective nonrecognition. Dugard ably summarizes the case in favor of accepting the notion of *jus cogens* and extending it to the law of recognition on pages 137–52, but the limits of the lecture form do not permit him to develop his thoughts well enough to persuade the skeptical.

Even those who agree with the general argument may not endorse the particular rules Dugard relies upon. He attempts to extend the taint of illegal origins to all entities that issue from the use of force by one state against another, even if the initial use was defensive. Yet, as long as the international system remains anarchical, it is not unreasonable to deny aggressors the means of further aggression. Reducing territory or dividing one state into two may sometimes be the only way to maintain a durable peace in the long term. Defining a "self-determination unit" as a territorial entity within previously established colonial boundaries (pp. 104, 110–11) begs all the hard questions. With decolonization virtually complete, problems stemming from secessionist conflicts will necessarily dominate future UN debates. A boundary-centered definition of self-determination provides no guidance for evaluating the competing claims in such cases (as Dugard admits on p. 162). Singling out systematic racism as grounds for denying statehood also confines legal doctrine to the simpler issue on which there is already consensus. Dugard shies away from imposing any other human rights–related tests, for the good reason that they would be very hard to apply.

These criticisms are not intended to deny the skill with which Dugard has researched and presents his case. They are meant, however, to warn that consensus on these matters is not as great as it seems in his presentation. Dugard rightly notes that the law on recognition of states is undergoing thorough change. Yet his focus on the United Nations means that he misses the real sources of change: interdependence and the implications of emerging human rights law. To understand these changes and help create doctrines appropriate to them, legal scholars must study the patterns of interaction developing among various types of actors and the legal doctrines being forged by governments as they cope with the new problems thus created, rather than focus exclusively on UN discussions.

M. J. PETERSON
University of Massachusetts, Amherst

International Arbitration: Three Salient Problems. By Stephen M. Schwebel. Cambridge: Grotius Publications Limited, 1987. Pp. xviii, 303. Index. £33; $59.

This revision of the first of the Hersch Lauterpacht Memorial Lectures, delivered at Cambridge University by Judge Stephen Schwebel of the International Court of Justice, has permitted the inclusion in the volume of extended quotations from, or analyses of, more than 40 international arbitrations, ranging from well-known arbitrations such as the *Jay Treaty* cases and the *Delagoa Bay Railway* case, through cases like the *BP, TOPCO* and *LIAMCO* oil cases against Libya, to more recent cases before the Iran–United States Claims Tribunal.

The fortunate result has been to provide the reader with a wealth of materials resembling something of a casebook but more of a carefully documented short treatise on each of the three salient problems examined: the severability of the arbitration agreement (ch. I); whether governmental repudiation of an agreement to arbitrate is a denial of justice (ch. II); and the authority of international arbitral tribunals in which an arbitrator refuses to participate (ch. III). Each of the problems is set forth with admirable clarity in a schematic treatment comprising the question, the theory, the practice, the views of commentators and the conclusions of Judge Schwebel. The questions are considered in the light of public international law and the law of international commercial arbitration, with some reference to national arbitration laws.

The first problem deals with the question whether, where a treaty or contract contains a clause providing for arbitration of disputes arising thereunder, the termination, nullification or suspension of the treaty or contract necessarily vitiates the arbitration clause. The argument, based on logic, that if the treaty or agreement is terminated, the arbitral clause falls with it, writes Schwebel, yields to the experience provided by practice and practical requirements, which have supported the severability of the arbitration clause from the substantive agreement in order to fulfill the original intention of the parties. Moreover, the rule of *la compétence de la compétence* is too firmly established in the law of international tribunals to be challenged today and provides a court with the jurisdiction to determine the initial or continuing validity of an arbitral agreement. A comparative survey of the rules adopted for international public law or commercial arbitrations and the international cases (here surveyed by the author) support the practice of the severability and survival of agreements to arbitrate even where the substantive agreement containing them falls. Discussion of the issues is of value to students of public international law and to private international lawyers.

The second problem treated in the lectures is whether the refusal by a state that has contracted with an alien that disputes under the contract shall be submitted to arbitration constitutes a denial of justice under international law. Subsidiary questions discussed are whether a state's contrary legislation—either specific or of a generally applicable nature—or pleas of nonexhaustion of local remedies or sovereign immunity provide a valid defense to a charge of denial of justice flowing from a refusal to arbitrate. Even more subsidiary is discussion of whether the alien himself, rather than his state, is entitled to seek an arbitral decision on the issue.

In examining these questions, Schwebel devotes considerable attention to the skeptical views expressed by Dr. F. A. Mann in his 1967 article *State Contracts and International Arbitration* in the *British Year Book of International Law,* as well as to cases like *Losinger, Anglo-Iranian Oil* and a dozen others, some of which, though tangential, he believes throw light on the issues. He clearly concludes "that a denial of justice springs from a State's repudiation of its arbitral obligations towards an alien" (p. 108) and that the local remedies rule and sovereign immunity are inapplicable. With perhaps more hesitation, the author favors the right of an alien to "base a claim in an arbitral proceeding with a State on international law, conventional and customary," including invocation of a denial of justice (p. 141).

The final problem—dealt with comprehensively in over 150 fascinating pages—examines "the authority of truncated international arbitral tribunals"—that is, the question whether an arbitral tribunal from which the arbitrator designated by one party has withdrawn (on instructions of his government or not), or is otherwise absent and not replaced, can deliver a binding award or decisions.

Where the arbitral agreement does not explicitly permit majority decisions, one party has too often sought to frustrate the arbitral process by withdrawing its arbitrator when it appeared that an unfavorable decision was likely to ensue. Even where the arbitration agreement provides for replacement of an arbitrator, delays have proved stultifying.

The problem becomes acute when international arbitration continues to be regarded in 19th-century terms as subject to the diplomatic control of each party rather than as an adjudication based upon the application of law by a court. As Schwebel points out in elaborate detail, the International Law Commission endeavored in the draft on arbitral procedure and the model code fostered by the late Professor Georges Scelle to eliminate the loopholes in arbitral practice, but the reluctance of many states in the General Assembly to yield control over the process of arbitration has slowed the development.

As for practice, one is tempted to linger over the insights provided by Schwebel in his observations on the *Jay Treaty* cases, *Republic of Colombia v. Cauca,* the *Hungarian Optants* case, the *Lena Goldfields* arbitration and the *Sabotage* cases, inter alia, as well as the recent information he produces on the *Buraimi* arbitration and the episodes before the Iran–United States Claims Tribunal, but space will not permit it here.

The thoughtful and carefully documented analyses of so many well-known arbitrations on these pages provide a fresh and original treatment of recurrent problems of international arbitration.

HERBERT W. BRIGGS
Board of Editors

Mezhdunarodnye sudebnye uchrezhdenya (International Judicial Institutions). By M. L. Entin. Moscow: "Mezhdunarodnye Otnoshenya," 1984. Pp. 174. 1 ruble, 60 kopecks.

The book bears the subtitle "The Role of International Arbitration and Judicial Organs in the Settlement of Interstate Disputes." Apart from international arbitration institutions, it deals mainly with the International Court of Justice and the Court of Justice of the European Communities, concentrating on developments in the 1970s and early 1980s. Soviet publications on international adjudication are sycophantically extolled (pp. 5, 33).

The chapter on international arbitration offers some elementary information but is interspersed with historical and political biases or even fabrications. For example, on pages 10–11, the antiwar provisions of the League of Nations Covenant and the 1928 Kellogg-Briand Pact are attributed to the "consistent fight of the USSR for the triumph of the ideals of a democratic world, self-determination of nations and international cooperation on an equal basis." Then cowed and weak, the USSR considered the Pact a propagandistic asset. Although it was the first country to ratify the Pact (though, of course, it was not one of the original states parties), it had no scruples about violating the Pact in 1939 (by its invasions of Poland and Finland). The author's attitude toward the League of Nations, as is usual in Soviet publications, is very hostile.[1]

On page 162, one reads that the court of arbitration, which may be created within the framework of the Commission of Mediation, Conciliation and Arbitration of the Organization of African Unity, "is obliged to settle disputes presented to it on the basis of principles of justice." In the next sentence, one reads about "fixing the principles of justice as the only or main basis for peaceful settlement." However, the Protocol of the Commission of Mediation, Conciliation and Arbitration of 1964,[2] provides in Article XXIX that the *compromis* may specify the law the parties wish to be

[1] *See also* my previous reviews at 77 AJIL 712 (1983) and 79 AJIL 850 (1985).
[2] *Cf.* 3 ILM 1116 (1964).

applied by the tribunal or, if they so agree, adjudication *ex aequo et bono;* if there is no pertinent provision in the *compromis,* Article XXX provides for different sources of international law to be applied (*ex aequo et bono* is mentioned only at the end, to be invoked "if the parties agree").

Among recent arbitration cases, there is a reference to the decision by the court of arbitration of 1977 in the *Beagle Channel* dispute, "ratified" by Queen Elizabeth II, and declared to constitute the award in accordance with the 1902 Santiago General Treaty of Arbitration. Chile's "fascist regime" is criticized, while Argentina's refusal to observe the award is not, and the kind of regime that prevailed there at that time is not mentioned. The Falkland Islands war is referred to, without mentioning, however, that the USSR made possible, by its abstention, the adoption of Resolution 502 of April 3, 1982 by the UN Security Council, determining that there had been a breach of the peace and demanding the immediate withdrawal of the Argentine forces.

One chapter is devoted to the Court of Justice of the European Communities. Of course, most of the latter's jurisdiction does not concern the settlement of disputes between states. This being the case, the attempt to deal comprehensively with the Court goes beyond the book's subtitle. Anyway, this chapter is very weak. There is heavy-handed party propaganda such as the following: "According to its sociopolitical aim, the Court is intended to protect the interests of the 'senior partners' of the Community and their multinational corporations . . . " (p. 110). Judgments going against the interests of multinationals—especially against the abuse of a dominant position within the Common Market prohibited by Article 86 of the EEC Treaty (e.g., cases 13/77 and 6/72[3])—and indicative of a general expression of proconsumer orientation (e.g., cases 27/76 and 85/76[4]) seem to be completely unknown. Also unknown—or too hard to admit—are the numerous cases decided by the Court in favor of "the weaker party" in areas such as social policy, social security for migrant workers, workers' rights and fundamental rights and freedoms.

On pages 113–14 there is mention of the settling of disputes between member states, as well as between these states and the organs of the Communities. That disputes between these organs alone are settled by the Court is probably not known to the author, though there are such cases (see, e.g., cases 81/72, 70/74, 218/82;[5] in a recent case, 34/86,[6] one organ that sued another organ was supported by three of the member states).

On the whole, Entin's knowledge of the decisions of the European Court of Justice seems to be extremely limited. Save for two decisions of the sixties, cited from the *Recueil de la Jurisprudence de la Court,* all the remaining ones are obviously quoted from two brochures distributed free of charge by the Information Offices of the European Communities and, evidently for this

[3] 1977 ECR 2115 and 1973 ECR 215, respectively.

[4] 1978 ECR 207 and 1979 ECR 461, respectively.

[5] 1973 ECR 575, 1975 ECR 795 and 1983 ECR 4063, respectively.

[6] Judgment of July 3, 1986, 47 Common Mkt. L.R. 3, 94 (1986).

reason, stop short at 1976. This goes against the author's promise on page 5 that he is going to concentrate on decisions of the seventies and early eighties.

The crudely negative appraisal of the work of the PCIJ is indefensible on any academic basis: "Essentially it [was] converted into a 'political organ' of the League of Nations and the capitalist states ruling it, and served the purpose of legitimizing imperialistic policy" (p. 32). The USSR, we are reminded, never recognized its competence, even after joining the League in 1934.

The ICJ is appraised less negatively, as an organ with "great democratic potential, capable of exerting a positive influence on the development of international relations" (*id.*). But the ICJ "handed down a number of judgments and consultative opinions, discrediting it in the eyes of public opinion and in the eyes of states" (p. 41). In the seventies, according to Entin, the ICJ "tried to rehabilitate itself" (p. 52). These alleged "rehabilitation efforts" are referred to again on page 59.

An extremely cursory review follows of the Court's judgments, advisory opinions and consultative conclusions on appeals from the decisions of the UN Administrative Tribunal between 1971 and 1982. Most of them are criticized by Entin; numerous dissenting opinions by Judge Morozov are quoted approvingly, without exception. Even concerning the *Gulf of Maine* case, the author echoes Morozov by criticizing the fact that the Chamber composed to hear this dispute between Canada and the United States was formed of judges "representing exclusively the bourgeois system of law" (p. 87).

On the whole, Entin maintains that

> [t]he practice of the ICJ in the seventies, the existence of individual positive elements notwithstanding, does not provide a basis for the conclusion that the Court had overcome the difficulties that characterized its activities in the previous period. . . . [I]n many cases, the activity of the Court did not correspond to the aims and tasks that were assigned to it by the UN Charter [p. 106].

If this is so, one may wonder whether even the 1986 Judgment in the *Nicaragua* case "rehabilitated" the ICJ in Entin's and some of his comrades' eyes. In a declaration by TASS on Nicaragua, the Judgment was referred to in just one sentence.[7]

Naturally, the decision will be praised in Soviet legal publications. But universal international adjudication is, in general, not treated very seriously by Entin and his like. As he stresses, "the Court does not enjoy the trust of the majority of states" (p. 34). Indeed, one may conclude that the ICJ would fully serve its purpose only if it were similar, say, to the Supreme Court of the USSR, especially in its totally "homogeneous" composition of obedient party members. Only then would those unspecified "certain conditions" alluded to by Entin be fulfilled, causing the ICJ "to serve as an important

[7] *Cf.* Pravda, June 30, 1986, at 5.

and useful instrument for settling disputes among states and for the defense of a *democratic* international legal order" (p. 4, italics added).

Entin's work, as it stands, should never have been published. Perhaps now, a few years later, the author himself regrets it. However that may be, occasional new winds seem to have started blowing in the USSR in this field as well: a 1986 article by E. Evgenyeva and F. Koshevnikov[8] represents a much more serious look at the ICJ.

Fair warning, though, is necessary. Mikhail Gorbachev's so-called new thinking, as applied to the realm of international law, is sometimes nothing more than a cover for the old, hard party line. In a recent article entitled *International Law or the Law of the Fist: New Thinking versus "Neo-Globalism,"* signed "V. Vereshchetin, Professor,"[9] the author dogmatically accuses the West, particularly the United States, of all possible violations of the basic principles of international law, including the right to self-determination and the *pacta sunt servanda* principle. Not the slightest Soviet violation, anywhere or ever, is even alluded to. In this case it is not "new thinking," but rather old doctrinal arrogance that is evident.

The basics of the Soviet system being as they are, much stronger impulses and much broader *glasnost* from above would be needed for a real breakthrough. Unfortunately, many "international" statements by the chief architect of the Soviet "new thinking" voiced, e.g., in Gorbachev's lengthy interview for *L'Unità*,[10] are not encouraging. The Cold War, one reads, was imposed by the West. When confronted with direct pertinent questions, he has not the least bit of self-criticism to offer on the 1968 aggression against Czechoslovakia. He maintains that the USSR has no spheres of influence whatsoever (even Afghanistan is allegedly no exception), does not aim at the creation of such spheres, and that opinions to the contrary are "deeply erroneous." If such pronouncements continue, probably not many basic changes can be expected in Soviet literature on international law.

RICHARD SZAWLOWSKI
Vancouver, B.C.

Negotiating World Order: The Artisanship and Architecture of Global Diplomacy. Edited by Alan K. Henrikson. Wilmington: Scholarly Resources Inc., 1986. Pp. xxx, 265. Index. $30.

A frequent criticism of blueprints for world order has been that "they don't tell us how to get there from here." This book, a product of the Negotiating World Order Project of the Fletcher School of Law and Diplomacy, is about the role of negotiation, or diplomacy, in the search for international order. The introductory framework set out by the editor, Alan K. Henrikson, involves a three-by-three matrix. On one axis are structures of world order—international, supranational and hegemonic. On the

[8] *Cf.* Evgenyeva & Koshevnikov, *The Role of the UN International Court in the peaceful solution of disputes,* SOVETSKOE GOSUDARSTVO I PRAVO, Oct. 1986, at 108 (in Russian).

[9] *Cf.* Pravda, Apr. 17, 1987, at 4.

[10] *Cf.* Pravda, May 20, 1987, at 1, 3–4.

other axis are the processes by which the orders are generated—negotiated, imposed and automatic (pp. xxi–xxii).

Actually, the book is about negotiations concerning international orders or more or less issue-specific regimes, rather than an encompassing world order or world government. The study is thus consonant with recent scholarship on efforts "to avoid anarchy, not through the construction of an ideal model of international governance, but by recognizing the validity of both realist and functionalist explanations of state behavior."[1] It is consistent also with recent scholarship showing that the pursuit of national self-interest assumed in Realist theory is not necessarily at odds with the development of regimes.[2]

The study converges on the now nearly standard definition of regime enunciated by Stephen Krasner[3] by defining "a world order" as "a regular . . . pattern . . . of relationships among nations that serves as a foundation for confident expectations about the future," encompassing principles, norms, rules and procedures (pp. xvi–xvii). "Order" reduces to "regime." Indeed, the two terms are used interchangeably (e.g., p. xvii). It is not apparent what benefit there is in preferring the term "order" to "regime." By substituting "regime" for "order" wherever the latter word occurs, the reader will be swimming in the currents of contemporary scholarship and avoiding the canonical evil of "nonadditivity."

The bulk of the work consists of 14 case studies by a well-selected group of thoughtful, senior men, all, except the editor, experienced negotiators. The studies are presented in four groups organized according to types of "bases of world order": (1) "Natural and Technological": food and health (Jean Mayer); acid rain (John Roberts); the sea (T. T. B. Koh); international communications (Leonard Marks); (2) "Cooperative and Strategic": the United Nations, collective security and peacekeeping (Brian Urquhart); "Star Wars" (Gerard C. Smith); nuclear nonproliferation (Joseph S. Nye, Jr.); the Madrid CSCE conference (Max Kampelman); (3) "Regional": the North Atlantic Alliance (Alan Henrikson); the OAS (Alejandro Orfila); ASEAN (Leonard Unger); (4) "Economic": international commodity markets (Gamani Corea); GATT (Gardner Patterson); and the international debt issue (Nathaniel Samuels).

The chapters were originally presented as lectures. They seem not to have been written in response to Henrikson's theoretical interest, and his introduction seems to have been a separate enterprise. Only some of the case studies provide evidence to fit the boxes of the matrix (p. 229) in the final chapter, in which Henrikson sums up and draws conclusions. He relies on historical sources and other writings for much of that. All the same, the case

[1] G. M. Lyons, The United Nations at Risk: Solutions and Prognoses (preliminary draft paper prepared for the 1987 Annual Meeting of the International Studies Association).

[2] Notably, R. O. Keohane, After Hegemony: Cooperation and Discord in the World Political Economy (1984); and R. Axelrod, The Evolution of Cooperation (1984).

[3] *See* Krasner, *Structural Causes and Regime Consequences: Regimes as Intervening Variables,* 36 Int'l Org. 185 (1982).

studies contain a good deal of information about the negotiations and the regimes with which they deal. They are generally of high quality, as is to be expected of such distinguished contributors. And the final chapter sets forth an interesting set of insights about the nature of the contemporary interactions between the processes and the resulting orders.

The case studies adequately document, and the concluding chapter appropriately underscores, the complexity of these interactions and the processes by which they occur. Unhappily, a compulsion for symmetry led Henrikson to search beyond the case studies for examples to fill all nine boxes of his matrix. Not all are fully convincing. Does the Islamic Conference, which he cites (pp. 225, 229) as an example of a supranational structure arrived at automatically, fit the original definition of an "order" given above—essentially, the anticipation of regularity in the future behavior of those who make up the order? Is the Islamic Conference, in short, a regime? Does that term fit the theoretical "pentapolarity" attributed by Richard Nixon and Henry Kissinger to the global power structure, which Henrikson describes (pp. 221–22, 229) as a structure of peace that remains "international," or basically pluralistic and egalitarian, but comes about automatically? The typology that figures prominently in the theoretical framework and in the conclusions seems less than totally persuasive. Moreover, some of the categories appear at best remotely relevant to the real issues of regime construction that confront us now and for the near term. How does it help to be told that the Versailles Treaty was an "imposed international" order (pp. 220, 229) or that, because of its "self-equilibrating character," the underlying regional balance gives NATO some qualities of automaticity—a dubious conclusion at best—although overall it is an example of a "negotiated hegemonic" structure (pp. 225–26, 229)?

The case studies, however, produce a richer crop than that, one that Henrikson's concluding chapter admirably harvests, when they focus on the conditions, catalysts and modalities of regime construction, maintenance and implementation. What emerges most clearly is the richness and variety of the experience. Only a few points can be noted here.

One important condition, among others (pp. 231–34), is the prior existence of the necessary knowledge to require and support a negotiated arrangement to deal with a problem. Jean Mayer emphasizes the importance of such knowledge as a condition for the development of international health regimes (p. 3), as does Leonard Marks for agreements affecting communication (pp. 52–53). Similarly, John Roberts emphasizes that the lack of shared understanding has been an obstacle to a Canadian-U.S. agreement on the control of acid rain (p. 25). These insights have to do with shared technological knowledge that either creates a problem or makes its solution possible, perhaps both. That is consistent with the recent focus of scholars on the importance of "consensual knowledge" as a basis for viable international agreements.[4] The process of seeking such consensus may itself

[4] *See, e.g.*, Haas, *Words Can Hurt You: Or, Who Said What to Whom About Regimes, id.* at 207; and Puchala, *The United Nations and Ecosystem Issues: Institutionalizing the Global Interest,* in POLITICS IN THE UNITED NATIONS SYSTEM 214 (L. S. Finkelstein ed. 1988).

be heavily political, as Nye demonstrates in the case of the International Nuclear Fuel Cycle Exercise (p. 86).

A second point is the importance attached by several of the authors to the need for changes in attitudes if further progress is to be made. Mayer (p. 15) and Urquhart (p. 59) agree on this with respect to the broad issues of world peace and security, and Corea makes the same point, in virtually identical language, about commodity negotiations (p. 177). The role of key individuals in bringing about such change is also a recurring theme (pp. 4, 36, 234).

When it comes to negotiations themselves, several points stand out. One is the importance attached to consensus as the decision mode, if reliable agreements are to be reached among states that remain sovereign. This was true of the negotiations on communication as described by Marks, trade as described by Patterson, and the law of the sea as described by Koh. Henrikson probes further in terms of Abba Eban's earlier distinction[5] between diplomacy, which requires "the adversary's agreement," and parliamentary process, which does not (p. 217). He concludes that this dichotomy does not penetrate deeply enough and that the fundamental issue is whether diplomacy, which seeks to engender confidence, can succeed in the absence of the world law and global institutions that he sees as the purpose of parliamentarianism (p. 217). His striking observation is that "[a]rchitecture is more necessary than artifice" (p. 218).

Is bilateralism or multilateralism the better way? The studies provide many examples of the need for both and of how the methods are dependent on each other. Nye's chapter on nuclear nonproliferation is particularly suggestive of the need for relying on concentric circles of participants, ranging from the bilateral, through small, to larger multilateral settings. The UNCLOS experience is consistent with that, as is GATT's. The importance of privacy in the early stages of seeking the grounds for agreement is emphasized in several of the chapters.

One paradox emerges from the volume and it deserves a concluding word. Several of the studies emphasize the importance of recognizing that the key to success is voluntary agreement because of the persistence of sovereignty. Mayer goes further and argues that an impediment to successful regimes in the fields of health and nutrition is that some countries lack the attributes of modern nationhood. In his words, "international agreements . . . require the solidity of established nations" (pp. 3–4). The emphasis on sovereignty is not wrong. Recent confirmation is to be found in Secretary of the Treasury Baker's observation that "[o]ne of the most difficult jobs in the world is coordinating economic policy. Of necessity, a country's domestic agenda has to come first unless you're going to cede sovereignty, and we're not going to do that."[6] Yet Mayer's own chapter shows the necessity of transcending sovereignty, both to produce the willingness of states to agree (pp. 5–6) and to ensure the fulfillment of what has been

[5] *See* A. EBAN, THE NEW DIPLOMACY: INTERNATIONAL AFFAIRS IN THE MODERN AGE (1983).

[6] Kilborn, *Can the Big Seven Learn to Waltz?*, N.Y. Times, May 31, 1987, §3 (Business), at 1, col. 1. This review was written in June 1987.

agreed (pp. 7–8). International governmental and nongovernmental organizations, indeed, individual opinion shapers, have critical roles to play in these respects. There are many instances of international regimes that could not exist, or work, if the rule of sovereignty prevailed and if the sole actors were the governments involved.

The point is important, especially in view of Henrikson's stress on the urgency of developing international "structure" and the emphasis in the volume on the need for attitudinal change if there is to be progress in that direction. This process certainly entails what Robert Keohane has recently called "changes in countries' definition of their own interests."[7] While many such changes must be internally generated, consistently with the rule of sovereignty, can there be success without internationally generated penetration of the walls of sovereignty to induce the international consensual understandings on which international agreements must rest?

LAWRENCE S. FINKELSTEIN
Northern Illinois University

La Plataforma Continental y su límite exterior. By Orlando Rubén Rebagliati. Buenos Aires: Editorial Universitaria de Buenos Aires, 1985. Pp. xv, 211.

"The Continental Platform and Its Outer Limit" follows the evolution of international law relating to the delimitation of the outer limit of coastal state sovereignty over the continental shelf. In doing so, the author, Orlando Rubén Rebagliati, pays particular attention to the development of this doctrine from the perspective of his home country, Argentina.

Following a brief introduction, the author discusses the significance of the outer edge of the continental shelf in both a geological and a geomorphological sense. He then proceeds to discuss the seabed enclosed by this boundary: the natural, living and mineral resources located therein and the interests of the coastal state in those resources.

Having established a context for discussion, the author, throughout the bulk of the study, undertakes a historical review of the outer limit of the continental shelf under international law. Rebagliati discusses in historical progression the early evolution of the concept of the continental shelf in the Americas (ch. 4); the work of the International Law Commission and the subsequent 1958 Conference on the Law of the Sea (ch. 5); the creation of the UN Deep Seabed Committee, various national interpretations of the 1958 Geneva Convention on the Continental Shelf and various unilateral national extensions of the shelf (chs. 6, 7 and 8); and the work of the Third UN Conference on the Law of the Sea (ch. 9). Notes to the text are collected at the end of the book, together with a rather extensive bibliography of Spanish and English sources. Annexes 1–8 reproduce major international agreements relating to the delimitation of the outer boundary of the conti-

[7] *See* R. O. Keohane, The Study of International Regimes and the Classical Tradition in International Relations (paper delivered at the 1986 Annual Meeting of the American Political Science Association).

nental shelf and a number of national declarations of Argentina (Annex 1: Decree 1.386 of January 24, 1944; Annex 3: Decree 14.708 of October 11, 1946; and Annex 4: Law 17.094 of December 29, 1966). Annexes 9–13 contain various maps depicting the offshore zones of Argentina and the physical structure of the underlying continental platform.

The work is a historical narrative and does not attempt explicitly to evaluate the end point at which we have arrived. Rebagliati's review of Latin American practice is particularly valuable. Among other things, he properly reminds us that Argentina's Decree of January 24, 1944 predates the Truman Proclamation. There is in the work at times, however, an undercurrent of natural law that is somewhat disquieting. In his conclusions, Rebagliati acknowledges the political compromise of the Third UN Conference on the Law of the Sea by which jurisdiction over the contiguous seabed is granted even to those coastal states that lack a continental shelf: "That compromise purports to close a question that remained open for many years and hopes to satisfy the interests of countries that possess a broad continental margin and those that lack it . . . ." However, the author does not appear to acknowledge equally that coastal state jurisdiction over the continental shelf generally is the result of a political choice and not the consequence of some natural right. For example, the author writes that

> the institution of the continental shelf [at UNCLOS III] ran the risk of disappearing in the new judicial concept of the exclusive economic zone, through the adoption of a maximum limit of . . . up to 200 miles. The institution of the continental shelf surpassed that last test and by doing so reached its own limit which takes into account the geomorphological reality.

Boundaries reflect political choices; that such boundaries may coincide with natural divisions does not alter the premise. When the notion of a common heritage of mankind over the deep seabed was proposed in 1967, the international right of coastal states to assert sovereignty over the adjacent seabed was generally thought to extend outward to a depth of 200 meters or further if the depth "admits of the exploitation of the natural resources of the said areas." The notion of a common heritage in part was a reaction to the potential of this definition to allow greater offshore claims by coastal states as technology permitted exploitation at greater distances. At the time of the proposal, the United Nations estimated on the basis of this definition that significant outlying petroleum deposits (physically on the continental shelf) likely lay beyond national jurisdiction and consequently would be a part of the common heritage. Ultimately, the coastal states in UNCLOS III chose to extend their jurisdiction over the contiguous continental shelf as far as could be said to be "naturally" possible, rather than reserving a portion of such areas as common heritage. The fact that the continental shelf is a "natural" extension of the continent should not disguise this political choice. The often unspoken assumption that coastal states possess a natural right to contiguous shelf area obscures the political choices that were made and confuses the political and legal analysis that should be made if competing offshore claims exist.

"The Continental Platform and Its Outer Limit" is a thorough historical review of the development of international law on the issue. It is particularly valuable for those wishing to understand better the positions of Latin America generally and Argentina specifically.

DAVID D. CARON
University of California, Berkeley

Permanent Sovereignty Over Natural Resources in International Law: Principle and Practice. Edited by Kamal Hossain and Subrata Roy Chowdhury. New York: St. Martin's Press, 1984. Pp. xx, 194. Index. $27.50.

Permanent sovereignty over natural resources was a leading theme of the debate about the "New International Economic Order" (NIEO) and the legal articulation of the Third World's goals of economic and political emancipation, revision of the international economic law formulated by the Western powers and acquisition of control over, and a maximal share in, the wealth derived from natural resources. Its heyday coincided with the peaking of world market prices of minerals in the 1970s, with the emergence of powerful state mining enterprises as a result of nationalizations and the renegotiation of investment arrangements, and with a sharp, antagonistic and as yet unresolved North/South debate. Much of the steam behind permanent sovereignty has evaporated: metal prices have fallen to their lowest levels in decades, the myth of ever-rising petroleum prices no longer holds true and state enterprises have not proven to be the cradle of economic development or the source of national wealth. These circumstances have repercussions on the legal debate. Kamal Hossain, former minister of law, foreign affairs and petroleum of Bangladesh, and Subrata Roy Chowdhury, a senior Indian government lawyer, both active in the International Law Association, combine extensive legal and political experience, which allows them to look at the issues with maturity, sobriety and an interest in building the consensus required for effective international law. They have assembled in the book under review a very interesting collection of essays by members of various national committees on permanent sovereignty of the International Law Association.

Hossain succinctly summarizes the major legal issues (pp. ix–xx): the legal implications of Resolution 3281 (as an opinion *de lege ferenda* or lawmaking?); the contemporary international law on nationalization; the right of governments to disregard contractual commitments to investors and home states assumed by previous governments, through legislation or renegotiation; the legal effect of stabilization clauses; and the juxtaposition of *rebus sic stantibus* and *pacta sunt servanda.* The most salient feature of this summary is the effort to delineate ground for consensus and hence for a universally accepted international law. This effort is noteworthy since the 1970s were characterized by the Third World's breaking away from the international law espoused by the West. Then the emphasis of the Third World was on unfettered national sovereignty. There is no trace of this attitude in Hossain and Chowdhury, and their professional and international legal experience may distinguish this mature position from the radicalism more typical of Third World doctoral candidates. In taking this stance, both authors seek to join with "like-minded" writers from Western countries (e.g., I. Brownlie, O. Schachter, R. Geiger, M. Muller and R. Dolzer) who have attempted to make the international law debate more a joint search for consensus than a face-off between radical demands and unyielding resistance to them.

Chowdhury assigns to permanent sovereignty the status of *jus cogens,* based on the almost unanimously voted Resolution 1803 of 1962 and the following sequence of reiterating resolutions. It then becomes essential to make this very general principle operative in particular circumstances. The implication of Chowdhury's position only becomes clear in the context of his discussion of specific issues. The first issue is that of compensation for nationalization. Between the Hull rule ("effective, full, and prompt") and the 1974 Charter rule ("compensation exclusively under the rules of the nationalizing state"), the author assumes "appropriate compensation" to be the current rule of international law. He thereby implicitly (but also explicitly) rejects the influence of the Calvo Doctrine on the formulations of the Charter (Art. 2(2)(c)). Appropriate compensation cannot be negated by exclusive application of national law; this standard is to be made operational by the "pertinent circumstances" method. The author's result is more practical and more likely to be generally acceptable than either the Hull rule or the Calvo Doctrine: it is in tune with actual compensation practice (as contrasted with the paper practice of investment treaties) and with modern arbitration cases. It provides sufficient scope for lawyers, arbitrators and negotiators to find an equitable solution by looking at the specific circumstances of an individual case. Chowdhury rejects the many propositions to make a technical accounting method (net present value, book value) a standard of law, as these methods are often but a label for subjective judgments, dependent on techniques developed for another purpose in a particular economy and lacking sufficient leeway for the traditional lawyering skills of balancing and combining general principles and the specific facets of individual cases.

The second issue tackled is the legal validity of stabilization clauses in investment agreements purporting to restrain the legislative power of the contracting state. According to a strict view of permanent sovereignty as *jus cogens* (propounded by Jiménez de Aréchaga), such promises by governments contradict the inalienability of permanent sovereignty and are *ultra vires* and void. Chowdhury's position is more sophisticated and more practical: while supporting in principle the argument of *jus cogens* and *ultra vires,* he recognizes that stabilization provisions may be "acceptable under certain conditions" (p. 31) and that their "breach . . . has legal consequences and will give right . . . to compensation" (p. 39). He demands "careful scrutiny" if a clause "amounts to an alienation of sovereignty." The author's perspective is most reasonable: few would deny that it is excessive to prevent a country from introducing modern standards of environmental protection applicable to offshore oil extraction into a contract of 30 years' duration; no developed country would suffer such limits on its legislative sovereignty and, in particular, common law countries emphasize that the legislature's sovereignty cannot be fettered. On the other hand, it is equally hard to deny that enacting a new tax one year after the start of commercial production from a high-risk mining project, disrupting its financial equilibrium and affecting its viability and debt service, seems a breach of good faith. In addition, credible assurances of contract and fiscal stability reduce political risk, and hence attract otherwise unavailable investment and increase the government's taxing power. Thus, the practical solution lies in a balanced view of the specific circumstances. While this may not be as predictable as a clear test accepting or rejecting the stabilization clause, it reminds lawyers and negotiators to be more prudent as to the effect of a watertight contractual arrangement supposed to be immutable for a generation.

Renegotiation obtained by a state based on its legislative powers is viewed by Chowdhury as a corollary of nationalization. As such, renegotiation entitles one to compensation. Here, being an international public lawyer, the author in our view might have benefited from looking more closely at contract law. Renegotiation is first a matter of contract law, and contract law provides a number of remedies allowing, or triggering, a right to renegotiate. Renegotiation becomes a matter of concern for international law when the free consent to renegotiate a new quid pro quo, this essential element of freedom unaffected by government action (threatened or actual), is substantially affected. The line between "normal" and "coerced" renegotiation is often hard to draw.

While the Charter of 1974 (Art. 2(2)(c)) can be read as excluding any arbitration and as favoring exclusive national jurisdiction (i.e., as an incorporation of the Latin American Calvo Clause), Chowdhury locates a "gap" in the Charter and fills it by reference to Resolution 1803, recognizing international dispute settlement. In Chowdhury's view—which is not too explicit or too clear—submission to international arbitration by governments cannot be assailed by reference to permanent sovereignty. Resolution 1803 could only be invoked against arbitration if such submission were not a product of the free will of equal bargaining partners.

Chowdhury's interpretation and application of permanent sovereignty to specific controversial issues is eminently reasonable. It mellows the one-sidedness of both the Calvo Doctrine and the strict sanctity-of-contract schools and produces criteria that lawyers, arbitrators and negotiators can apply to specific circumstances. In addition, unlike some elaborate academic theories of international law, which are tainted by ideology, his method is close to real business practices, which the author attempts to understand, incorporate and use as much as possible.

The Dutch contribution to the book (Paul Peters, Nico Schrijver and Paul de Waart) demonstrates that traditional international law is still alive. The authors basically repeat the classic reasoning of Arbitrator Dupuy in the *Texaco / Calasiatic v. Libya* case: an unqualified principle of *pacta sunt servanda* applies to investment agreements; and stabilization clauses not only are fully effective, but also—without so stipulating—make international law applicable (p. 123). All that is left to permanent sovereignty is to "underline, with regard to natural resources, the importance of a spirit of cooperation" (p. 125). This reasoning—in consistency and quality quite a decline from Dupuy's famous restatement of classic doctrine—seems to rest on two pillars. First, the Dutch group asserts that the main objective of the NIEO was to promote foreign investment (pp. 94, 109). The only reference to this assertion, completely contrary to the anti–transnational corporation and anti–foreign investment philosophy that the Third World adopted in UN forums in 1974, is an oblique reference to a minor paper by a small office of the UN Secretariat (UNCTC) and to the Brandt report (p. 133 n.90), both documents that by necessity had to accommodate the official Western view. Similar sloppiness occurs when the Dutch team asserts that the "*ius cogens*" concept was supported only by Libya (p. 95). In a confusing discussion of the Vienna Convention on the Law of Treaties—not per se applicable to investment contracts—the authors assume without question the applicability of *pacta sunt servanda* but execute a bizarre dance around *rebus sic stantibus,* which they consider as "normally" not an applicable consideration but as a reason "to stimulate the parties to review . . . the terms of their contract."

The second main pillar of their argument is an analysis of 183 bilateral investment treaties. In spite of both spirited attacks by the authors on their countryman M. Muller for ignoring this practice and a section entitled "Significance of the Bilateral Investment Treaties," it is not clear what conclusions the authors draw from that practice, apart from their remark that it negates the effect of permanent sovereignty resolutions. A close look at the facts presented by the Dutch group indicates, to the contrary, that most of these treaties do not include the leaders of the Third World (India, Brazil, Mexico, Argentina, Algeria and Nigeria) as parties and that 92 percent of them do not deal with the alteration of investment terms by subsequent legislation. The few references given (p. 120) apparently opt for full effect to be given to such legislation. One can speculate—the authors do not—about why there is so much reluctance to deal with this issue; the most likely response is that few governments, if any, were ready to have their legislative sovereignty restricted by such treaties.

The authors' understanding of the motivation behind bilateral treaties is not particularly realistic. Governments of developing countries do not enter into them because they wish to state a view on international law, but because they expect—probably mostly in vain—some benefit in the form of additional investment and are therefore ready to recognize in a limited context and with a limited scope what they are otherwise not ready to accept. The Dutch paper does not contribute very much, and it misses the opportunity to restate the Dupuy position in a carefully, consistently and reasonably argued modern way.

The last contribution, by David Flint, presents the views of Australia, a resource-rich country. He aligns himself largely with Chowdhury. On renegotiation, Flint considers the widespread business practice of renegotiation to be more indicative of current state practice than the few arbitral awards. In fact, it is hard to see how one can compare the opinions of a few old men with the actions of a large number of governments. He considers the effect of the Charter as at least derogating from the universal validity of postulated principles of traditional international law.

The result of this worthwhile collection is to delineate at least the contours of a possible consensus on international investment law. In addition, one should consider permanent sovereignty as a defense of the weaker members of the international community against exploitation of this weakness. It is hard to see how India or Brazil could rely on it. But the principle might still be used to control the contract-making power of often short-lived and not very legalistic governments in favor of the more permanent national interest they are supposed to serve. It might accordingly have a useful function in reminding negotiators that making unusual deals with weak, inexperienced and corrupt governments, particularly where fairness as judged by contemporary industry practices is not manifest, is a shaky business with little claim to sanctity of contract. Apart from this defensive function, there is a cooperative dimension to the principle: permanent sovereignty may not just be a matter for nations, but also for mankind. Resources should be developed in the interest of mankind. This environmental and cooperative dimension of permanent sovereignty deserves more emphasis than the dimension frequently found in the writings of international jurists, in which considerations of investment security and national sovereignty are used to repeat hollow clashes.[1]

THOMAS W. WÄLDE*
United Nations

Nationalisations Imposées—Nationalisations Négociées. By Marie-Chantal Boutard-Labarde. Paris: Presses Universitaires de France, 1984. Pp. 157.

This book does not precisely cover what its title suggests. Regrettably, it does not compare the substantive conditions of "imposed" nationalizations with those informally agreed upon in voluntary transfers of ownership from an alien to a host country. At the current time, such a comparison would serve a special purpose in the continuing discussion of the proper sources and the proper substance of the rules on compensation. This study rather

[1] I am grateful for the reference to this "cooperative dimension" of permanent sovereignty to a member of the Bangladesh committee of the ILA during a presentation on permanent sovereignty in Dhaka.

* Since 1981 the author has been responsible for the biannual reports of the Secretary-General on "permanent sovereignty over natural resources." This review represents solely the personal views of the author and not necessarily those of the United Nations.

focuses on legal techniques and mechanisms invented and applied by developing states that lack the financial, economic, commercial or technical resources required for a comprehensive takeover and the subsequent management of the enterprise concerned. Mainly during the "decade of nationalizations" in the 1970s, the politically inspired call for "economic decolonization," as reflected in the Charter of Economic Rights and Duties of States (1974), prompted nationalization programs accompanied by such domestic circumstances. There are no accurate statistics on numbers, areas and techniques of expropriations of aliens for that period, but the typical developing state nationalizing a foreign business had not, or not yet, acquired the money and expertise to take over the business and run it in an efficient manner. Boutard-Labarde is concerned with the legal infrastructure of these nationalization programs, i.e., the types of cooperative schemes involved in the progressive acquisition of ownership, the commercial elements of management and the technical expertise for industrially advanced projects. The first section of the book also addresses matters of "imposed nationalizations," with a certain emphasis on institutions designed to determine the amount of compensation. On the whole, this short treatment remains very much on the surface of the legal issues, and no contribution is made to the scholarship on the matters touched upon.

The chapters dealing with the voluntary transfer of ownership and with postnationalization schemes of cooperation with alien owners deserve more attention. Even though most of the materials and information relied upon have been treated or published previously (see mainly the 1975 Hague lectures by Ahmed El-Kosheri[1]), the author has collected a few documents so far not generally accessible. In the light of the widespread reluctance of the parties concerned to reveal any details in this area, this achievement deserves praise.

With regard to the transfer of property, various types of sales to the host country of alien-held projects (*la formule classique de transfert*) and certain less orthodox approaches are presented. Concerning commercial and technical aspects of the nationalized business, the author first distinguishes and describes mainly instances of cooperation with the previous owner and arrangements with a new partner. The author subsequently discusses various approaches to the acquisition of commercial and technical know-how by those countries that opted for the acquisition of partial ownership rights, whether in the form of minority, majority or parity interests. An annex contains four agreements (three of them previously published) entered into by Peru, Iraq and state-owned entities from the Congo and Morocco that illustrate some of the legal techniques discussed. It is not clear why these arrangements in particular were chosen.

As for the scope of the literature surveyed and discussed, contributions in languages other than French seldom rank prominently in this study. Following the mainstream of French scholarship in international law, the major

[1] El-Kosheri, *Le Régime juridique créé par les accords de participation dans le domaine pétrolier,* 145 Recueil des Cours 219 (1975 IV).

strength of the study pertains to the elegance, at times extravagance, of its classifications and systematizations. Beyond this distinct contribution, the study does not rise above the descriptive. No effort is made to analyze the issues that are of more practical concern from a lawyer's perspective: indirect expropriation, the borderline between forced and voluntary sales, or stabilization clauses. The "new forms of investments" such as service contracts, production-sharing arrangements and franchise contracts, to which the author in part refers, were generally favored in investment programs in the period reviewed. They were not restricted, as the reader of this book might believe, to postnationalization strategies. The only special element in the latter arrangements has been, in the pertinent jargon, the various "sweeteners" for the investors as compromise elements in the complex negotiations dealing simultaneously with the consequences of nationalizations and the possibilities for further cooperation.

During a period of sluggish growth for the world economy, with the attendant slowdown of exports, and as excessive debt and tightened conditions confront developing countries in the international financial markets, the political symbolism inherent in many nationalization programs in the past decade has lost much of its special appeal. The drive toward expropriation of the 1970s thus seems unlikely to be repeated in the near future. From the academic point of view, this book will retain some interest because of the broad basis of the compiled material and the plausibility of the categories on which it has been organized.

RUDOLF DOLZER
Max Planck Institute for Comparative Public Law and International Law, Heidelberg

Closed Borders: The Contemporary Assault on Freedom of Movement. By Alan Dowty. New Haven and London: Yale University Press, 1987. Pp. xvii, 270. Index. $20.

The freedom to move among states, celebrated in human rights conventions and exercised by people throughout history, is fundamental to our sense of self-determination and well-being. Yet all states, even the most liberal, limit this freedom to some degree; many flagrantly violate it. In this timely book, Alan Dowty, a political scientist at Notre Dame, delivers a status report on the restrictions that states have imposed on emigration. (He also discusses limits on immigration, but the analysis on this point is relatively summary and unilluminating.)

Dowty traces the history of national restrictions on emigration from classical slavery through medieval serfdom, mercantilist edicts, mass expulsions and forced colonizations, to the modern era. He shows how these techniques have been used to consolidate political power, unify national cultures, hoard valued economic skills and export dissent. A "liberal interlude," heralded by Locke, Adam Smith and the public law writers, occurred during the 18th and 19th centuries. Many restrictions on movement were relaxed in most western European countries, with the notable exception of underpopulated

France. But the resulting migration flows to America and within Europe led to the imposition of new controls on immigration after World War I, reducing the practical value of the freedom to emigrate, which by then was widely proclaimed.

A "new serfdom" was established between the world wars as harsh regimes, armed with new techniques of human and border control and collectivist theories of national domination and racial purity, coerced and limited movement. As Dowty puts it, "most who moved did not want to, and most who wanted to move could not" (p. 56). World War II flooded Europe and Asia with refugees and left economic devastation in its wake, creating new migratory pressures. These were further exacerbated by the postwar struggles against the colonial empires and the Soviet domination of Eastern Europe, which often led to oppressive policies of political consolidation. New forms of nationalism, collectivist ideology and repression were established, of which the Berlin Wall, Soviet exit restrictions and the expulsion of the boat people of Southeast Asia are only among the most vivid examples. Indeed, as Dowty emphasizes, perhaps the most striking pattern of the contemporary assault on freedom of movement is that many states, especially Marxist regimes, combine mass expulsions with restricted emigration.

In broad outline, at least, these developments are familiar. Dowty's approach is essentially descriptive and hortatory. He relies almost entirely upon existing sources such as UN data and published studies; the book contains few fresh facts or insights and breaks no new analytical ground. What he does do, however, is to bring together in one volume the major elements of this tragic story: the historical patterns, the evolution and persistent violation of legal principles favoring free movement, the changing pressures to restrict it and the political constraints within which any enduring solution must operate.

The value of this contribution is exemplified by one of Dowty's few extended analytical passages—his critique of the "brain drain" argument, which is often used to justify limiting emigration. He notes that this concern originated in Europe, not the Third World; that many countries that decry the brain drain simultaneously encourage low-skill workers to leave; that many states with high rates of emigration also experience high economic growth rates; that many developing states are scarcely affected by a brain drain; that many of the professionals who wish to migrate (as in Haiti, where almost 75 percent of the skilled manpower has left since 1950) are responding to political pressures, not just economic opportunity; that the problem is less the pull of the developed societies than the push of inadequate demand for those skills at home; and that there is little correlation among states between actual brain drain and efforts to limit emigration. Dowty concludes that the issue is primarily a symbolic one, deployed by some developing nations in an effort to extract political and economic concessions from their more industrialized competitors.

Less satisfactory is Dowty's final chapter. He begins by asking an important question: why has the right of free movement, which is so flagrantly violated, attracted so little public attention? His answers seem convincing.

The most crucial is that "*all* states find the implications of free movement somewhat disturbing. If some nations do not want to lose people, others do not want to gain them" (p. 223). He goes on, however, to dismiss the industrialized nations' concerns about large-scale immigration. Labor migrations, he says, "are usually temporary and (in theory) controllable" (p. 226), an assertion that is flatly contradicted by the European guest-worker programs and American experience. He also says that other potential immigrants are not numerous, a statement that cannot be verified so long as existing restrictions remain in place.

Dowty concludes that "constraint of free movement does not appear to serve any legitimate social or national interest" (*id.*). He may be correct that permitting free emigration would help rather than harm source countries, especially if they also pursued economic development and national integration through policies emphasizing free markets and competitive politics. But his broad, unequivocal claim is highly debatable as applied to immigration. In a world of easy transportation, vastly different wealth levels and social policies among states, and extremely fragile balances among rivalrous cultural and social groups, it seems fatuous to deny that societies do indeed have legitimate interests in limiting who may enter and become members. This may or may not be regrettable, depending upon how one evaluates the effects on the labor market and balances the imperatives of national self-definition and social cohesion in the receiving states and the imperatives of flight from the source states. What seems clear is that freedom of movement will become firmly established in the pantheon of precious human rights only when we are able to reconcile the receiving states' genuine national interests. Unfortunately, as this valuable book grimly documents, we seem to be moving away from, rather than toward, that noble goal.

PETER H. SCHUCK
Yale Law School

New Horizons in International Criminal Law. Edited by M. Cherif Bassiouni. Published by the International Association of Penal Law, 1985. Pp. 156.

This book is a report on an international conference sponsored by the International Institute of Higher Studies in Criminal Sciences[1] (ISISC) on the "New Horizons in International Criminal Law." The participants came from 24 countries and covered a wide range of legal systems. Among them were representatives of 55 universities and academic institutions; ministries of 12 countries, including ten from ministries of justice, one from a ministry of the interior and one from a ministry of defense; and five international

[1] The institute is located in Syracuse, Sicily and is a public foundation with academic purposes. It was founded in 1972 to provide specialized postgraduate educational and training programs and to conduct other scholarly activities in the criminal justice sciences. It was developed as a joint effort of the International Association of Penal Law, which is the scientific sponsor, and of the City, Province and Chamber of Commerce of Syracuse and the Sicilian Region, which are the financial sponsors.

organizations. The book includes reports on the various items on the agenda, the conclusions and recommendations of the conference, and three appendixes.

The editor served as the conference chairman and participated in the sessions. He recognizes that in view of the caliber of the participants, the publication of all the papers and interventions would have had a more scholarly impact.[2] However, it was decided at the conference that the needed policy impact could be attained by having every reporter write an account of his or her topic. The reports are concise, well written and cover the highlights of the papers and interventions.

The following topics were covered during the conference: *The Origins, Development, and Expanding Scope of International Criminal Law* (Farook Hassan, Willamette University); *The Codification of International Criminal Law* (Daniel Derby, Touro College); *International Criminal Law and Human Rights* (Anthony D'Amato, Northwestern University); *New Horizons in the Regulation of Armed Conflicts* (Jacques Verhaegen, Catholic University of Louvain); *Protection of the Environment* (Alfonso Stile, University of Naples); *The International Penal Aspects of Protection of National and Archaeological Treasures* (Shoshana Berman, District Court of Israel); *Expansion of Extraterritorial Penal Jurisdiction* (Michele Rusca, Federal Ministry of Justice and Police, Fribourg); *Expanding Scope of Extradition and Judicial Assistance and Cooperation in Penal Matters* (Julian Schutte, Ministry of Justice, The Hague); and *Enforcement Models of International Criminal Law* (Robert A. Friedlander, Ohio Northern University).

The need to identify the existing international criminal law is stressed. The report of Professor Bassiouni on his research concerning the existing conventions within the domain of international criminal law[3] (he found 312 treaties that deal in various ways with about 22 different areas within the broad field of international criminal law by using eight characteristics) represents a valuable contribution to the definition of the scope of the existing law. It may be used as a basis for determining what should be included in the future. But his work is only a beginning; additional study of this subject and the methodology to be used is needed. Professor C. Lombois (University of Paris II) questioned whether the eight characteristics used by Bassiouni were of equal validity and whether the 22 subjects in the field were of the same importance.

Suggestions of fields in which future attention is needed are reported under each topic (e.g., the current advances in technology such as computers, genetics and scientific—but unlawful—medical experimentation, identification of the global interests of the world community in combating criminal activities and the violations that warrant penal sanctions). There are cautions against overcriminalization and suggestions for using measures

[2] He indicates that these materials are already finding their way into academic and scholarly publications.

[3] A full report of his research may be found in M. C. BASSIOUNI, INTERNATIONAL CRIMES: DIGEST/INDEX OF INTERNATIONAL INSTRUMENTS, 1815–1985 (1986). Reviewed at 80 AJIL 998 (1986).

other than penal sanctions for controlling some international criminal activities. Views on the desirability of establishing an "International Criminal Code" are reported. The discussions on this point, in large measure, track the "Draft International Criminal Code" prepared by Bassiouni between 1978 and 1980.[4]

Various means by which international criminal law may be created and the problems connected with them are set forth. The treatment of the advantages of proceeding by way of bilateral rather than multilateral treaties and of whether the treaties should be general or limited to specific crimes is noteworthy. It is refreshing that some participants acknowledged the ease with which signatures to, and even ratification of, treaties may be obtained, as opposed to the difficulty in securing their implementation.

The concern caused by the ineffective implementation of existing conventions is mirrored by the characterization by Professor Sharon Williams (York University) of the Genocide Convention as "a toothless mosquito." Various enforcement models of international criminal law are discussed. Professor Gerhard O. W. Mueller (Rutgers University) suggests an inventory of existing enforcement models relating to international criminal law, and offers 13 possible approaches to enforcement ranging from the use of the International Court of Justice to the codification of enforcement models for the development of international criminal law.[5]

The possibility of merging various Council of Europe conventions on international cooperation into a single document is presented by Ekkehard Muller-Rappard (Council of Europe). The discussion of the comprehensive legislation of Switzerland, Austria and the Federal Republic of Germany covering the four main kinds of assistance in penal matters (i.e., extradition, mutual assistance in criminal matters, transfer of proceedings and the transfer of the enforcement of criminal judgments) could be of great assistance to all involved in drafting legislation on the subject. The report of the presentation of Professor B. James George (New York Law School) on the approach of U.S. authorities to the conclusion and application of treaties on mutual assistance, extradition and the transfer of prisoners states, "These policies are based on reciprocity rather than on confidence in the standards of practice in other states." This is at least incomplete in view of the unilateral enactment by the United States of legislation on assistance to foreign and international tribunals and to litigants before such tribunals.[6]

In Appendix I the editor gives an excellent description of the activities in the field of criminal justice of the United Nations, its specialized agencies and the specialized institutes affiliated with the United Nations; other regional multinational organizations; and nongovernmental organizations.

[4] The draft was submitted to the sixth UN congress in Caracas (1980) and is under consideration by the International Law Commission as part of the work on the Draft Code of Offences Against the Peace and Security of Mankind. *See* UN Doc. A/CN.4/SR.1823, at 3 (1984).

[5] With reference to the codification model, he cites the 1975 United Nations Standard Minimum Rules for Treatment of Prisoners as establishing a viable model for future expansion.

[6] 28 U.S.C. §1782 (1982).

In Appendix II he reports on the joint scientific activities of the International Association of Penal Law and its Institute of Higher Studies in Criminal Sciences with the United Nations and the Council of Europe.

Appendix III consists of the General Report of the International Association of Penal Law on New Dimensions of Criminality and Crime Prevention in the Context of Development: Challenges for the Future;[7] and the editor's commentary to the UN Guiding Principles for Crime Prevention and Criminal Justice in the Context of Development and a New International Economic Order.

The book is an excellent guide to the problems of attaining the dream of an enforceable international criminal law. It should be in the library of all who have a general interest in the subject.

WILLIAM SUMNER KENNEY
Of the District of Columbia Bar

Studies and essays on international humanitarian law and Red Cross principles in honour of Jean Pictet. By Christophe Swinarski. Geneva: International Committee of the Red Cross; The Hague: Martinus Nijhoff Publishers, 1984. Pp. lviii, 1143. Index. Dfl.150; $50.

This volume, containing 82 essays by experts in international humanitarian law, was published in honor of Jean Pictet's 70th birthday. The authors bear witness to the importance of Pictet as the foremost jurist of the International Committee of the Red Cross (ICRC) and guiding force behind the Geneva Conventions of 1949 and their Additional Protocols of 1977. The editor of this collection, Christophe Swinarski, is a senior legal officer of the ICRC in Geneva; his own contribution focuses on the notion of the neutral organization in international law.

This impressive and doubly weighty volume (figuratively and literally, because of its 1,201 pages) is divided into five sections covering (1) problems relating to the 1949 Geneva Conventions, (2) problems relating to the 1977 Protocols, (3) general problems of international humanitarian law, (4) problems of international human rights and of public international law in relation to international humanitarian law, and (5) theory and practice of the international Red Cross movement. Forty-two essays are in French, 31 in English, 5 in German and 4 in Spanish, thus reflecting the international impact of the Red Cross. Although Western European authors predominate, there are distinguished contributors from Latin America (Julio Barberis, Héctor Gros Espiell, Hernán Montealegre), Asia (Shigeki Miyazaki, Nagendra Singh, Enrique Syquia, Masayuki Takemoto), the Middle East (Georges Abi-Saab, Iqbal Al-Fallouji, Yoram Dinstein, Shabtai Rosenne), Africa (Medard Rwelamira) and Eastern Europe (Remigiusz Bierzanek, Igor Blishchenko, Bernhard Graefrath, Manfred Lachs,

[7] Prepared by Professor Mueller and submitted to a preparatory congress for the Seventh United Nations Congress on the Prevention of Crime and the Treatment of Offenders.

Stanislaw Nahlik, Konstantin Obradovic, Sava Penkov). American authors are also represented. The brief contribution by W. Hays Parks, Chief of International Law, Office of the Judge Advocate General of the Army, on Pictet's commentaries to the Geneva Conventions of 1949, the longer piece by George Aldrich, U.S. arbitrator on the Iran–United States Claims Tribunal, on the 1977 Geneva Protocols, and the reflections on humanitarian law by David Forsythe, Professor of Political Science at the University of Nebraska, are worth noting.

In such an extensive work, it is difficult to select which essays to discuss. This reviewer was particularly impressed by the study of René Kosirnik, Chief of the ICRC's legal department, on the protection of refugee camps in times of armed conflict. After describing the attacks on the Namibian refugee camp of Kassinga (Angola) and on the Palestinian refugee camps of Sabra and Chatila (Lebanon), he reviews the work of Felix Schnyder, former UN High Commissioner for Refugees, on the preparation of a declaration prohibiting military attacks on refugee camps. Kosirnik notes with regret that "*Realpolitik*" prevented a consensus on its adoption. Nevertheless, the Geneva Conventions and the Additional Protocols apply and should prevent the repetition of such massacres. He refers to Article 51(2) of Protocol I, which provides that "the civilian population as such, as well as individual civilians, shall not be the object of attack. Acts of violence the primary purpose of which is to spread terror among the civilian population are prohibited"; and to Article 51(6), which states, "Attacks against the civilian population or civilians by way of reprisals are prohibited."

Jiří Toman, deputy director of the Henry Dunant Institute in Geneva, provides a scholarly and concise account of the legal and institutional framework established for the protection of cultural property in international armed conflict. After mentioning the adoption of the Hague Convention at a 1954 conference held under the auspices of UNESCO (the Convention entered into force in 1956), Toman traces the developments leading to the adoption of the Convention Concerning the Protection of the World Cultural and Natural Heritage (which entered into force in 1975) and analyzes the most important provisions of both Conventions, the mandate of UNESCO in the protection of cultural property in time of war and the role of the ICRC.

The thoughtful piece by Sean MacBride, one of the founders of Amnesty International, focuses on the legality of weapons for societal destruction, and recalls that immediately after the atomic bombs fell on Hiroshima and Nagasaki, the ICRC sent a circular letter to all national Red Cross Societies drawing their attention to the vast new dangers created by nuclear weapons. It is obvious that nuclear weapons, which cannot distinguish between civilian populations and combatants, come within the prohibition contained in Article 48 of Additional Protocol I. Logically, it would seem that humanitarian law requires immediate nuclear disarmament.

Some of the most stimulating articles in this collection are devoted to the relationship of international human rights law and humanitarian law. According to Dr. Pictet, "International humanitarian law, in the broad sense, is constituted by all the international legal provisions, whether of statute or common law, ensuring respect for the individual and promoting his development." Thus, humanitarian law goes beyond "the law of The Hague," or law of war proper, which determines the rights and duties of belligerents in the conduct of operations and limits the means of doing harm, and "the law of Geneva," which is intended to safeguard military personnel placed *hors de combat* and persons not taking part in hostilities. In his high-spirited essay, Enrique Syquia, Professor at the Catholic University of the Philippines, argues that the law of The Hague and the law of Geneva are both parts of the law of armed conflict, itself only a component of international humanitarian law, which should be understood as also including the whole field of human rights in peacetime. Syquia welcomes the progressive interrelation of the law of war and human rights law and honors Pictet as one of the originators of this process.

As in every collection of articles, there are some that deserve less praise. A few authors, for instance, have succumbed to the temptation to politicize issues in the light of an East-West confrontation. Others are rather weak in their research and methodology. For instance, and notwithstanding the importance of the subject matter, the essay by Mr. Patrnogic, *Some reflections on humanitarian principles applicable to relief actions,* appears to have been hastily assembled from better argued and generally available published sources. No footnotes are given. Some portions of this chapter, including entire paragraphs as well as lines of argument, seem to have been drawn, without due acknowledgment, from prior publications of Dr. Peter Macalister-Smith, a well-known writer, whose 1980 thesis, *International Humanitarian Assistance,*[1] and articles, *Human Rights and Disaster Relief* (1980) and *The EEC and International Humanitarian Assistance* (1981), analyzed the issues more extensively and cogently than is done here.

Although a certain overlapping is inevitable in a collective publication of this nature, some important topics seem to have been overlooked, like the relevance of international humanitarian law to compulsory population transfers and the related phenomenon of mass exoduses for economic and other reasons. An article on the 1981 UN Declaration on the Elimination of All Forms of Intolerance and of Discrimination Based on Religion or Belief[2] would have been welcome considering the many domestic and international conflicts that originate in religious fanaticism.

The volume ends with an extensive subject index in English, accompanied by a table of corresponding terms from French, German and Spanish into English. A 20-page list of international agreements and a 34-page bibliography are also included.

As Denise Bindschedler-Robert noted in her foreword,

> there are very few jurists in our times whose careers have been as exceptional as Jean Pictet's; who have, like him, been able not only to guide the process of codification but also to participate in it, to inter-

[1] Reviewed at 79 AJIL 1113 (1985).
[2] GA Res. 36/55 (Nov. 25, 1981).

> pret the law thus created, and furthermore be called upon to take part in its application.

Pictet deserves our praise and admiration.

ALFRED-MAURICE DE ZAYAS

A Guide to the Civil Jurisdiction and Judgments Convention. By Alan Dashwood, Richard Hacon and Robin White. Deventer: Kluwer Law and Taxation Publishers, 1987. Pp. xlii, 604. Index. Dfl.265; £94.50; $129.

The guide begins with 60 pages of commentary describing the scope of the EEC's Convention on Jurisdiction and the Enforcement of Judgments in Civil and Commercial Matters and explaining the Convention's rules regarding jurisdiction, recognition and enforcement of judgments, and certain peripheral matters. The remainder of the book consists of an annotated text of the Convention, as well as various related documents and the crucial preparatory reports by Jenard and Schlosser.

Only the United Kingdom's implementing legislation is provided, although the authors express the wish that future editions include the legislation of other contracting states. The excellent annotations focus on the preparatory reports and decisions of the European Court; national decisions are ignored except with regard to the UK implementing legislation. For other national decisions, readers are referred to the European Court's *Digest of Case Law relating to the European Communities,* Series D. American readers will note that the guide gives due respect to complaints about one of the Convention's most troublesome aspects: that while under Articles 3 and 4, EEC domiciliaries are protected from exorbitant bases of jurisdiction, a judgment against a person not domiciled in one of the contracting states *must* be enforced even if it is based upon the exercise of exorbitant jurisdiction.

The authors correctly point out that the Convention "represents the most substantial achievement to date of the Member States of the European Community in carrying through the programme of legal reconstruction Article 220 of the EEC Treaty enjoins upon them." This book meets the need for an English-language reference source concerning the Convention and will be very helpful to those who would otherwise lack access to the basic documents and preparatory reports. Those who have access to those documents (found in the *Official Journal of the European Communities*) may be disappointed to find that most of the guide's 604 pages are committed to reproducing them.

DAVID G. LITT
University of Chicago

Biographical Dictionary of Modern Peace Leaders. Editor-in-Chief, Harold Josephson. Westport and London: Greenwood Press, 1985. Pp. xxvii, 1133. Index. $85.

Harold Josephson's *Biographical Dictionary of Modern Peace Leaders* is a companion volume to the *Biographical Dictionary of Internationalists,* reviewed in this *Journal* in 1984.[1] *Peace Leaders* provides biographical descriptions of about seven hundred people who have been identified in some way with peace movements during the years from 1800 more or less up to the present.

While this book complements the earlier volume (numerous individuals are cross-referenced in the two books), it has a slightly different focus. "Peace leaders," as a group, are generally defined as people who have been outside the conventional foreign policy/international affairs establishments. Therefore, statesmen, e.g., presidents, prime ministers, secretaries of state and foreign ministers, were categorized as "internationalists" rather than as "peace leaders." This definition is confused by the inclusion of Chou En-lai, Tomáš G. Masaryk, Jawaharlal Nehru, Tsar Nicholas II and several others who are most commonly remembered in the context of their service to their governments. Perhaps more typical of the people described in *Peace Leaders* are Bertha von Suttner, Frederic Passy, Romain Rolland, Dietrich Bonhoeffer, Erich Maria Remarque, Norman Angell, G. D. H. Cole, Bertrand Russell, Mohandas Gandhi, Leo Tolstoy, Alfred Nobel, Albert Schweitzer, Susan B. Anthony, Andrew Carnegie, William Lloyd Garrison and Martin Luther King, Jr. These people—clergymen, feminists, civil rights activists, humanitarians, philanthropists, philosophers, writers—shared a moral indignation at the suffering and injustice caused by war, and their response was to protest against the conditions they saw through their writings or teachings or through the organizations they founded or joined. Two examples may serve to illustrate the difference in focus of the two books: there are over one hundred women listed in *Peace Leaders* for their work as pacifists, feminists and socialists, as opposed to about 30 women in *Internationalists;* by contrast, *Peace Leaders* cites only 58 practicing lawyers, as opposed to nearly 150 in *Internationalists,* where international law and governmental and diplomatic machinery were categories that provided a broader scope for people within the legal profession.

The two books will serve as a useful set of reference works in any international law collection.

F. M. CARROLL
St. John's College
University of Manitoba

Der Warschauer Pakt und seine bilateralen Bündnisverträge: Analyse und Texte. By Alexander Uschakow and Dietrich Frenzke. Berlin: Berlin Verlag Arno Spitz, 1987. Pp. 418. Indexes. DM 48.

Uschakow and Frenzke, authors of many books and studies on the Soviet Union and Eastern Europe (Ost-Europa Institut at the University of Cologne), have added a volume to the documentation and analysis of the Soviet system. Uschakow is responsible for part 1—the Warsaw Pact and the trea-

[1] Reviewed at 78 AJIL 999 (1984).

ties on the stationing of Soviet troops in Poland, East Germany, Hungary and Czechoslovakia. Frenzke deals with the system of bilateral alliances between the Warsaw Pact countries and those between the members of the Warsaw Pact and third states—China, Finland, Mongolia, North Korea, Vietnam and Afghanistan (1978). The People's Republic of China can no longer be regarded as a member of the Soviet collective security system, as it has denounced its alliance with the Soviet Union.

Although formally the Warsaw Pact is a European system of collective security, it is more than that. It includes not only the Asian socialist states, but also socialist countries elsewhere. Certainly, Cuba and the one-party states in Africa are assured assistance by the Soviet Union and other socialist states under the doctrine of socialist internationalism.

Formally, the Warsaw Pact is an answer to NATO. In fact, due to a number of factors, it is far more than that. It coordinates Eastern Europe militarily and economically (through government ownership of industry) and is part of the general political division of Europe into two systems.

In their analysis of the Soviet system of collective security, the authors discuss a number of important issues, including the most recent changes in the Soviet doctrine of international law. Contrary to the trend that marked the theoretical works of Soviet publicists in the 1970s (the basic unity of the general system of international law), socialist international law is again stressed. Of extreme interest for general Soviet studies is the study of the terminology used in the Soviet alliances, both the Warsaw Pact and the bilateral treaties. One might continue listing various aspects of the analytical parts of the volume; however, the limited space available for this review restricts these remarks. This publication is an important reference tool for the diplomat, and for students of both Soviet political and social institutions and international law.

KAZIMIERZ GRZYBOWSKI
Duke University

Supreme Courts and Judicial Law-Making: Constitutional Tribunals and Constitutional Review. By Edward McWhinney. Dordrecht, Boston, Lancaster: Martinus Nijhoff Publishers, 1986. Pp. xvi, 305. Index. Dfl.165; $67; £45.75.

This book deals with judicial review of the constitutionality of governmental, especially legislative, action, the tribunals invested with that function, and a selection of important cases decided over the last several decades by such tribunals in a number of countries, particularly the United States, Canada, India, Germany, France and Japan. It also includes extensive references to the International Court of Justice and its jurisprudence. It is, at the same time, a very personal book—one that quite often centers on the author's personality, contributions to teaching, advising and writing, and even his "personal friendships" and "frequent exchange of letters" (p. v) in the area of, or with judges and others involved in, constitutional review.

The book represents, in some way, the author's return to the comparative analysis of a topic on which he has written extensively, especially during the 1950s and 1960s. This might explain why it reveals a certain aloofness—or should I say sovereign disinterest?—vis-à-vis the formidable stream of scholarship on the subject over the last 20 years. This aloofness, however, as well as other features mentioned below, should be seen in the light of the fact that the book is, essentially, the outgrowth of lectures in New Delhi in 1983 and Tokyo in 1984 (p. vi). One is led to wonder, however, how far Europeans will accept one of the recurring themes in Professor McWhinney's volume, namely, that there was a "reception and borrowing" of the U.S. system of judicial review not only in India and Japan, but also in Europe (see, e.g., pp. xiii *ff.*, 2 *ff.*, 19, 37, 51, 290–91). This statement seems open to question for a number of reasons. It is widely known, and certainly known to an expert like McWhinney, that (1) the "Kelsenian" model of judicial review introduced in Austria in 1920 was highly original and anything but "borrowed" from the American model; (2) that the Austrian system had *its own* distinctive evolution in 1929 and in the post–World War II period, after the tragic interruption under the totalitarian regime and the *Anschluss;* (3) that the German and Italian post–World War II systems, and, later, the Yugoslavian, Cypriot, Turkish and, more recently, Spanish and Portuguese systems, have been influenced by the Austrian-Kelsenian model no less, indeed surely more, than by the American; (4) that the American precedent (and the "ghost," evoked by it, of *gouvernement des juges*) was, if anything, most influential in preventing the adoption of judicial review in France until, at least, 1971–1974 (and this is still so in Belgium, Holland and elsewhere), and continues to inspire many of the arguments in France *against* an expansion, or even the simple preservation, of the limited system that has existed since the 1970s (compare pp. 19–20); and finally, (5) that historical antecedents of judicial review did exist in Europe centuries before *Marbury v. Madison.* Also, the author himself recognizes at one point (p. 167) that in certain areas constitutional adjudication in Germany "actually anticipated, by some years, developments in the United States" (compare also p. 285).

One might wonder, as well, whether an American audience will be able to understand why lengthy discussions on such topics as "constitutional text and constitutional construction, judicial self-restraint and judicial activism" (ch. V), "the courts and the constitutional *Grundnorm*" (ch. VI), and "judicial law-making for societies in transition" (ch. XII) are pursued by the author with no mention at all of the great debate that has been raging in recent years in America.[1] In the same vein, American readers might be puzzled to find in McWhinney's book an extensive (indeed, quite valuable) discussion of such a topic as the doctrine of "substantive due process" in the case law of the U.S. Supreme Court and the "disappearance into history" of

[1] The most recent books by U.S. authors referred to in those three chapters are one by Roscoe Pound (1942), one by Paul Freund (1949) and one by H. J. Abraham (1962), in addition to a third (1979) edition of a book by W. F. Murphy and C. H. Pritchett and a study on West Germany (1976) by Donald Kommers.

that doctrine after 1937 (p. 221), while no mention at all can be found of what to many appears as a novel emergence of that (or a similar) doctrine more recently.[2] Also, a new model of "economic rights" that pushes toward a resurrected doctrine of economic substantive due process is preached by the "law and economics" movement.[3]

This having been said, this reviewer nevertheless feels he should pay tribute to all that is interesting and valuable in the book—and, more generally, in McWhinney's many contributions to the subject. He has a remarkable knowledge of constitutional courts and their *causes célèbres* in a number of countries; their structure, organization and internal practice (see ch. II, where salient differences among courts are rightly attributed to basic differences in the civil law–common law families); and the rules concerning appointment, tenure and removal of constitutional judges, as well as the respective roles of Chief and Associate Justices (chs. III and IV). Also, the book contains praiseworthy discussion of the relationship between constitutional courts and the constituent, the governmental and the electoral processes (chs. VII, VIII and IX). A wealth of data is offered in these chapters as well as in chapters X and XI, which deal, in a most interesting comparative way, with the several constitutional courts' approaches to economic interests and social and moral policy (including abortion, race discrimination and affirmative state action). Less widely known constitutional systems, such as the Indian and the Japanese, are often focused upon, and this is surely a further positive characteristic of the book, as is its most challenging and on the whole successful and thought-provoking effort at a comparative analysis of developments in a number of highly diverse countries.

To be sure, some readers might find it an impossible task, challenging, perhaps, but futile, to attempt to compare such different countries as, say, the United States and India. I do not share this kind of objection, however; rather, I agree with most of what McWhinney says on this matter at pages v–vi and 279 *ff.* Certainly, a common point of departure—a *tertium comparationis*—must exist for any comparison to be tenable. But this point may well consist in a "problem of life" common to the systems in question, no matter how diverse the social, economic, cultural and legal contexts within which the common problem has to be solved. The problem shared by all the countries involved in McWhinney's comparison is that of assuring a system of "limited government" and effective protection of certain basic rights and values vis-à-vis the political power—and the worth of any comparative analysis is indeed to see how one and the same (or similar) problem is faced by different, even profoundly different, peoples with different, or perhaps at times similar, tools and techniques.

On the theoretical side, I suppose that many would agree with the author's opinion that discussion of the "myth" of the noncreativity of the

[2] *See, e.g.*, Ely, *The Wages of Crying Wolf: A Comment on Roe v. Wade,* 82 YALE L.J. 920 (1973) (especially pp. 937 *ff.*).

[3] See, e.g., for a recent summary, J. BARRON, C. T. DIENES, W. MCCORMACK & M. H. REDISH, CONSTITUTIONAL LAW: PRINCIPLES AND POLICY 398 *ff.* (3d ed. 1987).

judicial process has lost much of its interest today (p. xii), in many countries at least, and that the real problems now are, rather, those of "ways of rendering [judicial lawmaking] responsible" and of "relating it to contemporary constitutional conceptions of popular sovereignty" (*id.*). One important way of doing this, of course, is to adopt appropriate rules and practices concerning selection, behavior and accountability of judges, and these are, as indicated, quite properly central themes in this book. I must dissent, however—in part at least—with such statements as that, still in 1956 (this key year coinciding with the publication of McWhinney's first book on the topic), "Outside the U.S. . . . what the American Legal Realist had called the 'basic legal myth' still persisted" (p. 269), and that it was only later that "the American Legal Realist lessons [were] 'received' outside the United States" (p. 270). Without in any way wishing to diminish the widespread influence of American legal realism, I believe that here again the concept of "reception" is used in a much too loose and possibly misleading way. McWhinney knows too well the history of legal ideas in Europe to dismiss such important streams of legal thought—partly preceding and indeed themselves influencing American legal realism—as the German *Interessenjurisprudenz* and *Freie Rechtslehre,* Gény's *libre recherche scientifique* (see pp. 95 and 283) and Scandinavian realism. On the other hand, I wonder whether it is not an exaggeration to speak of a "reception" of American legal realism even in the common law world. This is especially true—I think the author would agree—for England and Australia, where the "myth" still prevails in large sectors of scholarship and judicial doctrine (compare p. 5 on what McWhinney calls the traditional "unspeculative" British approach to the nature of the judicial process, and p. 91 for a hint on Australia).

McWhinney proudly confirms, page after page, his adherence to the basics of American legal realism, a position that might seem old-fashioned to a vociferous, but mostly unconstructive and often narcissistic, contemporary trend in American legal thinking. Another aspect that seems quite positive to this reviewer is the author's openness in manifesting a sympathetic stance vis-à-vis certain basic values, often of a transnational import—"liberal-egalitarian" values of our "new era of participatory democracy" (p. 292) or "social-democratic" values in the European terminology so often adopted by McWhinney (compare, e.g., pp. 214, 226–27, 237 *ff.*, 265–66, 279)—as well as vis-à-vis those ideals of international coexistence and "imperative principles" of a novel *jus gentium* (see, e.g., p. 168) that have been the theme of much of his well-known writing in public international law.

It seems clear to me that the author enjoyed writing this book, as well as delivering the lectures from which it stemmed. It is, at times, a summation of his commitment, scholarly and otherwise, in this area. It is also a proud reconfirmation of his ideals and beliefs—quite valuable ones in my opinion. Whether his readers share this enjoyment might depend on circumstances. Some might be irritated by that very aloofness mentioned above. Others, including this reviewer, might find that, in the final analysis, there is not so much really new in the "newest debate" on judicial review—a debate whose deep roots lie, after all, in that very ancient *problématique* that has been defined with many different formulas in different times, but is, at bottom, simply the problem (1) of the pluralism of laws and legal orders, hence of the validity of one such law and legal order vis-à-vis another, "higher" one; (2) of the entrustment of the judgment on validity to appropriate institutions; and (3) of the legitimacy of such entrustment. (Let me note, incidentally, that within this framework it becomes understandable that McWhinney deals with the International Court of Justice alongside constitutional courts; indeed, I wonder why he overlooks other transnational courts such as the European Court of Justice, whose "constitutionalization" process has represented one of the most remarkable developments in post–World War II Europe, and the European and Inter-American Courts of Human Rights.) Other epochs have called this *problématique* the struggle between "natural," or even "divine," and "positive" or "human" laws. Less metaphysically, perhaps, but more realistically, we now call it the (possible) conflict between the *constitutional* and the *ordinary* law, both of these being human and passing (as everything human, alas, is passing), yet the former being somewhat less temporary, somehow more "principled" or "valuable," than the latter. Which explains, of course, also the more "political," or if one prefers, more value-laden character of the judicial process whenever its involvement is with such higher law.

MAURO CAPPELLETTI
Stanford and Florence

Technology Control, Competition and National Security: Conflict and Consensus. Edited by Bernard L. Seward, Jr. Lanham, New York, London: University Press of America; Charlottesville: Center for Law and National Security, 1987. Pp. xxii, 312. $29.75, cloth; $16.50, paper.

This volume presents the proceedings of the fourth annual seminar of the Center for Law and National Security at the University of Virginia School of Law, held in October 1985. It is a collection of 19 short papers, of about ten pages on average, arranged in several thematic sections. The introduction by Bernard L. Seward, Jr., summarizes each of the papers. The volume also contains the text of the Export Administration Act as amended by the Export Administration Amendments Act of 1985 (EAAA), part of the Defense Department's 1985 report on Soviet acquisition of Western technology and a bibliography.

The book's coverage is somewhat narrower than the words "technology control" might suggest, for it is almost exclusively concerned with American export controls under the Export Administration Act. The section on legal issues includes brief treatments of a few other areas such as the arrangements governing the transfer of military technology between Japan and the United States and the release of technical data under the Freedom of Information Act, but these are incidental to the volume's major themes.

Because the seminar on which this collection is based was held soon after passage of the EAAA, a number of papers include discussions of that Act. Most of these, however, amount to little more than recitations of the major provisions. The most interesting discussion is by Paul Freedenberg, who describes how the interaction of political factions and interest groups affected the drafting of several important provisions.

Many of the papers address the need for international cooperation in technology controls. Representatives of industry argue that the growing foreign availability of advanced technology has made many American controls costly and meaningless. Administration spokesmen and foreign government officials, on the other hand, stress progress in strengthening CoCom, the organization that coordinates Western technology controls, and what they see as a growing awareness among CoCom member governments of the dangers posed by Soviet acquisitions of technology. The recent Toshiba case, however, casts grave doubt on many of these optimistic assertions. Another perennial issue, the extraterritorial application of American trade controls, is addressed by the foreign contributors; Thomas Harris reviews the issue best, from the British perspective.

The central theme of the collection, made clear by its title, is the conflict between "national security" and "competition" in export control policy. To maintain its security in a bipolar world, the United States must curtail the flow of militarily significant technology to the Soviet Union, restricting even some West-West transactions to limit diversion. At the same time, however, the United States needs to minimize restraints on technology trade if its firms and economy are to prosper in the face of worldwide competition and continue producing the technological innovations on which the American military depends to offset Soviet numerical superiority. All the authors represented here recognize this dilemma; they differ over how to resolve it.

Representatives of the Departments of Commerce, Defense and State argue for restricting technology exports. Their argument is based on evidence that the Soviet Union is making concerted efforts to acquire Western technology, legally and illegally, and that its efforts have already led to important military advances. As presented here, the argument is forceful, but contains no surprises; administration officials have made essentially the same presentation scores of times in recent years.

Representatives of American industry take the opposite side of the argument. The best paper here is by Edward Law. Law challenges the notion that Western commercial technology has been the basis for significant Soviet military advances, stresses the need for export profits to fund research and development, and argues for integrating the Western economies through two-way technology trade. Law and Allen Frischkorn, Jr., also stress the absence of data on the effectiveness and cost of technology controls and the lack of any accepted method for balancing cost and risk.

The most valuable portions of this book are the contributors' proposals for changes in the export control system. The more interesting suggestions are found in a section of the book called "Building a Policy Consensus"—notably in papers by Hylan Lyon, Jr., and Stephen Merrill, the latter a reprinted chapter from a 1985 report of the Center for Strategic and International Studies—and in the papers of the industry representatives. These private sector authors do not share a true consensus even among themselves—let alone with the representatives of the Reagan administration—but certain themes emerge repeatedly.

The most common theme, sounded by Lyon, Frischkorn, Merrill and others, is that export controls should in principle focus on pure technology—the information and "know-how" needed to design, build and use sophisticated products—rather than on the products themselves. This sort of know-how is the foundation of the U.S. advantage in military technology; product exports alone can rarely convey it; and firms that depend on know-how can be counted on to cooperate in efforts to protect it. Only a few products, such as "keystone" manufacturing, inspection and testing equipment and items susceptible to reverse engineering, need to be controlled.

The same authors urge that controls extend only to "critical" technologies or those that would make "revolutionary" contributions to Soviet military systems. The Defense Department's Militarily Critical Technologies List was supposed to identify such crucial control points, but has instead become a compendium of modern technology.

A second theme is administrative feasibility: technology export controls that cannot be effectively administered should be abandoned. This principle, however, conflicts with the first: a licensing system in which middle-level officials must identify and evaluate complex, intangible and constantly changing proprietary technologies is manifestly impractical. Merrill, Law and the other advocates of pure technology controls thus urge a number of second-best strategies: that controls focus only on "keystone" equipment, on know-how in tangible form or on easily regulated transactions like turnkey projects.

Almost all of these proposals stem from the lengthy debate over implementation of the 1976 Bucy Report, an ambitious attempt by the Defense Science Board to devise a coherent technology control policy. Lyon and Frischkorn, however, bypass that debate with their suggestion that the licensing approach itself should be replaced, in the context of West-West trade, by a system based wholly on the certification of corporate security practices.

The regulatory strategies suggested here would all shrink the present control system dramatically. In considering them, it is probably not irrelevant to bear in mind that the authors from industry, at least, represent major exporting companies. The value of these proposals, on the other hand, lies precisely in the authors' evident familiarity with the techniques and management of modern high-tech manufacturing. The same familiarity leads to other tantalizing observations relevant to technology control policy; Lyon notes, for example, that know-how, traditionally an attribute of the human mind, is increasingly incorporated into hardware.

Unfortunately, the value of the authors' expertise is not fully realized in this collection. The papers are so brief, and cover so much ground, that they can provide little of the necessary technical background; the ideas themselves are often fired out in machine-gun fashion. Obscure prose sometimes compounds the problem. A volume that made it possible for experts of this caliber, with editorial assistance, to explain and develop their ideas fully would be a major contribution to technology control policy.

KENNETH W. ABBOTT
Northwestern University School of Law

Załatwianie Międzynarodowych Sporów Gospodarczych. By Andrzej E. Lebiecki. Gdańsk: INP Gdańsk University, 1981. Pp. 105. English summary.

The purpose of his study, as Lebiecki explains in the closing chapter, is to demonstrate that international economic disputes represent a separate category in international law, deserving special treatment. Their methods of settlement, characterized by a search for new approaches that bypass judicial procedures, set these disputes apart from other international conflicts and traditional instruments used in their peaceful resolution. Moreover, at the origin of economic disputes is pecuniary damage or a loss of economic advantage suffered by one party. Consequently, a peaceful monetary settlement of such conflicts is always possible.

The book is based on the dissertation Dr. Lebiecki presented to Gdańsk University in connection with his appointment to the Department of International Relations.

His study opens with a broad review of literature and principles defining internationality of disputes and the usual differentiation between those that are justiciable and the others, political in nature, that are not suitable for settlement by judicial decisions. As Lebiecki points out, socialist jurisprudence rejects this division as illogical, and that particularly applies to economic conflicts. For Lebiecki, these disputes chiefly arise in connection with international trade, foreign financial transactions including capital movements and world natural resources.

The next chapter is devoted to a general discussion of various, including coercive, methods used in efforts to settle international disputes.

Chapter 3 is taxonomic and brief. It outlines in a tutorial style four general categories of instruments available for the peaceful resolution of international economic conflicts.

The centerpiece of Lebiecki's book is chapter 4. Here he examines the function and effectiveness of individual settlement instruments as they apply to disputes on foreign trade, international monetary transactions and access to, and trade in, natural resources. In this context he analyzes first the impact on international economic disputes of some specialized world and regional economic organizations, like the GATT and the European Economic Community. He then points to a similar role played by international economic conferences, as exemplified by UNCTAD and international maritime compacts, as well as by international commodity agreements. But it is the GATT that Lebiecki finds the most successful and effective instrument for resolving conflicts of economic interests peacefully.

In conclusion, the author stresses the need for having an internationally codified convention on the settlement of economic disputes. It could serve, Lebiecki suggests, as a framework for resolving economic conflicts, in general, as well as a guide for drawing individual agreements on the settlement of specific economic disputes, in particular.

From the above, it seems clear that the theoretical scope of Lebiecki's inquiry is far too broad to be dealt with adequately in this book of rather modest size. As a result, some of its parts are more or less summaries of international legal, notably, Anglo-American, opinions and literature, with which he is obviously very well acquainted. Interestingly, only a few references to Soviet sources can be found.

Also, one may wonder why the author neglected to consider, even briefly, the effects multinational enterprises have on international economic disputes, potential or actual. And a still more baffling gap in Lebiecki's discussion, of significance to various regional cooperative approaches to international economic conflicts, is his complete failure to say anything about a mechanism established for that purpose within the CMEA (the Soviet bloc Council for Mutual Economic Assistance). Readers might also have been interested in comparing the results of Communist legal theory and practice to actual settlements of economic disputes within their own orbit. There is an English summary but no index.

JAY G. POLACH

The CMEA Uniform Law for International Sales (2d rev. ed.). By Iván Szász. Dordrecht, Boston, Lancaster: Martinus Nijhoff Publishers; Budapest: Akadémiai Kiadó, 1985. Pp. viii, 292. Index. Dfl.125; $50; £31.75.

Ivan Szász, Director General of the Legal Department of the Hungarian Ministry of Foreign Trade, has expanded and updated his earlier studies of the legal rules that govern sales of goods among the socialist countries that are members of the Council for Mutual Economic Assistance (CMEA).[1] These rules, called "General Conditions of Delivery of Goods" (GCDG), in form are standardized contracts but may fairly be termed uniform laws for international sales.[2]

The author's careful and scholarly study can help lawyers outside the CMEA anticipate what they will meet in negotiations and settlements involving East-West trade. The book will also be useful to a wider body of

[1] The CMEA was founded by Eastern European countries but now includes Albania, Cuba and Mongolia.

Szász's initial study was published in 1974 in Hungarian and in 1976 in English as *A Uniform Law on International Sale of Goods.* For reviews, see Harmathy, 19 ACTA JURIDICAE SCIENTIARUM HUNGARICAE 431 (1977); Strohbach, 26 STAAT UND RECHT 651 (1977); and Dutoit, 7 REV. SOCIALIST L. 223 (1981). The current version was reviewed by J. Hazard in 14 INT'L J. LEGAL INFO. 87 (1986).

[2] The mooted question of the freedom of enterprises in CMEA to modify the "General Conditions" is discussed at pp. 53–56.

readers for the insights it provides on the reciprocal relationship between economic planning and commercial law.

Szász, a respected representative of Hungary in the United Nations Commission on International Trade Law (UNCITRAL), places CMEA international sales law in worldwide perspective. The first chapter, "Unification of Law—An Exigency of Our Age," illumines the forces that in recent decades have produced a multifold expansion of international trade and describes the remarkable range of measures that have been developed to reduce the uncertainty resulting from divergent national rules. If Szász were writing today, he could expand the list to include the 1985 Hague Convention on the Law Applicable to Contracts for the International Sale of Goods (uniform conflicts rules) and the entry into force on January 1, 1988, of the 1980 UN Convention on Contracts for the International Sale of Goods.[3] The latter Convention's uniform substantive sales law and the CMEA rules occupy separate, but closely linked, fields. By ratifying the UN Convention, CMEA countries are expected to make use of an option to exclude the Convention from sales among the CMEA states, leaving it applicable to transactions with the rest of the world.[4]

What is the effect of CMEA's economic planning on the contractual obligations of economic enterprises? Contracts for international trade are, of course, subject to substantial governmental constraints. As Szász explains (p. 60), governments agree on the delivery or exchange of specified quantities of commodities by their "economic enterprises." If these enterprises are reluctant to supply the commodities on terms specified in these agreements, the government will require its enterprises to enter into contracts to fulfill the government's obligations to the other CMEA member. When this requirement results in loss to the enterprise, must the government make the loss good? In Hungary, this right has been recognized by statute (p. 61).

The exigencies of carrying out economic plans leave their marks on the rules of the CMEA General Conditions (GCDG). For example, when nonperformance is threatened, the rules emphasize penalties to coerce performance (p. 157) rather than, as in a market economy, avoidance of the contract and purchase from another supplier. Similarly, when goods are defective, emphasis is placed on repair or replacement rather than rejection (p. 162). Other interesting examples will be found by those concerned with East-West trade.

Questions of a more general nature arise from the author's call for unification of "municipal" contract law within CMEA (pp. 220–26). One may

[3] Following Senate consent (98:0), the United States on Dec. 11, 1986, deposited its instrument of ratification of the 1980 Sales Convention. Other states that have accepted this Convention (by ratification, accession or comparable action) include Argentina, Austria, China, Egypt, Finland, France, Hungary, Italy, Lesotho, Mexico, Sweden, the Syrian Arab Republic, Yugoslavia and Zambia. *See* Honnold, Book Review, 81 AJIL 540 (1987); and J. HONNOLD, UNIFORM LAW FOR INTERNATIONAL SALES UNDER THE 1980 UNITED NATIONS CONVENTION (1982) (text of the Convention at p. 469).

[4] United Nations Convention on Contracts for the International Sale of Goods, Apr. 11, 1980, UN Doc. A/CONF.97/18, *reprinted in* 19 ILM 671 (1980), Art. 94. *Cf.* Art. 90.

wonder whether the development of a clearer body of contract law would assist in current tendencies toward further use of market forces within an area of economic planning.

JOHN O. HONNOLD
University of Pennsylvania Law School, Emeritus

The Islamic Conception of Justice. By Majid Khadduri. Baltimore and London: The Johns Hopkins University Press, 1984. Pp. xvi, 256. Index. $25; £22.50.

The stated purpose of this distinguished Islamic scholar's inquiries, which have resulted in his latest study of Islamic law, is to discover the Islamic theory or conception of justice by reviewing the writings of Muslim scholars. He examines the development of Islamic justice from the rise of Islam in the 7th century in terms of its separate, but interrelated, political, theological, philosophical, legal and social concepts. What emerges is not so much a definitive exposition of the subject as a collection of three substantial and important essays. The first is a review of Muslim authorities on an essential issue that split and continues to rend the Islamic community: succession, broadly, if not euphemistically, defined as "political justice." Next, in the chapters on theological, philosophical and ethical justice, Professor Khadduri discusses revelation and reason as contending sources of law. At the same time, he introduces four Islamic philosophers from a period we Westerners call the Dark Ages, but which Muslims could fairly claim as an age of enlightenment, the several centuries during which Islam carried the lambent torch of Western civilization from the Romans and the Greeks to the Byzantines and the Renaissance Europeans. The philosophy of Ibn Rushd, one of the four seminal philosophers considered, for example, borrows from and builds on Platonic and Aristotelian concepts in concluding that justice can be realized only in a state founded on virtues, which, in turn, can be learned from both reason and revelation. It was communicated to European thinkers by his Jewish disciples, of whom Maimonides was one. The third essay should find wide readership among international lawyers and students of Middle East politics. Representing nearly half of this short, but tightly written, book, it is both a critical evaluation of Islamic legal procedure and an examination of the need for and method of modernization of this oldest of the world's four extant major legal traditions.

Khadduri tells us that legal justice is justice according to substantive and procedural law. While the substantive Islamic law of rights and wrongs is just, Islamic procedure, "the external aspect of the Law by virtue of which substantive justice is realized" (p. 144), is not. Why? It is flawed. Khadduri makes a compelling case that Islamic procedure lacks uniformity and consistency, in part because Islam does not recognize *stare decisis,* but mainly because Islam's process is "partly judicial and partly administrative [read bureaucratic fiat] in character" (p. 150). Early efforts to reform procedural law failed because the divergent schools of Islamic jurisprudence, which had evolved from the schism of political justice into the *Sunni* and *Shi'i*, advanced their differences at the cost of uniformity in the legal system. Inequities owing to procedural inconsistency were relieved not by reform and uniform application of the procedural law, but by resort to legal fictions, or *hiyal*, that extreme subordination of substantive to procedural justice (not unknown to the common law) where an act is deemed lawful when it expressly contravenes the substantive law. This situation, Khadduri writes, only exacerbated the need for reform, a process begun by the Ottoman Turks that continues to this day.

In Islam, law plays a greater role than it does in Western societies. Islamic law governs the life of every Muslim in every way. Law and religion are one. The Koran serves as the basic constitutional document and regulates all aspects of life, from the proper clothes to be worn and food to be eaten, to specific penalties for certain crimes. Islamic law therefore has had a greater influence on the societies it serves than has Western law on European societies, with two major exceptions. First, and this is a fundamental weakness of the system, Islamic law does not concern itself with the whole field of public law. It is a system of private law. Second, because of the conservative interpretation of its revelational sources, conservative to the extent that in the 10th century consensus was deemed so infallible that further independent interpretation was ended, growth of the legal tradition stopped until Muslim thinkers reexamined the classical conception of Islamic justice and became aware that "its relevance to reality was significantly outdistanced by the material advantages which man derived from the standards of justice in Western society" (pp. 195–96).

This fascinating topic of reform and modernization of a legal tradition that in recent years has produced such variations as Qaddafi's anarchic form of Islamic socialism[1] and Khomeini's revived fundamentalism at the other extreme[2] is the subject of the concluding chapters. It has become what the author calls today's big debate in Muslim legal circles. The debate has eschewed consideration of political, theological, philosophical and ethical justice and has focused on legal justice, concentrating on reform of procedural law and modernization through the transplantation of Western legal concepts. Discounting the disestablishment of Islamic law (e.g., Turkey), reform and modernization efforts have divided the Islamic legal system into three groups. First are those countries (Saudi Arabia, Yemen and Aden) that follow traditional Islamic law without fundamental change. Next are those that continue the Islamic legal tradition as modified by the Ottomans

[1]

> Popular congresses are the only means to achieve popular democracy. Any system of government other than popular congresses is undemocratic. All the prevailing systems of government in the world today are undemocratic, unless they adopt this method. Popular congresses are the end of the journey of the masses' movement in its quest for democracy.

M. Gadaffi, The Green Book: The Solution of the Problem of Democracy, "The Authority of the People" 26 (undated).

[2] For a discussion of Iran's legal system today, see S. H. Amin, Middle East Legal Systems (1985), briefly reviewed at 80 AJIL 1057 (1986).

(Iraq, Syria and Jordan are representative). Finally, there are those countries (such as Egypt, Lebanon, Algeria and Morocco) that have adopted the French civil code as their model. Khadduri leaves the reader with the languishing thought that a new standard of political justice acceptable to the community is needed to replace the present dichotomy of two levels of political justice, one of such Western characteristics as parliamentary democracy, civil codes and judicial procedures, the other of traditional *Shari'a*. No such new standard has emerged to take their place. Perhaps Khadduri's provocative criticism of Islamic procedure will stimulate further debate on the heretofore elusive standard.

JOSEPH L. BRAND
Of the Ohio and District of Columbia Bars

Japanese-U.S. Business Negotiations: A Cross-Cultural Study. By Don R. McCreary. New York, Westport and London: Praeger Publishers, 1986. Pp. viii, 121. Index. $35.

This book is a short, but dense, study of negotiations between Japanese and U.S. businessmen, done by a linguist primarily for linguists. It is a scholarly treatise that attempts to show the relevance of the theories of Vygotsky and the "Soviet school of psycholinguists" to bicultural negotiations. Vygotskyan theorists are particularly relevant, McCreary argues, because they "view language and cognitive development as socially derivative" (p. 7). He states that this is quite different from Piaget's widely accepted "individualistic theory of cognitive development," in which culture and social life play a less significant role (*id.*). Using the Vygotskyan approach, McCreary discusses certain phenomena characteristic of U.S.-Japanese business negotiations within their social and cultural contexts.

Although the title is enticing to American businessmen and lawyers who have dealings with Japan, the content will likely be disappointing, at least until a third of the way into the text. The tone is stiff and scholarly, reading much like a doctoral dissertation. Until actual examples of negotiation and particular characteristics of Japanese approaches to it are discussed, beginning in chapter 4, the book will be practically impenetrable to the average reader. If the reader can persevere, however, there are some interesting and useful observations and "how to's" in the book, especially toward the end.

The book is composed of a mere 75 pages of text and a 30-page appendix containing transcripts from a U.S.-Japanese negotiation and a U.S. domestic negotiation. These transcripts serve as raw material for observations made in the text. Following the introduction and two chapters, entitled "A Soviet Psycholinguistic Perspective" and "Relevance of Vygotsky's Theories to Japanese Society," the book begins to make some worthwhile points for nonlinguists in chapters entitled "Cross-Cultural Japanese-U.S. Negotiation," "*Haragei*—A Communicative Strategy for Japanese," "*Tatemae* vs. *Honne* and 'Yes' vs. 'No'" and "Closing a Negotiation" (which, unfortunately, never really tells the reader how to close one). A brief conclusion recaps what was said in the previous chapters.

To my knowledge, this is the only linguistic study of Japanese negotiations that has appeared in print. Graham and Sano's *Smart Bargaining: Doing Business with the Japanese*[1] is definitely an easier book for nonlinguists to study negotiation tactics with the Japanese, but it is not intended to be a scholarly treatise and, though insightful, lacks the analytical quality of McCreary's work. Imai's books about Japanese negotiations are also more approachable, but even more lacking in scholarly content.[2] There are numerous other writings on how to negotiate with the Japanese, usually chapters in books about doing business in Japan,[3] but also a large number of articles.[4]

The best parts of the book deal with actual Japanese psychological and sociocultural phenomena and how they affect negotiating style. Of particular note are McCreary's discussions of *amae* (dependence), *haragei* (negotiating "without the use of direct words," p. 45) and *tatemae* vs. *honne* ("a superficial facade of apparent truth vs. the actual truth," p. 59) and their effect on negotiations. His chapter on *haragei* is especially enlightening, and has some engaging examples and useful points. One is a description of a Japanese business executive who goes through an extended (up to 30 minutes) ritual finding and lighting his cigarettes in order to keep from breaking his silence when an impasse is reached in a negotiation (p. 53). Another is the author's listing of the communicative content of various aspects of Japanese "body language and other paralinguistic features":

> searching eye contact (seeks agreement or harmony), constant smiling (a facade—particularly without eye contact), the audible exhalation of breath through the nose (resignation), the forced exhalation of an extended sibilant as in *saaa* (generally disagreement), sucking in breath through the teeth (consternation or worry), or even closing the eyes (consideration—not sleepiness) [p. 52].

Although many of his best points are borrowed from other sources, McCreary succeeds in bringing them together rather well.

McCreary undoubtedly has experience in Japan, but I would have a stronger feeling of confidence in the book if the author more clearly demonstrated that he speaks Japanese (only one citation to a Japanese-language source in a lengthy bibliography) and that he has had first-hand experience in business negotiations with the Japanese (the negotiation transcripts in the appendix are from a film and a videotape produced by others).

[1] J. L. Graham & Y. Sano, Smart Bargaining: Doing Business with the Japanese (1984).

[2] M. Imai, Never Take Yes for an Answer (1975), and Sixteen Ways to Avoid Saying "No" (1981).

[3] E.g., B. DeMente, How to Do Business in Japan (1984), and M. Zimmerman, How to Do Business with the Japanese (1985).

[4] E.g., VanZandt, *How to Negotiate in Japan,* Harv. Bus. Rev., November–December, 1970, at 45; and Graham, *Negotiators Abroad—Don't Shoot from the Hip, id.,* July–August, 1983, at 160. Although Graham's article is about negotiating in other cultures generally, he clearly has Japan in mind.

The book is written on an important topic, is thoughtful and makes many good points, but it will likely have little impact on the average reader's knowledge of negotiation with the Japanese because of its strictly linguistic focus and difficult writing style. The purpose of the book is stated in the last sentence:

> When holistic strategies that operate throughout conversational frames or entire discourses are brought to light, academics in fields such as medicine and law are drawn into the study, which can only widen its scope and increase the societal value of linguistics as an autonomous discipline contributing to the improvement of humanity [p. 75].

While this is certainly a noble objective, the very sentence illustrates why McCreary will probably fail to draw people other than linguists into his endeavor.

WALTER L. AMES
Brigham Young University

BRIEFER NOTICES

Derecho Internacional Codificado. Derecho de Gentes: Recopilación Sistemática de Textos y Tratados. By José Ramón Remacha. (Pamplona: Editorial Aranzadi, 1984. Pp. 1136. Indexes.) This compilation of treaties and declarations of the United Nations contains the basic documents of public international law. Dr. Remacha has systematically organized and identified materials on international law that have exerted a major influence on, and thus greatly regulated, relations between and among nations. The book is divided into five parts, each preceded by an introduction that provides the reader with guidance to the materials contained therein. Part I sets forth what the author has called the "Basic Principles of the Relations Between Nations" and focuses on friendship and cooperation in accordance with the Charter of the United Nations, sovereignty over natural resources and the establishment of a "New International Economic Order." Part II, which makes up the bulk of the book, identifies the agreements and documents that constitute the law of the sea, space law, consular and diplomatic law, the law of treaties, jurisdiction and international arbitration. Part III sets forth the agreements establishing the principal international political, economic and military organizations. Part IV focuses on international human rights and draws together the key international documents of the United Nations, Europe, North and South America, and Africa. Part V sets forth the principal agreements on the law of armed conflict, including those that provide for humanizing norms and the protection of victims during war. Finally, indexes are provided of key words and phrases and of the signatories to each of the treaties. This reference work is recommended as a comprehensive and well-organized source of public international law to those working in the field.

DIANA V. LOPEZ
Of the New York Bar

International Business Transactions and Economic Relations. By J. G. Castel, A. L. C. de Mestral and W. C. Graham. (Toronto: Emond Montgomery Publications Ltd., 1986. Pp. xxii, 925. Index. $119.50.) This book represents a Canadian attempt at a problem that has troubled teachers in the United States: how does one present in a single course the basics of international business law? Stretching from the basics of treaty law to the details of antidumping proceedings is a great strain for both teacher and student. The Canadian volume exhibits the same coverage problems as its U.S. counterparts. American teachers will not likely resort to a collection that takes a Canadian viewpoint. Still, they should find much in it that is interesting and unfamiliar. It is good for Americans to think of our country as one that engages in dumping rather than simply being dumped upon (pp. 322–29). The Canadian response to U.S. attempts to enforce American laws abroad is well set out here (pp. 497–509). Canadian law on commercial arbitration, technology licensing and letters of credit differs from ours in significant detail, which is set forth in these materials.

BOOKS RECEIVED*

International Law—General

Recueil des Cours de l'Académie de Droit International de La Haye, 1986. Vols. I, II, III and IV. (Vols. 196, 197, 198 and 199 of the collection.) Dordrecht, Boston, Lancaster: Martinus Nijhoff Publishers, 1987. Vol. I: pp. 400; vol. II: pp. 419; vol. III: pp. 400; vol. IV: pp. 519. Dfl.165; $72.50; £57.50.

Akehurst, Michael. *A Modern Introduction to International Law* (6th ed.). London and Boston: Allen and Unwin, 1987. Pp. 315. Index. $14.95, paper.

Bledsoe, Robert L., and Boleslaw A. Boczek. *The International Law Dictionary.* Santa Barbara and Oxford: ABC-Clio, 1987. Pp. xii, 422. Index. $37.50.

Bos, Adriaan, and Hugo Siblesz (eds.). *Realism in Law-Making: Essays on international law in honour of Willem Riphagen.* Published under the auspices of the T.M.C. Asser Instituut. Dordrecht, Boston, Lancaster: Martinus Nijhoff Publishers, 1986. Pp. xix, 298. Index. Dfl.165; $75.50; £54.50.

Annuaire Français de Droit International. Vol. XXXII, 1986. Paris: Editions du Centre National de la Recherche Scientifique, 1987. Pp. 1255. Indexes. F.650.

Janis, Mark W. *An Introduction to International Law.* Boston and Toronto: Little, Brown and Company, 1988. Pp. xvi, 299. Index. $14, paper.

Matthews, James M. (ed./comp.). *Kime's International Law Directory, 1987.* London: Kime's International Law Directory Limited, 1987. Pp. 1128.

Morin, Jacques-Yvan, Francis Rigaldies and Daniel Turp. *Droit International Public: Notes et documents. Tome I: Documents d'intérêt international.* Montreal: Les Editions Thémis, 1987. Pp. xix, 1006.

International Economic Law & Relations

Gruson, Michael, and Michael Kutschera. *Legal Opinions in International Transactions: Foreign Lawyers' Response to US Opinion Requests.* London: Graham & Trotman; New York: International Bar Association, 1987. Pp. 80. £36.50; $67.

Holmes, Frank (ed.). *Economic Adjustment: Policies and Problems.* (Papers presented at a seminar held in Wellington, New Zealand, February 17–19, 1986.) Washington: International Monetary Fund, 1987. Pp. x, 281. $16.

* Mention here neither assures nor precludes later review.

Mahari, Julian. *Zuständigkeitskonflikte zwischen Rechtsordnungen: Essays in English and German on the Present Confusion in International Economic Law.* Bern: Verlag Stämpfli & Cie AG, 1987. Pp. 124. Sw.F.38; DM 45.

Oppermann, Thomas, and Ernst-Ulrich Petersmann (eds.). *Reforming the International Economic Order: German legal comments.* Berlin: Duncker & Humblot, 1987. Pp. 264. DM 98.

Law of the Sea & Maritime Law

Dahmani, M. *The Fisheries Regime of the Exclusive Economic Zone.* Dordrecht, Boston, Lancaster: Martinus Nijhoff Publishers, 1987. Pp. ix, 188. Dfl.145; $71.50; £44.75.

Hafner, Gerhard. *Die seerechtliche Verteilung von Nutzungsrechten: Rechte der Binnenstaaten in der ausschließlichen Wirtschaftszone.* Vienna and New York: Springer-Verlag, 1987. Pp. xv, 533. Indexes. DM 172.

International Organizations and the Law of the Sea: Documentary Yearbook 1985. Volume 1, 1985. Issued by The Netherlands Institute for the Law of the Sea (NILOS). London: Graham & Trotman; Dordrecht: Martinus Nijhoff, 1987. Pp. viii, 645. Index. Dfl.275; $132.50; £93.50.

Rozakis, Christos L., and Petros N. Stagos. *The Turkish Straits.* Dordrecht, Boston, Lancaster: Martinus Nijhoff Publishers, 1987. Pp. xviii, 200. Index. Dfl.125; $60; £38.75.

Weil, Prosper. *Perspectives du droit de la délimitation maritime.* Paris: Pedone, 1988. Pp. ix, 319. F.200.

Westerman, Gayl S. *The Juridical Bay.* New York: Oxford University Press; Oxford: Clarendon Press, 1987. Pp. xii, 290. Indexes. $39.95.

Terrorism

Alexander, Yonah (ed.). *The 1986 Annual on Terrorism.* Dordrecht, Boston, Lancaster: Martinus Nijhoff Publishers, 1987. Pp. vii, 358. Dfl.175; $89; £53, paper.

Human Rights

Kokott, Juliane. *Das interamerikanische System zum Schutz der Menschenrechte.* Berlin, Heidelberg, New York, Tokyo: Springer-Verlag, 1986. Pp. xii, 166. English summary. DM 78.

Environment & Natural Resources

Anand, R. P., Rahmatullah Khan and S. Bhatt. *Law, Science and Environment.* New Delhi: Lancers Books, 1987. Pp. xxxix, 297. Rs.275.

International Organizations

Baratta, Joseph Preston (comp.). *Strengthening the United Nations: A Bibliography on U.N. Reform and World Federalism.* New York, Westport, London: Greenwood Press, 1987. Pp. viii, 351. Indexes. $45.

Hamacher, Peter. *Die Maxime audiatur et altera pars im Völkerrecht: Ein Beitrag zum Internationalen Verfahrensrecht unter besonderer Berücksichtigung der Rechtsgutachten des (StIGH) IGH.* Vienna and New York: Springer-Verlag, 1986. Pp. xiv, 257. Index. DM 90.

McWhinney, Edward. *The International Court of Justice and the Western Tradition of International Law.* Dordrecht, Boston, Lancaster: Martinus Nijhoff Publishers, 1987. Pp. xiv, 158. Index. Dfl.125; $60; £38.75.

Schwob, Jacques. *Les Organes intégrés de caractère bureaucratique dans les organisations internationales.* Brussels: Etablissements Emile Bruylant, 1987. Pp. xi, 398. Index. BF 2,840.

The United Nations and the Maintenance of International Peace and Security. Published under the auspices of the United Nations Institute for Training and Research. Dordrecht, Boston, Lancaster: Martinus Nijhoff Publishers, 1987. Pp. xviii, 431. Index. Dfl.130; $64; £40.

Cultural Property

Merryman, John Henry, and Albert E. Elsen. *Law, Ethics, and the Visual Arts* (2d ed.). Vols. 1 and 2. Philadelphia: University of Pennsylvania Press, 1987. Pp. xxiv, 756. Index. $89.95.

U.S. Law & Foreign Relations

Perusse, Roland I. *The United States and Puerto Rico: Decolonization Options and Prospects.* Lanham, New York, London: University Press of America, 1988. Pp. xiii, 177. Index. $24.50, cloth; $11.75, paper.

Schwartz, Herman (ed.). *The Burger Years: Rights and Wrongs in the Supreme Court, 1969–1986.* New York: Penguin Books, 1988. Pp. xxv, 293. Index. $8.95, paper.

Foreign Relations of the United States, 1952–1954. Volume XII: East Asia and the Pacific. Part 2. (Dept. of State Pub. 9550.) Washington: U.S. Govt. Printing Office, 1987. Pp. xv, 763. Index.

Foreign Relations of the United States, 1955–1957. Volume III: China, Microfiche Supplement. Washington: Department of State, 1987. 30 microfiches.

Foreign Relations of the United States, 1955–1957. Volume VIII: South Asia. (Dept. of State Pub. 9538.) Washington: U.S Govt. Printing Office, 1987. Pp. xvii, 511. Index.

Foreign Relations of the United States, 1955–1957. Volume IX: Foreign Economic Policy; Foreign Information Program. (Dept. of State Pub. 9604.) Washington: U.S. Govt. Printing Office, 1987. Pp. xxvi, 628. Index.

Zucker, Norman L., and Naomi Flink Zucker. *The Guarded Gate: The Reality of American Refugee Policy.* San Diego, New York, London: Harcourt Brace Jovanovich, Publishers, 1987. Pp. xx, 342. Index. $22.95.

Regional & Foreign Law & Politics

Feldbrugge, F. J. M. (ed.). *The Distinctiveness of Soviet Law.* Dordrecht, Boston, Lancaster: Martinus Nijhoff Publishers, 1987. Pp. xix, 272. Index. Dfl.185; $91; £56.95.

Moinuddin, Hasan. *The Charter of the Islamic Conference and Legal Framework of Economic Co-operation among its Member States.* Oxford: Clarendon Press; New York: Oxford University Press, 1987. Pp. xx, 322. Index. $67.

International Relations & Politics

Wight, Nancy (ed.). *Law and Current World Issues.* Columbia Law School Symposium, 1986. New York, London, Rome: Oceana Publications, Inc., 1987. Pp. vii, 174. $35.

INTERNATIONAL LEGAL MATERIALS*

CONTENTS

VOL. XXVII, NO. 1 (January 1988)

PAGE

LEGISLATION AND REGULATIONS

Federal Republic of Germany: Act on the Revision of the *Private International Law*

Introductory Note 1

I.L.M. Content Summary 4

Text 6

Switzerland: Statute on *International Arbitration*

Introductory Note 37

I.L.M. Content Summary 42

Text 43

TREATIES AND AGREEMENTS

Belgium–Federal Republic of Germany–Italy–Netherlands–United Kingdom–United States: Agreement regarding *Inspections relating to the Treaty between the U.S. and the U.S.S.R. on the Elimination of Their Intermediate-Range and Shorter-Range Missiles*

I.L.M. Background/Content Summary 58

Text 60

U.S. Department of State Analysis 67

German Democratic Republic–United States: Exchange of Notes regarding *Inspections under the Treaty between the U.S. and the U.S.S.R. on the Elimination of Their Intermediate-Range and Shorter-Range Missiles*

I.L.M. Background 73

Text 73

Union of Soviet Socialist Republics–United States: Agreement on the *Establishment of Nuclear Risk Reduction Centers*

I.L.M. Background/Content Summary 76

Text 78

Union of Soviet Socialist Republics–United States: Treaty on the *Elimination of Their Intermediate-Range and Shorter-Range Missiles*

I.L.M. Background/Content Summary 84

Text of Treaty 90

Text of Memorandum of Understanding regarding the *Establishment of a Data Base* 98

U.S. Photographs 129

Soviet Photographs 132

U.S. Site Diagrams 138

Soviet Site Diagrams 149

Exchange of Letters regarding Six U.S. *On-Site Inspections of Former Silos for SS–4 Missiles* 182

Text of Protocol on *Elimination* 183

Text of Protocol on *Inspections* 190

U.S. Department of State Analysis 199

* ILM subscription, $100; concessionary rate to ASIL members, $50. Address orders to ILM, 2223 Massachusetts Ave., NW, Wash., D.C. 20008. Outside U.S., please add $5.50.

OTHER DOCUMENTS
Union of Soviet Socialist Republics–United States: Joint *Statement from the Washington Summit*
I.L.M. Content Summary 255
Text 256
United States: Letter of Transmittal to the U.S. Senate from the President and Letter of Submittal from the Secretary of State concerning the *INF Treaty*
I.L.M. Content Summary 262
Text 263
Western European Union: Platform on *European Security Interests*
I.L.M. Background/Content Summary 269
Text 270

RECENT ACTIONS REGARDING TREATIES TO WHICH THE UNITED STATES IS A PARTY 273
RECENT ACTIONS REGARDING TREATIES TO WHICH THE UNITED STATES IS NOT A PARTY 277
NOTICE OF OTHER RECENT DOCUMENTS (not reproduced) 280

VOL. XXVII, NO. 2 (March 1988)

TREATIES AND AGREEMENTS
Canada–United States:
Free-Trade Agreement
I.L.M. Background/Content Summary 281
Text 293
Memorandum of Understanding on *Drug Enforcement*
I.L.M. Background/Content Summary 403
Text 404
Memorandum of Understanding on *Administration and Enforcement of Securities Laws*
I.L.M. Background/Content Summary 410
Text 412
Protocol Amending the Treaty on *Extradition*
I.L.M. Content Summary 422
Text 423
Latin American States: Treaty of *Institutionalization of the Latin American Parliament*
Introductory Note 430
I.L.M. Content Summary 430
Text 431
Mexico–United States:
Framework Understanding on *Bilateral Trade and Investment*
I.L.M. Background/Content Summary 438
Text 439
Mutual Legal Assistance Cooperation Treaty
I.L.M. Content Summary 443
Text 447
New Agreement on *Textiles*
I.L.M. Background/Content Summary 451
Text 455
Switzerland–United States: Memorandum of Understanding on *Mutual Assistance in Criminal Matters and Ancillary Administrative Proceedings*
I.L.M. Background/Content Summary 480
Text 481

JUDICIAL AND SIMILAR PROCEEDINGS

American Arbitration Association Construction Industry Arbitration Tribunal: Award in the Matter of the Arbitration between Philip Morris International Finance Corporation and Overseas Private Investment Corporation (*Inconvertibility Claim in the Dominican Republic*)

I.L.M. Content Summary 487

Award 488

Colombia: Supreme Court Decision on *Law concerning the Extradition Treaty between Colombia and the United States*

Introductory Note 492

I.L.M. Content Summary 497

Decision 498

Inter-American Court of Human Rights: Advisory Opinion on *Habeas Corpus in Emergency Situations*

I.L.M. Content Summary 512

Advisory Opinion 513

OTHER DOCUMENTS

Bank for International Settlements: Committee on Banking Regulations and Supervisory Practices' Consultative Paper on *Proposals for International Convergence of Capital Measurement and Capital Standards*

Introductory Note 524

I.L.M. Content Summary 527

Consultative Paper 530

United Kingdom: Bank of England's Explanatory Paper on *Proposals for International Convergence of Capital Measurement and Capital Standards*

I.L.M. Content Summary 562

Explanatory Paper 563

RECENT ACTIONS REGARDING TREATIES TO WHICH THE UNITED STATES IS A PARTY 571

RECENT ACTIONS REGARDING TREATIES TO WHICH THE UNITED STATES IS NOT A PARTY 575

NOTICE OF OTHER RECENT DOCUMENTS (not reproduced) 576

STATE IMMUNITY: SOME RECENT DEVELOPMENTS

Christoph Schreuer

Professor of International Law, University of Salzburg

Suits against States and State-owned corporations in foreign courts are a major feature of international transactions and activities. In recent years treaties, national legislation and numerous judicial decisions have led to significant development in this important area of the law.

This book examines the principal international and national aspects of these new features. It will be of considerable interest to practitioners dealing with transnational cases, to government officials, to those interested in the machinery of international trade and to scholars of international law.

224 pp., including Index and Table of Cases — Published January 1988
Price: Hardback £28.00 (US $55.00) — ISBN 0 949009 14 8

THE INTERNATIONAL LAW COMMISSION

Sir Ian Sinclair, Q.C.

formerly Legal Adviser to the Foreign and Commonwealth Office
formerly Member of the International Law Commission

The International Law Commission is the principal United Nations organ concerned with the preparation of proposals for the progressive development and codification of international law.

This present study examines the constitution and working methods of the Commission; reviews the activity of the Commission since 1949 in the codification process; and analyses the contribution which the work of the Commission has made to the development of general international law.

185 pp., including Index — Published August 1987
Price: Hardback £28.00 (US $55.00) — ISBN 0 949009 10 5

AIR MAIL POSTAGE £5.00 (US $8.00)
Orders can be placed through local bookshops or order directly from:

GROTIUS PUBLICATIONS LIMITED
P.O. BOX 115, Cambridge CB3 9BP
United Kingdom

RECENT RELEASES

SELECTED INFORMATION MATERIALS

★

DEPARTMENT OF STATE

PUBLICATIONS

Digest of United States Practice in International Law, 1980

The Department of State's *Digest of United States Practice in International Law, 1980* will be available after May 1 at the U.S. Government Printing Office (xxx, 1134 pp.). The eighth in the annual series, the 1980 *Digest* includes the final 3 weeks of President Carter's administration in January 1981, and indicates developments in certain fields subsequent to the period of coverage.

Describing legal, diplomatic and other responses by the United States to Iran's continuing, lawless detention of the American hostages captured in 1979, the volume conveys the totality of the U.S. response to the crisis. It sets out actions undertaken by the President and the executive branch, including appearances by the U.S. Government in domestic litigation and before the International Court of Justice. It summarizes the negotiations that led to the resolution of the crisis, under the catalytic effect of an impending change in U.S. Presidents, and explains the legal issues considered in formulating the Algiers Declarations, including the establishment of the Iran–United States Claims Tribunal at The Hague.

The 1980 *Digest* details measures undertaken to curb foreign government–sponsored (Libyan) terrorism within the United States, which culminated in the closing of the Libyan People's Bureau in Washington. In another area involving Libya, the *Digest* discusses the U.S. Government's support, *amicus,* in judicial proceedings brought by an American corporate claimant to enforce a foreign arbitral award obtained against Libya (the *LIAMCO* case).

Other government participation in domestic litigation involved interpretations of the Foreign Sovereign Immunities Act and the act of state doctrine, as well as various provisions of the Immigration and Nationality Act. In regard to the latter, the United States succeeded in revoking the naturalization of a former Nazi death camp guard; this resulted in his deportation and in a number of successful similar efforts. A challenge to the constitutionality of that Act's legislative veto provision, which would have required deportation of an East Indian individual seeking adjustment of status, was also successful (the *Chadha* case).

The volume outlines the legal and other problems presented by the 1980 Mariel boatlift from Cuba and by the waves of illegal migrants from Haiti. It also relates government efforts to exclude common crimes of violence from the political offense exception to extradition, initially in arguments before U.S. extradition magistrates and courts (and, finally, through renegotiation of key extradition treaty provisions).

Lastly, the 1980 *Digest* traces the enlargement of the U.S. role in Middle East peacekeeping, which was to result in the establishment of the Multinational Force and Observers.

Earlier volumes:

- ☐ 1979: Digest of U.S. Practice in International Law $22.00 (Stock No. 044-000-01937-0) (1933 pp.)
- ☐ 1978: Digest of U.S. Practice in International Law $26.00 (Stock No. 044-000-01762-8) (1802 pp.)
- 1977: Digest of U.S. Practice in International Law (out of print) (Stock No. 044-000-01720-2) (1158 pp.)
- ☐ 1976: Digest of U.S. Practice in International Law $16.00 (Stock No. 044-000-01645-1) (850 pp.)
- ☐ 1975: Digest of U.S. Practice in International Law $17.00 (Stock No. 044-000-01605-2) (947 pp.)
- ☐ 1974: Digest of U.S. Practice in International Law $15.00 (Stock No. 044-000-01566-8) (2d printing) (796 pp.)
- ☐ 1973: Digest of U.S. Practice in International Law $14.00 (Stock No. 044-000-01525-1) (618 pp.)

Send orders to: Superintendent of Documents
U.S. Government Printing Office
Washington, D.C. 20402

LIFE MEMBERS OF THE AMERICAN SOCIETY OF INTERNATIONAL LAW 1987–1988

Gerald Aksen
Stanley Anderson
Masahiko Asada
Calvin A. Behle
Richard S. S. Bright
John C. Brooks
Ian Brownlie
John Carey
Chin-Yung Chao
Stephen S. F. Chen
Max Chopnick
J. G. Clarke
H. Alberta Colclaser
Carter K. Combe
Rebecca J. Cook
Jorge Antonio De Marzi
Dermott J. Devine
John E. Donnelly
Peter D. Ehrenhaft
Robert Eikel
Richard J. Erickson
Eleanor H. Finch
Richard I. Fine
Roger D. Fisher
Stefan Forch
Carl Mason Franklin
Gaudencio Garcia
Moti Lal Govila
Robert T. Greig
Joseph P. Griffin
Richard Kennedy Guelff
Judith R. Hall
Robert D. Hayton
Dan F. Henderson
Robert E. Herzstein
Gary N. Horlick
Christopher C. Joyner
William S. Kenney
Yoshito Kita
Elizabeth Lay
Monroe Leigh
Frankie Fook-lu Leung
Cynthia C. Lichtenstein
Mrs. Brunson MacChesney
Myres Smith McDougal
Samuel Pyeatt Menefee
John M. Metzger
Clifford L. Michel
James A. R. Nafziger
Andre W. G. Newburg
J. D. Nyhart
Hisashi Owada
Mauricio Perez-Badell
Hernán Pérez Loose
Ellis L. Phillips
Jane M. Picker
Robert J. Radway
Charles S. Rhyne
Elliot L. Richardson
Alfred P. Rubin
Mark Sandstrom
Tetsuo Sato
Oscar Schachter
Cabot Sedgwick
Yukio Shimada
William I. Shore
Anne Patricia Simons
Dwight J. Simpson
Owen Meredith Smaw
Earl A. Snyder
Jane Sommerich
John H. Spencer
Henry J. Steiner
Edward P. Torrey
Tullio Treves
J. W. Van Der Zanden
L. W. Wadsworth
Edith Brown Weiss
Elmer E. Welty
Ulrich Woelker
C. U. Zachrisson
Peaches Zaphiriou

ANNUAL PATRON, SUPPORTING, AND CONTRIBUTING MEMBERS OF THE AMERICAN SOCIETY OF INTERNATIONAL LAW 1987–1988

ANNUAL PATRON

Eli Whitney Debevoise

SUPPORTING

Mitchell Brock
Charles N. Brower
Alexander D. Calhoun
William Gilbert Carter
Anthony A. D'Amato
Robert MacCrate
William B. Matteson
Covey T. Oliver
George M. Pavia
Walter S. Surrey
Peter W. Thornton
Peter D. Trooboff
Jack G. Wasserman
Basil S. Yanakakis

CONTRIBUTING

Richard L. Abbott
Richard B. M. Abrams
Richard C. Allison
Manuel R. Angulo
Steven Wright Baker
J. Truman Bidwell
Roman A. Bninski
John Arthur Boyd
George W. Brandt
Aron Broches
David Carliner
C. J. Chen
Donald E. Claudy
Philip F. Cohen
John P. Corrigan
Samuel S. Cross
Michael Danaher
John L. A. De Passalaqua
George C. Denney
James M. Denny
Edward A. Dragon
Malcolm T. Dungan
Richard A. Eastman
Aly H. Elghatit
F. Javier Fabregat
Philip A. Faix, Jr.
Stanley F. Farrar
Benjamin B. Ferencz
John Basil Gantt
David G. Gill
Michael A. Gleim
Joseph Gold
L. F. E. Goldie
Thomas R. Graham
Ernest A. Gross
James V. Hackney
Herbert J. Hansell
Joel B. Harris
Thomas E. Haven
H. Healy
Cecil Hunt
Oliver T. Johnson
Joseph S. Kaplan
Charles J. Keever
Lee A. Kimball
Paul L. Laskin
James Leitner
Robert T. Lemon, II
Edwin Deane Leonard
Jacques L. Leroy
David M. Levitan
George N. Lindsay

Carlos A. Lopez-Guevara
G. Lorinczi
Ralph M. McDowell
A. F. Maulsby
Gerald D. Morgan
Frank E. Nattier
Franz M. Oppenheimer
Guillermo F. Peroni
Jose Martins Pinheiro Neto
Willis L. M. Reese
A. R. Richstein
Bruce L. Rockwood

James F. Sams
J. P. Schwebel
Charles M. Spofford
Samuel A. Stern
Isaac N. P. Stokes
Robert M. Thomas, Jr.
Robert B. von Mehren
Paul C. Warnke
John Stowell Williams
F. L. Wiswall
Richard Young

AMERICAN SOCIETY OF INTERNATIONAL LAW
2223 MASSACHUSETTS AVENUE, N.W., WASHINGTON, D.C. 20008-2864, (202) 265-4313
Be sure to check membership type on reverse side.

Name (please print) ______________________
Mailing Address ______________________
Street, P.O. Box, etc. ______________________
City, State, Zip ______________________
Country ______________ Phone ______________

Member, U.S. Bar?______ State:______ Year______

School, Firm or Other Affiliation:______________
(name & address)
____

Please start my membership January 1, ________. Membership is on a calendar year basis, and includes the *Journal* and the *Newsletter.* Check below for special rate on *Proceedings* or *International Legal Materials.*

☐ *Proceedings of the Annual Meeting,* at $15.
☐ *International Legal Materials.* Subscription at special member rate of $50 (plus $5.50 for mailing outside U.S.A.) for six issues per year.

VERIFICATION OF STUDENT STATUS. I hereby certify that the above applicant is regularly registered in

School:______________________ Completion year:______________

Signed______________________ Title______________ Date______________

$__________ **Amount Enclosed** (U.S. Dollars) Signature______________________

- ✂

AMERICAN SOCIETY OF INTERNATIONAL LAW
2223 MASSACHUSETTS AVENUE, N.W., WASHINGTON, D.C. 20008-2864, (202) 265-4313
Be sure to check membership type on reverse side.

Name (please print) ______________________
Mailing Address ______________________
Street, P.O. Box, etc. ______________________
City, State, Zip ______________________
Country ______________ Phone ______________

Member, U.S. Bar?______ State:______ Year______

School, Firm or Other Affiliation:______________
(name & address)
____

Please start my membership January 1, ________. Membership is on a calendar year basis, and includes the *Journal* and the *Newsletter.* Check below for special rate on *Proceedings* or *International Legal Materials.*

☐ *Proceedings of the Annual Meeting,* at $15.
☐ *International Legal Materials.* Subscription at special member rate of $50 (plus $5.50 for mailing outside U.S.A.) for six issues per year.

VERIFICATION OF STUDENT STATUS. I hereby certify that the above applicant is regularly registered in

School:______________________ Completion year:______________

Signed______________________ Title______________ Date______________

$__________ **Amount Enclosed** (U.S. Dollars) Signature______________________

- ✂

AMERICAN SOCIETY OF INTERNATIONAL LAW
2223 MASSACHUSETTS AVENUE, N.W., WASHINGTON, D.C. 20008-2864, (202) 265-4313
Be sure to check membership type on reverse side.

Name (please print) ______________________
Mailing Address ______________________
Street, P.O. Box, etc. ______________________
City, State, Zip ______________________
Country ______________ Phone ______________

Member, U.S. Bar?______ State:______ Year______

School, Firm or Other Affiliation:______________
(name & address)
____

Please start my membership January 1, ________. Membership is on a calendar year basis, and includes the *Journal* and the *Newsletter.* Check below for special rate on *Proceedings* or *International Legal Materials.*

☐ *Proceedings of the Annual Meeting,* at $15.
☐ *International Legal Materials.* Subscription at special member rate of $50 (plus $5.50 for mailing outside U.S.A.) for six issues per year.

VERIFICATION OF STUDENT STATUS. I hereby certify that the above applicant is regularly registered in

School:______________________ Completion year:______________

Signed______________________ Title______________ Date______________

$__________ **Amount Enclosed** (U.S. Dollars) Signature

Membership Status *(Check one)**

☐ **Regular Membership:**
$70 a year. Persons, regardless of nationality or profession, resident in a member country of the OECD (see below).

☐ **Special Membership:**
$30 a year. Persons *not* resident in a member country of the OECD (see below).

☐ **Intermediate Membership:**
$30 a year. Persons who are under 30 years of age at the time of application for membership may be Intermediate Members for the first three consecutive years of membership.
Date of Birth ______________________

☐ **Student Membership:**
$20 a year, and certification of student status (see form on reverse).

The member countries of the OECD are Australia, Austria, Belgium, Canada, Denmark, Federal Republic of Germany, Finland, France, Greece, Iceland, Ireland, Italy, Japan, Luxembourg, Netherlands, New Zealand, Norway, Portugal, Spain, Sweden, Switzerland, Turkey, United Kingdom, United States.

*Includes $30 allocation for *The American Journal of International Law*

☐ **Contributing Membership:**
$100 a year.

☐ **Supporting Membership:**
$200 a year.

☐ **Annual Patron:**
$500 a year. Any individual or organization eligible for membership may become an Annual Patron for a contributio of at least $500.

☐ **Retired Membership:**
$25 a year. Persons who are age 70 and older, and retired.

☐ **Corporate Membership:**
$1,500 a year. Any corporation, partnership, association, or other organization acceptable to the Executive Council is eligible for Corporate Membership.

☐ **Life Membership:**
$1,000 payment.

☐ **Patron:**
One-time contribution of $5,000.

Membership Status *(Check one)**

☐ **Regular Membership:**
$70 a year. Persons, regardless of nationality or profession, resident in a member country of the OECD (see below).

☐ **Special Membership:**
$30 a year. Persons *not* resident in a member country of the OECD (see below).

☐ **Intermediate Membership:**
$30 a year. Persons who are under 30 years of age at the time of application for membership may be Intermediate Members for the first three consecutive years of membership.
Date of Birth ______________________

☐ **Student Membership:**
$20 a year, and certification of student status (see form on reverse).

The member countries of the OECD are Australia, Austria, Belgium, Canada, Denmark, Federal Republic of Germany, Finland, France, Greece, Iceland, Ireland, Italy, Japan, Luxembourg, Netherlands, New Zealand, Norway, Portugal, Spain, Sweden, Switzerland, Turkey, United Kingdom, United States.

*Includes $30 allocation for *The American Journal of International Law*

☐ **Contributing Membership:**
$100 a year.

☐ **Supporting Membership:**
$200 a year.

☐ **Annual Patron:**
$500 a year. Any individual or organization eligible for membership may become an Annual Patron for a contributi of at least $500.

☐ **Retired Membership:**
$25 a year. Persons who are age 70 and older, and retired.

☐ **Corporate Membership:**
$1,500 a year. Any corporation, partnership, association, or other organization acceptable to the Executive Council is eligible for Corporate Membership.

☐ **Life Membership:**
$1,000 payment.

☐ **Patron:**
One time contribution of $5,000.

Membership Status *(Check one)**

☐ **Regular Membership:**
$70 a year. Persons, regardless of nationality or profession, resident in a member country of the OECD (see below).

☐ **Special Membership:**
$30 a year. Persons *not* resident in a member country of the OECD (see below).

☐ **Intermediate Membership:**
$30 a year. Persons who are under 30 years of age at the time of application for membership may be Intermediate Members for the first three consecutive years of membership.
Date of Birth ______________________

☐ **Student Membership:**
$20 a year, and certification of student status (see form on reverse).

The member countries of the OECD are Australia, Austria, Belgium, Canada, Denmark, Federal Republic of Germany, Finland, France, Greece, Iceland, Ireland, Italy, Japan, Luxembourg, Netherlands, New Zealand, Norway, Portugal, Spain, Sweden, Switzerland, Turkey, United Kingdom, United States.

☐ **Contributing Membership:**
$100 a year.

☐ **Supporting Membership:**
$200 a year.

☐ **Annual Patron:**
$500 a year. Any individual or organization eligible for membership may become an Annual Patron for a contribu of at least $500.

☐ **Retired Membership:**
$25 a year. Persons who are age 70 and older, and retired.

☐ **Corporate Membership:**
$1,500 a year. Any corporation, partnership, association, c other organization acceptable to the Executive Council is eligible for Corporate Membership.

☐ **Life Membership:**
$1,000 payment.

☐ **Patron:**
One-time contribution of $5,000.

American Journal of International Law

July 1988
Vol. 82 No. 3

Published by
American Society of International Law

PATRONS OF THE SOCIETY

ARTHUR H. DEAN (deceased)
HERMAN PHLEGER (deceased)
GENEVIEVE E. TILLAR (deceased)
W. ROBERT MORGAN
BRUNSON MACCHESNEY (deceased)
ALONA E. EVANS (deceased)
JOHN N. HAZARD
JOHN R. STEVENSON
ARTHUR R. ALBRECHT
ALWYN V. FREEMAN (deceased)
EDWARD DUMBAULD
KEITH HIGHET
STEPHEN M. SCHWEBEL
WILLIAM D. ROGERS
SEYMOUR J. RUBIN
JOHN LAWRENCE HARGROVE
FRANK A. BAUMAN
RICHARD W. EDWARDS, JR.
ALMESHAL HUSSAM

In Memoriam

DR. JAMES BROWN SCOTT
HENRY C. MORRIS
ARTHUR K. KUHN
ALEXANDER FREEMAN
STANLEY P. SMITH

PATRONAGE, GIFTS AND BEQUESTS

Upon donation to the Society of $5,000 or more by gift or bequest, any member of the Society or individual eligible for membership may be elected a Patron of the Society. Upon donation of at least $5,000 in the name of a deceased person, such person may be elected a Patron posthumously.

Gifts and bequests may be made in the name of the American Society of International Law, Washington, D.C. Such contributions are deductible from federal returns for income, estate and gift tax purposes. The Society is incorporated by Act of Congress approved September 20, 1950 (64 Stat. 869).

MANLEY O. HUDSON MEDAL

The American Society of International Law bestows from time to time without regard to nationality a gold medal to commemorate the life work of Manley O. Hudson. Such awards are made for preeminent scholarship and achievement in international law and in the promotion of the establishment and maintenance of international relations on the basis of law and justice. Medals have been awarded to Manley O. Hudson (1956), Lord McNair (1959), Philip C. Jessup (1964), Charles De Visscher (1966), Paul Guggenheim (1970), Myres S. McDougal (1976), Eduardo Jiménez de Aréchaga (1978), Richard Reeve Baxter (1981), Oscar Schachter (1981), Hardy Cross Dillard (1982), Suzanne Bastid (1984), Marjorie M. Whiteman (1985) and Leo Gross (1986).

The AMERICAN JOURNAL OF INTERNATIONAL LAW (ISSN 0002-9300) is published quarterly, in January, April, July and October, and is supplied to all members of the American Society of International Law. Annual subscription rate to nonmembers is $50.00, plus $5.00 postage outside U.S.A. Available back numbers of AJIL will be supplied at $15.00 each.

EDITORIAL OFFICE:
NEW YORK UNIVERSITY SCHOOL OF LAW
40 WASHINGTON SQUARE SOUTH
NEW YORK, N.Y. 10012

BUSINESS OFFICE:
2223 MASSACHUSETTS AVENUE, N.W.
WASHINGTON, D.C. 20008-2864

Second-class postage paid at Washington, D.C. and at additional mailing office. POSTMASTER: If undeliverable, send notice on Form 3579 to the American Journal of International Law, 2223 Massachusetts Ave., N.W., Washington, D.C. 20008-2864.

Printed by Lancaster Press, Lancaster, Pa. 17603

AMERICAN JOURNAL OF INTERNATIONAL LAW

VOL. 82 | July 1988 | NO. 3

CONTENTS

PAGE

Jan Mayen in Perspective — *Elliot L. Richardson* 443

Which Law Applies to the Afghan Conflict? — *W. Michael Reisman & James Silk* 459

Advancing the Freedom of Religion or Belief Through the UN Declaration on the Elimination of Religious Intolerance and Discrimination — *Donna J. Sullivan* 487

International Discovery after Aerospatiale: The Quest for an Analytical Framework — *David J. Gerber* 521

Notes and Comments

Further Thoughts on the Chambers Procedure of the International Court of Justice — *Shigeru Oda* 556

Waldemar A. Solf (1913–1987) — *Harry H. Almond, Jr.* 562

Correspondence 564

The Francis Deák Prize 565

Contemporary Practice of the United States Relating to International Law — *Marian Nash Leich* 566

Judicial Decisions — *Monroe Leigh* 580

Current Developments

Inter-American Commission on Human Rights Finds United States in Violation — *Donald T. Fox* 601

Second Session of the UN Committee on Economic, Social and Cultural Rights — *Philip Alston & Bruno Simma* 603

Book Reviews and Notes — *Edited by Detlev Vagts*

Review Article: McClendon, J. Stewart, and Rosabel E. Everard Goodman (eds.). *International Commercial Arbitration in New York;* Redfern, Alan, and Martin Hunter. *Law and Practice of International Commercial Arbitration;* Thieffry, Patrick, and Christine Lecuyer-Thieffry. *Le Règlement des litiges civils et commerciaux avec les Etats-Unis* (William W. Park) 616

De Lupis, Ingrid Detter. *The Concept of International Law* (Christopher Osakwe) 631

Boyle, Francis A. *World Politics and International Law* (Dean N. Menegas) 635

De Lupis, Ingrid Detter. *International Law and the Independent State* (2d ed.) (Christopher Osakwe) 640

Sinclair, Ian. *The International Law Commission* (Herbert W. Briggs) 643

Rigaux, Marie-Françoise. *La Théorie des limites matérielles à l'exercice de la fonction constituante* (Gillian White) 645

Zoller, Elisabeth. *Enforcing International Law Through U.S. Legislation* (Michael J. Glennon) 648

Gray, Christine D. *Judicial Remedies in International Law* (Elisabeth Zoller) 648

Yambrušic, Edward Slavko. *Treaty Interpretation: Theory and Reality* (Francis A. Boyle) 650
Kaiser, Karl, and Hans-Peter Schwarz (eds.). *Weltpolitik: Strukturen—Akteure—Perspektiven* (Rudolf Bernhardt) 650
Kohona, Palitha Tikiri Bandara. *The Regulation of International Economic Relations Through Law* (Mark Roy Sandstrom) 651
Long, Olivier. *Law and its Limitations in the GATT Multilateral Trade System* (John H. Jackson) 653
Woolcock, Stephen, Jeffrey Hart and Hans van der Ven. *Interdependence in the Post-Multilateral Era: Trends in U.S.-European Trade Relations* (R. Michael Gadbaw and Rosemary E. Gwynn) 654
Ebert, Klaus Wolfgang. *Rechtliche Beschränkungen des Technologietransfers im Außenwirtschaftsverkehr* (Wolfgang Fikentscher) 657
Pablo-Romero Gil-Delgado, María Concepción. *La inversión directa en el régimen de las inversiones extranjeras* (José de la Rosa and Rick Silberstein) 659
Levis, Mirta Noemí (ed.). *Régimen jurídico de las inversiones extranjeras en los países de la ALADI.* 9 binders (Ewell E. Murphy, Jr.) 662
Zartman, I. William (ed.). *Positive Sum: Improving North-South Negotiations* (Tom J. Farer) 665
Wöhlcke, Manfred. *Ein Dritter Weg für die Dritte Welt?* (Konrad Ginther) 668
Foreign Relations of the United States, 1952–1954. Volume VI: Western Europe and Canada. 2 parts (Elmer Plischke) 670
Frigo, Manlio. *La Protezione dei beni culturali nel diritto internazionale* (John Henry Merryman) 674
Dinstein, Yoram (ed.). *Israel Yearbook on Human Rights.* Volume 13, 1983 (Christina M. Cerna) 675
Dinstein, Yoram (ed.). *Israel Yearbook on Human Rights.* Volume 14, 1984 (Christina M. Cerna) 677
Levie, Howard S. (ed.). *The Law of Non-International Armed Conflict: Protocol II to the 1949 Geneva Conventions* (George H. Aldrich) 679
Bossuyt, Marc J. *Guide to the "Travaux Préparatoires" of the International Covenant on Civil and Political Rights* (Hurst Hannum) 680
Collected Edition of the "Travaux Préparatoires" of the European Convention on Human Rights. Vols. VI, VII and VIII (Hurst Hannum) 680
Fraser, Arvonne S. *The U.N. Decade for Women: Documents and Dialogue* (Rita E. Hauser) 682
Sethi, S. Prakash (ed.). *The South African Quagmire: In Search of a Peaceful Path to Democratic Pluralism* (William R. Cotter) 684
Kly, Y. N. *International Law and the Black Minority in the U.S.* (Robert A. Williams, Jr.) 688
Gorman, Robert F. *Coping with Africa's Refugee Burden: A Time for Solutions* (Dietrich Kappeler) 690
Briefer Notices: Sobrino Heredia, 692; Gorove (ed.), 693.
Collected Essays: *Realism in Law-Making: Essays on international law in honour of Willem Riphagen,* 693; *Questions of International Law: Hungarian Perspectives.* Vol. 3, 694; *Annuaire Français de Droit International.* Vol. XXXII, 1986, 694; *Chinese Yearbook of International Law and Affairs.* Vol. 6 (1986–87), 695.
Books Received 696
International Legal Materials. Contents, Vol. XXVII, No. 3 (May 1988) 702

The American Journal of International Law

The views expressed in the articles, editorial comments, book reviews and notes, and other contributions which appear in AJIL are those of the individual authors and are not to be taken as representing the views of the Board of Editors or the American Society of International Law.

Manuscripts in triplicate may be sent to the Editor in Chief of AJIL, Professor Thomas M. Franck, New York University School of Law, New York, N.Y. 10012. All footnotes should be typed double space at the end of the manuscript. Please do not make multiple submissions to other journals. Persons making submissions are invited to indicate whether their manuscript is available on an IBM-PC diskette. AJIL uses WordPerfect 4.2. Subscriptions, orders for back numbers, correspondence with reference to AJIL and books for review should be sent to the AMERICAN JOURNAL OF INTERNATIONAL LAW (ISSN 0002-9300), 2223 Massachusetts Avenue, N.W., Washington, D.C. 20008-2864.

The American Society of International Law

The American Society of International Law was organized in 1906 "to foster the study of international law and to promote the establishment and maintenance of international relations on the basis of law and justice."

Society membership is open to all persons of whatever nationality and profession who are interested in its objectives. Dues are: regular, $70; special category, $30 for persons *not* resident in a member country of the Organisation for Economic Co-operation and Development; intermediate, $30; student, $20. Membership application form is printed at the back of each issue of AJIL.

JAN MAYEN IN PERSPECTIVE

*By Elliot L. Richardson**

On October 22, 1981, the Governments of Iceland and Norway approved an agreement for the joint management of the resources of the Jan Mayen continental shelf.[1] Incorporating the recommendations of a three-member conciliation commission, the Agreement obviated the need to draw a line demarcating the right to exploit the nonliving resources in the disputed area. The proliferation of boundary disputes during the intervening 7 years makes this an appropriate time to look at the potential benefits of using this approach in other maritime boundary disputes. After reviewing the stages in the resolution of the *Jan Mayen* dispute and the terms of the Agreement, this essay will discuss other situations in which the joint development approach has been used, the factors affecting its success and some examples of current delimitation disputes where this approach may be applicable.

I. The Jan Mayen Fishing Agreement

The island of Jan Mayen lies 550 nautical miles from Tromsø, Norway, and 292 nautical miles from Iceland. At 53 kilometers in length and 15–20 kilometers in width, its total area covers 373 square kilometers. It is entirely volcanic in origin, the last eruption having been reported in 1970.

Now used only as a meteorological station, Jan Mayen has a year-round population of 30 to 40. It received very little attention until 1978 when Icelandic fishermen made a large catch of capelin off its shores. The sudden realization of the island's resource potential raised questions as to Jan Mayen's right to an exclusive economic zone (EEZ) and continental shelf, as contemplated for islands in provisions of the Law of the Sea Convention then being drafted.[2] Although Norway's title to Jan Mayen was established

* Of the District of Columbia Bar. The author served as Chairman of the Conciliation Commission on the Continental Shelf Area between Iceland and Jan Mayen. He was assisted in the preparation of this article by Camille M. Antinori, now with the Strategic Analysis Division of the Department of Commerce.

[1] Agreement on the Continental Shelf between Iceland and Jan Mayen, *done* Oct. 22, 1981, Iceland-Norway, *reprinted in* 21 ILM 1222 (1982).

[2] United Nations Convention on the Law of the Sea, *reprinted in* UNITED NATIONS, OFFICIAL TEXT OF THE UNITED NATIONS CONVENTION ON THE LAW OF THE SEA WITH ANNEXES AND INDEX, UN Sales No. E.83.V.5 (1983). The Convention was adopted on Apr. 30, 1982, and open for signature from Dec. 10, 1982, to Dec. 9, 1984, during which time it received 159 signatures. Currently, it has 34 of the 60 ratifications required to bring it into force. OCEANS POL'Y NEWS, September 1987, at 1. Article 121 provides that islands are entitled to a territorial sea, an economic zone and a continental shelf. *See* Iceland: Law No. 41 Concerning the Territorial Sea, the Economic Zone and the Continental Shelf, June 1, 1979, *reprinted in* 18 ILM 1504 (1979).

by a 1929 Act of the Norwegian Parliament,[3] Norway did not claim a 200-mile fishing zone or EEZ around the island in 1977 when it established an EEZ adjacent to its mainland coast.

Following the 1978 capelin catch, Norwegian fishing interests persuaded their Government to repair this omission. Norway's action drew immediate objections from Iceland, and the two Governments entered into negotiations that were held in 1979 and 1980. These negotiations led to the Fishing Agreement of May 1980, which established a Joint Fisheries Commission charged with setting species catch quotas.[4] The Agreement recognized that Iceland should have the full extent of its 200-mile EEZ between Jan Mayen and Iceland, while giving Jan Mayen an EEZ extending to 200 miles only where it is not constricted by Iceland's zone.[5]

There remained conflicting claims by the two Governments over the continental shelf surrounding the island. Invoking the theory of natural prolongation, Iceland asserted that the seabed between Iceland and Jan Mayen constituted part of the Icelandic continental shelf, while Norway insisted that it was an extension of Jan Mayen. The shelf area of prime interest to both parties was the part at the most exploitable depths, the Jan Mayen Ridge, a north-south trending feature marked by depressions and plateaus at water depths ranging from 200 meters to 1,600 meters.[6] Because of these conflicting claims, Article 9 of the 1980 Fishing Agreement provided for the establishment of a conciliation commission to which delimitation of the continental shelf would be referred. The commission was directed to submit, within 5 months of its appointment, unanimous recommendations, taking into account a "broad scope of considerations," including Iceland's strong economic interest in the sea area, the existing geographical and geological factors, and other special circumstances. Although these recommendations would not be binding, the parties committed themselves to pay reasonable regard to them.[7]

II. The Conciliation Commission's Report

The conciliation commission was formally established on August 16, 1980, with Ambassador Hans Andersen as conciliator for Iceland, Ambassador Jens Evensen as conciliator for Norway, and the author as Chairman. Since each of us was the head of our country's delegation to the Third

[3] Law No. 2 Concerning Jan Mayen, Feb. 27, 1930, *reprinted in* I.C.5 Ministry of Foreign Affairs, Norwegian Laws and Acts, Selected for the Foreign Service (1980).

[4] Agreement Concerning Fishery and Continental Shelf Questions, May 28, 1980 (entered into force June 1980), 1980 Overenskomster med fremmede stater 912. *See* Churchill, *Maritime Delimitation in the Jan Mayen Area,* 9 Marine Pol'y 16 (1985).

[5] Agreement Concerning Fishery and Continental Shelf Questions, *supra* note 4, preamble. *See also* Iceland: Law Concerning the Territorial Sea, the Economic Zone and the Continental Shelf, *supra* note 2.

[6] Conciliation Commission on the Continental Shelf Area between Iceland and Jan Mayen, Report and Recommendations to the Governments of Iceland and Norway (1981), *reprinted in* 20 ILM 797 (1981) [hereinafter Report].

[7] Agreement Concerning Fishery and Continental Shelf Questions, *supra* note 4, Art. 9.

United Nations Conference on the Law of the Sea, we were aware that customary international law was far from completely crystallized with respect to the principles governing continental shelf delimitation between neighboring states. To avoid becoming mired in that issue, we decided instead to explore the feasibility of a special zone of joint exploration and development covering the most promising resource potential of the disputed area. If Iceland and Norway would consent to cooperate within that zone in accordance with a mutually agreed regime, the focus would be placed where it belonged: on a fair division of the resources at stake, rather than on the determination of an artificial line.[8]

The key to gaining acceptance for this approach, in the commission's view, would be a solid factual basis for its recommendations. Without adequate knowledge about the location, size, accessibility and likely presence of the area's potential resources, we could not convincingly justify and explain the terms and specifications of the proposed regime. It would not do, moreover, for experts in either country to be able to shoot holes into our findings.[9]

The commission's first meeting took place during a Law of the Sea Conference session in Geneva. Serving on the U.S. delegation at the time was Dr. Manik Talwani, Director of the Lamont-Doherty Geological Observatory at Columbia University. As it happened, Dr. Talwani was an expert on the geomorphology of the Jan Mayen continental shelf. He was also intimately familiar with the work of all the other scientists whose research had focused on the shelf. It might be mutually beneficial, he suggested, both to the commission and to the interested scientists, if the latter could be assembled at the Lamont-Doherty Geological Observatory for an exchange of information on their recent findings. The commission unanimously agreed that this would be a perfect opportunity to obtain the factual data that it recognized as essential.

Convened as a scientific advisory committee to the commission and chaired by Dr. Talwani, a group of nine scientists from the United States, the Federal Republic of Germany, France, Norway and Iceland met at the observatory from December 8 to 10, 1980.[10] Their principal aims were:

[8] An approach addressed to the realities underlying cooperation in solving delimitation disputes was anticipated by Judge Jessup. North Sea Continental Shelf Cases (FRG/Den.; FRG/Neth.), 1969 ICJ REP. 3, 67–84 (Judgment of Feb. 20) (Jessup, J., sep. op.).

[9] The value of having adequate knowledge of a disputed area is illustrated by the Danish-Swedish continental shelf dispute in the Kattegatt. Despite Swedish protests, a Danish company proceeded with exploratory drilling in 1983, only to find no commercially exploitable resources in the disputed zone. This discovery relaxed the political tension, although the delimitation is still pending. *See* Lagoni, *Interim Measures pending Maritime Delimitation Agreements,* 78 AJIL 345, 363–64 (1984).

[10] In addition to Dr. Talwani, the members of the special scientific advisory committee were Dr. Karl Hinz (Bundesanstalt für Geowissenschaften und Rohstoffe, Federal Republic of Germany), Dr. Lucien Montadert (Institut français du Pétrole), Dr. Olav Eldholm (University of Oslo, Norway), Mr. E. Bergsager (Norwegian Petroleum Directorate), Dr. Gudmundur Palmason (National Energy Authority, Iceland), Dr. Lewis Alexander (Geographer of the United States), Dr. N. Terence Edgar (U.S. Geological Survey) and Mr. John Mutter, rapporteur (Lamont-Doherty Geological Observatory).

> (1) to examine how the Jan Mayen Ridge, which is the most prominent feature in this region containing sedimentary rocks, is related morphologically and geologically to the island of Jan Mayen and Iceland; [and]
>
> (2) to examine existing geological and geophysical data with a view towards obtaining the distribution of possible prospective areas for hydrocarbons in the region lying between Jan Mayen and eastern Iceland.[11]

The scientific advisory committee based its conclusions on an examination of the origin and evolution of the Jan Mayen Ridge and on a bathymetric and lithologic mapping of the area. With regard to its first aim—the relationship between the Jan Mayen Ridge and the island of Jan Mayen and Iceland—the committee found the concept of natural prolongation to be inapplicable:

> The concept of natural prolongation can be considered in two different senses, morphological and geological. Morphologically the northern part of Jan Mayen Ridge can be considered a southward extension from the shelf of Jan Mayen. On the other hand, Jan Mayen Ridge cannot morphologically be considered an extension from the Icelandic shelf.
>
> However, geologically Jan Mayen Ridge is a microcontinent that predates both Jan Mayen and Iceland which are composed of younger volcanics; therefore the ridge is not considered a natural geological prolongation of either Jan Mayen or Iceland.[12]

With regard to the second aim—the ridge area's hydrocarbon potential—the committee was unenthusiastic but emphasized the need for further exploration:

> The hydrocarbon potential of the northern part of the Jan Mayen Ridge . . . is regarded as more favorable mainly because it has a larger areal extent than the southern part. It should be stated that the southern part is less understood and appears to be more complex than the northern part.
>
> . . . .
>
> . . . However, considered in comparison with known oil-producing areas worldwide, the overall potential cannot be considered good, based on the existing fragmentary data. We emphasize that detailed further exploration could change this assessment.[13]

Having armed itself with the best possible data, the commission reverted to its mandate: to draw on a "broad scope of considerations" in formulating its recommendations. As previously noted, it was also charged with taking into account "Iceland's strong economic interests in these sea areas, the existing geographical and geological factors and other special circumstances."[14] Although acknowledging the numerous examples of state practice and court decisions developing the concept of natural prolongation in

[11] Report, *supra* note 6, at 806–07.
[12] *Id.* at 813–14.
[13] *Id.* at 818.
[14] *Id.* at 823.

the context of continental shelf delimitations, the commission followed its scientific advisory committee in finding these precedents inapplicable.[15]

Taking into account both the fact that Iceland had already been granted a 200-mile EEZ embracing a considerable area beyond the median line and the uncertainty as to the area's resource potential, the commission decided not to propose a demarcation line for the continental shelf different from the EEZ line. It gave special consideration to four other factors: (1) Iceland's total dependence on hydrocarbon imports; (2) the low hydrocarbon potential of the shelf around Iceland, placing it in a shelf-locked, disadvantaged status; (3) the fact that the Jan Mayen Ridge area was the only area between Jan Mayen and Iceland with any such potential; and (4) the inaccessibility of the resource due to the limitations of present technology and its distance from the market, which meant that only a large find would make it commercially exploitable.[16]

This was the route by which the commission came to its recommendation of a joint development zone "covering substantially all of the area offering any significant prospect of hydrocarbon production."[17] The zone is a rectangular area covering 45,475 square kilometers and containing the most promising hydrocarbon potential. Iceland's EEZ overlaps the southwest corner of the rectangle by about 12,725 square kilometers. The remaining area north of Iceland's EEZ comprises about 32,750 square kilometers.[18]

The commission next decided that cooperation should begin at the predrilling stage, during which Norway would bear the cost of carrying out seismic surveys through the Norwegian Petroleum Directorate. Iceland and Norway would collaborate on the plans for such surveys, with Iceland participating through its equivalent of the Norwegian Directorate. If the results so justified, oil companies would be invited to buy the seismic surveys and to bid for exploration permits. Any resulting profits would be divided equally between the two countries.[19]

At this point, the commission had a variety of forms of joint cooperation agreements to consider in structuring the control of licensing should oil companies wish to bid for exploration and drilling rights. Such agreements differ from each other with respect to ownership of hydrocarbons and performance and control provisions, as well as in their approaches to funding and risk capital. The models considered included concession contracts with joint venture arrangements, service contracts, production-sharing contracts and entrepreneur contracts.[20] Since Norway's national petroleum company, Statoil, had extensive experience in concession contracts with joint venture arrangements, the commission selected this model.

During the development stage in the special zone, combined Icelandic-Norwegian participation would constitute at least 50 percent of a joint

[15] *Id.* at 822, 824.

[16] *Id.* at 826.

[17] *Id.*

[18] The area was defined by a series of coordinates as the zone between 70°35′ and 68° north latitude, and 10°30′ and 6°30′ west longitude. Agreement on the Continental Shelf, *supra* note 1, 21 ILM at 1223.

[19] Report, *supra* note 6, at 830–31.

[20] *Id.* at 832–34.

venture. Norwegian legislation would apply in the area north of the Icelandic EEZ boundary, and Icelandic legislation would apply in the area south of this boundary. Each country would have the option of participating in negotiations with private companies bidding in the other party's sector, of joining any joint venture group and of acquiring a fixed percentage interest of 25 percent or less if it so wished.[21]

The commission felt that at the early development stage when the risks were greatest, the financial burden should not be borne by the states but by private companies with deep-water experience.[22] The states should therefore seek to have their share of the early drilling costs "carried" by the private companies until a commercial find was made, at which time the Governments would reimburse the oil companies. Recognizing that Iceland had less extensive experience in joint ventures than Norway, the commission recommended slightly different terms for each of the two sectors of the special zone. In Norway's sector, if the oil companies would not be willing to carry the Governments' share of exploration costs, Iceland would have the option of not joining the joint venture until a commercial find was made; if Iceland then decided to participate, it would reimburse Norway for its share of the costs incurred. In Iceland's sector, Norway would not have a corresponding right to withhold the decision to participate until a find was made.[23]

Unitization procedures[24] would be implemented in all three areas holding the possibility of transboundary hydrocarbon deposits: (1) within the special zone across Iceland's EEZ boundary line, (2) across the special zone southward into Iceland's EEZ, and (3) across the zone northward on Norway's side. However, as a slight concession to Iceland, any transboundary deposit lying to the north on Norway's side would be considered as falling wholly within the special zone, which in effect would extend the zone into Norwegian jurisdiction.[25]

III. Other Applications of the Joint Management Approach

The merit of a joint development zone, as opposed to a division of territory, lies in minimizing the potential for conflict, often by eliminating com-

[21] *Id.* at 836–39. [22] *Id.* at 837.

[23] *Id.* at 838. In making these technical recommendations, the commission benefited from the special expertise of Ambassador Evensen, whose experience in the North Sea negotiations had familiarized him with the legal, scientific and commercial aspects of the methods of petroleum development.

[24] Unitization procedures usually allow each party to maintain jurisdiction on its side of the boundary line while the field is exploited as a single unit subject to well-defined installations and apportionment of reserves. The procedures are intended to promote good oil-well practice.

[25] Report, *supra* note 6, at 839. Although not immediately recommending them, the commission also suggested including in a future agreement other fields of cooperation such as transfer of technology, long-term petroleum supply agreements to Iceland, access to scientific and practical training, and other spheres of activity not involving resources. *Id.* at 840.

petition over the ownership of resources. Letting both countries have access to the resources of a disputed area on the basis of a mutually accepted regime sidesteps the thorny problems inherent in resolving the issue of delimitation, especially where the resources are unknown.[26] It converts the otherwise intractable issue of ownership into a question of distribution and of quantity: how much can each state be assured of obtaining from the disputed area? Joint development promotes international cooperation in the management of common resources, encourages their rational use and guards against the possibility of conflict over future discoveries in the border region. This approach to dispute resolution is more naturally arrived at by the more flexible method of negotiation between the parties than through a formal adjudicative process. It can thus take into consideration a wide range of political and economic interests that would not necessarily be relevant in a claim as of right.

The Jan Mayen Agreement well illustrates these advantages, but it is by no means the only example of the value of the joint development approach. The situations where it has been used can be divided into two basic categories: those involving already discovered common deposits and those involving common deposits that may be discovered in the future.[27] Depending on the particular legal and factual circumstances, degrees of cooperation can range from requiring only periodic consultation between countries on the changing status of a commercially productive common resource,[28] to arrangements in which an international body is charged with determining the overall management of the area concerned, as has been proposed for Antarctica and its continental shelf.[29]

[26] Article IV of the Antarctic Treaty of 1959 is a prime example of sidestepping of the sovereignty question while research activities proceed. The Treaty establishes a regime for managing Antarctica but does not resolve the problems arising from the refusal of the United States, the USSR, Japan and others to recognize any territorial claims. Instead, Article IV simply freezes the parties' claims. Antarctic Treaty, *done* Dec. 1, 1959, 12 UST 794, TIAS No. 4780, 402 UNTS 71. A similar solution seems likely in the Antarctic mineral regime currently being negotiated. *See infra* note 29.

[27] *See* Onorato, *Apportionment of an International Common Petroleum Deposit,* 17 INT'L & COMP. L.Q. 85 (1968); Lagoni, *Oil and Gas Deposits Across National Frontiers,* 73 AJIL 215 (1979); Reid, *Petroleum Development in Areas of International Seabed Boundary Disputes: Means for Resolution,* 3 OIL & GAS: L. & TAX'N REV. 214 (1984/85).

[28] An example is the agreement between Austria and Czechoslovakia over the division of common gas fields lying in the Zwerndorf-Vysoká frontier area. *See* Agreement Concerning the Working of Common Deposits of Natural Gas and Petroleum, Jan. 23, 1960, Austria-Czechoslovakia, 495 UNTS 125. *See also* Lagoni, *supra* note 27, at 223.

[29] Since 1982, the parties to the 1959 Antarctic Treaty have been negotiating a legal regime that would govern the possibility of minerals development in Antarctica, including potential hydrocarbons on the surrounding continental margin. Although the draft regime is not a public document, a copy of its text has been published by Greenpeace. One of the most up-to-date descriptions of this proposed international management regime can be found in R. Tucker Scully's The Antarctic Mineral Resource Negotiations: A Report (paper presented at the 20th Annual Meeting of the Law of the Sea Institute, Miami, July 23, 1986). *See also* Joyner, *The Antarctic Minerals Negotiating Process,* 81 AJIL 888 (1987).

A comparison of the Jan Mayen Agreement with the United Kingdom–Norway Frigg Field Agreement of 1976[30] and the France-Spain Bay of Biscay Agreement of 1974[31] points up the adaptability of joint arrangements to differing circumstances. In all three agreements the parties retain jurisdiction over the installations and operations on their side of a boundary demarcation. The Frigg Field Agreement, however, governs the activities in an already developed reservoir unitized and operated by a single "unit operator." It allows for changes in apportionment of resources between the two countries in accordance with periodic reassessments by the Frigg Field Consultative Commission. The Bay of Biscay Agreement was made in anticipation of future exploration and created a special rectangular zone of cooperation similar to the Jan Mayen special zone. A difference between the Jan Mayen Agreement and the Bay of Biscay Agreement is the provision in the latter for "equal sharing," under which each state is allowed to nominate companies for bidding rights whenever a permit is being granted by the state governing the other side of the dividing line. This provision also encourages applicants for the concession to enter into *accords d'association* with applicants nominated by the other state. Both states are thus on an equal footing even though the licensed area is under the management of one operator. This arrangement is, in fact, essentially similar to that called for by the Jan Mayen Agreement since equal rights to the resources of the special zone are afforded to both parties.[32]

The success of the economic approach reflected in these agreements depends on the adaptability of the resource to a cooperative arrangement. Relevant factors are the nature of the resource, its significance to the concerned countries and the degree of benefit to be gained from coordinating their efforts. Jan Mayen's fishery resources are substantial and the fishing industry is much more important to Iceland than to Norway.[33] A joint fishing agreement between Iceland and Norway would thus be possible only if, like the Jan Mayen EEZ delimitation, it tilted heavily toward Iceland.

[30] Agreement Relating to the Exploitation of the Frigg Field Reservoir and the Transmission of Gas Therefrom to the United Kingdom, United Kingdom–Norway, May 10, 1976, 1977 Gr. Brit. T.S. No. 113 (Cmd. 7043).

[31] Convention sur la délimitation des plateaux continentaux des deux Etats dans le golfe de Gascogne (golfe de Biscaye), Jan. 29, 1974, France-Spain, *reprinted in* 80 REVUE GÉNÉRALE DE DROIT INTERNATIONAL PUBLIC 368 (1976). For additional agreements on maritime delimitation and fishing, see UN Doc. ST/LEG/SER.B/16, at 407 (1974).

[32] Lagoni, *supra* note 27, at 223–26. Another kind of cooperative agreement is that of the Ems-Dollart Treaty between Holland and the Federal Republic of Germany, which encourages concessionaires in the Ems River Estuary, long claimed by both countries, to enter into joint operations on either side of the boundary. The Treaty also adopts the common approach for the exploration and exploitation of the area. Supplementary Agreement to the Treaty Concerning Arrangements for Cooperation in the Ems Estuary (Ems-Dollart Treaty), Apr. 8, 1960, Netherlands–Federal Republic of Germany, 509 UNTS 104.

[33] "Fifteen percent of Iceland's population is employed in the fishing industry, while the earnings of fisheries amount to some 17 percent of the gross national product. Of the country's total exports, fish products account for 75 percent, and of this 95 percent is caught in Icelandic waters." W. ØSTRENG, INTERNATIONAL EXPLOITATION OF 'NATIONAL' OCEAN MINERALS (Fridtjof Nansen Institute, Study No. R:007, 1983).

Although the discovery of oil in the Jan Mayen Ridge would also be more important to Iceland than to Norway, which already has North Sea oil, the low hydrocarbon potential of the disputed area relieved a certain amount of tension and eased the way for a cooperative regime.

Sharing a common Nordic heritage, moreover, undoubtedly helped to bring Iceland and Norway together and facilitated communication between them. Norway's interest in keeping Iceland within the NATO fold may also have reinforced Norway's conciliatory attitude.[34] Indeed, an element of interdependence may be a general indicator of the likelihood of success of a cooperative approach.[35] This is not to say that sharing similar politico-strategic objectives or economic ideologies is a prerequisite for cooperation. On the contrary, even though the economic and political ideologies of China and Japan diverge widely, they have been jointly developing the Bohai region of the Yellow Sea for several years.[36]

Things can go wrong, of course, even where the circumstances favoring a joint management scheme seem propitious. Although joint management was the obvious and sensible way of resolving the boundary dispute between the United States and Canada in the Gulf of Maine, a 1979 fishing agreement signed by both countries was rejected by the Senate under pressure from the New England fishing lobby.[37] The two countries were thus obliged to submit the division of one of the most important fishing areas in the world to the International Court of Justice on the basis of complex and sometimes inconsistent or conflicting geological, geomorphological and ecological data.[38] The Court's delineation of a single maritime boundary was disappointing to the United States, which thereby lost access to part of Georges Bank, with the consequent disruption of the fishing patterns followed by New England fishermen for more than 300 years.[39] The outcome all too completely vindicated the position of Lloyd Cutler, the U.S. negotiator of the 1979 fishing agreement, who had argued:

[34] Østreng discusses the "Keflavik card" as a political factor influencing the formulation of the Norwegian negotiating standpoint *before* negotiations with Iceland actually took place. If tensions rose to the point where Iceland pulled out of NATO, as it had threatened to do in the "Cod Wars" with the United Kingdom, the United States would have been left without a base in the entire Norwegian Sea, which is of vital importance for surveillance of the Kola Peninsula. Nor could Norway have relocated the base on its territory. To do so would be in violation of its self-imposed military policy of "reassurance" for the Soviets, whereby Norway does not allow stationing of foreign troops on its soil during peacetime. Incidentally, the Norwegians mediated the "Cod Wars" dispute, which would have put them in an awkward position if they took a hard stance in the *Jan Mayen* dispute. *Id.* at 16–20.

[35] *Id.* at 31.

[36] *Id.*

[37] Agreement on East Coast Fishery Resources, Mar. 29, 1979, United States–Canada (not ratified by the United States). Linked to the Agreement was the Maritime Boundary Settlement Treaty with Canada, later ratified by both sides, calling for submission of the dispute to the International Court of Justice. Maritime Boundary Settlement Treaty, Mar. 29, 1979, United States–Canada, TIAS No. 10,204 (entered into force Nov. 20, 1981).

[38] Clain, *Gulf of Maine—A Disappointing First in the Delimitation of a Single Maritime Boundary,* 25 VA. J. INT'L L. 521 (1985).

[39] Delimitation of the Maritime Boundary in the Gulf of Maine Area (Can. v. U.S.), 1984 ICJ REP. 246 (Judgment of Oct. 12).

> [I]f we had no fisheries agreement, and in an adjudication of the boundary the U.S. position was fully upheld, we would be under no obligation to allow Canada access to any of the fisheries resources of Georges Bank, and we could have a free hand in the management of those fisheries. On the other hand, what if the Canadian position prevailed? In that case U.S. fishermen would be barred from the northeastern third of Georges Bank, an important area for scallops, cod, haddock and many other species. Moreover, because in that circumstance all the stocks on Georges Bank would be transboundary in nature, we would still have to manage the entire Georges Bank jointly with Canada. The Fishery Agreement provides insurance against the inherent risks of the boundary adjudication.[40]

In his analysis of the *Gulf of Maine* case, an American commentator expressed the hope that "*The Gulf of Maine Case* will stand as an example of how *not* to proceed in a delimitation dispute, and that nations will follow the much wiser alternative chosen in *The Jan Mayen Case.*"[41]

Where the strategic location of a region is even more significant than its natural resources, a system of joint jurisdiction within the disputed area is not likely to be acceptable to the parties. For example, a joint management approach is not likely in the Barents Sea between Norway and the Soviet Union because of its proximity to the home base of the Soviet Northern Fleet on the Kola Peninsula. Incidents of Soviet noncompliance with the provisional fisheries agreement of January 1978, generally known as the "grey zone" agreement,[42] also diminish the likelihood that the Norwegians would be willing partners with the Soviets in a zone of joint jurisdiction. Such incidents have included the boarding by Soviet patrols of fishing vessels operating under Norwegian licenses, in violation of the provisions of the agreement allowing third-party fishing in the grey zone. However, in militarily sensitive areas like the Barents Sea that are also prime fishing grounds, some degree of cooperation in fishing arrangements and conservation is almost unavoidable if continued activity is to be assured.

Where both strategic considerations and strained relations between the parties are involved, the lure of the resource has little chance of overcoming the obstacles to negotiation. Greece and Turkey, for example, have made several abortive attempts to negotiate the delimitation dispute involving the continental shelf in the Aegean Sea. At least for the time being, the longstanding friction between these two countries will continue to be an insuperable barrier to accommodating their common interest in exploiting the hydrocarbons believed to lie in parts of the disputed area.[43]

[40] *United States–Canadian Fishing Agreements: Hearings Before the Subcomm. on Fisheries and Wildlife Conservation and the Environment of the House Comm. on Merchant Marine and Fisheries,* 96th Cong., 1st Sess. 40, 43 (1979) (statement of Lloyd N. Cutler), *quoted in* Clain, *supra* note 38, at 603.

[41] Clain, *supra* note 38, at 605 (emphasis in original).

[42] Østreng, *Regional Delimitation Arrangements in the Arctic Seas: Cases of Precedence?,* 10 MARINE POL'Y 132, 143 (1986).

[43] Greece unsuccessfully requested interim measures of protection and the Court held that it lacked jurisdiction to entertain the Greek Application. Aegean Sea Continental Shelf (Greece

The relations between the parties also affect one of the most important components of petroleum exploration and development: technological input, a commodity that is often guarded jealously by private companies and subject to strict export restrictions based on national security interests. The issue turns on the extent to which one party views the other as a competitor or threat to its national security. There are many joint ventures, of course, in which these factors do not get in the way. In some that involve states on an unequal footing with respect to technological expertise, the more developed country carries a greater burden. Australia and Indonesia, Saudi Arabia and Sudan, and Japan and China are a few examples.[44]

Joint management zones can also be useful as a temporary solution to the delimitation problem. Article 83(3) of the Law of the Sea Convention provides that, pending an agreement on delimitation, "the States concerned, in a spirit of understanding and co-operation, shall make every effort" to reach a provisional arrangement without prejudice to the final agreement. This obligation to cooperate arises in the interval between the acknowledgment that a dispute exists and its final resolution.[45] While states may not always manage to establish interim arrangements, success in doing so allows resource exploitation to proceed peacefully and precludes one state from violating what may later prove to be the other state's territory or resources.[46] Interim arrangements can take an elementary form, such as the division of jurisdiction, or reach the level of some sort of joint management regime. In either case, the parties should be aware that the interim arrangement can have a "norm-creating" role. It follows that the terms they accept for such an arrangement should not deviate significantly from what they would deem acceptable on a permanent basis.[47]

IV. Potential Joint Development Zones

As previously noted, the indicators of the potential for a successful alternative to continental shelf delimitation are the adaptability of the resources

---

v. Turk.), 1976 ICJ Rep. 3 (Interim Protection Order of Sept. 11); and Aegean Sea Continental Shelf (Greece v. Turk.), 1978 ICJ Rep. 3 (Judgment of Dec. 19). The dispute has been going on since 1976. Turkey maintained that Greece had refused to participate in meaningful negotiations even to the extent of refusing to attempt to agree on the definition of the area in question. Observations of the Government of Turkey on the Request by the Government of Greece for Provisional Measures of Protection, 1976 ICJ Pleadings (Aegean Sea Continental Shelf) 69, 70, para. 10 (Observations submitted in 1976). *See also* Lagoni, *supra* note 9, at 355; The Maritime Dimension 184–85 (R. P. Barston & P. Birnie eds. 1980).

[44] W. Østreng, *supra* note 33, at 31–32.

[45] "Considering the object and purpose of the obligation, one has to endorse the opinion that it must arise as soon as the claims overlap. Otherwise, one of the states concerned could prejudice the negotiations before they actually started." Lagoni, *supra* note 9, at 364. The obligation would remain if negotiations reached a deadlock or were discontinued, or if one of the parties issued notice that a dispute had arisen. *Id.*

[46] *See generally id.*

[47] North Sea Continental Shelf Cases, 1969 ICJ Rep. at 42. *See also* W. Østreng, *supra* note 33, at 137, 141–44.

to joint management, the likelihood of a cooperative relationship between the parties, and their willingness to balance control and share technology. These same considerations apply to other jurisdictional disputes for which joint management could be an advantageous solution. While there are many situations involving one or more of these indicators,[48] those in the Gulf of Paria, the Bering Sea, the Beaufort Sea and the Rockall-Faeroe plateau are useful examples of the potential for joint development zones.

The Gulf of Paria

Among the many common interests shared by Venezuela and Trinidad and Tobago are fishing, and, to a lesser extent, hydrocarbon exploration and development. The islands of Trinidad and Tobago are situated off the Venezuelan coast, and their EEZs overlap with Venezuela's. The St. Clair–Paria Pérez Treaty of 1942, better known as the Gulf of Paria Treaty,[49] concluded by Venezuela and the United Kingdom on behalf of Trinidad and Tobago, establishes the boundaries between the submarine areas of the gulf. According to Kaldone Nweihed, this Treaty has the distinction of being "the first contractual instrument in international law to enshrine the delimitation of submerged territory, anywhere in the world."[50] The EEZs and continental shelves of the two countries, however, go beyond the Gulf of Paria both to the northwest and southeast of Trinidad and Tobago. Trinidadians' fears that Venezuela's vigorous Caribbean policy might lead to a dominant political relationship strengthened their desire to reach an agreement on the areas not covered by the Gulf of Paria agreement.

The controversy that arose over poaching by Trinidadian fishermen in Venezuelan waters in the 1960s was often depicted in terms of a dispute between an "oil-rich neighbor and poor fishermen denied access to their means of subsistence."[51] Trinidad and Tobago and Venezuela signed a fishing agreement on December 12, 1977, superseding the 1942 Treaty. This Agreement, after setting out formal expressions of friendship, solidarity and cooperation, established two common fishing areas to which fishing boats of either party have access. One area, the Northern Area, lies north of Trinidad and west of Tobago. The second area, the Southern Area, lies south of Trinidad and north of Venezuela. A Fishery Commission estab-

[48] Potential areas for the application of the joint development approach that are not discussed here are the Timor Gap between Australia and Indonesia, the Gulf of Thailand and the Gulf of Tonkin. *See* Valencia & Miyoshi, *Southeast Asian Seas: Joint Development of Hydrocarbons in Overlapping Claim Areas,* 16 OCEAN DEV. & INT'L L. 211 (1986). *See also* Dzurek, *Boundary and Resource Disputes in the South China Sea,* 5 OCEAN Y.B. 254 (1985); Park, *China and Maritime Jurisdiction: Some Boundary Issues,* 22 GER. Y.B. INT'L L. 119 (1979). Offshore industry in Africa is still in its early stages, and few delimitation agreements have, as yet, been concluded. The joint development approach may be useful in this region as the need arises in the future.

[49] Treaty Relating to the Submarine Areas of the Gulf of Paria, Feb. 26, 1942, United Kingdom–Venezuela, 205 LNTS 121.

[50] Nweihed, *EZ (Uneasy) Delimitation in the Semi-enclosed Caribbean Sea: Recent Agreements Between Venezuela and Her Neighbors,* 8 OCEAN DEV. & INT'L L. 1 (1980).

[51] *Id.* at 16.

lished by the Agreement regulates specific conditions regarding the parties' fishing activities in the common areas, such as types of boats permitted, pricing of fish caught and percentage of the catch to be sold in Trinidad and Tobago. The Fishery Commission also has the power to present recommendations to the Governments of both parties concerning measures necessary for the proper management of resources in the common areas.[52] The Fishing Agreement provides for the parties' cooperation in joint oceanographic and fishery enterprises, the protection of species, research and antipollution controls.

Negotiations for the permanent delimitation of the maritime areas extending from the Gulf of Paria into the Atlantic and the Caribbean continue to this day.[53] While only a partial solution to the delimitation dispute over the Caribbean areas is close to conclusion, it would still be advantageous to establish a joint development zone in areas with hydrocarbon potential.[54] The areas with hydrocarbon-bearing subsoil already contain operating oil wells and both countries have state-run oil industries, a circumstance that would facilitate the negotiation of a contractual arrangement. A joint development zone would appeal to Trinidad and Tobago because it would assure them of receiving technical assistance in petroleum development from Venezuela. For Venezuela, a joint development zone could bring political benefits in addition to economic returns: improved relations with its neighbors could be a byproduct of Venezuela's role as the leading contributor to the region's economic development.

The Bering Sea

Since 1981, the United States and the Soviet Union have been holding intermittent negotiations concerning the boundary in the Bering Sea set by the 1867 Convention Treaty on the Cession of Alaska. This maritime boundary, the longest in the world at over 1,800 nautical miles, crosses the highly promising hydrocarbon-bearing subsoil of the Navarin Basin, where the U.S. Minerals Management Service has conducted lease sales near the disputed zone. Geologically, the Navarin Basin extends into the eastern Siberian coast, making the discovery of a transboundary deposit very likely in the near future as this region is developed. Prior agreement on unitization procedures would be the first and most basic step toward eventual

[52] Fishing Agreement, December 1977, Venezuela–Trinidad and Tobago, Bilateral Treaties of Trinidad and Tobago (1979), Gazeta Oficial de la República de Venezuela, June 7, 1978.

[53] Telephone interview with Andrés Aguilar Mawdsley, Permanent Representative of Venezuela to the United Nations (June 1986).

[54] A report of the Inter-American Dialogue refers to the principle of joint exploitation as particularly appropriate for the Caribbean: "Joint regimes—which would harmonize with a tradition of integration between political units [in the] region—could reduce costs, and might make it easier for outside countries and agencies to render technical assistance." INTER-AMERICAN DIALOGUE, THE AMERICAS AT A CROSSROADS 50 (Woodrow Wilson International Center for Scholars, 1983).

exploitation of the resource. The United States and the Soviet Union have a history of environmental cooperation in the Bering Sea region, which improves the prospect of cooperative management in fisheries, pollution and preservation of marine mammals.[55] Although restrictions on technology transfer would be an obstacle to joint petroleum development schemes, and the countries can hardly be considered mutually dependent, each Government has an interest in developing the resources and creating an example of peaceful coexistence on the basis of a mutually accepted regime.[56]

The Beaufort Sea

The rich hydrocarbon potential of the Beaufort Sea has been known since the Prudhoe Bay discovery in 1968, but a dispute between the United States and Canada stemming from overlapping claims has stalled further exploration and production. The disputed zone covers part of the Diapir Basin; the United States has conducted lease sales but prohibited drilling there because of the dispute, and Canada has granted oil concessions nearby. The United States favors the principle of equidistance for the delimitation because it would allow the use of the convex U.S. coastline near the border to gain more continental shelf territory in the exploitable regions. Taking the sector-theory approach, Canada has called for a delimitation using the 141st west meridian running north in the direction of the pole.[57]

The traditional mutual dependence of the economies and policies of the United States and Canada should make them ideal partners in a joint development scheme, and a negotiated agreement may remove some of the sting left by the *Gulf of Maine* dispute. However, reluctance by the United States to grant any credence to the sector-theory claim may limit willingness to compromise on the issue. A joint development zone would not only allow operations to proceed, but also free the United States from trying to explain why it uses the 1867 Convention line as a maritime boundary in the west with the Soviet Union but not in the east with Canada, where the Convention prescribes the 141st west meridian.[58] It might also set an interesting precedent for a United States–Soviet agreement in the Bering Sea. Negotiations with Canada are now being considered. In any case, unitization proce-

[55] Agreement on Cooperation in the Field of Environmental Protection, Dec. 4, 1972, United States–USSR, 23 UST 3544, TIAS No. 7512.

[56] Antinori, *The Bering Sea: A Maritime Delimitation Dispute Between the United States and the Soviet Union,* 18 OCEAN DEV. & INT'L L. 1 (1987).

[57] Note, *Delimiting Continental Shelf Boundaries in the Arctic: The United States–Canada Beaufort Sea Boundary,* 22 VA. J. INT'L L. 221, 243–44 (1981). There is a distinction, however: the U.S.-USSR delimitation pursuant to the 1867 Convention line was a maritime boundary covering the sea, while the U.S.-Canada line is described by the bilateral treaties as running "as far as the Frozen Ocean" ("jusqu'au" in the French version). *Id.* at 227–28.

[58] Russia's cession of its interest in Alaska to the United States in the 1867 treaty specifically provided for continued use of the 141st meridian boundary. Art. I, Cession of Alaska, Mar. 30, 1867, United States–Russia, 15 Stat. 539, TS No. 301, 11 Bevans 1216. *See also* Note, *supra* note 57, at 228.

dures and cooperation in pollution control, which has been a subject of controversy with Canada in the past, will be a necessity in this oil-rich region.

The Rockall-Faeroe Plateau

The Rockall-Faeroe plateau in the North Sea is one of a number of unexplored frontier areas with potential oil and gas deposits.[59] Since 1974, Britain, Denmark and Ireland have laid claims to the continental shelf surrounding Rockall on the basis that it forms a natural prolongation of their land territories. Rockall measures 80 by 100 feet at the base, has an approximate area of .000241 square miles, and is both uninhabited and uninhabitable, supporting only a light put there by Great Britain in 1972.[60] Such an excrescence, while above water at high tide, is vulnerable to definition as a "rock" under Article 121(3) of the Law of the Sea Convention, entitling it only to a 12-mile territorial sea; in that event, it would have no right to an EEZ or a continental shelf.[61] British sovereignty over Rockall is undisputed. A tribunal has been established to settle the Irish and British continental shelf claims but not the Danish claim.[62] Propositions based on the natural prolongation theory are tenuous for all three claimants because geological evidence does not readily establish that the plateau is linked to the European continent or to the Faeroe Islands.[63]

Instead of establishing a tribunal aimed at a partial solution, Ireland, the United Kingdom and Denmark might agree to replace the bilateral tribunal with a commission like the Jan Mayen Commission. Such a commission could evaluate all three countries' claims and map out an area for joint exploitation where two or three of the countries' continental shelf claims overlap; it would not attribute to Rockall either an EEZ or a continental shelf. Such an agreement, while allowing Denmark and Ireland to share in the United Kingdom's superior oil and gas technology, would also benefit Anglo-Irish relations.

V. CONCLUSION

The strength of the Jan Mayen Agreement derives from the careful assessment of the parties' interests by the conciliation commission, its practical approach to surveying the disputed area, and its formulation of a framework for mutual cooperation. This and other joint management schemes, by

[59] *North Sea Oil,* ECONOMIST, Feb. 18, 1984, at 74 (U.S. ed.).

[60] Brown, *Rockall and the Limits of National Jurisdiction of the UK (Part 2),* 2 MARINE POL'Y 275, 289 (1978).

[61] *See* Law of the Sea Convention, *supra* note 2, Art. 121(3).

[62] *Britain and Ireland; the other border,* ECONOMIST, July 5, 1980, at 62.

[63] There is substantial geological evidence that Rockall and the Faeroe Islands are linked by an unbroken extent of submerged continental crust, thus establishing a basis for a claim of natural prolongation. Brown, *supra* note 60, at 284.

creating flexibility for the adjustment of competing claims over resources, relegate the establishment of a jurisdictional boundary to a secondary position. The feasibility of such an approach in a particular maritime delimitation dispute can be assessed in the light of the unique aspects of that situation, among them the political relationship of the disputants, the resource potential involved, and each party's technological capability and expertise. At a time when quarrels over delimitation are proliferating as a result of the expansion of coastal states' maritime jurisdiction and increasing need for resources, the cooperative approach offers an alternative consistent with both the relevant principles of international law and the rational accommodation of the parties' political and economic interests. The Jan Mayen Agreement has features capable of constructive adaptation to the future resolution of other disputes.

WHICH LAW APPLIES TO THE AFGHAN CONFLICT?

*By W. Michael Reisman and James Silk**

Soviet armed forces have been directly engaged in combat in Afghanistan for more than 8 years.[1] The level of international protest, sanctions and media coverage diminished after the initial outcry over the large-scale Soviet intervention in December 1979. With the conclusion in many diplomatic and professional quarters that the Soviet presence in Afghanistan would be of long duration, the focus of international disapproval shifted from the question whether the Soviet *presence* in Afghanistan was lawful or not to whether Soviet *conduct* in Afghanistan was lawful or not: from *jus ad bellum* to *jus in bello*.

Access to Afghanistan has been extremely limited, but various individuals, commissions and credible international organizations have reported extensive abuses of human rights by Soviet forces there; most of the reports are based largely on refugee testimony.[2] While the practices of the Soviet occupation and campaign have emerged with increasing clarity, the question of which law these practices are to be tested against is still controversial.

* W. Michael Reisman is Wesley Newcomb Hohfeld Professor of Jurisprudence, Yale Law School. James Silk expects to receive a J.D. from Yale University in 1989.

The authors gratefully acknowledge the comments and criticism of colleagues on the Board of Editors and of several scholars in Europe. The authors are, of course, solely responsible for the contents.

[1] By the time this article is published, it is possible that the Soviet Union will, at least, have begun to withdraw its troops from Afghanistan. But even should the Soviet Union have begun its withdrawal, important legal and humanitarian issues arising from the conflict will continue to present themselves to the international community. The particular question we address here will not be rendered moot for a number of reasons. First, a Soviet withdrawal would require at least several months to complete. If the Geneva Conventions apply to the conflict that has torn Afghanistan since December 1979, they will continue to apply as long as Soviet troops remain involved in hostilities there. Second, even if all Soviet involvement in fighting ceases, at least part of the Conventions will apply as long as a situation of occupation continues. Finally, the resolution of the question of what law applies to the Afghan conflict has implications for the application of humanitarian law to similar situations.

[2] *See, e.g.*, AMNESTY INTERNATIONAL, VIOLATIONS OF HUMAN RIGHTS AND FUNDAMENTAL FREEDOMS IN THE DEMOCRATIC REPUBLIC OF AFGHANISTAN (1979); AMNESTY INTERNATIONAL, AFGHANISTAN: TORTURE OF POLITICAL PRISONERS (1986); AMNESTY INTERNATIONAL, 1980–1987 AMNESTY INTERNATIONAL REPORT (chapter on Afghanistan) (annual); HELSINKI WATCH, TEARS, BLOOD AND CRIES: HUMAN RIGHTS IN AFGHANISTAN SINCE THE INVASION, 1979–1984 (1984); HELSINKI WATCH/ASIA WATCH, TO DIE IN AFGHANISTAN (1985); HELSINKI WATCH/ASIA WATCH, TO WIN THE CHILDREN: AFGHANISTAN'S OTHER WAR (1986); INTERNATIONAL AFGHANISTAN-HEARING, FINAL REPORT (1984); Ermacora, Report on the situation of human rights in Afghanistan prepared in accordance with Commission on Human Rights resolution 1985/38, UN Doc. E/CN.4/1986/24; and Report of the Independent Counsel on International Human Rights on the Human Rights Situation in Afghanistan, 42 UN GAOR C.3 (Agenda Item 12), UN Doc. A/C.3/42/8 (1987).

An important issue is whether to apply the four Geneva Conventions of 1949 in their entirety,[3] as well as the ensemble of customary and conventional law commonly known as the "law of The Hague," or only common Article 3 of the Geneva Conventions, which applies to "armed conflict not of an international character."[4] The consequences of the resolution of this issue are hardly negligible. If the more detailed code were deemed to apply, much more of the behavior of all the parties to the conflict, some of which has been reported in the inquiries cited above, would become legally cognizable.

Though concerned with the appraisal of a particular conflict, the present inquiry is undertaken with the conviction that the policy issues it addresses are of major continuing importance. Analysis of the Afghan situation leads to conclusions that may have consequences for the application of humanitarian law to an increasingly important species of armed conflict, the full implications of which could not have been anticipated when the Geneva Conventions were drafted.

I.

The Geneva Conventions of August 12, 1949, provide in great detail for the protection of the diverse victims of war. Each Convention deals with a different category of victim. The third and fourth Conventions cover the treatment of prisoners of war and the protection of civilians in time of war.[5] The four Conventions have several General Provisions in common, in particular, common provisions setting out the contingencies for their application.[6] Common Article 2 establishes the criteria for the application of the Conventions to armed conflict. It states:

> In addition to the provisions which shall be implemented in peacetime, the present Convention shall apply to all cases of declared war or of any other armed conflict which may arise between two or more of the High Contracting Parties, even if the state of war is not recognized by one of them.
>
> The Convention shall also apply to all cases of partial or total occupation of the territory of a High Contracting Party, even if the said occupation meets with no armed resistance.

[3] Convention for the Amelioration of the Condition of the Wounded and Sick in Armed Forces in the Field [hereinafter First Convention], Aug. 12, 1949, 6 UST 3114, TIAS No. 3362, 75 UNTS 31; Convention for the Amelioration of the Condition of the Wounded, Sick, and Shipwrecked Members of Armed Forces at Sea [hereinafter Second Convention], Aug. 12, 1949, 6 UST 3217, TIAS No. 3363, 75 UNTS 85; Convention Relative to the Treatment of Prisoners of War [hereinafter Third Convention], Aug. 12, 1949, 6 UST 3316, TIAS No. 3364, 75 UNTS 135; Convention Relative to the Protection of Civilian Persons in Time of War [hereinafter Fourth Convention], Aug. 12, 1949, 6 UST 3516, TIAS No. 3365, 75 UNTS 287 [hereinafter Geneva Conventions].

[4] Common Article 2 defines the applicability of the four Conventions. Common Article 3 sets forth the obligations of parties involved in noninternational conflicts. *Id.*

[5] *Id.*

[6] Common Article 1 states a general obligation: "The High Contracting Parties undertake to respect and to ensure respect for the present Convention in all circumstances." *Id.*

> Although one of the Powers in conflict may not be a party to the present Convention, the Powers who are parties thereto shall remain bound by it in their mutual relations. They shall furthermore be bound by the Convention in relation to the said Power, if the latter accepts and applies the provisions thereof.[7]

The first paragraph of Article 2 is the most straightforward, applying the Conventions to armed conflicts between states. While this includes what was, until World War II, thought of as "normal" war—i.e., declared war—it also includes "any other armed conflict" between states party to the Conventions, "even if the state of war is not recognized by one of them." This paragraph represents an advance over earlier conventions, which were more formalistic. As Jean Pictet states in his *Commentary* on the Conventions, "There is no need for a formal declaration of war, or for the recognition of a state of war, as preliminaries to the application of the Convention. The occurrence of *de facto* hostilities is sufficient."[8] The application of Article 2(1) does not rest on judgments about the lawfulness of particular uses of force.[9]

The second paragraph of Article 2 "was intended to fill the gap left by paragraph 1."[10] The whole of the Conventions is to be applied whenever all or part of the territory of a party is occupied, even when the occupation "meets with no armed resistance." The language is unqualified. Professor Schindler writes, "Whenever a State intervenes with its armed forces in another State, be it to alter the regime of that State or to exercise other acts of sovereign power, this is held to be an occupation within the meaning of Article 2(2)."[11] Pictet makes it clear that paragraph 2 was designed to protect the interests of protected persons in occupations achieved without hostilities when the government of the occupied country considered that armed resistance was useless. "It does not refer to cases in which territory is occupied during hostilities; in such cases the Convention will have been in force since the outbreak of hostilities or since the time war was declared."[12] Between them, then, paragraphs 1 and 2 of common Article 2 appear to

[7] *Id.*

[8] 3 THE GENEVA CONVENTIONS OF 12 AUGUST 1949. COMMENTARY 22–23 (J. Pictet ed. 1952–60) (4 vols., one on each Convention) [hereinafter Pictet].

[9] In this regard, it is consistent with the view that "[a]ny use of force which can be attributed to a State according to the rules of State responsibility will result in the applicability of the laws of war under international law." Schindler, *The Different Types of Armed Conflicts According to the Geneva Conventions and Protocols*, 163 RECUEIL DES COURS 119, 131 (1979 II).

[10] 4 Pictet, *supra* note 8, at 22.

[11] Schindler, *supra* note 9, at 132.

[12] 4 Pictet, *supra* note 8, at 21. Pictet adds:

> The application of the Convention to territories which are occupied at a later date, in virtue of an armistice or a capitulation, does not follow from [paragraph 2], but from paragraph 1. An armistice suspends hostilities and a capitulation ends them, but neither ends the state of war, and any occupation carried out in wartime is covered by paragraph 1. It is, for that matter, when a country is defeated that the need for international protection is most felt.

Id. at 22.

apply the Conventions to all occupations in fact of one state party by the forces of another state.

Common Article 3 establishes a minimum set of protections that apparently apply to all other conflicts in which one party to the Conventions is engaged. Common Article 3 states:

> In the case of armed conflict not of an international character occurring in the territory of one of the High Contracting Parties, each Party to the conflict shall be bound to apply, as a minimum, the following provisions:
>
> (1) Persons taking no active part in the hostilities, including members of armed forces who have laid down their arms and those placed *hors de combat* by sickness, wounds, detention, or any other cause, shall in all circumstances be treated humanely, without any adverse distinction founded on race, colour, religion or faith, sex, birth or wealth, or any other similar criteria.
>
> To this end, the following acts are and shall remain prohibited at any time and in any place whatsoever with respect to the above-mentioned persons:
>
> (*a*) violence to life and person, in particular murder of all kinds, mutilation, cruel treatment and torture;
>
> (*b*) taking of hostages;
>
> (*c*) outrages upon personal dignity, in particular humiliating and degrading treatment;
>
> (*d*) the passing of sentences and the carrying out of executions without previous judgment pronounced by a regularly constituted court, affording all the judicial guarantees which are recognized as indispensable by civilized peoples.
>
> (2) The wounded and sick shall be collected and cared for.
>
> An impartial humanitarian body, such as the International Committee of the Red Cross (ICRC), may offer its services to the Parties to the conflict.
>
> The Parties to the conflict should further endeavour to bring into force, by means of special agreements, all or part of the other provisions of the present Convention.
>
> The application of the preceding provisions shall not affect the legal status of the Parties to the conflict.[13]

Common Article 3 represents an important regulation of so-called noninternational conflict but is far from the functional equivalent of the legal regime applied by common Article 2. Unlike the plenary Conventions, which contain more than three hundred substantive articles (excluding the common articles), Article 3 sets forth general obligations but explicitly forbids only the most flagrant violations of humanitarian norms. Some scholars have contended that, even if observed by the parties to a conflict, the safeguards of Article 3 allow those parties, subject to other international legal prohibitions, to engage in practices forbidden by the plenary Conven-

[13] Geneva Conventions, *supra* note 3.

tions.[14] Moreover, Article 3, unlike the plenary Conventions, does not mandate supervision by a neutral "Protecting Power" or an organization such as the International Committee of the Red Cross (ICRC).[15] An impartial humanitarian body may offer its services to the parties, but they are under no obligation to accept the offer.[16] Although the ICRC may invoke Article 3 when thus offering its services, the provision adds little to the ICRC's general claim of a power to intervene in internal disturbances.[17] Pictet's conclusion seems quite balanced. He says, "It is true that [Article 3] merely provides for the application of the principles of the Convention and

[14] A relatively extreme interpretation in this regard may be found in Farer, *Humanitarian Law and Armed Conflicts: Toward the Definition of "International Armed Conflict,"* 71 COLUM. L. REV. 37, 39–40 (1971). Farer cites examples of the inferior position of noncombatants under Article 3. For example, captured participants may not be tortured, but Article 3, according to him, does not prevent them from being executed for "treason." Also, if their punishment is limited to detention, the form of detention may, *pace* Farer, approach barbarity without manifestly violating established humanitarian law if the full protection of the third Convention does not apply. Without the protection of the Conventions, Farer says, civilians may be compelled by belligerents to serve in effect as slave labor. For discussion of other scholarly views on this issue, see *infra* note 17.

[15] Article 8, common to all but the fourth Convention, provides:

> The present Convention shall be applied with the cooperation and under the scrutiny of the Protecting Powers whose duty it is to safeguard the interests of the Parties to the conflict. . . . The Parties to the conflict shall facilitate to the greatest extent possible the task of the representatives or delegates of the Protecting Powers.

First, Second and Third Conventions, *supra* note 3. *See also* Third Convention, Art. 126 (mandating permission for delegates of the protecting powers and the ICRC to visit places where prisoners of war are held and to interview prisoners without restriction on the duration and frequency of such visits); and Fourth Convention, Art. 143 (mandating permission for delegates of the protecting powers and the ICRC to visit all places where protected persons are and to interview such persons without restriction on the duration and frequency of such visits).

[16] Farer, *supra* note 14, at 39.

[17] Schindler, *supra* note 9, at 147. Others have identified a variety of deficiencies in common Article 3. *See, e.g.*, Cassese, *A Tentative Appraisal of the Old and the New Humanitarian Law of Armed Conflict*, in THE NEW HUMANITARIAN LAW OF ARMED CONFLICT 461, 492–93 (A. Cassese ed. 1979) (Article 3 covers only nonparticipants and persons who have laid down their arms; it does not regulate combat or protect civilians against the effects of hostilities. There are gaps in Article 3's humanitarian provisions. It does not define "noninternational armed conflict" or entrust to any international authority "the task of verifying whether or not a domestic disorder is in progress which should be deemed to fall under the purview of its provisions." The application of its provisions remains largely at the discretion of the parties to the conflict); Baxter, *Ius in Bello Interno: The Present and Future Law,* in LAW AND CIVIL WAR IN THE MODERN WORLD 518, 521–29 (J. N. Moore ed. 1974) (It is difficult to make distinctions between "armed conflict not of an international character" and other forms of domestic violence that may not rise to the level required for application of common Article 3. Whether or not Article 3 binds insurgents has been controversial. Its terms are so general that they cannot serve as an adequate guide to the conduct of belligerents); K. SUTER, AN INTERNATIONAL LAW OF GUERRILLA WARFARE 17 (1984) (Article 3's "lack of clear applicability to guerrilla warfare in general and guerrillas in particular" causes confusion); Draper, *Humanitarian Law and Internal Armed Conflicts,* 13 GA. J. INT'L & COMP. L. 253, 264 (1983) (The lack of "juridical precision" in the term "armed conflicts not of an international character" makes it difficult to apply Article 3).

not for the application of specific provisions, but it defines those principles and in addition lays down certain imperative rules."[18]

The 1977 Protocols Additional to the Geneva Conventions left intact the distinction between international and noninternational conflicts in international humanitarian law, while narrowing appreciably the range of the second concept. Article 1(3) of Protocol I makes the Protocol applicable "in the situations referred to in Article 2 common to those [Geneva] Conventions." Protocol I also applies its provisions and the Conventions to what is commonly referred to as "wars of national liberation," a term of art referring to "armed conflicts in which peoples are fighting against colonial domination and alien occupation and against racist régimes in the exercise of their right of self-determination."[19]

Protocol II applies to noninternational conflicts, but not to all those covered by Article 3 of the Conventions. Article 1(1) applies Protocol II "to all armed conflicts which are not covered by Article 1 [of Protocol I]" but then imposes several additional conditions that make Protocol II apply to a narrower range of phenomena than does common Article 3 of the 1949 Conventions. Its application depends on the control of territory by the group opposing the established government and on that group's ability to apply the Protocol. Furthermore, it only applies to conflicts between the government and insurgents. Protocol II is to apply automatically if its requirements are met; it requires no declaration.[20] But important humanitarian activities of relief societies such as the ICRC are "subject to the consent of the High Contracting Party concerned."[21] Perhaps most salient to the present inquiry is the fact that the relevant parties to the Afghan conflict have ratified the

[18] 1 Pictet, *supra* note 8, at 48.

[19] Art. 1, paras. 3 and 4, Protocol Additional to the Geneva Conventions of 12 August 1949, and Relating to the Protection of Victims of International Armed Conflicts [hereinafter Protocol I], *opened for signature* Dec. 12, 1977, INTERNATIONAL COMMITTEE OF THE RED CROSS, PROTOCOLS ADDITIONAL TO THE GENEVA CONVENTIONS OF 12 AUGUST 1949, at 3 (1977), 16 ILM 1391 (1977). Schindler concludes that "these provisions have small chances ever to be applied." Schindler, *supra* note 9, at 144. He notes that the Protocol was really aimed at wars of liberation from European colonialism and that "alien occupation" has been interpreted to include only a few situations. *Id.* at 137-38. The Protocol can only come into effect if the authority representing the liberation effort issues a declaration invoking it and consenting to comply with applicable international law. Protocol I, *supra*, Art. 96. Even if the Afghan resistance were likely to issue such a declaration, it is doubtful whether it would be valid. The language of the Protocol suggests that only an authority with a certain degree of organization and discipline may be able to issue a declaration. Thus, a declaration would probably not be valid for a resistance that is actually composed of many liberation movements. *See* Schindler, *supra* note 9, at 140, 143. The fact that the various mujahidin groups control large amounts of territory and have coalesced with varying success may not meet the standard of Protocol I. Finally, during most of the conflict, the Soviet Union, its allies and the Afghan regime have viewed the opposition as composed of counterrevolutionaries seeking to undo the already successful national liberation that put the regime in power.

[20] Art. 1, para. 1, Protocol Additional to the Geneva Conventions of 12 August 1949, and Relating to the Protection of Victims of Non-International Armed Conflicts [hereinafter Protocol II], *opened for signature* Dec. 12, 1977, INTERNATIONAL COMMITTEE OF THE RED CROSS, *supra* note 19, at 89, 16 ILM 1442 (1977).

[21] *Id.*, Art. 18(2).

1949 Geneva Conventions but not the Protocols Additional to the Conventions.

II.

The "distinction" between international wars and internal conflicts is no longer factually tenable or compatible with the thrust of humanitarian law, as the contemporary law of armed conflict has come to be known. One of the consequences of the nuclear stalemate is that most international conflict now takes the guise of internal conflict, much of it conducted covertly or at a level of low intensity. Paying lip service to the alleged distinction simply frustrates the humanitarian purpose of the law of war in most of the instances in which war now occurs.

This fact has long been appreciated.[22] But eliminating the legal distinction has been impossible for obvious political reasons; a majority of states are unwilling either to subject what they consider their "internal" affairs to international scrutiny or to create an international regime that might grant recognition to current or future domestic rebel groups. In 1971 and 1972, the ICRC proposed applying the rules of international humanitarian law, or at least those on the treatment of prisoners of war and internees, to civil wars where foreign troops intervened. The suggestion was rejected by many government experts; they feared that it would encourage the parties in a

[22] According to Cassese, the body of the law of war existing before the drafting of Protocols I and II, including the Geneva Conventions, has been "worn out by the 'new reality' of international and civil wars in the last few years. The new features of wars are well known." His list is extensive:

> the multiplication of struggles of national liberation, which are still formally treated as "internal armed conflicts" . . . while the international community, through the pronouncements of the U.N. General Assembly, has for some time come to consider them international conflicts; the spread of previously unknown or little-used methods of warfare such as guerrilla warfare . . . and electronic or ecological warfare as well as the recourse to increasingly cruel and sophisticated weapons . . . ; the staggering increase in civil wars, often fomented from abroad or manipulated by great Powers; the ever-greater risks to which the civilian population . . . is exposed, both in international and in civil wars; the inefficiency of the existing machinery for supervising the implementation of the laws of warfare; and finally, the failure of States to bring to trial all those who so often violate the laws of war in the course of armed conflicts.

Cassese, *supra* note 17, at 461–62.

Schindler has also described the problems in distinguishing between international and noninternational armed conflicts since 1949. The conception, under the Geneva Conventions, of wars of national liberation as noninternational has gradually changed since 1960. With the General Assembly's recognition of the right of self-determination for colonial peoples, the claim was put forward that wars of national liberation are to be considered international conflicts. Also, according to Schindler, there has been a large increase in noninternational armed conflicts "as a result of the growing number of States and of the instability of many regimes. Non-international conflicts are mostly carried out with greater cruelty than international ones." The "rudimentary rules" of common Article 3 have been inadequate to protect people in these conflicts. Foreign interventions in civil wars, which, Schindler notes, have increased, "show that non-international and international conflicts have increasingly mingled." Schindler, *supra* note 9, at 126-27.

See also Baxter, *supra* note 17, at 521-23; Draper, *supra* note 17, at 253-54.

civil war to seek foreign intervention so as to bring the Conventions into effect[23] or, in the case of insurgent groups, to enhance their legal status.[24] At the deliberations that produced the Protocols, an effort to abandon the distinction and to create a single law for international and internal conflicts was defeated.[25]

As a result, two laws of war hover like brooding omnipresences over each conflict. The whole of the law of Geneva and the law of The Hague applies to conflicts between an established government and a state intervening on behalf of the opposition; it also applies to conflicts between states intervening on behalf of the opposing sides in a civil war. It applies as well to belligerent occupations. However, aside from those customary norms that are independent of conventional instruments, only the conventional regime of Article 3 and, perhaps, Protocol II, if and insofar as it is deemed to be customary international law, will apply to an armed conflict between a government and its opposition.[26] The relationship between the opposition and the forces of a state intervening on behalf of the established government creates a more ambiguous legal situation.[27]

This latter problem must be addressed in determining which international humanitarian law applies to the conduct of Soviet forces and of Afghan resistance forces. We propose to examine in detail the facts of the conflict before assessing the application of Articles 2 and 3 to them. As will become clear, the facts of the intervention largely determine which of the alternative international legal regimes applies.

III.

The war in Afghanistan has never been either purely internal or purely international. Any determination is further complicated by the lack of neutral accounts of the conflict. Afghanistan is caught up in the politics of

[23] Schindler, *supra* note 9, at 150.

[24] Gasser, *Internationalized Non-International Armed Conflicts: Case Studies of Afghanistan, Kampuchea, and Lebanon*, 33 AM. U.L. REV. 145, 146 (1983).

[25] *Id.*

[26] *See* Schindler, *supra* note 9, at 150; and Gasser, *supra* note 24, at 147. For purposes of this discussion, the point is moot if Protocol II is not customary law, for Afghanistan is not party to the instrument.

[27] Schindler opines that only the rules for noninternational conflicts would apply because insurgents are not subjects of international law. Schindler, *supra* note 9, at 150. Schindler, in other work, has suggested the possibility of a different view. *See id.* n.35; and Schindler, *Die Anwendung der Genfer Rotkreuzabkommen seit 1949*, 22 ANNUAIRE SUISSE DE DROIT INTERNATIONAL 75, 95 (1965). *See also* D. BINDSCHEDLER-ROBERT, A RECONSIDERATION OF THE LAW OF ARMED CONFLICTS 52–53 (1971); Wilhelm, *Problèmes relatifs à la protection de la personne humaine par le droit international dans les conflits armés ne présentant pas un caractère international*, 137 RECUEIL DES COURS 311, 356–59 (1972 III); Bothe, *Völkerrechtliche Aspekte des Angola-Konflikts*, 37 ZEITSCHRIFT FÜR AUSLÄNDISCHES ÖFFENTLICHES RECHT UND VÖLKERRECHT 572, 590–92 (1977). The circularity here is lamentably characteristic of law. The relationship is not international because insurgents are allegedly not international subjects. They are not international subjects because the war is not international. Of course, the entire body of contemporary human rights law is premised on the susceptibility to international law of the relation between a government and its nationals.

East-West rivalry, and most reports of the conflict there rely, to a large degree, on sources with a clear preference for or tie to one side or the other in the larger rivalry. Accounts by the Soviets and the Afghan regime are very different factually from Western accounts. The former present a history that justifies or legitimates the Soviet intervention; the latter tend to establish the factual predicate for proving the illegality of the Soviet intervention. But the problem is not very different, or more daunting, than the ascertainment of the facts in any legal controversy. Indeed, there is substantial consensus on those key facts that are particularly pertinent to our inquiry.

The Soviet Union has played a significant role in Afghanistan for some time. Tsarist Russia had competed with Britain for influence in Afghanistan, particularly in the late 19th century. As early as 1919, the new Soviet Government sent material and technical aid to Afghanistan.[28] While Soviet influence diminished after 1929, Afghanistan benefited from trade with the Soviet Union, particularly in the 1920s and 1930s. After 1950, favorable trade agreements contributed to a rapid increase in trade with the Soviet Union.[29] When a 1953 coup brought Mohammad Daoud Khan to power in Afghanistan, its reliance on Soviet economic, technical and military aid increased rapidly.[30]

Daoud resigned in 1963, and King Zahir Shah introduced a new constitution that became law on October 1, 1964. The country was governed under it for the next 10 years. Perhaps stimulated by talk of a new constitution, a variety of political groups became more active after 1963. In January 1965, a group of Marxists formed the People's Democratic Party of Afghanistan (PDPA). The new democracy underwent political polarization in the mid-1960s, with factions on the extreme left and right gaining strength. PDPA split into two main factions on the left while, on the right, Islam-inspired groups attracted support. Religious demonstrations against the trend toward secularism and student strikes over demands at Kabul University in 1970 were seen as signs of the Government's weakness. At the same time, the parties of the left were recruiting members and gaining strength.[31]

In July 1973, a coup put Prime Minister Daoud back in power. The presence among his backers of many who were associated with the two main

---

On a related issue, see the excellent study by Louise Doswald-Beck on the lawfulness of military intervention at the invitation of the government of the state into which troops are sent. Doswald-Beck, *The Legal Validity of Military Intervention by Invitation of the Government*, 56 BRIT. Y.B. INT'L L. 189 (1985). She examines situations where the troops of one state enter another state to support a government that has lost or is in danger of losing control over the country. In particular, she analyzes the situation in Afghanistan, the reliance of the USSR on outside interference as its justification for intervening and other states' condemnation of the intervention as interference in the internal affairs of another country. *Id.* at 230–34.

[28] L. DUPREE, AFGHANISTAN 451 (2d printing 1978). For the history of Afghanistan up to the Saur Revolution, see generally *id.* at 430–666; J. COLLINS, THE SOVIET INVASION 8–45 (1986); A. HYMAN, AFGHANISTAN UNDER SOVIET DOMINATION, 1964–83, at 41–71 (1984); H. BRADSHER, AFGHANISTAN AND THE SOVIET UNION 13–73 (1985).

[29] L. DUPREE, *supra* note 28, at 493–94.

[30] A. HYMAN, *supra* note 28, at 28–30.

[31] *See generally id.* at 54–60; L. DUPREE, *supra* note 28, at 559–658.

PDPA splinter parties, Parcham and Khalq, led to suspicion in the West that the coup was pro-Soviet. But Daoud soon replaced Khalqi and Parchami supporters. He also closed down the independent press, which led to the publication of underground, antigovernment leaflets by the left and the religious right. A crackdown on fundamentalist Muslim groups in 1974 sent a small number of fundamentalists into exile in Pakistan, from which, in the summer of 1975, they organized attacks inside Afghanistan.[32] In 1977, Khalq and Parcham joined forces in response to their common disappointment with Daoud. A series of assassinations in late 1977 and early 1978 was indicative of the overall political instability of the country.[33] At the same time that Daoud was removing Khalq and Parcham members from positions of importance, Afghanistan was decreasing its dependence on the Soviet Union for foreign aid. In foreign policy, too, the Daoud Government was taking positions that were increasingly opposed to Soviet interests.[34]

The arrests of left-wing leaders in April 1978 prompted a quick, bloody coup on April 27, styled the Saur Revolution, which was led by the PDPA. Daoud was killed, and Radio Kabul announced that power was in the hands of the Revolutionary Council of the Armed Forces. Insecure because of its lack of popular support, the PDPA regime was nevertheless determined to transform Afghanistan rapidly. Officials who sympathized with the old regime were reportedly pressured to resign and even tortured in efforts to identify enemies of the new regime.[35]

From the beginning, three bitter rivals emerged as the dominant political figures in the new regime: Nur Mohammad Taraki, the President, and Hafizullah Amin, both Khalqi, and Babrak Karmal, a Parchami. The Khalqis, dominant in numbers and in the military, predominated and soon began to purge the Parcham leadership. The regime was also busy arresting other suspected enemies. By August, the Khalq party was completely in control, with all the key Parcham leaders exiled abroad as ambassadors. Karmal and the other Parcham leaders remained in Eastern Europe after they were dismissed as ambassadors there by the Afghan Government.[36]

The Taraki regime pushed ahead with ambitious reforms in the countryside, but corruption, insensitivity to deep rural traditions and poorly

[32] A. HYMAN, *supra* note 28, at 66–68. [33] *See id.* at 61–71.

[34] A. ARNOLD, AFGHANISTAN: THE SOVIET INVASION IN PERSPECTIVE 62–66 (1985). Collins believes that Daoud's pursuit of a nonaligned foreign policy perhaps annoyed the Soviet Union and that the Soviets began in late 1976 to prepare for an eventual post-Daoud Afghanistan, but that "there is no substantive evidence that they began to plot his ouster." J. COLLINS, *supra* note 28, at 38–41.

[35] A. HYMAN, *supra* note 28, at 75–78. Collins evaluates the evidence and concludes that "there is no substantive proof that the Soviets planned, directed, or participated in the coup." He acknowledges that Soviet urging was important in the reunification of Khalq and Parcham. J. COLLINS, *supra* note 28, at 48-52.

[36] Hyman suggests that claims of Soviet management of the coup were inconsistent with the fighting between Khalq and Parcham and the widespread purges, which were of no benefit to the Soviet Union. Also, it was assumed that the Soviets preferred the Parcham faction to Khalq, which was considered more independently nationalist. Thus, the ascendancy of Khalq calls into question Soviet control of the Government in Kabul. A. HYMAN, *supra* note 28, at 81–85.

planned land reform offended rather than attracted the rural poor, who were instead recruited by local elites to oppose the regime with armed resistance. By the summer of 1979, resistance reached the level of civil war.[37] The kidnapping and killing of the U.S. ambassador in February 1979 embarrassed the regime and drew into question the Government's control over the country. An uprising in the western, conservative city of Herat in mid-March turned into a major crisis for the Government. Some soldiers joined the uprising, which was eventually put down by bombing and strafing from Russian-built planes, tanks and helicopters. Among the heavy casualties, estimated to be as many as 5,000, were several hundred Khalqi officials and army officers killed by the people and some 50 Soviet citizens, military advisers and their families, who were tortured and killed by the angry mobs.[38] The incident led to changes in the Government, and Amin emerged with greater powers. Despite attempts to restore confidence in the Government, stability continued to decline as localized armed resistance spread.[39]

After the Saur Revolution, the number of Soviet advisers in Afghanistan increased quickly.[40] While Taraki denied dependence on the Soviet Union, Soviet advisers, particularly the ambassador, were thought to exercise a great deal of power. Yet it seemed that, by rejecting Soviet advice on moderating their political strategy, Taraki and Amin were asserting their independence from the Soviet Union. Nevertheless, the Soviet Union defended the regime, particularly with military aid against the growing resistance. Indeed, Soviet aid to the Khalq regime increased through 1979, and included training the Afghan secret police.[41]

The widespread terror, unrealized economic expectations among the poor, the introduction of a red flag and the painting red of buildings in Kabul, various insults to the Muslim faith, the personality cult of President Taraki, nepotism, the abuse of power to settle personal grudges and further personal ambition, and, most of all, the brutality of the regime increasingly alienated even those who initially sympathized with the revolution.

By the end of 1978, Peshawar, just across the border in Pakistan, had become a center of opposition activity. Attacks by Afghan fundamentalist groups from western Pakistan, as well as local resistance, were becoming

[37] *See id.* at 85–92; J. COLLINS, *supra* note 28, at 65.

[38] That only Soviet citizens were killed, while other Eastern Europeans were spared, is for Hyman evidence of the strong anti-Soviet feelings behind the uprising. "The growing dependence of the Taraki regime on Soviet advisers, arms and finances, when combined with the openly avowed sympathies of Khalq leaders for the 'Great Northern Neighbor' (as the Soviet Union was styled) had resulted in popular suspicion that Russian communists now ruled Afghanistan." A. HYMAN, *supra* note 28, at 99–101. *See also* H. BRADSHER, *supra* note 28, at 101–02.

[39] A. HYMAN, *supra* note 28, at 101–05.

[40] According to Hyman, there were about 3,000 Soviet advisers working in the ministries, on civil projects and with the armed forces at the end of Daoud's regime. He estimates that about one-third of the estimated 4,500 Soviet advisers in Afghanistan by April 1979 were assigned to the armed forces. *Id.* at 105.

[41] Hyman cites evidence that Soviet advisers were, at least, involved in brutal acts against real or imagined opponents of the regime in prisons and interrogation centers. *Id.* at 105–08.

more and more serious. Refugees from the border areas streamed into Pakistan, where camps were established and aid provided by the Pakistani Government. In one reported incident in a border village, Afghan soldiers, with Soviet advisers present, allegedly massacred most of the male inhabitants above the age of 12.[42] As the fighting grew, more refugees fled to Pakistan, and more men joined in the fight against the regime.

By the summer of 1979, not only was rural resistance more successful than the Taraki regime had expected; Kabul was also "seething with resentment."[43] In June, a large organized demonstration was put down by heavily armed troops. In the aftermath, the level of repression increased. The following month, the regime rounded up suspected opponents, who later disappeared. The spreading guerrilla war was taxing the Government and sapping the morale of the army. The Soviet Union provided massive new amounts of military equipment, especially air power. But the growing Soviet presence through 1979 alienated many Afghan officers, even Khalqi. At the time of the Saur Revolution, Afghanistan had a conscript army of about 80,000,[44] but it was shrinking, and the draft of fresh conscripts could no longer be enforced.[45]

Amin assumed greater power in July and tried to reverse the growing alienation of the army's officers and troops. An unsuccessful rebellion within the army and a rash of guerrilla attacks led in mid-September to Amin's taking over as the undisputed leader of the regime. Taraki and Amin escaped injury in a violent gunfight, but within weeks, in mysterious circumstances, Taraki was dead. It is thought that, despite expressions of confidence, the Soviet Union had serious doubts about Amin from the beginning.[46] But, apparently in return for improvements in his regime's policies toward the population, the Soviet Union continued its support. The country's dependence on the Soviet Union and the Soviet influence had not diminished. In fact, during the first months of the Amin regime, there was a buildup of Soviet forces in Afghanistan, and Soviet officers were involved in the Afghan army down to the company level. By the fall of 1979, the Government's reliance on Soviet military help had become even more pro-

[42] Estimates of the number of the dead vary from 640, J. COLLINS, *supra* note 28, at 59–60, to 1,170, A. HYMAN, *supra* note 28, at 126.

[43] A. HYMAN, *supra* note 28, at 148. [44] *Id.* at 147.

[45] *See id.* at 149–52; J. COLLINS, *supra* note 28, at 65.

[46] A. HYMAN, *supra* note 28, at 153–55. A correspondent in Karachi reported early in October that Russian exchanges with Amin indicated "grave doubts about Amin being able to stabilize the Afghan situation." The account went on, "According to informants with connections among the ruling Khalq party the Russians [a]re reported to have then given Amin 30 days to establish his authority throughout the land or make way for the Afghan extremists of the Parchamite party salted away in Eastern Europe, notably Karmal and Anita Ratziban." Daily Telegraph (London), Oct. 8, 1979, at 5, col. 3. A week later, an article with a Kabul dateline reported, "Diplomatic circles in Kabul were given the impression that Mr. Amin would either establish his authority within that time [30 days] or be replaced by the extremist Russian-backed Parchamites." *Id.*, Oct. 15, 1979, at 6, col. 6. Tensions between Amin and the Soviet Union were again reported early in November. *Id.*, Nov. 5, 1979, at 5, col. 1.

nounced, with Soviet pilots flying missions in jet fighters and helicopter gunships.[47]

While Amin continued to show signs of wanting to move Afghanistan away from its dependence on the Soviet Union, it was already impossible. His regime was too unpopular, both within the country and among possible alternative foreign supporters, and the Soviets were exercising effective control over the Government. Some 1,500 Soviet officials were working in the civilian ministries, and between 3,500 and 4,000 Soviet officers and technicians were in the armed forces. An estimated half of the 8,000 officers and noncommissioned officers in the Afghan army at the time of the coup had been purged for political reasons by October 1979.[48]

By September 1979, there were some 250,000 Afghan refugees in Pakistan and Iran. Amin's efforts at reconciliation were a failure. The war was still spreading and there was a wave of guerrilla attacks in Kabul itself.[49] By early December, the Soviet official media and government communications began to omit personal references to Amin.[50] On December 19, Amin moved with a force of trusted guards from the House of the People in the city to a palace outside Kabul. By this time, Soviet forces had been built up just across the border in the Soviet Union.[51]

[47] A. HYMAN, *supra* note 28, at 155–57. Early in November, the *Daily Telegraph* of London reported that 20 Soviet battalions had been rushed into Afghanistan to protect Afghan bases from Muslim rebels. The report suggested that the USSR had concluded that it was beyond Amin's capability to control the Muslim resistance. According to the same report, the Afghan army, once some 100,000 strong, was down to less than half that number, many troops having joined the Muslim rebels. Daily Telegraph (London), Nov. 3, 1979, at 6, col. 3.

[48] H. BRADSHER, *supra* note 28, at 123. Diplomatic sources, in mid-November, reported an increased infusion of Soviet arms and indicated that while the number of Soviet advisers had remained around 3,000, there had been a significant qualitative change. The Soviet Union had top political and military officials in advisory positions. One source said that there was evidence of Soviet organization and command of the military and that Russians were piloting aircraft, including helicopter gunships, and operating tanks. The Times (London), Nov. 17, 1979, at 7, col. 5. Estimates of the number of Soviet advisers in Afghanistan varied throughout this period. At the end of October, intelligence reports were cited estimating that there were 3,000 Soviet military specialists and 3,500 civilian advisers in Afghanistan. The same report noted that the Soviet Union had built a military complex in Afghanistan at Farah, some 65 miles from Iran, and enlarged an air base at Shindand. According to the report, the USSR had committed large sums to boosting the Afghan economy, had signed trade contracts worth £100 million and planned to supply the internal security forces with £3.3 million of equipment. Daily Telegraph (London), Oct. 31, 1979, at 4, col. 3. According to a *Times* article from Delhi, Amin had asked for outside help so he could cut his dependence on the Soviet Union. Pakistani President Zia ul-Haq told the reporter that Amin had approached his Government early in December with "frantic messages for an immediate meeting." Diplomatic sources in Kabul said that Amin had also approached the United States. The Times (London), Feb. 14, 1980, at 7, col. 6.

[49] A. HYMAN, *supra* note 28, at 157–58. By mid-December, Russian troops were said by Western sources to be defending key positions around Kabul. The Times (London), Dec. 19, 1979, at 7, col. 4.

[50] H. BRADSHER, *supra* note 28, at 124–25.

[51] *Id.* at 178–79. U.S. government officials, several days after the coup, said that Amin had been too independent and had rejected the introduction of Soviet troops to fight the Afghan rebels. The officials stated that the United States first considered that an invasion was possible after the increase in the Soviet military presence on Dec. 8 and 9; a "special brigade" arrived at

On December 24, Soviet troops began landing at the Kabul airport and at other air bases in Afghanistan. The airlift of troops into Kabul continued until, by the morning of December 27, an estimated 5,000 Soviet soldiers were in the city.[52] At the same time, Soviet troops and tanks were crossing into Afghanistan.[53] Meanwhile, Soviet advisers already in Afghanistan reportedly told their Afghan troops that an exercise was on and ordered them to turn in their ammunition for blanks; they also had batteries removed from tanks to be winterized.[54]

On the evening of the 27th, Soviet troops attacked Amin's palace complex, where they encountered loyal Afghan troops.[55] During this fighting, a speech by Babrak Karmal declaring that he had been elected Prime Minister and that Amin had been executed was broadcast on the frequency of Radio Kabul. But Western intelligence evidence indicates that the speech was prerecorded and broadcast from a Soviet transmitter in Soviet Central Asia, overpowering the actual Radio Kabul signal, which continued its normal broadcast.[56] It is not clear exactly how Amin died, but accounts agree that

---

the Bagram air base, then moved to Salang Pass, the route of invasion from the Soviet Union, and secured it from rebel control. N.Y. Times, Jan. 2, 1980, at A14, col. 4.

[52] A. HYMAN, *supra* note 28, at 159; H. BRADSHER, *supra* note 28, at 179. The massive airlift of Soviet troops into Kabul was reported in the West by Dec. 27. The U.S. Department of State said that the USSR had concentrated five divisions along the Afghan border and estimated that between 4,000 and 5,000 troops were in Afghanistan. People leaving from the Kabul airport on Dec. 26 reported seeing at least 12 Soviet transport planes land and unload armored vehicles and combat troops. The Times (London), Dec. 27, 1979, at 1, col. 3.

[53] A. HYMAN, *supra* note 28, at 159.

[54] H. BRADSHER, *supra* note 28, at 179–80; A. ARNOLD, *supra* note 34, at 93–95. The *Sunday Times* of London gave a similar account. According to an eyewitness report and a "highly-placed Afghan now in New Delhi," Amin was deceived during the final stages of the coup. The Soviets had advised him to move from the presidential palace downtown to the fortified Darulaman Palace 2 miles out to be "closer to 'protection' of the Soviet embassy." From there, Amin's contact with the Afghan army was tenuous. Then, Afghan officers guarding the radio station with 20 tanks were told by Russians that these tanks were being replaced with new Soviet models, but that since fuel was scarce, their diesel had to be transferred. Once the tanks were immobilized, the Afghans' radio transmitter was seized, and an attack launched on Darulaman Palace. Sunday Times (London), Jan. 6, 1980, at 17, col. 1.

[55] H. BRADSHER, *supra* note 28, at 180.

[56] *Id.*; A. HYMAN, *supra* note 28, at 165; A. ARNOLD, *supra* note 34, at 78; E. GIRARDET, AFGHANISTAN: THE SOVIET WAR 15 (1985). The first press reports of the coup relied on U.S. State Department sources. They cited eyewitness accounts of Soviet troops leading the assault on Kabul's radio station, fighting gun battles in armored personnel carriers in Kabul, fighting near the presidential palace and taking Afghan prisoners. Amin was reported executed on the 27th. Radio Kabul announced the sentence and execution of Amin and the election of Karmal as the new President and General Secretary of the People's Democratic Party. But the news account said that Tashkent Radio in the USSR, monitored by Reuters in Tehran, had broadcast a speech by Karmal. In another Radio Kabul broadcast monitored in Tehran, the Afghan Revolutionary Council was reported to have announced its support for Karmal. *Afghanistan President Executed after Soviet-backed Coup*, The Times (London), Dec. 28, 1979, at 1, col. 7. *See also Afghan President Is Ousted and Executed in Kabul Coup, Reportedly with Soviet Help—An Exile Takes Over*, N.Y. Times, Dec. 28, 1979, at A1, col. 6. No conclusions were drawn at that time about the whereabouts of Karmal, but the fact that his speech was only monitored on Radio Tashkent provided an early suggestion that something was amiss. A *New York Times* report from

he was dead by the end of the 27th.[57] Just after midnight, TASS, the Soviet news agency, broadcast a report that Karmal had spoken over Radio Kabul "on behalf of and on the instructions of" the PDPA Central Committee, the Revolutionary Council, and the Afghan Government, but did not explain how these instructions were given.

Only at 2:40 A.M. on December 28 did Radio Kabul broadcast an announcement that it said was from the Revolutionary Council's secretariat, naming Karmal council president and, thus, President of Afghanistan. That was followed by a broadcast demand for Soviet support, "including military aid," to defend Afghanistan and the Saur Revolution against continued aggression by foreign enemies. The announcement invoked the December 5 Treaty of Friendship.[58] A short time later, an announcement from "the

---

Islamabad on Dec. 29 said, "Diplomats here monitoring broadcasts from Radio Kabul and receiving information from embassies and other channels, were puzzled that Mr. Karmal had made no public appearances, even on television, since his takeover." The report then stated that the broadcast of Karmal's speech by Radio Tashkent several hours before it was first broadcast in Kabul suggested that it had been "taped, and rais[ed] the question of the whereabouts of Mr. Karmal, who is thought to have been in exile in Eastern Europe, under Soviet protection, for at least a year." *Id.*, Dec. 30, 1979, at A10, col. 3. On Jan. 1, the State Department said there was evidence of Soviet participation in the coup, including reliable indications that the initial radio reports were prerecorded tapes broadcast from the USSR. When those reports were being broadcast, the Department said, Radio Kabul was transmitting its normal programs. U.S. officials believed the reports were actually broadcast from the Soviet border city of Termez. The Times (London), Jan. 2, 1980, at 1, col. 1.

[57] A. HYMAN, *supra* note 28, at 169. The *Times* of London reported, however, that Soviet forces killed Amin: he had died in a small building near Darulaman Palace when six armored personnel carriers directed a "torrent of machine gun bullets" at the President's offices. "Popular—though not government—belief has it that Soviet troops fired the fatal rounds at the politically bankrupt dictator . . . ." The Times (London), Jan. 18, 1980, at 14, col. 1. According to another report, "Afghan sources confirm that . . . Hafizullah Amin was killed in cold blood by the Russians on the night of December 27." Sunday Times (London), Jan. 20, 1980, at 1, col. 3. However, the Afghan Interior Minister, speaking at a news conference in January, made a statement that contradicted earlier announcements in both Kabul and Moscow that Amin had been killed shortly after the coup. "It appeared to fix Dec. 29 as the date when Mr. Amin was put to death." N.Y. Times, Jan. 22, 1980, at A10, col. 3.

[58] H. BRADSHER, *supra* note 28, at 181. Moscow radio announced the coup within hours, carrying extracts of Karmal's statement. In its first report, however, the *Times* of London said, "In spite of the unusually speedy announcement there is no evidence that the Soviet Union engineered the reported coup against President Amin, but it can only be pleased with his overthrow." The Times (London), Dec. 28, 1979, at 4, col. 3. The first mention of Karmal's speech in the *New York Times* came in an article that said the text of a speech by Karmal broadcast over Radio Kabul had been distributed in English, by TASS, the Soviet press agency. N.Y. Times, Dec. 28, 1979, at A13, col. 3. Bradsher's account seems to differ from the reports in the Western press on Dec. 28 that announcements by Radio Kabul of Amin's downfall and Karmal's election were monitored on the 27th. *See supra* note 56. The USSR justified its airlift of troops into Afghanistan by saying that it had responded to an urgent request for help from the Afghan Government. TASS said that, on the basis of the Treaty of Friendship, the new Government had "approached the Soviet Union with an insistent request for urgent political, moral and economic aid, including military aid." But in later versions of the statement, TASS added a phrase to this description of the request: "which the Government of the Democratic Republic of Afghanistan repeatedly requested from the Government of the Soviet Union

revolutionary tribunal," which was never further identified, said that Amin had been sentenced to death and executed. The Karmal regime and Soviet spokesmen have maintained that the action against Amin was carried out by Afghan forces, but Westerners in the city at the time said that Soviet soldiers alone were involved in the assault on the palace.[59] Although Karmal later put forward conflicting accounts, he is not known to have been in Kabul until his first public appearance there on January 1.[60]

---

previously." This made the airlift seem less related to the coup. The Times (London), Dec. 29, 1979, at 1, col. 7. The TASS statements that the Afghan Government had requested aid in a Dec. 28 broadcast did not answer the questions already being asked about when and by what authorities the request was made since the Karmal Government came to power well after the airlift of Soviet troops began. N.Y. Times, Dec. 29, 1979, at A6, col. 6. In January, a Hungarian press agency dispatch from Kabul cited Karmal as having said that the Afghan Revolutionary Council had asked the USSR for help even before Amin was overthrown, but that Moscow had acted only when help was urgently needed. N.Y. Times, Jan. 11, 1980, at A6, col. 2.

In February, Karmal was quoted as having said, in an interview with the "pro-Moscow Indian newspaper Patriot," that Soviet troops had intervened 10 days before the coup. This was said to be the first admission that Soviet forces were in the country when Amin was overthrown. Karmal said that the PDPA had forced Amin to call for Soviet troops during the second week of December. *Id.*, Feb. 8, 1980, at A10, col. 1.

[59] H. BRADSHER, *supra* note 28, at 182. A Soviet statement in *Pravda* acknowledged that Soviet troops went to Afghanistan to help repel outside aggression, but denied that they had played any part in internal Afghan events. N.Y. Times, Dec. 31, 1979, at A1, col. 4. U.S. administration officials later said that elements of the Soviet airborne division that had landed at the Kabul airport on the 27th moved quickly across the city in armored vehicles and, after a brief, but violent, clash, wiped out the Afghan guard at Darulaman Palace, and captured and shot President Amin. *Id.*, *supra* note 51.

[60] Bradsher cites reports that Karmal arrived in a Soviet military plane at about 2:00 A.M. Dec. 28, which would have meant that he left Soviet Central Asia about the time Amin was killed. H. BRADSHER, *supra* note 28, at 186. Karmal later claimed to have secretly entered Afghanistan before the invasion and organized supporters within PDPA against Amin. According to Bradsher, Karmal gave several different versions of the time of this return—between August and mid-November and even later. *Id.* at 174. Karmal claimed that by the second week of December, an overwhelming majority of the PDPA Central Committee and the Revolutionary Council had successfully pressured Amin to request Soviet military assistance. Thus, Soviet troops entered Afghanistan beginning on Dec. 17 at the request of the Government. In Karmal's version, a majority of the Central Committee and Revolutionary Council had tried Amin, decided to execute him and elected Karmal to power before Dec. 27. Bradsher points out the inconsistencies in this and Soviet accounts of the request for troops and the election of Karmal. Among these inconsistencies was a Radio Kabul report on Dec. 28 that the PDPA Politburo had met and elected Karmal General Secretary and that the Revolutionary Council had elected him President that day. There was no mention, until much later, of Karmal's earlier secret election to the posts. *Id.* at 176. On Dec. 28, Radio Kabul said that the USSR had "acted in response to an official request from Afghanistan." The report on this broadcast pointed out that the Soviet buildup of troops preceded the new Afghan Government. It also said that Karmal had reportedly returned to Kabul during the week of the coup. N.Y. Times, Dec. 29, 1979, at A1, col. 3. At least one report at the time of the coup said that Karmal was believed to have returned to Kabul from Soviet Central Asia with other Afghan exiles among the Soviet troops airlifted into Afghanistan in the days before the action. The Times (London), Dec. 29, 1979, at 4, col. 1. The *New York Times* said that while President Karmal had not been seen in public by Dec. 31, he had been reliably reported to have met in private with some government supporters and at least one Eastern European ambassador. N.Y.

IV.

According to diplomats and to travelers who had driven to Pakistan, Kabul was, by December 31, "virtually a Soviet garrison town" with troops patrolling the streets. Soviet troops were also reported to have moved out of Kabul to take control of most of the rest of Afghanistan, and a force estimated at 15,000 by U.S. officials reportedly crossed into Afghanistan on December 29.[61] The Afghan Air Force was said to be dominated by the Soviet Air Force, most combat aircraft being flown by Soviet pilots.[62]

As the new year began, the Afghan Government appeared to be largely in Soviet hands.[63] By mid-January, the Soviet Union was reportedly in effective control of Afghanistan. The number of Soviet civilian advisers had increased dramatically since the coup, and they were said to be running the ministries.[64] Soviet troops had disarmed the Afghan army and then selec-

---

Times, Jan. 1, 1980, at A1, col. 2. U.S. officials stated that Karmal was flown to Kabul on Sunday, Dec. 30. *Id.*, *supra* note 51. The *Times* of London reported that Karmal made his first public appearance on Jan. 4. The Times (London), Jan. 5, 1980, at 4, col. 1. On Jan. 10, Soviet officials presented Karmal to foreign reporters. When asked why the Revolutionary Council, presided over by President Amin, would have called in Soviet troops if Amin was an American agent as Karmal had claimed, Karmal responded that the Revolutionary Council that requested Soviet help was the one over which he presided. N.Y. Times, Jan. 12, 1980, at A5, col. 1. (The article contended that Karmal was flown into Afghanistan by the Russians the day of the coup.)

[61] The Times (London), Dec. 31, 1979, at 6, col. 5. President Carter received intelligence reports that an additional 15,000 to 20,000 Soviet troops, including an airborne division, had crossed into Afghanistan around Dec. 29, raising the total number of Soviet military personnel there to between 25,000 and 30,000. N.Y. Times, Dec. 30, 1979, at A1, col. 6.

[62] The majority of some 160 combat aircraft in the Afghan armed forces was reportedly flown by Soviet pilots. There were also reports that at least two squadrons of fighters had been flown in to help combat the Afghan rebels. And all the M–24 helicopters being used against the rebels were flown by Soviet crews. All of the command, control and maintenance functions were reported to be in Soviet hands. N.Y. Times, Dec. 28, 1979, at A1, col. 5.

[63] A Western European diplomatic source said that Afghan functionaries at the Foreign Ministry were showing up for work, but not attempting to do anything. Other sources said the Ministries of the Interior and of Education were controlled by Russians. Soviet tanks were guarding Radio Kabul, and Soviet sentries were at the post and telegraph office and the Interior Ministry. The Times (London), Jan. 3, 1980, at 1, col. 7. Soviet troops were reported to have spread out all over Afghanistan, setting up encampments that "reportedly have an air of permanence. The Soviet forces are believed generally to be in control." Soviet forces had reportedly taken control of all civilian airports and the air bases at Kandahar and Shindand. N.Y. Times, Jan. 8, 1980, at A1, col. 3. A U.S. Defense Department analysis, though, said that the depleted Afghan army was doing most of the fighting, with Soviet troops largely in a supporting role; and that the USSR appeared to be giving top priority to rebuilding the Afghan army, which had been reduced from about 100,000 troops a year earlier to some 25,000. This account differed from the State Department's and from some press reports from the region, which indicated that Soviet forces were bearing the brunt of the combat. *Id.*, Jan. 9, 1980, at A5, col. 1.

[64] According to the *Sunday Times*, a senior Afghan government official said that a Soviet adviser had told him not to come to the office except to get paid and that the same thing was happening to "hundreds of my colleagues." An estimated 4,000 civilian advisers had been flown into Afghanistan since the Soviet troops had entered. The arriving advisers were not subjected to passport or customs checks. Each of Karmal's 19 ministers was reported to have at least two Russian advisers attached and ever present. The report said, "The Russians have

tively rearmed less than half of it. There were an estimated 70,000 Soviet troops in Afghanistan, supported by 1,750 tanks, 2,100 armored personnel carriers and two air divisions with 400 fighters, bombers and helicopters.[65] At the end of February, when martial law was declared, it reportedly gave effective government authority to the Soviet commander in Kabul.[66]

From fewer than 10,000 before December 1979, the number of Soviet troops in Afghanistan climbed to an estimated 85,000 by March 1980.[67] By April, Karmal was said by some observers to have lost any grasp that he had on the Soviet army. Government sources in Afghanistan said he was a "virtual prisoner" of the Russians.[68] After mass desertions, the Afghan

---

taken over the policy-making and executive functions in most departments, though these are still notionally exercised by Afghan civil servants." The state security bureau KAM was reportedly dismantled and rebuilt around 640 Soviet intelligence officers. The report said that the Soviets were using the Afghan army as "cannon fodder" against the Muslim rebels. Sunday Times (London), *supra* note 57. *See also* N.Y. Times, Jan. 23, 1980, at A6, col. 1 (analysts said Soviet administrators, including many KGB officers, were directing the "reorganization of the government bureaucracy"). A report from Rawalpindi, Pakistan, said, "Journalists leaving Afghanistan, other travelers and diplomats here reading cablegrams from Kabul all say the Karmal Government shows no signs of actually functioning." Karmal was reported at a summer palace near Kabul under Soviet guard. Statements, relayed through Moscow, were issued on his behalf. N.Y. Times, Jan. 27, 1980, §1, at 12, col. 1. Afghans who managed to slip into Pakistan at the end of January said, "Russians give orders and Afghans follow them." At some government buildings, Afghans reportedly entered by one door, where they were searched, while Russians passed freely in and out through another. Russians were also said to write the news scripts for radio and television and to monitor Afghan broadcasts to be sure they were read correctly. N.Y. Times, Feb. 2, 1980, at A5, col. 1.

[65] Diplomats in Kabul estimated Soviet troop strength at 80,000 to 85,000, made up of an advisory group in command of Afghan army units, helicopter and jet fighter pilots, an airborne division and five motorized rifle divisions. At the same time, the Afghan army was said to be disintegrating, its numbers now estimated by Western military analysts as less than 40,000. N.Y. Times, Jan. 17, 1980, at A12, col. 1. Another report said that intelligence sources discounted press reports of between five and seven full Soviet divisions in Afghanistan and believed the total number of Soviet troops in Afghanistan to be about 50,000, with others mobilized just inside the Soviet Union. The Times (London), Jan. 18, 1980, at 14, col. 1. The U.S. Defense Department revised its estimate of Soviet troop strength down to 70,000 in February and estimated that another 30,000 were mobilized on the Soviet side of the border. The Times (London), Feb. 22, 1980, at 7, col. 3.

[66] "The decree imposing martial law on Friday in effect gave government authority to the Soviet commander in Kabul, and reports yesterday said he appeared to have taken over." N.Y. Times, Feb. 27, 1980, at A1, col. 3.

[67] J. COLLINS, *supra* note 28, at 79; STAFF OF SENATE COMM. ON FOREIGN RELATIONS, 98TH CONG., 2D SESS., HIDDEN WAR: THE STRUGGLE FOR AFGHANISTAN 12 (Comm. Print 1984). The U.S. State Department said there were 85,000 Soviet troops in Afghanistan, another 35,000 along the border in the Soviet Union. The Times (London), Apr. 19, 1980, at 5, col. 8.

[68] The reporter, Chhotu Karadia, who had interviewed Karmal, said that, except for a dozen sentries at the main gate, the security of the People's House was in Russian hands. He said that Karmal's bodyguard, doctor and six chief advisers were Russians. He also cited such direct measures of Soviet control over the Afghan population as the replacement of English as the second language in schools with Russian, and of local television programs with Russian ones. Sunday Times (London), Apr. 20, 1980, at 1, col. 4.

army was reduced to fewer than 40,000 men by the end of May 1980.[69] Reports continued that Soviets were in control of most government departments. Furthermore, the Soviet Union was providing almost the entire food supply of Afghanistan and dominating the economy.[70]

By early 1981, defections and casualties had reduced the Afghan army to an estimated 10,000 to 15,000 effective fighting troops.[71] With forced conscription, the number was back up to as many as 50,000 by 1983, still far fewer than the 100,000 estimated to have made up the army prior to the invasion. But the morale of the remaining soldiers was low, men were fleeing the cities to avoid conscription, conscripts were deserting at rates of several thousand per month and many of the army's officers regularly collaborated with the resistance.[72] In addition, by that time, more than 115,000 Soviet troops were in Afghanistan, and Soviet advisers ran the Afghan army.[73] Clearly, the bulk of the fighting against resistance groups,

[69] An increase was also noted in the number of dependents of Soviet military personnel brought into Afghanistan, as well as in the number of Soviet engineers engaged in large improvement and construction projects at military bases. The Times (London), May 29, 1980, at 1, col. 1. At the end of June, the *Times* defense correspondent estimated that the Afghan army had between 40,000 and 50,000 troops. *Id.*, June 27, 1980, at 8, col. 1. In September, their number was estimated to be 35,000, according to a diplomatic source in Delhi. They were described as a demoralized and unreliable force of questionable loyalty, whose capacity and morale were continuing to deteriorate. While they were poorly equipped, the Russian troops were supplied with new equipment and vehicles. Although Soviet troop strength was commonly estimated at more than 100,000, this source said it was between 80,000 and 85,000. However, the number of civilian advisers had increased and there were more than 1,000 civilian families in Kabul. According to this source, Soviet advisers held key positions in all the ministries and controlled telecommunications, and Soviet editors controlled Radio Kabul and the Farsi and English daily newspapers. *Id.*, Sept. 11, 1980, at 7, col. 1.

[70] According to a U.S. government analysis, Soviet officials occupied the senior positions in every Afghan ministry except the Foreign Ministry where they held the post of deputy director. All decisions were Soviet. The most Soviet-dominated ministry was said to be the Ministry of Information and Culture; virtually all information releases were produced by Soviet staff. A Soviet adviser assigned to the education system had begun preparing textbooks immediately after the December revolution. The Times (London), May 30, 1980, at 7, col. 7. Also, "a virtual blizzard of economic, trade, and technical assistance agreements" was said to be tying the Afghan economy tightly to that of the USSR and the Eastern European countries. "Afghan judges, lawyers, teachers, medical workers, scientists, and even truck drivers are being sent to the Soviet Union to absorb—and presumably bring back—Soviet systems, methods, and skills." Christian Sci. Monitor, Mar. 4, 1981, at 3, col. 1.

[71] H. BRADSHER, *supra* note 28, at 282–83.

[72] A. HYMAN, *supra* note 28, at 198–99, 213.

[73] H. BRADSHER, *supra* note 28, at 282–83. The Area Handbook Series report on Afghanistan says that estimates of Soviet troop strength in the mid-1980s ranged from 105,000 to 150,000, but were usually around 118,000. D. Seekins, *Government and Politics*, in R. NYROP & D. SEEKINS, AFGHANISTAN, A COUNTRY STUDY 209, 250 (Area Handbook Studies No. DA Pam 550–65, 1986). According to Hyman, Soviet forces in 1983 included many squadrons of warplanes and more than 400 helicopter gunships. Soviet military and civilian advisers conducted the war and the administration, all of which was financed by the Soviet Union. "So heavy was the Karmal government's dependence on the USSR that by any objective standards its very independence could be questioned." A. HYMAN, *supra* note 28, at 213. Hyman also

whose numbers have been estimated at about 100,000, has been carried out not by Afghan, but by Soviet, troops.

While resistance forces have controlled, or threatened to control, significant parts of the territory of Afghanistan, and Soviet forces have been content to hold the main towns, roads and military bases, one area is apparently under complete Soviet domination. By June of 1980, Soviet forces had sealed off the Wakhan corridor from Afghanistan, leaving it accessible only from Soviet Central Asia. The corridor, a long, narrow finger of land extending from the northeast corner of Afghanistan, between the Soviet Union and Pakistan, and touching China at its tip, was created in 1895 to separate tsarist Russia from Britain's Indian empire. By establishing Soviet garrisons at the two main passes into China and Pakistan, occupying the entrance to the corridor from Afghanistan, improving the road to the Soviet frontier and mining the passes from China and Pakistan to stop arms movements, the Soviet Union effectively cut the corridor off. The area's main inhabitants, the Kirghiz tribesmen, had already fled into Pakistan a year earlier. Most of the rest are members of the Ismaili minority, which has traditionally suffered at the hands of the dominant Sunni tribesmen of Afghanistan. They were reportedly passive after the 1978 coup, even welcoming the change.[74]

By November, the official Pakistani news agency reported that the Soviet Union was in the process of annexing the Wakhan corridor, moving large numbers of troops into the area and improving its communication infrastructure.[75] Pakistan's President Zia stated publicly that the corridor was "now under the Soviet Union." It was reported in March 1981 that he had told an Indian journalist that an estimated 5,000 Soviet troops occupied the Wakhan.[76] The area was being administered directly by military authorities in the Soviet Union, rather than by the Soviet military command in Afghanistan, diplomatic sources said.[77]

On June 16, 1981, the Soviet Union and Afghanistan signed a treaty formally delineating their border along the Wakhan corridor.[78] An Afghan resistance leader said that Karmal had agreed to a border adjustment in the Wakhan area when he visited Moscow in June 1981. According to the

---

notes the extent of Soviet economic assistance to Afghanistan, particularly citing projects which "have had the effect of integrating the Afghan economy into the Soviet Central Asian system." *Id.* at 207.

[74] *Russia amputates an Afghan finger*, ECONOMIST, Aug. 9, 1980, at 32, col. 1.

[75] Christian Sci. Monitor, Nov. 6, 1980, at 2, col. 2; N.Y. Times, Nov. 16, 1980, at A4, col. 4.

[76] While reports of the Soviet occupation of the Wakhan corridor had been coming from Pakistan since 1980, diplomatic sources said reliable confirmation had been received only more recently. Christian Sci. Monitor, *supra* note 70.

[77] There were reports that the Soviets had been building underground bunkers and permanent barracks, improving an east-west road to China and widening a north-south road leading to a pass on the Pakistan border. *Id.*

[78] *Fingerwork*, ECONOMIST (U.S. ed.), July 4, 1981, at 33, col. 2. This treaty has apparently not yet been submitted to the United Nations for registration and publication in the *UN Treaty Series*.

resistance leader, "the official Kabul radio had spoken of an 'annexation' of part of the Wakhan district." He also reported that Soviet Tadjiks were being moved into the corridor to replace the local Afghan population, which had been relocated further west.[79] By late 1982, if not earlier, the Soviet Union had effectively annexed the Wakhan corridor.[80]

V.

Despite the obviously substantial role of Soviet forces in the Afghan war, the question whether or not the conflict can be called international for purposes of applying international humanitarian law has not been resolved decisively. The ICRC offered its services to Afghanistan in 1979 and 1980. Before the events of December 1979, the ICRC had categorized the conflict as noninternational.[81] In January 1980, Karmal received an ICRC delegation and assured the ICRC "that he would respect the principles of the Geneva Conventions under all circumstances and that all armed forces in Afghan territory would comply with their obligations under the Conventions."[82] The ICRC was given authorization to assist political and "security" prisoners and prisoners of war. But in mid-June 1980, after some limited activities, the ICRC delegates were forced to leave Afghanistan.[83] The ICRC continued to seek permission to carry out its humanitarian activities, but, through 1986, its requests were rejected by the Afghan Government.

The ICRC also made appeals to the Soviet Union in 1980, pointing out "the responsibility, under international humanitarian law, of States whose armed forces participated in an armed conflict, even on the basis of a treaty or other agreements."[84] Later that year, a Soviet spokesman told an ICRC mission that humanitarian problems caused by the Afghan conflict did not concern the Soviet Union because its forces had not participated in any combat.[85] The ICRC also called regularly on the resistance groups to conform to the provisions of Article 3.[86] Appeals to the Afghan and Soviet Governments in 1981 were similarly rejected; the Afghan authorities stated that "the Geneva Conventions had no bearing on the situation in their country."[87]

In April 1986, however, the Government of Afghanistan received an ICRC mission for talks on a proposed program of visits to detainees. In

[79] N.Y. Times, July 3, 1982, at A2, col. 3. Western intelligence analysts also reported such a population exchange. *Id.*, Dec. 26, 1983, at A8, col. 3.

[80] "Intelligence experts said this strip, called the Wakhan corridor, had in effect been annexed by the Soviet Union." *Id.*, Dec. 8, 1982, at A5, col. 1. After discussing the tenacious resistance the Soviet Union was encountering throughout Afghanistan, the *Washington Post* said, "An exception is the Wakhan corridor and Pamir region—the sparsely populated northeastern panhandle that stretches to the Chinese border—which the Soviets have virtually annexed, according to diplomats and correspondents who have recently visited the area." Wash. Post, Oct. 21, 1983, at A1, col. 2, A14, col. 1.

[81] Gasser, *supra* note 24, at 150.

[82] 1980 ICRC ANN. REP. 47.

[83] *Id.* at 44–45.

[84] *Id.* at 45.

[85] *Id.*

[86] *Id.*, and following ICRC ANN. REPS.

[87] 1981 ICRC ANN. REP. 37.

August and September, the Government confirmed that it had agreed in principle to ICRC visits to people "captured bearing arms or arrested on account of the events."[88] In January 1987, the ICRC returned to Afghanistan and began establishing programs in Kabul to provide medical and orthopedic assistance to those wounded in the war and medical assistance to the civilian population. The Afghan Government also authorized the ICRC to visit all prisoners in Afghan prisons, in accordance with standard ICRC procedures, but a visit to Pul-I-Charki prison, begun in March, "had to be interrupted the same month, after completion of the first stage."[89] Negotiations were continuing for the resumption of ICRC prison visits.

The ICRC made no determination of the legal character of the conflict. Hans-Peter Gasser suggests that the new Government's consent to the Soviet presence "may have put an end to the conflict between those two countries."[90] We will examine below the immediate and longer term implications of these legal and factual conclusions. Gasser also recommends that the Afghan Government and Soviet forces fighting the insurgents "should be equally committed to respecting at least" common Article 3, pointing out that even a treaty that may make the Soviet intervention legal cannot affect the applicability of international humanitarian law to the armed conflict.[91] But, Gasser writes, "In view of the opposing interests of the different parties to the conflict, it would be wishful thinking to postulate the application of the whole body of international humanitarian law to the relations between the intervening power and the insurgents."[92] Gasser adds, though: "Nevertheless, humanitarian policy demands protection for all actual and potential victims of the conflict. Among the top priorities must be achieving greater respect for the civilian population, treating captured combatants similarly to prisoners of war, and guaranteeing respect for the protective emblem. This is precisely what the ICRC attempts."[93]

The special rapporteur appointed in 1984 by the United Nations Commission on Human Rights to examine the human rights situation in Afghanistan, Felix Ermacora, considered the legal status of the conflict in his report of February 1985. Noting the extraordinary nature of the hostilities and the fact that the parties have not acceded to the Protocols, he concludes that the

[88] 1986 ICRC ANN. REP. 49–50.

[89] ICRC BULL., No. 142, November 1987.

[90] Gasser, *supra* note 24, at 151. Gasser points out that his article does not analyze what happens

> when a new government is installed after the arrival of a foreign power. Suffice it to state that the government currently established in Kabul is the only government claiming to represent the country—there is no government in exile—and that the international community has recognized it de facto: it is represented in the United Nations.

Id. at 151–52 n.15.

[91] *Id.* at 152.

[92] *Id.*

[93] *Id.* In our view, a conclusive characterization of the nature of the conflict and the law that applies is legally sound and consistent with the policy of contemporary international law. Specialized institutions with continuing responsibilities may sometimes find cogent reasons *not* to reach a conclusion on such a matter even when the facts warrant it, believing that the purposes of humanitarian law will better be served in some cases by a certain unclarity. For a particularly sensitive and candid examination of the issue, see *id.* at 157–59.

conflict is "one of a non-international character within the meaning of article 3 of the Geneva Conventions."[94] This is not, however, a conclusion that only Article 3 applies; the special rapporteur reiterates that it is difficult to conclude whether the conflict is international or noninternational, but that Afghanistan and the Soviet Union, as parties to the Geneva Conventions, are "*at least* bound by common article 3."[95] Whether or not the Conventions in their entirety apply thus remains an unanswered question for him. Ermacora notes violations of even the limited provisions of Article 3 and the inability of the opposition to ensure the application of international norms by its forces.[96]

VI.

Scholars, writing as scholars, are entitled to reject factitious distinctions in legal instruments, but scholars, writing as jurists who seek to apply those instruments, must accept the terms as given. The terms "international" and "noninternational" conflicts import a bipartite method that attempts to provide only two factual reference points on a spectrum of possibilities. *Eo ipso*, they represent a decision that some conflicts, no matter how violent, will not be considered international. The method is not one that comports easily with the manifest policy of the contemporary law of armed conflict. That corpus of law seeks to introduce as many humanitarian restraints as possible into conflict, without judgments about its provenance or about the justice of either side's cause. In the contemporary context, the distinctions may vouchsafe incremental gains in the actual acceptance of humanitarian law. Yet, of central importance here, the bipartite factual approach may yield the conclusion that a conflict is not international and thus is insulated from the plenary application of the law of armed conflict—even though that particular conflict may be more violent, extensive and consumptive of life and value than an "international" one.

In our view, the armed conflict in Afghanistan is subject to the plenary application of the Geneva and Hague laws, by virtue of common Article 2, paragraph 1, or, alternatively, common Article 2, paragraph 2. Our review of the facts has persuaded us that the Government of the Democratic Republic of Afghanistan (DRA) after December 27, 1979, could no longer be deemed to be an independent government. The factual record indicates that the alleged invitation issued to the Soviet Union to enter Afghanistan did not emanate from the Government of Afghanistan at that time. On the contrary, it was issued within the Soviet Union by an Afghan who had no official position in the Government. On the basis of this "invitation," Soviet forces invaded Afghanistan, attacked the presidential palace, killed the President, and installed in his place the person who had "invited" them in the first place.[97]

[94] Ermacora, *supra* note 2, at 42–43.

[95] *Id.* at 47 (emphasis added).

[96] *Id.* at 47–48.

[97] *See* section III *supra*.

To suggest that this sort of stratagem can transform an invasion by one state's military forces into the territory of another from an armed conflict into either an internal war or no war at all is to signal the end of a large part of the law of armed conflict. If concocted scenarios like this were to be taken at face value, any state could maintain a stable of political would-bes and has-beens of varying national pedigrees. At the appropriate time, one with the right nationality would be saddled and bridled and brought to the ring to issue the necessary "invitation." Once the armed forces of the foreign state had invaded his country, destroyed the existing government and put him in its place, the new leader, now clothed with authority, would then retroactively validate his government's "invitation."

Imagine the outcry, for example, if the United States were to claim that General Somoza had issued an invitation to U.S. troops from Managua, when he was actually broadcasting from Miami (or Ferdinand Marcos from Manila, when actually in Honolulu), and the United States then accepted the invitation by invading Nicaragua, killing Daniel Ortega, bringing Somoza back and keeping him in power with an enormous expeditionary force of U.S. troops involved in combat against Nicaraguans, all the while maintaining that the conflict was an internal one. This scenario would be absurd.[98] The initial outrage over the invasion itself would be followed by rejection of the U.S. "claim" that the conflict was internal. The analogy with Afghanistan, obviously, is imperfect, but it illustrates the predicament that designating such conflicts as "noninternational" leads to.

There is no way of excluding the operation of common Article 2, paragraph 1, together with the corpus of the Hague law, in the Afghan situation. No matter how the facts are viewed, forces of the Soviet Union entered Afghanistan and engaged in combat with loyal Afghan government forces, which brought about a change of government. The claim that the existing Amin Government invited Soviet troops to bring about its own downfall lacks any credibility. The Soviet Union quickly expanded its role in fighting the Afghan resistance forces until that role was not only predominant, but, in terms of administration and command, nearly complete. Thus, the situation in Afghanistan must be characterized as an armed conflict that became an occupation.[99] Pictet rejects the notion that the Conventions do not apply

[98] Such scenarios are further complicated when the "new" government is generally deemed to be competent to perform many international and intergovernmental functions, including, for example, holding a seat in organizations and maintaining embassies abroad. This kind of recognition, which is driven by the trend to recognize on de facto grounds, complicates further the status of insurgents under humanitarian law. We cannot consider these issues within the confines of this article. Their intractability is symptomatic of the unclarity of this part of international humanitarian law.

[99] Pictet makes it very clear that the transition from invasion to occupation has no effect on the application of the Conventions. They apply throughout. He says, "There is no intermediate period between what might be termed the invasion phase and the inauguration of a stable regime of occupation." 4 Pictet, *supra* note 8, at 60. Pictet's discussion of this point is in regard to the Fourth Convention, *supra* note 3, Article 6, and the relations between the occupying power and civilians. Similar reasons, however, call for the continuity of the application of the plenary Conventions through the transition from invasion to occupation.

to an armed conflict in which both parties deny the existence of a state of war. "Even in that event it would not appear that they could, by tacit agreement, prevent the Conventions from applying. It must not be forgotten that the Conventions have been drawn up first and foremost to protect individuals, and not to serve State interests."[100]

Thus, where the forces of one state enter the territory of another, engage in hostilities, however limited, with the forces of that state's government and install a new, compliant government, an international conflict is constituted. When the outside forces transform their role into one of occupation, paragraph 1 of common Article 2 continues to operate according to its terms.

Common Article 2, paragraph 2 of the Conventions brings into operation the plenary law of war in cases of partial or total occupation of a contracting state's territory even if there is no resistance. The language used is mandatory ("the Convention shall also apply").[101] If state *A*'s military forces occupy part of the territory of state *B* without resistance from the government of state *B*, the situation would not fulfill the contingency of common Article 2, paragraph 1, because it is not a "declared war," or any other armed conflict, between two or more of the high contracting parties.[102] As a result, the situation would not call into operation the plenary laws of war under Article 2, paragraph 1. But this situation would meet the requirement of common Article 2, paragraph 2, whose operation would achieve the same effect as the operation of paragraph 1.

If the claim is made that Soviet forces entered Afghanistan without resistance from Afghan government forces—discounting the factual accounts of the events in Kabul on December 27, 1979—and that there was therefore no armed conflict between two parties to the Convention, it would preclude operation of common Article 2, paragraph 1. But this rendition of the facts of the Soviet intervention would simply move the situation into the gap that paragraph 2 was designed to fill; the Conventions would still apply.[103]

Even assuming that the DRA, throughout the period in question, has been an independent government, and even assuming that this independent government existed before December 24, 1979, and even assuming that, freely and entirely of its own accord, it invited Soviet forces into Afghanistan, the factual record confirms that parts of Afghanistan are under "partial or total occupation" by Soviet forces.[104] Adam Roberts has concluded: "The evidence from conventions, practice, judgments and writings all points unambiguously to the conclusion that the generic term 'military occupation' (or just 'occupation'), though by no means infinitely elastic, is a very broad one."[105] He also notes that the ICRC and the United Nations have often asserted that international humanitarian law is applicable to particular situations, "irrespective of the issue as to whether they count as

[100] *Id.* at 21.

[101] *See supra* text accompanying note 7.

[102] *Id.*

[103] *See supra* notes 10–12 and accompanying text.

[104] *See* section IV *supra.*

[105] Roberts, *What Is a Military Occupation?*, 55 BRIT. Y.B. INT'L. L. 249, 299 (1984).

international armed conflicts and/or occupations."[106] After a brief, but cogent, description of the Afghan situation,[107] Roberts concludes, "The international element in such conflicts appears to be so marked that the better developed body of international law governing international armed conflicts and occupations may well be viewed as applicable."[108] Roberts also notes the disadvantages of an approach that tends to limit the application of the law relating to occupations to cases of classic belligerent occupation. Most important for our purposes, such an approach "goes against a large body of practice and court opinion [and] would leave many activities of armed forces outside their own country in something of an international legal limbo."[109] These concerns are clearly relevant to the situation in Afghanistan. Under the circumstances, we believe, the four Geneva Conventions must apply to the conflict by virtue of common Article 2.

It is appalling to realize that the *lex lata* seems to view an invitation by a government to another government to occupy its territory against the wishes of the inhabitants as not triggering the plenary application of the Geneva Conventions, no matter what the resistance or deprivation of rights suffered. *De lege ferenda*, that factual situation should lead to the opposite legal conclusion. As Pictet noted in a different, but relevant, context: "[H]ere once more the interests at stake (namely, human lives), and the upholding of the principles on which civilization is based, are too important to be circumscribed by rigid rules."[110] Textual arguments can be marshaled

[106] *Id.* at 302.

[107] Roberts writes:

> Take, for example, a deeply divided and weak country, facing civil war. It has an unpopular government with a clear external ideological orientation, which invites in a sympathetic superpower ally. That ally then largely dominates indigenous political developments, and there are even allegations that it had complicity in the assassination of the embarrassingly unpopular head of the government which had invited it in. It also gets deeply involved in counter-insurgency operations against the regime's opponents. This is a rough approximation of the situation in Afghanistan since the Soviet intervention of December 1979.

Id. at 278.

[108] *Id.* Roberts identifies

> some markers which may help to indicate the existence of an occupation, or may suggest the need for the law on occupations to be applied. These include: (i) there is a military force whose presence in a territory is not sanctioned or regulated by a valid agreement, or whose activities there involve an extensive range of contacts with the host society not adequately covered by the original agreement under which it intervened; (ii) the military force has either displaced the territory's ordinary system of public order and government, replacing it with its own command structure, or else has shown the clear physical ability to displace it; (iii) there is a difference of nationality and interest between the inhabitants on the one hand and the forces intervening and exercising power over them on the other, with the former not owing allegiance to the latter; (iv) within an overall framework of a breach of important parts of the national or international legal order, administration and the life of society have to continue on some legal basis, and there is a practical need for an emergency set of rules to reduce the dangers which can result from clashes between the military force and the inhabitants.

Id. at 300–01. The situation in Afghanistan is marked by each of these conditions.

[109] *Id.* at 304.

[110] 1 Pictet, *supra* note 8, at 30.

and some cases may be brought into point, but the drafters of the Convention either rejected or intentionally overlooked this situation. However, this lacuna, while appropriate for high priority on the lawmaker's agenda, is not relevant to the Afghan case. There, as the record shows, the "invitation" was self-issued; the Government of Afghanistan did not extend it. Where a bona fide invitation *has* been extended, it violates reason and conscience to insist that the invitation legitimates the foreign occupation or makes it not an occupation, even when it ceases to have popular support or real indigenous governmental support, indeed even when the country rises in resistance.

The factual continuum that was adopted as the method for determining which of two laws applies to armed conflicts plainly contemplates the possibility of a noninternational conflict in which there will be participation, e.g., at the invitation of the local government, of the military forces of a third state. Presumably, such participation could include joint military operations, the use of military advisers sent by the foreign state and, possibly, independent exercises by the forces of the foreign state under the general direction of the local government. The calculus that emerges from Article 2 does not have a quantitative threshold beyond which the outside force becomes dominant, making an erstwhile noninternational conflict international.

We submit that where outside forces are in effective control of the conflict and have incorporated local forces into their own operations, the conflict has been factually internationalized. While the evidence in the Afghan conflict on this particular matter is not unequivocal, our study of the record leads us to conclude that Soviet generals have directed the operations of the Afghan armed forces, both land and air (insofar as Afghan forces are an effective element in the conflict), and not vice versa. Furthermore, the number of Soviet troops active in Afghanistan has, throughout, far outweighed the number of Afghan army troops. Finally, Soviet officials have been in effective control of, at least, the most important ministries of the Afghan Government.

Conclusion

We conclude that key facts of the Soviet intervention in Afghanistan do, indeed, make the conflict an international one according to the provisions of common Article 2 of the Conventions. Therefore, the Conventions in their entirety, together with the ensemble of law of armed conflict, are applicable for judging the conduct of the parties to the conflict.

First, Soviet forces invaded Afghanistan and removed the Amin Government from power. They were resisted by loyal Afghan government troops. The evidence that Karmal was in the Soviet Union at the time, that his broadcast originated in Soviet Central Asia, and that he only entered Afghanistan after Soviet troops were in control of Kabul and Amin dead belies the claim that the Soviet military was invited by the existing Government. Thus, it would appear that, from the time of the invasion, the conflict met the criteria of the first paragraph of Article 2, applying the Conventions to conflicts between states. Even if the Afghan Government offered no resistance, neither did it offer a legitimate invitation. Thus, the Conventions would apply by virtue of the second paragraph of common Article 2.

Second, the Soviet participation in the conflict against the resistance absorbed the Afghan army's participation. All accounts of the increase in Soviet troop strength following the intervention in December 1979 and the parallel disintegration of the Afghan army, as well as the control of the army and civilian ministries by Soviet advisers, lead to one conclusion: the Soviet presence in Afghanistan, whether or not there was a bona fide invitation by the existing Afghan Government, has been an occupation of the territory of another state within the meaning of common Article 2. Again, the Conventions must apply.

ADVANCING THE FREEDOM OF RELIGION OR BELIEF THROUGH THE UN DECLARATION ON THE ELIMINATION OF RELIGIOUS INTOLERANCE AND DISCRIMINATION

*By Donna J. Sullivan**

In 1981, 19 years after efforts to elaborate protections for religious freedom were formally begun in the United Nations,[1] the Declaration on the Elimination of All Forms of Intolerance and of Discrimination Based on Religion or Belief (the Declaration) was adopted by consensus.[2] The long delay in achieving agreement on the text reflects well-known political struggles in the United Nations[3] but may also be attributed in part to the

* Member of the California Bar; Assistant to the Director, Jacob Blaustein Institute for the Advancement of Human Rights. The views expressed are solely those of the author. This article was developed from a lecture delivered at the 1987 Meller Conference at the New York University School of Law.

[1] See GA Res. 1781, 17 UN GAOR Supp. (No. 17) at 33, UN Doc. A/5217 (1962), requesting that the Economic and Social Council (ECOSOC) prepare a draft declaration and a draft convention on the elimination of religious intolerance. The Sub-Commission on Prevention of Discrimination and Protection of Minorities (hereinafter Sub-Commission) had earlier appointed a special rapporteur, Arcot Krishnaswami, to study religious rights. His report presented an analysis of norms and state practice, A. KRISHNASWAMI, STUDY OF DISCRIMINATION IN THE MATTER OF RELIGIOUS RIGHTS AND PRACTICES, UN Doc. E/CN.4/Sub.2/200/Rev.1, UN Sales No. 60.XIV.2 (1960), and draft principles prepared by the Sub-Commission on the basis of the report. *Id.*, Ann. I [hereinafter Draft Principles].

[2] GA Res. 36/55, 36 UN GAOR Supp. (No. 51) at 171, UN Doc. A/36/51 (1981).

[3] General Assembly Resolution 1781, *supra* note 1, was transmitted by ECOSOC to the Commission on Human Rights (hereinafter Commission) and the Sub-Commission. In 1964 the Sub-Commission transmitted a preliminary draft declaration to the Commission. *See* 37 UN ESCOR Supp. (No. 8), para. 294, UN Doc. E/3873 (1964) [hereinafter 1964 Sub-Commission Draft Declaration]. The working group formed in the Commission considered only 6 of the 14 articles in the Sub-Commission's draft. The Commission forwarded that draft, together with a modified text proposed by the working group, *id.*, para. 296 [hereinafter 1964 Commission Draft Declaration], to ECOSOC for referral to the General Assembly.

The General Assembly did not consider the preliminary drafts but asked ECOSOC to invite the Commission to begin work on a draft convention to be submitted to the Assembly together with the draft declaration. In 1965 the Sub-Commission presented a preliminary draft convention to the Commission, which the latter considered over the following two years. In 1967 ECOSOC transmitted the Commission's draft convention, consisting of a preamble and 12 articles on which the Commission had achieved agreement, to the General Assembly. For the text, see Note by the Secretary-General: Elimination of All Forms of Religious Intolerance, UN Doc. A/8330, Ann. III (1971) [hereinafter 1967 Draft Convention].

The General Assembly discussed the draft convention in 1967, but thereafter postponed consideration of the convention and decided in 1972 to accord priority to the completion of a draft declaration. GA Res. 3027, 27 UN GAOR Supp. (No. 30) at 72, UN Doc. A/8730 (1972). Work on the draft declaration progressed with difficulty in the Commission from 1974 until a text was adopted in 1981; it was transmitted by ECOSOC to the General Assembly in the same year.

For the history of the Declaration and the draft convention, see Liskofsky, *The UN Declaration on the Elimination of Religious Intolerance and Discrimination: Historical and Legal Perspectives,* potential for controversy inherent in the subject matter itself. Against the historical backdrop of civil strife, international warfare and ideological conflict fueled by religion, the Declaration stands as a milestone in the progressive development of human rights norms.

Although it lacks, of course, the nature of an international agreement, the Declaration is "regarded throughout the world as articulating the fundamental rights of freedom of religion and belief."[4] The Declaration gives specific content to the general statements of the rights to freedom of religion or belief and freedom from discrimination based on religion or belief contained in the major human rights instruments. Because it is enunciated in normative terms, elevating the rights and freedoms in question to normative status, the Declaration has a certain legal effect, "under the criteria deriving from international legal decisions."[5] That the United Nations General Assembly intended that it be normative and not merely hortatory is apparent from its Articles 4 and 7. Under Article 4, states are required to "make all efforts to enact or rescind legislation" and to take other effective measures to prohibit discrimination on the basis of religion or belief.[6] Article 7 imposes a more categorical obligation, by providing that "[t]he rights and freedoms set forth in the present Declaration shall be accorded in national legislation in such a manner that everyone shall be able to avail himself of such rights and freedoms in practice." There is no consensus on whether the prohibition of discrimination on grounds of religion or belief already constitutes a norm of customary law.[7] As the Declaration acquires

---

in RELIGION AND THE STATE: ESSAYS IN HONOR OF LEO PFEFFER 441, 460–63 (J. Wood ed. 1985); Lerner, *Toward a Draft Declaration Against Religious Intolerance and Discrimination*, 11 ISR. Y.B. HUM. RTS. 82 (1981); M. MCDOUGAL, H. LASSWELL & L. CHEN, HUMAN RIGHTS AND WORLD PUBLIC ORDER 677–84 (1980); Clark, *The United Nations and Religious Freedom*, 11 N.Y.U. J. INT'L L. & POL. 197 (1978); Claydon, *The Treaty Protection of Religious Rights: U.N. Draft Convention on the Elimination of All Forms of Intolerance and of Discrimination Based on Religion or Belief*, 12 SANTA CLARA LAW. 403 (1972). *See generally* Lerner, *The Final Text of the U.N. Declaration Against Intolerance and Discrimination Based on Religion or Belief*, 12 ISR. Y.B. HUM. RTS. 185 (1982).

[4] UN Doc. E/CN.4/1988/44/Add.2, at 1 (statement by the United States Government). *See also* UN Doc. E/CN.4/Sub.2/1987/26, at 48–49 (asserting that declarations adopted by the General Assembly imply "obligations of conduct" and contain "values" governing conduct that cannot be taken away by political action, although they do not give rise to "rights" from a strict legal standpoint).

[5] UN Doc. E/CN.4/AC.39/1988/L.2, at 5 (analytical compilation of views regarding the significance of the Declaration on the Right to Development, prepared by the Secretary-General).

[6] Article 4 of the Declaration states:

> 1. All States shall take effective measures to prevent and eliminate discrimination on the grounds of religion or belief in the recognition, exercise and enjoyment of human rights and fundamental freedoms in all fields of civil, political, social and cultural life.
>
> 2. All States shall make all efforts to enact or rescind legislation where necessary to prohibit any such discrimination, and to take all appropriate measures to combat intolerance on the grounds of religion or other beliefs in this matter.

[7] Section 702 of the *Restatement (Third) of Foreign Relations Law of the United States* (1988) does not include religious discrimination among the customary norms that it lists. See, however,

concrete material content through its implementation, it will contribute to the acceptance of the customary law status of this important principle.

The recent creation of implementing mechanisms in the United Nations has intensified the need for careful analysis of the Declaration. In 1986 the Commission on Human Rights entrusted a special rapporteur, Angelo d'Almeida Ribeiro, with the task of examining incidents of religious intolerance and discrimination, reporting on compliance with the standards stated in the Declaration and recommending remedial measures.[8] Following a review of Ribeiro's first report, which revealed the frequency and gravity of violations of religious freedom, the Commission extended his mandate.[9] The special rapporteur's second report, submitted in 1988, focused on the role of governments in violations of the Declaration; Ribeiro concluded that the broad geographic distribution of the allegations of violations he had received "highlight[ed] the nearly universal nature of the problem of intolerance and discrimination based on religion or belief."[10]

In addition, the Sub-Commission on Prevention of Discrimination and Protection of Minorities appointed a special rapporteur, Elizabeth Odio Benito, to report on the causes and current dimensions of religious intolerance and discrimination on grounds of religion or belief and to propose remedial measures.[11] Both of the special rapporteurs have recommended reopening the question of drafting a convention on this subject,[12] an undertaking that was initiated together with the work on a draft declaration but subsequently abandoned.[13] The purpose of this study is therefore twofold:

---

comment *j*. Although generalized references to the freedom of religion or belief appear in the Universal Declaration of Human Rights, Art. 18, GA Res. 217A, UN Doc. A/810, at 71 (1948), the International Covenant on Civil and Political Rights, Art. 18, GA Res. 2200, 21 UN GAOR Supp. (No. 16) at 52, UN Doc. A/6316 (1966), and regional human rights instruments, the Declaration is the only instrument that addresses the subject in specific terms. For a compilation of the general provisions relevant to the freedom of religion or belief and freedom from discrimination based on religion or belief contained in international and regional instruments, see UN Doc. E/CN.4/L.1417 (1979).

[8] Comm'n on Human Rights Res. 1986/20, UN Doc. E/CN.4/1986/65, at 66. For discussion in the Commission concerning the need for such a special rapporteur, see UN Doc. E/CN.4/1986/SR.50/Add.1, at 9–14. Several representatives to the Commission objected to the appointment on the ground that the special rapporteur's proposed mandate would overlap with that of the special rapporteur appointed by the Sub-Commission in 1983, who was authorized to study the causes and current dimensions of religious intolerance and discrimination.

[9] Ribeiro, Implementation of the Declaration on the Elimination of All Forms of Intolerance and of Discrimination Based on Religion or Belief, UN Doc. E/CN.4/1987/35 [hereinafter 1987 Ribeiro report].

[10] UN Doc. E/CN.4/1988/45, at 2 [hereinafter 1988 Ribeiro report].

[11] Sub-Comm'n Res. 1983/31, UN Doc. E/CN.4/Sub.2/1983/43, at 98. The final report by Special Rapporteur Odio Benito was issued as UN Doc. E/CN.4/Sub.2/1987/26 [hereinafter Odio Benito report]. *See also* UN Doc. E/CN.4/Sub.2/1985/28 (progress report by Special Rapporteur Odio Benito).

[12] 1988 Ribeiro report, *supra* note 10, at 25, 27; 1987 Ribeiro report, *supra* note 9, at 27; Odio Benito report, *supra* note 11, at 52–53, 57. *See also* UN Docs. E/CN.4/1988/44 and Adds. 1–7 (comments by member states regarding establishment of a working group to draft a binding instrument).

[13] *See* note 3 *supra*.

to suggest interpretive approaches to the Declaration that might be useful in the process of implementation, with a focus upon those areas in which conflict is likely to occur; and to identify problems raised by the text of the Declaration that might be addressed in a convention if the effort to draft a binding instrument is revitalized.

I. Preliminary Observations

The norms stated in the Declaration hold a striking potential for conflict with other rights; consequently, the task of applying the Declaration to concrete situations will challenge human rights advocates to devise interpretive approaches that will maximize the protection afforded to all the rights implicated. Two general features of the Declaration are likely to affect the resolution of such conflicts. First, it is directed primarily toward actions taken by governments, or by individuals who do not subscribe to a given religion or belief, against individuals who do hold and practice that belief. Interactions among members of the same religious groups are therefore not easily analyzed under the Declaration. Second, application of the Declaration is most straightforward when the belief or practice under consideration corresponds to a typically Western model of religion, in which religious institutions and authority are structurally separable from political and other social institutions.[14] The greater degree to which religious power may be structurally distinct from political power under this model than it is under other systems does not necessarily imply a formal separation of church and state. Indeed, the protections offered in the Declaration are not premised upon the separation of church and state and are clearly distinguished in this regard from First Amendment rights under the United States Constitution.[15]

Detailed analysis of the Declaration should focus primarily on Articles 1 and 2, which state its central principles. Article 1 affirms the right to free-

[14] This model contrasts, for example, with the status of religion in the state structure of Iran. For a historical discussion of the relationship of Shiism to the governance of people, see N. Keddie, Religion and Politics in Iran: Shi'ism from Quietism to Revolution (1984). On Islamic ideology and revolutionary potential in the contemporary Middle East, see generally From Nationalism to Revolutionary Islam (S. Arjomand ed. 1984). *See also* R. Howard, Human Rights in Commonwealth Africa 107–13 (1986) (on the relationship between political authority and religion in Commonwealth Africa).

[15] Compare Art. I(d) of the 1967 Draft Convention, *supra* note 3, stating that "neither the establishment of a religion nor the recognition of a religion or belief by a State nor the separation of Church from State shall by itself be considered religious intolerance or discrimination." For discussions of the need to address church-state relations in the Declaration, see, e.g., UN Docs. E/3925/Add.1, at 7, 9 (1964); E/3925/Add.2, at 5 (1964); A/C.3/SR.2011, at 14 (1973); A/C.3/SR.2013, at 23 (1973); E/CN.4/1145, at 12, 17 (1973); E/CN.4/1146, at 8 (1973).

Special Rapporteur Krishnaswami concluded that the formal or legal characteristics of church-state relations do not necessarily bear a causal connection to whether violations of the freedom of religion or belief, or discrimination, will occur or the frequency and seriousness of such violations. A. Krishnaswami, *supra* note 1, at 64–65. *See also* Odio Benito report, *supra* note 11, at 19–21 (summarizing data received from 29 countries regarding church-state relations).

dom of thought, conscience and belief, and the right to manifest one's religion or belief. Article 2 prohibits discrimination on the basis of religion or belief. Neither provision defines "religion" or "belief," nor are these terms defined elsewhere in the Declaration.[16] Although none of the definitions that were proposed at various stages of the drafting process won acceptance, the *travaux préparatoires* reveal general agreement that "theistic, non-theistic and atheistic beliefs" are all embraced by the phrase "religion or belief."[17]

The constitutions of many countries similarly fail to define these terms. Of course, in some countries, such as the United States, the development of case law has compensated for the lack of constitutional definitions.[18] In fact, the omission of definitions of religion and belief from the Declaration may prove more conducive to the protection of freedom of religion and belief than would any definitions that could be agreed upon, for several reasons.[19] First, it would be difficult to formulate a definition of religion, and still more difficult to devise one for belief, broad enough to be acceptable to a large number of states but sufficiently specific to expand the protections afforded. A definition detailing descriptive elements or enumerating types of belief systems protected might well deter acceptance of the norms themselves;

[16] Art. I(a) of the 1967 Draft Convention, *supra* note 3, did include a definition of these terms: "For the purpose of this Convention: (a) the expression 'religion or belief' shall include theistic, non-theistic and atheistic beliefs . . . ."

In the absence of a definition within the Declaration itself, Special Rapporteur Odio Benito suggested the following working definition of "religion": " 'religion' can be described as 'an explanation of the meaning of life and how to live accordingly.' Every religion has at least a creed, a code of action and a cult." Odio Benito report, *supra* note 11, at 4.

[17] During drafting discussions, it was asserted that "religion or belief" should be understood to include, inter alia, monotheism, polytheism, atheism, agnosticism, free thought and animistic beliefs. *See, e.g.*, UN Doc. E/3925, Annex, at 1, 3–4 (1964); 1978 UN ESCOR Supp. (No. 4) at 62, UN Doc. E/1978/34. Conversely, some governments identified systems of thought that should be specifically excluded from the definition such as racism, Nazism and apartheid, UN Doc. A/C.3/L.2033 (1973), and theories on subjects such as philosophy, history, politics, art and science. Analytical Presentation of the Observations received from Governments Concerning the Draft Declaration on the Elimination of All Forms of Religious Intolerance, Note by the Secretary-General, UN Doc. A/9135, at 11 (1973) [hereinafter Observations of Governments]. The view that the phrase "religion or belief" was well understood to refer to both religious and nonreligious beliefs prevailed, and proposed definitions (which continued to be offered as late as 1981) were rejected. *See, e.g.*, UN Docs. E/3925/Add.1, at 10 (1964); A/9135, at 10–11 (1973); E/CN.4/1146/Add.3, at 1 (1974); 1981 UN ESCOR Supp. (No. 5) at 149, UN Doc. E/1981/25.

[18] *See generally* R. MILLER & R. FLOWERS, TOWARD BENEVOLENT NEUTRALITY: CHURCH, STATE AND THE SUPREME COURT (rev. ed. 1982); L. PFEFFER, RELIGIOUS FREEDOM (1977).

For a case study of approaches used by U.S. courts to identify and define practices entitled to protection as religious freedoms, compare Native American Church of New York v. United States, 468 F.Supp. 1247 (S.D.N.Y. 1979), *aff'd*, 633 F.2d 205 (2d Cir. 1980) (regarding peyotism as a Native American religion), with Leary v. United States, 383 F.2d 851, *reh'g denied*, 392 F.2d 220 (5th Cir. 1967), *rev'd on other grounds*, 395 U.S. 6 (1968) (rejecting First Amendment claims regarding LSD brought by a primate of the Neo-American Church).

[19] For a discussion of descriptive and dictionary definitions of religion, see NEW SOUTH WALES ANTI-DISCRIMINATION BOARD, DISCRIMINATION AND RELIGIOUS CONVICTION 7–12 (1984).

states might argue that the definition does not encompass the religious practices and belief systems prevailing in their territories or might enter reservations that would eviscerate the protections offered. Any definition that purports to describe all the beliefs protected might be cited as a basis for denying protection to genuinely held beliefs that do not correspond to one or more of its particulars.[20]

Second, if these terms were defined, states might be tempted routinely to label as spurious all expressions of belief and practices that do not conform to the details of the definitions. Examination of the substantive content of beliefs for the purpose of conferring "legitimate religious" status upon them may undermine the basic purposes of the Declaration.

Attempts to define "religion or belief" thus offer little prospect for improvement in the standards of protection for the freedom of religion and belief. Rather, in the implementation of the Declaration (and in the drafting work on a convention, if it is resumed), the parameters of the conduct and expression protected by the substantive provisions of the Declaration must be carefully examined. Those parameters are broadly delineated by the twin principles of the freedom to manifest religion or belief, stated in Article 1 and elaborated in Article 6, and the freedom from discrimination based on religion or belief, set forth in Article 2. This analysis of the Declaration focuses on Article 1, with particular attention to its limitations clause, the scope of the prohibition of discrimination in Article 2, and selected problems of normative conflict.

II. The Scope of Article 1

Article 1 of the Declaration states:

> 1. Everyone shall have the right to freedom of thought, conscience and religion. This right shall include freedom to have a religion or whatever belief of his choice, and freedom, either individually or in community with others and in public or private, to manifest his religion or belief in worship, observance, practice or teaching.
>
> 2. No one shall be subject to coercion which would impair his freedom to have a religion or belief of his choice.
>
> 3. Freedom to manifest one's religion or beliefs may be subject only to such limitations as are prescribed by law and are necessary to protect public safety, order, health or morals or the fundamental rights and freedoms of others.

The freedom of thought, conscience and religion set forth in Article 1 should be distinguished from the freedom to manifest religion or belief. As has been observed regarding the nonderogable Article 18 of the Interna-

[20] *See* UN Doc. E/3925, Annex, at 7 (1964); 1981 UN ESCOR Supp. (No. 5) at 140, UN Doc. E/1981/25 (noting that any attempt to enumerate beliefs covered by the phrase "religion or belief" would necessarily be incomplete and thereby defeat the aim of universal application).

tional Covenant on Civil and Political Rights (the Political Covenant),[21] no limitations upon the freedom of thought and the freedom to have a religion or belief are permissible.[22] In contrast, the freedom to manifest one's religion or belief may be subject to restraints imposed to protect other human rights and the various societal interests recognized by the Political Covenant and other human rights instruments.[23]

Coercion

The prohibition of coercion which would impair the freedom to have a religion or belief of one's choice, stated in paragraph 2, clearly forbids the use or threat of physical force to compel believers (or nonbelievers) to recant or to convert.[24] The general wording of this provision, however, does not elucidate what other conduct, conditions or forms of communication would constitute coercion.[25] The municipal law of several countries incor-

[21] Article 18 of the Covenant, *supra* note 7, provides:

> 1. Everyone shall have the right to freedom of thought, conscience and religion. This right shall include freedom to have or to adopt a religion or belief of his choice, and freedom, either individually or in community with others and in public or private, to manifest his religion or belief in worship, observance, practice and teaching.
>
> 2. No one shall be subject to coercion which would impair his freedom to have or to adopt a religion or belief of his choice.
>
> 3. Freedom to manifest one's religion or beliefs may be subject only to such limitations as are prescribed by law and are necessary to protect public safety, order, health, or morals or the fundamental rights and freedoms of others.
>
> 4. The States Parties to the present Covenant undertake to have respect for the liberty of parents and, when applicable, legal guardians to ensure the religious and moral education of their children in conformity with their own convictions.

[22] *See* Partsch, *Freedom of Conscience and Expression*, in THE INTERNATIONAL BILL OF RIGHTS: THE COVENANT ON CIVIL AND POLITICAL RIGHTS 208, 213–14 (L. Henkin ed. 1981); T. VAN BOVEN, DE VOLKENRECHTELIJKE BESCHERMING VAN DE GODSDIENSTVRIJHEID 270, 275 (1967). *See also* A. KRISHNASWAMI, *supra* note 1, at 27.

[23] *See* Kiss, *Permissible Limitations on Rights*, in Henkin (ed.), *supra* note 22, at 290; Siracusa Principles 1–38, UN Doc. E/CN.4/1985/4, Annex, at 3–6. *Cf.* European Convention for the Protection of Human Rights and Fundamental Freedoms, Art. 9, 213 UNTS 221 (1950); American Convention on Human Rights, Art. 12, *reprinted in* ORGANIZATION OF AMERICAN STATES, HANDBOOK OF EXISTING RULES PERTAINING TO HUMAN RIGHTS IN THE INTER-AMERICAN SYSTEM 27, OEA/Ser.L/V/II.65, Doc. 6 (1985) [hereinafter American Convention].

[24] *See, e.g.*, 1988 Ribeiro report, *supra* note 10, at 5 (reporting allegations that Baha'is in Iran have been tortured and executed in an effort to force them to recant their faith).

[25] The draft principles prepared by the Sub-Commission included a more specific definition of coercion: "No one shall be subjected to *material or moral coercion* likely to impair his freedom to maintain or to change his religion or belief" (emphasis added). Draft Principles, *supra* note 1, pt. I(3).

On the need for a more specific definition, see, e.g., 34 UN ESCOR Supp. (No. 4) at 57–58, UN Doc. E/1978/34 (discussing a proposal to include a fuller statement of the various kinds of coercion, such as legal, economic and administrative coercion); *see also* 36 UN ESCOR Supp. (No. 6) at 72, UN Doc. E/1979/36 (definition proposed by Cyprus).

porates more specific definitions of coercion, in measures forbidding, for example, "open and overt acts or threats,"[26] "physical or moral compulsion"[27] and the "use of violence, intimidation or force"[28] for the purpose of making people change their beliefs. If the aim of protecting the right to have a religion or belief, which lies at the core of the Declaration, is to be achieved, "coercion" should be interpreted to include mental or psychological means of compulsion as well as physical means. In addition, the prohibition of coercion should extend to such practices as conditioning the receipt of benefits or services from the government upon the renunciation or acceptance of religious beliefs.[29]

Coercive forms of persuasion, which attack the intellectual and psychological aspects of belief, should be encompassed by the prohibited forms of coercion.[30] In two common situations, such "moral" coercion generates conflict between principles stated in the Declaration itself. Proselytizing activities, the first of these, by their very nature attempt moral compulsion to some degree.[31] Proselytizing may set the rights of those whose religious faith encourages or requires such activity in opposition to the rights of those targeted to be free from coercion to change their beliefs. The latter right is not a legitimate basis for denying believers the freedom to engage in *non-coercive* forms of proselytizing, such as mere appeals to conscience or the display of placards and billboards. The right to freedom of expression for those who proselytize should be considered in weighing protections for the rights of those whom they attempt to convert.[32]

The coercive effect of services provided in conjunction with missionary or proselytizing activities, such as medical or educational assistance, was noted by Arcot Krishnaswami in his key study of religious intolerance and discrimination.[33] These forms of inducement to conversion are obviously of special

[26] UN Doc. E/CN.4/1986/37/Add.4, at 1 (Mauritius).

[27] UN Doc. E/CN.4/1986/37, at 12 (Cyprus).

[28] *Id.* at 39 (Spain).

[29] *See, e.g.*, 1988 Ribeiro report, *supra* note 10, at 5 (reporting allegations that Baha'i children in Iran are denied admission to the state school system unless they formally convert to Islam).

[30] *See* Draft Principles, *supra* note 1, pt. I(3).

[31] *Cf.* UN Doc. CCPR/C/SR.202, at 7 (1980) (statement by representative of Mongolia, characterizing the very holding of religious services as a form of religious propaganda).

[32] Regarding the legal restrictions imposed by some countries on proselytizing, see 1987 Ribeiro report, *supra* note 9, at 11. *See also* Odio Benito report, *supra* note 11, at 13. The right to propagate religion is legally protected in some countries. *See, e.g.*, UN Doc. E/CN.4/1987/37, at 29 (Pakistan). *Cf.* UN Doc. E/CN.4/SR.319, at 6–7 (1952) (regarding the need to check interpretations of Art. 18(2) of the Political Covenant, *supra* note 21, prohibiting coercion, that would jeopardize the freedom of teaching, worship and observance or preclude persuasive methods).

Article 12(1) of the American Convention, *supra* note 23, explicitly affirms the right to "disseminate" one's religion or beliefs.

[33] A. Krishnaswami, *supra* note 1, at 41. *See also* T. van Boven, *supra* note 22, at 274 (arguing that the freedom to change one's religion or belief "does not constitute a license to proselytize by offering attractive social and material profits or by exerting undue pressure upon persons in a vulnerable position"); 36 UN GAOR (73d plen. mtg.) at 1219, UN Doc. A/36/PV.73 (1981) (regarding "impermissible material incentives").

concern to countries with histories of colonial domination linked to missionary activities,[34] although the problem of economic inducements is not limited to that context.

A desire to avoid the implicit approval of proselytizing was one of the considerations underlying the omission from the Declaration of an explicit reference to the freedom to change one's religion or belief.[35] Because the basic freedom to hold a religion or belief is not subject to limitation, in a situation of conflict the right to engage in coercive forms of proselytizing as an expression of religious belief must yield to the right of individuals to hold a belief of their choice without impairment.

The right of individuals to maintain their own beliefs is central to the concerns that motivated the drafting of the Declaration itself. This principle necessarily entails not only the right to retain a belief, but also the freedom to choose a belief without coercion, including the right to reject one's current belief and accept another. Although explicit reference to the right to change beliefs was dropped from the Declaration,[36] that right remains implicit in the right to have a religion or belief. Moreover, Article 8, the savings clause of the Declaration, preserves the standards set forth in the Universal Declaration of Human Rights (the Universal Declaration)[37] and the International Covenants on Human Rights by stating that "[n]othing in the present Declaration shall be construed as restricting or derogating from any right defined in the Universal Declaration of Human Rights and the International Covenants on Human Rights." The Universal Declaration affirms the freedom to change beliefs and the Political Covenant refers to the freedom to adopt a religion or belief.[38]

Nonetheless, the parameters of the right to change one's religion or belief remain uncertain, as illustrated by the difficulty of evaluating the treatment to be accorded apostates and heretics under the Declaration, a second area implicated by the prohibition of coercion. Apostasy and heresy present potential conflicts between the right of individuals to believe what they choose and the right of religious groups to promulgate doctrine as a part of religious practice. Such conflict illustrates the difficulty encountered in attempting to reconcile competing religious interests. History is replete with examples of religious persecution perpetrated in the guise of punishment

[34] *See, e.g.*, Nsereko, *Religion, the State and the Law in Africa*, 28 J. CHURCH & ST. 269, 273 (1986) (noting that "the majority of African states cannot dispense with the church's role in education. Therefore, many African states permit churches to operate schools and allow religion to be taught as a subject in public schools").

[35] *See* Clark, *supra* note 3, at 200; *see, e.g.*, UN Doc. A/C.3/SR.2009, at 4 (1973) (statement by Saudi Arabian representative characterizing proposed reference to the right to change religions as designed to benefit missionary religions).

Regarding opposition to inclusion of the right to change religions in the Universal Declaration, see N. ROBINSON, THE UNIVERSAL DECLARATION OF HUMAN RIGHTS 128–29 (1958). Regarding objections to its inclusion in the Political Covenant on the ground that it would encourage missionary activities, see, e.g., UN Doc. A/C.3/SR.367, para. 41 (1951).

[36] *See* UN Docs. A/36/684, at 2–3 (1981); A/C.3/36/SR.43, at 2 (1981).

[37] *See* note 7 *supra*.

[38] 36 UN GAOR (73d plen. mtg.) at 1218–19, UN Doc. A/36/PV.73 (1981).

for heresy. If religious and secular authorities overlap and attempt to suppress the expression of belief by alleged heretics through punitive measures, such as stripping them of secular privileges or property rights (as in the case of the Baha'is in Iran), it is again the right of individuals to adhere to, or to change, their beliefs that should be accorded greater weight.[39]

Morals and the "Fundamental" Rights of Others

Like Article 18 of the Political Covenant (from which it was drawn), Article 1 of the Declaration permits restraints prescribed by law and necessary for the protection of public safety, order, health or morals and the fundamental rights and freedoms of others. Given the breadth and vagueness of these terms, analyses of specific restrictions must guard against interpretations that would eviscerate the safeguards created and magnify uncertainties concerning the resolution of conflicts. Of the bases for restriction recognized, "public morals" and the "fundamental rights and freedoms of others" may be singled out for comment as bearing particularly interesting relationships to the freedom of religion or belief. The first of these, restraints based upon public morals, may, because of the inherent vagueness of the concept of morals,[40] be abused to challenge the principles upon which the Declaration is based through attacks on the expression of beliefs and practices that diverge from the norm or majoritarian values.[41]

The reference in Article 1(3) to the "fundamental rights and freedoms of others" as a basis for limiting the freedom to manifest religion also poses problems of interpretation. Like Article 18 of the Political Covenant, para-

[39] *See* A. KRISHNASWAMI, *supra* note 1, at 38; 1987 Ribeiro report, *supra* note 9, at 15. *See also id.* (characterizing the practice of forbidding the members of a community considered heretical to claim kinship with the majority religion as an infringement of Art. 1).

[40] Article 29(2) of the Universal Declaration recognizes morality as a basis for restrictions, as do all the limitation clauses in the Political Covenant. *See* Kiss, *supra* note 23, at 303–04.

In Handyside v. U.K., 24 Eur. Ct. H.R. (ser. A) (1976), the European Court found that it was impossible to find a uniform European concept of "morals" in the domestic law of the European states. The Court observed that views on the requirements of morals "var[y] from time to time and from place to place, especially in our era which is characterized by a rapid and far-reaching evolution of opinion on the subject." *Id.* at 22. *Accord*, Dudgeon v. U.K., App. No. 7525/76, Eur. Comm'n H.R., Report of Mar. 13, 1980, *aff'd*, 45 Eur. Ct. H.R. 21 (ser. A) (1981). *See also* Communication No. 61/1979, *Hertzberg v. Finland*, International Covenant on Civil and Political Rights, Human Rights Committee, Selected Decisions under the Optional Protocol (2d–16th sessions), UN Doc. CCPR/C/OP/1, at 124, 126 (1985).

Of the 29 states providing data to Special Rapporteur Odio Benito, 15 indicated that legislative or constitutional limitations upon the freedom to manifest religion or belief currently include "morals." Odio Benito report, *supra* note 11, at 29.

[41] *See, e.g.*, UN Docs. E/CN.4/1988/43, at 10–11 (response from Government of Colombia, noting that the constitutional provision guaranteeing the freedom to practice any religion not contrary to Christian morality reflects the fact that Catholicism has historically been the religion professed by the majority of Colombians); E/CN.4/1987/37, at 13 (response from Government of Panama, noting that Christian morality is included, with public order, as one of two grounds for imposing limitations on the freedom to practice all religions, in recognition of the fact that Catholicism is the majority religion).

graph 3 refers to the "fundamental" rights and freedoms, and not merely the rights and freedoms, of others.[42] The phrase "fundamental rights" does not occur elsewhere in the Declaration. A similar phrase, "fundamental human rights," appears in paragraph 5 of the Preamble to the Universal Declaration, paragraph 1 of the Preamble to the Convention on the Elimination of All Forms of Discrimination Against Women[43] (the Discrimination Against Women Convention) and Article 5(2) of the Political Covenant. Articles 2, 3 and 4,[44] and preambular paragraphs 1 and 3 of the Declaration employ the phrase "human rights and fundamental freedoms," as do several articles of the Charter of the United Nations, and paragraph 6 of the Preamble and Article 26(2) of the Universal Declaration. The use of the term "fundamental" to qualify "freedoms" (rather than "rights") is the formulation most common among the major international human rights instruments. Article 7 of the Declaration speaks of "rights and freedoms" without any qualifying term, a phrase that also appears in the other instruments mentioned above.

Because the phrase "fundamental rights" appears only in paragraph 3 of Article 1, it arguably narrows the range of human rights that will serve as legitimate bases for restrictions to include only those human rights considered to be "fundamental."[45] However, as Professor Meron recently argued in his cogent examination of the concept of a hierarchy in human rights norms, the use of the term "fundamental" to imply a hierarchical relationship between fundamental rights and other rights may be misleading.[46] As he pointed out, the terms "human rights" and "fundamental rights" are used interchangeably in international and regional human rights instruments. This inconsistency in terminology and, except for a small number of *jus cogens* rights, the absence of any general agreement on the greater importance of some human rights vis-à-vis others suggest that there is no substantive or definable legal distinction between those human rights that are "fundamental" and those that are not. The characterization of some

[42] The limitations clause of the Draft Principles, *supra* note 1, employed the wording in Article 29(2) of the Universal Declaration, which cites the "rights and freedoms" of others as grounds for limitations. Article XII of the 1967 Draft Convention, *supra* note 3, permitted limitations based on the "individual rights and freedoms of others."

[43] GA Res. 34/180, 34 UN GAOR Supp. (No. 46) at 193, UN Doc. A/34/46 (1979).

[44] For the text of Article 4, see note 6 *supra*. For Article 2, see text *infra* at p. 501. Article 3 is couched in hortatory language:

> Discrimination between human beings on grounds of religion or belief constitutes an affront to human dignity and a disavowal of the principles of the Charter of the United Nations, and shall be condemned as a violation of the *human rights and fundamental freedoms* proclaimed in the Universal Declaration of Human Rights and enunciated in detail in the International Covenants on Human Rights, and as an obstacle to friendly and peaceful relations between nations [emphasis added].

[45] T. MERON, HUMAN RIGHTS LAW-MAKING IN THE UNITED NATIONS: A CRITIQUE OF INSTRUMENTS AND PROCESS 181–82 (1986).

[46] *Id.* at 178–89; *see also* Meron, *On a Hierarchy of International Human Rights*, 80 AJIL 1 (1986).

rights as fundamental seems to rest primarily upon subjective views of their importance.[47]

Because the catalog of those rights possessing "fundamental" status is itself subject to differing interpretations, the objectivity suggested by hierarchical terminology proves deceptive when analysis of a particular situation of conflict is attempted. Indeed, the freedom of religion itself is described in the Declaration not as a "fundamental human right" but as a "human right and fundamental freedom" (Preamble, paragraph 3), which again echoes the dominant phrase in the Charter of the United Nations. A conflict might arise, for example, if Article 11 of the Discrimination Against Women Convention, which prohibits discriminatory employment practices, were applied to a business engaged in some activity barred to women by religious doctrine. Normative conflicts between the Declaration and the Convention are not resolvable under the savings clause of either instrument.[48] International state practice reveals that there is no consensus on the fundamental status of women's right to employment, yet this right is vital to the aims of the Convention. A conflict between women's right to employment and the right to observe religious teachings thus cannot be resolved by determining in the abstract that the employment right does or does not have fundamental status.

Although the savings clause of the Declaration, Article 8, appears to regulate conflicts between religious rights and other rights, it provides only that nothing in the Declaration shall be construed as restricting or derogating from any right defined in the Universal Declaration or the Covenants, and does not address conflict with other instruments. Moreover, Article 8 does not even provide sufficient guidance for the resolution of conflicts involving rights stated in the instruments that are specified. For example, restrictions upon proselytizing, which may be permissible under the Declaration to protect the rights of those targeted by the proselytizing activities,

[47] T. MERON, *supra* note 45, at 156, 178–83.

On the use of "fundamental" in the limitations clause of Article 18 of the Political Covenant, from which Article 1(3) of the Declaration was drawn, see UN Doc. E/CN.4/SR.319, at 4, 14 (1952) (regarding UK proposal, later defeated, to delete "fundamental" because "the intention was to refer rather to *personal* rights and freedoms"; *id.* at 4 (emphasis added)). *See also id.* at 64 (uniform limitations clause for the Political Covenant proposed by the Secretary-General, omitting the word "fundamental" from the reference to the rights and freedoms of others).

[48] T. MERON, *supra* note 45, at 77–78, 153–54.

Article 11 of the Convention, *supra* note 43, requires states to ensure for women, on a basis of equality with men, the same rights, inter alia, to employment opportunities (including application of the same criteria for selection), free choice of profession and employment, promotion, job security and all benefits and conditions of service, and equal remuneration, including benefits.

For the text of Article 8, the savings clause of the Declaration, see text at note 37 *supra*. Article 23, the savings clause of the Discrimination Against Women Convention, provides: "Nothing in the present Convention shall affect any provisions that are more conducive to the achievement of equality between men and women which may be contained: (a) In the legislation of a state party; or (b) In any other international convention, treaty or agreement in force for that state."

may conflict with the freedom of expression guaranteed in Article 19 of the Political Covenant. This conflict is more apparent than real, however, because Article 19 itself permits restrictions on the freedom of expression that are necessary for respect of the rights or reputations of others.[49]

The Boundary Between Religion and Politics

Arguments that the conduct restricted by the state is not religious in nature or that the individuals and groups affected are not engaged in religious activities are often advanced as a means of circumventing the broadly framed requirements of paragraph 3. All too frequently, a state seeking to suppress religious freedoms characterizes the activities of religious groups and leaders as impermissible political action or subversion.[50] The absence of a definition of religion or belief may facilitate such denials of the true basis for restrictions or oppression by the state, but probably has little substantive effect upon whether states will commit such abuses.

Governments do have a legitimate interest in controlling violence against the state or disruptions of public order, and may do so by using methods consistent with other human rights obligations. Nonetheless, governmental violations of religious freedoms and persecution of religious leaders and groups under the pretense of restraining impermissible political activity are far more prevalent than is the use of a religious identity to camouflage actions motivated by purely partisan political concerns. Although national security as a rationale for restrictions was omitted from the Declaration,[51] limitations necessary to protect public safety and order are authorized by paragraph 3. Given the vagueness of these terms, there is a risk that states will cite them to justify restrictions on religious freedom imposed for reasons tantamount to national security interests, by arguing that a religious group is engaged in political activities that endanger public safety and order.[52]

[49] The limitations clause of Article 19 of the Covenant, *supra* note 7, provides:

> 3. The exercise of the [freedom of expression] carries with it special duties and responsibilities. It may therefore be subject to certain restrictions, but these shall only be such as are provided by law and are necessary:
>
> (a) For respect of the rights or reputations of others;
> (b) For the protection of national security or of public order (*ordre public*), or of public health or morals.

[50] *See, e.g.*, 1987 Ribeiro report, *supra* note 9, at 13; UN Doc. E/CN.4/1987/SR.25, at 6, 8.

[51] *Cf.* 1967 Draft Convention, *supra* note 3, Art. XI (providing that "[n]othing in this Convention shall be interpreted as giving to any person, group or institution the right to engage in activities aimed at prejudicing national security, national sovereignty or friendly relations between nations").

Of the 29 states providing data to Special Rapporteur Odio Benito, 5 indicated that limitations on the basis of security were in effect. Odio Benito report, *supra* note 11, at 29. *See generally* Kiss, *supra* note 23, at 295–97 (regarding national security as a ground for limitations).

[52] *See, e.g.*, UN Doc. A/C.3/36/SR.32, at 13 (1981) (statement by representative of Australia, asserting that the draft Declaration did not give individuals or groups the right to participate in political activities against the interests of the state).

Not only is the distinction between religious and political activity subject to frequent abuse by states, but it also highlights a theoretical uncertainty concerning the scope of the beliefs protected by the Declaration. Many religious doctrines or beliefs dictate standards of social conduct and responsibility, and require believers to act accordingly. For those adherents who follow such precepts of social responsibility, the distinction between religious and political activities may be artificial.[53] For example, pacifist religious convictions may prompt an individual to participate in public protest, to refuse to pay taxes used for military expenses and to attempt to influence decisions made by political leaders. Religious beliefs inevitably assume political significance in such circumstances.

Indeed, the intensity with which believers commonly assert their faith, the highly organized character of many religious groups and the magnitude of their followings lend those groups formidable political power.[54] Moreover, the structural separation of secular and religious authority is obviously not a universal feature of societies, as demonstrated by Iran.[55] Finally, political beliefs are presumably subsumed within the general category of "beliefs" to which the Declaration extends and are protected under that rubric.[56] As Professor Partsch and others have observed regarding Article 18 of the Political Covenant, the freedom of thought that is affirmed in Article 1 of the Declaration embraces political and social thought.[57]

Article 6, which sketches the contours of the basic right to religious freedom broadly stated in Article 1, enumerates rights that are for the most part equally relevant to nonreligious beliefs.[58] Paragraphs (c) and (h), which

[53] *See* Woods, *Church Lobbying and Public Policy*, 28 J. CHURCH & ST. 183, 189 (1986); van Boven, *Religious Liberty in the Context of Human Rights*, 37 ECUMENICAL REV. 345, 350–51 (1985).

[54] *See* UN Doc. E/CN.4/Sub.2/1985/28, at 12.

[55] *See* note 14 *supra*.

[56] For national views concerning the scope of "belief," see, e.g., UN Doc. E/CN.4/1986/37, at 22 (response of the Government of the Federal Republic of Germany, noting that associations whose purpose is the cultivation of a philosophical ideology have the same status as religious bodies); *id.* at 37 (response of the Government of Spain, reporting that activities or study relating to psychic phenomena or to humanistic or spiritualistic values are not protected manifestations of belief); Observations of Governments, *supra* note 17, at 4 (response of the Government of Austria, stating that "belief" encompasses only those beliefs of a transcendental character and does not include every philosophy, particularly not purely political philosophy); *id.* at 11 (response of the Government of Sweden, excluding theories on subjects such as philosophy, history, politics and science from the purview of "belief"); UN Doc. A/C.3/SR.2012, at 12 (1973) (statement by representative of the German Democratic Republic, rejecting the view of the Austrian Government that "belief" refers only to "transcendental" philosophies); *accord id.* at 13 (statement by representative of the Netherlands).

[57] Partsch, *supra* note 22, at 213–14; Lillich, *Civil Rights*, in 1 HUMAN RIGHTS IN INTERNATIONAL LAW: LEGAL AND POLICY ISSUES 115, 159 n.243, 245 (T. Meron ed. 1984).

[58] Article 6 stipulates that, subject to the provisions of Article 1(3),

> the right to freedom of thought, conscience, religion or belief shall include, *inter alia*, the following freedoms:
>
> (a) To worship or assemble in connection with a religion or belief, and to establish and maintain places for these purposes;

detail rights regarding the use of ritual articles and materials and the observation of holidays and days of rest, primarily concern religious belief. The remaining rights enumerated in Article 6, however (including, for example, the freedoms to assemble and maintain places for assembly, to write and distribute publications, and to engage in national and international communication in matters of belief), obviously apply to nonreligious as well as religious belief. Article 6 thus protects a limited number of practices that are generally significant to both religious and nonreligious beliefs. Discussion of the extensive range of practices implicated by the freedom to manifest religion or belief, but not mentioned in Article 6, is beyond the scope of this article.[59]

III. The Scope of the Prohibition of Discrimination and Intolerance

The Prohibition of Discrimination

The companion principle to the freedom to manifest religion is the right to be free from discrimination on grounds of religion or belief, stated in Article 2, which provides:

> 1. No one shall be subject to discrimination by any State, institution, group of persons, or person on grounds of religion or other beliefs.
>
> 2. For the purposes of the present Declaration, the expression "intolerance and discrimination based on religion or belief" means any distinction, exclusion, restriction or preference based on religion or belief and having as its purpose or effect nullification or impairment of the recognition, enjoyment or exercise of human rights and fundamental freedoms on an equal basis.

The wording of Article 2(2) is borrowed from the definition of racial discrimination in Article 1 of the International Convention on the Elimina-

---

(b) To establish and maintain appropriate charitable or humanitarian institutions;

(c) To make, acquire and use to an adequate extent the necessary articles and materials related to the rites or customs of a religion or belief;

(d) To write, issue and disseminate relevant publications in these areas;

(e) To teach a religion or belief in places suitable for these purposes;

(f) To solicit and receive voluntary financial and other contributions from individuals and institutions;

(g) To train, appoint, elect or designate by succession appropriate leaders called for by the requirements and standards of any religion or belief;

(h) To observe days of rest and celebrate holidays and ceremonies in accordance with the precepts of one's religion or belief;

(i) To establish and maintain communications with individuals and communities in matters of religion and belief at the national and international levels.

[59] For discussion of the wide range of practices associated with religion or belief, factors that may justify restrictions on those practices and specific protections required for certain freedoms of religion or belief, see A. Krishnaswami, *supra* note 1, at 43–62. The Draft Principles, *supra* note 1, part II, and the 1967 Draft Convention, *supra* note 3, Article III, included fuller listings of the specific rights encompassed by the freedom of religion or belief than that contained in Article 6 of the Declaration.

tion of All Forms of Racial Discrimination (the Racial Discrimination Convention).[60] Like the Convention, the Declaration prohibits distinctions which have adverse effects on human rights in addition to those which are implemented for the purpose of impairing or nullifying such rights. In barring unintentional as well as intentional acts of discrimination, Article 2 expands the protection afforded by permitting the inference of purpose from effect.[61] As is true of racial discrimination, discrimination on grounds of religion or belief may be ingrained in socioeconomic and cultural institutions. A prohibition upon acts having a discriminatory effect as well as those having a discriminatory purpose may thus be essential to eliminating certain forms of discrimination.[62]

Finally, by prohibiting acts that have a discriminatory effect as well as purpose, the Declaration reaches not only the discriminatory imposition of civil, political, economic, legal or social disabilities, but also the extension of benefits to some religious groups and not others. For example, if governments grant tax-exempt status to certain religious groups only, other groups will be required to devote financial resources to tax payments that otherwise would have been available to fund their religious activities. Such schemes thus have a discriminatory effect upon the groups not allotted benefits.

Paragraph 2 of Article 2 does not explicitly address the intended reach of the prohibition of discrimination. However, if paragraph 1 of Article 2 is read in conjunction with Article 3 and paragraph 1 of Article 4,[63] the prohibition must be interpreted to apply to both public and private action. Paragraph 1 of Article 2 forbids discrimination by "any State, institution, group of persons, or person." This formulation echoes Article 2(1) of the United Nations Declaration on the Elimination of All Forms of Racial Discrimination (the Racial Discrimination Declaration), which proscribes discrimination by any "State, institution, group or individual."[64] The conduct of "private," nongovernmental institutions and groups as well as that of governmental authorities thus falls within the scope of Article 2. As the word "person" in the singular indicates, acts of discrimination committed

[60] *Opened for signature* Mar. 7, 1966, 660 UNTS 195, *reprinted in* 5 ILM 352 (1966). Article 1(1) of the Racial Discrimination Convention defines racial discrimination as

> any distinction, exclusion, restriction or preference based on race, colour, descent, or national or ethnic origin which has the purpose or effect of nullifying or impairing the recognition, enjoyment or exercise, on an equal footing, of human rights and fundamental freedoms in the political, economic, social, cultural or any other field of public life.

[61] T. MERON, *supra* note 45, at 11–16; Greenberg, *Race, Sex and Religious Discrimination in International Law,* in 2 Meron (ed.), *supra* note 57, at 307, 322 (1984).

[62] On the nexus between racial discrimination and discrimination on the ground of religion or belief, see *infra* pp. 507–10.

[63] For the text of Article 3, see note 44 *supra*. For the text of Article 4, see note 6 *supra*.

[64] GA Res. 1904, 18 UN GAOR Supp. (No. 15) at 35–37, UN Doc. A/5515 (1963). *Cf.* Racial Discrimination Convention, *supra* note 60, Art. 2(1)(d) (requiring states parties to prohibit and eliminate racial discrimination by "any *persons, group or organization*"); Discrimination Against Women Convention, *supra* note 43, Art. 2(e) (requiring states parties to take "all appropriate measures to eliminate discrimination against women by any *person, organization or enterprise*") (emphasis added).

by one individual against another are encompassed by Article 2.[65] The language of Article 3 confirms this interpretation, by condemning discrimination "between human beings."[66] Moreover, in a departure from the definition set forth in the Racial Discrimination Convention, Article 2(2) omits the clause in the latter that extends the prohibition of discrimination to the "political, economic, social, cultural or any other field of *public life*."[67] (Other provisions of the Racial Discrimination Convention nevertheless demonstrate that the intention was to reach private action as well.) Consequently, interpersonal and familial relationships are subject to the strictures of Article 2.

The legislative history reveals some disagreement over the inclusion of antidiscrimination provisions applicable to private institutions and individuals. One government, for example, commenting upon the drafts prepared by the Sub-Commission[68] and the Commission,[69] stated that the phrase " 'institutions, groups or individuals' [might] be deleted because there may be private religious institutions who [*sic*] can't be compelled in this regard."[70] The phrase "discrimination by any State, institution, group of persons, or person" in Article 2(1), taken together with Article 4, which obliges states to prevent and eliminate discrimination through legislative and other measures, clearly requires states to regulate nongovernmental conduct irrespective of whether national law authorizes such regulation. Moreover, the phrase "public life" was included in proposed versions of the definition of discrimination that reproduced the definition contained in the Racial Discrimination Convention, but was deleted from the final version of Article 2(2).[71]

In contrast, the obligation to take positive measures against religious discrimination, stated in Article 4, extends only to states and not to individuals.[72] Here the legislative history indicates that the drafters rejected

[65] Questionnaires prepared in connection with Special Rapporteur Odio Benito's study requested information from governments regarding measures taken to eliminate intolerance and discrimination, "whether proceeding from official circles or individuals or groups of persons." UN Doc. E/CN.4/Sub.2/1984/28, Ann. I, at 2.

Cf. T. MERON, *supra* note 45, at 18–23, 61–63 (on the application of the Racial Discrimination Convention and the Discrimination Against Women Convention to nongovernmental, private contexts). *See also* Meron, *The Meaning and Reach of the International Convention on the Elimination of All Forms of Racial Discrimination*, 79 AJIL 283 (1985).

[66] Article 1 of the Racial Discrimination Declaration, *supra* note 64, also refers to discrimination "between human beings."

[67] The definition of discrimination contained in the 1967 Draft Convention, *supra* note 3, Article I(b), did include the qualifying phrase "any other field of *public life*" (emphasis added).

[68] *See* 1964 Sub-Commission Draft Declaration, *supra* note 3, Art. 2.

[69] *See* 1964 Commission Draft Declaration, *supra* note 3, Art. III.

[70] Observations of Governments, *supra* note 17, at 12 (India); *accord* UN Doc. A/C.3/SR.2013, at 6 (1973) (statement by representative of the Byelorussian Soviet Socialist Republic, expressing agreement with proposal for deleting this phrase, on the same ground advanced by the Government of India). *See also* UN Doc. E/3925/Add.2, at 11 (1964).

[71] *See, e.g.*, 1979 UN ESCOR Supp. (No. 6) at 70, UN Doc. E/1979/36.

[72] *Cf.* UN Doc. E/CN.4/1146/Add.1, at 4 (1974) (proposed article stating that "no organization or *individual* shall have the right to invoke this Declaration if they impair the rights of citizens") (emphasis added).

proposed wording that required "particular efforts" to be made by "everyone to prevent and eliminate discrimination on the ground of religion or belief."[73]

Like the Racial Discrimination Declaration and Convention and the Discrimination Against Women Convention, the Declaration extends the prohibition of discrimination beyond conduct attributable to the state. The Declaration therefore applies to religious communities themselves; although they are not bound to take positive measures to eliminate discrimination, their conduct is governed by the prohibition of discrimination based on religion or belief.

The necessarily broad reach of Article 2 carries with it the potential for conflicts between principles set forth in the Declaration and obligations imposed by other human rights instruments or between principles stated in the Declaration itself. Consider the example of a religious custom or precept forbidding marriages between members of that faith and members of a different faith. On the one hand, the proscription of marriage outside the faith may be vital to preserving the identity of the religious community and may even be an important doctrinal feature of the faith. On the other hand, this practice constitutes discrimination on the basis of religion against a would-be spouse of another faith, and infringes the associational and privacy rights of both individuals. Because the state is obliged to eliminate discrimination, the application of Article 2 to the private context encourages, and indeed requires, the state to regulate interpersonal and intrareligious affairs to some degree.

Intolerance

The definition set forth in Article 2(2) refers not to discrimination alone, but to "intolerance and discrimination." Article 4(2) suggests a distinction between the two in calling for legislative action to prohibit discrimination while exhorting states to take "all appropriate measures" to combat intolerance.[74] Earlier drafts of the Declaration employed the two terms separately and the word "discrimination" was added to the title of the instrument at a later stage.[75] Two general views have been taken of the meaning of "intolerance" and its significance in the Declaration. The first, that the term lacks juridical meaning and refers to prejudice or a state of mind, was advanced during the drafting process,[76] and has been emphasized subsequently in discussions of educational measures to promote the Declaration.[77] The sec-

[73] 1980 UN ESCOR Supp. (No. 3) at 111–12, UN Doc. E/1980/13.

[74] For the text of Article 4, see note 6 *supra*.

[75] GA Res. 3267, 29 UN GAOR Supp. (No. 31) at 88, UN Doc. A/9631 (1974).

[76] *See, e.g.*, UN Docs. E/3925, Annex, at 3 (1964) (defining "intolerance" as a mental attitude or psychological state); A/4134, at 5 (1973) (stating that "intolerance" refers primarily to a subjective attitude).

[77] *See, e.g.*, United Nations Seminar on the Encouragement of Understanding, Tolerance and Respect in Matters Relating to Freedom of Religion or Belief, UN Doc. ST/HR/SER.A/16, at 7 (1984) (defining tolerance as acceptance by individuals of the right of others to hold different views, i.e., an act of understanding) [hereinafter 1984 Geneva Seminar]; Odio Benito report, *supra* note 11, at 64.

ond view, that intolerance refers to conduct manifesting hatred or prejudice based on religion or belief as well as to a state of mind, underlies descriptions of various human rights violations, such as attacks upon the physical integrity of the person, as intolerance.[78]

As defined in Article 2(2), intolerance is synonymous with discrimination and the two terms have been used interchangeably.[79] Yet linking intolerance with discrimination, which has a clear legal meaning, seems gratuitous if the former bears no independent relationship to the aims of the Declaration. The view that intolerance describes the emotional, psychological, philosophical and religious attitudes that may prompt acts of discrimination or violations of religious freedoms is persuasive. Where intolerance fuels such conduct as killing or the destruction of property, these acts constitute violations of substantive international human rights, such as the right to life, and, in most cases, violations of national law. If intolerance motivates deprivations of the freedom to manifest religion or belief, these acts again constitute violations of substantive rights protected by the Declaration itself.[80]

The distinction between intolerance and discrimination may be usefully analogized to the distinction between racial prejudice and racism. Attitudes of hatred and fear toward religious groups may be rooted in phenomena such as histories of conflict between religious communities and the competing interests underlying those conflicts, religious doctrines that condemn nonbelievers and condone their oppression or eradication, state propaganda against religious belief, and racial or ethnic conflict.[81] So understood, intolerance is not a particular type of violation of religious freedom or of discrimination, but the attitudes that may motivate such violations.

From this interpretation it follows that educational measures to eradicate intolerance are of vital significance. Educational activities obviously lie within the scope of the "appropriate" measures contemplated by Article 4(2), although no express reference to such activities appears in the Declara-

[78] *See, e.g.*, Clark, *supra* note 3, at 209; Clark, *The United Nations Declaration on the Elimination of All Forms of Intolerance and of Discrimination Based on Religion or Belief*, 31 CHITTY'S L.J. 23, 34 n.9 (1983); 1987 Ribeiro report, *supra* note 9, at 12, 14–15; Odio Benito report, *supra* note 11, at 3–4.

[79] *See, e.g.*, 1987 Ribeiro report, *supra* note 9, at 11–13; UN Doc. E/CN.4/1986/SR.30/Add.1.

The 1967 Draft Convention included the following tautological definition of "intolerance": "the expression religious intolerance shall mean intolerance in matters of religion or belief . . . ." 1967 Draft Convention, *supra* note 3, Art. I(c). Similarly, the questionnaire prepared in connection with Special Rapporteur Odio Benito's study, which requested information from governments regarding legislative or other measures taken to combat intolerance and discrimination, defined both intolerance and discrimination as "distinction, exclusion, restriction or preference." UN Doc. E/CN.4/Sub.2/1984/28, Ann. I, at 28.

[80] *See* 1988 Ribeiro report, *supra* note 10, at 24 (regarding the relationship between religious intolerance and infringements of various human rights, such as the right to life); UN Doc. E/CN.4/1987/SR.23, at 7 (regarding the relationship between violations of religious freedoms and violations of other human rights).

[81] *See* UN Doc. E/CN.4/Sub.2/1985/28, at 12.

tion.[82] Efforts to promote and implement the Declaration should compensate for the omission of a provision explicitly calling for educational measures by emphasizing the importance of such activities.

A second approach to combating intolerance, which was proposed during drafting but rejected, is to prohibit the expression of ideas based on religious hatred and the incitement of hatred and discrimination based on religion or belief.[83] The link between eliminating intolerance and such a prohibition is implicit in those proposed definitions that described intolerance as "any *expression* or act of discrimination or hatred"[84] or as "acts which stir up hatred against or persecution of individuals or groups" (as well as discrimination against them).[85] A prophylactic measure of this type appears in Article 4 of the Racial Discrimination Convention.[86]

As Article 4 of the Declaration makes clear, states are obliged not only to punish discrimination, but also to take preventive measures against it. A bar upon expressions of hatred and incitement to hatred, acts of violence or discrimination may constitute an effective preventive means of promoting the goals of the Declaration, but may require restrictions that conflict with the freedoms of expression and association. The arguments for and against such a provision should therefore be considered carefully if a convention is drafted at some time in the future. In any event, generalities concerning the desirability of a provision of this type are of little value. In some countries, discriminatory propaganda and invective may constitute incitement to violence and discrimination giving rise to a clear and present danger that religious freedoms will be violated; while in others, political and legal institutions may defuse the often serious threat to human rights created by such expression.[87]

Remedial Measures

The lack of specific guidance concerning measures to prevent discrimination is matched by lacunae concerning measures to provide redress for

[82] *Cf.* Racial Discrimination Declaration, *supra* note 64, Art. 8 (calling for "all effective steps . . . in the fields of teaching, education and information with a view to eliminating racial discrimination"); Declaration on the Elimination of Discrimination Against Women, GA Res. 2263, 22 UN GAOR Supp. (No. 16) at 35, UN Doc. A/6716 (1967) [hereinafter Discrimination Against Women Declaration], Art. 3 (calling for measures to "educate public opinion" for the purpose of abolishing prejudice and customary and other practices based on the idea of women's inferiority); Racial Discrimination Convention, *supra* note 60, Art. 7 (calling for effective measures, "particularly in the fields of teaching, education, culture and information, with a view to combatting prejudices which lead to racial discrimination").

[83] The 1964 Sub-Commission Draft Declaration, *supra* note 3, did incorporate such a provision, in Article XIV(2) and (3), as did the 1967 Draft Convention, *supra* note 3, in its Article IX.

[84] 1979 UN ESCOR Supp. (No. 6) at 70, UN Doc. E/1979/36 (emphasis added).

[85] Odio Benito report, *supra* note 11, at 4.

[86] *See* Positive Measures Designed to Eradicate All Incitement to, or Acts of, Racial Discrimination: Implementation of the International Convention on the Elimination of All Forms of Racial Discrimination, UN Doc. CERD/2, UN Sales No. E.85.XIV.2 (1986); T. Meron, *supra* note 45, at 23–35.

[87] *See* Greenberg, *supra* note 61, at 323–24.

existing discrimination: the Declaration makes no mention of the right to equality before the law or any obligation to provide effective remedies for violations of the principles of the Declaration. The guarantee of equality before the law is essential to securing human rights as well as equal rights under national law. The guarantee of equal protection is, of course, affirmed in the Universal Declaration (Article 7) and the Political Covenant (Article 26). Moreover, the Declaration does not state a right to effective administrative and judicial remedies for harm suffered as a result of discrimination on the basis of religion or belief and violations of the freedom of religion or belief.[88] Judicial and administrative remedies serve not only to redress the harm suffered, but also to deter future acts of discrimination. In addition, such remedies further the implementation of the Declaration by providing individuals with an avenue for its enforcement even when the state is inactive.[89] The development of such measures should be emphasized in implementation of the Declaration and the right to effective remedies should eventually be incorporated into a convention.

The Nexus Between Religious and Racial Discrimination

As a whole, the Declaration affords more specific, and therefore more rigorous, protection to the freedom to manifest belief than to the freedom from discrimination. The antidiscrimination provisions are less detailed than those found in other declarations addressing discrimination. The Discrimination Against Women Declaration, for example, spells out particular practices from which discrimination is to be eliminated in fields such as education (Article 9) and employment (Article 10).[90]

[88] The 1964 Commission Draft Declaration, *supra* note 3, Article III(2), provided: "Everyone has the right to effective remedial relief by the competent national tribunals against any acts violating the rights set forth in this Declaration or any acts of discrimination he may suffer on the grounds of religion or belief. . . ." The 1967 Draft Convention similarly addressed the availability of remedies, requiring states to

> ensure to everyone within their jurisdiction effective protection and remedies, through the competent national tribunals and other State institutions against any acts, including acts of discrimination . . . , which violate his human rights and fundamental freedoms contrary to this Convention, as well as the right to seek from such tribunals just and adequate reparation or satisfaction for any damage suffered as a result of such acts.

1967 Draft Convention, *supra* note 3, Art. X. Examples of provisions asserting a right to effective remedies appear in several international human rights instruments, including the Universal Declaration, *supra* note 7 (Art. 8), the Political Covenant, *supra* note 7 (Art. 2(3)), and the Racial Discrimination Declaration, *supra* note 64 (Art. 7(2)).

[89] Special Rapporteur Ribeiro has emphasized the need to make effective remedies available to victims of intolerance and discrimination based on religion or belief; he recommended that the Declaration be disseminated widely among those responsible for protecting the right to freedom of religion or belief, such as judges, lawyers and civil servants. 1988 Ribeiro report, *supra* note 10, at 28.

[90] Article 9 of the Discrimination Against Women Declaration, *supra* note 82, lists, inter alia, equal conditions of access to educational institutions of all types, the same choice of curricula and equal opportunities to benefit from scholarships as areas in which all appropriate measures shall be taken to ensure equal rights for women. Similarly, Article 10 enumerates specific

Religion is often a central component of ethnic group identity, inextricably enmeshed in the political, cultural and socioeconomic life of the community.[91] Of course, ethnic or racial identity and religious affiliations are not always congruent, as illustrated by the Baha'is.[92] Even in the latter circumstance, however, religious groups are often readily distinguishable from the broader community, by virtue of the manner in which belief is translated into daily custom (such as dress and dietary practices) and socioeconomic life (such as housing patterns and participation in particular types of economic enterprises). In this way, religion, like race, renders groups and individuals vulnerable to discrimination.

Furthermore, it is sometimes impossible to separate the religious elements from "racial" or "ethnic" components of group identity.[93] This difficulty is illustrated by a case in which the Norwegian Supreme Court reviewed a conviction for the circulation of leaflets that vilified Norwegian immigration policy regarding Islamic foreign workers, Islamic immigrants themselves

---

employment rights, including, inter alia, remuneration, leave with pay and retirement privileges, to be guaranteed, by all appropriate measures, on a basis of equality with men. *See also* Racial Discrimination Declaration, *supra* note 64, Art. 3 (citing areas in which states should make particular efforts to prevent discrimination). Of course, the obligations in the Discrimination Against Women and Racial Discrimination Conventions are elaborated in even greater detail than are the provisions of the two declarations.

The 1964 Commission Draft Declaration, *supra* note 3, did list fields of activity and specific rights, such as the right to take part in government, as to which "particular efforts" must be made to eliminate discrimination (Art. IV(2)). In subsequent drafting discussions, proposals to incorporate references to specific areas in which states should make particular efforts to eliminate discrimination were rejected. *See, e.g.*, 1980 UN ESCOR Supp. (No. 3) at 110, UN Doc. E/1980/13 (listing employment and civil rights, access to citizenship, and the enjoyment of such political rights as participation in elections). Employment rights were singled out for attention in many of these proposals. *See, e.g., id.* at 110–11. Objections to enumerating specific rights were based on the opinion that a partial listing would suggest that states need not exert efforts to eliminate discrimination with regard to rights not mentioned. *See* UN Doc. A/C.3/SR.2013, at 8–9 (1973); Observations of Governments, *supra* note 17, at 14; UN Doc. E/3925, Annex, at 2 (1964).

[91] *See* UN Doc. E/CN.4/1987/SR.23, at 2, 7–8; 1987 Ribeiro report, *supra* note 9, at 3; Odio Benito report, *supra* note 11, at 46. At the 1984 Geneva Seminar, participants emphasized that "on many occasions, religion and not language [is] the primary factor in the preservation of the identity and the unity of a group." 1984 Geneva Seminar, *supra* note 77, at 9.

[92] *See* UN Doc. E/CN.4/Sub.2/1985/SR.18, para. 17 (statement by Egyptian representative characterizing Baha'ism as "a faith or opinion" and not a religion, since Baha'is are "Iranian by race and by culture"); *see also* F. CAPOTORTI, STUDY ON THE RIGHTS OF PERSONS BELONGING TO ETHNIC, RELIGIOUS AND LINGUISTIC MINORITIES, UN DOC. E/CN.4/Sub.2/384/Rev.1, at 43, UN Sales No. E.78.XIV.1 (1979).

[93] For example, Special Rapporteur Ribeiro received allegations that ethnic Turks in Bulgaria have been persecuted on religious grounds, by means including the penalization of Islamic religious practices, the destruction of Muslim graveyards and mosques, and employment discrimination. The Government of Bulgaria, however, has refused to acknowledge the Turkish ethnic nature of the Muslim community of Bulgaria and has denied that there is a Turkish minority there. 1988 Ribeiro report, *supra* note 10, at 4, 8, 18.

For an example of processes by which religious communities themselves determine membership within the community, see Elon, *The Ethiopian Jews: A Case Study in the Functioning of the Jewish Legal System*, 19 N.Y.U. J. INT'L L. & POL. 535 (1987).

and the Islamic religion.[94] The author of the leaflets had treated the religious beliefs of the immigrants as the hallmark of their racial and ethnic identity and had explicitly invoked racial categories and racist attitudes.[95] In concluding that the vilification of the behavior and character of the immigrants exposed them to hatred and contempt and was therefore punishable under Norwegian penal law, the Court explained that the denigrating statements "hit out at a group which is easily identifiable, and which, on account of its alien nature, is particularly vulnerable to contempt and prejudice."[96]

The difficulty of disentangling racial or ethnic characteristics from religious ones should not result in the denial of protection. In two recent cases, the United States Supreme Court rejected the argument that Jews and Arabs cannot invoke the protection of civil rights statutes because those measures apply only to racial discrimination and Jews and Arabs are not racial, but religious or ethnic, groups. In *Saint Francis College v. Al-Khazraji*[97] and *Shaare Tefila Congregation v. Cobb*,[98] the Court noted that the concept of "race" is fluid, and has been extended to national origin or mere common ancestry.[99] Concluding that Jews and Arabs were among those considered at the time the civil rights statutes were drafted to be distinct "races," the Court stated that a distinctive physiognomy is not essential to qualify for protection under the statutes.[100]

By acknowledging the fluidity of the concept of "race," this approach takes account of the interrelationship of racial, religious and ethnic identities. Indeed, physiological traits, linguistic traditions, religious beliefs, and the distribution of political and economic power—all may contribute to the formation of racial identity as defined by members of the group, and as perceived by the surrounding society. Concepts of "race" have varied his-

[94] The case was reported to the UN Committee on the Elimination of Racial Discrimination (CERD). *See* Judgment No. 134 B/1981, *reprinted in* UN Doc. CERD/C/107/Add.4, at 14 (1984).

[95] *Id.* at 20–21.

[96] *Id.* at 24. In connection with the Norwegian judgment, members of CERD discussed whether Article 1 of the Racial Discrimination Convention applies to religious discrimination. Some members believed attacks on identifiable ethnic or national groups would breach the Convention but attacks on a specific religion would not. Others disagreed, stating that good grounds could be found for extending the Convention to cover attacks against religion. 39 UN GAOR Supp. (No. 18), para. 509, UN Doc. A/39/18 (1984).

Special Rapporteur Ribeiro has recommended that the procedures established by CERD be used to monitor the implementation of international standards concerning questions of discrimination or intolerance in matters of religion or belief. 1988 Ribeiro report, *supra* note 10, at 28. In a similar vein, the Government of Ecuador submitted the following statement in response to the request for information on national legislation regarding freedom of religion or belief: "if any person in Ecuador considers that his rights [as stated in the Declaration] are being jeopardized . . . , he may put his case before the Ecuadorian courts or before the *Committee on the Elimination of Racial Discrimination* . . . " (emphasis added). UN Doc. E/CN.4/1988/43/Add.1, at 8.

[97] 107 S.Ct. 2022 (1987).

[98] 107 S.Ct. 2019 (1987).

[99] *Al-Khazraji*, 107 S.Ct. at 2026–28.

[100] *Id.* at 2028. *See also* H. SANTA CRUZ, RACIAL DISCRIMINATION 4–5, UN Doc. E/CN.4/Sub.2/307/Rev.1, UN Sales No. E.76.XIV.2 (rev. ed. 1977) (regarding the relationship between racial and religious discrimination).

torically with socioeconomic changes and among different political systems. The characterization of "race" as a biological construct has been criticized by scientists, who argue that racial classifications are primarily sociopolitical, and not biological, in nature.[101]

In addition, protections for the rights of religious groups have been discussed in the United Nations under the rubric of minority protections.[102] Concern for the rights of religious groups qua minorities, the protean nature of the concept of "race" and the often central role of religion in forming ethnic identities point to the need for thorough and specific safeguards against discrimination on the basis of religion or belief. Activities to promote the aims of the Declaration, to investigate compliance with its standards and to guide its implementation should stress this need. If a convention is drafted, detailed antidiscrimination provisions applicable to such critical areas as employment and education should be included.

IV. Normative Conflicts Involving the Declaration

Conflicts that arise between the rights stated in the Declaration and other human rights may be best addressed by identifying those factors significant to a balancing of the rights and interests involved, rather than by relying upon ill-defined concepts of hierarchically ordered norms.[103] A balancing approach that takes into account particularized facts concerning those factors generally relevant to conflict situations can provide a framework for resolving conflicts between norms.

One of the primary factors to be assessed is the significance of a particular religious practice to the underlying religion or belief. A second, conversely, is the importance of the countervailing, nonreligious practice or interest to the right upon which it is premised. Third, the duration of the restrictions must be considered.[104] A final factor to be analyzed is the degree to which each practice interferes with the other or with the underlying rights and interests; that is, does the conflict result in only a slight degree of interfer-

[101] *See, e.g.*, S. Gould, The Mismeasure of Man (1981); A. Montagu, Man's Most Dangerous Myth (1974); Science and the Concept of Race (M. Mead, T. Dobzhansky, E. Tobach & R. Light eds. 1968). On the difficulty of defining and identifying racial groups for purposes of human rights instruments, see UN Doc. E/CN.4/Sub.2/1984/31, at 4. Regarding the related question of the definition of "minority" under Article 27 of the Political Covenant, see Sohn, *The Rights of Minorities*, in Henkin (ed.), *supra* note 22, at 276–82; F. Capotorti, *supra* note 92, at 5–12.

[102] *See, e.g.*, UN Docs. E/CN.4/1987/SR.23, at 7; E/CN.4/1987/SR.46, at 10. *See also* UN Doc. E/CN.4/1987/WG.5/WP.1 (compilation of proposals on the definition of "minority" in connection with the deliberations of the working group considering drafting a declaration on the rights of persons belonging to national, ethnic, religious and linguistic minorities). *But see* T. van Boven, *supra* note 22, at 272 (regarding problems associated with the special protection of religious liberty under a minority system).

[103] For a discussion of the concept of hierarchy and conflicts, see text at notes 45–49 *supra*.

[104] *See* A. Krishnaswami, *supra* note 1, at 36.

ence, or is either of the practices totally barred and the exercise of the underlying rights extensively restricted or foreclosed?[105]

Such assessments should eschew, as far as possible, inquiries into whether a practice is legitimately religious in nature, since such judgments may impose majoritarian values concerning the features characteristic of "bona fide" religions upon beliefs that do not share those traits.[106] Evaluation of the relationship between a religious practice and the substantive content of doctrine or belief should not extend beyond a determination that a significant relationship between belief and practice does exist.

A similarly particularized analysis is appropriate in assessing state-imposed restraints upon the freedom to manifest religion that are based on the other grounds listed in paragraph 3 of Article 1. Krishnaswami has emphasized the impossibility of identifying legitimate restrictions in the abstract. Nonetheless, he has suggested that some manifestations of religion or belief are "so obviously contrary to morality, public order, or the general welfare that public authorities are always entitled to limit them or even to prohibit them altogether."[107] Practices such as human sacrifice, self-immolation, mutilation of oneself or others, and reducing others to slavery or prostitution may thus be restricted without constituting discrimination against the perpetrators because the restrictions are "founded in the superior interests of society."[108] Certain practices, like human sacrifice, are clearly subject to restriction and prohibition, but such restrictions should be based upon the rights and freedoms of others, rather than the "superior interest of society." Because the concept of the "superior interest of society" unjustifiably assumes that the diverse groups within society subscribe to a homogeneous value system, it is preferable to ground the necessary prohibition of such practices as human sacrifice in the rights and freedoms of others.

[105] In the case of the discriminatory employment practice described in the text at note 48 *supra*, the relevant questions include: How significant is the practice of barring women from certain jobs to the religious doctrine or tradition? How important is women's access to those jobs to the elimination of employment discrimination? What is the relationship between the discriminatory employment practice and the larger goal of eliminating discrimination in all sectors of society? Does the employment bar apply to all jobs or only a few positions within the business? Is it a permanent, year-round restriction, or one that applies temporarily or only at certain times of the year?

For an example of the resolution of such conflicts under U.S. law, see Bollenbach v. Monroe-Woodbury Cent. School Dist., 659 F.Supp. 1450 (S.D.N.Y. 1987) (holding that the school district's refusal to assign women bus drivers to routes serving Hasidic male students, as an accommodation to the Hasidic belief in strict separation of the sexes, violates both the First Amendment and title VII of the 1964 Civil Rights Act). *See also* Parents' Ass'n of P.S. 16 v. Quinones, 803 F.2d 1235 (2d Cir. 1986) (holding that a city plan to provide physically segregated accommodations, instruction in English as a second language and only female teachers for female Hasidic students within a public school attended primarily by Latino children violated the First Amendment).

[106] *See, e.g.*, NEW SOUTH WALES ANTI-DISCRIMINATION BOARD, *supra* note 19, at 202–26 (regarding controversy over the religious status of beliefs held by certain minority religions such as the Scientologists).

[107] A. KRISHNASWAMI, *supra* note 1, at 43. [108] *Id.*

Conflicts Involving Children's Rights

Given the need for particularized evaluation of conflicts under the Declaration, a provision intended to regulate them would probably be of limited utility.[109] Some conflicts arising within the context of the Declaration itself, however, might have been avoided in the drafting process, as illustrated by the potential for conflict between Article 5 and other provisions.[110] Article 5 provides that the parents (or legal guardians) have the right to organize family life in accordance with their religion or belief and that children have a right of access to a religious education that is consistent with the wishes of their parents. Decisions concerning children's education in religion or belief are to be guided by the "best interests of the child"[111] (paragraph 2). The only restriction upon the control that parents (or other custodians) may exercise over their children's upbringing in matters of religion or belief is an injunction against practices that are "injurious to [their] physical or mental health or to [their] full development" (paragraph 5).

[109] *Cf.* Draft Principles, *supra* note 1, pt. IV(1), providing that "[i]n the event of a conflict between the demands of two or more religions or beliefs, public authorities shall endeavor to find a solution reconciling these demands in a manner such as to ensure the greatest measure of freedom to society as a whole."

[110] Article 5 states:

> 1. The parents or, as the case may be, the legal guardians of the child have the right to organize the life within the family in accordance with their religion or belief and bearing in mind the moral education in which they believe the child should be brought up.
>
> 2. Every child shall enjoy the right to have access to education in the matter of religion or belief in accordance with the wishes of his parents or, as the case may be, legal guardians, and shall not be compelled to receive teaching on religion or belief against the wishes of his parents or legal guardians, the best interests of the child being the guiding principle.
>
> 3. The child shall be protected from any form of discrimination on the ground of religion or belief. He shall be brought up in a spirit of understanding, tolerance, friendship among peoples, peace and universal brotherhood, respect for freedom of religion or belief of others, and in full consciousness that his energy and talents should be devoted to the service of his fellow man.
>
> 4. In the case of a child who is not under the care either of his parents or of legal guardians, due account shall be taken of their expressed wishes or of any other proof of their wishes in the matter of religion or belief, the best interests of the child being the guiding principle.
>
> 5. Practices of a religion or beliefs in which a child is brought up must not be injurious to his physical or mental health or to his full development, taking into account article 1, paragraph 3, of the present Declaration.

[111] *Cf.* Declaration of the Rights of the Child, Principle 7, GA Res. 1386, 14 UN GAOR Supp. (No. 16) at 19, UN Doc. A/4354 (1959). The second paragraph of Principle 7 provides that "[t]he best interests of the child shall be the guiding principle of those responsible for his education and guidance; that responsibility lies in the first place with his parents." In contrast, Article 18(4) of the Political Covenant, *supra* note 7, makes no reference to considerations other than the convictions held by parents or guardians: "The States Parties to the present Covenant undertake to have respect for the liberty of parents and, when applicable, legal guardians to ensure the religious and moral education of their children in conformity with their own convictions."

Because the Declaration fails to define "child" or to specify the age at which children are entitled to decide matters of religion or belief for themselves, parental rights under the Declaration may conflict with their children's rights if the children's preferences in these matters differ from those of their parents.[112] Such conflicts are not reconcilable under the limitations imposed by Article 5 unless the practices or beliefs urged by the parents are injurious or detrimental to the children's "full development."

Parental rights concerning children's religious education and upbringing should be construed primarily as the responsibility to safeguard children's religious freedoms.[113] By citing the duties to shield children from discrimination, injurious practices and beliefs, and compulsory religious education against parental wishes, the Declaration places the rights of children within the framework of special protections for children as articulated in other human rights instruments.[114] The proscription of practices harmful to children's health and "full development" clearly expresses this protective posture and reflects the drafters' concern that religious practices endorsed by parents, such as the refusal of blood transfusions, could threaten children's health or even survival.[115]

Although Article 5 reflects the laudable desire to deter interference by the state or attempts to convert children, especially orphans, from the beliefs held by their parents,[116] it generates considerable potential for conflict between parental rights and children's rights to freedom of religion or belief. In such conflicts, the child's right to freedom of belief should be weighed against parental rights under Article 5, in an analysis that con-

[112] The failure to address the rights of children themselves was noted during drafting discussions. *See, e.g.*, UN Doc. A/C.3/SR.2011, at 15 (1973) (comments by the representative of Japan). *See also* Observations of Governments, *supra* note 17, at 17 (response by the Government of Sweden).

Regarding the need to define "child" or to specify the age at which a child is entitled to make decisions concerning religion or belief, see, e.g., UN Docs. A/C.3/SR.2010, at 9 (1973); A/C.3/SR.2013, at 9–11 (1973); E/CN.4/1146/Add.3, at 4 (1974); and Observations of Governments, *supra*, at 17.

The Human Rights Committee has raised questions concerning the age at which children have the right to exercise the freedom of religion or belief under the Political Covenant. *See, e.g.*, 36 UN GAOR Supp. (No. 40) at 76, UN Doc. A/36/40 (1981); 37 UN GAOR Supp. (No. 40) at 15, UN Doc. A/37/40 (1982).

For an example of situations in which such conflicts may arise, see UN Doc. E/CN.4/1988/43/Add.1, at 8 (summary of the membership rules of the established Church of Denmark, giving children between the ages of 15 and 18 the right to join or resign from the church if the child's custodian provides a declaration of consent).

[113] For a proposed formulation of Article 5 stressing parental responsibility, see UN Doc. E/CN.4/1146/Add.3, at 4 (1974).

[114] *See, e.g.*, Declaration of the Rights of the Child, *supra* note 111; Political Covenant, *supra* note 7, Art. 24; International Covenant on Economic, Social and Cultural Rights, Art. 10(3), GA Res. 2200, 21 UN GAOR Supp. (No. 16) at 49, UN Doc. A/6316 (1966).

[115] *See* UN Doc. E/3925/Add.1, at 6–7 (1964) (asserting the need for a proscription upon exposing children to harmful religious practices in light of such phenomena as substituting a "laying on of hands" for medical treatment); *see also* 1981 UN ESCOR Supp. (No. 5) at 141, UN Doc. E/1981/25.

[116] *See generally* A. KRISHNASWAMI, *supra* note 1, at 39–40; Liskofsky, *supra* note 3, at 481.

siders, inter alia, the child's age and maturity,[117] the nature of the practice or belief at issue, and any influence or coercion exercised upon the child by sources outside the family. The potential for such conflict might have been lessened had Article 5 specified the age at which children may decide matters of religious practice and belief for themselves,[118] or required states to prescribe an age of majority for these matters in national legislation.[119] It may therefore be worthwhile for the drafters of a future convention to address this question.

Religious Law and Human Rights Law

Although the rights to establish religious courts and administer religious law are not stated in the Declaration, religious tribunals and the implementation of religious law are manifestations of religious belief to which the protections of Article 1 should apply.[120] Nevertheless, the extent to which religious law may be administered without restrictions by the state or without limitations derived from other human rights obligations may vary with the substantive content of the law itself, and with the scope of the subject matter and personal jurisdiction vested in the religious courts.

Religious law may incorporate elements hostile to various human rights, infringing upon those rights to differing degrees. At one end of the spectrum, for example, may be dress codes for women that have the effect of reinforcing societal beliefs that relegate women to inferior status in public life. At the other end of the continuum are the extreme violations of such rights as the freedom from torture and the right to life by practices such as mutilation and *suttee*. Other conflicts between religious tenets and human rights fall at different points along this spectrum. For example, rules of procedure, such as evidentiary laws that assign lesser weight to testimony by women, may infringe substantive rights by impairing the ability to obtain

[117] The working group on a draft convention on the rights of the child has discussed the need for a general provision regarding the "evolving capacities of the child," or a reference to those capacities in articles addressing particular rights. UN Doc. E/CN.4/1987/25, at 24–27.

[118] *See, e.g.*, Convention on Consent to Marriage, Art. 2, *opened for signature* Dec. 10, 1962, 521 UNTS 231 (entered into force Dec. 9, 1964) (national legislation shall specify a minimum age for marriage).

[119] For an example of national legislation regulating children's rights to exercise religious freedoms, see the discussion of the Religious Education Act of Austria, in UN Docs. CCPR/C/6/Add.7, at 27–28 (1981); E/CN.4/1988/43/Add.1, at 3. Under the Act, parents may determine the religion of their children until they are 12 years old, at which time the children may no longer be given against their will a religious education different from that previously received. At age 14, children have the right to decide for themselves what their religion will be, and state authorities must protect their choices if necessary. *See also* 41 UN GAOR Supp. (No. 40) at 44, UN Doc. A/41/40 (1986) (discussion of Finnish legislation under which children belong to the religious community of their parents until age 15, when they may join another religious community if they so desire); 36 UN GAOR Supp. (No. 40) at 76, UN Doc. A/36/40 (1981) (questions raised by the Human Rights Committee regarding provision in Norwegian Constitution giving children over the age of 15 the right to join or resign from the Church of Norway).

[120] T. MERON, *supra* note 45, at 155–56; F. CAPOTORTI, *supra* note 92, at 70–71.

legal protection for those rights. Attempts to resolve conflicts between religious law and human rights norms may be fruitless where religious doctrine insists upon the immutability of the sacred law or its supremacy over human rights norms.[121]

A major area of conflict between religious law and human rights law is that of women's rights. Conflicts between the norms contained in the Declaration and those appearing in the Discrimination Against Women Declaration and Convention are inevitable.[122] The formal requirements of religious law, interpretations of that law and social custom derived from it may all infringe women's rights. Analyses of specific situations of conflict should take account of the sometimes substantial divergence between legal theory and practice and of factors such as the effect of class distinctions among women within the same religious community.[123] However, certain broad principles relevant to the principal types of conflicts can usefully be delineated. Religious tenets governing rights associated with the life of the family, particularly those pertaining to marriage and divorce, inheritance and personal status, frequently set religious law in opposition to the prohibition of discrimination against women. Compare, for example, Articles 5 and 10(c) of the Discrimination Against Women Convention with Article 5(2) of the Declaration.[124] In some cases, religious law governing family relations and personal status in their entirety, and not merely particular practices, may be inconsistent with the basic concept of women's equality.[125]

[121] *See generally* UN Doc. E/CN.4/Sub.2/1987/35; 37 UN GAOR Supp. (No. 40) at 66–67, 72, UN Doc. A/37/40 (1982) (regarding the applicability of the principles underlying the Universal Declaration to Islamic societies). *See, e.g.*, UN Docs. A/C.3/36/SR.29, at 6 (1981); A/C.3/37/SR.67, at 9–11 (1982) (asserting the supremacy of Islamic law over international human rights norms governing the death penalty).

[122] Greenberg, *supra* note 61, at 330. For example, the freedom to teach a religion or belief (Art. 6(e)) may conflict with obligations under the Discrimination Against Women Convention if religious doctrine incorporates ideas based on stereotyped roles for the sexes or denies women admission to religious training academies. *See, e.g.*, UN Doc. E/1987/L.20, at 21–22, 25.

[123] *See, e.g.*, M. HOOKER, ISLAMIC LAW IN SOUTH-EAST ASIA 34–35 (1984) (observing that with regard to Southeast Asia, evidence is conflicting on the extent to which Islamic law can be considered an accurate expression of actual legal practice and that analysis of the evidence depends upon what is meant by "Islam").

[124] Article 5 of the Discrimination Against Women Convention, *supra* note 43, requires states to take appropriate measures to modify social and cultural patterns and practices based on stereotyped roles for men and women. In education, Article 10(c) calls for the elimination of "any stereotyped concept of the roles of men and women at all levels and in all forms of education by encouraging coeducation . . . [and] by the revision of textbooks and school programmes." Under Article 5(2) of the Declaration, however, children should not be compelled to receive teaching intended to eliminate stereotyped gender roles if such stereotyped roles are a feature of the belief system in which their parents wish to educate them.

[125] For example, Egypt has entered a reservation to Article 16 of the Discrimination Against Women Convention, *supra* note 43 (concerning the equality of men and women in all matters relating to marriage and family matters), which emphasizes the "sacrosanct nature of the firm religious beliefs which govern marital relations in Egypt and which may not be called into question." 39 UN GAOR Supp. (No. 45), para. 190, UN Doc. A/39/45 (1984). In reviewing this reservation, members of the Committee on the Elimination of Discrimination Against

Article 15 of the Discrimination Against Women Convention guarantees women equality with men before the law and legal capacity identical to that of men in civil matters, but the status of women before religious tribunals or secular courts applying religious law is not clarified by this guarantee.[126] Religious laws governing personal status obviously determine not only the religious rights of women, but also important legal rights, including those regulating economic resources.[127] Under the Shiite law of inheritance, as incorporated in Iranian law, for example, a husband inherits his share of his wife's estate without any distinction between real and movable property. In contrast, a widow cannot inherit any real property but receives only her share of the value of the buildings and household effects (not a share of the buildings and effects themselves).[128]

Discriminatory measures regulating marriage and divorce may impose strictures affecting women's position, both within and beyond the religious community, that are as inimical to women's equality as are measures directly

---

Women (CEDAW) queried whether "complementarity" and equivalency of rights between men and women under Islamic law were being equated with the concept of equality. *Id.* at 26. At its sixth session, CEDAW asked the United Nations "to promote or undertake studies on the status of women under Islamic laws and customs and in particular on the status and equality of women in the family on issues such as marriage, divorce, custody and property rights and their participation in [the] public life of the society." UN Doc. E/1987/L.20, at 88–89. *See also* UN Doc. CEDAW/C/L.3/Add.28 (1988) (clarifying the reasons for this request in response to criticisms voiced in the General Assembly and ECOSOC).

See also UN Docs. A/C.3/37/SR.56, at 16 (1981) (statement by Iranian representative characterizing provisions in the Universal Declaration and the Covenants regarding matters such as marriage as violations of the freedom to practice one's religion or belief); CCPR/C/SR.203, at 7–8 (1980) (statement by Iraqi representative asserting that personal status laws must be in conformity with the *Shari'a*).

[126] T. MERON, *supra* note 45, at 79. Article 6 of the Discrimination Against Women Declaration, *supra* note 82, calls for measures to ensure for women equal rights with men under civil law, including equality in legal capacity and equal rights to acquire, administer and inherit property, but qualifies this guarantee with the excessively vague caveat that such measures must be "[w]ithout prejudice to the safeguarding of the unity and the harmony of the family."

[127] On the status of women in Islamic family law, see generally J. ESPOSITO, WOMEN IN MUSLIM FAMILY LAW (1982). On Islamic family and personal status law, see generally J. NASIR, THE ISLAMIC LAW OF PERSONAL STATUS (1986); K. HODKINSON, MUSLIM FAMILY LAW: A SOURCEBOOK (1984). *See, e.g.*, UN Doc. E/1987/L.20, at 81–84 (regarding the effect of *Shari'a* personal status law in matters such as land tenure and inheritance, and the importance of control over land, as the basic resource, in rural Bangladesh).

[128] J. NASIR, *supra* note 127, at 223–24. *See generally* D. POWERS, STUDIES IN QUR'AN AND HADITH: THE FORMATION OF THE ISLAMIC LAW OF INHERITANCE (1986). The Unified Arab Draft Law for Personal Status, recently completed by the Ministerial Committee of the First and Second Congresses of the Arab Ministers of Justice, incorporates similarly discriminatory inheritance provisions. Under Article 251, for example, a husband receives one-half of his wife's estate if she has no descendants, while Article 252 provides that a wife receives only one-quarter of the husband's estate if he has no descendants. *Id.* at 304.

See, e.g., UN Doc. CCPR/C/SR.730, at 11 (1987) (statement by member of the Human Rights Committee characterizing Art. 91 of Iraq's Personal Status Act, concerning inheritance by daughters, as discrimination on the basis of sex). Inheritance provisions of this type appear to conflict with Article 6(a) of the Discrimination Against Women Declaration, *supra* note 82, which calls for women's right to inherit property on a basis of equality with men. See, however, note 126 *supra*.

restricting access to material resources. It has been suggested that the refusal to grant a religious divorce to a woman for reasons involving sex discrimination would not violate Article 15 of the Convention (mandating equality before the law) unless her ability to obtain a civil divorce was impaired by that refusal.[129] Yet consider the example of a Jewish wife whose husband withholds the bill of divorce (the *get*) required by Jewish law. Under Jewish law, a divorce is not final until the husband presents his wife with a *get* before a rabbinical court.[130] An observant Jewish woman who is neither living with her husband nor divorced under Jewish law cannot remarry, because without a *get*, the second relationship would be adulterous, and any children born of the remarriage would be considered illegitimate.[131] Such formidable disabilities render the availability of a civil divorce inconsequential for those women who wish to remain within the religious community.

The availability of secular remedies does not obviate the need to eliminate sex discrimination within religious law and practice. To conclude otherwise would require women, in effect, to choose between freedom from discrimination and participation in the religious community.[132] Some state legislatures in the United States have attempted to remedy the situation of observant Jewish women whose husbands will not grant them a religious divorce by making the religious divorce a precondition for the acquisition of a civil divorce. These efforts have been characterized by some observers as secular resolutions of a religious inequity that properly demands a religious remedy.[133]

Beyond the areas of substantive conflict, like women's rights, the operation of religious law must be circumscribed by an important principle limiting its secular effects and jurisdictional scope: namely, that where civil effect is accorded to religious laws, religious ceremonies and the decisions of religious tribunals, religious tribunals should not have personal jurisdiction over individuals who are not adherents of the faith represented by the tribunal.[134]

[129] T. MERON, *supra* note 45, at 157.

[130] MAIMONIDES, *Sefer Nashim, Hilkot Gerushin* 1:1, in MISHNEH TORAH (O. Yosef & S. Frankel pubs. 1977); *see generally* R. BIALE, WOMEN IN JEWISH LAW: AN EXPLORATION OF WOMEN'S ISSUES IN HALACHIC SOURCES 70–101 (1984).

[131] MAIMONIDES, *supra* note 130, *Sefer Kedusha, Hilkot Issurai Biah* 15:1; R. BIALE, *supra* note 130, at 101–13.

[132] For a historical review of women's participation in religious communities in the United States, see 1–3 WOMEN AND RELIGION IN AMERICA (R. Ruether & R. Keller eds. 1981, 1983, 1986).

[133] *See, e.g.*, N.Y. DOM. REL. LAW §253 (McKinney 1986); *see also* R. BIALE, *supra* note 130, at 99, 111–12; Meislin, *Pursuit of the Wife's Right to a* 'Get' *in United States and Canadian Courts*, 4 JEWISH L. ANN. 250 (1981). In recognition of the importance of reform from within the religious community, the New York Board of Rabbis recently called upon rabbis to apply sanctions against former husbands who refuse to grant religious divorces and to urge couples to sign prenuptial agreements stating that in the event of civil divorce they will grant a religious divorce. American Jewish Committee, Press Release No. 87-960-160, July 22, 1987, at 3.

[134] For a discussion of circumstances in which Jewish law concerning personal status may be applied to non-Jews, see Shava, *The Rabbinical Courts in Israel: Jurisdiction over Non-Jews*, 27 J. CHURCH & ST. 99 (1985).

In a multireligious state that recognizes the concurrent or exclusive jurisdiction of religious tribunals over personal status or other matters, a system of coexisting religious courts with personal jurisdiction over the members of their respective communities in these matters may arise.[135] If such states have no secular law of personal status, atheists or agnostics, as well as adherents of religions that are not recognized by the state or that have no religious tribunals, may be bound by legal standards contrary to their belief as a result of jurisdictional gaps.[136] Jurisdictional conflicts between different religious tribunals, like those occurring in a legal dispute between spouses in an interfaith marriage, may pose similar threats to the individual's religious and other rights. Gaps in the subject matter jurisdiction of secular courts may thus prove restrictive rather than protective of religious freedoms.[137]

V. Concluding Observations

This overview of the Declaration suggests that certain protections not included among its provisions may be necessary to guarantee those freedoms that are established, and that several of its provisions are cast in somewhat broad or vague language. If a convention is prepared at some time in the future, the challenge for the drafters will be to incorporate provisions that overcome these problems while retaining the positive elements of the Declaration. Among the key changes that seem necessary are a narrowing of the grounds on which states would be permitted to restrict manifestations of religion or belief; the elaboration of antidiscrimination measures; and the addition of provisions on remedies, reporting obligations and means for the international scrutiny of the respect accorded the rights concerned and their implementation. There is also a need to clarify the status of religious courts, i.e., the extent to which they represent a protected manifestation of the freedom to practice religion and the extent to which they must comply with such human rights obligations as the prohibition of discrimination on the basis of sex.

The Declaration stands as a major advance in the development of international norms governing the subjects that it addresses. The lengthy process leading to its adoption testifies to the complexity and sensitivity of the issues raised by these subjects.[138] New standard-setting efforts in this field should

[135] *See, e.g.*, R. Eisenman, Islamic Law in Palestine and Israel (1978). For example, in Israel, some personal status matters lie within the exclusive jurisdiction of the religious courts of the recognized religious communities and others are within the concurrent jurisdiction of the religious courts and the civil district courts. Shava, *supra* note 134, at 99, 101–02.

Jurisdictional conflicts between secular courts and religious courts may arise under systems of concurrent jurisdiction. *See, e.g.*, UN Doc. E/1987/L.20, at 74, 77 (regarding possible conflict between the canonic law and the civil law of marriage and divorce enacted in Colombia). *See also* H.C. 301/63, Schtreit v. Chief Rabbi of Israel, 18(1) Piskei Din 598, 608 (1964); H.C. 232/81, Vilozni v. Rabbinical Court, 36(2) Piskei Din 733, 738 (1982) (stating the rule that the Supreme Court of Israel will not sit in appeal over the decisions of the religious courts).

[136] *See, e.g.*, Shava, *supra* note 134.

[137] *See* A. Krishnaswami, *supra* note 1, at 53.

[138] 1988 Ribeiro report, *supra* note 10, at 25.

be approached with caution. The special rapporteur for the Commission on Human Rights has recommended the establishment, within the Commission, of an open-ended working group to consider the possibility of preparing a convention.[139] Although some governments have endorsed the creation of an open-ended working group charged with preparing a draft convention,[140] several others have voiced opposition to this course on the grounds that it would divert attention and resources from the activities of the Commission's special rapporteur and undermine the status of the Declaration itself.[141]

A convention would offer the obvious advantage of creating binding legal obligations, a particularly significant advance for those states that lack adequate constitutional or legislative protections for the rights and freedoms in question. Moreover, as noted by the Commission's special rapporteur, "the mandatory nature of the provisions of such an instrument would impose on States Parties a number of requirements, such as the submission of reports on the application of its provisions, which might encourage greater respect for religious rights and freedoms by such States."[142]

A major factor militating against the advisability of undertaking new standard setting in the near future is the danger of weakening the considerable normative force of the Declaration. Since in many countries religious freedoms are viewed as analogues of political rights and therefore sometimes as suspect, it is possible that a consensus could not be achieved for standards even higher than those provided by the Declaration and that only a less protective instrument could be adopted. A binding instrument, however, should raise the level of protection, building on the principles set forth in the Declaration, and drawing on the information and experience gained through the special rapporteur's activities and the implementation procedures established under the Political Covenant and the Racial Discrimination Convention (since the latter instruments address areas relevant to the Declaration).[143]

Certainly, the preparation of a convention would prove a protracted endeavor. If an open-ended working group is created for this purpose, the implementation activities of the Commission's special rapporteur should continue with unabated support. Efforts to promote the Declaration through public education should be encouraged and a prominent role in those efforts should be assumed by nongovernmental organizations and religious communities. Information gathered by the special rapporteurs of the Commission (Ribeiro) and the Sub-Commission (Odio Benito) can pro-

[139] *Id.*

[140] *See* UN Docs. E/CN.4/1988/44, at 4; E/CN.4/1988/44/Add.3.

[141] *See, e.g.*, UN Docs. E/CN.4/1988/44/Add.2, at 2; E/CN.4/1988/44, at 3–4.

[142] 1988 Ribeiro report, *supra* note 10, at 25.

[143] Special Rapporteur Ribeiro has recommended that attention be given to utilizing the "machinery now available for monitoring the implementation of international standards concerning questions of discrimination or intolerance in matters of religion or belief [, including the procedures established by] the Committee on the Elimination of Racial Discrimination and the Human Rights Committee." *Id.* at 28.

vide valuable guidance for devising the legal protections and educational measures most likely to be effective in eradicating religious discrimination and violations of the freedom of religion and belief.

Given the risks associated with undertaking the preparation of a binding instrument, a focus on improving means to implement the Declaration may be the better course at this time. For example, the General Assembly might create a reporting system and authorize the Economic and Social Council to set up a working group to review those reports and to continue the monitoring and investigatory activities begun by the two special rapporteurs. Indeed, the Commission might consider assigning these activities, rather than drafting responsibilities, to a working group of its own.

Should the work on a convention proceed, those who seek to ensure religious rights and freedoms must avoid politicization of the issue as far as possible.[144] Only with the support of a large number of countries across a broad sociopolitical spectrum is there reason to hope that the product of the drafting process will be both legally sound and transformed into practice by states parties. Most important, great care must be exercised to ensure that a convention, if one is drafted, does not erode the achievements of the Declaration, and that the Declaration will continue to apply to states that do not become parties to the convention.

[144] *See* T. van Boven, *supra* note 22, at 276; UN Doc. E/CN.4/1986/SR.50/Add.1, at 10, 12 (regarding the need for consensus in the area of freedom of religion).

INTERNATIONAL DISCOVERY AFTER AEROSPATIALE: THE QUEST FOR AN ANALYTICAL FRAMEWORK

*By David J. Gerber**

When a United States court orders the discovery of information located outside United States territory, it is employing state power "extraterritorially"[1]—i.e., to coerce conduct within foreign territory.[2] Such extraterritorial applications of U.S. discovery rules often conflict with basic principles of justice in the state where the information is located, and they may also harm legally protected interests of that state.[3] As a result, extraterritorial discovery has led in recent years to conflicts between the United States and foreign countries that have impaired the effectiveness of U.S. litigation,[4] imposed unnecessary costs and unfairness on litigants in U.S. courts and interfered with the policies of both the United States and foreign states.[5]

To reduce these conflicts and their concomitant harms, a legal framework must be developed that can effectively accommodate the various public and private interests involved. Both the structure and the substance of this framework must respond to fundamentally new legal problems created by U.S. extraterritorial discovery practices.[6]

* Associate Professor of Law, IIT/Chicago-Kent College of Law. The author wishes to thank the Marshall Ewell Faculty Research Fund of IIT/Chicago-Kent College of Law for financial support in the preparation of this article. He also wishes to thank Andre Fiebig for valuable research assistance.

[1] The term "extraterritorial" refers to the location of the required conduct. References to "foreign" or "international" discovery are imprecise, because they do not specify the nature of the nondomestic element. For example, "foreign" discovery may refer to conduct on foreign territory or to some other foreign element such as the nationality of a witness.

[2] The coercive effect of such an order derives from the expectation that failure to obey the order will lead to the imposition of sanctions. The fact that the order does not itself contain such sanctions does not make it any less coercive.

[3] The central conflicts arise from two facts. First, the United States permits the use of state power to *search* for information rather than merely to secure identified information. Second, it authorizes private attorneys to direct this power with minimal judicial supervision. For detailed discussion, see Gerber, *Extraterritorial Discovery and the Conflict of Procedural Systems: Germany and the United States,* 34 AM. J. COMP. L. 745 (1986). For a penetrating comparative analysis of procedural systems, see M. DAMASKA, THE FACES OF JUSTICE AND STATE AUTHORITY (1986).

[4] For discussion of the development of the problem, see Gerber, *supra* note 3, at 746–47.

[5] *See, e.g.,* RESTATEMENT (THIRD) OF FOREIGN RELATIONS LAW OF THE UNITED STATES §442 Reporters' Note 1 (1988) ("No aspect of the extension of the American legal system beyond the territorial frontier of the United States has given rise to so much friction as the requests for documents in investigation and litigation in the United States") [hereinafter RESTATEMENT (THIRD)].

[6] Developing such a framework is made particularly difficult by the fact that disputes concerning U.S. discovery procedures generally arise in U.S. courts, and therefore U.S. courts must develop and apply legal principles to resolve international conflicts caused by U.S. policies.

In *Societe Nationale Industrielle Aerospatiale v. U.S. District Court (S.D. Iowa)*,[7] the United States Supreme Court directly addressed extraterritorial discovery issues for the first time in some 30 years.[8] Recognizing the need for an accommodation of U.S. and foreign interests, the Court mandated that lower courts permit extraterritorial discovery only after a "particularized analysis" of those interests based on principles of fairness and mutual cooperation. The Court failed, however, to provide an analytical framework that could be used to achieve the goals it established. As a result, the opinion threatens to lead to conceptual chaos and may exacerbate rather than reduce current conflicts.

This article develops an analytical framework designed to achieve the goals established in *Aerospatiale.* It first reviews the *Aerospatiale* opinion, focusing on its decisional mandate to lower courts. It then examines the prerequisites for the effective evaluation of extraterritorial discovery and constructs from the *Aerospatiale* case, as well as from other principles of domestic and international law, a framework for analyzing extraterritorial discovery requests.

I. *AEROSPATIALE* AND EXTRATERRITORIAL DISCOVERY

The specific issue in *Aerospatiale* was whether litigants in United States courts were required, at least under certain circumstances, to use the Hague Convention on the Taking of Evidence Abroad in Civil or Commercial Matters (the Hague Evidence Convention)[9] to obtain evidence located within signatory states.[10] In resolving this issue, however, the Supreme Court established certain general principles to be applied to all requests for extraterritorial discovery. The specific issue was thus imbedded in fundamental issues involving the relationships between the U.S. legal system and most other legal systems.[11]

[7] Societe Nationale Industrielle Aerospatiale v. United States Dist. Court for the S. Dist. of Iowa, 107 S.Ct. 2542 (1987) [hereinafter *Aerospatiale*].

[8] The last major Supreme Court case on this issue was Societe Internationale pour Participations Industrielles et Commerciales, S.A. v. Rogers, 357 U.S. 197 (1958).

[9] Convention on the Taking of Evidence Abroad in Civil or Commercial Matters, *done* Mar. 18, 1970, 23 UST 2555, TIAS No. 7444, 847 UNTS 231. This treaty was expressly intended to "bridge the gap" between U.S. and foreign procedures by providing mechanisms through which United States courts could acquire evidence located in foreign countries without resorting to U.S. discovery rules.

The most important procedure created by the Convention permits a signatory state to request information from a court in another signatory state, and it establishes an international legal obligation on the requested state to provide the requested information. For discussion, see 1 B. RISTAU, INTERNATIONAL JUDICIAL ASSISTANCE (CIVIL AND COMMERCIAL) 192–257 (1986).

[10] States that are currently parties to the Convention include: Barbados, Cyprus, Czechoslovakia, Denmark, Finland, France, the Federal Republic of Germany, Israel, Italy, Luxembourg, Monaco, the Netherlands, Norway, Portugal, Singapore, Sweden, the United Kingdom and the United States. *See* 8 MARTINDALE-HUBBELL LAW DIRECTORY 12–21 (1987).

[11] Numerous nonparty organizations and countries filed amicus curiae briefs, including the Italy-America Chamber of Commerce, Inc.; the Motor Vehicle Manufacturers Association of

THE FACTS AND OPINIONS

The plaintiffs in *Aerospatiale* were United States citizens who had been injured in a plane crash in Iowa. They sued the manufacturer of the airplane, Société Nationale Industrielle Aérospatiale[12] (Aérospatiale) for injuries resulting from the crash and allegedly attributable to defects in the airplane. Aérospatiale is a French corporation wholly owned by the Government of France.[13]

After initial discovery by both sides pursuant to the Federal Rules of Civil Procedure,[14] a second set of discovery requests by the plaintiff was rejected by defendants, who sought a protective order on the grounds that they were "French corporations, and the discovery sought can only be found in a foreign state, namely France."[15] Defendants argued that any discovery within the territory of France had to be conducted, at least initially, according to the procedures of the Hague Evidence Convention.

Denial of defendants' motion was appealed to the U.S. Court of Appeals for the Eighth Circuit,[16] which affirmed the decision of the lower court.[17] The court of appeals held that the Convention not only was not mandatory, but also was not applicable to persons subject to the jurisdiction of the court.[18]

In a five-to-four opinion, the Supreme Court agreed with the lower courts that the Convention was not mandatory and that, therefore, U.S. discovery rules could be used to obtain information located outside the United States.[19] The Court held that the Convention itself neither stated nor implied that it was the exclusive means of obtaining foreign information; nor was there any other basis for finding such an obligation.[20] On this issue the

---

the United States, Inc.; the Product Liability Advisory Council, Inc.; Volkswagen AG; the Federal Republic of Germany; Switzerland; France; the United Kingdom; the United States; and the Securities and Exchange Commission.

[12] A second defendant was the Société de Construction d'Avions de Tourism[e].

[13] Defendants apparently did not argue that they were immune from jurisdiction under the doctrine of foreign sovereign immunity. *See* Foreign Sovereign Immunities Act of 1976, 28 U.S.C. §§1330, 1602–1611 (1982).

[14] Delay in raising the Hague Evidence Convention issue may have caused that argument to appear as something of an afterthought. Moreover, the possibility of cutting off discovery already begun obviously entails potential unfairness to one of the litigants. This also happened in another case on the same issue that had reached the Supreme Court the preceding year. *See In re* Anschuetz & Co., 754 F.2d 602 (5th Cir. 1985), *remanded,* 107 S.Ct. 3223 (1987).

[15] *Aerospatiale,* 107 S.Ct. at 2546.

[16] The magistrate denied the motion with respect to all discovery requests, except the request for oral depositions to be taken on French territory. Jones v. Societe Nationale Industrielle Aerospatiale, Civ. 82-435 C, App. to Pet. for Cert. 25a (July 31, 1985) (LEXIS, Genfed library, Briefs file).

[17] *In re* Societe Nationale Industrielle Aerospatiale, 782 F.2d 120 (8th Cir. 1986).

[18] *Id.* at 125.

[19] *Aerospatiale,* 107 S.Ct. at 2554.

[20] *Id.* at 2553.

Court was unanimous,[21] and its conclusion reflected the weight of opinion of lower courts[22] as well as scholars.[23]

The Supreme Court disagreed with the court of appeals, however, on the scope of application of the Convention. The Court held that application of the Convention was not affected by the jurisdictional status of the person from whom information was sought. The Convention was thus applicable both to persons subject to the jurisdiction of the court and to those who were not.[24]

The remaining issue was whether, and under what conditions, there was an obligation to use the Convention. In answering this question, the Court established the fundamental principle that the use of U.S. discovery procedures to obtain information outside the United States was subject to considerations of comity and fairness.[25] Again, the Court was unanimous on this point.[26]

The Court divided, however, over whether the principle of comity required that the procedures of the Convention be used *before* discovery could be ordered under U.S. law. According to the majority, comity did not require a presumption in favor of first resort to the Convention.[27] The Court found no basis for such a requirement, and it expressed concern that such a presumption might "be unduly time-consuming and expensive, as well as less certain to produce needed evidence than direct use of the Federal Rules."[28] The majority opinion held, therefore, that the use of U.S. discovery rules must be subjected to "prior scrutiny in each case of the particular facts, sovereign interests, and likelihood that resort to those procedures [of the Convention] will prove effective."[29]

The dissent vigorously disagreed. Justice Blackmun argued that international comity required that the Convention be used prior to resort to U.S.

[21] *Id.* at 2558 (Blackmun, J., dissenting).

[22] *See, e.g.,* Work v. Bier, 106 F.R.D. 45 (D.D.C. 1985); International Soc'y for Krishna Consciousness v. Lee, 105 F.R.D. 435 (S.D.N.Y. 1984); Slauenwhite v. Bekum Maschinenfabriken GmbH, 104 F.R.D. 616 (D. Mass. 1985); and Graco Inc. v. Kremlin, Inc. & SKM, 101 F.R.D. 503 (N.D. Ill. 1984). *But see, e.g.,* Schroeder v. Lufthansa German Airlines, 19 Fed. R. Serv. 2d 211 (N.D. Ill. 1983); and Pierburg v. Superior Court of Los Angeles County, 137 Cal. App. 3d 238, 186 Cal. Rptr. 876 (1982).

[23] *See, e.g.,* Amram, *Explanatory Report on the Convention on the Taking of Evidence Abroad in Civil or Commercial Matters,* 12 ILM 327 (1973); 1 B. RISTAU, *supra* note 9, at 253–55; and McLean, *The Hague Evidence Convention: Its Impact on American Civil Procedure,* 9 LOY. L.A. INT'L & COMP. L.J. 17, 62 (1986). *But see* Radvan, *The Hague Convention on Taking of Evidence Abroad in Civil or Commercial Matters: Several Notes Concerning Its Scope, Methods and Compulsion,* 16 N.Y.U. J. INT'L L. & POL. 1031 (1984); and Comment, *The Hague Convention on the Taking of Evidence Abroad in Civil or Commercial Matters: The Exclusive and Mandatory Procedures for Discovery Abroad,* 132 U. PA. L. REV. 1461 (1984).

For a summary of the foreign and domestic commentary on the exclusivity of the Convention, see McLean, *supra,* at 42–47.

[24] *Aerospatiale,* 107 S.Ct. at 2554.

[25] *Id.* at 2554–57.

[26] *Id.* at 2561–62, 2567 (Blackmun, J., dissenting).

[27] *Id.* at 2555–56.

[28] *Id.* at 2555.

[29] *Id.* at 2556.

discovery rules, except where fairness dictated otherwise.[30] He contended that such a presumption was necessary to achieve some degree of predictability about requests for extraterritorial discovery and that an open-ended, unstructured balancing test would lead to unfairness to litigants and harm to the international legal system.[31]

THE COURT'S DECISIONAL MANDATE

The *Aerospatiale* decision requires that trial courts apply a "particularized analysis" of all the facts to requests for extraterritorial discovery. This analysis is to be based on several general principles mentioned in the opinion that identify decision-making objectives.

Comity

The focal point of the mandated analysis is the principle of comity.[32] According to the Court, "Comity refers to the spirit of cooperation in which a domestic tribunal approaches the resolution of cases touching the laws and interests of other sovereign states."[33] Comity thus requires U.S. courts to evaluate requested extraterritorial discovery in relation to the legitimate interests of foreign states that would be affected.

The Court provided little guidance, however, as to how content is to be ascribed to the principle of comity. The only references in this regard in *Aerospatiale* are to the *Restatement of Foreign Relations Law of the United States (Revised).*[34] The Court stated that the types of factors to be considered in a comity analysis are "suggested" by section 437 of that document,[35] which represents the application of the standard of jurisdictional reasonableness to extraterritorial discovery. The list of factors includes items as diverse as "whether the information originated in the United States" and "the extent to which . . . compliance with the request would undermine important interests of the state where the information is located."[36]

[30] *Id.* at 2561–62, 2567–68 (Blackmun, J., dissenting).

[31] *Id.* at 2569 (Blackmun, J., dissenting).

[32] *See generally* Yntema, *The Comity Doctrine,* 65 MICH. L. REV. 9 (1966). The Supreme Court case most often cited for the concept of comity is Hilton v. Guyot, 159 U.S. 113 (1895).

[33] *Aerospatiale,* 107 S.Ct. at 2555 n.27.

[34] RESTATEMENT (REVISED) OF FOREIGN RELATIONS LAW OF THE UNITED STATES (Tent. Draft No. 7, 1986). Although the latter version was used by the Court, references below will be to the recently published *Restatement (Third), supra* note 5. For an evaluation of the new provisions concerning extraterritoriality, see Fox, *Extraterritoriality, Antitrust, and the New Restatement: Is "Reasonableness" the Answer?,* 19 N.Y.U. J. INT'L L. & POL. 565 (1987).

[35] *Aerospatiale,* 107 S.Ct. at 2555 n.28 (§437 is §442 of the RESTATEMENT (THIRD), *supra* note 5).

[36] Section 442 of the RESTATEMENT (THIRD), *supra* note 5, provides, in relevant part:

> In deciding whether to issue an order directing production of information located abroad, and in framing such an order, a court or agency in the United States should take into account the importance to the investigation or litigation of the documents or other information requested; the degree of specificity of the request; whether the information originated in the United States; the availability of alternative means of securing the

When used in conjunction with the Reporters' Notes and in the context of the conceptual framework of the *Restatement,* this section provides useful guidance in analyzing requests for extraterritorial discovery. Without this framework, however, reference to the listed factors is of little value, and the opinion does not indicate that courts should follow the approach of the new *Restatement.*

Fairness to Litigants

The *Aerospatiale* decision also requires courts to consider fairness to litigants in ruling on extraterritorial discovery requests. In particular, the Court required close scrutiny of discovery requests to prevent "abuses" of the discovery rules.[37] For example, according to the Court, "American courts, in supervising pretrial proceedings, should exercise special vigilance to protect foreign litigants from the danger that unnecessary, or unduly burdensome, discovery may place them in a disadvantageous position."[38] The Court did not, however, indicate the relationship of fairness considerations to the comity test, and it gave no guidance as to how fairness was to be analyzed.

Evidentiary Necessity and Procedural Efficiency

While comity and fairness to litigants were presented as factors that might lead a court to restrict the application of U.S. discovery rules, the Court also identified two factors—evidentiary necessity and procedural efficiency—that tend to support application of those rules. In concluding that comity did not require first resort to the Convention, the Court stated that use of the Convention could be rejected where it was likely to be unnecessarily costly and time-consuming and where it might not yield information necessary to the litigation.[39] Again, however, the Court did not provide any guidance as to how these concepts were to be applied.

The "particularized analysis" called for by the Supreme Court is thus largely unstructured and exceptionally vague. The Court not only refused to "articulate specific rules to guide this delicate test of adjudication,"[40] but also failed to provide significant conceptual guidance for the analysis. Although several concepts are mentioned as relevant, they are not presented as part of a coherent framework of analysis. They represent goals of analysis but provide little guidance for courts seeking to achieve them.

> information; and the extent to which noncompliance with the request would undermine important interests of the United States, or compliance with the request would undermine important interests of the state where the information is located.

The version used by the Court was substantially the same.

[37] *Aerospatiale,* 107 S.Ct. at 2556.

[38] *Id.* at 2557.

[39] *Id.* at 2555–57.

[40] *Id.* at 2557.

II. Criteria for an Effective Analytical Framework

The Supreme Court's laconic treatment of the analysis to be applied by lower courts to extraterritorial discovery requests might suggest to some that those courts may consider any interests of any state or party and "balance" them on whatever basis they choose. Such an interpretation of the Court's mandate, however, is likely to preclude attainment of the Court's goals. To achieve them, an analytical framework must be developed that meets two principal criteria. First, it must be sufficiently structured to provide effective guidelines for decision making and thus afford a reasonable degree of predictability. Second, it must be sufficiently comprehensive to include all relevant international as well as domestic law principles and relate to the full range of interests affected by extraterritorial discovery.[41]

Structure and Predictability

The degree of structure in an analytical framework depends on the extent to which there is general agreement among judicial decision makers concerning (1) the content of the legal concepts included in the framework and (2) the relationships among those concepts.[42] A structured analytical framework thus provides the decision maker with reasonable clarity regarding both of these factors.

As used here, the term "structure" does not imply fixed rules specifying the legal consequences of particular conduct. It refers to the analytical principles that are to be used in making judicial decisions.[43] Moreover, owing to the large number of competing interests involved in extraterritorial discovery, fixed rules are not likely to be appropriate for use in that context.

The degree of structure in an analytical framework has three consequences that largely determine its effectiveness regarding extraterritorial discovery orders:[44] first, it provides guidance for the judge and thus affects

[41] The Court's failure in the opinion to provide a structured framework of analysis does not mean that the Court intended that it be unstructured; the opinion simply does not provide guidance on the issue.

[42] The assumption here is not that legal concepts have inherent or logically discernible content, or that such concepts can be given fixed and unambiguous content. I do assume, however, that legal processes can and regularly do ascribe content to individual concepts and that this content reasonably can be ascertained by using the methods and conventions of the social institutions in which those processes operate. The so-called deconstructionist critique of legal reasoning does not, therefore, undermine the assumptions on which my analysis is based. For discussion of one version of the deconstructionist view, see Kennedy, *Form and Substance in Private Law Adjudication,* 89 Harv. L. Rev. 1685, 1725–37 (1976).

[43] For discussion of the distinction between rules and principles, see R. Dworkin, *The Model of Rules I,* in Taking Rights Seriously 14 (1981).

[44] This assertion does not assume a passive judicial decision maker who is somehow "bound" by the content of the principles. It does assume, however, that conscious application by a judge of a particular set of concepts to a given fact situation will significantly influence the outcome of the decision.

the predictability of judicial decision making;[45] second, it affects the way lawyers present arguments to courts and the characteristics of those arguments; and third, it influences the conduct of those who may be affected by the court's decision. The higher the degree of decisional predictability, the greater the probable effect on that conduct.[46]

Reducing State-Level Conflict

A structured framework of analysis is likely to reduce incentives for foreign states to obstruct the policy objectives of the United States by enacting or strengthening blocking legislation and by refusing to enforce judgments of U.S. courts. Such measures often stem from fear that foreign interests will not be fully and fairly considered in U.S. courts;[47] lack of a structured framework is likely to enhance that fear because it suggests that the judge may decide on the basis of subjective and/or possibly biased criteria.

A structured framework not only reduces this perceived subjectivity but also furnishes foreign states with a significant amount of information about the factors that are likely to influence judicial decisions and how those factors will be evaluated. Where the framework requires consideration of foreign interests, for example, the foreign state can be confident that they will be considered, and it can anticipate the analysis that will be applied. This confidence is likely to reduce pressure to enact countermeasures.

Conceptual structure also tends to narrow the range of conflict. It reduces the incentives for foreign states to make broad claims of sovereignty in the hope that a judge may consider some of them convincing. Instead, it encourages states to concentrate their efforts in support of interests that are identified as relevant by the analytical framework, and this, in turn, will tend to clarify and narrow the issues involved in the controversy. Moreover, without such a structure, foreign states may believe that confrontational tactics

[45] The role of structure in cases involving transnational legal claims must be assessed differently from its role in purely domestic disputes. In the domestic context, those affected by a judicial decision are subject to the authority of the state and cannot take legal action to interfere with the state's regulatory objectives. Moreover, they are presumed to have consented to the authority of the judge, and as members of the polity in which the judge acts they are presumed to be in a position to respond effectively to improper use of judicial discretion. Consequently, the potential adverse impact of ad hoc decision making is minimized.

In the extraterritorial discovery context, however, foreign states can and do take legal measures (e.g., blocking legislation) that obstruct the ability of the United States to accomplish its objectives. Moreover, those states have not consented to the authority of the U.S. judge. As a result, the degree of structure in the applicable analytical framework becomes a critical determinant of the response of foreign states to extraterritorial discovery practices, because it is the central source of information concerning the probable actions of the judge.

[46] For discussion of the need for predictability in applying comity principles, see Note, *Predictability and Comity: Toward Common Principles of Extraterritorial Jurisdiction*, 98 HARV. L. REV. 1310 (1985).

[47] *See, e.g.*, Heck, *U.S. Misinterpretation of the Hague Evidence Convention*, 24 COLUM. J. TRANSNAT'L L. 231, 278 (1986); H. STEINER & D. VAGTS, TRANSNATIONAL LEGAL PROBLEMS 611 (2d ed. 1976); and Wilkey, *Transnational Adjudication: A View from the Bench*, 18 INT'L LAW. 541, 542–43 (1984).

will be viewed as indicia of seriousness, which could lead them to *demonstrate* their objections to discovery through protests, blocking legislation and related measures.[48]

Increasing Fairness to Litigants

Conceptual structure is also likely to correlate with fairness to litigants. Blocking legislation and related confrontational measures increase the costs and risks of litigation, reduce the predictability of outcomes and often place litigants in the position of having to choose between violating United States law and violating foreign law. Consequently, reducing incentives for foreign states to obstruct U.S. discovery tends to improve fairness to litigants.

Increased structure also tends to reduce both unintentional and intentional judicial bias. A judge acting without a structured analytical framework may be more responsive to the demands of domestic litigants and U.S. interests merely because he understands them better than he does foreign interests.[49] Conceptual structure counteracts this unintentional bias by identifying relevant issues and relating them to a coherent framework of analysis. A structured framework also tends to counteract pressure on the judge to protect domestic interests and litigants, because it provides authority to which the judge can refer in support of potentially unpopular decisions.

Furthermore, a structured framework of analysis increases the information available to litigants. Where litigants can reasonably predict judicial responses to discovery requests, they can make informed evaluations of whether to incur the costs and risks involved in the proceedings.

Increasing the Effectiveness of U.S. Litigation

Finally, a structured framework of analysis should improve the efficiency and effectiveness of U.S. litigation involving extraterritorial discovery. In an amorphous decision-making context, litigants on both sides have an incentive to make as many and as varied arguments as possible because they cannot predict what will influence the judge's decision.[50] The result is often inefficient litigation encumbered by marginally relevant arguments and burdened by attendant delays and elevated costs. The problem is particularly severe in the context of extraterritorial discovery, for there are few limits on the variety of arguments that might conceivably relate to the general goals of comity and fairness. Where guiding principles are well articulated, there is less incentive for overargument, and the delays and costs of litigation are correspondingly contained.

[48] *See infra* text accompanying notes 145–50.

[49] *See Aerospatiale,* 107 S.Ct. at 2560 (Blackmun, J., dissenting); Heck, *supra* note 47, at 279; H. Steiner & D. Vagts, *supra* note 47, at 611; and Wilkey, *supra* note 47, at 542–44.

[50] *See* Langbein, *The German Advantage in Civil Procedure,* 52 U. Chi. L. Rev. 823, 830–32 (1985).

COMPREHENSIVENESS

To be effective, the analytical framework for evaluating extraterritorial discovery must also be comprehensive. Such discovery may involve many principles from international as well as from domestic law. Because of the many uncertainties in the law on this subject, the applicability of these principles is frequently unclear, and they often appear to conflict. Potentially applicable principles must therefore be identified and integrated into a framework that provides guidance in resolving these conflicts.

In *Aerospatiale* the Supreme Court failed to locate the principles it discussed in either a conceptual or a factual context.[51] It did not make clear the relationship between the principles announced in the case and other potentially applicable legal principles. As a result, some may mistakenly assume that *Aerospatiale* is the sole source of authority on extraterritorial discovery and that factors not identified in the case are not relevant to the analysis. The opinion, however, refers only to some of the applicable legal principles.

The most egregious omission is the Court's failure to discuss the role of customary international law.[52] Customary international law establishes the rights or entitlements of states, and thus it provides the necessary framework for evaluating the justifiable expectations of states about the conduct of other states.[53] Clearly, therefore, customary international law must play a central role in effectively analyzing issues regarding extraterritorial discovery. Moreover, customary international law is part of United States law;[54] consequently, U.S. courts are required to apply it, unless otherwise directed by Congress or, in some cases, the Executive.[55]

The comity analysis required by *Aerospatiale* is implicitly based on concepts of customary international law, but the opinion fails to identify them as

[51] Such a discussion was not necessary to resolve the case, and the Court therefore cannot be faulted for failing to include it. Considering the paucity of guidance concerning the principles of analysis to be used in such cases, however, one must regret the Court's failure to clarify the situation.

[52] The Court also failed adequately to identify the relationship between the principles it was enunciating and existing case law. Although many of the issues in previous cases have either been resolved or rendered irrelevant by *Aerospatiale,* those cases remain an important source of guidance on, e.g., the application of international law to discovery and the evaluation of fairness in extraterritorial discovery. For a digest of such cases, see Note, *Hague Evidence Convention: A Practical Guide to the Convention, United States Case Law, Convention-Sponsored Review Commission (1978 & 1985), and Responses of Other Signatory Nations: With Digest of Cases and Bibliography,* 16 GA. J. INT'L & COMP. L. 73, 99, App. A (1986).

[53] For discussion of the entitlement concept, see D'Amato, *The Concept of Human Rights in International Law,* 82 COLUM. L. REV. 1100, 1113 (1982).

[54] *See, e.g.,* The Paquete Habana, 175 U.S. 677, 700 (1900); The Over the Top, 5 F.2d 838, 842 (D. Conn. 1925); and Trans World Airlines v. Franklin Mint Corp., 466 U.S. 243, 252–53 (1983). For discussion of the relations between national and international law, see, e.g., 2 E. NEREP, EXTRATERRITORIAL CONTROL OF COMPETITION UNDER INTERNATIONAL LAW, ch. VII (1983); and Dickinson, *The Law of Nations as Part of the National Law of the United States,* 101 U. PA. L. REV. 26, 792, pts. I & II (1952–53).

[55] *See generally* Henkin, *International Law as Law in the United States,* 82 MICH. L. REV. 1555, 1567 (1984).

such. The central concept in the Court's comity analysis, for example, involves the "sovereign interests" of foreign states[56] and necessarily implies reference to the public international law concept of sovereignty to determine its content.[57] Similarly, according to *Aerospatiale,* U.S. courts must limit discovery that is unjustifiably "intrusive" on the interests of foreign states.[58] To assess whether particular action is intrusive, however, one must determine the sphere of protection to which the state is entitled, and this sphere of protection is established by international law.

III. Toward an Analytical Framework

Given the Supreme Court's failure to provide a structured and comprehensive framework for analyzing requests for extraterritorial discovery, this section attempts to do so through the use of elements provided by the *Aerospatiale* case, as well as other relevant principles of domestic and international law.

The basic framework can be stated succinctly. Where an order for extraterritorial discovery would violate either United States standards of procedural fairness or established norms of international law, it must be modified to avoid such violations. Where the United States Government reasonably requests that discovery be modified to avoid serious harm to U.S. foreign relations interests, the court must so limit discovery. In all other cases, the court must weigh the need for the requested information against the harm to the sovereign interests of foreign states that may result, and it must limit discovery to the extent necessary to avoid unjustified harm to those interests.

PRIVATE INTERESTS: FAIRNESS AND THE LITIGANT

The Separation of Public and Private Interests

Effective analysis of extraterritorial discovery requests requires that a fundamental distinction be made between private and public interests. The *Aerospatiale* decision considers both sets of interests,[59] but it fails to identify their distinct roles; as a result, some might mistakenly suppose that they can be mixed together in the decisional process.

The private interests of litigants in U.S. courts are protected by a standard of procedural fairness that is applicable to all discovery requests, regardless of where the information is located.[60] Application of this fairness stand-

[56] *Aerospatiale,* 107 S.Ct. at 2555–56.

[57] An argument that sovereign interests can be determined without reference to international law would be hard to sustain, because without reference to international law there would be no basis for ascribing content to the concept.

[58] *Aerospatiale,* 107 S.Ct. at 2556.

[59] *Id.* at 2542, 2555.

[60] This requirement of fairness derives from the Due Process Clause of the Fourteenth Amendment to the U.S. Constitution. *See generally* Burger King Corp. v. Rudzewicz, 471 U.S. 462, 474 (1985); World-Wide Volkswagen Corp. v. Woodson, 444 U.S. 286, 292 (1980);

ard is required by United States law, and a court has no authority to compromise it by reference to international or state interests.

Even if there were authority to "balance" private and state interests, there would be no principled basis on which to do so. Protection of a litigant's right to fair treatment is based on values that are not related to state and international interests, and therefore cannot be balanced against them. Moreover, any attempt to balance the fairness interests of a particular litigant against international and state interests on a general scale of "importance" not only would be unprincipled, but also would necessarily be biased in favor of state interests.[61]

Consequently, application of the fairness standard must be an independent element of the analysis, and a request for discovery abroad must be denied or modified where it would violate fairness standards under U.S. law.

Application of the Fairness Standard

Where information is located outside the United States, the fairness standard may require consideration of factors that generally would not be present in the domestic context.[62] The most important such factor relates to the ability of a foreign state to control sources of information within its territory. For example, a U.S. court must decide whether it would be fair to penalize a litigant for failure to comply with a discovery order where, under the law of the foreign state, such compliance would lead to the imposition of sanctions.[63]

International Shoe Co. v. Washington, 326 U.S. 310, 316 (1945). *See also* Maier, *Interest Balancing and Extraterritorial Jurisdiction,* 31 AM. J. COMP. L. 579, 582 (1983); and Newman, *Rethinking Fairness: Perspectives on the Litigation Process,* 94 YALE L.J. 1643 (1985).

Fairness is also specifically called for in the discovery context in Fed. R. Civ. P. 26(c), which states, in relevant part, that a court "may make any order which justice requires to protect a party or person from annoyance, embarrassment, oppression, or undue burden or expense." *See generally* Kerschbaumer v. Bell, 112 F.R.D. 426, 427 (D.D.C. 1986).

[61] A court applying an unstructured "balancing" analysis based on an undefined standard of "importance" to a conflict between the interests of a state and those of an individual would in most cases presumably find that the interests of the state were more "important," because a state's conduct typically has more numerous and significant effects on persons and institutions than an individual's.

[62] *See, e.g.,* Heck, *supra* note 47, at 252 ("U.S. law recognizes that discovery abroad is different from domestic proceedings and therefore may have to be exercised more restrictively"); Lowenfeld, *Sovereignty, Jurisdiction, and Reasonableness: A Reply to A. V. Lowe,* 75 AJIL 629, 634 (1981); and R. von Mehren, *Transnational Litigation in American Courts: An Overview of Problems and Issues,* 3 DICK. J. INT'L L. 43, 50 (1984).

[63] In some cases, the fairness doctrine may be applied after a discovery order has been entered. The Supreme Court indicated in Societe Internationale pour Participations Industrielles et Commerciales, S.A. v. Rogers, 357 U.S. 197 (1958), that this may be a more appropriate procedural context for evaluating certain issues.

Evaluation of fairness issues need not, however, be confined to this procedural context, and there may be significant waste and unfairness in doing so. Where a court reasonably believes, for example, that foreign blocking legislation would be applied to prevent compliance with its

In analyzing fairness, a court must consider the actual impact of the foreign blocking legislation on the particular litigant. Consequently, the court must consider factors such as whether the statute is regularly enforced[64] and, in some cases, whether the litigant has made a good faith effort to avoid the impact of the legislation.[65] It must also consider the penalties for violation of the legislation.[66] Where the foreign litigant cannot reasonably comply with an order of a U.S. court, it would generally be unfair to impose a penalty for noncompliance.[67]

The fairness analysis must include, in addition, the increased costs, risks and compliance burdens that may result from the foreign location of persons or documents. For example, the costs and risks incurred by sending large numbers of documents all the way to the United States to be examined for long periods may substantially disadvantage a foreign litigant.[68] Moreover, the foreign location of persons or documents may expose the litigant to unfair manipulation by an opponent in the U.S. litigation; the Supreme Court, however, has specifically directed lower courts to protect litigants against such manipulation.[69]

Fairness is necessarily a relational concept. It requires evaluation of the needs of those seeking extraterritorial discovery as well as of those resisting it. Where the fairness analysis involves burdens on the requested party rather than ability to comply, those burdens must be evaluated in light of the requesting party's need for the discovery. A demonstrated need for specific information justifies greater burdens on the requested party than the pursuit of unspecified information that might merely lead to usable evidence.[70]

The relational aspect of the fairness test also requires consideration of the actions of the requesting party. For example, attempts by a litigant to use the foreign location of information to gain an advantage over an opponent should constitute a waiver of fairness protections. This aspect of the fairness test is likely to be particularly important in two contexts. Fairness protections should not be available to a litigant that has attempted to avoid obligations under U.S. law by intentionally placing documents in foreign terri-

---

order, requiring the litigant to attempt to evade its application is likely to be both wasteful and useless.

[64] *See, e.g.*, Garpeg, Ltd. v. United States, 583 F.Supp. 789, 797 (S.D.N.Y. 1984); Compagnie Francaise d'Assurance pour le Commerce Exterieur v. Phillips Petroleum Co., 105 F.R.D. 16, 30 (S.D.N.Y. 1984); and Graco Inc. v. Kremlin, Inc. & SKM, 101 F.R.D. 503, 514 (N.D. Ill. 1984).

[65] *See, e.g.*, United States v. Vetco, Inc., 644 F.2d 1324, 1332 (9th Cir. 1981), *cert. denied*, 454 U.S. 1098 (1981); and United States v. First Nat'l City Bank, 396 F.2d 897, 905 (1968).

[66] Where the penalty involves a fine, ability to pay may also be a factor. A $5,000 fine, for example, may be a significant factor for a small firm but a bagatelle for a large firm.

[67] The foreign party presumably cannot comply where the situs state uses force to prevent compliance, as well as where the penalties for violating the statute would involve loss of personal freedom or significant financial burdens.

[68] *Aerospatiale*, 107 S.Ct. at 2567. [69] *Id.*

[70] The degree of specificity in requesting information is critical. Requests for specific information—e.g., documents relating to a particular conversation—generally also entail fewer burdens on the requested party than broader discovery requests.

tory.[71] Moreover, they should not be available to a party that utilizes U.S. discovery rules but resists their application to itself.[72]

United States courts consistently have required that fairness considerations be part of the analysis of extraterritorial discovery.[73] They have held, for example, that the effect of foreign blocking legislation on a litigant's ability to comply with a discovery order must be considered in assessing the propriety of sanctions against that party for failure to comply.[74] Moreover, the foreign location of documents has led courts to order the use of alternative means of obtaining information where the burdens of complying with the discovery request were excessive.[75] Consequently, there is not only ample case law to support the consideration of such issues, but also guidance concerning the factors to be evaluated.

THE APPLICATION OF PUBLIC INTERNATIONAL LAW NORMS

A second component of the analysis asks whether the requested extraterritorial discovery would violate an established norm of public international law.[76]

Claims that U.S. extraterritorial discovery violates customary international law are based on a fundamental postulate of international law, which provides that a state may not "interfere" with the "sovereignty" of another state—i.e., its control over conduct within its territory.[77] The principle of noninterference is thus central to the controversy over extraterritorial discovery.

At issue here is the extent to which specific applications of this principle have been established as norms of state conduct under international law. Several such norms are well established. For example, an agent of a state may not act on its behalf within foreign territory without the consent of the

[71] *See, e.g., In re* Anschuetz & Co., 754 F.2d 602, 607 (5th Cir. 1985), *remanded,* 55 U.S.L.W. 3852 (1987); and Cooper Indus. v. British Aerospace, Inc., 102 F.R.D. 918, 920 (S.D.N.Y. 1984). *See generally* Sadoff, *The Hague Evidence Convention: Problems at Home of Obtaining Foreign Evidence,* 20 INT'L LAW. 659, 664–65 (1986).

[72] *See, e.g.,* International Soc'y for Krishna Consciousness v. Lee, 105 F.R.D. 435, 446 (S.D.N.Y. 1984).

[73] *See, e.g.,* McLaughlin v. Fellows Gear Shaper Co., 102 F.R.D. 956 (E.D. Mo. 1984). *See generally* Rosdeitcher, *Foreign Blocking Statutes and U.S. Discovery: A Conflict of National Policies,* 16 N.Y.U. J. INT'L L. & POL. 1061 (1984).

[74] *See, e.g.,* Graco Inc. v. Kremlin, Inc. & SKM, 101 F.R.D. 503, 513 (1984); and *In re* Uranium Antitrust Litigation, 480 F.Supp. 1138, 1147 (N.D. Ill. 1979).

[75] *See, e.g.,* Philadelphia Gear Corp. v. American Pfauter Corp., 100 F.R.D. 58, 61 (E.D. Pa. 1983); and Laker Airways v. Pan American World Airways, 103 F.R.D. 42 (D.D.C. 1984).

[76] The Court's failure to discuss this issue in *Aerospatiale* may have been based on the assumption that no such customary law norms were involved in the case, and therefore that there was no need to address the point.

[77] For discussion of the noninterference principle, see Gerber, *Beyond Balancing: International Law Restraints on the Reach of National Laws,* 10 YALE J. INT'L L. 185, 209–20 (1985). *See generally* I. BROWNLIE, PRINCIPLES OF PUBLIC INTERNATIONAL LAW 310 (3d ed. 1979); and T. LAWRENCE, THE PRINCIPLES OF INTERNATIONAL LAW 120 (P. Winfield 7th rev. ed. 1923).

foreign sovereign.[78] Consequently, a U.S. court may not send police or military forces onto foreign territory to enforce a U.S. judgment.[79] Similarly, it is well established that a state may not send its agents onto foreign territory to seize documents for review,[80] nor may it order depositions within a foreign state.[81]

The current controversy relates primarily to whether existing norms of conduct prohibit U.S. courts from requiring (1) that documents located within a foreign state be made available for inspection within foreign territory (extraterritorial document inspection), and (2) that persons or materials located in foreign territory be made available for inspection in the United States (information removal). Many foreign governments consider that both actions violate international law.[82] While United States courts have divided over the legality of extraterritorial document inspection orders,[83] they generally have not considered removal orders to be violations.[84]

[78] *See, e.g.*, I. BROWNLIE, *supra* note 77, at 306–07. According to Hans Kelsen:

> That the territory enclosed by the boundaries of a state legally belongs to this state or—as it is usually characterized—that it is under the territorial supremacy or sovereignty of this state means that all individuals staying on this territory are, in principle, subjected to the legal power of that state and only of that state.

H. KELSEN, PRINCIPLES OF INTERNATIONAL LAW 317–18 (R. W. Tucker 2d rev. ed. 1966).

[79] *See, e.g.*, 1 M. WHITEMAN, DIGEST OF INTERNATIONAL LAW 225 (1963); Mann, *The Doctrine of Jurisdiction in International Law*, 111 RECUEIL DES COURS 1, 127–58 (1964 I); and Oxman, *The Choice Between Direct Discovery and Other Means of Obtaining Evidence Abroad: The Impact of the Hague Evidence Convention*, 37 U. MIAMI L. REV. 733, 751 (1983).

[80] *See, e.g.*, 6 M. WHITEMAN, *supra* note 79, at 160–83 (1968); and Ings v. Ferguson, 282 F.2d 149, 151 (2d Cir. 1960).

[81] *See generally* 1 B. RISTAU, *supra* note 9, at 90–93; Lorenzen, *Territoriality, Public Policy and the Conflict of Laws*, 33 YALE L.J. 736 (1924); Oxman, *supra* note 79, at 749–52; and Note, *Limitations on the Federal Judicial Power to Compel Acts Violating Foreign Law*, 63 COLUM. L. REV. 1441 (1963). *See also, e.g.*, Work v. Bier, 106 F.R.D. 45, 48 (D.D.C. 1985); and Graco Inc. v. Kremlin, Inc. & SKM, 101 F.R.D. 503, 513 (N.D. Ill. 1984).

[82] *See, e.g.*, Brief for the Republic of France at 16, *Aerospatiale*, 107 S.Ct. 2542 (1987); Brief for the Federal Republic of Germany at 13, *id.*; and Brief for the Government of Switzerland at 8, *id.*

[83] For cases refusing orders for extraterritorial document inspection on sovereignty grounds, see, e.g., Compagnie Francaise d'Assurance pour le Commerce Exterieur v. Phillips Petroleum Co., 105 F.R.D. 16, 35 (S.D.N.Y. 1984); Philadelphia Gear Corp. v. American Pfauter Corp., 100 F.R.D. 58, 60 (E.D. Pa. 1983); TH. Goldschmidt A.G. v. Smith, 676 S.W. 2d 443, 445 (Tex. App. 1984) ("[discovery orders] that conflict with West German reservations under the Convention . . . impinge upon the sovereignty of the Federal Republic of Germany and should not be issued in ordinary circumstances"); and Volkswagenwerk A.G. v. Superior Court, 123 Cal. App. 3d 840, 850, 176 Cal. Rptr. 874, 883 (Ct. App. 1981) (discovery orders executed in West Germany "would violate West German judicial sovereignty").

For cases holding that such orders would not violate foreign sovereignty, see, e.g., International Soc'y for Krishna Consciousness v. Lee, 105 F.R.D. 435, 449 (S.D.N.Y. 1984); and Graco Inc. v. Kremlin, Inc. & SKM, 101 F.R.D. 503, 520 (N.D. Ill. 1984).

[84] *See, e.g.*, *In re* Messerschmitt Bolkow Blohm GmbH, 757 F.2d 729 (5th Cir. 1985), *remanded*, 107 S.Ct. 3223 (1987); *In re* Anschuetz & Co., 754 F.2d 602, 615 (5th Cir. 1985), *remanded*, 107 S.Ct. 3223 (1987) ("If Anschuetz is not voluntarily forthcoming in Germany, the court can order documents and the examination of witnesses to occur in the United States to avoid any infringement upon German sovereignty"); and International Soc'y for Krishna Consciousness v. Lee, 105 F.R.D. 435, 449 (S.D.N.Y. 1984).

Not unexpectedly, these differences in result depend on the analysis applied. Three basic theories have been used to determine whether extraterritorial discovery orders violate international law.

The Concept of Judicial Sovereignty

United States courts generally have analyzed the role of international law by reference to the concept of judicial sovereignty.[85] According to this view, an order by a U.S. court relating to information within a foreign state interferes with the rights of that state by usurping a governmental function that is there reserved to the judiciary.[86]

The notion of judicial sovereignty was developed to conceptualize foreign opposition to U.S. extraterritorial discovery practices.[87] It is an aspect of the general concept of sovereignty, and thus quintessentially part of international law. However, because courts and commentators often have failed explicitly to recognize this fact, the concept is often used with little or no international law analysis to support its application.[88]

The concept consistently has been held to prohibit the ordering of depositions on foreign soil.[89] Cases on extraterritorial document inspection, however, are less clear. Some courts have held that orders for such inspection violate foreign judicial sovereignty,[90] while others have distinguished depositions from document inspection on the ground that the latter is only

[85] *See, e.g., In re* Societe Nationale Industrielle Aerospatiale, 782 F.2d 120, 123–24 (8th Cir. 1986); Boreri v. Fiat S.p.A., 763 F.2d 17, 19 (1st Cir. 1985); Compagnie Francaise d'Assurance pour le Commerce Exterieur v. Phillips Petroleum Co., 105 F.R.D. 16, 26 (S.D.N.Y. 1984); and Volkswagenwerk A.G. v. Superior Court, 123 Cal. App. 3d 840, 852, 176 Cal. Rptr. 874, 881 (1981).

[86] *See, e.g., Report of United States Delegation to Eleventh Session of Hague Convention on Private International Law,* 8 ILM 785, 806 (1969) [hereinafter *1969 Delegation Report*].

[87] For description of the development of this concept, see Gerber, *supra* note 3, at 775–79. *See also* Oxman, *supra* note 79, at 761–65; and *Report of the Special Commission on the Operation of the Hague Convention of 18 March 1970 on the Taking of Evidence Abroad in Civil or Commercial Matters (July 1985),* 24 ILM 1668, 1678 (1985) [hereinafter *1985 Special Commission Report*]. In drafting the Convention, this concept of judicial sovereignty was "constantly borne in mind." *1969 Delegation Report, supra* note 86, at 806.

[88] *See, e.g.,* Lowrance v. Michael Weining, GmbH, 107 F.R.D. 386, 388–89 (W.D. Tenn. 1985); and Cooper Indus. v. British Aerospace, Inc., 102 F.R.D. 918, 920 (S.D.N.Y. 1984).

[89] *See, e.g.,* Work v. Bier, 106 F.R.D. 45, 56–57 (D.D.C. 1985); International Soc'y for Krishna Consciousness v. Lee, 105 F.R.D. 503, 520 (N.D. Ill. 1984); Cooper Indus. v. British Aerospace, Inc., 102 F.R.D. 918, 920 (S.D.N.Y. 1984); and Volkswagenwerk Aktiengesellschaft v. Superior Court, 33 Cal. App. 3d 508, 509, 109 Cal. Rptr. 219, 220 (1973). For discussion of the difficulties of taking depositions in a foreign state, see Smit, *International Aspects of Federal Civil Procedure,* 61 COLUM. L. REV. 1031, 1053–59 (1961); and Jones, *International Judicial Assistance: Procedural Chaos and a Program for Reform,* 62 YALE L.J. 515, 522–34 (1953).

[90] *See, e.g.,* McLaughlin v. Fellows Gear Shaper Co., 102 F.R.D. 956, 959 (E.D. Pa. 1984) (court declined to order compliance because "some of the requests for production of documents, because of their sweeping character, may very well require of persons located in West Germany, efforts which would be substantially equivalent to producing evidence in that country"); and Philadelphia Gear Corp. v. American Pfauter Corp., 100 F.R.D. 58, 60 (E.D. Pa. 1983).

ancillary to the judicial process.[91] Nevertheless, this distinction is difficult to maintain, and U.S. courts recently have tended to avoid ordering document inspection and to order instead that documents be produced in the United States.

The reason is that the concept of judicial sovereignty does not prohibit removal orders. Orders requiring that persons be deposed or documents produced in the United States consistently have been held not to represent the exercise of judicial functions on foreign territory.[92] As a result, reliance on the concept of judicial sovereignty has led U.S. courts to assume that objections to discovery under international law can be avoided by ordering that discovery take place in the United States.[93] The question remains whether this concept of usurpation properly defines the scope of the principle of noninterference.

The Locus of State Conduct

Judicial sovereignty may also be viewed as merely one application of the broader principle of international law that proscribes conduct by one state within the territory of another without the latter's consent.[94] This principle is a fundamental postulate of international law,[95] and it is based directly on state practice.

If this broader standard is applied to extraterritorial discovery, the issue is whether a U.S. attorney acting under authority of a U.S. court order is acting as an agent of the United States, and there can be little doubt that he is. Consequently, under this analysis, orders for extraterritorial document inspection are prohibited. Removal orders are permitted, however, because they do not involve conduct by agents of the United States on foreign territory.

[91] *See, e.g., In re* Anschuetz & Co., 754 F.2d 602, 611 (5th Cir. 1985), *remanded,* 107 S.Ct. 3223 (1987); and *In re* Societe Nationale Industrielle Aerospatiale, 782 F.2d 120, 124–25 (8th Cir. 1986).

[92] *See, e.g., In re* Messerschmitt Bolkow Blohm GmbH, 757 F.2d 729, 732 (5th Cir. 1985), *remanded,* 107 S.Ct. 3223 (1987); *In re* Anschuetz & Co., 754 F.2d 602, 615 (5th Cir. 1985), *remanded,* 107 S.Ct. 3223 (1987); International Soc'y for Krishna Consciousness v. Lee, 105 F.R.D. 503, 521 (N.D. Ill. 1984); Lowrance v. Michael Weining, GmbH, 107 F.R.D. 386, 388 (W.D. Tenn. 1985); and Cooper Indus. v. British Aerospace, Inc., 102 F.R.D. 918, 920 (S.D.N.Y. 1984).

[93] *See, e.g., In re* Anschuetz & Co., 754 F.2d 602, 615 (5th Cir. 1985), *remanded,* 107 S.Ct. 3223 (1987); *In re* Messerschmitt Bolkow Blohm GmbH, 757 F.2d 729, 732 (5th Cir. 1985), *remanded,* 107 S.Ct. 3223 (1987); and Graco Inc. v. Kremlin, Inc. & SKM, 101 F.R.D. 503, 521 (N.D. Ill. 1984) ("Nor does the court agree that the Convention requires deference to a country's judicial sovereignty over documents, people, and information—if this really is how judicial sovereignty is to be understood—when they are to be produced in this country").

[94] For discussion of this principle, see G. VON GLAHN, LAW AMONG NATIONS 119–21 (5th ed. 1986); 1 L. OPPENHEIM, INTERNATIONAL LAW 265–70 (Lauterpacht 5th ed. 1937); H. KELSEN, *supra* note 78, at 357; E. DE VATTEL, LE DROIT DES GENS 138–43 (1758) (G. Gregory trans. 1964); and Maier, *supra* note 60, at 582–86.

[95] *See, e.g.,* S.S. "Lotus" (Fr. v. Turk.), 1927 PCIJ (ser. A) No. 10 (Judgment of Sept. 7), 2 M. O. HUDSON, WORLD CT. REP. 20, 35 (1935).

Coercing Foreign Conduct: The Extension of State Power

A third theory used to ascribe content to the principle of noninterference asserts that a state may not coerce conduct within another state without the latter's consent,[96] at least where such conduct violates basic principles of the latter state's legal system. Here the concern is not with the locus of the state's conduct, but with the extension of its power to cover private conduct occurring in foreign territory.

The broadest extension of this analysis would find a violation of the principle of noninterference wherever a state attaches significant sanctions to conduct on foreign territory.[97] This argument is undermined, however, by the fact that some foreign states also attach legal consequences to the failure of a party to produce information located abroad, and such practices generally have not been considered to violate the noninterference principle.[98]

According to a narrower version of this analysis, a violation occurs only where the required conduct violates fundamental principles of the foreign legal system.[99] The rationale is that where a state requires conduct on foreign territory that is substantially consistent with fundamental principles and procedures of the situs state, there can be no interference with that state's legal order because the protections established by that state continue to be applied. Interference occurs only where those protections are denied.

In the context of discovery, the argument has been advanced that U.S. procedures violate international law because they deny fundamental protections to which persons are entitled under the laws of the situs state.[100] In particular, it has been argued that a violation may occur where U.S. procedures coerce the production of information without a prior determination by a judge that the information is directly relevant to the litigation.[101]

[96] According to Kelsen:

> That the legal power of the state is limited to its own territory does not mean that no act of the state may legally be carried out outside this state's territory. The limitation refers in principle to coercive acts in the wider sense of the term, including also the preparation of coercive acts. These acts must not be executed on the territory of another state without the latter's consent. Without such consent they constitute a violation of international law.

H. KELSEN, *supra* note 78, at 310–11.

[97] *See, e.g.,* Brief for the Government of Switzerland at 3, *Aerospatiale,* 107 S.Ct. 2542 (1987); and Brief for the Government of the United Kingdom of Great Britain and Northern Ireland at 17, *id.*

[98] *See, e.g.,* P. SCHLOSSER, DER JUSTIZKONFLIKT MIT DEN VEREINIGTEN STAATEN 17–22 (1985).

[99] *See, e.g.,* Stiefel, *"Discovery"-Probleme und Erfahrungen im Deutsch-Amerikanischen Rechtshilfeverkehr,* 25 RECHT DER INTERNATIONALEN WIRTSCHAFT 509, 514–20 (1979); and Rio Tinto Zinc Corp. v. Westinghouse Elec. Corp., [1978] 1 All E.R. 434, 448, [1978] 2 W.L.R. 81, *reprinted in* 17 ILM 38, 43 (1978).

[100] This argument is sometimes based on the private international law concept of *ordre public.* For discussion of *ordre public,* see, e.g., O. KAHN-FREUND, GENERAL PROBLEMS OF PRIVATE INTERNATIONAL LAW 282–85 (1980); Forde, *Ordre Public,* 29 INT'L & COMP. L.Q. 259 (1980); and Paulsen & Sovern, *Public Policy and the Conflict of Laws,* 56 COLUM. L. REV. 969 (1956).

[101] *See, e.g.,* Corning Glass Works v. ITT, 20 ILM 1025, 1029 (1981) (Munich Ct. App. 1980).

The primary significance of applying the coercion analysis is that under that analysis removal orders may violate the principle of noninterference, whereas removal orders do not violate international law under the other theories. It is generally agreed that under international law there are limits on the extent to which a state may coerce conduct within the territory of a foreign state.[102] The content of these limits has not been defined, however, and their application to extraterritorial discovery remains unclear.

Analysis of extraterritorial discovery orders under international law thus yields the following conclusions: a U.S. court would violate a norm of customary international law by ordering depositions on foreign territory and probably by ordering extraterritorial document inspection, but there are no established norms that specifically prohibit removal orders. Substantial uncertainty remains, however, over the application of the principle of noninterference to extraterritorial discovery, largely because recent changes in U.S. discovery procedures and the expanded application of those procedures to foreign information have created a new factual situation,[103] and settled principles of law have not yet developed in response to that situation.

COMITY AND BALANCING

United States courts have long recognized that the exercise of U.S. jurisdiction may infringe on legally protected interests of foreign states, and they have employed the concept of comity as a mechanism for minimizing such conflicts.[104] The function of this third element of the analytical framework is thus to provide a means of regulating conflicts between states over extraterritorial discovery.[105] Comity balancing is often viewed as an essentially unstructured, hence discretionary, process,[106] but a decision-making process of this type is not appropriate for accommodating state interests.[107] Consequently, comity is used here as an analytical tool for resolving conflicts in the international legal system.

The Objectives of Comity Balancing

To develop analytical content in a balancing framework, the objectives must be clearly identified, because they provide the basis for evaluating

[102] *See, e.g.,* Mann, *supra* note 79, at 137.

[103] For discussion of this development, see Gerber, *supra* note 3, at 746–47.

[104] *See generally* Yntema, *supra* note 32; and Maier, *Extraterritorial Jurisdiction at a Crossroads: An Intersection Between Public and Private International Law,* 76 AJIL 280 (1982). For judicial treatment of the concept, see, e.g., First Nat'l City Bank v. Banco Nacional de Cuba, 406 U.S. 759, 768 (1972); Laker Airways v. Sabena, Belgium World Airways, 731 F.2d 909, 937 (D.C. Cir. 1984); United States v. First Nat'l City Bank, 396 F.2d 897, 902 (2d Cir. 1968); and Ings v. Ferguson, 282 F.2d 149, 151–52 (2d Cir. 1960).

[105] According to one commentator: "The weighing of state interests, including the interests of the individual, is thus a process compelled by international customary law. Whether the weighing of state interests standard in and of itself is a rule of international law, is immaterial." 2 E. NEREP, *supra* note 54, at 558.

[106] For discussion, see Gerber, *supra* note 77, at 204–06.

[107] *See supra* text accompanying notes 47–48.

competing interests and the mechanism for comparing those evaluations. With respect to extraterritorial discovery, the objective of comity balancing should be to accommodate the legally protected interests of the United States, on the one hand, and of foreign states affected by the discovery, on the other. Extraterritorial discovery creates conflicts between these two sets of interests, and comity thus requires that each state accept limits on its own entitlements so as not unnecessarily or unreasonably to harm the entitlements of the other.[108]

The comity analysis should aim to achieve compromises among conflicting interests. In an individual case, the standard should be whether the harm caused to the legal interests of a foreign state by a particular discovery order is justified by the need to protect an equal or greater U.S. interest that cannot be protected with reasonable cost by less harmful means.

The frame of reference for the comity analysis is systemic.[109] No state can secure evidence abroad without at least the tacit cooperation of the situs state. States are therefore dependent on each other to accomplish the purely domestic function of providing a fair and reasonable procedure for resolving civil disputes. Where the legal principles governing extraterritorial discovery reflect a reasonable accommodation of the legal interests of all states involved, cooperative state relationships will continue effectively to furnish access to information abroad. Where there is no such accommodation, the necessary cooperation between states will be impaired, and litigation involving evidence abroad will be rendered either unjust or ineffective or both.[110] The system of state relationships performs a function that no state could achieve by itself, and this function justifies limitations on the policies of individual states.

The Interests to Be Balanced

Effective balancing also requires standards for determining which interests are to be balanced. The starting point for analyzing this issue must be the recognition that the "interests" in question cannot refer to the subjective interests of states—i.e., states cannot have whatever protections they

[108] *See generally* Maier, *supra* note 104, at 303–20; and Meessen, The International Law on Taking Evidence from, Not in, a Foreign State: The *Anschuetz* and *Messerschmidt* Opinions of the United States Court of Appeals for the Fifth Circuit, Petitioners' Brief in Response to the Solicitor General's Brief for the United States, Anschuetz & Co. v. Mississippi River Bridge Auth., 107 S.Ct. 3223, App. 4 (1987) (cert. granted and case remanded in light of *Aerospatiale*).

[109] In recent years, the systemic aspects of the comity doctrine have been developed primarily by Professor Harold Maier. *See, e.g.*, Maier, *supra* note 104, at 281–85. *See also* Maier, *Extraterritorial Discovery: Cooperation, Coercion and the Hague Convention*, 19 VAND. J. TRANSNAT'L L. 239, 252–55 (1986).

[110] Where a foreign state prohibits compliance with U.S. procedures, it may render those proceedings unfair by making it unreasonable to expect litigants to comply with the court's order. A foreign state may also physically prevent information—e.g., documents—from leaving its territory and thus render ineffective the procedures of the requesting state. In both cases the actions of the situs state prevent the requesting state from achieving the objective of providing fair and effective procedures.

choose. A state may have a wide range of general "interests" in the outcome of any litigation. For example, it may wish to protect persons or enterprises from costs, inconvenience or the necessity of disclosing valuable information,[111] but legal analysis is possible only where there is a standard for evaluating these interests.

Lack of analysis of this issue has allowed room for the assumption that the interests to be balanced are somehow determined or at least influenced by the desires of the states themselves, but the fallacy of this reasoning is obvious. There is no objective means of measuring the subjective interests of states; consequently, a balancing test that attempted to measure them would have no content and would necessarily be discretionary.[112]

The standards for determining which interests are relevant to the comity analysis must therefore be objective; that is, the determination of whether an interest is to be included must be based on objectively ascertainable criteria. This means, first, that the only interests that should be relevant to the comity analysis are the legal interests of the states involved, because only legal interests are objectively ascertainable. Second, only public international law provides a reference framework for applying the comity test, because it alone defines the legal interests of states vis-à-vis each other.[113]

International law is not only the sole means of achieving objectivity in the comity analysis, but also the sole source of generally accepted principles defining the rights, obligations and legitimate expectations of states. If the objective of comity balancing is to accommodate the legitimate interests and expectations of states, it must be guided by international law principles. The issue here is not whether existing norms of conduct under international law have been violated.[114] Rather, a court is asked to look to the principles and processes of international law to determine which interests of states are legally protected. International law is thus used to render guidance in achieving domestic legal objectives.[115]

[111] *See, e.g.*, Gerber, *The Extraterritorial Application of the German Antitrust Laws*, 77 AJIL 756, 776–79 (1983).

[112] Foreign subjective interests may be relevant to the analysis of extraterritorial discovery, but only in a separate context. *See infra* text accompanying notes 151–53. On the problems of trying to combine objective and subjective elements in the same analysis, see Maier, *supra* note 60, at 582–88.

[113] National legal systems cannot provide objectivity in the international context, because they do not regulate the relationships among states and because each is subject to alteration by the state in which it operates.

[114] For discussion of that issue, see text at notes 76–103 *supra*.

[115] Such uses of international law have long been neglected, perhaps as a result of the positivist focus on the existence or nonexistence of specific norms, as well as on the separation of international law analysis from domestic legal analysis. Recently, attention has begun to be paid to the related issue of the role of "international soft law"—i.e., international principles that do not have the force of norms. *See, e.g.*, Baxter, *International Law in "Her Infinite Variety,"* 29 INT'L & COMP. L.Q. 549 (1980); and G. VAN HOOF, RETHINKING THE SOURCES OF INTERNATIONAL LAW 179–91 (1983). *See also* Weil, *Vers une normativité relative en droit international?*, 86 REVUE GÉNÉRALE DE DROIT INTERNATIONAL PUBLIC 5 (1982), *modified, expanded and translated in* 73 AJIL 413 (1983).

United States regulatory interests. A state is entitled under international law to regulate its system of civil procedure as it wishes, provided that in so doing it does not unjustifiably harm the protected interests of foreign states.[116] The interests protected are what may be called "regulatory interests"—the right of a state to control its own domestic policies. For purposes of the comity analysis, therefore, the United States has a legally protected interest in applying its own discovery rules, and it is this interest that is to be balanced against any protected interests of other states.

The U.S. regulatory interest in applying discovery procedures extraterritorially derives from the role of discovery in the U.S. procedural system, which is to secure information for civil litigation.[117] Consequently, the U.S. regulatory interest in any requested discovery is a function of the importance of that information to the litigation; the more important the information is in a given case, the greater the interest of the United States in acquiring it.

Further analysis reveals that discovery actually performs two distinct functions in the U.S. system. One is to obtain reasonably identified evidence for use in proving contested facts (evidence gathering); the other is to *search* for information that may be used to identify such evidence (evidence seeking).[118] These functions represent different degrees of regulatory interest. Where information has been reasonably identified as directly relevant to the outcome of the litigation—i.e., where the source of the information (witness or document) is needed as evidence[119]—the U.S. interest is higher than where it is sought merely to determine whether it might eventually yield admissible evidence.[120]

The distinction between these two functions is important, because one is in accord with the practice of other states, while the other is not. Most states use state power to coerce persons subject to their jurisdiction into producing reasonably identified evidence.[121] Foreign states generally do not, however, allow state power to be used to search for evidence, at least not to the extent that this is done in the United States.[122]

[116] *See, e.g.,* I. BROWNLIE, *supra* note 77, at 298–99.

[117] *See generally* Brazil, *The Adversary Character of Civil Discovery: A Critique and Proposals for Change,* 31 VAND. L. REV. 1295, 1298–1303 (1978).

[118] *See generally* Hickman v. Taylor, 329 U.S. 495, 507 (1947); Lyell Theatre Corp. v. Loews Corp., 91 F.R.D. 97, 99 (W.D.N.Y. 1981) ("The purpose of discovery has been succinctly stated as 1) to narrow the issues; 2) to obtain evidence for use at trial; and 3) to secure information about the existence of evidence"); and Nutt v. Black Hills Stage Lines, Inc., 452 F.2d 480 (8th Cir. 1971). *See also* 8 C. WRIGHT & A. MILLER, FEDERAL PRACTICE AND PROCEDURE §2001 (1970).

[119] The concept of relevance used in the United States often differs dramatically from similar concepts employed in other legal systems. For discussion, see, e.g., Gerber, *supra* note 3, at 761–63.

[120] This is also the position of the new *Restatement. See* RESTATEMENT (THIRD), *supra* note 5, §442 comment *a.*

[121] *See, e.g.,* R. SCHLESINGER, H. BAADE, M. DAMASKA & P. HERZOG, COMPARATIVE LAW 425–33 (5th ed. 1987).

[122] For extensive discussion of the differences between the permissible scope of U.S. discovery and acceptable use of coercive power in the United Kingdom, see, e.g., Rio Tinto Zinc

The interests of foreign states. The interests of foreign states that are to be included in the comity analysis are identified in the *Aerospatiale* decision as "*sovereign* interests."[123] The language specifies that not all interests of a foreign state are to be considered in the analysis, but only those that relate to its sovereignty—i.e., those as to which it is entitled to protection under international law. The opinion thus implicitly requires the use of international law to determine whether interests are sovereign for purposes of the comity analysis.

Claims that U.S. extraterritorial discovery practices impinge on the sovereign interests of foreign states are based on the principle of noninterference.[124] In this context, however, that principle is not used as a source of accepted norms that prohibit defined conduct. Instead, it identifies state interests that may be harmed by particular conduct, thus requiring a balancing of those interests against the interests of the state causing the interference.

Consequently, the principle of noninterference performs two separate, but related, functions in analyzing extraterritorial discovery. It identifies certain state conduct as interference with the rights of a foreign state. In some cases, norms of customary international law have developed that prohibit such conduct, regardless of the interests of the regulating state. With regard to other types of conduct, no such norms have emerged, and a balancing analysis is necessary to determine whether the interference is justified.[125]

Where a U.S. court orders conduct within foreign territory, such an order necessarily interferes with that state's control over its own territory. Where the interference does not violate an existing norm of customary law, the issue is the *degree* of "interference" or "intrusion" that results. This point was made by the Supreme Court in *Aerospatiale* when it said that some orders are "more intrusive" than others.[126] The more the conduct interferes with the situs state's right to control information and persons within its territory, the more serious is the resulting harm for purposes of the comity analysis.

Examples drawn from the opinion illustrate the point.[127] Where the requested discovery merely consists of requests for admissions or interroga-

---

Corp. v. Westinghouse Elec. Corp., [1978] 1 All E.R. 434, [1978] 2 W.L.R. 81, *reprinted in* 17 ILM 38 (1978). For further discussion, see Gerber, *supra* note 3, at 757–69.

[123] *See, e.g., Aerospatiale,* 107 S.Ct. at 2556 (emphasis added).

[124] *See* text at notes 77–103 *supra.*

[125] Although the use of international law that I here advocate—namely, as the central informing principle for domestic comity analysis—is in many ways new, it is clearly supported by modern trends in international law scholarship, particularly by the writings of Professors Myres McDougal, Michael Reisman and other associated scholars of the "Yale school of international law." McDougal and his colleagues have focused attention on the breadth of the international law process and on the interrelatedness of legal and other social processes, and the analysis I am here proposing draws on those insights. *See, e.g.,* McDougal & Reisman, *The Prescribing Function: How International Law Is Made,* 6 YALE STUD. WORLD PUB. ORD. 249 (1980).

[126] *Aerospatiale,* 107 S.Ct. at 2556.

[127] *Id.* at 2555–56.

tories, there would typically be minimal harm to the protected interests of the foreign state.[128] An order to respond in writing to questions generally has little, if any, impact on a state's territorial prerogatives, and therefore such requests typically will encounter little difficulty in a comity analysis.[129]

In contrast, where private documents are required to be made available for inspection within the state or to be removed from the state, there may be considerable interference with the control that the foreign state is entitled to exercise over its territory, depending on the nature of the documents, the number of documents sought and the degree of specificity with which they are identified. As indicated by the Supreme Court,[130] such extensive interference may not be justified by the importance of the documents to the litigation. In each case, therefore, the degree of harm to the legally protected interests of a foreign state must be weighed against the importance of the requested information to the litigation.

Alternative Means of Discovery: The Hague Evidence Convention

The comity analysis also requires consideration of alternative means of obtaining information. Where information can be obtained with reasonable cost and convenience by means that would entail significantly less harm to foreign sovereign interests than discovery procedures, the objective of minimizing harm to protected state interests requires that the former means be used instead of or prior to the latter.

The only significant potential alternative to discovery is the Hague Evidence Convention.[131] Because the United States is a party to the Convention, the procedures it prescribes must be evaluated in the comity analysis if the situs state is also a party. As the Supreme Court held in *Aerospatiale,* a court may require those procedures to be used before resort is had to U.S. discovery rules where the Convention provides a reasonably efficient and convenient means of acquiring the information sought.[132]

Use of the Convention entails no harm to protected interests of a state party because, by definition, that state has agreed to it.[133] Consequently, where these procedures can reasonably be expected to perform the functions otherwise performed by discovery procedures without undue inconvenience to the requesting party, the harm to foreign interests that would result from using discovery procedures cannot be justified. In each case, two issues require analysis: (1) how effective and convenient the procedures of

[128] The degree of harm will depend primarily on the scope of the interrogatories and the type of information requested. The broader the range of the interrogatories and the more politically or economically sensitive the information, the greater the degree of interference.

[129] Interrogatories may, of course, also raise issues of fairness to the litigant that must be analyzed separately. *See* text at notes 62–75 *supra.*

[130] *Aerospatiale,* 107 S.Ct. at 2557.

[131] Information may be obtained from foreign territory through use of letters rogatory, but they do not oblige the situs state to provide the requested information and therefore cannot be viewed as a reasonable alternative to U.S. discovery procedures.

[132] *Aerospatiale,* 107 S.Ct. at 2555.

[133] *Id.* at 2563 (Blackmun, J., dissenting).

the Convention would be in providing the requested information, and (2) how important the requested information is to the litigation.

For many purposes, the Convention clearly does offer a convenient and effective alternative to United States discovery.[134] Where a U.S. court properly requests information, the foreign court generally is required to supply it. In most cases, therefore, the litigant can reasonably rely on production. Moreover, the procedures, for the most part, are easily understood and their effectiveness in a particular case can reasonably be predicted. Finally, the costs of using them are minimal,[135] and compliance burdens are generally limited.[136]

Nevertheless, two potentially significant limitations detract from the utility of the Convention as an alternative to U.S. discovery procedures. First, under the Convention, parties may not search for information to the extent possible under the U.S. rules. Most states take the position that its procedures may only be used to acquire information that a judge has determined to be directly related to issues involved in the litigation.[137]

While this requirement may limit the scope of investigation in some cases, this reduction in scope may be offset by an increase in the ability of the foreign judge to acquire relevant information.[138] Moreover, such limitations in scope are often more apparent than real, because they merely require the United States attorney to specify and identify the requested information more clearly than would be necessary under U.S. rules.[139]

The second limitation concerns the examination of documents under the Convention. Although by its terms the Convention applies to the examination of documents, most states have filed reservations under Article 23 declaring that they "will not execute Letters of Request issued for the purpose of obtaining pre-trial discovery of documents as known in Common

[134] For general discussions of the practical advantages of using the Convention, see, e.g., Augustine, *Obtaining International Judicial Assistance under the Federal Rules and the Hague Convention on the Taking of Evidence Abroad in Civil and Commercial Matters: An Exposition of the Procedures and a Practical Example: In re Westinghouse Uranium Contract Litigation,* 10 GA. J. INT'L & COMP. L. 101 (1980); Platto, *Taking Evidence Abroad for Use in Civil Cases in the United States—A Practical Guide,* 16 INT'L LAW. 575 (1982); and *1969 Delegation Report, supra* note 86, at 806–07. For discussions of the practical aspects of using the Convention to obtain information in particular states, see Borel & Boyd, *Opportunities for and Obstacles to Obtaining Evidence in France for Use in Litigation in the United States,* 13 INT'L LAW. 37 (1979); Collins, *Opportunities for and Obstacles to Obtaining Evidence in England for Use in Litigation in the United States, id.* at 27; and Shemanski, *Obtaining Evidence in the Federal Republic of Germany: The Impact of the Hague Evidence Convention on German-American Judicial Cooperation, 17 id.* at 465 (1983).

[135] *See* 1 B. RISTAU, *supra* note 9, at 225–28. *See also* Note, *The Hague Convention on the Taking of Evidence Abroad in Civil or Commercial Matters—A Comparison with Federal Rules Procedures,* 7 BROOKLYN J. INT'L L. 365, 396–97 (1981).

[136] Technical problems, e.g., translation, associated with gathering information from foreign sources may arise in using the Convention, but such problems are not necessarily greater or lesser than they would be if discovery procedures were used.

[137] *See, e.g.,* 1 B. RISTAU, *supra* note 9, at 229–35.

[138] For discussion of the advantages of having a civil law judge do the questioning, see Langbein, *supra* note 50, at 826–30.

[139] *See, e.g.,* Heck, *supra* note 47, at 234–35; and Shemanski, *supra* note 134, at 470.

Law countries," at least under certain circumstances.[140] This restricts the utility of the Convention, but only to a limited extent. First, not all parties have filed such reservations.[141] Second, many of the reservations are limited in scope, often allowing documents to be acquired where they can be shown to be directly relevant to issues in the litigation.[142] Finally, information about the contents of documents generally can be acquired through oral examination.[143] This oral information can often serve to establish the relevance—hence the accessibility—of the documents themselves.

The comity analysis requires that use of the Convention as an alternative to U.S. discovery procedures be assessed in the context of specific informational needs. Consequently, where particular information is not likely to be obtainable with reasonable convenience through the procedures of the Convention, an additional level of analysis is required.[144] Here the test would be whether the need for the requested information outweighs any harm to the sovereign interests of the situs state that would result from the use of U.S. discovery procedures.

The Expression of Sovereign Interests and the Subjectivism Fallacy

The majority opinion in *Aerospatiale* refers on two occasions to "sovereign interests *expressed* by foreign states."[145] These references implicate an ele-

[140] Art. 23, Hague Evidence Convention, *supra* note 9. *See generally* Note, *supra* note 52, at 73, 84–87.

[141] States that have made reservations include Denmark, Finland, the Federal Republic of Germany, France, Italy, Luxembourg, the Netherlands, Norway, Portugal, Singapore, Sweden and the United Kingdom. 8 MARTINDALE-HUBBELL LAW DIRECTORY 15–21 (1987).

[142] According to the reservation of the United Kingdom, for example:

> In accordance with Article 23 Her Majesty's Government declare that the United Kingdom will not execute Letters of Request issued for the purpose of obtaining pre-trial discovery of documents. Her Majesty's Government further declare that Her Majesty's Government understand "Letter of Request issued for the purpose of obtaining pre-trial discovery of documents" for the purposes of the foregoing Declaration as including any Letter of Request which requires a person:
>
> a. to state what documents relevant to the proceedings to which the Letter of Request relates are, or have been, in his possession, custody, or power; or
>
> b. to produce any documents other than particular documents specified in the Letter of Request as being documents appearing to the request court to be, or to be likely to be, in his possession, custody or powers.

Declarations and Reservations of the United Kingdom, *id.* at 19.

For other reservations with similar provisions, see those of France, Luxembourg, the Netherlands, Norway, Portugal, Singapore and Sweden. *Id.* at 15–21.

[143] There are typically few limits on the right to question witnesses about the contents of documents. In Germany, for example, a witness is required to refresh his recollection about the content of documents, if necessary to have them with him, and to answer fully about their contents. *See generally* Martens, *German Civil Procedure and the Implementation of the Hague Evidence Convention,* 1 INT'L LITIGATION Q. 115, 120 (1985). For discussion of similar procedures in the United Kingdom, see J. LEVINE, DISCOVERY: A COMPARISON BETWEEN ENGLISH AND AMERICAN CIVIL DISCOVERY LAW WITH REFORM PROPOSALS 61–67 (1982).

[144] For information that is not reasonably and conveniently available under the Convention, the analysis is essentially the same as in cases where the situs state is not a party to the Convention.

[145] *Aerospatiale,* 107 S.Ct. at 2555, 2557 (emphasis added).

ment of subjectivism in the analysis that is not only misplaced and misleading, but also inconsistent with an effective analytical framework. As discussed above,[146] a comity analysis can only be effective where it is based on the objective evaluation of legally protected interests; the manner in which they are expressed should not be relevant.

Although "expression" is not explained by the Court, there are two ways that it can come into play. A state may "express" its interests by enacting blocking legislation and by attempting to influence U.S. litigation, whether through appeals to the Department of State[147] or through appearance as amicus curiae.[148] Since an unstructured analysis does not differentiate between objective and subjective issues, one might argue that such actions indicate the intensity of the state's concern and should be accorded weight in the balancing process.

The Supreme Court appears to have envisioned that the expression of interests could be used as a convenient and easily applicable filter to reduce the number of situations in which foreign interests must be considered, which, in turn, would reduce both burdens on the courts and the number of cases in which foreign sovereign interests could "block" the application of U.S. discovery rules. A court can readily determine whether a foreign state has "expressed" its interests and thus can easily filter out many cases.

A structured analytical framework, however, obviates the need for this type of artificial and easily avoidable conceptual filter.[149] In particular, an objective comity analysis gives weight to foreign interests according to readily ascertainable standards and only in a balancing context. The inclusion of subjective elements in the comity analysis would destroy its integrity by requiring courts to attempt to evaluate subjective interests and relate them to objective interests. Moreover, there is no basis for judicial evaluation of such subjective factors, and there is no basis for comparing them or relating them to objective factors.[150]

In addition to rendering judicial decision making discretionary, the inclusion of subjective factors in the analysis of discovery requests would create incentives for foreign states to "express" their interests through blocking legislation and attempts to influence U.S. litigation. Any such response would further impede U.S. policy and interfere with the effectiveness of U.S. litigation.

[146] *See* text at notes 111–15 *supra.*

[147] For discussion, see Oxman, *supra* note 79, at 148 n.39; and Contemporary Practice of the United States, 73 AJIL 669, 678 (1979).

[148] On the use of statements by foreign governments, see Comment, *The Sovereign Compulsion Defense in Antitrust Actions and the Role of Statements by Foreign Governments,* 62 WASH. L. REV. 129, 146–49 (1987).

[149] These references appear to be part of the Court's response to the previous practice of utilizing the foreign sovereign compulsion defense to analyze blocking legislation. For discussion, see text at notes 156–172 *infra.*

[150] A state's position may, of course, be relevant to the analysis of state practice under customary international law, because customary international law develops through the responses of states to the actions of other states. A state's actions, however, are only relevant under certain circumstances and only when related to the actions of other states. For a leading discussion of the formation of customary international law, see, e.g., A. D'AMATO, THE CONCEPT OF CUSTOM IN INTERNATIONAL LAW (1971).

FOREIGN RELATIONS INTERESTS OF THE UNITED STATES

While the degree of importance attached by a foreign state to particular conduct or litigation should not be a factor in the comity analysis, a foreign state's subjective concerns may affect the foreign relations of the United States. Consequently, where the U.S. Government considers that an extraterritorial discovery order would harm important foreign relations objectives and asks the court to limit discovery accordingly, the court should normally accede to the request. This treatment of foreign relations issues accords with U.S. law, which requires that the courts generally defer to the executive branch in matters relating to U.S. foreign relations.[151]

In contrast to the comity analysis, this component of the proposed analytical framework does not involve the accommodation of conflicting state interests. It is based on the recognition, however, that at times discovery practices will affect the foreign relations interests of the United States, and it provides a means of considering such political issues. The subjective concerns of a foreign state are taken into account, if at all, by the responsible political officials of the United States Government.[152]

When the analysis is structured in this way, the courts are not placed in the position of having to make political judgments. Political issues are relevant only if the U.S. Government has determined that a particular discovery order should be modified. In those presumably rare cases, the court has only two functions. It must assure that the Government has reasonable grounds for its request, and it must fashion discovery orders that minimize any harm to the fairness rights of individual litigants.[153]

ANALYSIS OF FOREIGN BLOCKING STATUTES

Because foreign states can easily impede U.S. policy by enacting and enforcing blocking legislation,[154] the treatment of such legislation is central to effective analysis of extraterritorial discovery practices. Unfortunately,

[151] *See, e.g.,* United States v. Belmont, 301 U.S. 324, 330 (1937); Oetjen v. Central Leather Co., 246 U.S. 297, 302 (1918); Tel-Oren v. Libyan Arab Republic, 726 F.2d 774, 801–08 (D.C. Cir. 1984), *cert. denied,* 470 U.S. 1003 (1985); and United States v. First Nat'l City Bank, 396 F.2d 897, 901 (2d Cir. 1968) ("[C]ourts must take care not to impinge upon the prerogatives and responsibilities of the political branches of the government in the extremely sensitive and delicate area of foreign affairs"). *See generally* Berger, *The Presidential Monopoly of Foreign Relations,* 71 MICH. L. REV. 1 (1972).

[152] For a discussion of government decision making involving these issues, see Maier, *Resolving Extraterritorial Conflicts, or "There and Back Again,"* 25 VA. J. INT'L L. 7, 25–33 (1985).

[153] In effect, this will require judges to keep discovery orders as narrow as is consistent with legitimate government purposes.

[154] According to one court, "A blocking statute is a law passed by the foreign government imposing a penalty upon a national for complying with a foreign court's discovery request." *In re* Anschuetz & Co., 754 F.2d 602, 614 n.29 (5th Cir. 1985). For discussion of blocking legislation, see, e.g., 1 J. ATWOOD & K. BREWSTER, ANTITRUST AND AMERICAN BUSINESS ABROAD §4.17 (1981). As of 1986, 15 states had enacted legislation designed to counter U.S. efforts to secure the production of documents within their territories. *See* RESTATEMENT (THIRD), *supra* note 5, §442 Reporters' Note 1. For a list of such legislation, see *Bibliography—International Discovery,* 16 N.Y.U. J. INT'L L. & POL. 1217, 1223–26 (1984).

however, judicial analysis of blocking legislation has been fundamentally flawed,[155] and the *Aerospatiale* decision did not significantly improve the situation. The Supreme Court's misguided analysis of this issue can be understood only in light of the conceptual framework to which the Court was responding.

Prior to *Aerospatiale,* blocking legislation was analyzed primarily by application of the so-called foreign sovereign compulsion defense.[156] Originally developed in the context of antitrust enforcement, this doctrine provides that conduct compelled by a foreign sovereign is immune from prosecution in the United States.[157] The defense has been viewed as an extension of the act of state doctrine,[158] and it also has been supported on grounds of fairness and comity.[159]

Applying the basic idea behind this doctrine to extraterritorial discovery,[160] the courts have held that discovery orders must be modified so as not to require a national or resident of a foreign state to engage in conduct on foreign territory that is prohibited by that state.[161] The foreign sovereign compulsion defense thus has served as a convenient conceptual device to limit the reach of U.S. discovery jurisdiction.

Use of the defense to analyze discovery issues, however, suffers from a fundamental conceptual flaw because it does not provide a mechanism for

[155] *See, e.g.,* Note, *Foreign Nondisclosure Laws and Domestic Discovery Orders in Antitrust Litigation,* 88 YALE L.J. 612 (1979); Note, *Limitations on the Federal Judicial Power to Compel Acts Violating Foreign Law,* 63 COLUM. L. REV. 1441 (1963); Comment, *Ordering Production of Documents from Abroad in Violation of Foreign Law,* 31 U. CHI. L. REV. 791 (1964); and Note, *Compelling Production of Documents from Abroad in U.S. Antitrust Litigation: Recent Developments in the Law Concerning the Foreign Illegality Excuse for Non-Production,* 14 VA. J. INT'L L. 747 (1974). *See also 1985 Special Commission Report, supra* note 87, at 1675.

[156] For discussion of this defense, see Meal, *Governmental Compulsion as a Defense under United States and European Community Antitrust Laws,* 20 COLUM. J. TRANSNAT'L L. 51 (1981); Rosdeitcher, *Foreign Blocking Statutes and U.S. Discovery: A Conflict of National Policies,* 16 N.Y.U. J. INT'L L. & POL. 1061 (1984); Timberg, *Sovereign Immunity and Act of State Defenses, Traditional Boycotts and Economic Coercion,* 55 TEX. L. REV. 1, 20–27 (1976); and Note, *International Law—Extraterritoriality—Antitrust Law—Development of the Defense of Sovereign Compulsion,* 69 MICH. L. REV. 888 (1971).

[157] *See, e.g.,* Interamerican Refining Corp. v. Texaco Maracaibo, 307 F.Supp. 1291, 1296–99 (D. Del. 1970) (proof of compulsion by Venezuelan regulatory authorities served as a defense to U.S. antitrust action).

[158] *See, e.g.,* Timberlane Lumber Co. v. Bank of America, 549 F.2d 597 (9th Cir. 1976); and United States v. Watchmakers of Switz. Information Center, Inc., 1963 Trade Cas. (CCH) 70,600, 77,456 (S.D.N.Y. 1963). For discussion, see Meal, *supra* note 156, at 77–82.

[159] *See, e.g.,* United States v. Vetco, Inc., 691 F.2d 1281 (9th Cir.), *cert. denied,* 454 U.S. 1098 (1981) (on fairness); United States v. First Nat'l City Bank, 396 F.2d 897, 902 (2d Cir. 1968); and Application of Chase Nat'l Bank, 297 F.2d 611, 613 (2d Cir. 1962) (on comity).

[160] The same basic justifications have been used regarding discovery. *See, e.g.,* Compagnie Francaise d'Assurance pour le Commerce Exterieur v. Phillips Petroleum Co., 105 F.R.D. 16, 35 (S.D.N.Y. 1984); and Schroeder v. Lufthansa German Airlines, 39 Fed. R. Serv. 2d 211, 212 (N.D. Ill. 1983).

[161] *See, e.g.,* United States v. First Nat'l Bank of Chicago, 699 F.2d 341, 345 (7th Cir. 1983); United States v. Vetco, Inc., 691 F.2d 1281, 1287–88 (9th Cir.), *cert. denied,* 454 U.S. 1098 (1981); and FTC v. Compagnie de Saint-Gobain-Pont-a-Mousson, 636 F.2d 1300 (D.C. Cir. 1980).

accommodating conflicting interests. By merely prohibiting discovery where foreign legislation satisfies certain conditions, the doctrine refers only to the interests of the situs state and does not reflect those of the requesting state. Even more importantly, it does not consider the effects of such legislation on individual litigants.

Indeed, use of this analysis encourages foreign states to enact blocking legislation; it appears to have played a significant role in the increase of such statutes.[162] Consequently, use of the doctrine not only has been analytically flawed, but also has tended to increase the harm that it should have diminished.

To minimize the consequences of using this flawed analysis, United States courts have severely restricted the scope of application of the doctrine.[163] For example, it has been held that the defense applies only if the defendant can show that it has in good faith taken all reasonable steps to avoid application of the foreign statute.[164] Moreover, the defense has been held to apply only where compliance with the discovery request would require violation of a penal statute[165] that is regularly enforced.[166]

In *Aerospatiale* the Supreme Court implicitly rejected use of the foreign sovereign compulsion defense to analyze blocking legislation. Arguing that "blind obedience" to blocking legislation would subject U.S. courts to "control" by foreign states,[167] the Court held that such legislation did not automatically block U.S. discovery orders. Instead, the Court included blocking legislation within the "particularized analysis" of discovery requests.

In rejecting foreign sovereign compulsion as the conceptual tool for analyzing blocking legislation, the Court eliminated a major obstacle to effective analysis of this issue. The Court went on, however, to undermine much of the improvement this step entailed and to create new uncertainty. Apparently still responding to the conceptual framework it was rejecting,[168] the

[162] For discussion, see 1 E. NEREP, *supra* note 54, at 589–603 (1983).

[163] On the limitations of the defense, see Timberg, *supra* note 156, at 23–27; and Comment, *supra* note 148, at 134–44.

[164] *See* United States v. First Nat'l Bank of Chicago, 699 F.2d 341, 346 (7th Cir. 1983); United States v. Vetco, Inc., 644 F.2d 1324, 1332 (9th Cir. 1981); and Graco Inc. v. Kremlin, Inc. & SKM, 101 F.R.D. 503, 516 (N.D. Ill. 1984). *See also* Timberg, *supra* note 156, at 23.

[165] *See, e.g.*, Societe Internationale pour Participations Industrielles et Commerciales, S.A. v. Rogers, 357 U.S. 197, 211 (1958) ("It is hardly debatable that fear of criminal prosecution constitutes a weighty excuse for nonproduction"). *But see* RESTATEMENT (THIRD), *supra* note 5, §441 comment *c* (which indicates that the foreign sovereign compulsion defense applies where "the requirement or prohibition by the first state is backed by criminal or civil liability or both").

[166] *See, e.g.*, Application of Chase Manhattan Bank, 297 F.2d 611, 613 (2d Cir. 1962); and Remington Products, Inc. v. North Am. Phillips Corp., 107 F.R.D. 642, 643 (D. Conn. 1985).

[167] *Aerospatiale,* 107 S.Ct. at 2556 n.29.

[168] One part of the Court's analysis involved a fundamental misunderstanding of the international jurisdictional issue. According to the Court, "[T]he language of the statute, if taken literally, would appear to represent an extraordinary exercise of *legislative jurisdiction* by the Republic of France over a United States District Judge . . ." (emphasis added). *Id.* The

Court stated that blocking legislation could only be considered "to the extent that its terms and its enforcement identify the nature of the sovereign interests in nondisclosure of specific kinds of material."[169] The Court apparently intended to use this interest-specification requirement to distinguish between "substantive rules of law" and legislation designed to frustrate U.S. discovery efforts.[170] But the Court failed to recognize that such a requirement is unnecessary where blocking legislation is subsumed in a particularized analysis of all the facts of a given situation.

The Court also failed to perceive a basic inconsistency in its reasoning. At the same time that the *Aerospatiale* opinion established a restrictive and formalistic interest-specification requirement virtually eliminating blocking legislation from consideration in the comity analysis,[171] it required courts to consider fairness to litigants. Yet blocking legislation often has a direct impact on the fairness of discovery orders, and thus the interest-specification requirement may be inconsistent with the objective the Court intended to promote. The lack of conceptual structure in the *Aerospatiale* analysis appears to have concealed from the Court this fundamental flaw in its approach to blocking legislation.

Where, as proposed here, blocking legislation is treated primarily as an issue of fairness to litigants,[172] such inconsistency and confusion are eliminated. The analysis focuses instead on the point of impact of blocking legislation on a particular fact situation—namely, its effect on the fairness of the proceedings—and it reduces incentives for foreign states to use blocking legislation to impede U.S. policy.

IV. Concluding Perspectives

Extraterritorial Discovery and American Law

Where a U.S. court applies discovery procedures to information located in a foreign state, domestic policy objectives can be achieved only with the cooperation of that state. In addition to being able to prohibit compliance with extraterritorial discovery orders, foreign states have every right to

---

concept of legislative jurisdiction refers, however, to the legal capacity of a state to attach legal consequences to particular conduct. The French blocking statute merely attaches legal consequences to the actions of individuals subject to its jurisdiction. It does not purport to attach legal consequences to the conduct of a U.S. judge.

169 *Id.*

170 This distinction derives from the new *Restatement. See* RESTATEMENT (THIRD), *supra* note 5, §442 Reporters' Note 5.

171 Existing blocking statutes do not typically meet the interest-specification requirements. *See, e.g.,* Law Concerning the Communication of Documents or Information of an Economic, Commercial, Industrial, Financial or Technical Nature to Aliens, Whether Natural or Juristic Persons, No. 80-538, 1980 J.O. 1799 (France); and Protection of Trading Interests Act, 1980, ch. 11 (United Kingdom). For discussion, see Lowe, *Blocking Extraterritorial Jurisdiction: The British Protection of Trading Interests Act, 1980,* 75 AJIL 257 (1981); Herzog, *The 1980 French Law on Documents and Information, id.* at 382; and Toms, *The French Response to the Extraterritorial Application of United States Antitrust Laws,* 15 INT'L LAW. 585 (1981).

172 *See* text at notes 62–75 *supra.*

prevent it. This interdependence of states fundamentally alters the legal context in which U.S. courts must operate; to achieve procedural fairness, U.S. courts must exercise their power to order extraterritorial discovery on the basis of principles that effectively accommodate the interests of foreign states.

In its *Aerospatiale* decision, the United States Supreme Court recognized the need to establish principles of restraint that would reflect both the international context of extraterritorial discovery and the interests of foreign states and litigants. It also generally recognized that achieving its goals would require reference to the legitimate expectations of states under international law. The Court failed, however, to provide a conceptual framework within which these goals could be pursued effectively. Moreover, the Court failed to recognize that achieving U.S. goals regarding extraterritorial discovery requires not only appropriate substantive principles, but also appropriate analytical methods.

The analytical framework proposed in this article is designed to achieve the goals of accommodation and effective justice that were identified in *Aerospatiale.* Both the structure and the substance of the proposed framework are specifically adapted to the new legal context created by U.S. extraterritorial discovery practices.

The proposed framework responds to the methodological requirements of this context by providing sufficient conceptual structure to allow analytical clarity as well as reasonable predictability and flexibility in decision making. It provides for analytical clarity by identifying the interests, policies and principles involved in the often complex legal and factual situations created by extraterritorial discovery requests and by relating them to a coherent decision-making framework. It thus separates issues that tend to be mixed together. The foreign relations interests of the United States, the need for accommodation with foreign states, fairness concerns and international law norms—all involve distinct policy goals and thus require separate analysis related to the ends to be served. Where these complexes of issues are not separately identified and courts are asked merely to balance interests on an undefined and unstructured basis, the underlying objectives are unlikely to be given consistently adequate consideration.

The framework of analysis proposed here responds to the need to accommodate foreign interests by providing information to foreign states concerning the factors that courts will consider in reaching decisions on extraterritorial discovery. It assures those states that their interests will be evaluated according to a particular set of principles and allows them reasonably to assess probable judicial responses to particular situations and to actions they might take—e.g., the enactment of blocking legislation.

The substantive principles that inform the analysis are also specifically adapted to the legal context of extraterritorial discovery. The issue of blocking legislation is analyzed, for example, at its specific point of impact on those affected, namely, by reference to its effect on the ability of a litigant to comply with a U.S. discovery order.

Of particular importance is the analysis of comity. Whereas comity is frequently either applied without conceptual structure or given content by reference to vague "general interests," here its content is derived from the only set of principles whose use can make it effective—i.e., principles of international law. This use of international law is unfamiliar because it treats international law not as a source of specific norms of conduct that either are or are not violated, but as an informing principle for domestic decision making. It recognizes that international legal processes determine the expectations of states regarding the activities of other states and therefore must be the cornerstone of any domestic legal analysis that attempts to accommodate those expectations.

ACHIEVING AN EFFECTIVE FRAMEWORK OF ANALYSIS

Achieving widespread acceptance of an analytical framework such as the one proposed here may be as difficult as it is important. The sheer range of factors that may be affected by judicial decisions involving extraterritorial discovery may be an obstacle to the rapid development of a cohesive framework of analysis by the lower courts. An order applying U.S. discovery rules to information located abroad may affect several types of state interests of the United States, a variety of foreign state interests and the interests of actual and potential foreign and domestic litigants. Courts operating without a structured and comprehensive framework of analysis may be inclined to make ad hoc decisions based on factors that appear important in the particular case. Judicial development of a principled analysis may therefore be quite slow.

Judicial structuring will also be impeded by the general lack of opportunity for appellate review of discovery orders. Appellate court opinions are the primary means of developing legal principles in the U.S. system, but lower court rulings relating to extraterritorial discovery will typically be subject to review only where they are without reasonable foundation.[173] As a consequence, appellate opinions may not perform their normal role in developing conceptual structure.[174]

Under these circumstances, inductive generalizations based on limited trial court experience may be particularly misleading. For example, factors not considered or misunderstood in a series of trial court decisions may erroneously be omitted from general principles based on those decisions. Similarly, erroneous interpretations of factual situations by lower courts may be perpetuated in future cases.

[173] *See* 8 C. WRIGHT & A. MILLER, *supra* note 118, §2006; and 15 *id.* §3914 (1976). *See also* Greyhound Lines, Inc. v. Miller, 402 F.2d 134, 143 (8th Cir. 1968).

[174] Legal scholarship may aid in the development of structure. Because legal commentators are not subject to the constraints imposed by particular fact situations, they can more easily focus on the development of the principles of analysis. Legal literature may thus be a central source of information about what lower courts are doing, as well as a means of identifying patterns in the resulting data.

Given these obstacles to developing an effective analytical framework through adjudication alone, achieving the goals of *Aerospatiale* may require that elements of structure be prescribed through legislation and/or international cooperation. It must be emphasized that the objective is not to provide fixed rules, but to establish general principles that can guide the adjudicative process.

The most direct and effective means of establishing such principles would be to include them in the Federal Rules of Civil Procedure and in analogous state procedural codes. Many of the relevant principles—e.g., the requirement of procedural fairness—are not open to serious question. Consequently, the main effect of prescribing a framework of analysis would be to clarify the applicability of the principles, to establish their interrelationships and, in so doing, to facilitate their effective use.[175]

Analytical principles may also be established through international cooperation. For example, the United States could make agreements with foreign governments on either a bilateral or a multilateral basis concerning principles to be applied to the evaluation of discovery requests.[176] The agreements could designate the framework for analyzing discovery requests involving particular countries or identify the state interests to be considered.

REDUCING CONFLICTS: RESTRAINTS AND ALTERNATIVES

Under the current international legal system, the development of effective legal principles to accommodate the interests affected by the extraterritorial application of U.S. discovery procedures must occur, if at all, in the courts of the United States, because they are virtually the only judicial forums for evaluating these issues. The effort to develop an effective framework of analysis under U.S. law thus becomes particularly critical. Nevertheless, accommodation by means of U.S. litigation is likely to be difficult, costly and time-consuming, owing to the extent and variety of conflicting interests and the inherent limitations on the effective adjudication of such issues by national courts. Consequently, the need to fashion an analytical framework that can perform this function effectively should not obscure the importance of efforts to reduce the need for such litigation.

Through bilateral and/or multilateral agreements states themselves can provide or improve alternatives to U.S. discovery procedures and thus re-

[175] An additional benefit of the process of prescribing general principles is that it may be combined with policy analysis of the importance of pursuing particular objectives. Congress and/or the Supreme Court can face the full range of issues and ask how U.S. state power should be employed in the context of extraterritorial discovery.

[176] For example, foreign governments could provide information on their own interests and procedural systems, and thus make U.S. proceedings less burdensome, less costly and more effective. In addition, foreign states could enter into agreements with the United States about procedures and principles they would apply to U.S. letters of request, and thus allow U.S. courts more effectively to evaluate the consequences of requiring use of the Hague Evidence Convention.

duce incentives for the extraterritorial application of those procedures and perhaps even limit its permissible scope.[177] In particular, the Hague Evidence Convention could be revised to improve its attractiveness to U.S. litigants, and its use could even be required under specified circumstances.[178]

* * * *

The United States has chosen to utilize procedures to obtain information located abroad for use in civil litigation that most foreign countries consider unacceptable, at least under some circumstances. Nevertheless, because the United States depends on the cooperation of foreign states to achieve its domestic objectives, the analysis applied by its courts must reflect this interdependence.

To the extent, therefore, that the U.S. legal system develops an effective mechanism for accommodating the interests affected by the extraterritorial application of U.S. discovery procedures, the system of international relationships on which the United States depends for achieving its policy goals will be improved and impediments to its policies will be reduced. To the extent, however, that U.S. courts treat decisions on extraterritorial discovery as exercises in discretionary justice and/or consistently favor U.S. litigants or interests, United States extraterritorial discovery practices will continue to be a source of unfairness, conflict, uncertainty and waste.

177 For discussion of different interpretations of the Hague Evidence Convention and suggestions for possible improvements, see Gerber, *supra* note 3, at 779–88.

178 For example, the signatory states could narrow the scope of permissible reservations under Article 23, which would clarify a source of conflict, eliminate confusion and uncertainty, and increase the usefulness of the Convention for American litigators.

NOTES AND COMMENTS

Further Thoughts on the Chambers Procedure of the International Court of Justice

1. The Statute of the International Court of Justice provides for various kinds of Chambers. The special Chambers for dealing with "particular categories of cases; for example, labour cases and cases relating to transit and communications," set up on an ad hoc basis (Art. 26, para. 1), originated in the similar Chambers contemplated by the Statute of the Permanent Court of International Justice, which were preconstituted to meet possible postwar requirements for the implementation of the Treaty of Versailles and the other Treaties of Peace, but were never employed in that Court's history of nearly 20 years. There is another type of Chamber, that of summary procedure (Art. 29), which was also inaugurated by the old Court but was employed only once in its history.[1] Neither of these two types of Chambers has ever been resorted to in the International Court of Justice. The Chamber that Judge Schwebel discusses in his recent *Journal* article is an *ad hoc* Chamber for dealing with a particular case, which may be formed at any time by the Court (Art. 26, para. 2), but no such Chamber was known to the old Court.[2]

2. One of the main problems of the *ad hoc* Chamber, as Judge Schwebel points out,[3] is related to Article 17, paragraph 2 of the 1978 Rules of Court, which provides: "the President shall ascertain [the parties'] views regarding the composition of the Chamber, and shall report to the Court accordingly."[4] This provision may be traced to Article 26, paragraph 1 (then a newly introduced provision) of the 1972 Rules of Court, which stated: "the President shall consult the agents of the parties regarding the composition of the Chamber, and shall report to the Court accordingly."[5] Criticism of this procedure seems to spring from the apprehension—already evident in the softening from "consult" to "ascertain"—that, if the requirement of the President's inquiry regarding the composition of the *ad hoc* Chamber is meant to signal to the parties that they should propose names of judges, the Court will be dictated to by the parties in the election of the Chamber.

3. As a preliminary to the elections of the Chamber for the case of *Delimitation of the Maritime Boundary in the Gulf of Maine Area,* the Chamber for the *Frontier Dispute* (Burkina Faso/Mali) case and two other recently constituted Chambers, the President did ascertain the views of the parties

[1] Treaty of Neuilly, Article 179, Annex, Paragraph 4 (Interpretation), 1924 PCIJ (ser. A) No. 3 (Judgment of Sept. 12); Interpretation of Judgment No. 3, 1925 PCIJ (ser. A) No. 4 (Judgment of Mar. 26).

[2] Schwebel, *Ad Hoc Chambers of the International Court of Justice,* 81 AJIL 831, 838–43 (1987).

[3] *Id.*

[4] *Reprinted in* 73 AJIL 748, 753 (1979).

[5] *Reprinted in* 67 AJIL 195, 203 (1973).

"regarding the *composition* of the Chamber," as the Order for the constitution of each Chamber clearly indicated.[6] The question whether the parties' views concerning the *names* of the judges to constitute the Chamber were ascertained was not expressly addressed by the terms of the respective Orders (Constitution of Chamber), though it could hardly have been otherwise. Furthermore, it is not on official record whether in fact all of these Chambers were composed in accordance with the views of the parties. In the *Gulf of Maine* case, the only authentic indication available with regard to the election of this Chamber was given by my declaration attached to that Order (Constitution of Chamber) of January 20, 1982, where I stated that "it should in my view have been made known that the Court, for reasons best known to itself, has approved the composition of the Chamber entirely in accordance with the latest wishes of the Parties."[7] In connection with the case of the *Land, Island and Maritime Frontier Dispute* (El Salvador/Honduras), Judge Schwebel observed, in quoting my declaration appended to the Order (Constitution of Chamber) of May 8, 1987, that that declaration "may imply that, in this case, [the] process [of election], in [Oda's] view, was not [judicially impartial]."[8]

4. On what ground does the Court under Article 17, paragraph 3 of the Rules of Court elect the judges to compose a Chamber? While, under the Statute of the old Court, consideration of representation of "the main forms of civilization and the principal legal systems of the world" (Art. 9 of the 1920 PCIJ Statute) was to have been assured for the Chambers for labor cases and the cases relating to transit and communications, these requirements were not retained for special Chambers of a similar nature under the International Court of Justice. Moreover, these factors were not relevant from the outset for the Chambers of Summary Procedure of the old Court; the present Court does not seem to take account of any such factor in electing the standing members of the Chamber of Summary Procedure each year. For an *ad hoc* Chamber (this being an innovation of the present Court), these representative requirements are not mentioned either in the Statute or in the Rules of Court.

In the case of all four of the *ad hoc* Chambers that have been constituted during recent years, consideration of "the main forms of civilization and the principal legal systems of the world" apparently was not in the minds of the parties in proposing the judges to sit on the Chamber or of the Court as a whole in electing the Chamber. Excluding national and *ad hoc* judges, the Chamber for the *Gulf of Maine* case had three Western European judges (from France, the Federal Republic of Germany and Italy); the Chamber for

[6] Delimitation of the Maritime Boundary in the Gulf of Maine Area (Can. v. U.S.), Constitution of Chamber, 1982 ICJ REP. 3 (Order of Jan. 20); Frontier Dispute (Burkina Faso/Mali), Constitution of Chamber, 1985 ICJ REP. 6 (Order of Apr. 3); Elettronica Sicula S.p.A. (ELSI) (U.S./Italy), Constitution of Chamber, 1987 ICJ REP. 3 (Order of Mar. 2); Land, Island and Maritime Frontier Dispute (El. Sal./Hond.), Constitution of Chamber, 1987 ICJ REP. 10 (Order of May 8).

[7] 1982 ICJ REP. at 10 (Oda, J., declaration).

[8] Schwebel, *supra* note 2, at 848.

the *Frontier Dispute* (Burkina Faso/Mali) case, one African (Algeria), one Eastern European (Poland) and one Latin American (Argentina); the Chamber for the *Elettronica Sicula S.p.A. (ELSI)* case (U.S./Italy), two Asians (India and Japan) and one Western European (United Kingdom) (one of the Asians was the then President of the Court); and the Chamber for the *El Salvador/Honduras* case, one Latin American (Brazil), one Asian (Japan) and one Western European (United Kingdom). This record suggests that no consistent geographical consideration has guided the choice of the judges of the Chambers. It may also be asked, when there are five main regions according to United Nations practice, by what criteria is the Court to choose three judges from among these five regions?

5. What, then, should the decisive factor be in electing the judges to constitute an *ad hoc* Chamber, if it is not to be the consideration of "representation of the main forms of civilization and the principal legal systems of the world"? Should it be the political beliefs or the personal abilities of the judges? Or can the consideration that, for reasons of the equitable apportionment of work among judges, a judge should not sit in more than one Chamber at one time be a ground for rejecting a judge? There is no basis for the Court to disregard the wishes of the parties on the grounds of, for example, the personal resistance of some judges to other judges in the Court. I myself cannot believe that anything other than the views of the parties can reasonably be taken into account by the Court in composing the Chamber.

6. Irrespective of whether the parties' views that "the President shall ascertain" under Article 17, paragraph 2 of the Rules of Court should or should not include the actual names of the judges to constitute the Chamber, the parties cannot be denied the opportunity of expressing their views on the concrete composition of the Chamber. I am not suggesting that the Court should relinquish its ultimate power to elect judges of its choice, as corroborated by Article 17, paragraph 3 of the Rules of Court. A judge proposed by the parties may be unable to sit on a Chamber because of health or other legitimate reasons, or may be disqualified under Article 24 of the Statute. Yet there is a clear and cogent probability that, if the parties to any dispute decide to come to an *ad hoc* Chamber instead of the full Court, this will be because, as in the case of an arbitration, they do not want to see the dispute adjudged by a court whose composition may not wholly suit them.

7. If the selection of the judges in the Chamber is made in disregard of the wishes of the parties, they will certainly go to arbitration instead, as the agreements between Canada and the United States in the *Gulf of Maine* case indicated in terms.[9] While the parties to a case brought before the full Court may be held to a binding acceptance of jurisdiction, this is not possible for parties whose acceptance is conditional pending the formation of a Chamber. The jurisdiction of a Chamber has always been based on the

[9] Treaty to Submit to Binding Dispute Settlement the Delimitation of the Maritime Boundary in the Gulf of Maine Area, Canada–United States, with annexed agreements, Mar. 29, 1979, TIAS No. 10,204, Art. II.

immediate consensus of the parties, as the Statute clearly indicates in Article 26, paragraph 3 that "[c]ases shall be heard and determined by the chambers . . . if the parties so request." There is little which can be done to prevent that consensus from dissolving if the parties are dissatisfied with the results of the election held within the Court. I stated my views on the procedure for the election to the Chamber in my declaration in the *El Salvador/Honduras* case as follows:

> The Court, being sovereign in judicial proceedings, is free to choose any composition it likes; yet the possibility must also be borne in mind that sovereign States have the legal right to withdraw a case if they prefer a composition different from that determined by the Court. In practical terms, therefore, it is inevitable, if a chamber is to be viable, that its composition must result from a consensus between the Parties and the Court. To ensure that viability, it accordingly behoves the Court to take account of the views of the Parties when proceeding to the election.[10]

In fact, this view is nothing new. Judge Jiménez de Aréchaga suggested in his 1972 article, which Judge Schwebel rightly quoted:

> [I]t is difficult to conceive that in normal circumstances those Members who have been suggested by the parties would not be elected. For that it would be necessary for a majority of the Members of the Court to decide to disregard the expressed wishes of the parties. This would be highly unlikely since it would simply result in compelling the parties to resort to an outside arbitral tribunal or even to abandon their intention to seek a judicial settlement of the dispute.[11]

Where they are not prepared to resort to the full Court, the alternatives facing the parties in dispute are: namely, to choose either an *ad hoc* Chamber, whose judges they themselves name, or an arbitration, whose institution is established by the parties.

8. In sum, I submit that an *ad hoc* Chamber of the International Court of Justice may in some measure be equated to an arbitral tribunal that may be set up by an agreement of the states in dispute, although, unlike an arbitration, where the rules of procedure may be determined for each individual case, the proceedings of an *ad hoc* Chamber are governed by the firmly established procedure of the Court and, in addition, the expenses borne by the parties may be less onerous because of the use of the full facilities of the Court. However, the most important difference is that a case submitted to an *ad hoc* Chamber is adjudged in the same way as proceedings before the full Court and is concluded with a judgment that has the same effect as one rendered by the full Court. The *ad hoc* Chamber, a new institution employed by the International Court of Justice, should be examined from this point of view. In other words, it should be asked if it is appropriate for an *ad hoc* Chamber, which in its genesis and orientation so resembles an arbitral

[10] 1987 ICJ REP. at 13 (Oda, J., declaration).

[11] Jiménez de Aréchaga, *The Amendments to the Rules of Procedure of the International Court of Justice*, 67 AJIL 1, 2–3 (1973), *quoted in* Schwebel, *supra* note 2, at 841.

tribunal, to be able to give a judgment, elements of which, like the judgments of the Court as a whole, constitute jurisprudence of the Court.

9. In this regard, it may be pertinent to examine the manner in which the concept of an *ad hoc* Chamber, unknown to the Permanent Court of International Justice, was introduced in the Statute of the new Court. At the Committee of Jurists that met in Washington in April 1945 to reexamine the Statute of the Court, the Statute of the old Court was only modestly revised.[12] The United States submitted a proposal, containing an additional paragraph in Article 26, which read: "The Court may from time to time form one or more chambers for dealing with particular cases or with particular categories of cases. . . . If the parties so request, cases will be heard and determined by such chambers."[13] In the introductory note to this document, the following explanation was given for this particular provision: "Provision is made for the establishment of chambers, superseding the special chambers provided for by Articles 26 and 27 of the present Statute." The United Kingdom made the following suggestion regarding Chambers: "*Articles 26 and 27.* As the special chambers for labour and transit cases have never been employed, it is suggested that these provisions should be replaced by conferring a general faculty on the Court to constitute special chambers in such cases as may seem appropriate."[14]

The committee, under the chairmanship of Green H. Hackworth, who later became a judge and President of the Court, held discussions on the Chamber, in which he explained that

> in the United States proposals Article 26 of the present Statute is omitted and . . . two short paragraphs are substituted.
>
> . . . .
>
> The Chairman thought . . . Articles 26 and 27 of the Statute have never been used. Under the United States proposals, chambers of the Court are made available to deal with any type of case. He suggested that the relevant articles of the United States proposals should be read together before reaching a decision.
>
> . . . .
>
> Ambassador Castro (El Salvador) . . . agreed to the United States proposal on the understanding that labor cases may freely be brought before the Court on the same footing as other cases . . . .
>
> . . . .
>
> Minister Novikov (Soviet Union) considered that the American proposal was intended to deal with all classes of cases and, therefore, should be supported.[15]

The Chairman appointed a subcommittee to submit a report on this article.[16] The subcommittee unanimously recommended that Article 26 should be revised as follows:

[12] 14 UNCIO Docs. (1945).

[13] Doc. Jurist 5, G/5, *id.* at 323, 334.

[14] Doc. Jurist 14, DP/4, *id.* at 314, 317.

[15] Doc. Jurist 46(22), G35, *id.* at 117, 122–23.

[16] *Id.* at 124.

> The Court may from time to time form one or more chambers, composed of . . . judges, for dealing with particular cases or with particular categories of cases, such as labor cases and cases relating to transit and communications. If the parties so request, such cases will be heard and determined by those chambers.[17]

The committee continued its debate.

> [Judge Hudson] thought the subcommittee was proposing a wholly different system when it provided for *ad hoc* appointment of chambers with the approval of the parties. . . .
>
> . . . .
>
> . . . [Judge Hudson] thought that there might be an advantage in having *ad hoc* chambers if the number of judges available fell below a quorum for the full Court.
>
> . . . .
>
> Mr. Bathurst (United Kingdom), Rapporteur of this subcommittee, explained its report. The subcommittee recommended that the provisions in Articles 26 and 27 for labor, transit, and communication chambers should be replaced by a general provision permitting the Court to establish chambers to deal with particular cases or particular classes of cases. . . .
>
> Ambassador Cordova (Mexico) said . . . that it might be desirable to distinguish between *ad hoc* chambers in which the number of judges was left open and chambers to deal with particular classes of cases for which the number of judges might be fixed.
>
> . . . .
>
> Judge Hudson suggested the desirability of adopting Ambassador Cordova's suggestion regarding chambers. . . .
>
> Dr. Moneim-Riad Bey (Egypt) felt that it was necessary to distinguish between pre-existing and *ad hoc* chambers and to fix a minimum number of members for chambers.
>
> . . . .
>
> . . . Dr. Moneim-Riad Bey (Egypt) suggested that the question of *ad hoc* and fixed chambers should be further considered.
>
> . . . .
>
> Articles 26, 27, 29, and 30 were approved as a whole, subject to the consideration of the Drafting Committee.[18]

These were the principal points that were made at the Washington Committee of Jurists concerning the nature of the *ad hoc* Chamber.

10. The drafting of the provision of the Statute in 1945 concerning an *ad hoc* Chamber, as described above, does not provide sufficient explanation of the basis upon which this institution was to be formed, or of the manner in which it was to be resorted to, especially since the Chamber for dealing with particular categories of cases and the five-judge Chamber of Summary Procedure were retained from the old Court. While the American and Soviet statements, quoted above, contained in the *travaux préparatoires* may suggest otherwise, perhaps it may not be incorrect to assume that an *ad hoc* Chamber

[17] Doc. Jurist 23, G/17, *id.* at 282.

[18] Doc. Jurist 57, G/45, *id.* at 199–202.

was envisaged principally to adjudge minor cases that might not be required to go through the complete proceedings of the full Court. This idea seems to linger in the 1978 Rules of Court, Article 92 of which states: "1. Written proceedings in a case before a Chamber shall consist of a single pleading by each side. . . . 3. Oral proceedings shall take place unless the parties agree to dispense with them, and the Chamber consents."[19]

As shown below, however, the practice has proved otherwise. The *Gulf of Maine* case (1984), the first dealt with by an *ad hoc* Chamber, required three rounds of written pleadings exchanged between Canada and the United States, amounting to nearly 15,000 pages of written documents in total, and as many as 26 sittings for oral arguments. The *ad hoc* Chamber's Judgment went on record as a piece of jurisprudence concerning maritime delimitation comparable to other law of the sea cases such as the *North Sea Continental Shelf Cases* (1969), the *Tunisia/Libya* case (1982) and (later) the *Libya/Malta* case (1985), all of which were adjudged by the full Court.[20] To look no further than the first *ad hoc* Chamber case, therefore, it is clear that the jurisprudential impact of the new institution cannot be overlooked. Such considerations, however, go well beyond my present theme.

11. As a Member of the Court, I feel it appropriate to abstain from developing any basic criticisms directed at the very institution of an *ad hoc* Chamber. I content myself, therefore, with reiterating that states come to an *ad hoc* Chamber, by agreement, because they feel free to indicate their choice of judges from among the Members of the Court. At the same time, they are perfectly entitled to enjoy the full services and facilities of the Court and have their *ad hoc* Chamber render a judgment of the International Court of Justice.

SHIGERU ODA*

WALDEMAR A. SOLF (1913–1987)

The death of Waldemar Solf on June 20, 1987, brought to a close a multifaceted career that included stints as practicing lawyer in Chicago, field artillery officer in World War II, supervisor of the U.S. Army's international legal affairs and professor of international law. While he was a member of the army's Judge Advocate General's Corps (JAG), Solf served in Germany, and also in South Korea where he was Staff Judge Advocate of the Eighth U.S. Army/U.S. Forces Korea/United Nations Command and the U.S. Strike Command. He later served in the United States as the Chief Judicial Officer, U.S. Army Judiciary, and then as the Chief, Military Justice Division, Office of the Judge Advocate General.

[19] *See* 73 AJIL at 777–78.

[20] North Sea Continental Shelf Cases (FRG/Den.; FRG/Neth.), 1969 ICJ REP. 3 (Judgments of Feb. 20); Continental Shelf (Tunisia/Libyan Arab Jamahiriya), 1982 ICJ REP. 18 (Judgment of Feb. 24); Continental Shelf (Libyan Arab Jamahiriya/Malta), 1985 ICJ REP. 13 (Judgment of June 3).

* Member of the International Court of Justice; Honorary Member, American Society of International Law.

After 2 years of teaching international law at American University, Solf rejoined the JAG as a civilian and for 10 years served as Chief of the International Law section in the International Affairs Division. He was assigned to be a U.S. delegate to the International Committee of the Red Cross's Diplomatic Conference on the Reaffirmation and Development of International Humanitarian Law Applicable in Armed Conflicts. He retired again in August 1979, and then became Adjunct Professor of Law at Washington College of Law, American University.

Solf's participation in the ICRC conferences, extending from 1972 to their conclusion in 1977, and in the follow-on conferences leading to prohibitions on conventional weapons, was marked by the painstaking research that he engaged in for all of his efforts. This research enabled him to become an effective dialectician who could deftly promote his positions. Solf was also an effective participant on the delegations: he was widely respected, in great demand for the luncheon and dinner sessions where the shaping of perceptions so often takes place. From the outset, he strongly supported the institutional mechanism—the establishment of the protecting power—that would provide enforcement of the Geneva Conventions and monitor compliance. He also supported the U.S. efforts to abolish the reservations to the Conventions—particularly those that would make a prisoner of war, when captured, prima facie a war criminal until evidence was adduced otherwise.

Solf's numerous articles and participation were a major factor in the development of the law of war, significant in large measure because his research was effectively coupled with his broad and pragmatic experience in the practice of this field of law. He also was an active participant in the development of the law relating to terrorism and other international crimes, extradition, and, of course, military law and military justice. In recognition of his work in the ICRC conferences and in general, he received the Exceptional Civilian Service Award in 1978 and the Meritorious Civilian Service Award in 1975. He received recognition as well for his prominent role in several professional associations.

In addition, he was a superb teacher, both of students in the classroom and as a colleague or friend, discussing the difficult points that are inherent in the law of war. He insisted that the law regulating states in war was the law of war and avoided the ambiguous expression "international humanitarian law" because he saw that the law of war itself was aimed at reducing the "unnecessary suffering" that arises out of the hostilities. Solf observed that the "law of Geneva" was addressed to the protection of noncombatants in situations outside the hostilities. Hence, in his view, much of the Geneva law was intended to promote and effectuate the enforcement of the rights of the noncombatants—human rights in the larger sense.

In apt conclusion to his work on the law of war, Solf became a consultant to the ICRC, and also joined with Professors Karl Joseph Partsch and M. Bothe in completing the text, *New Rules for Victims of Armed Conflicts*, on the Geneva Protocols of 1977. Together with Captain J. Ashley Roach (USN), he updated the *Index of International Humanitarian Law*, which was published after his death. His death cut short the completion of an excellent text for teaching the law of war, which he was coauthoring with Professor Robert

Goldman of Washington College of Law. This text draws upon the Jessup problem of 1978, of which Solf was one of the authors. In general, the Jessup problems offer a unique model that others may yet choose to follow, for they provide perspective on the often sequential nature of the issues we face in international law.

We have relatively few experts in the law of war, so critical to the development of global order, who can couple work of impeccable scholarship with the experience of the practitioner. Wally Solf was one of these few.

HARRY H. ALMOND, JR.*

CORRESPONDENCE

The *American Journal of International Law* welcomes short communications from its readers. It reserves the right to determine which letters should be published and to edit any letters printed. Letters should conform to the same format requirements as other manuscripts.

TO THE EDITOR IN CHIEF:

May 5, 1988

I would like to respond to Professor Alain Pellet's letter in the April 1988 issue (82 AJIL 331) lamenting the fact that out of 2,880 footnotes in a recent volume of the *American Journal of International Law*, only 41 cited references in French. Professor Pellet concludes that the American authors "certainly deprive themselves of the indispensable comparative dimension," and that "navelism" of this sort "might be the way empires collapse."

Professor Pellet might do well to inquire why foreign sources are conspicuous by their relative absence in AJIL footnotes. A look upward at the text of recent essays in our *Journal* reveals sharp controversy over the legality of actions taken and positions asserted by the Government of the United States. There has been not only robust criticism of the legality of what our Government has done, but challenge as well to the versions of the facts that have been officially reported. For instance, some of our colleagues—at personal risk—have traveled to Nicaragua to report on what the contras have been doing with U.S. aid. In addition, some of our colleagues have participated in legal actions against the Government of the United States in our courts and in international courts.

The essays that result from this kind of legal activism—whether they support or challenge the Government's position—challenge comfortable assumptions about the nature and sources of international law. As French thinkers historically have been among the first to realize, sharply contested expositional positions help articulate and stimulate the development of doctrine.

Frankly, I do not see very much that is new or challenging in French scholarship at the present moment. When we were having our clashes over

* Institute of National Strategic Studies, National Defense University.

Grenada and Nicaragua, why were the French journals not debating the facts and legality of the *Greenpeace* affair? Where was the debate over France's withdrawal from the general compulsory jurisdiction of the International Court of Justice after the *Nuclear Tests* cases? Are international lawyers in France collectively timid about criticizing their own Government? Or are the editors of French journals unwilling to publish iconoclastic essays submitted by unestablished authors? The absence of critical examination of issues such as *Greenpeace* in the leading French journals of international law not only discourages American scholars from reading and citing those journals, but also removes an opportunity for French scholars to engage in the intellectual challenge of reexamining the conceptual underpinnings of public international law as interpreted on the continent.

ANTHONY D'AMATO*

THE FRANCIS DEÁK PRIZE

The Board of Editors takes great pleasure in announcing that the Francis Deák Prize for 1988 has been awarded to the French scholar, Elisabeth Zoller, for her article, *The "Corporate Will" of the United Nations and the Rights of the Minority*. The winning article appeared in the July 1987 issue of the *Journal* at page 610.

The prize, which is given annually in memory of Francis Deák, honors meritorious scholarship by younger AJIL authors. The Board of Editors is grateful to the Institute for Continuing Education in Law and Librarianship and to its President, Mr. Philip F. Cohen, whose continued generosity has made it possible to grant an award to the recipient of the prize. The Board also wishes to extend its congratulations to Professor Zoller for her outstanding scholarship.

* Of the Board of Editors.

CONTEMPORARY PRACTICE OF THE UNITED STATES RELATING TO INTERNATIONAL LAW

MARIAN NASH LEICH*

The material in this section is arranged according to the system employed in the annual *Digest of United States Practice in International Law,* published by the Department of State.

RECOGNITION OF GOVERNMENTS

(U.S. *Digest,* Ch. 2, §3)

Economic Measures Against the Illegal Noriega Regime in Panama

On February 25, 1988, President Eric Arturo Delvalle of Panama dismissed from his post as Commander of the Panama Defense Forces General Manuel Antonio Noriega, against whom (and others) United States grand juries in Miami and Tampa had returned indictments on February 4, 1988, for violations of U.S. narcotics laws (in sum, by facilitating the transit of narcotics shipments from Colombia to the United States through Panama and by participating or conspiring to participate in various money-laundering schemes in Panama).[1]

Even prior to the investigations that had led to the indictments in Miami and Tampa, concern had grown within the executive branch and Congress about deteriorating political and human rights conditions in Panama. This concern was directed not only toward the dominant role of the Panama Defense Forces in Panamanian Government operations, but also toward their use of excessive measures in quelling demonstrations, their intimidation of political opponents, including their alleged complicity in the unsolved murder (and decapitation) of an insistent critic, Dr. Hugo Spadafora, and the reported widespread corruption of their officers.[2]

On June 30, 1987, the American Embassy in Panama had been attacked during a demonstration orchestrated by the Panamanian Government, with resultant damages of $106,000. The United States Government informally withheld disbursement of assistance to Panama until the Panamanian Government paid for the damages to the Embassy. Payment was made on July 29, but in the meantime consensus had been reached at high levels of the executive branch that military and economic assistance should continue to be withheld until Panamanian authorities (in particular, the Panama De-

* Office of the Legal Adviser, Department of State.

[1] For a summary of the indictments, see Dept. of Justice news release, Feb. 5, 1988, also in Dept. of State File No. P88 0056-1708.

[2] *See Situation in Panama: Hearings Before the Subcomm. on Western Hemisphere Affairs of the Senate Comm. on Foreign Relations,* 99th Cong., 2d Sess. (1986). *See in particular id.* at 38–43, *reprinted in* AMERICAN FOREIGN POLICY: CURRENT DOCUMENTS, 1986, at 792–95.

fense Forces) ended their abuses of human rights and democratic governmental processes were restored. Secretary of State George P. Shultz made the suspension public at a news conference on August 6, 1987.[3]

Noriega, following his own dismissal by President Delvalle, thereupon brought about the purported dismissal of President Delvalle and Vice President Roderick Esquivel by a rump session of the Panamanian National Assembly (meeting for 10 minutes in the early morning hours of February 26, 1988). He also brought about the purported appointment by the Cabinet Council of Manuel Solís Palma as "Minister in Charge of the Presidency of the Republic."[4]

On March 1, 1988, President Delvalle, who had gone into hiding in Panama, issued a proclamation advising all persons and parties engaging, or considering engaging, in transactions with the Government of the Republic of Panama or with the Republic of Panama that any contracts, agreements or other transactions entered into with the Noriega regime or any public agency or entity purporting to act on its behalf were neither recognized by nor binding upon the Government of the Republic of Panama or the Republic of Panama, and that any persons or parties entering into them did so at their own risk. Any debts or other obligations incurred by the Noriega regime or any public agency or entity purporting to act on its behalf were neither recognized by nor binding upon the Government of the Republic of Panama and the Republic of Panama. Any taxes, fees or other payments paid to the Noriega regime or any public agency or entity purporting to act on its behalf would not be credited as a payment to the Government of the Republic of Panama, and any person or party making such payments would be reassessed therefor, "as appropriate," by the Government of the Republic of Panama. The final operative paragraph of the proclamation stated:

> 4. Payments of debts, taxes, fees or other obligations due and owing to the Republic of Panama, the Government of the Republic of Panama or any public agency or entity thereof should be held, until further notice, in escrow in trust for the Republic of Panama.[5]

On March 2, 1988, counsel representing the lawful Government of Panama began filing suits in several jurisdictions in the United States to establish title to the Panamanian Government's bank deposits and to prevent banks holding those deposits from turning them over to the Noriega regime.

In a note dated March 2, 1988, the Embassy of the Republic of Panama at Washington notified the Department of State that Ambassador Juan

[3] *See* DEPT. ST. BULL., No. 2127, October 1987, at 11, 13. For a further statutory prohibition on assistance to Panama, see p. 574 *infra*.

[4] On Feb. 25 and 26, 1988, the White House issued statements reiterating the "unqualified support of the United States for civilian constitutional rule in Panama." *See* 24 WEEKLY COMP. PRES. DOC. 263, 265 (Feb. 29, 1988). See also the statement of Ambassador Richard T. McCormack, U.S. Permanent Representative to the Organization of American States, Feb. 27, 1988, before a Special Session of its Permanent Council, OEA/Ser.G, CP/Acta 729/88 (1988).

[5] For the text, see Dept. of State File No. P88 0058-1104.

Bautista Sosa was the sole person having authority to receive, control or dispose of any property held in any Federal Reserve Bank or any insured bank from or for the account of the Republic of Panama or any central bank thereof, including Banco Nacional de Panamá and Caja de Ahorros. On the same date, Acting Secretary of State John C. Whitehead certified, in accordance with section 25(b) of the Federal Reserve Act, as amended (12 U.S.C. §632 (1982)), "to any Federal Reserve bank or to any insured bank" that he recognized and accepted the authority of Ambassador Sosa with respect to such property.[6]

On March 2, 1988, Judge Lloyd F. MacMahon of the Southern District of New York issued a temporary restraining order, in *Republic of Panama v. Republic National Bank of New York,*[7] enjoining the defendant bank from debiting any account of the Republic of Panama. The plaintiff subsequently filed an amended complaint naming Bankers Trust Co., Irving Trust Co. and Marine Midland Bank as defendants. The same day, March 2, Republic agreed to transfer all funds in the account of the Republic of Panama to the Federal Reserve Bank of New York, and the action against Republic was dismissed. On March 3, 1988, the court granted a temporary restraining order that enjoined the three remaining defendants from debiting any account of the Republic of Panama unless approved by Ambassador Sosa, and also enjoined payment on any letters of credit or like instruments in the name of the Republic of Panama or any of its agencies or instrumentalities. After Irving Trust Co. stipulated with the plaintiff not to pay against any account of the Republic of Panama except payments under outstanding letters of credit, the action was dismissed against Irving.

On March 7, 1988, Judge MacMahon extended the temporary restraining order against Bankers Trust Co. and Marine Midland Bank for 10 more days, and took under advisement the plaintiff's application for a preliminary injunction. In an opinion dated March 15, 1988, the court granted the preliminary injunction, recognizing the "well-established" rule of judicial deference to the executive branch in regard to questions of recognition. "As a corollary" to that deference in determining "whom to accredit as repre-

[6] *Id.* Nos. P88 0059-0376 and P88 0059-0373. The certification related to and included all gold, silver, currency, credits, deposits, securities, choses in action, and any other form of property, the proceeds thereof, and any right, title, or interest therein, theretofore or thereafter received by any Federal Reserve bank or insured bank, from or for the account of the Government of Panama or any of its agencies or instrumentalities, including Banco Nacional de Panamá, as its fiscal agent. The certification encompassed the following premises: that Panama is a foreign state recognized by the United States Government; that Ambassador Sosa is its Ambassador to the United States and is recognized by the Secretary of State as its accredited representative; that Ambassador Sosa had certified to the Secretary of State in the note dated Mar. 2, 1988, referred to in the text *supra,* his full control and authority to receive, control, and dispose of any and all such property; and that the Secretary of State accepted and recognized Ambassador Sosa's full power and authority in these respects.

On Apr. 1, 1988, Acting Secretary of State Whitehead delegated his authority to make section 25(b) certifications with respect to Panama to the Assistant Secretary of State for Inter-American Affairs, effective Apr. 4, 1988. 53 Fed. Reg. 12,092 (1988).

[7] No. 88 Civ. 1427 (LFM) (S.D.N.Y. Mar. 2, 1988).

sentatives of a foreign state," it held, U.S. courts would not hear suits by governments from which official recognition had been withheld.[8]

Subsequently, on March 25, 1988, President Delvalle issued Executive Decree No. 16, in regard to payment of Panamanian income taxes falling due on March 31, 1988. It extended the due date to April 30, required all tax payments to be made only through deposits to the order of the Government of the Republic of Panama in the Federal Reserve Bank of New York, and provided that any income tax payment made in a manner different from that prescribed would not be deemed good payment. Acting on behalf of President Delvalle, Ambassador Sosa then asked the Internal Revenue Service to announce that all payments of Panamanian income taxes in accordance with Executive Decree No. 16 would be entitled to the foreign tax credit provided for in sections 901 and 902 of the Internal Revenue Code of 1986.

Following consultations among the Departments of State and the Treasury and the Federal Reserve Bank of New York, Government of Panama Account No. 2 was opened at the bank for the purpose, inter alia, of receiving tax payments made pursuant to Executive Decree No. 16, subject to an irrevocable instruction from Ambassador Sosa that no payments be made therefrom, unless the Secretary of State, or his lawful delegate, have first notified the bank in writing that "constitutional order has been restored in Panama." On April 1, 1988, the Internal Revenue Service issued Notice No. 88-47, stating, in part, that

> income taxes due to the Government of Panama which are paid into [Government of Panama Account No. 2 at the Federal Reserve Bank of New York] will be considered paid to the Government of Panama, and will therefore be creditable foreign taxes if all other requirements of sections 901 and 902 of the Code are satisfied.[9]

AIRCRAFT CRIMES

(U.S. *Digest,* Ch. 8, §3)

Multilateral Conventions—Montreal Protocol

On May 6, 1988, Secretary of State George P. Shultz submitted a report to President Reagan on the Protocol for the Suppression of Unlawful Acts of Violence at Airports Serving International Civil Aviation, done at Montreal on February 24, 1988, which supplements and extends the Convention

[8] *See* Republic of Panama v. Republic Nat'l Bank of New York, 681 F.Supp. 1066 (S.D.N.Y. 1988). *See also* Republic of Panama v. Citizens & S. Int'l Bank, 682 F.Supp. 1544 (S.D. Fla. 1988); Republic of Panama v. First Nat'l Bank of Boston, No. 88–0518–H (D. Mass.) (in which District Judge Edward F. Harrington granted a temporary restraining order on Mar. 3, 1988; the case was settled prior to a hearing on the application for a preliminary injunction and dismissed on Mar. 11, 1988).

[9] IRS BULL., No. 1988-16, Apr. 18, 1988, at 27–28.

for the Suppression of Unlawful Acts Against the Safety of Civil Aviation (Sabotage), done at Montreal on September 23, 1971.[1]

The United States played a leading role in negotiation of the Protocol, preparation of which began late in 1986, after the Assembly of the International Civil Aviation Organization (ICAO) unanimously called for a new international instrument to suppress unlawful acts of violence at airports serving international civil aviation. The ICAO Assembly's action followed several terrorist incidents at international airports, in particular the attacks in December 1985 at the Rome and Vienna airports that resulted in the deaths of 20 persons, including 5 Americans. A subcommittee of the ICAO Legal Committee and the full Legal Committee met in January 1987 and April–May 1987, respectively, to develop the Protocol. Its final text was adopted by consensus by 81 nations at an International Conference on Air Law, held under ICAO auspices at Montreal, February 9–24, 1988.

The Secretary's report reads in part as follows:

> The Protocol is an important instrument that will enhance international cooperation in combatting acts of terrorist violence. . . .
>
> . . . .
>
> The Protocol will . . . encompass unlawful acts of violence committed at airports serving international civil aviation, even where such acts do not endanger the safety of aircraft in flight. Pursuant to Article I of the Protocol, as between the parties to the Protocol, the Montreal Convention and the Protocol will be read and interpreted as a single instrument.
>
> The Montreal Convention, now in force for 137 nations, was the third major step taken by the international community to deal with terrorist attacks and other criminal acts against civil aviation. The Convention on Offenses and Certain Other Acts Committed on Board Aircraft, signed at Tokyo on September 14, 1963, entered into force in 1969. The Convention for the Suppression of Unlawful Seizure of Aircraft (Hijacking Convention), signed at the Hague on December 16, 1970, entered into force in 1971. The United States is a party to all three of these Conventions.
>
> The major provisions of the Protocol are as follows:
>
> Paragraph 1 of Article II sets forth the offenses covered by the Protocol and will be Article 1, paragraph 1 *bis* for the parties to the Montreal Convention as supplemented by the Protocol. This article states that any person commits an offense if he unlawfully and intentionally, using any device, substance or weapon (a) performs certain acts of violence at an international airport or (b) destroys or seriously damages the facilities of an international airport or aircraft not in service located thereon, or disrupts service at that airport. To be an offense under this provision, the Protocol requires that these acts endanger or be likely to endanger safety at an airport serving international civil aviation.

[1] 24 UST 564, TIAS No. 7570 (entered into force for the United States Jan. 26, 1973).

Paragraph 2 of Article II provides that the words "or paragraph 1 *bis*" will be inserted after the words "paragraph 1" in paragraph 2(a) of Article 1 of the Convention. Through this amendment, the supplemented Montreal Convention will also include as offenses (a) attempts to commit any of the acts listed in paragraph 2 of Article II of the Protocol and (b) complicity in such acts or attempts.

Article III of the Protocol adds a paragraph 2 *bis* to Article 5 of the Convention. Under this new paragraph, each party agrees to take measures to establish jurisdiction over the offenses mentioned in the Protocol, where an alleged offender is present in its territory and it does not extradite him pursuant to Article 8 of the Convention.

Articles IV through VII set out the procedures for signature, ratification, accession and entry into force of the Protocol. . . .

Because the Protocol includes an offense not currently part of U.S. domestic law, it will require implementing legislation before the United States can become a party. This legislation is now being prepared.[2]

ECONOMIC SANCTIONS

(U.S. *Digest,* Ch. 10, §12)

Measures Against the Illegal Noriega Regime in Panama

On February 29, 1988, President Reagan signed the certifications regarding major illicit drug-producing or major drug-transit countries required by section 481(h)(2)(A) of the Foreign Assistance Act of 1961, as amended.[1] The provision mandates the withholding of United States assistance to such countries unless the President determines, and so certifies to Congress at the time of submitting an annual international narcotics control report, that during the previous year the country in question has cooperated fully with the United States, or has taken adequate steps on its own, in preventing narcotic or other psychotropic drugs and other controlled substances produced or processed, in whole or in part, in that country, or transported through it, from being sold illegally within that country's jurisdiction to U.S. Government personnel or their dependents, or from being transported, directly or indirectly, into the United States. The certification must also address the country's cooperation in preventing and punishing the laundering in the country of drug-related profits or drug-related monies. If

[2] Dept. of State Files L/T. On May 20, President Reagan forwarded the Protocol for the Suppression of Unlawful Acts of Violence at Airports Serving International Civil Aviation to the Senate for advice and consent to ratification. S. TREATY DOC. NO. 19, 100th Cong., 2d Sess. (1988).

For the Convention on Offenses and Certain Other Acts Committed on Board Aircraft, *done* Sept. 14, 1963, see 20 UST 2941, TIAS No. 6768, 704 UNTS 219. For the Convention for the Suppression of Unlawful Seizure of Aircraft, *done* Dec. 16, 1970, see 22 UST 1641, TIAS No. 7192.

[1] Anti-Drug Abuse Act of 1986, Pub. L. No. 99-570, §2005, 100 Stat. 3207, 3207-61–63 (1986) (codified at 22 U.S.C. §2291(h)(2)(A)).

the country does not otherwise qualify for certification under these standards, assistance may be obligated and expended, nevertheless, if the President certifies that the vital national interests of the United States require provision of that assistance. Either type of presidential determination may be disapproved by Congress by joint resolution within a 45-day period of continuous session after receipt of the President's certification (22 U.S.C. §2291(h)(4)(A)).

In Presidential Determination No. 88-10, signed February 29, 1988, the President determined, among other things, that four major producing and/or major transit countries, among them Panama, did not meet the standards set forth in section 481(h)(2)(A).[2]

Subsequently, on March 11, 1988, President Reagan discussed measures that he would place in effect against the "illegitimate Noriega regime" until democratic government was restored in Panama. Certain payments due Panama from the Panama Canal Commission were to be placed in escrow. Trade preferences available to Panama under the Generalized System of Preferences (GSP) and the Caribbean Basin Initiative (i.e., under the Caribbean Basin Economic Recovery Act) would be suspended.[3] The Immigration and Naturalization Service and the U.S. Customs Service would intensify their scrutiny of Panamanians in order to apprehend drug traffickers and money launderers. All sources of funds due or payable to the Republic of Panama from the United States Government were to be inventoried, for the purpose of determining those that should be placed in escrow for the Delvalle Government on behalf of the Panamanian people. The President concluded:

> We have welcomed the recent statements issued by President Delvalle, the political parties and the Civilian [Civic] Crusade of Panama calling for a government of national reconciliation. We support their goal of restoring democratic government and constitutional order. Once Panamanians achieve this goal, the United States is fully prepared to work with the Government of Panama to help quickly restore Panama's economic health. The United States has been, and remains, committed to fulfilling faithfully its obligations under the Panama Canal treaties. We are also prepared to resume our close

[2] 53 Fed. Reg. 11,487 (1988).

[3] Proclamation No. 5779, *id.* at 9,850, dated Mar. 23, 1988, denied until further notice the preferential tariff treatment afforded under the Generalized System of Preferences and the Caribbean Basin Economic Recovery Act to articles otherwise eligible for such treatment that are imported from Panama.

The President's action was undertaken pursuant to §802(a) under title VIII of the Trade Act of 1974, 19 U.S.C. §2492(a), as added by title IX (Denial of Trade Benefits to Uncooperative Major Drug Producing or Drug-Transit Countries) of the Anti-Drug Abuse Act of 1986, *supra* note 1, 100 Stat. 3207-164. The provisions of title VIII, known as the Narcotics Control Trade Act, authorize restrictive tariff treatment to be given products of uncooperative major producing or drug-transit countries. Under §803 of the Trade Act of 1974, as added by Pub. L. No. 99-570, no allocation may be made of any limitation imposed on the quantity of sugar (that may be imported into the United States) to any country having a government that is involved in the trade of illicit narcotics or that is failing to cooperate with the United States in narcotics enforcement activities as defined in §802(b), as determined by the President.

working relationships with the Panamanian Defense Forces once civilian government and constitutional democracy are reestablished.[4]

On April 8, 1988, President Reagan imposed economic sanctions, including the blocking of assets, against the Noriega regime in Panama. Acting under his constitutional authority and under the International Emergency Economic Powers Act, the National Emergencies Act, and 3 U.S.C. §301, the President found in Executive Order No. 12,635, Prohibiting Certain Transactions with Respect to Panama, that the policies and actions in Panama of Manuel Antonio Noriega and Manuel Solís Palma constitute an unusual and extraordinary threat to the national security, foreign policy and economy of the United States; and he declared a national emergency to deal with that threat. The operative provisions of the order follow:

> *Section 1.* I hereby order blocked all property and interests in property of the Government of Panama that are in the United States, that hereafter come within the United States, or that are or hereafter come within the possession or control of persons located within the United States. For purposes of this Order, the Government of Panama is defined to include its agencies, instrumentalities and controlled entities, including the Banco Nacional de Panama and the Caja de Ahorros.
>
> *Sec. 2.* Except to the extent provided in regulations which may hereafter be issued pursuant to this Order:
>
> (a) Any direct or indirect payments or transfers from the United States to the Noriega/Solis regime of funds, including currency, cash or coins of any nation, or of other financial or investment assets or credits are prohibited. All transfers, or payments owed, to the Government of Panama shall be made into an account at the Federal Reserve Bank of New York, to be held for the benefit of the Panamanian people. For purposes of this Order, the term "Noriega/Solis regime" shall mean Manuel Antonio Noriega, Manuel Solis Palma, and any agencies, instrumentalities or entities purporting to act on their behalf or under their asserted authority.
>
> (b) Any direct or indirect payments or transfers to the Noriega/Solis regime of funds, including currency, cash or coins of any nation, or of other financial or investment assets or credits, by any United States person located in the territory of Panama, or by any person organized under the laws of Panama and owned or controlled by a United States person, are prohibited. All transfers, or payments owed, to the Government of Panama by such persons shall be made into an account at the Federal Reserve Bank of New York, to be held for the benefit of the Panamanian people. For purposes of Section 2(b), "United States person" is defined to mean any United States citizen, permanent resident alien, juridical person organized under the laws of the United States, or any person in the United States.
>
> *Sec. 3.* Sections 1 and 2 shall not be deemed to block property or interests in property of the Government of Panama, including, but not limited to, accounts established at the Federal Reserve Bank of New

[4] 24 WEEKLY COMP. PRES. DOC. 328 (Mar. 14, 1988).

York as described in section 2, with respect to which transactions are authorized by, or on behalf of, the recognized representative of the Government of Panama as certified by the Secretary of State, or are otherwise authorized in regulations which may hereafter be issued pursuant to this Order. Section 2 shall not be deemed to prohibit interbank clearing payments.

Sec. 4. The measures taken pursuant to this Order are intended to extend the effectiveness of actions initiated in cooperation with the Government of Panama and its President, Eric Arturo Delvalle, and are not intended to block private Panamanian assets subject to the jurisdiction of the United States or to prohibit remittances by United States persons to Panamanian persons other than the Noriega/Solis regime.

Sec. 5. This Order shall take effect at 4:00 p.m. Eastern Daylight Time on April 8, 1988, except as otherwise provided in regulations issued pursuant to this Order.

Sec. 6. The Secretary of the Treasury, in consultation with the Secretary of State, is authorized to take such actions, including the promulgation of rules and regulations, and to employ all powers granted to me by the International Emergency Economic Powers Act, as may be necessary to carry out the purposes of this Order. The Secretary of the Treasury may redelegate any of these functions to other officers or agencies of the Federal Government.

Sec. 7. Nothing contained in this Order shall confer any substantive or procedural right or privilege on any person or organization, enforceable against the United States, its agencies or its officers, or the Federal Reserve Bank of New York or its officers.[5]

The economic measures described above were undertaken by the President under his constitutional authority and under the statutory authorizations and mandates referenced, after Noriega had sought to depose President Delvalle. Prior to the events of February 1988, however, Congress had enacted statutory prohibitions against the obligation or expenditure of any U.S. assistance to Panama, including any assistance appropriated and previously obligated, "unless" the President made certain certifications regarding political and human rights conditions within Panama. (The suspension of such assistance made public by Secretary of State Shultz on August 6, 1987,[6] had been effected through administrative measures taken by the executive branch.)

Section 570 of the Foreign Operations, Export Financing, and Related Programs Appropriations Act[7] provides:

ASSISTANCE FOR PANAMA

SEC. 570. (a) Unless the President certifies to Congress that—

(1) the Government of Panama has demonstrated substantial progress in assuring civilian control of the armed forces and that

[5] 53 Fed. Reg. 12,134–35 (1988). [6] *See* p. 567 *supra*.

[7] Pub. L. No. 100-202, §101(e), 101 Stat. 1329-131 (1987).

the Panama Defense Forces and its leaders have been removed from non-military activities and institutions;

(2) the Government of Panama is conducting an impartial investigation into allegations of illegal actions by members of the Panama Defense Forces;

(3) a satisfactory agreement has been reached between the governing authorities and representatives of the opposition forces on conditions for free and fair elections; and

(4) freedom of the press and other constitutional guarantees, including due process of law, are restored to the Panamanian people;

then no United States assistance (including any such assistance appropriated and previously obligated) shall be obligated or expended for Panama in this fiscal year and any fiscal year thereafter, and none of the funds appropriated or otherwise made available in this Act, or any other Act, shall be used to finance any participation of the United States in joint military exercises conducted in Panama during the period January 1, 1988, through December 31, 1988.

(b) It is the sense of the Congress that if the conditions described in paragraphs (1) through (4) of subsection (a) have been certified as having been met, then not only will United States assistance be restored, but increased levels of such assistance should be considered for Panama.

(c) For purposes of this section, the term "United States assistance" means assistance of any kind which is provided by grant, sale, loan, lease, credit, guaranty, or insurance, or by any other means, by any agency or instrumentality of the United States Government, including—

(1) assistance under the Foreign Assistance Act of 1961 (including programs under title IV of chapter 2 of part I of such Act);

(2) sales, credits, and guarantees under the Arms Export Control Act;

(3) sales under title I or III and donations under title II of the Agricultural Trade Development and Assistance Act of 1954 of nonfood commodities;

(4) other financing programs of the Commodity Credit Corporation for export sales of nonfood commodities;

(5) financing under the Export-Import Bank Act of 1945; and

(6) assistance provided by the Central Intelligence Agency or assistance provided by any other entity or component of the United States Government if such assistance is carried out in connection with, or for purposes of conducting, intelligence or intelligence-related activities except that this shall not include activities undertaken solely to collect necessary intelligence;

except that the term "United States assistance" does not include (A) assistance under chapter 1 of part I of the Foreign Assistance Act of 1961 insofar as such assistance is provided through private and voluntary organizations or other nongovernmental agencies, (B) assistance which involves the donations of food or medicine, (C) disaster relief assistance (including any assistance under chapter 9 of part I of the Foreign Assistance Act of 1961), (D) assistance for refugees, (E) assistance under the Inter-American Foundation Act, (F) assistance necessary for the continued financing of education for Panamanians in the

> United States, or (G) assistance made available for termination costs arising from the requirements of this section.
>
> (d) The Secretary of Treasury shall instruct the United States Executive Directors to the Multilateral Development Banks (the International Bank for Reconstruction and Development, the International Finance Corporation, and the Inter-American Development Bank) to vote against any loan to Panama, unless the President has certified in advance that the conditions set forth in subsection (a) of this section have been met.[8]

Section 571 of that Act was also specifically directed against political and human rights abuses within Panama. It reads, in part:

> ELIMINATION OF THE SUGAR QUOTA ALLOCATION OF PANAMA
>
> SEC. 571. (a) IN GENERAL.—Notwithstanding any other provision of law, no sugars, sirups, or molasses that are products of Panama may be imported into the United States after the date of enactment of this Act during any period for which a limitation is imposed by authorities provided under any other law on the total quantity of sugars, sirups, and molasses that may be imported into the United States: *Provided*, That such products may be imported after the beginning of the last week of any quota year if the President certifies that for the entire duration of the quota year, freedom of the press and other constitutional guarantees, including due process of law, have been restored to the Panamanian people.
>
> (b) REALLOCATION OF QUOTA AMOUNTS.—For any quota year for which the President does not certify for the entire duration of the quota year, freedom of the press and all other constitutional guarantees, including due process of law, have been restored to the Panamanian people, no later than the last week of such quota year, the United States Trade Representative shall reallocate among other foreign countries the quantity of sugar, sirup, and molasses products of Panama that could have been imported into the United States before the date of enactment of this Act under any limitation imposed by other law on the total quantity of sugars, sirups, and molasses that may be imported into the United States during any period.
>
> . . . .
>
> (d) CERTIFICATION.—The provisions of subsections (a) and (b), and the amendments made by subsection (c) of this section, shall cease to apply if the President certifies to Congress pursuant to section 570(a) of this Act.[9]

On April 29, 1988, President Reagan decided to exempt certain types of payments[10] by United States persons in Panama from the economic sanc-

[8] *Reprinted in* 1 HOUSE COMM. ON FOREIGN AFFAIRS AND SENATE COMM. ON FOREIGN RELATIONS, 101ST CONG., 2D SESS., LEGISLATION ON FOREIGN RELATIONS THROUGH 1987, at 546–47 (Jt. Comm. Print 1988).

[9] *Id.* at 547–48.

[10] These included payments by individuals other than income tax payments (individuals who make their own social security payments may continue to do so); travel-related payments by individuals, including departure fees and ticket taxes, or by U.S. firms in connection with the provision of travel services to individuals, e.g., landing fees and fuel; payments for postal

tions against Panama effected by Executive Order No. 12,635. Payments other than those specified in Treasury regulations must be made to the specially designated account at the Federal Reserve Bank of New York in accordance with Treasury guidelines to be issued. Payments that must be paid into the specially designated account include corporate and individual income taxes, social security taxes (when paid by corporations or agencies of the U.S. Government but not by individuals who ordinarily pay such taxes directly), direct taxes and fees (e.g., port fees, export fees, import duties and related expenses), direct payments of excise taxes collected as agent for the Government of Panama and rental fees. Additionally, individuals may not make payments, directly or indirectly, for or on behalf of U.S. firms.[11]

ENVIRONMENTAL AFFAIRS

(U.S. *Digest*, Ch. 11, §1)

Whaling—Japanese Violation of IWC Moratorium

In accordance with section 201(e) of the Magnuson Fishery Conservation and Management Act of 1976, as amended (the Packwood-Magnuson Amendment, 16 U.S.C. §1821(e) (1982)) and section 8 of the Fishermen's Protective Act of 1967, as amended (the Pelly Amendment, 22 U.S.C. §1978), Secretary of Commerce C. William Verity certified to President Reagan on February 9, 1988, that nationals of Japan were conducting whaling operations that diminish the effectiveness of the International Whaling Commission's conservation program.

Secretary Verity's certification was based upon the fact that the Government of Japan had issued special permits for scientific research to its nationals, which allows them to kill Southern Hemisphere minke whales for that purpose, notwithstanding the adoption by the International Whaling Commission (IWC) of resolutions regarding such permits at its annual meeting in June 1987.[1] The Secretary's certification discussed the Commission's actions on this issue, in part as follows:

> In a general resolution (IWC/39/24), the IWC requested its Scientific Committee to review all such programs and to report whether the programs satisfy certain scientific criteria. In that resolution, the IWC also recommended that member governments not issue permits for programs that, in the view of the IWC, do not satisfy the criteria "and therefore are not consistent with the Commission's conservation policy."

---

services and for telephone, telegraph and other telecommunication services; payments for utilities including electricity, water and similar municipal services; payments of indirect taxes (i.e., those normally collected in the purchase of goods and services such as sales and excise taxes) and certain administrative fees paid in connection with basic business activity (Treasury regulations to be issued will specify which administrative fees can be paid).

[11] Dept. of the Treasury news release, Apr. 30, 1988, Dept. of State File No. P88 0063-0941. For the Panamanian Transaction Regulations, see 53 Fed. Reg. 20,565 (1988).

[1] Res. IWC/39/24 and IWC/39/45, INTERNATIONAL WHALING COMMISSION, CHAIRMAN'S REPORT OF THE 39TH MEETING, 22–26 JUNE 1987, Apps. 1 and 4 (1987).

> In a resolution concerning Japan's proposed research program (IWC/39/45), the IWC (1) adopted the view that Japan's program does not satisfy the applicable criteria; and (2) recommended that Japan not issue the special permit for the program until the serious uncertainties in the program identified by the IWC Scientific Committee have been resolved to the satisfaction of that Committee. In December 1987, the IWC Scientific Committee held a special meeting to review a revised research program submitted by Japan in the interim. The report of the Scientific Committee reveals that Japan did not succeed in satisfying the Committee that the defects in its program had been cured. On December 22, 1987, the IWC circulated a resolution for a postal vote due February 14, 1988, recommending that Japan not take whales under its revised scientific research program. Nevertheless, the Government of Japan proceeded to issue the permit and, pursuant to that permit, nationals of Japan have begun killing Southern Hemisphere minke whales. Under these circumstances, I have determined, and hereby certify, that nationals of Japan are conducting whaling operations that diminish the effectiveness of the IWC conservation program.[2]

In identical letters to the Speaker of the House of Representatives (Congressman James C. Wright, Jr.) and the President of the Senate (Vice President George H. W. Bush) dated April 6, 1988, the President reported in accordance with the Pelly Amendment on his action regarding the certification, as well as on the reasons for his decision not to prohibit—in accordance with his discretionary authority under the Pelly Amendment—the import of all Japanese fish products into the United States. The President's letter read in part:

> Shortly after the Secretary's certification, the IWC adopted a second resolution on February 14, 1988, recommending that Japan not proceed with its revised research program. Japan has continued its whaling activities notwithstanding this second resolution.
>
> Given the lack of any evidence that Japan is bringing its whaling activities into conformance with the recommendations of the IWC, I am directing the Secretary of State under the Packwood-Magnuson Amendment to withhold 100 percent of the fishing privileges that would otherwise be available to Japan in the U.S. Exclusive Economic Zone. Japan has requested the opportunity to fish for 3,000 metric tons of sea snails and 5,000 metric tons of Pacific whiting. These requests will be denied. In addition, Japan will be barred from any future allocations of fishing privileges for any other species, including Pacific cod, until the Secretary of Commerce determines that the situation has been corrected.
>
> The sanctions being imposed are the strongest possible under the Packwood-Magnuson Amendment. The immediate and prospective effects of a 100 percent reduction of fishing allocations, coupled with

[2] Dept. of State, Exec. Secretariat Log No. 8804258, attachment. *See also U.S. Whaling Policy*, DEPT. OF STATE, GIST, October 1987.

On the postal vote, see IWC Circular Communications, Dec. 22, 1987, and Feb. 15, 1988, IWC Refs. RG/VJH/16800 and RG/VJH/16891, respectively.

Presidential review in the near future, is the most effective means of encouraging Japan to embrace the IWC conservation program. Therefore, I will not impose at this time the sanctions available under the Pelly Amendment against Japanese fish products imported into the United States. I am asking Secretary Verity, in cooperation with Secretary Shultz, to monitor Japanese whaling practices during the next few months and to report to me no later than December 1, 1988.

I also am directing the Secretary of Commerce and the Secretary of State to continue consultations with our IWC partners to ensure that we bring to a halt all whaling that diminishes the effectiveness of the IWC's conservation program, specifically including that under Japan's contested research program. Our actions taken today and in the future should encourage all nations to adhere to the conservation programs of the IWC.[3]

In *Japan Whaling Association v. American Cetacean Society,*[4] the Supreme Court, reversing on certiorari both the Court of Appeals for the District of Columbia Circuit and the District Court for the District of Columbia, held by five to four that the Secretary of Commerce was not mandatorily required to certify Japan under the Packwood-Magnuson or Pelly Amendments, where Japan had agreed with the United States (in 1984)[5] to cease commercial whaling altogether by 1988, in return for the "short-term continuance of a specified level of limited whaling by Japan." The Court ruled that the construction placed on the statutes by the Secretary of Commerce —that there were circumstances in which he might withhold certification, despite a country's departures from the IWC schedules (quotas), without violating his duty—was "also" a reasonable construction of the language used in both the Packwood-Magnuson and the Pelly Amendments. The Court concluded that this construction "neither contradicted the language of either Amendment, nor frustrated congressional intent."[6]

[3] 24 WEEKLY COMP. PRES. DOC. 438 (Apr. 11, 1988).

[4] 106 S.Ct. 2860 (1986), *rev'g* American Cetacean Soc'y v. Baldrige, 604 F.Supp. 1398 (D.D.C.), 604 F.Supp. 1411 (D.D.C.), 768 F.2d 426 (D.C. Cir. 1985).

[5] *See* 79 AJIL 434 (1985).

[6] 106 S.Ct. at 2871.

JUDICIAL DECISIONS

MONROE LEIGH

Political asylum—deportation—standard of judicial review—motion to reopen proceedings

IMMIGRATION AND NATURALIZATION SERVICE v. ABUDU. 108 S.Ct. 904. U.S. Supreme Court, March 1, 1988.

The Immigration and Naturalization Service (INS) petitioned the Supreme Court to review a court of appeals decision (1) reversing the order of the Board of Immigration Appeals (BIA) denying respondent's motion to reopen deportation proceedings, and (2) remanding for an evidentiary hearing on respondent's asylum and withholding of deportation claims. This case arose in 1981 when the INS initiated deportation proceedings against respondent, Assibi Abudu, a native and citizen of Ghana who had overstayed a student visa and had pleaded guilty to drug charges. During the deportation proceedings, respondent expressly declined to seek asylum as a refugee.[1] The immigration judge ordered the respondent deported on July 1, 1982, and the BIA dismissed his appeal on August 14, 1984. The respondent filed a petition for review of the deportation order in the U.S. Court of Appeals for the Ninth Circuit and a motion with the BIA requesting a reopening of his deportation proceeding to enable him to apply for asylum and withholding of deportation. The BIA denied respondent's motion to reopen and the respondent then appealed to the Ninth Circuit. The appellate court consolidated the respondent's petitions for review and affirmed the deportation order, but reversed the order denying the motion to reopen the deportation proceeding and remanded for further evidentiary hearings. The U.S. Supreme Court (per Stevens, J.) unanimously reversed the appellate court's order and *held:* that the court below had erred in subjecting the BIA decision to a standard of review stricter than the appropriate abuse-of-discretion standard.

In its review of the decision below, the Court initially clarified the question presented. The regulations issued by the INS to implement the Immigration and Nationality Act (the Act) provide that the party filing a motion to reopen deportation proceedings must demonstrate to the BIA "that evidence sought to be offered is material and was not available and could not have been discovered or presented at the former hearing."[2] If the

[1] Instead, respondent argued that his marriage to a U.S. citizen made him eligible for adjustment of status under 8 U.S.C. §1255(a). The immigration judge denied the application for adjustment of status because respondent's drug conviction constituted a nonwaivable ground of excludability (*see* 8 U.S.C. §1182(a)(23) (1982)), and the BIA affirmed this determination.

[2] 8 C.F.R. §3.2 (1988).

motion to reopen includes a request for asylum, the proof of new evidence must include a "reasonable" explanation by the alien of "the failure to request asylum prior to the completion of the . . . deportation proceeding."[3] Further, the movant must establish prima facie eligibility for asylum under section 208 or withholding of deportation under section 243(h) of the Act.

While the BIA based its denial of respondent's motion to reopen on both new evidence/reasonable explanation and prima facie grounds, either of which would have sufficed according to the Court,[4] the appellate court apparently blended the two grounds into one.[5] The questions presented in the petition for certiorari also did not clearly separate the BIA's two grounds for denial, but the Court relied on the formulation of the question in the petitioner's reply memorandum to clarify the narrow issue before the Court: "to determine the standard a Court of Appeals must apply when reviewing the BIA's conclusion that an alien has not reasonably explained his failure to assert his asylum claim at the outset."[6] The Court declined to consider the standard of review for a BIA denial of a motion to reopen based on the ground that the movant had not established a prima facie case for relief.

With respect to the standard of review of the BIA's decision, the Court held that the appellate court had erroneously analogized the respondent's motion to reopen to a motion for summary judgment. In its opinion, the appellate court stated that a motion to reopen deportation proceedings may be granted if it "presents 'proof that will support the desired finding [of a prima facie case] . . . until it is contradicted or overruled by other evidence.' "[7] As is the case in the review of motions for summary judgment, the appellate court stated that "inferences are to be drawn in favor of the party whose entitlement to further proceedings is at stake: . . . the alien seeking reopening under 8 C.F.R. 3.2."[8]

The Court criticized the appellate court's comparison of the motion to reopen to a motion for summary judgment as unsupported by precedent and contrary to decisions reached by other courts of appeals and by other panels in the Ninth Circuit. Precedent has established the proposition that "the BIA has discretion to deny a motion to reopen even if the alien has made out a prima facie case for relief."[9] The Court suggested that these "prior glosses on §3.2 have served as support for an abuse-of-discretion standard of review for the [cases in which] the BIA simply refuses to grant relief that is itself discretionary in nature, even if the alien has surmounted

[3] *Id.* §208.11.

[4] 108 S.Ct. 904, 908.

[5] The appellate court "did not discuss, as a separate matter, the 'failure to explain' ground in the BIA's decision," and also stated in its opinion that "the sole issue [in this case] is whether petitioner presented a *prima facie* case for reopening." *Id.* at 910 (quoting Abudu v. INS, 802 F.2d 1096, 1100 (9th Cir. 1986) (case below)).

[6] *Id.* at 911.

[7] *Abudu,* 802 F.2d at 1101 (quoting Maroufi v. INS, 772 F.2d 597, 599 (9th Cir. 1985)).

[8] *Id.*

[9] 108 S.Ct. at 912 (citing INS v. Jong Ha Wang, 450 U.S. 139, 144 n.5 (1981); INS v. Rios-Pineda, 471 U.S. 444, 449 (1985); INS v. Phinpathya, 464 U.S. 183, 188 n.6 (1984)).

the requisite thresholds of prima facie case and new evidence/reasonable explanation."[10] Since the new evidence/reasonable explanation evidentiary requirements of sections 3.2 and 208.11 must be satisfied by the alien before the BIA reaches the ultimate decision on discretionary relief from deportation, the Court reasoned that the BIA's decisions regarding the evidentiary requirements are also subject to an abuse-of-discretion standard of review.[11]

To support its legal analysis, the Court suggested that a motion to reopen deportation proceedings should be analogized to a petition for rehearing or a motion for a new trial on the basis of newly discovered evidence. In these cases, although granting the petition or motion is generally disfavored, the public interest in judicial efficiency must be balanced with the interest in giving the parties a fair opportunity to develop and present their cases. The Court has applied this principle to motions to reopen deportation proceedings in the past, quoting with approval a dissenting opinion in a case before the Ninth Circuit that stated that the INS "has some latitude in deciding when to reopen a case" and that the INS "should have the right to be restrictive" to prevent the "endless delay of deportation by aliens creative and fertile enough to continuously produce new and material facts sufficient to establish a prima facie case."[12]

The Court extended its analogy by demonstrating that the application of the stricter standard of review of motions for summary judgment to motions to reopen has been rejected by precedent and by the "tenor" of the INS regulations, which "plainly" disfavor motions to reopen.[13] Therefore, for the purpose of a motion to reopen deportation proceedings, the alien bears the same heavy burden of proof as the moving party in a motion for a new trial in a criminal case. In addition, the Court indicated that it would grant extra latitude (i.e., more deference) to INS decisions, which, unlike other adjudications by administrative agencies, often implicate questions of foreign relations.[14] For all the foregoing reasons, the Court concluded that the BIA did not abuse its discretion when it held that the respondent had not reasonably explained his failure to apply for asylum prior to the completion of his initial deportation proceeding.

The Court's decision to apply the abuse-of-discretion standard of review to BIA decisions regarding requests for asylum raised in a motion to reopen deportation proceedings reaffirms the policy on judicial review established by the Administrative Procedure Act, which provides that decisions rendered by executive agencies must be upheld unless they represent an abuse of discretion.[15] The decision does not establish a new principle regarding

[10] *Id.* [11] *Id.* at 912–13.

[12] *Jong Ha Wang,* 450 U.S. at 144 n.5 (quoting Judge Wallace's dissenting opinion in Villena v. INS, 622 F.2d 1352, 1362 (9th Cir. 1980) (en banc)).

[13] 108 S.Ct. at 914. The INS regulations regarding motions to reopen deportation proceedings establish the procedure in the negative, i.e., "Motions to reopen in deportation proceedings *shall not be granted* unless . . . ." 8 C.F.R. §3.2 (emphasis added). *See also id.* §242.22.

[14] 108 S.Ct. at 914–15. [15] 5 U.S.C. §706 (1982).

review of INS decisions but, rather, clarifies that the abuse-of-discretion standard of review applies to all aspects of adjudications regarding postdeportation proceedings.

Sovereign immunity—federal jurisdiction—whether alleged tortious conduct abroad causes a direct effect in the United States

MARTIN v. REPUBLIC OF SOUTH AFRICA. 836 F.2d 91.
U.S. Court of Appeals, 2d Cir., December 29, 1987.

Appellant sued the Republic of South Africa and two South African Government–owned hospitals in the U.S. District Court for the Southern District of New York for negligence and medical malpractice. Appellant, who is a black American citizen, alleged that the defendants had caused his permanent disability by delaying medical treatment to him because of his color following an automobile accident in South Africa. Appellant alleged that, because of this delayed medical treatment, he had returned to the United States permanently disabled, subject to continuing medical complications and dependent on government aid for his subsistence. The district court dismissed the complaint on the grounds that it lacked subject matter jurisdiction and personal jurisdiction over the defendants. It held that the defendants were entitled to sovereign immunity under the Foreign Sovereign Immunities Act (28 U.S.C. §§1330, 1602–1611 (1982)) (the Act) since their conduct did not cause a "direct effect in the United States" within the meaning of section 1605(a)(2) of the Act.[1] The U.S. Court of Appeals for the Second Circuit (per Timbers, J.) affirmed and *held:* that South Africa's acts did not have a "direct effect in the United States" for the purposes of the Act.

In interpreting the phrase "direct effect in the United States," the court found the legislative history unhelpful. The House report indicated that a "direct effect" in the United States would be such as would subject the defendant's action to U.S. jurisdiction in accordance with section 18 of the *Restatement (Second) of Foreign Relations Law of the United States* (1965).[2] This, the court concluded, was "inapposite"[3] since, as the Court of Appeals for the Fifth Circuit had noted in *Zernicek v. Brown & Root, Inc.*,[4] section 18 appeared to relate not to sovereign immunity but to the extent to which a state may enact substantive rules of law governing conduct outside its terri-

(a) A foreign state shall not be immune from the jurisdiction of courts of the United States or of the States in any case—

. . .

(2) in which an action is based . . . upon an act outside the territory of the United States in connection with a commercial activity of the foreign state elsewhere and that act causes a direct effect in the United States.

28 U.S.C. §1605(a)(2) (1982).

[2] *See* H.R. REP. NO. 1487, 94th Cong., 2d Sess. 6 (1976), *reprinted in* 1976 U.S. CODE CONG. & ADMIN. NEWS 6604, 6618.

[3] 836 F.2d 91, 94.

[4] 826 F.2d 415, 417 (5th Cir. 1987).

tory that has effects within its territory. For this reason, the Second Circuit had held in *Texas Trading & Milling Corp v. Federal Republic of Nigeria* that, in construing the "direct effect" clause, the courts should not be constrained to follow the "substantial" and "foreseeable" factors of section 18 of the *Restatement (Second).*[5]

The court therefore based its holding on the language of the statute, and subsequent case law, in particular the *Texas Trading* case. That case had concerned a contract for three American companies to supply cement to Nigeria. Payment was to be made through a New York bank. Nigeria repudiated the contract, and the companies sued Nigeria in the United States. The Second Circuit held that the district court had subject matter jurisdiction. The effect of the breach was "direct," as "financial loss" had been sustained. It was "in the United States" because the plaintiffs were to have presented documents and collected money in the United States but were precluded from doing so by Nigeria's breach of contract. No injury was sustained until the plaintiffs were denied payment, in the United States, from the New York bank.

In the present case, however, the "effects" of South Africa's acts occurred in South Africa, where the appellant became quadriplegic. Appellant was not in the United States at the time of the accident and, indeed, did not return to the United States until more than a year after the date of the accident. *Texas Trading* was therefore distinguishable.[6] The court found the present facts to be similar to those in *Zernicek,* in which the Fifth Circuit held that continuing sickness caused by exposure to radiation overseas was not a "direct" effect within the meaning of the Act.[7] The Second Circuit had also noted that all courts that have considered a claim for personal injuries sustained in a foreign state have dismissed the claim because they presented insufficiently direct effects.[8]

The court rejected appellant's contention that this holding created a distinction between corporations and individuals. The "plain language" of the Act led the court to conclude that South Africa's conduct did not cause a direct effect in the United States.[9]

In terms of the statutory language, the court's holding seems to be logical: an injury to a natural person outside U.S. jurisdiction does occur abroad, not "in" the United States. Even if the person is a U.S. citizen who returns to the United States and requires lifetime care, the continuing effects are

[5] 647 F.2d 300, 311 (2d Cir. 1981), *cert. denied,* 454 U.S. 1148 (1982).

[6] The *Texas Trading* court had noted that in cases involving personal injury abroad, it was "easy to locate the 'effect' outside the United States." 647 F.2d at 312 n.35.

[7] 826 F.2d at 419.

[8] *See* Tucker v. Whitaker Travel, Ltd., 620 F.Supp. 578, 586 (E.D. Pa. 1985), *aff'd,* 800 F.2d 1140 (3d Cir.), *cert. denied,* 107 S.Ct. 578 (1986) ("Whatever pain and pecuniary loss plaintiffs suffer in the United States are indirect consequences of the accident [overseas]"); and Upton v. Empire of Iran, 459 F.Supp. 264, 266 (D.D.C. 1978), *aff'd,* 607 F.2d 494 (D.C. Cir. 1979) ("The common sense interpretation of a 'direct effect' is one which has no intervening element, but, rather, flows in a straight line without deviation or interruption").

[9] 836 F.2d at 95.

"indirect" rather than "direct." This decision, as well as the Fifth Circuit's decision in *Zernicek* and several lower court rulings, should serve to establish that personal injuries suffered abroad may not be pursued under the Foreign Sovereign Immunities Act. Although the court stated that no distinction exists in the relevant law between individuals and corporations, it remains possible that failure to pay an American corporation overseas can create an effect "in the United States" for purposes of the Act.[10]

Viewed in relation to the body of case law created in recent years by the Second Circuit, the court's decision in this case reflects a trend different from that found in the Second Circuit's decisions under the Alien Tort Claims Act. The Second Circuit has held that under the Alien Tort Claims Act aliens can pursue claims for torture against other aliens based on injuries incurred abroad.[11] In a recent decision involving Amerada Hess, the Second Circuit has also held that foreign corporations may pursue claims against foreign sovereigns under the Alien Tort Claims Act for injuries suffered abroad on the high seas without regard to the Foreign Sovereign Immunities Act.[12] If the *Amerada Hess* decision, now pending before the Supreme Court, is upheld, aliens—but not U.S. citizens—would be able to pursue claims against foreign sovereigns in U.S. courts for personal injuries occurring outside the United States.

Foreign Sovereign Immunities Act—act of state doctrine—treaty exception

DAYTON v. CZECHOSLOVAK SOCIALIST REPUBLIC. 834 F.2d 203. U.S. Court of Appeals, D.C. Cir., December 8, 1987.

Appellants, former Czechoslovakian citizens who became United States citizens after their property was expropriated, filed a lawsuit against Czechoslovakia and a Czechoslovakian trading company (Centrotex) seeking compensation for the nationalization of their textile production plants in Czechoslovakia in October 1945. Plaintiffs received partial payment under a claims settlement agreement but sought full recovery through this lawsuit. The district court denied plaintiffs' motions for entry of default judgment against Czechoslovakia and dismissed the complaint. The U.S. Court of Appeals for the District of Columbia Circuit (per Ginsburg, J.) affirmed the district court's judgment and *held:* that defendants were immune from suit under the provisions of the Foreign Sovereign Immunities Act of 1976 (28 U.S.C. §§1330, 1602–1611 (1982)) (FSIA).

The court first determined that appellees, the Czechoslovak Socialist Republic and Centrotex, were entitled to immunity unless one of the statutory

[10] This point was expressly left open in *Texas Trading,* as was the case of failure to pay a foreign corporation in the United States. 647 F.2d at 312 & nn. 34 & 35.

[11] Filartiga v. Pena-Irala, 630 F.2d 876, 880 (2d Cir. 1980), *summarized in* 75 AJIL 149 (1981).

[12] Amerada Hess Shipping Corp. v. Argentine Republic, 830 F.2d 421 (2d Cir. 1987), *summarized in* 82 AJIL 126 (1988), *cert. granted,* 56 U.S.L.W. 3718 (U.S. Apr. 18, 1988) (No. 87-1372).

exceptions to immunity was applicable. Adopting the district court's reasoning, the court rejected appellant's theory that the Government of Czechoslovakia had waived the sovereign immunity of Centrotex when it provided the company with the capacity to sue and be sued. On this issue the district court had referred to Congress's intention "to extend sovereign immunity to all foreign state instrumentalities endowed with the capacity to sue and be sued when it enacted the FSIA," as well as to "the legislative history to §1603 [which] establishes that entities with the capacity 'to sue and be sued' were included within the protection of §1604."[1] Therefore, the court of appeals agreed that "no intelligent waiver" can be "fairly extracted from endowment of a state trading company with the capacity to sue and be sued."[2]

The court also found that the expropriated property exception in section 1605(a)(3) did not apply. Neither the expropriated textile plants, nor any properties exchanged for these plants, were present in the United States, nor did appellee Centrotex own or operate such properties.[3]

Even though the court rejected the claim on the basis of the FSIA, the court also noted that the "act of state doctrine" would preclude judicial review in any event. Under that doctrine, in the " 'absence of a treaty or other unambiguous agreement regarding controlling legal principles, courts in the United States will generally refrain from examining the validity of a taking by a foreign state of property within its own territory.' "[4] The court held that the act of state doctrine applied even though appellee Czechoslovakia had not participated in this lawsuit, because the doctrine " 'is a judicial policy of restraint, [and its] application . . . cannot be "waived" by the foreign state.' "[5]

The court rejected appellants' argument that the treaty exception should apply. Noting that this exception requires "a treaty or other unambiguous agreement," the court considered the 1946 Agreement, in which the parties agreed to "provide adequate and effective compensation to the nationals of one country with respect to their rights or interests in properties which may have been or may be nationalized or requisitioned by the Government of the other country."[6] Since the Agreement refers only to nationals and " 'contains no reference to *when the property owners became* [*United States*] *nationals for the purpose of being included in settlement coverage*,' "[7] it was unclear whether the Agreement applied to appellants. This lack of clarity caused the court to conclude that the Agreement was insufficient "to dislodge the act of state doctrine."[8]

[1] 672 F.Supp. 7, 9–11 (D.D.C. 1986).
[2] 834 F.2d 203, 205.
[3] *Id.* at 206.
[4] *Id.* (quoting RESTATEMENT OF FOREIGN RELATIONS LAW OF THE UNITED STATES (REVISED) §469 (Tent. Draft No. 7, 1986)).
[5] *Id.* (quoting RESTATEMENT (REVISED), *supra* note 4, §469 comment *e*).
[6] Agreement Relating to Commercial Policy, Nov. 14, 1946, United States–Czechoslovakia, 61 Stat. 2431, TIAS No. 1569, 7 UNTS 119.
[7] 834 F.2d at 206 (quoting Plaintiffs' Memorandum in Opposition to the Motion to Dismiss the Complaints at 21–22) (emphasis in original)).
[8] *Id.*

This case confirms that U.S. private claimants face substantial legal obstacles in U.S. courts when seeking compensation for foreign expropriations. Private claimants may turn instead to the U.S. Government to espouse their claims or to Congress for legislation vesting blocked assets.

Bankruptcy—act of state doctrine—misappropriation of trade secrets—international comity—constructive trust

REMINGTON RAND CORP. v. BUSINESS SYSTEMS, INC. 830 F.2d 1260.
U.S. Court of Appeals, 3d Cir., October 5, 1987.

Appellee, Remington Rand Corp., filed an adversary action in U.S. bankruptcy court alleging that appellant, Business Systems, Inc., B.V., had misappropriated its trade secrets in a certain typewriter. In 1978 appellee had acquired the know-how to produce the SR–101 electronic typewriter, which it then licensed to its Dutch subsidiary. In 1981 appellee sought reorganization under chapter 11 of the United States Bankruptcy Code. At the same time, the Dutch subsidiary entered "suspension of payments"—the equivalent of reorganization under Dutch law. While appellee was successfully reorganized, its subsidiary was declared bankrupt. The Dutch trustees in bankruptcy sold the subsidiary's manufacturing plant, together with the know-how to produce the SR–101, to appellant. The bankruptcy court held appellant and its U.S. affiliate liable for misappropriating the know-how to produce the SR–101 and made recommendations to the district court on appropriate relief. The district court ordered appellant to return the misappropriated documents and imposed a constructive trust on all products and proceeds derived therefrom no matter where those products were located, to secure any damages ultimately awarded to appellee. The district court later awarded over $200 million to appellee. On appeal, the United States Court of Appeals for the Third Circuit (per Aldisert, J.) affirmed in part and reversed in part and *held:* (1) that the district court's finding of liability on misappropriation accorded with Dutch law and was not in error; (2) that neither the act of state doctrine nor international comity precluded the district court from entertaining appellee's suit; (3) that requiring the return of the know-how documents to appellee was an appropriate remedial measure; (4) that international comity required vacating the constructive trust imposed on appellant's non-U.S. assets; and (5) that the district court's assessment of damages should be vacated and remanded for further proceedings in accordance with the opinion.

The Third Circuit first addressed on appeal whether the district court's ruling on misappropriation was proper. The district court had concluded that under Dutch law, appellants' liability depended upon two elements: "(1) some inappropriate act by [the] Dutch trustees, and (2) some inappropriate act by or imputed to [appellant]."[1] The court of appeals concluded, as had the district court, that judging the appropriateness of the Dutch trustees' actions required recourse to Dutch law. After reviewing a number

[1] 830 F.2d 1260, 1263.

of legal sources, the Third Circuit concluded that misappropriation of trade secrets constituted a tort under Dutch law, and that the trustees in bankruptcy had therefore committed an inappropriate act by transferring the know-how to produce the SR–101 without compensating appellee.[2] As to the second element of liability, the district court had adopted the bankruptcy court's determination that under both New Jersey and Dutch law, the conduct of appellant was inappropriate since it had known or should have known of the know-how–licensing agreement when it purchased the assets of appellee's subsidiary from the Dutch trustees in bankruptcy. The court of appeals concluded that this finding was not clearly erroneous. Both elements of liability having been met, the Third Circuit held that the district court had not erred in ruling appellant liable to appellee for misappropriation of trade secrets.

The court of appeals next focused on appellant's argument that the act of state doctrine precluded appellee's suit. The court observed that acts of bankruptcy trustees were not " 'considered policy determination[s] by a government to give effect to its political and public interests,' "[3] and thus did not "rise to the dignity of acts of a foreign sovereign"[4] requiring deference under the act of state doctrine. The application of that doctrine had therefore been properly rejected by the district court.

Appellant argued alternatively that since a Dutch court had approved the trustees' sale of the know-how, the doctrine of international comity barred any examination of the propriety of that transaction. The bankruptcy court had rejected that argument on the basis of its findings that the purchase agreement between appellant and the trustees exceeded the Dutch court's order, and that the Dutch court neither knew of, nor participated in, the negotiation of the purchase agreement. On appeal, appellant alleged that the bankruptcy court's failure to consider the SR–101 know-how as an asset authorized to be sold was an improper interpretation of the Dutch court's order. The court of appeals concluded that appellant had failed to establish that the bankruptcy court's findings were clearly erroneous, and thus held that the courts below had not abused their discretion in refusing to abstain from hearing appellee's claims on the grounds of comity.[5]

Appellant also argued on appeal that the district court's equitable relief order was inconsistent with principles of comity since at the time of the order, appellant was in bankruptcy proceedings in the Netherlands. With respect to the district court's order that appellant turn over to appellee the

[2] Specifically, the court found that the trustees' actions violated the Netherlands Civil Code, Article 1401, which, according to the Dutch Supreme Court, proscribes any act that "conflicts with . . . the duty of good care to be observed in social intercourse with regard to another's person or goods." *Id.* at 1264 (quoting Lindenbaum v. Cohen, 1919 NJ 161 (HR)).

[3] *Id.* at 1265 (citing Mannington Mills, Inc. v. Congoleum Corp., 595 F.2d 1287, 1294 (3d Cir. 1979)).

[4] *Id.*

[5] The court of appeals alternatively held that the bankruptcy and district courts had not erred in denying comity to the Dutch court order since appellant did not have notice of, or an opportunity to be heard at, the Dutch proceedings, and was thus denied due process.

misappropriated trade-secret documents, the court of appeals, like the court below, rejected appellant's argument. According to the court, compliance with the order did not offend principles of comity since the question of ownership of the documents had been fully litigated in district court, and there had been no contrary court ruling in the Netherlands.[6] Much more problematic for the court of appeals, however, was the constructive trust placed on all typewriters, parts and proceeds of appellant—"the most controversial aspect of the district court's . . . order."[7]

At the outset, the Third Circuit stressed the tension in the case that resulted from appellant's having entered "suspension of payments" status in the Netherlands after the commencement of the litigation in the United States. From appellant's standpoint, the court noted, the constructive trust unfairly granted appellee priority over similarly situated creditors in the Netherlands. Indeed, for this very reason, the appellant's Dutch trustee had refused to obey the district court's order and had concluded that the constructive trust order did not affect the rights of Dutch banks under their security agreements with appellant. From appellee's perspective, on the other hand, the constructive trust represented the only realistic means of recovering on its judgment against appellant. Resolving these opposing considerations, the court noted, required resort to "general precepts of transnational business affairs, especially those that apply to commercial reorganizations or bankruptcies."[8]

Supporting the extension of comity to the bankruptcy proceedings in the Netherlands, according to the court of appeals, was American bankruptcy law's fundamental principle—shared by Dutch law—that assets be distributed equally among creditors of similar standing.[9] Moreover, the court observed, the U.S. Bankruptcy Code[10] expressly recognizes an American policy of favoring comity for foreign bankruptcy proceedings. A consideration undercutting the extension of comity, however, was the obligation of the district court to prevent " 'forcing American creditors to participate in foreign proceedings in which their claims will be treated in some manner inimical to this country's policy of equality.' "[11]

Applying these principles to the facts before it, the court concluded that that portion of the constructive trust order attaching appellant's assets in the United States should be upheld since it raised no comity concerns. To the extent the court's order imposed a constructive trust operating directly on appellant's property outside the United States, however, it "ha[d] the capacity to disregard the underlying reasons for comity, to interfere with the orderly administration of bankruptcy in The Netherlands, and to provoke a confrontation between the courts of the two countries."[12] As a conse-

[6] 830 F.2d at 1269.

[7] *Id.* at 1270.

[8] *Id.* at 1271.

[9] *Id.*

[10] 11 U.S.C. §304 (1982).

[11] 830 F.2d at 1271 (quoting Banque de Financement v. First Nat'l Bank of Boston, 568 F.2d 911, 921 (2d Cir. 1977)).

[12] *Id.* at 1272.

quence, the Third Circuit ruled, the order attaching foreign assets could be sustained only as a last resort.

According to the court of appeals, the proper procedure in these circumstances was as follows.[13] First, after retrial of the damages proceedings,[14] appellee should reduce any damages award it receives to judgment, and then seek a declaratory judgment from the Dutch bankruptcy court as to whether the American judgment will stand on equal terms in appellant's bankruptcy proceedings with a judgment obtained in the Netherlands. If the Dutch court accords full force and effect to the American judgment, the district court will then have to determine whether any of appellant's assets attached in the United States should be forwarded to the Netherlands for distribution. If, however, the Dutch court fails either to rule on appellee's declaratory judgment in a timely fashion, or to accord the district court's judgment appropriate respect, the district court will be free to enter appropriate remedies—including, presumably, the reimposition of that portion of the constructive trust attaching appellant's foreign assets. According to the court of appeals, its solution "would afford appropriate protection to an American creditor, yet also acknowledge the primary role of the Dutch court in equitably distributing the available funds."[15]

Indeed, the stepwise solution of the court of appeals to "this vexing problem of private international law" strikes an appropriate balance between protecting the interests of those seeking recourse to U.S. laws and giving due deference to the judicial proceedings of another nation—precisely the considerations that must be taken into account when applying the doctrine of international comity. Whether comity will ultimately be extended in this case, however, depends in the first instance on whether the Dutch bankruptcy court will recognize appellee on the same footing as

[13] This procedure was first described in the early English case of *Solomons v. Ross,* "[k]nown from a scant note in 1 H. Bl. 131 n., 126 Eng. Rep. 79 n. (1764), more fully reported in a note to *Neale v. Cottingham* (Irish Ch. 1770), *reported in* Wallis-Lyne, *Irish Chancery Reports* 54, 59 n. (1839)." 830 F.2d at 1273 n.5. In *Solomons v. Ross,* a Dutch trustee in bankruptcy laid claim to assets of an insolvent Dutch debtor that had been attached in London by an English creditor. The English court relinquished the assets to the Dutch trustee after receiving assurances that foreign and domestic creditors would be treated on equal terms under Dutch bankruptcy law.

[14] At the first trial on damages, appellant argued that it could have recreated the know-how to produce the SR-101 from scratch in just 6 months, and that its tort liability must therefore be limited to only the "head start" it received by misappropriating the trade secrets. The district court refused to allow appellant to raise this "lead time valuation defense" as a sanction for failing to obey the court's constructive trust order. In view of its determination that the constructive trust was too far-reaching, the court of appeals held that the sanctions formerly imposed against appellant—the imposition of attorneys' fees and the denial of the lead time valuation defense—must be overturned. Accordingly, it ordered that the district court reassess damages, after giving appellant the opportunity to interpose the lead time valuation defense. On remand, however, the district court recently held that because appellant's head start precluded appellee from entering the market, and because "appellee was denied and continues to be denied possession of the know-how documents despite the Orders of this Court," the head start defense was not available to appellant as a matter of law. Kilbarr Corp. v. Business Sys., Inc., 679 F.Supp. 422 (D.N.J. 1988).

[15] 830 F.2d at 1273.

appellant's Dutch creditors. If it does, then the focus will return to the district court, which will have to determine whether comity should be observed by relinquishing appellant's U.S. assets to the Dutch bankruptcy court.

Arbitration—enforcement of international award in U.S. courts—access to U.S. courts by nonrecognized government—federal question jurisdiction—New York Convention

MINISTRY OF DEFENSE OF THE ISLAMIC REPUBLIC OF IRAN v. GOULD, INC. No. CV 87-03673-RG.
U.S. District Court, C.D. Cal., January 14, 1988.

Petitioner, the Ministry of Defense of the Islamic Republic of Iran (Iran), brought suit in federal district court against respondents Gould, Inc., Gould Marketing, Inc. and Gould International, Inc. (collectively, Gould), seeking enforcement of an award of $3,640,247.13 it had obtained in 1984 against respondent Gould Marketing, Inc. from the Iran–United States Claims Tribunal in The Hague. The respondents moved to dismiss, arguing (1) that the unrecognized Government of Iran has no right of access to United States courts, and (2) that there is no legal mechanism for enforcement of Tribunal awards by U.S. courts. District Judge Richard A. Gadbois, Jr., denied the motion to dismiss, *holding* that the express determination of the executive branch that Iran could sue in U.S. courts was dispositive on the access issue, and that while the case did not fall within the court's federal question jurisdiction, the legislative implementation of the Convention on the Recognition and Enforcement of Foreign Arbitral Awards (New York Convention)[1] confers jurisdiction to enforce awards by the Tribunal.

In late 1981, respondent Gould Marketing's corporate predecessor brought claims at the Tribunal seeking over $4 million in contract damages and termination costs arising out of the disruption of a contract for the sale of various electronic equipment and services to the Iranian Ministry of Defense.[2] After briefing and a hearing on the merits, the Tribunal determined that prepayments already made by Iran, together with counterclaims asserted by Iran against Gould Marketing, exceeded the amounts due to Gould Marketing for work performed and costs incurred. The result was a net award in favor of Iran in the amount of $3,640,247.13.[3]

[1] *Done* June 10, 1958, 21 UST 2517, TIAS No. 6997, 330 UNTS 38 (entered into force Dec. 29, 1970).

[2] *See* Gould Marketing, Inc. v. Ministry of Defence of the Islamic Republic of Iran, 6 IRAN-U.S. CLAIMS TRIBUNAL REP. 272, 274, 286 (1984 II), *summarized in* 79 AJIL 148 (1985).

[3] 6 IRAN-U.S. CLAIMS TRIBUNAL REP. at 287. This was an extremely unusual result at the Tribunal. Only eight other contested cases at the Tribunal have resulted in awards against a private U.S. party, generally involving nominal awards of $2,000 to $15,000 for costs. Besides Gould, only two other American claimants received substantial adverse monetary awards, and both of these involved large advance payments, some portion of which the claimants conceded was payable to Iran. *See* Harris International Telecommunications, Inc. v. Islamic Republic of Iran, AWD 323-409-1 (Nov. 2, 1987) (Chamber 1) ($833,949.44 awarded to Iran); FMC Corp. v. Islamic Republic of Iran, AWD 292-353-2 (Feb. 12, 1987) (Chamber 2) ($8,659,750.50 awarded to Iran).

Gould Marketing refused to pay Iran the amount of the award. Rather than seek to enforce the award directly against Gould Marketing, Iran initially sought redress by means of a claim at the Tribunal against the United States. In that action, known as *Case A/21,* Iran sought an order compelling the United States to satisfy judgments awarded against all American nationals that refuse voluntarily to pay, much as Iran is required, by means of the Security Account established in the Algiers Accords,[4] to satisfy awards of the Tribunal against Iranian entities. In its decision in *Case A/21,* the Tribunal rejected Iran's claim, relying on the representations of the United States that U.S. courts were available for enforcement of the Tribunal's awards in Iran's favor. The Tribunal stated that it would reconsider the claim if Iran were ultimately denied such access.[5] Iran thereafter brought the present action in a U.S. court against Gould Marketing and its corporate affiliates for the enforcement of the award.

Gould moved to dismiss the petition on two grounds. First, it argued that the present Government of the Islamic Republic of Iran should be denied access to the courts of the United States because the United States has not recognized that Government as the legitimate representative of the Iranian state. Second, Gould argued that federal district courts lack subject matter jurisdiction over suits to enforce the Tribunal's awards because such suits cannot be considered to be "civil actions arising under . . . the laws . . . of the United States," as required for "federal question" jurisdiction under 28 U.S.C. §1331. In addition, Gould contended that jurisdiction does not arise from the New York Convention since two necessary elements, a signed agreement to arbitrate and the use of the substantive law of the forum state, are absent.[6]

The United States intervened in the case,[7] filing a statement of interest supporting Iran's claim for enforcement and refuting Gould's defenses. The United States asserted that it was in its interest that the Tribunal's awards be enforceable (1) to fulfill the international obligations set forth by the Tribunal in *Case A/21;* (2) to encourage Iran to continue to meet its obligations under the Algiers Accords, including replenishment of the Security Account; (3) to establish the enforceability of the Tribunal's awards under the New York Convention in case U.S. claimants should have to seek enforcement of awards against Iran in national courts; and (4) to promote generally the recognition and enforcement of duly rendered international awards in

[4] Paragraph 7 of the Declaration of the Democratic and Popular Republic of Algeria, Jan. 19, 1981, *reprinted in* 75 AJIL 418, 420, created a Security Account funded with $1 billion in Iranian assets that had been frozen during the hostages crisis. Awards to successful American claimants are paid out of the Security Account. No specific provision for the payment of awards in favor of Iranian claimants was made in the Accords.

[5] Islamic Republic of Iran v. United States, DEC 62–A/21–FT, at 11 (May 4, 1987) (Full Tribunal).

[6] Gould also raised procedural defenses based on the form of the pleadings. No. CV 87–03673–RG, slip op. at 7, *reprinted in* INT'L ARB. REP., January 1988, at C.

[7] The U.S. appearance was pursuant to 28 U.S.C. §517, which authorizes the Attorney General to "attend to the interests" of the United States in any pending suit.

commercial cases.[8] The United States urged the court to accord Iran full access, arguing that the grant or denial to a foreign sovereign of the right of access to the courts of the United States is a matter in the sole discretion of the executive branch, and stating that implicitly by its past conduct and expressly by its present intervention the United States had determined that such access should be accorded to Iran.[9] It also urged the court to accept Iran's assertion that the court had jurisdiction over suits to enforce awards by the Tribunal on both federal question and New York Convention grounds.

The court's brief order first rejected Gould's access argument.[10] Recognizing that, traditionally, access to the courts has been reserved to nations enjoying recognition by and diplomatic relations with the United States, the court held that the question of access is ultimately in the "exclusive power of the Executive Branch."[11] It accepted the Government's statement of interest on the matter as dispositive.

Turning to the issue of its jurisdiction to adjudicate this dispute, the court refused the request of Iran and the United States that it exercise general federal question jurisdiction under 28 U.S.C. §1331. It held that a suit to enforce an award by the Tribunal could be said to arise under the laws of the United States only if the Algiers Accords establishing the Tribunal were considered part of the law of the United States. Since the declaration establishing the Tribunal was implemented as an executive agreement rather than as a formal treaty with the consent of the Senate, it can be considered the law of the United States for jurisdictional purposes only "if it is self-executing and requires nothing further to implement it."[12] Relying on an earlier decision by the Court of Appeals for the Ninth Circuit expressly finding the Algiers Accords not to be self-executing,[13] the court held Iran's petition to be outside its general federal question jurisdiction.[14]

The court, however, found a sufficient source for its jurisdiction under the New York Convention. The court first noted that the implementing legislation provides that actions arising under the Convention "are deemed to arise under the laws of the United States."[15] It then rejected both of Gould's arguments that the Convention is inapplicable. First, it dismissed

[8] Statement of Interest of the United States, in Ministry of Defense of the Islamic Republic of Iran v. Gould, Inc., Case No. CV 87-03673-RG, at 3-6 (C.D. Cal. filed Sept. 2, 1987).

[9] The United States recently filed similar statements of interest in two other cases in which American defendants disputed Iran's right to access to U.S. courts. *See* Statement of Interest of the United States in Organization for Investment, Economic and Technical Assistance of Iran v. Shack & Kimball, Civ. No. 85-0437 (NHJ) (PJA) (D.D.C. filed Mar. 1, 1988); Brief for Amicus Curiae the United States of America in National Petrochemical Co. of Iran v. The M/T Stolt Sheaf, No. 87-9022 (2d Cir. filed Feb. 29, 1988).

[10] The court made no reference to the prior contrary holding of the U.S. District Court for the Southern District of New York. *See* National Petrochemical Co. of Iran v. The M/T Stolt Sheaf, 671 F.Supp. 1009 (S.D.N.Y. 1987), *appeal docketed,* No. 87-9022 (2d Cir. Dec. 4, 1987).

[11] Slip op. at 3 (relying on Pfizer v. Government of India, 434 U.S. 308 (1978)).

[12] *Id.* at 4.

[13] Islamic Republic of Iran v. Boeing Co., 771 F.2d 1279 (9th Cir. 1985).

[14] Slip op. at 5.

[15] *Id.* at 6 (citing 9 U.S.C. §203 (1982)).

the contention that the Accords are not an "agreement in writing" between the parties establishing the arbitration as required by the Convention. While Gould did not sign that agreement, "[t]he question whether the Executive can bind U.S. persons to such an arrangement as if they were signatories is quite effectively dispatched by the *Dames & Moore* decision."[16] It also rejected the suggestion that to be enforceable under the Convention, an award must have been based on the arbitration law of a contracting state, in this case the Netherlands, rather than on international law. Conceding that the argument had some appeal, it nevertheless decided to resolve the "form v. substance tension" in favor of "the overriding judicial interest in effective arbitral proceedings."[17]

The district court's rather summary order will likely not long remain the final exposition of the issues raised in this case, as it may soon be superseded by at least two appellate proceedings. The court granted both parties' requests for certification of the jurisdictional questions to the Ninth Circuit Court of Appeals[18] and an appeal of a different case involving the issue of Iran's access to U.S. courts is now pending in the Second Circuit.[19] Nevertheless, as the first opinion in these circumstances by a court that had the benefit of the strongly stated interest of the United States in the case, the decision points up the issues that are likely to be central to all such cases, and joins a series of cases arising from the Iranian hostage crisis that have involved the balance of private interests and the Executive's plenary foreign affairs authority.

Alien Tort Claims Act—jurisdiction—default judgment—misappropriation of public funds by deposed ruler

JEAN-JUSTE v. DUVALIER. No. 86-0459 Civ.
U.S. District Court, S.D. Fla., January 8, 1988.

Plaintiffs, two citizens of Haiti, filed a complaint individually and on behalf of the Haitian people against defendants, Jean-Claude Duvalier and Michelle Bennett Duvalier, the deposed rulers of Haiti. The complaint alleged that the defendants had misappropriated vast amounts of public monies for their own personal use. Jurisdiction was alleged under the Alien Tort Claims Act (28 U.S.C. §1350 (1982)) and "under the law of nations."[1] After defendants failed to respond to the complaint, the U.S. District Court

[16] *Id.* (citing Dames & Moore v. Regan, 453 U.S. 654 (1981)). The absence of the signature of President Carter or President Reagan on the Accords was also held to be irrelevant. *Id.*

[17] *Id.* at 7.

[18] Ministry of Defense of the Islamic Republic of Iran v. Gould, Inc., No. CV 87-03673-RG (C.D. Cal., order filed Feb. 17, 1988).

[19] *See* note 10 *supra.*

[1] Plaintiffs' First Amended Complaint alleged jurisdiction under the Universal Declaration of Human Rights, the American Convention on Human Rights, the Charter of the United Nations, the Charter of the Organization of American States, the International Covenant on Civil and Political Rights, the International Covenant on Economic, Social and Cultural Rights, and the Declaration on Social Progress and Development.

for the Southern District of Florida entered a default judgment and awarded plaintiffs over half a billion dollars. The court cited no evidence showing that it had subject matter jurisdiction over the case, or that defendants were present in the United States or even that any of the assets allegedly stolen were present in the United States.

However, the court observed that defendants had been served while in exile in France. The court found that service of process was conducted in accordance with French laws in the appropriate manner.

In addition, the court noted that "[d]espite appropriate service of process, the Defendants failed to answer the Complaint, enter an appearance, or even seek a limited appearance challenging the jurisdiction of this Court."[2] Therefore, on September 2, 1986, the court entered a default judgment. Without discussing the possible legal challenges to the court's jurisdiction, or the controversial issues surrounding the Alien Tort Claims Act or the developing international law of human rights, the court concluded that it "is satisfied it does have jurisdiction in this case under the laws of the United States of America."[3]

Turning to the amount of the award, the court noted that extensive documentary and testimonial evidence of defendants' illegal activities had been presented to the court. This evidence included expert testimony about canceled checks and other bank transactions, as well as affidavits of former government officials. On the basis of this evidence, the court concluded that the defendants had "misappropriated more than $504,000,000 from public monies and the Haitian treasury alone."[4] Evidence indicated that additional monies had been taken by means of corrupt schemes such as direct bribes, kickbacks on state contracts and on licensing arrangements, tax breaks, and tax holidays for favored corporations. In addition, the individual plaintiffs offered evidence about the violation of their "rights . . . under the Duvalier regime."[5]

Based on the detailed evidence of damages, the court entered a final judgment against defendants pursuant to Federal Rule of Civil Procedure 55(b)(2). Plaintiffs were awarded $504 million, to be distributed to the Haitian people under an "Economic Development Plan for Haiti" developed by the court. The individual plaintiffs were awarded $1.75 million. Plaintiff Gérard Jean-Juste was awarded $1 million "resulting from his inability to practice his religion freely and subsequent exile from his homeland."[6] Plaintiff Etzer LaLanne was awarded $750,000 "resulting from the deprivation of human rights as a result of physical and emotional torture incurred under the Duvalier regime."[7]

This order contains no analysis or discussion of the important legal issues raised by the complaint in the case. Even though the defendants did not respond to the lawsuit, a more detailed discussion of the jurisdictional issues

[2] No. 86-0459 Civ., slip op. at 1.

[3] *Id.*

[4] *Id.* at 2.

[5] *Id.* at 3.

[6] *Id.* at 4.

[7] *Id.*

would have been preferable. If this case becomes accepted law, it seems likely that the U.S. courts will become a Mecca for human rights claims from all over the world and that these claims will be pressed to default judgments irrespective of proof of territorial or other contacts usually required before U.S. courts exercise jurisdiction.

It remains to be seen whether the judgment in this case will be enforceable.

War Powers Resolution—discretion to exercise jurisdiction—political question doctrine

LOWRY v. REAGAN. 676 F.Supp. 333.
U.S. District Court, D.D.C., December 18, 1987.

Over a hundred members of the U.S. House of Representatives brought suit seeking (1) a declaration that the War Powers Resolution (50 U.S.C. §§1541–1548 (1982)) (the Resolution) required the President to file reports concerning incidents in the Persian Gulf, and (2) an order requiring the President to submit a report concerning continued use of U.S. forces in the Persian Gulf. Under the Resolution, the filing of such a report would trigger the 60-day period after which the troops would have to be recalled unless Congress acted to extend that period. The U.S. District Court for the District of Columbia (per Revercomb, J.) granted defendant's motion to dismiss and *held:* the constraints of equitable discretion and the political question doctrine made exercise of jurisdiction inappropriate in this case.

The court began by describing the relevant provisions of the Resolution, which—as the court noted—was enacted over a presidential veto on November 7, 1973. The Resolution requires the President to consult with Congress "in every possible instance" before introducing U.S. military forces into hostilities and, in any event, to submit a written report to Congress within 48 hours of introducing U.S. forces "into hostilities or into situations where imminent involvement in hostilities is clearly indicated by the circumstances."[1] The Resolution also requires the President to withdraw U.S. forces 60 days after such a report is filed unless Congress extends the period beyond that time.

Turning to the facts in this case, the court described various military incidents involving U.S. forces in the Persian Gulf. The court observed that Congress had debated various responses to this situation but had not enacted any provision into law.

The court next briefly summarized the parties' arguments. Plaintiffs argued that summary judgment was appropriate because the facts were drawn entirely from government sources and thus could not be disputed. Applying the statute to these undisputed facts, plaintiffs maintained that the reporting requirement had been triggered by the hostilities. Without challenging the

[1] 50 U.S.C. §1543(a)(1) (1982).

facts presented by plaintiffs, defendant contended—relying upon the doctrines of standing, political question and equitable discretion—that the case should be dismissed because it did not present a justiciable controversy. Defendant also maintained that because a private right of action cannot be implied under the Resolution, plaintiffs had failed to state a claim for which relief could be granted.

Accepting some—but not all[2]—of defendant's arguments, the court concluded that "exercise of federal jurisdiction in these circumstances would be both inappropriate and imprudent."[3] Invoking the doctrine of "remedial discretion," and relying upon the absence of congressional consensus, the court refused to intervene in a dispute among members of Congress. "This Court declines to accept jurisdiction to render a decision that, regardless of its substance, would impose a consensus on Congress."[4]

Moreover, the court held that the political question doctrine precluded judicial determination of the issues presented. Again, the court relied upon the absence of congressional consensus as a basis for its decision. "Because this Court concludes that the volatile situation in the Persian Gulf demands . . . a 'single-voiced statement of the Government's views,' the Court refrains from joining the debate on the question of whether 'hostilities' exist in that region."[5]

Despite the holding dismissing these congressmen's claims, the court expressly stated by way of dicta that certain types of cases arising under the Resolution may be ripe for judicial review. The court observed that "[j]udicial review of the constitutionality of the War Powers Resolution is not, however, precluded by this decision. A true confrontation between the Executive and a unified Congress, as evidenced by its passage of legislation to enforce the Resolution, would pose a question ripe for judicial review."[6] The court concluded its opinion by noting that "[a]lthough adjudication of constitutional questions should not be encouraged, the courts nonetheless would have the responsibility of resolving the constitutionality of this provision if it were properly presented."[7]

By dismissing this case but going out of its way to note that a different case could be justiciable, the court offered some guidance for future cases. The congressional consensus the court would require for judicial review is likely to result in a presidential decision on purely political grounds to withdraw troops long before judicial review can be rendered. This call for political consensus in Congress may serve the judiciary well as it attempts to fulfill its responsibilities.

[2] The court refused to consider the standing issue. 676 F.Supp. 333, 337 n.26. Moreover, the court concluded that if it had decided to exercise jurisdiction, "the availability of constitutional review indicates that the apparent absence of a private right of action is not fatal to this Court's equitable disposition of this case." *Id.* at 339.

[3] *Id.* at 337.

[4] *Id.* at 339.

[5] *Id.* at 340 (quoting Baker v. Carr, 369 U.S. 186, 211 (1962)).

[6] *Id.* at 339.

[7] *Id.* at 341.

ICSID Arbitral Decision

Arbitration—contracts—international shipping—obligation of good faith performance—speculativeness of damages for future lost profits

Maritime International Nominees Establishment v. Republic of Guinea. Case No. ARB/84/4.

International Centre for Settlement of Investment Disputes, January 6, 1988.

Claimant Maritime International Nominees Establishment (MINE), a corporation that entered into an agreement (the Convention) with respondent Republic of Guinea in 1971 for the formation of a company to exploit Guinea's substantial bauxite deposits, registered a claim with the International Centre for Settlement of Investment Disputes (ICSID) alleging that Guinea had breached the Convention by acting in bad faith to prevent performance of the agreement. Guinea countered that MINE was responsible for the venture's failure. MINE went to ICSID for relief after the United States Court of Appeals for the District of Columbia Circuit held that a U.S. district court lacked jurisdiction to enforce a $27 million award rendered in favor of MINE by the American Arbitration Association. The three-member ICSID tribunal *held:* that Guinea had violated the Convention and was liable to MINE for damages and interest totaling nearly $12.25 million.[1]

The tribunal began by reviewing the history of efforts to mine and transport Guinea's huge deposits of bauxite (which is refined into aluminum) and the protracted litigation spawned by the failure of the company, SOTRAMAR, which was formed by MINE and Guinea pursuant to the Convention. Guinea had previously granted a group of major Western bauxite refiners the right to mine and purchase Guinea's bauxite, as well as the right to transport 50 percent of the bauxite freight; Guinea retained the other 50 percent of freight rights, upon which Guinea hoped to build a merchant marine flying the Guinean flag. Guinea then entered into the Convention with MINE for the establishment of SOTRAMAR, which was 49 percent owned by Guinea and 51 percent by MINE. Two and one-half years later, SOTRAMAR had failed to execute any contracts for shipment of bauxite to the bauxite refiners, and Guinea had negotiated a contract with a shipping consortium called AFROBULK to carry the freight originally intended for SOTRAMAR. After MINE learned of this arrangement, MINE began its efforts to obtain damages for Guinea's alleged bad faith in impeding SOTRAMAR's success and then entering into a freight agreement with a third party.

The tribunal found that although Guinea was unsophisticated in matters of international shipping while MINE was experienced and well financed,

[1] The tribunal awarded Guinea $210,000 for its counterclaim, finding that MINE had improperly attached Guinea's property in other forums, in disregard of ICSID's exclusive jurisdiction over the dispute. The tribunal awarded Guinea less than its full expenses incurred in defending the attachments, however, because MINE's conduct was partially excused by other factors.

the Convention was a valid contract binding on both parties. "In hindsight," the tribunal observed, "the Convention failed because both parties had inflated expectations of what could be accomplished" with the freight rights retained by Guinea under its agreement with the bauxite refiners.[2] But Guinea breached the Convention, the tribunal held, by secretly entering into the agreement with AFROBULK to transport the bauxite that should have been transported by SOTRAMAR. The tribunal rejected Guinea's argument that the AFROBULK contract was necessitated by the failure of MINE to perform its obligations under the Convention. Guinea had never suggested to MINE that SOTRAMAR undertake the type of short-term freight arrangement that Guinea reached with AFROBULK. Moreover, MINE had repeatedly sought authority from Guinea to move forward with various charter and affreightment arrangements in order to make SOTRAMAR succeed, but Guinea did not act: "Guinea was simply not attuned to the shipping market, and it did not appreciate that moving ahead without proper planning could be fatal."[3] Guinea's secret negotiation of the AFROBULK freight contract was held to have breached the Convention because it violated the principle of good faith performance of contracts set forth in the French Civil Code.[4]

With respect to damages, the tribunal rejected MINE's projections of future lost profits by SOTRAMAR, finding those projections too speculative in light of the fact that SOTRAMAR was a new venture that had never earned any profits at all. However, the tribunal accepted the general principle that MINE was entitled to be compensated in some manner for profits it would have earned had Guinea not breached the Convention. Accordingly, the tribunal awarded MINE damages measured by the revenues derived by Guinea during the 2 years that its agreement with AFROBULK was in effect, and projected those revenues over a 10-year period during which the bauxite refiners could reasonably be assumed to have continued to purchase bauxite. Adding a substantial sum for simple interest and costs, and offsetting an amount awarded to Guinea on its counterclaim,[5] the tribunal awarded MINE approximately $12.25 million.

The tribunal's decision provides a straightforward application of contract principles to a complex set of facts. Ultimately, the decision stands for the simple proposition that contracting parties—both private parties and states—must act in good faith both to further the purposes of, and to refrain from hindering, the contract. As to damages, the decision reflects the tribunal's unwillingness to accept complex projections of future lost profits for a venture with no track record to serve as a basis for such projections. Finally, the decision exemplifies the kinds of difficulties that can arise in the context of commercial efforts to exploit natural resources in developing countries.

[2] Case No. ARB/84/4, slip op. at 29, *reprinted in* INT'L ARB. REP., January 1988, at A.

[3] Slip op. at 32.

[4] The tribunal cited Article 1134 of the French Civil Code, without engaging in any discussion or explanation of its choice of law. The tribunal cited no other statutes or decisions.

[5] *See* note 1 *supra*.

Corrigendum

In the report of the decision of the Iran–United States Claims Tribunal in *Mobil Oil Iran Inc. v. Islamic Republic of Iran,* AWD 311-74/76/81/150-3 (July 14, 1987) (82 AJIL 136 (1988)), the words "lost profits" in the quotation from the Partial Award on page 140 at note 15 should be replaced with "alleged losses other than [damages for claimants' advances, investments, and withheld natural gas liquid and crude oil products]." The Tribunal modified the language quoted in the AJIL report in a formal Correction to Award dated July 17, 1987, but did not otherwise change the English text of the Partial Award.

CURRENT DEVELOPMENTS

Inter-American Commission on Human Rights Finds United States in Violation

The Inter-American Commission on Human Rights recently decided[1] that the United States Government had violated two provisions of the American Declaration of the Rights and Duties of Man. The proceeding involved two cases of persons convicted of crimes committed before their 18th birthdays, one in South Carolina and one in Texas. After all state and federal appeals were exhausted, the U.S. Department of State replied to the Commission's request for a stay of execution that "under the U.S. federal system, there are no domestic legal grounds for executive intervention in the implementation of the sentence."[2] The Governor of South Carolina refused a request from the Organization of American States to stay execution and the Governor of Texas did not bother to reply.

With the support of the American Civil Liberties Union and the International Human Rights Law Group, David Weissbrodt presented a brief to the Commission on behalf of the now deceased petitioners, to which the U.S. Government replied. On March 27, 1987, the Commission adopted its resolution by a vote of five to one.[3]

The decision of the Commission in this case found the United States to have violated human rights standards applicable in the inter-American system even though the United States had not ratified the American Convention on Human Rights and, when transmitting it for ratification, had specifically reserved on the issue of juvenile punishment.

The Commission held that the execution of these two individuals for crimes committed before they were 18 years of age violated Article I of the American Declaration of the Rights and Duties of Man, which states: "Every human being has the right to life . . . ." Petitioners had argued that the American Declaration should be read in the light of its purpose and other interpretive terms of the Vienna Convention on the Law of Treaties as expressing a norm of customary international law that prohibits the execution of minors. The Commission rejected this argument on the ground that the United States cannot be bound by "customary law" when it clearly does not, in this respect, accept such a binding principle. However, the Commission went further and held that the rule prohibiting execution of juvenile offenders had acquired the authority of *jus cogens*, a norm of international law from which no derogation is permitted. Unfortunately, the Commission did not elaborate on the notion of a regional *jus cogens*, or compare it to the notion of peremptory norm stated in Article 53 of the Vienna Convention,

[1] Res. 3/87, Case No. 9647, OAS/Ser.L/VII.71, Doc. 9 (1987).

[2] *Id.* at 149.

[3] *Id.* at 150.

which defines *jus cogens* as a "norm accepted and recognized by the international community of States as a norm from which no derogation is permitted." Instead, the Commission found it sufficient that such a norm is accepted by the member states of the OAS, including the United States, although the latter disputes that a consensus exists on the age of majority.

The Commission also concluded that the United States had violated Article II of the American Convention (right to equality before the law) by failing to preempt actions of its constituent states regarding the right to life and thus permitting "a pattern of legislative arbitrariness." The Commission noted that because of the diversity of state practice, the death penalty could be applied to children as young as 10 years of age who committed a crime in one state, while in others it would be inapplicable even for adults committing the same crime.

The American Declaration of the Rights and Duties of Man, which the United States was held to have violated, is, of course, not a treaty. It was promulgated as Resolution XXX by the Ninth International Conference of American States, which adopted the Charter of the Organization of American States. The United States ratified the OAS Charter and is a member of the Organization. The introduction to Resolution XXX states that although the protection of human rights provided by American states under their domestic law was appropriate under existing conditions, international protection for such rights should be strengthened as conditions become more favorable; and it urges that "the international protection of the rights of man should be the principal guide of an evolving American law."[4]

The process of interpreting this "evolving guide" has been carried out by the Inter-American Commission on Human Rights. Since its organization in 1960, the Commission has consistently interpreted its powers broadly in light of its mandate to further respect for the human rights set forth in the American Declaration.[5] Although the original Statute granted by the OAS Council to the Commission did not provide jurisdiction over individual complaints,[6] the Commission ruled that it had power to investigate such complaints and to make recommendations to particular governments. In the face of the Council's repeated denials of requests to revise the Commission's Statute in this regard, the Second Special Inter-American Conference directed the inclusion of an amendment that, in effect, would ratify the Commission's interpretation of its powers.[7]

The Commission is not an international tribunal and its decision is not binding, as it would be if it were a decision of the Inter-American Court of Human Rights and the United States had ratified the American Convention

[4] Res. XXX, 6 NINTH INTERNATIONAL CONFERENCE OF AMERICAN STATES, ACTAS Y DOCUMENTOS 297 (1953) [hereinafter Declaration]; *see* Fox, *The Protection of Human Rights in the Americas*, 7 COLUM. J. TRANSNAT'L L. 222 (1968).

[5] On the evolution of the concept of the binding character of the Declaration, see Buergenthal, *The Revised OAS Charter and the Protection of Human Rights*, 69 AJIL 828 (1975).

[6] OAS/Ser.L/V/I.1 (Sept. 26, 1960).

[7] Res. XXII of the Second Special Inter-American Conference, OAS/Ser.L/V/II.14, Doc. 33 (1966); *see* Fox, *Doctrinal Development in the Americas: From Non-Intervention to Collective Support for Human Rights*, 1 N.Y.U. J. INT'L L. & POL. 44, 55 (1968).

and accepted the jurisdiction of the Court. However, the recommendation is an interpretation by an authorized body of independent experts of an international agreement to which the United States is a party and thus should be persuasive to U.S. courts interpreting the Eighth Amendment in the light of "evolving standards of decency."[8]

Finally, the Commission's recommendation raises the issue of United States ratification of the American Convention on Human Rights.

At the meeting of foreign ministers in 1959 when a treaty was first proposed to permit American states to take collective measures in support of human rights, the United States stated that it could not participate in such an endeavor.[9] This isolationist position was reversed a decade later and a U.S. delegation participated actively in drafting the proposed San José treaty, which became the American Convention on Human Rights. The Convention entered into force in 1978 and has now been ratified by 18 members of the Organization of American States. When the treaty was submitted for ratification by President Carter, the Senate did not act favorably and it has not been resubmitted.

Will the Commission's recommendation provide further substance to the specter of foreign intervention in matters of U.S. domestic policy?[10] Perhaps such a reaction would be offset by the observation that even if the United States chooses not to ratify the Convention, it may have acquired certain limitations on its freedom of disposition in human rights matters by virtue of membership in the OAS. As an international organization dedicated to the promotion of human rights and representative democracy, the OAS has a legitimate claim on the respect of its member states.

DONALD T. FOX*

SECOND SESSION OF THE UN COMMITTEE ON ECONOMIC, SOCIAL AND CULTURAL RIGHTS

Introduction

The second session of the United Nations Committee on Economic, Social and Cultural Rights, which took place in Geneva from February 8 to 26, 1988, marked a turning point in international efforts to promote the reali-

[8] Gregg v. Georgia, 428 U.S. 153 (1976). On June 27, 1988, the Supreme Court decided (5-3) that at least minors under the age of 16 at the date of the crime could not be executed under state laws that did not set a minimum age. Four members of the majority concurred that "evolving standards of decency" would make the execution of such persons unconstitutional. Thompson v. Oklahoma, N.Y. Times, June 30, 1988, at A17, col. 1 (U.S. June 29, 1988) (No. 86-6169). In its October 1988 term, the Court will determine whether capital punishment of minors violates the constitutional ban on cruel and unusual punishment (*High v. Zant,* No. 87-5666; *Wilkins v. Missouri,* No. 87-6026). This Eighth Amendment ban is not as broad as Article XXVI of the American Declaration forbidding cruel, infamous or unusual punishment.

[9] Res. VIII, Fifth Meeting of Consultation of Ministers of Foreign Affairs, Final Act, OEA/S.C/II.S (1960).

[10] *See* Fox, *The American Convention on Human Rights and Prospects for United States Ratification,* 3 HUM. RTS. 243 (1973).

* Of the New York Bar.

zation of those rights.[1] In formal terms, the mandate of the Committee of 18 independent experts is to assist the Economic and Social Council (ECOSOC)[2] in carrying out its responsibilities relating to the implementation of the International Covenant on Economic, Social and Cultural Rights,[3] to which there are now 91 states parties.[4]

In practice, however, the Committee has moved substantially beyond this formal advisory role and has begun to emerge as the principal forum in which the implications of the concept of economic, social and cultural rights are being explored. This development reflects an important transition from the sterile formalism that tended to characterize earlier UN efforts to deal with economic rights.[5] It has been facilitated by several different factors. The first is the emergence of a certain shared understanding on the part of the members of the Committee, which has in turn enabled the gradual growth of that sense of esprit de corps which is virtually indispensable to the effective functioning of such a group. This process had been impeded at the Committee's first session by the reluctance of the expert from the USSR, E. Sviridov, to embrace any significant procedural innovations. However, in a significant demonstration of the potential international repercussions of *perestroika,* Sviridov's resignation was tendered prior to the opening of the second session. This and other developments led to a major improvement in the political climate affecting the work of the Committee and enabled it to continue to operate on the basis of consensus, a prospect that had seemed highly improbable at the conclusion of the first session.[6] The second factor is the extent to which the notion of a "constructive dialogue" has been maintained as the basis of all of the Committee's deliberations. The result has been to remove, or at least reduce, the threat of politicization of its work and to provide reassurance to states parties to the Covenant that they will be treated fairly and constructively rather than in an adversarial manner. The third factor is a willingness by the Committee to begin its efforts to give substance to the theory (and rhetoric) of economic, social and cultural rights

[1] *See generally* Alston & Simma, *First Session of the UN Committee on Economic, Social and Cultural Rights,* 81 AJIL 747 (1987).

[2] The Committee was established pursuant to ESC Res. 1985/17. For its first report, see Committee on Economic, Social and Cultural Rights, Report on the First Session (9–27 March 1987), 1987 UN ESCOR Supp. (No. 17), UN Doc. E/1987/28.

[3] GA Res. 2200, 21 UN GAOR Supp. (No. 16) at 49, UN Doc. A/6316 (1966) [hereinafter Covenant].

[4] Committee on Economic, Social and Cultural Rights, Report on the Second Session (8–26 February 1988), 1988 UN ESCOR Supp. (No. 4), UN Doc. E/1988/14, para. 1 [hereinafter Committee's Second Report].

[5] *See* Alston, *Out of the Abyss: The Challenges Confronting the New UN Committee on Economic, Social and Cultural Rights,* 9 HUM. RTS. Q. 332 (1987).

[6] Alston & Simma, *supra* note 1, at 749. Because members of the Committee are experts elected by the Economic and Social Council, and because there is no provision for the nomination of a replacement or alternate of the same nationality, the Soviet expert could only have been replaced by a special election of the Council. Since the resignation was not tendered in time for that to happen, the seat of the Soviet expert remained vacant throughout the session. An experienced Soviet diplomat did, however, follow all of the Committee's meetings.

by going back to reexamine the fundamental premises of UN action in this field. A fourth factor that has enabled the Committee to begin to develop into an effective advocate of economic rights is the acceptance by states[7] (and by the members of the Committee themselves) of the principle that, for most intents and purposes, the Committee should be treated on the same footing as the Human Rights Committee, which monitors compliance with the "other" Covenant, dealing with civil and political rights.[8] Finally, it is clear that the advent of *perestroika* in the economic, social and cultural fields in Eastern Europe has begun to reduce the fundamental East-West ideological differences that for so long have bedeviled international efforts in this field. As a result, there is a greater sense of shared challenges and a reduced desire to seek to exploit the difficulties or inadequacies of any particular socioeconomic system.

The principal achievements of the Committee's second session were procedural rather than substantive. This is to be welcomed, however, since greatly improved procedures are an indispensable prerequisite to the achievement of more significant substantive results in this field. The procedural innovations that were adopted emerged both from formal discussions on the Committee's methods of work (in the framework, initially, of a working group and, subsequently, of the Committee as a whole) and from the precedents that were established indirectly in examining 15 reports submitted by some 13 states parties.[9] The analysis that follows focuses more on the future evolution of the Committee's work in the light of decisions taken at the 1988 session than on the precise details of the deliberations. In particular, the outcomes of its "evaluation" of the reports of specific states parties are only noted insofar as they are relevant to the issues the Committee is likely to emphasize, and the procedures it is likely to adopt, in the future.

Improving the Understanding of the Normative Content of Economic Rights

It is generally recognized that the precise normative content of most of the rights contained in the Covenant is substantially less well understood, or identifiable, than is the case for the majority of civil and political rights. Among the reasons for this situation are the vast scope of some of the rights

[7] Thus, in December 1987, the General Assembly specifically invited the Committee, in considering its future work, to pay "particular attention to practices followed by other treaty bodies." GA Res. 42/102, para. 5 (Dec. 7, 1987).

[8] The Human Rights Committee was established in accordance with Article 28(1) of the International Covenant on Civil and Political Rights, GA Res. 2200, 21 UN GAOR Supp. (No. 16) at 52, UN Doc. A/6316 (1966). For reviews of its work, see Nowak, *The Effectiveness of the International Covenant on Civil and Political Rights: Stocktaking after the First Eleven Sessions of the UN Human Rights Committee,* 1 HUM. RTS. L.J. 136 (1980); Nowak, *UN Human Rights Committee: Survey of Decisions Given up till July 1984,* 5 *id.* at 199 (1984); and Nowak, *UN Human Rights Committee: Survey of Decisions Given up till July 1986,* 7 *id.* at 287 (1986).

[9] The states parties whose reports were examined are Zaire (3 reports), Austria and Chile (2 reports each), and Bulgaria, the Byelorussian SSR, Denmark, Mongolia, Norway, Romania, Sweden and Yugoslavia.

concerned (e.g., the right to an adequate standard of living), their relative novelty, the difficulty of rendering some of them justiciable or otherwise implementing them through "traditional" means, the relative lack of experience with such rights at the national level, the complexity of the relationship between the obligations incumbent upon states and the availability of financial resources, the absence of detailed international standards (except with respect to labor rights), and the poverty of studies that have been undertaken of specific economic rights qua rights.

At its second session, the Committee recognized that the normative content of each of the relevant rights must be spelled out more clearly for it to lay the foundations for the effective exercise of its basic monitoring and catalytic functions. It addressed this need by adopting two new activities, one of which has long been undertaken by the Human Rights Committee, while the other is entirely novel. They are, first, the elaboration of "general comments" and, second, the holding of an annual in-depth discussion on a specific right or article of the Covenant.

The stated purposes of the general comments are:

> to make the experiences gained so far through the examination of . . . reports available for the benefit of all States parties in order to promote their further implementation of the Covenant; to draw the attention of the States parties to insufficiencies disclosed by a large number of reports; to suggest improvements in the reporting procedures; and to stimulate the activities of the States parties, the international organizations and the specialized agencies concerned.[10]

The proposal could be adopted unanimously for several reasons. Perhaps the most important is the precedent set by the very effective use of general comments by the Human Rights Committee as a means of communicating to states its understanding of the various rights and its perception of the specific issues on which states parties should report.[11] Although some of the specific comments it has adopted have been criticized by certain states, the criticism has been directed not at the practice of adopting comments per se but at the alleged *ultra vires* scope of some additional topics chosen for elaboration.[12]

Another reason for the noncontroversial nature of the proposal is that no attempt was made to suggest that the comments should be used as a vehicle for criticizing the performance of a particular state, as has been proposed in the Committee on the Elimination of All Forms of Discrimination Against

[10] Committee's Second Report, *supra* note 4, para. 369.

[11] For a description of the principles governing the work of the Human Rights Committee in the formulation of general comments, see Report of the Human Rights Committee, 39 UN GAOR Supp. (No. 40) at 106–09, UN Doc. A/39/40 (1984).

[12] Particular criticism was directed at the Committee's general comment 14(23), *reproduced in* Report of the Human Rights Committee, 40 UN GAOR Supp. (No. 40) at 162–63, UN Doc. A/40/40 (1985) ("the designing, testing, manufacture, possession and development of nuclear weapons are among the greatest threats to the right to life which confront mankind today"). For the Committee's response to the criticism, see *id.* at 6, paras. 26–27.

Women (CEDAW).[13] Indeed, such a proposal was carefully avoided because of (1) the extent to which it could jeopardize the important principle involved; (2) the fact that specific "violations" are perhaps less likely to emerge in the context of economic rights than of discrimination against women; and (3) the decision to permit individual members of the Committee to make concluding observations at the end of the examination of each state's report,[14] in the course of which any appropriate criticisms can readily be placed on record.

The procedure for drafting general comments[15] is to be, in several respects, more flexible than that followed by the Human Rights Committee. In the first place, proposals may be made and drafts circulated by members at any time, whether the Committee is in session or not. There is thus no possibility that a proposal will be vetoed before it even gets off the ground. The agreed procedure also makes no specific reference to the need for a general comment to be adopted by consensus (i.e., unanimity), which seems appropriate. Although in principle it would be undesirable to have to adopt a general comment by majority vote, the possibility for any single persistent objector to foil the will of the rest of the Committee should not be entrenched through absolute insistence upon "consensus."

The second means by which the Committee will seek to develop understanding of the normative content of the rights in the Covenant is through the holding of an annual "general discussion" focused on a particular right or cluster of rights contained in a single article.[16] The rationale underlying this decision accords closely with the vision expressed by many of the framers of the Covenant, who wanted the supervisory function to be used primarily as a means of exchanging information among states, highlighting shared problems and difficulties, and encouraging the emulation of successful practical initiatives designed to ensure respect for the relevant rights.[17] The Committee is not currently playing any of these roles effectively. Although it and its predecessor together have examined almost 170 reports by states parties,[18] there has never been any attempt to draw broad conclusions

[13] At its sixth session, in 1987, CEDAW decided that the "suggestions and general recommendations" that it is empowered to make under Article 21 of the Convention on the Elimination of All Forms of Discrimination Against Women (GA Res. 34/180, 34 UN GAOR Supp. (No. 46) at 193, UN Doc. A/34/46 (1979)) could, "in an appropriate case," be "based on the examination of a report and information received from a State party." This proposal was adopted despite the objections of several experts that recommendations should be addressed not to a single state party but "to all States parties in a general way." *See* Report of the Committee on the Elimination of Discrimination Against Women, 42 UN GAOR Supp. (No. 38), paras. 57–60, UN Doc. A/42/38 (1987).

[14] *See* text at notes 44–46 *infra*.

[15] Committee's Second Report, *supra* note 4, para. 370. The procedure draws upon that followed by the Human Rights Committee and by CEDAW.

[16] *Id.*, para. 365.

[17] *See generally* Annotations on the Text of the Draft International Covenants on Human Rights: Prepared by the Secretary-General, UN Doc. A/2929, at 116–25 (1955) [hereinafter Annotations].

[18] Committee's Second Report, *supra* note 4, para. 368.

of general utility and applicability from the experience. There has thus been no context in which the Committee could seek to synthesize the results of its work or to reflect on the emergence of any consistent patterns with respect to problems, achievements or other dimensions of the experience of states. The 1-day "general discussion" will enable members of the Committee not only to draw upon the wealth of information provided in the accumulated reports of states parties, but also to reflect upon and discuss any other relevant reports or materials, whether from UN, governmental or NGO sources, dealing with the specific right in question. The discussion could also be used as an opportunity to request specific inputs to the Committee from any or all of these sources.

The new mechanism is clearly not designed to focus on the specific problems confronted by, or the violations alleged to have been committed by, an individual state party to the Covenant. The desired outcome is more akin to an improved understanding of the central issues by the members of the Committee themselves, the states parties and all others with an interest in the substance of the Committee's work. While the general discussion will not necessarily be linked in any way to the elaboration of "general comments," it would nevertheless seem logical for the former to give rise, from time to time, to specific proposals for general comments and to serve as an occasion for debating preliminary suggestions as to their content.

To avoid any suggestion that the Committee will be "wasting" time on its general discussions that could otherwise be used to examine states' reports, the Committee agreed to schedule its discussion day during the final week of each session, by which time it is too late (for logistical reasons) to consider states' reports.[19] It also agreed that the focus of its first general discussion, to be held in 1989, would be Article 11 of the Covenant,[20] which deals, inter alia, with the rights to food and housing. The Committee will thus have an important and unprecedented opportunity to examine and discuss the report of the special rapporteur of the Sub-Commission on Prevention of Discrimination and Protection of Minorities on the right to adequate food[21] and to react to various resolutions by the General Assembly and the Commission on Human Rights dealing with the right to housing.[22]

Improving the Quality and Relevance of States' Reporting

The quality of the Committee's output is linked inextricably to the quality of the inputs it receives. The most important input of all is the report that must be provided from time to time by states parties to the Covenant de-

[19] *Id.*, para. 365. The logistical constraints are attributable to the need for the Secretariat and the rapporteur to draft a summary of the examination of each report, for the summary to be typed and translated, and for a review of each draft by the full Committee prior to adoption.

[20] *Id.*

[21] Eide, Report on the Right to Adequate Food as a Human Right, UN Doc. E/CN.4/Sub.2/1987/23.

[22] E.g., Comm'n on Human Rights Res. 1987/22, 1987 UN ESCOR Supp. (No. 5) at 71, UN Doc. E/1987/18; and GA Res. 42/146 (Dec. 7, 1987).

tailing "the measures which they have adopted and the progress made in achieving the observance of the rights recognized"[23] and providing an indication of "factors and difficulties affecting the degree of fulfilment of obligations."[24] At its second session, the Committee adopted a fundamentally different approach to these reports and recommended the abandonment of the existing system, in which each individual state report deals with a different cluster of rights (those contained in Articles 6 to 9, 10 to 12, or 13 to 15).[25] After the initial cycle was completed, these reports were due once every 3 years; hence, a complete reporting cycle was spread over 9 years.[26] As a result, a state that reported in 1988 on, say, the right to work, would not be expected to do so again until 1997 at the earliest. The Committee found at least three major problems in this system. In the first place, the division of articles (or rights) into three clusters means that at no stage does the state have to provide a global overview of the situation with respect to economic, social and cultural rights. Instead, the reports are divided up, quite arbitrarily in some respects, which conceals how closely the various rights are interrelated (such as the right to social security in Article 9, and the right to an adequate standard of living in Article 11). Consequently, the Committee is given only a partial, and inevitably inadequate, glimpse of the actual situation in the reporting state. Second, the reporting burden placed on states (both rich and poor) is enormous, since a new report must be submitted every 3 years. Under the circumstances, the backlog of overdue reports is hardly surprising.[27] Third, the Committee itself is called upon to review an excessive number of reports. This cumbersome and time-consuming system thus holds a number of built-in incentives to delay reporting, providing states with a ready-made justification for consolidating several reports into one.

The existing system was originally justified by considerations that are no longer valid. In essence, the rationale was to separate the rights into clusters that coincided with the range of concerns of given UN specialized agencies. Thus, by putting Articles 6 to 9 together (dealing with different aspects of the right to work and social security), almost all of the International Labour Organisation's concerns could be taken care of in a single report. Similarly, by bracketing Articles 13 to 15 (dealing with education, science and culture), only UNESCO needed to be involved with that part of the reporting cycle. But this accommodating timetable for reporting is now an anachronism since in practice the specialized agencies either have been accorded (in

[23] Covenant, *supra* note 3, Art. 16(1). [24] *Id.*, Art. 17(2).

[25] This reporting program had been established by ESC Res. 1988 (LX), para. 1, 60 UN ESCOR Supp. (No. 1) at 11, UN Doc. E/5850 (1976).

[26] ESC Decision 1985/132, 1985 UN ESCOR Supp. (No. 1) at 42, UN Doc. E/1985/85.

[27] According to information provided to the Committee by the Centre for Human Rights, a total of 136 reports were overdue as of Feb. 8, 1988. Of 91 states parties, 63 have overdue reports. The statistical breakdown was as follows. Out of these 63 states, 56 have the initial reports overdue: 25 have all 3 reports overdue; 12 have 2 overdue; and 19 have 1 overdue. Out of these 63 states, 15 have their second periodic report overdue; 3 states have 2 overdue reports, and 12 have 1 overdue report. Committee's Second Report, *supra* note 4, Ann. 1.

the case of the ILO), or have only been prepared to accept (in the case of the others), a rather insignificant and formalistic supervisory role.[28]

The Committee has thus opted to call upon states to submit a single report dealing with the whole Covenant once every 5 years.[29] This should reduce the total number of reports submitted, ease the workload of the national officials charged with preparing the reports, facilitate the Committee's appreciation of the overall situation in the state concerned and make the whole reporting process much more comprehensible to the public at large. It will also make it possible to synchronize the reporting schedule with that established under other treaties and to organize it so that different states can be designated to report in different years, which will facilitate the consideration of reports within a year of their preparation (in contrast to the lengthy delays sometimes experienced under the present system).

Two other means of improving the reports of states parties were also considered. It was decided that the Committee would undertake, at its third session, a concerted effort to revise and simplify the guidelines that are provided to assist states in determining what information should be provided.[30] In addition, the Committee suggested that states seek to involve appropriate nongovernmental groups in the process of preparing the reports.[31] At the second session, Norway[32] indicated that such input is already being made, and Bulgaria[33] announced that it would follow that approach in the future.

Enhancing the Dialogue between the Committee and Individual States Parties

The principal assumption underlying the "monitoring" of states' compliance with the obligations of the Covenant is that a "constructive dialogue" between the members of the Committee and the representative(s) of the state party will occur when the latter's report is presented to the Committee. Under existing procedures, a "dialogue" of sorts does indeed take place. Whether or not it is "constructive" is a different matter. That term has at least two connotations in this context: (1) the opposite of destructive, in the sense that the relationship should not be adversarial; and (2) focused and productive, in the sense of enabling the Committee to act as a catalyst to improve the existing situation.

At its second session, the Committee made considerable gains over the performance of its predecessor (the Economic and Social Council's Sessional

[28] *See generally* Alston, *supra* note 5, at 362–67.

[29] Committee's Second Report, *supra* note 4, para. 351. Some concern was expressed by a few members that the requirement of a single 5-yearly report would not be in accordance with the provisions of Article 17(1) of the Covenant, which provides that states parties "shall furnish their reports in stages, in accordance with a programme to be established by the Economic and Social Council." The *travaux préparatoires* of the Covenant make it clear, however, that this wording was not intended to restrict the Council's discretion in any way. *See* Annotations, *supra* note 17, at 118.

[30] Committee's Second Report, *supra* note 4, para. 352.

[31] *Id.*

[32] UN Doc. E/C.12/1988/SR.15, para. 5.

[33] UN Doc. E/C.12/1988/SR.19, para. 63.

Working Group of Governmental Experts)[34] in the first sense of maintaining a civil and nonadversarial dialogue. This advance was illustrated in particular by the case of Chile, which presented two separate reports (dealing, respectively, with Articles 10 to 12, and 13 to 15). When Chile had first appeared before the Committee's predecessor, in 1981, its report was in effect rejected outright. In a perfect display of the double standards that seem unavoidably to plague some of the UN human rights endeavors, the representatives of the USSR, the German Democratic Republic, Bulgaria and Libya persuaded the Committee to invite the Chilean Government to submit additional information without having posed a single question to the government representative or cited any specific facts (except indirectly by reference to UN reports whose content was not specifically discussed).[35] This time around, the Government was presented with a comprehensive and detailed set of questions that provided evidence for the concerns expressed by members of the Committee. To its credit, the Government responded in considerable detail, although its responses did little to dispel the grave doubts evinced by the Committee.[36]

Similarly, in dealing with three reports submitted by Zaire, and presented by the Minister for the Protection of Citizens' Rights and Freedoms, the Committee succeeded in maintaining a constructive dialogue despite the following clear convictions of several members: the requirement that a married woman obtain her husband's permission to work outside the house violated Article 3 of the Covenant; the deliberate abolition of *free* primary education constituted a clear violation of Article 13; the absence of any detailed plan to restore it contravened Article 14; and the automatic membership of all citizens in the People's Movement for the Revolution was inconsistent with the principles governing freedom of association.[37]

To enhance the constructiveness of the dialogue, in the second sense of the term, the Committee adopted a variety of procedural innovations designed to achieve a more streamlined, focused and productive discussion. First, it proposed the establishment of a working group that would "identify in advance the questions which might most usefully be discussed with the representatives of States parties."[38] The objectives are to eliminate some of the duplication in questioning that the present ad hoc system inevitably produces, to reduce the likelihood that issues of major importance will accidentally be overlooked and to give the representative at least some advance warning of the issues most likely to be pursued by the Committee. The Committee also authorized its Chairperson, after consultation with members of the working group, to ask states parties for additional information before their reports are considered where the reports fail to deal with

[34] *See generally* Commentary, *Implementation of the International Covenant on Economic, Social and Cultural Rights: ECOSOC Working Group,* ICJ REV., No. 27, December 1981, at 26.

[35] UN Doc. E/1981/WG.1/SR.7, paras. 11–34.

[36] UN Docs. E/CN.12/1988/SR.12, paras. 36–64; and E/CN.12/1988/SR.13, paras. 1–48.

[37] UN Docs. E/CN.12/1988/SR.16–19.

[38] Committee's Second Report, *supra* note 4, para. 361.

outstanding issues raised when the previous report was examined,[39] or are clearly incomplete in terms of the types of information requested in the reporting guidelines.[40]

The Committee's second session saw a substantially more constructive use of available sources of information, other than those contained in the governments' reports. For example, considerable use was made of statistical information provided by the Secretariat at the Committee's request;[41] direct reference was made to information emanating from NGO sources;[42] and information provided by the ILO was taken directly into account in questions posed by members.[43] As a result, there is every reason to believe that the Committee will eventually be able to draw upon a sufficiently diverse, precise and authoritative range of information to ensure that the dialogue with states parties proceeds on the basis of much more than the government's own version of the situation.

In addition, the Committee succeeded in making far more effective use of the limited time available to it by imposing strict time limits of 15 minutes for the introduction of the state party's report; 90 minutes for questioning by the Committee; 60 minutes, preferably at a subsequent meeting, for a reply by the state party; and 15 minutes for "concluding observations" by members of the Committee.[44] These rules proved highly conducive to more precise and incisive questioning by members and provided an incentive for government representatives to provide additional information or responses to the Committee in writing. Moreover, the final period of 15 minutes represents an innovation of major importance since it allows individual members to indicate the extent to which they were satisfied (or otherwise) with the preceding dialogue. At the second session, this opportunity was used very unevenly; some states' reports "escaped" almost without any substantive concluding observations, while others were subjected to lengthy and detailed comments. This unevenness was principally a function of the novelty of the technique,[45] which may be expected to work much more

[39] *Id.*, para. 359.

[40] *Id.*, para. 360. This provision is modeled on the practice of CEDAW. *See* its 1987 report, *supra* note 13, para. 49.

[41] In accordance with ESC Res. 1987/5, para. 13 (May 26, 1987).

[42] E.g., UN Doc. E/C.12/1988/SR.13, para. 23. In 1987 the Committee became the first of the UN human rights treaty–monitoring bodies to be able to receive information from NGOs. The procedure was established by ESC Res. 1987/5, *supra* note 41, in para. 6 of which the Council invited

> non-governmental organizations in consultative status with the Council to submit to it written statements that might contribute to full and universal recognition and realization of the rights contained in the International Covenant on Economic, Social and Cultural Rights, and requests the Secretary-General to make those statements available to the Committee in a timely manner.

[43] E.g., UN Doc. E/C.12/1988/SR.13, para. 12.

[44] Committee's Second Report *supra* note 4, para. 364.

[45] The Committee recognized this problem when it agreed to insert a paragraph to the following effect in its summary of its examination of Austria's report:

> In the course of the adoption of the present summary it was noted that there appears to be an imbalance in the extent and nature of the concluding observations made with respect

smoothly at future sessions. The opportunities afforded by the new procedure for implicit performance evaluations stand in marked contrast to the bland, but misleading, practice followed at the Committee's first session, where the Chairperson, purportedly on behalf of the Committee, offered an identical concluding expression of thanks with respect to each and every state party's report, regardless of its adequacy.[46]

Conclusion

In the broader scheme of things, the second session of the Committee on Economic, Social and Cultural Rights represented a major breakthrough in the effort to treat those rights as though they were in practice, and not only in UN theory, equal in importance to civil and political rights. As in all areas of international relations, and particularly in human rights, the roles played by the two superpowers were critical elements in this development. On the Soviets' part, the spirit of "openness" (*glasnost*) and "restructuring" (*perestroika*) led not only to the resignation of the former Soviet expert prior to the session,[47] but also, and more importantly, to a significantly more open and progressive approach to the issues on the part of the other experts from Eastern Europe.[48] This change reflects two developments of fundamental long-term significance for the future of economic, social and cultural rights. The first is the growing reliance on market mechanisms in economic decision making, as a result of which the differences between capitalist and socialist approaches to the rights in question are being greatly reduced. The second is the increasing justiciability of economic and social rights in the USSR. For example, in response to recognition of the fact that "instances of violation of rights, especially of labor, housing, and certain others, and of violation of the procedure for handling and resolving complaints . . . are still quite widespread,"[49] a new law has been introduced giving any Soviet citizen "the right to appeal to court if he considers that his rights have been violated by the actions of an official."[50] The law, which entered into force

---

to the report of Austria compared to those made with respect to the reports of some other States considered at this session. It was explained that this is attributable not to the particular details of the report of Austria and of its presentation but to the relative newness of the procedures adopted by the Committee in making concluding observations.

Id., para. 48.

[46] "In concluding the consideration of the report, the Chairman thanked the representative of the State party for having co-operated with the Committee in a spirit of constructive dialogue and with the common objective of implementing the rights recognized in the Covenant." Report on the First Session, *supra* note 2, paras. 35, 66, 85, 114, 149, 169, 220, 259 and 297.

[47] *See supra* note 6. The USSR subsequently nominated Professor V. Kusnetzov for election to the Committee.

[48] Mr. W. Neneman from Poland and Mr. V. Mrachkov from Bulgaria.

[49] Remarks by a deputy of the Supreme Soviet, *quoted in* Izvestia, July 2, 1987, at 5, and *cited in* Quigley, *The New Soviet Law on Appeals: Glasnost' in the Soviet Courts,* 37 INT'L & COMP. L.Q. 172, 173 n.3 (1988).

[50] Law on the Procedure for Appealing in Court the Unlawful Actions of Officials that Infringe the Rights of Citizens, VEDOMOSTI VERKHOVNOGO SOVETA SSSR, No. 26, 1987, item 389, Art. 1. *See* Quigley, *supra* note 49, at 172.

on January 1, 1988,[51] brings some aspects of the Soviet approach to economic rights much closer than ever before to those of most Western countries. This convergence can only augur well for further development of a perceived commonality of interest across the East-West divide.

The influence of the other superpower on the work of the Committee, of course, is much less visible. Since the United States has failed to ratify the Covenant, it is not in a position to nominate an expert for election to the Committee. Had the present U.S. administration been able to do so, the consensus in the Committee might have been jeopardized by an unproductive debate over whether economic rights are really human rights at all. Given the administration's recent repudiation[52] of the 1969 Declaration on Social Progress and Development,[53] which had long been seen by most development and human rights experts as the single most important and coherent statement of Western liberal values on the subject, it is difficult to lament the U.S. absence. By the same token, however, it is regrettable that the United States has abdicated its opportunity to influence the shape of UN action in this field, which, whether or not a particular American administration approves, will have an abiding impact on international attitudes and perceptions.

Against this background, the Committee's second session was notable for its movement away from the automatic taking of positions by members in accordance with their geopolitical or ideological affiliations. While such an approach is inevitably characteristic of the UN political organs in the human rights field, it is anathema to the healthy development of an effective expert committee. Thus, at its second session, the Committee abandoned the practice of rotating the membership of the Bureau on geopolitical lines, worked through a sessional working group that was effectively open-ended rather than being finely tuned along regional lines, and held debates in which members consistently took positions that failed to accord exactly with those expected of them on the basis of their national origins.

The final observation to be made on this session concerns the manner in which the Committee coped with its unique hybrid role as an entity responsible for treaty supervision that is answerable not to the states parties to the

[51] *Id.* n.2(a).

[52] In November 1987, the U.S. representative (Ms. Byrne) told the Third Committee of the General Assembly

> that the United States would no longer adhere to the Declaration on Social Progress and Development. The Declaration had been adopted at a time when ideas about the role of Government in social development and in providing social welfare were very different. The United States had learned that Government, even in the richest countries, could not alone provide massive social welfare programmes on a scale such as that suggested in the Declaration. Individual needs varied so greatly that centralized social welfare schemes were often counterproductive to the effort to allow all individuals to become self-sufficient and independent. In the United States, the contribution of the private sector and of State and local Governments to social progress and development were an essential part of all effective social programmes.

UN Doc. A/C.3/42/SR.32, para. 1 (1987).

[53] GA Res. 2542 (XXIV), 24 UN GAOR Supp. (No. 30) at 49, UN Doc. A/7630 (1969).

treaty but to one of the principal political organs of the United Nations, the Economic and Social Council. At its first session, members tended, somewhat inconsistently, to emphasize one role *or* the other, depending on the circumstances. By the end of its second session, however, it had become clear that the Committee could consistently have the best of both worlds. Thus, on the one hand, there is a clear consensus that it should seek to emulate, as far as appropriate, the practices and procedures of the "independent" treaty-based supervisory bodies such as the Human Rights Committee. On the other hand, its formal status as a subsidiary organ of the Council means that the most divisive political issues can be fought out within the Council while the Committee gets on with the rest of its work in a relatively nonpoliticized context.[54]

PHILIP ALSTON & BRUNO SIMMA*

[54] It is also worthy of note that the Committee's status as a subsidiary organ of ECOSOC insulates it, to some extent, from the full force of the UN financial crisis, which has significantly affected the work of some of the other supervisory committees. *See* Gaer, *Financial Crisis at the UN,* HUM. RTS. INTERNET REP., No. 5/6, 1987, at 58.

* Dr. Alston is Associate Professor of International Law at the Fletcher School of Law and Diplomacy, and Lecturer on Law at Harvard Law School. He served as rapporteur of the Committee on Economic, Social and Cultural Rights at its first and second sessions. Dr. Simma is Professor of International Law at the University of Munich and the University of Michigan and a member of the Committee on Economic, Social and Cultural Rights.

BOOK REVIEWS AND NOTES

EDITED BY DETLEV VAGTS

REVIEW ARTICLE

NATIONAL LEGAL SYSTEMS AND PRIVATE DISPUTE RESOLUTION

International Commercial Arbitration in New York. Edited by J. Stewart McClendon and Rosabel E. Everard Goodman. New York: The World Arbitration Institute; Dobbs Ferry, N.Y.: Transnational Publishers, Inc., 1986. Pp. xvi, 326. Index. $35, cloth; $25, paper.

Law and Practice of International Commercial Arbitration. By Alan Redfern and Martin Hunter. London: Sweet & Maxwell, 1986. Pp. xliii, 462. Index. $173. £64.

Le Règlement des litiges civils et commerciaux avec les Etats-Unis. By Patrick Thieffry and Christine Lecuyer-Thieffry. Paris: Jupiter, 1986. Pp. xiv, 399. Index. F.290.

Arbitration of transnational commercial disputes has become a business. Countries and cities vie for a greater share of the fees paid to arbitrators and attorneys, particularly at the seat of an arbitration.[1] The marketing strategy of some nations includes reform of arbitration law, which members of the local bar have energetically publicized.[2]

Idiosyncrasies of national law come into play in nonjudicial dispute resolution when one party to the controversy regrets having agreed to binding arbitration, or sees the arbitration as unfolding in an unfair manner. The unhappy contender may invoke the procedural and/or substantive norms of several jurisdictions to vitiate or to modify the arbitral process. The efficiency and fairness of international arbitration thus depend on how national legal systems deal with arbitral agreements, proceedings and awards.

[1] This rivalry coincides with a trend toward "lawyerizing" in nonjudicial dispute resolution. For a poignant description of the "end of innocence" of international commercial arbitration, see Jan Paulsson's note at 1 ARB. INT'L 2 (1985). For a critique of "the legalization of the arbitration process," see J. AUERBACH, JUSTICE WITHOUT LAW 109–14 (1983).

[2] When, in 1979, England enacted legislation to limit judicial review of arbitration awards rendered in London, Lord Cullen of Ashborn estimated that this reform would bring England £500 million of "invisible exports" such as arbitrators' and lawyers' fees. 392 PARL. DEB., H.L. (5th ser.) 99 (1979). *See* Park, *Judicial Supervision of Transnational Commercial Arbitration,* 21 HARV. INT'L L.J. 87 (1980). The French, in 1981, and the Belgians, in 1985, modernized their arbitration law in an attempt to keep and/or to capture a share of the dispute resolution market. The Swiss recently amended their federal conflicts-of-law procedure to permit foreign parties to limit judicial annulment of an award. *See* Loi fédérale sur le droit international privé, Arts. 176–95 (text of Dec. 18, 1987) (not yet in force).

Three books by American, British and French practitioners provide differing perspectives on the interaction of judge and arbitrator. Seeking to attract to New York some of the cases that have traditionally gone to London, Paris and Geneva, the World Arbitration Institute[3] has produced a collection of essays on federal and state arbitration law. Two British solicitors have examined the legal aspects of international arbitration in a general survey that goes beyond the law of the sceptered isle. The French contribution comes from two Paris lawyers who have written about aspects of both arbitration and litigation in the United States.

I. THE VIEW FROM NEW YORK

The essays edited by McClendon and Goodman present a valuable guide to the nitty-gritty of commercial arbitration in New York. They cover the agreement to arbitrate, commencement of the proceedings, appointment of an arbitrator, hearings, interim measures, applicable law and challenge to awards. Extensive notes to cases make it a particularly useful tool for both practitioners and scholars. Appendixes include portions of relevant federal and state statutes, the 1958 New York Arbitration Convention and the rules of major arbitral institutions active in New York. Surprisingly, the book gives no statistics indicating whether consumers of international arbitration favor New York over other cities. Experience with arbitration under the Rules of the International Chamber of Commerce would lead to the suspicion that the book attempts to reverse a disappointing track record rather than to prolong a successful run.[4]

The Yankee peddlers showing arbitral shoppers the wares offered in the Big Apple are 14 talented lawyers of enviable credentials and reputation, well-known and well respected by arbitration connoisseurs worldwide. Except for one of the editors, all practice with major American firms. As is frequent in cooperative ventures, the essays are not of even quality. Nor are they always responsive to the book's audience.

Foreign readers might have expected sharper focus on the interplay of state and federal law. Several essays suggest that one need not worry about the complexity of the federal system because state law applies to international arbitration "only to the extent that its provisions are not more restrictive" than those of federal law (pp. 7, 19 and 41). The meaning of "not more restrictive," however, is less than self-evident, especially with respect to provisional measures such as pre-award attachment, which may defeat some objectives of arbitration while furthering others.[5] Authorities are di-

[3] "World" may seem rather impertinent. The institute is a program of the American Arbitration Association established "to foster the use of New York City as a venue" for international commercial arbitration (p. xiii).

[4] *See* W. CRAIG, W. PARK & J. PAULSSON, INTERNATIONAL CHAMBER OF COMMERCE ARBITRATION App. I, table 7 (1984). During the years surveyed (1980–1982), the United States was established as the place of arbitration in less than 5% of the cases, as compared with 33% for France, 27% for Switzerland and 9% for the United Kingdom.

[5] Pre-award attachment in support of arbitration increases the winner's chances of enforcing the award, but it interjects national court proceedings that the parties intended to avoid. *Compare* McCreary Tire & Rubber v. CEAT, 501 F.2d 1032 (3d Cir. 1974) (holding that the

vided (as one essay acknowledges on pp. 99–113) on whether a federal court must grant attachments available under the law of the state where it sits. Moreover, disputes often end up in state courts in circumstances where it may not be clear, until after years of expensive appeals, that state law is preempted by federal statute.[6] Particularly uncertain is the impact of a state law with no corresponding provision in the Federal Arbitration Act. Scholars and practitioners must acknowledge that the contours of federal preemption here are ill-defined.[7]

Not all of the essays make clear the distinctions between the different stages and aspects of the arbitral process. Elliptical references to enforcement of foreign awards (a topic excluded from the book's coverage) appear in a section on *vacatur* of local awards (pp. 136–42) without explanation of its nexus to the section's subject. In one chapter, a treaty defense to recognition of awards dealing with nonarbitrable subject matter is presented as a justification for a court's refusal to enforce an agreement to arbitrate (p. 34), without explanation of the problematic mechanism by which a defense to an award works its way back into the part of the treaty dealing with agreements to arbitrate.

Arbitration is consensual, and the arbitration clause itself requires considerably more attention than parties usually give to future disputes when preparing for the trip home. The thoughtful essay by Aksen and Connolly explores the essential and useful elements of the agreement to arbitrate. Such a clause ought to be drafted with an eye to reducing uncertainties on the day when there will be a dispute, and perhaps an award. Therefore, several matters dealt with here are treated in later chapters.[8] Any work where the same material is spread among different authors risks inadvertent inconsistency. The careful reader might wonder whether overlapping statements on currency fluctuation[9] and time limitations[10] are reconcilable. The

---

New York Convention prohibits attachment), *with* Carolina Power & Light v. Uranex, 451 F.Supp. 1044 (N.D. Cal. 1977) (permitting attachment).

[6] In *Cooper v. Ateliers de la Motobecane,* a dispute between a French and an American corporation, to be arbitrated in Zurich, was tied up in New York courts for several years in deciding whether conditions precedent to arbitration had been met and whether a prejudgment attachment was available. *See* 49 N.Y.2d 741, 404 N.E.2d 741, 427 N.Y.S.2d 619 (1980), and 57 N.Y.2d 408, 442 N.E.2d 1239, 456 N.Y.S.2d 728 (1982).

[7] For a recent discussion of federal preemption in arbitration, see Loumiet's Introductory Note to the Florida International Arbitration Act, 26 ILM 949 (1987).

[8] For example, interest (pp. 28, 155), currency fluctuations (pp. 29, 129) and time bars (pp. 38, 48) are all treated twice.

[9] On page 29, we find the statement, "Unless otherwise specified, U.S. courts convert awards made in foreign currency into dollars at the exchange rates prevailing on the date of entry of judgment when the obligation is performable in a foreign country." However, on page 129, different authors state that the "judgment day rule" is applied if foreign law governs. Is the reader to take these two statements as being consistent when the obligation to be performed abroad has been subjected to U.S. law by the parties' explicit choice?

[10] On page 38, the authors state that New York law requires courts to compel arbitration if the claim is not barred by the New York state statute of limitations. A different author writes (p. 48) that the New York state statute of limitations will *not* apply to international arbitrations. The reader is left to wonder why the first author omitted telling us that his statement was irrelevant to the book's topic.

next edition might note that the effect of bankruptcy on arbitration is becoming more complicated; several recent cases have permitted international arbitrations to proceed despite the automatic stay provided for by the Bankruptcy Code.

McClendon's description of commencement and administration of arbitration includes discussion of institutional rules and appointment of arbitrators. Of the issues that may arise at the commencement of arbitration (pp. 47–54), at least two are worth exploring in greater detail: What does it mean for an agreement to be "inoperative"? At what point does participation in litigation constitute waiver of the right to arbitrate?

The selection of an arbitrator is often the most critical single decision by a party. Themes related to the arbitrators themselves are developed in the thorough and scholarly contribution by Hoellering. In a follow-up article, Hoellering might examine in greater depth issues related to the arbitrator's ethics and independence. When—if at all—may parties talk to an arbitrator outside the proceedings? About what? May an arbitrator be nominated by the same party in several arbitrations? Hoellering might also devote more attention to the national balance of the arbitral tribunal, and the degree of confidence in transnational arbitration by nationals of countries whose elites are not integrated into the emerging caste of professional arbitrators.

Foreign fears of American-style discovery account for much of the reluctance to choose New York as an arbitral situs. This concern is explored in the well-researched chapter on procedure, where Stein and Wotman extensively document the proposition that courts in New York will ordinarily deny requests for discovery. However, not all peculiarities of American procedure can be avoided. The authors note that the right to cross-examine witnesses (on which the continental and the Anglo-American approaches diverge) is deemed an essential element to a fair hearing, and thus prevents arbitrators from adopting an entirely inquisitorial system. In the same chapter on procedure, Newman and Nelson further explore judicial assistance to the arbitral process. They provide a thorough examination of consolidation of multiparty arbitration and an excellent section on measures of interim protection such as attachment. Care is taken to point out differences between state and federal statutes, divisions among the federal circuits and the interaction of statutory and institutional rules.

The unsigned chapter on applicable substantive law draws a rather extreme conclusion about choice of law: that the right to choose an arbitral forum implies the parties' right to choose "any substantive law they wish" (p. 117). However, dicta by the Supreme Court in *Mitsubishi* (discussed on the same page as the above assertion) stressed that national law may limit the parties' choice when public interests are involved. In holding antitrust matters arbitrable in an international dispute, the Court warned that it would condemn, as against public policy, a choice-of-law clause that operated as a "prospective waiver" of the right to pursue statutory claims.[11]

[11] *See* Mitsubishi v. Soler Chrysler-Plymouth, 473 U.S. 614, 637 n.19 (1985).

Increasingly, arbitrators face a double bind: whether to give effect to the will of the parties, or to protect the reputation of the arbitral process by refusing to let it be used to evade the mandatory norms of a country with a vital interest in the subject matter of the dispute. The parties' choice-of-law clause may well be ineffective when it would operate to avoid imperative rules of the place of performance—often called *lois de police*—such as competition law, currency controls, and boycott, environmental protection and bribery regulations.[12] In applying these norms, the arbitrator does not serve as an officer of the court; rather, he acts to maximize the award's effectiveness by exhibiting sensitivity to the vital national interests of the place of enforcement.

Parties obtaining awards in New York will want to know whether the award will be recognized abroad where the loser has assets. The book has two excellent chapters to help practitioners ensure that such awards will be enforceable. McLaughlin, Brill and Rostow provide a thorough summary of procedures for review, confirmation and *vacatur* of awards. Unfortunately, the section on judicial challenge to awards blurs the important distinction between vacating an award and refusal to confirm.[13] The scholarly chapter by Layton and Sherman continues to develop themes related to confirmation and enforcement of the award, including special considerations regarding enforcement against a foreign state.

* * * *

The reviewer's major disappointment with the book is that public policy issues were not refracted through the practitioners' eyes. The book's narrow perspective pays little attention to the social and commercial implications of transnational arbitration. The essays pass without comment over the policy implications of matters such as currency fluctuations,[14] interest,[15] punitive damages[16] and reasoned awards,[17] and provide little analysis of the

[12] *See* Mayer, *Mandatory Rules of Law in International Arbitration,* 2 ARB. INT'L 274 (1986).

[13] The section entitled "Grounds for Vacating Awards" (pp. 136–47) deals with challenge to awards rendered in the United States by referring to New York Convention defenses to enforcement of foreign awards. Although these treaty defenses constitute grounds for withholding confirmation of awards rendered locally, *vacatur* of an award has a broader effect under Article V(1)(e) of the New York Convention than does refusal to confirm. *Vacatur* permits refusal to enforce the award abroad. The distinction is not always clear when courts deal simultaneously with actions to vacate and to confirm arbitration awards. *See* Northrop v. Triad, 811 F.2d 1265 (9th Cir. 1987).

[14] The judgment date rule (mentioned on pp. 29 and 129) can be harsh on creditors when there has been a depreciation of currency between the breach of contract and the award.

[15] New York's statutory interest rate (mentioned on pp. 28 and 155) seems less neutral, and thus less just, than the market rate.

[16] The holding of *Garrity v. Lyle Stuart,* that punitive damages are reserved for courts (discussed at pp. 127–28), opens the door to the multiple adjudication and judicial proceedings that the parties expected to avoid by arbitration. The 11th Circuit has held *contra* in a case involving the U.S. Arbitration Act. *See* Willoughby v. Kajima Int'l, 776 F.2d 269 (11th Cir. 1985), *aff'g* 598 F.Supp. 353 (N.D. Ala. 1984).

[17] It is stated (p. 29) that though customary in international arbitration, awards that include reasons are not the general practice in the United States. The reader might want to know whether this is good or bad. Reasoned awards make heightened demands on the intellectual

justification for international arbitration's privileged legal status, by virtue of which rules applied to domestic disputes are often rejected in the international arena.

International commercial arbitration provides a neutral playing field on which transnational economic law is enforced. Its role in the process of creating global wealth is justified by neither speed nor cost, but rather primarily as a means of avoiding the "hometown justice" of the other party's judicial system. In a purely domestic context, an unenforceable arbitration clause may result in a trial in Philadelphia rather than an arbitration in New York. In an international context, the alternative judicial proceedings may be in a foreign language before a hostile judge of a country where political influence makes a fair trial problematic.

This special need for neutrality has led to application of different rules to domestic and international arbitration in matters such as subject matter arbitrability[18] and confirmation of awards.[19] The reader can legitimately ask how this privileged status affects larger societal interests, and whether it should be extended. Particularly interesting would have been an evaluation of the appropriate limits of national judicial meddling with the arbitration. One might argue that in international arbitration, the scope of judicial review of awards should be narrower than in domestic cases.

Understanding the genesis, evolution and justification of a rule facilitates a grasp of its operation. A glimpse at the policy context of international arbitration's special legal status would help the reader to grapple more effectively with the description of cases and statutes. The study of rules without consideration of their policy underpinnings may create a type of "voodoo jurisprudence,"[20] in which words are assumed to have power to change behavior regardless of their impact on society and the enforcement mechanism on which they depend.

A proper mix of the analytic and the descriptive is admittedly difficult. Yet the quality of objective intellectual curiosity that American lawyers would like to project abroad includes concern for how law affects both the participants in the arbitral process and the communities in which the participants operate.

Finally, the book would be more geared to its audience if it contained a comparative dimension,[21] giving the reader an idea of what makes New York a better (or worse) place to arbitrate than Geneva, London or Paris.

---

rigor and integrity of the arbitral process. They also stimulate the development of a *lex mercatoria* in which awards become part of an objective corpus of international arbitral case law. On the other hand, reasons may serve as dangerous invitations to judicial annulment of the award, where a losing party is seeking a peg on which to hang a challenge to the award.

[18] *See* Mitsubishi v. Soler Chrysler-Plymouth, 473 U.S. 614 (1985) (antitrust); and Scherk v. Alberto-Culver, 471 U.S. 506 (1974) (securities regulation).

[19] *See* 9 U.S.C. §207 (1982) (providing a 3-year statute of limitations for confirmation of awards in international disputes, as opposed to 1 year in domestic cases).

[20] *See* W. M. Reisman's review of installment 7 of the *Encyclopedia of Public International Law,* 81 AJIL 263, 269 (1987).

[21] For example, in discussing laches on page 53, reference might have been made to the abundant English law on time bars and court sanctions imposed on dilatory parties. *See, e.g.,* M. Mustill & S. Boyd, Commercial Arbitration 130, 159–87 and 433–34 (1982).

Flat descriptions of state and federal law are only partially responsive to the World Arbitration Institute's self-asserted purpose of showing that New York is "a good place to arbitrate an international dispute" (p. xi).

II. A British Perspective

Alan Redfern and Martin Hunter have produced the best general treatment of trends in international commercial arbitration yet to be published in English. Their beautifully written and solidly structured *vade mecum* is a pleasure to read, and should be part of the library of every international lawyer. These two London lawyers do more than address practitioners about how to serve clients. They also provide teachers with a useful pedagogical tool, and give scholars an erudite and learned analysis of the evolution of international arbitration.[22] Practical advice is married with doctrinal analysis in a well laid-out map of the rules, laws and practices through which lawyers must navigate in commercial arbitrations containing an international element.

The complex interface of treaty, statute and arbitration rules (both institutional and ad hoc) unfolds without giving any one legal system or set of rules so much detail as to be tedious. The laws of several countries illustrate each topic, but without an overambitious attempt at a systematic or comprehensive contrast of historical peculiarities.

The first-rate introduction presents a topographical survey of the legal playing field for transnational arbitration, and carefully distinguishes the functions of three principal legal systems: the law applied to the merits of the dispute, the law governing the arbitration itself, and the law(s) affecting the recognition and enforcement of the arbitration agreement and award. A fourth legal system, it might have been added, comes into play when arbitrators subject procedural matters such as evidence to a particular national law. The reader is reminded of the differences between agreements to arbitrate future disputes and agreements to arbitrate existing quarrels. Useful definitions are suggested for "international" and "commercial" as applied to arbitration.

The disadvantages of arbitration include delay due to inadequate power to discipline recalcitrant parties, and expense from the arbitrator's fees and administrative costs. These defects are noted, and the reader is mercifully spared the silly marketing hype found in many books on arbitration. Logic and experience are combined to explore theories relating to the *lex arbitri,* the law governing the arbitration itself. Responding to suggestions that arbitration be detached from the law of the place of the proceedings, Redfern and Hunter describe the fashion for "a-national," "delocalized" or

[22] Notable examples of their academic bent include speculation that the origins of the "delocalisation theory," which would cut arbitration loose from the law of the place of the proceedings, lie in the state immunity doctrine announced in the 1958 *Aramco* award (p. 58). Historical material is provided on the 1923 Geneva Protocol, the 1928 Bustamante Code and the background (from 1899!) of the role of the United Nations in arbitration. Ironically, one of the coauthors has on occasion complained about the academic approach to the study of international commercial arbitration. *See* Hunter, Book Review, 51 ARBITRATION 290, 293 (1985).

"floating" arbitration (pp. 55–60) in a learned chapter that compares the "delocalization" doctrine with the theory that an arbitration is controlled by the law of its territorial seat.[23]

Conceding the "understandable desire for uniformity in the regulation of international commercial arbitration" (p. 56), the authors insist that to make arbitration independent of the law of its seat would "attach too much significance to the wishes of the parties and not enough to the framework of national laws within which [the arbitration] must take place" (p. 98). The authors' sophisticated and nuanced analysis of the *lex arbitri* takes into account the viewpoints of both claimant and defendant, and gives local law more than a grudging tolerance as a necessary evil in ensuring the award's enforceability.[24] Unlike commentators who focus solely on the winner's concerns—finality and speed—the authors also acknowledge the potential loser's interest in a fair consideration of all issues.

The authors' enthusiasm for the "seat theory" may be excessive when they suggest that an award, to be enforceable, must absorb the nationality of the state where the arbitration takes place (pp. 57–58 and 64). Although the New York Convention allows a state to refuse to enforce awards that do not conform to the law of the place of arbitration, this denial of recognition is permissive, not mandatory.[25] And the 1961 European Arbitration Convention permits refusal of recognition of an award set aside where made only if annulment was for one of the reasons specified in the Convention.

Teasing questions about the interplay of different legal systems make the treatise an intellectual delight. The chapter on beginning an arbitration mentions the conflict that arises when the proper law of the contract and the law of the place of arbitration impose different time limits for bringing a claim (p. 149). The authors admit to honest agnosticism on such issues, which they put into a box awaiting further light.

Outlining professional standards for arbitrators, the authors rightly note the need for "experience" (p. 196). They might also have noted that experience can have unfortunate dimensions when large fees exert too much influence on professional arbitrators. Some arbitrators may be so eager for new appointments that they relax rigor and integrity; a junior arbitrator

[23] Much ink has been spilled in the debate on whether international arbitration should be set free from procedural norms of the place of the arbitral seat. For a summary of the discussion on "floating awards" and "drifting arbitration," see Park, *Lex Loci Arbitri and International Commercial Arbitration,* 32 INT'L & COMP. L.Q. 21 (1983); and the reply by Paulsson, *Wings of Silence, id.* at 53.

[24] *Cf.* Craig, *International Ambition and National Constraints in I.C.C. Arbitration,* 1 ARB. INT'L 49 (1985).

[25] The English version of Article V(1) of the Convention states that an award "may" be refused recognition and enforcement if set aside under the law of the place where rendered. Theoretically, national courts of a party to the Convention could enforce an annulled award, although this does not happen in practice. The equally authoritative French text is more ambiguous: "La reconnaissance et l'exécution de la sentence ne seront refusées . . . que si . . . la sentence a été annulée ou suspendue . . ." (Recognition and enforcement will not be refused . . . unless . . . the award was annulled or suspended).

may defer to a more senior member of the international arbitration mafia in the hope of being recommended in another case.

The authors show considerable conceptual precision in their detailed analysis of the ethical qualifications of arbitrators. The domestic practice of expecting an arbitrator to be an advocate for his nominating party is contrasted with the international custom of more neutrality. Although not all of the authors' nuances are easy to follow, helpful distinctions are made among "independence," "impartiality" and "neutrality" (pp. 171–72). An arbitrator is "non-neutral" if he sees himself as an advocate; he lacks "independence" if he has a direct financial interest in the outcome; and he is "partial" if his beliefs and convictions predispose him toward a particular outcome. In an international commercial dispute, an arbitrator should always be financially and professionally independent, and he is expected to be less of an advocate, and thus more neutral, than in a domestic arbitration. Some developing countries nevertheless nominate employees or consultants of state agencies as their arbitrators.

Minds new to a subject grasp concrete examples more readily than abstract generalities. Therefore, students will benefit from the detailed presentation of the facts of vital awards and cases such as *Aramco, Texaco* and *S.P.P.* (pp. 58–59 and 328–33). The excellent index, outline and tables of cases and awards conspire to make this treatise a good companion to any set of teaching materials. Six appendixes provide the UNCITRAL Model Law, the UNCITRAL Rules, the IBA Rules of Evidence, the New York Convention, an ad hoc ("one-off") arbitration clause and a submission agreement.

The reviewer's enthusiasm abated in the chapter on the role of the United Nations in sponsoring treaties, laws and rules. The book would be worth its price even without these somewhat superfluous 45 pages. The material might have been integrated elsewhere, and the space saved devoted to more on the drafting of terms of reference.

Many good one-liners attest to the authors' humor and culture. Some common law jurists are unfamiliar with *amiable composition* (decision according to fairness rather than law), a two-edged sword that may substantially reduce the loser's opportunity to challenge an award. To illustrate the Anglo-American experience gap, the authors tell of an English lawyer who knew a little French, and thought that an *amiable compositeur* was a "friendly printer." The section on arbitrability contains a derivative reference to Baron von Münchhausen's pigtail.

Occasionally, broad assertions beg for specific supporting authority. A statement that the word "controversies" in an arbitration clause has been held in the United States to have "the widest possible meaning" (p. 116) is unsubstantiated.[26] The announcement that "in most jurisdictions" the arbitrators have no inherent power to strike a claim by reason of dilatory conduct (pp. 136–37) is supported only by reference to English and Hong Kong law.

[26] Reference might have been made to the cases cited in S.A. Mineracao Da Trindade-Samitri v. Utah Int'l, 745 F.2d 190 (2d Cir. 1984).

Certain controversial subjects need more critical discussion. In particular, the procedural aspects of the Third World's "New International Economic Order" (pp. 81–84) pose more problems than the book suggests. The Charter of Economic Rights and Duties of States would remove investment disputes from the jurisdiction of international arbitration in favor of host state tribunals. To permit compensation for nationalized assets to be determined solely by the host state would permit one party in a dispute to decide its own case, and reduce the stability and security necessary for foreign private investment.

These quibbles, however, are minor. With grace, elegance and style, Redfern and Hunter have written a superb general treatise on how arbitration law affects international dispute resolution.

III. A French Look at American Procedure

Patrick Thieffry and Christine Lecuyer-Thieffry approach both arbitration and litigation in a single volume. This intriguing Gallic contribution to the literature on international dispute resolution covers a broad range, examining, first, rules of American civil procedure, and then the recognition and enforcement of foreign judgments and awards in the United States.

The title, translated as "Resolution of Civil and Commercial Disputes with the United States," may lead the reader to expect more analogies and contrasts than the book delivers. It is intended to give the Francophonic reader an awareness of concepts, cases and statutes relating to American jurisdiction and judgments. The reader may be stimulated to think about similarities and differences between the parallel adjudicatory processes of arbitration and litigation; but he will have to draw his own conclusions.

The authors begin with a "preliminary chapter" outlining differences between French and American business law (such as consideration, frustration and the trust), jurisdictional principles and arbitration law. The book thereafter divides into two parts. The first summarizes basic rules of American civil procedure, with chapters on jurisdiction, hearings and judgments. The second part sketches American principles related to foreign judgments (including reference to the Uniform Foreign Money Judgment Recognition Act and the *Restatement (Second) of Conflict of Laws*) and recognition and enforcement of arbitral awards.

A useful table indicates bilateral Franco-American treaties and certain multilateral conventions ratified by the United States. Seven appendixes set forth, in English, American statutes and arbitral rules. These omit the Rules of the International Chamber of Commerce, perhaps because the French reader will have them available. It should be noted, however, that Franco-American controversies are as likely to be dealt with under the Rules of the International Chamber of Commerce as under the Rules of the more domestically oriented American Arbitration Association.

Another curious gap (p. 43) is any serious analysis of the French procedural peculiarities that affect Franco-American disputes. The "exorbitant" jurisdictional provisions of Articles 14 and 15 of the French *Code civil* grant French courts competence over disputes merely on the basis of the French nationality of the plaintiff or the defendant. Although these rules may be abrogated by contract (including a choice-of-forum clause), their competing jurisdiction will influence resolution of disputes between businesses in Paris and New York, particularly when Americans forget them at the time of contract negotiations.

The 10 pages devoted to recourse against awards under chapter I of the Federal Arbitration Act should be expanded. A Pandora's box is opened when courts attempt to draw a fine line between a normally unreviewable legal error of an arbitrator and his deliberate or inadvertent refusal to apply the chosen law. "Excess of authority" and "manifest disregard of law" are slippery concepts by which courts deal with a fundamental disaccord between how the arbitrator was authorized to decide and how he in fact did decide.

Dissenting opinions, not permitted in French courts, are an important difference between continental and Anglo-American procedure and might have been studied in a comparative book. Continental arbitrators are sometimes surprised when Anglo-American colleagues insist on memorializing their reasons for refusing to join the majority. The value of a dissenting opinion as a stimulus to rigorous legal reasoning must be weighed against its potential abuse by a minority arbitrator to impair the enforceability of an award.

The authors suggest that American civil procedure should be avoided, if possible, because of its complexity (p. 169). The advantages and disadvantages of the proposed alternative—arbitration—beg more focused analysis than the book provides. What the authors call the "permeability of the American territory" on international arbitration raises the question *how* American litigation differs from arbitration.[27] Rigorous comparison of these competing adjudicatory mechanisms could provide insight into the way the commercial community's values and goals are reflected in the application of arbitration treaties and statutes. Perhaps the adage that parties are presumed to know the law should not apply to the same extent in arbitration as in litigation. The search for a neutral forum may override the goal of legal predictability. A comparison might also give to the practical-minded some guidance on the merits of competing tactics and strategies for compelling production of documents in arbitration and litigation.

International and domestic adjudication are disparate beasts. The opposing sides of a controverted international transaction usually seek a political and procedural neutrality that is problematic in a national court. Thus it would be interesting to explore which procedural safeguards of American law French businessmen expect to obtain, and which they hope to avoid, when arbitrating in the United States. Are cross-examination and discovery bargained for in the same way as the right to have awards vacated for arbitrator misconduct?

[27] The authors' "permeability" notion (p. 169) may not be entirely consistent with their statement (p. 172) that "arbitration . . . can be detached from any context of state sovereignty" (l'arbitrage . . . peut être détaché de tout lieu de souveraineté).

The book's topic might also be a springboard for contrasting the relative expense and speed of transnational adjudication with its domestic counterparts. Perhaps the American Arbitration Association provides quicker and cheaper decisions than are available under federal appellate procedure. Can the same be said of arbitration in Europe when compared with local courts? In some countries, a right to judicial recourse against an award on its legal merits may substantially delay arbitration.

The reviewer's temptation to ask why the authors wrote a different book from the one he would have written should not obscure the value of the work. Although readers would have benefited from more comparisons between arbitration and litigation, and between French and American procedure, the manual performs a useful service in introducing French lawyers to the complexities of adjudication of disputes with Americans.

IV. The Constraints of National Legal Systems

Sound Policy or Just a Nuisance?

The books under review all deal with how national legal regimes influence an adjudicatory process intended to avoid national courts. The powers of an arbitrator, as Redfern and Hunter note, arise from a "complex amalgam of the will of the parties, the law of the place of arbitration and the law of the place where recognition or enforcement of the award may be sought" (p. 209). Whether the last two components of this amalgam are imperatives of sound policy, or merely a nuisance to the arbitrator, is open to debate. Paradoxically, court intervention in arbitration results from the business community's wish that agreements to renounce recourse to courts should be binding. When the disappointed loser of an arbitration resists enforcement of the award, or when one party wavers in its willingness to go forward with proceedings as agreed, courts that enforce the agreement or award inescapably impose some measure of their own national law.

The practitioner will pay attention to national legal systems principally to maximize the award's enforceability, or to increase the scope of judicial review if his client expects to lose. The legislator and the student of policy, however, will ask deeper questions about the intersection of national law and international arbitration.

Ensuring respect for the consensual nature of arbitration occasions much of the interface between judge and arbitrator. A legal system will not normally support an arbitrator who decides the dispute differently from the way the parties agreed he should. When protecting parties from overreaching arbitrators, however, courts may also look after the interest of those who are not party to the arbitration agreement, including the public.

Countries that act in the arbitral process will want to protect three types of interests: societal welfare affected by the content of the award; parties' rights affected by an arbitrator's unfairness or excess of authority; and the evolution of a country's substantive law, which may stagnate if courts are not fertilized with disputes about new problems. Thus, courts have historically restricted private adjudication of "nonarbitrable" subjects that implicate vital public interests. Courts may refuse to enforce arbitration agreements or awards that contravene imperative substantive norms related to matters such as free commercial competition.[28] Courts will also ask whether the arbitrator has respected the procedure the parties bargained for and whether the arbitration has infringed nonwaivable due process rights. These rights may be of more limited scope in international arbitration than in domestic litigation. For example, in New York, cross-examination, but not discovery, is considered an essential element of a fair arbitration hearing. And to further development of local law, some categories of arbitration may be subject to a mandatory right of appeal. In England, for example, predispute exclusion of appeal is not possible with respect to disputes governed by English law in the commodities, shipping and insurance areas, where English law has long been preeminent.

International businessmen resort to arbitration above all for its neutrality, both political and procedural. Neutrality means, first, the avoidance of "hometown justice": judicial xenophobia or hostile interference by the opposing side's government. Neutrality also means a minimum of procedural idiosyncracy. Cross-examination may appear non-neutral to continental businessmen even if the judge is fair. The prospect of American-style discovery probably increases, rather than diminishes, the Frenchman's sense of uncertainty.

Ironically, ensuring the political neutrality of a non-national forum complicates the realization of procedural neutrality. Judicial enforcement of arbitration agreements and awards insinuates into the arbitral process an element of a national legal system that the parties intended to avoid. When the U.S. Supreme Court compelled arbitration of the now famous dispute between Mitsubishi and one of its American distributors, the Court insisted that the distributor's antitrust counterclaim be considered under the Sherman Act, despite the Swiss choice-of-law clause in the contract. Judicial support of arbitration against recalcitrant parties gives businessmen the bargained-for non-national forum at the expense of interjecting some of the peculiarities of the enforcement system.

Of the several legal orders on which the bindingness of international arbitration depends, the role of the arbitral seat is the most frequently questioned. This is also the legal system that can most easily be manipulated by the contracting parties (or the supervisory arbitral institution) when they select the situs of the arbitration.

The understandable desire to further a more uniform system of international dispute resolution tempts one to ask whether arbitration should not be detached from the law of its situs. This attractive concept of delocalized arbitration would seem to promote the wishes of the parties without necessarily violating the vital interests of the arbitral seat, which, in a transnational dispute, rarely coincides with the parties' citizenship or residence.

[28] See the "prospective waiver" and "second look" doctrines announced in *Mitsubishi,* 473 U.S. at 637 n.19.

The arbitration usually will have its economic or social impact outside the borders of the place of the proceedings. Only if local substantive law applies to the merits of the dispute will the arbitration affect the country of the proceedings, and this only tangentially in its removal from courts of disputes that otherwise might have fertilized the evolution of local law.

It would be misguided, however, to eliminate all scrutiny of the award by courts at the seat of the arbitration. Unless a defective award is subject to challenge where rendered, at least for violation of minimum standards of procedural fairness, the loser might unfairly be forced to defend against enforcement wherever it has assets. In particular, a person that never signed the arbitration agreement—for example, a corporation or a country joined to the arbitration merely because of its relationship to the other defendant—should have a chance to litigate the arbitrator's jurisdiction at the time of the award. A country that assists arbitration indirectly by allowing the proceedings to go forward should control the fairness of the process. The very fact that an award is rendered within the territory of a signatory to the New York Convention gives the award presumptive validity before the courts of all other states adhering to the Convention. As Redfern and Hunter note, "it would be unusual for a state to lend its support to arbitral tribunals operating within its jurisdiction without [attempting] to ensure that certain minimum standards of justice are met, particularly in procedural matters" (pp. 42–43).

The wishes of the parties themselves are not always served by arbitral autonomy. Whether a national legal framework can be called favorable to arbitration depends in large part on whether one is a potential winner or loser. The party that expects to win will look for speed, economy and finality. The party that fears losing because its arguments are not self-evident looks for judicial review, to ensure that all aspects of the case have been fairly considered. No national legal system is likely to reconcile satisfactorily the inconsistent aims of both winner and loser, claimant and defendant.

The Limits of Arbitral Autonomy

The arbitrator in a transnational dispute must look over his shoulder at national norms imposed by the parties' residence, the seat of the arbitration and the locus of the loser's assets. Not only must he be attentive to more than one legal system, but he must juggle dictates that are not always consistent. Application of the parties' chosen law may lead to an unenforceable award if it violates the public policy of the country of performance. But an arbitrator who ignores the parties' choice of law, in order to respect mandatory norms of the country of performance, may invite challenge at the place of arbitration for excess of authority.

The extent of the arbitrator's dilemma in navigating among legal mandates of several countries might be illustrated by a fictional story about a joint venture to market foreign minerals in the United States. Through one of its thinly capitalized subsidiaries, an American enterprise contracted with a foreign state agency to purchase minerals for 20 years at a fixed price. The parties agreed that any dispute "relating to the interpretation of the contract" would be decided according to "principles of English law," and that all disputes "arising out of the contract" would be settled by arbitration in Ruritania under the Rules of the International Chamber of Commerce.

The sale of the minerals in the United States was embargoed, and the profitability of the venture put into doubt. Considering that the trade sanctions constituted *force majeure,* the Americans terminated the contract. The state agency insisted that the minerals be sold in Europe, and commenced arbitration against the doubtfully capitalized subsidiary (which quickly slipped into bankruptcy) and also against its parent. The American defendants assert that the arbitral tribunal is incompetent because the parent never signed the arbitration agreement and because the Bankruptcy Code provides an automatic stay of proceedings against the subsidiary. Consider how the arbitrator must sail precariously through the straits of inconsistent legal systems on the following issues:

(1) The Ruritanian court reviewing an interim award on the arbitrators' jurisdiction may refuse to stop the arbitration against the subsidiary even if it has been enjoined by an American judge.

(2) Whether the parent corporation can be joined to the arbitration on an *alter ego* theory could be subject to inconsistent decisions in a Ruritanian court and by an American judge ultimately called on to enforce the award.

(3) A Ruritanian court might uphold appointment of an arbitrator (challenged for improper links with one of the parties) although an American court could later refuse to enforce the award because the arbitrator lacked the independence required by the party-selected arbitral rules.

(4) If the arbitrators apply English law only to "interpretation" of the contract, but not to the quantum of damages, the award may be annulled in Ruritania for excess of authority. Thereafter, jurisdictions where the loser has assets will not be obliged to enforce the award. But American courts may refuse enforcement if the arbitrators do not consider American public policy.[29]

(5) The defendants may bring an action for damages against the arbitrators for allowing the arbitration against the parent.

(6) The award's *res judicata* effect may be tested under the law in the claimant's home country, which forbids state agencies to submit future disputes to arbitration.

(7) Public international law principles of sovereign immunity of any country where the state agency has assets will arise if the arbitrators accept an American counterclaim.

[29] The first part of Article V of the New York Convention provides that an award annulled where rendered may be refused recognition abroad. Under the second part of Article V, a country may refuse enforcement of a foreign award that violates its public policy.

The arbitrator's bind is all the more poignant because the timing of judicial intervention does not necessarily correspond to the relevant stages of the arbitration. American power exercised at the award stage may inhibit arbitrators during hearings. Or American courts may refuse to compel the defendant to participate in the arbitration at its commencement because the law that will later govern the merits of the dispute operates as a "prospective waiver" of mandatory norms of the performance.

* * * *

Professor René David has defined arbitration as dispute resolution in which a private agreement, not state power, invests the decision maker with authority.[30] While eminently correct in emphasis, the definition needs completion with the observation that state power gives arbitration its binding character. By allowing an award to be made within its territory, the seat of the arbitration gives the award an "international currency" that facilitates enforcement against assets found in jurisdictions that adhere to the New York Convention.

Review of awards by the seat of the arbitration takes forms so diverse as to defy taxonomy. However, almost all forms of review derive from a sense of national responsibility to control the integrity of a process that receives state support. A nation that gives the arbitrator power to bring about legal consequences takes upon itself an obligation to ensure respect for the limits imposed on the arbitrator's authority and for fundamental procedural rights. The winner's interest in finality, privacy and economy must be weighed against the loser's concern for a fair proceeding.

No national legal system is likely to resolve all these tensions between judge and arbitrator, or between winners and losers. However, the books under review should contribute to a dialogue among practitioners and policymakers that will advance understanding, and perhaps partial accommodation, of national interests and the arbitrator's impulse toward autonomy.

WILLIAM W. PARK
Boston University

The Concept of International Law. By Ingrid Detter De Lupis. Stockholm: Norstedts Förlag, 1987. Pp. 145.

Right from the time that Jeremy Bentham coined the term "International Law" to refer to the law of nations, every theoretical formulation of the basis and essence of that law has been open to challenge. Austinian positivists questioned the validity of the term "law" as applied to the law of nations. The monists and dualists debated whether international law and municipal law are integral parts of the same legal order. More recently, the debate

[30] R. DAVID, L'ARBITRAGE DANS LE COMMERCE INTERNATIONAL 9 (1982).

seems to have shifted to the twin issues of what entities may be properly considered subjects of international law and whether the principle of the universality of international law would permit regional derogations from certain of its norms. Throughout these debates the only point on which scholars seem to agree is that modern international law is the product of Christian civilization and that it was originally conceived as a set of rules designed to govern the conduct of the Christian states of Western Europe.

All existing theories of international law, when judged in terms of their ideological orientation, tend to fall into three general groups: traditional Western, belligerent socialist[1] and dissident Third World. Now, for the first time in the history of modern international law, we have a new theory that apparently sheds all ideological constraints and seeks to capture the true character of the changing law of nations in all its complexities. Professor Ingrid Detter De Lupis has produced a richly textured book on the theory of modern international law. It is deeply pondered and scrupulously researched. It is a compelling, mind-expanding account of how rules of international law are created. It posits a revealing theory of the foundations of international legal obligations. It paints a fresh and infinitely more complex portrait of international law than we have previously seen.

What is particularly interesting about De Lupis's theory is that many of its key elements are bound to appeal to both socialist and Third World nations. For example, her idea that regional and universal international laws constitute two coexistent concentric circles is particularly appealing to apologists of the socialist theory of international law.[2] Her notion that international customary law is an exaggerated fallacy fits well with the political agenda of the Third World nations.

There are four components to De Lupis's theory. The first reformulates the norm-creating process in international law. The second rethinks the basis of international legal obligations. The third debunks the notion of international customary law. The fourth constructs a new taxonomic model for international legal rules. I regard the first three elements as the core of her thesis. The thrust of the book is captured in a single, isolated, declarative sentence: "However, at present there is some uncertainty as to the present state of international law and it has become increasingly noticed that the theory itself of international law is in a state of anarchy" (p. 17).

The author attributes this anarchy to the fact that proponents of the competing schools of thought—the normativists and the social process adherents—seem to be talking at each other rather than with each other. In

[1] The socialist theory of international law is essentially a "fighting" rather than a "thinking" theory. A representative sample may be found in G. Tunkin, Theory of International Law (W. Butler trans. [with an introduction] 1974).

[2] For a discussion of the Soviet perspective on the parallel existence of socialist international law and general international law, see Osakwe, *Socialist International Law Revisited,* 66 AJIL 596 (1972); Hazard, *Renewed Emphasis upon a Socialist International Law,* 65 *id.* at 142 (1971); W. Butler, *"Socialist International Law" or "Socialist Principles of International Relations"?, id.* at 796.

her view, the social process school dispenses with the debate over who may be the proper subjects of international law, but provides little guidance on the normative value of the international legal system. On the other hand, she thinks that the normativists provide few guidelines on the participation of nonstates in the international arena. In her words, "the social process school now appears to lack normativity and the normative school to lack universality" (p. 19). The author views herself as a normativist of sorts, but regards her brand of normativism as not incompatible with social process theory. In her words, "international law is not a process but a normative system laying down rules and obligations. But this normative system may be created and continuously revised by a process in the way the social process school suggests. And the normative system may be more dynamic than the additional normativists contend" (p. 17).

The author challenges the validity of some of the entrenched institutions of all modern theories of international law. She thinks, for example, that existing theories of international law tend to equate subjects of international law with the creators of that law. In her view, there are clear distinctions among actors, persons and creators. Creators make the law, actors act under it, and legal persons are given rights and duties under the system. All three categories are bound by international law. As such, they are all latent subjects of international law. They are active subjects insofar as they all enjoy certain direct rights under international law. All subjects are potential actors. But it is only when they presume to act in a way relevant to the international sphere that they become actors (p. 129).

The author then goes on to challenge the conventional theory of obligations in international law. She rejects both the "consent theory" and the *grundnorm* approach as absurd (p. 121). She finds some merit in the theories of social obligation as developed by Scelle, but concludes that these are equally wanting. Rather, she opines that the basis of obligation in international law varies according to the nature of the rule. She devises a tripartite formula by which an international rule is binding by virtue of either logical necessity or social necessity or consent (pp. 122–23). In her view, the inherent maxims of international law (such as *pacta sunt servanda, nemo debet esse judex in propria causa* and *res judicata*) are binding by virtue of logical necessity. On the other hand, prophylactic rules (such as those concerning prohibition of the use of force) are binding by virtue of social necessity. She does concede, however, that consent is the most common basis for obligation in the international society (p. 123).

The author saves her strongest criticism for what she calls the fallacies of customary law. She regards the psychological element of *opinio juris* as nebulous (p. 112). She dubs Cheng's paradoxical concept of instant customary law as an unacceptable contradiction in terms (pp. 112–13). In her view, all modern writers on international law exaggerate the role of custom (p. 115). It is her contention that outside the realm of territorial claims by prescription, customary law has no foundation or justification in modern public international law (p. 116).

Perhaps the author's most innovative idea is her "theory of interactivism" in which she explains the formulation of new rules of international law. She believes that international legal rules are brought about as a result of the legal acts of the members of the international society (p. 87). She further asserts that for a rule to flow from an act, the act must be internationally relevant and the actor must be competent to act (p. 116). She cautions, however, that even though all norms in the international society are the product and result of legal acts, not all acts create norms. In her words, rules are "usually produced by the juxtaposition of complex acts of varying type and form in converging patterns. The essence of this mechanism of interactivism is that participating acts are all individually relevant in the international society but it is together that they are capable of producing norms of behavior" (p. 88).

Ancillary to her thesis is a new theory on the taxonomy of international legal rules. In her view, rules of international society can be classified in a hierarchical order according to their immediate linkage to a hypothetical goal of international law. Using this criterion, De Lupis comes up with the following categories of rules: intrinsic, entrenching and supplementing. Intrinsic rules are subdivided into inherent maxims and general principles. By contrast, entrenching rules are broken down into prophylactic and stabilizing rules. Within the category of supplementing rules, she includes promotional and consequential rules.

Thoughtful as this book may be, it is not without blemish. Some of the good ideas put forward by the author are left hanging in thin air. For example, absent further clarification, one is at a loss to understand the author's reasons for drawing a distinction between "fundamental human rights" (which she fails to define) and "socioeconomic rights" in her formula for determining the spheres of operation between general and particular international law. She thinks that international law rules regarding the former group of rights are universally binding, but not rules relating to the latter (p. 37). Also, her contention that international customary law has some applicability in the realm of territorial claim by prescription is not fully explained, particularly in light of her generally well-argued contention that customary law is fundamentally a nebulous fiction. Furthermore, the book, in my opinion, contains one noteworthy, albeit nonfatal, structural flaw. By pursuing so many facets of the theory of international law, the author runs the occasional risk of losing the drive and focus that a single narrative line might have had. What I consider to be the most important elements of her thesis seem to fade around the edges, whereas the most minor feature of her theory, i.e., the taxonomy of international legal rules, comes on loud and strong.

Despite these reservations, De Lupis's book is a fascinating and provocative contribution to the continuing search for a more perfect theory of international law. What is particularly impressive about her efforts is her ability to interweave variations of old ideas with creations of her own imagination. Indeed, the author has produced the closest thing to a consensus theory of modern international law. In the eyes of the socialist and Third World nations, De Lupis's theory has the additional advantage of cleansing traditional international law of two of its many original sins.

CHRISTOPHER OSAKWE
Christ Church College, Oxford

World Politics and International Law. By Francis A. Boyle. Durham: Duke University Press, 1985. Pp. xi, 366. Index. $14.75, paper.

American political scientists since World War II have postulated that international law and organizations are generally irrelevant to world politics. Hans Morgenthau's realist-school works of the early postwar era introduced and crystallized the concept.[1] In a precursor to his vaunted *Politics Among Nations,* Morgenthau announced that "the legalistic approach to essentially political problems is but an aberration from the true laws of politics."[2] He later discussed the "iron law of international politics, that legal obligations must yield to the national interest."[3] For years, only Louis Henkin's *How Nations Behave* has offered a lawyer's comprehensive rebuttal.[4]

From his perspective as both political scientist and international lawyer, Francis Boyle directly disputes Morgenthau's view. *World Politics and International Law* contends that international law and international politics are inextricably intertwined. Labeling problems "essentially political" ignores this symbiotic relationship. The observance of law does not conflict with the national interest: it is *part* of the national interest. Boyle urges nations in general, and the United States in particular, to pay more attention to law in international affairs.

Part I is a thorough historical review. Boyle presents the early American international legal positivists as men acutely aware of the "dynamic interrelationship between power and law in international affairs" (p. 22). He describes their impressive list of achievements from 1898 to 1917, the point at which a radically different Wilsonian legalism-moralism took precedence for a short time. That and the ensuing isolationism led to the Second World War. The renaissance of international legal positivism in the immediate postwar era brought about the proud achievement of the United Nations.

Boyle then describes the replacement of positivism by the power-politics realism of his mentor, Hans Morgenthau. It has been the power politics of the realists following the Korean War that has produced "a series of unmitigated disasters for the United States government" (p. 56). Boyle discusses how Morgenthau abandoned his own theory in later life, opening the

[1] Realists have a power-politics view of the world, in which states are rational, unitary actors engaged in a utilitarian calculus designed to extend and solidify their power.

[2] Morgenthau, *Diplomacy,* 55 YALE L.J. 1067, 1078 (1946).

[3] H. MORGENTHAU, IN DEFENSE OF THE NATIONAL INTEREST 144 (1951).

[4] L. HENKIN, HOW NATIONS BEHAVE: LAW AND FOREIGN POLICY (2d ed. 1979).

door for Boyle's own "functionalist" approach (one suggested years earlier by Morgenthau himself but abandoned in favor of realism). But, he asserts, Morgenthau's followers—Kissinger, Brzezinski, Haig, Reagan, *et al.*—still cling to the realist approach, with the results presented at length in part III.

Boyle focuses on the law of force and its effects during international crises. In a crisis, "[i]nternational politics is and becomes international law, while international law is and becomes international politics" (p. 81). He eschews the standard realist focus on legality per se:

> [T]he primary emphasis of a functionalist analysis is upon the operational process of management, not upon the . . . promulgation and enforcement of rules. The cardinal task of functionalism is thus to analyze the ability of international law and organizations to contribute to the successful management of international crises and the peaceful resolution of the underlying disputes [p. 131].

Boyle proposes a five-step method by which public international lawyers and international political scientists can jointly analyze the interaction between international law and politics in times of crisis (p. 78). They must gather descriptive statements from case studies; derive sets of theoretical propositions from the statements; construct a general theoretical model; formulate and test predictive hypotheses; and then make recommendations on the promulgation of new law, the improvement of organizations and the alteration of national decision-making procedures.

Part II is the analytical core of Boyle's work. It is well structured and clear. He concentrates on the second step of his method, deriving a set of theoretical propositions concerning the roles of international law and organizations in an international crisis. His single case study is Israel's daring 1976 military raid against Palestinian terrorists who had hijacked a passenger jet and forced it down at Entebbe airport in Uganda. The raiders rescued the hostages and, as retaliation against Uganda's complicity with the hijackers, destroyed the Ugandan Air Force on the ground.

Boyle initially identifies five functions that international law and organizations served in the Entebbe case: the *definition* of applicable standards, as perceived by the actors; their service as elements of *decision* in Israeli crisis management; the *adjudication* of the dispute between the actors; the *resolution* of the crisis; and the *redefinition* of standards in light of the actors' experiences (p. 82). Focusing upon each function in turn, he derives 33 separate propositions from the Entebbe facts. The first proposition is that "[i]n time of international crisis, governmental decision makers will define their vital national interests to include considerations of international law and vice versa" (p. 157).

One can separate Boyle's five functions into two groups. Definition, adjudication and redefinition are all essentially prescriptive functions. They deal with the stock question of an international legal positivist: Did the Israeli raid violate international law? The positivist who seeks a simple yes-or-no answer, Boyle contends, is missing the point. Instead, international law and organizations directly and clearly affected Israeli and Ugandan perceptions of the legality and rightness of certain actions, and of their own interests (definition). The UN Security Council provided a forum for the actors to test their interpretations of the law, and a forum for the international community to react to the actions taken (adjudication). The events propelled the solidification of international opinion against hostage taking, and the consequential change in international law to include a convention against hostage taking (redefinition).

Thus, international law is and becomes international politics and vice versa. Boyle makes his case regarding the prescriptive functions. In these interpretive phases of the crisis, though, international law and organizations merely outlined the standards, forums and procedures relevant to the situation. The active phases of the crisis, where states make their moves against the background of the aforementioned information, relate to law's functions of decision and resolution.

Boyle's case in the active phases is weaker. His key proposition in the decision stage is that "[i]n time of international crisis, a government will initially pursue those viable options it perceives to be the 'least violative' of the international legal order" (*id.*). (Building up to a general theoretical model, Boyle goes on to list a half-dozen other international crises, from the Cuban missile crisis to the Iranian hostage affair, where the "least violative" principle played a role (p. 160).) Although the proposition amply refutes the argument that law is totally irrelevant to international politics, it says very little more. "Initially" and "viable" are loaded words. Boyle makes clear that Israeli decision makers agreed early on that a raid was the only truly viable option because they perceived that the very existence of their state was in question. He stresses that they worked through legal channels first, asking France, the UN Secretary-General and the International Civil Aviation Organization to intercede. But after those formal steps, none of which were ever really expected to succeed, a raid was inevitable. The Israelis had a good faith belief in the legality of their actions, but would have taken them in any case.

Likewise, in the resolution stage, international law and organizations seemed important only when convenient. Uganda submitted its complaint to the Security Council as a face-saving ploy. It had decided that the political and military costs of carrying out its threat of retaliation against Israel were too high; at the United Nations, Uganda could depend upon the inevitable majoritarian condemnation of Israel by the anti-Israel general membership, even if the Security Council took no action. The primary proposition from the resolution stage is that "[a] party to an international crisis will resort to a competent political/legal forum when it believes that a peaceful and satisfactory resolution of the dispute is possible there" (p. 158). This should not surprise even the most cynical of political scientists. "Satisfactory" is a loaded term; international organizations are denied any role at all in many situations.

In both the decision and resolution stages, public opinion and perceived vital national interests were key considerations, while international law and organizations played attenuated roles. Boyle argues convincingly, in the abstract, that a "dialectical interaction" generally exists between vital national interests and international law, where states will construe the former to incorporate the latter (p. 79). At Entebbe that symbiosis was not evident. Israel believed that its raid was legal. Idi Amin had no regard for international law whatsoever, resorting to the Security Council in pure self-interest (p. 123). By sheer fortuity, the dictates of international law and the authority of international organizations coincided somewhat with the actors' chosen courses. Boyle's functionalist analysis here works to undermine his fundamental thesis.

While part II has an international focus, part III concentrates on the interplay between the national and international legal and political dimensions of crises. Through a critique of all the main foreign policy initiatives of the Carter and Reagan administrations between 1979 and 1984, it means to show how a functionalist approach can improve American foreign policy. Analyzed in depth are the Iranian hostage crisis, the U.S. response to the Israeli invasion of Lebanon, arms control issues, and the troubles in Grenada, Nicaragua and El Salvador. Boyle finds errors ranging from the use of flawed decision-making processes to wanton disregard for international law. The "elementally lawless" Reagan administration carried out a "comprehensive and malicious assault upon the integrity of the international legal order" (p. 290). Closer attention to and use of international law and organizations, Boyle concludes, would have avoided or mitigated most of America's foreign affairs troubles during the period.

Boyle's legal reasoning is generally sound. Critical passion, however, sometimes leads him to implausible conclusions. For instance, he presents "hypothetical legal arguments" to defend the Iranian students' seizure of the American Embassy: the extensive American intelligence activity in the Embassy could have given the students reasonable apprehension of an imminent American-sponsored coup d'état, making the seizure a legitimate exercise of Iran's right of self-defense under the UN Charter (p. 188). In his zeal, he neglects to consider that major revelation of this activity surfaced only after the seizure and subsequent pillaging of the Embassy, and that Iran had nonviolent legal remedies available (namely, expulsion of the offending diplomats and/or severance of diplomatic relations). This latter oversight is especially glaring in a book dedicated to the rule of law. Boyle also carries arguments to unconstructive extremes, as where he contends that the United States should bring Israeli leaders to trial in the United States as suspected war criminals with regard to the Sabra and Chatila refugee camp massacres (p. 236).

Boyle's presentation is seriously marred by its often crass tone. He descends from articulate analysis of literature and recounting of events to bemoaning "the rape of Grenada" by the "demented" Reagan administration (p. 290). President Carter is "foolish," lost in "positivistic delusions of self-righteousness" (pp. 191, 199). Boyle derides the "rotting morass" (p. 57) of realist power politics, spitting out "Machiavellian" as a derogatory adjective with a frequency and bitter tone more familiar to inflammatory ideological tracts than to reasoned political science discourse.

This tendency to vitriolic attack goes well beyond artistic license to detract from the work as a whole, distracting the reader from the more commendable analysis and conclusions. It also might cause even the most tolerant of readers with different analytical persuasions or subtler biases to question the value of the entire work. Had Boyle implied a belief that reasonable people may differ with him, readers with other political views would accept, or at least give a fair hearing to, his analysis in spite of the disagreements. Boyle forces such readers to discount his analysis because of the differences. A close reading of the well-researched text does not support the book's prima facie appearance of irrationality and knee-jerk bias, but the initial impression leaves its mark.

Although Boyle probes deeply into Entebbe, he lacks breadth of scope in describing current practices. Boyle's post–World War II analysis is limited to Entebbe and a half decade of American national security issues. From the book's tone, one expects to see a detailed argument that, even beyond the Reagan administration, the United States brazenly violates key principles of international law on a routine basis. But Boyle shows no interest in describing the broad contours of the situation. Moreover, he gives little indication that his elegantly drawn functionalist analysis bears any relevance to past events in U.S. foreign policy as they actually unfolded. Given the depth of his research, these omissions seem contrived: if the United States in practice has generally obeyed international law since World War II, presentation of this fact might weaken the urgency of Boyle's plea for change.

The omissions create the risk of misdirection in the exhaustive derivation of a set of theoretical propositions from the Entebbe case. If the law is usually obeyed, an accurate general theoretical model would take that fact into account. Boyle's and the reader's time would be better spent deriving theoretical propositions from a case where the law was clearly obeyed.

On the other hand, Boyle's strategy perhaps serves best to focus the reader's attention. Improvements in international law and organizations and in national decision making are needed most where the system fails. In this case, Boyle's proposition that international law and organizations are relevant to the conduct of international relations could be proved in the main by systematically citing examples of such relevance. Part I takes this proof through the formation of the League of Nations after World War I, but no farther, implying that the proposition does not ring true in more contemporary times. Rather than focusing upon one group of recent failures in American foreign policy, Boyle might have devoted part III to an analysis of the overall postwar relevance of international law and organizations. Parts II and III are not complementary—one of the two is time better spent elsewhere.

Boyle writes with a lawyer's weakness for leaving key legal terms undefined (he discusses the codification of customary international law at length without attempting a definition), which may discourage a nonlegal audience. The format and overall language, though, are those of a sophisticated political scientist. The study is well documented. Boyle does not totally succeed in bridging the communication gulf between lawyers and political scientists, but he lays a strong foundation for future work.

That Boyle's functionalist analysis, as developed to date, has left blank areas in the intricate mosaic of foreign affairs is not surprising. His list and description of functions may need amending as analysis of more cases fills out the picture, to ensure that theory matches experience. Others would do well to take up his five-step research method as a guide for further study. *World Politics and International Law* is a significant step toward a truer understanding of the interrelationship between international law and world politics.

DEAN N. MENEGAS
Of the New York Bar

International Law and the Independent State (2d ed.). By Ingrid Detter De Lupis. Brookfield, Vt.: Gower Publishing Company, 1987. Pp. xxvi, 252. Indexes. $49.95.

The notion that the sovereignty of the independent state is less wholesome today than it has traditionally been is an axiom of modern international law. Even though a state can still lay claim to sovereign powers within its territory, its freedom to legislate on matters that were once deemed to lie within its reserved domain has been substantially circumscribed. What is particularly remarkable about this new phenomenon of truncated legislative supremacy is that it was essentially accomplished with the specific consent of the state itself and by virtue of the operation of general international law. Thus, what was once regarded as an oxymoron, i.e., the concept of limited sovereignty, has now become a permanent fixture on the landscape of the contemporary law of nations.

In its traditional meaning, sovereignty presupposes supremacy or superiority of the sovereign. It is an attribute of all independent states that manifests itself in both their external and their internal conduct. The corollaries of sovereignty are equality, independence and exclusive jurisdiction over a defined territory. Under modern international law, however, the sovereignty of a state is encumbered with so many fetters that the state can no longer lay claim to absolute sovereignty over all persons and property within its territory. It is this dilemma of the modern law of nations, i.e., how to reconcile state sovereignty with the limitations placed upon it, that constitutes the thrust of Professor Ingrid Detter De Lupis's analysis in this essay.

The book, which is a second edition, is written in the form of a glossatorial commentary on the various aspects of international law that intersect with the independence of a state. In her discussions the author remains steadfastly faithful to the texts of the relevant treaties and conventions on the given subject. Among the many areas of international law dealt with are the law of the sea, international human rights law, the law of treaties, air and space law, the international law of armed conflicts, diplomatic and consular law, the law of international organizations and international environmental law. Two issues are central to the theme of the book. The first is the extent to which rules of international law encroach on the exercise of sovereignty in a state's own territory. The second concerns the guarantees that international law provides to ensure that the independence of a state is not reduced by treaties that it concludes under external pressure. In her analysis of the latter topic, the author shows particular concern for the needs of the developing countries.

The author's discourse opens with the axiomatic statement that a state enjoys full sovereignty and self-determination over its territory and over all persons and property in that territory unless international law contains specific rules to the contrary. In her opinion, there is a presumption in favor of full sovereignty of a state over its territory and the burden of proof rests with the party that claims that the territorial sovereignty of a state has been restricted. The author opines that sovereignty embodies two things: independence and self-determination. The former entails the right to remain free from outside interference. The latter denotes the positive elements of the same rule, i.e., the right to secede from colonial rule, the right to be the supreme power within the territory of the state and the right to form a representative government (p. 227).

De Lupis feels, however, that there are certain exceptions to sovereignty. These exceptions fall into two groups: those relating to the territory itself and those relating to individuals and property in that territory (p. 228). In her view, these exceptions either are imposed on the state by general international law or are self-inflicted through treaty law. The author's carefully reasoned opinion is that treaties that are procured through military coercion (imposed treaties) are void under international law because they do not take effect at all. However, an exception to this rule could be made with regard to boundary treaties (pp. 227, 229). The author further concludes that to be valid, a treaty that imposes territorial restrictions on a state's sovereignty must be free of coercion and must have the full and free consent of the aggrieved state. Such consent must not be construed as following automatically from state succession, even if the treaty concerns the land itself and thus is technically in rem (p. 229). De Lupis states quite categorically that there are no servitudes in international law. In her words, "there are certainly no servitudes which survive state succession" (*id.*).

For purposes of her subsequent analysis, the author distinguishes an "imposed treaty" from an "unequal treaty." The former is induced by military coercion, whereas the latter is concluded freely but on unequal terms (p. 195). In the author's opinion, not all unequal treaties are void. "To regard [all unequal treaties] as void would merely endanger the rule of *pacta sunt servanda* . . ." (p. 195). However, she does not articulate any formula by which to determine when an unequal treaty is void or voidable. She then goes on to distinguish "unequal treaties" from "potentially unequal treaties" (p. 197). The latter term has a built-in ambiguity even though De Lupis defines it as those treaties that need the continuous consent of the host state to be valid (p. 198). She makes the point quite succinctly that potentially unequal treaties are not void per se under international law (p. 199). From this analysis she postulates what she calls the continuous consent theory, according to which a state may at any time notify the other contracting party that it no longer consents to the potentially unequal treaty. Such notice may be served either by the state that entered into the original treaty or by its successor.

De Lupis thinks that her new theory is better than the *rebus sic stantibus* doctrine, which she perceives as a great threat to the stability of international law (p. 198). Whereas *rebus sic stantibus* exposes all treaties to the threat of subsequent invalidation, her continuous consent theory permits a state to invalidate only a limited group of treaties, i.e., those that delegate to others sovereign functions within a state's territory. Examples of such treaties are military base agreements, other in rem agreements, capitulation treaties and treaties that delegate legislative functions to an international organization. Because of the limited scope of the treaties to which the continuous consent theory applies, the latter poses less threat to the principle of *pacta sunt servanda* than does *rebus sic stantibus.*

Still on the question of treaties induced by coercion, the author acknowledges that contracting parties are also subjected to other forms of nonmilitary coercion such as economic or political pressure. In fact, she feels that virtually all treaties contain some elements of these latter types of pressure (p. 227). From this observation she reasons that agreements concluded under economic or political pressure are neither void nor voidable under international law (*id.*). On this point, as well as on the question of the invalidity of unequal treaties, the author is bound to disappoint her client states—developing countries—which feel that an international agreement that is induced by unlawful economic or political pressure ought to be voidable at the least. Third World nations will also find more sympathy for their cause in the prevailing Soviet theory, that all unequal treaties, including what De Lupis calls potentially unequal treaties, are void *ab initio.*[1]

The author makes other interesting observations in her book. For example, in her discussions of "Other Restrictions of Sovereignty Relating to Territory," she asserts that "territorial sovereignty cannot imply a right to take action within a territory when such action is likely to cause damage to neighboring states" (p. 94). In her view, this principle "could also be held to imply that a state must not pollute, or allow pollution of its own groundwater which, in case considerable damage is caused, may have disastrous effects on neighboring states" (p. 95). Put quite simply, the author thinks that under general international law, even in the absence of any applicable treaty law, a state may not pollute its rivers, ground water or international rivers because any such pollution is bound to have a deleterious effect on the welfare of other states.

With regard to the restrictions on state sovereignty vis-à-vis private individuals, the author asserts that it is no longer true to say that only aliens in a country enjoy certain minimum rights under international law. In her view, even nationals have such rights by virtue of general international law rules of human rights (p. 101). In fact, the author dismisses as too vague the

[1] The best articulation of the prevailing Soviet doctrine on unequal treaties may be found in Talalaev & Boiarshinov, *Neravnopravnye Dogovory kak Forma Uderzhaniia v Kolonial'noi Zavisimosti Novykh Gosudarstv Azii i Afriki* (Unequal Treaties as a Form for Prolonging the Colonial Dependence of the New States of Asia and Africa), 1961 SOVIET Y.B. INT'L L. 156. *See also* A. TALALAEV, IURIDICHESKAIA PRIRODA MEZHDUNARODNOGO DOGOVORA (The Juridical Nature of an International Treaty) 218 (1963).

notion that aliens should be subjected to a "minimum standard." Rather, it is more realistic to apply the safeguards of human rights to protect aliens and nationals alike in a state's territory (p. 126). The author, however, qualifies her view somewhat by stipulating that international law guarantees equal protection of the law to aliens and nationals alike only with regard to what she calls fundamental human rights (*id.*). She fails to spell out when a human right becomes fundamental.

The author's discussion of this entire problem raises more questions than it resolves. At various points in the analysis, she uses different incongruous terms to refer to the rights that aliens and nationals supposedly enjoy on an equal basis. She speaks of them variously as "the most fundamental human rights" (*id.*), "the human rights enumerated in the Universal Declaration of Human Rights" (*id.*), "an individual's general human rights" (p. 129), "fundamental rights of individuals" (p. 130) and "basic human rights" (p. 133). It should be noted that among the human rights that are listed in the Universal Declaration of Human Rights is the right to own property (Art. 17). But De Lupis asserts elsewhere in her book that the right to own real property is not a fundamental right (p. 126). Other rights listed in the Universal Declaration include the right to vote (Art. 21), the right to social security benefits (Art. 22) and the right to free education (Art. 26). It is not clear to me whether the author is suggesting that under general international law a state is obligated to treat its nationals and aliens equally with regard to this latter group of rights.

Not intended as a "think piece," the book breaks no new ground and postulates no fresh theory of state sovereignty. Rather, it offers a current restatement of the conventional viewpoint on many aspects of modern international law. A commendable feature is the fact that the author makes a good faith effort to draw upon Western as well as non-Western sources. At a time when it is fashionable for Western commentators to treat Soviet doctrine with benign neglect, De Lupis devotes more than token attention to the prevailing Soviet doctrine of international law even though she quite often disagrees with it.

CHRISTOPHER OSAKWE
Christ Church College, Oxford

The International Law Commission. By Ian Sinclair. Cambridge: Grotius Publications Limited, 1987. Pp. viii, 177. Index. £28; $49.

This volume embodies the Hersch Lauterpacht Memorial Lectures delivered by Sir Ian Sinclair at the University of Cambridge in 1985—that is, prior to the irresponsible behavior of the UN General Assembly in failing to reelect him (and Willem Riphagen) to the Commission in 1986. For almost 40 years the work of the International Law Commission has been illuminated by the contributions of its British members—Brierly, Lauterpacht, Fitzmaurice, Waldock, Vallat, Sinclair. It is true that members of the ILC serve, not as "representatives" of their countries but as "persons of recognized competence in international law" (Art. 2, ILC Statute). Failure to observe this requirement is traceable to the vicious electoral quota system imposed by the General Assembly to further the "representation of the main forms of civilization and of the principal legal systems of the world" on the Commission (Art. 8), while minimizing the further provision of Article 8 that "persons to be elected to the Commission should individually possess the qualifications required" by Article 2.

Sinclair summarizes the establishment of the Commission to promote "the progressive development of international law and its codification" (Art. 1) and the subsequent politicization of membership. The size of the Commission has been increased to 34 members in order to pass around the pie (there are not 34 "principal legal systems" and the function of the Commission is *international* law). One wonders whether more than a dozen members of the current Commission are "persons of recognized competence in international law." A much smaller Commission composed of such qualified persons might better achieve the purposes for which the Commission was established. Sinclair does not go so far in his analysis and appears to accept the rationalization that if a state has a member of its nationality on the Commission, it will be more inclined to vote for a finished draft—a correlation that has yet to be established. He notes the absenteeism of members. An examination of the daily Summary Records of the Commission shows on the average at least 10 members absent each day—for which "justification" is advanced that they have more important work at home.

Despite these serious shortcomings, Sinclair concludes that the Commission—particularly in its earlier years—has made unrivaled contributions to the codification and progressive development of international law. In an informative section, he shows how the International Court of Justice and its members have been influenced by the Commission's work. In assessing its accomplishments, Sinclair faithfully examines the fate (the ultimate disposition) of the drafts adopted (e.g., how many were adopted by states in convention form and how many have been ratified or failed to attract support), but limitations of space have prevented him from giving sufficient detail or including actual texts to enlighten the reader about the specific provisions of the particular drafts on which he comments.

Nevertheless, he shows how the Commission prepared the way for the UN Convention on the Law of the Sea in formulating what became the 1958 Geneva Conventions on the Law of the Sea (retained with amplifications in the UN Convention); and how the Commission provided the basis for the current law of diplomatic and consular relations and has achieved a signal success in its work on the law of treaties. On state succession, the work of the Commission was largely overtaken by the contemporaneous behavior of successor states, although it may have had some impact on practice. The major work of the Commission on state responsibility is not completed, but it fully justifies the time it has consumed.

On the contrary, the Commission has wasted an exorbitant number of hours on topics such as the status of the diplomatic bag and the Draft Code of Offences against the Peace and Security of Mankind. The latter attempts to draft in one code juridical provisions (which states are reluctant to accept) against aggression, terrorism, genocide, colonialism, apartheid, war crimes and, perhaps, drug trafficking. A pet project of some people in the UN General Assembly, it promises to be as useless (except for propaganda purposes) as the Helsinki Accords.

From his experience on the Commission and a comprehensive examination of its methods of work, Sinclair is able to make a number of valuable suggestions for improvement: more careful selection of topics likely to result in general acceptance; return to the Commission's former practice of not insisting that every topic on the agenda be discussed at each short session; deciding in advance on whether the result should always be a draft convention.

While this book appears designed for readers who already have considerable knowledge of the Commission and its completed drafts, it provides the informed insights and reflections of a person of recognized competence in international law and is a welcome contribution to the literature on the Commission.

HERBERT W. BRIGGS
Board of Editors

La Théorie des limites matérielles à l'exercice de la fonction constituante. By Marie-Françoise Rigaux. Brussels: Maison Ferdinand Larcier, s.a., 1985. Pp. 335.

This highly theoretical study examines the interrelationship among different legal orders from the perspective of material limits (in the sense of limits *ratione materiae*) on the exercise of constitutional power within a state. While purporting to be of general application, it is apparent that the prototype envisaged by Mme. Rigaux is the state whose political and legal system is based upon a written constitution, whether unitary or federal. Her examples are drawn overwhelmingly from three European countries, Belgium, France and the Federal Republic of Germany, and to a lesser extent, Greece.

Among the varieties of material limits considered is a large category comprising external limits originating in another legal order (ch. 3 of title II, pp. 139–98). Part of this chapter discusses the ways in which the exercise of the constitutional function of a component state in a federation is subordinated to the federal constitution (pp. 143–49). For example, Article 4, section IV of the U.S. Constitution requires the states to adopt a republican form of government. In federal states, Rigaux perceives a third type or level of legal order whose function is to govern and maintain the structural relationship between the federal and the provincial orders. The exercise of constitutional competence by the states or provinces, as well as by the federal legislator, is constrained by limits imposed by this third order, but the states are not directly subordinated to the federation. The third order guarantees the pluralist form of sovereignty that the people have chosen, if only by implication, by agreeing on a federal structure. A federal constitutional court provides the concrete expression of the guarantee, for example, in its task of interpreting and maintaining a provision such as Article 79(3) of the German *Grundgesetz,* which prohibits any revision relating to the organization of the federation in *Länder* or to the participation of the *Länder* in the legislative process (pp. 83, 148). Here Rigaux takes issue with Kelsen and the Vienna school whose theories of the *Rechtstaat* or *l'Etat de droit* have served to inspire centripetal tendencies in some constitutional analyses.

The greater part of this lengthy chapter is devoted to the subordination of the holder of the constitutional function to the international legal order (section 3, pp. 149–98). The author examines the interaction between a state's constitution and international law, including particular treaties, general customary international law and the constitutions of certain international organizations. There are four subsections: the first deals with provisions giving primacy to, or incorporating the general rules of, international law such as the celebrated Article 25 of the *Grundgesetz;* second, there are constitutional powers limited by treaty provisions affecting the future exercise of constitutional aspects of sovereignty such as provisions respecting the form of government of a state or guaranteeing the rights of minorities or limiting the exercise of external sovereignty, as in the cases of permanent neutrality. The third subsection treats limitations on constitutional power that may be imposed by membership in an organization, and the fourth discusses tacit limitation by general rules of international law, including, but not limited to, *jus cogens.* This reviewer was disappointed by the skeletal analysis and discussion of the domestic jurisdiction limitation in the UN Charter, and of the nature of states' obligations under the Charter to secure human rights and freedoms. Moreover, one lapidary sentence on page 179 on the effect of ratification of the European Convention on Human Rights does nothing to clarify the issue of the legal effect of the Convention on the law of a dualist party such as the United Kingdom. Rigaux falls into error in her next example, the OAS, as she refers to the exclusion of the state of Cuba from that organization (p. 180). But she offers the comment that both the OAS and the Organization of Central American States, with their provisions of "constitutional legitimacy" obliging members to maintain certain democratic principles and not to recognize governments established in their countries by coup or revolution, illustrate the permeability of the internal state order by the international legal order, whose authority the states recognize by belonging to such an organization.

The doctrine of the supremacy of European Community law over inconsistent national law receives some attention (pp. 182–83, 289–91), focusing upon the *Simmenthal* case. Rigaux's thesis is that the interconnection between the two orders can operate only to limit the exercise of member states' autonomy, and that the enactment of conflicting laws gives rise to responsibility. But we may also recognize "a greater authority" in particular Community provisions in areas where the legal order of a member state has accepted the loss of part of its prerogatives. This reviewer admits to considerable difficulty in following the purported distinction between a limit on the exercise of sovereign legislative authority and the loss or abandonment of part of that authority. Rigaux seems anxious to refute any global proposition as to the primacy of Community law, and to affirm that the EEC is a collaborative association of states for the realization of certain objectives, but she is compelled to admit that respect for rules belonging to the Community sphere "reduces the efficacy" (p. 291) of national rules having the same object or subject matter. What precisely is meant by reducing the efficacy of legal rules remains a mystery. Important steps in the argument cry out for greater precision of language and additional concrete examples.

Some rules of general international law can produce limitations on the constitutional competence of state organs, provided that certain conditions are satisfied. National legal orders may be subject to certain rules of international law, for example, respect for fundamental human rights (pp. 188–90) and the principle of self-determination of peoples (pp. 190–95). The reasoning is hard to pin down, and one has to turn to the final part of the book, part II, title III, for a treatment of the validity of such external limitations, or the conditions that must be satisfied for these limitations to acquire obligatory force. Rigaux formulates a principle of reticulatory normativity of external limits ("le principe de la normativité réticulaire des limites hétéronomes") and seeks to apply it to the examples and arguments selected in the earlier chapter (see pp. 286–302). To have a limiting effect on national constitutional organs, the international rule must be temporary and capable of future amendment or abrogation; the material limitation affects the liberty of the national constituent and not its legal capacity, which means that an inconsistent national provision is valid in terms of the national system but may give rise to state responsibility. However, in the case of a rule of *jus cogens,* the capacity of the national organ may be restricted in terms of its own national law (pp. 302–06). Authority for these various validating conditions is sought in doctrine, in arguments from principle and, to a limited extent, in state practice, including the preparatory work of the Vienna Convention provisions on *jus cogens.* This reviewer was not entirely satisfied that the author sustained her main thesis, but the arguments arouse interest and call for further empirical testing and theoretical review.

This book is based on Rigaux's doctoral thesis and carries the unmistakable stamp of a mind trained in the civil law and attracted by generalized and abstract theories of law and the state. The work exemplifies a legitimate and distinctive approach and methodology that offer some illuminating insights into the relationship between different and distinct legal orders, but it is not an intellectual milieu in which a pragmatic and fairly positivist common law–trained international lawyer can feel at home. The book contains a useful bibliography and a detailed table of contents, but no index or lists of cases or treaties cited.

GILLIAN WHITE
University of Manchester

Enforcing International Law Through U.S. Legislation. By Elisabeth Zoller. Dobbs Ferry: Transnational Publishers, Inc., 1985. Pp. xiv, 189. Index. $35, cloth.

In this book, Elisabeth Zoller, professor of law at the University of Strasbourg, identifies and categorizes acts of Congress that seem to respond to violations of international law by other states. Following this mammoth undertaking, she attempts to draw conclusions that might constitute "a general theory of unilateral remedies in peacetime" (p. 4).

The reasons given for studying U.S. legislation and only U.S. legislation (this is not a comparative review of national legislation enforcing international law) as evidence of customary international law seem questionable. These are that the "usually wide authority of executives in foreign affairs" does not characterize the U.S. system,[1] and that the United States is "the only state in the world that has systematically made its unilateral peacetime remedies public by legislation" (p. 3). One wonders whether U.S. legislation is, as the author asserts, "an exemplification of enforcement mechanism [*sic*] in international law" (p. 4).

The volume of statutes collected and analyzed is impressive. But often the author does not examine the admittedly elusive, but necessarily central, issue of *purpose:* whether Congress intended to enforce an international norm by enacting the law in question, or whether the President intended to do so by enforcing it. Indeed, virtually no attention is paid to any practice that may exist on the part of the United States with respect to the statute in question. Where the relevant international norm derives from treaty law, purpose can perhaps be inferred. In the case of customary norms, however, one is seldom sure whether Congress or the Executive acted with any knowledge of, let alone concern about, the rule purportedly enforced.

Nonetheless, the work should have considerable utility as an idea-generator for governmental officials putting together option papers. One can quibble about the author's categorization of certain laws, but overall the analysis is a huge and creative first step in exploring a largely uncharted area of international law.

MICHAEL J. GLENNON
Board of Editors

Judicial Remedies in International Law. By Christine D. Gray. Oxford: Clarendon Press; New York: Oxford University Press, 1987. Pp. xix, 250. Index. $57.

This book was originally formulated as a Ph.D. thesis submitted at Cambridge University. It deals with one aspect of the consequences of breaches

[1] Much of the analysis seems based on a simplistic premise: that "the President has no general retaliatory authority." He may, the author claims, "act only under a delegation which, falling short of being embodied in the Constitution, may be given only by the legislative branch" (pp. 10–11). The President's constitutional power over recognition, diplomatic relations and treaty negotiation is not considered.

of international law. As Ian Brownlie indicates in the preface, "International lawyers always pay tribute to the principle of judicial settlement of disputes, but in recent times most writers have tended to avoid touching on the particular questions falling under the fairly loose headings of the 'judicial function' or 'state responsibility'."

Christine Gray addresses the nature and role of judicial remedies in international law. The scope of the study is impressive, both in the range of arbitral and judicial bodies dealt with, and in the variety of remedies examined. The author considers the approach of arbitral tribunals, the World Court, the European Court of Justice, human rights courts, administrative tribunals and international commercial tribunals to the question of judicial remedies. Her goal is to find out whether these various bodies have developed common rules in the field of remedies. She eventually comes to the conclusion that they have not. Thus, it becomes impossible to refer to a coherent international law of remedies. One may wonder, however, how any other conclusion could have been reached in light of the diversity of the judicial remedies examined. For the international arbitral practice alone she considers negative injunctions, *restitutio in integrum,* specific performance, declaratory judgments, damages, punitive damages, nominal damages and interest (pp. 11–33). She also examines interim measures of protection (pp. 69–79) and advisory opinions by the World Court (pp. 111–18), as well as rulings by the European Court of Justice (pp. 120–48). Nonetheless, the book is a useful reminder of the diversity of means by which international law may be adjudicated by international tribunals.

A recurrent argument in the book is that the primacy (or even the possibility) in international law of the remedy of *restitutio in integrum*—as adopted by the Permanent Court of International Justice in the *Chorzów Factory* case—finds no support in arbitral and judicial practice. Gray justifies her position by invoking the rarity of *restitutio in integrum* awards in arbitral practice and its refusal in certain cases (pp. 14–15), and by pinpointing that in the *Chorzów Factory* case, "not only was restitution not requested by the claimant state . . . , but also the treaty which the Court had to apply gave the injured party the treaty right to demand restitution in kind" (p. 96). There is force to these arguments. However, they fail to take into account that restitution, like Janus, has two faces: restitution in kind and restitution by equivalence ("payment of a sum corresponding to the value which a restitution in kind would bear").[1]

Gray is apparently not optimistic about the role of judicial remedies in international law. She rightly raises "the question of the limits on what can be expected from and achieved by [such remedies]" (p. 210). However, she leaves open the daunting question of what could replace them.

ELISABETH ZOLLER
University of Strasbourg

[1] Factory at Chorzów, 1927 PCIJ (ser. A) No. 17, at 47.

Treaty Interpretation: Theory and Reality. By Edward Slavko Yambrusic. Lanham, New York, London: University Press of America, 1987. Pp. xi, 298. $28.50, cloth; $15.75, paper.

This book would be an important starting place for anyone interested in doing research on treaty interpretation either in the abstract or in reference to a particular case. The first part consists of a good comparative analysis of state practice with respect to the interpretation of treaties: the common law tradition (the United States, the United Kingdom), the jurisprudence of the continental civil code (Austria, France, Germany) and the socialist law approach (the USSR). On this point, the author's conclusions are that in state practice the primary emphasis is upon the will of the parties as expressed in the text of the treaty, but that there exist no obligatory rules of treaty interpretation that states share in common.

In light of these findings, the author then proceeds to analyze the jurisprudence of the International Court of Justice with respect to treaty interpretation up to about the time of the adoption of the Vienna Convention on the Law of Treaties in 1969. Here the author concludes that the Court considered "the so-called canons of interpretation merely as guides to the logical process of the interpreter's reasoning rather than the obligatory norms to be followed and applied by the Court" (p. 144). For this reason, the author faults the Court for failing to provide certainty, objectivity and predictability in its jurisprudence of treaty interpretation.

The third part of the book examines the *travaux préparatoires* of Articles 31 and 32 of the Vienna Convention. In the author's opinion, the International Law Commission likewise failed to provide the international community with a general rule of treaty interpretation. Hence his conclusion that Articles 31 and 32 are not declaratory of customary international law on this subject (pp. 245–46). At the end of this exhaustive analysis, the author argues persuasively for Professor McDougal's contextual approach to the interpretation of treaties.

FRANCIS A. BOYLE
University of Illinois College of Law

Weltpolitik: Strukturen—Akteure—Perspektiven. Edited by Karl Kaiser and Hans-Peter Schwarz. Stuttgart: Klett-Cotta, 1985. Pp. 742. Index.

This is not a book on international law in general, nor does it contain a collection of essays on specific international legal problems, but it should be useful to all those who are interested in the general background and the most important spheres of international politics in our time. It tries to give a reliable picture of global, as well as many regional, political problems. Such an undertaking could hardly be successful without the cooperation of first-rate authors. The editors have assembled such a collection of competent authors. Only a few of them can be considered specialists in international law (Wilhelm Grewe, Boris Meissner, Wolfgang Graf Vitzthum); the great majority of the articles are written by political scientists. Even where problems of international law are touched on (e.g., in the articles on nuclear weapons, arms control, oceans, space, human rights), no discussion of legal problems can be found—this proves once more the neglect of international law by many political scientists.

All in all, 45 authors contributed to this work, which is divided into two parts: global problems and regional problems. In the first part, we find chapters on structural problems of the international community, for example, on the relevance of the power factor in the system of sovereign states, and on the most important challenges of our time—East-West relations, economic problems, the proliferation of arms, human rights. In the part on regional problems, there are articles on the relations among Western states, the socialist system and the Near East; other chapters deal with Asian problems, Africa and Latin America.

On average, each chapter is less than 20 pages. This excludes any thorough discussion of the problems, but in the aggregate a fair survey is afforded. If the articles were not written by well-informed authors, the book would not deserve a review in this *Journal.* A Western and conservative approach dominates the book, but this does not diminish its merits.

It does not make sense here to go into details. Some chapters and subchapters are superficial and some statements are even wrong. For instance, one author asserts in his short remarks on the question of an international law of the environment (pp. 214 *ff.*) that no rule of international law inhibits transfrontier pollution. One sentence on page 331 touches upon the American intervention in Grenada; Namibia is dealt with in another chapter in only a few pages (pp. 654 *ff.*) and without adequate discussion of the international law aspects.

The book is recommended for those who seek a global survey of the main political problems of our time. For specialists, especially scholars and practitioners of international law, neither the articles themselves nor the bibliographical references provide sufficient guidance or information.

RUDOLF BERNHARDT
Max Planck Institute for Comparative Public Law and International Law, Heidelberg

The Regulation of International Economic Relations Through Law. By Palitha Tikiri Bandara Kohona. Dordrecht, Boston, Lancaster: Martinus Nijhoff Publishers, 1985. Pp. xxii, 280. Index. Dfl.150; $49.50; £41.75.

Palitha T. B. Kohona completed this book while working for the Australian Department of Foreign Affairs. He did most of his research at Cambridge University while writing his Ph.D. thesis on international economic relations. Although the book evidences a great deal of thought on the author's part, its rather abstract content does not make it of practical use to attorneys who wish to familiarize themselves with the specific legal and structural aspects of the various international economic organizations. Nevertheless, the book is valuable to anyone generally interested in international relations. It offers general information on numerous organizations and provides a very comprehensive bibliography.

Kohona's thesis is that "international economic regimes," in their growth, are influencing the domestic policies of individual states to an increasingly substantial degree, and that this influence is by and large consented to by the individual states involved. The author attributes the development of "international economic regimes" to the consent of the member states. Kohona argues that this consent is given in the commonly shared belief that all groups and nations affected by world economic change must be effectively represented through active participation, and that economic relations should be governed by rules derived from norms accepted by all groups of nations involved.

Kohona contends that groups and nations that share this representation-oriented outlook have engaged in economic relations, and have reached agreements that, in turn, have promoted the growth of international economic law. To ensure that the objectives of the underlying agreements are attained, the groups and nations concerned have created organizations that determine new policies, adopt norms of conduct, implement decisions and resolve disputes. In exercising these functions, such organizations have ushered in the creation and evolution of "international economic regimes." According to the author, states consent to that development in the hope of achieving their mutually beneficial goals more effectively and efficiently. In return, states must surrender a certain degree of sovereignty in that they must work out internally how they will implement the policies adopted by an organization.

One criticism that could be raised about the book is that the author presents an overly abstract theory of international relations. He places too much emphasis, it seems, on the theoretical structure of membership in international organizations and the consent of nations to such membership and its attending rights and obligations. Very little discussion is provided concerning the international economic forces themselves that have led to the establishment of international agreements and have shaped those agreements and the institutions under which they are administered. It is the specific, and varying, need of individual countries to respond to the growing economic interrelationship and interdependence of nations that has caused them to consider membership in international economic organizations and determines the scope of the economic matters dealt with by such organizations. Any discussion of international economic organization that ignores or minimizes these factors provides a less than complete characterization of the numerous and widely differing international economic institutions.

A second comment is that the book is focused heavily on the perspective of developing countries. The internal workings of international organizations are analyzed almost exclusively from this viewpoint. Such a perspective may be appropriate for organizations like UNIDO and UNCTAD, which deal almost exclusively with issues of primary relevance to developing countries, but it provides less insight into how and why other organizations, such as the OECD, function. Membership in these other organizations is drawn significantly or almost entirely from industrialized nations, and the problems they seek to resolve are those of trade and investment primarily between industrialized countries. Between those two types of organizations is yet a third category covering organizations such as the GATT, which attempt to deal with problems affecting both groups of nations. In such organizations, it would be more appropriate to consider the economic perspectives of both the industrialized and the developing countries, whose viewpoints in many cases conflict, and the manner in which the organizations attempt to balance these conflicting points of view.

These criticisms notwithstanding, the book is helpful in that it puts international economic law into some perspective. The author concludes that norms of conduct adopted by international organizations can serve only as points of reference; that they are enforceable only insofar as individual member states consent; and that, consequently, dispute resolution should not follow any universal rules or strictly legal procedure if social, political or cultural conflicts are to be avoided. Rather, dispute resolution in international economic affairs should be oriented toward a more ad hoc approach by which the conflicting parties reach mutually acceptable terms that apply only to their specific situation.

MARK ROY SANDSTROM
Of the District of Columbia Bar

Law and its Limitations in the GATT Multilateral Trade System. By Olivier Long. Dordrecht, Boston, Lancaster: Martinus Nijhoff Publishers, 1985. Pp. xi, 145. Index. Dfl.100; $38.50; £27.75.

"[O]n the international plane there is only one system which provides in legal form a framework of rules and procedures governing international trade and trade relations and which embodies legal rights and obligations between its member countries. This system is the General Agreement on Tariffs and Trade (GATT) . . ." (p. 4).

In this short but precise book, Olivier Long, former director general of GATT (1968–1980) and professor at the Graduate Institute of International Studies in Geneva, provides us with an English translation of his Hague Academy lectures on the GATT (delivered in 1983). Beginning with the definition of GATT quoted above, this book is an exceptional and valuable work, and not merely a set of reminiscences by a person who has had direct and central experience with the institution he describes. It is a truly scholarly attempt to reflect on the meaning of some of those experiences. The manner of presentation is concise and well organized. It reflects extensive reading in the related literature, as well as extensive discussions about the manuscript among a number of GATT officials. This is clearly the most authoritative short overview of the GATT as a legal institution.

The GATT is truly a perplexing institution. It became what it was never intended to be—the central international organization for world trade—after the 1948 charter of the International Trade Organization failed to come into force. Thus, the GATT has had to exist without the many institutional clauses found in normal organization charters. These deficiencies are noted by the author, who describes many of the fascinating circumstances of practice and evolution that have allowed the GATT to exist as a pragmatic and reasonably effective legal order. Particularly to be noted are excellent accounts of the troublesome Multifibre Agreements (p. 32), the legal questions of preferences for developing countries (p. 31), voting and consensus decision making (p. 55) and the procedures for dispute settlement (p. 65). While the opinions and perspectives of the author will certainly not be universally accepted, they are well stated and carefully thought out.

After an opening chapter on "The Legal Framework" of GATT, in which the author surveys the history of GATT and provides an overview of its rules, Long proceeds to an examination of the GATT as a "Forum for Negotiations." He then turns to a chapter on decision making and organizational structure, entitled "The Functioning of GATT." A fourth chapter deals with "supervising" the GATT, focusing on the dispute settlement process, and presenting some judgments (which, of course, can be debated) such as that the GATT Contracting Parties' "main objective is to produce recommendations designed to protect this balance [of advantage], rather than have recourse to sanctions" (p. 71).

After an excellent chapter on the evolution of a GATT legal structure to promote economic development, the author turns to his conclusions. Let some of his words carry the flavor:

> In a multilateral trade treaty such as the General Agreement the legal rules provide what the member countries expect from them: the assurance of a reasonable degree of certainty in the conventional conditions under which international trade takes place, and transparency in the conduct by member countries of their trade relations.
>
> The rules and procedures of the GATT are such that they can evolve and be modified in response to changes in the economic and political conditions that influence trade relations [p. 107].

As the world moves forward into the eighth and most complex trade negotiation sponsored by GATT, a negotiation that not only will likely be the last in this century, but also could frame the structure of trade well into the next century, Long's book will be both a delightfully short introduction for those new to the subject and an authoritative source of information and judgment, particularly about the legal institutional aspects of GATT.

JOHN H. JACKSON
Board of Editors

Interdependence in the Post-Multilateral Era: Trends in U.S.-European Trade Relations. By Stephen Woolcock, Jeffrey Hart and Hans van der Ven. Cambridge: Center for International Affairs, Harvard University; Lanham: University Press of America, 1985. Pp. xxv, 138. $19.50, cloth; $7.75, paper.

As its title suggests, the authors of this book believe that we have entered an era in which multilateral efforts to resolve trade disputes are doomed to failure. The premise of the book is that differences in national approaches to trade and the formulation of industrial policy (as illustrated by case studies of U.S. and EC policy with respect to three industrial sectors—steel, automobiles and "telematics") are so great that the establishment of an effective multilateral regime to govern international trade is a virtual impossibility, at least outside the tariff area. The authors focus in particular on the growing use by individual nations of a variety of industrial targeting measures, including nontariff barriers on imports. They conclude that competing sovereign national interests and approaches are likely to prevent the achievement of any coordination of multilateral policy or effective multilateral resolution of the trade conflicts such measures create.

Despite its gloomy forecast about multilateralism, *Interdependence in the Post-Multilateral Era* makes a valuable contribution to the literature on international trade relations. The authors' effort to integrate a "micro" political/economic analysis of individual cases with a "macro" view of international trade relations marks an important direction in trade policy analysis. The particular strength of the book lies in its three trade policy case studies. Each of the authors has chosen an industrial sector that has been the subject of trade friction between the United States and the European Communities, and has analyzed the policies adopted by them in these areas in terms of their implications for U.S.-EC relations and, by extension, the international trading system. These studies are useful, and quite insightful, in describing the origins and dimensions of these trade disputes and the policies that have evolved in the United States and the European Communities to address them.

The book also offers a number of thought-provoking observations about the nature of trade and trade policy in the late 1980s. The authors implicitly recognize that although "industrial policy" remains a dirty word in U.S. government circles, U.S. trade policy is increasingly a sectoral policy, which observers from other countries have difficulty distinguishing from industrial policy. Because the "industrial policy" label has become associated in this country with notions of unfair trade and unacceptable levels of government intervention in the marketplace, the United States has tended to take an ad hoc, rather than a consciously coordinated, approach to microeconomic policy, with trade measures frequently forced to carry the burden of achieving essentially microeconomic policy goals when other measures would be more appropriate. However, the official U.S. government view remains that the role of trade policy is a limited one—to eliminate unfair trading practices, and occasionally to allow limited protection for domestic industries to permit them to adjust to foreign competition—and that trade policy should not properly be used as a tool to promote any particular form of, or direction for, economic development.

The European Communities, on the other hand, have been more forthright about employing whatever measures are deemed necessary (e.g., trade restrictions, subsidization, forced rationalization) to foster or preserve important industrial sectors. Trade policy in the Communities, then, is viewed as a subset of overall competition policy rather than as an independent branch of policymaking with limited applications. When trade conflicts arise between the United States and the European Communities, the differences in their views regarding the proper role of trade policy in the overall policy process inevitably create difficulties in achieving a satisfactory resolution of any particular dispute.

Although few would quarrel with these observations, not all would agree with the authors' reasoning that this state of affairs precludes the possibility that the multilateral regime (GATT) can address trade problems outside the tariff area with any degree of effectiveness. One suspects that the authors were unduly influenced by the pundits and cynics of the day, and are overly skeptical as a consequence. The authors' pessimism may also derive from their focus on the differences in national policies that inhibit policy coordination, and a consequent tendency to overlook or minimize the importance of the areas of mutual interest that promote dispute resolution.

One consequence of this focus on the negative aspects of the cases examined is a tendency to offer criticisms that are not entirely justified. Particularly in the case study on steel, the book criticizes U.S. and EC trade policy actions without sufficient consideration of whether, under existing economic and political conditions, a particular action did or did not represent the best achievable alternative. Granted, there is room to criticize the woodenness of U.S. trade laws and the U.S. policy process, and one can easily paint a picture of a U.S. Government operating at the mercy of domestic steel interests to the detriment of the international trading system. However, this perspective fails to recognize that the solutions crafted in the steel case were designed not only to conform with U.S. obligations under the GATT, but also to take account of European economic and political realities. The trigger price mechanism (TPM) was, after all, designed to allow (often heavily subsidized) European producers to compete against the more efficient Japanese in the U.S. market, rather than subjecting them to the rigors of the U.S. countervailing duty law, a result that would have excluded certain EC producers from the U.S. market entirely. In this context, the study's criticisms of U.S. trade laws and of the details of administering the TPM obscure a central point, namely, the important areas of mutual interest that enabled the United States and the European Communities to reach agreement on measures to address the problem.

Similarly, the analysis of the telematics case would benefit from a more extensive focus on areas of mutual interest, as well as on problem areas. By looking narrowly at the issues surrounding deregulation of telecommunications markets, the study fails to take account of the growing recognition in both the United States and the European Communities that there are large areas of mutual U.S.-EC interest, not only in the telecommunications sector, but across the entire spectrum of electronics products and services, from semiconductors to computers, and from informatics to high-definition television. This growing awareness of common interests and of the need to avoid trade conflicts can be seen in a number of recent positive initiatives such as the U.S.-EC High Technology Working Group and the willingness of the European Communities to entertain comments on the EC Green Paper on telecommunications deregulation. These initiatives suggest that there are strong undercurrents that could be channeled to promote policy coordination if the issues were properly conceptualized and packaged.

All of this, quite naturally, leads to a consideration of the multilateral system and GATT. The "macro" conclusions drawn by the authors regarding the implications of their analysis for the multilateral trading system are less compelling than the "micro" analysis of the individual case studies. In part, this is because insufficient attention is devoted to developing an overall framework to tie the case studies together, with the result that the book's conclusions and policy prescriptions come across as something of an afterthought.

It appears, moreover, that the standards by which the authors have evaluated prospects for managing trade conflicts multilaterally are unduly restrictive. The GATT system itself recognizes that free trade notions must often be modified to take account of the fundamental economic realities that frequently prevent the development of optimal trade policies. In a world in which sovereign nations are unprepared to cede control over their commercial policies, the GATT cannot realistically be expected to replace sovereign nations in their policymaking function. This does not, however, necessitate the conclusion that there is no useful role to be played by such a multilateral regime. The GATT can (and should) continue to play its traditional role as a forum for developing agreement on the ground rules for international trade and for arbitrating disputes regarding their application. (That interpretation and enforcement of the international rules must, of necessity, begin at the national level is not an argument for doing away with GATT.) Beyond its traditional role, the GATT can also continue to expand what has become (in the new Uruguay Round of negotiations in particular) its de facto function as a promoter of mutual interests and appropriate national trade policies. In this latter function lies the most promising direction for effective multilateral management of international trade relations in an increasingly complex world.

The most telling criticism of U.S. trade policy since the late 1960s and early 1970s is that the United States quite simply does not have one. The studies in this book help one to understand why. In this regard, they make an invaluable contribution to the effort to reconcile the "micro" view of industrial efforts to address foreign competition with the "macro" view of the appropriate role of trade in overall economic policy.

R. MICHAEL GADBAW
Of the District of Columbia Bar
ROSEMARY E. GWYNN
Of the District of Columbia Bar

Rechtliche Beschränkungen des Technologietransfers im Außenwirtschaftsverkehr. By Klaus Wolfgang Ebert. Baden-Baden: Nomos Verlagsgesellschaft, 1986. Pp. 381. DM 87.

Although most German doctoral dissertations in fields such as law, medicine and economics are not published by a regular publishing house but are printed in upgraded mimeograph form at the candidate's expense, K. W.

Ebert's thesis, which was accepted by the University of Hamburg (I) Faculty of Law, was issued by the renowned publisher Nomos Verlagsgesellschaft.

The author's subject is the legal restrictions on the transfer of technology in foreign trade, primarily in German law. His last chapter, however, deals with the applicability of foreign embargo provisions to the business of German subsidiaries of U.S. corporations, and to German licensees of foreign licensors. The purpose of the book is to engage in a legal discussion of the *politically* motivated restrictions of recent years. Ebert focuses on the question whether, and if so, to what degree, the transfer of militarily important technology to states of the Warsaw Pact has been restricted. Another subject that interests the author is the restrictions concerning the transfer of nuclear technology for civil use to states that might employ resulting nuclear material in the construction of nuclear weapons. He also deals with restrictions that affect the transfer of technology to states whose political system the Federal Republic of Germany, and/or the United Nations, disapproves of; such restrictions may be designed to effectuate possible changes in these systems.

The author starts from the premise that the German economic and legal order, as a rule, entitles any person freely to transfer the technical know-how he possesses. He describes the exceptions provided by German law with respect to the international transfer of technology, including the possibilities of judicial review of the constitutionality of acts of state that may be invoked by the concerned persons and corporations. This approach is taken only to the law of the Federal Republic of Germany and excludes the regulations and administrative practice of the European Communities; of all other countries, the United States is mentioned merely in connection with the extraterritorial effects of U.S. law in Germany.

The book consists of six parts. The first part discusses the forms of technical knowledge and the factual and legal possibilities for its transfer. The second covers the reasons for, and the forms of restrictions on, the transfer of technology in the foreign trade law (*Außenwirtschaftsrecht*) of the Federal Republic of Germany. In the third chapter, the author deals with restrictions on transfer in cases he identifies by what he calls an absolute interest of secrecy. Here some provisions of the German penal code, and restrictions and limitations based on the patent law, are investigated.

A longer fourth chapter deals with the *Außenwirtschaftsgesetz* (AWG, foreign trade law) and discusses, in technical detail, the implementation of this statute with reference to the transfer of technology if the reasons for such restrictions are one or more of the *political* reasons mentioned above. Another long chapter discusses the rights of the concerned to sue in cases of legal or administrative restrictions for (1) revocation of the administrative act; (2) indemnification under patent law; and (3) indemnification under constitutional law (Art. 14 of the German Constitution, *Grundgesetz*). Finally, the last chapter deals with the extraterritoriality of transfer restrictions. The author discusses the problems of the evasion of embargoes, particularly by detours through third countries (*Umweghandel*). Here a short description of U.S. law, the NATO recommendations and a detailed presentation of the German situation are offered. Then the admissibility of direct extraterritorial restrictions under international law is briefly examined. The two last subchapters deal with extraterritorial restrictions originating in the Federal Republic and directed against foreign enterprises, and with the reverse problem of the applicability of foreign embargo provisions on German corporations. It is here that some decisions of the German Supreme Court (Bundesgerichtshof) of 1960 and 1962 and an older decision of the Reichsgericht are discussed. In his summary, the author again cites the principle of territoriality, which invalidates many attempts to influence foreign enterprises by embargo provisions. Moreover, the author makes the point that many such provisions have little practical effect.

The book may serve as an introduction to the legal problems of embargo provisions. It presents the principles and offers, in this respect, not much new material. The Anglo-American reader will expect more case material. The book makes useful suggestions on the interpretation of the German foreign trade law with regard to embargoes.

WOLFGANG FIKENTSCHER
University of Munich

La inversión directa en el régimen de las inversiones extranjeras. By María Concepción Pablo-Romero Gil-Delgado. Pamplona: Ediciones Universidad de Navarra, S.A., 1986. Pp. ix, 214.

Ms. María Concepción Pablo-Romero Gil-Delgado, in her Spanish-language work, "Direct Investment within the Ambit of Foreign Investment Laws," takes on a subject of great practical importance in many countries and special significance in the country where her book was published, Spain. Spain joined the European Economic Community on January 1, 1986. Membership has meant that Spain must adjust many of its laws, including its foreign investment laws, to Community norms during the transitional period that terminates on January 1, 1992. The need to adjust implies changes in the laws that rule both investments made by foreigners in Spain and investments that are made from Spain to other countries, both of which include the concept of direct investment. This book is not an attempt to tackle and analyze direct investment regimes throughout the world. In the author's words, it is an attempt to shed light on the concept of direct investment.

To achieve her purpose, the author selects a variety of countries that operate under different circumstances and summarizes their approach to legislation and control of direct investments. Her orientation is decidedly tilted toward the Spanish situation; almost half the book is dedicated to an analysis of Spanish legislation on direct investment. That, however, does not prevent her from presenting a balanced and scholarly work.

Pablo-Romero begins her study with a survey of economic theory concerning investments and their definition. On the macroeconomic level, an investment is considered to be an increase in the totality of capital goods, a "real investment." On the financial level, an investment is the application of accumulated savings in the hopes of obtaining a profit. Of course, the author notes, a financial investment can be a real investment. The interplay of these two points is returned to when analyzing specific laws.

The author provides a short history of foreign investment; how it evolved from mainly long-term projects to an increase in short-term movements of capital. She then investigates the factors that influence a country's position with regard to direct investments from abroad and foreign investments in general. She mentions the political situation (i.e., degree of stability) and balance of payments as factors that influence the way a country regulates its foreign investments. Especially important for her is economic development. She states that the latter perhaps is the main reason a country would take a restrictive position with regard to foreign investment.

Other economic factors also affect the foreign investment regime of a country. Countries that export capital do so for different reasons from those of countries that import it. Countries are exporters of capital, according to the author, because they must maintain or expand markets. These actions, of course, carry with them the corresponding risks: poor communications because of long distances, together with increased expenses and possible political risks.

Countries import capital because of the favorable effects on their balance of payments. It enables them to import technology and achieve commercial balance. Recurrent mention is made of the negative effects of capital importation such as the risk of economic interdependence to the point of weakening the economic policy of the government, inflation, the shutting down of weak national industries or businesses, and a sense of loss of sovereignty when foreign investors control certain aspects of the national wealth. The negative effects are the reasons, according to the author, that countries have foreign investment laws. The laws are designed, she writes, to prevent the fearful situation of "economic colonialism." These laws control more what goes on in a country than what goes on outside it because of the obvious limits on the application of domestic laws abroad.

Pablo-Romero uses the experiences of several of the countries in the Andean Common Market, Mexico and Argentina to support her argument concerning economic colonialism. It is not so clear that her argument is as accurate with regard to the European countries, whose foreign investment laws she reviews, especially those of France, Italy and the Common Market regime in general. Portugal and Spain, on the other hand, depending on the specific point in time, could be said to be "subjects" of economic colonialism.

The author believes that countries receiving capital from abroad "are conscious of its advantages and disadvantages and they establish legislative bases that permit the foreign capital to aid, within the legal order, their economic development." She chooses to review European and Latin American countries with foreign investment regimes because of their geographic and historical connection with Spain. She examines the foreign investment law of Portugal because its situation is similar to that of Spain. It also is a country trying to adapt its legal regime to that of the EEC.

There are, of course, basic differences between the Community countries and the Latin American countries that influence their foreign investment regimes. The author lists the differences that she finds the most significant: in general, the EEC countries are both importers and exporters of capital, while those of Latin America are mainly importers; the EEC countries are more stable politically than those of Latin America; and, finally, except for Portugal, the EEC countries are economically autonomous, while such autonomy does not exist in Latin America. She finds the Spanish situation to be in the middle; somewhere between a full member of the EEC and a Latin American nation.

In her overview of each foreign investment law, Pablo-Romero begins by signaling its main purpose. After a detailed analysis, she summarizes the most important points developed from her analysis. For the author, four things are to be emphasized in the study of direct investment legislation: the breadth allowed for direct investments in the various economic sectors of the country, the legal and physical persons who may make the investment, the types of capital admitted and the system of control. These points are addressed in her discussion of the various foreign investment laws, which is systematic, detailed and amply reinforced by references to scholarly works and official publications. It is interesting to discover through her research, for example, that the drafters of the Andean Foreign Investment Code, whose purpose is to assure the development of the national private sector and limit foreign influence, are often "the representatives of foreign capital in their own country."

Countries of the EEC are concerned, as exporters of capital, that their citizens' investments be protected. This is done, she says, by relying on the internal law of the foreign country and reinforcing those guarantees with treaties. At the same time, the EEC countries are also concerned with domination and control of their national economy.

From her study of the Latin American and European regimes, the author derives her own definition of a direct investment: an entrepreneurial investment in which the investor engages in an entrepreneurial activity, whether derived from ownership of the business assets or from control of the business activity that is the target of the investment. Control can exist because the investor has a majority of the capital of the business or because the target is a subsidiary that together with its parent forms an economic group.

With this definition in hand, the author undertakes a comprehensive study of Spanish legislation on direct investment. She provides a historical background of Spanish law regarding foreign investment. Legal, social and political influences are touched upon. Then the author takes up the present (1986) legislation in Spain, analyzing the main features of the law and its regulation. Her analysis is complete, ranging from an investor's access to the various Spanish markets and Spanish investments abroad, to classification of the type of investments and the intricate aspects of management and control with regard to indirect investments. She says that the Spanish foreign investment system is based on control, limiting access to certain markets such as mining, banking and insurance. Spanish investments abroad are regulated to make Spanish products competitive with other products in the market.

Pablo-Romero ends her analysis of the concept of direct investment in Spanish law by comparing it to EEC law. The comparison serves a useful purpose in that the year the book was published was the first year of Spanish membership in the Common Market. It provides a bridge to an analysis of the new laws on foreign investment that Spain has passed since 1986 in an attempt to adjust Spanish legislation to Community norms. These new laws greatly change the legal landscape of foreign investments in Spain and Spanish investments abroad. One hopes that Pablo-Romero will at some future date extend her excellent analysis to include the new law.

JOSÉ DE LA ROSA
Of the Madrid Bar
RICK SILBERSTEIN
Of the California Bar

Régimen jurídico de las inversiones extranjeras en los países de la ALADI. Edited by Mirta Noemí Levis. Buenos Aires: Instituto para la Integración de América Latina, Banco Interamericano de Desarrollo, 1985. 9 binders. $50/set; $8/binder.

Since World War II, foreign investment seeking to enter Latin America has encountered many obstacles. The most formidable barrier was the xenophobia of the foreign investment laws of the investment-receiving nations. A minor, but not inconsequential, deterrent was the absence of a readily available, up-to-date, bilingual compendium of those laws. Presumably, commercial publishers considered that the market for such a publication was too small, or, more specifically, that existing and prospective investments were too concentrated, by industry or nation, to support a loose-leaf service covering all industrial sectors of every nation.

In the 1970s the Institute for the Integration of Latin America (INTAL), a division of the Inter-American Development Bank, took commendable first steps toward correcting that omission with the publication of loose-leaf collections of Latin American laws governing foreign investment[1] and the transnational licensing of technology.[2] The work here reviewed (hereinafter *Inversiones*) is the first revision of INTAL's 1976 collection of foreign investment laws. INTAL has separately revised, in a format similar to that of *Inversiones,* its 1977 collection of technology-licensing laws.[3]

[1] INSTITUTO PARA LA INTEGRACIÓN DE AMÉRICA LATINA, BANCO INTERAMERICANO DE DESARROLLO, RÉGIMEN DE LAS INVERSIONES EXTRANJERAS EN LOS PAÍSES DE LA ALALC (1976).

[2] INSTITUTO PARA LA INTEGRACIÓN DE AMÉRICA LATINA, BANCO INTERAMERICANO DE DESARROLLO, RÉGIMEN DE LA TRANSFERENCIA DE TECNOLOGÍA EN LOS PAÍSES DE AMÉRICA LATINA (1977).

[3] INSTITUTO PARA LA INTEGRACIÓN DE AMÉRICA LATINA, BANCO INTERAMERICANO DE DESARROLLO, RÉGIMEN JURÍDICO DE LA TRANSFERENCIA DE TECNOLOGÍA EN LOS PAÍSES DE LA ALADI (1986).

Inversiones consists of nine loose-leaf paperback binders containing the foreign investment norms of the 11 nations that constitute the Asociación Latinoamericana de Integración (ALADI).[4] For six of the ALADI nations (Argentina, Brazil, Chile, Mexico, Paraguay and Uruguay), those norms are expressed only in national legislation. For the remaining five (Bolivia, Colombia, Ecuador, Peru and Venezuela), which belong to the Andean Common Market (ANCOM), the norms also include ANCOM undertakings pursuant to the Treaty of Cartagena, notably Decision 24,[5] by which the ANCOM nations agreed to impose specific minimum restrictions on foreign capital.

Subject to that difference, the national presentations of *Inversiones* are usefully uniform. The foreign investment rules of each nation are divided into (1) "Basic Norms" (general legislative and regulatory requirements), (2) "Procedural Norms" (administrative provisions, including helpful reproductions of application forms), (3) "Sectoral Norms" (restrictions on foreign investment in particular industrial sectors) and (4) "International Agreements" (investment-related treaties such as those that support programs of the Overseas Private Investment Corporation (OPIC), the International Centre for Settlement of Investment Disputes (ICSID) and the Multilateral Investment Guarantee Agency (MIGA)).

Classifying foreign investment norms into those standard categories highlights the idiosyncracies of the ALADI nations, sustaining the truism that Latin America is not a homogeneous entity but a propinquity of diverse peoples. Legislation of the ANCOM nations, to be sure, reflects the obligatory uniformities of Decision 24; and nearly all the ALADI nations declare certain industrial sectors—chiefly oil and gas, mining, finance, nuclear energy and domestic transport—off limits to foreign enterprise. But within those similarities, differences abound. Mexico's foreign investment statute[6] is the most immutable of them all, with policy variations reflected not in subsequent decrees but by General Resolutions of the Mexican Foreign Investment Commission. Argentina and Brazil are conspicuous for legislative meticulousness concerning taxes and exchange controls. Paraguay takes pains to forbid foreign equity in sugar cane and alcohol, as do Bolivia and Mexico in forestry, Brazil and Colombia in publishing and news media, Venezuela in the dehydration of milk and Peru in the production of anchovy flour and oil, and the sale of cotton and rice. Even in legislative verbosity the ALADI members occupy a broad spectrum, the entire compilations varying from the 289 pages of changeful Brazil to the 40 of laconic Uruguay.

[4] In English, Latin American Integration Association (LAIA); formerly, Asociación Latinoamericana de Libre Comercio (ALALC), or Latin American Free Trade Association (LAFTA).

[5] Régimen común de tratamiento a los capitales extranjeros y sobre marcas, patentes, licencias y regalías, adopted Dec. 31, 1970, *reproduced with amendments in Eng. trans. in* 16 ILM 138 (1977).

[6] Ley para promover la inversión mexicana y regular la inversión extranjera, Diario Oficial [D.O.], Mar. 9, 1973, at 5.

It is particularly helpful that *Inversiones* appears in loose-leaf form with frequent supplements. Since *Inversiones* was first published, the ANCOM nations have made a historic reassessment of foreign enterprise. On May 11, 1987, they signed Decision 220,[7] which abrogates Decision 24 and releases each ANCOM nation to deal with foreign investment essentially as it sees fit. In the history of foreign investment in Latin America that was an epochal event, the most significant counterxenophobic initiative since World War II. During the presidency of Miguel de la Madrid, Mexico has made more modest, but similarly oriented, changes, culminating on February 3, 1988, in the promulgation of a single, liberalized General Resolution.[8] Those departures merit prompt and widespread publicity.

Inversiones is a needed and useful work. Dr. Levis and her national collaborators are to be congratulated on a painstaking and lucid presentation. Without misprizing their efforts in the least, two suggestions are offered for the enhancement of the publication.

The first suggestion is that in future loose-leaf supplements *Inversiones* take a closer look at the international agreements that support foreign investment in the ALADI nations. *Inversiones* shows their only adherents, as of September 1, 1987, to be Argentina (OPIC), Bolivia (OPIC), Chile (OPIC), Ecuador (OPIC), Paraguay (ICSID and a bilateral arrangement with France) and Uruguay (OPIC). As of July 1, 1987, however, a standard compilation reported such agreements in effect also with Brazil (OPIC) and Colombia (OPIC); included Ecuador as an adherent of ICSID and MIGA, and Paraguay as an adherent of OPIC; and listed Bolivia, Chile, Colombia and Uruguay as having signed, but not ratified, MIGA.[9] Those and subsequent instances of adherence to international agreements confirm the current investment-receptive trend in Latin America, and deserve recognition.

The second suggestion is that the *Inversiones* materials be presented in English as well as in their native Spanish or Portuguese. A few years ago, that suggestion would have been the special pleading of a monolingual United States as the source of preponderant foreign investment in Latin America. Today, if the United States is a diminishing source of new foreign capital in Latin America, English is nevertheless the international commercial language of Japan and other investment sources that are economically positioned to take up the slack. Presenting Latin American investment laws to them in English would significantly increase the outreach of this valuable publication.

EWELL E. MURPHY, JR.
Of the Texas Bar

[7] Sustitución de las decisiones 24 y conexas sobre el régimen común de tratamiento a los capitales extranjeros y sobre marcas, patentes, licencias y regalías, Gaceta Oficial del Acuerdo de Cartagena, May 18, 1987, at 15.

[8] D.O., Feb. 3, 1988, at 19.

[9] INSTITUTE FOR TRANSNAT'L ARB., NEWS & NOTES, No. 3, July 1987.

Positive Sum: Improving North-South Negotiations. Edited by I. William Zartman. New Brunswick and Oxford: Transaction Books, 1987. Pp. 314. Index. $29.95, cloth; $14.95, paper.

I. William Zartman is a skillful, shrewd and sophisticated political scientist, an authority on Francophonic Africa who has progressively broadened the focus of his work to include the whole complex of issues implicated in North-South negotiations over the international economic system. He has also contributed to the substantial literature on the theory of negotiations.[1]

This book stems from his dual interests. It is not simply another analytic or hortatory work on the substantive issues that make up the North-South agenda. Its focus rather is on the negotiating process itself, on the way in which the parties have packaged issues and organized themselves for bargaining in diverse arenas, and on the dynamics of those bargaining sessions. More specifically, its purpose is to test some 16 hypotheses about North-South negotiations that have emerged from earlier process-oriented studies such as Robert Rothstein's *Global Bargaining* (1979), Roger Hansen's *The "Global Negotiation" and Beyond* (1981) and the Commonwealth Group of Experts' *The North-South Dialogue: Making It Work* (1982). Among those hypotheses are the following:

(1) "Negotiation is bound to fail when the parties' definitions of the problem diverge."

(2) "When one side possesses primarily negative power (i.e. only veto power but no positive incentives or trade-offs for the other party), a mutually favorable outcome is unlikely and an unfavorable atmosphere prevails, making matters worse."

(3) "Global forums keep results low because of the need to pace the slowest member and combine all interests."

(4) "Specific functional negotiations are fruitful and mutually productive; global negotiations are not, because of the broad demands and the complex agenda."

(5) "Negotiations fail where demands of one side and the concessions of the other are imbalanced, and succeed only where equal trade-offs are possible."

(6) "Concessions are made by the party with the lowest tolerance for breakdown or conflict (critical-risk factor), which lies permanently on the Southern side."

(7) "In the absence of an ability to produce constraints (sticks), only rewards (carrots) or moral obligations can produce results for the South."

In addition to testing the various hypotheses, Zartman asked his authors to look "for other possible explanations of success and failure." Zartman recognizes in his analytically rich introduction that measuring success in

[1] I. W. Zartman & M. Berman, The Practical Negotiator (1982); and The Negotiation Process (I. W. Zartman ed. 1978).

negotiations is a highly problematic enterprise because (1) the nature of the process dictates that, if an agreement is reached, there is no absolute winner or loser, and (2) "all judgments of negotiated outcomes are based on contingent benefits" (pp. 10–11). Evaluations attempted years later may be very different from those made immediately following negotiations. And even the former will be contingent since we can never be certain that outcomes were the result of the negotiations themselves rather than of exogenous factors. Nevertheless, Zartman plainly believes that useful, albeit provisional, judgments can be made by comparing results against opening positions, by taking seriously the parties' own assessment (if they sign, he presumes, each side must feel it is better off with than without an agreement) and by independently verifying their assessments.

The bulk of the book consists of eight cases, each with its own analyst, selected in light of the various elements in the hypotheses being tested. In order of appearance they are as follows: (1) the effort lasting from 1974 to 1979 to create a new commodities regime, the so-called Integrated Program; (2) the effort in the United Nations Committee of the Whole (the COW) from 1977 to 1980 to forge agreement in principle on the shape of a "New International Economic Order"; (3) the Third UN Conference on the Law of the Sea; (4) the effort from 1975 to 1979 to negotiate a new international wheat agreement; (5) the Third Multifibre Arrangement; (6) the World Administrative Radio Conference of 1979; (7) the Lomé Conventions; and (8) the debt negotiations of 1974–1980. Thus, they include global negotiations with broad and with relatively narrow agendas, regional negotiations with a broad agenda of redistributional issues and negotiations with a single, well-defined subject and a limited set of particularly concerned participants. Zartman contends that three (nos. 3, 6 and 7 above) can be characterized as "successful," two (the COW and the wheat negotiations) as "failures" and the remaining three as "mixed" in that, although an agreement was signed, "the benefits remain under dispute" (p. 11).

Though the essays vary considerably in subtlety and elegance, the authors employ a common set of perspectives and analytic categories. And all begin with

> an appreciation of the essential nature of negotiation as a process of joint decision making that combines conflicting positions into a common outcome [where it is successful], a process in which each party is required to give something from its initial positions to attain an outcome that is mutually (although usually unequally) beneficial and is preferable to nonagreement, i.e. to unilateral attempts at a solution [p. 6].

In his concluding chapter, Zartman summarizes the salient features of most North-South negotiations and elaborates the lessons that he believes these studies yield. To close students of the negotiations, the features enumerated are familiar: southern participants tend to arrive with an inadequate technical grasp of the issues. The northerners, with their vastly greater infrastructure for research and reservoir of technically trained personnel, have an immense advantage here. Sensitivity to the disparity reinforces the South's tendency to distrust northern initiatives, to maintain hard positions and to rely on moral exhortation rather than on persuasive demonstrations of common interest in reaching agreements. But the northern countries have only occasionally attempted either to share information or otherwise to help their southern counterparts to compete on a level playing field; they have, moreover, frequently employed technical discourse to frustrate progress in the belief that any agreement genuinely responsive to southern interests would almost certainly injure northern ones. (The cases indicate that this view of North-South relations is particularly prominent among the largest northern states; several of the smaller ones have argued in favor of a much less rigid zero-sum perspective.)

Both sides work hard to achieve intrabloc unity. Particularly on the southern side, the demands of unity inhibit the sensitive adjustment of positions as negotiations unfold. In general, neither side exhibits much appreciation of the guides to effective negotiation elaborated in the scholarly literature. "The basis for any agreement," Zartman writes, "is a *formula,* a conscious attempt to arrive at a joint definition of the problem and the solution and to combine relevant portions of both parties' positions into a common justification of terms of trade" (p. 283). He sees the law of the sea negotiations as

> a unique, almost-textbook case of building formulas. Negotiations began when the opening formula of "extended underwater national resource jurisdiction in exchange for narrow territorial sea plus rights of passage" became understood. Discussions then proceeded to devise formulas for the various issue areas covered in the negotiations. The most crucial of them was the imaginative bridging of the competing redistributive and equity formulas for deep-sea mining [p. 284].

Successful formula building requires the identification of potential trade-offs. Since in many issue areas the South is short of items to trade, the conventional wisdom favoring narrowly focused discussions needs qualification. "Almost every one of the case studies," as Zartman reads them, demonstrates "unexploited possibilities of trade-offs, inducements, benefit sharing, compensations on details, and even procedural institutional concessions to make changes appear less threatening that dragged down the search for a productive agreement" (p. 285).

Another key to successful negotiations—above all, where the preconditions for a fundamental change of regimes (new power configurations, new consensus on goals and/or new possibilities opened up by new knowledge) are absent, as in the case to date of North-South relations—is for the party seeking change to accept the virtues or at least the inevitability of *incrementalism,* in terms of both substance and participants, if there is to be progress. The South must, in other words, be willing to find success in small adjustments in the distributive structure and must not allow its negotiating position to be hostage to the interest in maintaining a common front. The North, for its part, should be far more generous in sharing informational resources or in assisting the South in developing resources of its own. And both should recognize the virtues of a mediator, not excluding one with links to the North but with an institutional interest in successful negotiations (the Commission for the European Communities played a sort of mediatory role in the Lomé negotiations).

All of these ideas make a great deal of sense. But would their adoption in the various cases have produced very different results? The authors of the eight studies focus on process. They do not attempt to pursue the admittedly very difficult question of to what extent, if any, a different outcome would have better served the interests of the North, or would at least have helped the South without actual detriment to its negotiating partner. The deep assumption of this volume is that latent in present conditions are adjustments in the structure of international economic relations that, if negotiated into being, would serve northern as well as southern interests better than the status quo. Intuitively, I believe Zartman and his colleagues are right. Despite its virtues, this volume does not provide systematic support for that belief.

TOM J. FARER
Board of Editors

Ein Dritter Weg für die Dritte Welt? Nachholende Nationenbildung im Schnittpunkt entwicklungspolitischer und hegemonialer Interessen. By Manfred Wöhlcke. Baden-Baden: Nomos Verlagsgesellschaft, 1985. Pp. 254. DM 29.

Will Third World nations have to take the capitalist market-oriented route or the socialist road in order to catch up on development, or is there a "third road" to nation building and development? This question cannot be easily separated from the question whether there ought to be a "third road" and in whose security interest it would be.

Considering both the elusiveness of a concept like the "third road" and the heterogeneous nature of the group of states labeled the "Third World," any attempt to give an answer to this question in general and prescriptive terms is an ambitious undertaking. At the end of Manfred Wöhlcke's book, here under review, the author pleads for a better understanding on the part of Western nations of those countries that have opted for a "third road" to nation building and development (p. 156a). The book is an important attempt at what one could call "consciousness-raising" and "conscience-raising" with regard to the pitfalls of a worldview that either allows for no alternatives to bloc loyalty or is blind to the potential for innovation in the Third World. Wöhlcke's intention is to clarify whether and to what extent, without endangering the security interests of the West, a "third road" is politically conceivable as a development alternative (p. 13).

In the first two chapters (pp. 29–108), Wöhlcke takes issue with the theory of modernization and gives, instead of an analytical definition, what he calls a "synoptical portrayal" of the concept of the "third road." He illustrates the concept by reference to the policy programs of a select group of Third World states and is generally less concerned with empirically tested hard facts and their analysis than with exploring the meaning of policies and strategies, revealing the "third road" as a new world concept of the intellectual superstructure of modern international relations. Wöhlcke distinguishes several dimensions of the "third road." On the internal level, it is national integration and identity, and self-reliant development; on the level of external relations, it is national emancipation, nonalignment and socioeconomic delinking, and regional economic cooperation (p. 25).

His concern is, and for this he relies on "empirical background knowledge" (p. 12), to improve the design for societal evolution. He points out that a dependent capitalist development model leads in most instances to structural heterogeneity and to a crippled economy; for support he draws largely from Dieter Senghaas's writings such as *Von Europa lernen. Entwicklungsgeschichtliche Betrachtungen* (1982). He then portrays the concept of the "third road" as a necessary alternative and corrective to the model of dependent capitalist development (p. 60). Its "leitmotif" is twofold: self-reliant participatory development (pp. 64 *ff.*), which requires internal structural reform, and, as the external corrective, South-South cooperation and regional integration, although Wöhlcke sees difficulties in realizing the latter.

All in all, Wöhlcke's design of a "third road" implies a new vision of the world that would allow the developing state more freedom in defining its development and alliance policies. Although Wöhlcke probably does not want to offer more than an impulse to rethinking international relations, it is urgently needed in the face of the fading debate on a new international economic order and the "global dialogue" that is gradually giving way to a "policy dialogue" on a bilateral or interregional level. The focus of the debate on development is more and more on the internal policy performance of the Third World state. The question of the "third road" is therefore a timely one and it includes the issue of "national integration and identity," which Wöhlcke treats in a separate chapter. Under the title "State and Nation" (pp. 83–108), Wöhlcke pleads for a balance between efficiency- and participation-criteria, if a strong and centralized state is not to be counterproductive with respect to development. His thoughts and ideas in this chapter are less persuasive than in the preceding chapters. One would have hoped that the dual nature of the developing state, which has been described amply in the past, would have been treated in greater depth. Still, the way in which Wöhlcke poses the question, "Is there a third road for the Third World?," will prompt the international lawyer into reconsidering the paradigm underlying his own approach to Third World issues in international law.

The main thesis of Wöhlcke's last chapter, on foreign policy and the security issue (pp. 109–56a), is that the pressure for development and emancipation in the Third World cannot be contained forever and that, therefore, channeling the pressure into a "third road" still acceptable to the West is preferable to a status quo policy (p. 149). To argue this point, he explains nonalignment as a strategy directed for historical-political reasons primarily against the West, which is often wrongly dramatized by Western observers as a political choice in favor of the Soviet Union. Wöhlcke suggests, however, that it may well be in the West's own security interest even to support, in certain cases, a shift from a dependent capitalist development model towards a "third road" alternative, if revolutionary turmoil can thus be avoided (p. 154).

The bibliography in the appendix would have benefited from annotation and less arbitrary selection, though, with documents on Third World development theory and programming, one has to start somewhere. The book seems to have been written in haste: there is a reference to a chapter that does not exist, and the underlying theory could have been better streamlined. This does not, however, in any way diminish the importance and relevance of the book, which, one hopes, will attract a broad readership. A "third road" for the Third World is both a difficult and an ambitious undertaking, which will demand imagination and perseverance.

KONRAD GINTHER
University of Graz

Foreign Relations of the United States, 1952–1954. Volume VI: Western Europe and Canada. Parts 1 and 2. Washington: U.S. Govt. Printing Office, 1986. (Dept. of State Pubs. 9489 and 9490.) Pp. xliv, 2176. Index in part 2.

This volume, like others in the 1952–1954 *Foreign Relations* series, bridges the last year of the Truman administration and the early years of the Eisenhower presidency. A compilation of one thousand sequentially numbered documents, it is composed of two parts. Part 1 (pp. 1–1,137) focuses on U.S. multilateral diplomacy, especially the historic developments relating to European integration, as well as several meetings of American chiefs of mission stationed in Europe, and U.S. bilateral relations with the United Kingdom. Part 2 (pp. 1,139–2,144) continues documentation on bilateral relations with other European countries, the Vatican and Canada. This anthology does not encompass either U.S. relations with Germany and Austria, which are treated in considerable depth elsewhere,[1] or general economic and political matters, overall national security affairs and Western European security issues, which are treated in separate volumes.[2]

The documents provided in this compendium consist of the customary notes, telegrams, messages and memorandums (of summaries of conversations and statements "for the record"), together with letters, reports and other papers and diplomatic communications that flowed primarily within and among U.S. government agencies in Washington and between the Department of State and its missions abroad (including U.S. representatives to the North Atlantic Treaty Organization [NATO] and the European Coal and Steel Community). The documents also embrace other types of policymaking records and such special collections as presidential exchanges with

[1] *See* FOREIGN RELATIONS OF THE UNITED STATES, 1952–1954. VOLUME VII: GERMANY AND AUSTRIA. Reviewed at 81 AJIL 994 (1987).

[2] For these, see FOREIGN RELATIONS OF THE UNITED STATES, 1952–1954. Vols. I, II and V, reviewed, respectively, at 79 AJIL 857 (1985), *id.* at 1135 and 78 AJIL 1025 (1984).

Prime Minister Churchill, other European leaders and the Pope, and records pertaining to several bilateral summit and ministerial meetings.

Substantively, the initial segment of part 1 (pp. 1–635) constitutes the Department of State's impressive documentary contribution to U.S. encouragement of the second stage of the historic West European movement toward economic and political integration in the post–World War II era.[3] Concerned not only with the launching of the European Coal and Steel Community (the treaty was ratified in 1952), it also deals with issues of economic (including agricultural), political and defense integration by means of treaties to "federalize" the "Community of Six" through the establishment of the European Defense Community and the European Political Community. These treaties, signed respectively in 1952 and 1953, were never ratified.

Specific matters relating to these developments involve the policies and positions of Belgium, Britain, Luxembourg, the Netherlands, Italy and France. These include such factors as the planning process, the principle of supranationality, organizational structure, memberships and observerships, headquarters sites, interrelations with other agencies (principally NATO and the Western European Union), treaty ratification and U.S. diplomatic representation. A possible "common market," trade liberalization and balance of payments are also touched upon.

The next segment (pp. 636–92) contains agendas, chronological reports or minutes, and summaries of results for five meetings of selected U.S. chiefs of European missions (a practice begun by the Department of State in 1949). These sessions were convened to discuss East-West relations, the unity of Western Europe within the framework of the Atlantic Community, a West German contribution to European defense and U.S. economic and military assistance. They were attended by representatives of the Department of State and American emissaries to European countries, NATO and the European Coal and Steel Community. They were held in London, Luxembourg, Copenhagen, and again at London for American emissaries to Western Europe, and in Vienna for envoys to East European countries and Berlin.

The final segment of part 1 (pp. 693–1,137) concerns bilateral diplomacy with the United Kingdom and presents two types of materials. On the one hand, they deal with such substantive issues as U.S.-UK foreign policy coordination, Britain's relations with other European powers, Britain's role in European integration, atomic weapons tests, the NATO Atlantic Command, U.S. economic and military assistance, and various regional problems.

Other portions of this segment concentrate on top-level diplomacy (the Truman-Churchill meeting in Washington, January 5–18, 1952; the Eisen-

[3] The first phase involved the establishment of the Council of Europe, the Brussels Pact, the Organization for European Economic Cooperation and the European Coal and Steel Community—foreshadowing the attempt to integrate the "Community of Six." A later stage was characterized by the birth of the European Economic Community (EEC) and the European Atomic Energy Community (EURATOM).

hower-Churchill meeting in Washington, June 25–29, 1954; Eisenhower's summit communications with the British Prime Minister) and ministerial visits (Secretary of State Acheson to London, February 13–19, 1952; Foreign Minister Eden to Washington, March 4–7, 1953; and Secretary Dulles to London, April 11–13, 1954). The documentation pertains both to preliminary negotiations and to the conduct and results of meetings, including "agreed minutes," joint declarations and public announcements.

Part 2, which continues documentation on U.S. bilateral diplomacy, consists of separate segments on France, Iceland, Ireland, Italy, Portugal, the Scandinavian countries, Spain and Canada. Information on relations with several other countries—namely, Greece, Luxembourg, the Netherlands, Switzerland, Turkey and West Germany—is interspersed without separate country-by-country treatment. Aside from the problems of integration, North Atlantic Alliance affairs and U.S. economic and military assistance, the principal topics dealt with are the following (countries at issue in parentheses): UN membership (Ireland, Italy and Spain); contributing to the defense of Europe (especially France); U.S. military bases and other facilities (Iceland, Spain and Portugal/Azores); neutrality in East-West affairs (Ireland, Sweden and Switzerland); consideration of an Export-Import Bank loan (France); and the role of a domestic Communist Party and the Trieste issue (Italy); as well as other categories designated simply as "relations with" individual countries. In addition, part 2 also provides materials on the summit visits to Washington by French Premiers René Mayer (March 1953) and Pierre Mendès-France (November 1954), and exchanges during September 1953 respecting a possible visit by Premier Joseph Laniel.

The final segment (pp. 2,022–144) is devoted to U.S. relations with Canada. One of the principal issues concerned the St. Lawrence Seaway and Power Project, which had previously been subscribed to by the President and the Canadian Prime Minister in an agreement in 1941, but had not been approved by Congress. When Canada decided to view the agreement as defunct and to proceed unilaterally with the project, revised authorization for the venture was negotiated and embodied in an exchange of notes, with the backing of the Wiley-Dondero Act, signed by the President on May 13, 1954.[4] Specific aspects involved the development of water potential of the St. Lawrence River, construction responsibility, joint administrative machinery, cost allocations and tolls.

Other issues in Canadian-American affairs included the possibility of the outbreak of general war (resulting from the Korean War), joint defense arrangements and the actions of the Canadian-American Permanent Joint Board on Defense (established on the basis of the Ogdensburg Agreement of August 17, 1940), the use by the United States of bases in Canada, the polar electronic early warning system and such cooperative ventures as the Joint Canadian-U.S. Military Study Group, the Canada-U.S. Scientific Advisory Team and the creation of a Joint Economic and Trade Committee.

[4] The 1941 agreement remained unapproved by Congress for more than a decade. President Eisenhower and Queen Elizabeth II participated in dedicating the St. Lawrence Seaway, at Montreal, in June 1959.

A small portion of part 2 (pp. 2,002–21) is devoted to the attempt to launch formal American diplomatic relations with the Vatican (which had existed from 1848 to 1864, when the United States commissioned chargés d'affaires and ministers to the Holy See). In 1951, to regularize the informal practice of commissioning Myron C. Taylor to serve as presidential special emissary during World War II and until 1949, President Truman nominated Mark Clark to be appointed as American ambassador. Because of congressional and public opposition, the nomination was withdrawn from the Senate in January 1952, at Clark's request.[5] Documents concerning this development embody summit exchanges between the President (both Truman and Eisenhower) and Pope Pius XII, and commentary by Myron Taylor and others.[6]

Those interested in high-level U.S. policymaking and coordination will welcome the inclusion of National Security Council (NSC) papers embracing eight NSC "documents" (concerned with overall policy toward Iceland, Italy and Spain, and the Canadian-American early warning system, the St. Lawrence Seaway and North American continental defense) and six memorandums of council discussions prepared by NSC staff members. Other records of this type include several documents of the National Advisory Council, a National Intelligence Estimate on short-term development in French policy and a number of papers from or about the Operations Coordinating Board (of the NSC), the Joint Chiefs of Staff and the National Advisory Council on international monetary problems. This collection also embodies documentation pertaining to such agencies as the Economic Commission for Europe, the Export-Import Bank and the Economic Cooperation Administration and its successor agencies—the Mutual Security Agency and the Foreign Operations Administration.

In terms of selectivity, organization, treatment and content, this compendium characterizes the traditionally superior standards of the Office of the Historian of the Department of State in producing the *Foreign Relations* series, and is welcomed by all who are interested in the diplomatic relations of the United States in Western Europe during the early 1950s. To assist the user, its editors supplement the textual materials with a liberal supply of explanatory, descriptive and cross-referencing editorial notes and documentary footnotes. They also provide an inventory of some 325 abbreviations, symbols and acronyms, a 20-page catalog of persons with their official titles and ranks, a short list of official and unofficial published volumes including several key memoirs (those of Acheson, Eisenhower and Truman), a complete list of unpublished resources with their archival designations (which, in

[5] For commentary on this matter, see review of FOREIGN RELATIONS OF THE UNITED STATES, 1951. VOLUME IV: EUROPE: POLITICAL AND ECONOMIC DEVELOPMENTS, 80 AJIL 772, especially at 774 (1986).

[6] A practical temporary solution to the matter was worked out by means of unilateral representation in Washington by the Vatican's Apostolic Delegate. Eventually, formal diplomatic relations were regularized in 1984. Also, in addition to Woodrow Wilson's audience with the Pope in 1919, every President, beginning with Eisenhower, has had one or more such audiences during summit trips to Europe.

addition to the central files of the Department of State, were used to prepare this compilation) and a comprehensive, 30-page, double-columned index.

As in the past, under the supervision of William Z. Slany (Historian, Department of State), the editors brought to these volumes their high standards and considerable skill in coping with voluminous, complex and dispersed documentary resources, which they have distilled for the public domain in a compact, reliable and readily usable way.

ELMER PLISCHKE
University of Maryland, Emeritus
American Enterprise Institute

La Protezione dei beni culturali nel diritto internazionale. By Manlio Frigo. Milan: Dott. A. Giuffrè Editore, 1986. Pp. vii, 435. Author index. L. 28.000.

For readers who have an interest in the topic, this is an important book, a scholarly contribution to the literature on the international law of cultural property.[1] Frigo begins his study with a brief orienting discussion of the history of, and fundamental conceptions at work in, the international law of cultural property. He places special emphasis on the Italian experience, but since Italy has long been a major source nation (and, in ancient and Renaissance times, was a major importer), and since Italian cultural property law is more highly developed than other national schemes, the emphasis is more helpful than limiting.

In his second chapter, Frigo traces the development of the law protecting cultural property in war, culminating in the Hague Convention for the Protection of Cultural Property in the Event of Armed Conflict of 1954.[2] Chapter III describes the legal framework of the protection of cultural property in peacetime and chapter IV deals with the illicit trade in, and the movement for "repatriation" of, cultural objects. Chapter V is a formal discussion, in the style of Italian legal science, of legal concepts in the field and would be of little interest to most readers. Chapter VI discusses private international law questions raised by the international traffic in cultural property.

[1] Other recent significant works include S. WILLIAMS, THE INTERNATIONAL AND NATIONAL PROTECTION OF MOVABLE CULTURAL PROPERTY: A COMPARATIVE SURVEY (1978); P. BATOR, THE INTERNATIONAL TRADE IN ART (1982), originally published as *An Essay on the International Trade in Art,* 34 STAN. L. REV. 275 (1982); the symposium on International Art Law in 15 N.Y.U. J. INT'L L. & POL. 757 (1983); L. PROTT & P. O'KEEFE, LAW AND THE CULTURAL HERITAGE. VOL. I: DISCOVERY AND EXCAVATION (1984); R. FRAOUA, LE TRAFIC ILLICITE DES BIENS CULTURELS ET LEUR RESTITUTION (1985). *Cf.* Merryman with Elsen, *Hot Art: A Reexamination of the Illegal International Trade in Cultural Objects,* J. ARTS MGMT. & L., No. 3, Fall 1982, at 5, *reprinted in* THE PENAL PROTECTION OF WORKS OF ART 151 (S. Berman ed. 1983); Merryman, *Thinking about the Elgin Marbles,* 83 MICH. L. REV. 1880 (1985); Merryman, *Two Ways of Thinking about Cultural Property,* 80 AJIL 831 (1986); J. H. MERRYMAN & A. ELSEN, LAW, ETHICS AND THE VISUAL ARTS, chs. 1 and 2 (2d ed. 1987).

[2] 249 UNTS 240.

I disagree with Frigo on a number of substantive matters: e.g., for employing the euphemism "protection" of cultural property when what is really meant is "retention"—i.e., prohibition of export; for inadequately distinguishing objects that can be moved about without damage or the loss of information, expressive power or beauty from objects that all would agree should be left in place; for accepting too easily the notion of a "national cultural patrimony" and its implications; but this is not the place for a debate with the author.[3] Such differences are bound to exist in a field as highly charged politically and as conceptually and analytically underdeveloped as this one.

Despite these differences of outlook with the author, I think he has written an admirable book. Frigo's research is impressive—his footnotes contain treasures until now undiscovered. He explores questions in depth, exposing layers of meaning and difficulty. Like most Italian legal scholarship, the writing is complex, full of qualifiers and dependent clauses, in the pursuit of precision and nuance. The result is a rich discussion that illuminates interesting questions of law and policy affecting "the common cultural heritage of all mankind."[4] This book is another good reason to learn to read Italian.

JOHN HENRY MERRYMAN
Stanford Law School

Israel Yearbook on Human Rights. Volume 13, 1983. Edited by Yoram Dinstein. Published under the auspices of the Faculty of Law, Tel Aviv University. Pp. 374.

For the Western world, institutionalized international concern for the fate of the victims of human rights abuses dates from the end of the Second World War. Consequently, an Israeli journal on human rights is particularly appropriate to deal with such issues as war crimes and crimes against humanity, not to mention the more pervasive problems of racial discrimination and minority rights, and the more specifically local problems unique to the state of Israel. Even articles in the last category, such as Shabtai Rosenne's *Recognition of Israel by the Security Council in 1948,* could be of

[3] The Fraoua book, cited in note 1 and generously (in my opinion, overgenerously) reviewed by Professor Nafziger in volume 80 of this *Journal* at p. 751, is a much worse offender. More a tract than a study, it attempts to establish that contemporary international law already imposes, or, if it does not, should impose, two kinds of obligations: (1) an obligation on other nations to recognize and enforce source-nation cultural property export restrictions, and (2) an obligation on foreign holders of cultural objects to "repatriate" them to their nations of origin. Although both theses are zealously advanced in UNESCO and other international forums by source nations, neither is or is likely soon to become a rule of international law. A mild form of the first thesis is the principal concern of the 1972 UNESCO Convention on the Means of Prohibiting and Preventing the Illicit Import, Export and Transfer of Ownership of Cultural Property, 823 UNTS 231, *reprinted in* 10 ILM 289 (1971). Of the major market nations, only the United States and Canada have become parties. The second thesis has attracted even less international acceptance.

[4] The quoted phrase occurs in the Preamble to the 1954 Hague Convention, *supra* note 2.

interest to non-Israeli readers who want to know more about the history of this period.

The lead article, by Professor Leo Gross, is a historical consideration of the failure of the United Nations to adopt a Code of Offences Against the Peace and Security of Mankind. Following the Second World War, the United Nations sought to criminalize the Nuremberg offenses, such as "genocide," in an international criminal code. In spite of the fact that a draft code was prepared by the International Law Commission (ILC) in 1954, this draft was shelved for 20 years pending UN adoption of a definition of "aggression." Also in 1954, the General Assembly established the order for the consideration of what were considered three interrelated topics: (1) the definition of aggression, (2) the Code of Offences, and (3) the creation of an international criminal court.

Subsequently, the 1974 UN definition of aggression was criticized by states as being insufficiently precise to be used in a code of offenses that sought to impose criminal penalties on a person who failed to disobey the orders of his own government. The ILC also took the position that the code would have to take into account new international crimes that were recognized as such after 1954. Gross sees this as an additional problem in achieving adoption of the code. He suggests that the prospective adoption and enforcement of a sweeping list of crimes suggests the eventual criminalization of international relations, fueling the already confrontational politics of the United Nations and dooming the prospects for a code.

Considering the parallel development of human rights law on the regional level and the empowerment of regional human rights courts in the Americas and in Europe to adjudicate responsibility for international crimes such as torture and "disappearances," these regional tribunals may be blazing the trail for the eventual acceptance of an international criminal court.

The article by Professor Yoram Dinstein on the *Laws of Land Warfare* is the latest in his series on the rules of international humanitarian law, which, given their didactic format, appear destined to be reissued as manuals for use by Israeli combatants.

This volume does not shrink from criticizing the Israeli Government. Judge Eli Nathan of the District Court of Jerusalem, in his article on *Israeli Civil Jurisdiction in the Administered Territories,* suggests that a set of 1969 Israeli Justice Ministry regulations, which prescribe that service of Israeli court documents be carried out in the "Administered Territories" (Judea and Samaria) by the same procedure applicable to the service of documents within Israel, violates the law of belligerent occupation. Nathan argues that an extension of civil jurisdiction constitutes an extension of sovereignty, and that the law of belligerent occupation (the fourth Geneva Convention and the fourth Hague Convention of 1907) provides that the belligerent occupant does not acquire sovereignty over occupied territory.

Both Professor Giorgio Sacerdoti and Eliezer Yapou deal with the rights of minorities. Mr. Yapou reviews the incorporation of human rights standards in the Italian-Yugoslav territorial accords following the Second World War to guarantee protection of the ethnic minorities. Professor Sacerdoti compares the affirmative action programs on behalf of disadvantaged minority groups under the League of Nations and under the United Nations. The nondiscrimination clauses of current multilateral human rights treaties guarantee equality before the law, but Sacerdoti suggests that affirmative action programs are still necessary to achieve de facto equality.

His most provocative point deals with what he terms the "internal" dimension of the right of self-determination. He suggests that peoples seeking independence from colonial domination is the predominant, but not the sole, manifestation of this right. Since minorities can be considered as "peoples," he states that there is "slowly emerging at the international level" a claim for internal self-determination, which comprises the exercise of fundamental human rights and, in particular, the right to political participation within the larger state.

Some of the other articles in this volume that warrant mention are Nathan Lerner's review of the 15-year history of the UN Committee on the Elimination of Racial Discrimination, and Rowell Genn's survey of the limitations placed on the freedoms of expression and association in the European human rights system, in order to prevent and punish incitement to hatred and to restrict the activities of organizations that foster racial hatred.

On the subject of racial hatred, Stephen Roth, in his article entitled *Anti-Semitism and International Law,* points out a curious irony of history, *viz.* that anti-Semitism has reemerged in spite of the fact that the international human rights movement is a reaction to the atrocities committed against the Jews. Anti-Semitism, he maintains, has been ignored in international law, as compared with the number of international instruments that seek, for example, to outlaw other forms of discrimination such as apartheid.

Last, one should not fail to mention Justice Haim Cohn's elegantly written article, *On the Meaning of Human Dignity,* aptly defined as "the goal to which the rule of human rights law aspires." In a doubtless controversial defense of the right to suicide, Cohn eloquently defends an individual's right to decide when life is no longer worth living, arguing that human dignity is vindicated in the exercise of that choice.

CHRISTINA M. CERNA
Of the District of Columbia Bar

Israel Yearbook on Human Rights. Volume 14, 1984. Edited by Yoram Dinstein. Published under the auspices of the Faculty of Law, Tel Aviv University. Pp. 327.

This volume of the *Yearbook* is less satisfying to the non-Israeli reader than its predecessor. It deals with many of the same issues discussed in the earlier volume such as war crimes, racial discrimination and, again, an article that calls for recognition of the right to commit suicide. The lead piece, however, is excerpted from a speech given by the President of Israel, Chaim Herzog, entitled "Judaism, Law and Justice." Its tone has less to do with law and human rights than with a defense of Israel, exemplified by President

Herzog's claim to "represent a nation which gave to this world the concept of the Rule of Law." Israel's enemies are afflicted with "moral bankruptcy," which is "emphasized by the attitude of so many towards the people and country of Israel."

Three other articles seem to have little other purpose than to defend Israel's human rights record. Israel, as everyone knows and these authors point out, has been in an almost continuous state of hostility with its Arab neighbors since its creation in 1948. Consequently, a state of emergency has been in force since 1948 and official press censorship exists. Ze'ev Chafets, the director until 1982 of the Israel Government Press Office, in his article *Press and Government in Israel,* roundly defends the press freedom that exists in Israel.

Over 70 pages of this volume are devoted to an examination of administrative detention orders in Israel. The first of these two articles, entitled *The Judicial Review of Administrative Detention Orders in Israel,* by Professor Harold Rudolph of the University of Witwatersrand in Johannesburg, traces the history of this practice. Administrative detention was introduced by the British mandatary Government in 1945 and absorbed into Israeli law when independence was obtained in 1948, by means of the declaration of the state of emergency.

In 1979 the Israeli Parliament enacted a new set of emergency regulations that superseded the 1945 regulations. One of the most important changes in the new regulations was that the administrative detention order may only be issued by the Minister of Defense if an *objective* standard is satisfied to show that the detention is required for national security reasons. Previously, the grounds for detention were left to the *subjective* discretionary power of the military commander. These 1979 emergency regulations stipulate that administrative detention orders be subject to mandatory judicial review, and the District Court shall set aside a detention order if it is not proven that the detention was carried out for objective reasons of state security. Rudolph reviews the practice of the Israeli courts in this area and criticizes cases where the court has abdicated its responsibility, having appeared "unwilling to impose its views on the Israeli military authorities," and praises other decisions where the court has found a detention order not to be justified in law, and therefore ordered it set aside.

The second of the two articles is entitled *A Contemporary Model of Emergency Detention Law. An Assessment of the Israeli Law,* by Professor Shimon Shetreet of the Hebrew University. As expressed in the title of his article, Shetreet considers the 1979 Israeli Emergency Powers (Detention) Law a model law and in conformity with international human rights standards.

Another article that deals with controversial subject matter is Professor L. C. Green's *War Crimes, Extradition and Command Responsibility.* Green, of the University of Alberta, discusses, inter alia, the command responsibility of the Israeli military authorities for the Phalangist attack on the PLO refugee camps at Sabra and Chatila, Lebanon, in September 1982. The Phalangists, who massacred approximately three hundred inhabitants of these camps, were under the control of the Israeli military authorities, who did not prevent the massacre, although they had reason to expect it would take place and did nothing to stop it once they learned that it was under way. An Israeli commander acknowledged that the Israeli military system "showed insensitivity" in its failure to act. An Israeli governmental Commission of Inquiry absolved Israel of "direct responsibility" for the atrocities. Green sets forth the case but offers no judgment of his own, deferentially concluding that "any disciplinary or punitive acts against individual members of the Israeli forces . . . will depend upon Israeli law."

Last, an excellent short piece that warrants mention is Professor Pieter van Dijk's article on *The Right to Development and Human Rights—A Matter of Equality and Priority.* Van Dijk suggests that the right to development should mean that on the national and international level a priority must be set "for combatting poverty and fulfilling basic needs." This priority in favor of the poorest countries is based upon the principle of solidarity, which together with the principles of freedom and equality underlie the concept of the "New International Economic Order." Van Dijk recognizes the difficulty in obtaining the consent of states to turn these moral obligations into legal ones.

CHRISTINA M. CERNA
Of the District of Columbia Bar

The Law of Non-International Armed Conflict: Protocol II to the 1949 Geneva Conventions. Edited by Howard S. Levie. Dordrecht, Boston, Lancaster: Martinus Nijhoff Publishers, 1987. Pp. xiii, 635. Index. Dfl.275; $134; £100.

In 1977 the Geneva Diplomatic Conference on the Reaffirmation and Development of International Humanitarian Law Applicable in Armed Conflicts adopted two Protocols to the nearly universally accepted 1949 Geneva Conventions.[1] Protocol I deals with the law applicable in international armed conflicts and builds upon and develops the law set forth in those Conventions, as well as in the fourth Hague Convention of 1907 and its annexed Regulations Respecting the Laws and Customs of War on Land and customary international law. Containing 102 articles and two annexes, Protocol I represents a major step in the development of the law of war and in the protection of the victims of war, both combatants and noncombatants. Protocol II deals with the law applicable in noninternational armed conflicts and builds upon the slim base of one article—Article 3—common to the four Geneva Conventions of 1949. Protocol II contains 28 articles designed to secure minimum standards of humanitarian treatment for all persons involved in or affected by civil wars or other noninternational armed conflicts within a state.

[1] The texts of the two Protocols can be found in UN Doc. A/32/144 (1977), Anns. I and II, *reprinted in* 16 ILM 1391 (Protocol I) and 1442 (Protocol II) (1977) and *in* 72 AJIL 457 (Protocol I) and 502 (Protocol II) (1978).

In this new book, Professor Levie does for Protocol II what, from 1979 to 1981, he did for Protocol I when he published a four-volume history of the 1974–1977 negotiations, entitled *Protection of War Victims.* His technique is to assemble all available materials from the official records of the conference, plus certain unpublished conference documents made available to him, and, dealing in turn with each provision of the Protocol, set forth all relevant documents chronologically, with editorial comment where necessary, so that the reader can follow the negotiation of any particular provision from the original proposals by the International Committee of the Red Cross to the finally adopted text. The result is a valuable, indeed almost indispensable, research tool for anyone concerned with the history of any provision of the Protocol and the views of those involved in its negotiation.

Levie's new volume on Protocol II is a timely arrival in view of the recent decision by the Reagan administration to seek advice and consent of the Senate to its ratification, but, unfortunately, in the view of this reviewer, not to seek ratification of Protocol I.[2] This compilation of negotiating history is most useful and understandable if used in conjunction with more narrative commentaries such as the *Commentary on the Additional Protocols* by the International Committee of the Red Cross (1987) and *New Rules for Victims of Armed Conflicts* by Bothe, Partsch and Solf (1982). Given the facts that Protocol II was negotiated in parallel with Protocol I and that its overly elaborate draft provisions were drastically pruned during the final session of the Diplomatic Conference, the conference documents set forth in Levie's book are occasionally inadequate by themselves to explain fully why changes were made. Nevertheless, any serious effort to interpret Protocol II would be virtually impossible without recourse to this book, which should become a standard reference work for scholars concerned with the law applicable to civil wars or to the protection of human rights.

GEORGE H. ALDRICH
Board of Editors

Guide to the "Travaux Préparatoires" of the International Covenant on Civil and Political Rights. By Marc J. Bossuyt. Dordrecht, Boston, Lancaster: Martinus Nijhoff Publishers, 1987. Pp. xxvi, 851. Dfl.475; $210; £167.50.

Collected Edition of the "Travaux Préparatoires" of the European Convention on Human Rights. Vols. VI, VII and VIII. Council of Europe. Dordrecht, Boston, Lancaster: Martinus Nijhoff Publishers, 1985. Vol. VI: pp. xix, 298. $66.50. Vol. VII: pp. xxxi, 354. $75. Vol. VIII: pp. xix, 226. $60. Index in each vol.

Publication of these two lengthy and expensive works is yet another indication of the coming of age of human rights as a separate discipline of

[2] *See* President Reagan's Message of Jan. 29, 1987, Transmitting Protocol II to the Senate, S. TREATY DOC. NO. 2, 100th Cong., 1st Sess. (1987), *reprinted in* 81 AJIL 910 (1987).

international law. As noted in an earlier review of a collection of the jurisprudence of the European Court and Commission on Human Rights,[1] the substantive content of international human rights in Europe is now extensive, and the European human rights machinery has addressed fundamental issues ranging from torture and arbitrary detention to more esoteric (if, nonetheless, important) examinations of the requirements of due process and fair trials. While the system of protection established under the International Covenant on Civil and Political Rights is only little more than a decade old, the Human Rights Committee is now beginning to arrive at significant interpretations of the Covenant's provisions through "general comments" under Article 40 of the Covenant, review and questioning of state parties' periodic reports under the same article and opinions issued in response to individual communications filed under the Optional Protocol to the Covenant.[2]

The different organizational approaches adopted in these two works are perhaps reflected in their titles: the "collected edition" of the European *travaux préparatoires* is a chronological collection of discussions in the various bodies that considered the European Convention and its first Protocol, while the "guide" to the Covenant contains an article-by-article summary of the relevant debates in the United Nations. The latter is by far the more helpful for practitioners, as it permits ready identification of the different positions taken by states on the same substantive issue at all stages of the drafting process.

Much of the *Guide* is drawn directly from UN documents, and its summaries are taken from an annotated text of the draft Covenant prepared by the Secretary-General for the General Assembly in 1955 (UN Doc. A/2929) and subsequent reports of the Assembly's Third Committee. Bossuyt has inserted specific references to the relevant summary records (which total over five thousand pages), including identification of the country that adopted a particular position. Discussions of each article are divided according to the major substantive points,[3] and all references are further classified as "discussions" or "proposals-decisions." A good brief introduction to the methodology and organization of the *Guide* enables the reader to use it with a minimum of complication.

The bilingual (English and French) *Collected Edition* is much more difficult to use as an analytical aid, although its reproduction of debates in the order in which they occurred does offer a certain historical flavor that one cannot

[1] 79 AJIL 1108 (1985).

[2] While President Carter signed the Covenant and submitted it to the Senate for its advice and consent in 1978, the Reagan administration has regrettably refused to encourage its ratification pending a purported "review," which has now taken 7 years and has, in fact, been moribund for some time. *Cf.* U.S. RATIFICATION OF THE HUMAN RIGHTS TREATIES: WITH OR WITHOUT RESERVATION? (R. Lillich ed. 1981).

[3] For example, materials on Article 1 are organized under the headings of general debate, political principle or legal right, Charter provisions, all peoples and all nations, meaning of self-determination, permanent sovereignty over natural wealth and resources, obligations of all states and the problem of minorities.

appreciate as easily in the *Guide*. Unfortunately, an initially envisaged general index to the entire eight-volume set was abandoned; thus, the only indexes are found at the end of each volume and refer only to that volume. Most of the index entries refer to individual speakers, although broad references to various substantive rights are also included; there is no reference by number to the articles of the Convention as finally adopted.

Minor mistakes occur in both works, although they are not so numerous as to detract from the overall utility of the volumes. The European materials quoted in the *Collected Edition* would be undoubtedly difficult to consult directly (even in Strasbourg); the UN reports and summary records referenced in the *Guide* are more readily available in major depository libraries, although cross-references between the reports and the discussions collected in the summary records would be nearly impossible to find without substantial effort by an individual researcher.

The cost of both of these works—over $200 for the *Guide* and several hundred dollars for all eight volumes of the *Collected Edition*—ensures that they will be purchased primarily by libraries, and the limited usefulness of the format found in the latter will lessen its attraction for all but the most specialized European or human rights collections. However, the Bossuyt volume is an important work, and the status of the International Covenant on Civil and Political Rights as the most widely ratified general human rights instrument should justify the *Guide*'s inclusion in serious international law collections. One wishes that a similar reference work for the International Covenant on Economic, Social and Cultural Rights were also available.

Even a cursory review of the debates summarized in the two works exposes the illusion that one can easily identify the "intent of the parties" with respect to an ambiguous treaty provision, and one should bear in mind that any *travaux préparatoires* are only supplementary means of interpretation, as confirmed in Article 32 of the Vienna Convention on the Law of Treaties. While this will not deter those with LEXIS, research assistants or junior associates at their disposal from ferreting out even the most obscure remark that might support a particular interpretive position, the availability of works such as the *Guide* and the *Collected Edition* does not obviate the need for sound legal reasoning and good faith when one seeks to implement human rights treaties.

HURST HANNUM
Of the District of Columbia Bar

The U.N. Decade for Women: Documents and Dialogue. By Arvonne S. Fraser. Boulder and London: Westview Press, 1987. Pp. xi, 235. Index. $18.85.

This splendid book not only is a contribution to knowledge about the growing worldwide feminist movement, it adds to our understanding of the dynamics of international conferences held under the auspices of the United

Nations on subjects ranging from the environment to population. These conferences are marked by a high level of public interest and involvement in the proceedings, and have given rise to parallel informal gatherings of nongovernmental persons that have often been more noteworthy than the official conference itself.

As an active U.S. nongovernmental person, the author participated in the three conferences of the past decade dedicated to women's issues; this reviewer was a delegate to the first such gathering held in Mexico City in 1975. Following upon the recommendations of that conference, the UN General Assembly established the UN Decade for Women (1976–1985) and thus put women's issues on the international agenda. Indeed, the symbol of the UN Decade, the dove of peace with the women's sign and an equal sign in the body of the dove, was thereafter noted even in remote places of the less-developed world. Clearly, a new consciousness and confidence among women has emerged in many countries. Networks and organizations of women were spawned by the Decade's activities, and dialogue among them transcended national boundaries.

The First Women's Conference in Mexico City, which ran for 2 weeks, was the largest meeting in history to deal with women's concerns. Almost all UN members participated. At the same time, a parallel nongovernmental Tribune was held, which constituted a highly sophisticated lobby, aimed at influencing not only the outcome of the conference, but also national governments, the media and the public. Over six thousand women affiliated with a multiplicity of private organizations converged on Mexico City from all over the globe. The Tribune put out a daily newspaper and held 192 informal sessions. This gathering mobilized women worldwide in a more dramatic fashion than the official delegations and, despite its chaotic nature, it was the true source of a spreading feminist dialogue.

The conference adopted a "World Plan of Action" by consensus vote, with heavy emphasis on the needs of women in the developing world. The proceedings were marred by political resolutions introduced at a late stage, particularly those dealing with "Zionism is Racism" and opposition to apartheid in South Africa. These subjects were hardly germane to the feminist agenda, and their intrusion led to greater unity among the women as they sought to protect that agenda from extraneous issues.

By the time the next conference was held in Copenhagen, in 1980, the delegates included many women far more knowledgeable about dealing with the UN system and with governments. New international groups arose after the Mexico City conference, many of which sent participants to the nongovernmental forum held parallel to the conference, which registered over eight thousand people. The "Program of Action" adopted in Copenhagen was specific in content and concrete in scope. The 1979 Convention on the Elimination of All Forms of Discrimination Against Women was signed at a ceremony marking the opening of the conference. Unfortunately, political statements (referring to Zionism, apartheid and Palestinian women) were inserted in the international section of the Program of Action; as a result, on the document as a whole, the United States, Canada, Israel and Australia cast negative votes. The national section was adopted by consensus.

The last half of the Decade for Women culminated in the 1985 Nairobi conference. The final report of the conference itself acknowledged the contribution of women's organizations and the shared understanding held by women worldwide on their agenda of concerns. At Nairobi, unlike at previous conferences, the nongovernmental forum preceded the official gathering; consequently, its determinations greatly influenced the final report. The host country, Kenya, desirous of a successful result, was able to have the phrase equating Zionism with racism eliminated from the final report. Nairobi was thus reported in the world press as a triumph. The report, entitled "Forward Looking Strategies for the Advancement of Women to the Year 2000," conveyed the progress made from a sense of the oppression of women, which marked Mexico City, to a new spirit of independence and hope, culminating in Nairobi.

Arvonne Fraser traces this extraordinary UN Decade with precision and a sense of achievement. Her book merits reading by all concerned with social progress on an international scale.

RITA E. HAUSER
Of the New York and District of Columbia Bars

The South African Quagmire: In Search of a Peaceful Path to Democratic Pluralism. Edited by S. Prakash Sethi. Cambridge, Mass.: Ballinger Publishing Company, 1987. Pp. xvi, 444. $29.95.

This is a collection of 37 essays by 41 authors, focused on the role of multinational corporations in South Africa and designed to "bring . . . together, for the first time, and in one place, the authoritative views of the spokespersons for major interest groups and political and public opinion" (p. xiii). The book is only partially successful in meeting this laudable goal. It would certainly be useful for those new to the question of whether American and other foreign firms should remain in South Africa. However, those more familiar with these issues will find only a few chapters with fresh insights and even much of that is outdated, considering the pace of events during the tense past 2 years in South Africa. Most of the essays were written in early 1986. Many, in fact, appeared in the spring and summer 1986 issues of *Business and Society Review.* Since that time a state of emergency has been reimposed, the major black opposition groups working for peaceful change have been banned and their leaders jailed, press censorship has increased and the white voters have turned increasingly to the most conservative candidates, including some who proudly display neo-Nazi symbols. Given these changes, the prospect for greater moderation on the part of the whites, which is the premise of so many of the essays, appears increasingly remote.

Another shortcoming of the book is its lack of balance. It is part of the Ballinger series Business in a Global Environment and has a distinctly pro-business (and proinvestment) bias. The editor, S. Prakash Sethi, concludes in chapter 1 that American corporations should stay in South Africa, on the ground that economic boycotts "would end up hurting the United States and its companies without having much effect in bringing about desired changes in South Africa" (p. 15). In fact, he advocates that the United States increase its foreign aid to South Africa in order to help the white South Africans bear the "immense economic cost" necessary to achieve a "peaceful transition to a democratic post apartheid . . . South Africa." He finds U.S. foreign aid to South Africa, $20 million in 1985, totally insufficient: "Even as guilt money, its pettiness is embarrassing if not deplorable" (p. 17). Sethi is, however, somewhat critical of the Sullivan code and, drawing upon the interesting study by Karen Paul (ch. 37), concludes that the "Sullivan principles reporting system [managed by Arthur D. Little, whose Reid Weedon, Jr., defends the reports in chapter 36] . . . is so flawed that one cannot state with a high degree of certainty that the data indeed purport to show what actually is occurring in those companies" (p. 23). Nevertheless, Sethi advocates that companies stay in South Africa and increase their pressures on the South African Government and their assistance to black workers and community support activities.

Curiously, neither Sethi's long introductory chapter nor any of the other articles mentions that in May 1985, Leon Sullivan, the author of the Sullivan principles, had warned companies that they had only 2 more years to demonstrate that corporate engagement in South Africa would bring about the end of apartheid. In May 1987, Sullivan made good on his warning, withdrew his leadership from the Sullivan principles program and advocated that U.S. companies withdraw.

Given the editor's strong personal bias, he should have taken special pains to be certain that the important voices and best arguments supporting disinvestment were well represented. Unfortunately, they are not: 19 authors favor and only 8 oppose continuing multinational investment. Moreover, virtually all of the authors are white. There are *no* black American leaders and only three black South Africans represented. Of those, Bishop Desmond Tutu favors disinvestment and economic sanctions (ch. 13), while Chief Mangosuthu Gatsha Buthelezi favors continued investment (ch. 14). The third black author, A. J. Thembela, Vice Rector for Academic Affairs and Research at the University of Zululand, is highly critical of the South African Government for its disgraceful underfunding of black education, but takes no position on whether U.S. firms should stay in South Africa (ch. 21). The figures supplied by Thembela leave little doubt that the gap between black and white education in South Africa remains enormous despite the assertion of the South African minister for black education (ch. 20) that the Government "has accepted the responsibility to offer effective education and to work purposefully toward equal education opportunities in the shortest possible time" (p. 227).

Sethi explains that he tried to get the views of the African National Congress, the Congress of South African Trade Unions and representatives of the black press in South Africa, but that "unfortunately, these efforts were not successful because of limitations of time and the inability or unwillingness of the participants to prepare the necessary material'' (p. xiv). This may be because Sethi's own credibility was never established within the urban black community in South Africa. Indeed, many of his contacts seem to have been made through an executive of an American oil company, a professor of political science at the Rand Afrikaans University, and the Deputy Consul-General of South Africa in New York (p. xv).

While it is sometimes very difficult to obtain contributions from black South Africans opposed to U.S. investments (because the security laws may subject them to detention for such advocacy), it is very easy to obtain contributions from leading black Americans who have been active here in the efforts to have U.S. companies disinvest. It is surprising that there are no articles by—or, apparently, even an attempt to obtain articles from—individuals such as Randall Robinson, head of TransAfrica and the Free South Africa Movement; members of the Congressional Black Caucus such as Congressmen Mickey Leland and Bill Gray; Roger Wilkins, Senior Fellow, Institute for Policy Studies; Mary Frances Berry, former member of the U.S. Civil Rights Commission; Willard Johnson, professor of political science at MIT; or Leon Sullivan himself. The absence of these and other voices from both countries makes this a far less balanced and useful book than it could have been.

Despite these reservations, several chapters do illuminate current prospects for change in South Africa and the role that American investment (or the absence thereof) might play in the future. Senator Nancy Kassebaum (ch. 3) has a balanced essay that ends with this important observation:

> Arguments about disinvestment are less relevant than such questions as whether the United States should give greater recognition to the ANC, what initiatives we should press South Africa to take in the next six months to establish a modicum of trust on the black side, and how the United States can better present its political position to black South Africans [p. 52].

"A Democratic Blueprint for South Africa'' (ch. 8), by Arend Lijphart and Diane R. Stanton of the University of California at San Diego, contains a number of interesting suggestions on how a postapartheid government might be structured, although Colin Eglin, leader of the opposition Progressive Federal Party in South Africa, despairs of the possibility for meaningful dialogue between blacks and whites in the near future (ch. 7). He notes that South Africa's State President, P. W. Botha, gave an encouraging speech to Parliament in January 1986, which seemed to commit the Government to power sharing, negotiations with black leaders, the restoration of black citizenship and the removal of the influx control system. But Eglin reports that "within a week, hopes were dashed'' when Botha reprimanded his foreign minister "for suggesting that the consequence of the government's new policy was that a black South African could possibly become State President'' (p. 87).

The essay by Patrick O'Meara and N. Brian Winchester of the African Studies Program at the University of Indiana (ch. 10) is particularly useful in describing current realities: "Despite the escalating violence of the recent past it should not be forgotten that whites are still firmly in control in South Africa and they are unlikely to surrender their privileges easily" (p. 111). They warn "that the military and security forces could stage what they see as a preemptive coup d'état" (p. 113) and conclude, as do so many of the other authors, that the white majority must enter "into sincere negotiations with authentic black leaders over significant and meaningful political, economic and social transformation" (p. 119). But they caution that

> [t]he willingness of the ANC to negotiate and co-exist with whites is predicated on a relatively speedy transfer of power. If this struggle is a protracted one, the more militant members of the leadership of the ANC may predominate, and given its radical orientation and links with the South African Communist Party, . . . a different scenario [would result]. . . . The tragedy of white South Africa is that it has not learned the Rhodesian lesson: that earlier, voluntary, negotiated settlement is much preferable to a later, rampant, maelstrom [p. 122].

Part II of the book, "An Overview and Historical Perspective," contains only two chapters. "The Legal Structure of the Apartheid State" (ch. 11) gives a very useful history of the role that law has played in sustaining apartheid, beginning not with the ascendancy to power in 1948 of the Afrikaner-dominated Nationalist Party, but rather with apartheid laws enacted in the 17th century. While noting that petty apartheid—minor segregation laws—has been relaxed in a number of areas, the authors, Lawrence Boulle, dean of the University of Natal Law School and Jacky Julyan, a lecturer at Natal, observe that there has been no real relaxation in "the racially based political system. . . . The resolution of the apartheid predicament will ultimately be found not in state reform but in a political settlement" (p. 147).

The second chapter in part II is "The Religious Rationale of Racism," by Oliver Williams, professor of management at the University of Notre Dame. He examines the policies of the Dutch Reformed Church, whose white members, he notes, "are the power brokers of government policy in the Republic" (p. 154). Unfortunately, the Williams article, ending with "Prospects for Change," was written before the dramatic decision by the Dutch Reformed Church to renounce its previous position that the Bible sanctions white control of the inferior black.

The balance of the book (parts III–VIII) has a number of chapters debating the likely effectiveness of economic pressures, on the one hand, or increased corporate involvement in South Africa, on the other. Two of the best pieces supporting the continued investment of U.S. firms are by Herman Nickel (ch. 16), former U.S. Ambassador to South Africa, and Sal Marzulo (ch. 34), a manager in the Mobil Oil Corporation who has been a leader in the industry support group of Sullivan companies urging American firms to increase their contributions to black community development and black education.

Other chapters worth noting provide contrasting views on investment by two British authors (chs. 30 and 31) and interesting articles on the history of

U.S. church involvement in the antiapartheid campaign (chs. 25 and 26). "The Apartheid Debate on American Campuses," by Joseph Murphy, chancellor of the City University of New York (ch. 27), an article on actions taken by states and cities with respect to apartheid (ch. 28), and a review of the "social investing" movement where certain mutual funds have constructed South Africa–free portfolios (ch. 29) are also worthwhile.

There are two excellent articles on threats to freedom of the press in South Africa (chs. 23 and 24), by Anthony Heard, editor of the *Cape Times*, and by Harold Packendorf, editor of the Afrikaans *Die Vaterland*. John Barratt, director general of the South African Institute of International Affairs, has written an exceptionally thoughtful and balanced piece (ch. 19), "Can External Leverage Pressure South Africa?" Finally, Michael Sutcliffe, senior lecturer in the Department of Regional Planning, University of Natal (ch. 15), points out that it is extremely hard to determine just what black South Africans think about foreign investment. He discusses a series of recent surveys of black workers that point to different conclusions, each of which seems to suffer from important sampling bias and other errors.

While *The South African Quagmire* has rewarding chapters, it remains an incomplete and unbalanced treatment of the efficacy of the opposing approaches of constructive corporate involvement and disinvestment. Moreover, given recent events in South Africa, it is not clear whether either strategy can have much impact on that increasingly polarized and violent situation. The growing strength of the radical right among the white electorate and the suppression of moderate black opposition groups such as the United Democratic Front may mean that internal positions are hardening to the point where external economic influence will become marginal to the play of the terrible forces that are gathering but have not yet been unleashed in South Africa. If this occurs, the book will also become largely irrelevant as a guide to either public or private decision making in the United States.

WILLIAM R. COTTER
Colby College
Of the New York Bar

International Law and the Black Minority in the U.S. By Y. N. Kly. Atlanta: Clarity Press; Ottawa: Commoners' Publishing Society Inc., 1985. Pp. xxvi, 125.

Professor Y. N. Kly's *International Law and the Black Minority in the U.S.* will disturb and provoke many readers, minority and nonminority alike. Kly's book challenges pat assumptions about the inevitability of achieving racial harmony in U.S. society through traditional legal and political mechanisms, skepticism about the capacity of international law to effect change in the behavior of nations toward their own citizens, and the normal civic religion professing faith in the ideal that in the United States all men and women are created equal. *International Law and the Black Minority in the U.S.*, with its emphasis on international human rights law as a viable alternative for securing as yet unsecured minority rights, represents an important contribution to the discourse of dissent articulated by a growing number of black and other minority intellectuals on the capacity of the legal and political system of the United States to effect a truly equal status for its national minorities.

Kly's sweeping critique of the past, present and future of U.S. race relations in the context of contemporary international human rights law is organized around two principal theoretical constructs: what he calls the U.S. view of collective rights (USVCR) as it concerns national minorities (most particularly the black minority), and the international law view of collective rights (ILVCR) of minorities. According to Kly, the USVCR emphasizes civil and individual rights of minorities and assumes their eventual assimilation or integration into the dominant national culture. The ILVCR, on the other hand, emphasizes official recognition of the legal and political existence of national minorities and the acceptance of "special measures" or affirmative action designed to enable the minority to attain a political, economic and social equal-status relationship with the majority (p. xxiii).

In elaborating the significance of these two constructs, Kly's book draws heavily on the work of Harvard Law School Professor Derrick Bell (Bell is cited no less than half a dozen times in this 150-page work) and his central thesis that the most significant political advances for American blacks have resulted from policies that had the effect of serving the interests and convenience of whites rather than remedying racial injustices against blacks (p. 75). Kly applies this thesis to the history of U.S. black-white relations to suggest that the U.S. minority rights system "treats its national minorities in a manner which often corresponds to the constituent elements of imperialism and colonialism: domination, exploitation, and inequality" (p. viii). Thus, the U.S. view of minority rights permits a system of domestic colonialism in violation of contemporary international human rights law, most particularly, the general legal principles embodied in Article 27 of the United Nations Covenant on Civil and Political Rights. This central text of international human rights law states: "In those states in which ethnic, religious or linguistic minorities exist, persons belonging to such minorities shall not be denied the right, in community with the members of their group, to enjoy their own culture, to profess and practice their own religion, or to use their own language" (p. xxii).

Kly argues that Article 27 requires that a government grant official recognition to its national minorities and special measures for them. Until the United States accepts these two obligations, Kly asserts, the credibility of U.S. human rights foreign policy and solutions to the problems of blacks and other minorities in the United States will continue to be impeded.

Part 1 of Kly's book elaborates the international law concept of minority collective rights, citing Switzerland, a country with three national minorities, French, Italian and Romanche, spread out among the 25 cantons of the Swiss confederation, as an example of a modern Western state that has instituted effective minority protection institutions. Besides the concrete example of the multilingual Swiss state, Kly sketches a brief history of minority rights in Western state practice, beginning with the 17th and 18th centuries, when a number of treaties between European countries incorporated clauses relating to the rights of religious minorities. This process continued and developed through the 19th and early 20th centuries, culminating in Article 27, "the essence," according to Kly, of the ILVCR (p. 36).

Part 2 analyzes the U.S. concept of collective rights of minorities and its divergence from the ILVCR. Kly's survey of the history of black-white relations in America is divided into four parts: the slavery period (1776–1865), Reconstruction (1868–1895), the apartheid period (1895–1960) and the era of Martin Luther King, Jr. (1960–1975). It leads him to conclude that there has never existed any clear-cut, legally articulated minority policy in the United States, certainly not one that would meet the requirements of official recognition and special measures mandated by Article 27 and international human rights law. Instead, Kly argues, the USVCR is "highly flexible and pragmatic" (p. 87), thus assuring that the "maxim that majority self-interest will prevail over minority rights is in no danger of becoming antiquated" (p. 49). Suggesting that legislative initiatives such as the 1964 and 1968 Civil Rights Acts were but "a pragmatic response intended merely to stave off further minority protest," Kly joins a growing chorus of black and other American intellectuals of color who have offered negative assessments of the civil rights movement of the recent past and of the prospects for improvements in race relations in the United States for the near future (see, for example, Derrick Bell's new book, *And We Are Not Saved* [1987]). Kly's unique contribution is to place the past, present and future of U.S. race relations within the broader context of international human rights law, thus permitting an assessment of the USVCR of minorities according to the evolving norms of a legal discourse on national minorities liberated from a history of "intentional enslavement, extermination and gross exploitation" (p. 92). Kly's strategic placement of the USVCR within the more widely accepted normative discourse of international human rights law provides not only an alternative vision of race relations in the United States, but also, even more importantly, an alternative *solution.* Kly's unique perspective is worthy of consideration and debate by minority and nonminority individuals alike, intrigued by the possibility that the rule of law is more likely to be discovered in universal declarations of human rights than in more parochial interpretations.

ROBERT A. WILLIAMS, JR.
University of Arizona
Lumbee Indian Tribe

Coping with Africa's Refugee Burden: A Time for Solutions. By Robert F. Gorman. Dordrecht, Boston, Lancaster: Martinus Nijhoff Publishers; UNITAR, 1987. Pp. xiv, 206. Index. Dfl.80; $35.50; £26.25.

This book deals with the thorny question of combining assistance to refugees with development efforts so as to enable the beneficiaries to become self-sufficient. Such an approach is relevant for two categories of refugees: those who are able to return to their country of origin and must rebuild an existence there, and those who cannot be expected to return in the foreseeable future and thus should be helped to settle down in the country of asylum. In both cases the local population, infrastructure and environment are likely to be affected. The idea of going beyond assisting refugees in camps and making them self-sufficient is of relatively recent origin. Efforts to put it into practice have lately been hampered by the drought disasters that have struck much of Africa and, in particular, many of the countries with a sizable refugee population. This turn of events led to the provisional abandonment of long-term solutions in favor of immediate and massive disaster relief.

In the first chapter, the author relates the gradual emergence of the concept that refugee relief could be combined with development, which led to the first International Conference on Assistance of Refugees in Africa (ICARA I). The second chapter describes the various steps that led to ICARA II and provides a brief account of the conference itself. The third chapter describes the role of the various, mostly UN, agencies in the preparation and implementation of ICARA II and highlights some of the coordination problems that had to be faced and that sometimes continue to hamper efficient action. The fourth chapter deals with donor country response to ICARA II. It describes the internal difficulties faced by many of them, especially the United States and the Federal Republic of Germany, as well as the evolution of attitudes in other donors such as the United Kingdom, Japan and the European Economic Community. The fifth chapter relates the views and attitudes of the host countries and the problems many of them encounter in implementing development programs designed for refugees. Chapter 6 describes the roles of the nongovernmental organizations. Chapter 7 draws the balance of achievements and unresolved problems and provides some recommendations on how the latter could be handled.

The great merit of this study lies in the fact that it was written by someone with considerable inside knowledge of the workings of both donor and recipient countries and the various international institutions involved. It shows how the dichotomy between relief and development assistance is usually reflected in the organizational setup at both the national and the international levels. At the latter, as far as the United Nations is concerned, this dichotomy is compounded by the fact that one principal agency, the United Nations Development Programme, is headquartered in New York, whereas the other, the United Nations High Commissioner for Refugees, has its seat in Geneva. As a result, much time and impetus is lost because of friction between ministries and offices, to the detriment of the programs and those who are meant to benefit from them. In addition, chapter 5 shows how the drought disasters and consequent worldwide relief effort not only have distracted government agencies from giving much attention to development programs for refugees, but also have kept most important nongovernmental relief agencies completely out of such efforts as they were totally absorbed by the ongoing emergency actions. Consequently, only a few minor agencies have become involved in development programs within the ICARA framework.

What might have been given more attention is the fact that drought, famine and man-made economic calamities have given rise to mass movements across international borders. The people involved have often become inextricably mixed up with refugee populations, which makes the sorting out of the latter, for purposes of repatriation and settlement projects, extremely hard in countries like Sudan and Ethiopia.

DIETRICH KAPPELER
University of Nairobi

BRIEFER NOTICES

Las Relaciones de cooperación para el desarrollo CEE–Estados ACP. By José Manuel Sobrino Heredia. (Santiago de Compostela: Universidad de Santiago de Compostela, 1985. Pp. 273.) This excellently documented book traces the history of the trade preferences agreed to by the European Economic Community in favor of a large number of states, mostly former European colonies. Professor Sobrino Heredia has produced a solid work. The historical account of the EEC's cooperation policy is thorough and complete, and the progress made from the timid "association" themes in the Treaty of Rome to the much more advanced ideas of economic cooperation embodied in the Lomé Conventions is well described and contrasted. The book starts with a general introduction to the European system of cooperation for economic development (ch. I). Chapter II contains a competent legal analysis of Article 238 and part IV of the EEC Treaty. In chapter III Sobrino Heredia analyzes the Lomé Conventions, both historically and substantively, with particular reference to the enlargement of the EEC in the 1970s. This chapter is perhaps the best in the book. While the approach is, in this reviewer's judgment, too generous to the Lomé process, the author exhibits knowledge and understanding of this complex area of international law. Chapter IV adds a much-needed commentary about the EEC cooperation policy in the light of the recent accession of Spain and Portugal. In the appendix, the author includes a brief analysis of the 1984 Lomé III Convention, which was signed when the book was already in print.

Perhaps a criticism of the book is its excessive emphasis on historical events to the detriment of economic and policy analysis. The main conceptual tension in the idea of economic cooperation is that between the antithetical purposes of political altruism and economic self-interest. The author discusses only marginally how this tension is dealt with by the Lomé process. In the author's defense, one should add that the willingness to deal overtly with moral and political issues is quite uncommon in current international legal scholarship.

The foregoing criticism, however, does not overshadow the merits of the book. This work is a major contribution to the Spanish legal literature on the EEC.

FERNANDO R. TESÓN
Arizona State University

The Teaching of Space Law Around the World. Edited by Stephen Gorove. ([L.Q.C. Lamar Society of International Law, Monograph Series No. 4, University of Mississippi Law Center, 1986.] Pp. 93. Index. $26.) This short, but concentrated, book adds a new element to the growing field of space law. For lawyers, political scientists and commercial space specialists interested in designing and teaching a course on space law, it serves as a guide to some of the concepts, syllabuses and materials now being offered in courses in the United States, Canada, Eastern and Western Europe, Argentina, the Soviet Union and China. While doing so, it provides the user with a glance at the history of space law and the materials and writings available to the prospective student. The author has included contributions from some of the leading academic figures in space law, each describing his own institution's space law program.

The author is well equipped to compile such a book since the University of Mississippi Law School was a pioneer in offering a space law course as a regular part of its academic program. A comparison of the programs included in the book gives the reader a feel for the currently evolving nature of space law as an academic subject. For some, it is closely connected with air law; for others, it is a separate and distinct subject. Mention is made in a number of places of a 1932 article by Vladimir Mandl—referred to by some as the "father of space law"—in which he said that state sovereignty does not extend to outer space. The subject of jurisdiction and territorial rights in space is a theme throughout the programs.

Although one has to compile the bibliography oneself from each of the programs, the book is a rich source of bibliographical listings on space law. This, added to the variety of topics covered and the history and ideas presented, makes this a valuable book for anyone thinking of developing and teaching a course on space law.

COLLEEN DRISCOLL SULLIVAN
Common Heritage Institute
Villanova University

COLLECTED ESSAYS

Realism in Law-Making: Essays on international law in honour of Willem Riphagen. Edited by Adriaan Bos and Hugo Siblesz. (Published under the auspices of the T.M.C. Asser Instituut. Dordrecht, Boston, Lancaster: Martinus Nijhoff Publishers, 1986. Pp. xix, 298. Index. Dfl.165; $75.50; £54.50.)

W. G. Belinfante, *State Immunity To-Day;* R. J. Dupuy, *Les Conflits sur les Lois de la Mer;* A. Fattal, *La Convention d'Armistice Libano-Israélienne de 1949 au Regard du Droit des Gens;* H. Golsong, *Dispute Settlement in Recently Negotiated Bilateral Investment Treaties—the reference to the ICSID additional facility;* G. Jaenicke, *The Role of Proportionality in the Delimitation of Maritime Zones;* P. H. Kooijmans, *Who Tolled the Death-Bell for Compulsory Jurisdiction? Some comments on the judgment of the ICJ in the case concerning military and paramilitary activities in and against Nicaragua;* G. Ladreit de Lacharrière, *Aspects du Relativisme du Droit International;* M. Lachs, *Law in the World of Today;* G. Lagergren, *Iran–United States Claims Tribunal;* M. C. W. Pinto, *The Duty of Co-Operation and the United Nations Convention on the Law of the Sea;* P. Reuter, *Du Consentement des Tiers aux Normes d'un Traité;* S. Rosenne, *UNCLOS III—*

The Montreux (Riphagen) Compromise; J. G. Sauveplanne, *Developments in Private International Law: A Retrospective Look at the Boll Case;* H. G. Schermers, *Preliminary Rulings under the European Convention on Human Rights?;* S. M. Schwebel, *United Nations Resolutions, Recent Arbitral Awards and Customary International Law;* I. Sinclair, *The Impact of the Unratified Codification Convention;* L. B. Sohn, *Unratified Treaties as a Source of Customary International Law;* T. Treves, *Notes on Transit Passage Through Straits and Customary Law;* C. C. A. Voskuil, *Party Autonomy in Matters of International Judicial Jurisdiction in the Netherlands—Farewell to the principle of sovereignty.*

Questions of International Law: Hungarian Perspectives. Volume 3. Edited by Hanna Bokor-Szegö. (Dordrecht, Boston, Lancaster: Martinus Nijhoff Publishers; Budapest: Akadémiai Kiadó, 1987. Pp. 274. Dfl.125; $59; £41.25.)

E. Ustor, *In Memoriam Gyorgy Haraszti;* H. Bokor-Szegö, *Identity and Succession of States in Modern International Law;* A. Bragyova, *Reflections on Immunity of States from the Point of View of International Law;* J. Bruhacs, *The Problem of the Definition of an International Watercourse;* G. Herczegh, *International Law in a Multicultural World;* P. Katona, *Ad hoc Arbitration Rules: Similarities and Differences. A Comparative Review;* V. Lamm, *Some Remarks about Non-Appearance before the International Court of Justice;* F. Madl, *Principal Elements of the New Regulation of Foreign Trade in Hungary;* I. Meznerics, *Guarantees for Investments in International Law and in Other International Schemes;* K. Nagy, *The Problem of Reparation in International Law;* A. Prandler, *The Unchanging Significance of the United Nations Charter and Some International Legal Aspects of its Application;* L. Reczei, *Leasing;* E. Ustor, *Most-Favored-Nation Clauses in Treaties of Commerce: The Question of an Implied Customs Union Exception Rule;* L. Valki, *The Social Functions of International Law;* S. Vida, *Intellectual Property and the Code of Private International Law.*

Annuaire Français de Droit International. Vol. XXXII, 1986. (Paris: Editions du Centre National de la Recherche Scientifique, 1987. Pp. 1255. Indexes. F.650.)

B. Stern, *Quelques observations sur les règles internationales relatives à l'application extraterritoriale du droit;* D. Simon and L. A. Sicilianos, *La contre-violence unilatérale—Pratique étatique et Droit international;* S. Regourd, *Raids antiterroristes et développement récents des atteintes au principe de non-intervention;* H. Labayle, *Droit international et lutte contre le terrorisme;* A. Ch. Kiss, *L'accident de Tchernobyl: ses conséquences au point de vue du Droit international, les Conventions du 26 septembre 1986.*

P. M. Eisemann, *L'arrêt de la CIJ dans l'affaire des activités militaires et paramilitaires au Nicaragua et contre celui-ci;* J. Cl. Gautron, *Création d'une chambre au sein de la Cour internationale de Justice, mesures et médiation provisoires dans le différend frontalier entre le Burkina-Faso et le Mali;* E. Decaux, *L'arrêt de la Chambre de la Cour internationale de Justice dans l'affaire du différend frontalier Burkina-Faso c. République du Mali;* H. Dipla, *L'affaire concernant le filetage à l'intérieur du golfe du Saint-Laurent entre le Canada et la France;* P. Rambaud, *L'annulation des sentences Klockner et Amco;* V. Coussirat-Coustère, *Les arrêts rendus par la Cour européenne des Droits de l'homme en 1985;* C. Chanet, *Les requêtes individuelles présentées contre la France devant la Commission et la Cour européennes des Droits de l'homme (1981–1985);* G. Cohen-Jonathan and J. P. Jacqué, *Activités de la Commission européenne des Droits de l'homme;* J. Boulouis, *Jurisprudence de la Cour de Justice des Communautés européennes;* J. Schwob, *Jurisprudence du Tribunal administratif des Nations Unies;* D. Ruzié,

Jurisprudence du Tribunal administratif de l'Organisation internationale du Travail.

M. Bertrand, *Planification, programmation, budgétisation et évaluation à l'ONU;* Y. Beigbeder, *La crise financière des Nations Unies et les travaux du Comité des Dix-huit;* V. Y. Ghebali, *L'évolution du corps commun d'inspection des Nations Unies;* Ph. Manin, *La Convention de Vienne sur les accords entre Etats et organisations internationales ou entre organisations internationales;* T. Treves, *Innovations dans la technique de codification du Droit international—La préparation de la Convention de Vienne sur les traités passés par les Organisations internationales;* P. Tavernier, *L'année des Nations Unies 1986—problèmes juridiques;* J. Dauchy, *Travaux de la Commission juridique de l'Assemblée générale des Nations Unies (XLIe session);* J. Dehaussy, *Travaux de la Commission du Droit international;* D. Prémont, *Etat d'acceptation du Pacte international relatif aux droits civils et politiques et du protocole s'y rapportant;* Y. Sandoz, *Analyse juridique de la décision de suspendre la délégation gouvernementale sud-africaine de la XXVe Conférence internationale de la Croix Rouge.*

D. Carreau, Th. Flory and P. Juillard, *Chronique de droit international économique;* S. Courteix, *La coopération nucléaire internationale de la République populaire de Chine;* J. Conquy Beer-Gabel, *Le Programme intergouvernemental d'informatique de l'UNESCO;* C. A. Colliard, *Les principes régissant la télédétection spatiale.*

D. Momtaz, *La Convention des Nations Unies sur les conditions de l'immatriculation des navires;* R. Jeannel, *L'incident de pêche franco-espagnol du 7 mars 1984 dans le golfe de Gascogne;* R. Goy, *Le tunnel sous la Manche;* J. Chappez, *Les cables sous-marins de télécommunications;* J. Barberis, *L'exploitation hydro-électrique du Parana et l'accord tripartite de 1979.*

G. Isaac, *L'insertion du Parlement européen dans le système juridictionnel des Communautés européennes;* J. de la Rochère, *Transport aérien européen—problèmes de concurrence;* M. F. Labouz, *Le principe d'égalité hommes-femmes dans la jurisprudence récente de la Cour de Justice des Communautés européennes.*

G. Burdeau, *Les engagements internationaux de la France et les exigences de l'Etat de droit;* J. Fr. Flauss, *Note sur le retrait par la France des réserves aux traités internationaux;* A. Lewin, *Les années France-Brésil, projet conventionnel ou nouveau mode de relations internationales?;* J. Charpentier, *Le règlement de l'affaire Greenpeace;* J. Ph. Arnold, *La protection sociale des Français servant dans les organisations internationales intergouvernementales.*

Chinese Yearbook of International Law and Affairs. Volume 6 (1986–87). Edited by Hungdah Chiu with the assistance of Jaw-ling Joanne Chang. (Taipei: Chinese Society of International Law, 1987. Pp. viii, 517. Index. $15. Distributed by the Occasional Papers/Reprints Series in Contemporary Asian Studies, Baltimore, Md.)

Kuen-chen Fu, *Equitable Considerations Taken into Account in International Ocean Boundary Delimitation Cases;* Cing-Kae Chiao, *The Protection of Labor Welfare in the Republic of China, with Special Reference to the Labor Standards Law of 1984 (with Text of the Labor Standard Law);* Ruey-Long Lin, *Protection of Intellectual Property in the Republic of China;* David S. Chou, *International Status of the Republic of China;* Ying-jeou Ma, *Two Major Legal Issues Relating to the International Status of the Republic of China;* David Chemin Cheng, *A Communist Chinese Armed Attack on Taiwan: Some Inquiries of International Law and Politics;* John K. T. Chao, *Legal Implications of a Pacific Blockade of Taiwan;* R. B. Greenburgh, *Sovereign Debt and the Republic of China.*

BOOKS RECEIVED*

International Law—General

Bos, Maarten, and Ian Brownlie (eds.). *Liber Amicorum for the Rt. Hon. Lord Wilberforce, PC, CMG, OBE, QC.* Oxford: Clarendon Press; New York: Oxford University Press, 1987. Pp. vi, 251. Index. $59.

Butler, W. E. (ed.). *International Law and the International System.* Dordrecht, Boston, Lancaster: Martinus Nijhoff Publishers, 1987. Pp. 208. Dfl.125; $49.50; £38.50.

International Economic Law & Relations

Bianca, C. M., and M. J. Bonell (eds.). *Commentary on the International Sales Law: The 1980 Vienna Sales Convention.* Milan: Giuffrè, 1987. Pp. xvii, 886. Index. L. 100,000.

Delaume, Georges R. *Law and Practice of Transnational Contracts.* New York, London, Rome: Oceana Publications, Inc., 1988. Pp. xxxvi, 409. Index. $75.

Ffrench, H. Leigh. *International Law of Take-Overs and Mergers: The EEC, Northern Europe, and Scandinavia.* New York, Westport, London: Quorum Books, 1986. Pp. viii, 390. Indexes. $55. (See review of earlier vols. at 80 AJIL 1020 [1986].)

———. *International Law of Take-Overs and Mergers: Southern Europe, Africa, and the Middle East.* New York, Westport, London: Quorum Books, 1987. Pp. viii, 264. Indexes. $49.95. (See review of earlier vols. at 80 AJIL 1020 [1986].)

Frazer, Tim. *Monopoly, Competition and the Law: The Regulation of Business Activity in Britain, Europe and America.* Sussex: Wheatsheaf Books; New York: St. Martin's Press, 1988. Pp. xvii, 265. Index. $39.95.

Freedman, Warren. *Foreign Plaintiffs in Products Liability Actions: The Defense of Forum Non Conveniens.* New York, Westport, London: Quorum Books, 1988. Pp. vii, 162. Indexes. $45.

——— (ed.). *Products Liability: An International Manual of Practice.* Binder I. London, Rome, New York: Oceana Publications, Inc., 1987. 2 binders projected. $250/set.

Howell, Thomas R., William A. Noellert, Janet H. MacLaughlin, and Alan Wm. Wolff. *The Microelectronics Race: The Impact of Government Policy on International Competition.* Boulder and London: Westview Press, 1988. Pp. xxi, 278. Index. $27.50.

Hudec, Robert E. *Developing Countries in the GATT Legal System.* Aldershot, Eng., and Brookfield, Vt.: Gower, 1987. Published for the Trade Policy Research Centre, London. Pp. xix, 259. £12.95.

Lillich, Richard B. (ed.). *The Valuation of Nationalized Property in International Law.* Volume IV. Charlottesville: University Press of Virginia, 1987. Pp. xvii, 238. Index. $30.

Sauvant, Karl P. *International Transactions in Services: The Politics of Transborder Data Flows.* Boulder and London: Westview Press, 1986. Pp. xxiii, 372. $38.50.

———. *Trade and Foreign Direct Investment in Data Services.* Boulder and London: Westview Press, 1986. Pp. xv, 223. Index. $30.50.

Secchi, Carlo, and Giorgio Sacerdoti. *L'Uruguay Round del GATT.* Milan: Università Commerciale Luigi Bocconi, 1987. Pp. xi, 169.

UNCITRAL Legal Guide on Electronic Funds Transfers. Prepared by the Secretariat of the United Nations Commission on International Trade Law. New York: United Nations, 1987. Pp. 150. $17.

Will, Michael R. *Internationale Bibliographie zum UN-Kaufrecht.* Saarbrücken: Europa-Institut der Universität des Saarlandes, 1987. Pp. 56. DM 10.

Zheng, Henry R. *Legal Structure of International Textile Trade.* New York, Westport, London: Quorum Books, 1988. Pp. xi, 228. Index. $45.

Law of the Sea & Maritime Law

Alexander, Lewis M. *Navigational Restrictions Within the New LOS Context: Geographical Implications for the United States.* Peace Dale, R.I.: Offshore Consultants, Inc., 1986. Pp. xii, 396.

* Mention here neither assures nor precludes later review.

Brown, E. D., and R. R. Churchill (eds.). *The UN Convention on the Law of the Sea: Impact and Implementation.* Proceedings of the Law of the Sea Institute, Nineteenth Annual Conference. Co-sponsored by the Centre for Marine Law and Policy, University of Wales Institute of Science and Technology. Honolulu: The Law of the Sea Institute, University of Hawaii, 1987. Pp. xiii, 639. Index.

The Law of the Sea—being a series of articles first published in ACTA JURIDICA 1986. Published under the auspices of the Faculty of Law, University of Cape Town. Cape Town and Johannesburg: Juta & Co., Ltd., 1986. Pp. ix, 226. R64.

Regional compendium of fisheries legislation (Indian Ocean Region). Volume II. Prepared by the Legislation Branch, FAO Legal Office, with the assistance of the International Centre for Ocean Development. Rome: Food and Agriculture Organization of the United Nations, 1987. Pp. vi, 543. $49.50. Distributed by UNIPUB.

Seeberg-Elverfeldt, Niels-Jürgen. *Die Streitbeilegung im Tiefseebergbaurecht: Die Probleme nach der Seerechtskonvention unter besonderer Berücksichtigung des Rechtsschutzes Privater.* Baden-Baden: Nomos Verlagsgesellschaft, 1986. Pp. xvi, 185. DM 47.

Sobarzo, Alejandro. *Régimen Jurídico del alta mar* (2d ed.). Mexico: Editorial Porrúa, S. A., 1985. Pp. xvi, 495. Index.

Use of Force & Law of War

Bailey, Sydney D. *War and Conscience in the Nuclear Age.* New York: St. Martin's Press, 1988. Pp. xviii, 210. Index. $32.50.

Calogeropoulos-Stratis, S. *Le Recours à la force dans la société internationale.* Lausanne: Editions L.E.P., Loisirs et Pédagogie; Paris: Librairie Générale de Droit et de Jurisprudence, 1986. Pp. 191.

Dinstein, Yoram. *War, Aggression and Self-Defence.* Cambridge: Grotius Publications Limited, 1988. Pp. xxx, 292. Indexes. £52; $95.

Kirkpatrick, Jeane J. *Legitimacy and Force. Volume One: Political and Moral Dimensions.* New Brunswick and Oxford: Transaction Books, 1988. Pp. xxiii, 486. $34.95, cloth; $16.95, paper.

Kirkpatrick, Jeane J. *Legitimacy and Force. Volume Two: National and International Dimensions.* New Brunswick and Oxford: Transaction Books, 1988. Pp. xxiii, 421. $34.95, cloth; $16.95, paper.

LaCroix, W. L. *War and International Ethics: Tradition and Today.* Lanham, New York, London: University Press of America, 1988. Pp. x, 305. Index. $28.50, cloth; $15.25, paper.

Reisman, W. Michael, and Andrew R. Willard (eds.). *International Incidents: The Law That Counts in World Politics.* Princeton: Princeton University Press, 1988. Pp. xii, 278. Index. $35, cloth; $12.95, paper.

Solf, Waldemar A., and J. Ashley Roach (eds.). *Index of International Humanitarian Law.* (Rev. ed. of Jiri Toman's *Index of the Geneva Conventions for the Protection of War Victims of 12 August 1949.)* Geneva: International Committee of the Red Cross, 1987. Pp. xxvi, 283.

Human Rights

Brownlie, Ian. *The Human Right to Food.* London: Commonwealth Secretariat, 1987. Pp. 17.

Ergec, Rusen. *Les droits de l'homme à l'épreuve des circonstances exceptionnelles: Etude sur l'article 15 de la Convention européenne des droits de l'homme.* Brussels: Editions Bruylant; Editions de l'Université de Bruxelles, 1987. Pp. xv, 427. BF 2,850.

European Convention on Human Rights: Collected Texts, 1987. Dordrecht, Boston, Lancaster: Martinus Nijhoff Publishers, 1987. Pp. xi, 236. Dfl.170; $78; £56.75.

Ferencz, Benjamin B., in cooperation with Ken Keyes, Jr. *PlanetHood: The Key to Your Survival and Prosperity.* Coos Bay, Or.: Vision Books, 1988. Pp. 188. $2.50.

Frankowski, Stanislaw J., and George F. Cole (eds.). *Abortion and Protection of the Human Fetus: Legal Problems in a Cross-Cultural Perspective.* Published under the auspices of The Institute of International and Comparative Law, The University of Santa Clara. Dordrecht, Boston, Lancaster: Martinus Nijhoff Publishers, 1987. Pp. xv, 334. Dfl.175; $86; £53.95.

Jaspers, A.Ph. C. M., and L. Betten (eds.). *25 Years European Social Charter.* Deventer: Kluwer Law and Taxation Publishers, 1988. Pp. viii, 181. Dfl.80; £24; $42.

Rayner, Mary. *Turning a Blind Eye? Medical Accountability and the Prevention of Torture in South Africa.* Washington: Committee on Scientific Freedom and Responsibility, American Association for the Advancement of Science, 1987. Pp. vi, 96.

Aliens & Refugees

Frowein, Jochen Abr., and Torsten Stein (eds.). *Die Rechtsstellung von Ausländern nach staatlichem Recht und Völkerrecht / The Legal Position of Aliens in National and International Law / Le régime juridique des étrangers en droit national et international.* 2 vols. Berlin, Heidelberg, New York: Springer-Verlag, 1987. Pp. xlvi, 2135. Index. DM 480.

Reiterer, Michael. *The Protection of Refugees by Their State of Asylum.* Vienna: Wilhelm Braumüller, 1984. Pp. 114. Index.

Ressler, Everett M., Neil Boothby, and Daniel J. Steinbock. *Unaccompanied Children: Care and Protection in Wars, Natural Disasters, and Refugee Movements.* New York and Oxford: Oxford University Press, 1988. Pp. x, 421. Index. $49.95, cloth; $18.95, paper.

Wölker, Ulrich. *Zu Freiheit und Grenzen der politischen Betätigung von Ausländern: Der politische Gebrauch der Meinungs-, Versammlungs- und Vereinigungsfreiheit der Ausländer nach innerstaatlichem Recht, Völkerrecht und Europarecht.* Berlin, Heidelberg, New York: Springer-Verlag, 1987. Pp. xxi, 264. English and French summaries. Index. DM 98.

Conflicts & Disputes

Gustafson, Lowell S. *The Sovereignty Dispute over the Falkland (Malvinas) Islands.* New York and Oxford: Oxford University Press, 1988. Pp. xiii, 268. Index. $36.

Terrorism

Mickolus, Edward F. (comp.), with Peter A. Flemming. *Terrorism, 1980–1987: A Selectively Annotated Bibliography.* New York, Westport, London: Greenwood Press, 1988. Pp. ix, 314. Indexes. $55.

International Labor Law

Ben-Israel, Ruth. *International Labour Standards: The Case of Freedom to Strike.* A study prepared for the International Labour Office. Deventer: Kluwer Law and Taxation Publishers, 1988. Pp. vii, 133. Index. Dfl.75; £23; $39.

Environment & Natural Resources

Barberis, Julio A., for the Legislation Branch, FAO Legal Office. *International groundwater resources law.* Rome: Food and Agriculture Organization of the United Nations, 1986. Pp. vii, 67. $6. Distributed by Bernan-Unipub.

Munro, R. D. (chairman), and J. G. Lammers (rapporteur). *Environmental Protection and Sustainable Development: Legal Principles and Recommendations.* Adopted by the Experts Group on Environmental Law of the World Commission on Environment and Development. London, Dordrecht, Boston: Graham & Trotman/Martinus Nijhoff, 1987. Pp. xxi, 196. Dfl.99; $49; £33.95.

Qing-nan, Meng. *Land-Based Marine Pollution: International Law Development.* London, Dordrecht, Boston: Graham & Trotman/Martinus Nijhoff, 1987. Pp. xvi, 254. Index. Dfl.135; $66.50; £46.50.

Rodman, Kenneth A. *Sanctity Versus Sovereignty: The United States and the Nationalization of Natural Resource Investments.* New York: Columbia University Press, 1988. Pp. xvii, 403. Index. $45.

Antarctica

Orrego Vicuña, Francisco. *Antarctic mineral exploitation: The emerging legal framework.* Cambridge and New York: Cambridge University Press, 1988. Pp. xv, 615. Index.

——— (comp.). *Antarctic Bibliography—with particular reference to the legal and political issues of co-operation and the regime on mineral resources.* Santiago: Institute of International Studies of the University of Chile, 1987. Pp. 155.

Peterson, M. J. *Managing the Frozen South: The Creation and Evolution of the Antarctic Treaty System.* Berkeley, Los Angeles, London: University of California Press, 1988. Pp. xi, 283. Index. $35.

Air & Space Law

Anand, R. P., K. B. Ganesan, Shri V. Pattanayak, S. S. Sidhu, Rahmatullah Khan, N. K. Singh and S. Bhatt (eds.). *Recent Developments in Civil Aviation in India.* New Delhi: Lancers Books, 1987. Pp. 243. Index. Rs.150; $20.

Dempsey, Paul Stephen. *Law and Foreign Policy in International Aviation.* Dobbs Ferry: Transnational Publishers, Inc., 1987. Pp. xvii, 468. Index. $65.

Singh, J. N. *Outer Space, Outer Sea, Outer Land and International Law.* New Delhi: Harnam Publications, 1987. Pp. xi, 296. Rs.180.

Sovereign Immunity

Schreuer, Christoph H. *State Immunity: Some Recent Developments.* Cambridge: Grotius Publications Limited, 1988. Pp. xxiii, 200. Index. £28; $55.

Intellectual Property

Gadbaw, R. Michael, and Timothy J. Richards (eds.). *Intellectual Property Rights: Global Consensus, Global Conflict?* Boulder and London: Westview Press, 1988. Pp. xxi, 412. $58.

International Organizations

Finkelstein, Lawrence S. (ed.). *Politics in the United Nations System.* Durham and London: Duke University Press, 1988. Pp. xvi, 503. Indexes. $65, cloth; $22.50, paper.

Jhabak, Kasturchand M. *The Emerging Role of Security Council as an Instrument of International Peace.* n.p., 1987. Pp. 134.

Köhler, Peter A. *Sozialpolitische und sozialrechtliche Aktivitäten in den Vereinten Nationen.* Baden-Baden: Nomos Verlagsgesellschaft, 1987. Pp. 1232. Index. DM 189.

Papacostas, Alkis-B. N. *L'Organisation Internationale.* Athens, 1986. Pp. 221. In Greek.

Treaty Law

Bowman, M. J., and D. J. Harris (comps./anns.). *Multilateral Treaties: Index and Current Status.* Fourth Cumulative Supplement. Nottingham: University of Nottingham Treaty Centre, 1987. Pp. 120. £15.

Ginsburgs, George. *A Calendar of Soviet Treaties, 1974–1980.* Dordrecht, Boston, Lancaster: Martinus Nijhoff Publishers, 1987. Pp. xix, 666. Dfl.425; $210; £131.

Remiro Brotons, Antonio. *Derecho Internacional Público. II. Derecho de los Tratados.* Madrid: Tecnos, 1987. Pp. 550. Indexes.

Sciso, Elena. *Gli Accordi Internazionali Confliggenti.* Bari: Cacucci Editore, 1986. Pp. xvi, 406. Indexes. L. 32,000.

Private International Law

Proceedings of the Extraordinary Session, 14 to 30 October 1985: Diplomatic Conference on the law applicable to contracts for the international sale of goods. Edited by the Permanent Bureau of the Hague Conference on private international law. The Hague: Netherlands Government Printing Office, 1987. Pp. 801.

U.S. Law & Foreign Relations

Diebold, William, Jr. (ed.). *Bilateralism, Multilateralism and Canada in U.S. Trade Policy.* Cambridge, Mass.: Ballinger Publishing Company, 1988. Pp. xviii, 206. Index. $16.95.

Farer, Tom. *The Grand Strategy of the United States in Latin America.* New Brunswick and Oxford: Transaction Books, 1988. Pp. xxxii, 294. Index. $39.95.

Forsythe, David P. *Human Rights and U.S. Foreign Policy: Congress Reconsidered.* Gainesville: University of Florida Press, 1988. Pp. xii, 224. Index. $24.

House, H. Wayne (ed.). *Restoring the Constitution, 1787–1987: Essays in Celebration of the Bicentennial.* Dallas: Probe Books, 1987. Pp. xiii, 350. Indexes.

Sanchez, James Joseph. *Index to the Tower Commission Report.* Jefferson, N.C., and London: McFarland & Company, Inc., Publishers, 1987. Pp. vi, 57. $8.95.

Development

Akinrinade, Olusola, and J. Kurt Barling (eds.). *Economic Development in Africa: International Efforts, Issues and Prospects.* London: Pinter Publishers, 1987. Pp. x, 266. Index. $30. Distributed by Columbia University Press.

Anthony, Constance G. *Mechanization and Maize: Agriculture and the Politics of Technology Transfer in East Africa.* New York: Columbia University Press, 1988. Pp. xiv, 178. Index. $25.

El-Naggar, Said (ed.). *Adjustment Policies and Development Strategies in the Arab World.* Papers presented at a seminar held in Abu Dhabi, United Arab Emirates, February 16–18, 1987. Washington: International Monetary Fund, 1987. Pp. ix, 200. $12.

Martirena-Mantel, Ana María (ed.). *External Debt, Savings, and Growth in Latin America.* Washington: International Monetary Fund; Buenos Aires: Instituto Torcuato di Tella, 1987. Pp. xv, 207. $12.

Shihata, Ibrahim F. I. *MIGA and Foreign Investment: Origins, Operations, Policies and Basic Documents of the Multilateral Investment Guarantee Agency.* Dordrecht, Boston, Lancaster: Martinus Nijhoff Publishers, 1988. Pp. xvi, 540. Index. Dfl.295; $152; £89.50.

Snyder, Francis, and Peter Slinn (eds.). *International Law of Development: Comparative Perspectives.* Abingdon, Eng.: Professional Books, 1987. Pp. ix, 322. Index. £27.50, cloth; £19.50, paper.

Telecommunications

Communications (Includes Telecommunications). Thesaurus Acroasium, Volume XV (Session 1984). Thessaloniki: Institute of Public International Law and International Relations of Thessaloniki, 1987. Pp. 530. $125.

Regional, Foreign & Comparative Law & Politics

Antieau, Chester James. *The Practice of Extraordinary Remedies: Habeas Corpus and the Other Common Law Writs.* 2 vols. New York, London, Rome: Oceana Publications, Inc., 1987. Pp. xxxiv, 844. Index in vol. 2. $175/set.

Butler, W. E. (ed.). *Yearbook on Socialist Legal Systems, 1987.* Dobbs Ferry, N.Y.: Transnational Publishers, Inc., 1988. Pp. x, 404. $67.

Butler, William E., Peter B. Maggs, and John B. Quigley, Jr. (eds.). *Law After Revolution.* New York, London, Rome: Oceana Publications, Inc., 1988. Pp. xiii, 247. $40.

De Vree, Johan K., Peter Coffey and Richard H. Lauwaars (eds.), in collaboration with Max Jansen, Alfred E. Pijpers and Edmond L. M. Völker. *Towards a European Foreign Policy: Legal, Economic and Political Dimensions.* Records of a Colloquium held by the Europa Institute of the University of Amsterdam on the Occasion of its 25th Anniversary. Dordrecht, Boston, Lancaster: Martinus Nijhoff Publishers, 1987. Pp. xii, 388. Index. Dfl.185; $95; £52.

Dickson, Michael G., Wolfgang Rosener and Paul M. Storm (eds.). *Security on Movable Property and Receivables in Europe: The principal forms of security in the European Community (except Greece) and Switzerland.* Published for the Association Européenne d'Etudes Juridiques et Fiscales. Oxford: ESC Publishing Limited, 1988. Pp. 227. £27.50.

Greiter, Ivo. *How To Get Your Money in Foreign Countries: A Survey of Court Costs and Lawyer's Fees in 151 Countries.* Deventer: Kluwer Law and Taxation Publishers, 1988. Pp. ix, 253. Dfl.145; £43.50; $72.50.

Hanami, T., and R. Blanpain (eds.). *Industrial Conflict Resolution in Market Economies: A study of Canada, Great Britain and Sweden.* Deventer: Kluwer Law and Taxation Publishers, 1987. Pp. xii, 253. Index. Dfl.148; £44.50; $77.

Mény, Yves, and Vincent Wright (eds.), with the editorial assistance of Martin Rhodes. *The Politics of Steel: Western Europe and the Steel Industry in the Crisis Years (1974–1984).* Berlin and New York: Walter de Gruyter, 1987. Pp. ix, 811. Index. DM 298.

Moser, Michael J. (ed.). *Foreign Trade, Investment, and the Law in the People's Republic of China* (2d ed.). Hong Kong, Oxford, New York: Oxford University Press, 1987. Pp. x, 603. Index. $45.

Schneider, Eberhard. *Moskaus Leitlinie für das Jahr 2000: Die Neufassung von Programm und Statut der KPdSU.* Munich: Günter Olzog Verlag, 1987. Pp. 124.

Simmonds, Kenneth R., Brian H. W. Hill and Sigvard Jarvin (eds.). *Commercial Arbitration Law in Asia and the Pacific.* Paris: ICC Publishing SA; New York, London, Rome: Oceana Publications, Inc., 1987.

Spanger, Hans-Joachim, and Lothar Brock. *Die beiden deutschen Staaten in der Dritten Welt: Die Entwicklungspolitik der DDR—eine Herausforderung für die Bundesrepublik Deutschland?* Wiesbaden: Westdeutscher Verlag, 1987. Pp. 428.

Streeten, Paul (ed.). *Beyond Adjustment: The Asian Experience.* Washington: International Monetary Fund, 1988. Pp. xii, 274. $15.

Thomas, James Burrows. *Judicial Ethics in Australia.* North Ryde, N.S.W.: The Law Book Company Limited, 1988. Pp. xxxii, 126. Index. $25.

Waterkamp, Dietmar. *Handbuch zum Bildungswesen der DDR.* Berlin: Berlin Verlag Arno Spitz, 1987. Pp. 438. Index.

Miscellaneous

House, Peter W., and Roger D. Shull. *Rush to Policy: Using Analytic Techniques in Public Sector Decision Making.* New Brunswick and Oxford: Transaction Books, 1988. Pp. xi, 219. Index. $34.95.

Pannick, David. *Judges.* Oxford and New York: Oxford University Press, 1987. Pp. vii, 255. Index. $21.95.

INTERNATIONAL LEGAL MATERIALS*

CONTENTS

VOL. XXVII, NO. 3 (May 1988)

PAGE

TREATIES AND AGREEMENTS

Afghanistan–Pakistan–Union of Soviet Socialist Republics–United States: Accords on the *Peaceful Resolution of the Situation in Afghanistan*

I.L.M. Background/Content Summary ... 577

Afghanistan-Pakistan Agreement on the Principle of Mutual Relations, in Particular on Non-Interference and Non-Intervention ... 581

U.S.-U.S.S.R. Declaration of International Guarantees ... 584

Afghanistan-Pakistan Agreement on the Voluntary Return of Refugees ... 585

Agreement on the Interrelationships for the Settlement of the Situation relating to Afghanistan ... 587

Association of Southeast Asian Nations: Agreements and Statements from the Third Summit

I.L.M. Background/Content Summary ... 596

Manila Declaration of 1987 ... 603

Joint Press Statement ... 605

Protocol Amending Treaty of *Amity and Cooperation in Southeast Asia* ... 609

Treaty of *Amity and Cooperation in Southeast Asia* ... 610

Agreement for the *Promotion and Protection of Investments* ... 612

Revised Basic Agreement on *ASEAN Industrial Joint Ventures* ... 615

Protocol on *Improvements on Extension of Tariff Preferences* under the ASEAN Preferential Trading Arrangements ... 619

Memorandum of Understanding on *Standstill and Rollback on Non-Tariff Barriers* among ASEAN Countries ... 622

Contracting Parties to the Convention for the *Prevention of Marine Pollution from Land-Based Sources:* Protocol Amending the Convention

I.L.M. Background/Content Summary ... 625

Text of Protocol ... 626

International Civil Aviation Organization: Protocol for the *Suppression of Unlawful Acts of Violence at Airports Serving International Civil Aviation*

I.L.M. Background/Content Summary ... 627

Text of Protocol ... 628

International Labour Conference: Conventions Adopted at Its Seventy-fourth (Maritime) Session

I.L.M. Background/Content Summary ... 631

Convention concerning *Seafarers' Welfare at Sea and in Port* ... 633

Convention concerning *Health Protection and Medical Care of Seafarers* ... 641

Convention concerning *Social Security for Seafarers* (Revised) ... 649

Convention concerning the *Repatriation of Seafarers* (Revised) ... 661

International Maritime Organization: Convention and Protocol from the International Conference on the *Suppression of Unlawful Acts against the Safety of Maritime Navigation*

I.L.M. Background/Content Summary ... 668

* ILM subscription, $100; concessionary rate to ASIL members, $50. Address orders to ILM, 2223 Massachusetts Ave., NW, Wash., D.C. 20008. Outside U.S., please add $6.50.

Convention for the Suppression of Unlawful Acts against the Safety of Maritime Navigation 672
Protocol for the Suppression of Unlawful Acts against the Safety of Fixed Platforms Located on the Continental Shelf 685

International Maritime Satellite Organization: Amendments to the *Convention and Operating Agreement of INMARSAT*
I.L.M. Background/Content Summary 691
Amendments to Convention 693
Amendments to Operating Agreement 694

Sweden–Union of Soviet Socialist Republics: Agreement on *Principles for the Delimitation of Sea Areas in the Baltic Sea*
I.L.M. Background/Content Summary 695
Agreement 695

United Nations: Protocols to the 1979 Convention on *Long-Range Transboundary Air Pollution*
I.L.M. Background/Content Summary 698
Protocol on *Long-Term Financing of the Co-operative Programme for Monitoring and Evaluation of the Long-Range Transmission of Air Pollutants in Europe* (EMP) ... 701
Protocol on the *Reduction of Sulphur Emissions* or Their Transboundary Fluxes by at Least 30 per cent 707

DOCUMENTS ON THE CONTROVERSY SURROUNDING THE CLOSING OF THE PALESTINE LIBERATION ORGANIZATION OBSERVER MISSION TO THE UNITED NATIONS
I.L.M. Contents and Introductory Note 712
U.S. *Foreign Relations* Appropriations Act for 1988 and 1989 (Includes the *Anti-Terrorism Act* of 1987) 715
U.N. *General Assembly Resolutions* concerning Controversy 770
U.N. *Secretary-General's Reports* concerning Controversy 779
U.S. Complaint Filed in the U.S. District Court for the Southern District of New York (*United States v. Palestine Liberation Organization*) and Response to Court's Request about Arbitration 789
I.C.J. Order and Advisory Opinion on the *Applicability of the Obligation to Arbitrate* under Section 21 of the U.N. Headquarters Agreement of 26 June 1947 800

OTHER DOCUMENTS
Second International Conference on the Protection of the North Sea: Ministerial Declaration Calling for *Reduction of Pollution* 835

RECENT ACTIONS REGARDING TREATIES TO WHICH THE UNITED STATES IS A PARTY 849
RECENT ACTIONS REGARDING TREATIES TO WHICH THE UNITED STATES IS NOT A PARTY 856
NOTICE OF OTHER RECENT DOCUMENTS (not reproduced) 857

LIFE MEMBERS OF THE AMERICAN SOCIETY OF INTERNATIONAL LAW 1987–1988

Gerald Aksen
Stanley Anderson
Masahiko Asada
Calvin A. Behle
Richard S. S. Bright
John C. Brooks
Ian Brownlie
John Carey
Chin-Yung Chao
Stephen S. F. Chen
Max Chopnick
J. G. Clarke
H. Alberta Colclaser
Carter K. Combe
Rebecca J. Cook
Jorge Antonio De Marzi
Dermott J. Devine
John E. Donnelly
Peter D. Ehrenhaft
Robert Eikel
Richard J. Erickson
Eleanor H. Finch
Richard I. Fine
Roger D. Fisher
Stefan Forch
Carl Mason Franklin
Gaudencio Garcia
Moti Lal Govila
Robert T. Greig
Joseph P. Griffin
Richard Kennedy Guelff
Judith R. Hall
Robert D. Hayton
Dan F. Henderson
Robert E. Herzstein
Gary N. Horlick
Christopher C. Joyner
William S. Kenney
Yoshito Kita
Elizabeth Lay
Monroe Leigh
Frankie Fook-lu Leung
Cynthia C. Lichtenstein
Mrs. Brunson MacChesney
Myres Smith McDougal
Samuel Pyeatt Menefee
John M. Metzger
Clifford L. Michel
James A. R. Nafziger
Andre W. G. Newburg
J. D. Nyhart
Hisashi Owada
Mauricio Perez-Badell
Hernán Pérez Loose
Ellis L. Phillips
Jane M. Picker
Robert J. Radway
Charles S. Rhyne
Elliot L. Richardson
Alfred P. Rubin
Mark Sandstrom
Tetsuo Sato
Oscar Schachter
Cabot Sedgwick
Yukio Shimada
William I. Shore
Anne Patricia Simons
Dwight J. Simpson
Owen Meredith Smaw
Earl A. Snyder
Jane Sommerich
John H. Spencer
Henry J. Steiner
Edward P. Torrey
Tullio Treves
J. W. van der Zanden
L. W. Wadsworth
Edith Brown Weiss
Elmer E. Welty
Ulrich Woelker
C. U. Zachrisson
Peaches Zaphiriou

SUPPORTING AND CONTRIBUTING MEMBERS OF THE AMERICAN SOCIETY OF INTERNATIONAL LAW 1987–1988

SUPPORTING

Mitchell Brock
Charles N. Brower
Alexander D. Calhoun
William Gilbert Carter
Anthony A. D'Amato
Robert MacCrate
William B. Matteson
Covey T. Oliver
George M. Pavia
Walter S. Surrey
Peter W. Thornton
Peter D. Trooboff
Jack G. Wasserman
Basil S. Yanakakis

CONTRIBUTING

Richard L. Abbott
Richard B. M. Abrams
Richard C. Allison
Manuel R. Angulo
Steven Wright Baker
J. Truman Bidwell
Roman A. Bninski
John Arthur Boyd
George W. Brandt
Aron Broches
David Carliner
C. J. Chen
Donald E. Claudy
Philip F. Cohen
John P. Corrigan
Samuel S. Cross
Michael Danaher
John L. A. De Passalaqua
George C. Denney
James M. Denny
Edward A. Dragon
Malcolm T. Dungan
Richard A. Eastman
Aly H. Elghatit
F. Javier Fabregat
Philip A. Faix, Jr.
Stanley F. Farrar
Benjamin B. Ferencz
John Basil Gantt
David G. Gill
Michael A. Gleim
Joseph Gold
L. F. E. Goldie
Thomas R. Graham
Ernest A. Gross
James V. Hackney
Herbert J. Hansell
Joel B. Harris
Thomas E. Haven
H. Healy
Cecil Hunt
Oliver T. Johnson
Joseph S. Kaplan
Charles J. Keever
Lee A. Kimball
Paul L. Laskin
James Leitner
Robert T. Lemon, II
Edwin Deane Leonard
Jacques L. Leroy
David M. Levitan
George N. Lindsay
Carlos A. Lopez-Guevara
G. Lorinczi
Ralph M. McDowell
A. F. Maulsby
Gerald D. Morgan
Frank E. Nattier
Franz M. Oppenheimer
Guillermo F. Peroni
Jose Martins Pinheiro Neto
Willis L. M. Reese
A. R. Richstein
Bruce L. Rockwood
James F. Sams
J. P. Schwebel
Charles M. Spofford
Samuel A. Stern
Isaac N. P. Stokes
Robert M. Thomas, Jr.
Robert B. von Mehren
Paul C. Warnke
John Stowell Williams
F. L. Wiswall
Richard Young

AMERICAN SOCIETY OF INTERNATIONAL LAW

Be sure to check membership type on reverse side.

______________________________ Member, U.S. Bar?______ State:______ Year______

ame (please print)

______________________________ Firm, School or Other Affiliation:______________

ailing Address

______________________________ Signature:______________________________

treet, P.O. Box, etc.

____

ity, State, Zip

____

ountry Phone

Please start my membership January 1, ________. Membership is on a calendar year basis, and includes the *Journal* and the ASIL *Newsletter.* Check below for special rate on *Proceedings* or *International Legal Materials.* Student members receive, in addition to these materials, the International Law Students Association *NEWSLETTER.*

] *Proceedings of the Annual Meeting,* at $15.

] *International Legal Materials.* Subscription at special member rate of $50 (plus $6.50 for mailing outside U.S.A.) for six issues per year.

ERIFICATION OF STUDENT STATUS. The following form may be completed by a professor or administrative officer of your school.
hereby certify that the above applicant is regularly registered in (school):

______________________________ Completion Year__________

igned______________________ Title______________ Date__________

$__________ **Amount Enclosed** (U.S. Dollars)(Include Contributions and Publications Order Payment).

AMERICAN SOCIETY OF INTERNATIONAL LAW

Be sure to check membership type on reverse side.

______________________________ Member, U.S. Bar?______ State:______ Year______

ame (please print)

______________________________ Firm, School or Other Affiliation:______________

ailing Address

______________________________ Signature:______________________________

treet, P.O. Box, etc.

____

ity, State, Zip

____

ountry Phone

Please start my membership January 1, ________. Membership is on a calendar year basis, and includes the *Journal* and the ASIL *Newsletter.* Check below for special rate on *Proceedings* or *International Legal Materials.* Student members receive, in addition to these materials, the International Law Students Association *NEWSLETTER.*

] *Proceedings of the Annual Meeting,* at $15.

] *International Legal Materials.* Subscription at special member rate of $50 (plus $6.50 for mailing outside U.S.A.) for six issues per year.

ERIFICATION OF STUDENT STATUS. The following form may be completed by a professor or administrative officer of your school.
hereby certify that the above applicant is regularly registered in (school):

______________________________ Completion Year__________

igned______________________ Title______________ Date__________

$__________ **Amount Enclosed** (U.S. Dollars)(Include Contributions and Publications Order Payment).

AMERICAN SOCIETY OF INTERNATIONAL LAW

Be sure to check membership type on reverse side.

______________________________ Member, U.S. Bar?______ State:______ Year______

ame (please print)

______________________________ Firm, School or Other Affiliation:______________

ailing Address

______________________________ Signature:______________________________

treet, P.O. Box, etc.

____

ity, State, Zip

____

ountry Phone

Please start my membership January 1, ________. Membership is on a calendar year basis, and includes the *Journal* and the ASIL *Newsletter.* Check below for special rate on *Proceedings* or *International Legal Materials.* Student members receive, in addition to these materials, the International Law Students Association *NEWSLETTER.*

] *Proceedings of the Annual Meeting,* at $15.

] *International Legal Materials.* Subscription at special member rate of $50 (plus $6.50 for mailing outside U.S.A.) for six issues per year.

ERIFICATION OF STUDENT STATUS. The following form may be completed by a professor or administrative officer of your school.
hereby certify that the above applicant is regularly registered in (school):

______________________________ Completion Year__________

igned______________________ Title______________ Date__________

$__________ **Amount Enclosed** (U.S. Dollars)(Include Contributions and Publications Order Payment).

Membership Status *(Check one)*

☐ **Regular Membership:**
$70 a year. Persons, regardless of nationality or profession, resident in a member country of the OECD (see below).

☐ **Special Members:**
$30 a year. Persons *not* resident in a member country of the OECD (see below).

☐ **Intermediate Members:**
$30 a year. Persons who are under 30 years of age at the time of application for membership may be Intermediate Members for the first three consecutive years of membership.
Date of Birth ____________________

Student Members (Mark appropriate box.)

☐ $20 a year, and certification of student status (see form on reverse). Includes free membership in International Law Students Association.

☐ $10 a year with certification of membership in International Law Students Association.

The member countries of the OECD are Australia, Austria, Belgium, Canada, Denmark, Federal Republic of Germany, Finland, France, Greece, Iceland, Ireland, Italy, Japan, Luxembourg, Netherlands, New Zealand, Norway, Portugal, Spain, Sweden, Switzerland, Turkey, United Kingdom, United States.

☐ **Contributing Members:**
$100 a year.

☐ **Supporting Members:**
$200 a year.

☐ **Annual Patron:**
$500 a year. Any individual or organization eligible for membership may become an Annual Patron for a contribution of at least $500.

☐ **Corporate Members:**
$1,500 a year. Any corporation, partnership, association, or other organization acceptable to the Executive Council is eligible for Corporate Membership.

☐ **Life Members:**
$1,000 payment (during 1988).

☐ **Patron:**
One-time contribution of $5,000.

☐ **Retired:**
$25 a year. Persons who are retired and who are 70 years of age or older.

Check Interest Groups in which you would l to participate, and enclose fee listed.

☐ $5 a year. Antarctica Law, Politics and Reso Policy (31)
☐ $5 a year. Dispute Resolution in Internatio Commercial Contracts (32)
☐ $5 a year. Indigenous Rights (33)
☐ $7.50 a year. International Economic Law (
☐ $5 a year. International Environmental Law
☐ $5 a year. International Human Rights (36)
☐ $5 a year. International Organizations (37)
☐ $5 a year. Private International Law (38)
☐ $5 a year. Law in the Pacific Region (39)
☐ $10 a year. International Space Law (40)
☐ $5 a year. Women in International Law (41
☐ $5 a year. Wildlife Law (42)

Membership Status *(Check one)*

☐ **Regular Membership:**
$70 a year. Persons, regardless of nationality or profession, resident in a member country of the OECD (see below).

☐ **Special Members:**
$30 a year. Persons *not* resident in a member country of the OECD (see below).

☐ **Intermediate Members:**
$30 a year. Persons who are under 30 years of age at the time of application for membership may be Intermediate Members for the first three consecutive years of membership.
Date of Birth ____________________

Student Members (Mark appropriate box.)

☐ $20 a year, and certification of student status (see form on reverse). Includes free membership in International Law Students Association.

☐ $10 a year with certification of membership in International Law Students Association.

The member countries of the OECD are Australia, Austria, Belgium, Canada, Denmark, Federal Republic of Germany, Finland, France, Greece, Iceland, Ireland, Italy, Japan, Luxembourg, Netherlands, New Zealand, Norway, Portugal, Spain, Sweden, Switzerland, Turkey, United Kingdom, United States.

☐ **Contributing Members:**
$100 a year.

☐ **Supporting Members:**
$200 a year.

☐ **Annual Patron:**
$500 a year. Any individual or organization eligible for membership may become an Annual Patron for a contribution of at least $500.

☐ **Corporate Members:**
$1,500 a year. Any corporation, partnership, association, or other organization acceptable to the Executive Council is eligible for Corporate Membership.

☐ **Life Members:**
$1,000 payment (during 1988).

☐ **Patron:**
One-time contribution of $5,000.

☐ **Retired:**
$25 a year. Persons who are retired and who are 70 years of age or older.

Check Interest Groups in which you would to participate, and enclose fee listed.

☐ $5 a year. Antarctica Law, Politics and Res Policy (31)
☐ $5 a year. Dispute Resolution in Internatic Commercial Contracts (32)
☐ $5 a year. Indigenous Rights (33)
☐ $7.50 a year. International Economic Law
☐ $5 a year. International Environmental La
☐ $5 a year. International Human Rights (36
☐ $5 a year. International Organizations (37
☐ $5 a year. Private International Law (38)
☐ $5 a year. Law in the Pacific Region (39)
☐ $10 a year. International Space Law (40)
☐ $5 a year. Women in International Law (4
☐ $5 a year. Wildlife Law (42)

Membership Status *(Check one)*

☐ **Regular Membership:**
$70 a year. Persons, regardless of nationality or profession, resident in a member country of the OECD (see below).

☐ **Special Members:**
$30 a year. Persons *not* resident in a member country of the OECD (see below).

☐ **Intermediate Members:**
$30 a year. Persons who are under 30 years of age at the time of application for membership may be Intermediate Members for the first three consecutive years of membership.
Date of Birth ____________________

Student Members (Mark appropriate box.)

☐ $20 a year, and certification of student status (see form on reverse). Includes free membership in International Law Students Association.

☐ $10 a year with certification of membership in International Law Students Association.

The member countries of the OECD are Australia, Austria, Belgium, Canada, Denmark, Federal Republic of Germany, Finland, France, Greece, Iceland, Ireland, Italy, Japan, Luxembourg, Netherlands, New Zealand, Norway, Portugal, Spain, Sweden, Switzerland, Turkey, United Kingdom, United States.

☐ **Contributing Members:**
$100 a year.

☐ **Supporting Members:**
$200 a year.

☐ **Annual Patron:**
$500 a year. Any individual or organization eligible for membership may become an Annual Patron for a contribution of at least $500.

☐ **Corporate Members:**
$1,500 a year. Any corporation, partnership, association, or other organization acceptable to the Executive Council is eligible for Corporate Membership.

☐ **Life Members:**
$1,000 payment (during 1988).

☐ **Patron:**
One-time contribution of $5,000.

☐ **Retired:**
$25 a year. Persons who are retired and who are 70 years of age or older.

Check Interest Groups in which you wo to participate, and enclose fee listed.

☐ $5 a year. Antarctica Law, Politics and Policy (31)
☐ $5 a year. Dispute Resolution in Intern Commercial Contracts (32)
☐ $5 a year. Indigenous Rights (33)
☐ $7.50 a year. International Economic L
☐ $5 a year. International Environmenta
☐ $5 a year. International Human Rights
☐ $5 a year. International Organizations
☐ $5 a year. Private International Law (3
☐ $5 a year. Law in the Pacific Region (3
☐ $10 a year. International Space Law (4
☐ $5 a year. Women in International Lav
☐ $5 a year. Wildlife Law (42)

WAR, AGGRESSION AND SELF-DEFENCE

Yoram Dinstein

Professor of International Law and Yanowicz Professor of Human Rights, Tel Aviv University

This book re-examines the topics of war, aggression and self-defence, as well as related issues, such as collective security and the use of force short of war.

The first part deals with such questions as: What is war? When does it commence and terminate? What is the difference between peace treaties, armistice agreements and cease-fires? Where can war be waged and what is the meaning of neutrality?

The focus of the discussion in the second part is the contemporary prohibition of the use of force and its standing as *jus cogens*. The meaning of aggression is explored. The concept of crimes against peace, which evolved in the *Nuremberg* trial, is examined. Some controversial implications of the illegality and criminality of war are analyzed.

The third part explores the concept of self-defence. The scope of armed attack, prior to the exercise of the right of self-defence, is investigated, distinguishing between attacks launched by a foreign State and those that are carried out from its territory by armed bands. Special attention is given to such disputed points as the legality of armed reprisals and the protection of nationals abroad.

324 pp., including Index, Table of Cases and Table of Treaties
Price: Hardback £52.00 (US $95.00)

Published February 1988
ISBN 0 949009 15 6

CHERNOBYL: LAW AND COMMUNICATION

edited by

Philippe J. Sands

Research Fellow in International Law at St. Catharine's College and Research Associate at the Research Centre for International Law, University of Cambridge

Chernobyl: Law and Communication brings together in full the up-to-date texts of the most important materials necessary for a comprehensive examination of the international law and communication issues arising from nuclear accidents with trans-boundary effects.

The texts reproduced include multilateral and bilateral treaties, non-binding acts of international organizations and private associations of scholars, and national legislation. Each text is introduced by a Note summarizing its background and main provisions, and is accompanied by a select bibliography.

In his Introduction the editor discusses the current law by reference to the texts. Both the texts and his conclusions will be a convenient reference work for those interested in international law, as well as in communication, environmental and nuclear issues.

346 pp., including Index
Price: Hardback £38.00 (US $75.00)

Published April 1988
ISBN 0 949009 22 9

Air Mail Postage £5.00 (US $8.00) per volume

Order from any bookshop or direct from
GROTIUS PUBLICATIONS LIMITED
P.O. Box 115, CAMBRIDGE, CB3 9BP, ENGLAND

Presenting
The American Law Institute's
long-awaited, comprehensive, two-volume

Restatement of the Law Third, Restatement of the Foreign Relations Law of the United States

covering both international law as it applies to the United States and domestic law that has substantial impact on the foreign relations of the United States.

Completely supersedes the 1965 Restatement and contains greatly expanded coverage of many topics, including:

- Jurisdiction
- International Dispute Settlement
- Cooperation in Law Enforcement
- The Law of the Sea and of the Environment
- Human Rights
- Selected Areas of International Economic Law
- The International Law of Remedies

The culmination of nearly a decade of labor by leading authorities in the field:

Chief Reporter
Louis Henkin, Columbia University School of Law, New York, New York

Associate Reporters
Andreas F. Lowenfeld, New York University School of Law, New York, New York
Louis B. Sohn, University of Georgia School of Law, Athens, Georgia
Detlev F. Vagts, Harvard Law School, Cambridge, Massachusetts

Destined to have a profound effect on the future course of both international and U.S. law and to become a basic and necessary reference source for practitioners, judges, government officials, and scholars.

$150.00 plus postage and handling ($2.25 for delivery within the U.S.; $5.90 for 4th class bulk rate delivery outside of the U.S.) 1987, 2 volumes: vol. 1 xxviii, 641 pp.; vol. 2 xxiv, 561 pp., hardbound, Order No. 5898.

Also available from The American Law Institute: **Federal Income Tax Project—International Aspects of United States Income Taxation,** *$90.00 plus postage and handling ($3.50 for delivery within the U.S.; $3.95 for 4th class bulk rate delivery outside of the U.S.) 1987, 499 pp., hardbound, Order No. 5897.*

To order, write The American Law Institute
attn: C. Lerner
4025 Chestnut Street
Philadelphia, Pennsylvania 19104

American Journal of International Law

October 1988
Vol. 82 No. 4

Published by
American Society of International Law

PATRONS OF THE SOCIETY

PATRONAGE, GIFTS AND BEQUESTS

Upon donation to the Society of $5,000 or more by gift or bequest, any member of the Society or individual eligible for membership may be elected a Patron of the Society. Upon donation of at least $5,000 in the name of a deceased person, such person may be elected a Patron posthumously.

Gifts and bequests may be made in the name of the American Society of International Law, Washington, D.C. Such contributions are deductible from federal returns for income, estate and gift tax purposes. The Society is incorporated by Act of Congress approved September 20, 1950 (64 Stat. 869).

MANLEY O. HUDSON MEDAL

The American Society of International Law bestows from time to time without regard to nationality a gold medal to commemorate the life work of Manley O. Hudson. Such awards are made for preeminent scholarship and achievement in international law and in the promotion of the establishment and maintenance of international relations on the basis of law and justice. Medals have been awarded to Manley O. Hudson (1956), Lord McNair (1959), Philip C. Jessup (1964), Charles De Visscher (1966), Paul Guggenheim (1970), Myres S. McDougal (1976), Eduardo Jiménez de Aréchaga (1978), Richard Reeve Baxter (1981), Oscar Schachter (1981), Hardy Cross Dillard (1982), Suzanne Bastid (1984), Marjorie M. Whiteman (1985) and Leo Gross (1986).

The AMERICAN JOURNAL OF INTERNATIONAL LAW (ISSN 0002-9300) is published quarterly, in January, April, July and October, and is supplied to all members of the American Society of International Law. Annual subscription rate to nonmembers is $50.00, plus $5.00 postage outside U.S.A. Available back numbers of AJIL will be supplied at $15.00 each.

EDITORIAL OFFICE:
NEW YORK UNIVERSITY SCHOOL OF LAW
40 WASHINGTON SQUARE SOUTH
NEW YORK, N.Y. 10012

BUSINESS OFFICE:
2223 MASSACHUSETTS AVENUE, N.W.
WASHINGTON, D.C. 20008-2864

Second-class postage paid at Washington, D.C. and at additional mailing office. POSTMASTER: If undeliverable, send notice on Form 3579 to the American Journal of International Law, 2223 Massachusetts Ave., N.W., Washington, D.C. 20008-2864.

Printed by Lancaster Press, Lancaster, Pa. 17603

AMERICAN JOURNAL OF INTERNATIONAL LAW

VOL. 82 **October 1988** **NO. 4**

CONTENTS

PAGE

Legitimacy in the International System *Thomas M. Franck* 705
Self-Executing Treaties *Jordan J. Paust* 760

Agora: The U.S. Decision Not to Ratify Protocol I to the Geneva Conventions on the Protection of War Victims (Cont'd)
The Rationale for the United States Decision *Abraham D. Sofaer* 784

Notes and Comments
Perestroika and International Law *John Quigley* 788
Correspondence 797

Contemporary Practice of the United States Relating to International Law *Marian Nash Leich* 803

International Decisions *Peter D. Trooboff* 816

Book Reviews and Notes *Edited by Detlev Vagts*
Recueil des Cours de l'Académie de Droit International de La Haye, 1983. 5 vols. (Alfred P. Rubin) 841
Gutiérrez Espada, Cesáreo, and Alfonso-Luis Calvo Caravaca. *Textos de Derecho internacional público* (Laura Bocalandro) 853
Bourguignon, Henry J. *Sir William Scott, Lord Stowell: Judge of the High Court of Admiralty, 1798–1828* (David J. Bederman) 854
Spinedi, Marina, and Bruno Simma (eds.). *United Nations Codification of State Responsibility* (Gordon A. Christenson) 858
Mériboute, Zidane. *La Codification de la succession d'Etats aux traités: Décolonisation, sécession, unification* (Keith Highet) 862
Wegen, Gerhard. *Vergleich und Klagerücknahme im internationalen Prozeß* (Ignaz Seidl-Hohenveldern) 865
Empell, Hans-Michael. *Die Kompetenzen des UN-Menschenrechtsausschusses im Staatenberichtsverfahren (Art. 40 des Internationalen Paktes über bürgerliche und politische Rechte)* (Julia B. Kokott) 868
Arend, Anthony Clark (ed.). *The United States and the Compulsory Jurisdiction of the International Court of Justice* (E. Lauterpacht) 870
Franck, Thomas M. *Judging the World Court* (E. Lauterpacht) 870
Thoolen, Hans, and Berth Verstappen. *Human Rights Missions: A study of the fact-finding practice of non-governmental organizations* (Diane F. Orentlicher) 873
Meron, Theodor. *Human Rights in Internal Strife: Their International Protection* (Howard S. Levie) 876
Gorbachev, Mikhail. *Perestroika. New Thinking for Our Country and the World* (Richard Szawlowski) 878
Feldbrugge, F. J. M. (ed.). *The Distinctiveness of Soviet Law* (John N. Hazard) 886

Blishchenko, I. P. (ed.). *Osvobodivshiesia strany i mezhdunarodnoe pravo* (John N. Hazard) 887
Soviet Year-Book of International Law, 1986 (John N. Hazard) 889
Cançado Trindade, Antônio Augusto. *Repertório da Prática Brasileira do Direito Internacional Público.* Vols. IV and V (G. E. do Nascimento e Silva) 891
Shen Yu, and Wei Jiajui. *Guojifa Xin Lingyu Jianlun* (Hungdah Chiu) 892
Liu Ding. *Guoji Jingifa* (Hungdah Chiu) 892
Shen Daming, Feng Datong and Zhao Hongxun. *Guoji Shangfa.* 2 vols. (Hungdah Chiu) 892
Liu Longheng. *Guoji Shuifa* (Hungdah Chiu) 893
Yao Meizhen. *Guoji Touzifa* (Hungdah Chiu) 893
Shen Yu. *Guoji Huobifa Gailun* (Hungdah Chiu) 893
Shen Daming, and Feng Datong. *Guoji Maoyifa* (Hungdah Chiu) 893
Qiu Zaiyu, and Zhang Jincao. *Xiandai Guojifa Jichu* (Hungdah Chiu) 894
Zhu Lisun *et al. Guoji Gongfa* (Hungdah Chiu) 894
Hu Wenzhi *et al. Guojifa Gailun* (Hungdah Chiu) 894
Wei Min *et al. Guojifa Gailun* (Hungdah Chiu) 894
de Vries, Margaret Garritsen. *Balance of Payments Adjustment, 1945 to 1986: The IMF Experience* (Charles P. Kindleberger) 895
Winham, Gilbert R. *International Trade and the Tokyo Round Negotiation* (Gary Hufbauer) 898
Bassiouni, M. Cherif (ed.). *International Criminal Law. Vol. II: Procedure; vol. III: Enforcement* (Burrus M. Carnahan) 899
Triggs, Gillian D. (ed.). *The Antarctic Treaty regime: Law, Environment and Resources* (Christopher C. Joyner) 903
von Münch, Ingo. *Internationales Seerecht* (Thomas F. Marsteller and Peter K. Hahn) 909
Foreign Relations of the United States, 1952–1954. Vol. XII: East Asia and the Pacific. Parts 1 and 2 (Elmer Plischke) 911
Blanchard, Margaret A. *Exporting the First Amendment: The Press-Government Crusade of 1945–1952* (Colleen Roach) 913

Briefer Notices: Simmonds, Hill and Jarvin (eds.), 918; Kirkpatrick (2 vols.), 918; Greiter, 918.
Books Received 919
International Legal Materials. Contents, Vol. XXVII, No. 4 (July 1988) 924
Table of Cases 926
Index 928

The American Journal of International Law

The views expressed in the articles, editorial comments, book reviews and notes, and other contributions which appear in AJIL are those of the individual authors and are not to be taken as representing the views of the Board of Editors or the American Society of International Law.

Manuscripts in triplicate may be sent to the Editor in Chief of AJIL, Professor Thomas M. Franck, New York University School of Law, 40 Washington Square South, New York, N.Y. 10012. All footnotes should be typed double space at the end of the manuscript. Please do not make multiple submissions to other journals. Persons making submissions are invited to indicate whether their manuscript is available on an IBM-PC diskette. AJIL uses WordPerfect 4.2. Subscriptions, orders for back numbers, correspondence with reference to AJIL and books for review should be sent to the AMERICAN JOURNAL OF INTERNATIONAL LAW (ISSN 0002-9300), 2223 Massachusetts Avenue, N.W., Washington, D.C. 20008-2864.

The American Society of International Law

The American Society of International Law was organized in 1906 "to foster the study of international law and to promote the establishment and maintenance of international relations on the basis of law and justice."

Society membership is open to all persons of whatever nationality and profession who are interested in its objectives. Dues are: regular, $70; special category, $30 for persons *not* resident in a member country of the Organisation for Economic Co-operation and Development; intermediate, $30; student, $20. Membership application form is printed at the back of each issue of AJIL.

OFFICERS OF THE SOCIETY, 1988–1989

LEGITIMACY IN THE INTERNATIONAL SYSTEM

*By Thomas M. Franck**

INTRODUCTION

The surprising thing about international law is that nations ever obey its strictures or carry out its mandates. This observation is made not to register optimism that the half-empty glass is also half full, but to draw attention to a pregnant phenomenon: that most states observe systemic rules much of the time in their relations with other states. That they should do so is much more interesting than, say, the fact that most citizens usually obey their nation's laws, because the international system is organized in a voluntarist fashion, supported by so little coercive authority. This unenforced rule system can obligate states to profess, if not always to manifest, a significant level of day-to-day compliance even, at times, when that is not in their short-term self-interest. The element or paradox attracts our attention and challenges us to investigate it, perhaps in the hope of discovering a theory that can illuminate more generally the occurrence of voluntary normative compliance and even yield a prescription for enhancing aspects of world order.

Before going further, however, it is necessary to enter a caveat. This essay attempts a study of why states obey laws in the absence of coercion. That is not the same quest as motivates the more familiar studies that investigate the sources of normative obligation.[1] The latter properly focus on the origins of rules—in treaties, custom, decisions of tribunals, *opinio juris*, state conduct, resolutions of international organizations, and so forth—to determine which sources, qua sources, are to be taken seriously, and how seriously to take them. Our object, on the other hand, is to determine why and under what circumstances a specific rule is obeyed. To be sure, the source of every rule—its *pedigree*, in the terminology of this essay—is *one* determinant of how strong its pull to compliance is likely to be. Pedigree, however, is far from being the only indicator of how seriously the rule will be taken, particularly if the rule conflicts with a state's perceived self-interest. Thus, other indicators are also a focus of this essay insofar as they determine the capacity of rules to affect state conduct.

* Editor in Chief. The author acknowledges the generous support of the Filomen D'Agostino and Max E. Greenberg Research Fund of New York University School of Law, the very helpful advice of his colleagues Paul Chevigny, Ronald Dworkin, David W. Kennedy, David Richards, Alfred Rubin, Michael Sharpston and Roberto Unger, and the unstinting research assistance of Steven Hawkins, Laurie Oberembt and William Richter. Particular thanks are due to several colleagues on the Board of Editors, and Ag. R.-J. Dupuy of the Collège de France, who have made profoundly useful suggestions.

[1] *See especially* Schachter, *Towards a Theory of International Obligation*, 8 VA. J. INT'L L. 300 (1968).

This essay posits that, in a community organized around rules, compliance is secured—to whatever degree it *is*—at least in part by perception of a rule as legitimate by those to whom it is addressed. Their perception of legitimacy will vary in degree from rule to rule and time to time. It becomes a crucial factor, however, in the capacity of any rule to secure compliance when, as in the international system, there are no other compliance-inducing mechanisms.

Legitimacy is used here to mean that quality of a rule *which derives from a perception on the part of those to whom it is addressed that it has come into being in accordance with right process*. Right process includes the notion of valid sources but also encompasses literary, socio-anthropological and philosophical insights. The elements of right process that will be discussed below are identified as affecting decisively the degree to which any rule is perceived as legitimate.

I. Why a Quest for Legitimacy?

Why study the teleology of law? What are laws *for*? What causes obedience? Such basic questions are the meat and potatoes of jurisprudential inquiry. Any legal system worth taking seriously must address such fundamentals. J. L. Brierly has speculated that jurisprudence, nowadays, regards international law as no more than "an attorney's mantle artfully displayed on the shoulders of arbitrary power" and "a decorous name for a convenience of the chancelleries."[2] That seductive epigram captures the still-dominant Austinian positivists' widespread cynicism towards the claim that the rules of the international system can be studied jurisprudentially.[3]

International lawyers have not taken this sort of marginalization lying down. However, their counterattack has been both feeble and misdirected, concentrating primarily on efforts to prove that international law is very similar to the positive law applicable within states.[4] This strategy has not been intellectually convincing, nor can it be empirically sustained once divine and naturalist sources of law are discarded in favor of positivism.

That international "law" is not law in the positivist sense may be irrefutable but is also irrelevant. Whatever label is attached to it, the normative structure of the international system is perfectly capable of being studied with a view to generating a teleological jurisprudence. Indeed, international law is the *best* place to study some of the fundamental teleological issues that

[2] J. Brierly, The Outlook for International Law 13 (1944) (quoting Sir Alfred Zimmern).

[3] Austin believed that law was the enforced command of a sovereign to a subject. J. Austin, The Province of Jurisprudence Determined (1832); *see also* Janis, *Jeremy Bentham and the Fashioning of "International Law,"* 78 AJIL 405, 410 (1984). This Austinian view has been widely shared by critics. See, however, H. L. A. Hart, The Concept of Law, ch. 10 (1961); and Williams, *International Law and the Controversy Concerning the Word 'Law,'* 22 Brit. Y.B. Int'l L. 146 (1945).

[4] For the best recent exposition of this view, see A. D'Amato, *Is International Law Really Law?*, in International Law: Process and Prospect 1 (1987).

arise not only in the international, but also in national legal systems. This makes it odd that it is not more frequently used as a field for investigation.

Up to a point, the Austinians are empirically right. The international system of states *is* fundamentally different from any national community of persons and of corporate entities. It is not helpful to ignore those differences or to cling to the reifying notion that states are "persons" analogous to the citizens of a nation. Some of the differences are of great potential interest. In a nation, Machiavelli noted, "there cannot be good laws where there are not good arms."[5] In the international community, however, there are ample signs that rules unenforced by good arms are yet capable of obligating states and quite often even achieve habitual compliance. The Austinians, beginning with a defensible empirical observation about the difference between national laws and international rules, deduce from the difference that rules governing conduct which are not "law" in the positivist sense cannot usefully be studied as a system of community-based obligations. It is *this* deduction—not the empirical observation—which is wrong.

Indeed, it is precisely the curious paradox of obligation in the international rule system that should whet our speculative appetite, provoking the opening, not the closing, of jurisprudential inquiry. *Why should rules, unsupported by an effective structure of coercion comparable to a national police force, nevertheless elicit so much compliance, even against perceived self-interest, on the part of sovereign states?* Perhaps finding an answer to this question can help us to find a key to a better, yet realistic, world order. The answer, if there is one, may also incidentally prove useful in designing more widely obeyed, less coerced, laws for ordering the lives of our cities and states.

A series of events connected with the role of the U.S. Navy in protecting U.S.-flagged vessels in the Persian Gulf serves to illustrate the paradoxical phenomenon of uncoerced compliance in a situation where the rule conflicts with perceived self-interest. Early in 1988, the Department of Defense became aware of a ship approaching the gulf with a load of Chinese-made Silkworm missiles en route to Iran. The Department believed the successful delivery of these potent weapons would increase materially the danger to both protected and protecting U.S. ships in the region. It therefore argued for permission to intercept the delivery. The Department of State countered that such a search and seizure on the high seas, under the universally recognized rules of war and neutrality, would constitute aggressive blockade, an act tantamount to a declaration of war against Iran. In the event, the delivery ship and its cargo of missiles were allowed to pass. Deference to systemic rules had won out over tactical advantage in the internal struggle for control of U.S. policy.

Why should this have been so? In the absence of a world government and a global coercive power to enforce its laws, why did the U.S. Government, with its evident power to do as it wished, choose to "play by the rules" despite the considerable short-term strategic advantage to be gained by seizing the Silkworms before they could be delivered? Why did preeminent

[5] N. MACHIAVELLI, THE PRINCE 71 (L. de Alvarez rev. ed. 1981).

American power defer to the rules of the sanctionless system? At least part of the answer to this question, quietly given by the State Department to the Department of Defense, is that the international rules of neutrality have attained a high degree of recognized legitimacy and must not be violated lightly. Specifically, they are well understood, enjoy a long pedigree and are part of a consistent framework of rules—the *jus in bello*—governing and restraining the use of force in conflicts. To violate a set of rules of such widely recognized legitimacy, the State Department argued, would transform the U.S. posture in the gulf from that of a neutral to one of belligerency. That could end Washington's role as an honest broker seeking to promote peace negotiations. It would also undermine the carefully crafted historic "rules of the game" applicable to wars, rules that are widely perceived to be in the interest of all states.

Such explanations for deferring to a rule in preference to taking a short-term advantage are the policymaker's equivalent of the philosopher's quest for a theory of legitimacy. Washington voluntarily chose to obey a rule in the Persian Gulf conflict. Yet it does not always obey all international rules. Some rules are harder to disobey—more persuasive in their pull to compliance—than others. This is known intuitively by the legions of Americans who deliberately underreport the dutiable price of goods purchased abroad, and by the aficionados who smuggle Cuban cigars into the country behind pocket handkerchiefs, but would not otherwise commit criminal fraud. That some rules *in themselves* seem to exert more pull to compliance than others is the starting point in the search for a theory of legitimacy.

The questions raised by such examples of obedience and disobedience, however, are more interesting when examined in the context of the international than of the national community. It is the voluntariness of international compliance that heightens the mystery and lures us with the possibility of discovery. Thus, while the Austinians are right in pointing to important differences between the place of law in national society and the place of rules in the society of nations, those differences do not justify the closing of the international rule system to jurisprudential inquiry.

Indeed, such inquiry into the international system ought to be aided by the insights developed by the study of national and subnational communities. Research into the teleology of national legal systems has led the way to a recognition of the role of legitimacy, as distinct from coercion, as the key to legal order and systematic obedience. While most students of national systems, except perhaps for a few utopians such as Foucault,[6] agree with Machiavelli that governance requires *some* exercise of power by an elite supported by coercive force, few any longer believe the Austinians' claim that this necessary condition is also a sufficient one. Having reached this

[6] Foucault rejects all notions of dominance, whether embodied in theories of sovereignty (divine rule, autocracy, "public rights" and so forth) or embraced in "mechanisms of discipline," including, for example, "power that is tied to scientific knowledge." He visualizes, instead, a new form of "right," which is antidisciplinarian and divorced from concepts of sovereignty. M. FOUCAULT, POWER/KNOWLEDGE: SELECTED INTERVIEWS AND OTHER WRITINGS 106–08 (C. Gordon ed. 1980).

conclusion, most students of law, power and structure in society have sought to identify other characteristics that conduce to the rule of law. Ronald Dworkin identifies three such characteristics: *fairness*, *justice* and *integrity* (the last being a principled, more sensitive variant of consistency).[7] Jürgen Habermas emphasizes the role of discursive validation, following the tradition of Aeschylus and Aristotle.[8] Important scholarship on contract theory has demonstrated that coercion need not be an essential element in ensuring the efficacy of a contract, which is more accurately seen as self-enforcing obligation.[9] In fact, much recent work focusing on the phenomenon of obedience and obligation in national societies concerns itself primarily with noncoercive factors conducing to consensual compliance.

While some such studies have emphasized the role of strategic concepts that gain voluntary compliance by mutualizing advantage, others, beginning with the seminal work of Max Weber,[10] have emphasized the role of *legitimacy* and *legitimation*. Weber's analysis stressed process legitimacy. He hypothesized that rules tend to achieve compliance when they, themselves, comply with secondary rules about how and by whom rules are to be made and interpreted. In his view, a sovereign's command is more likely to be obeyed if the subject perceives both the rule and the ruler as legitimate. Somewhat different concepts of legitimacy have been developed by Habermas[11] and by neo-Marxist philosophers.[12] Oscar Schachter, working in the field of international normativity, has elucidated and emphasized the

[7] R. DWORKIN, LAW'S EMPIRE 176–224 (1986).

[8] According to Habermas:

> Legitimacy means that there are good arguments for a political order's claim to be recognized as right and just; a legitimate order deserves recognition. *Legitimacy means a political order's worthiness to be recognized.* This definition highlights the fact that legitimacy is a contestable validity claim; the stability of the order of domination (also) depends on its (at least) de facto recognition. Thus, historically as well as analytically, the concept is used above all in situations in which the legitimacy of an order is disputed, in which, as we say, legitimation problems arise. One side denies, the other asserts legitimacy. This is a *process* . . . .

J. HABERMAS, COMMUNICATION AND THE EVOLUTION OF SOCIETY 178–79 (T. McCarthy trans. 1979).

[9] Kronman, *Contract Law and the State of Nature,* 1 J. L., ECON. & ORG. 5 (1985).

[10] Weber postulates the validity of an order in terms of its being regarded by the obeying public "as in some way obligatory or exemplary" for its members because, at least in part, it defines "a model" which is "binding" and to which the actions of others "will in fact conform." At least in part, this legitimacy is perceived as adhering to the authority issuing an order, as opposed to the qualities of legitimacy that inhere in an order itself. This distinction between *an* order (command) and *the* order (authority) is easily overlooked but fundamental. 1 M. WEBER, ECONOMY AND SOCIETY: AN OUTLINE OF INTERPRETIVE SOCIOLOGY 31 (G. Roth & C. Wittich eds. 1968). For a critique, see Hyde, *The Concept of Legitimacy in the Sociology of Law,* 1983 WIS. L. REV. 379.

[11] "What are accepted as reasons and have the power to produce consensus . . . depends on the *level of justification* required in a given situation." J. HABERMAS, *supra* note 8, at 183.

[12] Hyde, for example, believes that the concept of legitimacy should be abandoned and replaced by investigation of "rational grounds for action." Hyde, *supra* note 10, at 380. *See also* Bos, *Friede Durch Volkerrecht—Oder Durch Volkerlegitimitat?,* 17 NEDERLANDS TIJDSCHRIFT VOOR INTERNATIONAAL RECHT 113 (1970).

role of "competence and authority" in endowing a rule with capacity to obligate.[13] All have in common, however, their emphasis on noncoercive factors as conducing to rule-compliant behavior.

It thus appears that, despite its residual Austinian propensities, national jurisprudence has quite a bit to say to the international system precisely because there is empirical evidence that, in both systems, noncoercive factors play an important part in conducing to rule/law-compliant behavior. The special value to both national and international jurisprudential inquiry of studying the international system, however, lies in its unalloyed noncoercive state. While the dependence of the international system on voluntary compliance is often (and justly) perceived as a weakness, it happens to afford a singular opportunity. Critics of efforts to study legitimacy as a noncoercive factor conducing to compliance in national legal systems have been able to argue that this factor necessarily eludes researchers because it cannot be isolated from other, authoritarian, elements compelling obedience.[14] That critique loses its force, however, in the international context. Thus, the operation of the noncoercive element, or, specifically, *legitimacy*, becomes easier to isolate and study in the interstate system than in societies of persons, where the coercive sovereign always lurks in the background.

Yet there is a stronger motivation for studying legitimacy in the international system than the academic objective of creating a bridge from national to international speculative jurisprudence. A teleology that makes legitimacy its hypothetical center envisages—for purposes of speculative inquiry—the possibility of an orderly community functioning by consent and validated obligation, rather than by coercion. This is surely the realistic approach to an international jurisprudential teleology: one that examines the objective properties of the global rule system so as to study whether and how it may advance or perfect itself in accordance with the propensities of those observable properties. That inquiry begins with the unexplained, yet evident, paradox that autonomous actors systematically engage in rule-determined conduct, not infrequently in the face of a strong countervailing desire to pursue realizable short-term gratification in violation of the rules.

Admittedly, the rule system of the community of states is far from perfected: absence of rules and disobedience continue to be important dissonant features. But it is too readily assumed that these deficiencies are attributable primarily to the lack of an Austinian sovereign with police powers. The weakness of this explanation is its failure to account for significant deviance: that many rules are obeyed much of the time. What if, instead, rule disobedience, or a rule void, were attributable—in whole or in part—not to the absence of coercive power to enforce the rules but to the perceived lack of legitimacy of the actual or proposed rules themselves and of the rule-making and rule-applying institutions of the international system? Put another way, perhaps failure to obey the rules can best be studied through a better understanding of its opposite: voluntary deference to them.

[13] Schachter, *supra* note 1, at 309.

[14] Hyde, *supra* note 10, at 411–17, 422–25.

That might be rather good news. Since the world is not about to create a global supersovereign with overriding enforcement powers, it might be encouraging to know that these are not the prerequisites of a developed, functioning international community. It would be even more helpful to know that the global system of rules could be further refined and developed, even in the absence of the Austinian factors, by augmenting the legitimacy of rules and institutions. It would spur the social imagination to realize that the creation of a global regime with enforcement power might only be the final culmination of a process capable of gradually perfecting the community, not the sine qua non for system building.

If such a noncoercive, or voluntarist, community were a reasonable goal of the study of legitimation, the resulting society of states would still not resemble the modern nation. In place of coercion, there is only the claim to compliance, based on social entitlement, which a legitimate rule makes on, and on behalf of, all members of the community. In this sense, the international community more closely resembles a membership club with house rules. Membership confers a desirable status, which is manifested when the members have internalized socially functional and status-rooted privileges and duties. Membership is reinforced by valid governance, shared experience, reciprocal gestures of deference and recognition, common rituals, mature common expectations and the successful pursuit of shared goals. Obedience to law, in contrast, at least in part is a recognition of the coercive power of the organized state.

In both the state and the voluntarist international system, obedience to commands is evidence of the existence of an organized community. The international community, however, does not closely resemble the modern state, precisely because the activist state exists to issue and enforce sovereign commands, while the more passive international community exists to legitimize, or withhold legitimacy from, institutions, rules and its members and their conduct. The legitimacy of a rule, or of a rule-making or rule-applying institution, is a function of the perception of those in the community concerned that the rule, or the institution, has come into being endowed with legitimacy: that is, in accordance with right process.

What "right process" means in practice is the subject of the remainder of this essay. Pursuing this line of inquiry, we will focus most of our attention on the legitimacy of *rules*, although attention will also have to be paid to the legitimacy of those institutions and processes through which the rules come into being. In our inquiry we will begin with the rules themselves: their literary structure, origins, internal consistency, reasonableness, utility in achieving stated ends and connection to the overall rule system, and the extent to which their origins and application comport with the international community's "rules about rules." It is the underlying hypothesis of this essay that rules, to varying degrees, contain the determining elements of their own legitimacy.

If legitimacy can be studied, it can also be deliberately nourished. There lies the practical rationale of this inquiry. Someday, perhaps, the international system will come to have law and legal institutions that mirror their domestic counterparts. But that is not now, and it is not likely to be in the foreseeable future. H. L. A. Hart put it more gently: "though it is consistent with the usage of the last 150 years to use the expression 'law' here, the absence of an international legislature, courts with compulsory jurisdiction, and centrally organized sanctions ha[s] inspired misgivings, at any rate in the breasts of legal theorists."[15] Such misgivings, however, are not a cause for despair, nor should they be the end of the road of theoretical inquiry. On the contrary, the misgivings are valid but, for that very reason, are precisely the right starting point in the search for those elements which conduce to the growth of an orderly voluntarist international community and system of rules.

Four elements—the indicators of rule legitimacy in the community of states—are identified and studied in this essay. They are *determinacy*, *symbolic validation*, *coherence* and *adherence* (to a normative hierarchy). To the extent rules exhibit these properties, they appear to exert a strong pull on states to comply with their commands. To the extent these elements are not present, rules seem to be easier to avoid by a state tempted to pursue its short-term self-interest. This is not to say that the legitimacy of a rule can be deduced solely by counting how often it is obeyed or disobeyed. While its legitimacy may exert a powerful pull on state conduct, yet other pulls may be stronger in a particular circumstance. The chance to take a quick, decisive advantage may overcome the counterpull of even a highly legitimate rule. In such circumstances, legitimacy is indicated not by obedience, but by the discomfort disobedience induces in the violator. (Student demonstrations sometimes are a sensitive indicator of such discomfort.) The variable to watch is not compliance but the strength of the compliance pull, whether or not the rule achieves actual compliance in any one case.

Each rule has an inherent pull power that is independent of the circumstances in which it is exerted, and that varies from rule to rule. This pull power is its index of legitimacy. For example, the rule that makes it improper for one state to infiltrate spies into another state in the guise of diplomats is formally acknowledged by almost every state, yet it enjoys so low a degree of legitimacy as to exert virtually no pull towards compliance.[16] As Schachter observes, "some 'laws,' though enacted properly, have so low a degree of probable compliance that they are treated as 'dead letters' and . . . some treaties, while properly concluded, are considered 'scraps of paper.' "[17] By way of contrast, we have noted, the rules pertaining to belligerency and neutrality actually exerted a very high level of pull on Washington in connection with the Silkworm missile shipment in the Persian Gulf.

The study of legitimacy thus focuses on the inherent capacity of a rule to exert pressure on states to comply. This focus on the properties of rules, of course, is not a self-sufficient account of the socialization process. How rules

[15] H. L. A. HART, *supra* note 3, at 209.

[16] Permissible activities of diplomats are set out in Article 3 of the Vienna Convention on Diplomatic Relations, Apr. 18, 1961, 23 UST 3227, TIAS No. 7502, 500 UNTS 95. Obviously, these do not include espionage.

[17] Schachter, *supra* note 1, at 311.

are made, interpreted and applied is part of a dynamic, expansive and complex set of social phenomena. That complexity can be approached, however, by beginning with the rules themselves. Those seemingly inert constructs are shaped by other, more dynamic forces and, like tree trunks and seashells, tell their own story about the winds and tides that become an experiential part of their shape and texture.

II. Determinacy and Legitimacy

What determines the degree of legitimacy of any particular rule text or rule-making process? Or, to ask the same question another way: what observable characteristics of a rule or of a rule-making institution raise or lower the probability that its commands will be perceived to obligate? It is to such questions that the remainder of this analysis is addressed. One could approach the social phenomenon of noncoerced obedience directly, through such various openings as are afforded by the study of myths, game theory or contractarian notions of social compact. Instead, these and other socializing forces will be approached indirectly, through a unifying notion of *rule legitimacy*; that is, by approaching dynamic social forces through those rules which the society chooses to obey or to regard as obligatory. It should be borne in mind, however, that the norm-centered question—what is it about the properties of a rule that conduces to voluntary compliance?—is merely the lawyer's approach to larger sociological, anthropological and political questions: what conduces to the formation of communities and what induces members of a community to live by its rules?

Let us begin by examining the literary properties of the text itself that conduce to voluntary compliance or induce a sense of obligation in those to whom the rule is addressed.

Perhaps the most self-evident of all characteristics making for legitimacy is textual *determinacy*. What is meant by this is the ability of the text to convey a clear message, to appear transparent in the sense that one can see through the language to the meaning. Obviously, rules with a readily ascertainable meaning have a better chance than those that do not to regulate the conduct of those to whom the rule is addressed or exert a compliance pull on their policymaking process. Those addressed will know precisely what is expected of them, which is a necessary first step towards compliance.

To illustrate the point, let us compare two textual formulations defining the boundary of the underwater continental shelf. The 1958 Convention places the shelf at "a depth of 200 metres or, beyond that limit, to where the depth of the superjacent waters admits of the exploitation of the natural resources of the said areas."[18] The 1982 Convention on the Law of the Sea, on the other hand, is far more detailed and specific. It defines the shelf as "the natural prolongation of . . . land territory to the outer edge of the continental margin, or to a distance of 200 nautical miles from the baselines from which the breadth of the territorial sea is measured," but takes into

[18] Convention on the Continental Shelf, Art. 1, Apr. 29, 1958, 15 UST 471, TIAS No. 5578, 499 UNTS 311.

account such specific factors as "the thickness of sedimentary rocks" and imposes an outermost limit that "shall not exceed 100 nautical miles from the 2,500 metre isobath," which, in turn, is a line connecting the points where the waters are 2,500 meters deep.[19] The 1982 standard, despite its complexity, is far more determinate than the elastic standard in the 1958 Convention, which, in a sense, established no rule at all. Back in 1958, the parties simply covered their differences and uncertainties with a formula, whose content was left in abeyance pending further work by negotiators, courts, and administrators and by the evolution of customary state practice.[20] The vagueness of the rule did permit a flexible response to further advances in technology, a benefit inherent in indeterminacy.

Indeterminacy, however, has costs. Indeterminate normative standards not only make it harder to know what conformity is expected, but also make it easier to justify noncompliance. Put conversely, the more determinate the standard, the more difficult it is to resist the pull of the rule to compliance and to justify noncompliance. Since few persons or states wish to be perceived as acting in obvious violation of a generally recognized rule of conduct, they may try to resolve the conflicts between the demands of a rule and their desire not to be fettered, by "interpreting" the rule permissively. A determinate rule is less elastic and thus less amenable to such evasive strategy than an indeterminate one.

A good example of this consequence of determinacy is afforded by the recent litigation between Nicaragua and the United States before the International Court of Justice. From the moment it became apparent that Nicaragua was preparing to sue the United States, State Department attorneys began to prepare the defense strategy. One option considered was invoking the "Connally reservation," which, as part of the U.S. acceptance of the jurisdiction of the International Court of Justice, specifically barred the Court from entertaining any case that pertains to "domestic" matters *as determined by the United States*.[21] Yet the American lawyers chose not to use this absolute defense.[22] Instead, they tried in various other ways to challenge the Court's authority. They argued that the dispute was already before the Organization of American States and the UN Security Council; that it was

[19] United Nations Convention on the Law of the Sea, Art. 76, *opened for signature* Dec. 10, 1982, UN Doc. A/CONF.62/122, *reprinted in* UNITED NATIONS, OFFICIAL TEXT OF THE UNITED NATIONS CONVENTION ON THE LAW OF THE SEA WITH ANNEXES AND INDEX, UN Sales No. E.83.V.5 (1983), 21 ILM 1261 (1982).

[20] For a legislative history and analysis of the provisions of the 1958 Convention, see Whiteman, *Conference on the Law of the Sea: Convention on the Continental Shelf*, 52 AJIL 629 (1958).

[21] 92 CONG. REC. 10,694 (1946).

[22] As I have written elsewhere:

> That the Connally Reservation did not license the United States to refuse to litigate *any* case for *any* reason whatsoever, that a "good faith" caveat was to be implied, is to be given some support by the fact that Connally was not invoked by U.S. lawyers to withdraw the Nicaraguan case from the I.C.J.'s jurisdiction.

Franck & Lehrman, *Messianism and Chauvinism in America's Commitment to Peace Through Law*, in THE INTERNATIONAL COURT OF JUSTICE AT A CROSSROADS 3, 17 (L. Damrosch ed. 1987).

not a legal dispute at all, but a political one;[23] that Nicaragua, having failed to perfect its acceptance of the Court's compulsory jurisdiction, had no right to implead the United States. The failure of the lawyers to use the Connally shield is all the more remarkable because, whereas the reservation gave the United States a self-judging escape from the Court's jurisdiction, all the other defenses left the key jurisdictional decision up to the Court, which rejected every one.[24] Had the U.S. Government simply faced the Court with a "finding" that the mining of Nicaragua's harbors was a "domestic" matter for the United States, that would have ended the litigation. Instead, the United States went on to lose, not only on the matter of jurisdiction, but also, eventually, on the merits.[25]

Why was the Connally shield rejected? The answer, surely, lies in its determinacy. Anyone reading its language would instantly understand that the reservation, while rather open-ended, nevertheless was not intended to cover such matters as the CIA's alleged mining of the harbors of a nation with which the United States was not at war. Although the term "domestic matter" is not so determinate as to bar all differences of interpretation—that, after all, is why its interpretation was reserved to the U.S. Government and not left to the Court—*no* reasonable interpretation of the concept could be stretched to cover the events in question. The U.S. legal strategists, anxious to do everything possible to stay out of court, nonetheless were unwilling to subject their client to the obloquy that would have ensued had the Connally shield been deployed. Interest gratification, convenience and advantage were sacrificed so as not to be seen as absurd.

Such foreboding of shame and ridicule is an excellent guide to determinacy. If a party seeking to justify its conduct interprets a rule in such a way as to evoke widespread derision, then the rule has determinacy. The violator's evidently tortured definition of the rule can be seen to exceed its range of plausible meanings.

Thus, while it may be true in theory, as Wittgenstein has charged, that no "course of action could be determined by a rule because every course of action can be made out to accord with the rule,"[26] some rules are less malleable, less open to manipulation, than others. Although Wittgenstein's point has merit—and has recently been wittily adumbrated by Professor Duncan Kennedy[27]—in practice, determinacy is not an illusion. No verbal formulas are entirely determinate, but some are more so than others.

[23] The United States announced that the case involved "an inherently political problem that is not appropriate for judicial resolution." Department Statement, Jan. 18, 1985, DEP'T ST. BULL., No. 2096, March 1985, at 64, 64, *reprinted in* 24 ILM 246, 246 (1985), 79 AJIL 438, 439.

[24] Military and Paramilitary Activities in and against Nicaragua (Nicar. v. U.S.), Jurisdiction and Admissibility, 1984 ICJ REP. 392 (Judgment of Nov. 26).

[25] Military and Paramilitary Activities in and against Nicaragua (Nicar. v. U.S.), Merits, 1986 ICJ REP. 14 (Judgment of June 27).

[26] L. WITTGENSTEIN, PHILOSOPHICAL INVESTIGATIONS 81, para. 201 (G. E. Anscombe trans. 1953).

[27] Kennedy, *Towards a Critical Phenomenology of Judging*, 36 J. LEGAL EDUC. 518 (1986).

The degree of determinacy of a rule directly affects the degree of its perceived legitimacy. A rule that prohibits the doing of "bad things" lacks legitimacy because it fails to communicate what is expected, except within a very small constituency in which "bad" has achieved a high degree of culturally induced specificity. To be legitimate, a rule must communicate what conduct is permitted and what conduct is out of bounds. These bookends should be close enough together to inhibit incipient violators from offering self-serving exculpatory definitions of the rule. When almost everyone scoffs at such an exculpation, the outer boundary of the rule's determinacy has been established.

There is another sense in which determinacy increases the legitimacy of a rule text. A rule of conduct that is highly transparent—its normative content exhibiting great clarity—actually *encourages* gratification deferral and rule compliance. States, in their relations with one another, frequently find themselves tempted to violate a rule of conduct in order to take advantage of a sudden opportunity. If they do not do so, but choose, instead, to obey the rule and forgo that gratification, it is likely to be because of their longer term interests in seeing a potentially useful rule reinforced. They can visualize future situations in which it will operate to their advantage. But they will only defer the attainable short-term gain if the rule is sufficiently specific to support reasonable expectations that benefit can be derived in a contingent future by strengthening the rule in the present instance.

Let us consider the case of a foreign ambassador's son who has murdered someone in Washington, D.C. He is about to be "booked" by the District police when a message arrives from the State Department demanding his release. The Secretary of State announces that the culprit is to be sent home. Hearing of this, the public understandably is outraged; members of Congress complain to the President. Patiently, the Secretary of State explains that "almost all" states "almost always" act in accordance with the universal rules of diplomatic immunity, which protect ambassadors and their immediate family from arrest and trial.[28] Although in this instance, the Secretary continues, the rule does seem to work an injustice, in general it operates to make diplomacy possible. By gratifying popular outrage and violating the rule this time, the United States would weaken the rule's future utility, its reliability in describing and predicting state behavior. Alternatively, by acting in compliance with the rule, even at some short-term cost to its self-interest, the United States will reinforce the rule text and thus its future utility in protecting U.S. diplomats and their families abroad.[29] Indeed, a study by a committee of the British House of Commons—conducted after a shot from

[28] Vienna Convention on Diplomatic Relations, *supra* note 16, Arts. 31, 37.

[29] The Department of State, on Aug. 5, 1987, submitted its views on a " 'bill to make certain members of foreign diplomatic missions and consular posts in the United States subject to the criminal jurisdiction of the United States with respect to crimes of violence.' " The Department (Ambassador Selwa Roosevelt) "could not support the proposed legislation because it would be detrimental to U.S. interests abroad." If enacted, the law "would place the United States in violation of its international obligations" and would invite more harmful reciprocal action. Contemporary Practice of the United States, 82 AJIL 106, 107 (1988). For the text of Ambassador Roosevelt's statement, see also DEP'T ST. BULL., No. 2127, October 1987, at 29.

the Libyan embassy ("People's Bureau") on April 17, 1984, killed an on-duty London policewoman—came to something very like this conclusion despite the inflamed state of public opinion.[30]

Note, however, that this thoughtful argument by the Secretary against interest gratification only makes sense if the son's immunity is seen as part of a clearly understood normative package, that other countries will refrain from arresting members of the families of U.S. ambassadors on real or trumped-up charges. Such expectations of reciprocity are important threads in the fabric of the international system; but before an expectation of reciprocity can arise, there must be some mutual understanding of what the rule covers, what events constitute "similar circumstances." If the contents of the rule are vaguely defined and fuzzy—if some countries in some instances have extended immunity to the ambassador's children while others have not, or have done so only if no capital crime is involved, or only if the child was actually working for the embassy, or have not extended immunity to second sons, or daughters or stepchildren—the impetus for gratification deferral in the instant case would diminish. The demand for the trial of the ambassador's son might then be both reasonable and irresistible. It could quite easily be defended as not violating a "real" rule. The argument could also be made that bringing the son to trial would create no more hazards for American diplomats abroad than were already posed by the vagueness of the rule. If a norm is full of loopholes, there is little incentive to impose on oneself obligations that others can evade easily.

An excellent example of this cost of indeterminacy is offered by the rules prohibiting and defining aggression that were approved in 1974 by the General Assembly after some 7 years of debate. Among the actions branded as aggression is the "sending by or on behalf of a State of armed bands, groups, irregulars or mercenaries, which carry out acts of armed force against another State." Almost in the same breath, however, the text states that nothing in the foregoing "could in any way prejudice the right to self-determination, freedom and independence . . . of peoples forcibly deprived of that right . . . ; nor the right of these peoples . . . to seek and receive support." To confuse matters further, another article declares that no "consideration of whatever nature, whether political, economic, military or otherwise, may serve as a justification for aggression"; and yet another adds that in "their interpretation and application the above provisions are interrelated and each provision should be construed in the context of the other provisions."[31] Interrelated they may be, but like a tangled skein. Do they prohibit or encourage aid by one country to an insurgent movement in

[30] H.C. Foreign Affairs Committee, First Report, The Abuse of Diplomatic Immunities and Privileges, Report with Annex; Together with the Proceedings of the Committee; Minutes of Evidence Taken on 20 June and 2 and 18 July in the Last Session of Parliament, and Appendices (1984). *See also* Higgins, *The Abuse of Diplomatic Privileges and Immunities: Recent United Kingdom Experience*, 79 AJIL 641 (1985).

[31] Definition of Aggression, GA Res. 3314, 29 UN GAOR Supp. (No. 31) at 142, UN Doc. A/9631 (1974).

another? It is not that the individual mandates and caveats are opaque, but that, seeking to reconcile irreconcilable positions, they contradict one another. Such a muddled obligation, one would expect, could have little effect on the real-world conduct of states; and one would be right.

It happens—by way of contrast—that, in international practice, the rules protecting diplomats, as codified by the Vienna Convention, have a very high degree of specificity,[32] and they are almost invariably obeyed. So, too, are the highly specific rules, in another Vienna Convention, on the making, interpreting and obligation of treaties.[33] Among other subjects covered by determinate rules that exert a strong pull to compliance and, in practice, elicit a high degree of conforming behavior by states are jurisdiction over vessels on the high seas, and in territorial waters and ports,[34] jurisdiction over aircraft,[35] copyright and trademarks,[36] and international usage of posts,[37] telegraphs, telephones[38] and radio waves.[39] There is also a high degree of determinacy in the rules governing embassy property,[40] rights of passage of naval vessels in peacetime,[41] treatment of war prisoners[42] and the duty of governments to pay compensation—even if not as to the *measure* of that compensation—for the expropriation of property belonging to aliens.[43]

[32] *See* Vienna Convention on Diplomatic Relations, *supra* note 16, Arts. 27, 28.

[33] *See* Vienna Convention on the Law of Treaties, Arts. 6, 55, *opened for signature* May 23, 1969, UNTS Regis. No. 18,232, UN Doc. A/CONF.39/27 (1969), *reprinted in* 8 ILM 679 (1969), 63 AJIL 875 (1969).

[34] United Nations Convention on the Law of the Sea, *supra* note 19.

[35] Convention on Offenses and Certain Other Acts Committed on Board Aircraft, Sept. 14, 1963, 20 UST 2941, TIAS No. 6768, 704 UNTS 219.

[36] Universal Copyright Convention, July 24, 1971, 25 UST 1341, TIAS No. 7868 (revised version of 216 UNTS 132).

[37] *See* UNIVERSAL POSTAL UNION CONST., July 10, 1964, 16 UST 1291, TIAS No. 5881, 611 UNTS 7.

[38] *See* Telegraph and Telephone Regulations, with appendices, annex, and final protocol, Apr. 11, 1973, 28 UST 3293, TIAS No. 8586.

[39] *See* International Telecommunication Convention, Oct. 25, 1973, 28 UST 2495, TIAS No. 8572.

[40] *See* Vienna Convention on Diplomatic Relations, *supra* note 16, Art. 22 (which provides for inviolability of diplomatic missions and imposes a special duty on states to protect premises of missions on their territory). *See also* Convention on the Prevention and Punishment of Crimes Against Internationally Protected Persons, Including Diplomatic Agents, Dec. 14, 1973, 28 UST 1975, TIAS No. 8532, 1035 UNTS 167 (which criminalizes violent attacks upon the official premises of internationally protected persons).

[41] The right of innocent passage was specifically provided for in Article 14 of the Geneva Convention on the Territorial Sea and Contiguous Zone, Apr. 29, 1958, 15 UST 1606, TIAS No. 5639, 516 UNTS 205, and by Article 17 of the UN Convention on the Law of the Sea of 1982, *supra* note 19.

[42] *See* Convention Relative to the Treatment of Prisoners of War, Aug. 12, 1949, 6 UST 3316, TIAS No. 3364, 75 UNTS 135. For a complete treatment of war prisoners, see N. RODLEY, THE TREATMENT OF PRISONERS UNDER INTERNATIONAL LAW (1987).

[43] As to compensation for expropriated property, there is agreement in principle, but disagreement as to the measure of compensation. *See, e.g.*, Charter of Economic Rights and Duties of States, Dec. 12, 1974, Art. 2(2)(c), GA Res. 3281, 29 UN GAOR Supp. (No. 31) at 50, UN

What is interesting about these examples is that the high degree of textual determinacy goes together with a high degree of rule-conforming state behavior. When determinacy is absent, it is unlikely that states will have compunctions about not complying with the rule. Indeed, some rules are probably written with low determinacy so that noncompliance will be easy.

A good example is the abortive effort by the United Nations to draft a code for the prevention and punishment of terrorism. In 1972, at the initiative of Secretary-General Kurt Waldheim, the General Assembly tried its hand at devising a set of rules requiring states to act in concert against what was perceived as a global problem.[44] Two years of negotiations demonstrated the difficulty of coming to a commonly acceptable definition of the activity to be prohibited.[45] The Government of Senegal, for example, proposed on behalf of the Non-Aligned Group that the prohibition should include "acts of violence and other repressive acts by colonial, racist and alien régimes against peoples struggling for liberation, for their legitimate right to self-determination, independence and other human rights and fundamental freedoms." The same group urged an exception in favor of those committing terrorist acts on behalf of "the inalienable right to self-determination and independence of all peoples under colonial and racist régimes and other forms of alien domination," in recognition of "the legitimacy of their struggle, in particular the struggle of national liberation movements."[46] The Soviet Union demanded exemption from the prohibition on terrorism for "acts committed in resisting an aggressor in territories occupied by the latter, and action by workers to secure their rights against the yoke of exploiters."[47]

Understandably, the United States and other Western countries took the position that these exculpatory caveats, if adopted, would shape a definition

---

Doc. A/9631 (1974). *See also* Resolution on Permanent Sovereignty over Natural Resources, GA Res. 1803, 17 UN GAOR Supp. (No. 17) at 15, UN Doc. A/5217 (1962). Article 4 of the latter states in part concerning expropriation: "In such cases the owner shall be paid appropriate compensation, in accordance with the rules in force in the State taking such measures in the exercise of its sovereignty and in accordance with international law." *But see* Resolution on Permanent Sovereignty over Natural Resources, GA Res. 3171, 28 UN GAOR Supp. (No. 30) at 52, UN Doc. A/9030 (1973). Article 3 "affirms" that "each State is entitled to determine the amount of possible compensation and the mode of payment, and that any disputes which might arise should be settled in accordance with the national legislation of each State carrying out such measures."

[44] UN Docs. A/8791 and A/8791/Add.1 (1972).

[45] *See, e.g., Ad Hoc* Committee on International Terrorism, Observations of States Submitted in Accordance with General Assembly Resolution 3034 (XXVII), UN Docs. A/AC.160/1 and Adds. 1–2 (1973).

[46] UN Doc. A/AC.160/3/Add.2, at 3 (1973).

[47] UN Doc. A/AC.160/2, at 7 (1973). However, Ambassador Oakley has reported a new Soviet "awareness that distinctions must be made between so-called liberation movements and groups whose objectives and operations are primarily directed toward producing terror, and whose targets are often unrelated to their putative 'liberation' goals." Oakley, *International Terrorism*, 65 FOREIGN AFF. 628 (1987).

of terrorism that would exacerbate, rather than ameliorate, the problem. The loopholes would be so large as to permit unimpeded passage for almost any act of violence claimed to be directed against a wicked regime. On the other hand, few governments would be willing to implement a prohibition on all politically motivated violence against every regime, no matter how repressive. Even the United States has put forward the "Reagan Doctrine,"[48] with its sophisticated distinctions that exculpate external support for "good" insurgents against "bad" regimes, while excoriating support for "bad" insurgents against "good" regimes.[49]

The Reagan Doctrine was merely the most recent restatement of the "just war" notion, evolved by Christian thinkers in the time of Emperor Constantine to reconcile their pacifist theology with imperial military needs,[50] and reinterpreted by Augustine,[51] Aquinas[52] and Grotius.[53] Each version has sought to define the circumstances in which war is permissible, against the background of a more general prohibition. These efforts appeal to common sense and human decency. As long as there is no Austinian world sovereign and centralized world police force, there will be good (defensive) wars and bad (aggressive) wars. Articles 2(4) and 51 of the United Nations Charter[54] likewise seem to bless this distinction. The problem is to distinguish good violence from bad without the benefit of a papal decision.

This problem—how to tell the sheep from the goats—operates whenever a rule tolerates exculpatory distinctions. While simple rules inherently suffer from lack of humanity, reason and texture, more complex ones tend to be hard to apply or to make exculpation too easy. Thus we have a literary conundrum. In consequence of making a simple, but irrational, rule more complex, sensible and humane, the text may become too elastic to secure compliance. For example, applying the proposed international norms known as the Reagan Doctrine, Ambassador Jeane Kirkpatrick has argued that U.S. support for the Nicaraguan contras is permissible, but Soviet and Cuban support for the Sandinistas is not, because the contras are democrats fighting a totalitarian regime while the Sandinistas are totalitarians used by

[48] See Address by Ambassador Kirkpatrick, National Press Club (May 30, 1985), which in effect gave new life to the "just war" doctrine.

[49] On this policy, see Franck, *Porfiry's Proposition: Legitimacy and Terrorism*, 20 VAND. J. TRANSNAT'L L. 195, 218 (1987). *See infra* text accompanying note 55.

[50] F. RUSSELL, THE JUST WAR IN THE MIDDLE AGES 12 (1975).

[51] *Id.* at 18–20.

[52] T. AQUINAS, SUMMA THEOLOGIAE, Question 40, Art. 1 (T. Heath trans. 1972).

[53] *See* H. GROTIUS, ON THE LAW OF WAR AND PEACE (L. Loomis trans. 1949); Edwards, *The Law of War in the Thought of Hugo Grotius*, 19 J. PUB. L. 371 (1970). Grotius expressly contemplated intervention by a third state to protect the natural law rights of the citizens of another state. *See* bk. II, ch. XXV of H. GROTIUS, *supra* (entitled "On the Causes of Undertaking War on Behalf of Others").

[54] UN CHARTER. Article 2(4) seeks to curb aggressive wars by imposing the obligation on states to refrain from the threat or use of force against the territorial integrity or political independence of any state, while Article 51 provides support for the inherent right of individual or collective self-defense in case of armed attack.

Russians and Cubans to colonize Nicaragua.[55] A rule that lends itself to that interpretation, however humane and rational its intent, is unlikely to inhibit any state from pursuing every opportunity for short-term interest gratification. It will be dismissed from serious consideration by states as they weigh their options.

Determinacy thus poses a dilemma. As defined, the term "determinacy" has been used to indicate the clarity of the message transmitted by a rule to those at whom it is directed as a command. We have argued that greater clarity conduces to compliance. Now, however, it has become apparent that "clarity" is far from identical with simplicity. For example, the UN Charter, in Articles 2(4) and 51, sets out a simple rule pertaining to the use of force. It says, in substance, that a state may not use force against another except to respond to an *actual armed attack*. This rule, on its face, seems to enjoy a high level of determinacy. And in most instances of conflict, the rule also makes sense. It is usually possible, in these days of outer space sensing devices, to provide persuasive proof of which state initiated hostilities. Even without such evidence, the answer can usually be determined by looking to see which party is winning after the first day of fighting. Nevertheless, despite its superficial clarity, the rule—under certain circumstances—does not satisfy the test of genuine determinacy: it does not send a clear message as to its meaning in such a way as to promote compliance. This is because a literal reading of the law will produce absurd obligations at the margins of its application. Thus, the rule would seem to compel a state threatened by a nuclear attack to wait until it had actually been hit ("armed attack") before being permitted to use force in self-defense.[56] The rule would also require a tiny state like Israel or Singapore to wait until after an armed attack before striking back, even though it might well have been overrun in that first offensive. In Mr. Bumble's words, "If the law supposes that, the law is a ass—a idiot." Such a rule lacks essential legitimacy, because it is easy to

[55] Address by Ambassador Kirkpatrick, *supra* note 48. The Reagan doctrine is not the only 20th-century attempt to revive the just war doctrine. The Soviet Union has long maintained that "[j]ust wars . . . are not wars of conquest but wars of liberation, waged to defend the people from foreign attack and from attempts to enslave them, or to liberate the people from capitalist slavery, or, lastly, to liberate colonies and dependent countries from the yoke of imperialism." COMMISSION OF THE CENTRAL COMMITTEE OF THE C.P.S.U., HISTORY OF THE COMMUNIST PARTY OF THE SOVIET UNION (BOLSHEVIKS) 167–68 (1939). The modern non-aligned movement has also upheld the just war doctrine, one result being the provisions of Protocol I to the Geneva Conventions. *See, e.g.*, Art. 1(4), Protocol Additional to the Geneva Conventions of 12 August 1949, and Relating to the Protection of Victims of International Armed Conflicts, *opened for signature* Dec. 12, 1977, INTERNATIONAL COMMITTEE OF THE RED CROSS, PROTOCOLS ADDITIONAL TO THE GENEVA CONVENTIONS OF 12 AUGUST 1949, at 3 (1977), *reprinted in* 16 ILM 1391 (1977). This position was dramatically put forth in a 1973 General Assembly resolution: "colonial peoples have the inherent right to struggle by all necessary means at their disposal against colonial Powers and alien domination in exercise of their right of self-determination." GA Res. 3103, 28 UN GAOR Supp. (No. 30) at 142, UN Doc. A/9030 (1973). *See also* GA Res. 2105, 20 UN GAOR Supp. (No. 14) at 3, UN Doc. A/6104 (1965). For a case study, see Dugard, *SWAPO: The Jus ad Bellum and the Jus in Bello*, 93 S. AFR. L.J. 144 (1976).

[56] *See* Franck, *Who Killed Article 2(4)?*, 64 AJIL 809, 820–22 (1970).

predict that in at least some situations no state would abide by its strictures. If a patently absurd result—a *reductio ad absurdum*—accrues from the only possible application of the evident meaning of a simple rule in circumstances requiring a more calibrated response, then it becomes evident that the rule will not be taken seriously in those circumstances, and perhaps also not in others.

If simplicity of text is an invitation to *reductio ad absurdum*, which undermines the determinacy of a rule, and if complexity imposes an elasticity that deprives it of determinate meaning, what can be said about determinacy that is not self-contradicting? There is an answer to this riddle, but it requires attention to detail and, in particular, to content. A simple, straightforward rule—"red light to port, green light to starboard"—will have a high level of determinacy if the problem to which it is addressed is widely recognized as essentially binary: that is, capable of being resolved by an objective test of compliance involving a choice between only two options. A true-false test is binary in this sense. Most traffic regulations also are of this kind. So are prohibitions on specific acts as to which there is general agreement that no exculpatory exceptions are ever admissible. One example is aerial hijacking.[57] The United States, however ruefully, has prosecuted a gunman who seized an aircraft to escape from Eastern bloc oppression,[58] because it felt obliged to discharge its obligation under the Hague Convention either to prosecute or to extradite hijackers.[59] The binary view of hijacking—it either *is* or *is not*, but no excuse will avail—is also manifest in the accord signed by the United States and Cuba in 1973,[60] and in the 1978

[57] [Tokyo] Convention on Offenses and Certain Other Acts Committed on Board Aircraft, Sept. 14, 1963, 20 UST 2941, TIAS No. 6768, 704 UNTS 219; [Hague] Convention for the Suppression of Unlawful Seizure of Aircraft, Dec. 16, 1970, 22 UST 1641, TIAS No. 7192 [hereinafter Hague Convention]; [Montreal] Convention for the Suppression of Unlawful Acts Against the Safety of Civil Aviation, Sept. 23, 1971, 24 UST 564, TIAS No. 7570.

[58] This scenario most notably occurred when an East German hijacked a Polish airliner to West Berlin. As an outgrowth of the historical and jurisdictional freak that is Berlin, the hijacker was charged with crimes under West German law but prosecuted by the United States and tried in an American court. The U.S. ambassador to West Germany appointed a New Jersey federal district judge, Herbert Stern, to preside over the trial. *See* H. STERN, JUDGMENT IN BERLIN (1984). Judge Stern, applying U.S. constitutional law, determined that the defendant was entitled to a jury trial (despite the anomaly that juries generally do not exist under German law). United States v. Tiede, 86 F.R.D. 227 (U.S. Ct. Berlin 1979). Impaneling a jury of West Berliners to judge an East German "refugee" raised the specter that the jury would refuse to convict the defendant in the American tradition of jury nullification. *See* Lowenfeld, *Hijacking, Freedom, and the "American Way,"* 83 MICH. L. REV. 1000, 1005 (1985). In other words, the jury would in effect graft a complex clause upon the linear law of the Hague Convention. In the end, the jury did acquit the defendant of hijacking but convicted him of hostage taking. H. STERN, *supra*, at 350. Judge Stern, affronted throughout the trial by the American prosecutor's stance that the Constitution was inapplicable to West Berlin and skeptical that parole (which he thought appropriate) would be granted, sentenced the hostage taker to time served (9 months) and released him from custody. *Id.* at 369–70.

[59] Hague Convention, *supra* note 57, Arts. 7, 8.

[60] Memorandum of Understanding on Hijacking of Aircraft and Vessels and Other Offenses, Feb. 15, 1973, United States–Cuba, 24 UST 737, TIAS No. 7579.

Bonn Declaration adhered to by Canada, France, Italy, Japan, the United Kingdom, the United States and the Federal Republic of Germany,[61] which imposes collective measures against states that refuse to extradite or prosecute hijackers.[62] Similarly, there appears to be near-universal belief that an objective binary test should apply to hostage taking[63] and violence against diplomats.[64] Even Islamic and Soviet authorities joined in the UN Security Council[65] to condemn the Iranian violations of U.S. diplomatic immunity in Tehran in 1979, a decision that was reaffirmed by a nearly unanimous International Court of Justice.[66] It is not difficult to visualize other narrow

[61] *International Terrorism*, DEP'T ST. BULL., No. 2018, September 1978, at 5 [hereinafter Bonn Declaration].

[62] *Id.* This language tracks Articles 7 and 9(2) of the Hague Convention, *supra* note 57. The Bonn Declaration in effect grafts an enforcement mechanism upon the norms embodied in the Hague Convention. However, imposition of sanctions under the Bonn Declaration is not premised on violation of the Hague Convention. Accordingly, sanctions might be taken against a state that had refused to sign the Hague Convention, not on the basis of the duty to prosecute or extradite (assuming, as is likely, that that is not a duty under customary international law), but on the basis that the support of international terrorism violates international law. *See* Levitt, *International Counterterrorism Cooperation: The Summit Seven and Air Terrorism*, 20 VAND. J. TRANSNAT'L L. 37 (1987). *See also* Chamberlain, *Collective Suspension of Air Services with States Which Harbour Hijackers*, 32 INT'L & COMP. L.Q. 616, 628–32 (1983); Busuttil, *The Bonn Declaration on International Terrorism: A Non-Binding International Agreement on Aircraft Hijacking*, 31 INT'L & COMP. L.Q. 474 (1982). Specifically, the Seven would (1) "take immediate action to cease all flights to that country," and (2) "initiate action to halt all incoming flights from that country or" (3) "from any country by the airlines of the country concerned." Bonn Declaration, *supra* note 61.

[63] International Convention Against the Taking of Hostages, Dec. 17, 1979, GA Res. 34/146, 34 UN GAOR Supp. (No. 46) at 245, UN Doc. A/34/46 (1979). The negotiations for the Hostages Convention reveal the opposition that a straightforward rule, even one for a compartmentalized activity, faces. Attempts at a reformulation of the Convention ranged in sophistication. Several delegations suggested the Convention should only protect "innocent" hostages. *See, e.g.*, UN Doc. A/32/39, at 38 (1977) (statement of Egypt); *id.* at 40 (statement of Guinea, using Ian Smith as an illustrative guilty hostage). The Tanzanian delegate proposed an exculpatory clause and provided an umpire: "For the purposes of the Convention, the term 'taking of hostages' shall not include any act or acts carried out in the process of national liberation against colonial rule, racist and foreign regimes, by liberation movements recognized by the United Nations or regional organizations." UN Doc. A/AC.188/L.5 (1977). The Pakistani delegate wished to condition invocation of the Hostages Convention against national liberation movements on the target state's acceptance of both the Geneva Conventions and the 1977 Protocols. UN Doc. A/C.6/34/SR.62, at 2 (1979).

[64] Convention on the Prevention and Punishment of Crimes Against Internationally Protected Persons, including Diplomatic Agents, *supra* note 40. *See also* Convention to Prevent and Punish the Acts of Terrorism Taking the Form of Crimes Against Persons and Related Extortion that Are of International Significance, Feb. 2, 1971, 27 UST 3949, TIAS No. 8413. The latter, an OAS version of the Internationally Protected Persons Convention, specifically condemns all physical attacks on diplomats, "regardless of motive" (Art. 2). This protection afforded diplomats can be analogized to the 11th-century Peace of God doctrine, which declared certain classes, especially the clergy, exempt from all violence. F. RUSSELL, *supra* note 50, at 34.

[65] SC Res. 461, 34 UN SCOR (Res. & Dec.) at 24, UN Doc. S/INF/35 (1979).

[66] United States Diplomatic and Consular Staff in Tehran (U.S. v. Iran), 1980 ICJ REP. 3 (Judgment of May 24).

categories of international offenses that could be defined without exculpatory caveats: offenses against children,[67] the use of biological[68] and chemical weapons,[69] and offenses against nonbelligerent civilians.[70]

Issues that cannot be reduced to simple binary categories invite regulation by more complex rule texts which, while avoiding the problem of *reductio ad absurdum*, suffer the costs of elasticity. A rule finely calibrated to reflect complex considerations, embodying a textured system of regulatory and exculpatory principles, may suffer legitimacy costs because it invites disputes as to its applicability in any particular case. These costs, however, can be reduced by introducing a forum in which ambiguity can be resolved case by case. Such a legitimate forum mitigates the textual elasticity of the rule by introducing process determinacy. One example is a provision in the 1982 Law of the Sea Convention that deals with the allocation of continental shelf shared by two or more riparian states. The shelf should be apportioned, the rule says, "on the basis of international law . . . in order to achieve an equitable solution."[71] The evidently nonbinary quality of this rule, the vagueness of the notion of an "equitable solution," has been redressed effectively in a series of interpretations by the International Court of Justice. The judges have noted that the treaty sets "a standard, and it is left to the States themselves, or to the courts, to endow this standard with specific content."[72] This the Court has set out to do. In a 1969 opinion, the judges had ruled that there should be some relation "between the extent of the continental shelf areas appertaining to the coastal State and the length of its coast measured in the general direction of the coastline."[73] In a 1982 case between Tunisia and Libya[74] and a 1985 dispute between Libya and Malta,[75] they gave quite specific content to an "equitable solution." In this

[67] The rights of children were recently codified in the Draft Convention on the Rights of the Child, UN Doc. E/CN.4/1986/39. In addition, these rights are treated in the Declaration of the Rights of the Child, GA Res. 1386, 14 UN GAOR Supp. (No. 16) at 19, UN Doc. A/4354 (1959); the Universal Declaration of Human Rights, GA Res. 217A (III), UN Doc. A/810, at 71 (1948), Arts. 25, 26; the International Covenant on Civil and Political Rights, GA Res. 2200, 21 UN GAOR Supp. (No. 16) at 52, UN Doc. A/6316 (1966), Arts. 6, 14, 23, 24; and the International Covenant on Economic, Social and Cultural Rights, GA Res. 2200, *id.* at 49, Arts. 10, 12. *See* Bennett, *A Critique of the Emerging Convention on the Rights of the Child*, 20 CORNELL INT'L L.J. 1 (1987).

[68] Convention on the Prohibition of the Development, Production and Stockpiling of Bacteriological (Biological) and Toxin Weapons and on Their Destruction, Apr. 12, 1972, 26 UST 583, TIAS No. 8062.

[69] Protocol for the Prohibition of the Use in War of Asphyxiating, Poisonous or Other Gases, and of Bacteriological Methods of Warfare, June 17, 1925, 26 UST 571, TIAS No. 8061, 94 LNTS 65.

[70] Convention Relative to the Protection of Civilian Persons in Time of War, Aug. 12, 1949, 6 UST 3516, TIAS No. 3365, 75 UNTS 287.

[71] United Nations Convention on the Law of the Sea, *supra* note 19, Art. 83(1).

[72] Continental Shelf (Libyan Arab Jamahiriya/Malta), 1985 ICJ REP. 13, 30–31 (Judgment of June 3).

[73] North Sea Continental Shelf (FRG/Den.; FRG/Neth.), 1969 ICJ REP. 3, 54 (Judgment of Feb. 20).

[74] *See* Continental Shelf (Tunisia/Libyan Arab Jamahiriya), 1982 ICJ REP. 18, 35 (Judgment of Feb. 24).

[75] 1985 ICJ REP. at 44.

way, the elastic rule text has gained determinacy, just as the papacy once gave content to the vague notion of "just" wars.

Process determinacy is not solely the prerogative of courts. Any institution that is seen to be acting legitimately may be used for the purpose. "Acting legitimately" means here that those it addresses perceive the forum itself as having come into being in accordance with right process. In practice, the legitimacy of a forum can be tested in the same way as that of a rule: by reference to the determinacy of its charter, its pedigree, the coherence of its mandate and its adherence to the normative institutional hierarchy of international organization. Nowadays, the UN General Assembly and Security Council, as well as organs of regional organizations, sometimes play this clarifying role. They will only succeed, however, if they are seen to be acting in accordance with their specific mandate and the general principles of fairness; that is, in a disinterested, principled fashion and not simply to gratify some short-term self-interest of a faction. Moreover, each rule-decision emanating from a legitimate forum is itself subject to the test of its perceived legitimacy: its determinacy, coherence, and so forth.

To summarize: the legitimacy of a rule is affected by its degree of determinacy. Its determinacy depends upon the clarity with which it is able to communicate its intent and to shape that intent into a specific situational command. This, in turn, can depend upon the literary structure of the rule, its ability to avoid *reductio ad absurdum* and the availability of a process for resolving ambiguities in its application.

III. Symbolic Validation and Legitimacy

As determinacy is the linguistic or literary-structural component of legitimacy, so *symbolic validation, ritual* and *pedigree* provide its cultural and anthropological dimension. As with determinacy, so here, the legitimacy of the rule—its ability to exert pull to compliance and to command voluntary obedience—is to be examined in the light of its ability to communicate. In this instance, however, what is to be communicated is not so much content as *authority*:[76] the authority of a rule, the authority of the originator of a validating communication and, at times, the authority bestowed on the recipient of the communication. The communication of authority, moreover, is symbolic rather than literal. We shall refer to these symbolically validating communications as cues.

These three concepts—symbolic validation, ritual and pedigree—are related, but not identical. The *symbolic validation* of a rule, or of a rule-making process or institution, occurs when a signal is used as a cue to elicit compliance with a command. The cue serves as a surrogate for enunciated reasons for such obedience. The singing of the national anthem, for example, is a vocal and (on public occasions) a visual signal symbolically reinforcing the citizen's relationship to the state, a relationship of rights and duties. This

[76] Schachter, *supra* note 1, at 309–11. Schachter uses the terms "competence and authority" to cover some of the same matters. In his formulation, "whether a designated requirement is to be regarded as obligatory will depend in part on whether those who have made that designation are regarded by those to whom the requirement is addressed (the target audience) as endowed with the requisite competence or authority for that role." *Id.* at 309.

compliance reinforcement need not be spelled out in the actual words of the anthem (as it is not in the commonly used stanza of the American one). The act of corporate singing itself is a sufficient cue to validate the fabric of regularized relationships that are implicated in good citizenship. We are not really singing about bombs bursting in the night air, but about free and secret elections, the marketplace of ideas, the rule of valid laws and impartial judges.

Ritual is a specialized form of symbolic validation marked by ceremonies, often—but not necessarily—mystical, that provide unenunciated reasons or cues for eliciting compliance with the commands of persons or institutions. The entry of the mace into the British House of Commons is intended to call to mind the Commons's long and successful struggle to capture control of lawmaking power from the Crown. It functions as a much more direct, literal kind of symbolic validation than the "Star-Spangled Banner." Ritual is often presented as drama, to communicate to a community its unity, its values, its uniqueness in both the exclusive and the inclusive sense.

All ritual is a form of symbolic validation, but the converse is not necessarily true. *Pedigree* is a different subset of cues that seek to enhance the compliance pull of rules or rule-making institutions by emphasizing their historical origins, their cultural or anthropological deep-rootedness. An example is the practice of "recognition." When a government recognizes a new regime, or when the United Nations admits a new state to membership, this partly symbolic act has broad significance. It endows the new entity with a range of entitlements and duties, the concomitants of sovereignty. The capacity of states, and, nowadays, perhaps also of the United Nations, to confer sovereignty and its incidents in this fashion derives not from some treaty or other specific agreement but from the ancient practice of states and groupings of states, which legitimizes the exercise of this power.[77] The time-honored recognition practices by which status is conferred symbolically include such subsets as recognition "de facto" and "de jure," recognition of states and governments, the opening of diplomatic relations, and, in the United Nations, admittance to membership and acceptance of delegates' credentials. Along similar lines, Professor Schachter has observed that a body of rules produced by the UN legislative drafting body, the International Law Commission, will be more readily accepted by the nations "after [the Commission] has devoted a long period in careful study and consideration of precedent and practice." Moreover, the authority will be greater if the product is labeled *codification*—that is, the interpolation of rules from deep-rooted evidence of state practice—"than if it were presented as a 'development' (that is, as new law),"[78] even though the Commission (as a subsidiary of the General Assembly) is equally empowered by the UN Charter to promote "the progressive development of international law and its codification."[79] The compliance pull of a rule is enhanced by a demonstrable lineage. A new rule will have greater difficulty finding compliance, and even evidence of its good sense may not fully compensate for its lack of

[77] For a discussion of the origins of recognition policy and procedure, see 1 L. OPPENHEIM, INTERNATIONAL LAW 124–52 (H. Lauterpacht 8th ed. 1955).

[78] Schachter, *supra* note 1, at 310.

[79] UN CHARTER art. 13(1)(a).

breeding. Nevertheless, a new rule may be taken more seriously if it arrives on the scene under the aegis of a particularly venerable sponsor such as a widely ratified multilateral convention, or a virtually unanimous decision of the International Court of Justice.

Symbolic validation, ritual and pedigree are part of the legitimation strategy of all communities, all compliance-inducing rule systems. A study of the legitimacy of imperial authority in ancient China observes that rituals and symbols, "by endowing authority with mystical values and legitimacy, serve not merely to reflect authority but also to recreate and reinforce it. By such means the extent to which people are persuaded to accept a given authority goes far beyond the obedience normally elicited by force."[80] Similar observations have derived from the study of Aztec legitimation strategy, which was found to employ a social tactic making extensive symbolic resources available to achieve "political socialization."[81] For example, the government made a point of distributing food to the citizenry at certain state ceremonies. Feeding as Christian sacrament is also a symbolic validation of status as members of the mystical body of Christ, of hierarchic authority structure within that community, and serves as a renewal of commitment and obligation.

"Political legitimacy," a study of ancient China notes, "can be said to adhere to a regime and its authorities when the governed are convinced that it is right and proper to obey them and to abide by their decisions."[82] This conviction was cued symbolically in Aztec society by priests who provided "supernatural sanction for legitimate state authority,"[83] rather as did the Roman Pontifex Maximus.[84] But, in many societies, ritual and pedigree will have their symbolic roots in the cultural and political, rather than the religious, experience. In a posttheistic society, ritual is not discarded; rather, politics and history are substituted for magic and myth as the compliance-inducing or status-securing cue.

For example, in Britain the rule that a parliamentary bill becomes law only after receiving the assent of the Crown[85] certainly no longer relates to the divine right of monarchs. Although the Queen's title still claims that she rules "by the grace of God," it is not widely believed either that the Queen rules or, for that matter, that there is a God, particularly one involved in

[80] H. WECHSLER, OFFERINGS OF JADE AND SILK 21 (1985).

[81] Kurtz, *Strategies of Legitimation and the Aztec State*, 23 ETHNOLOGY 301, 309 (1984).

[82] H. WECHSLER, *supra* note 80, at 10. [83] Kurtz, *supra* note 81, at 306.

[84] The Pontifex's task, originally, was to legitimate political authority by appeasing the river god Tiber over whose banks the civil authorities had built a useful, but undeniably intrusive, bridge.

[85] When presenting bills for royal assent, the Speaker of the House of Commons pays homage to the Crown with the formula: "Be it enacted by the Queen's most Excellent Majesty, by and with the advice and consent of the Lords Spiritual and Temporal, and Commons, in this present Parliament assembled, and by the authority of the same, as follows . . . ." O. PHILLIPS, A FIRST BOOK OF ENGLISH LAW 118–19 (7th ed. 1977). The Crown's right to refuse assent to bills that have properly passed through both Houses of Parliament is "practically obsolete." A. DICEY, INTRODUCTION TO THE STUDY OF THE LAW OF THE CONSTITUTION 114 (9th ed. 1939). In fact, when the Unionists posited in 1913 that the reference to assent restored a real right of veto, the theory was criticized as "obviously absurd" and was said to have troubled the king. E. RIDGES, CONSTITUTIONAL LAW 106 (8th ed. 1950).

British government. A utilitarian explanation for the survival of the historic ritual of royal assent would have to look elsewhere.

Oddly, the very obsolescence of the practice of royal assent helps keep it alive. The act of seeking the Queen's signature on legislation, even when it is clear that she has no choice but to grant it, is not meaningless. It signifies the Government's acceptance of all the accumulated encrustation of customs that define and restrict British governmental powers and practices. The Speaker of the House, for example, assures the Queen that the bill has had its customary three readings in Parliament and has passed both Houses.[86] While meaning little in itself, since the governing party usually can command the parliamentary majority necessary to do what it wants, the ritual of three readings[87] symbolizes the governing party's subordination to orderly, unhurried parliamentary procedure. In an era of relentless bureaucratic momentum, these quaint historical-political rituals provide a delay for reflection and debate between the drafting of a bill and its implementation. The result is that the rituals of three readings and monarchial assent symbolically validate, cuing public compliance and serving to certify the legitimacy of the new law.

Of course, a bad law does not become a good one for having been anointed by parliamentary ritual and having received the blessing of pedigreed authority. A citizen who believes a law to be evil probably will not be induced to think otherwise by symbolic cues. Nevertheless, when decisions to comply or defy are made by those to whom a command is addressed, such cues, with their symbolic validation of its legitimacy, may tip the scales on the side of obedience.

The three-readings ritual is the secular analogue of the church's practice of "publishing the banns" of a proposed marriage on three successive Sundays before the actual nuptials are consecrated.[88] Even in this rational era, the publication of banns also has its residual validating force, which derives not from belief in the divine, but from faith in the evolutionary history that the ritual symbolizes. Just as the House of Commons's three readings celebrate the continuity of parliamentary democracy, the publication of banns symbolizes commitment to the social status of matrimony conferred by both the church and the acquiescent congregation. Both rituals constitute a recommitment to the society's procedural rules of recognition, the "rules of

[86] When a bill is presented to the Crown for assent, it bears an endorsement signed by the Speaker of the House certifying that the provisions of the Parliament Act have been complied with. Parliament Act, 1911, 1 & 2 Geo. 5, ch. 13, §2(2), *reprinted in* SELECT STATUTES, CASES AND DOCUMENTS 350, 352 (C. Robertson ed. 1935).

[87] For a full discussion of this ritual as it applies to the enactment of both public and private bills by the House of Commons and the House of Lords, see S. A. DE SMITH, CONSTITUTIONAL AND ADMINISTRATIVE LAW 265–71 (3d ed. 1977).

[88] The calling of banns is the public and official announcement of persons who intend to marry and is meant to discover whether the parties are free to marry and whether any impediment to their lawful and valid marriage may exist. The tradition that no marriage was to be celebrated until after a triple publication of the church's banns originated in the 8th century and was extended over all Christendom by Pope Innocent III in 1215. ENCYCLOPEDIC DICTIONARY OF RELIGION 357 (1979).

the game," about which more will be said below. These *secondary* rules about rules are particularly important because they are the yardstick by which all *primary* or substantive rules and commands can be tested. The legitimacy of secondary rules is particularly dependent on the length of their pedigree. They must be difficult to change if they are to be perceived as valid and able to validate. Thus, the secondary rules, as well as the primary rules made in accordance with them, derive their legitimacy in part from the rootedness of the former deep in the history and culture of the community. For this reason, a bill that did not undergo three readings and was not presented for the assent of the Crown would undoubtedly be perceived by Britons as lacking legitimacy, not because those rituals are believed to be powerful in themselves, but because the Government's failure to perform them would be seen as a repudiation of the ancient democratic essence of the British parliamentary system, of which the rites and pedigree are still potent cues.

As we have noted, validating cues are not a modern, or a western, invention. Pedigree is a particularly universal form of symbolic validation. Most societies make some form of linguistic connection between the concepts "old" and "venerable." In the ancient Aztec state, the rulers' hereditary relation to the Toltec dynasty "was the sacred source of legitimate power and authority,"[89] supplemented by a host of "pedigree nobles."[90] So, too, in the China of 1000 B.C., where the Mandate of Heaven doctrine endowed an ancient imperial series of rulers with historically pedigreed and ritually validated power that rested on an orderly system, or line, of succession.[91]

Ritual, too, is a pandemic validator of authority. The fundamental purpose of ritual in ancient China was to create a form of procedural legitimacy that Max Weber would have understood.[92] The point is illustrated by the story of Kao-tsu (206–195 B.C.). When Kao-tsu founded the Han dynasty, he and his followers were "rough and ready fellows" and, to put them at ease, the emperor abolished the "elaborate and bothersome" *Ch'in* ritual code. Unfortunately, this made a "shambles of court audiences" as the members of his court went about "getting drunk, hurling insults at one another, and hacking up the wooden pillars of the palace with their swords. To introduce some decorum . . . , Kao-tsu was moved to appoint an erudite named Shu-sun T'ung to provide him with a court ritual consonant with his modest personal capacity for performing ceremonial." The experiment proved a great success. The ritual "served as a powerful tool for dignifying and strengthening the ruler's position and for controlling the behavior of subordinates. It emphasized the large gap between the position of emperor and that of mere bureaucrat, prevented former associates from presuming upon past friendships, and helped keep subordinates agreeably subservient."[93]

In the modern state system, ritual and other kinds of symbolic validation play much the same role as in ancient and medieval national societies, inte-

[89] Kurtz, *supra* note 81, at 306. [90] *Id.* at 308.

[91] H. WECHSLER, *supra* note 80, at 12–15.

[92] *See supra* note 10 (for Weber's perception that legitimacy in part stems from the authority issuing an order, rather than from the order itself).

[93] H. WECHSLER, *supra* note 80, at 25.

grating by inclusion and exclusion, seducing subjects into obeying rules and rulers, validating the exercise of power and generally contributing to the legitimization of the institutions and rules of the society. As a less-developed system, international society is underendowed with such symbolic validation, but what there is serves approximately the same legitimizing function as in ancient China, in the Aztec nation[94] and in modern parliamentary democracies.[95]

Despite their paucity, there are significant examples of attempts by the international system to legitimize itself through ritual and pedigree. One of the oldest and most universal was by using marriage between children of heads of state as symbolic emphasis for a practical political and social compact between nations, sometimes merely reifying the concept of a "family" of allied nations, at other times leading to—legitimizing—actual political union or federation. The practice was common not only among medieval European royal houses, but also in Asia, Africa and the precolonial Americas. For example, in Aztec Mexico, the "head of state established alliances with neighboring states through marriage. . . . Acamapichtli is reputed to have married twenty daughters of the chiefs of the clans that comprised Aztec society."[96]

One of the newest examples of symbolic international system legitimation is the creation of supranational agencies such as the United Nations Development Programme,[97] the International Bank for Reconstruction and Development[98] (the "World Bank"), the World Health Organization,[99] the Food and Agriculture Organization[100] and the United Nations International Children's Emergency Fund.[101] Their role is to distribute benefits to the deserving and the needy, either in tandem, or in competition, with the unilateral donations still given by one country to another.

The purpose of these agencies is largely and usefully instrumental. Nevertheless, the form of the organization is heavily symbolic. The World Bank, for example, could as well have been set up with only the 12 to 16 chief industrial nations as members, since they contribute almost all its working capital. Instead, the symbolic mingling of donors and recipients in the bank's governing organs and bureaucracy is intended to purge the assistance given of the aura of direct dependence between recipient and donor, a relationship in which gratitude has often been superseded by bitterness. By symbolic multilateralization, gratitude is directed to the agency, all of whose

[94] *See supra* text accompanying note 81.

[95] *See supra* text accompanying notes 86–87.

[96] Kurtz, *supra* note 81, at 308.

[97] *See* GA Res. 2029, 20 UN GAOR Supp. (No. 14) at 20, UN Doc. A/6014 (1965).

[98] Articles of Agreement of the International Bank for Reconstruction and Development, *opened for signature* Dec. 27, 1945, 60 Stat. 1440, TIAS No. 1502, 2 UNTS 134.

[99] WORLD HEALTH ORGANIZATION CONST., July 22, 1946, 62 Stat. 2679, TIAS No. 1808, 14 UNTS 186.

[100] UN FOOD AND AGRICULTURE ORGANIZATION CONST., Oct. 16, 1945, 12 UST 980, TIAS No. 4803.

[101] The United Nations International Children's Emergency Fund was founded by GA Res. 57, 1 UN GAOR (Res. pt.2) at 90, UN Doc. A/64/Add.1 (1946).

members participate, in most cases, as theoretical equals. This equality of participation is itself the symbolic representation of a confluence between sovereignty and interdependence that holds together the "community" of states.

The distribution of benefits by a global agency, with its own officials and symbols, also helps to create a sense of social solidarity—a primitive version of loyalty—between recipients (both persons and governments) and the international system (the "United Nations Family") of which the donor agency is a part, rather in the same way as did the Aztec rulers' ritual distribution of foodstuffs to subjects. This symbolic, as well as utilitarian, function of multilateral, institutionalized benevolence is familiar to anthropologists and sociologists who study the formation of national societies. In Aztec society, the "[c]onstruction and maintenance of temples and other public buildings appeased the gods, organized people's labor according to state directives and supported priests and other state functionaries."[102] The Pharaohs similarly sought to serve both personal and socializing objectives in the construction of the pyramids.[103] This concept of legitimization through the symbolism of public works has not been unknown, either, to American politicians from "Boss" Curley of Boston[104] to Nelson D. Rockefeller of New York.[105] It is also understood by the fledgling bureaucracy of the international system.

There are many other examples of ritual and other symbolic reinforcement of legitimacy in the international system. Thus, the United Nations Organization is authorized to fly its own flag, not only at headquarters, but also over regional and local offices around the world.[106] The flag has been used at the instigation of the Secretary-General to immunize such UN battle-front operations as clearing sunken ships from the Suez Canal in 1956

[102] Kurtz, *supra* note 81, at 310.

[103] Although many consider the pyramids to be solely the product of slave labor, evidence has been advanced indicating that the labor was in fact compensated. Thus, it is "probably nearer the truth [to] regard these monuments as vast public works providing economic security for a good part of the population." H. JANSON, THE HISTORY OF ART 40 (rev. ed. 1969). Erected as part of vast funerary districts, the pyramids were the scene of great religious festivities, both during and after the Pharaoh's lifetime. *Id.* at 38. At least as far as Old Kingdom pyramids are concerned, Pharaohs equipped their tombs as a "kind of shadowy replica of [their] daily environment for [their] spirit[s] . . . . [T]he Egyptian tomb was a kind of life insurance, an investment in peace of mind." *Id.* at 35.

[104] *See* J. DINNEEN, THE PURPLE SHAMROCK (1949) (which details the life of James Michael Curley, four-time mayor of Boston). *See also* E. O'CONNOR, THE LAST HURRAH (1956) (which, although fictional, is said to be based on Curley's life and career).

[105] In formulating the project for the Albany Mall, Governor Nelson Rockefeller suggested modeling New York's capitol on the palace of the Dalai Lama at Lhasa, Tibet. The revised version of the mall's plan incorporated architectural and symbolic elements from Lhasa, Washington, D.C., Brasília, Versailles, Rockefeller Center and St. Petersburg, and was meant to be "the most spectacularly beautiful seat of government anywhere in the world." Krinsky, *St. Petersburg-on-the-Hudson: The Albany Mall* (citing FORTUNE, June 1971, at 92), in M. BARASCH & L. SANDLER, ART THE APE OF NATURE 771, 778 (1981).

[106] The General Assembly adopted and authorized the use of the United Nations flag on Oct. 20, 1947. *See* GA Res. 167, 2 UN GAOR (96th plen. mtg.) at 338–39, UN Doc. A/414 (1947).

and protecting members of the Palestine Liberation Organization being evacuated from Lebanon in 1983.[107] The United Nations also issues stamps,[108] which not only are accepted for mail delivery by member states, but also generate a tidy independent income—some $8.6 million in 1986–1987.[109] Peacekeeping forces and truce observers under UN command and wearing UN symbols are stationed between hostile forces in Kashmir,[110] the Golan Heights,[111] Cyprus,[112] Lebanon[113] and Iran-Iraq.[113a] They are lightly armed, if at all, and palpably unable to defend themselves in the event of renewed hostilities; but, with their distinctive emblems, they have come to symbolize the world's interest in the continuance of an agreed truce or armistice. The blue and white helmets and arm bands also symbolize a growing body of rules applicable to peacekeeping operations, manifesting and reinforcing the authority of forces that usually are neither as numerous, nor as well armed, as those they must keep pacified. Their role is purely, but effectively, symbolic of the desire of bitter enemies—and the international community—to have respite from combat. Yet their token presence has a far more inhibitory effect on the behavior of states than can be explained by their minimal coercive power.[114] It is their perceived legitimacy, symbolically validated, that serves as their shield and usually induces more powerful forces to defer to their intangible authority.

The United Nations and its agencies also maintain headquarters and regional facilities that are accorded limited extraterritoriality and immuni-

[107] For the Secretary-General's operation to remove ships sunk in the Suez Canal during the 1956 war, see 1956 UN Y.B. 53–55; and GA Res. 1121, 11 UN GAOR Supp. (No. 17) at 61, UN Doc. A/3386 (1956). The Secretary-General also authorized, with the "support" of the Security Council, the flying of the UN flag on ships that would evacuate armed elements of the PLO from Tripoli. *See* UN Docs. S/16194, S/16195, 38 UN SCOR (Res. & Dec.) at 5–6, UN Doc. S/INF/39 (1983).

[108] The United Nations Postal Administration was established on Jan. 1, 1951. *See* GA Res. 454, 5 UN GAOR Supp. (No. 20) at 57–58, UN Doc. A/1775 (1950).

[109] The estimated 1986–1987 net revenue from the sale of postage stamps was $8,667,700. *See* Advisory Committee on Administrative and Budgetary Questions, First Report on Proposed Programme Budget for the Biennium 1986–1987, 40 UN GAOR Supp. (No. 7) at 209, UN Doc. A/40/7 (1985).

[110] The origin of the United Nations Military Observer Group in India and Pakistan (UNMOGIP) is found in a resolution of the UN Commission for India and Pakistan. *See* 3 UN SCOR Supp. (Nov. 1948) at 32, UN Doc. S/1100, para. 75 (1948). The Security Council subsequently authorized its operation. *See* SC Res. 91, para. 7, 6 UN SCOR (Res. & Dec.) at 1, 3, UN Doc. S/INF/6/Rev.1 (1951).

[111] The Security Council established the UN Disengagement Observer Force (UNDOF) for the Golan Heights on May 31, 1974. *See* SC Res. 350, 29 UN SCOR (Res. & Dec.) at 4, UN Doc. S/INF/30 (1974).

[112] The United Nations Force in Cyprus (UNFICYP) was formed by the Security Council on Mar. 4, 1964. *See* SC Res. 186, 19 UN SCOR (Res. & Dec.) at 2–4, UN Doc. S/INF/19/Rev.1 (1964).

[113] The United Nations Interim Force in Lebanon (UNIFIL) was created by the Security Council on Mar. 19, 1978. *See* SC Res. 425, 33 UN SCOR (Res. & Dec.) at 5, UN Doc. S/INF/34 (1978).

[113a] *See* Report of the Secretary-General, UN Doc. S/20093 (Aug. 7, 1988); SC Res. 619 (Aug. 9, 1988) (creating the force); GA Res. 42/233 (Aug. 17, 1988) (funding the force).

[114] For a discussion of the noncoercive role of UN peacekeeping forces, see B. URQUHART, A LIFE IN PEACE AND WAR 287–88, 342–43 (1987).

ties.[115] These have symbolic as well as practical significance. The extension of diplomatic immunity to top UN officials, privileges usually reserved for representatives of states, symbolizes the emergence of the Organization as an autonomous international actor, pedigreed in its own right. The functions and privileges of the agencies' resident representatives in various countries do not differ greatly, in practice, from those of ambassadors. Although it is not widely known, the Organization also levies an income tax[116] (staff assessment) on its employees who, with the exception of Americans, are immune from national taxation in recognition of the fact (noted by the U.S. Supreme Court in the domestic federal context[117]) that the right of states to tax federal instrumentalities must be limited because it necessarily encompasses the right to destroy.

A few more examples. Symbols of pedigree and rituals are firmly imbedded in state diplomatic practice. The titles ("ambassador extraordinary and plenipotentiary"), prerogatives and immunities of ambassadors, consuls and others functioning in a representative capacity are among the oldest of symbols and rites associated with the conduct of international relations. The sending state, by the rituals of accreditation, endows its diplomats with pedigree. They become, in time-honored tradition, a symbolic reification of the nation ("full powers" or *plenipotentiary*), a role that is ritually endorsed by the receiving state's ceremony accepting the envoy's credentials. These ceremonies, incidentally, are as old as they are elaborate and are performed with as remarkably faithful uniformity in Communist citadels as in royal palaces.[118] Once accredited and received, an ambassador *is* the embodiment of the nation. The status of ambassador, once conferred, carries with it inherent rights and duties that do not depend on the qualities of the person, or on the condition of relations between the sending and receiving states, or on the relative might of the sending state. To insult or harm this envoy, no matter how grievous the provocation, is to attack the sending state. Moreover, when an envoy, acting officially, agrees to something, the envoy's state is bound, usually even if the envoy acted without proper authorization.[119] The host state normally is entitled to rely on the word of an ambassador as if his or her state were speaking.

[115] *See* Convention on the Privileges and Immunities of the United Nations, *adopted* by the General Assembly Feb. 13, 1946, 21 UST 1418, TIAS No. 6900, 1 UNTS 1 (entered into force for the United States Apr. 29, 1970). *See also* Agreement Regarding the Headquarters of the United Nations, June 26, 1947, United States–United Nations, 61 Stat. 3416, TIAS No. 1676, 11 UNTS 11 (entered into force Nov. 21, 1947). *See further* Convention on the Privileges and Immunities of the Specialized Agencies, *approved* by the General Assembly Nov. 21, 1947, 33 UNTS 261.

[116] To rectify the inequalities it perceived in its original system of compensation, the United Nations subjected UN salaries to a tax assessed at a rate comparable to the employee's national income tax liability. GA Res. 239 (III), UN Doc. A/703, at 3 (1948), *as amended* by GA Res. 359 (IV), UN Doc. A/1949, at 1 (1949).

[117] McCulloch v. Maryland, 17 U.S. (4 Wheat.) 316, 347 (1819).

[118] *See* M. McCaffree & P. Innis, Protocol, The Complete Book of Diplomatic, Official and Social Usage 87–104 (1985).

[119] Legal Status of Eastern Greenland (Den. v. Nor.), 1933 PCIJ (ser. A/B) No. 53 (Judgment of Apr. 5).

The venerable ritual practices of diplomacy are almost universally observed, and the rules that govern diplomacy are widely recognized as imbued with a high degree of legitimacy, being both descriptive and predictive of nearly invariable state conduct and reflecting a strong sense of historically endowed obligation. When the rules are violated—as they have been by Iran and Libya in recent years[120]—the international community tends to respond by rallying around the rule, as the Security Council[121] and the International Court of Justice[122] demonstrated when the Iranian regime encouraged the occupation of the U.S. Embassy in Tehran. Violations of the elaborate rules pertaining to embassies and immunities usually lead the victim state to terminate its diplomatic relations with the offender.[123] The offended state—as Britain demonstrated after the St. James Square shooting—usually takes care not to retaliate by means that the rules do not permit.[124]

Related to the pedigreeing process of diplomatic accreditation, with its symbolic status of privileges and immunities, is the prevalent idea of sovereign immunity. That set of rules and practices has its roots in the medieval notion that the "king can do no wrong" and the monarch's claim that "I am the state." Nowadays, most governments can be sued in their own courts. Until at least the 1920s, however, nations, among themselves, generally continued to treat as sacrosanct not only foreign governments, but also all property of recognized foreign states and those activities and enterprises carried on in the foreign government's name.[125] Only in the last three

[120] For a discussion of the Iranian hostages incident, see Gross, *The Case of United States Diplomatic and Consular Staff in Tehran: Phase of Provisional Measures,* 74 AJIL 395 (1980). For an analysis of the Libyan violations, see Higgins, *supra* note 30.

[121] SC Res. 457, 34 UN SCOR (Res. & Dec.) at 24, UN Doc. S/INF/35 (1979) (adopted unanimously).

[122] *See* United States Diplomatic and Consular Staff in Tehran (U.S. v. Iran), Provisional Measures, 1979 ICJ REP. 7 (Order of Dec. 15); United States Diplomatic and Consular Staff in Tehran (U.S. v. Iran), 1980 ICJ REP. 3 (Judgment of May 24); United States Diplomatic and Consular Staff in Tehran (U.S. v. Iran), 1981 ICJ REP. 45 (Order of May 12).

[123] See, e.g., *France Breaks Iran Ties and Isolates Embassy,* N.Y. Times, July 18, 1987, at 1, col. 3, which followed the grant of sanctuary by the Iranian Embassy in Paris to a nondiplomat wanted for questioning in connection with terrorist activities.

[124] The British limited their reaction to the shooting of a policewoman from the premises of the Libyan People's Bureau to expulsion of the perpetrators and closing of the Bureau. *See* Higgins, *UK Foreign Affairs Committee Report on the Abuse of Diplomatic Immunities and Privileges: Government Response and Report,* 80 AJIL 135 (1986).

[125] In the *Steamship Pesaro* case, the U.S. Supreme Court refused to recognize the difference between ships held and used by a government for a public purpose and ships used by a government in trade. The latter "are public ships in the same sense that war ships are. We know of no international usage which regards the maintenance and advancement of the economic welfare of a people in time of peace as any less a public purpose than the maintenance and training of a naval force." Berizzi Bros. Co. v. S.S. Pesaro, 271 U.S. 562, 574 (1926). The Court expounded upon this doctrine in *The Navemar,* holding that, "[a]dmittedly a vessel of a friendly government in its possession and service is a public vessel, even though engaged in the carriage of merchandise for hire . . . ." Compania Espanola de Navigacion Maritima, S.A. v. Navemar, 303 U.S. 68, 74–76 (1938). For similar holdings in British cases, see The Jassy, 1906 P. 270; and The Gagara, 1919 P. 95.

decades have most nations begun to limit the immunity from suit of foreign governments and state commercial entities. While many nations now have restricted this status-based right of immunity by withdrawing it from purely *commercial* property and activities of foreign governments,[126] immunity continues to be granted to all officials and property engaged in *governmental* (public, or noncommercial) undertakings.[127] In practice, this means that immunity protects such officials, state property and governmental activity from legal action or, at a minimum, from the execution of a judgment against them.

Symbolically validated rules like these, precisely because they are old, or have been encrusted with quaint forms and rituals, seem easy prey to functionalist critique. They sometimes work an injustice, and they often appear anachronistic. On the other hand, a new rule, even if agreed upon, might not have the same capacity to obligate. To the extent that the legitimacy of a rule is dependent on symbolic validation, there is reason—albeit not invariably a decisive one—to leave the rule alone.

Symbols, ritual and pedigree are factors that cannot be made to order and rules endowed with them need to be husbanded. "No one makes up ritual or symbol any more than anyone makes up language," a study of ancient Chinese ritual has shown.

> Ritual and symbol arise without intention or adaptation to conscious purpose; they seem to be collective products worked out . . . over long periods of time. . . . Ironically, it appears that rituals and symbols must in some way already be regarded as "legitimate" in order for them to confer legitimacy on those who employ them.[128]

IV. Coherence and Legitimacy

Symbolic validation, like determinacy, serves to legitimize rules. But like determinacy, symbolic validation is not quite as simple a notion as it may initially appear. For example, as traditional Chinese practice makes clear, ritual invoked to enhance the capacity of a rule to compel compliance will

[126] The United States officially promulgated this policy in 1952, when the Department of State, by means of the "Tate letter," declared its adherence to the "restrictive theory" of sovereign immunity. Under this theory, immunity would be recognized with regard to sovereign or public acts (*jure imperii*) but not with respect to private acts (*jure gestionis*). Letter from Jack B. Tate, Acting Legal Adviser, Department of State, to Philip B. Perlman, Acting Attorney General, May 19, 1952, *reprinted in* 26 DEPT. ST. BULL. 984 (1952). For current European treatment of immunity, see the European Convention on State Immunity and Additional Protocol, 1972 ETS 74, *reprinted in* 11 ILM 470 (1972).

[127] Foreign Sovereign Immunities Act of 1976, 28 U.S.C. §§1330, 1602–1611 (1982). *See also* Higgins, *Recent Developments in the Law of Sovereign Immunity in the United Kingdom*, 71 AJIL 423 (1977). For judicial discussion of current U.S. practice and its history, see Broadbent v. Organization of Am. States, 628 F.2d 27 (D.D.C. 1980). U.S. application of the "commercial" activity concept under the doctrine of restrictive immunity is discussed in *id.* at 33–35; and the immunity accorded international organizations under the rubrics of restrictive and absolute immunity is treated in *id.* at 30–33.

[128] H. WECHSLER, *supra* note 80, at 35.

only succeed if the rituals are themselves legitimate and are strictly observed. Similarly, a pedigree only confers actual rights and duties when the standards for pedigreeing are applied *coherently*. When, on the contrary, symbols, ritual and pedigree are dispensed capriciously, the desired effect of legitimization may not accrue.

Both determinacy and symbolic validation are connected to a further variable: coherence. The effect of incoherence on symbolic validation can be illustrated by reference to diplomatic practices pertaining to the ritual validation of governments and states. The most important act of pedigreeing in the international system is the deep-rooted, traditional act that endows a new government, or a new state, with symbolic status. When the endowing is done by individual governments, it is known as *recognition*.[129] The symbolic conferral of status is also performed collectively through a global organization like the United Nations when the members vote to admit a new nation to membership,[130] or when the General Assembly votes to accept the credentials of the delegates representing a new government.[131]

These two forms of validation are important because they enhance the status of the validated entity; that is, the new state or government acquires legitimacy, which, in turn, carries entitlements and obligations equal to those of other such entities. Such symbolic validation cannot alter the empirically observable reality of power disparity among states and governments, nor, properly understood, does it give off that cue. It does, however, purport to restrict what powerful states legitimately may do with their advantage over the weak. It is a cue that prompts the Soviets, however reluctantly, to do a lot of explaining when they invade Afghanistan. The pedigreed statehood of Afghanistan, together with the determinacy of the rules against intervention by one state in the internal affairs of another, then combine to render those Soviet explanations essentially unacceptable, global scorn evidencing the inelastic determinacy of the applicable rules. The practices of symbolic equality conferred by recognition also stipulate that the leader of tiny Bhutan must receive exactly the same number of volleys fired in salute as does the head of state of its huge neighbor, China. Recognition, as validation, has the effect of cuing the equal capacity of rich and poor, strong and weak, for acquiring rights and duties. It creates a presumption against all purported interpretations of existing rules—and against proposed new rules—that would make arbitrary distinctions between the rights and duties of different states or governments. Symbolic equality thus both affirms and reinforces real equality. Weaker nations, in particular, believe that ritual incantation of their symbolically validated status, at a minimum, has reduced somewhat the option of the powerful to treat the weak as tributary or

[129] For U.S. practices, see L. GALLOWAY, RECOGNIZING FOREIGN GOVERNMENTS: THE PRACTICE OF THE UNITED STATES (1978). An excellent treatment of recognition in general can be found in H. LAUTERPACHT, RECOGNITION IN INTERNATIONAL LAW (1947).

[130] J. DUGARD, RECOGNITION AND THE UNITED NATIONS (1987).

[131] See *infra* note 140 for illustrations of the converse, attempts to deny or rescind recognition by opposing delegates' credentials.

vassal states in contravention of the rights inherent in their status as states.[132]

These important benefits only accrue if the validation is effective; and it is only effective if the forms and standards have been followed.

Each kind of pedigreeing has its own rules and standards. No cue, no amount of ritual behavior, can achieve symbolic validation if its prescribed procedures are not followed or its public standards are violated. Graham Greene's "whisky priest" may have lost his faith,[133] but as long as he follows the rites, he remains an effective validator. Prescribed standards are the essential element in symbolic validation. For example, in 1948, the International Court of Justice was asked by the General Assembly to designate the test for admitting candidate states to UN membership.[134] The Court replied, essentially, by reciting the rules established by Article 4 of the UN Charter: that an applicant must be a state, peace loving, willing to accept the obligations of the Charter, able to carry them out, and willing to do so. The Court further explained that these were "not merely . . . the necessary conditions, but also . . . the conditions which suffice."[135] In other words, nations that objectively satisfy that standard are entitled to have their status validated. The standard is itself pedigreed by its inclusion in the UN Charter, the world's most inclusive multilateral treaty, and by its deep historical rootedness in analogous national recognition practices.[136]

Similarly, the legal adviser to the Secretary-General prepared a memorandum explaining the rules applicable to accepting or rejecting the credentials of a delegation when there is doubt about their validity, for example, during a civil war when there may be two adversary claimants. In such situations, too, UN members should be guided by Charter Article 4, the legal adviser said. Moreover,

> [w]here a revolutionary government presents itself as representing a State, in rivalry to an existing government, the question at issue should be which of these two governments in fact is in a position to employ the resources and direct the people of the State in fulfilment of the obligations of membership. In essence, this means an inquiry as to whether the new government exercises effective authority within the territory of the State and is habitually obeyed by the bulk of the population.[137]

[132] For example, a pledged word commits powerful as well as weak governments. There is widespread recognition by states, antedating the UN Charter, that a commitment equally obligates powerful, as weaker nations. *See* Legal Status of Eastern Greenland (Den. v. Nor.), 1933 PCIJ (ser. A/B) No. 53, at 22 (Judgment of Apr. 5).

[133] Greene shows that even though a priest may fall into a secularized life style, he retains his spiritual powers. A "whisky priest" is "a damned man putting God into the mouths of men," owing to his authority to perform communion. *See* G. GREENE, THE POWER AND THE GLORY 83 (1940).

[134] Admission of a State to the United Nations (Charter, Art. 4), 1948 ICJ REP. 57 (Advisory Opinion of May 28).

[135] *Id.* at 62, 63.

[136] *See* 1 L. OPPENHEIM, *supra* note 77, at 124–52.

[137] Letter to Trygve Lie, Mar. 8, 1950, Legal Aspects of the Problems of Representation in the United Nations, 5 UN SCOR Supp. (Jan.–May 1950) at 18, 22–23, UN Doc. S/1466 (1950).

Governments that do are eligible; those that do not are not. These standards are also rooted in venerable national recognition practices.

These standards for symbolic validation at the United Nations, like any rules, leave room for differences of interpretation in borderline cases where "willingness to carry out obligations" and "control over territory and population" are not wholly self-evident. Nevertheless, the standards have a fairly high degree of formal determinacy and are not difficult to understand, making it possible to dismiss bogus, self-serving interpretations. For example, it is surely not permissible to vote to deny membership to a new state on the ground that its president is black or that its inhabitants are poor. The standards also explain why even ardent Palestinian and Sahrawian representatives have not yet sought membership in the United Nations.

When the symbolic validation proceeds legitimately in accordance with its own prescription—when these rules are followed—it succeeds in its purpose. If validation is withheld in conformity with the same standards, the rejected candidate will be denied the hallmark of effective statehood. The legitimate refusal of governments, individually, and collectively in the United Nations, to validate the Bantustan "homelands"—which clearly do not meet the standard—has undoubtedly contributed to those pseudo-nations' failure to achieve the status of membership and equality in the international community.[138] Problems arise, however, when the standards are not applied coherently; that is, when they are applied to some but not to others equally entitled, or when the standards cease to be connected to principles of general applicability. For example, the United States Government led the fight that, for years, allowed the Nationalist regime on Taiwan, and not the Communist regime in Beijing, to occupy the Chinese seat in UN organs, on the ground that this "is a privilege and not a right."[139] The United States meant that symbolic validation could be withheld from the Beijing Government, even though it obviously met the traditional criteria, because those could be overridden by political considerations. More recently, African and Arab members of the General Assembly have led efforts to reject the credentials of the delegations from South Africa and Israel[140]

[138] The General Assembly condemned the establishment by South Africa of Bantu homelands (Bantustans) as an attempt artificially to divide the African people into "nations" according to their tribal origins, with the aim of weakening the African front in its struggle for its inalienable and just rights. GA Res. 2775E, 26 UN GAOR Supp. (No. 29) at 42, UN Doc. A/8429 (1971). The resolution passed by the resounding vote of 110 in favor, 2 opposed, with 2 abstentions. *See also* Report of the Secretary-General, UN Doc. A/8388 (1971) (transmitting consensus adopted on Sept. 13, 1971, by joint meeting of the Special Committee on *Apartheid*, the Special Committee on the Situation with regard to the Implementation of the Declaration on the Granting of Independence to Colonial Countries and Peoples, and the United Nations Council for Namibia); Dugard, *South Africa's "Independent" Homelands: An Exercise in Denationalization*, 10 DEN. J. INT'L L. & POL'Y 11 (1980) (for the development of the Bantustan policy).

[139] State Department Memorandum, *U.S. Policy on Nonrecognition of Communist China*, 39 DEP'T ST. BULL. 385 (1958).

[140] GA Res. 3207, 29 UN GAOR Supp. (No. 31) at 2, UN Doc. A/9631 (1974) (resolution on South Africa). When, in 1982, the Arab bloc decided to challenge the credentials of the

even though there is no question that these do meet the criteria for representing their respective countries. The General Assembly, with the support of the United States and a majority of Western and Third World nations, has also continued to seat the delegation of the Kampuchean regime headed by Prince Sihanouk even though it fails to control any significant part of the territory of the country it claims to represent. At least those who are responsible for the Kampuchean result have sought to justify themselves by proposing a new general rule: that a regime, even if it is in effective control, should not be rewarded for having been installed by foreign aggression.[141] That new rule may eventually acquire pedigreed legitimacy, but it has not done so as yet.

When the process of symbolic validation is abused by failure to follow its own procedural rules and standards, a divergence is likely to occur between the real world and the symbolic world, to the detriment of the status-validating processes and symbols. They may cease to be taken seriously. For example, at a time when the Chinese Communist regime was still being excluded from the United Nations, Secretary-General Dag Hammarskjöld nevertheless engaged in numerous important negotiations with Chou En-lai, Beijing's foreign minister.[142] The head of the UN Secretariat, it seems, did not feel constrained by the members' decision denying validation to the Communist authorities. Similarly, Hammarskjöld's successor, U Thant, vigorously pressed his negotiations with Hanoi during the Vietnam War,[143]

Israeli delegation, the United States announced it would boycott any UN body that excluded the Israelis and would also withhold its contribution amounting to 25% of the UN budget. T. FRANCK, NATION AGAINST NATION 217 (1985). Most recently, Oman, acting on behalf of 20 Arab states, proposed an amendment to exclude the credentials of Israel from General Assembly approval. The General Assembly voted not to act on this amendment. *Credentials Committee Reports Adopted*, UN CHRON., No. 1, February 1987, at 16. *See also* Halberstam, *Excluding Israel from the General Assembly by a Rejection of its Credentials*, 78 AJIL 179 (1984).

[141] Credentials of Representatives to the Forty-first Session of the General Assembly: First Report of the Credentials Committee, UN Doc. A/41/727, para. 12 (prov. ed. 1986).

> The representative of the United States of America stated that the credentials of the representatives of Democratic Kampuchea were in order, fulfilled the requirements of rule 27 of the rules of procedure, had already been accepted by the General Assembly in the past and should be accepted at the current session. The suggested alternative was a regime brought to power by a foreign military invasion and that was clearly not representative in any way, shape or form of the Kampuchean people.

Id.

[142] The Secretary-General conducted a series of talks with Chou En-lai "in the name of the United Nations" (*see* GA Res. 906, 9 UN GAOR Supp. (No. 21) at 56, UN Doc. A/2890 (1954)) in order to discuss the release of four U.S. fighter pilots shot down near the Yalu River between October 1952 and January 1953, while they were flying missions for the UN Command during the Korean War. See 2 PUBLIC PAPERS OF THE SECRETARIES-GENERAL OF THE UNITED NATIONS: DAG HAMMARSKJÖLD (1953–1956), at 415–59 (1972), for details of the Secretary-General's mission. *See also* T. FRANCK, *supra* note 140, at 136–37.

[143] In 1964 U Thant secretly informed President Johnson that he could arrange a meeting between the United States and North Vietnam. Believing he had secured the President's blessing, he proceeded to use his good offices to arrange a meeting in Rangoon. But when the United States failed to respond once the meeting had been agreed to by the North Vietnamese,

even though the UN political organs had never validated the nation of North Vietnam, let alone its governmental representatives.[144] The refusal to seat the South African delegates to the General Assembly likewise has not prevented Secretary-General Pérez de Cuéllar from negotiating with Pretoria over such matters as the future of illegally occupied Namibia.[145] With whom else, after all, *could* he negotiate that question?

To recapitulate: an act of recognition, the symbolic validation of a state or regime, has the capacity to bestow, symbolically, rights and duties on the recognized entity when, *but only if*, it is done in accordance with the applicable principled rules and procedures. Such pedigreed recognition, and its corporate UN equivalent, is everywhere accorded great weight. On the other hand, when the rules and standards for validation are violated, or are themselves unprincipled and capricious, then symbolic validation fails in its objective of bestowing status. Moreover, when validation is seen to be capricious, a failure to validate will do more to undermine the legitimacy of the validating process than of the state or government thus deprived of symbolic validation.

The failure of mystical ritual to do what it is invoked for is usually explained metaphysically. The excommunicate priest who elevates the host before the altar in a fraudulent Eucharist is left holding only bread and wine because his invalid orders cannot effect the miracle of transubstantiation. But failed validation can often be explained rationally. For example, the Ukraine has not been transformed into a sovereign and equal state by its membership in the United Nations. Membership held at variance with the Organization's own standards does not validate the Ukraine's statehood.[146] Similarly, when the United Nations wishes to engage in relief activities in Kampuchea, its officials do not deal with the symbolically validated government of Prince Sihanouk but, rather, with the "unrecognized" regime actually in control. The perverse use of validation, in both instances, fails to give or withhold status for reasons that are practical, rational and not in the least

---

Thant felt humiliated by the U.S. Government and leaked his story to the world. T. FRANCK, *supra* note 140, at 154–58.

[144] The People's Republic of China was admitted to the United Nations on Oct. 25, 1971, and Vietnam acquired membership only in 1977.

[145] For an account of how the Security Council directed Secretary-General Waldheim " 'to initiate as soon as possible contacts with all parties concerned' " so that the people of Namibia might exercise their right to self-determination and independence, see D. SOGGOT, NAMIBIA: THE VIOLENT HERITAGE 53–54 (1986).

[146] Despite the fact that the Soviet Constitution guarantees individual republics the right to secede from the Soviet Union, it was widely known that the Ukraine, like each of its sister republics, was considerably less independent than any American state and thus was otherwise ineligible for UN membership. Nonetheless, the West ultimately acceded to the Soviet request to admit two republics as UN members because it was viewed as a reasonable price to pay for Soviet participation in the United Nations. T. FRANCK, *supra* note 140, at 21. For a detailed history of the negotiations leading to the West's disposition of Stalin's initial request for membership for all 16 Soviet republics, see R. RUSSELL, A HISTORY OF THE UNITED NATIONS CHARTER 435, 533, 536–37, 539 n.49, 584, 597–98, 636 (1958).

metaphysical. If the valid procedural rules or standards are not applied, it is to be expected that no legitimacy will be conferred.

The costs to its legitimacy of applying a rule incoherently arise in three related, but different, senses. First, incoherence nullifies the flawed act of validating or withholding validation. Second, it undermines the standards, rules and processes for bestowing status or validity. Third, it derogates from the legitimacy of the institution that is charged with validating. Thus, in the UN context, when the General Assembly fails to follow the Organization's own rules, standards or procedures for accrediting delegates, it damages the claim of the whole UN system to be taken seriously as the symbolic bestower of status.

Dworkin has pointed out that coherence (he uses the term "integrity")[147] is a key factor in explaining why rules compel.[148] He observes that a rule is coherent when like cases are treated alike in application of the rule and when the rule relates in a principled fashion to other rules of the same system. Consistency requires that a rule (or, as we have noted, a ritual or standard), whatever its content, be applied uniformly in every "similar" or "applicable" instance. The opposite is what Dworkin calls "checkerboarding."[149]

There is another aspect of coherence. It encompasses the further notion that a rule, standard or validating ritual gathers force if it is seen to be connected to a network of other rules by an underlying general principle. This latter aspect of coherence merits closer examination.

Let us imagine that it has been generally agreed that the $1,010 billion debt of Third World states[150] should be retired by the borrowers' paying the lenders half the total amount owed. Both sides regard this compromise as the best deal they can get in present circumstances. The problem is one of coverage. How is the 50 percent repayment formula going to be implemented in practice? Who will repay what? Suppose it were suggested that states whose names begin with the letters *A–M* should repay their entire debt, while those whose names start with *N–Z* pay nothing. Such a rule has determinacy. Although some will fare better than others, no borrower state will be worse off with the compromise than without it. The compromise is also better for the lenders than being repaid nothing, and better for the borrowers than having to repay everything. Yet any such "checkerboard" compromise is likely to be rejected by both borrowers and lenders because of its manifest incoherence. Its incoherence makes it facially illegitimate.

To be legitimate, Dworkin points out, such a compromise must "aim to settle on some coherent principle whose influence then extends to the natural limits of its authority."[151] That means the compromise must connect what it does with some *rational principle of broader application*. The alphabetic

[147] R. DWORKIN, *supra* note 7.

[148] *Id.* at 190–92.

[149] *Id.* at 179.

[150] INTERNATIONAL BANK FOR RECONSTRUCTION AND DEVELOPMENT, WORLD DEBT TABLES, EXTERNAL DEBT OF DEVELOPING COUNTRIES, 1985–86, at xi (1986).

[151] R. DWORKIN, *supra* note 7, at 179.

compromise asserts a principle that distinguishes between countries—those which must repay and those to be forgiven—by means of a general principle that cannot be defended on any rational basis. The alphabetic compromise, like the flipping of a coin, is an admission that no rational principle can be found that will produce the desired result. Thus, the decision is left to chance: the "draw" of the alphabet. This establishes no generalizable rule, no principle to justify the basis for making a decision. It lacks coherence because it lacks nexus: both in logic and, more important, in practice. It fails to connect to a rational principle in general use. It establishes no basis for a continuing pattern of systemic interaction; it connects the particular decision to no sense of ongoing community. Even if there were other debt crises in the future, the alphabetic approach would merely become more indefensible as it lost its one vestigial merit: its randomness. Nothing in international life is ever resolved, or likely to be solved, by recourse to the alphabetic principle except seating arrangements at multinational conferences.

A coherent half-loaf compromise could be achieved by applying any one of various coherent, principled approaches. For example, debt forgiveness could be distributed on a sliding scale based on national income or on per capita productivity, the inverse of the scale of assessment used to tax UN members. Or each debtor's indebtedness could be reduced by a fixed percentage, as in a bankruptcy reorganization. Or all repayments could be stretched out in accordance with a schedule based on rise in productivity. Any of these methods of implementing the half-loaf compromise connects with a principle of distribution that commends itself rationally and has been, and will be, applied elsewhere. Coherence requires that the rule applied to a dispute about the distribution of debt relief should employ distinctions that are acceptable (or, at least, not unacceptable) in solving not only future instances of the same problem but also quite different distributive problems.

Dworkin illustrates the potency of coherence as a factor in legitimacy by asserting that a half-loaf regulation is even less acceptable than no loaf at all when it produces a checkerboard result. "Even if I thought strict liability for accidents wrong in principle," he has written, "I would prefer that manufacturers of both washing machines and automobiles be held to that standard rather than that only one of them be. I would rank the checkerboard solution not intermediate between the other two [no strict liability and universal strict liability] but third, below both, and so would many other people." Such "compromises are wrong, not merely impractical."[152] They are lacking in legitimacy.

A rule taxing only property with even-numbered addresses would be incoherent and lack legitimacy. The same rule would be perfectly coherent if odd-numbered properties, all being on the same side of each street, had received a 20-year tax abatement in return for yielding several feet of their frontal property to the city for the widening of roadways. A "selective service" lottery for induction into the armed services employs a purely random military draft, which may be justified as the fairest way to allocate a

[152] *Id.* at 182.

social burden in some circumstances. In other words, before a rule that is facially inconsistent in its application can be adjudged incoherent, it is necessary to determine not only that it applies unequally but also that no reasonable principle of general application can justify the inequality. If a rule is unequally applied, its legitimacy is placed in question. If the inequality is also unprincipled, the legitimacy of the rule—its capacity to obligate—will be severely depleted.

The idea that coherence is a key indicator of legitimacy may be illustrated further by reference to three recent developments in the international community: the emergence of a "right" to *self-determination*; the development of a notion of *state equality*, as exemplified by the voting system of the United Nations; and the entrenchment of free and nondiscriminatory terms of trade—the *most-favored-nation* system—in the General Agreement on Tariffs and Trade. Each has undergone a crisis of legitimacy occasioned by challenges to its normative coherence. Let us examine how each has attempted to meet that challenge and thus to protect its legitimacy.

The notion that national or ethnic groups are entitled to "self-determination" had its origins in the settlements made at the end of World War I. The U.S. delegation to the Versailles Peace Conference was firmly instructed to apply ethnic criteria to resolve all European territorial disputes and, to that end, President Woodrow Wilson saw to it that his team included historians, geographers and ethnologists.[153] Throughout the negotiations, Wilson insisted that settlements be based on "facts,"[154] by which he meant "racial aspects, historic antecedents, and economic and commercial elements."[155] Note, however, in passing, that this general principle need not be accepted as *just*. The legitimacy of a rule is conditioned by its coherence, but a rule may be quite coherent (in our sense of the term), as well as highly determinate and symbolically validated, and yet be thought unjust. Wilsonian self-determination, for example, may be legitimate yet work an injustice by transferring territories and resources in accordance with a general principle of ethnicity while ignoring considerations of economic well-being and the distributive claims of poor people.[156]

The Wilsonian principle achieved considerable coherence in the immediate period following World War I. Insistence on its application led to a plebiscite in Schleswig, which had been annexed by Prussia in 1864.[157] In 1920, Northern Schleswig voted to revert to Denmark, a verdict accepted by the Peace Conference.[158] The same principle governed the creation of Czechoslovakia, in accordance with the wishes of Wilson's Secretary of State Lansing, "that all branches of the Slav race should be completely freed from German and Austrian rule."[159] Similarly, the principle was used by Wilson

[153] R. S. BAKER, WOODROW WILSON AND WORLD SETTLEMENT 109 (1922).

[154] *Id.* at 187. [155] *Id.*

[156] Franck & Hawkins, *Rawls' Theory of Justice in International Context*, 10 MICH. J. INT'L L. (1988).

[157] S. WAMBAUGH, PLEBISCITES SINCE THE WORLD WAR 14 (1933).

[158] 2 A HISTORY OF THE PEACE CONFERENCE OF PARIS 205 (H. W. V. Temperley ed. 1920).

[159] 4 *id.* at 261 (1921).

to oppose efforts by France to create a buffer Rhenish Republic[160] between itself and Germany. Wilson's chief adviser, Colonel House, was scornful of the French, who "do not seem to know that to establish a Rhenish Republic against the will of the people would be contrary to the principle of self-determination."[161] The compromise accommodated some elements of both French geopolitics and American moralism. A Saar buffer was established. However, it was not to be independent but administered through the League of Nations. Although the inhabitants were not allowed to be represented in the German Reichstag, their schools, language, laws and German nationality were left untouched.[162]

The principle of self-determination was also used in drawing the boundaries of an independent Poland on incontrovertible historical and ethnic grounds.[163] Wilson succeeded in his demand that the new Polish state "should be erected" to "include the territories inhabited by indisputably Polish populations."[164] Finally, Upper Silesia was divided by the League Council in 1921 along strictly ethnic lines.[165]

The coverage, in practice, of the concept of self-determination after World War I should not be exaggerated by dwelling exclusively on these dramatic instances. The rule was extended only—and, at that, imperfectly—to the European territories of the vanquished powers. It was not applied, for example, to the dispute between Sweden and Finland over the Aaland Islands.[166] The commission of inquiry appointed to settle that problem instead declared that "the principle had not yet attained the status of a positive rule of international law."[167] On the other hand, Britain claimed to be motivated by self-determination in the partition of Ireland.[168]

After World War II, however, the self-determination principle came to be applied even more generally. The United Nations Charter for the first time expressed a general obligation of states to help enable inhabitants of all dependent non-self-governing territories to make a meaningful choice of national destiny. By joining the United Nations, its members accepted "a sacred trust" to "develop self-government, to take due account of the political aspirations of the peoples, and to assist them in the progressive development of their free political institutions."[169] Some colonial territories that previously belonged to Germany or Japan were placed under a formal

[160] THE INTIMATE PAPERS OF COLONEL HOUSE 334 (C. Seymour ed. 1928).

[161] *Id.* at 345.

[162] 2 Temperley (ed.), *supra* note 158, at 182.

[163] R. S. BAKER, *supra* note 153, at 110–11.

[164] *Id.*

[165] D. FLEMING, THE UNITED STATES AND WORLD ORGANIZATION 153 (1938).

[166] L. BUCHHEIT, SECESSION 71 (1978). [167] *Id.*

[168] Linking the issue of Ireland to self-determination, Balfour wrote: "No one can think that Ulster ought to join the South and West who thinks that the Jugo Slavs should be separated from Austria. No one can think that Ulster should be divorced from Britain who believes in self-determination." Balfour, The Irish Question, Nov. 25, 1919, PRO CAB 24/93, *quoted in* T. G. FRASER, PARTITION IN IRELAND, INDIA AND PALESTINE 27 (1984). For Lloyd George's comments, see T. G. FRASER, *id.* at 38.

[169] UN CHARTER art. 73.

trusteeship system supervised by the United Nations, which aimed "to promote . . . progressive development towards self-government or independence as may be appropriate," in accordance with "the freely expressed wishes of the peoples concerned."[170]

The principle now applied equally to all: to colonies and to Europe, to victors and to vanquished. The first article of the Charter, enumerating the Organization's "Purposes and Principles," specifies an all-embracing obligation of members to develop "friendly relations among nations based on respect for the principle of equal rights and self-determination of peoples."[171] This casts the principle in terms of universal coverage. The term "peoples," moreover, recognizes the importance of the ethnic dimension in determining *who* is entitled to invoke self-determination. No boundary separates "peoples" entitled from "peoples" not entitled. Coherence was achieved and the rule acquired powerful legitimacy.

This is not merely a matter of theory or words. Very few rules of the international system have had as dramatic an impact. Beginning with India, Burma and the Gold Coast, Britain conceded self-determination to nearly one billion persons, with France, the Netherlands, Belgium, Spain and Portugal, albeit at first reluctantly, following suit. With a host of new nations seeking validation, UN membership nearly doubled between 1960 and 1980.[172] This was achieved almost entirely by voluntary compliance in deference to a legitimate rule, rather than by coercion.

The coherence of the rule, however, did not last. Even as these dramatic events were occurring, the same principle of self-determination was being denied all of Eastern Europe. Territories largely inhabited by Latvians, Poles, Germans, Romanians, Hungarians and Slovaks were arbitrarily annexed by neighboring states, and their populations often put to flight. Somewhat later, some of the very nations of a Third World that had just benefited from the application of self-determination refused to join in censuring the Soviet Union and Warsaw Pact nations during the invasion of Hungary in 1956 and of Czechoslovakia in 1968.[173] Nor was the principle disregarded only in Europe. No sooner had India become independent than its armed forces denied self-determination to the princely state of Kashmir, which might well have been entitled to it on ethnic, religious and legal grounds.[174] So, too, neither independent Nigeria nor the Organization of African Unity felt any obligation to permit self-determination to the ethni-

[170] *Id.* art. 76(b).

[171] *Id.* art. 1, para. 2.

[172] UN membership rose from 82 members at the beginning of 1960, 1959 UN Y.B. 539, to 154 by the end of 1980, 1980 UN Y.B. 1347.

[173] Saudi Arabia, Syria, Yemen, Yugoslavia, Afghanistan, Burma, Ceylon, Egypt, India, Indonesia, Iraq, Jordan, Libya and Nepal abstained from voting on a resolution condemning the 1956 Soviet invasion of Hungary. GA Res. 1004, ES-2 UN GAOR (564th plen. mtg.) at 7, 20, UN Doc. A/PV.564 (1956). Algeria, India and Pakistan abstained from voting on a Security Council resolution condemning the 1968 Soviet invasion of Czechoslovakia. 23 UN SCOR (1443d mtg.) at 28–29, UN Doc. S/PV.1443 (1968).

[174] India Independence Act, 1947, 10 & 11 Geo. 6, ch. 30.

cally and religiously distinct Ibo "nation" when it sought statehood for Biafra.[175]

Thus, the principle of self-determination began its descent into incoherence—in the sense of inconsistency of application—almost from the moment of its greatest apparent ascendance. Increasing incoherence became textually evident in 1960 with the General Assembly's adoption of the Declaration on the Granting of Independence to Colonial Countries and Peoples.[176] Drafted by the newly independent former colonies of Africa and Asia, it reiterated, on the one hand, "that all peoples have an inalienable right to complete freedom"[177] and demanded immediate implementation of this right "without any conditions or reservations in accordance with their freely expressed will and desire"[178] and regardless of "political, economic, social or educational preparedness."[179] On the other hand, the right was now to be applicable only to "territories which have not yet attained independence." The right was also offset by a new rule against any "attempt aimed at the partial or total disruption of the national unity and the territorial integrity of a country."[180]

The declaration thus revived the notion of the sanctity of existing boundaries and resistance to secession that informed the U.S. Civil War[181] and the decision in the Aaland Island case, but had briefly been disestablished by the notion of self-determination after World War I. In place of a coherent rule, there was now checkerboarding, with self-determination doctrinally sanctioned for some cases and prohibited for others. Not only has the coverage of self-determination shrunk, but also its boundaries—where it is applicable and where not—have become indistinct and incoherent. The standards for granting or withholding the right seem to lack connection to any underlying rational general principles.

This incoherence can be demonstrated by searching for applicable general principles that would justify the inconsistencies in the actual state practice since 1960. For example, Algeria was granted self-determination at the insistence of the world community, while Biafra was not. Is Algeria different from Biafra because the former is separated from France by water, while the latter is a contiguous part of the Nigerian landmass? Surely, this is not a

[175] Biafra declared its independence on May 30, 1967, but only five nations recognized its claim to independence. Neither the United Nations nor the OAU supported Biafran independence and the United Nations never even considered the issue. Nanda, *Self-Determination in International Law*, 66 AJIL 321, 326–27 (1972). *See also* 66 ASIL PROC. 58, 175 (1972).

[176] GA Res. 1514, 15 UN GAOR Supp. (No. 16) at 66, UN Doc. A/4684 (1960).

[177] *Id.*, Preamble.

[178] *Id.*, Art. 5.

[179] *Id.*, Art. 3.

[180] *Id.*, Art. 5.

[181] See, e.g., comments by President Lincoln:

> My paramount object in this struggle *is* to save the Union . . . . If I could save the Union without freeing *any* slave I would do it, and if I could save it by freeing *all* the slaves I would do it; and if I could save it by freeing some and leaving others alone I would also do that.

Letter from Abraham Lincoln to Horace Greeley, Aug. 22, 1862, *reprinted in* 5 THE COLLECTED WORKS OF ABRAHAM LINCOLN 388 (R. Basler ed. 1953).

principled distinction capable of being generalized. Many nations—the United States, the Philippines, Canada, Indonesia, India, China and the Soviet Union—have provinces or regions separated from the rest of their territory by salt water. Thus, the distance from Hawaii to Los Angeles is five times greater than that from Marseilles to Algiers. Understandably, an ultramarine principle has never been accepted in practice to define the boundaries of self-determination. No government is likely to accept a distinction that would allow the Canadian province of Prince Edward Island to enjoy the right of self-determination but not Quebec.

Other principles for making distinctions between those entitled and those not, encounter equal difficulty. A differentiation between oppressed "peoples" (entitled) and others (not entitled) has a certain moral attraction. But it is not generalizable and certainly fails to account for the actual behavior of states during the past 25 years in supporting or ignoring demands for self-determination. For example, even before their independence, the populations of Nigeria, India, Senegal and the Ivory Coast had far more say in their government than is currently enjoyed by the people of Latvia, Eritrea and the southern Sudan. Yet the international community has championed self-determination for the former, but not for the latter.

Likewise, attempts to introduce an economic variable to rationalize the "checkerboard" application of self-determination tends to be unsuccessful. It has been argued that Biafrans and other Nigerians have fared better by remaining united than they would have done had they separated.[182] But a strong case can also be made that Algeria and France would have prospered more had they remained together. And Katanga has surely suffered economically as a result of its continued union with Zaire, a denial of self-determination that was actually enforced by the United Nations.[183] The economic factor not only does not rationalize actual state practice, it is also probably bad theory. That economic considerations should or ever *will* trump political, cultural and ethnic ones is a very questionable basis for any agreed general principle.

A more defensible distinction makes self-determination applicable only to "peoples" who are treated *unequally* by government. This principle would

[182] An independent and united Nigeria was perceived to be a "model for Africa," a "key" to that continent's future stability and prosperity, because of its material wealth and rich culture. The "progressive Balkanization" of Nigeria, with its concomitant vast waste of human and social resources, was viewed with great anxiety as a tragedy for all Africa. 283 PARL. DEB. (5th ser.) 1367–76 (1967).

[183] The United Nations completely rejected the claim that Katanga was a sovereign independent nation. *See, e.g.*, SC Res. S/5002, 16 UN SCOR (Res. & Dec.) at 3, UN Doc. S/INF/16/Rev.1 (1961). The United Nations found itself at odds with Katanga. On Apr. 3, 1961, Katanga adopted a Decree on the State of Enmity with the United Nations, *reproduced in* J. GERARD-LIBOIS, KATANGA SECESSION 335–37 (R. Young trans. 1966), which, inter alia, forbade Katangans to enter into relations of any nature whatsoever with the United Nations or its agents. See also C. C. O'BRIEN, TO KATANGA AND BACK (1962), in which the author, a former representative of the United Nations in Katanga and former member of the Secretary-General's executive staff, offers a case history of UN experiences with Katanga.

explain why the inhabitants of a colony ruled by Britain or France might be entitled to self-determination, while Latvians or Biafrans were not. Even though preindependence Algeria did elect members to the French Assembly and Senate, the system of communal "colleges" then in operation gave a European vote ten times more weight than an Arab one.[184] Biafrans, by contrast, enjoyed the same rights as other Nigerians. Paradoxically, this basis for distinction may deny the right of self-determination to groups that are more oppressed than some to whom the right would accrue. Latvians, deprived of many basic freedoms, would have no right because they are treated no differently than other disempowered Soviet citizens. Thus, "peoples" of nations that treat everyone equally badly would have no right, while "peoples" treated quite well would be entitled to secede if they were not accorded quite as many rights as the most privileged of that populace.

Moreover, this theoretical basis for determining entitlement to self-determination, while coherent, and also rather congruent with prevailing state conduct, is hard to apply in practice. Once a secessionist movement is in full operation, its ethnic group is almost certain to encounter discriminatory treatment, as is demonstrated by the rise of anti-Tamil sentiment in Sri Lanka in tandem with the spread of Tamil insurrection. Secessionism and discrimination mutually reinforce one another, and it is difficult in particular instances to determine whether secessionism *caused* or *was caused by* unequal treatment.

Difficult or not, the search for a coherent general principle of coverage, or boundary, is important. If it fails, the once-dynamic right of self-determination will fall into incoherence and desuetude. As a rule of state conduct, it began to lose its power to obligate when it became a checkerboard of incoherent practice.

Coherence, in this sense, is fundamental to understanding why a rule text has sufficient legitimacy to affect the conduct of states. The power of coherence to validate derives from the phenomenon we have already identified: that the status of states is symbolically validated by admission into the community of states. It is by symbolic recognition of their membership in that community that states are confirmed in their equal capacity for rights and obligations. Coherence derives from—is the operational manifestation of—that community of rules. Dworkin, although focusing on a community of persons rather than of nations, explains *why* legitimacy is "grounded in" coherence.[185] Coherence demonstrates that states relate through more than random interactions; that they consciously accept responsibilities derived "from a more general responsibility" that is based on membership in a community. Thus, in the community of nations, each state must "treat discrete obligations that arise only under special circumstances, like the obligation to help a friend who is in great financial need, as derivative from and expressing a more general responsibility active throughout the association in different ways."[186] This concern, in principle, must be "an *equal*

[184] E. BEHR, THE ALGERIAN PROBLEM 38 (1961).

[185] R. DWORKIN, *supra* note 7, at 194. [186] *Id.* at 200.

concern for all members."[187] However, the concern is not incompatible with distinctions, so long as each distinction "fits a plausible conception of equal concern."[188] A plausible conception of equal concern is another way of describing a generalizable principle for determining the coverage of a rule-based obligation.

To take another example of such a search: the UN Charter, in Article 2, sets forth "the principle of the sovereign equality of all . . . Members." Article 27, however, provides that the five permanent members of the Security Council—Britain, China, France, the United States and the USSR—shall have a veto over substantive decisions. If states did not regard the United Nations as an aspect of a global community, this seeming contradiction would not matter. Life is full of contradiction. It only matters when a contradiction rises to the level of an incoherence that invalidates and illegitimatizes an aspect of the system of rules of a community to which the state belongs and by reference to which the state defines *its own legitimacy*. Does the contradiction between the voting procedure of the Charter and its rule of state equality invalidate the rules, the UN-based community and, thus, even the individual legitimacy of the members? To ask the question is to understand why states are reluctant to let the Charter fall into incoherence. Instead, they strive to find a reconciling "neutral principle,"[189] a rational distinction that could restore coherence and validate the "checkerboarding." The best one available is this: while all states are equal, some states, because of their special wealth and power, have greater obligations and responsibilities. Consequently, they may also be entitled to an enhanced vote in certain matters.

Unfortunately, this coherent conceptual justification for the privileges granted the "Big Five" in 1945 is not rationally defensible in 1988. In 1945, they really were the world's major powers, having vanquished the Axis and inherited the postwar leadership. Their special status had a certain plausibility, since the success of any important Security Council action would depend on their cooperation. Today, however, Britain, France and China are middle powers, and their role in the world and in the Organization has become no more important than that of some important states without the veto such as the Federal Republic of Germany, Brazil, Nigeria, India and Japan. The privilege bestowed by the rules has thus lost its rational persuasiveness as a boundary, a standard for making distinctions that connects with a rational general principle.

Apparently, this problem of incoherence, with its concomitant dangers, is recognized. While it has not been possible to amend the Charter, Britain, France and China, although casting occasional negative votes in the Council, have made it a practice not to do so except in the company of a majority, or of either the United States or the USSR.[190] In this way, they have contributed to the de facto remission of their veto power.

[187] *Id.* [188] *Id.* at 201.

[189] For a noteworthy attempt to establish a theoretical basis for such a quest in another area of law, see Wechsler, *Toward Neutral Principles of Constitutional Law*, 73 HARV. L. REV. 1 (1959).

[190] U.S. Mission to the United Nations, List of Vetoes Cast in Public Meetings of the Security Council (Apr. 14, 1988). Only once did the People's Republic of China stand alone in its veto in

This example illustrated that coherence mandates a connectedness between various component parts of a rule or code; between several applications of a rule in various instances; and between the general principles underlying a rule's application and those implicated in other rules. The General Agreement on Tariffs and Trade of 1947[191] further illustrates these aspects of coherence. Its most basic provision is the most-favored-nation clause, which prohibits members from giving benefits to some trading partners not given to all.[192] As long as this rule is applied consistently in practice, it appears to be coherent and, thus, legitimate. In recent years, however, it has become evident that the MFN provision, if applied consistently to all nations, would undermine rather than advance GATT's underlying purpose by diminishing the trade prospects of some 50 less-developed member countries. GATT therefore adopted a Generalized System of Preferences for these special cases.[193] It allows developed states temporarily to permit preferential access to products of only some states, particularly the "least developed."[194] While GSP is inconsistent with MFN, it coheres with the underlying purpose of GATT, which is to increase trade for all nations. It thus advances the real objectives of GATT. Also, it establishes a standard for distinction between the members to whom MFN is applicable and those temporarily benefited by GSP. That standard connects coherently with boundaries commonly used in other sets of regulations to demarcate coverage. Redistributive principles such as those which underlie GSP are commonplace in the international rule system and justify distinctions that, although creating superficial inconsistencies within rules and the application of rule systems, nonetheless leave the rules coherent and legitimate. The checkerboarding, in other words, is redeemed by being seen as based on a principle that both is consistent with the real intent of the specific rule and connects with that skein of principles integrating various other rules of the international system.

To summarize: coherence, and thus legitimacy, must be understood in part as defined by factors derived from a notion of community. Rules become coherent when they are applied so as to preclude capricious checkerboarding. They preclude caprice when they are applied consistently or, if inconsistently applied, when they make distinctions based on underlying general principles that connect with an ascertainable purpose of the rules and with similar distinctions made throughout the rule system. The result-

---

the Security Council. *Id.* at 9. France has vetoed alone only twice since 1946. *Id.* at 10–11. All United Kingdom vetoes during the last 15 years have been cast with the United States. *Id.* at 12–13.

[191] General Agreement on Tariffs and Trade [hereinafter GATT], Oct. 30, 1947, 61 Stat. (5), (6), TIAS No. 1700, 55–61 UNTS.

[192] *Id.*, Art. 1(1).

[193] GATT Contracting Parties, Decision of Nov. 28, 1979, Differential and More Favorable Treatment Reciprocity and Fuller Participation of Developing Countries, GATT, BASIC INSTRUMENTS AND SELECTED DOCUMENTS, 26th Supp. 203 (1980). *See also* J. JACKSON & W. DAVEY, LEGAL PROBLEMS OF INTERNATIONAL ECONOMIC RELATIONS 1149 (2d ed. 1986).

[194] Decision of Nov. 28, 1979, *supra* note 193, paras. 1 and 6.

ant skein of underlying principles is an aspect of community, which, in turn, confirms the status of the states that constitute the community. Validated membership in the community accords equal capacity for rights and obligations derived from its legitimate rule system.

By focusing on the connections between specific rules and general underlying principles, we have emphasized the horizontal aspect of our central notion of a community of legitimate rules. However, there are vertical aspects of this community that have even more significant impact on the legitimacy of rules.

V. Adherence (to a Normative Hierarchy) and Community

Professor Hart's observation, noted above, that the international arena lacks a "legislature, courts with compulsory jurisdiction, and centrally organized sanctions" leads him to deduce "that the rules for states resemble that simple form of social structure, consisting only of primary rules of obligation, which, when we find it among societies of individuals, we are accustomed to contrast with a developed legal system."[195] Although he acknowledges that international law does have many substantive "primary" rules, such as those specific rights and duties typically enumerated in treaties or developed through customary usage, he nevertheless concludes that the system is primitive, if not illusory, because it lacks those crucial procedural "secondary" rules which permit a rule to change and adapt through legislation and the decision of courts. An even more serious disqualification of the international system, Hart alleges, is its lack of "a unifying rule of recognition specifying 'sources' of law and providing general criteria for the identification of its rules."[196] By a "unifying rule of recognition," Hart means an international equivalent of the U.S. Constitution, or the British rule of parliamentary supremacy, both of which are "ultimate" in that they test the validity of all other rules by standards that are not themselves subject to being tested by reference to any superior rule.

Hart identifies the essential elements of a developed system of rules and then concludes that they are missing at the international level. He thus finds the international community to be the approximate equivalent of a small primitive tribe that has primary rules of obligation about such matters as land and kinship, but no system of governance that allocates and regulates social roles or facilitates, by an established process, the making, changing, application and reinterpreting of these random substantive primary rules.

In effect, Hart considers the international system to be primitive because individual rules lack *adherence* to a rule hierarchy. This is a much more sophisticated critique of the international rule system than the simple Austinian one, which focuses on the absence of a system of coercion. Hart does note the lack of institutionalized coercion but puts greater critical emphasis on the failure of international rules to adhere to a hierarchic rule structure.

[195] H. L. A. Hart, *supra* note 3, at 209. [196] *Id.*

Adherence—a term Hart does not use—is used here to mean the vertical nexus between a single *primary rule of obligation* ("cross on the green; stop on the red") and a pyramid of secondary rules about how rules are made, interpreted and applied: rules, in other words, about rules. These may be labeled *secondary rules of process*. Primary rules of obligation that lack adherence to a system of secondary rules of process are mere ad hoc reciprocal arrangements. They are not necessarily incapable of obligating parties that have agreed to them. They may even connect coherently with the underlying principles of distinction found in other rules to create a horizontal skein that is an aspect of community. But the degree of legitimacy of primary rules that only cohere is less than if the same rule were also connected to a pyramid of secondary rules of process, culminating in an ultimate rule of recognition. A rule, in summary, is more likely to obligate if it is made within the procedural and institutional framework of an organized community than if it is strictly an ad hoc agreement between parties in the state of nature. The same rule is still more likely to obligate if it is made within the hierarchically structured procedural and constitutional framework of a sophisticated community rather than in a primitive community lacking such secondary rules about rules.

Hart's critique of the community of states as small and primitive is still widely accepted. Even those who think that the system is at a more sophisticated stage of development might well concede that Hart's misgivings are not wholly unjustified. The recurrence of wars, other conflicts and unremedied injustices invites the appellation "primitive."

The misgivings, however, need to be kept in perspective. Of course, there *are* lawmaking institutions in the system. One has but to visit a highly structured multinational negotiation such as the decade-long Law of the Sea Conference of the 1970s to see a kind of incipient legislature at work. The Security Council, the decision-making bodies of the World Bank and, perhaps, the UN General Assembly also somewhat resemble the cabinets and legislatures of national governments, even if they are not so highly disciplined and empowered as the British Parliament, the French National Assembly or even the U.S. Congress. Moreover, there *are* courts in the international system: not only the International Court of Justice, the European Community Court and the regional human rights tribunals, but also a very active network of quasi-judicial committees and commissions, as well as arbitral tribunals established under such auspices as the Algiers agreement ending the Iran hostage crisis.[197] Arbitrators regularly settle investment disputes under the auspices and procedures of the World Bank and the International Chamber of Commerce. Treaties and contracts create jurisdiction for these tribunals and establish rules of evidence and procedure.[198]

[197] *See* Declaration of the Government of the Democratic and Popular Republic of Algeria Concerning the Settlement of Claims by the Government of the United States of America and the Government of the Islamic Republic of Iran, DEP'T ST. BULL., No. 2047, February 1981, at 3, *reprinted in* 75 AJIL 422 (1981), 20 ILM 230 (1981).

[198] The World Bank approved the Convention on the Settlement of Investment Disputes Between States and Nationals of Other States, Mar. 18, 1965, 17 UST 1270, TIAS No. 6090,

The international system thus appears on close examination to be a more developed community than critics sometimes allege. It has an extensive network of horizontally coherent rules, rule-making institutions, and judicial and quasi-judicial bodies to apply the rules impartially. Many of the rules are sufficiently determinate for states to know what is required for compliance and most states obey them most of the time. Those that do not, tend to feel guilty and to lie about their conduct rather than defy the rules openly. The system also has means for changing, adapting and repealing rules.

Most nations, most of the time, are both rule conscious and rule abiding. Why this is so, rather than that it is so, is also relevant to an understanding of the degree to which an international community has developed in practice. This silent majority's sense of obligation derives primarily not from explicit consent to specific treaties or custom, but from *status*. Obligation is perceived to be owed *to a community of states as a necessary reciprocal incident of membership in the community*. Moreover, that community is defined by secondary rules of process as well as by primary rules of obligation: states perceive themselves to be participants in a structured process of continual interaction that is governed by secondary rules of process (sometimes called rules of recognition), of which the UN Charter is but the most obvious example. The Charter is a set of rules, but it is also about how rules are to be made by the various institutions established by the Charter and by the subsidiaries those institutions have created, such as the International Law and Human Rights Commissions.

In addition, obligation is owed not only to the rules of the game, but also *to the game itself*. This is symptomatic of a community organized by a pyramid of secondary rules at whose apex is an ultimate rule or set of rules of recognition. The ultimate rule defines the community. If the game were football, the ultimate rule of recognition would be the one justifying the statement that what is being played is not baseball or tennis, but football. Thus, when the umpire calls a "foul," the legitimacy of that judgment derives ultimately from those rules which define the activity as football rather than some other sport. In the international system, the game of nations does have its own ultimate, defining set of rules by which the validity of all subsidiary rules—secondary procedural as well as primary substantive—may be tested.

A community is sophisticated when it has such an *ultimate rule of recognition*. In the United States, France, Germany and many other countries this is in the form of a written constitution. In the United Kingdom, however, the existence of an ultimate rule of recognition must be established deductively, since there is no written law defining the community. Nevertheless, it is

---

575 UNTS 159, which established the International Centre for Settlement of Investment Disputes. *See* Broches, *The Convention on the Settlement of Investment Disputes: Some Observations on Jurisdiction*, 5 COLUM. J. TRANSNAT'L L. 263 (1966). For U.S. implementing legislation, see Convention on the Settlement of Investment Disputes Act of 1966, Pub. L. No. 89-532, §2, 80 Stat. 344 (codified at 22 U.S.C. §§1650, 1650a (1982)). Under certain circumstances, parties to a dispute may arbitrate in the International Chamber of Commerce Court of Arbitration.

demonstrable that parliamentary supremacy qualifies as an ultimate rule of recognition because it owes its legitimacy only to public acquiescence, or to the corporate act of social commitment sometimes metaphorically described as a social contract. Its validity, unlike all the community's other secondary and primary rules, cannot be tested by reference to any other law. No statute makes Parliament supreme, nor can any law curb that supremacy. Indeed, if an act stipulated that it could only be repealed by a two-thirds majority, Parliament could delete that two-thirds requirement by a simple majority vote.[199] The rule of parliamentary supremacy defines the legitimacy of all other laws, but its own legitimacy is undefined, and thus *ultimate*. The rule is autochthonous: one "sprung from the earth itself."

Both the British Parliament and the U.S. Constitution are repositories of ultimate power unfettered by superior authority. Both the rule of parliamentary supremacy in Britain and the rules embodied in the Constitution of the United States are ultimate secondary rules of process by which the legitimacy of all primary rules of obligation may be tested and established. A rule of ultimate recognition operates with such extraordinary power to validate a subsidiary pyramid of rules—both other secondary rules of a procedural nature and primary rules of obligation—because the ultimate rule is accepted by a community that is defined by that rule. The ultimate set of rules also defines the status of each member of the community; that is to say, each member's status derives from the recognition of membership. Rejection of the ultimate rule by the members constitutes revolution and is the only option for discarding the ultimate rule (which, in some states but not in others, may be changed—as distinct from being overthrown—but only in strict accordance with its own terms). Acquiescence, on the other hand, is demonstrated tautologically, by compliance. Ultimate rules of recognition cannot be validated by reference to any other rule. All other secondary rules of the community are inferior to, and validated by, the ultimate rule or set of rules.

It is the nature of community, therefore, both to empower authority and to circumscribe it by an ultimate rule or set of rules of recognition that exists above, and itself is not circumscribed by, the system of normative authority. Does such a notion of community exist internationally, among states? Do nations recognize an ultimate rule or set of rules of recognition or process by which the legitimacy of all other international rules and procedures can be tested, a rule not itself subject to a higher normative test of its legitimacy, a rule that simply *is*, because it is accepted as font of the community's collective self-definition?

If the international community were merely a playing field on which states engaged in various random, or opportunistic, exchanges or interac-

[199] In perhaps the most eloquent statement of Parliament's unlimited legislative authority, Sir Edward Coke has declared that its "power and jurisdiction . . . is so transcendent and absolute, that it . . . hath sovereign and uncontrollable authority in the making, confirming, enlarging, restraining, abrogating, repealing, reviving, and expounding of laws." E. COKE, FOURTH INSTITUTE 36, *quoted in* A. DICEY, INTRODUCTION TO THE STUDY OF THE CONSTITUTION 41 (9th ed. 1939).

tions, it would be easy to conclude that this was a truly primitive aggregation, a rabble, lacking the organizing structure of secondary rules of process and, of course, an ultimate secondary rule. This, rather than any absence of coercive force, would indeed justify the appellation "primitive." The international community, however, demonstrably is not like that. States—whatever their occasional rhetorical excesses—recognize that they are not sovereign. They accept that they are members of a sophisticated community with secondary rules and with what amounts to a constitution or ultimate rules of recognition. States also recognize that they derive validation from membership in this community.

The nonsovereignty of states and the existence of a set of ultimate community rules can be demonstrated by examining the way treaties operate from the perspective of those that become parties to them. It is quite wrong to think that treaties bind states *because* they have consented to them. If states were sovereign, the mere act of entering into a treaty could not "bind" them in any accurate sense. States are not bound only because they agree to be bound, in the sense in which neighbors in an apartment building might informally agree, for their mutual convenience, to turn off their television sets by 10 o'clock every evening. Those neighbors are at liberty to disregard their obligation whenever it does not suit their purpose. Nor are states obligated by treaties the way individuals are bound by a contract. In municipal law, contracts are binding because their sanctity is prescribed and enforced by the state.[200] True, most contracts operate without recourse to state sanctions, but the sanctions remain in reserve.

Treaties thus do not exactly fit either model. They are not like the free-will agreement among neighbors, which is valid only as long as it continues to suit everyone's purpose; and they are not contracts made under the authority of a sovereign and enforceable by the full authority of the state, through either compelled specific performance or an award of damages. Treaties obviously cannot be binding in the sense of being sanctioned by an Austinian sovereign; but a treaty also cannot be said to be binding only because two or more sovereign states voluntarily agree to carry it out. "Sovereign" means *unbindable.* A treaty ratified by a truly sovereign state could only *declare*, never *bind*, that state's free will. If the state were indeed sovereign, then, no matter what it had signed, it would nevertheless remain free to terminate its consent at any time, just as the sovereign British Parliament cannot legislate a law that can only be amended by a two-thirds major-

[200] While the term "contract" is susceptible of many definitions, whatever else a contract may entail, it is agreed that it is "a promise, or set of promises, for breach of which the law gives a remedy, or the performance of which the law in some way recognizes as a duty." 1 WILLISTON ON CONTRACTS §1 (3d ed. 1957); RESTATEMENT (SECOND) OF CONTRACTS §1 (1981). *See also* 1 A. CORBIN, CONTRACTS §3 (1963) (which defines a contract to include "a promise enforceable at law directly or indirectly"). In some jurisdictions, courts will routinely mandate specific performance of the promise. *See, e.g.*, Dawson, *Specific Performance in France and Germany*, 57 MICH. L. REV. 495 (1959). The Anglo-American legal system, however, prefers to impose damages at least equal to the value of the breached promise. *See, e.g.*, J. CALAMARI & J. PERILLO, THE LAW OF CONTRACTS 580–604 (1977).

ity. If states were sovereign, entering into a treaty would be nothing more than evidence of their state of mind for the time being.

Notably, states never claim this. They act, instead, as if they were bound. They believe themselves to be bound—which can only be understood as evidence of their acquiescence in something demonstrable only circumstantially: an ultimate rule of recognition. In the international community "sovereignty"—however fragile—resides in the rule, and not in the individual states of the community. States seem to be aware of this rule's autochthony. They act in professed compliance with, and reliance on, the notion that when a state signs and ratifies an accord with one or more other states, then it has an obligation, superior to its sovereign will. The obligation derives not from consent to the treaty, or its text, but from membership in a community that endows the parties to the agreement with status, including the capacity to enter into treaties.

The most recent instance of this perception of an international rule superior to the specific acquiescence of any particular state is to be found in the advisory opinion rendered by the International Court of Justice on April 26, 1988, at the request of the United Nations General Assembly.[201] At issue was a conflict between provisions of a U.S. law that required the closing of the Observer Mission of the Palestine Liberation Organization,[202] and the obligation assumed under the UN Headquarters Agreement.[203] The Court stated unequivocally that it was "the fundamental principle of international law that it prevails over domestic law,"[204] that "the provisions of municipal law cannot prevail over those of a treaty."[205] The U.S. judge (Stephen M. Schwebel) added that "a State cannot avoid its international responsibility by the enactment of domestic legislation which conflicts with its international obligations" under a treaty.[206] Unanimously, the Court accepted that clear limitation on the sovereignty of states imposed by membership in the international community.

In Hart's words, the "view that a state may impose obligations on itself by promise, agreement, or treaty is not . . . consistent with the theory that states are subject only to rules which they have thus imposed on them-

[201] GA Res. 42/229B (Mar. 2, 1988).

[202] The Observer Mission status was created by GA Res. 3237, 29 UN GAOR Supp. (No. 31) at 4, UN Doc. A/9631 (1974). The closure of the mission is required by the Anti-Terrorism Act of 1987, title X of the Foreign Relations Authorization Act, 1988 and 1989, Pub. L. No. 100-204, tit. X, §1001, 101 Stat. 1331, 1406 (codified at 22 U.S.C.A. §§5201–5203 (West Supp. 1988)).

[203] *See* Agreement Regarding the Headquarters of the United Nations, June 26, 1947, *supra* note 115.

[204] Applicability of the Obligation to Arbitrate under Section 21 of the United Nations Headquarters Agreement of 26 June 1947, 1988 ICJ REP. 12, 34, para. 57 (Advisory Opinion of Apr. 26).

[205] Greco-Bulgarian "Communities," 1930 PCIJ (ser. B) No. 17, at 32 (Advisory Opinion of July 31).

[206] 1988 ICJ REP. at 42 (Schwebel, J., sep. op.).

selves."[207] Rather, "*rules* must already exist providing that a state is bound to do whatever it undertakes by appropriate words to do."[208] This hypothetical notion itself is actually set out in the text of a global treaty defining the law of treaties,[209] a document establishing a body of secondary rules of process. Even so, the binding force of the treaty codifying the law of treaties cannot emanate from the agreement of the large majority of states that have ratified it. It must come from some ultimate, generally accepted unwritten rule of recognition that is fundamental to any real understanding of the nature of international obligation.

If there is an ultimate set of secondary rules of process that embodies an abstract sovereignty and confers legitimacy in the international community, what are its other provisions? As with the foregoing rule, *pacta sunt servanda*, the other components of an ultimate rule of recognition can only be hypothesized and demonstrated circumstantially by habitual state deference. Thus, the rule that treaties are binding is itself modified by the rule that treaties are *void ab initio* if they are against the community's basic public policy, that is, if they violate the community's ultimate (peremptory) norms.[210] A treaty to commit genocide, for example, would be invalid for this reason. A related notion that appears to qualify as part of the ultimate rule of recognition pertains to the binding obligation imposed on state conduct by global custom. There is widespread acknowledgment by states that they are obligated by international customary rules, whether or not they agree in any specific instance with the import of a rule. This was recently reiterated by the International Court of Justice in the case brought by Nicaragua against the United States, where the latter was held to be obligated by an extensive array of customary norms despite an evident desire to pursue its self-interest in a manner incongruent with those rules.[211]

There are other parts of the ultimate rule that can be deduced from the practice of states in adhering to it *as an incident of statehood* rather than as a consequence of their specific consent. For example, new states are deemed to acquire the universal rights and duties of statehood not because they have agreed but because they have joined the community.[212] Similarly, new states may "inherit" rights and duties from a "parent" state[213] not by virtue of

[207] H. L. A. HART, *supra* note 3, at 219. [208] *Id.*

[209] Vienna Convention on the Law of Treaties, *supra* note 33, Art. 26.

[210] *Id.*, Art. 53.

[211] Military and Paramilitary Activities in and against Nicaragua (Nicar. v. U.S.), Merits, 1986 ICJ REP. 14 (Judgment of June 27).

[212] It is a well-established principle that a new state to the international community is automatically bound by the rules of international conduct existing at the time of admittance. *See* 1 L. OPPENHEIM, *supra* note 77, at 17–18. Even Tunkin concedes that if it enters "without reservations into official relations with other states," a new state is bound by "principles and norms of existing international law." *See* Tunkin, *Remarks on the Juridical Nature of Customary Norms of International Law*, 49 CAL. L. REV. 419, 428 (1961).

[213] There has been wide debate over the rights and obligations a successor state can inherit from its parent. The 19th-century doctrine of universal succession maintains that all the rights and duties of the parent pass to the successor. *See* O. UDOKANG, SUCCESSION OF NEW STATES

their consent but as a concomitant of status. Successor governments, too, automatically inherit rights and obligations.[214]

One more example of a part of the ultimate rule of recognition is the previously noted notion of state equality. UN Charter Article 2(1) specifically restates this rule, and no state since Hitler's Germany has claimed anything to the contrary. All states are bound by a rule of state equality as a concomitant of their membership in the community of nations. In the words of U.S. Chief Justice John Marshall in an 1825 decision, *The Antelope*, "No principle of general law is more universally acknowledged than the perfect equality of nations."[215]

It is therefore circumstantially demonstrable that there are obligations that states acknowledge to be necessary incidents of community membership. These are not perceived to obligate because they have been accepted by the individual state but, rather, are rules in which states acquiesce as part of their own validation; that is, as an inseparable aspect of "joining" a community of states that is defined by its ultimate secondary rules of process. It is even possible to conclude that the members of the global community acknowledge—for example, each time they sign a treaty or recognize a new government—*that statehood is incompatible with sovereignty*. They acknowledge this because they must, so as to obtain and retain the advantages of belonging to an organized, sophisticated community, advantages only available if ultimate sovereignty resides in a set of rules of universal application. That is why states behave as if such rules existed and obligated.

To put the matter another way, a "community" of states exists. It has at least some important secondary rules of recognition. These rules are "associative obligations," to use Dworkin's term,[216] which fasten onto all states because of their status as validated members of the international community. Only by stretching the notion of "consent" beyond its natural limits can these specific associative obligations be said to have been assumed consensually, even though they may sometimes be restated in a treaty. Dworkin rightly points out that "associative" rules of obligation are interpretive,[217] defining what a member owes others in the community in general. Thus, the obligation to honor treaties is acquired associatively, rather than by specific consent; and it is owed generally towards all members of the community. This is universally acknowledged. It is inconceivable, for example,

---

TO INTERNATIONAL TREATIES 122–24 (1972). At the other extreme is negativist theory, which holds that a successor inherits no rights and obligations, but begins with a tabula rasa. *See* D. O'CONNELL, STATE SUCCESSION IN MUNICIPAL LAW AND INTERNATIONAL LAW 14–17 (1967). The truth lies somewhere in between, with certain rights and duties of the parent devolving upon the successor. *See* 1 L. OPPENHEIM, *supra* note 77, at 120. Hart further points to evidence that changes in a state's circumstance may automatically accord it new rights and duties, for example, when it acquires new territory giving it a coastline. H. L. A. HART, *supra* note 3, at 221.

[214] Tinoco Case (Gr. Brit. v. Costa Rica), 1 R. Int'l Arb. Awards 369 (1923), *reprinted in* 18 AJIL 147 (1924).

[215] The Antelope, 23 U.S. (10 Wheat.) 66, 122 (1825).

[216] R. DWORKIN, *supra* note 7, at 196.

[217] *Id.* at 197.

that a state would announce that it would no longer be bound by treaties or custom. The obligation, moreover, cannot be extinguished by renouncing a consent that was never given, but only by extinguishing the status that is the real basis of the obligation.

According to Dworkin, a true community, as distinguished from a mere rabble, or even a system of random primary rules of obligation, is one in which the members

> accept that they are governed by common principles, not just by rules hammered out in political compromise. . . . Members of a society of principle accept that their political rights and duties are not exhausted by the particular decisions their political institutions have reached, but depend, more generally, on the scheme of principles those decisions presuppose and endorse. So each member accepts that others have rights and that he has duties flowing from that scheme . . . .

Nor are these rights and duties "conditional on his wholehearted approval of that scheme; these obligations arise from the historical fact that his community has adopted that scheme, . . . not the assumption that he would have chosen it were the choice entirely his."[218]

Moreover, the community "commands that no one be left out, that we are all in politics together for better or worse."[219] And its legitimizing requirement of rule integrity "assumes that each person is as worthy as any other, that each must be treated with equal concern according to some coherent conception of what that means."[220]

Does that accurately describe the social condition of the nations of the world in their interactive mode? The description does not assume harmony or an absence of strife. According to Dworkin, an "association of principle is not automatically a just community; its conception of equal concern may be defective."[221] What a rule community, a community of principle, does is to validate behavior in accordance with rules and applications of rules that confirm principled coherence and adherence, rather than acknowledging only the power of power. A rule community operates in conformity not only with primary rules but also with secondary ones—rules about rules—which are generated by valid legislative and adjudicative institutions. Finally, a community accepts its ultimate secondary rules of recognition not consensually, but as an inherent concomitant of membership status.

In the world of nations, each of these described conditions of a sophisticated community is observable today, even though imperfectly. This does not mean that its rules will never be disobeyed. It does mean, however, that it is usually possible to distinguish rule compliance from rule violation, and a valid rule or ruling from an invalid one. It also means that it is not necessary to await the millennium of Austinian-type world government to proceed with constructing—perfecting—a system of rules and institutions that will exhibit a powerful pull to compliance and a self-enforcing degree of legitimacy.

[218] *Id.* at 211.
[219] *Id.* at 213.
[220] *Id.* at 214.
[221] *Id.*

SELF-EXECUTING TREATIES

*By Jordan J. Paust**

The distinction found in certain cases between "self-executing" and "non-self-executing" treaties is a judicially invented notion that is patently inconsistent with express language in the Constitution affirming that "*all* Treaties . . . shall be the supreme Law of the Land."[1] Indeed, such a distinction may involve the most glaring of attempts to deviate from the specific text of the Constitution. For some 40 years after the formation of the Constitution, President George Washington's recognition in 1796 that "*every* Treaty [properly ratified] . . . thenceforward becomes the law of the land" was widely shared.[2] Yet today not all treaties are thought to be capable of operating as supreme federal law of their own effect.

It may prove profoundly informative to rediscover the predominant expectations of the Framers concerning the domestic legal effects of treaties and to ask whether certain present distinctions make constitutional sense. To that end, this paper will examine the following questions: When did the judicially created distinction first occur? How has it actually been used in the Supreme Court's history? Should the distinction be retained? What sort of criteria have been articulated with respect to the difference between a "self-executing" and a "non-self-executing" treaty, and how do these relate to the views of the Framers and to our constitutional history? Although a treaty may be non-self-executing according to its own terms, should any other treaty be inherently non-self-executing? What are the implications regarding a proper separation of powers and a responsible judiciary?

"ORIGINAL INTENT"—PREDOMINANT VIEWS OF THE FRAMERS

The year before the Constitutional Convention, on October 13, 1786, John Jay, as Secretary of Foreign Affairs of the Confederation, reported to Congress that a treaty "made, ratified and published by Congress, . . . immediately [became] binding on the whole nation, and superadded to the laws of the land. . . . Hence [it was to be] . . . received and observed by every member of the nation . . . ."[3] By unanimously adopting Jay's his-

* Professor of Law, University of Houston Law Center.

[1] *See* U.S. CONST. art. VI, cl. 2 (emphasis added). *See also id.* art. III, §2, cl. 1 ("The judicial Power shall extend to *all* Cases . . . arising under . . . Treaties . . .") (emphasis added).

[2] *See* President Washington, Message to the House of Representatives, Mar. 30, 1796, *reprinted in* 3 THE RECORDS OF THE FEDERAL CONVENTION OF 1787, at 371 (M. Farrand ed. 1937) (emphasis added). The President added: "when ratified, ["all" treaties] become obligatory. . . . [T]he assent of the House of Representatives is not necessary." *Id. See also* note 29 *infra.*

[3] Jay, report to Congress, Oct. 13, 1786, *quoted in* 1 C. BUTLER, THE TREATY-MAKING POWER OF THE UNITED STATES 268 n.4, 270 (1902). Jay also made these points after becoming Chief Justice in 1789. *See* notes 36–37 *infra.*

toric report,[4] Congress affirmed this early expectation that all treaties would be self-executing and superadded immediately to the laws of the land.

Jay's report also reflected the expectation that treaties would be national acts creating a supreme law of the land "independent of the will and power of" state legislatures[5] and that they were to be applied in all courts hearing causes or questions arising from or touching on such law.[6] With respect to the concept of national preemption, now termed federal preemption, Jay added: "the legislatures of the several states cannot of right pass any act or acts for interpreting, explaining or construing a national treaty, or any part or clause of it; nor for restraining, limiting or counteracting the operation or execution of the same."[7] Yet, as noted above, judicial power certainly applied, and "[a]ll doubts, in cases between private individuals, respecting the meaning of a treaty, like all doubts respecting the meaning of a law," were to be resolved by the judiciary.[8]

Soon afterward, Jay's report was referred to by Judge James Iredell of North Carolina (who later joined the U.S. Supreme Court), Iredell recognizing, much like the Secretary, " 'that a treaty when once made pursuant to the sovereign authority, *ex vi termini* became immediately the law of the land' " and was " 'binding upon those who delegated authority for that purpose,' " i.e., the people.[9] Indeed, recommendations during the 1787 Convention that treaties be ratified or sanctioned by congressional legislation, since they "are to have the operation of laws," were defeated.[10] Draft phrases such as "enforce treaties" were also considered "superfluous, since treaties were to be 'laws' " and thus were directly enforceable.[11] A proposal by James Madison that there be two types of treaties (i.e., those requiring only action by the Senate and the President, and those also requiring House action before they could take effect as law) was also rejected[12]—further

[4] 1 C. BUTLER, *supra* note 3, at 389. Nearly the same phrases as those quoted in the text at note 3 *supra* and at notes 5–7 *infra* were adopted in a resolution of the Continental Congress of Mar. 21, 1787. 12 J. CONG. 24 (1801).

[5] *See* 1 C. BUTLER, *supra* note 3, at 274 n.4. *See also* note 13 *infra*. Similarly, Jay wrote: "Under the national government, *treaties* and articles of treaties . . . will *always* be *expounded* . . . and *executed* . . . ." THE FEDERALIST NO. 3, at 98 (B. Wright ed. 1961) (emphasis added).

[6] *See* 1 C. BUTLER, *supra* note 3, at 270 n.4 and 275 n.4. *See also* Hamilton v. Eaton, 11 F. Cas. 336, 337 (Sitgreaves), 340 (Ellsworth) (C.C.D.N.C. 1792) (No. 5,980). Oliver Ellsworth had been a member of the Constitutional Convention (1787) and would join the Supreme Court in 1796. *See* J. NOWAK, R. ROTUNDA & J. YOUNG, CONSTITUTIONAL LAW 1109 (3d ed. 1986).

[7] *See* 1 C. BUTLER, *supra* note 3, at 274 n.4.

[8] *See id.* at 270 n.4.

[9] *See id.* at 389 (quoting a pamphlet written by Iredell). Iredell would make similar points later (*see* note 17 *infra*) and after joining the Supreme Court in 1790 (*see* notes 36, 40 *infra; cf.* note 46 *infra*).

[10] *See* J. MADISON, NOTES OF DEBATES IN THE FEDERAL CONVENTION OF 1787, at 520 (recommendation of Gouverneur Morris on Aug. 23), 597 (recommendation, quoted in part in the text above, by James Wilson on Sept. 7) (1966 ed.) (1840); 2 Farrand (ed.), *supra* note 2, at 297 (Mercer), 538 (Wilson); *see also* THE FEDERALIST NO. 64, at 421–24 (Jay).

[11] *See* J. MADISON, *supra* note 10, at 517.

[12] *See* 2 Farrand (ed.), *supra* note 2, at 394.

evidence that there was to be one type of treaty law, that which is immediately operative as supreme federal law when approved by the Senate and ratified by the President.

That this expectation predominated among the Framers can be seen as well in the *Federalist* papers and in the various debates on ratification of the Constitution in the states. For example, the *Federalist* recognized that "treaties of the United States, to have any force at all, must be considered as part of the law of the land. Their true import, as far as respects individuals, must, like all other laws, be ascertained by judicial determinations."[13] A later paper declared that the treaty power "ought to exist without limitation . . . [, with] no constitutional shackles."[14] During the 1788 debates on ratification in North Carolina, Mr. Lenoir affirmed that the treaty power is a "legislative power given to the President" and Senate, since treaties "are to be the supreme law of the land."[15] Iredell, who was supported by a similar remark by Porter,[16] added: "When treaties are made, they become as valid as legislative acts . . . [and] the law of the land."[17] Also in North Carolina, William Davie stated: "It was necessary that treaties should operate as laws on individuals. They ought to be binding upon us the moment they are made. They involve in their nature not only our own rights, but those of foreigners [and should be protected by the federal judiciary]."[18] Treaties, Davie added, "are the supreme law of the land to their respective citizens or subjects."[19]

[13] THE FEDERALIST NO. 22, at 197 (Hamilton). Hamilton asserted also that federal judicial power extends to "cases arising upon treaties and the law of nations," without mentioning any distinction among types of treaties and later quoting Article III, §2, "*all* cases . . . arising under" (emphasis added). *Id.*, NO. 80, at 501, 503 (Hamilton). *See also id.*, NO. 64, at 423–24 (Jay):

> [T]reaties, when made, are to have the force of laws . . . . [and] have as much legal validity . . . as if they proceeded from the legislature . . . .
>
> . . . They are just as binding, and just as far beyond the lawful reach of legislative acts now, as they will be at any future period, or under any form of government.

Jay implicitly added that this power need not involve the full legislature, yet it was a power "by which the citizens are to be bound and affected," and he noted: "It will not be in the power of the President and Senate to make any treaties by which they and their families and estates will not be equally bound and affected with the rest of the community . . . ." *Id.* at 424, 425. He articulated these points again as Chief Justice. *See* notes 36–37 *infra.* On Jay's point that the President is bound, see, e.g., Paust, *The President* Is *Bound by International Law,* 81 AJIL 377 (1987).

[14] THE FEDERALIST NO. 23, at 200 (Hamilton). The treaty power, of course, is that of the President and Senate.

[15] *See* 4 THE DEBATES IN THE SEVERAL STATE CONVENTIONS ON THE ADOPTION OF THE FEDERAL CONSTITUTION 27 (J. Elliot ed. 1941) (1830). George Mason of Virginia had opposed the new constitution, in part because the federal treaty power was "in many Cases, an exclusive Power of Legislation." *See* G. MASON, OBJECTIONS TO THE CONSTITUTION OF GOVERNMENT FORMED BY THE CONVENTION (1787), *reprinted in* 2 THE COMPLETE ANTIFEDERALIST 11 (H. Storing ed. 1981), 2 Farrand (ed.), *supra* note 2, at 639. Similarly, Cato had opposed ratification, characterizing treaties as "legislation." *See* Letters of Cato, N.Y.J., September 1787–January 1788, *reprinted in* Storing (ed.), *supra,* at 122.

[16] *See* 4 Elliot (ed.), *supra* note 15, at 115.

[17] *Id.* at 28.

[18] *Id.* at 158.

[19] *Id.* at 119.

In South Carolina, John Rutledge affirmed that "*every* treaty was law paramount, and must operate. . . . [T]his treaty is binding in our courts and in England." "Now supposing," he continued, "any [subsequent] law had passed . . . , would not the treaty be a sufficient bar to any local or municipal laws?"[20] His colleague Charles Pinckney noted that treaties under the new Constitution were to be "paramount to the laws of the land," would create individual rights and duties, and would have the force of law.[21] In Pennsylvania, James Wilson affirmed that Article III, section 2 of the new Constitution "will show the world that we make the faith of treaties a constitutional part of the character of the United States; that . . . the judges of the United States will be enabled to carry it into effect."[22] "There is no doubt," Wilson added, that "under this Constitution, treaties will become the supreme law of the land . . . . [T]reaties are to have the force of laws . . . ."[23] Similar points were made by James Madison[24] and George Nicholas[25] in Virginia. Although some had argued that the consent of the House should be required in the case of "commercial" treaties,[26] no such limitation on the treaty power was ultimately proposed or adopted.

After ratification, the predominant expectations of the Framers were reaffirmed by the first President.[27] As noted by Mr. Murray that same year (1796) in the House of Representatives while referring to the "explicitness of the instrument itself" (i.e., to the patent command of the text of the Constitution), "nothing . . . is left for expedience or sophistry . . . . [A]s a treaty, it is the supreme law of the land . . . nothing that we can rightfully do, or refuse to do, will add or diminish its validity, under the Constitution and law of nations."[28] Thus, it could be written in a constitutional law treatise in 1825: "[T]he people of course excluded from all interference with it, those parts of the government which are not described as partaking of it [e.g., the House]. . . . The immediate operation of the treaty must

[20] *Id.* at 267–68 (emphasis added). Rutledge was appointed to the Supreme Court in 1789 and had been one of the signers of the Constitution. *See* J. NOWAK, R. ROTUNDA & J. YOUNG, *supra* note 6, at 1111.

[21] *See* 4 Elliot (ed.), *supra* note 15, at 277–79.

[22] 2 *id.* at 490. Wilson, who had signed the Declaration of Independence and the Constitution and would join the Supreme Court in 1789 (*see* J. NOWAK, R. ROTUNDA & J. YOUNG, *supra* note 6, at 1112), would make similar points as a Justice. *See* notes 36–37 *infra.*

[23] 2 Elliot (ed.), *supra* note 15, at 506.

[24] *See* 3 *id.* at 501, 514, 532.

[25] *See id.* at 502, 506.

[26] *See id.* at 365 (Grayson of Virginia), 511 (Corbin of Virginia).

[27] *See* text at note 2 *supra.* Hamilton, in a draft for the President's message, had written: "the House of Representatives . . . have no legal power to refuse its execution because it is a law." *See* WORKS OF ALEXANDER HAMILTON 566 (J. C. Hamilton ed. 1851), *quoted in* L. HENKIN, FOREIGN AFFAIRS AND THE CONSTITUTION 161 (1972). The treaty power was simply too important to be left with the full Congress, or even with Congress and the Executive. *See also* notes 1, 2, 4, 5 and 13 *supra,* and note 29 *infra.*

[28] *See* 4 Elliot (ed.), *supra* note 15, at 435. *But see* Gallatin, 4 ANNALS OF CONG. 744–46 (1796). For views similar to Murray's, see, e.g., notes 13–15, 27 *supra;* 4 ANNALS OF CONG. 485 (Havens), 595–96 (J. Smith) and 1243 (Ames), *quoted in* Lobel, *The Limits of Constitutional Power: Conflicts Between Foreign Policy and International Law,* 71 VA. L. REV. 1071, 1098–99 (1985); *see also id.* (Hamilton, Findley, Williams, Coit).

therefore be to overrule all existing legislative acts inconsistent with its provisions."[29]

These historic patterns of expectation demonstrate that most of the Framers intended all treaties *immediately* to become binding on the whole nation, superadded to the laws of the land; to be observed by every member of the nation; to be applied by the courts whenever a cause or question arose from or touched on them; and to prevail over and preempt any inconsistent state action. In these ways at least, all treaties (to the extent of their grants, guarantees or obligations) were to be self-executing. Additionally, it would have made no sense to argue that a particular treaty was not self-executing unless one agreed that whether or not a treaty was self-executing was to be tested by the language of the treaty considered in context (with the possible exception posed by some exclusive congressional power expressly documented as such in the new Constitution).

These recaptured views of the Founders are certainly consistent with the actual text of the Constitution and would require acknowledgment, in modern parlance, that all treaties are self-executing except those (or the portions of them) which, by their very terms, require domestic implementing legislation. According to this viewpoint, as the words of the Constitution affirm, each treaty is supreme law of the land, especially for use by the judiciary[30] and for supremacy purposes.[31] Each treaty is law; but if a treaty provision expressly requires domestic implementing legislation before it becomes directly operative, that is merely a condition of such law. Further, as explained below, merely because the full Congress (i.e., the House and Senate) has an express power to make a law should not be relevant to whether a treaty is self-executing, since the President and Senate also have an express power to make treaty law and each treaty is supreme law of the land.

Early Cases

The earliest federal cases addressing the domestic effect of treaties made no mention of any distinction between self-executing and non-self-executing treaties. Not surprisingly, the language in early judicial opinions mirrored the predominant expectations of the Framers noted above. In 1792, for example, Judge Oliver Ellsworth, who would join the U.S. Supreme Court 4 years later, wrote that a treaty, "being ratified and made . . . became a complete national act and law of every state."[32] Judge Sitgreaves, writing in

[29] W. Rawle, A View of the Constitution of the United States 57–61 (1825), *quoted in* 1 C. Butler, *supra* note 3, at 397; *see also* 1 J. Kent, Commentaries on American Law 286–87 (1826) (general expectations that a treaty "is as much obligatory upon Congress as upon any other branch of the government, or upon the people at large. . . . The House of Representatives are not above the law"); letter from Secretary of State Livingston to Mr. Serurier, June 3, 1833, *reprinted in* 2 F. Wharton, A Digest of the International Law of the United States 67 (1866).

[30] *See* U.S. Const. art. III, §2, cl. 1; *see also* text at notes 6, 8, 13, 18, 20 and 22 *supra.*

[31] *See* U.S. Const. art. VI, cl. 2; *see also* McLaughlin, *The Scope of the Treaty Power in the United States,* 42 Minn. L. Rev. 709, 731 (1958) ("the phrasing used was calculated to assure that all treaties were included").

[32] Hamilton v. Eaton, 11 F. Cas. 336, 340 (C.C.D.N.C. 1792) (No. 5,980).

the same case, declared that "the treaty consequently became obligatory on the people . . . when made and duly ratified," which "was alone sufficient" for its "validity and legality" within the United States with respect to judicial decision making.[33]

In 1801 Chief Justice Marshall declared broadly: "If the law [there, a treaty] be constitutional, . . . I know of no court which can contest its obligation."[34] And in 1809 the Chief Justice wrote: "*Whenever* a right grows out of, or is protected by, a treaty, . . . it is to be protected."[35] In fact, in several federal cases decided up until 1829, treaty law was accepted as operating directly as supreme federal law in the face of inconsistent state law,[36] or more generally for other purposes.[37] Moreover, it was early recognized that statutes should be interpreted so as to be consistent with international law, a recognition that was not hinged upon whether or not a treaty was self-executing or directly operative.[38] And it was recognized, at least since 1796, that federal judges, as state judges under the Supremacy

[33] *Id.* at 337. *See also* Penhallow v. Doane's Admin., 3 U.S. (3 Dall.) 54, 94 (1795) (Paterson, J.) ("when rightfully exercised," constitutional power as to treaties is "equally binding upon those from whom the authority was derived," i.e., the people).

[34] United States v. The Schooner Peggy, 5 U.S. (1 Cranch) 103, 110 (1801) (Marshall, C.J.). Just before he joined the Court, Marshall, as a member of the House of Representatives, defended the actions of President Adams under a treaty by noting: "The treaty . . . is a law . . . . Congress, unquestionably, may prescribe the mode, and Congress may devolve on others the whole execution of the contract; but till this be done, it seems the duty of the Executive department to execute the contract by any means it possesses." 10 ANNALS OF CONG. 613–14 (1800).

[35] Owings v. Norwood's Lessee, 9 U.S. (5 Cranch) 344, 348–49 (1809) (Marshall, C.J.) (emphasis added). As Secretary of State, Marshall had also decried the failure of certain British judges to apply international law, thus "converting themselves from judges into mere instruments of plunder." *See* 2 AMERICAN STATE PAPERS (FOREIGN RELATIONS) 386–87, 486–90 (1832).

[36] *See, e.g.*, Carneal v. Banks, 23 U.S. (10 Wheat.) 181, 189 (1825) (Marshall, C.J.); Chirac v. Chirac, 15 U.S. (2 Wheat.) 259, 271, 274–76 (1817) (Marshall, C.J.); Martin v. Hunter's Lessee, 14 U.S. (1 Wheat.) 304, 340–41, 360 (Story, J.), 370–71 (Johnson, J.) (1816); Fairfax's Devisee v. Hunter's Lessee, 11 U.S. (7 Cranch) 603, 627 (1813) (Story, J.); Owings v. Norwood's Lessee, 9 U.S. (5 Cranch) 344, 348–49 (1809) (Marshall, C.J.); Hopkirk v. Bell, 7 U.S. (3 Cranch) 454, 458 (1806); Ware v. Hylton, 3 U.S. (3 Dall.) 199, 236–37 ("any treaty"), 244–45 (Chase, J.), 249, 256 (Paterson, J.), 272, 276–77, 279 (Iredell, J.), 281 (Wilson, J.), 282, 284 (Cushing, J.) (1796); Hamilton v. Eaton, 11 F. Cas. at 337–38, 340; Gordon v. Kerr, 10 F. Cas. 801, 802 (C.C.D. Pa. 1806) (No. 5,611) (Washington, Circuit Justice); Fisher v. Harnden, 9 F. Cas. 129, 130–31 (C.C.D.N.Y. 1812) (No. 4,819) (Livingston, Circuit Justice), *aff'd*, 14 U.S. (1 Wheat.) 300 (1816). *See also* Georgia v. Brailsford, 3 U.S. (3 Dall.) 1, 4 (1794) (Jay, C.J.) (alien's individual right "revived at the peace, both by the law of nations and the treaty of peace").

[37] *See, e.g.*, American Ins. Co. v. 356 Bales of Cotton, 26 U.S. (1 Pet.) 511, 542 (1828) (Marshall, C.J., opinion); United States v. Robins, 27 F. Cas. 825, 833 (D.C.D.S.C. 1799) (No. 16,175); United States v. Cooper, 25 F. Cas. 631, 641–42 (C.C.D. Pa. 1800) (No. 14,865) (Chase, Circuit Justice); Henfield's Case, 11 F. Cas. 1099, 1100–01 (Jay, C.J.), 1120 (Wilson, J.) (C.C.D. Pa. 1793) (No. 6,360); 1 Op. Att'y Gen. 57, 58 (1795); *see also* Talbot v. Jansen, 3 U.S. (3 Dall.) 133, 159–61 (1795) (Iredell, J.); 1 Op. Att'y Gen. 566, 570–71 (1822).

[38] *See, e.g.*, Murray v. The Charming Betsy, 6 U.S. (2 Cranch) 64, 117–18 (1804) (Marshall, C.J.); Talbot v. Seeman, 5 U.S. (1 Cranch) 1, 43 (1801) (Marshall, C.J.); 1 Op. Att'y Gen. 52, 53 (1794); 1 Op. Att'y Gen. 26, 27 (1792).

Clause,[39] are equally "bound by duty and oath" to apply treaty law.[40] Indeed, in 1809 Chief Justice Marshall affirmed: "The reason for inserting that clause [Art. III, §2, cl. 1] . . . was, that all persons who have real claims under a treaty should have their causes decided . . . ."[41]

Ever since these cases, the supremacy of international law over state law has been complete and in no Supreme Court decision has that supremacy had to depend upon the status of a treaty as self-executing law.[42] Of course, nothing in the written Constitution requires that a treaty be self-executing in order to be supreme law of the land. By express terms, "all" treaties made under the authority of the United States "shall" have that status.[43] Indeed, it is difficult to imagine that something shall be supreme federal "law of the land" but not operate directly as "law" except by believing in one of the most transparent of judicial delusions. That sort of vision has been applied by the Supreme Court only with regard to competing congressional power (i.e., of the full Congress, including the House), for example, when a constitutionally required power of Congress was thought to be at stake.[44] It first occurred, moreover, nearly 40 years after the formation of the Constitution, without any evident precedent and in seeming contrast to the predominant expectations of the Framers and early judicial opinions noted above.

The Judicial Invention

The first Supreme Court opinion that actually used the phrase "self-executing" did not appear until 1887.[45] Yet Chief Justice Marshall had invented the concept in 1829 when opining that a treaty "is carried into

[39] *See* U.S. CONST. art. VI, cl. 2.

[40] *See* Ware v. Hylton, 3 U.S. (3 Dall.) at 237, 244 (Chase, J.), 261 (Iredell, J.), 272 (*cf. id.* at 273); Paust, *Rediscovering the Relationship Between Congressional Power and International Law: Exceptions to the Last in Time Rule and the Primacy of Custom,* 28 VA. J. INT'L L. 393, 434–35, and references cited (1988).

[41] *See* Owings v. Norwood's Lessee, 9 U.S. (5 Cranch) at 348–49. Importantly, the Chief Justice declared the next year that our judicial tribunals "are established . . . to decide on human rights." Fletcher v. Peck, 10 U.S. (6 Cranch) 87, 133 (1810) (Marshall, C.J., opinion).

[42] *See* Paust, *supra* note 40, at 430, 431–33 n.79, and references cited; *see also* Henkin, *The Constitution and United States Sovereignty: A Century of* Chinese Exclusion *and its Progeny,* 100 HARV. L. REV. 853, 867 n.65 (1987); Gordon v. Kerr, 10 F. Cas. 801, 802 (C.C.D. Pa. 1806) (No. 5,611) (seemingly non-self-executing treaty "is supreme" over state constitution); 6 Op. Att'y Gen. 291, 293 (1854); B. WESTON, R. FALK & A. D'AMATO, INTERNATIONAL LAW AND WORLD ORDER 192 (1980); L. SOHN & T. BUERGENTHAL, INTERNATIONAL PROTECTION OF HUMAN RIGHTS 947 (1973); Wright, *National Courts and Human Rights—The* Fujii *Case,* 45 AJIL 62, 69 (1951); RESTATEMENT (THIRD) OF FOREIGN RELATIONS LAW OF THE UNITED STATES §115 comment *e* (1987) [hereinafter RESTATEMENT (THIRD)] (stating that *any* U.S. treaty or international agreement "supersedes inconsistent State law or policy . . . . Even a non-self-executing agreement . . . may sometimes be held to be federal policy superseding State law or policy"). *But see id.* ("non-self-executing agreement . . . not effective as law").

[43] U.S. CONST. art. VI, cl. 2.

[44] *See* Paust, *supra* note 40, at 431–33 n.79, and references cited; notes 99, 104–05 and 107 *infra.*

[45] Bartram v. Robertson, 122 U.S. 116, 120 (1887) (Field, J., opinion). Justice Field used the phrase a year later in a more oft-cited opinion. Whitney v. Robertson, 124 U.S. 190, 194 (1888) (Field, J., opinion).

execution . . . whenever it operates of itself,"[46] the notion being that some treaties do not operate of themselves but require domestic legislation to carry them "into execution." This judicial invention, considered in historical context and with reference to other words in Marshall's 1829 opinion, was relatively proper. Later commentators, however, have distorted his meaning and created tests concerning self-executing and non-self-executing treaties that are patently inconsistent with the text of the Constitution, the predominant expectations of the Framers and early judicial opinions. What Marshall actually declared and his evident criterion are worth examining.

Marshall knew that in some countries a treaty is "not a legislative act" and "does not generally effect, of itself, the object to be accomplished . . . but is carried into execution by" legislation or other exercises of "sovereign power."[47] He added, however, that "[i]n the United States a different principle is established. Our constitution declares a treaty to be the law of the land. It is, consequently, to be regarded in courts of justice as equivalent to an act of the legislature, whenever it operates of itself . . . ."[48] Therefore, even though Marshall still maintained that every treaty was "the law of the land,"[49] his suggestion that some treaties did not operate of themselves represented a new twist, perhaps, with respect to precedent—but, in context, a minor new twist. After all, *the* criterion as to whether or not a treaty, as law, was to be "carried into execution" was to be the treaty itself. It was to be carried into execution "*whenever* it operates *of itself*," and it was not to be self-executory if its terms so indicated.[50] Thus, it was the language of such supreme federal law, considered in context, that was to be determinative.

[46] Foster v. Neilson, 27 U.S. (2 Pet.) 253, 314 (1829) (Marshall, C.J.). *See also id.* (treaties that "the legislature must execute").

[47] *Id.* Marshall had primarily in mind the practice in Great Britain. *Id.* For evidence of a subsequent British practice, see Preuss, 45 ASIL PROC. 82, 85–87 (1951); United States v. Rauscher, 119 U.S. 407, 417 (1886).

In fact, most nation-states ratify treaties through a legislative process, thus obviating much of the concern about "self-executing" status or shifting attention to the intent of the legislature upon ratification. *Cf.* Iwasawa, *The Doctrine of Self-Executing Treaties in the United States: A Critical Analysis,* 26 VA. J. INT'L L. 627, 638–41 & n.57 (1986). *See also* RESTATEMENT (THIRD), *supra* note 42, §111 Reporters' Note 5 ("few other states distinguish between self-executing and non-self-executing treaties"); T. FRANCK & M. GLENNON, FOREIGN RELATIONS AND NATIONAL SECURITY LAW 274–75 (1987); Henry, *When Is a Treaty Self-Executing?,* 27 MICH. L. REV. 776, 779 (1929); Lillich, *Invoking International Human Rights in Domestic Courts,* 54 U. CIN. L. REV. 367, 373 (1985); Preuss, *supra,* at 87–96, and references cited; P. DE VISSCHER, DE LA CONCLUSION DES TRAITÉS INTERNATIONAUX 122, *passim* (1943). Professor Iwasawa also explains the many different meanings of "self-executing" and related phrases here and abroad and some of the confusion generated by the use of such phrases. *See* Iwasawa, *supra,* at 635–49, and references cited.

[48] 27 U.S. (2 Pet.) at 314.

[49] *See* notes 34–38 *supra.* As a member of the House, the year before he joined the Court, Marshall had also recognized that the President was bound by a treaty because it was supreme federal law. *See* 10 ANNALS OF CONG. 614 (1800), *also in* United States v. Robins, 27 F. Cas. 825, 836, 867 (D.C.D.S.C. 1799) (No. 16,175).

[50] *See* 27 U.S. (2 Pet.) at 314 ("when the terms . . .—when either of the parties engages . . . , [when] the treaty addresses"); *see also id.* at 314–15:

> Do *these words* act directly . . . or *do they* pledge the faith of the United States to pass acts which shall ratify and confirm them?

This viewpoint was relatively consistent with prior patterns of expectation, and it would be expressed later in connection with criteria utilized to test self-executory effect.[51] Again, in this sense, all treaties, to the extent of their grants, guarantees or obligations, were to be self-executing. Those that were not were those which, by their terms, required domestic implementing legislation. Law was to operate as law unless the law itself specified that domestic implementing legislation was necessary to produce direct legal effect. Applying this general test (hereinafter termed the language of the treaty criterion), Marshall found that a specific portion of a treaty between the United States and Spain protecting private land titles (couched in the terms "shall be ratified and confirmed") was not directly operative.[52] Four years later, however, he reversed himself after construing the terms of the same treaty differently: "*They* may import that they 'shall be ratified and confirmed' *by* force of *the instrument itself.*"[53] In effect, Marshall had retained

---

> . . . .
>
> . . . *It does not say,* that those grants are hereby confirmed. *Had such been its language,* it . . . would have repealed those acts of congress which were repugnant to it; *but its language* is, that those grants shall be ratified and confirmed . . . . By whom shall they be ratified and confirmed? [emphasis added].

[51] *See, e.g.,* Warren v. United States, 340 U.S. 523, 526–27 (1951); Valentine v. United States, 299 U.S. 5, 10–11 (1936); Jones v. Meehan, 175 U.S. 1, 10 (1889); Baldwin v. Franks, 120 U.S. 578, 703–04 (1887) (Field, J., dissenting); Edye v. Robertson, 112 U.S. 580, 598–99 (1884); Dainese v. Hale, 91 U.S. 13, 18–19 (1875); Owings v. Norwood's Lessee, 9 U.S. (5 Cranch) at 348–49; Cardenas v. Smith, 733 F.2d 909, 918 (D.C. Cir. 1984); Benjamins v. British European Airways, 572 F.2d 913, 916–19 (2d Cir. 1978); Z. & F. Assets Realization Corp. v. Hull, 114 F.2d 464, 470 (D.C. Cir. 1940), *aff'd,* 311 U.S. 470 (1941); *Ex parte* Toscano, 208 F. 938, 942 (S.D. Cal. 1913); United Shoe Mach. Co. v. Duplessis Shoe Mach. Co., 155 F. 842, 845 (5th Cir. 1907); United States v. Enger, 472 F.Supp. 490, 542 & n.23 (D.N.J. 1978); Noel v. Linea Aeropostal Venezolana, 144 F.Supp. 359, 360 (S.D.N.Y. 1956); Indemnity Ins. Co. of N. Am. v. Pan Am. Airways, 58 F.Supp. 338, 340 (S.D.N.Y. 1944); Five Per Cent Cases, 6 Ct. Cust. App. 291, 328–31 (1915), *rev'd on other grounds,* 243 U.S. 97 (1917); *see also* Ware v. Hylton, 3 U.S. (3 Dall.) at 244 (Chase, J); People of Saipan v. United States Dep't of Interior, 502 F.2d 90, 101 (9th Cir.) (Trask, J., concurring), *cert. denied,* 420 U.S. 1003 (1974); Blandford v. State, 10 Tex. App. 627, 639–40 (1881); Commonwealth v. Hawes, 76 Ky. (13 Bush) 697, 702 (1878); M. S. McDougal & W. M. Reisman, International Law in Contemporary Perspective 1223 (1981) (*cf. id.* at 1229–30); 1 N. Redlich & B. Schwartz, Constitutional Law 3–107 (1983); B. Schwartz, Constitutional Law 102 (2d ed. 1979); 2 J. Story, Commentaries on the Constitution of the United States §423 (1833); 4 *id.* §1838 (4th ed. 1873); J. Sweeney, C. Oliver & N. Leech, The International Legal System 1069 (2d ed. 1981) (*but see id.* at 1076 (Riesenfeld's suggestion)); Bell & Foy, *The President, the Congress, and the Panama Canal: An Essay on the Powers of the Executive and Legislative Branches in the Field of Foreign Affairs,* 16 Ga. J. Int'l & Comp. L. Supp. 607, 627, 629 & n.97, 633 (1986); McDougal, Remarks, 45 ASIL Proc. 102 (1951); note 94 *infra; cf.* Henry, *supra* note 47, at 785, *passim;* Iwasawa, *supra* note 47, at 654–57, and references cited; Shelton, *Overview of International Human Rights Law in Domestic Courts,* 17 U.S.F. L. Rev. 12, 16 (1982). *See also* Henkin, *Lexical or "Political Question": A Response,* 101 Harv. L. Rev. 524, 533 (1987) (strong preference "to make treaties self-executing whenever the character of the undertaking permits, so that they will have full status immediately as law").

[52] *See* 27 U.S. (2 Pet.) at 314–15; note 50 *supra.*

[53] United States v. Percheman, 32 U.S. (7 Pet.) 51, 89 (1833) (Marshall, C.J.) (emphasis added) (adding that the "Spanish part of the treaty was not then [in *Foster*] brought to our view . . . . [It shows a] difference of expression in the same instrument, drawn up in the language

and reapplied a language of the treaty test. It was not a "political question" test,[54] and it was not a test that was hinged upon the existence of some concurrent congressional power.[55] Thus, under Marshall's test, no particular subject matter would render a treaty inherently non-self-operative.

Interestingly, Marshall cited no precedent for his invented distinction and proffered test, but could he have cited Justice Iredell's dissenting opinion in *Ware v. Hylton*?[56] Was Iredell arguing in *Ware* that, under the Constitution, certain treaty provisions are inherently "executory" "[w]hen . . . a treaty stipulates for any thing of a legislative nature, [because, in his view,] the manner of giving effect to this stipulation is by that power which possesses the Legislative authority"?[57] It is extremely doubtful that he was. First, Iredell was addressing a circumstance "independent of" and "previous to the ratification of the present Constitution."[58] Second, such a notion would have been completely at odds with his statements noted earlier concerning the immediate effect of treaties as supreme federal law under the new Constitution.[59] Third, he stated that his points about the operation of a treaty prior to the Constitution derived "considerable weight from the practice in Great Britain,"[60] which, after and with respect to the Constitution, would have been a strange precedential referent indeed.[61] Fourth, Iredell recognized that the very problem before the Court had led to the formation of the Supremacy Clause, which would thereafter control;[62] but he argued that his notion of "executory" treaty provisions should operate in such a manner that state law would control when something had been "done" or "executed" under state law *prior* to the creation of the Supremacy Clause.[63] Fifth, he understood that the distinction between "executed"

---

of each party"). *See also* Garcia v. Lee, 37 U.S. (12 Pet.) 511, 519 (1838) (Taney, C.J., opinion); United States v. Wiggins, 39 U.S. (14 Pet.) 334, 349 (1840) (Catron, J., opinion).

[54] *Contra* Dred Scott v. Sandford, 60 U.S. (19 How.) 393, 630 (1857) (Curtis, J.); Wright, *supra* note 42, at 64. All that Marshall said that was even close was that "*when the terms* . . . import a contract . . . to perform a particular act, *the treaty addresses itself* to the political, not the judicial department; and the legislature must execute the contract." 27 U.S. (2 Pet.) at 314 (emphasis added). *See also id.* at 315; notes 50, 53 *supra. See further* text at note 69 *infra;* Ware v. Hylton, 3 U.S. (3 Dall.) at 244 (Chase, J.) (stating that an article in a treaty is "a contract, on behalf of those courts"—thus, "contract" language does not require legislative action).

[55] In *Foster* and *Percheman,* Congress clearly had enacted relevant legislation under a relevant congressional power, but self-executory effect hinged on interpretation of the terms of the treaty itself. On the general point, see also L. HENKIN, *supra* note 27, at 149, 159 n.††; RESTATEMENT (THIRD), *supra* note 42, §111 Reporters' Note 6; notes 100 and 102 *infra.*

[56] 3 U.S. (3 Dall.) 199, 256 (1796) (Iredell, J., dissenting).

[57] *See id.* at 272.

[58] *See id.* at 271–72.

[59] *See* notes 9 and 17 *supra.*

[60] *See* 3 U.S. (3 Dall.) at 273 (Iredell, J., dissenting).

[61] *See* text at notes 47–48 *supra; see also* Respublica v. Cobbet, 3 U.S. (3 Dall.) 467, 473 (1798).

[62] *See* 3 U.S. (3 Dall.) at 276–77 (Iredell, J., dissenting) (adding: once the Constitution was ratified, the treaty would control "as if every act constituting an impediment . . . had been expressly repealed, and any further act passed, which the public obligation had before required").

[63] *See id.* at 277.

and "executory" provisions of a treaty was to be addressed "by considering various stipulations in the treaty" and whether, "from the nature of them, they require no further act to be done."[64] He did not consider the new powers of Congress in *Ware,* and he acknowledged that provisions of the treaty permitting fishing rights and the right to navigate the Mississippi were thereby "executed" (i.e., because of the words of the treaty and their nature, requiring no further act).

From the above, it is evident that Iredell's scheme, even if it was thought to be applicable after the enunciation of the Supremacy Clause of the new Constitution, involved a situation where a treaty is "executory" according to its own terms—for example, when by its terms it requires domestic implementing acts of legislation. It is then that "a treaty *stipulates for*" a legislative act, and "the manner of giving effect to *this* stipulation" would certainly be "by that power which possesses the Legislative authority."[65] As Justice Chase affirmed in the same case, "No one can doubt that a treaty may stipulate, that certain acts shall be done by the Legislature"; but he disagreed that the relevant portions of the treaty in question could be so interpreted.[66] In this sense, Chase and Iredell were using the same test with respect to "executory" treaty provisions, but that test was hinged upon the language of the treaty and did not involve—any more than Marshall's concept some 33 years later in *Foster*[67]—a more recent notion of inherently non-self-executing treaties based on an interpretation of powers conferred by the Constitution.

Before other postulated tests or criteria are addressed, it is worth noting that other writers have rightly recognized that Chief Justice Marshall's related criterion of "contract . . . to perform a particular act"[68] does "not itself provide a workable test to determine whether a provision in a treaty requires legislative action."[69] "In almost all treaties one of the 'parties engages to perform a particular act,' "[70] and such a test has not generally been applied. Similarly, "to take 'futurity of language' as the test makes little sense since the future tense is often used in treaties . . . and it in no way indicates that legislation is necessary."[71] Moreover, as the signatories rarely

[64] *See id.* at 272.

[65] *See id.* (emphasis added).

[66] *See id.* at 244.

[67] *See* text at notes 47–54 *supra.*

[68] *See* 27 U.S. (2 Pet.) at 314–15.

[69] *See* Schachter, *The Charter and the Constitution: The Human Rights Provisions in American Law,* 4 VAND. L. REV. 643, 645 (1951), *reprinted in* INTERNATIONAL HUMAN RIGHTS: PROBLEMS OF LAW AND POLICY 72 (R. Lillich & F. Newman eds. 1979). For similar views, see, e.g., Henry, *supra* note 47, at 777–78; Iwasawa, *supra* note 47, at 685; Wright, *supra* note 42, at 65 n.12. *But see* Robertson v. General Elec. Co., 32 F.2d 495, 500 (4th Cir. 1929) (using the "contract" approach without evident knowledge of *Percheman*).

[70] Schachter, *supra* note 69, at 645.

[71] *Id.,* adding: "The Supreme Court certainly does not consider either [of these supposed tests] as an indication that a treaty is not self-executing." *See also Ex parte* Toscano, 208 F. 938, 942 (S.D. Cal. 1913). *Cf.* 19 Op. Att'y Gen. 273, 278–79 (1889). For similar views, see, e.g., Henry, *supra* note 47, at 777–78; Iwasawa, *supra* note 47, at 685–86; Comment, *Self-Execution of United Nations Security Council Resolutions Under United States Law,* 24 UCLA L. REV. 387, 394 (1976) [hereinafter UCLA Comment]; Comment, *Criteria for Self-Executing Treaties,* 1968 U.

concern themselves with the details of domestic implementation, treaties are hardly ever addressed "to the political, not the judicial department," or to any domestic governmental apparatus.[72] Marshall, it may be recalled, had great difficulty applying these criteria to the particular treaty at stake,[73] and they seem to be no more useful today. Significantly, some of his earlier opinions lend support to Marshall's language of the treaty criterion. More importantly, he might well have expected, even after 1829, that treaties were to be self-operative, in his words, "[w]henever a right grows out of, or is protected by, a treaty" or persons "have real claims under a treaty."[74] This latter test (hereinafter termed the rights under a treaty test) would certainly guarantee that human rights treaties were self-operative,[75] unless a treaty expressly required domestic legislation implementing such rights before they could become operative.

Post-1829 Criteria and Separate Lines of Cases

After 1829, Marshall retained both the language of the treaty criterion and the rights under a treaty test. As mentioned, he used those criteria in 1833 in reinterpreting the treaty involved in *Foster.*[76] In 1835 he applied them again in holding that language in a treaty reading "they shall be maintained and protected in the free enjoyment of their liberty, property, and . . . religion" protected the right to property and meant, "then, [that it] is protected and secured by the treaty" in a direct or self-operative manner.[77] Justice Story, in his 1833 *Commentaries,* seemed to accept Marshall's language of the treaty criterion,[78] but he stressed that, in most cases, "treaties . . . should be held, when made, to be the supreme law of the land" and that it is "indispensable, that they should have the obligation and force of a law, that they may be executed by the judicial power, and obeyed like other laws."[79] For Justice Story, treaties "ought to have a positive binding efficacy, as laws,"[80] and he emphasized that the "difference

---

ILL. L.F. 238, 242 (1968) [hereinafter Ill. Comment]; Note, *Treaties—Scope of Treaty-Making Power—When Treaties Are Self-Executing,* 26 MICH. L. REV. 316, 320 (1928); note 51 *supra* and accompanying text. *But see* Robertson v. General Elec. Co., 32 F.2d 495, 500 (4th Cir. 1929); Ortman v. Stanray Corp., 371 F.2d 154, 157 (7th Cir. 1967). Marshall himself must have abandoned such a viewpoint. *See* note 53 *supra* and text at note 77 *infra.*

[72] The quoted phrase is Marshall's. 27 U.S. (2 Pet.) at 314. On the general point, see also Taylor v. Morton, 23 F. Cas. 784, 785 (C.C.D. Mass. 1855) (No. 13,799); L. HENKIN, *supra* note 27, at 158; Iwasawa, *supra* note 47, at 654, 661, 684. One notable exception is the guarantee of the right to an effective remedy in domestic tribunals contained in human rights instruments.

[73] *See* notes 50, 52 and 53 *supra.*

[74] *See* text at notes 35 and 41 *supra.*

[75] *See also* note 41 *supra.*

[76] *See* text at note 53 *supra.*

[77] *See* Delassus v. United States, 34 U.S. (9 Pet.) 117, 133 (1835) (Marshall, C.J., opinion). Marshall's treaty language test seems to have been used later in 4 Op. Att'y Gen. 201, 209–10 (1843). *See also* 21 Op. Att'y Gen. 347, 348 (1896); 19 Op. Att'y Gen. 273, 278–79 (1889); 6 Op. Att'y Gen. 748, 749–50 (1854).

[78] J. STORY, *supra* note 51, §423 ("when the terms . . . the treaty addresses . . .").

[79] *Id.* For relevant judicial opinions of Justice Story, see, e.g., notes 36 *supra* and 83 *infra.*

[80] J. STORY, *supra* note 51, §423.

between considering them as laws, and considering them as executory, or executed contracts, is exceedingly important. . . . If they are supreme laws, courts of justice will enforce them directly in all cases, to which they can be judicially applied . . . ."[81]

Very few courts, however, paid attention to Marshall's invented distinction between self- and non-self-operative treaties until the end of the 19th century.[82] Rather, two lines of cases at the Supreme Court level began to emerge: one line (hereinafter termed the invented distinction cases) accepted the general distinction between self- and non-self-operative treaties, while the other (hereinafter termed the law of the land cases) seems simply to have ignored it.[83] Exemplifying the second line of cases, in *Worcester v. Georgia* the Court declared: "So long as treaties and laws remain in full force, . . . the judicial power can exercise no discretion in refusing to give effect to those laws, when questions arise under them, unless they shall be deemed unconstitutional."[84] In *Strother v. Lucas,* there was a cite to *Foster,* but the Court stated flatly: "Treaties are the law of the land, and a rule of

[81] *Id.* Such direct enforcement is also known as direct incorporation, as opposed to indirect incorporation. *See also* text at notes 124–25 *infra.*

[82] For cases recognizing such a distinction after 1829, see, e.g., Terlinden v. Ames, 184 U.S. 270, 285, 288–89 (1902) (Fuller, C.J., opinion); Fong Yue Ting v. United States, 149 U.S. 698, 720 (1893); Chae Chang Ping v. United States, 130 U.S. 581, 600 (1889); Whitney v. Robertson, 124 U.S. 190, 194 (1888); Dred Scott v. Sandford, 60 U.S. (19 How.) 393, 630 (1857); United States v. Flint, 25 F. Cas. 1107, 1109 (C.C.D. Cal. 1876) (No. 15,121) (Field, Circuit Justice); *In re* Metzger, 17 F. Cas. 232, 233–35 (D.C.S.D.N.Y. 1847) (No. 9,511) (also recognizing that a treaty can enhance judicial power and that if it is "addressed to the judicial power [it can] become a rule of law of" itself and "must be observed and enforced" by the judiciary). *See also* Garcia v. Lee, 37 U.S. (12 Pet.) 511, 519 (1838); Turner v. American Baptist Missionary Union, 24 F. Cas. 344, 345 (C.C.D. Mich. 1852) (No. 14,251); *In re* Sheazle, 21 F. Cas. 1214, 1217 (C.C.D. Mass. 1845) (No. 12,734) (President can exercise "ministerial acts" to implement extradition treaty even though no congressional legislation exists); note 45 *supra.* However, in *Sheazle,* the court declared that state magistrates are "bound in *all* cases to respect *treaties* and the *rights* under them." 21 F. Cas. at 1216 (emphasis added).

[83] *See, e.g.,* La Abra Silver Mining Co. v. United States, 175 U.S. 423, 458, 461 (1899); Geofroy v. Riggs, 133 U.S. 258, 267 (1890); United States v. Raucher, 119 U.S. 407, 418 (1886); Chew Heong v. United States, 112 U.S. 536 (1884); Von Cotzhausen v. Nazro, 107 U.S. 215, 217 (1883); Hauenstein v. Lynham, 100 U.S. 483, 488–90 (1879); United States v. Forty-Three Gallons of Whisky, 93 U.S. 188, 197 (1876); Haver v. Yaker, 76 U.S. (9 Wall.) 32, 34 (1870); The New York Indians, 72 U.S. (5 Wall.) 761, 768, 770, 772 (1867); The Kansas Indians, 72 U.S. (5 Wall.) 737, 757, 759 (1866); Doe v. Braden, 57 U.S. (16 How.) 635, 657–59 (1853); The Passenger Cases, 48 U.S. (7 How.) 283, 413 (1849); Lessee of Pollard's Heirs v. Kibbe, 39 U.S. (14 Pet.) 353, 412 (1840) (Baldwin, J., concurring); Carver v. Jackson, 29 U.S. (4 Pet.) 1, 101 (1830) (Story, J., opinion); *In re* Lee Sing, 43 F. 359, 360–62 (C.C.N.D. Cal. 1890); *In re* Parrott, 1 F. 481, 507, 517 (1880); Baker v. City of Portland, 2 F. Cas. 472, 473 (C.C.D. Ore. 1879) (No. 777); 26 Op. Att'y Gen. 250, 251–53 (1907); and cases cited in notes 84–86 *infra.* In one such case it was also recognized: "Where a treaty admits of two constructions, one restrictive as to the rights, that may be claimed under it, and the other liberal, the latter is to be preferred." Hauenstein v. Lynham, 100 U.S. at 487 (citing Shanks v. Dupont, 28 U.S. (3 Pet.) 242, 249–50 (1830)). *See also* Paust, *Human Rights: From Jurisprudential Inquiry to Effective Litigation,* 56 N.Y.U. L. REV. 227, 240 & n.65 (1981).

[84] Worcester v. Georgia, 31 U.S. (6 Pet.) 515, 593 (1832) (Washington, J.). *See also* Hauenstein v. Lynham, 100 U.S. at 488 (Swayne, J., opinion) ("The *efficacy* of the treaty is declared and *guaranteed* by the Constitution" (emphasis added)).

decision in all courts. Their stipulations are binding on the United States . . . ."[85] And in an 1857 case, the Court declared that a ratified treaty "becomes the supreme law of the land, and the courts can no more go behind it for the purpose of annulling its effect and operation, than they can behind an Act of Congress."[86]

Prior to the 20th century, other judicial opinions seemed to follow this separate line of cases,[87] and the line has been maintained into this century. For example, in 1909 the Court made no mention of the distinction, while declaring that "[a] treaty, . . . by the express words of the Constitution, is the supreme law of the land, binding alike National and state Courts, and is capable of enforcement, and must be enforced by them in the litigation of private rights."[88] Some 15 years later, in *Asakura v. City of Seattle,* the Court seemed even less inclined to acknowledge such a distinction:

> The rule of equality established by [the treaty] cannot be rendered nugatory in any part of the United States by municipal ordinances or state laws. It stands on the same footing of supremacy as do the provisions of the Constitution and laws of the United States. It operates of itself without the aid of any legislation, state or national; and it will be applied and given authoritative effect by the courts.[89]

The same has been true of many subsequent cases.[90]

The *Restatement (Third) of Foreign Relations Law of the United States* seeks to explain away this separate line of cases,[91] but it still remains. Interestingly,

[85] Strother v. Lucas, 37 U.S. (12 Pet.) 410, 439 (1838) (Baldwin, J., opinion).

[86] Fellows v. Blacksmith, 60 U.S. (19 How.) 366, 372 (1857).

[87] *See, e.g.,* note 83 *supra.*

[88] Maiorano v. Baltimore & Ohio R.R., 213 U.S. 268, 272–73 (1909).

[89] 265 U.S. 332, 341 (1924). *See also* Paust, *supra* note 83, at 240 n.65. In view of the many cases that seem to have paid no attention to the question of self-executing versus non-self-executing status, it would be difficult to argue that the Court in *Asakura* "assumed without discussion" that the relevant treaty was self-executing unless such an "assumption" clearly were "the rule" (i.e., that *all* treaties are "assumed" to be self-executing). *See id.* (addressing Reporters' Note 5 to §131 of the RESTATEMENT OF FOREIGN RELATIONS LAW OF THE UNITED STATES (REVISED) (Tent. Draft No. 1, 1980) [hereinafter 1980 DRAFT RESTATEMENT]); *see also* RESTATEMENT (THIRD), *supra* note 42, §111 Reporters' Note 5; note 92 *infra.* No such "assumption" is evident, however, in the separate line of cases.

[90] *See, e.g.,* Zschernig v. Miller, 389 U.S. 429, 440–41 (1968); Baker v. Carr, 369 U.S. 186, 212 (1962); Kolovrat v. Oregon, 366 U.S. 187, 190–98 (1961); Clark v. Allen, 331 U.S. 503, 508 (1947) (Douglas, J., opinion); United States v. Pink, 315 U.S. 203, 231 (1942) (Douglas, J., opinion); Hines v. Davidowitz, 312 U.S. 52, 62–63 (1941); Bacardi Corp. of Am. v. Domenech, 311 U.S. 150, 161–62, 166 (1940); Santovincenzo v. Egan, 284 U.S. 30, 40 (1931); Nielsen v. Johnson, 279 U.S. 47, 52 (1929); Jordan v. Tashiro, 278 U.S. 123, 127–29 (1928); Cheung Sum She v. Nagle, 268 U.S. 336, 345–46 (1925); Filartiga v. Pena-Irala, 630 F.2d 876, 882–87 (2d Cir. 1980) (a case nonetheless grounded upon a federal statute and arguably thereby "executed," 28 U.S.C. §1350); Coriolan v. Immigration & Naturalization Serv., 559 F.2d 933, 996–97 (5th Cir. 1977); Kashani v. Immigration & Naturalization Serv., 547 F.2d 376, 379 (7th Cir. 1977); Perre v. United States, 525 F.2d 933, 935 (5th Cir. 1976); United States v. Steinberg, 478 F.Supp. 29, 33 (N.D. Ill. 1979); Chim Ming v. Marks, 367 F.Supp. 673, 676–81 (S.D.N.Y. 1973), *aff'd,* 505 F.2d 1170, 1171–72 (2d Cir. 1974) (per curiam), *cert. denied,* 421 U.S. 911 (1975); Kan Kam Lin v. Rinaldi, 361 F.Supp. 177, 179 n.1, 183–86 (D.N.J. 1973), *aff'd,* 493 F.2d 1229 (3d Cir.), *cert. denied,* 419 U.S. 974 (1974).

[91] *See* note 89 *supra.*

however, the new *Restatement* also seems to have used these and other cases as support for the general presumption that treaties are self-executing. The *Restatement* not only recognizes non-self-execution as an exception to the duty of courts to give effect to international law "as law,"[92] but also declares: "*In general,* agreements that can be readily given effect . . . are deemed self-executing, *unless* a contrary intention is manifest."[93] Furthermore, the *Restatement* basically adopts Marshall's criterion of the language of the treaty considered in context, as to self-executing status,[94] but adds that in some rare cases implementing legislation may be "constitutionally required."[95] In practice, the language of the treaty test has found significant acceptance,[96] and some cases have sought to elucidate other aspects of context that might be considered while focusing on language and probable intent.[97]

[92] *See* RESTATEMENT (THIRD), *supra* note 42, §111(3) and (4). The test of non-self-execution set forth in §111(4) strengthens such a presumption, since non-self-execution only exists "if the agreement manifests an intention that it shall not become effective as domestic law without the enactment of implementing legislation" or in a "rare" case (*see* note 95 *infra*) where legislation is "constitutionally required." *Id.* Since such agreements are rare, the presumption will be strong that treaties are self-executing. The newer version of Reporters' Note 5 retains this general presumption and also identifies a "strong presumption" of self-execution "if the Executive Branch has not requested implementing legislation and Congress has not enacted such legislation." *Id.* §111 Reporters' Note 5. *See also* Aerovias Interamericanas de Panama, S.A. v. Board of County Comm'rs, 197 F.Supp. 230, 248 (S.D. Fla. 1961) (presumed self-executing if no executive request for legislation), *rev'd on other grounds sub nom.* Board of County Comm'rs v. Aerolineas Peruanasa, 307 F.2d 802 (5th Cir. 1962), *cert. denied,* 371 U.S. 961 (1963); L. HENKIN, R. PUGH, O. SCHACHTER & H. SMIT, INTERNATIONAL LAW 202 (2d ed. 1987); Ill. Comment, *supra* note 71, at 243, 248. The new version of the *Restatement* adds: "Obligations not to act, or to act only subject to limitations, are generally self-executing." RESTATEMENT (THIRD), *supra,* §111 Reporters' Note 5 (citing and later quoting Commonwealth v. Hawes, 76 Ky. (13 Bush) 697, 702–03 (1878)).

[93] RESTATEMENT (THIRD), *supra* note 42, §111 Reporters' Note 5 (emphasis added). This presumption is recognized by others. *See, e.g.,* Amaya v. Stanolind Oil & Gas Co., 158 F.2d 554, 556 (5th Cir. 1947); N. REDLICH & B. SCHWARTZ, *supra* note 51, at 3–107; B. SCHWARTZ, *supra* note 51, at 102; Iwasawa, *supra* note 47, at 656, 668 n.184; Ill. Comment, *supra* note 71, at 248. *See also* Henkin, *supra* note 51.

[94] *See* RESTATEMENT (THIRD), *supra* note 42, §111(4) ("if the agreement manifests an intention that it shall not become effective as domestic law"), §111 Reporters' Note 5 (quoting Marshall), and *id.* ("unless a contrary intention is manifest"). This, of course, with the strong presumption noted in note 92 *supra.*

[95] *See* RESTATEMENT (THIRD), *supra* note 42, §111(4). *See also id.* §111 Reporters' Note 6. A previous draft recognized that such instances would be "rare." *See* RESTATEMENT OF FOREIGN RELATIONS LAW OF THE UNITED STATES (REVISED) §131(4) (Tent. Draft No. 6, 1985) [hereinafter 1985 DRAFT RESTATEMENT].

[96] *See* notes 51 and 82 *supra.*

[97] *See, e.g.,* People of Saipan v. United States Dep't of Interior, 502 F.2d 90, 97 (9th Cir. 1974) (citing M. MCDOUGAL, H. LASSWELL & J. MILLER, THE INTERPRETATION OF AGREEMENTS AND WORLD PUBLIC ORDER (1967)); Ill. Comment, *supra* note 71, at 239–41. For extensive treatment of related factors considered by the courts, see Iwasawa, *supra* note 47, at 653–75, 681–85, and references cited. *See also* Note, *When Are Treaties Self-Executing?,* 31 NEB. L. REV. 463, 467–71 (1952).

The infamous *Sei Fujii* case, an old opinion of the California Supreme Court, also adopted a language considered in context approach, while concluding that relevant treaty provisions were not obligatory and lacked specificity. *See* Sei Fujii v. California, 38 Cal. 718, 722–25, 242

From the above, it is evident that Marshall's approach and the *Restatement*'s presumption and general test can be compatible with the text of the Constitution and the predominant views of the Framers. Again, all treaties, to the extent of their grants, guarantees or obligations, are self-executing. Those that are not are those which, by their terms, require domestic implementing legislation or otherwise express an intention that they not be self-operative. Thus, non-self-execution is to be tested by the language of the treaty considered in context and, according to the *Restatement,* against a strong presumption of self-execution.[98]

The Role of Congressional Power

Need one stress that this rediscovered view rejects completely the current insistence that certain treaties are inherently non-self-executing because legislative power exists, for example, to regulate commerce, to define and punish crimes, and to appropriate money?[99] The Senate and President also

---

P.2d 617, 620–22 (1952). Use of these two bases for the court's conclusion that the treaty provisions were not self-executing was not really questioned as such, but the specific application and choices were questioned. *See, e.g.,* Wright, *supra* note 42. Further, subsequent events have obviated both prongs of the court's conclusion and it has been recognized that the degree of "specificity" needed for judicial application is not great. *See, e.g.,* Paust, *supra* note 83, at 239 & n.59; Schachter, *supra* note 69, at 652, 655.

The fact that a treaty addresses an obligation of signatories to assure that any necessary implementing legislation is forthcoming is not determinative. *See, e.g.,* Burke, Coliver, de la Vega & Rosenbaum, *Application of International Human Rights Law in State and Federal Courts,* 18 TEX. INT'L L.J. 291, 302 (1983); Iwasawa, *supra* note 47, at 658–61, and references cited; Ill. Comment, *supra* note 71, at 241 & n.20. First, whether or not legislation is "necessary" in the United States is the very question at stake. Second, such a treaty provision may well be directed at other countries where treaties cannot be self-executing. *See, e.g.,* Iwasawa, *supra* note 47, at 660–61 & nn.144, 152; Ill. Comment, *supra* note 71, at 241 & n.20. Third, such a clause may merely seek greater assurance of a directly operative effect in countries where legislation is not constitutionally "necessary." *See* Iwasawa, *supra,* at 660; American Convention on Human Rights, Art. 2, *opened for signature* Nov. 22, 1969, *reprinted in* ORGANIZATION OF AMERICAN STATES, HANDBOOK OF EXISTING RULES PERTAINING TO HUMAN RIGHTS IN THE INTER-AMERICAN SYSTEM, OEA/Ser. L/V/II.65, doc. 6, at 63 (1985); International Covenant on Civil and Political Rights, Art. 2(2), GA Res. 2200, 21 UN GAOR Supp. (No. 16) at 52, UN Doc. A/6316 (1966). In countries where the treaty can be self-executing, additional legislation is simply not "necessary." Legislation would also not be "necessary" further to "ensure" self-operative effect if prior legislation were already operative to "execute" the particular treaty or such treaties more generally (or portions of them), it being recognized that treaties could be "executed" by any form of legislation. Fourth, text writers have recognized that the legislative history of relevant human rights treaties demonstrates that the parties "never intended to deny their self-executing character by inserting domestic implementation clauses." Iwasawa, *supra,* at 660. Moreover, this recognition is strengthened by the fact that the right to an effective remedy in domestic tribunals for human rights deprivations is customary and is expressed elsewhere in the treaty as an independent right. *See, e.g.,* Paust, *On Human Rights: The Use of Human Right Precepts in U.S. History and the Right to an Effective Remedy in Domestic Courts,* 10 MICH. J. INT'L L. (1988); American Convention on Human Rights, *supra,* Art. 25. Further, language such as "undertakes to ensure" has a mandatory quality unlike words such as "could" or "may," which are usually discretionary.

[98] *See* notes 92–94 *supra.*

[99] For examples of this approach, see, e.g., E. CORWIN, THE PRESIDENT, OFFICE AND POWERS 1787–1957, at 195 (4th rev. ed. 1957); L. HENKIN, *supra* note 27, at 159 (re appro-

have an express power to make a treaty, which is supreme law of the land, and the mere existence of a concurrent power does not obviate either the existence or the exercise of another.[100] Indeed, to claim that certain treaties

---

priations, crime, war; *but see id.* at 149, 159 n.††, 160); H. STEINER & D. VAGTS, TRANSNATIONAL LEGAL PROBLEMS 584 (2d ed. 1976) (citing The Over the Top, 5 F.2d 838, 845 (D. Conn. 1925), re revenue matters and crime; actually, the case spoke of "fiscal" matters and appropriations, and the treaty involved was later found to be self-executing in Cook v. United States, 288 U.S. 102, 118–19 (1933)); R. ROTUNDA, MODERN CONSTITUTIONAL LAW 232 (2d ed. 1985); L. TRIBE, AMERICAN CONSTITUTIONAL LAW 167–68 (1978) (citing Turner v. American Baptist Missionary Union, 24 F. Cas. 344 (C.C.D. Mich. 1852) (No. 14,251)); 14 M. WHITEMAN, DIGEST OF INTERNATIONAL LAW 305 (1970); Anderson, *The Extent and Limitations of the Treaty-Making Power Under the Constitution,* 1 AJIL 636, 653 (1907); Dickinson, *Are the Liquor Treaties Self-Executing?,* 20 AJIL 444, 448–49 (1926) (*cf. id.* at 449–50); Evans, *Some Aspects of the Problem of Self-Executing Treaties,* 45 ASIL PROC. 66, 71, 74 (1951) (*but see id.* at 72–74) [hereinafter Evans I]; Evans, *Self-Executing Treaties in the United States of America,* 30 BRIT. Y.B. INT'L L. 178, 185, 187 (1954) (*but see id.* at 186–87, 190–91, also listing cases involving self-executing treaties) [hereinafter Evans II]; Henkin, *supra* note 42, at 868 n.70 (reading United States v. Hudson & Goodwin, 11 U.S. (7 Cranch) 32 (1812), too broadly re common law crime); Henry, *supra* note 47, at 780 (*but see id.* at 782 re crimes); Iwasawa, *supra* note 47, at 676–78 (*cf. id.* at 676–77); Riesenfeld, *The Doctrine of Self-Executing Treaties and* U.S. v. Postal: *Win at Any Price?,* 74 AJIL 892, 898 n.30 (1980); Schachter, *supra* note 69, at 645; Wright, *supra* note 42, at 68, 77–78; UCLA Comment, *supra* note 71, at 399–400 (re appropriations; *but see id.*, all others can be self-executing); Note, *supra* note 97, at 472–74 (*but see id.* at 471–74); *cf.* Paust, *After My Lai: The Case for War Crime Jurisdiction over Civilians in Federal District Courts,* 50 TEX. L. REV. 6, 9 n.10 (1971) (assumed better view at the time re crime), *reprinted in* 4 THE VIETNAM WAR AND INTERNATIONAL LAW 447, 450 n.10 (R. Falk ed. 1976); Wright, *Treaties and the Constitutional Separation of Powers in the United States,* 12 AJIL 64 (1918); British Caledonian Airways v. Bond, 665 F.2d 1153, 1160 (D.C. Cir. 1981); Hopson v. Kreps, 622 F.2d 1375, 1380 (9th Cir. 1980); Edwards v. Carter, 580 F.2d 1055, 1057 n.4 (Raoul Berger), 1058 (D.C. Cir.), *cert. denied,* 436 U.S. 907 (1978) (*but see id.* at 1057–58); Swearingen v. United States, 565 F.Supp. 1019, 1022 (D. Colo. 1983) (citing *Edwards*); Aerovias Interamericanas de Panama, S.A. v. Board of County Comm'rs, 197 F.Supp. 230, 246 (S.D. Fla. 1961) (citing *Turner,* 24 F. Cas. 344).

[100] *See* Edwards v. Carter, 580 F.2d at 1058–59 (discussed in text at notes 111–21 *infra*); Indemnity Ins. Co. of N. Am. v. Pan Am. Airways, 58 F.Supp. 338, 339–40 (S.D.N.Y. 1944); *see also* United States v. The Schooner Peggy, 5 U.S. (1 Cranch) 103, 103–10 (1801). Several treaties have had a self-executing or self-operative effect despite the existence of some concurrent congressional power. *See, e.g.,* Trans World Airlines v. Franklin Mint Corp., 466 U.S. 243, 252, *reh'g denied,* 467 U.S. 1231 (1984); Cook v. United States, 288 U.S. 102, 119 (1933); Charlton v. Kelley, 229 U.S. 447 (1913); Johnson v. Browne, 205 U.S. 309 (1907); Francis v. Francis, 203 U.S. 233, 241–42 (1906); Ward v. Race Horse, 163 U.S. 504 (1896); Chae Chan Ping v. United States, 130 U.S. 581, 600 (1889); Smith v. Canadian Pacific Airways, 452 F.2d 798, 801–02 (2d Cir. 1971); Vanity Fair Mills v. T. Eaton Co., 234 F.2d 633, 640 & n.9 (2d Cir. 1956); Master v. Cribben & Sexton Co., 202 F.2d 779, 783 (C.C.P.A. 1953); Pettibone v. Cook County, Minn., 120 F.2d 850, 854–55 (8th Cir. 1941); John T. Bill Co. v. United States, 104 F.2d 67, 73 (C.C.P.A. 1939); United States v. Garrow, 88 F.2d 318, 320 (C.C.P.A. 1937) (re customs); The Pictonian, 3 F.2d 145, 147 (E.D.N.Y. 1924) (re extension of criminal jurisdiction), *rev'd on other grounds,* 20 F.2d 353 (2d Cir. 1927); Hennebique Const. Co. v. Myers, 172 F. 869, 873–74 (Gray, J.), 887–88 (Archbald, D.J.) (3d Cir. 1909); Hannevig v. United States, 84 F.Supp. 743, 744–45 (Ct. Cl. 1949); Petition of Georgakopoulos, 81 F.Supp. 411, 413 (E.D. Pa. 1948); American Express Co. v. United States, 4 Ct. Cust. App. 146 (1913); United States v. Kelly, 2 Extrater. Cases 665, 669–70 (U.S.C. China 1923) (treaty prohibiting contraband trade can be self-executing for criminal sanction purposes); Ill. Comment, *supra* note 71, at 243; UCLA Comment, *supra* note 71, at 399–400; notes 34, 37, 51, 53, 55, 77, 83,

should be inherently non-self-executing merely because Congress has a relevant concurrent power is to ignore or subvert the separation of powers between the legislative and judicial branches, to rewrite the Constitution at the expense of the treaty power. It is the judiciary, not Congress, that has been granted the power (indeed, the textual commitment) under Article III of the Constitution to apply treaty law in cases or controversies otherwise properly before the courts.[101]

For these or related reasons, commentators and others have recognized that treaty provisions can be directly applicable despite the existence of a relevant congressional power,[102] and the same recognition has appeared in recent cases.[103] Nonetheless, the *Restatement* (*Third*) seeks to retain the possibility that a treaty may not be self-executing in a case where "implementing legislation is constitutionally required."[104] This test does not answer the question at stake, i.e., whether legislation *is* "constitutionally required." Thus, this test, as the new *Restatement* recognizes, might only apply where

---

86 and 90 *supra. See also* INS v. Stevic, 467 U.S. 407, 428 n.22 (1984); O'Donnell v. Great Lakes Dredge & Dock Co., 318 U.S. 36, 42 (1943); The Three Friends, 166 U.S. 1, 53 (1897) (crimes); Reichert v. Felps, 73 U.S. (6 Wall.) 160, 165–66 (1868); United States v. Moreno, 68 U.S. (1 Wall.) 400, 404, (1864); United States v. Worrall, 2 U.S. (2 Dall.) 384, 391 (Chase, J.), 395 (Peters, J.) (C.C.D. Pa. 1798); Robertson v. General Elec. Co., 32 F.2d 495, 500 (4th Cir. 1929); Morris v. United States, 161 F. 672, 675 (8th Cir. 1908); 7 Op. Att'y Gen. 746, 750 (1856); *cf.* United States v. Mason, 344 F.2d 673, 683–85 (2d Cir. 1965). *See further* United States v. Ragsdale, 27 F. Cas. 684, 686 (C.C.D. Ark. 1847) (No. 16,113).

[101] *See* note 1 *supra.* To decide otherwise would be to undermine both the treaty power and judicial power, and thus to disrupt the proper balance of power the Constitution sought to establish, by preventing the judiciary and the executive branch from accomplishing their constitutionally assigned responsibilities. For this reason also, appropriate concern for the separation of powers compels recognition that a court that refuses for some specious reason to apply international law denies its own validity. When human rights are at stake, such a court may also be denying or disparaging human rights within the meaning of the Ninth Amendment. *See* Paust, *Human Rights and the Ninth Amendment: A New Form of Guarantee,* 60 CORNELL L. REV. 231, 234–37, 249, 257–60, 266–67 (1975); note 41 *supra.*

[102] *See, e.g.,* Representative Marshall, *quoted in* note 34 *supra;* Anderson, *supra* note 99, at 653, 655, 657, 664; McDougal & Arens, *The Genocide Convention and the Constitution,* 3 VAND. L. REV. 683, 690–91 (1950) (*cf. id.* at 693 n.63); Hamilton (re taxes, *quoted in* Lobel, *supra* note 28, at 1098); Palmer, *The Federal Common Law of Crime,* 4 LAW & HIST. REV. 267, 276, 277 n.63 (1986) (also quoting Representative Marshall, 10 ANNALS OF CONG. 607 (1800)); note 55 *supra;* Ill. Comment, *supra* note 71, at 243; UCLA Comment, *supra* note 71, at 399–400 (*but see id.;* one exception involves appropriations). *See also* text at notes 10–11 and 26 *supra;* Talbot v. Jansen, 3 U.S. (3 Dall.) 133, 159–61 (1795) (Iredell, J.); 1 Op. Att'y Gen. 68, 69 (1797) ("law of nations" can be self-operative for criminal sanction purposes); J. HENDRY, TREATIES AND FEDERAL CONSTITUTIONS 92 (1955) (citing 5 G. HACKWORTH, DIGEST OF INTERNATIONAL LAW 16–17 (1943)); Dickinson, *supra* note 99, at 449–50 (re crimes); Dickinson, *The Law of Nations as Part of the National Law of the United States,* 101 U. PA. L. REV. 26, 36–38 (1952); Evans I, *supra* note 99, at 72–74 (re taxes, revenue, duties, commercial matters, trademarks); Evans II, *supra* note 99, at 190–91; Henry, *supra* note 47, at 782 (re crimes); McLaughlin, *supra* note 31, at 749; Nathanson, *The Constitution and World Government,* 57 NW. U.L. REV. 355, 362–64 & n.16 (1962); Paust, *supra* note 99; Note, *supra* note 97, at 471–74; *cf.* Marshall, *supra:* "But the Judicial power cannot extend to *political* compacts: so as to allow Courts to 'execute' such compacts" (emphasis added).

[103] *See* note 100 *supra.*

[104] *See* RESTATEMENT (THIRD), *supra* note 42, §111(4).

Congress is thought to have an exclusive power (i.e., not merely a concurrent power with respect to matters that can also be effectuated by treaty).[105] The *Restatement* even adds: "That a subject is within the legislative power of Congress does not preclude a treaty on the same subject."[106]

Yet the *Restatement* assumes that agreements involving the appropriation of funds do require congressional action.[107] More cautiously, the *Restatement* states that it has been "assumed" that agreements creating a state of war or a crime or calling for punishment of certain conduct require congressional implementing legislation,[108] adding that "[i]t has also been suggested" that treaties cannot "raise revenue" by imposing taxes or tariffs.[109] A Reporters' Note remarks more openly:

> There is no definitive authority for the rule set forth . . . that agreements on some subjects cannot be self-executing. . . . No particular clause of the Constitution conferring power on Congress states or clearly implies that the power can be exercised only by Congress and not by treaty. . . .
>
> The principle declared . . . is nevertheless generally assumed for the cases given.[110]

What the Reporters' Note nearly admits is that powers conferred on Congress by Article I, section 8 of the Constitution are merely concurrent powers, not exclusive powers. This recognition was even more evident in *Edwards v. Carter,* although there the circuit court was uncomfortable with the notion that none of the section 8 powers (especially the war power) were exclusive. As the majority found in *Edwards:*

> The grant of authority to Congress under the property clause states that "The Congress shall have Power . . . ," *not* that only the Congress shall have power, or that the Congress shall have *exclusive* power. In this respect the property clause is parallel to Article I, §8, which also states that "The Congress shall have Power . . ." Many of the powers thereafter enumerated in §8 involve matters that were at the time the Constitution was adopted, and that are at the present time, also commonly the subject of treaties. The most prominent example of this is the regulation of commerce with foreign nations, Art. I, §8, cl. 3, and appellants do not go so far as to contend that the treaty process is not a constitutionally allowable means for regulating foreign commerce. It thus seems to us that, on its face, the property clause is intended not to restrict the scope of the treaty clause, but, rather, is intended to permit

[105] *See id.* §111 comment *i* ("if the agreement would achieve what lies within the *exclusive* law-making power of Congress under the Constitution" (emphasis added)).

[106] *Id.* §111 Reporters' Note 6.

[107] *See id.* §111 comment *i* ("Thus . . . requires").

[108] *See id.* and §111 Reporters' Note 6. *But see* note 102 *supra.*

[109] *See* RESTATEMENT (THIRD), *supra* note 42, §111 comment *i. But see* note 102 *supra.*

[110] RESTATEMENT (THIRD), *supra* note 42, §111 Reporters' Note 6, adding: "But see the dissenting opinion in Edwards v. Carter . . . ." There are no Supreme Court opinions supporting such assumptions and relevant judicial opinions are extremely rare. *See* note 99 *supra. Cf.* note 116 *infra* on the *sui generis* power of Congress to declare war.

> Congress to accomplish through legislation what may *concurrently* be accomplished through other means provided in the Constitution.[111]

With respect to the war power conferred by Article I, section 8, clause 11, the court merely stated: "The *sui generis* nature of a declaration of war and the unique history indicating the Framers' desire to have both Houses of Congress concur in such a declaration, may place it apart from the other congressional powers enumerated in Art. I, §8 and in Art. IV, §3, cl. 2."[112]

Yet, with respect to exclusive powers of the full Congress (which cannot be fully effectuated domestically by a self-executing treaty alone), the court offered a distinction between section 8 powers (almost all of which are concurrent) and those conferred by certain portions of sections 7 and 9:

> There are certain grants of authority to Congress which are, by their very terms, *exclusive.* In these areas, the treaty-making power and the power of Congress are not concurrent; rather, the only department of the federal government authorized to take action is the Congress. For instance, the Constitution expressly provides only one method—congressional enactment—for the *appropriation of money:*
>
> No Money shall be drawn from the Treasury, but in Consequence of Appropriations made by Law.
>
> Art. I, §9, cl. 7. Thus, the expenditure of funds by the United States cannot be accomplished by self-executing treaty; implementing legislation appropriating such funds is indispensable. Similarly, the constitutional mandate that "all *Bills for raising Revenue* shall originate in the House of Representatives," Art. I, §7, cl. 1, appears, by reason of the restrictive language used, to prohibit the use of the treaty power to impose taxes.[113]

[111] 580 F.2d at 1057–58 (emphasis added), adding:

> The American Law Institute's Restatement of Foreign Relations, directly addressing this issue, comes to the same conclusion we reach:
>
> The mere fact, however, that a congressional power exists does not mean that the power is exclusive so as to preclude the making of a self-executing treaty within the area of that power.
>
> ALI Restatement of Foreign Relations Law (2d), §141, at 435 (1965).

580 F.2d at 1058.

[112] 580 F.2d at 1058 n.7. *See also* note 116 *infra.*

[113] 580 F.2d at 1058 (emphasis added), adding:

> These particular grants of power to Congress operate to limit the treaty power because the language of these provisions clearly precludes any method of appropriating money or raising taxes other than through the enactment of laws by the full Congress. This is to be contrasted with the power-granting language in Art. I, §8, and in Art. IV, §3, cl. 2. Rather than stating the particular matter of concern and providing that the enactment of a law is the only way for the federal government to take action regarding that matter, these provisions state simply that Congress shall have power to take action on the matters enumerated.

Id. at 1059.

In my opinion, this overall distinction (hereinafter termed the *Edwards* rationale) generally makes sense. Moreover, unlike the *Restatement*'s retained assumptions about inherently non-self-executing treaties, the *Edwards* rationale seems to leave very few exclusive powers to the full Congress and, thus, very few circumstances in which a treaty would be inherently non-self-executing. In particular, treaties creating an international crime or requiring punishments could be self-executing,[114] and so could treaties creating taxes or tariffs.[115] If it were not for its *sui generis* nature and history, the war power might also be thought to be nonexclusive.[116] If it were, every section 8 power, at least, would be nonexclusive and, thus, treaties implicating those powers could be self-executing. Significantly, a few of the Founders thought that such a nearly unrestrained and self-operative treaty power would exist, but that it would be balanced in part by an exclusive power of the House and Senate to appropriate money.[117]

Nonetheless, there are problems with some of the specific choices made by the *Edwards* court while applying the general rationale. Just because all "Bills" for raising revenue shall originate in the House,[118] it does not follow that revenue may be raised in no other way.[119] Further, is there a difference

[114] *See* U.S. CONST. art. I, §8, cl. 10; notes 100 and 102 *supra. See also* Note, *supra* note 97, at 473. *But see* note 99 *supra.*

[115] *See* U.S. CONST. art. I, §8, cls. 1 and 3; notes 100 and 102 *supra. But see* text at note 113 *supra* (*Edwards,* considering Art. I, §7, cl. 1 to prohibit taxes by treaty); note 99 *supra.*

[116] *Compare* U.S. CONST. art. I, §8, cl. 11, *with* text at note 112 *supra. See also* U.S. CONST. art. I, §8, cls. 12–15; P. BREST, PROCESSES OF CONSTITUTIONAL DECISIONMAKING 435 (1975) (recognizing that the Founders "rejected a resolution that would have lodged the war power in the president and Senate" (citing 1 Farrand (ed.), *supra* note 2, at 292, 300)); Iwasawa, *supra* note 47, at 677–78 & n.251; Murphy, *Treaties and International Agreements Other Than Treaties: Constitutional Allocation of Power and Responsibility Among the President, the House of Representatives, and the Senate,* 23 KANS. L. REV. 221, 224–30, 241–42, 245 (1975); 3 Falk (ed.), *supra* note 99, at 489–91 (1972); 4 *id.* at 535–818; THE FEDERALIST NO. 64, at 420 (Jay) ("power of making treaties is an important one, especially as it relates to war"); Paust, *supra* note 40, at 416–18 ("war power" exception to last-in-time rule accepts treaty-based international law as a restraint on congressional power); RESTATEMENT (THIRD), *supra* note 42, §111 Reporters' Note 6 ("The power of Congress to declare war is not characterized or designated in any way that would distinguish it from, say, the power to regulate commerce . . .").

A declaration of war is not the equivalent of legislation or a "law," but is the outcome of an exercise of a *sui generis* power. *See, e.g.,* Brown v. United States, 12 U.S. (8 Cranch) 110, 125–26 (1814) (Marshall, C.J., opinion). This might distinguish that portion of the "war power" so as to allow the conclusion that no treaty constitutionally could declare war, although treaties regulating the conduct of war certainly could be self-executing. *See also* 50 U.S.C. §§1541, 1547(a)(2) (1982) (§8(a)(2) of the War Powers Resolution: no authority to introduce forces shall be inferred "from any treaty . . . unless such treaty is implemented by legislation specifically authorizing the introduction of United States Armed Forces"). Further, there is significant judicial precedent to the effect that the war power (unlike others here mentioned) is vested in the full Congress. *See, e.g.,* The Prize Cases, 67 U.S. (2 Black) 635, 668 (1862); Brown v. United States, *supra;* Talbot v. Seeman, 5 U.S. (1 Cranch) 1, 28 (1801); Bas v. Tingy, 4 U.S. (4 Dall.) 37 (1800). *See also* Glennon, *United States Mutual Security Treaties: The Commitment Myth,* 24 COLUM. J. TRANSNAT'L L. 509 (1986); Paust, *Responding Lawfully to International Terrorism: The Use of Force Abroad,* 8 WHITTIER L. REV. 711, 718–19 n.21 (1986).

[117] *See* 4 Elliot (ed.), *supra* note 15, at 129 (Iredell), 438 (Lyman).

[118] U.S. CONST. art. I, §7, cl. 1; text at note 113 *supra.*

[119] *See also* notes 102 and 115 *supra.*

between section 8 powers and that mentioned in section 9, clause 7 of the Constitution? Under the latter, no money can be appropriated "but in Consequence of Appropriations made by Law." The word "Law" in section 9, clause 7 is not limited by the words "House" (as in section 7) or "Congress" (as in section 9, clause 1 ["not . . . by the Congress"] and section 8 ["no Person . . . without the Consent of Congress"]), or even "exclusive Legislation" (as in section 8, clause 17). Moreover, the word "Law" also appears in Article III, section 2, clause 1 ("The judicial Power shall extend to all Cases, in Law . . . , arising under . . . Treaties") and Article VI, clause 2 (e.g., "supreme Law of the Land," covering also "all Treaties"), which suggests that the appropriations power is not exclusive to Congress.[120]

If so, it may well be that no treaty is inherently non-self-executing in the face of some congressional power. Using the *Edwards* rationale (but not all of the conclusory dicta), one can see that, with the exception of the war power, no seemingly relevant congressional power is exclusive.[121] Thus, as the text of the Constitution and almost all of the Founders seem to affirm,[122] legislation is not constitutionally required in any seemingly relevant circumstance and, as the predominant view of the Framers demonstrates, all treaties are supreme federal law and, potentially, are directly operative. Treaties that are not directly operative are those which by their terms are not "self-executing." It is worth repeating that any judicial opinions to the contrary are extremely rare and less than authoritative.[123]

Legal Effects of Non-Self-Executing Treaties

It is important to note that even non-self-executing treaties can produce legal effects. Although such treaties cannot operate directly without implementing legislation, they can be used indirectly as a means of interpreting relevant constitutional, statutory, common law or other legal provisions.[124] Indirect incorporation of international law, moreover, is the most prevalent form of judicial incorporation.[125]

[120] *See also* Evans II, *supra* note 99, at 185 n.3 ("It is possible to argue, however, that . . . appropriations may be made by treaty" (citing Feidler & Dwan, *The Extent of the Treaty-Making Power,* 28 Geo. L.J. 187, 192 (1939)); Restatement (Third), *supra* note 42, §111 Reporters' Note 6 (might be "possible to conclude that since treaties are declared to be 'law' (Art. VI) and are treated as equal to an act of Congress for other purposes, an appropriation of funds through an international agreement is an appropriation 'made by law' "). *But see id.* §111 comment *i* (appropriation of funds listed as "exclusive law-making power of Congress").

[121] *But see* Restatement (Third), *supra* note 42, §111 Reporters' Note 6 (addressing Art. I, §8, cl. 17, "exclusive legislation," which might even be distinguished from the term "Law"); notes 112 and 116 *supra* (re war power as *sui generis*).

[122] *But see* text at note 117 *supra.*

[123] *See* note 111 *supra* and accompanying text; *see also* note 99 *supra.*

[124] *See, e.g.,* Iwasawa, *supra* note 47, at 687, 689–90 (& nn.323, 328), 692; Paust, *supra* note 40, at 403–05, and references cited; Paust, *supra* note 83, at 240–42, 244.

[125] *See* note 124 *supra.*

An early draft of the new *Restatement*[126] had mirrored an incorrect and overly broad statement in an opinion of the Court of Appeals for the Fifth Circuit that "treaties affect" domestic law only when they "are given effect by congressional legislation or are, by their nature, self-executing."[127] As argued in a prior writing, however, such assertions are clearly out of line with predominant trends in judicial decision and are fallacious for at least three reasons.[128] First, the self-executing treaty doctrine does not apply to customary international law.[129] The doctrine therefore poses no obstacle to the direct incorporation of customary norms for use in domestic litigation. Because non-self-executing treaties often are evidence of customary international law, these treaties can affect the municipal law of the United States. Second, although some decisions pay great attention to the self-executing treaty doctrine, usually so as to deny claims of incorporation, in another line of cases treaty provisions have been incorporated directly for judicial use without any mention of the doctrine.[130] Third, non-self-executing treaties are available for interpretive purposes and, thus, can at least affect domestic law indirectly.

CONCLUSION

From the above, it seems clear that the text of the Constitution, the predominant views of the Founders, and early and more modern trends in judicial decision all demand that certain notions of several text writers with respect to the inherently non-self-executing nature of certain types of treaties be abandoned. The constitutionally preferable view is that no treaty is inherently non-self-executing except those which would seek to declare war on behalf of the United States.[131] With the exception of the *sui generis* power of Congress to declare war, the mere existence of a congressional power does not mean that it is exclusive and would obviate any potentially self-executing effect of a treaty.

From these sources, it also seems clear that all treaties are self-executing except those (or the portions of them) which, by their terms considered in context, require domestic implementing legislation or seek to declare war on behalf of the United States. All treaties are supreme federal law, but some treaties, by their terms, are not directly operative. Finally, even non-self-executing treaties can produce and have produced domestic legal effects through indirect incorporation, by which a treaty norm is utilized as an aid in interpreting the Constitution, a statute, common law or some other legal provision.

[126] *See* 1980 DRAFT RESTATEMENT, *supra* note 89, §131(3) ("given effect only after"). Section 131(3) was changed in the 1985 draft to read: "not be given effect as law" and should have read "not be given effect directly as law." *See* 1985 DRAFT RESTATEMENT, *supra* note 95; Paust, *supra* note 40, at 403–04 n.14, 446–47.

[127] United States v. Postal, 589 F.2d 862, 875 (5th Cir.), *cert. denied,* 444 U.S. 832 (1979).

[128] *See* Paust, *supra* note 83, at 239–40.

[129] *See id.* at 240 n.63.

[130] *See* text at notes 83–90 *supra.*

[131] *See* note 116 *supra.*

The word "self-executing" may or may not be felicitous,[132] but awareness of the actual text of the Constitution, the predominant views of the Founders, early and more modern judicial opinions, and a proper separation of powers should prove a useful counter to ambiguity and the contrary "assumptions" of text writers. In this time of the bicentennial, it is appropriate to reaffirm the text of the Constitution and expectations of the Founders that all treaties will be the supreme law of the land.

[132] *See* McDougal, Remarks, 45 ASIL PROC. 102 (1951) ("this word 'self-executing' is essentially meaningless, and . . . the quicker we drop it from our vocabulary the better for clarity and understanding").

AGORA: THE U.S. DECISION NOT TO RATIFY PROTOCOL I TO THE GENEVA CONVENTIONS ON THE PROTECTION OF WAR VICTIMS (CONT'D)

The Rationale for the United States Decision

The October 1987 issue of the *Journal* contains an article written by Hans-Peter Gasser,[1] the Legal Adviser to the Directorate of the International Committee of the Red Cross (ICRC), on the U.S. decision not to ratify Protocol I (on international armed conflicts) to the 1949 Geneva Conventions on the Protection of War Victims. Unfortunately, the *Journal* did not include any response by the administration, but only the President's necessarily brief letter of transmittal to the Senate of January 18, 1987, recommending advice and consent to ratification of Protocol II (on noninternational conflicts).[2] The President's letter of transmittal was not intended to be an exhaustive statement of the U.S. objections to Protocol I, nor does it purport to be such.

The underlying assumption of Dr. Gasser's article is that the United States is somehow obligated to ratify or accede to Protocol I simply because it was adopted by the Geneva Conference. We disagree. We appreciate that Protocol I was the product of a substantial effort by the Swiss Government and the ICRC to alleviate the plight of victims of war. Nonetheless, each sovereign state must make its decision on whether to ratify such agreements based on a comprehensive assessment of their merits, including the consequences of ratification.

The United States would have preferred to ratify Protocol I, since it contains some sound and meritorious elements. The new provisions on the missing and dead and on protection of medical aircraft are in this category, and are largely designed to address problems experienced by members of the U.S. Armed Forces during the Vietnam conflict. We will support efforts to have these provisions observed and in time recognized as customary international law.

The enforcement provisions of the Protocol give no assurance, however, that these provisions would actually be complied with. Further, the Protocol also contains provisions that the United States cannot accept from a military, political or humanitarian standpoint. These problems were raised at the conference, and they should come as no surprise. The unfortunate fact is that Third World and other countries chose not to respect our strong views and those of our European allies, and thus chose to create a new legal regime that we find unacceptable.

[1] Gasser, *An Appeal for Ratification by the United States,* 81 AJIL 912 (1987).

[2] *Letter of Transmittal, id.* at 910. The President's letter of transmittal and Dr. Gasser's article constituted an *Agora* section entitled "The U.S. Decision Not to Ratify Protocol I to the Geneva Conventions on the Protection of War Victims."

The Joint Chiefs of Staff, after a careful and extensive study, concluded that Protocol I is unacceptable from the point of view of military operations. The reasons, spelled out in a detailed JCS report of more than a hundred pages, include the fact that the Protocol grants irregulars a legal status which is at times superior to that accorded regular forces; that it unreasonably restricts attacks against certain objects that have traditionally been legitimate targets; and that it eliminates significant remedies in cases where an enemy violates the Protocol. The total elimination of the right of reprisal, for example, would hamper the ability of the United States to respond to an enemy's intentional disregard of the limitations established in the Geneva Conventions of 1949 or Protocol I, for the purpose of deterring such disregard. Before ratifying any agreement that deals with U.S. national security, we must be satisfied that the terms of the agreement are reasonable and that they can be implemented without undue consequences in terms of U.S. casualties. Our Joint Chiefs of Staff have unanimously concluded that this is clearly not the case with respect to Protocol I. U.S. soldiers would have to pay the price for such unreasonable limitations through unnecessary casualties and charges of criminal activity.

From a political standpoint, the principal deficiency is that part of Protocol I which deals with so-called wars of national liberation. Traditionally, the law of war has recognized two general categories of armed conflicts—international armed conflicts (e.g., conflicts between sovereign states) and internal ones (e.g., civil wars). No distinction has ever previously been made under the law of war based on the cause for which one of the parties claims to be fighting. Rather, the law of war has had some degree of success in the world because it attempts to be objective in its categorization of conflicts rather than using subjective and hence political and controversial concepts. Neutral principles are vital in the laws of war, since no party is ever prepared to apply rules of warfare on the assumption that its opponent has been wronged, and particularly that the opponent is justifiably fighting to be "liberated."

As the record of the 1974 session of the Diplomatic Conference demonstrates, Third World states (which numerically dominated the conference) were not interested in applying the rules of international armed conflict to ordinary civil wars, but insisted on applying these rules to civil wars that involved causes they favored—the so-called wars of national liberation, specifically those being conducted by the Palestine Liberation Organization and the liberation movements of southern Africa. To accomplish this objective, they pushed through a provision—Article 1(4) of Protocol I—that treats as international armed conflicts those noninternational conflicts in which "peoples are fighting against colonial domination and alien occupation and racist régimes."

One result of this provision, if actually applied, would be that those fighting for such causes would theoretically obtain prisoner-of-war status if captured, and thus immunity from prosecution for belligerent acts. On the other hand, those fighting for less-favored political causes (at least from a Third World perspective) would be treated under the rules of internal conflicts, and would not receive POW status or immunity from prosecution for warlike acts. If one is dealing with a group like the PLO, elements of which often use terrorist tactics, this distinction becomes very important. Treating these terrorists as soldiers also enhances their stature, to the detriment of the civilized world community.

These problems are compounded by Article 44 of Protocol I, which allows irregular fighters to retain combatant and POW rights even though they do not comply with the traditional requirement of distinguishing themselves from the civilian population by carrying their arms openly and wearing some distinctive sign. (The only exception would be during attacks and military operations preparatory to an attack.) This provision would make it easier for irregulars to operate, and it would substantially increase the risks to the civilian population. Inevitably, regular forces would treat civilians more harshly and with less restraint if they believed that their opponents were free to pose as civilians while retaining their right to act as combatants and their POW status if captured. Innocent civilians would therefore be made more vulnerable by application of the Protocol. This is no advance for humanitarian law.

In addition, the Protocol eliminates one of the basic existing requirements that irregular groups must meet to qualify for combatant and POW status: that the group as such generally conduct its operations in accordance with the laws and customs of war. Instead, Protocol I provides that individual members of such groups must be accorded POW benefits (with very limited exceptions) even if the group as such (e.g., the PLO) displays a callous and systematic disregard for the law. This means in effect that liberation groups can enjoy many of the benefits of the law of war without fulfilling its duties, and with the confidence that the belligerent state has no real remedy under the Protocol to deal with this matter.

The experience of the last decade confirms the hypocrisy of the regime established by Article 1(4). Having achieved a political victory by "internationalizing" their own internal conflicts, so-called liberation groups have shown little interest in following through on the obligations of the Protocol. They have not acted in accordance with the existing requirements of customary international law, nor have they even bothered to file declarations with the Swiss Government accepting the obligations of the Protocol (as contemplated in Article 96). They have been content to cite the Protocol (e.g., in the United Nations) for the proposition that they must be accorded the benefits of humanitarian law (e.g., prisoner-of-war status) without fulfilling the duties expected. In practice, they have continued to make indiscriminate attacks on innocent civilians.

The *Journal* article complains that the U.S. decision deprives the world community of a "common framework" and "hinder[s] the development and acceptance of universal standards in a field where they are particularly needed."[3] This view fails to take into account the fact that the main problem with the current laws of war is not their substantive adequacy but the lack of

[3] Gasser, *supra* note 1, at 924.

observance of even the most basic principles, such as immunity for noncombatants from intentional attack. Sadly, many of those countries or entities demanding new rules appear to have little regard for the existing requirements of international law.

In addition, the charge in the article that the U.S. position is "political" and "partisan" is polemical.[4] The U.S. position is based on the merits of the Protocols, and our conclusion on whether they advance humanitarian law. From the standpoint of the United States, it is not sufficient that Protocol I was the product of enormous negotiating efforts over many years and that many countries have and will become a party. The approval of the United States should never be taken for granted, especially when an agreement deals with national security, the conduct of military operations and the protection of victims of war.

Finally, as the President stated in his transmittal letter, we must not, and need not, give recognition and protection to terrorist groups as the price for progress in humanitarian law. Article 1(4) of Protocol I creates "an unacceptable and thoroughly distasteful price"[5] for adherence. The United States is not willing to acquiesce in such a regime.

ABRAHAM D. SOFAER*

[4] *Id.*

[5] *Letter of Transmittal, supra* note 2, at 911.

* Legal Adviser, Department of State.

NOTES AND COMMENTS

PERESTROIKA AND INTERNATIONAL LAW

Soviet positions on international law and organizations are changing sharply under the influence of the policy of *perestroika* (restructuring) introduced by General Secretary M. S. Gorbachev. This development was brought to the attention of the American Society of International Law at its Annual Meeting in April 1988 by the noted Soviet international lawyer, G. I. Tunkin.[1]

Considering the dismissive attitude toward international law of the Soviet Union in its early years, the magnitude of the change is impressive. Stressing "the primacy of international law in politics,"[2] Gorbachev has initiated Soviet payment of back dues to the United Nations, encouragement of universal acceptance of the compulsory jurisdiction of the International Court of Justice, espousal of customary international law as "general international law" to be respected by all countries, and application by the USSR for observer status in the General Agreement on Tariffs and Trade (GATT); and he has even hinted that Soviet participation in the International Monetary Fund would be appropriate. One cannot but ask whether Soviet policymakers have turned the page to a new chapter in the history of Soviet attitudes toward international law and institutions. To find the answer, the new attitudes must be seen against the background of previous Soviet views, in particular, those that began to evolve in the 1950s.

CLASS STRUGGLE

Gorbachev describes early Soviet foreign policy as having aimed at creating conditions for the "construction of a new society in the country of the socialist revolution." Foreign policy, in his view, represented "a continuation of the class politics of the victorious proletariat."[3] Soviet analysts interpreted international law in those years as a reflection of the will of the ruling classes of states. Socialist states and capitalist states each produced a set of international legal norms.[4] "General" international law was formed by the

[1] Tunkin, Address at the Annual Meeting of the American Society of International Law, Washington, D.C. (Apr. 21, 1988). The references cited hereinafter are based on a tape recording of the Address.

[2] Gorbachev, *Real'nost' i garantii bezopasnogo mira* (Reality and Guarantees of a Secure World), Pravda, Sept. 17, 1987, at 1, col. 1, 2, col. 3. Translations from Russian-language sources are the author's.

[3] Gorbachev, *Oktiabr' i perestroika: revoliutsiia prodolzhaetsia* (October and Perestroika: The Revolution Continues), Izvestiia, Nov. 3, 1987, at 2, col. 1, 4, col. 3 (report to joint session of Central Committee of CPSU, Supreme Soviet of USSR, Supreme Soviet of RSFSR, 70th anniversary of October revolution).

[4] Kulski, *The Soviet Interpretation of International Law*, 49 AJIL 518, 518–23 (1955).

coincidence of norms from the two sets.[5] Class struggle, however, prevailed; international law was to be used by the USSR as part of that struggle.[6]

PEACEFUL COEXISTENCE EMERGES AS A LEGAL DOCTRINE

In the 1950s, Soviet attitudes began to change. The Government formulated the theory of peaceful coexistence, which minimized the role of class struggle between socialist and capitalist states and stressed the element of cooperation.[7] This departure did not find favor with China, which criticized peaceful coexistence as "revisionist" for postulating the possibility of cooperation.[8]

Nevertheless, the theory of peaceful coexistence continued to be refined in the Soviet Union and was applied by Tunkin to international law. Taking peaceful coexistence as the basis for international legal relations,[9] he argued that while socialist and capitalist states had different ideas about international legal norms, they could agree upon certain norms that he saw as forming a single body of international law. The agreement might be explicit (treaties) or tacit (customary law).[10] Tunkin thus rejected the prior theory of two separate bodies of international law for the socialist and capitalist states. His thesis provided a "theoretical foundation for the common legal system of the entire international community"[11] and facilitated relations with capitalist states on the basis of international law.[12]

Peaceful coexistence was viewed under this approach as a context in which capitalism and socialism vied with each other. The 1961 version of the Communist Party program characterized peaceful coexistence as "a specific form of the class struggle."[13] "The characteristic of the contemporary stage of development of international law from the standpoint of its economic base," according to a 1967 text, "is that its development occurs under the influence of two antagonistic systems—the capitalist and the socialist. Peaceful coexistence of states of these two opposing systems defines, in general, the level of development of general international law at this stage."[14]

[5] Quigley, *The New Soviet Approach to International Law*, 7 HARV. INT'L L.J. 1, 2–4 (1965).

[6] Hazard, *Pashukanis Is No Traitor*, 51 AJIL 385, 387 (1957).

[7] Quigley, *supra* note 5, at 8.

[8] Chiu, *Communist China's Attitude Toward International Law*, 60 AJIL 245, 245–46 (1966).

[9] Tunkin, *Co-Existence and International Law*, 95 RECUEIL DES COURS 1 (1958 III); Hazard, *Soviet Socialism as a Public Order System*, 53 ASIL PROC. 30, 33–34 (1959).

[10] Quigley, *supra* note 5, at 4–5.

[11] K. GRZYBOWSKI, SOVIET PUBLIC INTERNATIONAL LAW: DOCTRINES AND DIPLOMATIC PRACTICE 10–22 (1970).

[12] McWhinney, *Changing International Law Method and Objectives in the Era of the Soviet-Western Détente*, 59 AJIL 1, 3 (1965); E. MCWHINNEY, THE INTERNATIONAL LAW OF DÉTENTE 27 (1978) [hereinafter E. MCWHINNEY, DÉTENTE].

[13] PROGRAMMA I USTAV KOMMUNISTICHESKOI PARTII SOVETSKOGO SOIUZA (Program and Charter of the Communist Party of the Soviet Union) 101 (1964) (adopted at 22d Party Congress, 1961) [hereinafter PROGRAM]. This concept of peaceful coexistence is attributed to the Cold War by Evgenii Primakov, Director of the Institute of International Relations. *In the Same Boat*, NEW TIMES, No. 42, 1987, at 14, 15 (interview of Primakov).

[14] 1 KURS MEZHDUNARODNOGO PRAVA (Course in International Law) 31 (F. I. Kozhevnikov et al. eds. 1967).

Tunkin's position led to formulation of a law of peaceful coexistence during a decade and a half of détente with capitalist states.[15] Soviet scholars said that peaceful coexistence involved respect for sovereignty, nonaggression, noninterference in internal affairs and equality of states.[16] The USSR proposed codification of these concepts, resulting in the adoption by the United Nations General Assembly of the 1970 Declaration on Principles of International Law concerning Friendly Relations and Cooperation among States in Accordance with the Charter of the United Nations.[17] Soviet theorists saw the USSR as having achieved an international posture that permitted it to play a significant role in the development of international law; international law was losing its capitalist character.[18]

Peaceful coexistence was not viewed as static. "At one period it can significantly differ from peaceful coexistence at another period of development of international relations, both from the standpoint of its breadth and depth of collaboration and as regards its certainty." Peaceful coexistence as of 1967 was said to be "significantly different from the peaceful coexistence that existed before World War II."[19]

GORBACHEV'S "NEW THINKING" ON PEACEFUL COEXISTENCE

Gorbachev now moves Tunkin's position on peaceful coexistence a bit further by minimizing the aspect of class struggle and stressing the aspect of cooperation. Peaceful coexistence, he has said, "changed into a condition for the survival of all humanity." He characterizes the world as having become increasingly interdependent through "internationalization of economic connections," the technological revolution and the "qualitatively new role of the media." Greater cooperation is necessitated by problems of a worldwide order such as the increasing scarcity of resources, "ecological danger," the "crying social problems of the developing world" and, most important, nuclear weapons, which place humanity's survival "in doubt."[20]

The earlier formulation of peaceful coexistence as "the class struggle in the international arena" is now criticized on the grounds that it "does not reflect the actual meaning of the principle. It is a principle of interstate relations that should not be turned into an arena for class struggle."[21] At its

[15] E. MCWHINNEY, DÉTENTE, *supra* note 12, at 1–5, 23.

[16] McWhinney, *"Peaceful Co-Existence" and Soviet-Western International Law*, 56 AJIL 951, 954 (1962); E. MCWHINNEY, DÉTENTE, *supra* note 12, at 7.

[17] GA Res. 2625, 25 UN GAOR Supp. (No. 28) at 121, UN Doc. A/8028 (1971); E. MCWHINNEY, DÉTENTE, *supra* note 12, at 23; Hazard, *Codifying Peaceful Co-Existence*, 55 AJIL 109 (1961); Hazard, *Co-Existence Codification Reconsidered*, 57 AJIL 88 (1963); Hazard, *New Personalities to Create New Law*, 58 AJIL 952 (1964); Hazard, *Co-Existence Law Bows Out*, 59 AJIL 59 (1965); Freeman, *Some Aspects of Soviet Influence on International Law*, 62 AJIL 710, 715 (1968).

[18] Crane, *Soviet Attitude Toward International Space Law*, 56 AJIL 685 (1962). Quigley, *supra* note 5, at 14.

[19] Kozhevnikov (ed.), *supra* note 14, at 83–84.

[20] Gorbachev, *supra* note 3, at 2, col. 1.

[21] Vereshchetin & Miullerson, *Novoe myshlenie i mezhdunarodnoe pravo* (The New Thinking and International Law), SOVETSKOE GOSUDARSTVO I PRAVO (Soviet State and Law), No. 3, 1988, at 3, 5.

27th congress in 1986, the Communist Party deleted the characterization of peaceful coexistence as "a specific form of class struggle" from its program.[22] "The interests of mankind," Tunkin explained to the American Society of International Law, "must take precedence over national or class interests." Just as the Nazi threat forced the USSR and capitalist states to unite during World War II, so today the nuclear threat forces them to work together to avert war.[23] "What is new," said Tunkin, "is an idea that the primacy of international law in international politics is a precondition of human survival."

World War Is No Longer Inevitable

The traditional Soviet thesis about world war, prior to Khrushchev, was that wars between capitalist states were to be viewed as inevitable. Lenin interpreted World War I as a war between capitalist states vying for raw materials and territory for capital investment: "Capitalism now finds that the old national states are too cramped for it."[24]

That thesis was modified in 1956, when the Twentieth Party Congress declared that the growth of the socialist camp had made it possible to prevent the outbreak of intercapitalist wars.[25] In 1961 the party program stated:

> The growing counterweight of the forces of socialism over the forces of imperialism, of the forces of peace over the forces of war, means that even before the full victory of socialism on earth, with capitalism preserved in a part of the earth, there will be a realistic possibility of excising world war from the life of society.[26]

Gorbachev finds additional factors militating against world war. Since World War II, there has occurred "a modification of the contradictions" that "in the past inexorably led . . . to world wars among the capitalist states."[27] "Now," according to Gorbachev, "the situation is different. The lessons of the past war and fear of weakening oneself vis-à-vis socialism, which has become a worldwide system, have not allowed capitalism to take its internal contradictions to the limit." The contradictions have "turned into a technological race."[28]

[22] M. S. Gorbachev, Perestroika i novoe myshlenie dlia nashei strany i dlia vsego mira (Reconstruction and the New Thinking for Our Country and for the Whole World) 150 (1987); Program, *supra* note 13, at 101; *Programma Kommunisticheskoi Partii Sovetskogo Soiuza: Novaia redaktsiia, priniata XXVII s'ezdom KPSS* (Program of the Communist Party of the Soviet Union: New Edition, adopted by the XXVII Congress of the CPSU), Pravda, Mar. 7, 1986, at 3, 7.

[23] M. S. Gorbachev, *supra* note 22, at 150.

[24] Lenin, *Socialism and War* (1915), in The Lenin Anthology 183, 185–86 (R. Tucker ed. 1975).

[25] M. S. Gorbachev, *supra* note 22, at 147; Hazard, *supra* note 6, at 388.

[26] Program, *supra* note 13, at 99.

[27] Gorbachev, *supra* note 3, at 4, col. 4.

[28] *Id.*

The possibility of peace is enhanced, in Gorbachev's view, by the fact that capitalist states can develop economically "without militarization." Gorbachev cites the " 'economic miracle' in Japan, West Germany, and Italy. . . . The period of rapid development of the contemporary capitalist economy in a number of countries occurred with minimal military expenditures." In the United States after World War II, the economy "relied on militarism. At first, this stimulated it." But then, "this waste of resources turned into an astronomical state debt."[29]

Capitalist states still need the markets and resources of the Third World, where they have traditionally fought wars for control, but now the Third World is demanding a "New International Economic Order" to end unequal exchange with the developed world. Thus, "in this realm as well, the contradictions are undergoing modification."[30] Some Third World countries, "while maintaining features of underdevelopment, are approaching the level of the great powers in the world economy."[31] This growth will lead to a more secure world.

In addition, says Gorbachev, as a result of the restructuring of its economy, the Soviet Union will substantially increase its foreign trade. Its "scientific, technical and productive potential will become a qualitatively more significant part of the world economy. And this in a decisive way will broaden and strengthen the material base of an all-encompassing system of peace and international security."[32]

A final factor working toward world peace is the emergence in capitalist states since World War II of citizen movements in opposition to nuclear armaments, pollution, racial discrimination and poverty. Left-of-center political parties—socialist, social democrat and laborite—have also opposed militarism.[33] "The antiwar movement has become an influential factor in international life."[34]

War and Development

According to Anatolii Dobrynin, former Soviet ambassador to the United States, a "basic change in world social development" is that capitalism "has shown a much greater capacity for durability than was earlier imagined." This observation applies not only to developed, but also to Third World countries. Referring to the latter, Dobrynin said that the need now is for "a struggle for the path of progressive democratic development under the conditions of capitalism," relying on a broader social base than formerly.[35] From the point of view of the working class, Dobrynin claimed, this new strategy was justified because workers suffer most of all from the arms race, regional wars and failure to improve "North-South" economic relations.[36]

[29] *Id.*

[30] *Id.*

[31] *Id.* at 5, col. 1.

[32] *Id.* at 4, col. 4.

[33] *Id.* at 5, col. 2.

[34] M. S. Gorbachev, A Time for Peace 26 (1985).

[35] *Soveshchanie v Prage* (Meeting in Prague), Pravda, Apr. 13, 1988, at 4, col. 4 (speech of Dobrynin at meeting of Communist parties).

[36] *Id.* at 4, col. 5.

To achieve social change, Dobrynin stressed setting a good example. He said that, so far, socialism has not done this well: "Socialism at the present stage of its development has not fully manifested its advantages. It has not yet set, for the people of the West, a convincing example of thorough democratization of society and of radical, thorough-going resolution of economic problems." Then, in an apparent reference to Stalinism, he conceded that "[t]here have also been negative phenomena in the development of many socialist countries, beginning with ours. As a result, the attracting force of socialism was weakened."

This strategy places little emphasis on armed force. It seems to leave only a minor role for anticolonial wars (wars of national liberation). Dobrynin stated that "many Communist parties have already concluded that . . . it is necessary to follow a peaceful path of social reforms." Force, he said, is appropriate only as a countermeasure: "Interference by imperialism, force from rightist forces . . . may give rise to responsive—and fully justified—actions, including armed actions, by revolutionary forces." But he went on to ask: "How can one limit such a conflict within national bounds and not let it turn into a new kindling point of international tension?" Such force must be kept to a minimum because "social progress . . . is now possible only in conditions of international peace, only by observing the right of each nation to free determination of its fate, without outside interference."[37]

As for Gorbachev, he has asserted that peace is a condition for economic reform in the USSR. "Yes," he wrote, "we are interested in normal international conditions for our internal progress."[38] To achieve economic reform, the Soviet Union needs to reduce its military budget and commitments.[39] A desire for increased foreign trade is doubtless another factor.[40]

SOVIET-U.S. RELATIONS

Gorbachev believes that the antagonism between the United States and the Soviet Union has diminished in significance. He sees a "gradual, yet increasingly apparent, loss by the United States of its former economic and political domination and the erosion of its positions as compared with the new 'centers of force,' primarily Western Europe and Japan."[41] In addition, he finds that the Third World is increasingly independent politically of the United States.[42]

Gorbachev says that some U.S. officials and analysts regard hostility as "normal" and "view confrontation as almost natural." But "confrontation is not an innate defect in our relations; it is an anomaly. It is not inevitable that it should be maintained."[43] Now peaceful coexistence is seen as having

[37] *Id.*

[38] M. S. GORBACHEV, *supra* note 22, at 5.

[39] Lebahn, *Political and Economic Effects of Perestroika on the Soviet Union and its Relations to Eastern Europe and the West*, 39 AUSSENPOLITIK 107, 107–11 (1988).

[40] Grzybowski, *Soviet Theory of International Law for the Seventies*, 77 AJIL 862 (1983).

[41] M. S. GORBACHEV, *supra* note 34, at 32.

[42] M. S. GORBACHEV, *supra* note 22, at 186.

[43] M. S. GORBACHEV, *supra* note 34, at 67. *See also id.* at 87 ("There is no fatal inevitability of confrontation between the two countries").

entered an even more collaborative stage. As the aspect of class struggle declines, collaboration becomes "the most important component of the principle" of peaceful coexistence.[44] The former view of peaceful coexistence, according to Central Committee member V. A. Medvedev, was that the capitalist and socialist states moved "on parallel rails." That view he calls "an illusion. The interdependence of the world is such that these parallels inevitably will intersect." The two types of states "will interact closely" in "scientific-technical, economic and social spheres, in human relations and in solving global problems."[45]

Increased Reliance on the United Nations

From the increasing role of cooperation and the decreasing role of class struggle emerges a greater role for international law. The primacy of international law to which Gorbachev alludes "is a normative expression of the priority of general human values and interests."[46]

One area of initiative in international law is the role of the United Nations. Tunkin told the Society that while "world government is unattainable in the foreseeable future," there is a need for "effective international mechanisms of solving international problems and enforcing international law."

In a long public letter to the United Nations on the occasion of the opening of the General Assembly session in September 1987, Gorbachev called for increased reliance on the Organization. He suggested the creation of a United Nations mechanism to monitor arms limitation agreements, crisis situations and military preparations that might lead to aggression. He proposed that military observers be used more widely to contain conflicts. The permanent members of the Security Council should take particular responsibility for preventing regional wars and should themselves abstain from involvement, which, he said, is "one of the factors that fan regional conflicts."[47]

Gorbachev's letter advanced various other proposals. A tribunal should be established under United Nations auspices to investigate acts of international terrorism. The United Nations should take stronger measures to end apartheid, a "destabilizing factor" in international relations, and to implement the New International Economic Order, since a world suffering from starvation cannot be secure. To allow Third World states to improve their economies, their debt payments should be limited to a percentage of annual export earnings, and protectionist barriers of developed states should be eliminated.[48] "Ecological security" should be promoted by a system of annual reports to the United Nations on antipollution efforts.[49] A consulta-

[44] Vereshchetin & Miullerson, *supra* note 21, at 5.

[45] V. A. Medvedev, *paraphrased in Velikii oktiabr' i sovremennyi mir* (Great October and the Contemporary World), Izvestiia, Dec. 10, 1987, at 5, col. 6.

[46] Vereshchetin & Miullerson, *supra* note 21, at 3.

[47] Gorbachev, *supra* note 2, at 2, col. 1. *See also* Vereshchetin & Miullerson, *supra* note 21, at 7.

[48] Gorbachev, *supra* note 2, at 2, col. 1.

[49] *Id.* at 2, col. 2.

tive council of leading intellectuals should be created to advise the United Nations.[50]

In his address, Tunkin referred to a General Assembly resolution proposed in 1986 by the USSR and nine other socialist states entitled "Establishment of a Comprehensive System of International Peace and Security." The resolution called for a strengthening of United Nations processes and was supported by most Third World states, while most Western states abstained.[51] The resolution reflected ideas the USSR had presented to the Secretary-General in a memorandum on the development of international law. The memorandum stated that "international law . . . must go to an even higher level. It must become *a law of comprehensive security and collective State responsibility towards mankind*. The primary responsibility is to deliver the human race from the impending threat of nuclear annihilation." The memorandum called for an "obligation *on the part of nuclear Powers to renounce the possession of nuclear weapons* and any other weapons of mass destruction, on the basis of agreements on their total elimination." It also called for a greater role in the international system for non-nuclear states and renunciation of "spheres of vital interests" and "spheres of influence," concepts that it said were responsible for "subjugation and enslavement."[52]

In contrast to the USSR's traditional wariness of international adjudication,[53] Gorbachev urges greater use of the International Court of Justice. He recommends that all states recognize the compulsory jurisdiction of the Court under the optional clause. A set of criteria for the acceptance of that jurisdiction should be developed, and the permanent members of the Security Council should take the lead in doing so. More frequent requests for ICJ advisory opinions should be made by the General Assembly and the Security Council.[54] This view of the Court, which Tunkin characterized as new, is more favorable than that expressed in recent Soviet scholarship.[55] The Soviet Union has also indicated an intent to apply for membership in the International Monetary Fund and the GATT.[56]

Formerly, the Soviet approach to the creation of norms in international law tended toward positivism, a readiness to accept only that to which agreement was manifested.[57] This practice limited the creation of customary norms.[58] Now, however, the positivist approach appears to be softening.

[50] *Id.* at 2, col. 4.

[51] GA Res 41/92 (Dec. 4, 1986). Vote: 102-2-46 (France and the United States in the negative).

[52] Letter to the Secretary-General from the Deputy Minister for Foreign Affairs and Deputy Head of the delegation of the Union of Soviet Socialist Republics to the forty-first session of the General Assembly, Nov. 24, 1986, UN Doc. A/C.6/41/5 (1986) (emphasis in original).

[53] Zile, *A Soviet Contribution to International Adjudication: Professor Krylov's Jurisprudential Legacy*, 58 AJIL 359, 364–66 (1964).

[54] Gorbachev, *supra* note 2, at 2, col. 3.

[55] *See, e.g.*, M. L. ENTIN, MEZHDUNARODNYE SUDEBNYE UCHREZHDENIIA (International Judicial Institutions) (1984), *reviewed in* 82 AJIL 396 (1988) (by Richard Szawlowski).

[56] Tran, *Breaking into the Bank*, SOUTH, May 1988, at 13.

[57] INTERNATIONAL LAW 61–62 (G. I. Tunkin ed. 1986).

[58] Quigley, *supra* note 5, at 15–16.

Gorbachev advocates recognition of consensus resolutions of the General Assembly as "morally and politically binding."[59] In addition, the Soviets suggest that nongovernmental organizations be given a greater role in the United Nations.[60] They also claim that final acts of international conferences can create norms if they contain postulates that the parties intend to be normative.[61]

Assessment

The most concrete manifestation of the "new thinking" has been the radical Soviet suggestions for arms reduction, reflected in the 1987 intermediate nuclear force treaty[62] and in negotiations for a 50 percent reduction in long-range nuclear weapons.[63] Détente brought arms control. The new thinking has brought arms reduction. While this approach would seem to apply to the full range of international law issues, doctrinal positions have yet to be formulated. Consequently, the new thinking remains a framework. It is unclear what impact it may have on such matters as, for example, the Brezhnev doctrine.[64]

The ultimate impact of the new thinking on international relations will depend on the reaction of other states and on the future of the *perestroika* policy within the USSR. The reaction of the United States has been one of skepticism.[65] The Department of State says that the new thinking is "a set of tactical maneuvers designed to court world public opinion, throw rivals off balance, and gain the diplomatic high ground in Third World issues."[66]

The new thinking is probably more serious than that. The USSR is likely to continue to desire external calm for domestic economic reform. Promotion of the United Nations reflects the increasing support for Soviet views there and the increasing isolation of the United States. That situation is not

[59] Gorbachev, *supra* note 2, at 2, col. 4.

[60] Vereshchetin & Miullerson, *supra* note 21, at 7; Malinin, *Kontseptsiia vseob'emliushchei sistemy mezhdunarodnoi bezopasnosti i mezhdunarodnoe pravo* (The Concept of a Comprehensive System of International Security and International Law), PRAVOVEDENIE, No. 4, 1987, at 16, 21.

[61] Malinin, *supra* note 60, at 24.

[62] Treaty on the Elimination of Their Intermediate-Range and Shorter-Range Missiles, Dec. 8, 1987, United States–USSR, S. TREATY DOC. NO. 11, 100th Cong., 2d Sess. (1988), DEP'T ST. BULL., No. 2131, February 1988, at 24.

[63] DEP'T ST. BULL., No. 2123, June 1987, at 13 (news conference of Secretary of State Shultz, Apr. 15, 1987); *id.*, No. 2131, February 1988, at 6 (address by General Secretary Gorbachev), and at 20 (address by President Reagan).

[64] *Sovereignty and International Duties of Socialist Countries*, Pravda, Sept. 25, 1968, *reprinted in* 7 ILM 1323 (1968) (trans. N.Y. Times, Sept. 27, 1968).

[65] John C. Whitehead, Deputy Secretary of State, *U.S.-Soviet Relations*, DEP'T ST. BULL., No. 2122, May 1987, at 43.

[66] Michael H. Armacost, Under Secretary of State for Political Affairs, *U.S.-Soviet Relations: Testing Gorbachev's "New Thinking,"* DEP'T ST. BULL., No. 2126, September 1987, at 36, 38. *See, to same effect,* Weeks, *The Reagan Détente*, GLOBAL AFFAIRS, No. 2, 1988, at 89.

likely to change soon. The Soviets' new assessment of the international situation focuses on significant factors of international relations. The new thinking carries the USSR further in the direction first taken by its adoption of peaceful coexistence in the 1950s. It represents another step in the accommodation between the Soviet revolution and Western capitalism.

JOHN QUIGLEY*

CORRESPONDENCE

TO THE EDITOR IN CHIEF:

August 1, 1988

Judge Schwebel's article (81 AJIL 831 (1987)) directs attention to an interesting new aspect of the internal organization and practice of the Court that is, evidently, gaining in strength and developing its own constitutional customs and conventions in ways not necessarily anticipated by the drafters of the Court's Statute and of the successive revisions of the Rules of Court, but compatible, nevertheless, with the letter or the spirit of those Rules.

The Statute envisages—apart from the special Chamber of five judges to "hear and determine cases by summary procedure" allowed under Article 29—the creation of special Chambers "composed of three or more judges as the Court may determine, for dealing with particular categories of cases," here indicating, specifically, "labour cases and cases relating to transit and communications" (Article 26(1)). Judge Lachs, in reviewing the historical origins of the institution of special Chambers, going back to the old Permanent Court and to the Treaty of Versailles and, particularly, its Articles 336 and 376, and the provisions of the Peace Treaties dealing with questions of navigation, transit and communications, has made the case for *functional* specialization within the Court through the Chamber system, as a means of mobilizing specialist expertise.[1] One such functionally specialized panel suggested by Judge Lachs would have been devoted to the protection of the environment, particularly as to pollution of rivers and lakes on borders between states, and another to the law of the sea. If the statutory provision for special Chambers had been picked up, earlier, by the Court, and used in its original, functionally specialized intent, this might have headed off the current tendency, in recourse to the judicial process as a means of international third-party dispute settlement, to create international tribunals parallel to the International Court of Justice, specialized by subject matter, like the one provided by the Third United Nations Conference on the Law of the Sea in its Final Act. Judge Lachs seems right, in this regard, to signal the problems for the organic unity of international law posed by any such separate and autonomous, and potentially competing, international tribunals.[2]

* Professor of Law, Ohio State University. The author is indebted to Gordon Livermore, Associate Editor, *Current Digest of the Soviet Press*, Columbus, Ohio, for reference to recent statements by Soviet officials.

[1] Lachs, *The Revised Procedure of the International Court of Justice*, in ESSAYS ON THE DEVELOPMENT OF THE INTERNATIONAL LEGAL ORDER 21, 42 (Kalshoven, Kuyper & Lammers eds. 1980).

[2] *Id.* at 44.

The public debate surrounding the first special Chamber created by the Court, for the *Gulf of Maine* case,[3] has concerned the degree of deference to be accorded by the Court to the preferences of the parties as to the choice of the "three or more judges," from among the regular 15-member plenum of the Court, to make up the panel. The Court's Statute, by itself, appears conclusive: it is the "number of judges to constitute such a chamber" that the plenum of the Court is to determine "with the approval of the parties" (Article 26(2)). It is the Rules of Court that, *ex hypothesi*, could not overcome the language of the Statute; in their 1972 version and, again, in the 1978 revised version, the Rules introduce a new element of ambiguity. Article 26(1) of the 1972 Rules required the President of the Court to consult with the parties regarding the "composition of the Chamber"—this in addition to the requirement in Article 26(2) of the same Rules, which repeated the provision of Article 26(2) of the Statute as to the Court's determining the "number" of judges with the approval of the parties. Article 17(2) of the present, 1978, revised Rules of Court states the requirement under the previous Article 26(2) a little more strongly, perhaps, with its stipulation that "[w]hen the parties have agreed, the President shall ascertain their views regarding the composition of the Chamber, and shall report to the Court accordingly."

It is known—from the Institut de Droit International reunion in Dijon in August 1981—that the special Chamber originally proposed would not have been limited in its membership to Western Europe and North America, but would have been broadly representative in terms of both the principal legal systems of the world and the main political-geographic regions, and that its members would also have had a high degree of functional (law of the sea) specialization. In addition, it would *not* have included judges of the same nationalities as the two parties—a principle that carries extra weight if the Chamber is to be limited to five judges, and that seems only partly explained, in its application in the specific *Gulf of Maine* context, by U.S. Judge Richard Baxter's recusing of himself. After President Waldock's sudden death in the late summer of 1981, it was left to the then Acting President, Judge Elias, to conclude the arrangements for the panel for *Gulf of Maine*, for presentation for approval by the plenum of the Court. The task was further complicated, not merely by the fact that President Waldock would himself have presided over the special Chamber, but also by the sudden death of the distinguished Danish jurist, Professor Sørensen (not a member of the International Court), who had already agreed to serve on the Chamber.

The debate within the Court itself over the constitution of this Chamber—reflected not merely in the dissenting opinions of Judges Morozov and El-Khani, cited in Judge Schwebel's article, but also in Judge Oda's declaration accompanying the Court's Order[4]—seems to have assisted in the long-range dialectical development of the Court's own thinking: first, as to how much, if at all, to defer to the wishes of the parties on the choice of judges; and, second, as to how far it is an imperative of the constitution and practice of the Court today for it to be seen as broadly representative, in legal-sys-

[3] Delimitation of the Maritime Boundary in the Gulf of Maine Area (Can. v. U.S.), Constitution of Chamber, 1982 ICJ REP. 3 (Order of Jan. 20).

[4] *Id.* at 10.

temic and political-geographical terms, both in its decision making and in its opinion writing in support of decision. If the *Gulf of Maine* panel, as finally constituted, may be viewed by many as having been narrowly Eurocentrist in character and composition since limited, in its five judges, to Western European and North American jurists, every special Chamber constituted by the Court thereafter has been determinedly eclectic in legal-systemic terms, and immune, in consequence, from any political reproaches of "Eurocentrism" (i.e., Western Europe and, by extension, North America). Moreover, in the aftermath of *Gulf of Maine*, even where, as with the *Guinée/Guinée-Bissau* arbitration,[5] the parties have opted for a special arbitral tribunal rather than the International Court, and consequently have acted with absolutely no legal restrictions on their choice of members, they have restricted that choice to serving judges of the International Court of Justice and made sure that the membership represented various legal systems.

The preferred constitutional position would be for Article 26(2) of the Statute and Article 17(2) of the 1978 Rules to be interpreted as instituting a full consultation by the Court with the parties as part of the process of constituting special Chambers, and a pragmatic consensus between the Court and the parties that a broadly eclectic membership including respect for political-geographical representativeness is imperative. The *Gulf of Maine* experience, imperfect as it may have been, would thus be seen as part of a trial-and-error testing experience of which the present Court is the beneficiary.

Incidentally, the proposition advanced by Judge Schwebel in regard to the final Judgment in *Gulf of Maine*,[6] that it was not in fact (whatever the legal-cultural homogeneity of its members) narrowly Eurocentrist in its holding or in its supporting reasoning, should be augmented by a further one. The advantages of special panels or senates or chambers, specialist in terms of subject matter, within a larger tribunal, are sufficiently well-known and proven in the experience of continental European and European-influenced courts for the International Court's current experience with Chambers to continue to be useful and to be extended; and there is enough acquired experience, in continental European and European-influenced courts and also within the International Court itself, to guard against the political risks inherent in any system of selecting some judges, rather than others, from the full ranks of the Court.

It is, however, especially important in this regard that the opting for a special Chamber not be viewed as a convenient method by the states parties to a case of avoiding or bypassing the jurisdiction of the full Court, characterized as "political" for the purpose. Some public comments by the State Department in the aftermath of the earlier *Nicaragua* judgments[7] did seem

[5] Tribunal arbitral pour la délimitation de la frontière maritime Guinée/Guinée-Bissau (Award of Feb. 14, 1985).

[6] Delimitation of the Maritime Boundary in the Gulf of Maine Area (Can. v. U.S.), 1984 ICJ REP. 246 (Judgment of Oct. 12).

[7] Military and Paramilitary Activities in and against Nicaragua (Nicar. v. U.S.), Jurisdiction and Admissibility, 1984 ICJ REP. 392 (Judgment of Nov. 26); Military and Paramilitary Activities in and against Nicaragua (Nicar. v. U.S.), Declaration of Intervention, 1984 ICJ REP. 215 (Order of Oct. 4).

to imply such justifications for recourse to Chambers.[8] In contrast, nothing in the Canadian Government's public statements—either of the Trudeau Government, which agreed to the Chamber in *Gulf of Maine*, or of the successor Mulroney Government—derogates from long-standing policies of support for the International Court of Justice in its normal full jurisdiction as a prime means of international dispute settlement.

EDWARD MCWHINNEY*

TO THE EDITOR IN CHIEF:

July 18, 1988

Professor Barrie's arguments that the ASIL policy on divestment violates international law (82 AJIL 311 (1988)) are erroneous, for reasons going beyond Paul Szasz's excellent responding Comment (*id.* at 314). As the author of the underlying Note on the Society's divestment decision (81 AJIL 744 (1987)), and also as one who, like Professor Barrie, makes his daily bread teaching international law, I add a few words in reply.

In citing Chief Buthelezi's aphorism against burning down a house to rid it of a snake, Professor Barrie is too kind to both the snake and the house. An apter reference would have been to the historical necessity in many parts of East and southern Africa to burn down village huts and sometimes even whole villages to rid them of driver ants. This reflects the nature of apartheid to black, and increasingly to white, South Africans, not as a single creature but a deadly scourge of racism made pervasive by the Pretoria regime. All participants are obliged under the Convention on the Suppression and Punishment of the Crime of Apartheid (Annex to GA Resolution 3068 (XXVIII) of November 30, 1973) to help rid the international community of this crime, as apartheid is now defined by international law.

It was a recognition of "law," including obligations to desist from being either a joint tort feasor or an accessory to a crime, that helped produce the ASIL decision to desist from taking steps economically or symbolically to cooperate with or lend support to a governmental system that is both illegal and criminal under international law.

As Szasz well states, the principle of domestic jurisdiction is no longer a bar to the international scrutiny of human rights violations (82 AJIL at 317). Moreover, that principle's underpinning doctrine of sovereignty is no longer a bar to individual state action, provided that action is consonant with the United Nations Charter and other major global community policies, in response to massive human rights violations. This permissibility arguably extends to all participants under international law, including learned societies.

The illegality of apartheid and the obligation of states to act against it derive directly from the UN Charter. Thus, all General Assembly resolutions, such as those cited by both Barrie and Szasz, are governed, regarding

[8] *See, e.g.*, Statement of Department of State on U.S. Withdrawal from Nicaragua Proceedings, Jan. 18, 1985, *reprinted in part in* Contemporary Practice of the United States, 79 AJIL 438, 441 (1985).

* Professor of International Law and Relations, Simon Fraser University, Vancouver.

issues relating to apartheid, by authoritative interpretations of the Charter, including its Purposes and Principles. These interpretations, as regards the rights of black South Africans and permissible means of implementing them, have been, and are being, spelled out in a considerable body of General Assembly and Security Council resolutions specifically pertaining to South Africa and apartheid. South Africa is not a "normal" state entitled to enjoy "normal" discretionary internal actions of sovereignty, including the weighing under Article 29 of the Universal Declaration of Human Rights of the rights of its citizens as against their duties to the state. Decisions about the rights and duties of black South Africans have rightfully become the intense concern of the entire international community.

Further, the legality of economic pressure by one state against another is not limited to instances of self-defense and reprisal. Rather, economic pressure is encompassed within and permitted by the duty of all states to respond to the commission of an international crime by a regime, to respond to a system of government that is per se illegal under the Charter and international law, and illegitimate in its utter alienation from and brutality toward the great majority of its citizens. The duty to apply economic pressure has arisen as a consequence of the continuous actions and expectations under the Charter and other law of the international community condemning apartheid over the past 40 years. This duty exists notwithstanding the lack, as yet, of a Security Council resolution imposing economic sanctions. It would exist toward any state to which the global response in law and fact had been the equivalent, regarding duration of time and focus of objective, to that toward South Africa for its policy of apartheid. Its existence, accordingly, cannot be dismissed by invoking the illegality of random self-help economic measures of national policy convenience. A separate issue would be raised, however, if an outside state proposed to use military force under non-self-defense circumstances, absent appropriate authorization by the United Nations.

The recent reimposition of a state of emergency by Pretoria, long condemned as contrary to law and basic rights; its recent announcements of new plans to enforce the Group Areas Act more effectively; and the suppression of Nelson Mandela's birthday celebrations only, sadly, confirm the entire appropriateness of the duty to apply economic pressure in this case.

HENRY J. RICHARDSON III*

TO THE EDITOR IN CHIEF:

April 26, 1988

It may be that some of your readers would have preferred it if the comment on *Taking Treaties Seriously* (82 AJIL 67 (1988)) had appeared after the decision of the arbitration tribunal to be set up in accordance with the International Court of Justice's ruling on the United Nations request for an advisory opinion, for it may be that even that tribunal would not agree with your suggestions.

* Professor of Law, Temple University.

Of course treaties must be and, I believe, are taken seriously, but only in respect of what they are providing for. The effect of a treaty, as you know better than most, depends on "the ordinary meaning to be given to the terms of the treaty in their context and in the light of its object and purpose"—to repeat the extraordinary tautology in Article 31 of the Vienna Convention. From this point of view it is difficult to see how the closure of a mission can impede the transit of "persons" to or from the United Nations. The "persons" do not need a mission to enjoy unimpeded transit to or from the United Nations. Transit from or to a mission is a different matter not covered, apparently, by the Headquarters Agreement. The "persons" can stay, e.g., in a hotel from which they can transit to and to which they can transit from the United Nations. In other words the provision in the Headquarters Agreement to which you refer is concerned with the movement of "persons" to or from the United Nations; it has no bearing upon any other place of departure or destination or, indeed, the situation, accessibility or privileges of a mission.

Messrs. Lillich and Weston (82 AJIL 69 (1988)) similarly neglect the nature, scope, "object and purpose" of a treaty, when they repeat their often proclaimed view that so-called lump sum agreements may be relevant to the problem of the amount of compensation, in particular its justness. The suggestion that if I have to assess the "just" amount of compensation I should look to the amount extracted, frequently years after the event, from an impecunious or obstreperous debtor is untenable. It is submitted that the true standard is supplied by the three hundred treaties or so concerning the promotion and reciprocal protection of investments, which were concluded in the course of the last 30 years. The 34 treaties of this kind to which the United Kingdom is a party frequently speak of "just," sometimes of "prompt, adequate and effective," and in the case of China of "reasonable compensation." Whether it is just, adequate or reasonable, the term is invariably defined: compensation "shall amount to the market value [in the case of China "the real value"] of the investment expropriated immediately before the expropriation or impending expropriation became public knowledge, shall include interest at a normal commercial rate until the date of payment, shall be made without delay and shall be effectively realizable and freely transferable." Can it really be said that such clauses leave room for treating the fractions usually payable under lump sum agreements as providing the true or even a relevant standard sanctioned by customary international law?

Messrs. Lillich and Weston list the Agreement between the United Kingdom and China of June 5, 1987, concerning the Settlement of Mutual Historical Property Claims (Cm. 198). They do not list the treaty between the same states of May 15, 1986, concerning the Promotion and Reciprocal Protection of Investments (Cmd. 9821). What possible bearing can the former Agreement have on the construction of the terms "reasonable compensation" in Article 5 of the latter Agreement or on the term "just compensation" in customary international law? Treaties should indeed be taken seriously.

F. A. MANN

CONTEMPORARY PRACTICE OF THE UNITED STATES RELATING TO INTERNATIONAL LAW

MARIAN NASH LEICH*

The material in this section is arranged according to the system employed in the annual *Digest of United States Practice in International Law,* published by the Department of State.

INTERNATIONAL ORGANIZATIONS

(U.S. *Digest,* Ch. 2, §4.B)

Expulsion of Nicaragua's Permanent Representative to OAS

Following the expulsion on July 11, 1988, of the American Ambassador to Nicaragua, Richard Melton, and seven other members of the American Embassy at Managua, President Reagan ordered the departure of the Nicaraguan Ambassador to the United States, Dr. Carlos Tunnermann, and seven other Nicaraguan Embassy members. Ambassador Tunnermann was accredited, also, to the Organization of American States as the Permanent Representative of Nicaragua, and one of the other Embassy members, Major Pedro Sampson, Military Attaché, was accredited as Adviser to the Permanent Mission of Nicaragua to the Organization of American States.

On July 12, 1988, Under Secretary of State Michael Armacost summoned Ambassador Tunnermann to inform him that his activities and actions and those of Major Sampson constituted abuse of their privilege of residence in the United States and that their presence was no longer acceptable.[1] The

* Office of the Legal Adviser, Department of State.

[1] Article 3 of the Agreement between the United States of America and the Organization of American States, Relating to Privileges and Immunities, Mar. 20, 1975, 26 UST 1025, 1027–28, TIAS No. 8089, reads:

> In case of abuse of the privileges of residence in the United States by any person enjoying diplomatic privileges and immunities under the foregoing articles, the said privileges and immunities shall not be construed to grant exemption from the laws and regulations of the United States regarding the continued residence of aliens. However, no such person shall be required to leave the country otherwise than in accordance with the customary procedure applicable to diplomatic envoys accredited to the Government of the United States.

Authority for the expulsion of Ambassador Tunnermann and Major Sampson also existed under §8 of the International Organizations Immunities Act, 22 U.S.C. §288e(b) (1982).

See further Presidential Power to Expel Diplomatic Personnel from the United States, a memorandum opinion by Asst. Att'y Gen. John M. Harmon, Apr. 4, 1980, 4A OPINIONS OFFICE OF LEGAL COUNSEL 207 (1985). The question had been raised because of the contemplated expulsion of Iranian diplomatic and consular personnel from the United States, which President Carter announced on Apr. 7, 1980, in connection with the breakoff of diplomatic relations between the United States and Iran. *See* 1980 DIGEST OF UNITED STATES PRACTICE IN INTERNATIONAL LAW 333–35. In regard to the closure on May 6, 1981, of the People's Bureau (Embassy) of the Socialist People's Libyan Arab Jamahiriya, for a "general pattern of presence of six other named Nicaraguan diplomats accredited to the United States was no longer acceptable, the Under Secretary continued, and the Ambassador must arrange for his own departure and that of the named individuals within 72 hours (i.e., by 5:30 P.M. on July 15, 1988).[2] On behalf of the Secretary of State, Under Secretary Armacost handed Ambassador Tunnermann two diplomatic notes confirming the United States Government's decision: one in his capacity as Ambassador of Nicaragua to the United States, the other in his capacity as the Permanent Representative of the Republic of Nicaragua to the Organization of American States.[3]

On the same day, July 12, 1988, Ambassador Richard T. McCormack, the United States Permanent Representative to the Organization of American States, informed it of the U.S. Government's action to expel the two Nicaraguan diplomats, also accredited to the Organization, by identical notes to the Chairman of its Permanent Council, Ambassador Eladio Knipping Victoria, and the Assistant Secretary General in Charge of the General Secretariat, Ambassador Val T. McComie.[4]

A special meeting of the Permanent Council was called on July 14, 1988, at the request of the Permanent Representative of Nicaragua, Ambassador Tunnermann, "for information purposes." In a statement before the meeting that documented the most recent repressive actions by the Nicaraguan Government against its own people,[5] including its violation of pledges under the Esquípulas II Accord and the Sapoa Agreement,[6] Ambassador

---

unacceptable conduct," see *id.* at 326–33. None of the Iranian diplomats in 1980, nor the Libyan diplomats in 1981, were also accredited to an international organization.

On Feb. 11, 1978, the United States expelled the Permanent Representative of the Socialist Republic of Vietnam to the United Nations, Ambassador Dinh Ba Thi, for personal involvement in an espionage conspiracy against the United States. The Ambassador was not accredited to the United States Government, which did not have diplomatic relations with the Socialist Republic of Vietnam. *See* 1978 *id.* at 119–24.

[2] In addition to Ambassador Tunnermann and Major Sampson, the persons requested to depart were Manuel Cordero, Minister-Counselor (the second-ranking officer of the Embassy); Orlando Martín Vega Gutiérrez, Counselor; Mrs. Zelmira L. García, Counselor; Mrs. Sofía Clark D'Escoto, First Secretary; Angel R. Arce, Attaché; and Mrs. Maureen Sampson, Attaché.

[3] For the notes, see Dept. of State File Nos. P88 0088-2275 and 0088-2274.

[4] For the text, see *id.*, No. P88 0088-2273.

[5] Ambassador McCormack discussed the following examples, among others, of repressive Nicaraguan government actions: the shutdown on July 11, 1988, of Radio Católica, for an indefinite period; the suspension the same day of publication of the independent newspaper, *La Prensa*, for 15 days; the police attack on peaceful demonstrators in Nandaime on July 10, 1988, in which 43 were imprisoned, numerous others beaten and four leaders then "sentenced" by the police to 6 months in jail; the murder of Carlos García, a leader of the independent labor confederation, by police after illegally entering his home during the night of July 3, 1988; and threats by Defense Minister Ortega against the lives of the resistance delegation during negotiations under the Sapoa Agreement in June, made in the presence of OAS Secretary General João Clemente Baena Soares and Cardinal Miguel Obando y Bravo, Chairman of the Nicaraguan National Reconciliation Commission and Co-Chairman of the Verification Commission of the Sapoa Agreement. *See further* OAS Doc. OEA/SER.G, CP/INF.2706/88 (1988).

[6] The text of the Esquípulas II Accord (the Guatemalan Agreement for Peace in Central America), signed by the Presidents of Costa Rica, Guatemala, El Salvador, Honduras and

McCormack set out the legal basis for the departure of Ambassador Tunnermann and Major Sampson from the United States, in part, as follows:

> For the first time in the history of this Organization, the United States, as host country, had reason to invoke its rights under Article 3 of the March 20, 1975 Agreement Relating to Privileges and Immunities between the United States and the Organization of American States, to request the departure of diplomats accredited to the OAS in light of their abuse of their privilege of residence in the United States.
>
> . . . .
>
> The United States is committed to carrying out its obligations under the Charter as host country to the Organization of American States, its officers and employees and the accredited representatives of its member states. In return, OAS Missions and members of the General Secretariat are obliged not to abuse their privilege of residence through their conduct in the host country.
>
> Certain activities and actions of Ambassador Tunnermann and Major Sampson while serving in a diplomatic mission located in the United States constitute an abuse of their privilege of residence in the United States under the March 20, 1975 Agreement . . . .
>
> The Organization of American States can take pride in the fact that the United States has never before had any reason to use its legal authority to take actions against diplomats accredited to the OAS for abuse of their privilege of residence in the United States. Nonetheless, in the rare cases of those who do abuse their privilege of residence, the United States has the legal authority to protect its sovereignty and inherent rights as host country by taking appropriate action, based upon Article 3 of the March 20, 1975 Agreement Relating to Privileges and Immunities between the United States and the Organization of American States. I should note that in the United Nations context, the United States has been forced to invoke this principle some two dozen times.
>
> Some have asked why the United States waited until its Ambassador and diplomats in Managua were expelled by the Nicaraguan Government to order the departure of Ambassador Tunnermann and Major Sampson for abuses of their privilege of residence.
>
> Prior to the events of this week, the United States had information on which to base its request for their departure. Nevertheless, in the spirit of the Esquipulas Agreement, we deferred action in order to

---

Nicaragua on Aug. 7, 1987, at Guatemala City, may be found at DEPT. ST. BULL., No. 2127, October 1987, at 56, 26 ILM 1166 (1987). For the text of the Declaration of Esquípulas—"Esquípulas I"—signed by the five Presidents on May 25, 1986, at Esquípulas, Guatemala, see DEPT. OF STATE, AMERICAN FOREIGN POLICY: CURRENT DOCUMENTS, 1986, at 764, and UN Doc. S/18106 (May 28, 1986).

The Sapoa Agreement was the cease-fire agreement between the Nicaraguan resistance and the Sandinista regime, concluded Mar. 23, 1988. An English translation of the text may be found at DEPT. OF STATE, CENTRAL AMERICA REGIONAL BRIEF, NICARAGUA: NEGOTIATING DOCUMENTS OF THE SAPOA TRUCE 2 (1988).

avoid giving the Nicaraguan Government a pretext for taking the kinds of actions it perpetrated this week . . . .

It was important to have an Ambassador and a functioning Embassy in Managua. Obviously, Nicaragua's actions against our diplomats in Nicaragua and against the Nicaraguans who dare to speak out against repression of democracy and human rights in Nicaragua have removed the basis for such restraint on the part of the United States.

On July 11, without provocation, the Nicaraguan Government expelled the United States Ambassador and seven other Embassy officers from Nicaragua for engaging in normal diplomatic activities. The Embassy was in contact with major political groups, including the opposition, in Nicaragua as are foreign Embassies everywhere, including in the United States. The Sandinista Government's charges against our Ambassador and his staff are patently false and ridiculous.

These Sandinista actions are not directed only against the United States. They are calculated efforts to subdue, isolate, and intimidate the Nicaraguan people. We are outraged that the Sandinista Government has, once again, sought to turn its internal conflict with the Nicaraguan people into a bilateral issue with the United States.[7]

The special meeting closed without taking any action on the matter brought to its attention by the Permanent Representative of Nicaragua.[8]

Human Rights

(U.S. *Digest,* Ch. 3, §6)

Convention Against Torture and Other Cruel, Inhuman or Degrading Treatment or Punishment

On May 20, 1988, President Ronald Reagan forwarded to the Senate for its advice and consent to ratification, subject to certain reservations, understandings and declarations, the Convention against Torture and Other Cruel, Inhuman or Degrading Treatment or Punishment, adopted by the United Nations General Assembly unanimously on December 10, 1984,[1] and signed by the United States on April 18, 1988.

In his letter of transmittal, the President, in accordance with recommendations from the Department of State, stated his intent, when depositing the United States (instrument of) ratification, to make a declaration, pursuant to Article 28 of the Convention, that the United States does not recognize the competence of the Committee against Torture (provided for in Articles 17–24 of the Convention) to make confidential investigations pursuant to Article 20 of charges that torture is being systematically practiced in the United States. In addition, the President stated, he intended not to make declarations pursuant to Articles 21 and 22 of the Convention, which would

[7] Dept. of State File No. P88 0089-2068.

[8] OAS Doc. OEA/SER.G, CP/ACTA 745/88 (1988).

[1] GA Res. 39/46 (Dec. 10, 1984) (entered into force June 26, 1987).

recognize that Committee's competence to receive and consider communications from states and individuals alleging that the United States is violating the Convention. The President believed that a final U.S. decision to accept the competence of the Committee in this regard should be withheld until there had been an opportunity to assess its work (after a sufficient body of experience with the Committee had been developed). He noted the possibility of future U.S. acceptance of that competence, pursuant to Articles 20, 21 and 22 of the Convention, if experience with the Committee should prove satisfactory and if the United States should consider this step desirable.

The President's letter of transmittal was accompanied by a report on the Convention from Secretary of State George P. Shultz, dated May 10, 1988, with an attached memorandum that summarized the general background to the Convention and discussed its provisions, as well as the reservations, declarations and understandings recommended by the Departments of State, Justice and Defense. Portions of the Secretary's letter follow:

> The Convention marks a further significant step in the development during this century of international measures against torture and other inhuman treatment or punishment. The core provisions of the Convention establish a regime for international cooperation in the criminal prosecution of torturers relying on so-called "universal jurisdiction." Each State Party is required either to prosecute torturers who are found in its territory or to extradite them to other countries for prosecution. . . .
>
> The United States contributed significantly to the development of the final Convention, especially in proposing that the Convention focus on torture rather than on other relatively less abhorrent practices and that the Convention conform more closely to comparable articles of the Conventions on Hijacking, Sabotage, Protection of Diplomats, and Hostages, aiming at a strong and effective Convention that would gain the widest possible adherence. In October 1984, a Joint Resolution of Congress expressed support for the involvement of the U.S. Government in the formulation of international standards and effective implementing mechanisms against torture, particularly through the draft U.N. Convention against Torture.
>
> In view of the large number of States concerned, it was not possible to negotiate a treaty that was acceptable to the United States in all respects. Accordingly, certain reservations, understandings, and declarations have been drafted to reflect the federal system of the United States, to clarify the definition of "torture," to ensure that the provisions relating to extradition and deportation are consistent with U.S. treaty obligations and U.S. law, and to reserve both to the compulsory jurisdiction of the International Court of Justice and to the competence of the Committee against Torture to initiate investigations of the United States. In addition, a declaration that the Convention is not self-executing is recommended. With such a declaration, the provisions of the Convention would not of themselves become effective as domestic law. The Department of Justice is of the view that, with the

inclusion of the recommended reservations, understandings and declarations, no constitutional or other legal obstacles to United States ratification exist.[2]

DIPLOMATIC PRIVILEGES AND IMMUNITIES

(U.S. *Digest*, Ch. 4, §1)

Limitation on Use of Foreign Mission Incompatible with Status

Section 215 of the Foreign Missions Act, as added by section 128(a) of the Foreign Relations Authorization Act, Fiscal Years 1988 and 1989, Public Law No. 100-204,[1] was enacted in response to congressional concerns about the use of diplomatic or consular (foreign mission) premises, in particular, premises of Permanent Missions to the United Nations, that were entitled to inviolability under United States laws and treaties, by foreign individuals not entitled to residential immunity or by foreign state commercial enterprises not entitled to the immunity accorded to diplomatic or consular office premises.[2]

Section 215(a) prohibits a foreign mission from allowing an "unaffiliated alien" the use of any premise of that mission "which is inviolable under United States law (including any treaty) for any purpose which is incompatible with its status as a foreign mission, including use as a residence." Under section 215(b), a residence does not include "such temporary lodging" that the Secretary of State may permit by regulations. Section 215(c) authorizes the Secretary to waive the limitation on use established by section 215(a), and also to revoke such a waiver, 30 days after written notification of the waiver or of its revocation, as well as the reasons therefor, to the House Committee on Foreign Affairs and the Senate Committee on Foreign Relations. Section 215(d) requires the Secretary of State to submit a report concerning implementation of section 215 not later than 180 days after enactment and to submit such other reports concerning changes in implementation as may be necessary.[3]

[2] S. TREATY DOC. NO. 20, 100th Cong., 2d Sess. v–vi (1988).

Under Article 1(1) of the Convention, torture is defined as

> any act by which severe pain or suffering, whether physical or mental, is intentionally inflicted on a person for such purposes as obtaining from him or a third person information or a confession, punishing him for an act he or a third person has committed or is suspected of having committed, or intimidating or coercing him or a third person, or for any reason based on discrimination of any kind, when such pain or suffering is inflicted by or at the instigation of or with the consent or acquiescence of a public official or other person acting in an official capacity. It does not include pain or suffering arising only from, inherent in or incidental to lawful sanctions.

[1] 101 Stat. 1331, 1343 (1987) (to be codified at 22 U.S.C. §4315).

[2] *See* H.R. REP. NO. 34, 100th Cong., 1st Sess. 20–21 (1987).

[3] For the Department's report, see enclosures to letters from J. Edward Fox, Assistant Secretary of State for Legislative Affairs, to Vice President George Bush, President of the Senate, and to Speaker of the House James Wright, June 22, 1988, Dept. of State File Nos. P88 0089-1535, 1536, 1537 *ff.*

Section 215(e) defines the term "foreign mission" to include any international organization as defined in section 209(b) of the Foreign Missions Act (22 U.S.C. §4309(b) (1982)). It defines "unaffiliated alien," with respect to a foreign country, as an alien admitted to the United States as a nonimmigrant, who is not a member of the foreign country's mission or a member of such an individual's family.

Under section 128(b) of Public Law No. 100-204, the amendment of the Foreign Missions Act by the addition of section 215 became applicable to all foreign missions upon the date of enactment, except as to any nonimmigrant alien using a foreign mission as a residence or a place of business on that date. As to these individuals, the amendment was to apply beginning 6 months after the date of enactment, and the Secretary of State, upon a finding of hardship to the alien, might delay its effective date with respect to that person for not more than 6 (further) months.

In a circular note to the Chiefs of Mission at Washington, dated February 23, 1988, the Secretary of State summarized the provisions in question and asked that missions submit all requests for waivers of the statutory restrictions by March 31, 1988. They should, however, be aware, the note cautioned, that the Department intended to grant waivers on a "limited and exceptional basis." For foreign missions that had not received waivers, the restriction on the use of foreign mission property as a residence or as a place of business by prohibited individuals (i.e., unaffiliated aliens) was to take effect no later than June 22, 1988.[4]

In a further circular note to the Chiefs of Mission at Washington, dated June 13, 1988, the Secretary of State informed them that few requests for waivers had been received. The Department viewed the lack of such requests as an indication that the missions considered that the current use of their diplomatic or consular offices and residential premises was compatible with the "inviolable status and accepted use of such properties." The note requested, nevertheless, written confirmation from the missions that they considered themselves in compliance with the statutory provision.

The note also answered some inquiries that had been received from missions, as follows:

> The Department has received inquiries regarding the specific application of the statute, certain of which relate to the use of inviolable residential property by domestic servants and personal guests of members of the mission. The Chiefs of Mission are informed that the Department considers the use of diplomatic or consular residences by domestic servants as a compatible use not requiring a waiver by the Secretary, provided that such individuals are registered with the Department's Office of Protocol. With regard to personal guests, the regulations now under development in the Department will permit the temporary lodging of such individuals. The long term use of a diplomatic or consular residence by unaffiliated individuals, however, is restricted under the new law.

[4] *Id.*, No. P88 0089-1545. For a parallel circular note from the U.S. Mission to the United Nations to the Permanent Missions and the Permanent Observer Offices to the United Nations, Mar. 7, 1988, see *id.*, No. P88 0088-1179.

Also in response to inquiries the Chiefs of Mission are advised that the Department understands that the legislation is not intended to prevent traditional and accepted uses of diplomatic and consular office[s] and inviolable residential property. The legislation is compatible with Article 41(3) of the Vienna Convention on Diplomatic Relations and Article 55(2) of the Vienna Convention on Consular Relations which provide that "The premises of the mission must not be used in any manner incompatible with the functions of the mission . . . ." Thus, the use of diplomatic or consular office space by representatives of private commercial entities or by miscellaneous government offices who are engaged in activities that do not constitute accepted diplomatic or consular functions has always been considered an unacceptable use of mission premises.[5]

Interpretation of Treaties

(U.S. *Digest,* Ch. 5, §2)

INF Treaty

On May 27, 1988, by a vote of 93 to 5, the Senate gave its advice and consent to ratification of the Treaty Between the United States of America and the Union of Soviet Socialist Republics on the Elimination of Their Intermediate-Range and Shorter-Range Missiles, signed on December 8, 1987, at Washington on the occasion of the state visit of Mikhail Gorbachev, General Secretary of the Central Committee of the Communist Party of the Soviet Union. The resolution of ratification postulated the following condition, among others:

(1) Provided, that the Senate's advice and consent to ratification of the INF Treaty is subject to the condition, based on the Treaty Clauses of the Constitution, that—

(A) the United States shall interpret the Treaty in accordance with the common understanding of the Treaty shared by the President and the Senate at the time the Senate gave its advice and consent to ratification;

(B) such common understanding is based on:

(i) first, the text of the Treaty and the provisions of this resolution of ratification; and

(ii) second, the authoritative representations which were provided by the President and his representatives to the Senate and its Committees, in seeking Senate consent to ratification, insofar as such representations were directed to the meaning and legal effect of the text of the Treaty; and

(C) the United States shall not agree to or adopt an interpretation different from that common understanding except pursuant to Sen-

[5] *Id.*, No. P88 0089-1541. For a parallel circular note from the U.S. Mission to the United Nations to the Permanent Missions and the Permanent Observer Offices to the United Nations, July 6, 1988, see *id.*, No. P88 0088-2276.

ate advice and consent to a subsequent treaty or protocol, or the enactment of a statute; and

(D) if, subsequent to ratification of the Treaty, a question arises as to the interpretation of a provision of the Treaty on which no common understanding was reached in accordance with paragraph (2), that provision shall be interpreted in accordance with applicable United States law.[1]

In a statement issued the same day, President Reagan, while expressing appreciation for the Senate leadership's action in obtaining "timely approval" of the Treaty, noted, nevertheless, his "concerns about the constitutionality of some provisions of the resolution of ratification, particularly those dealing with interpretation," regarding which he would, he said, communicate with the Senate "in due course."[2]

After his return from the Moscow Summit Meeting with General Secretary Gorbachev, at which the two leaders exchanged their respective instruments of ratification of the Treaty on June 1, 1988, the President addressed the "one provision" giving him "serious concern," in a letter to the Senate, dated June 10, 1988, that read in part as follows:

The Senate condition relating to the Treaty Clauses of the Constitution apparently seeks to alter the law of treaty interpretation. The accompanying report of the Committee on Foreign Relations accords primacy, second only to the Treaty text, to all Executive branch statements to the Senate above all other sources which international forums or even U.S. courts would consider in interpreting treaties. It subordinates fundamental and essential treaty interpretative sources such as the treaty parties' intent, the treaty negotiating record and the parties' subsequent practices.

Treaties are agreements between sovereign states and must be interpreted in accordance with accepted principles of international law and United States Supreme Court jurisprudence. As a practical matter, the Senate condition only can work against the interests of the United States by creating situations in which a treaty has one meaning under international law and another under domestic law. Unilateral restrictions on the United States should be avoided, especially in a treaty affecting vital national security interests. With respect to U.S. law, the President must respect the mutual understandings reached with the Senate during the advice and consent process. But Executive statements should be given binding weight only when they were authoritatively communicated to the Senate by the Executive and were part of the basis on which the Senate granted its advice and consent to ratification. This is in accordance with the legal standards applied by our courts in determining legislative intent. I commend the thoughtful statements made during the Senate debate by Senators [Arlen] Specter, [William V.] Roth, [Jr., Pete] Wilson, and others which amplify these concerns.

This Administration does not take the position that the Executive branch can disregard authoritative Executive statements to the Senate,

[1] 134 CONG. REC. S6937 (daily ed. May 27, 1988).

[2] 24 WEEKLY COMP. PRES. DOC. 683 (June 6, 1988).

and we have no intention of changing the interpretation of the INF Treaty which was presented to the Senate. On the contrary, this Administration has made it clear that it will consider all such authoritative statements as having been made in good faith. Nonetheless the principles of treaty interpretation recognized and repeatedly invoked by the courts may not be limited or changed by the Senate alone, and those principles will govern any future disputes over interpretation of this Treaty. As Senator [Richard G.] Lugar pointed out during the debate, the Supreme Court may well have the final judgment, which would be binding on the President and Senate alike. Accordingly, I am compelled to state that I cannot accept the proposition that a condition in a resolution to ratification can alter the allocation of rights and duties under the Constitution; nor could I, consistent with my oath of office, accept any diminution claimed to be effected by such a condition in the constitutional powers and responsibilities of the Presidency.

I do not believe that any difference of views about the Senate condition will have any practical effect on the implementation of the Treaty. I believe the Executive branch and the Senate have a very good common understanding of the terms of the Treaty, and I believe that we will handle any question of interpretation that may arise in a spirit of mutual accommodation and respect. In this spirit I welcome the entry into force of the Treaty and express my hope that it will lead to even more important advances in arms reduction and the preservation of world peace and security.[3]

The Senate's resolution of ratification was made subject to the following, further conditions, declarations, and a declaration and understanding:

(a) CONDITIONS:

. . . .

(2) The advice and consent of the Senate to the ratification of the INF Treaty is further subject to the condition that in connection with the exchange of the instruments of ratification pursuant to Article XVII of the Treaty, the President shall obtain the agreement of the Union of Soviet Socialist Republics that the agreement concluded by exchange of notes in Geneva on May 12, 1988 between the United States and the Union of Soviet Socialist Republics as to the application of the Treaty to intermediate-range and shorter-range missiles flight-tested or deployed to carry or be used as weapons based on either current or future technologies and as to the related question of the definition of the term "weapon-delivery vehicle" as used in the Treaty, the agreed minute of May 12, 1988 signed by Ambassador Maynard W. Glitman and Colonel General N. Chervov reflecting the agreement of the Parties regarding certain issues related to the Treaty, and the agreements signed on May 21, 1988 in Vienna and Moscow, respectively, correcting the site diagrams and certain technical errors in the Treaty, are of the same force and effect as the provisions of the Treaty.

(3) That prior to the exchange of the instruments of ratification pursuant to Article XVII of the Treaty, the President shall certify that it is the common understanding of the United States and the Soviet

[3] *Id.* at 779, 780 (June 13, 1988). *See further* S. EXEC. REP. NO. 15, 100th Cong., 2d Sess. 87–108, 437–46 (1988).

Union that if either Party produces a type of ground-launched ballistic missile (GLBM) not limited by the Treaty using a stage which is outwardly similar to, but not interchangeable with, a stage of an existing type of intermediate-range GLBM having more than one stage, it may not produce any other stage which is outwardly similar to, whether or not it is interchangeable with, any other stage of an existing type of intermediate-range GLBM.

(b) DECLARATIONS:

(1) The Senate's advice and consent to ratification of the Treaty is further subject to the following:

Declaration.—The Senate declares that—

(A) because the incentive for Soviet noncompliance, and the difficulty of monitoring will be greater for any strategic arms reduction talks (START) agreement than for the INF Treaty, the United States should rely primarily on its own national technical means of verification rather than any cooperative verification scheme, such as the on-site inspection procedures agreed to in the INF Treaty;

(B) because the United States enjoys a comparative advantage in the development of nonnuclear technologies that can increase the nuclear threshold and reduce the likelihood of war and because START and the INF Treaty will increase the military need to rely more heavily on such nonnuclear capabilities, in any subsequent agreement between the United States and the Soviet Union regarding the reduction of Strategic Weapons, it should be the position of the United States that no restrictions should be established on current or future nonnuclear air- or sea-launched cruise missiles developed or deployed by the United States, or on nonnuclear ground launched cruise missiles of ranges not prohibited by the INF Treaty; and

(C) because the reductions contemplated under any START agreement would change the character and optimal mix of strategic nuclear forces that the United States will need to maintain stability, the United States Congress and the President should agree on the character of, and funding for, these forces before any START agreement, framework or otherwise, is signed or agreed to.

(2) Provided that the Senate's advice and consent to ratification of the INF Treaty is subject to the condition:

Declaration.—It shall be the declared policy of the United States of America that, as an integral factor in its decision to adhere to this Treaty, the United States intends to continue to negotiate with the Union of Soviet Socialist Republics a treaty effecting reductions in strategic nuclear forces of the Parties and, in conjunction with its NATO Allies, to negotiate a treaty establishing conventional stability in Europe. In so doing, it shall be guided by the following principles and considerations:

(A) a main object of such future treaties shall be international stability and reduction of the risk of war by obtaining general equivalence in the resultant strategic forces of the Parties;

(B) during any negotiations contemplated by this declaration, the United States shall act in close consultation with its Allies who are member states of the North Atlantic Treaty Organization and with such other states as appropriate;

(C) negotiations contemplated by this declaration shall also be conducted with close and detailed consideration of the advice of the United States Senate, and the Senate should be kept fully apprised of all significant proposals made to the Union of Soviet Socialist Republics and, with respect to such negotiations, the judgments and recommendations of the United States Senate shall be given full and highest consideration and due regard;

(D) the negotiations contemplated by this declaration shall also seek to secure regimes of effective verification and mechanisms for full compliance which build upon the verification regime and compliance mechanisms of the present Treaty, strengthening them appropriately for any subsequent treaty;

(E) in accordance with the Constitutional process of the United States, the United States shall, consistent with correctly construed principles of international law, not be bound to adhere to or observe any treaty contemplated by this declaration until ratification thereof pursuant to the advice and consent of the Senate. However, nothing in this declaration shall imply that the United States will take an action of such nature as to make impossible the performance of any future treaty contemplated by this declaration after the signing of such treaty and during the period in which there is a clear prospect of timely ratification thereof;

(F) the United States considers full and exact compliance with the present treaty and with all other existing arms control agreements between the Parties to be a major issue affecting (i) the proposals and attitudes of the United States with respect to the future treaties contemplated hereby and (ii) proportionate and appropriate responses with respect to such existing agreements;

(G) pursuant to this declaration, any joint statement by the United States of America with the Union of Soviet Socialist Republics of a framework for the negotiation of strategic arms treaties contemplated hereby, and such framework itself, shall serve for the purpose only of guiding the conduct of the negotiations which the United States herein has declared its desire to pursue expeditiously, and shall not constrain any military programs of the United States unless otherwise provided for in accordance with Section 33 of the Arms Control and Disarmament Act; and

(H) the capability of the United States of America to monitor any future treaty contemplated by this declaration shall be strengthened in order to increase the ability of the United States to detect violations thereof.

(c) DECLARATION AND UNDERSTANDINGS:

The advice and consent to ratification given by the Senate under this resolution of ratification is subject to the following declaration and understandings, which the President, using existing authority, shall communicate to the Union of Soviet Socialist Republics, in connection with the exchange of the instruments of ratification of the Treaty:

(1) the declaration that the Senate strongly believes that respect for human rights and fundamental freedoms is an essential factor to ensure the development of friendly relations and cooperation between the United States and the Soviet Union and calls upon the President to use every opportunity to stress the inherent link between respect for human rights and the achievement of lasting peace;

(2) the understanding that the President shall seek sustained and demonstrable progress by the Soviet Union in its implementation of the provisions of—

(A) the Final Act of the Conference on Security and Cooperation in Europe (hereafter referred to as the "Helsinki Final Act"),

(B) the Madrid Concluding Document of the Commission on Security and Cooperation in Europe, done September 9, 1983 (hereafter referred to as the "Madrid Concluding Document"),

(C) the Universal Declaration of Human Rights (also known as the "Universal Declaration"), and

(D) other international human rights agreements to which the Soviet Union is a signatory or party, including provisions relating to—

(i) the freedom of thought, conscience, religion, and belief, without regard to race, sex, language, religion, or national origin,

(ii) the recognition and respect for the rights of individuals, including those belonging to national minorities, to enjoyment and practice of their cultures, heritage, history, and national consciousness,

(iii) the right of freedom of movement for individuals within the Soviet Union and the right to leave the Soviet Union, without arbitrary and capricious barriers, and

(iv) the right of individuals to know and act upon their rights and duties in these agreements; and

(3) the understanding that the United States, through the Helsinki process, will expect full compliance, as evidenced by specific action, by the Soviet Union with its commitments in the field of human rights and fundamental freedoms and will seek to strengthen these commitments through review meetings and a balanced number of follow-up activities which will advance verifiable implementation of the human rights provisions of the Helsinki Final Act and the Madrid Concluding Document.[4]

[4] 134 CONG. REC., *supra* note 1, at S6937–38.

INTERNATIONAL DECISIONS

PETER D. TROOBOFF*

Editor's Note

For the past 7 years, Monroe Leigh has edited this section with the able assistance of his associates at Steptoe & Johnson. His fine eye for accuracy and his fairness remain as standards for his successors. The *Journal* acknowledges its great debt to him and to his firm.

We begin in this issue with a modified approach to preparing the section. We seek volunteers among skilled young lawyers in practice, government or international civil service, and teaching to assist by preparing case summaries. As in the past, we count upon our readers to send us important recent United States and foreign court judgments and arbitral awards.

P. D. T.

Hague Service Convention—scope and application—role of internal law

VOLKSWAGEN AKTIENGESELLSCHAFT v. SCHLUNK. 108 S.Ct. 2104. U.S. Supreme Court, June 15, 1988.

In this first decision by the United States Supreme Court on the scope and application of the Convention on the Service Abroad of Judicial and Extrajudicial Documents in Civil or Commercial Matters, better known as the Hague Service Convention,[1] petitioner, a West German company, challenged the respondent's attempt to serve process on petitioner by serving its wholly owned U.S. subsidiary in accordance with the state's rules rather than pursuant to the procedures of the Convention. The Circuit Court of Cook County, Illinois, found that the relationship between the German parent and the U.S. subsidiary was such that, under state-law rules of agency, the U.S. subsidiary was the parent's involuntary agent for service of process. Because service could thus be perfected entirely within the United States, the court held that it was not necessary to follow the procedures of the Hague Service Convention. The Illinois Appellate Court affirmed,[2] and the Illinois Supreme Court denied leave to appeal.[3] The U.S. Supreme Court (per O'Connor, J.) affirmed and *held:* (1) the Hague Service Conven-

* Mary Ellen O'Connell of the District of Columbia Bar assisted the Editor in the preparation of the summaries in this issue.

[1] *Opened for signature* Nov. 15, 1965, 20 UST 361, TIAS No. 6638, 658 UNTS 163 [hereinafter Convention].

[2] 145 Ill. App. 3d 594, 503 N.E.2d 1045 (1986).

[3] 112 Ill.2d 595 (1986).

tion is "mandatory" and preempts inconsistent state-law methods of service in all cases to which it applies;[4] (2) the Convention applies where there is occasion to transmit a document abroad to charge persons with formal notice of a pending action;[5] and (3) whether it is necessary to transmit a document abroad for such purposes is determined by the forum state's internal law.[6]

The Court began its analysis with the text of the treaty, observing that the Convention by its terms applies "in all cases, in civil or commercial matters, where there is occasion to transmit a judicial or extrajudicial document for service abroad."[7] But the Convention does not specify when there is "occasion to transmit" a document "for service abroad," and the Court accordingly examined the negotiating history of the Convention. The preliminary draft provided that the Convention was to apply "where there are grounds" to transmit documents to persons staying abroad. When one delegate proposed amending the section by adding the phrase "according to the law of the requesting state," several delegates expressed the view that such an amendment was unnecessary. They reasoned that the requesting state's law would necessarily determine whether "grounds exist" for transmitting documents abroad. The proposed amendment was rejected. However, the reporter explained that, under the formulation that was ultimately adopted, the law of the requesting state would determine when a document must be served abroad. The Court thus concluded that the forum's internal law governs whether the procedures of the Convention must be followed.

The Court rejected the petitioner's argument that such an interpretation would be inconsistent with the purpose of the Convention " 'to create appropriate means to ensure that judicial and extrajudicial documents to be served abroad shall be brought to the notice of the addressee in sufficient time.' "[8] This purpose could easily be circumvented, the petitioner argued, if the state parties remained free to authorize methods of serving process on foreigners that did not require the transmission of documents abroad. The Court acknowledged that one of the purposes of the Convention was to eliminate one such method of service, *notification au parquet,* pursuant to which service of process on foreign defendants could be accomplished by depositing documents with designated local officials. Under this procedure, the documents were thereafter to be transmitted to the defendant through diplomatic channels. Service was deemed complete upon the official's receipt of the documents, whether or not the documents were ultimately transmitted by the official or received by the defendant. The Court left open the question whether the Convention applies to *notification au parquet,* but observed that "there is no comparable evidence in the negotiating history that the Convention was meant to apply to substituted service on a

[4] 108 S.Ct. 2104, 2108.
[5] *Id.*.
[6] *Id.* at 2109–10.
[7] Convention, *supra* note 1, Art. 1.
[8] 108 S.Ct. at 2109–10 (quoting the Preamble to the Convention, *supra* note 1).

subsidiary . . ., which clearly does not require service abroad under the forum's internal law."[9]

The Court also rejected the petitioner's argument that service on its subsidiary necessarily required the transmission of documents abroad, as the subsidiary would have to transmit the documents to the parent if the latter were ultimately to receive actual notice of the action. The Court held that "[w]here service on a domestic agent is valid and complete . . . the Convention has no further implications. Whatever internal, private communications take place between the agent and the foreign principal are beyond the concerns of this case."[10]

In the end, the Court conceded that its interpretation "does not necessarily advance" the Convention's purpose of ensuring adequate notice to foreign defendants. At the same time, the Court doubted that any country would "draft its internal laws deliberately so as to circumvent the Convention in cases in which it would be appropriate to transmit judicial documents for service abroad."[11]

Justice Brennan, writing for himself and Justices Marshall and Blackmun, concurred in the judgment but disagreed with the majority's conclusion that the forum nation's internal law is dispositive of the applicability of the Convention. "Under the Court's analysis," Justice Brennan observed,

> a forum nation could prescribe direct mail service to any foreigner and deem service effective upon deposit in the mailbox, or could arbitrarily designate a domestic agent for any foreign defendant and deem service complete upon receipt domestically by the agent even though there is little likelihood that service would ever reach the defendant.[12]

The Court's interpretation, in Justice Brennan's view, conflicts with the primary purpose of the Convention, set forth in its Preamble, " 'to ensure that . . . documents to be served abroad . . . be brought to the notice of the addressee in sufficient time.' "[13] Relying on the Preamble, certain statements in the negotiating history that conflicted with the statements on which the majority relied, and the clear purpose of the Convention to eliminate *notification au parquet,* Justice Brennan concluded that the Convention "embod[ies] a substantive standard that limits a forum's latitude to deem service complete domestically."[14]

Justice Brennan acknowledged that the Convention does not precisely define the contours of the substantive standard, and he did not attempt to define them himself beyond quoting the statement in the final report that "[a]ll of the transmission channels (prescribed by the convention) *must have as a consequence the fact that the act reach the addressee in due time.*"[15] Because

[9] *Id.* at 2110.

[10] *Id.* at 2112.

[11] *Id.*

[12] *Id.* at 2114 (Brennan, J., concurring).

[13] *Id.* at 2113 (quoting the Preamble to the Convention, *supra* note 1).

[14] *Id.* at 2112.

[15] *Id.* at 2115 (quoting 3 CONFÉRENCE DE LA HAYE DE DROIT INTERNATIONAL PRIVÉ, ACTES ET DOCUMENTS DE LA DIXIÈME SESSION (NOTIFICATION) 367 (1965) (emphasis supplied by Justice Brennan)).

the method of service employed by the respondent was reasonably calculated to apprise the defendant of the action in due time, Justice Brennan had no trouble concluding that it did not run afoul of the Convention.

* * * *

Justice Brennan is plainly correct in his conclusion that the Convention does not permit service by mail on a defendant residing in another state party. Although discussed by neither opinion, Article 10 of the Convention is relevant to this issue. That section provides in pertinent part that, "Provided the State of destination does not object, the present Convention shall not interfere with—(a) the freedom to send judicial documents, by postal channels, directly to persons abroad." Most U.S. courts that have considered the question have concluded that this provision does not authorize formal service of process by mail.[16] Moreover, many of the parties to the Convention, including the Federal Republic of Germany, have objected pursuant to Article 10 even to the "sending" of judicial documents through the mails. Clearly, therefore, the Convention does not permit service by mail to persons within the territory of another state party, whether or not the forum state deems such service complete upon deposit in the mailbox.

Nevertheless, the majority opinion need not be interpreted as permitting service by mail. As the U.S. subsidiary was deemed petitioner's agent for purposes of service of process, service on the subsidiary could be considered the equivalent of service on the parent. Any subsequent communications between parent and subsidiary thus would arguably not constitute a "transmission" of documents within the meaning of the treaty. This rationale would distinguish service on an agent from any form of service requiring the delivery of judicial documents abroad by third parties, such as service by mail or *notification au parquet.*[17] To the extent, however, that forum law determines who an "agent" is for these purposes, Justice Brennan's concerns would remain well-founded.

Schlunk is the second decision in the course of a year in which the Supreme Court has interpreted narrowly an important multilateral treaty on international judicial assistance. Unlike the decision last Term in *Societe Nationale Aerospatiale v. United States District Court,*[18] however, the effects of this decision are likely to be felt more strongly by U.S. nationals being sued abroad than by foreign defendants being sued in the United States. Since aliens are

[16] *See, e.g.,* Hantover, Inc. v. Omet S.N.C. of Volentieri & C., No. 87–1140–CV–W–JWO (W.D. Mo. June 9, 1988); Pochop v. Toyota Motor Co., 111 F.R.D. 464 (S.D. Miss. 1986).

[17] The Court's opinion suggests a different distinction. The majority concluded that, if service is deemed completed domestically, subsequent communications abroad do not implicate the Convention if they are private in nature. Presumably, service by mail could be distinguished on the ground that it requires the intervention of public authorities (i.e., the postal authorities). This distinction, however, is unsatisfactory: should the result be any different if the services of a private courier were used? The distinction proposed in the text would distinguish service on an agent from forms of service requiring the intervention of any third party, whether public or private.

[18] 107 S.Ct. 2542 (1987), *summarized* in 81 AJIL 944 (1987).

entitled to the same due process guarantees in the United States as nationals, they need not apprehend forms of domestic service that are not reasonably calculated to result in actual notice.[19] As Justice Brennan observed, however, other nations are not bound by our Constitution, and U.S. citizens sued abroad must rely instead on the guarantees of the Convention. After the Court's decision in *Schlunk,* a U.S. national complaining of inadequate service may find foreign courts less receptive to any arguments based on the Hague Service Convention.

CARLOS M. VÁZQUEZ
Of the District of Columbia Bar

Act of state—extraterritorial exception—situs of debt

BANDES v. HARLOW & JONES, INC. 852 F.2d 661.
U.S. Court of Appeals, 2d Cir., July 19, 1988.

The former majority shareholders of Industria Nacional de Clavos y Alambres de Puas, S.A. (INCA), a large Nicaraguan steel company, sought to recover from Harlow & Jones, Inc. (H & J), a U.S. steel company, the purchase price of a shipment of undelivered steel billets. Following the Sandinista revolution, the Nicaraguan Government had "intervened" in INCA and it, too, demanded the funds that H & J interpleaded into the court. The district court rejected the claim of the Sandinista Government and allocated the funds to the benefit of all parties who held shares in the company prior to the intervention.[1] On cross-appeals by the claimants, a panel of the United States Court of Appeals for the Second Circuit (per Kaufman, J.) affirmed in part and reversed in part, and *held:* the act of state doctrine does not bar judicial resolution of the dispute over the funds; the actions of the Sandinista Government amounted to a taking without compensation that will not be enforced by the U.S. courts; and the district court's allocation of pro rata shares for all of the preintervention stockholders, including minority interests, was equitable.[2]

Since 1960, INCA has manufactured and sold steel products for Nicaraguan consumption and for export throughout Central America. INCA was operated by members of the Bandes family who collectively owned 72.9 percent of the company's shares. Another 18.2 percent was issued in 1976 to two Nicaraguan generals, one of whom was the brother of then-dictator

[19] *See* Mullane v. Central Hanover Bank & Trust Co., 339 U.S. 306 (1950). The petitioner in *Schlunk* did not challenge either the constitutionality of the method of service employed or the state's basis for personal jurisdiction over it, and the Supreme Court accordingly did not address those issues. *Compare* Cannon Mfg. Co. v. Cudahy Packing Co., 267 U.S. 333 (1925) (activities within forum state of a wholly owned subsidiary are not sufficient to subject parent corporation to forum's jurisdiction).

[1] 570 F.Supp. 955 (S.D.N.Y. 1983).

[2] Nos. 1146 and 1281, slip op. at 10–23 and 25.

Anastasio Somoza. The remaining 8.9 percent was held by more than 50 Nicaraguan businessmen.[3]

In late June 1979, toward the end of Nicaragua's civil war, the Bandes family fled to Honduras. Shortly thereafter, having prevailed in the war, the Sandinista revolutionary forces "intervened" and expropriated[4] INCA. On July 20, 1979, pursuant to Decree No. 3 of the Government Council,[5] the Attorney General of Justice of Nicaragua was empowered to intervene, requisition and confiscate the assets of the Somoza family and military personnel who had fled the country since December 1977. On July 22, 1979, Decree No. 10 was enacted, declaring that managers of businesses who abandoned or hindered the operation of the economy had committed a crime, and authorizing the state to intervene and take control of abandoned businesses. The holdings of the Bandes family and the Somoza regime's generals were thus intervened and the government intervenor was placed in control of INCA.[6]

In 1978, prior to the fall of the Somoza Government, INCA placed an order with H & J for 2,000 tons of steel billets for which it advanced \$460,000. The revolution followed and the steel was never delivered. After the Sandinista intervention of INCA, the Bandes family head, acting pursuant to a long-held general power of attorney from INCA, asked H & J to return to the family shareholders the \$460,000. He subsequently concluded a settlement with H & J for \$420,000, amounting to the purchase price, less the cost of recision and other setoffs owed by INCA to H & J. Two days before making payment to the Bandes family, H & J received a telex from the Nicaraguan intervenor stating that INCA was operating under the administration of the Nicaraguan Government and that the intervenor alone was authorized to represent the company in business transactions.

The Bandes family sued H & J in the Southern District of New York. H & J responded by depositing \$420,000 with the court and filing an interpleader complaint against the Bandes family and the government intervenor. Both claimants moved for summary judgment. The district court held that the act of state doctrine did not bar judicial resolution of the dispute and that the Sandinista Government's intervention of INCA amounted to a taking without compensation contrary to U.S. law and policy. The district court thus refused to recognize the intervenor's claim and

[3] *Id.* at 5–6.

[4] In the district court, the claimants disputed the meaning and legal significance of the term "intervention." The Bandes family maintained that the intervention constituted a permanent taking. The representative of the Nicaraguan Government argued that it was only a temporary measure. The appellate court, echoing the reasoning of the district court, held that "[b]ecause, during the nine years of this litigation, INCA has been solely controlled by the Sandinista Government without any attempt to indemnify the Bandes family, . . . the company has been expropriated to the extent of permanent ownership and control over the Bandeses's property." *Id.* at i n.1.

[5] The texts of the relevant Sandinista decrees are reprinted as notes to the district court's opinion. 570 F.Supp. at 957–59 nn.1–2 and 5–8.

[6] Later, the government intervenor held a general shareholders meeting and removed the Bandeses from their positions as officers of INCA. Slip op. at 6–7.

allocated the fund (which, including interest, had grown to nearly $900,000) to the benefit of the preintervention shareholders as follows: $171,759 plus interest to the preferred shareholders; nearly 73 percent of the balance to the Bandes family; and the remainder to the minority shareholders, including 18.2 percent reflecting the Somoza generals' pro rata portion.[7] Both claimants appealed.

The court of appeals affirmed in part and reversed in part.[8] Judge Kaufman held that the act of state doctrine—based on notions of comity, constitutional principles and a recognition of the practical limits of national jurisdiction—does not apply when property confiscated without compensation by a foreign sovereign is within the United States at the time of the foreign governmental action. In such circumstances, when another state attempts to seize property held here, U.S. jurisdiction is "paramount."[9]

The court found the situs of the H & J fund to be the United States because H & J is domiciled in Connecticut. Accordingly, "[t]he act of state doctrine . . . does not apply, and we may look to our own [U.S.] laws to determine the reach of the foreign sovereign's proscriptions."[10]

According to the court, acts of foreign states asserted to be applicable to property in the United States will be given effect only if they "are consistent with this nation's policies."[11] The court had "no doubt" that the intervention of INCA "was a 'taking' contrary to United States policy," as expressed in the Fifth and Fourteenth Amendments to the U.S. Constitution prohibiting confiscations without just compensation. Finding that "compensation was never considered when the Sandinistas seized control of INCA," the court refused to enforce the intervention and affirmed the denial of the government intervenor's claim.[12]

Turning to the claimants' challenges to the distribution of the funds, the court rejected them all and affirmed the district court's allocation. The Bandes family sought on appeal to recover the entire fund, focusing its objections solely on the amount reserved for the Somoza generals. The

[7] The district court allocated the funds "by creating the fiction of a corporate dissolution." *Id.* at 9. The district court also provided that notice would be sent to the unrepresented shareholders, and it held that any unclaimed amount would escheat to New York pursuant to that state's abandoned property law. N.Y. Aband. Prop. Law §§1200–1223 (McKinney 1944 & Supp. 1988). Slip op. at 9.

[8] For his effort in creating the fund for the minority and preferred shareholders, the district court awarded the Nicaraguan intervenor his attorney's fees and expenses amounting to $51,811.67 to be paid from the minority shareholders fund. Slip op. at 9. The court of appeals reversed the award of attorney's fees to intervenor because "he did nothing to create the common fund," and because of "the general policy in United States courts that each party bear the cost of his own counsel's compensation." *Id.* at 24–25.

[9] "[T]he foreign sovereign is acting beyond *its* enforcement capacity when it involves itself within our nation's jurisdiction." *Id.* at 12 (emphasis in original).

[10] *Id.*

[11] *Id.* (citing RESTATEMENT (SECOND) OF FOREIGN RELATIONS LAW OF THE UNITED STATES §43 (1965); RESTATEMENT (THIRD) OF FOREIGN RELATIONS LAW OF THE UNITED STATES §443 comment *b* (1987) [hereinafter RESTATEMENT (THIRD)]).

[12] *Id.* at 13.

Bandes family alleged that the generals themselves "confiscated" the stock from the family and that this wrongful act should not be enforced by U.S. courts. Terming this argument "disingenuous," the court found that INCA in fact had benefited "as a result of the influence wielded by the Somoza associates." The court held that the act of state doctrine barred an inquiry into the reasons for the Nicaraguan Government's conduct that, the Bandes family alleged, had forced the sale of INCA shares to the generals.[13]

The Nicaraguan intervenor claimed that the Bandes family should receive no part of the fund because the family's representative had failed to exhaust administrative remedies available in Nicaragua. The court held that these remedies were "illusory," noting that to avail himself of Nicaraguan remedies, the family head would have been required to appear in Nicaragua and answer criminal charges resulting from Decree No. 10, which had been enacted after his departure. Recognizing that U.S. constitutional prohibitions apply only domestically, the court held that "[n]onetheless, [it] should avoid extending the effects of another country's *ex post facto* legislation within [U.S.] borders."[14]

The government intervenor also argued that the interpleaded fund should be applied to repay preintervention debts owed by INCA. If this theory were accepted, the court noted, Nicaragua could collect INCA's extraterritorial debts and accomplish indirectly what the act of state doctrine would not allow to be accomplished directly. The court held that "United States policy demands that our court refuse that convolution."[15]

Finally, the intervenor maintained that confiscation during a time of emergency in Nicaragua was a legitimate act of government and hence not contrary to U.S. policy. The court declined to extend to another nation's attempted confiscations of property outside that nation's territory carefully circumscribed United States constitutional principles regarding the President's authority to seize property in times of national emergency.

* * * *

The Supreme Court of the United States has not passed on the applicability of the act of state doctrine to asserted expropriations by a foreign government of property located outside of the foreign state's territory at the time of taking. However, this case is in accord with the unanimous line of

[13] *Id.* at 14–16. The court also found "due process problems" in depriving the generals—who were not parties to the action—of property without affording them notice and the opportunity to defend their interests in court. Because the Bandes family accepted and enjoyed the benefits of state favoritism—a practice also contrary to U.S. policy—its members lacked "clean hands" to claim the portion of the fund reserved for the generals. In addition, the court affirmed the reservation of an amount for the unrepresented minority shareholders.

[14] *Id.* at 19.

[15] *Id.* at 22. The court relied on United Bank Ltd. v. Cosmic Int'l, Inc., 542 F.2d 868 (2d Cir. 1976), in which the Bangladesh confiscators argued that the situs of disputed debts was in Bangladesh because they were actually security for previous debts located there. The *United Bank* court disagreed, holding that the Bangladesh confiscators should not be allowed to accomplish indirectly what the act of state doctrine otherwise precluded. 542 F.2d at 876.

lower court decisions holding that the act of state doctrine is inapplicable to takings by a foreign state of property located outside of its territory.[16]

The lower courts have been divided on the issue of how the territorial exception to the act of state doctrine should be applied to various types of intangible property.[17] In this regard, the *Bandes* case contrasts with the 1985 decision of the U.S. Court of Appeals for the Ninth Circuit in *Tchacosh Co., Ltd. v. Rockwell International Corp.*,[18] in which a panel of that circuit applied the act of state doctrine to a claim for the debt owed by a U.S. company to an Iranian company that was expropriated by the revolutionary Government of Iran. The court there affirmed the lower court's grant of summary judgment dismissing a suit by the former owner on behalf of the expropriated company for payment for work performed in Iran. The Ninth Circuit panel rejected the argument in *Tchacosh* that the underlying claim was within the extraterritorial exception to the act of state doctrine even though the corporate headquarters and principal place of business of the defendant company were in the United States. In *Tchacosh* the U.S. debtor established a separate office in Iran, all the work was performed in Iran and all the accounts for the contract appear to have been kept there. Judge Kaufman's test in the instant case based on the domicile of the debtor appears more likely to be applied in the future to the locus-of-debt issue in act of state cases in the absence of the special facts in *Tchacosh*.

MICHAEL R. CALABRESE
Of the District of Columbia Bar

International judicial assistance—cooperation of United States courts with foreign investigations

In re REQUEST FOR ASSISTANCE FROM MINISTRY OF LEGAL AFFAIRS OF TRINIDAD AND TOBAGO. 848 F.2d 1151.
U.S. Court of Appeals, 11th Cir., July 7, 1988.

Appellant, Joseph Azar, appealed the district court's denial of his motion to quash a subpoena obtained by the U.S. Department of Justice at the request of the Minister of Legal Affairs of Trinidad and Tobago. The United States had sought the subpoena to obtain Azar's Florida bank records as part of a criminal investigation in Trinidad and Tobago.[1] On review,

[16] RESTATEMENT (THIRD), *supra* note 11, §443 comment *b*.

[17] *E.g., compare* Garcia v. Chase Manhattan Bank, N.A., 735 F.2d 645 (2d Cir. 1984) (act of state doctrine not applied in view of promise to pay at any branch worldwide), *with* Perez v. Chase Manhattan Bank, N.A., 61 N.Y.2d 460, 474 N.Y.S.2d 689, *cert. denied,* 469 U.S. 966 (1984) (act of state applied on the basis that debt could have been enforced or collected in Cuba). *See generally* Note, *The Act of State Doctrine: Resolving Debt Situs Confusion,* 86 COLUM. L. REV. 594 (1986).

[18] 766 F.2d 1333 (9th Cir. 1985).

[1] *In re* Request for Assistance from Ministry of Legal Affairs of Trinidad and Tobago, 648 F.Supp. 464 (S.D. Fla. 1986).

the Court of Appeals for the Eleventh Circuit (per Fay, J.) affirmed the district court's decision and *held* that 28 U.S.C. §1782 authorized the judicial assistance sought by the Minister of Legal Affairs even though there was no pending proceeding in Trinidad and Tobago.

The court characterized the appeal as presenting an issue of first impression, namely, "whether section 1782 requires that a proceeding be pending before a federal court may grant judicial assistance to a foreign official."[2] The panel decided the issue by reviewing the text and legislative history of 28 U.S.C. §1782(a), which provides that a district court may order a resident "to give his testimony or statement or to produce a document or other thing *for use in a proceeding* in a foreign or international tribunal."[3] Section 1782(a) also requires that the request for assistance come from "a foreign or international tribunal or upon the application of any interested person." In this case, the request came from the Minister of Legal Affairs, who was conducting a criminal investigation of possible violations of the Exchange Control Act[4] by Trinidad and Tobago nationals, but who had not initiated any judicial proceedings.

The court decided that the absence of a pending proceeding was not fatal to the request for judicial assistance, relying primarily on a 1964 amendment to section 1782. Prior to 1964, it was recognized that U.S. courts could not provide international judicial assistance until after the initiation of a judicial proceeding in the foreign country.[5] In 1964, however, Congress adopted a set of proposals submitted by a Commission on International Rules of Judicial Procedure, which Congress had previously established to evaluate the provisions of federal law relating to international judicial assistance.[6] The commission submitted to Congress several proposals[7] intended to encourage broader judicial cooperation and provide U.S. judicial assistance on "a wholly unilateral basis."[8]

The commission's proposals included a suggestion that Congress alter the language of section 1782, which at that time stated that the assistance must be used in a "judicial proceeding *pending* in any court in a foreign country."[9] The commission suggested that Congress drop the word "pending" and state simply that the assistance must be "for use in a proceeding in a foreign

[2] 848 F.2d 1151, 1152.

[3] 28 U.S.C. §1782(a) (1982) (emphasis added).

[4] Laws of Trinidad and Tobago, ch. 79:50.

[5] *See* Smit, *International Litigation Under the United States Code,* 65 COLUM. L. REV. 1015, 1026 n.72 (1965) (emphasis added).

[6] 848 F.2d at 1153; *see also In re* Letter Rogatory from the Justice Court, District of Montreal, Canada, 523 F.2d 562, 565 (6th Cir. 1975).

[7] Other proposals broadened §1782 to cover the production of documents (the section had previously applied only to depositions and testimony) and the use of evidence before administrative tribunals (it had previously applied only to the use of evidence before courts). 848 F.2d at 1151.

[8] *In re* Letter Rogatory, 523 F.2d at 565 (quoting Amram, *New Developments in International Judicial Assistance in the United States of America,* 32 J.B.A.D.C. 24, 28 (1965)).

[9] *See* Smit, *supra* note 5, at 1026 & n.72.

or international tribunal."[10] Congress adopted this change as part of the legislation it enacted in 1964.

The court concluded that Congress had specifically intended to eliminate from section 1782 the requirement that a proceeding must be pending. The panel relied in part on common canons of statutory interpretation,[11] as well as on the views of the reporter of the 1964 commission, who had subsequently stated that "[i]t is not necessary, however, for the proceeding to be pending at the time the evidence is sought, but only that the evidence is eventually to be used in such a proceeding."[12] The court embraced a similar (but not identical) rule, stating that "the determination to grant assistance turns not on whether the proceeding is pending but on whether the requested evidence will likely be of use in a judicial proceeding."[13]

Azar unsuccessfully argued that the statute demanded more, pointing to its requirement that the request for assistance come from "a foreign or international tribunal or upon the application of any interested person." Azar quoted 1964 legislative history that stated that the amendment to section 1782 extended judicial assistance by making it available to "international tribunals and litigants before such tribunals."[14] He contended that this indicated that the Minister of Legal Affairs could not be an "interested person" unless he were an actual litigant.[15]

The court rejected this argument in a paragraph, relying on a different portion of the legislative history, which stated that a request for judicial assistance could come from "an interested party, *such as a person designated by or under a foreign law,* or a party to the foreign or international litigation."[16] The court concluded that the congressional definition of an "interested person" therefore included a foreign government official such as the Minister of Legal Affairs. The court cautioned, however, that as between private parties, "a private individual may need to be a litigant in a pending proceeding in order to be an 'interested person.' "[17]

The court then decided that the Minister of Legal Affairs had satisfied its requirement that the requested evidence be of use in a judicial proceeding. The panel pointed to the facts that the documents were discoverable under the law of Trinidad and Tobago; that the Minister had requested production in a form that would ensure admissibility; and that he had stated why he wanted eventually to use the records in legal proceedings. On the basis of these indications, the court found that the district judge had correctly concluded that "a proceeding was probable and [had] properly assisted the Minister of Legal Affairs by ordering the production of the bank records."[18]

[10] 848 F.2d at 1154.

[11] *Id.* at 1154–55.

[12] Smit, *supra* note 5, at 1026.

[13] 848 F.2d at 1155.

[14] S. Rep. No. 1580, 88th Cong., 2d Sess. (1964), *reprinted in* 1964 U.S. Code Cong. & Admin. News 3782, 3788 (Report of the Senate Judiciary Committee).

[15] *See* 848 F.2d at 1155.

[16] S. Rep. No. 1580, *supra* note 14, 1964 U.S. Code Cong. & Admin. News at 3789 (emphasis added).

[17] 848 F.2d at 1155.

[18] *Id.* at 1156.

* * * *

The Eleventh Circuit decision presents the issue of whether a foreign government official is an "interested person" under 28 U.S.C. §1782(a) as a straightforward question. The result seems much less clear in light of the minimal legislative history supplied by Congress. The most that a supporter of the opinion can find in that history is that Congress stated that an "interested party" should include "a person designated by or under a foreign law."[19] However, whatever that means, it does not—without more—indicate that a government official engaged in a criminal investigation necessarily so qualifies.

The court in this case may well have been guided less by legislative history than by policy concerns regarding criminal investigations. The decision adapts the rules of judicial assistance to an era in which the international flow of funds has made it increasingly difficult to investigate violations of securities and exchange control laws.[20] Investigative agencies need access to financial records such as those involved in the *Azar* case not only ultimately to prosecute such violations, but also to determine at a preliminary stage who has violated the law and how. The court's decision thus aids law enforcement efforts by extending existing principles of international judicial assistance to encompass investigations of increasingly important criminal conduct.

At the same time, the decision may well create new practical difficulties. The "pending proceeding" requirement—whatever its failings—provides governments and courts with a bright-line rule that is easy to understand and administer. This clear rule is now replaced by a requirement that is less certain and susceptible to varying interpretations—that the evidence requested must likely be of use in a judicial or administrative proceeding.[21] The facts in this case seem clear enough; however, it is not difficult to imagine other instances in which there is no more than a remote chance that any proceeding will ultimately ensue or that the requested evidence will ever be used as stated.

At a minimum, the Eleventh Circuit's new rule will function properly (and without abuse) only if district courts apply it with caution and more than modest scrutiny. In particular, the Eleventh Circuit wisely recognized this fact by stating that "a private individual may need to be a litigant in a pending proceeding in order to be an 'interested party' " within the meaning of the statute.[22] In truth, one could go farther and state that, in the

[19] S. REP. NO. 1580, *supra* note 14, 1964 U.S. CODE CONG. & ADMIN. NEWS at 3788.

[20] Moreover, a series of exchange control violations is sometimes involved in the financing of large-scale illegal drug transactions.

[21] The court itself may have created some confusion in this regard. In its opinion it first described its test as one requiring that the requested evidence "be of use" in a proceeding (848 F.2d at 1155), but it then focused on whether the evidence would ultimately be used in such a proceeding (*id.* at 1156). The second test requires the court to assess the probability that there will be such a proceeding, whereas the first could be interpreted as requiring it to analyze solely the utility of the evidence should a proceeding go forward.

[22] *Id.* at 1155.

absence of very sound reasons, a private party should not be able to obtain judicial assistance unless it first becomes a litigant in a pending proceeding. Counsel to private parties could otherwise be tempted to use this procedure to gain useful competitive information or conduct so-called fishing expeditions. Restricted to government investigations, the Eleventh Circuit's decision assists criminal investigations in an area where such help is needed. If it is extended to private parties, however, it may well become impossible to put this genie back in a bottle.

BRADFORD L. SMITH
Of the District of Columbia Bar

Jurisdiction—Foreign Sovereign Immunities Act—commercial activity exception—direct effect

ZEDAN v. KINGDOM OF SAUDI ARABIA. 849 F.2d 1511.
U.S. Court of Appeals, D.C. Cir., June 24, 1988.

Plaintiff Zedan, an American citizen, brought suit in the United States District Court for the District of Columbia against the Kingdom of Saudi Arabia for breach of a contract guaranteeing wages and profits. While performance under the contract occurred in Saudi Arabia, plaintiff alleged that the jurisdictional requirements under the Foreign Sovereign Immunities Act of 1976 (28 U.S.C. §§1330, 1602–1611 (1982)) (FSIA) were satisfied by a recruitment call in California from a representative of the royal overseer of a private Saudi company. The district court granted the Saudi motion to dismiss. On appeal, the United States Court of Appeals for the District of Columbia Circuit (per Silberman, J.) unanimously affirmed and *held:* (1) that the telephone call did not have the requisite substantiality of contact with the United States; (2) that it was not sufficient to form the basis of a cause of action; and (3) that the alleged breach did not have sufficient direct effect in the United States to satisfy the exceptions to immunity under the FSIA.

Zedan apparently began work on the Riyadh Outer Ring Road in Saudi Arabia as an employee of the Arab Service Office. This entity, which Zedan did not allege to be an agency of the Saudi Government, sought his services through a representative of its royal overseer, Prince Sultan. Subsequently, Zedan entered into a 5-year employment contract with another private Saudi entity. When progress on the road lagged, the Saudi Ministry of Communications put Zedan in charge of the project and guaranteed payment of his salary and a share of the profits under his contract with the second private employer. The roadway was completed within 5 months and Zedan returned to the United States, allegedly without having been paid over $600,000 in salary and profits by Saudi Arabia.

The court of appeals explained that the first clause of section 1605(a)(2) of the FSIA withholds immunity from a foreign state if the cause of action is "based upon a commercial activity carried on in the United States by the foreign state." Section 1603(e) defines such activity to require "substantial contact with the United States." Zedan maintained that the recruitment telephone call satisfied the substantial contact test because an "unbroken connection" existed between that call and the alleged breach of the guarantee contract. The court noted that the substantial contact requirement of the FSIA is more rigorous than that suggested by a minimum contacts due process inquiry.[1] Here no part of the contract performance occurred in the United States. Relying on the legislative history of the FSIA, the court found the degree of contact "no more than that 'occasioned simply by U.S. citizenship or U.S. residence of the plaintiff.' "[2] Finally, the court disposed of the plaintiff's position on the first clause by finding that the link between the recruitment of Zedan in the United States and the act in Saudi Arabia giving rise to his subsequent claim was not "based upon" the act in the United States and, consequently, was "too attenuated" to satisfy that FSIA requirement.[3]

The court next addressed Zedan's contention that jurisdiction was provided for under the second clause of section 1605(a)(2), which withholds sovereign immunity for an act "performed in the United States in connection with a commercial activity of the foreign state elsewhere." Judge Silberman proceeded to endorse for the first time since the FSIA's enactment the statement in the legislative history that "the acts (or omissions) encompassed in this category are limited to those which in and of themselves are sufficient to form the basis of a cause of action."[4] The court held that, since the suit was based upon a contract entered into and performed in Saudi Arabia, no alleged act or omission in the United States formed the basis of the cause of action.

Under the third clause of section 1605(a)(2), a foreign sovereign is subject to the jurisdiction of the United States when an act outside the territory of the United States in support of a commercial activity of the foreign state elsewhere causes a direct effect in the United States. Zedan argued that his financial destitution in the United States resulted from the failure of Saudi Arabia to honor its agreement and, therefore, constituted such a "direct effect." The court distinguished what it described as "financial hardship fortuitously suffered *in the United States*" by virtue of the "happenstance of [Zedan's] travel arrangements"[5] from the required substantial and foreseeable direct effect of the alleged Saudi breach. The court emphasized that "something legally significant actually happened in the United States" in

[1] 849 F.2d 1511, 1513 (citing Maritime Int'l Nominees Establishment v. Guinea, 693 F.2d 1094, 1109 (D.C. Cir. 1982), *cert. denied,* 464 U.S. 815 (1983) (two business meetings in the United States between plaintiff and a representative of a foreign sovereign held not sufficient to satisfy the substantial contact test)).

[2] *Id.* (quoting H.R. REP. NO. 1487, 94th Cong., 2d Sess. 17 (1976), *reprinted in* 1976 U.S. CODE CONG. & ADMIN. NEWS 6604, 6615–16)).

[3] *Id.* at 1514: the court distinguished Gilson v. Republic of Ireland, 682 F.2d 1022, 1027 n.22 (D.C. Cir. 1982) (allegation that defendants colluded in the United States to entice plaintiff to travel to Ireland where defendants stole his expertise and patent rights presents sufficiently "direct causal connection" to satisfy "based upon" requirement).

[4] H.R. REP. NO. 1487, *supra* note 2, at 19.

[5] 849 F.2d at 1514 (emphasis in original).

each of the other cases finding that the third clause was satisfied, both of which were suits by corporations that had incurred financial losses in the United States.[6]

The court also reasoned that Zedan's situation resembled the line of cases construing the direct effects of personal injuries that U.S. citizens have suffered abroad by virtue of acts or omissions of foreign states or their instrumentalities. These cases have uniformly held that there is no direct effect in the United States when the wrongful conduct occurred in the foreign state and the U.S. consequences are limited to those associated with physical rehabilitation in the United States.[7] Here, Saudi Arabia's breach did not have a direct effect in the United States because the financial loss suffered by Zedan resulted from an intervening event—his return to the United States.[8]

* * * *

This case is a useful judicial refinement of the commercial activity exception to the FSIA and is noteworthy for its endorsement of the language in the House report narrowing the second clause, relating to acts in the United States connected with commercial activity abroad. In a potentially important footnote, Judge Silberman considers how the direct effect test would apply to an alleged breach of contract by a foreign sovereign calling for payment in the United States but involving performance wholly outside the United States. He states in dicta that breach of such a contract would have a substantial, direct and foreseeable effect in the United States only if it specified, "at the very least, . . . a particular location in the United States," and that it might have to set out "the particular bank through which payment was to be made."[9]

EDWARD M. LEIGH
Of the District of Columbia Bar

Aliens—request for asylum on account of persecution—attribution of political opinion to refugee by persecuting government

DESIR v. ILCHERT. 840 F.2d 723.
U.S. Court of Appeals, 9th Cir., May 26, 1988.

Plaintiff, a Haitian seeking asylum in the United States, filed a petition for habeas corpus in the United States District Court for the Northern District

[6] *Id.* at 1515 (citing Transamerican S.S. v. Somali Democratic Republic, 767 F.2d 998, 1004 (D.C. Cir. 1985) (detention of ship abroad, but demand for payment in the United States by agency of Somali Government and actual U.S. bank transfers sufficient to form basis for direct effect jurisdiction); and Texas Trading & Milling Corp. v. Federal Republic of Nigeria, 647 F.2d 300, 312 (2d Cir. 1981), *cert. denied,* 454 U.S. 1148 (1982) (direct effect found from refusal to pay letters of credit issued by U.S. bank and payable in the United States to financially injured claimant)).

[7] *See, e.g.,* Zernicek v. Brown & Root, Inc., 826 F.2d 415, 418 (5th Cir. 1987) (citing cases), *cert. denied,* 108 S.Ct. 775 (1988).

[8] 849 F.2d at 1515 (citing Upton v. Empire of Iran, 459 F.Supp. 264, 266 (D.D.C. 1978), *aff'd mem.,* 607 F.2d 494 (D.C. Cir. 1979)).

[9] *Id.* n.2.

of California, to overturn a denial of asylum by both an immigration judge and the Board of Immigration Appeals (BIA). The plaintiff sought asylum under section 101(a)(42)(A) of the Immigration and Nationality Act (8 U.S.C. §1101(a)(42)(A) (1982)) (INA) on the basis of "persecution or a well-founded fear of persecution on account of race, religion, nationality, membership in a particular social group, or political opinion." The district court upheld the BIA decision, which allowed deportation of the plaintiff because the incidents of persecution in Haiti were economically rather than politically motivated. The Court of Appeals for the Ninth Circuit (per Tang, J.) reversed, *holding* that the plaintiff had demonstrated persecution based on political opinion by showing a pattern of extortion by government officials, and remanded for a determination of whether the plaintiff would be persecuted upon his return to Haiti.[1]

The court of appeals first noted that an alien must satisfy both an objective and a subjective component of the test for fear of persecution. To satisfy the subjective prong, the alien must prove that he or she actually fears persecution. To satisfy the objective prong of the asylum test, the alien must create a record that includes "credible, direct and specific evidence" that establishes that persecution is a "reasonable possibility."[2]

The factual record developed before the immigration judge revealed that the plaintiff had been periodically beaten by the Haitian security forces, the Ton Ton Macoutes, because of his refusal to pay bribes for the privilege of fishing and selling curios to tourists. The plaintiff produced undisputed evidence that the Haitian security forces branded anyone resisting extortion as a political subversive. The immigration judge, the Board of Immigration Appeals and the district court accepted the plaintiff's portrayal of the facts as accurate. Yet, without exception, they held that the plaintiff's nonpayment of extortion did not spring from political motives but rather from economic motivation such as inability to pay. Further, the BIA found that the plaintiff had failed to show that the security forces interpreted his nonpayment of the bribes as politically motivated.

The court of appeals rejected this rationale and held that, in applying the asylum test, the motives and perspective of the persecutor—the Macoutes —are at least as important as those of the persecuted. Noting that the Haitian Government of deposed President Duvalier operated as "government by thievery," the court found that the former Government had established a security system that fostered corruption, extortion and violence. For most of the Ton Ton Macoutes, their sole source of income was extortion from ordinary Haitians. The court concluded that this system of extortion and terror directly benefited the Duvalier Government and that the Macoutes were an " 'organization created for political purposes.' "[3]

[1] The court took judicial notice of President Duvalier's flight from Haiti on February 6, 1986, and the disbanding by the successor Government of the security forces, the Ton Ton Macoutes, that had persecuted the plaintiff.

[2] 840 F.2d 723, 726.

[3] *Id.* at 727 (quoting Haitian Refugees Center v. Civiletti, 503 F.Supp. 442, 498–500 (S.D. Fla. 1980), *aff'd as modified sub nom.* Haitian Refugees Center v. Smith, 676 F.2d 1023 (5th Cir. 1982)).

The court characterized the plaintiff's refusal to accede to extortion as "more than arbitrary, personal actions." Rather, his refusal was the manifestation of a political opinion because it "resulted in his classification and treatment as a subversive."[4] An alien may have a legitimate claim to political persecution or fear of political persecution, the court found, as long as the relevant government regards political opinion as motivating the alien's actions. As the court added, "whether the political opinion is actually held or implied makes little difference where the alien's life is equally at risk."[5] Nonpayment of bribes to the Macoutes was a "political choice" in Duvalier's Haiti.

The court remanded for a determination of whether, in view of the changes in the Haitian Government, plaintiff now faces a clear probability of persecution should he be returned to Haiti. Plaintiff will have the opportunity to show his likely treatment in post-Duvalier Haiti.

* * * *

Desir v. Ilchert continues the trend in the Ninth Circuit toward finding political persecution on the basis of imputed political opinions.[6] It remains to be seen whether other circuits will follow this lead. The court of appeals correctly focused on whether the source of the persecution, i.e., the government security forces or other government actors, views the victim's actions as politically motivated. A citizen living under an oppressive regime may engage in conduct the local authorities regard as antigovernmental and that citizen may also intentionally avoid any overt expression of political motive in order to remain safe from persecution. Persecution may nonetheless be visited upon such a silent party on the basis of a supposed political opinion. It seems logical that in such cases the result under the "well-founded fear of persecution" standard should be no more restrictive than if the victim actually held and expressed political opinions. Indeed, this silent victim may be entitled to greater solicitude under the asylum test if persecuted by a regime with the characteristics that the court found to exist in Haiti under President Duvalier.

SUSAN BURKE
Of the Virginia Bar

[4] *Id.* at 727–28.

[6] The court discussed a number of relevant precedents, e.g., Bolanos-Hernandez v. INS, 767 F.2d 1277 (9th Cir. 1985) (refusal of former member of right-wing party and military groups to join guerrillas in El Salvador was conscious choice to remain politically neutral and constituted political opinion); Argueta v. INS, 759 F.2d 1395 (9th Cir. 1985) (death threat based on persecutors' erroneous belief that alien was member of guerrilla organization, coupled with affirmative choice to remain politically neutral, sufficient to establish clear probability of persecution based on political opinion); Del Valle v. INS, 776 F.2d 1407 (9th Cir. 1985) (refusal to join "death squad" and pursuit of studies and other community activities constituted choice to remain neutral and expression of political opinion under the Immigration and Nationality Act); Hernandez-Ortiz v. INS, 777 F.2d 509, 517 (9th Cir. 1985) (alien's actual political view, whether neutral or partisan, irrelevant; where government attributed certain political opinions to him, this constituted persecution on account of political opinion); Lazo-Majano v. INS, 813 F.2d 1432, 1435 (9th Cir. 1987) (alien persecuted because of political opinion imputed by persecutor).

Treaties—Agreement Between the United States and the United Nations Regarding UN Headquarters—reconciliation of provisions of U.S. statutes and treaties —congressional intent

UNITED STATES v. PALESTINE LIBERATION ORGANIZATION. No. 88 Civ. 1962 (ELP).
U.S. District Court, S.D.N.Y., June 29, 1988.

Plaintiff, the United States, brought an action in the U.S. District Court for the Southern District of New York against the Palestine Liberation Organization (PLO) and four individuals[1] seeking an injunction to close the PLO's Permanent Observer Mission (Mission) to the United Nations as violative of the Anti-Terrorism Act of 1987 (ATA).[2] The district court (per Palmieri, J.) entered summary judgment for defendants and *held:* (1) the ATA does not require the closure of the PLO's Mission to the United Nations; (2) the status of the PLO's Mission, an invitee of the United Nations, is protected by the Agreement Between the United States and the United Nations Regarding the Headquarters of the United Nations (Headquarters Agreement);[3] and (3) Congress did not intend the ATA to supersede the Headquarters Agreement.

The court first determined that it had jurisdiction over the case. In this regard, defendants had the requisite minimum contacts with the forum state, consistent with the requirements of due process under *International Shoe Co. v. Washington,*[4] to permit the court to assert personal jurisdiction over them. The PLO finances and maintains an office and telephone listing in New York and each of the individual defendants employed at the PLO's Mission maintains a "continuous presence" in New York. The PLO neither has nor claims the benefits of diplomatic immunity.

The court also concluded that it had subject matter jurisdiction over the dispute, finding that both the interpretation of the ATA as a matter of domestic law and reconciliation of the ATA with the international obligations of the United States are matters that fall within the mandate of the federal courts. The court rejected the argument of defendants that section 21 of the Headquarters Agreement provides a "rule of decision" that requires the United States to arbitrate disputes involving interpretations of the Headquarters Agreement, depriving the court of subject matter jurisdiction.[5]

[1] Individual defendants included the Permanent Observer of the PLO, who possesses an Algerian passport but whose citizenship is not divulged; the Deputy Permanent Observer of the PLO, a United States citizen; the Alternate Permanent Observer of the PLO, an Iraqi citizen; and an administrator at the Mission, a citizen of Great Britain.

[2] Foreign Relations Authorization Act for Fiscal Years 1988–1989, tit. X, Pub. L. No. 100-204, §1001, 101 Stat. 1331, 1406 (codified at 22 U.S.C.A. §§5201–5203 (West Supp. 1988)).

[3] June 26, 1947, 61 Stat. 3416, TIAS No. 1676, 11 UNTS 11, *authorized by* S.J. Res. 144, 80th Cong., 1st Sess., *set out in* 22 U.S.C. §287 note (1982).

[4] 326 U.S. 310, 320 (1945).

[5] Section 21(a) of the Headquarters Agreement, *supra* note 3, provides, in pertinent part: "Any dispute between the United Nations and the United States concerning the interpretation or application of this agreement or of any supplemental agreement, which is not settled by

First, the court found section 21 inapplicable on its face because its arbitration provisions govern disputes solely between the United Nations and the United States. The court pointed out that the United Nations had explicitly refrained from becoming a party to this litigation.[6] Second, the court concluded that it would exceed its constitutional powers granted under Article III if it ordered the United States to submit to arbitration. The manner in which the United States honored its treaty obligations and, in particular, whether to submit to the jurisdiction of an international tribunal, constituted a nonjusticiable "political question" within the purview of the executive branch. The court relied on a long line of cases, spanning nearly a century, that rejected jurisdiction over matters involving international obligations.[7]

The court then considered the central issue in the case—whether the ATA required the closure of the PLO Mission to the United Nations. The court described the United Nations headquarters in New York as an "international enclave"[8] and summarized provisions of the Headquarters Agreement that guarantee appropriate transit, entry and access to the facility. Section 11 of the Headquarters Agreement bars the United States from "impos[ing] any impediments to transit to or from the headquarters district" of persons invited to the headquarters by the United Nations on official business.[9]

The United Nations, from its incipiency, has invited various nonmember groups to participate in its proceedings and maintain "Permanent Observer Missions," including nonmember nations, intergovernmental organizations and other organizations, such as the PLO. For nearly 40 years, the United States has acquiesced in the presence of such observer missions and has refrained from impeding their function. The Department of State has never

---

negotiation or other agreed mode of settlement, shall be referred for final decision to a tribunal of three arbitrators . . . ."

[6] The court also rejected the argument of defendants that it should defer to an advisory opinion of the International Court of Justice finding a dispute between the United States and the United Nations subject to arbitration under section 21. Applicability of the Obligation to Arbitrate under Section 21 of the United Nations Headquarters Agreement of 26 June 1947, 1988 ICJ Rep. 12 (Advisory Opinion of Apr. 26), *reprinted in* 27 ILM 808 (1988). The Secretary-General argued before the ICJ that a dispute within the meaning of section 21 existed upon enactment of the ATA, in the absence of adequate assurances from the United States that the ATA would not affect the status of the PLO Mission. The United States argued that arbitration would not be "appropriate or timely" because it pledged not to take any action to close the Mission pending the outcome of the district court litigation. The ICJ agreed with the Secretary-General, finding that the United States had taken measures against the PLO Mission that could not be reconciled with the position of the Secretary-General. The ICJ also noted that the United Nations had not agreed to settle this dispute in U.S. court and had restricted its role in the district court suit to amicus curiae.

[7] *See, e.g.*, Goldwater v. Carter, 444 U.S. 996, 996–97 (1979) (vacating, with instructions to dismiss, an attack on the President's action terminating a treaty with Taiwan); Clark v. Allen, 331 U.S. 503, 509 (1947) (President and Senate may denounce a treaty and thus terminate its life); Chae Chan Ping v. United States, 130 U.S. 581, 602 (1889) (whether government can disregard an engagement with another nation is not for determination by the courts).

[8] No. 88 Civ. 1962 (ELP), slip op. at 3.

[9] Headquarters Agreement, *supra* note 3, §11.

disputed that this right of access includes maintenance of an office in which to organize and carry out official United Nations business.

In 1974 the United Nations invited the PLO "to participate in the sessions and the work of the General Assembly in the capacity of observer."[10] That same year, a U.S. district court dismissed a suit challenging the presence of a PLO representative in New York pursuant to that invitation, holding that "[t]his problem must be viewed in the context of the special responsibility which the United States has to provide access to the United Nations under the Headquarters Agreement."[11] The State Department took the position in that case that the Headquarters Agreement required the United States to provide access for the PLO. Since 1974, the PLO has functioned without interruption as a permanent observer to the United Nations and the United States has acted in a manner consistent with recognizing the PLO's rights as an invitee.

The ATA, which became effective on March 21, 1988, declares that the PLO is a "terrorist organization and a threat to the interests of the United States, its allies, and to international law and should not benefit from operating in the United States."[12] The ATA, inter alia, forbids the establishment or maintenance of "an office, headquarters, premises, or other facilities or establishments within the jurisdiction of the United States at the behest or direction of, or with funds provided by" the PLO, if the purpose is to further the PLO's interests.[13]

The court recognized that both statutes and treaties constituted the supreme law of the land and that the court must reconcile conflicts between them by giving effect to both wherever possible. The court, however, could not reconcile the ATA and the Headquarters Agreement insofar as they affected the status of the PLO Mission. When such a conflict cannot be resolved, a court may find that a later enacted statute such as the ATA takes precedence over an existing treaty obligation only if Congress "clearly and unequivocally" stated its intent to do so. The court cited considerable precedent for the proposition that, in the absence of such explicit congressional intent, the court must interpret the statute at issue in a manner consistent with existing treaty obligations.[14]

The court held that the ATA did not apply to the PLO Mission because Congress, in enacting the legislation, did not evince a clear and unequivocal intent to supersede the Headquarters Agreement. First, Congress did not mention either the PLO Mission or the Headquarters Agreement in the ATA. The court found the absence of specific references to the Mission and Headquarters Agreement in the ATA particularly significant because, prior to passage of the statute, the State Department had informed Congress of its

[10] GA Res. 3237, 29 UN GAOR Supp. (No. 31) at 4, UN Doc. A/9631 (1974).

[11] Anti-Defamation League of B'nai B'rith v. Kissinger, Civ. No. 74 C 1545, slip op. at 37 (E.D.N.Y. Nov. 1, 1974), *excerpted in* 1974 Digest of United States Practice in International Law 27, 28, *quoted in PLO*, slip op. at 6.

[12] 22 U.S.C.A. §5201(b) (West Supp. 1988).

[13] *Id.* §5202(3).

[14] *See, e.g.*, Weinberger v. Rossi, 456 U.S. 25, 32 (1982); Chew Heong v. United States, 112 U.S. 536, 602 (1884).

view that closure of the PLO Mission would be inconsistent with the obligations of the United States under the Headquarters Agreement.[15] Second, the ATA's provisions prohibiting maintenance of a PLO office applied "notwithstanding any provision of *law* to the contrary," but did not purport to apply notwithstanding any *treaty*.[16] Third, a review of the legislative history of the ATA indicated that no member of Congress had expressed a clear and unequivocal intent to supersede the Headquarters Agreement. The only debate on the issue focused on whether the United States had an obligation to provide access to the PLO, and every proponent of the ATA argued, under a misapprehension, that no such obligation existed under the Headquarters Agreement.

Although the court held that the ATA did not apply to the PLO Mission, it rejected the position of defendants that it strike the statute in its entirety. The court found that the statute remained a valid enactment of general application that restricted PLO activity within the United States, aside from the Mission.[17]

* * * *

On August 29, 1988, the United States announced it would not appeal the decision by the district court "in light of foreign policy considerations including the U.S. role as host to the United Nations Organization."[18] A possible ground for appeal by the United States would have been the district court's interpretation of the intent of Congress in enacting the ATA. The opinion recognizes that members of Congress expected that the ATA would lead to the closing of the PLO Mission and knew throughout their deliberations that the ATA posed a potential conflict with the Headquarters Agreement. The court of appeals, however, would have needed to find that the district court's careful and convincing review of the legislative history was erroneous in order to reverse the decision. Such an outcome would have been unlikely because Congress, if it wished, could reenact the ATA with a clear statement of intent. According to press accounts, the President personally resolved the issue of whether to appeal on the basis of the Secretary

[15] The court afforded "great weight" to the views of the executive branch in reaching its conclusion. The United Nations Secretariat and General Assembly also opined that the Headquarters Agreement protected the PLO Mission, and the court afforded these views "some weight," particularly because the UN position was consistent with that of the State Department. Slip op. at 26.

[16] 22 U.S.C.A. §5202(3) (West Supp. 1988) (emphasis added). Other parts of the Foreign Relations Authorization Act, of which the ATA was a part, specifically superseded treaty obligations and referred to "United States law (including any treaty)." 101 Stat. at 1343. *See* slip op. at 29.

[17] In a related case, Judge Palmieri construed the ATA as not prohibiting the opening of an information office to gather, write and disseminate materials on the subject of the Palestinian people, so long as such office did not accept any money from the PLO or purport to act in any kind of official capacity for the PLO. The court also held that the ATA, as narrowed, did not violate the First Amendment or bill of attainder clause of the U.S. Constitution. Mendelsohn v. Meese, No. 88 Civ. 2005 (ELP) (S.D.N.Y. June 29, 1988).

[18] N.Y. Times, Aug. 30, 1988, at A1, col. 8 (Justice Department statement).

of State's emphasis on foreign policy considerations, thereby overriding the Justice Department's views on proper construction of the ATA.

ERIC S. KOENIG
Of the District of Columbia Bar

Sovereign immunity—international organizations—act of state doctrine—recognition of foreign laws—arbitration clauses

INTERNATIONAL TIN COUNCIL v. AMALGAMET INC. 524 N.Y.S.2d 971. Supreme Court, New York County, January 25, 1988.

Petitioner, International Tin Council (ITC), brought an action to stay an American Arbitration Association arbitration that was initiated by respondent, Amalgamet Inc., and that arose out of petitioner's refusal to honor three contracts for the purchase of tin from respondent. Petitioner claimed that it was immune from suit in the United States by virtue of its status as an international organization under British law, and, in the alternative, that the arbitration clause in its contract with respondent was unenforceable. The Supreme Court of New York County (per Parness, J.) dismissed the petition, and *held* that petitioner lacked any basis under U.S. law for immunity from legal process and that petitioner had consented to the arbitration clause providing for arbitration in New York.

This case arose out of the October 1985 collapse of the world's tin market.[1] The International Tin Council, formed in 1960 and consisting of 22 member countries that consume or produce tin,[2] had entered into numerous contracts for tin and tin futures aimed at ensuring the worldwide availability of tin at stable prices.[3] ITC had agreed to purchase tin from Amalgamet at the high, precollapse prices, but refused to complete three purchases at those prices after the collapse reduced prices by over half. Amalgamet sought to enforce its claim for damages by demanding an arbitration pursuant to the arbitration clause found in each sale confirmation form, and ITC petitioned for a stay of the arbitration.

In considering ITC's arguments that it was immune from legal process and suit under U.S. law, the court analyzed and rejected four potential bases for immunity. First, the court found inapplicable the Foreign Sovereign Immunities Act (28 U.S.C. §§1330, 1602–1611 (1982)) (FSIA), since the FSIA covers foreign states and their instrumentalities, but not international organizations.[4] Second, the court reviewed the International Organizations

[1] *See generally* McFadden, *The Collapse of Tin: Restructuring a Failed Commodity Agreement,* 80 AJIL 811 (1986). The events of 1985 resulted in numerous civil cases in England regarding ITC contracts. *See, e.g.,* Shearson Lehman Bros. v. Maclaine Watson & Co., [1988] 1 W.L.R. 16; Maclaine Watson & Co. v. International Tin Council, [1987] 2 All E.R. 787; Standard Chartered Bank v. International Trade Council, [1986] 3 All E.R. 257.

[2] The ITC was created pursuant to Article IV of the Second International Tin Agreement, Sept. 1, 1960, 403 UNTS 3, "to administer the provisions and to supervise the operation" of the Agreement.

[3] *See id.,* Art. I (objectives of Second International Tin Agreement).

[4] The FSIA defines a "foreign state" as including "a political subdivision of a foreign state or an agency or instrumentality of a foreign state." An agency or instrumentality of a foreign state must be a separate legal person, an organ of a foreign state or political subdivision thereof or

Immunities Act (22 U.S.C. §288 (1982)) (IOIA), but noted that the ITC met neither of the two criteria for international organizations specified in the Act.[5] Third, the court considered the argument of ITC that its refusal to purchase Amalgamet's tin was an act of state. The court stated that the act of state doctrine concerns "certain international disputes . . . [that] should be resolved by the executive branch of the United States government rather than by the courts," adding that the doctrine "is involved where the dispute is intrinsically involved with some sovereign function of a foreign entity so that political as well as purely private commercial issues are implicated."[6] Citing several cases, the court stated that the act of state doctrine does not apply to purely commercial transactions.[7] It went on to conclude that ITC had failed to demonstrate how any sovereign rights would be sacrificed during a New York arbitration, especially given that the 1972 UK-ITC Headquarters Agreement[8] and the British law on the ITC's status[9] would permit an arbitration in England by a British corporation asserting a similar claim.

The court also found that general principles of comity could not form a sufficient basis for immunity in this case. The court asked whether it "should recognize under principles of international comity a law of the U.K. which grants immunity to a U.K. resident from a suit in contract but to none other."[10] The court again reviewed the Headquarters Agreement, noting that it was meant to provide immunity only within British territory; it allows suits to enforce arbitrations, and it requires ITC's contracts to contain arbitration clauses.[11] In refusing to find that comity required giving the British law extraterritorial effect, the court found it "presumptuous to suggest . . . that a U.S. court as a matter of comity deprive a U.S. corporation of the right to enforce a claim against ITC in the U.S., where the U.K. would permit same to be brought by its own citizens against ITC in the U.K."[12] The court added that, in any event, the arbitration clause in the confirmation form, by providing for settlement of disputes by arbitration in

---

owned by such a state or subdivision, and neither a U.S. citizen nor created under the laws of a third country. 28 U.S.C. §1603(a)–(b) (1982). *Cf.* International Ass'n of Machinists v. OPEC, 477 F.Supp. 553 (C.D. Cal. 1979), *aff'd on other grounds,* 649 F.2d 1354 (9th Cir. 1981), *cert. denied,* 454 U.S. 1163 (1982) (dismissing suit against OPEC members under FSIA when defendants were individual nations, but not OPEC as an organization, which had not been properly served).

[5] Section 1 of the IOIA defines an international organization as:

> a public international organization in which the United States participates pursuant to any treaty or under the authority of any Act of Congress authorizing such participation or making an appropriation for such participation, and which shall have been designated by the President through appropriate Executive order as being entitled to enjoy the privileges, exemptions, and immunities provided in this subchapter.

[6] 524 N.Y.S.2d 971, 974. [7] *Id.*

[8] Headquarters Agreement, Feb. 9, 1972, United Kingdom–International Tin Council, 834 UNTS 287. *See also infra* note 11.

[9] International Tin Council (Immunities and Privileges) Order, S.I. 1972, No. 120.

[10] 524 N.Y.S.2d at 975.

[11] Headquarters Agreement, *supra* note 8, Arts. 8, 23, 24 and 28.

[12] 524 N.Y.S.2d at 975.

New York, constituted a waiver of any immunity ITC might enjoy from U.S. jurisdiction.

The remainder of the court's opinion focused on ITC's argument that ITC was not bound by the arbitration clause in the sale confirmation form because it had not consented to the inclusion of the clause. First, the court rejected ITC's argument that the arbitration clause constituted an unconsented oral addition to the confirmation form, noting that the executed written confirmation letter used in over 35 previous transactions was the sole contract to govern these purchases. Second, the court quickly dismissed ITC's claim that the arbitration clause was hidden in the confirmation form, pointing to its prominent location on the form, the size and number of prior sales using the same clause, and the experience and sophistication of the parties to the contract.

* * * *

The New York court's decision is of marginal value in the rules it sets down for the immunity of international organizations from suits in U.S. courts. Although its dismissal of the applicability of the FSIA and IOIA to the ITC is obviously correct, its examination of the act of state doctrine is seriously flawed. First and most important, the act of state doctrine does not apply in this case, because the ITC is not a foreign sovereign. The doctrine pertains only to the governmental acts of a foreign state.[13] Second, this court, like others, discusses immunity and act of state interchangeably, neglecting to consider that the former is a jurisdictional defense based on international law while the latter is an affirmative defense containing elements of U.S. constitutional law, conflict of laws and comity. Its citation to a sovereign immunity case that analyzed the commercial activity exception to the FSIA (28 U.S.C. §1605(A)(2) (1982)), to demonstrate that the act of state doctrine is applicable in a purely commercial context,[14] is thus inappropriate. A better approach might thus have pointed out that ITC's activities can never be acts of state and, moreover, that default on a contract, regardless of its commercial nature, is not the type of conduct to which the act of state doctrine was meant to apply.[15]

The court's analysis of comity proves much more logical. The court applies a rule of reason in determining whether respect for foreign law requires holding ITC immune from suit in the United States. By emphasizing that ITC would be subject to suit in the United Kingdom under British law, the court can easily and sensibly hold that permitting a similar suit in New

[13] RESTATEMENT (THIRD) OF FOREIGN RELATIONS LAW OF THE UNITED STATES §443 (1987).

[14] Texas Trading & Milling Corp. v. Federal Republic of Nigeria, 647 F.2d 300 (2d Cir. 1981), *cert. denied,* 454 U.S. 1148 (1982).

[15] Alfred Dunhill of London, Inc. v. Republic of Cuba, 425 U.S. 682, 694–95 (1976). The commercial nature of the default of the instant case could have been considered an additional basis for rejecting the act of state doctrine, based on the plurality opinion in *Dunhill, id.* at 695–706 (opinion of White, J.).

York shows no disrespect for British law and thus cannot violate notions of comity. The court's conclusion—that an international organization of which the United States is not a member and that is based in another country is not immune from the application of U.S. law—is consistent with notions of comity, as well as with customary international law and the intent of Congress in enacting the International Organizations Immunity Act.[16]

STEVEN R. RATNER*
Attorney-Adviser
United States Department of State

[16] *See* RESTATEMENT (THIRD), *supra* note 13, §467 comments *a* and *f* and Reporters' Note 1.

* These views are those of the author and not necessarily those of the United States Government.

BOOK REVIEWS AND NOTES

EDITED BY DETLEV VAGTS

Recueil des Cours de l'Académie de Droit International de La Haye, 1983. 5 vols. (Vols. 179, 180, 181, 182 and 183 of the collection.) The Hague, Boston, London; Dordrecht, Boston, Lancaster: Martinus Nijhoff Publishers. Vol. I, 1984: pp. 412; vol. II, 1984: pp. 411; vol. III, 1984: pp. 409; vol. IV, 1984: pp. 469; vol. V, 1985: pp. 382.

The general course in 1983 was given by Professor Michel Virally (University of Law, Economy and Social Sciences of Paris). It constitutes the entire volume V (vol. 183 of the collection) and is titled *Panorama du droit international contemporain.*

Virally defines international law as a legal order, comparable to municipal legal orders, governing international society. He sees contemporary international law as differing from classical international law by replacing the older emphasis on political manipulation and the rigidity of obligations, particularly contained in treaties, with a bias toward change in directions determined ideologically. Three major contributors to channeling the ideological trends into conceptions of law are the Soviet Revolution of 1917, the decolonization of political groups seeking to justify their recent history and ambitions in terms of collective "peoples' " rights (*droits des peuples*), as distinguished from individual rights (*droits des hommes*), and the emergence of international public opinion as a major influence on state behavior.

Nonetheless, Virally holds the state still to be the key conception of the international legal and political orders. He defines the state by its effects rather than by natural law characteristics. It is the unit, however composed, that governs itself in the society of other such units; the fundamental conception is structured authority based on control of territory ("un *pouvoir institutionnalisé* . . . [qui] se présente donc fondamentalement comme *un pouvoir territorial,* dépendant de la maîtrise du territoire") (p. 48). It is created by the processes of history and politics in fact, but is brought into the international legal order by recognition. Virally characterizes recognition as unilateral by the recognizing state, juridical in that it has legal consequences desired by that state and totally discretionary (pp. 52–53). His overall conception thus seems to be mainstream modern positivism.

Troubles arise, however, in considering whether the "droit des peuples" to independence and self-governance has in recent years created a legal right to "recognition" as a state, at least when the facts that would justify such acceptation exist; whether "recognition" is legally as discretionary as first stated. Virally concludes his very clear and learned analysis of this point by finding that the rights of "peoples" involve rights of states under the existing international legal order, including the right to determine their own constitutions (pp. 65–66). Thus, he implies that state practice and practical political considerations are moving to minimize the legal effect of de jure labels attached at the discretion of third states; that those considerations bring about legal results based on a recognition implied by actions in disregard of the legal labels attached by policy in disregard of law. Furthermore, the impact of Article 73 of the UN Charter and its elaboration in various General Assembly resolutions has been to create a distinction in law between ethnic enclaves and political units in the Third World; i.e., between, on the one hand, Biafra, Katanga and the Kurdish areas, inter alia, and, on the other hand, former colonies of Western states. The latter have achieved a degree of international status by positive law; the former have not and must achieve statehood by other means, if they want it. In any case, in practice, the "droit des peuples" has been confined to victims of colonialism (pp. 69–70), and the concept of colonialism seems to have been confined to European and North American actions, presumably counting South Africa as a European state.

Turning to the concept of the state in international law, Virally regards the word as implying various legal results such as the capacity within the international legal order to conduct external relations. The principles involved are created by custom and the evolution of practice; they are to some degree codified in the UN Charter, various resolutions of the General Assembly and such frankly political accords as the Final Act of the Helsinki Conference of 1975.

To Virally, the state is the only unit of the international legal order whose rights and obligations are complete (p. 72). This leads to a discussion of those rights and obligations, which Virally relates to the legal word "sovereignty," a concept he finds defined within the system, but with a variable content. These rights include the exclusive authority of the state to make and enforce municipal law within its own territory (subject to some limits imposed and constantly modified by the international legal order) and the right to determine its internal and external policies for itself. The first section closes with a few pages devoted to the concept of equality under the law as an aspect of state sovereignty, noting that sovereign equality implies equality of rights derived from the fact of sovereignty, thus full reciprocity in reciprocal situations, and, most interestingly, a principle of unequal treatment for unequal situations. This last then becomes the basis for special rights of geographically disadvantaged and nonindustrialized states. It is not clear why he thinks these "rights" are legal and not merely moral or political.

There is a pedagogical problem with Virally's approach. It is full of self-references; limitations on the rights of states are said to exist in the system, and each explication is referred back to a general concept of the undefined "legal order." Thus, whatever its utility as a positivist model of the legal order itself, the approach seems very hard on students. On the other hand, failure to make the constant back-references would result in generalities that are clearly incorrect, or so laden with specific qualifications as to be incomprehensible. It is quite likely that what seems a sophisticated model to modern positivists will be useless to students who have not yet organized their thinking to be able to criticize any particular model of the international legal order and to scholars who find modern positivism a closed system not responsive to the demands of natural justice and other values they believe implicit in the concept of "law."

The next section explores in more detail the authority (*pouvoirs,* legal powers) of the state in the international legal order. Here the differences between the categorizations and vocabularies of civil lawyers and common lawyers begin to play a role of some significance. Virally is, of course, a French-trained civil lawyer. Thus, he begins by addressing the "titres de compétence" of the state, what we common lawyers might call the scope of legislative jurisdiction. The basic rules are territoriality and nationality, subject to exemptions based on treaty and general international law, such as the exemptions from territorial jurisdiction usually enjoyed by visiting foreign forces and diplomats. Then he reverses the usual formulation by suggesting that conflict-of-laws theory provides a kind of foreign application of national laws, subject to the obstacles to that application that might be a product of the foreign forum in which those laws are sought to be enforced.

In addition, he finds some bases in principle for the direct extensions of national law to nationals' property sited abroad and the acts of foreigners abroad. In this last regard, Virally repeats the usual nonsense about piracy being subject to universal jurisdiction without regard to the ingrained rules of standing, and treats the "codification" of the 1958 and 1982 law of the sea conventions as if it meant something. He also asserts, without discussion, that states have the authority to protect themselves by applying their criminal law to acts of foreigners abroad that threaten their vital interests, citing espionage as an example, as well as the more often-cited counterfeiting, immigration and customs laws. Oddly, he singles out the United States with regard to customs and immigration laws, as if those were legally doubtful extensions of prescriptive jurisdiction, and does not cite American adherence to contiguous zone treaties, which fix territorial limits to the extensions of enforcement jurisdiction for customs and immigration. He gives no examples of the overseas application of espionage laws to foreigners. On the other hand, he properly cites the United States as the principal proponent of expanded prescriptive jurisdiction on the basis of "effects" on various legally protected interests. He also notes that the American assertions seem to many to be excessive, that the "rule of reason" and "balance of interests" approaches are self-judging revivals of discredited earlier attempts to justify using national discretion as a basis for ignoring foreign interests, and that a number of countries have enacted blocking statutes to prevent the exercise of "effects doctrine" jurisdiction against persons in their territory. In the main, what seems to be lacking in this extraordinarily compact and sophisticated exposition is the support in depth for various propositions that are not self-evident, although, in a sense, they flow from Virally's fundamental premises. Having introduced conflict of laws in its choice-of-law phase as a type of extraterritorial jurisdiction, Virally assumes there are public law underpinnings for that prescriptive jurisdiction. What is lacking is a clear differentiation among prescriptive, enforcement and adjudicatory jurisdiction, and, to introduce a concept adverted to three times by the International Court of Justice and generally ignored by publicists, the relationship of all three phases of jurisdiction to *jus standi.*

Moving on to more forceful types of intervention, Virally notes the major positive documents and the inconsistent practice, ending with a discussion of minimum standards of justice and human rights. Again, the presentation is highly compressed, extremely clear and well organized, subtle and realistic. For example, in discussing assistance to an established government as possible "intervention," he points out that assistance is rendered legally by one state to another state, but when the requesting "government" reflects more the will of the invitee than of the people it is nominally governing, the legality of the "assistance" has been properly questioned.

Part I of the course concludes with a discussion of territory, including the law of the sea, airspace and outer space.

Part II is devoted to even more theoretical considerations and their practical implications: the lawmaking processes of the international legal order. Again, the text is so packed with insight and so tightly organized that a mere description would be nearly as long as the text itself. Once more, Virally places himself above the technical disputes, pointing out, for example, that the phrase *jus cogens* has been accepted in the Vienna Convention on the Law of Treaties, but that its actual content, if it has any, has not been agreed on. Again, there are points on which it is possible to wish for fuller analysis. For example, the word "comity" is identified with mere courtesy, "observé pour des raisons diverses, mais non juridiques" (p. 182); an assertion that would not surprise most American jurists, but would greatly surprise Lord Mansfield, who first used the term in its current sense, and Latinists who know that it relates to obligations that derive from membership in the community, much as modern naturalist jurists derive legal obligations from the basic structure of international society.[1]

The third and last part of Virally's course is devoted to what Wolfgang Friedmann called the law of cooperation: international organizations and problems of authority, "soft law [*droit doux*]" and even cooperation to maintain the peace. Again, the compact organization of the course prevents setting forth the detailed outline that those not fortunate enough to have access to the book would want. This time I must resist the temptation to try.

In a final chapter, Virally finds the talk of a revolution in the structure of the international legal order or its fundamental rules to be greatly exaggerated. The expansion of the community has changed its politics substantially, and the demand for changed rules of substance cannot be ignored, but the

[1] The word appears to have entered the common law via a Latin phrase used by Mansfield in holding the law of the place of contracting to be the proper law of the contract "*ex comitate et jure gentium.*" Robinson v. Bland, [1760] 2 Burrow 1077. "*Jure gentium*" at that time referred to a hypothesized universal substantive law whose traces still survive in modern admiralty law, but whose utility was undermined and whose supposed rules have been, in the main, superseded by the evolution of conflict-of-laws theory. This is not the place for a fuller analysis.

lawmaking process has not changed fundamentally. That raises yet another problem. The need for clarity and definitiveness in some substantive rules is dictated not by political pressures alone, but by changed technology, which has opened up new areas, such as outer space and the deep seabed, for human interaction. The basic problem is that lawmaking is a political process, and nobody is prepared to accept the assertions of others as legally binding. To some degree, the problem has been alleviated by the proliferation of international organizations with some lawmaking capacities, structured to provide their members with safeguards of their essential interests even if that means crippling the organizations' capacity to make law for all. But there is room for optimism when it is seen that the "areas of turbulence" are at the edges of the massive movements of international society, and that in the vital areas of international commerce and economic relations in general, the law is developing in an orderly fashion and doing its job.

It is patently impossible in a review to describe adequately a course as deep as this, as well written, as brilliantly organized and as comprehensive. Every paragraph embodies variations on the basic positivist model that raise questions too subtle to be answered in a general course; to criticize it, as I have done, for what appear to be unavoidable gaps or inconsistencies in the form of the course is as unfair to Virally as the failure to criticize would be to the readers of this *Journal.*

Julio A. Barberis (Catholic University of Buenos Aires) addressed *Nouvelles Questions concernant la personnalité juridique internationale.* Because "law" is an abstract conception built upon words, every legal term, including "international juridical personality," rests on definitions that derive their meaning from contexts and traditions that cannot be directly communicated but that each analyst defines for himself and tries to communicate by words to others. Two positivist definitions of "subject of international law" are set out: Kelsen's "pure theory" definition, which depends upon determining what "the law" defines as its subjects, i.e., to whom or what it addresses itself; and the "theory of responsibility" urged primarily by Eustathiades and Wengler, under which the term "subjects" properly applies only to those whose violations of norms the law punishes. The difference seems subtle, but could have major effects on the consideration of the legal status of such asserted "subjects" of the law as individuals and national liberation movements. Barberis prefers something in between: "subjects" of international law are those whose conduct is envisaged by the law directly and effectively as containing a right or an obligation.[2] He amusingly analogizes the distinction between the positivist and naturalist definitions of subject of the law to the realm of zoology, pointing out that the animal kingdom viewed objectively does not create natural distinctions between whales and ungulates among mammals, however useful those distinctions might be to zoologists. So the Holy See, as party to a bilateral treaty, is a subject of

[2] "En conséquence . . . l'on peut définir le sujet du droit international comme étant celui dont la conduite est prévue directement et effectivement par le droit des gens en tant que contenu d'un droit ou d'une obligation" (p. 168).

international law whatever its objective characteristics. This view leads quickly to a rejection of various hypothetical naturalist positions under which special subcategories of international law have been posited, such as, among others, a special law of international organizations, a humanitarian law of war applicable directly to individuals and a law of international transactions between governmental and private commercial parties. In this last area there is considerable controversy, and Barberis notes that some jurists posit the existence of a *lex mercatoria* or special category of "law merchant" applicable to those transactions. He rejects the category on the ground that, if it exists, its binding force would have to derive either from public international law or the municipal law of whatever national regulatory body is seized of the case. He cites the dicta of the Permanent Court of International Justice in the *Serbian Loans* case in support of his position, but does not delve more deeply into the sources or implications of the notion of an independent *lex mercatoria.*

The second part of the course focuses solely on "private persons," within which category he includes both physical persons and collective persons, corporations, as individuals before the law. He distinguishes four situations: (1) presentation by a state of a claim on its own behalf to protect its national (including corporations); (2) creation by the states involved of a settlement procedure, typically arbitration, by which the injured "person" is authorized to present his own claim either in his own name or as the legal creation of the complaining state; (3) creation by the states involved of a settlement commission or court to which injured individuals are given direct access, typically in the European and Latin American human rights institutions; and (4) general arrangements of international organizations such as the United Nations Human Rights Committee, which can receive private persons' petitions and give them some political weight, but is not empowered to settle any claims or resolve any legal issues. A completely different approach is also mentioned under which states have occasionally, by treaty, obligated themselves to accord specified rights to foreigners in their own municipal laws.

But, departing from this mere categorization, the most interesting settlement technique seems to be what Barberis calls "les accords quasi internationaux." By that he means arrangements directly between a state and a foreign person by which a tribunal is designated and given jurisdiction over contractual disputes. Typically, the two parties, the state and the foreign enterprise, are considered equal before the law and a choice-of-law clause directs the tribunal to the body of substantive law it should find and apply. This leads to a discussion far too complex to summarize here, setting into perspective such arbitral awards as *Lena Goldfields* and *Abu Dhabi,* the three Libyan oil expropriation cases and other well-known arbitrations. The approach is positivist, severely criticizing, for example, the assertion by arbitrator Mahmassani in *LIAMCO* of a rule of *jus cogens* forbidding contractual limits on a state's power to nationalize a foreign enterprise (p. 199). But it is not clear that Barberis has kept in mind the distinction between the legal power of a state to change property rights within its territory and a contractual obligation by the state not to do so, which might not diminish its power, but could change the legal result of exercising it.

Turning to physical persons, Barberis takes the usual positivist view that even "war crimes" are essentially a matter of the obligations of states to prevent or punish atrocities by their agents. He also believes that the notion that international law applies directly to individuals is overstated, even though it was applied in some cases by Allied tribunals immediately after World War II and is embedded in some international documents, like the 1977 Protocols to the 1949 Geneva Conventions.

Chapter 2 puts the international capacities of international organizations in the same positivist perspective. Barberis regards every actor in the international arena, whether a state, transnational religious organization, belligerent, liberation movement or functional organization, as a legal order or regime independent of every other, and the international legal order as that which regulates the interaction among these separate orders (pp. 224–25). The result is a dualist model of great complexity, but easier to relate to reality than the monist models posed by others. In their external relations, international organizations that are accepted as partners to treaties or correspondence by other subjects of the international legal order are governed by the rules of that order in those relations. But he is silent regarding the most difficult issues, e.g., whether a state that does not choose to correspond with an organization of which it is not a member must accept organizational registry as shielding the individual members of the organization from direct correspondence and international responsibility for the liabilities that a state of registry would normally have for its ships or aircraft. In that case, Barberis notes merely that some organizations may have ships and aircraft flying the organizations' flags (p. 232). Finally, in this section, he addresses public international enterprises, by which he means jointly administered facilities like Cointrin airport in Geneva (France-Switzerland) and the Terneuzen Canal (Netherlands-Belgium). He finds these facilities to be governed solely by the pertinent document(s) and the laws chosen by the states that created them.

The last chapter deals with national liberation movements. It begins by asserting that in 1817 the international legal order first applied the term "belligerent" to an organized fighting unit that was not the military arm of a state engaged in a war; the assertion is not footnoted and, given the ancient origins of the concept of the laws of war applying to nonstate actors, seems either a technical quibble or wrong.[3] Similarly, the assertion that Article 3 of the 1949 Geneva Conventions gives nongovernmental parties to an armed

[3] For example, the "pirates" defeated by Pompey the Great in 67 B.C. were considered by the Roman Senate to be subordinate to Rome and not independent, but were in fact treated as honorable enemies during and after the conflict. 5 PLUTARCH, PARALLEL LIVES OF GREEKS AND ROMANS 173–77 (C. B. Perrin, trans. 1917). While the privateers of James II and Louis XIV were treated as "pirates" under English law after the abdication of 1688, their defeated soldiers after the battle of the Boyne were treated as combatants and not as criminals. See the petition of John Golding and others to the House of Lords in 1693, 12 HOWELL'S STATE TRIALS 1270, 1275 *ff.* (1816).

conflict the status of subjects of international law (p. 241) seems difficult to reconcile with the terms of that article expressly denying that its provisions affect the legal status of the parties to the conflict. However, the discussion that follows, in which the author lists many UN General Assembly declarations purporting to give international legal status to named "national liberation" movements, is placed in much better perspective by reference to the basic requirement of *opinio juris,* as distinct from political passion and repetition, for the formation of a rule of customary law. Barberis finds that the resolutions play a role in the legal regime of the United Nations and have contributed politically to the evolution of legal rules in a broader context, particularly in the drafting by the International Committee of the Red Cross of the provision of Protocol I of 1977 to the 1949 Geneva Conventions that purports to apply the general law of war to armed conflicts in which peoples are fighting against colonial domination.

Attempting to find objective characteristics that distinguish "national liberation movements" from other subjects of the classical international law of war, Barberis ultimately finds two: (1) their status is constituted by recognition; and (2) they need not control any territory. Whether this categorization will serve a useful purpose in the international legal order, or is merely political or moral, seems to be a matter about which readers may disagree.

The practical importance of distinguishing political and moral considerations from legal considerations is a major underlying theme of the course by Derek Bowett (Cambridge University), *Contemporary Developments in Legal Techniques in the Settlement of Disputes.* It begins by pointing out why states are often reluctant to permit third parties to settle their disputes at all, and why the application of substantive rules of law is frequently believed to be inappropriate. Because the "legal process" itself frequently relies on compromise, "[t]he search for certainty is misguided, and predictability of result is a myth" (p. 191), states with real interests to protect must be reluctant to give discretion to any third party. Bowett overlooks the situation in which a government, expecting to lose, will nonetheless agree to third-party settlement in order to be able to blame the loss on factors beyond its control, thus disarming a vocal constituency that has made a domestic political issue of its supposed "legal" rights to the embarrassment of the government. But that minor exception does not take away from the major point. The rest of the course is a general *tour d'horizon* of the problems of judicial settlement, from the tendency of the legal approach to attach complete blame or complete vindication to complex patterns of facts in which neither side is entirely right or wrong by any objective measure, through the increasing practice of nonappearance (the article was written before the United States withdrew from the *Nicaragua* case[4]), to enforcement. It does not go deeply into any particular matter and seems to overgeneralize some very controversial conclusions, for example: "in most juris-

[4] Military and Paramilitary Activities in and against Nicaragua (Nicar. v. U.S.), Merits, 1986 ICJ REP. 14 (Judgment of June 27).

dictions, a Sovereign State's agreement to arbitrate is deemed to be a waiver of immunity . . . [and] is generally regarded as extending to enforcement and execution of any award" (p. 220).

Another *tour d'horizon* was given in a very different subject matter by Stephen Gorove (University of Mississippi), who lectured on *International Space Law in Perspective—Some Major Issues, Trends and Alternatives.* He finds that the Bogotá Declaration, by which equatorial states claimed sovereignty up to the 35,800 kilometer-high location of stationary orbits, has not affected the activities of the space states; that the easy "spacial" demarcation of 100–110 kilometers, plus the path of vehicles mounting into or returning from space, has been accepted by many states; and that the "functional" approach that fixes no boundary but determines the legal regime by the activity involved, has been accepted by many others, though no consensus has been reached. Reviewing the Moon Treaty and other documents, and measuring them against realities, he concludes that national sovereignty can be exercised in vehicles in free space by a state of registry and that the apparent prohibition on exercising sovereignty on celestial bodies will raise a host of legal and practical problems if and when human settlements are established. Those who believe that a state could not legitimately exercise national authority will have to suggest some other way of dealing with the obvious problems of governing a human community. Turning to resource exploitation, Gorove finds enough substance in the "common heritage of mankind" phrase as adopted in the Moon Treaty to raise legal questions certainly regarding exhaustible resources, and possibly regarding even inexhaustible solar radiation, whose utilization by mankind on earth now seems on the verge of feasibility. Similarly, interpreting the words of the treaties applicable to military uses of space raises another host of unanswerable questions, where the language chosen by the treaty framers sidestepped the difficult problems rather than resolving them. With regard to registration and liability, the international agreements also refer many questions back to national authorities, and the complex choice-of-law problems implicit in their terms, as well as the complex legal regimes of states, such as the United States with its federal system, leave much discretion to administrators and little certainty in the law.[5] Finally, Gorove addresses satellite communication. In what may have been premature optimism, he suggests that if INTELSAT can expand its domestic services, the needs of the less-developed countries might be accommodated without a radical change in the current organization of space activities. In sum, this is a masterful course, hitting the high spots in comprehensible detail without much oversimplification.

Le Contrôle par les organisations internationales de l'exécution des obligations des Etats was the title of the course given by Jean Charpentier (University of Nancy). The word "contrôle" is a term of art in French, meaning rather

[5] Some indication of the causes for this situation in the negotiating process are analyzed in Rubin, *Liability for Damages from Space Activities and the Need for Domestic Legislation,* 7 AFJAG L. REV. 30 (1965). I do not like to cite my own rather outdated work in a book review, but Gorove cites very little in this section and his bibliography is slim.

more than verification and less than supervision. Doctrinally, three types of *contrôle* exist: (1) unilateral *contrôle,* by which the organs of the state itself enforce international obligations, as when the courts apply international law to municipal relations (what Scelle, in a famous phrase, called "dédoublement fonctionelle"); (2) reciprocal *contrôle,* by which the parties to a treaty react to breaches, and states whose interests are threatened by the actions of another ultimately assert rights of self-defense, in some cases through agreement of the treaty members, like the Antarctic Treaty's provisions for any party to send observers to the bases of any other in the Antarctic; and (3) institutionalized *contrôle,* by which third parties, typically international organizations, are given the authority to oversee the obligations of members. An example would be the institution of a third-party "protecting power" under the 1949 Geneva Conventions relative to the protection of the victims of armed conflict or the publication by the International Labour Organisation of national data in its annual reports on matters of concern to the Organisation's Council. There follows a categorization of the sorts of matters states submit to the *contrôle* of international organizations, and a discussion of the legal basis for that submission (ultimately, consent of the state) and the relinquishment of authority by the *contrôle* organization. Techniques of *contrôle* are analyzed, principally, but not necessarily and not exclusively, involving the receiving of information from official and, if agreed, unofficial sources; inspections, if permitted; and various degrees of external communication, from private correspondence with the agents of the state being "*contrôled,*" through in-house reportage, to general publication. Finally, the effective limits of *contrôle* are set out and it is made clear that "enforcement" by international organizations is not involved in the concept. In a final overview, Charpentier concludes that *contrôle* serves four important functions: (1) it encourages the observance of the rules of international law; (2) it identifies areas in which the transition from "soft law" to positive law is proceeding and areas in which international organizations can encourage that movement by exercising their particular powers; (3) it institutionalizes the areas of developing international cooperation, making closer cooperation easier in areas of mutual concern; and (4) it provides states with a view of things detached from purely national interest, thus encouraging the development of public institutions capable of common use. In sum, this is a fine analysis of a potentially important subject that has been rather neglected in the English-language literature.

A subject less theoretical, but equally important, is *The Protection of Minorities before the United Nations,* which was the title of the course by Felix Ermacora (University of Vienna). But because the principal document of the UN period on which Ermacora relies to translate statements of moral obligation into legal obligation is the 1966 Covenant on Civil and Political Rights (Article 27 of which forbids parties to deny persons belonging to minorities "the right, in community with the other members of their group, to enjoy their own culture, to profess and practise their own religion, or to use their own language") and the Covenant is binding as a treaty on its parties, the course goes far beyond the special world of the United Nations.

Indeed, Ermacora extends it to include the special status of "indigenous peoples" agreed on by the parties to ILO Convention No. 107.

He begins by noting the special protection given by treaty to "minorities" in the minorities treaties and various other documents directly related to the political reorganization of Europe at the end of the First World War, pointing out that they have specific objects and are not related to "human rights" as the term is understood today. He proceeds to the difficulties of defining a "minority," adopting the definition proposed by the special rapporteur for the United Nations Commission on Human Rights, Francesco Capotorti:

> Minority means a group numerically inferior to the rest of the population of a State, in a non-dominant position, whose members—being nationals of the State—possess ethnic, religious or linguistic characteristics differing from those of the rest of the population and show, if only implicitly, a sense of solidarity, directed towards preserving their culture, traditions, religion or language.

As to the content of the "rights" minorities now possess in general international law, Ermacora generalizes from various treaties relating to group rights. He asserts that the basic rights have become part of the *jus cogens,* although he presents no clear argument for that view other than citing the dicta of the International Court of Justice in the *Barcelona Traction* case affirming generally that there exist obligations *erga omnes* in the international legal order. His language is careful, but might be misleading. For example, he concludes at one point (p. 327) that "national and racial, perhaps also religious, minorities could be considered peoples in the sense of an autonomous concept of the United Nations instruments. For them self-determination is inalienable." Yes, but not because they are "minorities" but because they are "peoples" within the sense of documents other than those being examined.

His conclusions seem well supported when they relate to moral values and disputable when translating those moral values into assertions of "law." He confirms the authority of the United Nations to consider the plight of minorities as defined by Capotorti, denies that there is a single body of international law containing provisions on their protection, but asserts that "there is direct and indirect protection on the international level," finding seven particular obligations for states toward their minorities, including the prohibition of genocide, restrictions on compulsory assimilation and prohibitions on discrimination on the basis of minority "characteristics." He declares these rules to be part of the *jus cogens* but then denies that minorities as such are subjects of international law. He does not grapple directly with the question of *jus standi* but asserts—undoubtedly correctly, but, again, possibly overbroadly—that there are organizations, both states and NGOs, through which minorities can claim "rights." In sum, this is a scholarly study of an area of public international law in transition, whose author sees perhaps a stronger direction of movement and greater specificity than seems supported by the direct evidence.

A special series of lectures was given in commemoration of the fourth centenary of the birth of Hugo Grotius. The first, *Le Droit international dans la conception de Grotius,* is a very learned review by Judge Roberto Ago (International Court of Justice) of the jurisprudential mind-set evident in *De jure belli ac pacis,* which concludes that the distinctions between natural and positive law theorists today can be traced, in a sense, to Grotius's use of both a priori and a posteriori forms of reasoning, and the logical power of both. It is at least comparable to, and much more compact than, Lauterpacht's seminal work, *The Grotian Tradition in International Law.*[6]

The lecture by Hartmut Schiedermair (University of Cologne), *The Influence of Grotius' Thought on the Ius Naturale School,* is also learned, but seems so steeped in the natural law tradition itself that its interpretations are of narrower interest. For example, Schiedermair concludes, in what seem absolute terms, that it is the similarity of the 20th century's ideological antagonisms with those of the 17th century that has revitalized the memory of Grotius's thought. There is no mention of less "objective" factors, such as the search, by those holding to a certain ideal of international organization, for a source of legal authority and substantive rules that would release them from the legal constraints of their charters, and let them legislate for the world without regard for the constituency groups that inhibit the discretion of democratically elected national officials.

Willem Riphagen ("Erasmus" University, Rotterdam) lectured on *Grotius and the New Law of the Sea.* This also seems to reflect a rather unbalanced perspective. Riphagen seems unaware that the great shift in Grotius's views about *mare liberum* came not merely in his advocacy of 1613–1615, but was reflected in mature thought by at least 1632, when he wrote that the sea is subject to appropriation (*imperium*), just as the land is, by human presence or physical domination by neighboring land.[7]

Judge Antonio Truyol Serra (Constitutional Court, Madrid) spoke about *Grotius dans ses rapports avec les classiques espagnols du droit des gens.* This learned lecture, too, is marred to some degree by what seems a misunderstanding of Suárez's positivism and a surprising silence with regard to Vitoria's principal antagonist in the great debate at Valladolid in 1550–1551: Juan Ginés de Sepúlveda, probably the leading spokesman for the cultural imperialist notion of the *mission civilisatrice,* against which Grotius, like Vitoria, posed a system based on legal equality.

The final lecture, by Robert Feenstra (University of Leiden), is titled *Grotius et le droit privé européen.* It is probably of more interest to historians of private international law than to readers of this *Journal.*

One other course, although not primarily in the public international law field, deserves special mention: *Contrats entre Etats ou entreprises etatiques et personnes privées; développements récents,* by Jean-Flavien Lalive (Geneva). After categorizing a number of legal models to explain the bindingness of contracts between multinational enterprises and foreign states, and examining in some detail the opinions of the arbitrators in a number of important

[6] 23 BRIT. Y.B. INT'L L. 1 (1946).

[7] *De jure belli ac pacis,* bk. II, ch. III, sec. xiii, para. 2. I have checked the 1632 edition but have been unable to find either the 1631 or 1625 first edition.

cases, particularly the three Libyan arbitrations and *Kuwait v. Aminoil* (1982), he criticizes the political approach urged by S. B. Asante and the separation of contractual from sovereign rights urged by Sir Gerald Fitzmaurice, to argue in favor of a *lex mercatoria* model of transnational contract law existing independently of other legal orders. This course can be read side by side with the second part of Barberis's course, to see how two very eminent authorities, viewing identical data, can construct equally persuasive and totally incompatible models. Those responsible for selecting arbitrators to determine disputes, particularly contractual and expropriation disputes, between multinational enterprises and foreign governments, would do well to ponder the differences in argument the two approaches imply, and the possibility that there is no legal certainty in this area.

In another course that straddles the distinctions between private and public international law, *The Extraterritorial Effects of Antitrust Laws,* J.-G. Castel (Osgood Hall, Toronto) reviews the self-imposed jurisdictional limits of the United States, Canada and the European Community, and the "claw-back" statutes of the United Kingdom, Canada, Australia and France, to propose choice-of-law rules as a means to rationalize the conflict of national laws relating to restrictive business practices. His proposal is largely an expansion of the approach already signaled in private enforcement actions and in the *Restatement (Third)* in the United States and he approves the list proposed by Professor Andreas Lowenfeld in the 1979 Hague lectures of 10 factors to be weighed in making the choice-of-law decision. He concludes by suggesting that uniform rules be worked out by the Hague Conference on Private International Law.

Primarily descriptive, but of undoubted interest to many readers of this *Journal,* is the course by A. O. Adede (United Nations), *Legal Trends in International Lending and Investment in the Developing Countries.* Other courses at the Hague Academy in 1983 were by Olivier Long (GATT), *La Place du droit et ses limites dans le système commercial multilatéral du GATT;* Octavian Capatina (University of Bucharest), *L'Entraide Judiciaire internationale en matière civile et commerciale;* Roger Jambu-Merlin (University of Law, Economy and Social Sciences of Paris), *La Loi Applicable aux accidents du travail en droit international et en droit communautaire;* Didier Opertti Badan (University of Montevideo), *L'Adoption Internationale;* and F. Gamillscheg (University of Goettingen), *Rules of Public Order in Private International Labor Law.*

In sum, 1983 was an extraordinary year for the Hague Academy. The courses as a whole were of unusual depth and interest.

ALFRED P. RUBIN
The Fletcher School of Law and Diplomacy

Textos de Derecho internacional público. By Cesáreo Gutiérrez Espada and Alfonso-Luis Calvo Caravaca. Madrid: Editorial Tecnos, 1986. Pp. 921.

Textos de Derecho internacional público, a recent Spanish sourcebook of documents on public international law, reflects a welcome approach to teaching public international law. In addition to presenting a diverse, up-to-date set of basic public international law texts, the book highlights the Spanish perspective on international law by the judicious inclusion of materials illuminating Spain's current practice in the field. The editors are clearly intent on emphasizing to users of the book that international law is a part of Spanish law, an outlook that seems to reflect the increasing self-confidence of Spain vis-à-vis its position in the international sphere.

With the exception of the law of armed conflicts and international institutions, the book covers most of the basic topics in public international law, including sources of international law, the relation between domestic and international law, state responsibility, self-determination as an element in the formation of new states, recognition and succession of states, international protection of the individual, jurisdiction and sovereignty over territory, sea and airspace, the peaceful settlement of disputes, the use of force, disarmament, and economic cooperation and development. For each of these topics, full texts and excerpts from international court decisions, conventions and UN resolutions are given. More recent texts include the 1986 Vienna Convention on Treaties between States and International Organizations and the decision of the International Court of Justice in *Nicaragua v. United States.* Each multilateral agreement includes a useful footnote listing the parties to it.

The Spanish perspective is developed by the inclusion of certain treaties that Spain has concluded and internal legislation pursuant to international norms. Refugee law, for example, is covered not only by the UN Refugee Convention and its Protocol, but also by the 1959 European agreement on visas, the relevant provision of the Spanish Constitution and the Spanish domestic laws and decrees regulating the rights to asylum and refuge. A similar approach is taken to the law of the sea, where Spain's bilateral treaties with France and Italy concerning continental shelf delimitation and fisheries, as well as relevant Spanish domestic laws and regulations, follow the law of the sea conventions (1958, 1982). Spain's membership in the EEC is acknowledged by the inclusion of European materials, particularly in the area of human rights and extradition. Also noteworthy, with respect to the distinctly Spanish perspective of the book, is the inclusion of the Agreement on Friendship, Defense and Cooperation between the United States and Spain in the section on territorial sovereignty.

This book stands as one of the very few well-conceived and up-to-date sourcebooks on public international law available in Spanish. It should be of great interest to scholars and students in Spain, and useful generally throughout the Spanish-speaking world.

LAURA BOCALANDRO
Of the New York Bar

Sir William Scott, Lord Stowell: Judge of the High Court of Admiralty, 1798–1828. By Henry J. Bourguignon. Cambridge: Cambridge University Press, 1987. Pp. xiv, 310. Index. $49.50, cloth.

Much of the municipal law of nations begins with Sir William Scott. His decisions were introduced into the American practice of international law by such authorities as Chancellor Kent,[1] Henry Wheaton,[2] Justice Joseph Story[3] and Chief Justice John Marshall.[4] To review the early history of the practical application of the law of nations in common law jurisdictions is, in essence, to chart the career and jurisprudence of William Scott, later Lord Stowell. Henry Bourguignon has offered, with a few self-imposed limitations, an outstanding judicial biography of this most interesting judge.

Bourguignon's book concentrates on Scott's decisions in prize and civil admiralty ("instance") cases. Excluded from consideration are those opinions that he rendered on such subjects as crimes encompassed within the admiralty's jurisdiction, slave cases[5] and those treating the finer points of civil practice and procedure. The author has decided to defer discussion of these matters for later publication (p. xi). Moreover, any details of Scott's contributions to other areas of civilian practice, including ecclesiastical law, are limited to those pertinent to the biographical sketch contained in the second chapter of the book.

The author devotes his first section to a discussion of the historical development of the Admiralty Court's jurisdiction. This was a wise vehicle for exposition. Without it, the modern reader, used to the integration of admiralty jurisdiction with that of equity and law, would have been befuddled by the bitter competition in post-Tudor England between the common lawyers practicing in the courts of law and the civilians working in the admiralty and church tribunals. Indeed, the fact that these rival practices of law were reconciled at all in Britain by the 19th century can be attributed to Scott's judicial restraint. Bourguignon rejects the theory, advanced by some,[6] that Scott had an abnormal fear that a common law court would issue a writ of prohibition, thus withdrawing jurisdiction over a matter from the admiralty. Instead, he correctly places this restraint in the context of over 200 years of jurisdictional conflict and Scott's inherent conservatism (p. 251).

Scott's most significant contribution to the law of instance and prize was that he ensured that most of his decisions were published. Before his time, precedent was established by an oral tradition, through the exchange of notes of arguments and proceedings by the close-knit group of civil lawyers. One can appreciate the real effort that was involved in "finding" the law in

[1] *See* 1 J. Kent, Commentaries on American Law 69–70 (1832).

[2] *See* H. Wheaton, A Digest of the Law of Maritime Captures and Prizes (1815); H. Wheaton, Elements of International Law (G. Wilson 8th ed. 1936).

[3] Story and Scott carried on a vigorous correspondence throughout their later lives. *See* 1 W. W. Story, Life and Letters of Joseph Story 307 (1851). *See also* R. Newmyer, Supreme Court Justice Joseph Story—Statesman of the Old Republic (1985).

[4] *See* The Venus, 12 U.S. (8 Cranch) 253, 299 (1814); B. Ziegler, The International Law of John Marshall (1939).

[5] As a consequence, such famous cases as the Le Louis, 2 Dod. 210 (Adm. 1817), dealing with the right of visit on the high seas for vessels suspected of engaging in the slave trade, are not discussed.

[6] *See* F. Wiswall, The Development of Admiralty Jurisdiction and Practice since 1800, at 33 (1970).

Scott's time. But it was there. Bourguignon's fine and painstaking research shows us how often precedent was actually used, and it conclusively refutes the suggestion that Scott fashioned modern admiralty law out of whole cloth. This is a major premise of the book and the author more than adequately proves it.

As for the substantive law that Scott practiced and then judged, Bourguignon's emphasis is rightly placed on prize. One chapter is, however, dedicated to explaining Scott's forays into such areas as suits for mariners' wages, for possession and salvage, for bottomry bonds (an early form of ship mortgage) and for damages arising from collisions and personal injury. It is apparent from this discussion that Scott had a keen insight into the very risky business of shipping, a discernment revealed in his adoption of the trade's motto, "[S]hips were made to plough the ocean, and not to rot by the wall" (p. 86).[7]

Scott was truly of the old mercantilist school, an economic system and political mentality that was being challenged during the Napoleonic period, and would later be utterly supplanted by the forces of the Industrial Revolution. It nevertheless provided the most cogent theory guiding Britain's prosecution of the war against France, a war nearly global in proportion and almost total in its commitment, and consumption, of national resources. Prize law was nothing more than the judicial determination of the propriety of captures at sea of the enemy's ships and cargoes. But although dressed in the garb of an unbiased proceeding governed by the law of nations, the prize cases that Scott presided over for 30 years unquestionably implicated such high state policies as treatment of neutral powers, the ways and means of preserving and expanding the colonial trade, and the most essential matter of winning the war against Napoleon.

Bourguignon divides his analysis of Scott's prize jurisprudence into a long chapter on the law of nationality, the determination of enemy character essential in any capture, and another section dealing with such doctrines as neutral rights and duties, contraband, blockade and colonial trade. The treatment of these subjects is quite good, if a bit mechanical with its consideration, in turn, of 18th-century precedent and Scott's contributions as an advocate and jurist.

Unfortunately, this doctrinal discussion is not illustrated with any assessment of Scott's impact on later courts and publicists, particularly in American practice. Prize law is portrayed as a historical relic. In one sense, of course, it is. The last prizes adjudicated in this country's courts were in 1948.[8] Owing to the nature of modern naval warfare, one can legitimately wonder if any lawyer will have recourse to cite Scott's prize decisions. In another sense, however, certain doctrines espoused by Scott, particularly in the law of nationality and domicile, continue to influence (some might say haunt) us today.[9]

[7] The Apollo, 1 Hag. 306, 312 (Adm. 1824).

[8] *See* United States v. The EUROPA, 80 F.Supp. 12 (S.D.N.Y. 1948); Ling v. 1,689 Tons of Coal, 78 F.Supp. 57 (W.D. Wash. 1948).

[9] Scott's opinion in The Young Jacob and Johanna, 1 C. Rob. 20 (Adm. 1798), had to be distinguished in that most sublime of decisions, The Paquete Habana, 175 U.S. 677, 693–94

Even though we are not privileged with the author's sense of how Scott's legal innovations were later received, he does give us a vision of their contemporaneous relevance. A peculiar glaucoma, however, clouds this vision in several ways. The first, and perhaps of most interest here, is Scott's addition to the understanding of international law. By education and professional affiliation, Scott seemed to be an enthusiastic advocate of the law of nations. But was he really? That he relied on the early publicists of our discipline, such men as Grotius, Vattel and Bynkershoek, is unquestioned. That he was rooted firmly in the natural law theories espoused by these writers and believed that they collectively established the "moral limits of international relations" (p. 141) is undoubted. What can be disputed is whether Scott viewed the law of nations as anything but a static and unchanging entity. An elemental theory of custom seemed to have eluded him. This is especially apparent from Scott's handling of blockade cases, an area of law that, arguably, he created (p. 205). Bourguignon conveys no sense of Scott's having any appreciation of his own role as a maker of international law.

A second problem is in assessing Scott's judicial temperament. This is essential since the author declares that Scott's "fame rests entirely upon his success as an admiralty judge" (p. 50). If success were measured by longevity or number of opinions, Scott would be deemed a great judge. If he were judged by his impartiality and ability to withstand political influence, he would be considered less favorably. Chief Justice Marshall's statement that it was "impossible to consider [Scott's prize decisions] attentively without perceiving that his mind leans strongly in favor of the captors"[10] shows the two sides of the man. It is apparent that Scott toadied for his peership, acted as a lackey for the Portland Government by speaking in Parliament for the controversial Orders-in-Council (p. 219) and generally comported himself in a rather nonjudicial way. He was a reactionary, to boot.

But he also believed in reason, the right reason that enabled nations to coexist under the rule of law. When Marshall spoke of Scott's mind, he meant it in that pure Enlightenment way. And Scott had a very different mind, assuredly, from that of Jeremy Bentham, who made our modern "international law,"[11] a neologism that Scott likely loathed. In Marshall's measure of Scott we have reason coupled with prejudice.

All this means, of course, is that Scott was a thoroughly 18th-century Englishman. No better or worse, for that matter, than William Blackstone or Samuel Johnson. Unfortunately, Scott found himself on the bench at a rather uncivilized time. He did his best, as Bourguignon explains, to accommodate his limited conception of the law of nations within a broad horizon of extraordinary lawlessness. Like those today who are expected to uphold the laws of war on the battlefield, Scott had an unenviable job.

(1900) (Gray, J.), which ruled that coastal fishing vessels may not be taken as prize. *See also id.* at 719 (Fuller, C. J., dissenting). Another example of Scott's influence is his decision in The Indian Chief, 3 C. Rob. 12, 29, 165 Eng. Rep. 367, 374 (Adm. 1801), which spawned a remarkable debate on the law of extraterritorial domicile.

[10] The Venus, 12 U.S. (8 Cranch) 253, 299 (1814).

[11] *See* Janis, *Jeremy Bentham and the Fashioning of "International Law,"* 78 AJIL 405 (1984).

Bourguignon's study should initiate a fruitful reconsideration of Scott's influence on today's international law. Although the book features some repetitiveness and disjointed writing (plainly the product of being written in segments), and also suffers from mediocre indexing and the lack of a table of cases, it will undoubtedly become the modern authority on Sir William Scott's prize jurisprudence. Bourguignon is no apologist. He does what we would expect of any self-respecting biographer: he comes to like his subject.

DAVID J. BEDERMAN
Of the Georgia Bar

United Nations Codification of State Responsibility. Edited by Marina Spinedi and Bruno Simma. New York, London, Rome: Oceana Publications, Inc., 1987. Pp. xi, 418. Index. $75.

Scholars and international lawyers are just beginning to understand the magnitude of the International Law Commission's work on state responsibility. We are deeply in debt to Marina Spinedi and Bruno Simma for giving us better access to this work through the volume of studies of important themes in the codification by eight young continental scholars. Funded by the Hague Academy of International Law in 1982, these studies present for the first time in one volume an in-depth analysis and appraisal of the most significant portions of the Commission's work to date.

The Commission's unabashed ambition for the progressive development and codification of state responsibility for internationally wrongful acts has astonished observers more for its persistent abstractness than for its apparent utility. As the editors caution, however, this tendency to yawn at the work misses completely the seriousness of the ILC's mission to embrace all of the rules and consequences governing the breach of any international obligation of the state. Apart from the great German and French codifications, one of the most comprehensive projects occurred when Emperor Theodosius II assembled his commission of nine learned publicists in A.D. 429 to collect the imperial edicts from the time of Constantine and codify them and the Novels. His decree stated that "the laws to be observed throughout the world should be arranged in a compendium of sixteen books." Shortly after the 9-year project was done, the Western Empire was undone. With greater hope, the editors see more in the ILC's work than most skeptical Americans have: "No other codification project," they write in the introduction, "goes so deeply into the 'roots', the theoretical and ideological foundations of international law, or has created comparable problems."

By design, the Commission's work does not codify the substantive rules of state responsibility, except in the separate project on strict liability. The main codification, however, builds a concealed structure of baroque complexity and detail, encasing many philosophical and political assumptions yet to be fleshed out. Doubt about the resulting strictures reminds one of Savigny's objections to the codification of German law in the Roman law tradition, fearing too soon an end to the creative spirit of German custom and a stultifying effect upon the growth of the law as part of the national spirit. While addressing the most important of the structural decisions of the ILC's codification project, the collection remains free from overt ideology except now and then to expose a political or theoretical assumption. Inescapably, we are led to a wonderfully rich, but concealed, dimension about political and economic values in an emerging global society. This discussion might ensue from any of the main topics studied such as the legitimacy of countermeasures and self-defense as responses to delicts, the difference in international responsibility between crimes and delicts, the new role of peremptory norms (seemingly pervasive) on the customary law of state responsibility, whether damages constitute part of the wrongful act, and the different consequences of moral, in contrast to material, damages. The ILC's work deserves this worthy inquiry, whether or not it is a premature gloss on deeper structural stirrings.

The ILC's project on state responsibility began in 1955 with the appointment of Dr. F. V. García-Amador, special rapporteur, to tackle a manageable topic with a narrow focus on injuries to aliens, a subject with much traditional content. After six reports and unease on the part of the Sixth Committee, the ILC broadened the work to its present scope, appointing Professor Roberto Ago as special rapporteur. He submitted eight reports on the comprehensive codification of the origin of responsibility without any substantive primary rules. By 1980, the Commission adopted on first reading his part 1, 35 articles heavily annotated with some of the densest commentary ever published by the Commission. It covered the subjective act of the state (attribution, wrongly considered a subject apt to glaze eyes) and objective breach of the rules of obligation (infuriatingly never defined, but eternally present). With Ago's election to the World Court, Professor Willem Riphagen took over, presenting seven reports that attempted greater clarity in defining regimes of responsibility, and began the work of part 2, on legal consequences of breach, including a possible part 3 on implementation and procedures for settlement of breaches of international obligation. Professor Gaetano Arangio-Ruiz succeeded Riphagen, no doubt aware of the need again to reappraise, possibly to strengthen, the remedies side of state responsibility.

Ten years ago, the ILC decided to treat separately the problem of strict liability for injurious activities not prohibited by international law. It appointed Mr. R. Quentin-Baxter special rapporteur, and from 1980 to 1984, he submitted five reports before his death. Mr. Julio Barboza has continued the work with three reports so far, including six draft articles in his latest report to the Commission in 1987.

Only one study in the book, responsibility for nuclear energy, analyzes in depth the substantive problem of the allocation of the risk of harm from hazardous activities when no wrong is present. Who bears the cost when highly technical industrial activities providing social goods result in transboundary harm to the human environment? This problem confronts difficult questions of both substance and process in allocating the costs of these activities. The author of this study, Angelo Miatello, concludes that states seem willing to codify the obligation to make compensation for such damage, at least in the abstract, relying on the *Trail Smelter* doctrine. The nuclear accident at Chernobyl illustrates how easy it is for a benign theory of responsibility (for example, separating moral and material damage) to allow a major power to pass on to other countries the social costs of serious and irreversible transborder damage, especially nuclear damage. Toxic pollution from major industrial powers, more insidiously diffuse but no less dangerous to the global environment, transfers the social costs of its harmful effects to later generations and to powerless people everywhere. Miatello's study does not appraise the Chernobyl accident, which occurred after the study was completed. The problems of acid rain and the effect of pollutants on the global climate also present this general question of allocating the cost of transborder harm to the human environment.

Wrongful acts, in contrast to those not prohibited, that involve nuclear energy and cause serious damage to the human environment would fall under the general codification, not as "ordinary" delicts but as "international crimes," according to Miatello. We see here glimpses of how difficult it is to produce a general and comprehensive codification of state responsibility without considering the substance of the rules of obligation. How does the difference between crimes and delicts help clean up the global environment? Though the editors did not include Miatello's study of nuclear energy for any such strategic purpose, I think it shows the inevitable linkages between the special project on strict liability for nonprohibited acts and the general project on responsibility for wrongful acts.

Where, for example, would the Bhopal incident fall? Is the United States responsible for failure to control by regulation the private export of a hazardous technology involving a complex manufacturing process? Is any such failure of duty wrongful? Would the United States have responsibility under the *Trail Smelter* theory for the transboundary risk of hazardous enterprise? What responsibility would India have? Indeed, one might argue that throughout the comprehensive law of state responsibility, the only significant theoretical question ought to be which polity or group of polities and their nationals should bear the social costs of activities attributed to the state under some duty. These costs would include the risks from ultrahazardous activities as well as risks of harm from other activities. The question of international obligation or duty is too metaphysical and moralistic if it fails to address that question. The function of satisfying moral damage or repairing material damage more closely resembles what Roscoe Pound called the general security interest in controlling private self-help and the function of compensation as buying off private feuds to keep the peace. It does not adequately consider the allocation of cost to future generations.

If we pose the problem initially as a question of the allocation of the social costs of certain internationally harmful activities, then we may lessen the propensity to invent a monopoly to authorize collective sanctions against "international crimes" by states, in other contexts called police actions or just wars or community-authorized countermeasures. Manfred Mohr's lucid study of the distinction between international delicts and international crimes from a socialist point of view strongly supports the position taken in Article 19 of part 1 of the general study and favors keeping it. The study of strict liability is strategic because it shows how the more comprehensive codification simply hides similar allocation-of-risk-of-harm decisions in the language of serious or not so serious moral and material damage. The paper by Attila Tanzi thus examines the ILC's proposal of responsibility without material damage and the forms for reparations, raising the question also addressed in other papers whether responsibility entails the duty to pay compensation or merely a set of secondary legal consequences among which are the possibility of moral satisfaction, the duty to entertain a diplomatic claim and the immediate duty to pay reparations for material damage.

Riccardo Pisillo Mazzeschi examines the important question of state responsibility for the breach of treaty and the relationship to the remedy for breach (suspension and termination) codified in the Vienna Convention on the Law of Treaties. Here is seen the influence of the Roman law that treats both contracts and delicts under the law of obligations in contrast with the contemporary distinction between treaty and customary international law. The consequence is an important one, for if treaty breach also entails international responsibility, then a regime of countermeasures might be available in addition to suspension or termination. The author believes the ILC here completes its otherwise imperfect work in the codification of treaty law.

The other studies develop a better understanding of the ILC's main doctrines than is available elsewhere in one place. The themes build toward a unified structure of responsibility within the fabric of the nation-state system. Much of this edifice rests upon a highly abstract foundation whose assumptions seem grounded in Kantian dualism. Subjective autonomy of will, making up an act of a state, finds expression in part 1, the articles determining the origin of responsibility when conduct is attributed to the state as the primary subject of international law. This identity of individual subjective will with the state as person through the doctrine of attribution constitutes the origin or the beginning point in the legal possibility of a state's responsibility for a wrongful act. The wrongfulness of the act occurs when the subjective act breaches an objective primary norm of obligation. At that moment when the subjective act encounters the objective regime resulting in breach of obligation, an internationally wrongful act springs into "existence" with new legal consequences. The secondary norms governing satisfaction, reparations or countermeasures create new obligations occasioned by breach.

Within this framework, the various studies analyze and appraise the doctrine. Two of the best papers are revisions of earlier published studies on countermeasures and self-defense in state responsibility. Denis Alland's work, especially, develops the linkages of the codification to political and legal theory, but with too little critical appraisal of the Kantian (Kelsen) and Hegelian (Jhering) assumptions identified. That paper stands out as one of the least technical and most valuable of the studies. Peter Malanczuk's study relates the doctrinal meaning of countermeasures and self-defense in the codification project to traditional concepts of sanctions (such as self-help, reprisal and retortion) and to UN law on the use of force. These areas need greater attention in light of the World Court decision in *Nicaragua v. United States* (decided after the study was written), now in its reparations phase, further developing the law of countermeasures and self-defense as part of state responsibility.

The problem of intertemporal law, taken up by Wolfram Karl, both in the moment and duration of the delict and in the question of time of damage and its extension into the future, suggests relativity between generations and between cultures and ideologies. Interestingly, *jus cogens superveniens* is introduced into his discussion with some skepticism over its intertemporal use such as in wars of national liberation and self-determination. "Only a fundamental change in the most basic convictions of international society should exempt a State from its responsibility for previous acts." Freeing slaves of a ship in harbor several hundred years ago formed an international wrong. Today, freeing slaves (freeing coerced labor?) would be not only lawful but also mandatory under principles of *jus cogens*.

Hazem Atlam's study criticizes the neutral principles argument of the equivalence of attribution of responsibility for conduct of insurrectional movements and for national liberation movements to later governments or states. Attribution of wrongful acts by a defeated government is not the same in each case. For successful insurrections, responsibility is attributed for acts of the defeated government. For successful liberation movements, Atlam argues that the succeeding government might not be responsible for the acts of the defeated government. Again, the ideological grounding of this criticism of the ILC draft articles reveals a consciousness that needs critical appraisal in scholarship.

Especially useful to scholars in reaching the deeper policy considerations are appendixes containing all draft articles to 1985 and synoptical tables of reference to all ILC and General Assembly proceedings on the various drafts and commentaries. A bibliography of 178 titles covers extant scholarly studies (mostly European) of the codification project by the ILC. A systematic classification of these studies provides an immediate aid to research, one of the most convenient references in the volume. A good index integrates subjects across the various studies.

This collection of papers by European scholars ought to spur American and other scholarship on this important codification. The editors in particular should be congratulated for presenting studies of the codification themes that no longer can find repose in the bureaucrat's drawer.

GORDON A. CHRISTENSON
University of Cincinnati College of Law

La Codification de la succession d'Etats aux traités: Décolonisation, sécession, unification. By Zidane Mériboute. Paris: Presses Universitaires de France, 1984. Pp. 272. F.135.

This is a well-conceived and detailed study of the history of the codification of the law of state succession as it relates to treaties, and will be useful to the French-reading scholar of the law of state succession as that law has now been embodied in and expressed by the Vienna Convention of 1978. It reviews the state practice on the question and contains a detailed review of the codification efforts of the International Law Commission and the discussions that took place in the Sixth Committee in the early part of the 1970s, which culminated in the 1978 Convention.[1] The book contains a solid exposition of the different and conflicting values and perceptions underlying the development of this important multilateral treaty and reflecting the contrasting schools of thought between north and south, east and west, during the period in question; it contains a lucid and carefully researched exposition of the debates and varying positions on the several important points in the Convention.

The book is essentially divided into three parts. First, a general introduction sets forth in summary form the principal theories of state succession in the matter of treaties espoused over the years and also the conflicting opinions as voiced in the International Law Commission. As is well known, the significant element that haunted each aspect of the Commission's work and the later travails of the delegations in the drafting of the actual Convention was the question how far a state should be bound by the undertakings of its predecessor: the so-called question of the *tabula rasa* or "*le principe de la table rase.*" This problem acquired peculiar importance and sensitivity following the massive decolonizations of the early 1960s, and, indeed, was the *fons et origo* of the codification effort itself. The dead hand of the former imperial and colonial powers was seen to persist in the tangled web of international agreements inherited by the newly independent states from their colonial masters, with the result that the debate over the law of state succession became imbued with complex ideological colorations in the two postcolonial decades of the 1960s and 1970s. This reviewer recalls, from personal experience, how even an advanced newly independent state such as Ghana was baffled and beset, in the early 1960s, by complex decisions about which treaty arrangements it wished to inherit and which it wished to disavow.

The introduction is followed by a detailed analysis of the law of state succession (in the matter of treaties) relating to the creation of a new state, normally by decolonization or a similar grant of independence, but also in instances of (subsequent) secession such as the cases of Pakistan (1947), Singapore (1965) and Bangladesh (1971). The fact that the vast majority of decolonizing situations occurred well before 1978 underscores the obvious recognition that history had already run its course as far as most newly independent states were concerned by the time the Convention was in fact signed.[2]

[1] Vienna Convention on Succession of States in Respect of Treaties, UN Doc. A/CONF.80/31 and Corr.1 (1978).

[2] "[O]n peut ajouter le fait que la partie de la Convention concernant les Etats nouvellement indépendants est inutile à l'heure actuelle, puisque la plupart des pays sont décolonisés" (p. 218).

This lends specific interest to the third part of Mériboute's study, which deals with the complex situations attending instances of annexation, union and dissolution of states. A businesslike conclusion follows. There is also a detailed and useful bibliography, and two annexes (the 1978 Convention and the 1974 draft articles proposed by the International Law Commission, given in their French form). The only glaring flaw is that there is no trace of an index;[3] this may perhaps be occasioned by the typically detailed continental table of contents, but it is, nonetheless, inexplicable in a work of this class, published by the Graduate Institute of International Studies in Geneva and the Presses Universitaires de France.

This book therefore occupies an interesting and important niche in the scholarship on the law of state succession. It is particularly important for at least two reasons. First, it contains a thorough study of the opposition of various points of view, in the ILC and the convention debates; objective and useful summaries of the negotiating positions of the various representatives and delegations; and useful references to the speakers and their specific interventions on the several issues at various times.[4] Mériboute also distinguishes between the kinds of rules applicable to different types of international obligations: institutional, lawmaking, normative, synallagmatic, bilateral and so forth.

Second, it is a work by a distinguished scholar from the Third World—in particular, from Algeria, a country whose travails for independence from its metropolitan power were long, bitter and hard fought. It therefore offers an interesting perspective, touching on a number of aspects of the views of states that were former colonial territories on the question of the degree to which they should be bound by decisions of their former colonial masters; it creates a natural interest and sympathy in the reader for the plight of the new countries. It is able to do this, moreover, because Mériboute is remarkably objective and free from evident bias of any kind. It is commendable for a scholar from the Third World to be able to deal with such a complex subject that has aroused so many sensitive reactions, in a manner that is completely free of "Third World rhetoric" and argumentative distortion of any sort.[5] It is reassuring to see how professional balance can overcome what must otherwise have been a strong predisposition toward a given point of view; it is instructive to observe that the author's message gets across far more effectively and thoughtfully when presented objectively and dispas-

[3] Continental scholars would do well to remember that a detailed work of scholarship is only as good as its index, and that the lack of one will necessitate more work on the part of the reader than is saved on the part of the author and his editor.

[4] Indeed, one cavil with the author's style is that *too much* is given to footnotes. This reviewer is pluperfectly allergic to end notes, and is therefore grateful for the author's use of notes at the foot of each page, but, nevertheless, in many instances, one can spot interesting matter submerged in the footnotes, as well as the secondary reference, that could probably have been embodied in the text.

[5] This contrasts quite sharply with another recent book on state succession by an Ethiopian scholar on a particular aspect of state succession and the "East African solutions": Yilma Makonnen's book on *International Law and the New States of Africa* (1983): *which see* at 364, 373–74, 406 and review (by this reviewer) at 80 AJIL 242, 245 and 245 n.8 (1986).

sionately than when clouded with rhetoric and bias. The injunction is again confirmed that it is usually best to let matters speak for themselves.

This is also one of the first overall surveys of the build-up to the work of the International Law Commission and the fate of its draft articles as they were amended through the Vienna conferences leading up to the 1978 Convention. It is certainly a useful book for the scholar of this area of the law, as well as for the student of the work of the ILC and the international treaty-making process since the Second World War. It is a relatively specialized overview, however, since the subject of which it provides such a useful survey is itself specialized. It is perhaps too detailed for the general reader, although the scope and accuracy of the scholarship appear to be excellent.[6] It contains brief summaries of the state practice in the field in the context of various aspects of state independence, and short résumés of the historical theory and practice relating to this subject. This is not enough solid food for the in-depth scholar of state succession outside the codification history of the 1970s, but the book contains sufficiently appetizing material, coupled with expansive references to secondary works and other sources, to serve as a useful guide in the area.

Mériboute's contribution is an excellent addition to the practitioner's bookshelf if he or she is concerned with the specifics of what has happened to the law of treaty succession since the 1960s, and specifically with the results and salient details of the codification effort of 1978. In summary, it is valuable not only as a compendium of what happened, but also as a sourcebook for further research into the primary sources of the debates and positions that led up to the codification achievement of 1978.

KEITH HIGHET
Of the New York Bar

Vergleich und Klagerücknahme im internationalen Prozeß. By Gerhard Wegen. Berlin: Duncker & Humblot, 1987. Pp. 484. DM 188.

This doctoral thesis from Tübingen is the first monograph on a topic of great practical importance—the various forms of settlement and discontinuance of international proceedings. The author analyzes with great subtlety the relevant rules of 40 treaties and draft projects that aim at establishing an international dispute settlement machinery for interstate litigation as well as for disputes involving private parties. In a first, general part, the author explains the basic characteristics that distinguish international proceedings from those before national tribunals. He avoids the mistake of most of the

[6] It is, however, regrettable that the publisher was not able to have the book properly proofread. Although its format is very polished, it contains a large number of typographical errors that distract even an English-speaking reader and that could have been easily avoided without too much more effort: the spelling, for example, of Professor D. P. O'Connell's name is given in at least two variants, an error that, in the matter of state succession scholarship, is inexcusable. This, like the lack of an index, is sheer inefficiency; one wishes that such an excellent study will, in a future edition, receive more careful polishing.

relatively few authors who, before him, have dealt with aspects of the problems discussed in his book. These authors approached their subject from the viewpoint of their domestic procedural law and used the latter as a basis for their comparison. Wegen realizes that the basis of international proceedings is radically different from that governing proceedings under domestic law. Whether the international adjudicating entity is permanent like the International Court of Justice or established ad hoc or semipermanent, i.e., established by individual acts in accordance with permanent rules, like the arbitral tribunals established pursuant to the ICSID Convention,[1] its authority to settle the dispute depends on the sovereign will of the litigants. The very existence of the tribunal will come to an end if the agreement between the parties establishing its jurisdiction is terminated either by a subsequent agreement by the parties or for other reasons, e.g., lapse of time. In such cases, the will of the parties may often lead to a *perpetuatio fori.* Thus, the Permanent Court of International Justice and the ICJ continued to hear and decide cases even after the end of the period for which the respondent had accepted the Court's jurisdiction in virtue of the optional clause. The author finds it remarkable (p. 88) that in all but one of these cases, the Court, on the merits, found for the respondent. In the case of semipermanent instances directly accessible also to private individuals, such termination poses the problem of the fate of cases still pending at that time. In some instances, the tribunal retained authority to wind up such cases; in others, the individual claimant was deprived of the remedy granted to him, e.g., in some minority treaties after World War I. The author mentions this problem (p. 76). A discussion in detail, however, would fall outside his terms of reference.

The author shows hard-boiled realism in doubting whether machinery conceived to enable international adjudicatory bodies to render an award in spite of nonparticipation of the impleaded party will, indeed, end the dispute between the litigants. International adjudication remains based on agreement between the litigants. Therefore, even a permanent international tribunal will lose its jurisdiction in a given case if the case is settled or discontinued. The author rejects (p. 177) the idea advanced, inter alia, by Georges Scelle, that the tribunal should continue the proceedings where the settlement reached would be contrary to international public policy.

According to the author, an arbitration clause will survive the fate of the rest of the treaty concerned. Such survival is said to result from the fact that the jurisdiction of the tribunal is based on an international agreement. According to Article 70(b) of the Vienna Convention on the Law of Treaties, the termination of a treaty does not affect any right, obligation or legal situation of the parties created through the execution of the treaty prior to its termination. The author's reliance on this rule implies that he qualifies an arbitration clause as executed rather than as an executory obligation (p. 93).

[1] Convention on the Settlement of Investment Disputes between States and Nationals of Other States, *done* Mar. 18, 1965, 17 UST 1270, TIAS No. 6090, 575 UNTS 159.

The author deems it redundant to end a dispute by a consent judgment, unless the parties in a dispute of a commercial nature are contemplating rendering the terms of the settlement executory in domestic courts.

As far as discontinuance is concerned, the author, after a careful analysis of the drafting history of the rules of procedure of the PCIJ and ICJ, and of the amendments thereto, rejects the view that such discontinuance must be based on an agreement between the parties. As long as the respondent party has not yet taken any step in the proceedings, the applicant may end the proceedings unilaterally. Otherwise, the respondent must acquiesce either explicitly or by implication. However, such activity or inactivity of the respondent is said not to amount to an agreement with the applicant (pp. 286–88). To this reviewer, this appears to be a rather formalistic distinction. An order of the ICJ concerning discontinuance is held to be *res judicata* only as to this procedural effect, but not as to the material points at issue between the parties (p. 300). This reviewer has always felt some sympathy with Spain's grievance that Belgium, by discontinuing the first proceedings in the *Barcelona Traction* case after Spain had submitted preliminary objections, gained an unfair advantage over Spain, which by Belgium's application had been induced to unmask its batteries. Again, this preoccupation falls outside the author's terms of reference.

The author, however, had to draw the line somewhere. His comparative effort merits high praise. After having explained the theoretical bases of any settlement and discontinuance, he thoroughly discusses all procedural problems that may arise in efforts to end proceedings by settlement or discontinuance. He begins by commenting on the authority to offer a settlement and ends with the order or consent judgment declaring the case settled or discontinued. For each such step, the author describes the solution found in the rules of procedure of the various tribunals, as well as the practice concerning the relevant rules and their discussion by commentators. He shows that no general principles of international procedural law can be deduced from this material, although there are many parallels in the solutions found by tribunals confronted with more or less similar situations. The field encompassed by the author is very wide and divergent. Yet he fits these elements neatly into the above-mentioned step-by-step system followed in this main part of his book. His deductive impetus leads him sometimes to establish distinctions that may appear hardly relevant to a pragmatic mind. However, insofar as parts of the matters dealt with by the author have been discussed at all by earlier commentators, these scholars, too, were trained in or influenced by the school of legal reasoning developed in Italy and France prior to World War I. Even if the facts of most leading cases thus are banished into the footnotes, Wegen's work is an outstanding contribution to international procedural law and will be a great help to any practitioner, not only in the field of interstate adjudication, but also in the much wider field of international arbitration.

IGNAZ SEIDL-HOHENVELDERN
University of Vienna

Die Kompetenzen des UN-Menschenrechtsausschusses im Staatenberichtsverfahren (Art. 40 des Internationalen Paktes über bürgerliche und politische Rechte). By Hans-Michael Empell. Frankfurt am Main, Bern, New York: Peter Lang, 1987. Pp. viii, 294. Sw.F.65.

This book tries to clarify the meaning of Article 40 of the International Covenant on Civil and Political Rights, which governs the Covenant's most important implementation mechanism: the state reporting procedure. In the first chapter, which serves as the introduction, the author gives some examples of the sometimes far-reaching "general comments" (Art. 40(4)) of the Human Rights Committee. For instance, the Committee has interpreted the right to life (Art. 6 of the Covenant) rather broadly to include a supreme duty of states to prevent wars, stating that the production, testing, possession, development and use of atomic weapons should be qualified as crimes against humanity.

The second chapter discusses whether and to what extent the Human Rights Committee has investigative competence or whether it is limited to requesting and reading the reports prepared by the states concerned (Art. 40(1)(a) and (b)). Another problem is how to deal with incomplete reports. The solution seems to be provided by Article 40(1)(b), according to which "the States Parties undertake to submit reports . . . whenever the Committee so requests." This can be understood as including requests for additional information if an incomplete report has been submitted. According to Empell's rather sophisticated analysis, subparagraphs (a) and (b) of Article 40(1) apply by analogy in case of incomplete reports. The author maintains that the Committee may request reports under Article 40(1)(b) "whenever" the situation in a country implies that there is a particular danger to human rights. He deduces this additional and unwritten requirement under Article 40(1)(b) from the principle of equal treatment of states.

As for the use of information other than that officially submitted by the states concerned, Empell suggests that "studying," as opposed to "examining," excludes any investigative functions. The Committee is limited to the material handed in by the states concerned. The Committee usually invites state delegates to discuss the reports. "Such a representative should be able to answer questions which may be put to him by the Committee and make statements on reports already submitted by his State, and may also submit additional information from his State" (Rule 68, sentence 4). Empell stresses, rightly, that the Rules of Procedure cannot confer any additional competence on the Committee. However, Rule 68 corresponds to an established state practice. Therefore, the author's thesis that only the individual member of the Committee, as opposed to the Committee as an institution, is entitled to discuss the reports with the state delegates seems overly sophisticated. In Empell's opinion, the Committee, as opposed to its members, is limited to taking cognizance of the information provided by the states concerned (p. 100).

Chapter 3 deals with potential reactions of the Human Rights Committee after studying the reports. Three important questions are raised: (1)

whether the term "its reports" in Article 40(4) of the Covenant refers to the reports submitted by the states or whether the Committee may prepare its own reports; and, if the latter, (2) what kinds of reports the Committee may work out; and (3) whether the "general comments" by the Committee include comments addressed to individual states or only comments addressed to the member states in general. Article 40(4) of the Covenant reads in part: "The Committee shall study the reports submitted by the States Parties to the present Covenant. It shall transmit *its reports,* and such general comments as it may consider appropriate, to the States Parties . . ." (emphasis added). On the basis of a convincing analysis of the wording, object and purpose, as well as of the preparatory work, of Article 40 of the Covenant, Empell adheres to the prevailing view that "its reports" refers to reports prepared by the Committee itself.

As for the content of "its reports," the author rejects the restrictive opinion that the Committee may only summarize the reports submitted by the states parties or that these would be identical to the Committee's annual reports. Empell compares the wording of Article 40(4) of the Covenant with the terminology of other humanitarian treaties. Usually, annual reports are clearly referred to as such. He infers that "its reports" includes particular reports by the Committee about the reports submitted by each of the states parties, taking into account the discussion with that state's representative. The reports focus on setting forth the facts, even though, as the author explains, the Committee may evaluate the human rights situation in the country concerned. However, this evaluation must not go so far as to state that there have been violations of the Covenant.

Empell distinguishes between the reports of the Committee and its "general comments" under Article 40(4) of the Covenant. "General comments" certainly exclude comments on concrete individual cases (p. 152). Moreover, the author holds that the preparatory work of the treaty, as well as general practice within the United Nations, supports the position that the term "general comments" was used in order to prevent singling out individual states. A comprehensive comparison with the meaning of similar terminology in other international reporting procedures confirms this view. Empell concludes that Rule 70(3) of the Committee, pursuant to which it may determine "that some of the obligations of that State Party under the Covenant have not been discharged," is void.

The next section deals with the object and purpose of the reporting procedure, which does more than simply provide states an opportunity to inform each other about human rights matters. The author, rather, adheres to the prevailing view that the Committee has supervisory functions. He points out that control is more effective if the reports are as concrete as possible. Therefore, Empell concludes that the Committee may criticize individual member states in its reports, which it has no right to do in its "general comments" (pp. 219, 231). According to Article 40(5), "States Parties . . . may submit to the Committee observations on any comments . . . made in accordance with paragraph 4." Empell applies Article 40(5) by analogy to the Committee's reports. This seems reasonable. The Committee's reports are of greater interest than its general comments because only the reports may refer to individual states.

In sum, the author has written a thoroughly researched dissertation on the state reporting procedure under Article 40 of the International Covenant on Civil and Political Rights. The book is stimulating because Empell points to so many questions that, probably owing to political considerations, remain unresolved, even though the Committee has now been operating for more than 10 years. His results are based on a careful analysis of the Committee's practice after discussing the different and often conflicting positions of its members and groups of members. The author also draws extensively on the preparatory work of Article 40 of the Covenant and demonstrates many useful parallels with other systems for the promotion or protection of human rights. It would be difficult to find another study on the subject as profound as this one.

JULIA B. KOKOTT
Max Planck Institute for Comparative Public Law and International Law, Heidelberg
Harvard Law School

The United States and the Compulsory Jurisdiction of the International Court of Justice. Edited by Anthony Clark Arend. Lanham, New York, London: University Press of America; Charlottesville: The Center for Law and National Security, 1986. Pp. ix, 250. $26.50, cloth; $14.25, paper.

Judging the World Court. By Thomas M. Franck. New York: Priority Press Publications, 1986. Published under the auspices of the Twentieth Century Fund. Pp. vii, 112. $8.50.

These two works are part of the continuing and necessary debate about the attitude the United States should adopt toward the International Court of Justice. Each contains a valuable substantive analysis of the problem, as well as suggestions for the future.

The first of the two works, *The United States and the Compulsory Jurisdiction of the International Court of Justice,* consists of papers and proceedings of a workshop sponsored by the Center for Law and National Security at Charlottesville, which was held in August 1985. In this, as in the second work, *Judging the World Court,* a single-author study by Professor Thomas Franck, the starting point is the fact that the United States continues to be bound by an extensive range of acceptances of the Court's compulsory jurisdiction by reason of the inclusion, in some 60 or so treaties to which the United States is a party, of dispute settlement provisions contemplating compulsory recourse to the International Court of Justice under Article 36(1) of the Court's Statute. As it is not within the power of the United States unilaterally to terminate these undertakings, the debate is limited to the question of the extent to which, if at all, the United States should reinstate its acceptance of the Court's compulsory jurisdiction under Article 36(2), the "optional clause."

The two principal approaches are both reflected in the Charlottesville papers. There are, first, those who favor the reestablishment, though to only a limited extent, of the U.S. acceptance of the optional clause. Thus, Professor Louis Sohn, starting from the position that there should be some U.S. acceptance of the optional clause jurisdiction, proposes a draft declaration that (among other things) would exclude from the Court's jurisdiction not, as in the past, "disputes which are essentially within the domestic jurisdiction of the United States of America as determined by the United States of America," but "disputes with regard to matters which, traditionally, in the practice of the United States" have been considered as essentially within its domestic jurisdiction. He also suggests the exclusion of disputes relating to "any question which affects the national security" of the United States or of a state party to a collective security arrangement to which the United States is also a party. A comparable stance is adopted by Professor Fred Morrison, who additionally identifies the need to exclude from the Court's jurisdiction disputes that "are properly exclusively within the jurisdiction of the Security Council." Other suggestions include that of Monroe Leigh to the effect that the United States should limit its acceptance of jurisdiction to cases that are to be brought before specially constituted Chambers.

The opposite school of thought is cogently represented by Professor Michael Reisman. He contends that, among other things, changes in the composition of the Court, the trend of its decisions and the unpredictability of their content warrant the conclusion that "at the present juncture of world policy trends, ICJ development and United States policy, the least destructive course for all concerned is withdrawal from the optional regime."

In his study, Franck pursues in greater detail and with a striking and instructive wealth of information the same general line as the majority of the participants in the Charlottesville workshop. It is both surprising and cheering to be reminded that the administration of Theodore Roosevelt was capable of negotiating no less than 27 agreements providing for the settlement of all classes of disputes by the Permanent Court of Arbitration, and comparably unsurprising to learn that their teeth were drawn by the Senate, which insisted that no case could be so tried without prior senatorial consent. Roosevelt thereupon withdrew the treaties from consideration.

The essence of Franck's study is that the United States needs "a sober inventory that sorts out those areas of United States foreign relations that require unfettered self-determination from those that could benefit from impartial conflict resolution." He concludes, therefore, that the United States should return to the general compulsory jurisdiction of the Court, though subject to a number of important qualifications. The most important would exclude disputes relating to armed conflict and similar or related situations. He also favors the increased use of Chambers and a greater use of the Court for declaring relevant principles of international law rather than firmly and directly resolving specific disputes. He identifies the importance of achieving symmetry, in terms of period of exposure and range of subject matter open to the Court's jurisdiction, between the obligations of the

United States and those of other states seeking to invoke against it the system of the optional clause.

This reviewer has little difficulty in agreeing with the majority view that it is regrettable that the United States as a world power with a commitment to both the existence and the full operation of international law should now be completely outside the operation of Article 36(2) of the Court's Statute; and it seems right to hope that the United States will in the not-too-distant future resume its place among the signatories of the optional clause. But the terms in which it does so must obviously be carefully chosen. Each of the two works under review contains specific proposals centering upon the identification of excluded classes of case. In assessing these, it is important to bear in mind that such exclusions will need to be applied as a preliminary matter, that is to say, at the jurisdictional stage before the Court enters into a consideration of the merits. Consequently, exceptions that are worded in such a way as to require the Court to examine the substance of the case *before* it can decide that it does not have jurisdiction, will not achieve the desired objective, namely, the exclusion of judicial scrutiny of the use of armed force by the United States. Thus, while there can be no objection to the exclusion suggested by Franck of "disputes relating to or connected with facts or situation of hostilities [or] armed conflict" because the identification of such disputes does not involve a detailed assessment of their character, the same cannot be said of the added exclusion of "individual or collective actions taken in self-defense [or] resistance to aggression." In order to decide whether an action was "taken in self-defense," or was by way of "resistance to aggression," the Court would have to look at the whole course of conduct between the parties, not for the purpose of deciding the legality of such conduct but merely for determining that it did not possess the jurisdiction to do so. The wording of the additional reservation, by directly linking the operation of the reservation to a review of the essentials of the episode, would thus appear to be self-defeating.

Both works have stressed the undesirability of "self-judging" reservations because of the possible invalidity with which such reservations may be tainted and the consequent weakening—on this ground and on that of reciprocity—of the declaration of which they form a part. But consideration may perhaps yet be given to the possibility of filing two declarations: one that, while full of positive content, completely excludes "armed conflict"-type disputes from the jurisdiction of the Court; the other, expressed to be without prejudice to the first, containing an acceptance of the Court's jurisdiction in respect of such cases involving armed conflict, etc., as the United States does not determine are, in the particular circumstances, not suitable for the exercise of the jurisdiction of the Court. The separation of this second, more controversial, declaration from the first would avoid any impairment of the operation of the first. Moreover, such a declaration, although admittedly significantly restricted by its limitation to "armed conflict"-type cases, would at least manifest the acceptance by the United States of the application of international law across the board to all its international activities.

The value of the works under review is that they are bound to stimulate constructive thought, whether along the lines just canvassed or along others. Moreover, each is a reflection of how the community of international lawyers in the United States is reacting to an episode that, with inescapable force, has obliged all of us, abroad as well as in the United States, to grapple with a question fundamental to the international order: to what extent does commitment to the rule of law also involve a willingness to accept the adjudication of all disputes?

E. LAUTERPACHT
Research Centre for International Law
University of Cambridge

Human Rights Missions: A study of the fact-finding practice of non-governmental organizations. By Hans Thoolen and Berth Verstappen. Dordrecht, Boston, Lancaster: Martinus Nijhoff Publishers, 1986. Pp. viii, 184. Dfl.95; $44; £31.50.

As foreign policy analysts begin to take the measure of Ronald Reagan's presidency, they will likely take note of a development few would have predicted at the beginning of his first term: the endurance of the human rights initiative launched by Jimmy Carter. Over the course of the Reagan presidency, the notion that human rights concerns have a proper place in U.S. policy has taken firm root—a remarkable development in view of the administration's outspoken hostility toward the principle when it entered office 8 years ago.

As the principle itself gained acceptance, the public debate over human rights policy shifted increasingly toward issues of fact: Do countries that receive U.S. aid respect fundamental rights? Have sanctions been any more effective than "constructive engagement" in promoting human rights in South Africa? Throughout this process, nongovernmental organizations (NGOs) concerned with human rights have played a key role in establishing the facts that policymakers rely upon. There has been an explosion of human rights reporting by NGOs in the 1980s, and these reports have found their way into the front pages of the news, the *Congressional Record* and embassy offices throughout the world.

Human rights reporting has become a distinct profession, but the professionals have not developed widely adopted standards respecting fact-finding procedures or guidelines concerning their reporting of facts. The authors of *Human Rights Missions: A study of the fact-finding practice of non-governmental organizations* seek to identify minimal standards for human rights fact-finding and reporting by NGOs, believing that adherence to such standards would increase the reliability—and hence the credibility—of NGO reporting. The guidelines they propose are based upon their analysis of human rights reports produced by NGOs over a 15-year period.

The research was limited to a statistical analysis of published reports whose preparation included a fact-finding visit to the country concerned.

One hundred eighty-seven NGO reports based upon field research undertaken between 1970 and 1984 were analyzed in accordance with a questionnaire containing 49 questions, further divided into over 100 subquestions.[1] A further 153 reports were collected after the statistical study was completed, but were nonetheless occasionally cited to illustrate points.

The bulk of *Human Rights Missions* consists of a question-by-question analysis of the results of the statistical analysis. The principal findings of the study are summarized near the end of the book, which concludes with recommendations to NGOs based upon the results of the research.

The study's most important limitations were self-imposed. The authors chose not to supplement their examination of the published reports of NGOs with interviews, press articles or any other relevant sources. As a result, the authors frequently acknowledge that their information is inconclusive, and at times they resort to speculation about the practices and deliberations that lay behind the published reports when interviews with NGO staff would have obviated the need to speculate.[2] Inevitably, some of the inferences drawn from sketchy information contained in published reports miss the mark or are incomplete.[3]

Some of the issues addressed by the study simply cannot be adequately probed on the basis of information supplied in published reports; this is especially true with respect to methodological questions surrounding the fact-finding process. Human rights reports often address some issues of methodology, but rarely do so in depth or comprehensively. Although the authors may have had to resolve difficult methodological issues in the course of formulating their conclusions, their principal objective in publishing the report typically is to write a persuasive account of the facts they have judged to be true. In this context, the authors may conclude that no substantial purpose would be served by revisiting in the final text the methodological issues that proved most vexing.

The other self-imposed limitation of particular consequence is the authors' decision to rely upon statistical analysis. Professionals engaged in human rights reporting will know that the enterprise has raised a raft of complex and politically sensitive issues that simply cannot be explored adequately through quantitative analysis.[4]

[1] The questionnaires were completed by the researchers on the basis of their own reading of the reports; they were not completed by the NGOs that published the reports.

[2] For example, noting that few reports refer to preliminary visits to the country in question, the authors speculate that "[i]t is fair to assume that this can be explained to a large degree by budgetary constraints" (p. 99).

[3] The authors conclude, for example, that governments are no more likely to cooperate with NGO delegates when contact has been made before the visit than when it has not. To reach this conclusion, they seem to have assumed that NGO reports consistently make mention of advance contacts in cases where they were established. In fact, many NGOs regularly make advance contacts but do not consider it necessary to refer to these in their reports.

[4] The limitations of the authors' approach are illustrated by the treatment of the practice of issuing press releases during on-site investigations. Applying its statistical analysis approach, the study reports the number of times that published reports indicate that delegates to the country concerned issued a press release during their visit. It does not—and, because of the authors' self-imposed limitations, cannot—explore in any depth the complex issues raised by this practice.

The discomfort of the authors themselves with the limitations they have placed on their study is most apparent in the presentation of their conclusions and recommendations. Much of what they present in these two sections reaches beyond what could be drawn from the results of their statistical analysis. As a result, their conclusions at times appear speculative,[5] and some of their recommendations will strike the reader as subjective.[6]

This does not wholly detract from the value of the conclusions. Some of the most interesting recommendations—such as the study's final suggestion that human rights NGOs annually publish a listing of countries that continue to deny them entry—cannot be said to have arisen directly from the authors' research.

And, despite the limitations in the authors' methodology, professional fact finders will derive useful insights from the raw data yielded by the study. Some questions of pressing concern to human rights NGOs do lend themselves to statistical analysis, and this study provides valuable information respecting some of those issues. For example, most NGOs do not have a standard practice of submitting reports to the government concerned for its review and comment in advance of publication. The issues surrounding this option are, in fact, a subject of frequent discussion in the board rooms of many NGOs. Their deliberations will be aided by this study's finding that the response rate of governments given the opportunity to respond to advance copies of reports is in the 50 percent range. Similarly, the study's findings concerning the frequency with which international NGOs translate their reports into the language of the country concerned—the rate is low —may prod some NGOs into examining their practice in this regard.

Many of the report's other findings will be of particular value to organizations that do not make a regular practice of human rights reporting but that occasionally undertake such an effort. To cite two examples: the study examines the frequency with which human rights reports (1) include a summary of conclusions separate from the main body of the report, and (2) refer to normative standards, such as those set forth in international human rights instruments, in assessing the practices in the country under study.

[5] This is especially evident in the report's concluding analysis of the geographical imbalance in NGO reporting on human rights violations. Possible reasons for the imbalance are repeatedly (and necessarily) introduced with language of speculation: "The reasons most likely to be offered by NGO's for not sending missions to other countries are that . . ." (p. 137); "We have the impression that other . . . considerations play an equally decisive role" (p. 138); "Another explanation . . . may be that . . ." (*id.*).

[6] An example is the authors' recommendation that NGOs make a greater effort to reflect in their reports "[n]uances in the degree of consensus or indications of what were difficult decisions" among mission delegates (p. 136). They offer the following reasoning:

> Although the fear for a loss of impact by the presentation of dissenting opinions may be founded on some negative experiences, we feel that the almost total absence of differences of opinion in the reports contributes equally to a loss of credibility. This unanimity becomes particularly unbelievable in cases where large and varied delegations visit a number of countries [*id.*].

Significantly, the authors' research did not include an attempt to determine any correlations between the extent to which a report's conclusions are presented as unanimous and the readers' perceptions of the report's credibility.

Established human rights organizations typically do both, but organizations less experienced in the practice of human rights reporting will benefit from the study's attention to these practices.

As these examples suggest, the study will likely raise the level of deliberate attention to issues of procedure within its target audience, even if the professionals to whom the book is directed disagree with many of its conclusions.

DIANE F. ORENTLICHER
Columbia University School of Law
Columbia University School of International and Public Affairs

Human Rights in Internal Strife: Their International Protection. By Theodor Meron. Cambridge: Grotius Publications Limited, 1987. Pp. xiii, 172. Index. £27; $48.

This volume is an expanded version of the Hersch Lauterpacht Memorial Lectures delivered by the author in March 1986 at the University of Cambridge Research Centre for International Law.

While this reviewer does not agree with the growing tendency to consider "humanitarian law," applicable in time of war, and "human rights law," applicable in time of peace, as being two entirely different sets of norms, Professor Meron's book is a welcome addition to the literature on the subject of the protection of the individual in time of civil war or, to use the modern euphemism, internal strife. The author states that his object is "to determine whether there exists a serious lacuna in the area where humanitarian law meshes with human rights law, i.e., in internal strife." He succeeds admirably in attaining that objective.

He begins by discussing in some detail the major areas in which there is convergence of the rules of humanitarian law and the rules of human rights law, listing those areas as (1) the prohibition of torture and cruel, inhuman or degrading treatment or punishment; (2) the prohibition of arbitrary arrest or detention; (3) the prohibition of discrimination on grounds of race, sex, language or religion; and (4) the requirement of the grant of due process. He then gives us areas where the protection granted is unique to one or the other set of norms, or is more far-reaching in one than in the other; some, such as the treaties prohibiting slavery, are of minimal applicability to the modern law of war.

In his discussion of the application of common Article 3 of the 1949 Geneva Conventions, the "mini-convention" relating to armed conflicts not of an international character, Meron states that that article "should no longer be regarded as a legal aberration." Unfortunately, as he points out, states apparently do not agree with that conclusion because of a latent fear that by so doing they will be granting the rebels some sort of recognition and thereby give them some sort of status that they would not otherwise have—this, despite the specific provision in the article by which a state's willingness to apply the humanitarian provisions thereof does not affect the legal status of the opposing sides. The reluctance of France to state that it would apply

Article 3 in the Franco-Algerian conflict, although it was finally overcome,[1] is typical of the attitude of most states when confronted by an organized rebellion.[2] This is also undoubtedly the reason that the many new African and Asian states lost interest in the drafting of what became the 1977 Protocol II, applicable to noninternational armed conflicts, once the activities of national liberation movements had, by mandate, been categorized as international armed conflicts. It is also the reason, as the author prognosticates, that the prospects for the application of Protocol II are poor. Indeed, going a step further, as of December 31, 1987, nine countries (Angola, Cuba, Cyprus, Mexico, Mozambique, Saudi Arabia, Syria, Vietnam and Zaire) had become parties to the 1977 Protocol I, but not to Protocol II.[3]

At various places throughout the book, the author discusses the problem of the right of derogation granted by various international instruments and frequently specifies with particularity which norms therein contained are "non-derogable."[4] Worthy of special mention is the author's statement, which is, unfortunately, all too true, that "[a]buse of the right of derogations is a world-wide phenomenon."

Chapter III is entitled "Pathology of Internal Strife." To the individual interested in understanding the ramifications of "internal strife," or "civil strife" or "civil war," this chapter is required reading. For example, in setting forth the problems that have evolved in the various attempts to define the term "internal strife" (and its synonyms), Meron points out how the extent of the opposition's organization, the duration of the strife, the intensity of the violence, the political motivation involved, and so on, are all factors that must be taken into account. Departing for the moment from the "humanitarian law–human rights law" thesis, he discusses the related definitional problems of the Overseas Private Investment Corporation (OPIC), a creation of the United States, and of the Multilateral Investment Guarantee Agency (MIGA), a creation of the World Bank, both of which are concerned with defining with adequate specificity the type of internal strife that is to fall within the ambit of their insurance coverage. Unfortunately, the use of a term such as "civil disturbance" in the MIGA contract, even though understood as meaning internal strife, is bound to cause confusion since the Diplomatic Conference that drafted Protocol II attempted to ensure that it would not be applicable to "internal disturbances."[5]

After discussing the role of the International Committee of the Red Cross (ICRC) in internal strife (ch. IV) and some of the innumerable meetings of experts seeking solutions to the various problems created by the existence of internal strife (ch. V), Meron ends his presentation with a chapter on "The Need for Remedies." Here I must disagree with the interpretation that he

[1] M. Bedjaoui, Law and the Algerian Revolution 213 (1961).

[2] The situations in Nicaragua, El Salvador and Afghanistan are discussed at pp. 47–50.

[3] International Committee of the Red Cross, Geneva Conventions of 12 August 1949 and Additional Protocols of 8 June 1977: Signatures, Ratifications, Accessions and Successions as at 31 December 1987.

[4] *See, e.g.*, pp. 23–26, 51–63, etc.

[5] Art. 1(2), 1977 Protocol II, *reprinted in* 16 ILM 1442, 1443 (1977).

has placed on three ICRC statements. He says that "internal strife is not covered by the existing humanitarian instruments" and that this has been acknowledged by the ICRC. If "internal strife" means what this reviewer would call "civil war," and that appears to be the substance of the entire book, then internal strife *is* covered by both common Article 3 of the 1949 Geneva Conventions and by the 1977 Protocol II, as Meron himself has cogently pointed out. Concerning the ICRC statements, the first is contained in a quoted report submitted by the ICRC to the 25th International Conference of the Red Cross where reference is made to "situations of internal tensions or unrest which are not covered by international humanitarian law"; the second is a footnote reference to a 1984 report of experts "concerning the protection of victims of situations not covered by international humanitarian law"; and the third is a speech given in 1983 by the then ICRC President, Alexandre Hay, in which he refers to "violence that ranges from simple internal tensions to more serious internal disturbances" (p. 136).[6] A close examination of all three of these documents makes it abundantly clear that what the authors are concerned with is not internal strife as understood throughout the book, but with what Article 1(2) of the 1977 Protocol, in excluding them from its coverage, refers to as "situations of internal disturbances and tensions, such as riots, isolated and sporadic acts of violence and other acts of a similar nature." There is no question that these situations, which fall far short of being internal strife, are not covered by existing international humanitarian law; and it is exceedingly doubtful that any state will become a party to an international instrument that permits international intervention in situations that every state, without exception, would consider to be exclusively a matter of domestic concern.[7]

Despite the foregoing difference of opinion, this reviewer recommends Meron's book without reservation.

HOWARD S. LEVIE
Saint Louis University Law School, Emeritus

Perestroika. New Thinking for Our Country and the World. By Mikhail Gorbachev. New York: Harper & Row, 1987. Pp. 254.

Perestroika was written very quickly by its busy author (and probably some ghostwriters) in the summer of 1987. That fall, publication started on an unprecedented worldwide scale in many languages. The U.S. edition was launched at the Soviet Embassy in Washington in November.[1] Publication in other languages followed and, in February 1988, even a Chinese "mass edition" was given its send-off at the Soviet Embassy in Beijing.[2] So far,

[6] Hay, *The ICRC and International Humanitarian Issues,* INT'L REV. RED CROSS, No. 238, Jan.–Feb. 1984, at 3, 9.

[7] For support of this position, see the negotiating history of Article 1 of Protocol II in H. LEVIE, THE LAW OF NON-INTERNATIONAL ARMED CONFLICT 23–90 (1987).

[1] Pravda, Nov. 5, 1987, at 11.

[2] Pravda, Feb. 26, 1988, at 7. Pravda, Mar. 26, 1988, at 4, reports on a second Chinese edition, a Spanish and an Arabic one.

Gorbachev's book, which, as he states (p. 10), was written at "the request of American publishers," has been a tremendous financial success—200,000 copies of the Dutch edition alone were sold in the first 3 months.[3] A totally different question is what influence this book, written in a very popular style, will exert on the world and especially on Western public opinion.

The book has two parts: the first, "Perestroika," is mainly devoted to its application at home, and the second, "New Thinking and the World," is devoted to international relations. This review will focus on part 2, some 120 pages. Writing in this *Journal,* one is tempted to start by noting that Gorbachev, a graduate of the Law Faculty of the University of Moscow, although writing about contemporary international relations, does not, even once, refer directly to international law; the term simply cannot be found, even where one would most expect it, e.g., in the reference to "asserting civilized standards in international relations" (p. 132). Nor is the main post–World War II treaty—the United Nations Charter—referred to at all, although the United Nations, and "its experience of streamlining international cooperation" is mentioned as "more important than ever before" (p. 140). The above may lead one to a pessimistic conclusion about the role played by international law in top-level Soviet thinking (and the impact Soviet law schools have on their students in that field!).

Regarding the premises for the Soviet "new thinking" in international relations, the book mentions such factors as the threats posed by nuclear weapons, environmental pollution, limited natural resources, the scientific, technical and information revolution, and problems of starvation, indebtedness and poverty in the Third World. All of this gives rise to a state of global interdependence. What one misses very much, though, is any clear admission that the main necessity for Soviet *perestroika,* in international relations as well as domestically, arises out of the catastrophic economic and social conditions that the ossified, dogmatic and corrupt Brezhnev regime brought about in the USSR. It was only in February 1988 that Gorbachev himself made this devastating statement:

> As is known, the speed of economic development in our country has decreased and reached a critical point. But even that speed, as it has now become clear, was achieved in great part on an unhealthy basis . . . oil trade on the world market at the high prices then prevailing, and the totally unjustified promotion of the sale of alcoholic beverages. If one purges the economic growth indicators of the influence of these factors, it transpires that during the period of, effectively, four five-year plans, we did not have an increase in the absolute growth of the national income, and at the beginning of the eighties it even started decreasing.[4]

This deep economic crisis, resulting in the Soviet Union's increasingly falling behind the West, was (and still is) coupled with social evils like drunk-

[3] Pravda, Feb. 20, 1988, at 4. Pravda, Mar. 26, 1988, at 4, reported that in Italy the book "still firmly holds first place on the list of the most popular publicistic books in the country."

[4] Speech at Plenum of Central Committee of the CPSU, Pravda, Feb. 19, 1988, at 2.

enness on a scale greater than ever before in Russian history and unheard-of environmental pollution. There was incredible waste, some of it catastrophic, such as the loss of 10 to 12 million hectares of prime agricultural land that, according to Gorbachev, was inundated to construct power stations.[5] The costly, and totally unsuccessful, intervention in Afghanistan, which, despite initial illusions, has dragged on for years, affecting millions of Soviet people, as well as other factors, demands radical revision of certain policies at home and changes in the country's approach to foreign policy. Considerably more funds must be directed toward internal reconstruction, even at the expense of "internationalistic aid" (as the intervention in Afghanistan used to be called) or of gigantic armament. There is also a desire to lure Westerners into joint ventures and to create an international climate propitious to more liberal imports from the West of "sensitive" technology. These, one strongly feels, are the most likely reasons for *perestroika* in Soviet thinking in international relations, much more so than concerns about the future of mankind, which is what the book tries to convey.

However that may be, one should now turn briefly to the promises made in *Perestroika,* intended to substantiate the alleged Soviet "new thinking" in international relations. One must distinguish between (1) the offer vis-à-vis the West and (2) what is in store for the members of the Eastern bloc. In the first, there is the promise of less militant relations. On page 147, the reader is reminded that the new 1986 program of the Communist Party of the Soviet Union (CPSU) abandoned the concept that "peaceful coexistence" is a specific form of the international class struggle.[6] There are declarations of a certain readiness to compromise "on equal terms." One reads that "we want to return to the true, original meaning of the words we use in international contacts. In declaring our commitment to honest and open politics, we do mean honesty, decency and sincerity" (p. 158) and, as Gorbachev maintains, "we follow these principles in our actions."

There is also repetition of such well-known principles, vital to international security, as equality of states and recognition of the right of every nation to "choose its own social system" (pp. 142–43, 226–27), which boils down to recognition of fundamental principles of international law. For the West, there is hardly anything new, let alone "revolutionary," in all this (*perestroika* is supposed to be "a revolution," p. 49). At most, Westerners may feel that such pronouncements by a Soviet leader confirm the political will to follow international obligations legally entered into by having become a state party to the UN Charter, the two International Covenants on Human Rights and other international agreements. But one must bear in

[5] At a meeting with leaders of the "mass media, ideological institutions and creative unions." Pravda, Jan. 13, 1988, at 2.

[6] The previous program of the CPSU (1961) read:

> Peaceful coexistence forms the basis for peaceful competition between socialism and capitalism on an international scale, and represents a specific form of the class struggle between them. While the socialist countries pledge themselves consistently to peaceful coexistence, they aim at unremitting strengthening of the positions of the socialist world system in its contest with capitalism.

mind that "every nation's" right to choose (and change) its sociopolitical system does not, in Soviet thinking, refer to every nation *tout court,* but only to every "non-socialist nation"—while you are welcome to switch from capitalism to Moscow-brand socialism, there is a clear *nyet* to movement in the opposite direction.

We must now have a look at whether *perestroika* offers "new thinking" to the smaller countries of the "Soviet bloc," especially the six members of the Warsaw Treaty Organization. Here it must be said at the outset that the self-criticism offered by the author on the character of past relations is minimal and extremely general. Concerning earlier periods, probably mainly under Stalin, one reads:

> Drawing on the Soviet experience, some countries failed duly to consider their own specifics. Even worse, a stereotyped approach was given an ideological tint by some of our theoreticians and especially practical leaders who acted as almost the sole guardians of truth. . . . As regards our friends in the socialist countries, they usually kept quiet, even when they noticed something of concern. Frankness was frowned upon, and could be "misunderstood," so to speak [pp. 162–63].

Concerning the situation at the eclipse of the Brezhnev era, one reads the following: "Indeed, beginning with the end of the 1970s, contacts between leaders of fraternal countries became more and more for show rather than for real business. There was less trust in them and their approach was more businesslike" (p. 164).

The worst aspect of these relations, the most flagrant breaches of international law by the USSR, are evidently to be considered all right. As to aggression or the threat thereof toward allied Warsaw Pact countries, Gorbachev simply states:

> Some socialist countries went through serious crises in their development. Such was the case, for instance, in Hungary in 1956, in Czechoslovakia in 1968, and in Poland in 1956 and then again in the early 1980s. Each of these crises had its own specific features. They were dealt with differently [p. 163].

What about the so-called principles of proletarian and socialist internationalism in relations with the smaller members of the "family"? What about those perversions of international law by Moscow, the "new and higher" kind of Communist "regional international law," with its notions of "*socialist* self-determination," "*socialist* sovereignty" and the "right and duty" to intervene, even militarily, whenever Big Brother feels that "socialism is threatened"? They have not been abandoned, or even criticized.

"Proletarian" and "socialist internationalism" are not referred to by name in *Perestroika.* But one reads: "It goes without saying that no socialist country can successfully move forward in a healthy rhythm without understanding, *solidarity* and mutually beneficial cooperation with the other fraternal nations, or at times even without their *help*" (p. 161) (including "invasion help"?) (emphasis added). Although later it says that "the entire framework of political relations between the socialist countries must be strictly based on absolute independence" (p. 165), just a few lines below one reads that "we are also firmly convinced that the socialist community will be successful only if every party and state cares for both its own and *common* interests" (emphasis added).

Lest one be totally confused or—worse still—carried away by the "absolute independence," one has to refer, in the final instance, to the CPSU program of March 1, 1986, adopted under Gorbachev. It is *this* document, meant to stay in force for decades, that is binding, and not what the General Secretary of the day says in a book. And here the party program is crystal clear. It confirms, in one place, "the construction of relations with other fraternal countries on the principles of socialist internationalism."[7] Elsewhere, it pronounces that "[i]n its relations with the fraternal parties the *CPSU adheres firmly to the principle of proletarian internationalism,* which organically contains within itself both revolutionary solidarity and the acknowledgement of the full independence and equality of each party."[8] In yet another place, the party program sums it up: "In its whole activity the CPSU unswervingly directs itself *by the tried-out Marxist-Leninist principles of proletarian, socialist internationalism.*"[9]

The matter is thus settled in accordance with very "*old* thinking." Should a "critical" situation develop, should Moscow, for instance, feel that one of the six countries of the Warsaw Pact is drifting toward Finlandization, there is no doubt that, though the level of tolerance would probably be higher than before, military force would be used as the *ultima ratio.*

On page 169, Gorbachev relates how, during his 1987 visit to Czechoslovakia, while talking to people on the street, one young man noted: " 'So it boils down to: "Speak the truth, love the truth, and wish others the truth." ' I added: 'And act according to the truth. This is the most difficult science.' "[10] The obvious problem is that some truths may be highly unpalatable and even "counterproductive" politically. As the caption of a cartoon in the leading Polish Marxist weekly *Polityka* went: "So what if it is the truth—if this truth runs against us?" Marxist-Leninist "dialectical relativism" certainly also applies here just as in the field of *glasnost.* As Gorbachev himself stated: "we are for *glasnost* without any provisos, without limits. But for *glasnost*—in the interests of socialism."[11]

If truth is applied as a yardstick, *Perestroika* shows serious gaps, partially by omission, partially by commission. Concerning the first, one does not find even one instance of bold self-criticism in international relations (in contrast to domestic questions). There is, for example, not one word about the destructive role played in so many countries by the Moscow-controlled Comintern (1919–1943). There is no word about the secret protocol to the Ribbentrop-Molotov treaty of August 23, 1939 (still not acknowledged, let

[7] Program of the CPSU in KOMMUNIST, No. 3, 1986, at 142.

[8] *Id.* at 148. [9] *Id.* at 152.

[10] Recounting this episode, Pravda, Apr. 10, 1987, also prints a passage where Gorbachev, answering a voice from the crowd that says the truth should be heard, stated: "The truth, the truth, otherwise you will not get anywhere. When there is no truth, it is unclear what to do."

[11] Pravda, Jan. 13, 1988, at 2.

alone published, in the USSR). As is known, this secret protocol gave the green light for Soviet aggression against Poland and Finland, as well as for the annexation of the Baltic countries and parts of Romania. Concerning the post–World War II era, the West is still presented as totally responsible for the "Cold War" and, in this connection, the question is posed with sanctimonious naiveté: "We also ask why the West was the first to set up a military alliance, NATO" (p. 149). Soviet treatment of Hungary, Czechoslovakia and Poland between 1956 and 1981, and the lack of any trace of self-criticism on all that, was mentioned above. The same lack applies to Afghanistan, where the freedom fighters are, incidentally, still called "counter-revolutionary bands" (p. 177). Under these circumstances, one must recognize as very "old thinking" (and tactics) what one reads on pages 202–03: "It is high time to put an end to the lies about the Soviet Union's aggressiveness."[12]

Perestroika, in its international aspects, seems much influenced by Lenin's 1920 brochure written in connection with the preparations for the second congress of the Comintern, *"Left-Wing" Communism—An Infantile Disorder* (not mentioned in the book). Two short quotations seem particularly appropriate: "the entire history of Bolshevism, both before and after the October Revolution, is *full* of instances of changes of tack, conciliatory tactics and compromises with other parties, including bourgeois parties!" And: "We must be able to . . . agree to make any sacrifice, and even—if need be—to resort to various stratagems, artifices and illegal methods, to evasions and subterfuges . . . ."[13]

Part 2 of *Perestroika* is a good illustration of the application of the teachings of the Master. There are even heavy-handed attempts (in spite of a denial) at driving a wedge between Western Europe and America:

> Sometimes . . . one has the impression that the independent policies of West European nations have been abducted, that they are being carried off across the ocean; that national interests are farmed out under the pretext of protecting security. A serious threat is hovering over European culture too. The threat emanates from the onslaught of "mass culture" from across the Atlantic [p. 208].

What is envisaged is the potential creation of a sort of international "people's front" of Communists with other leftist and even center parties, something that the Comintern tried to arrange in the midthirties in Western Europe on a national scale. There is even talk (if the teachings of the book are followed) of the prospect of a "golden age" for the whole world (p. 252)!

"Peaceful coexistence," as already mentioned, is now supposed to be devoid of elements of the international class struggle. But anyone who believes that this means, according to the "new thinking," that Moscow now

[12] Speaking of lies, consider the following by former Soviet Minister of Defense Sokolov, in Pravda, Feb. 23, 1987, at 2: "The whole heroic history of the Soviet Armed Forces confirms the consistency of their lofty destiny—to defend the socialist Fatherland. They have not attacked anybody in the past." See, in the same vein, the present incumbent, Yazov, in Pravda, Feb. 23, 1988, at 2.

[13] V. I. Lenin, Selected Works 543, 554 (1968).

accepts the idea that the West's socioeconomic status will remain basically unchanged for generations to come, is wrong. *Perestroika* does not, of course, declare that the West, according to Communist doctrine, is doomed anyway. But the 1986 program of the CPSU very traditionally declares that "[t]he general crisis of capitalism is deepening," and that "[i]mperialism is parasitical, decaying and moribund capitalism, the eve of the socialist revolution."[14]

What *Perestroika* offers on international relations is, on most points, very old and conservative, or ambiguous and unconvincing. But if this is so, then the *only* proof of genuine "new thinking" must lie in hard facts. And here, serious doubts must be registered. In 1954–1955, Khrushchev, without proclaiming a new era or publishing a bestseller, simply demonstrated practical "new thinking" and corrected many anomalies in Soviet foreign policy, to mention only some territorial decisions: giving Port Arthur back to China, signing the State Treaty with Austria and withdrawing Soviet troops from there, and relinquishing the naval base in Porkkala to Finland. In the case of Gorbachev's stewardship, 3 years in duration at this writing, there have been, as yet, few such acts. Military withdrawal from Afghanistan started in May 1988, but, apart from that, there are still "proxy soldiers" occupying Cambodia, unsettled Chinese and Japanese territorial claims, and many problems of a different character. A positive step of considerable caliber has been taken in the field of disarmament. But when thinking about the INF Treaty between the United States and the USSR, one should not forget the 1963 multilateral Test Ban Treaty, concluded under Khrushchev. Of course, new progress in nuclear disarmament may follow. But the build-up of conventional forces continues unabated under Gorbachev and, "perhaps most disturbingly of all, the Soviets have continued to build up their capability to conduct offensive operations."[15] There has been no practical application, so far, of what *Perestroika* advocates as to the "purely defensive character" (pp. 142–43) of the Warsaw Pact's military doctrine proclaimed by the Pact's summit in May 1987.

A relatively small but symbolic manifestation of "new thinking" vis-à-vis the rest of the world would be a change in the Soviet emblem. Recall that the present emblem, as described in Article 169 of the 1977 Soviet Constitution, "consists of a representation of a sickle and hammer against the background of the globe . . . with an inscription . . . 'Proletarians of All Countries, Unite!' " The handle of the sickle encompasses part of Western and Central Africa and the blade itself covers the Middle East and the hammer Europe. This emblem, symbolizing Communist expansionist ambitions worldwide, would hardly be tolerable in the basic law of a peace-loving country and continues to represent very old thinking.

Another serious problem is the lack of official admission of the murder of up to 15,000 Polish officers at Katyn and other places in 1940; apologies must be made, compensation paid to the victims' families and other steps taken.

[14] Program, *supra* note 7, at 106, 109.

[15] Galvin, *The INF Treaty—No Relief from the Burden of Defence*, NATO REV., Feb. 1988, at 2, 3.

New thinking must also be demonstrated in the interpretation of what is "essentially within the domestic jurisdiction of the Soviet government." During the Brezhnev era, human rights issues were considered off-limits to "foreign interference." In *Perestroika,* Gorbachev states: "I have said . . . that we are prepared to discuss in a humane spirit individual cases, but we are also determined to openly and extensively discuss the entire range of these problems" (i.e., human rights) (p. 205). Nonetheless, though progress may be noted in this realm, when it comes to Western broadcasts in the languages of the USSR, which, most of the time, center on broadly conceived human rights problems, and whose reception in the USSR must be treated, per se, as a realization of Article 19(2) of the International Covenant on Civil and Political Rights, they are attacked by Gorbachev as "the inflammatory American broadcasts from Munich" (p. 217). He lashed out at Western "radio voices" again in February 1988.[16] Shortly thereafter, escalating "old thinking," a "decisive protest" regarding the Voice of America was lodged by the Soviet Ministry of Foreign Affairs with the U.S. Embassy.[17] Western countries do not object to Soviet broadcasts in their languages. Nor should Moscow object to the reverse, if it wants anybody to believe what *Perestroika* says: "we criticize ourselves the way nobody has ever criticized us, West, East or anywhere else . . . because we are strong and we do not fear for our future" (p. 129).

A few final words. *Perestroika* in international relations, the offer of "civilized standards," "honest and open policies," etc., would, per se, sound encouraging. Unfortunately, coming, as it does, from a country that has demonstrated for decades so many actions counter to these principles and flagrant breaches of international law, it cannot be taken at face value. Concrete and meaningful international actions must take place. No "benefit of the doubt," no *in dubio pro Kremlo,* is warranted.

The book, as this review has tried to demonstrate, often lacks intellectual honesty and confirms ongoing "*old*" thinking in many places. It is very superficial, clearly written in haste to "inundate" the foreign public as quickly as possible. Some of its boasts are utopian, such as the claim that the success of *perestroika* at home would also "help the developing countries find ways to achieve economic and social modernization without having to make concessions to neocolonialism or throwing themselves into the cauldron of capitalism" (p. 131). There is also, in places, a certain tone of the self-appointed *praeceptor mundi.* It is already evident in the book's subtitle (its Russian original even reads "New Thinking for Our Country and the *Whole World*" (emphasis added)).

In February 1988, Gorbachev made this revealing admission, which one would look for in vain in this book: "I also have to stress: new thinking is based on Lenin's theory of imperialism, on V. I. Lenin's research on the nature of imperialism, which will never become 'good.' On this question we have not had and do not have any illusions."[18]

[16] Pravda, Feb. 19, 1988, at 3.

[17] Pravda, Mar. 1, 1988, at 5.

[18] Pravda, Feb. 19, 1988, at 3.

We, too, should harbor no illusions. Some improvement in the direction of more dialogue, more "civilized international standards" and limited disarmament may, in fact, be demonstrated by the other side. But genuinely peaceful and fully secure "coexistence" based on far-reaching confidence and good will, a "golden age," is difficult to imagine. For this, the very nature of the beast would have to be changed—an impossible dream!

RICHARD SZAWLOWSKI
Vancouver, B.C.

The Distinctiveness of Soviet Law. Edited by F. J. M. Feldbrugge. Dordrecht, Boston, Lancaster: Martinus Nijhoff Publishers, 1987. Pp. xix, 272. Index. Dfl.185; $91; £56.95.

A search for distinctive approaches to international law, sometimes called "comparative international law," is now routine among scholars specializing in ideological and regional attitudes toward the discipline. Pluralism arrived soon after World War II when the "socialist" camp became a major factor in the United Nations. Western statesmen no longer dominate the development of international law, or even its codification. This volume is to be welcomed as a well-informed effort of Western Sovietologists to discern the new trends.

As might be expected, the compendium of papers, selected from those presented to the Third World Congress for Soviet and East European Studies in 1985, is primarily devoted to socialist municipal law. International law norms are treated only as they concern extradition, judicial and administrative assistance, consular law and foreign trade law. In spite of this weighted balance, the volume is not without interest for readers of the *Journal,* for both Easterners and Westerners have often taken the position that foreign policy is but an extension of domestic policy. Marxist attitudes are not divided between external and internal application, even though the drama of exporting revolution seemed to survive well after the fire of revolution had gone out of Soviet domestic policy. Today, Mikhail Gorbachev has brought the external and domestic policies into balance, as he swings his support to UN peacekeeping to calm the world's tumult while the restructuring process at home is pressed.

Regrettably, the volume contains no contributions from Eastern Europeans or Chinese. The absence of inside evaluations of distinctiveness to be compared with those from the outside is not critical since Westerners now know a great deal about what is written by the socialists. It is known that all are not of one mind, for two schools have been vocal: one arguing that distinctiveness is so great that a new "socialist international law" has emerged, and the other denying such an evolution in spite of some variation in practice between East and West.

Dr. Henn-Jüri Uibopuu provides some indication of varying approaches, for he is himself an Estonian, long resident in Salzburg as a professor of international law. With his command of both Eastern and Western attitudes, his view is important when he concludes that Soviet consular law conforms to general international norms, even though it recognizes in its consuls much greater authority over Soviet nationals in the receiving state than classical law allows.

Extradition practice as exemplified in the treaties concluded suggests some variation to its author, Karin Schmidt of Cologne. Here the contrast is in attitudes toward political crime: the East recognizes no barrier to extradition within the socialist family of states, but when Western states are concerned, treaties draw the classical line. Yugoslavia, with its fence-sitting location, provides the variation. It recognizes no right to extradite political offenders, but the receiving state is always authorized by treaty to decide what is political.

Foreign trade law and its socialist variation are treated by Peter B. Maggs of the University of Illinois with his usual careful hand. Of course, all students of Soviet law know that state trading has left a heavy mark on institutions and practice. Indeed, Soviet authors have long stressed the distinction in infrastructure and contract law because of the state monopoly of foreign trade in the East. Maggs treats the steps in the development of infrastructure and concludes that one clear basis for it stands out: the Communist Party is determined to prevent foreigners from intervening either ideologically or institutionally in its monopoly of policymaking. Lenin distrusted capitalist traders, and his heirs have until recently shown no change of mind. Today, with joint ventures and in some socialist countries 100 percent foreign investment, the early Leninist rule can hardly remain intact.

The noted Dutch editor of the volume, who has already done so much through his Documentation Center in Leiden to provide studies on socialist law, has now added a thought-provoking series of papers on "distinctiveness."

JOHN N. HAZARD
Board of Editors

Osvobodivshiesia strany i mezhdunarodnoe pravo (The Liberated Countries and International Law). I. P. Blishchenko (chief ed.). Moscow: Mezhdunarodnye otnosheniia, 1987. Pp. 264. $3.75.

The colonial powers and, notably, the United States are made the scapegoats for the tragedy of the developing world in this first textbook to be published by the Lumumba University of Friendship of Peoples. Although a Western reader might have expected the book to be published in a language accessible to many of the Third World's peoples, it is printed, so far as indicated, only in Russian. This suggests that it was designed only for foreign students in the USSR who are being prepared to convey its message to their fellow students after their return home.

In spite of its sharp propagandistic tone, it incorporates a remarkably full record of the measures sponsored over the past 20 years by Soviet scholars and diplomats to restructure international law to suit the perceived needs of the Third World. This academic attentiveness to a record of notable facts might have been expected of an editorial committee headed by Dr. I. P. Blishchenko of the Soviet Ministry of Foreign Affairs and his two "readers," the noted Ukrainian international lawyer, I. I. Lukashuk, and his colleague, G. P. Zadorozhnyi of the Moscow State Institute of International Affairs. These are all very knowledgeable jurists.

Western scholars no longer overlook the lamentable state of the colonially oriented body of international law prior to the 1950s, but some will quarrel with this Soviet presentation. For example, it notes that although Japan and Europe lay in ruins after World War II, the war "did not hamper American concerns in profiting from war orders and shipments of goods, nor hamper banks from transforming the U.S.A. into the greatest world creditor" (p. 89). Not a word is said about the Marshall Plan's contribution to the reconstruction of Europe, a plan that was also offered to Eastern countries, but declined.

Praise is showered on the United Nations and some of its organs. Readers with long memories will recall the unending criticism of the United Nations by Eastern European statesmen until majorities began to appear in favor of Soviet initiatives. But there is no praise for financial agencies or the International Court of Justice. The authors take the traditional line of attack on these as being dominated by the West. Perhaps the support of the Soviet Union for dispute resolution by the International Court of Justice, its application for observer status in GATT and possibly even membership in, and support of, UN peacekeeping activities was too recent for the authors to digest and include.

Some hint of affirmative attitudes to the varied activities of the United Nations is given in a paragraph reading, "Art. 1, para. 3 of the Charter and other democratic provisions, set forth in the Charter, have made it possible to transform the U.N. into a leading international instrument of struggle, first against political colonialism, and, second, also against neocolonialism and foreign exploitation" (p. 93).

The lengthy chapter on the "New International Economic Order" (pp. 70–102) gives Western readers more of a basis for understanding its proposals than many other sources that omit detail. Third World students are told that opinions vary on what this program can achieve to satisfy their dreams. Apparently, there is a position that calls for radical restructuring of the economic life of the world through total abandonment of market economics, to be replaced by obligatory planning of world trade so as to favor Third World suppliers of raw materials. At the other end of the spectrum, there is a view favoring a less radical approach within the market system.

The authors seem to suggest to their students some caution in pressing their ideas, so as to avoid backlash. As they state,

> The deepening and democratization of the international law of collaboration must not conflict with international law [presumably, contemporary general international law]. In particular, socialist international law does not conflict with general international law, which is at the

> current time the most advanced form of development. So also the law of development does not deny the existence of general international law, but, emerges from it. It furthers the affirmation of social justice in interstate relations, legitimating the struggle of peoples for real equality, against economic dictatorship of the imperialist powers and their multinational corporations [p. 85].

This book may have been written too early, for today's Communist Party preaches cooperation, not struggle, and to the extent that struggle is to be carried on by the developing world, it must be kept within the framework of "law," rather than taking the nihilistic approach to regulation that was once favored.

In sum, this text can be helpful to Westerners trying to learn what is being taught foreign students in Soviet universities, and it can cast light upon what those students are expected to do when they return to their homelands. It draws the curtain away from a program that, until now, has not been so clearly explained to Western readers.

JOHN N. HAZARD
Board of Editors

Soviet Year-Book of International Law, 1986. Moscow: Publishing House "Nauka," 1987. Pp. 391. 5 rubles, 40 kopeks.

Academician G. I. Tunkin is celebrated on his 80th birthday in this 28th volume of the *Year-Book,* and well he might be, as founder of the Soviet Association of International Law and initiator of the *Year-Book* series, former member of the International Law Commission and member of the Institut de Droit International, and as formulator of the concept of an "international law of peaceful coexistence." For the Western world of internationalists, as well as for his colleagues, Tunkin has for decades been accepted as spokesman for Soviet academics, and even for Soviet diplomats, on suitable international law solutions for problems touching on Soviet interests.

His career is reviewed by his colleague R. A. Mullerson in a jubilee article. He places Tunkin with the two early architects of a Soviet philosophy of international law, E. B. Pashukanis and E. A. Korovin, and as a contemporary of V. N. Durdenevskii, V. M. Koretskii, F. M. Kozhevnikov, S. B. Krylov, D. B. Levin and M. Ya. Rapoport in developing the field. Mullerson sees Tunkin's major contribution of recent years as a redefining of international law as the product of a coordination of wills. Westerners will know that in developing that theory, Tunkin broke out of the straitjacket created by Pashukanis, who saw international law as a product of the will of the bourgeois ruling class, to be utilized by Soviet diplomats with care, on a "pick and choose" basis. Tunkin set the stage for the development of international law in a new era of vigorous innovative participation with Western scholars and diplomats in coordinating wills.

Tunkin himself leads the authors who present papers in this *Year-Book,* as he has done throughout most of the years of the *Year-Book*'s publication. For his jubilee, he has chosen to argue again for the renunciation of ages-old stereotypes of thinking and conduct in international life. He calls for the adoption of a model built upon the premise that peace is an indispensable condition for the survival of humanity and that law must prevent warfare, which would destroy mankind. As always, he adheres to the Communist Party program's position that peaceful coexistence does not require the cessation of class struggle for the minds of men. He continues in his paper to strike hard at "imperialists" and, most of all, at the United States. He has never been one to see the beam in his own country's eye. For him, the entry into Afghanistan was stimulated by an American threat to Soviet security.

In the same *Year-Book,* a colleague discloses one of the forms of struggle for the minds of men when he tells of a summer school conducted for diplomats of the developing world. It seems that the Foreign Office legal adviser, Dr. I. P. Blishchenko, served as dean in 1985 of a program that brought together 86 jurists from 41 countries to hear lectures on international law. A hint as to what they heard has been provided recently by a textbook edited by the dean. The substance of this book has been set forth in a review of the text in this *Journal.*[1] For Westerners, it will be seen as a continuation of the "struggle" approach.

As has been the case in prior years, the *Year-Book* contains many technically oriented articles of considerable value to Westerners searching for clues to current Soviet thinking. Two notable papers suggest measures to be taken during armed conflict to protect civilian objects. S. A. Egorov notes that there is no code covering either attacks from the air on objects in the sea or attacks from outer space. He is worried about attacks on nuclear power stations and nuclear ships, probably mindful of Chernobyl. V. Yu. Markov argues that oil spills have proven dangerous and that they would be worse if caused by military action. He proposes the creation of an International Committee on Neutralization of offshore fields and suspension during war of deliveries from them to belligerents.

Canadian and U.S. jurists will welcome praise for the use of a Chamber of the International Court of Justice to resolve their dispute over the boundary in the Gulf of Maine. This praise may suggest proposals for Chamber resolution of disputes in which the USSR is a party. Western scholars know that M. S. Gorbachev has sounded friendly toward use of the ICJ in recent comments, and the Chamber approach may be a way of narrowing the bench to judges thought to be impartial. Yu. V. Osintsev also praises the Chamber's search for "equity" in resolving the dispute, rather than relying on hard law. He even permits himself to say that the decision could be accepted as a precedent despite the specific exclusion in the Statute of the Court of the common law view that its decisions may be precedents. For the author, precedents may in some cases fill lacunae in the law.

Finally, G. A. Matveev's paper on proposals for revision of the Paris Convention on Protection of Industrial Property can be helpful to counsel advising clients who are entering upon joint ventures with Soviet enter-

[1] *See* review in this issue at p. 887.

prises. He argues that the "author's certificate," normally issued to Soviet citizens instead of a traditional patent, must be accepted on the same basis as patents in establishing priority in invention. He proposes amendment of the Paris Convention to put this principle in writing.

Tunkin must take satisfaction in the performance of his colleagues in the *Year-Books*. He has stimulated extensive writing in international law, as the bibliographies at the end of each *Year-Book* prove. The annual meetings of the association of which he is president bring together jurists from Eastern Europe as well as those of the USSR. If the current trend toward active participation in all phases of the work of the United Nations and its agencies continues, there may be a lessening of the "class struggle" approach in international law.

JOHN N. HAZARD
Board of Editors

Repertório da Prática Brasileira do Direito Internacional Público. 2 vols. By Antônio Augusto Cançado Trindade. Vol. IV (1899–1918): pp. 518; vol. V (general index): pp. 235. Brasília: Fundação Alexandre de Gusmão, 1986–1987.

With the publication of volume IV of his digest of Brazilian international law, Professor Cançado Trindade completes a solo task of monumental proportions. The fifth volume is a complete index of the four volumes that constitute the digest. It is worthy of note that this is the first digest published in Latin America or, to be more precise, in the Southern Hemisphere, and it is to be hoped that the example will be followed in other countries.

The volume under review covers the period 1899–1918 and is of special interest not only to experts in international law, but also to students of Brazil's diplomatic history, since Baron Rio-Branco, the country's foremost diplomat, headed the Ministry of Foreign Relations from 1902 until his death in 1912. During those 10 years, the annual report of the Foreign Ministry was abolished, and therefore many of the documents published are of special interest. The volume also covers the First World War, and the positions taken by Brazil as a neutral and as a belligerent are of special interest.

As in the previous volumes,[1] the book is divided into nine separate parts. In the introduction, the author writes that the most important chapters deal with space in international law, e.g., territory, international rivers and the law of the sea. The chapter on international rivers shows that in the beginning of the century the issue was of the utmost importance; conversely, the law of the sea was of scant interest.

The chapter on the codification of international law shows how codification progressed in Latin America. The first important steps were taken under the aegis of the inter-American system and culminated in the Conven-

[1] Reviewed by Edith Brown Weiss at 79 AJIL 1131 (1985).

tion on Private International Law and in conventions on diplomatic agents, consuls and treaties, all of which were signed at the 1928 Havana Conference. The first proposal made, in 1899, during the conference held in Mexico City, was put forward by the Brazilian delegate, José Hygino Duarte Pereira.

The speech made by Ruy Barbosa during the 1907 Peace Conference in The Hague, in which he defended the sovereign equality of states, is considered the most important Brazilian contribution to international law. It was received on that occasion with skepticism but is, at present, enshrined in the Charter of the United Nations.

This digest, like the previous ones, has frequent recourse to the opinions (*pareceres*) of the legal advisers of the Brazilian Ministry for Foreign Relations. Even though there are doctrinal misgivings regarding this source of international law, it should be stressed that most of the legal advisers whose opinions are mentioned were outstanding jurists in international law, such as Clovis Bevilaqua, Hildebrando Accioly and Haroldo Valladao; all were authors of important books on international law and their opinions quite often were capable of modifying the stand that the government was contemplating on a given subject.

Considering the importance of Cançado Trindade's digest, one can only wonder why the fourth volume only goes back as far as 1899 when, in this reviewer's opinion, it would have been more logical to begin with the proclamation of the Republic in 1889. During those 10 years, many important events took place and, from a legal point of view, the resolution of the question of the rights of Brazil to the Island of Trindade in the mid-Atlantic, in 1896, is of special interest.

Finally, reference must be made to the general index in volume V, which examines the four previous volumes and has the added advantage of containing translations in English and French of the indexes. I feel that Cançado Trindade should take one more step forward and publish an abridged version of the four volumes in English since it would reach a much larger body of readers than the Brazilian version.

With the completion of the digest, Cançado Trindade, who is the author of many books and articles on international law, can be expected to take his place among the principal experts on international law in Latin America.

G. E. do Nascimento e Silva

Guojifa Xin Lingyu Jianlun (A Concise Introduction to the New Areas of International Law). By Shen Yu and Wei Jiajui. [Changchun]: Jilin People's Press, 1984. Pp. 272.

Guoji Jingifa (International Economic Law). By Liu Ding. Beijing: Chinese People's University Press, 1984. Pp. 426.

Guoji Shangfa (International Commercial Law). 2 vols. By Shen Daming, Feng Datong and Zhao Hongxun. Beijing: External Trade Education Press, 1985. Vol. 1: pp. 360; vol. 2: pp. 240.

Guoji Shuifa (International Tax Law). By Liu Longheng. Beijing: Current Affairs Press, 1985. Pp. 167.

Guoji Touzifa (International Investment Law). By Yao Meizhen. [Wuhan]: Wuhan University Press, 1985. Pp. 451.

Guoji Huobifa Gailun (Introduction to International Monetary Law). By Shen Yu. Beijing: Law Press, 1985. Pp. 289.

Guoji Maoyifa (International Trade Law). By Shen Daming and Feng Datong. Beijing: Beijing University Press, 1985. Pp. 454.

The renewed Chinese interest in international law in the post-Mao period[1] is motivated by China's four modernization programs. One of the major means chosen to achieve modernization goals is to attract foreign investments, by introducing foreign technology transfer to China, forming joint ventures, conducting joint exploration of natural resources and expanding foreign trade. As a result, in addition to traditional public international law, Chinese scholars have begun to develop an interest in international economic and business law.

"A Concise Introduction to the New Areas of International Law," by Shen Yu and Wei Jiajui, contains 10 chapters, dealing respectively with the international law of development, international monetary law, international antitrust law, international product liability law, international environmental law, international economic organization law, international travel and tourism law, atomic energy law, international criminal law and legal problems of international arms control. While in the West the international law of human rights has become a popular subject, it is not even mentioned in Shen and Wei's book.

Liu Ding's "International Economic Law" deals primarily with international trade and technology transfer, but it also analyzes in detail legal problems relating to joint ventures and their protection under Chinese law and international law (pp. 261–380). Shen, Feng and Zhao's "International Commercial Law" is a textbook used for teaching college students majoring in international trade. The authors attempt to compare continental European and Anglo-American laws on international contracts, sales, agency, commercial organizations, negotiable instruments, carriage of goods by sea, marine insurance, industrial property, trade dispute arbitration and litigation involving foreign elements. Several important international trade conventions concluded under the auspices of the United Nations are also discussed and analyzed. Liu Longheng's "International Tax Law" is a concise discussion of the Chinese tax system as it applies to foreigners, the tax systems of the United States, Japan and a few Asian countries, and certain international tax agreements.

A comprehensive discussion of international investment law is provided in Yao Meizhen's "International Investment Law." Aside from providing an

[1] For details, see Chiu, *Chinese Attitudes Toward International Law in the Post-Mao Era, 1978–1987,* 21 INT'L LAW. 1127 (1987).

introduction to the investment policy, laws and guarantee systems of capitalist countries, this book discusses in detail socialist countries and China's policy and legislation on using foreign capital (pp. 95–204). Unfortunately, the book only deals briefly with the subject of how to settle foreign investment disputes in China (pp. 447–51).

Post-Mao China has participated in the International Monetary Fund, the World Bank, the International Development Association and the International Finance Corporation. It no longer rejects foreign borrowing for short-term or long-term purposes. However, there are very few Chinese works that deal with international monetary problems, especially their legal aspects. Shen Yu's "Introduction to International Monetary Law" fills this gap. It is primarily concerned with introducing the international monetary system—its organization, exchange controls, banking and related problems—to the Chinese reader, though in a few places, it also discusses briefly the Chinese foreign exchange system, the settlement of accounts and the gold reserve policy (pp. 63–66, 76–77 and 219–20).

Shen and Feng's "International Trade Law" deals with both private and public law aspects of international trade. It is divided into four parts and 14 chapters. Part 1 covers international sales of goods, including problems relating to contracts, shipping, insurance and payment. Part 2 discusses problems of international transfer of technology such as the concepts of industrial property, trademark and patent protection, and methods of transfering technology and licensing agreements. Part 3 deals with foreign trade control, trade agreements, the General Agreement on Tariffs and Trade and capitalist countries' antitrust or similar legislation. The last part covers the settlement of international trade disputes and includes a concise discussion of the Chinese law and practice in this area.

HUNGDAH CHIU
University of Maryland
School of Law

Xiandai Guojifa Jichu (Foundation of Modern International Law). By Qiu Zaiyu and Zhang Jincao. [Baoding]: Hebei University Teaching Materials Section, 1984. Pp. 316.

Guoji Gongfa (Public International Law). By Zhu Lisun *et al.* Beijing: Central Broadcasting Television University Press, 1985. Pp. 373.

Guojifa Gailun (Introduction to International Law). By Hu Wenzhi *et al.* [Hanzhou]: Zhejiang People's Press, 1986. Pp. 350.

Guojifa Gailun (Introduction to International Law). By Wei Min *et al.* Beijing: Guangming Daily Press, 1986. Pp. 413.

The first standard college textbook on international law published in the People's Republic of China appeared in 1981.[1] Several new textbooks have

[1] GUOJI FA (International Law) (Wang Tieya & Wei Min eds. 1981), reviewed by Hungdah Chiu in 77 AJIL 977 (1983).

come out since then. Qiu and Zhang's "Foundation of Modern International Law" is a textbook published for the use of law students at Hebei University. It contains 13 chapters, dealing respectively with the concept, nature, sources and relations between international law and municipal law (all grouped in the introductory chapter), fundamental principles, subjects, territories, law of the sea, airspace and outer space, residents (individuals), diplomatic and consular relations, law of treaties, international organizations, international economic law, peaceful settlement of international disputes and law of war and neutrality. The contents of Zhu Lisun's "Public International Law" are similar, except that there is no chapter on international economic law. Zhu's book is used for television college programs, so it has a printing of 153,000 copies and thus is the most widely distributed text on international law in China. Hu's "Introduction to International Law" has contents similar to Qiu and Zhang's book. Wei's "Introduction to International Law" omits chapters on international economic law and law of war and neutrality; however, it does treat each of its subjects in more depth. Wei's book is used for self-study programs of the People's Republic of China, but its first printing was only 12,600 copies.

While the contents of these books are generally similar to those of certain introductory books on international law published in the West, they all deny that individuals are subjects of international law (Qiu and Zhang, pp. 49–50; Zhu, p. 48; Hu, pp. 49–50; and Wei, pp. 74–79) and emphasize that state sovereignty is one of the fundamental principles of international law. All four books occasionally deal with certain Chinese practices of international law such as the nationality question, and they support Chinese positions on certain international issues such as condemning Vietnamese intervention in Cambodia. For teaching purposes, it appears that among the four textbooks, Wei's book is the best written. It also contains an extensive bibliography for further study, a list of dates when countries established diplomatic relations with the PRC and a list showing Chinese participation in multilateral conventions.[2]

HUNGDAH CHIU
University of Maryland
School of Law

Balance of Payments Adjustment, 1945 to 1986: The IMF Experience. By Margaret Garritsen de Vries. Washington: International Monetary Fund, 1987. Pp. xi, 336. Index. $14.50.

Margaret Garritsen de Vries has written alone, or with others, three fat multivolume books on the International Monetary Fund, covering the years 1945–1965, 1966–1971 and 1972–1978, plus a single volume of synthesis

[2] For a more complete list of conventions with China's participation, see Chiu, *Chinese Attitudes Toward International Law in the Post-Mao Era, 1978–1987,* 21 INT'L LAW. 1127, 1154–158 (1987).

covering the entire period 1945–1985. The book under review addresses one aspect of the Fund's work, balance-of-payments adjustment, which may be the prime issue faced by the Fund (p. 1). It combines analysis of the theory of such adjustment, especially as economists working on the Fund's staff have helped to shape and extend that theory, with a running account of adjustment problems of industrial and developing countries as they appeared to the Fund. There are many references to the longer studies: in chapter 6, for example, nine of 20 footnotes refer to Mrs. de Vries's earlier work (sometimes with colleagues). There is heavy quotation from IMF reports, speeches, studies and meetings. The book has a fairly extensive bibliography, appendix tables and suggestions for further reading.

It is a little hard to say whether the book is intended to be read straight through or to serve as a reference for particular subjects. For one who begins at the beginning and plows ahead, it should be noted that it can be read at two levels: as economic history, and as the history of economic thought on balance-of-payments adjustment. The economic history is to a considerable extent what was called in my youth "upsy-downsy"; this exchange rate or balance-of-payments surplus went up, that went down. The history of economic thought begins after World War II with the creation of the Fund and pays little or no attention to the automatic adjustment process thought to have existed under the price-specie-flow mechanism or the gold standard. Nor does it pay particular attention to the enormous literature produced outside the Fund. For example, there is no mention of Robert Triffin's *Gold and the Dollar Crisis* (1958), and the devaluations of sterling in 1949 and 1967 are dealt with in a few pages without reference to Alec Cairncross and Barry Eichengreen's *Sterling in Decline* (1983).

The basic problem facing the Fund has been the differences in view between the industrial countries, on the one hand, and the developing countries, on the other. In the former, deficits in balances of payments are for the most part the consequence of mistaken macroeconomic policy, and should be corrected by an exchange-rate change in the event that overvaluation arises from inflation, by reducing expenditure on consumption, investment and government (together called "absorption," meaning absorption of resources), or by restraining or reducing the money supply. Developing countries, in contrast, believe in "structural" deficits that arise in part from exogenous or outside events rather than domestic policy mistakes. The Fund and de Vries started out very partial to the three macropolicy schools —based on "elasticities" (the exchange rate), absorption (spending) or the money supply. During the period of fixed exchange rates, they wanted correction to take place first through fiscal and then monetary contraction. When, after 1971, this seemed not to have brought correction, and floating exchanges replaced the par-value system with which the Fund had started in 1946, they moved to dependence on elasticities introduced by floating exchange rates. This strong view is a little curious, however, since the Fund spent the first decade or so after its foundation on the sidelines, while the burden of moving to balance-of-payments adjustment was carried by the Marshall Plan, a program of assistance explicitly relying upon structural adjustment. There were economists in 1947 and 1948 (and a revisionist school has appeared today) who said that the balance of payments of Europe could readily be corrected by curbing inflation and adjusting the exchange rate—in its vulgar form, balancing the budget and devaluing to the purchasing-power-parity level. For the most part, however, both economists and governmental authorities relied on a diagnosis that stressed structural change.

The developing countries today, as for the last 40 years, insist that their troubles are not homemade but come from abroad, and that they are the result of declining export prices (terms of trade), restricted markets in the industrial countries, sharp increases in the prices of such a commodity as oil (in 1973 and 1979), and so on. They want more resources, and they want them unconditionally. De Vries states explicitly that she is not writing a book on conditionality, but the pressures of the Fund to restrain spending, control money supplies and insist on correction of overvalued (and multiple) exchange rates, and the resistance of developing countries to the Fund's "grandmotherly" scolding of them, are set forth at length.

Perhaps the greatest interest in the book is the Darwinian fashion in which this Cartesian instrument grew. The Fund was established with limited facilities, divided into fifths, available at limited intervals in limited amounts. First, there was the long delay from 1946 to perhaps 1958 before operations could really get going—in contrast with the originally contemplated 5-year transitional period. Bit by bit, more resources were drawn in by the General Arrangements to Borrow, and outside the Fund's jurisdiction, the swap arrangements of the Basel Agreement. Stand-by agreements provided for future contingencies, and back-to-back joining of separate tranches allowed increased borrowing. As new problems arose, new sorts of drawings were allowed: Compensatory Financing, the Special Drawing Right (a failed initiative that some observers now want to bring back), the Supplementary Financing Facility, the Structural Adjustment Facility, the Oil Facility, the Extended Fund Facility and the like. The Articles of Agreement originally provided for fixed exchange rates, alterable only under special conditions. With the breakdown of this system and the move to floating exchange rates, the Fund has successively worked on target zones, policy coordination, trigger consultations and surveillance.

I find particularly interesting an account of Managing Director H. Johannes Witteveen's speech of April 1976, warning the commercial banks and the borrowing developing countries on using bank credit to meet balance-of-payments deficits (pp. 128–29). His warning went unheeded and most historical accounts of the problem regard it as having surfaced for the first time in 1982 with the Mexican debt crisis. Even if the Fund recognized the signs of a forthcoming problem, the steps taken to meet it, and especially its recurrence in the second half of 1986 (pp. 257 *ff.*), have a painful ad hoc quality, involving loans from the Fund, the World Bank, the Inter-American Bank and commercial banks. Moreover, the initiative in the recent past seems to have passed from the Fund as such to the (now former) U.S. Secretary of the Treasury, James Baker. On page 284, the author notes that for developing countries, policy changes may be needed to raise current aggregate output, to change the structure of output, to increase rates of savings and investment, and to improve the return on investment. Changes would conceivably be needed not only in exchange-rate policy, but also in pricing policies, income policies, trade policies and specific aspects of taxation or public spending policies. A tall order! She goes on to say that the framework for determining these policies was undeveloped, which left "considerable scope for more thinking about the general strategy of adjustment programs, especially over the medium term." There is little comfort in that judgment.

In conclusion, two nitpicks: on page 81, the author states that in the absence of a good reserve asset, countries used the dollar. This reveals a failure of understanding. Throughout modern history, a leading currency has been used as both a vehicle and a reverse currency. Using the same currency—the Venetian ducat, Amsterdam rix-dollar, British pound sterling and U.S. dollar—for both purposes saves transaction costs, that is, it is economical. I do not mean to pin this misunderstanding specifically on de Vries: it is and has been general. But it involves a misunderstanding.

Secondly, and less substantively, I take strong exception to the expression on page 94, "infinitely more difficult." One could more concisely use the word "impossible."

CHARLES P. KINDLEBERGER
Massachusetts Institute of Technology, Emeritus

International Trade and the Tokyo Round Negotiation. By Gilbert R. Winham. Princeton: Princeton University Press, 1987. Pp. xiv, 449. Index. $45, cloth; $13.50, paper.

Gilbert Winham's definitive work on the GATT Tokyo Round (1973–1979) stands as a worthy sequel to Ernest Preeg's landmark study of the Kennedy Round (1963–1969).[1] Preeg's study gave a history of the negotiations, an analysis of the results and an evaluation of the significance of the Kennedy Round for future trade policy. By contrast, Winham spends far more time on the mechanics of the negotiation, how negotiating positions evolved and the horse-trading that took place.

Despite the successful conclusion of the Kennedy Round, an accumulation of unsolved problems soon threatened the liberal trading regime that was forged in the GATT agreement of 1947. As Winham notes: "On the trade side, the problem was not so much with the system as with an accumulation of injurious policy actions taken by various nations against the interests of others." The central task was to negotiate methods to make old rules apply more fairly, and to avert a pattern of retaliation that would unravel the fabric of the trading system. The trade setting of 1973 was thus very much like the trade setting of 1988.

[1] E. PREEG, TRADERS AND DIPLOMATS: AN ANALYSIS OF THE KENNEDY ROUND AND THE GENERAL AGREEMENT ON TARIFFS AND TRADE (1970).

In terms of size, the ensuing Tokyo Round was quite simply the largest commercial negotiation ever held. In terms of substance, it was the most important commercial negotiation since the early postwar conferences that constructed the Bretton Woods system. Prior GATT trade negotiations had dealt almost exclusively with tariff cuts and did not penetrate protectionism behind the borders. By comparison, the Tokyo Round exposed nontariff problems, even when it did not redress them.

The fact that Winham examined the Tokyo Round through the lens of political science means that, even in a very long book, many aspects get short shrift. There are no tables of trade statistics, no before-and-after tariff rates. There is no room for legal analysis. The subject matter of the six Tokyo Round codes is summarized in a bare eight pages in Appendix B.

Instead, Winham gives a very detailed phase-by-phase, subject-matter-by-subject-matter, account of the negotiating process. Chapters 3–7 are the heart of the book: "The Negotiation Launched, 1973–1974" (ch. 3), "Early Phase, 1974–1977" (ch. 4), "Middle Phase, 1977–1978" (ch. 5) and "End Phase, 1978–1979" (chs. 6 and 7).

Winham places the Tokyo negotiations in the larger setting of commercial policy since the 1930s—essentially the political economy of mercantilism. In this setting, negotiators represent producer interests, even though the greater purpose of their efforts—besides the thrill of the bargaining table and the delight of elegant cuisine—is consumer interests. Above all, each negotiator is mindful that his personal reputation depends on a "successful" outcome. Pity the forgotten negotiators who spent long years toiling on the failed Safeguards Code!

Some episodes are particularly well told. Chapter 7 gives an excellent exposition of the historical and political intricacies of the complex U.S. nontariff measure known as the "wine gallon" tax. Another example: at various points, Winham recounts Robert Strauss's bag of negotiating tricks. One memorable story recalls the ambassador's delivery of the so-called Strauss list of agricultural priorities, penned on the tablecloth of the Intercontinental Hotel in Geneva, to the horror of the maitre d', and the dismay of Finn Gundelach.

This is a book for both academic specialists and trade practitioners. It makes timely reading for those who will carry the Uruguay Round to its middle and end phases—especially the political ambassadors who will step into the shoes of Grey, Haferkamp, Strauss and Ushiba.

GARY HUFBAUER

International Criminal Law. Volume II: Procedure. Edited by M. Cherif Bassiouni. Dobbs Ferry: Transnational Publishers, Inc., 1986. Pp. xvii, 552. Indexes. $60.

International Criminal Law. Volume III: Enforcement. Edited by M. Cherif Bassiouni. Dobbs Ferry: Transnational Publishers, Inc., 1987. Pp. xvii, 313. Indexes. $35.

These are the last two volumes of Professor Bassiouni's three-volume series on international criminal law. (Volume I, *Crimes,* was reviewed in an earlier issue of this *Journal.*[1]) As stated in the introduction to each volume, Bassiouni's declared purpose in presenting the work is "to provide the scholar, researcher, practitioner and student with the necessary basis of understanding this important subject." Admittedly, "every topic contained in these volumes is not exhaustively covered."

Keeping in mind the caveat he himself has noted, Bassiouni has successfully achieved his purpose. His focus is on the *lex lata* rather than *de lege feranda,* and both volumes are more descriptive and analytical than critical of existing law and practice. The result is more an encyclopedia of international criminal law than a treatise.

Volume II (*Procedure*) covers extradition, prisoner exchange treaties and other means by which individual states cooperate to enforce both national and international criminal law. (Bassiouni refers to these means as "the indirect enforcement method.") Volume III (*Enforcement*) is concerned with "the direct enforcement model," i.e., the practice of international criminal courts. Both volumes include articles and essays by the editor and other authors as well as reprints of treaties, UN reports and other primary source materials.

Volume II is the most successful of the series, and will be of more interest to the practitioner than volumes I or III. Jurisdiction, extradition, transfer of prisoners, recognition of foreign penal judgments, taking evidence abroad and other topics related to international cooperation in penal matters are all touched upon in this volume. While each chapter has a different author, the editor has done an admirable job of tying these diverse essays into a unified and comprehensive volume. As in the first volume of the series, the work is strengthened by the inclusion of many primary source documents such as the European Convention on Transfer of Prisoners and U.S. statutes on extradition.

The law and policy of the United States are the chief focus of volume II, with Western European laws and agreements receiving almost equally comprehensive treatment. Discussion of Eastern European positions comes in a poor third.

From a purely American perspective, of course, the topics discussed in this volume include matters that have undergone exciting changes in the last 15 years. These developments include the negotiation of the first prisoner exchange treaties, the subsequent negotiation of bilateral agreements for international cooperation in penal matters, the elimination of the "political offense" exception in certain extradition treaties and the reevaluation, in the context of antiterrorism legislation, of the historic opposition of the United States to the passive personality principle of jurisdiction.

Though a few of these developments (e.g., the revision of the "political offense" provisions of the U.S.-UK extradition treaty) occurred too recently to be discussed in this work, most have been covered in a thorough and

[1] 81 AJIL 510 (1987).

scholarly manner. On a few topics, such as the U.S. law of international prisoner exchange, this volume is virtually the only treatise to deal with the matter.

Eastern European law is primarily represented by a valuable chapter surveying "Socialist" positions on jurisdiction, extradition and other aspects of international penal cooperation, written by Professor Gardocki of the University of Warsaw. This short article gives the reader a fascinating comparative look at topics not normally covered even in Western works on Eastern European law. Unfortunately, the look is little more than a glimpse.

Taken as a whole, volume II will be a valuable resource for scholars and students, and for those practitioners who find themselves faced with an occasional international criminal law problem. A specialist in international trade law, for example, might well need to consult this work when a client is suddenly faced with a question involving the effects and application of the European Convention on the International Validity of Criminal Judgments.

Volume III is the weakest of the three. One would expect that a work dealing with "the direct enforcement model" of international criminal law, through international prosecution before an international court, would look mainly to the future and focus on the problems and prospects for the success of such a model. Less than half of this volume is concerned with such issues, however, and this half consists (except for a five-page introduction by the editor) solely of reprints of documents from international organizations.

It is undeniably valuable to have access to these otherwise hard-to-find reports. Documents from international organizations are, however, notoriously subject to political considerations in the course of their drafting. This part of the volume would have been much more useful if these documents had been supplemented by commentaries from qualified scholars, both proponents and skeptics on the issue of an international criminal court. The approach of including both primary source documents and academic commentary is consistently followed elsewhere in these three volumes, and it is not clear why the editor chose to depart from this practice in part 2 of volume III.

Part 1 of volume III deals with historical examples of international prosecution. It also suffers from problems, but of a different nature from those that afflict part 2. The articles and essays in part 1 are generally thought-provoking and of high academic quality. Noteworthy, in this regard, are Bassiouni's essays on crimes against peace and crimes against humanity, and Professor Bierzaneck's treatment of the history of the definition of war crimes.

The problem is that this material has little to do with enforcement, the announced theme of the volume. Most of the essays in this part deal with the definition of offenses and other issues of substantive law, issues previously covered in volume I of this series. There may be a sound basis for placing this material in volume III, rather than in volume I, but the criteria governing that decision are not readily apparent. Those doing research on substantive aspects of war crimes, crimes against humanity and crimes against peace would be well-advised to consult both volumes. Similarly, Jordan

Paust's fine survey of American military practice on the defense of superior orders, and Christine van den Wijngaert's succinct essay on statutory limitations, are both more concerned with problems encountered in the national enforcement of international law than they are with the practice of international courts. They would thus have been more appropriately included in volume II, with other discussions of the "indirect enforcement method," than in volume III.

Volume III is at its weakest in its treatment of the International Military Tribunal for the Far East (the Tokyo Trial). In the context of the Pacific war, this Tribunal dealt with many of the same issues as the International Military Tribunal at Nuremberg, as well as with a number of interesting matters not raised at Nuremberg. Here, however, its work has been relegated to a two-page "Editor's Note," from which we learn little beyond the fact that Bassiouni does not think highly of the Tokyo Trial.

While the editor obviously has strong feelings about the Tokyo Trial, we are given almost no analysis to support them. He cites only two sources, both secondary, for the conclusion that the Tokyo Trial had a "decisively political flavor" and is, unlike Nuremberg, an example of "victor's justice." He charges the presiding judge with a lack of impartiality and the chief prosecutor with presenting questionable evidence, without providing examples of either type of impropriety. The note fails to mention that the defense succeeded in convincing the Tribunal to dismiss a significant number of the charges (though no defendant at Tokyo was acquitted of all charges).

In the documentary appendix, the editor quotes five pages (out of 1,200) from the majority judgment at Tokyo and 20 from Justice Roling's dissent. Again, this selection is skewed against the Tribunal's majority. It certainly does not give the reader an adequate basis for forming an independent opinion of the Tokyo Trial.

One reason given for this negative attitude toward the Tokyo Trial is that General MacArthur, as Supreme Allied Commander in occupied Japan, had a large role in setting up the Tribunal, approving the charges, appointing the judges and choosing the defendants. All that was true. The Charter of the Tribunal was, in fact, promulgated as a General Order issued by MacArthur. (The point is made because the "Editor's Note" erroneously suggests that the Charter of the Tokyo Tribunal was part of an international agreement, like the Charter of the International Military Tribunal at Nuremberg.[2])

By singling out the Tokyo Trial for criticism on this basis, the "Editor's Note" may leave the erroneous impression that other Allied war crimes tribunals were not similarly constituted. In reality, most Anglo-American war crimes tribunals (called "military commissions" by the Americans and "military courts" by the Commonwealth countries) were set up in much the same way in both theaters of war. The local Allied military commander

[2] The Charter of the International Military Tribunal for the Far East is reprinted in DOCUMENTS ON PRISONERS OF WAR 312 (H. Levie ed. 1979). For what it may be worth, a recent account of the Tokyo Trial by a journalist who covered it for United Press indicates that MacArthur was not personally enthusiastic about the trial. A. BRACKMAN, THE OTHER NUREMBERG 74 (1987).

selected the court members, convened the court, approved the charges and the accused, referred cases to trial and reviewed the findings and sentence. The source of these practices was not political prejudice. Rather, they were adopted by analogy to the court-martial procedures used in the British and American armed forces.

Finally, volume III displays evidence of hasty editing. As an example, an entire chapter seems to have been dropped from part 1, leaving behind a few enigmatic traces. "Chapter One" of part 1 is entitled "International Prosecution." Where part of a work is designated "Chapter One," the reader would expect a "Chapter Two" to follow. (Otherwise, why divide the work into chapters?) Here, there is nothing labeled "Chapter Two." After the documentary appendixes to chapter 1, however, there is a brief essay by Professor D'Amato entitled *National Prosecution for International Crimes.* Is this the elusive "Chapter Two," or at least an introduction to it? It certainly does not seem to belong in a chapter on international prosecutions, and if it is part of chapter 1, why does it appear after the appendixes? On the other hand, there would appear to be a lack of balance in a work that has a first chapter of 146 pages and a second chapter of 10 pages.

Again, in the documentary appendixes to part 1, chapter 1, the 1968 Convention on the Non-Applicability of Statutory Limitations to War Crimes and Crimes Against Humanity is wrongly titled the "Convention on the Nonapplicability of Statutory Limitations to War Crimes Against Humanity." This error appears both in the document itself and in the table of contents.

A certain number of typographical and textual errors are likely to appear in any volume of over three hundred pages. Where a work purports to reprint primary reference documents, however, the reader is entitled to assume that special care has been taken to ensure that those are accurately reproduced. A major error in the title of such a document must raise doubts about the accuracy of the documentary appendixes as a whole.

All in all, however, the weaknesses of volume III do not significantly undercut the value of the series as a whole. It should be noted that volume II is fully capable of standing alone as a reference work. Practitioners and others with little interest in the more theoretical aspects of international criminal law might well consider buying only that volume. Those who have a broader interest in the history, development, theory and current status of international criminal law will want to have access to the entire series. For them, all three volumes are recommended.

BURRUS M. CARNAHAN
Of the Illinois Bar

The Antarctic Treaty regime: Law, Environment and Resources. Edited by Gillian D. Triggs. Cambridge and New York: Cambridge University Press, 1987. Pp. xxi, 237. $54.50.

This volume contains papers prepared by 15 authors for the "Whither Antarctica?" Conference, sponsored in April 1985 by the British Institute of

International and Comparative Law. Collectively, these assessments by highly qualified experts ably elucidate the tangled nexus of legal, political and resource problems that complicate contemporary Antarctic affairs. As such, the book is a welcome addition to an expanding literature.[1]

The work is organized into five substantive parts, each of which is introduced by a brief, yet perceptively informative, commentary by the editor, Gillian Triggs. Part I deals with the physical environment and scientific research in the Antarctic. In the initial chapter, D. J. Drewry comprehensibly sets out the geographical situation and geophysical structure of the Antarctic region. The acquisition of greater geological knowledge about Antarctica in a resource-hungry world is assuming increasing importance. This thesis undergirds the contribution by R. M. Laws, who discusses scientific opportunities within the context of geophysical and biogeographical processes in the Antarctic. As Professor Laws plainly explains, the fragile ecological situation in the Antarctic is likely to influence the future course of scientific research there toward conservation and wise management of resources.

Legal issues affecting the Antarctic Treaty regime are treated in part II. Here the dilemmas associated with sovereignty in the Antarctic are articulated: who, if anyone, owns what territory, where, under what legal conditions, and with what attendant legal rights, on and offshore the continent? R. Trolle-Andersen supplies a useful, lucid analysis of the legal and political elements underpinning the Antarctic Treaty system. His conclusion is politically salient: Antarctica today remains a natural preserve of international peace and cooperation, a political reality engendered by the Antarctic legal regime. It would be imprudent, he concludes, to abandon this proven system hastily for some untried, more universal international regime. Similarly, Francisco Orrego-Vicuña examines the utility of the Antarctic Treaty system as an alternative for regulating resource-related activities in the region. As he rightly posits, the system of Antarctic agreements furnishes several demonstrated advantages for the international community. These include the openness of the Treaty to universal accession, its operation for unlimited duration, its preservation of the region as a nonmilitarized, nuclear weapons–free zone of peace, its inclusion of an on-site inspection system, its multiple efforts to protect the Antarctic environment, and its specific facilitation of international scientific cooperation and exchange of information. Professor Orrego-Vicuña makes compelling the argument that participation in Antarctic decision making is not arrogated as a right of certain states; rather, it has accrued to them from their acceptance of specific obligations over activities in the region. The Antarctic Treaty system thus should properly be viewed today as an evolving international organization, though it lacks much sophisticated institutionalization. As such, it has actually been strengthened, rather than debilitated, by the recent debate

[1] As indicated in the introduction, impetus for the present volume came from publication of the papers in ANTARCTIC RESOURCES POLICY: SCIENTIFIC, LEGAL AND POLITICAL ISSUES (F. Orrego-Vicuña ed. 1983).

over Antarctica and its governing regime. That is, the UN debates since 1983 have prompted the Antarctic Treaty Consultative Parties (ATCPs) to rethink and reevaluate their stake in the Antarctic Treaty system. The unmistakable upshot has been to convince them that the Treaty and its family of agreements was worth preserving. That remains a fundamental point not to be lost sight of in contemporary Antarctic affairs.

Of what relevance is Antarctica to the lawyer? Hazel Fox addresses this query from four stages of legal thinking that reveal ample opportunities for the international lawyer. As Lady Fox observes, Article IV of the Antarctic Treaty presents the most intriguing conundrum to the lawyer in that it provides a legally binding political compromise of delicate balance between select claims of sovereign territoriality and international nonrecognition of those assertions to title. Her thoughtful analysis of that double-edged provision, coupled with the distinct possibilities of some commercial development on the continent, the likelihood of ensuing jurisdictional conflicts and the patent need to clarify how private international criminal law applies to the continent, highlights prominent challenges that international lawyers will have to meet in devising a more practicable legal system for Antarctica.[2]

Complications that arise from conflicting juridical positions over sovereignty on the continent have compounded and protracted recent negotiations on Antarctic resources and environmental preservation. Gillian Triggs seizes upon this theme as she analyzes "some jurisdictional problems" relating to the Antarctic Treaty system. Critical issues treated include difficulties stemming from the "purgatory of ambiguity" associated with Article IV; legal questions regarding offshore jurisdictional rights in coastal zones; jurisdictional complications posed by a future International Sea-Bed Authority; problems of jurisdiction over Antarctic living marine resources; the limited participation in decision making under the Antarctic Treaty regime; and the implications underpinning the application of an approach to the region based on the principle of the "common heritage of mankind." Her discussion and assessments are well reasoned, balanced and insightful, and the issues are clearly presented. The main message gleaned from Professor Triggs's treatment, as well as from several other essays in the volume, is that problems do exist in the present Antarctic Treaty system, but that any reform by the Consultative Parties should proceed slowly, with patient circumspection and caution. So long as governments work through the present Treaty system to fashion a regime that protects the Antarctic region, the entire international community benefits. If the past is prologue, that deduction may be a fair appraisal.

The third part of this volume concerns protection of the Antarctic environment. John Gulland assesses the Antarctic Treaty system as a resource management mechanism, specifically by focusing on the Convention on the

[2] Potential problems associated with private international criminal law in Antarctica are not substantively discussed in this treatment. For a lucid account, see Carl, *The Need for a Private International Law Regime in Antarctica,* in THE ANTARCTIC LEGAL REGIME 65 (C. Joyner & S. Chopra eds. 1988).

Conservation of Antarctic Marine Living Resources (CCAMLR). Effective resource management patently remains dependent upon obtaining agreement from the parties on shared objectives and then acquiring adequate technical and scientific information on possible outcomes of management alternatives. As Dr. Gulland observes, Antarctic Treaty states are bound, in concerted interest and joint responsibility, to manage living resources south of the Antarctic convergence. Failure to cooperate fully in these efforts, as in the present case of the CCAMLR, undermines the practical prospects for effecting a successful conservation regime throughout the region.

M. W. Holdgate takes up this theme as he cogently assesses the prospects for regulated development and conservation of Antarctic resources. His central thesis holds that if development of Antarctica should occur, it must proceed in an orderly manner that builds and improves upon achievements already attained under the Antarctic Treaty system. Development must be made compatible with a viable conservation strategy, so that it "sustains the productivity of renewable resources and balances alternative uses, where they compete, in a fashion most beneficial to human welfare" (pp. 128–29). Thus is posed the fundamental query: are environmental regulations contained in the Antarctic Treaty system adequate in coverage and effective in implementation? Dr. Holdgate optimistically concludes that, on balance, they have been. Even so, a more precisely defined and applied conservation strategy is warranted for the Antarctic, especially one that takes into account the impending promulgation of a minerals regime there.

W. M. Bonner's chapter on recent developments in Antarctic conservation neatly complements Holdgate's views. As Dr. Bonner notes, the 1964 Agreed Measures on the Conservation of Antarctic Fauna and Flora do supply a practical code of conduct aimed at environmental protection, albeit admittedly only for the Antarctic land and ice shelves. For the circumpolar waters, the 1972 Seals Convention and the CCAMLR furnish the legally binding conservation ethic. Yet, as Bonner posits, "CCAMLR is a philosophical scientist's convention. It is certainly not a convention for fisheries managers" (p. 145). Monitoring and enforcement of regulations are not institutionally guaranteed. Thus, international environmental organizations such as the International Union of the Conservation of Nature, the Antarctic and Southern Ocean Coalition, and Greenpeace, as well as the Scientific Committee on Antarctic Research, must work to demonstrate the criticality of integrating environmental considerations into Antarctic policymaking.[3] In like fashion, the paper by James Barnes calls for adopting new approaches and ecological perspectives to protect the Antarctic environment. Highlights among the environmental objectives advocated by Dr. Barnes include the establishment of an Antarctic Environmental Protection Agency, greater scientific management of Southern Ocean fisheries (especially krill), a long-term moratorium on all minerals activities in the region, widespread acceptance of Antarctica as a world park and creation of an Antarctic fund

[3] For an insightful treatment, see Kimball, *The Role of Non-Governmental Organizations in Antarctic Affairs,* in Joyner & Chopra (eds.), *supra* note 2, at 33.

for research aimed at enhancing environmental protection in the area. Implicit in all these suggestions is the necessity of redirecting priorities and changing attitudes. Not surprisingly, it is easier to posit the scientific wisdom and rationality of environmentally sensitive policies than it is to convince 20 individual governments that their national interests are best served by adopting those policies for the benefit of all mankind.

Part IV informatively treats the Antarctic minerals regime as it had emerged up through 1985. At the outset, it is worth inquiring, why negotiations on a minerals regime now? If no minerals of appreciable commercial quantity are known to exist in the Antarctic, why have mineral negotiations been pursued so intensely by the Antarctic Treaty Consultative Parties over the past decade? Alan Watts pinpoints the answer in his contribution. As he astutely observes, considerable political and diplomatic advantage lies in negotiating a regulatory regime without precise knowledge of mineral deposits. Discovery and determination of substantial mineral deposits on, in or around the continent would undoubtedly make negotiations even more difficult, as the vested stakes of states became more sharply focused. Mr. Watts argues convincingly that the creation of a regime now demonstrates an attempt by the ATCPs to resolve problems before they occur, to seize the initiative instead of being relegated to a policy of prescriptive reaction. Watts goes on to address related significant questions: Why does such a regime have to be negotiated? Why should these negotiations be open only to Antarctic Treaty Consultative Parties? What problems have encumbered progress in the negotiations? What solutions appear foreseeable? As Watts intimates, answers to these queries remain inextricably linked to claims of national sovereignty and competing national interests in the Antarctic. Given that an Antarctic Minerals Convention was completed in June 1988, there is no doubt that national interests, sovereign claims and political priorities have been accommodated by the ATCPs through a concerted willingness to compromise and cooperate.

What are the commercial prospects for Antarctic minerals? The pithy conclusion reached by F. G. Larminie should be reassuring to environmentalists: "Virtually nil" (p. 176). How have the minerals negotiations proceeded and what will the new treaty regime look like? In a separate chapter, Dr. Triggs concisely examines the emerging regime's institutional structure, the system likely to be adopted for decision making, the probable means of regulatory enforcement, the role of third-party states and the conceivable distribution of any benefits derived from exploitation activities.

Part V deals with future management and regulation of policies concerning Antarctic affairs. In a succinct essay, John Heap considers the potential for harvesting icebergs for water and mining exploitable minerals in the Antarctic. Irrespective of eventual technological innovations, his conclusion for futuristic resource exploitation in the Antarctic is diplomatically perceptive and politically instructive: international appreciation of the role that territorial sovereignty plays in Antarctic affairs remains critical if resource activity there is to be regulated in a responsible and reasonable way. Given the twin experiences of negotiating the CCAMLR in the late 1970s and the minerals treaty during the 1980s, ample reason exists to take that warning seriously.

Ambassador Zain-Azraai, former Permanent Representative of Malaysia to the United Nations, takes a different tack from the other contributors. He critically examines the espoused "rights" of the ATCPs based on expertise and experience in the Antarctic, as contrasted with the "rights" of the international community to participate in deciding Antarctic policy priorities in view of all mankind's vested "interests" in the region. In the end, he advocates an "open-minded approach to reconcile the legitimate interests of all parties in the management of Antarctica." The presumption is that such an approach will facilitate resolution of the sovereignty conundrum by establishing a universal regime to manage activities on the continent. Such a noble vision, however, may well outstrip the political practicality and administrative feasibility of a universally directed oversight regime.

Alternative strategies for managing future Antarctic affairs is the subject of J. R. Rowland's piece, and he foresees two general options: (1) the continued evolution of the present Treaty system, and (2) the adoption of new institutional arrangements, the main models for which range from an ATCP-UN trusteeship system, or the negotiation of an entirely new international regime under UN auspices, to the creation of a special UN agency for dealing specifically with Antarctic minerals. As Mr. Rowland suggests, the latter arrangement might defuse the minerals issue. Even so, progress since 1985 in negotiating the ATCP minerals regime plainly indicates that it remained an option beyond realistic consideration by the ATCPs.[4] By way of conclusion, Triggs cogently summarizes the 1983 and 1984 General Assembly debates on the Question of Antarctica. This assessment prompts her to conclude that the United Nations "can be expected to maintain a watching brief on Antarctic activities and to play a closer role in the negotiations upon a minerals regime" (p. 233). Again, though perhaps the issue is arguable, events since 1985 strongly suggest that subsequent UN debates exerted scant influence upon the progress, process and substance of the minerals negotiations.

There is much to commend in *The Antarctic Treaty regime.* On balance, the presentations are politically objective, lucid and thoughtful. The book admirably achieves its stated purpose, namely, to update "the legal, resource and environmental issues presently [in 1985] under consideration within the Antarctic Treaty system and more recently, by the Secretary-General of the United Nations" (p. xv). This said, it must not be overlooked that Antarctic law and politics have surged on and that some technical information in the volume has been overtaken by subsequent events. This inevitability is evidenced by developments concerning the progressive negotiation of an Antarctic minerals agreement, the emergence of further questions about the political, practical and scientific efficacy of the CCAMLR, and the height-

[4] For more recent assessments, see F. Orrego-Vicuña, Antarctic Mineral Exploitation (1988); and Joyner, *The Evolving Antarctic Minerals Regime,* 19 Ocean Dev. & Int'l L. 73 (1988).

ening of widespread international concern over serious depletion of the ozone layer above the continent. Nonetheless, the legal premises in the volume remain substantively intact and relevant, as do the economic, political and environmental realities of the Antarctic situation.

This work embodies much more than the proceedings of a major conference. It supplies valuable insights and important commentary on the evolutionary process of managing Antarctic affairs. A perusal of its contents tells much about where diplomats, government officials and scientists have gone in fashioning Antarctic policy. Even more important for the international lawyer, the contributions also reveal where and why new policies are needed for regulating certain activities in the Antarctic. As a consequence, students, scholars and policymakers alike who are interested in Antarctic law and politics would be well-advised to consult the discerning presentations in this book. Those who do so will be handsomely rewarded for their efforts.

CHRISTOPHER C. JOYNER
The George Washington University

Internationales Seerecht. By Ingo von Münch. Heidelberg: R. v. Decker's Verlag, G. Schenck, 1985. Pp. v, 288. Index. DM 128.

This book is the 20th volume in a series of legal and social science publications. It attempts to bridge the gap between historical and modern maritime law in light of the Conference on the Law of the Sea (UNCLOS III). *Internationales Seerecht* is written predominantly in German, with two articles translated into English.

Von Münch achieves his goal by laying out the book in three major parts. The first is a detailed introduction to the law of the sea in historical perspective. There follows a series of essays written during UNCLOS III and the period leading up to it. This is done to show the reader the concerns of German international lawyers in the area of the law of the sea. The concluding section is a brief summation of the author's opinion of the results of UNCLOS III.

The introduction is broken up into 21 subsections. The first group examines historical matters relating to shipping. Among these are border problems, attacks on shipping, trade union effects, registration under flags of convenience, environmental concerns and the policing of the oceans. Most of the introduction deals with other uses of the oceans, with an emphasis on the exploitation of the seabeds. Von Münch goes into great detail here because, as later discussed, this seems to be the area of UNCLOS III that stirs up the most controversy.

The author discusses topics such as the effects of the exploitation of the ocean on neighboring countries, exclusive economic zones (EEZs), partitioning the continental shelf, the regulation of seabed exploration, the problems involved in technology transfers and using Antarctica as an international law model. The last subsection of the introduction is a 10-point analysis prepared to assist the West German Government in deciding whether to accede to the 1982 Convention on the Law of the Sea. This is a pro/con analysis giving the opinions of the German Committee of the International Law Association on the good and bad points of the Convention.

The second part, a collection of articles previously published elsewhere by von Münch, covers a wide range of topics and concerns during the 15-year period leading up to the conclusion of the Convention. The articles show a concern that any agreed-upon international law needs to be flexible to keep up with the changing needs of the world. They also show that while reflagging ships under flags of convenience did offer diplomatic protection to shipping, it did not take into account the needs of the sailors involved, which was the main concern of the maritime trade unions. Other articles discuss topics such as ownership of shipwrecks, the environmental/maritime connection and the problems relating to exploitation of the seabed.

The conclusion gives von Münch's opinions of and reservations about the signing of the Convention on the Law of the Sea. He concludes that some modernization of the international law of the sea is desirable, but he is skeptical as to whether the Convention is the correct approach. He notes that the strongest argument for signing is that this would allow the signatories to participate in the making of the final form of the international law. Von Münch is concerned that countries that agree only with the desire to modify the law (and not agreeing to the form of the then existing modifications) might later be seen as agreeing to a version not actually forming the basis of the agreement. In other words, once a party signs, it would quickly become so enmeshed in the process that disentanglement from a section to which it did not agree would be impossible.

The author further points out that the then existing version of the Convention does not decisively deal with the problem of the transfer of technology. He states that while this package is intended to benefit Third World countries, gaps in the laws could allow developed countries to avoid passing on the benefits of new technology to these countries. Other omissions could require that trade secrets be brought into the public domain. Both of these results are highly undesirable.

The last point that von Münch feels was left unanswered is the possibility that nations could overburden shipping by overregulating their exclusive economic zones. This could happen if a nation imposed high fees on ships passing through its territorial waters. Von Münch goes on to suggest that further refinement could successfully deal with all these problems and that signing at that time would be advisable. On the other hand, he posits that not signing, combined with inaction, could lead to problems more serious than those already existing.

Considering the breadth of this text and the treatment of the subject by others, the contribution of *Internationales Seerecht* lies in its West German perspective and its introductory and concluding sections where von Münch summarizes the salient points of concern in the 1982 Convention.

THOMAS F. MARSTELLER
Of the Houston Bar

PETER K. HAHN
University of Houston Law Center

Foreign Relations of the United States, 1952–1954. Volume XII: East Asia and the Pacific. Part 1. (Dept. of State Pub. 9390.) Washington: U.S. Govt. Printing Office, 1984. Pp. xiv, 1113. Index.

Foreign Relations of the United States, 1952–1954. Volume XII: East Asia and the Pacific. Part 2. (Dept. of State Pub. 9550.) Washington: U.S. Govt. Printing Office, 1987. Pp. xv, 763. Index.

This volume of the *Foreign Relations* series, which bridges the final year of the Truman administration and the early years of the Eisenhower presidency, coalesces developments in the Far East during the transitional period that links a number of critical diplomatic activities. These include the termination of World War II (with the signing of the Japanese Peace Treaty in September 1951), the end of the Korean War (with the signing of the Armistice in July 1953), the deterioration of the internal and international situation in Indochina (with the crisis at Dien Bien Phu in May 1954), and the Geneva Conference, which produced the cease-fire agreement dividing Vietnam (July 1954). American containment policy in the area is epitomized by the energizing of the ANZUS Pact (September 1951), the signing of the Manila Pact (September 1954), the establishment of the Southeast Asia Treaty Organization, and the framing of a series of bilateral collective defense treaties (signed by the United States with Japan, the Republic of Korea, Nationalist China and the Philippines (1951–1955)).

This anthology of 1,876 pages of records consists of two parts. Part 1 (pp. 1–1,085) focuses on U.S. policies toward the East Asian–Pacific area as a whole, with documents arranged chronologically throughout. Part 2 (pp. 1–748), which deals with American relations with four countries in the area—Burma, Indonesia, the Philippines and Thailand—contains 439 sequentially numbered documents that are arranged chronologically within each of the four segments. Both parts have their own lists of relevant unpublished archival resources, lists of abbreviations, symbols and acronyms, and comprehensive, double-columned indexes. Unlike others in the *Foreign Relations* series, this volume lacks the customary catalog of persons with their full names, official titles, ranks and positions.

Part 1 deals with five major topics. One of these concentrates on general U.S. objectives, policies and actions in the Far East. Another centers on economic aid and development programs. Documentation on these matters concerns unilateral American economic and military assistance arrangements (including action under the Mutual Security Acts of 1953 and 1954), U.S. relations with and the activities of the United Nations Economic Commission for Asia and the Far East (ECAFE) and the Colombo Plan for Cooperative Economic Development in South and Southeast Asia.

The remaining three topics involve defense and security affairs. These embody activities of the ANZUS (Australia, New Zealand and the United States) powers, the five-nation (Australia, France, New Zealand, the United Kingdom and the United States) military consultations to plan for collective action to constrain Communist China's aggression in the area, and the conclusion of the Southeast Asia Collective Defense Treaty and the establishment of the Southeast Asia Treaty Organization (SEATO). Commentary on the operation of ANZUS embraces planning studies on the development of operational machinery and procedures, and materials on participation in and the deliberations of the ANZUS Council and meetings of member military representatives, and on cooperation of ANZUS with ANZAM (the Australia–New Zealand–Malaya defense arrangement). Records concerned with five-power military consultations pertain to the establishment and functions of an ad hoc committee, a conference of diplomatic representatives that convened in three annual sessions in Washington and Pearl Harbor (1952–1954), and a five-power servicing Staff Agency.

These activities presaged the historic Manila Conference of September 1954, documentation concerning which covers the negotiations of both the preparatory working group and the formal ministerial-level sessions (which convened September 6–8), including verbatim accounts of its six plenary meetings at which the Southeast Asia Collective Defense Treaty, a Protocol to the Treaty and the Pacific Charter were signed by Australia, France, New Zealand, Pakistan, the Philippines, the United Kingdom and the United States (see pp. 852–98).

In addition to presenting materials on general U.S. policy developments and bilateral economic and military assistance arrangements with each of the four countries covered, part 2 furnishes documentation on particularized issues pertaining to each of them. To illustrate, the segment on Burma deals with the problem caused by the presence of Nationalist Chinese (Kuomintang) troops in Burma, their cooperation with the Karen rebellion, the operation of a UN peace observation mission, the evacuation of the Chinese troops and the establishment of an American Military Assistance Advisory Group (MAAG) mission. The segment on Indonesia focuses largely on its dispute with the Netherlands over West Irian/New Guinea, and U.S. efforts to remain neutral in the controversy. In the segment on Thailand, attention is paid to a possible Chinese Communist threat, Thai negotiations with Japan and the probability of establishing U.S. military bases and a joint MAAG mission in the country.

Because of the special relationship of the United States with the Philippine Republic, documentation on this country ranges more widely, from such internal matters as domestic politics and elections, rural development and the insurgency of the Huks, to revision of trade relations (under the bilateral treaty of 1946), implementation of the Mutual Defense Treaty (signed in 1951), the maintenance of U.S. military bases (under the Military Bases Agreement of 1947), and the functioning of the U.S.-Philippines Defense Council and a joint MAAG.

This compendium consists of the customary telegrams, messages, notes and memorandums (of statements "for the record" and summaries of conversations)—together with reports, letters, and other papers and diplomatic communications that flowed primarily within and among the Department of State and other U.S. government agencies in Washington and between the Department and its missions abroad. They also encompass other types of records, such as those relating to the Manila Conference. Those interested in high-level policymaking and coordination will appreciate the inclusion of information pertaining to the activities of the Joint Chiefs of Staff, the Foreign Operations Administration and the U.S. Information Agency, as well as an ample quantity of National Security Council papers. The latter embrace references to six "National Intelligence Estimates" and four "Special Estimates," more than a dozen NSC "actions," and some 30 references to NSC "documents," most of which concern drafts and refinements of policy statements on "U.S. Policies in the Far East," "U.S. Objectives and Courses of Action With Respect to Communist Aggression in Southeast Asia" and a "Review of U.S. Policy in the Far East." Memorandums of sessions of the National Security Council prepared by members of its Secretariat and documentation on NSC subsidiary agencies—the Planning Board and the Operations Coordinating Board—are also provided.

So far as selectivity, organization, treatment and content are concerned, this anthology characterizes the traditionally superior standards of the Office of the Historian of the Department of State in producing the *Foreign Relations* series, and will be appreciated by all who are interested in the diplomatic relations of the United States in the Far East during the early 1950s. To assist the user, its editors supplement the textual materials with a liberal supply of explanatory, descriptive and cross-referencing editorial commentary and documentary footnotes. As in the past, under the supervision of William Z. Slany (Historian, Department of State) and John P. Glennon (editor in chief), David W. Mabon (editor of part 1), Carl N. Raether and Harriet D. Schwar (editors of part 2) brought to this task their high standards of coping with voluminous, complex and dispersed documentary resources, and distilled them for the public domain in a compact, reliable and readily usable way.

Elmer Plischke
University of Maryland, Emeritus
American Enterprise Institute

Exporting the First Amendment: The Press-Government Crusade of 1945–1952. By Margaret A. Blanchard. New York and London: Longman, 1986. Pp. xiv, 448. Index. $39.95.

Exporting the First Amendment, by Margaret Blanchard, is an important, but flawed, book. It is important because of the historical period it covers and the extensive documentation it offers. However, it is essentially flawed because of its lack of analysis and the scant attention paid to some of the most significant issues related to its themes.

It is undeniably to the author's credit that she has chosen to examine one of the most important periods in the recent history of international communications: the post–World War II era. For, as demonstrated during the Iran-contra congressional hearings, it was during this postwar period that U.S. foreign policy built the structure for a world order whose contours are still operative even as we approach the 1990s. Of particular significance for international communications, it was during the post–World War II period that an intensive American campaign was launched to promote freedom of information throughout the world. This endeavor, backed by the U.S. press and the State Department, is examined in great detail in Professor Blanchard's book.

Given that the American efforts to "export the First Amendment" were pursued primarily within the UN system, one would assume that an in-depth analysis of this period would be especially enlightening with respect to the more recent debates on the New World Information Order. For, as this book itself acknowledges, the UNESCO polemics of the 1970s and 1980s brought into relief the same irreconcilably opposing views on freedom of information that were already in evidence in the early days of the United Nations. However, in spite of the obvious interest of this early historical period, and the abundant firsthand documentation cited, Blanchard has managed to miss the main points of the debate she has so assiduously studied. As background for this assessment, it should be mentioned that the author is by no means the first scholar to examine the postwar free-press crusade of the U.S. Government and newspaper industry. The most well-known writer, who looked at this period over 10 years ago, is Herbert Schiller of the University of California.[1] Schiller's basic thesis is that the postwar promotion of the free flow of information doctrine, and freedom of the press *à l'américaine,* corresponded to the economic and political needs of capitalist expansion. The conceptual contribution of Schiller to international communication debates in the 1970s and 1980s is such that almost every book on the debate over the New World Information Order, for example, cites him.

Therefore, it is troubling that Blanchard does not even cite Schiller's thesis (except in her bibliographic essay at the end of the book), particularly since he was the main pioneer in her own field of study. The reason for this omission is no mystery: the author has simply rejected out of hand his analysis of the press-government campaign of the mid-1940s. In its place, however, she offers very little of substance. This, then, is the main criticism of Blanchard's book: its failure to explain the motivating forces behind the postwar free-press crusade. What the author does offer are numerous statements of press and government officials explaining their cause. But valuable as such statements may be in understanding this period, by themselves they are certainly no substitute for analysis.

There are numerous examples of how the author has simply accepted at face value the rationale offered by the press and government officials for their promotion of the American way. This stance, taken throughout most of the book, is clearly spelled out in the introduction: "In general, the free press crusade was part of a larger effort by American diplomats and business leaders to create a world safe for democracy by remodelling that world in the image of the United States. Although tinged with self-interest, the free-press efforts were basically grounded in noble intentions." These "noble

[1] *See* H. SCHILLER, COMMUNICATION AND CULTURAL DOMINATION (1976).

intentions" are made explicit on numerous occasions. According to Blanchard, the press was primarily concerned with freedom to gather information throughout the world. The State Department had somewhat broader goals: freedom to spread information about the United States around the globe and to promote democracy by free reporting. Its specifically Cold War objectives were slightly modified versions of the above agenda: to fight communism and spread "truthful information" about the United States. A good example of her lack of analysis is to be found precisely in the treatment by Blanchard of the debate over the government information agencies set up after World War II. According to her account, the State Department responded to criticism that it was setting up "government propaganda agencies" by stating that it was only presenting "truthful information." Blanchard lets such an assertion stand, with neither comment nor analysis.

With regard to the press, the book does make brief allusions to the idea that perhaps (but only perhaps) the American private sector also had certain commercial gains in mind through promotion of U.S.-style freedom of the press. For example, readers are summarily informed that even during the days of the League of Nations, American press groups attempted to gain international acceptance for the U.S. Supreme Court decision of 1918 that news had a commercial value. During the UN debates, the commercial interests behind the free-press campaign are also briefly mentioned, but, again, only in passing. In what one can only assume is intended as "an objective rendering of the facts," the author does, for example, make reference to British and Indian criticism of commercial motivations behind the American free-press campaign. But such critiques are followed by neither comment nor analysis.

It is therefore not surprising that toward the end of the book, Blanchard's summary of the goals of the postwar press-government crusade obscures anything but a purely journalistic motivation: "Underlying most of the rhetoric in the international free-press campaign was an effort to protect American correspondents working in foreign countries. Generally, the protection centered on ensuring the individual's right to gather and disseminate information . . . ." The incompleteness of such an analysis is evident when one realizes that it does not even answer one of the most important questions raised throughout the book itself: the continuous and unrelenting opposition the U.S. press crusade encountered from both allies and enemies. In fact, explicit rejection of U.S. notions of freedom of information is certainly one of the most important themes stressed throughout *Exporting the First Amendment.* And yet, are we to suppose that countries as diverse as Britain, Mexico, France and India would criticize important aspects of such a "noble" cause if its main concern were, in truth, simply to assist American journalists in gathering and disseminating news? As numerous authors have pointed out in connection with the information debates of the 1970s and 1980s, the stakes of the "free flow" battle are obviously much higher. Past and present opposition to the values of the American First Amendment is based not only on different journalistic philosophies, but also on the important connection U.S. critics have established between American information ideology and the objectives of political and economic expansion.

A number of other related issues are also mishandled. Within the context of the freedom of information polemics at the United Nations, the author deals with U.S. objections to proposed international regulations assigning "responsibilities" to the press. As correctly presented in this book, the official U.S. position (which remained unchanged 30 years later at UNESCO) was that asking journalists to do anything except "report the facts" was incompatible with American notions of a free press. What Blanchard virtually ignores in her treatment of this question, however, is the important contribution to this debate made, during the mid-1940s, by the American Hutchins Commission on Freedom of the Press. In fact, the "social responsibility" theory of the press is almost unanimously attributed to the work of this commission. Although this theory was never officially accepted in the United States, it certainly came to the fore in UN discussions and, ironically, was later to be taken up by Third World and socialist countries in the UNESCO debates. Although the book does make reference to other facets of the Hutchins Commission's work, the commission's position on "social responsibility" lies buried in a footnote, which is all the more remarkable since Blanchard herself has written on this question.

Moreover, the author's tendency to accept official pronouncements as gospel truth leads her to the erroneous conclusion that, unlike other countries, this country has rejected press "responsibility" out of hand. In reality, although the "social responsibility" doctrine was never codified in the United States, there is ample evidence—including adjurations to the press by public officials, columns by editors such as William Randolph Hearst and scholarly studies of American newspaper values—that the social responsibility of the press has been and remains to this day one of the most important principles of American journalism.

Another flaw in this book is the absence of any in-depth analysis of First Amendment legislation in the United States. Indeed, one would rightfully expect that a book dealing with the exportation of the First Amendment would have at least given readers some indication of the extremely rich jurists' debates and court decisions relating to this principle. The author is to be faulted for giving no evidence whatsoever that she is even familiar with the long-standing and abundant literature on the First Amendment.

The international legal perspective is also given short shrift. For example, simply pointing out that the Soviet Union has systematically opposed American principles of a free press with notions of national sovereignty and government responsibility does little more than state the obvious. One might actually learn something about foreign news systems, however, if it were pointed out that freedom of the press is actually written into the Soviet Constitution, albeit in a very different form from what Americans are familiar with. Likewise, intellectual awareness is advanced very little by simply pointing out that in the UN debates, French diplomats called for government enforcement of a right of correction. What one would expect from a scholarly work is some historical, legal explanation of this position based upon references to the pervasive centralization of the French system of governance.

One of the most interesting, but undeveloped, "asides" of the book does, nonetheless, relate to international lawmaking in the field of communications. In the detailed examination of the draft UN Convention on Gathering and International Transmission of News, backed by the State Department and American press groups in the early days of the UN debates, it is stressed that the U.S. Government would, under no circumstances, accept the application of international legislation that might contravene national laws or journalistic principles. The implications of this position are particularly important for progressive legal groups in the United States that have recently supported the UN/UNESCO declarations on the New World Information Order. Part of the reasoning behind this support seems to be that recent legislation designed to curb freedom of information in the name of national security within the United States might be countered by calls for adherence to international norms of open access to information and unlimited freedom of the press.

What clearly emerges in the last—and best—chapter of Blanchard's book is that the U.S. Government has never been bothered by the overt contradictions between its demands for journalistic freedom at the international level and repressive legislation on the national front. Whereas in previous chapters the author adopts a neutral stance on her subject, in this chapter she takes a very convincing, engagé position. For instance, she implicitly condemns the anti-Communist legalistic maneuvers of the Cold War such as Truman's classification program: "American failure to protect communists holding jobs in the communications industry was not an aberration. In fact, Americans never willingly have shared freedom of expression with persons whose beliefs might alter their society" (p. 380). The final chapter also points out that, while certain sectors of the American press condemned these Cold War violations of American journalistic freedoms, no connection whatsoever, in any quarter, was ever made between the hypocrisy of this domestic action and American posturing at the international level. It is not without significance that this same "blind spot" would reappear in the debates of the New World Information Order of the 1970s and 1980s. Newspapers such as the *New York Times* and the *Washington Post* have freely criticized recent government attempts to control and censor information in the United States. Such condemnation, however, has never influenced to the slightest degree these newspapers' portrayal of the New World Information Order debate as a movement pitting American defenders of freedom of the press against Communist and Third World proponents of government-controlled information.

Unfortunately, the merits of this final chapter of *Exporting the First Amendment* do not outweigh its overall deficiencies. In addition to the substantive points raised above, this is a tedious book. The reader is constantly confronted with the inability of the author to synthesize large amounts of information, the end result being that her few inspired moments lie buried in mountains of verbiage. From an academic viewpoint, there are several lessons to be learned: a doctoral dissertation does not a good book make, and reams of documentation are no substitute for sound analysis. In a larger sense, the lesson of the book is that unless the political and commercial aspects of information are finally understood, history will repeat itself both in the United States and abroad.

COLLEEN ROACH
Fordham University

BRIEFER NOTICES

Commercial Arbitration Law in Asia and the Pacific. Edited by Kenneth R. Simmonds, Brian H. W. Hill and Sigvard Jarvin. (Paris: ICC Publishing SA; New York, London, Rome: Oceana Publications, Inc., 1987.) This book takes its place in a series published under the aegis of the International Chamber of Commerce that includes not only *Arbitration Throughout the World,* which dealt largely with arbitration in Western European countries, but also a study of international commercial arbitration by Clive Schmitthoff and one of ICC arbitration by W. Laurence Craig, William W. Park and Jan Paulsson.[1] It gives both summaries of the law on arbitration and texts of relevant statutes of 14 countries in the Far East and the Pacific. The reader now can resort to three different collections of national laws on arbitration for those countries, the rivals being the *International Handbook on Commercial Arbitration,* published by the International Council on Commercial Arbitration, and the Smit-Pechota *World Arbitration Reporter.* The latter two seem less complete but more compact. Users will likely differ as to how much data about a country's rules they will wish to have before they decide to designate it as the situs of possible arbitration or, alternatively, before they decide to consult local counsel about such a choice.

Legitimacy and Force. 2 vols. By Jeane J. Kirkpatrick. *Volume One: Political and Moral Dimensions.* Pp. xxiii, 486. *Volume Two: National and International Dimensions.* Pp. xxiii, 421. (New Brunswick and Oxford: Transaction Books, 1988. $60/set, cloth; $30/set, paper.) Whether as professor, think-tank tenant or U.S. ambassador to the United Nations, Dr. Kirkpatrick has played a leading role in formulating the conservative foreign policy pursued by President Reagan. Hence this collection of her more or less occasional, brief pieces is an important historical source even if its multifariousness precludes review or even listing of the many items.

How To Get Your Money in Foreign Countries: A Survey of Court Costs and Lawyer's Fees in 151 Countries. Prepared by Ivo Greiter. (Deventer: Kluwer Law and Taxation Publishers, 1988. Pp. ix, 253. Dfl.145; £43.50; $72.50.)

[1] Reviewed at 80 AJIL 268 (1986).

This is a book not about the higher theory of international law but about the gritty realities of international litigation practice. In tabular form, and for each country, it tells the reader whether the loser pays the costs, including attorneys' fees, or whether they remain with each party, how those costs are set and how great those costs are apt to be in collection cases. There is much unclarity and guesswork about the way in which foreign legal systems work[1] and the detailed factual information presented here will be useful for academics as well.

BOOKS RECEIVED*

International Law—General

The British Year Book of International Law 1985. Volume 56. Oxford: The Clarendon Press, 1986. Pp. viii, 556. Index. $116.

The British Year Book of International Law 1986. Volume 57. Oxford: The Clarendon Press, 1987. Pp. viii, 671. Index. $119.

Cassese, Antonio. *International Law in a Divided World.* Oxford: Clarendon Press, 1986. Pp. xv, 429. Index.

Conforti, Benedetto. *Diritto Internazionale* (3d ed.). Naples: Editoriale Scientifica, 1987. Pp. xiii, 432. Index. L. 35,000.

Delbrück, Jost, Wilhelm A. Kewenig and Rüdiger Wolfrum (eds.). *German Yearbook of International Law.* Volume 29, 1986. Berlin: Duncker & Humblot, 1987. Pp. 612. DM 212.

South African Yearbook of International Law. Volume 12, 1986–1987. Pretoria: VerLoren van Themaat Centre for International Law, University of South Africa. Pp. 319. Index. R25; $25.

International Economic Law & Relations

Aden, Menno. *Internationale Handelsschiedsgerichtsbarkeit: Kommentar zu den Verfahrensordnungen.* Heidelberg: Verlag Recht und Wirtschaft GmbH, 1988. Pp. 299. Index. DM 135.

Draetta, Ugo. Il Diritto dei contratti internazionali: La patologia dei contratti. Padua: CEDAM, 1988. Pp. xiv, 170. Author index.

Feketekuty, Geza. *International Trade in Services: An Overview and Blueprint for Negotiations.* Cambridge: Ballinger Publishing Company, 1988. Published with the American Enterprise Institute. Pp. xix, 355. Indexes. $26.95.

Hentzen, Matthias Klaus. *US-amerikanische Exportkontrollen: Die Systematik ihrer gesetzlichen Grundlagen.* Heidelberg: Verlag Recht und Wirtschaft GmbH, 1988. Pp. 334. Index. DM 116, paper.

Michigan Yearbook of International Legal Studies. Volume IX, 1988. *Symposium: Internationalization of the Securities Markets.* Ann Arbor: Michigan Yearbook of International Legal Studies, 1988. Pp. vi, 410. $40.

Mowery, David C. (ed.). *International Collaborative Ventures in U.S. Manufacturing.* Cambridge: Ballinger Publishing Company, 1988. Published with the American Enterprise Institute. Pp. xiv, 386. Index. $34.95.

Neri, Rita E. *U.S./Japan Foreign Trade: An Annotated Bibliography of Socioeconomic Perspectives.* New York and London: Garland Publishing, Inc., 1988. Pp. xv, 306. Indexes. $40.

Simmonds, Kenneth R., and Brian H. W. Hill (comps./eds.). *Law and Practice under the GATT.* New York, London, Rome: Oceana Publications, Inc., 1988. 1 binder. $100.

[1] Galanter, *Reading the Landscape of Disputes: What We Know and Don't Know (and Think We Know) About Our Allegedly Contentious and Litigious Society,* 31 UCLA L. Rev. 4 (1983).

* Mention here neither assures nor precludes later review.

Trade Policies for a Better Future: The 'Leutwiler Report', the GATT and the Uruguay Round. Dordrecht, Boston, Lancaster: Martinus Nijhoff Publishers, 1987. Pp. vii, 174. Dfl.105; $52.50; £32.

van Dijk, Pieter, Fried van Hoof, Albert Koers and Kamiel Mortelmans (eds.). *Restructuring the International Economic Order: The Role of Law and Lawyers.* Proceedings of the Colloquium, organized by the Department of International and Economic Law on June 12 and 13, 1986 on the occasion of the 350th anniversary of the University of Utrecht. Published in co-operation with the Netherlands Institute for Social and Economic Legal Research. Deventer: Kluwer Law and Taxation Publishers, 1987. Pp. viii, 270. Dfl.125; £43; $61.

Wallace, Cynthia Day (ed.). *Foreign Direct Investment and the Multinational Enterprise: A Bibliography.* Dordrecht, Boston, Lancaster: Martinus Nijhoff Publishers, 1988. Pp. xi, 355. Dfl.195; $100; £59.

Law of the Sea & Maritime Law

Arroyo, Ignacio (ed.). *Yearbook Maritime Law.* Volume II, 1985–1986. Deventer: Kluwer Law and Taxation Publishers, 1988. Pp. ix, 445. Dfl.175; £52; $90.

Conforti, Benedetto, Giampiero Francalanci, Angelo Labella and Daniela Romanò (eds.). *Atlas of the Seabed Boundaries.* Part Two. Milan: Dott. A. Giuffrè Editore, 1987. Pp. xv, 241. Treaty index. L. 35,000.

Hasselmann, Cord-Georg. *Die Freiheit der Handelsschiffahrt: Eine Analyse der UN-Seerechtskonvention.* Kehl am Rhein, Straßburg, Arlington: N. P. Engel Verlag, 1987. Pp. xx, 507. Index. English summary. DM 136.

Kittichaisaree, Kriangsak. *The Law of the Sea and Maritime Boundary Delimitation in South-East Asia.* Singapore, Oxford, New York: Oxford University Press, 1987. Pp. xv, 209. Index. $36.

Martínez Puñal, Antonio. *Los Derechos de los Estados sin litoral y en situación geográfica desventajosa en la Zona Económica Exclusiva (Participación en la explotación de los recursos vivos).* Santiago: Xunta de Galicia, 1988. Pp. 421. Summary in English.

Smith, Brian D. *State Responsibility and the Marine Environment: The Rules of Decision.* Oxford: Clarendon Press; New York: Oxford University Press, 1988. Pp. xviii, 281. Index. $65.

Use of Force & Law of War

Tesón, Fernando R. *Humanitarian Intervention: An Inquiry into Law and Morality.* Dobbs Ferry, N.Y.: Transnational Publishers, Inc., 1988. Pp. xv, 272. Indexes. $50.

Terrorism

Falk, Richard. *Revolutionaries and Functionaries: The Dual Face of Terrorism.* New York: E. P. Dutton, 1988. Pp. xxiii, 222. Index. $17.95.

Levitt, Geoffrey M. *Democracies against Terror: The Western Response to State-Supported Terrorism.* Published with The Center for Strategic and International Studies, Washington, D.C. New York, Westport, London: Praeger, 1988. Pp. xiv, 142. Index. $32.95, cloth; $9.95, paper.

Human Rights

Alston, Philip, and Maria Rodriguez-Bustelo. *Taking Stock of United Nations Human Rights Procedures.* Report of a January 1988 Workshop at Lake Mohonk, N.Y. Organized by the Fletcher School of Law and Diplomacy. Pp. 63.

Bindman, Geoffrey (ed.), for the International Commission of Jurists. *South Africa: Human Rights and the Rule of Law.* London and New York: Pinter Publishers, 1988. Pp. 159. Index. $37.50. Distributed by Columbia University Press.

Detzner, John A. *Tribunales Chilenos y derecho internacional de derechos humanos: La recepción del derecho internacional de derecho humanos en el derecho interno chileno.* Santiago: Comisión Chilena de Derechos Humanos, 1988. Pp. xxvii, 182.

García Bauer, Carlos. *Los Derechos Humanos en América.* Guatemala, 1987. Pp. 416.

Medina Quiroga, Cecilia. *The Battle of Human Rights: Gross, Systematic Violations and the Inter-American System.* Dordrecht, Boston, London: Martinus Nijhoff Publishers, 1988. Pp. xvii, 363. Index. Dfl.170; $95; £52.

Nikken, Pedro. *La Protección internacional de los derechos humanos: Su desarrollo progresivo.* Published under the auspices of the Instituto Interamericano de Derechos Humanos. Madrid: Editorial Civitas, S. A., 1987. Pp. 321.

Stormorken, Bjørn, and Leo Zwaak. *Human Rights Terminology in International Law: A Thesaurus.* Dordrecht, Boston, Lancaster: Martinus Nijhoff Publishers; Strasbourg: Human Rights Documentation Centre, Council of Europe, 1987. Pp. 234. Dfl.100; $52; £30.95.

International Labour Law

International Labour Law Reports. Volume 6. Dordrecht, Boston, Lancaster: Martinus Nijhoff Publishers, 1988. Pp. xxxiv, 409. Dfl.225; $123; £68.

Migration Law

Plender, Richard. *International Migration Law* (rev. 2d ed.). Dordrecht, Boston, London: Martinus Nijhoff Publishers, 1988. Pp. xxvii, 587. Index. Dfl.225; $123; £67.95.

Environment & Natural Resources

Sands, Philippe (ed.). *Chernobyl: Law and Communication. Transboundary Nuclear Air Pollution—The Legal Materials.* A publication of The Annenberg Washington Program in Communications Policy Studies of Northwestern University and the Research Centre for International Law, University of Cambridge. Cambridge: Grotius Publications Limited, 1988. Pp. xxxiii, 312. Index. £38; $75.

Utton, Albert E., and Ludwik A. Teclaff (eds.). *Transboundary Resources Law.* Boulder and London: Westview Press, 1987. Published in cooperation with the International Transboundary Resources Center and the *Natural Resources Journal,* University of New Mexico School of Law. Pp. viii, 321. $35.

Air & Space Law

Diederiks-Verschoor, I. H. Ph. *An Introduction to Air Law* (3d rev. and enlarged ed.). Deventer: Kluwer Law and Taxation Publishers, 1988. Pp. xxiv, 197. Index. Dfl.120; £35; $62.

International Organizations

Amerasinghe, C. F. *The Law of the International Civil Service (as Applied by International Administrative Tribunals).* Volume I. Oxford: Clarendon Press; New York: Oxford University Press, 1988. Pp. xxii, 635. $125.

Dembinski, Ludwik. *The Modern Law of Diplomacy: External missions of states and international organizations.* Dordrecht, Boston, Lancaster: Martinus Nijhoff Publishers; UNITAR, 1988. Pp. xv, 282. Index. Dfl.135; $74; £40.95.

Roberts, Adam, and Benedict Kingsbury (eds.). *United Nations, Divided World: The UN's Roles in International Relations.* Oxford: Clarendon Press; New York: Oxford University Press, 1988. Pp. xii, 287. Index. $59.

Private International Law

Boguslavskii, M. M. *Private International Law: The Soviet Approach.* Translated by David Winter and William B. Simons. Dordrecht, Boston, Lancaster: Martinus Nijhoff Publishers, 1988. Pp. ix, 261. Index. Dfl.165; $90; £49.50.

Czermak, Peter. *Der express trust im internationalen Privatrecht.* Frankfurt am Main, Bern, New York: Verlag Peter Lang, 1986. Pp. xxxiii, 323.

U.S. Law and Foreign Relations

Arend, Anthony Clark. *Pursuing a Just and Durable Peace: John Foster Dulles and International Organization.* New York, Westport, London: Greenwood Press, 1988. Pp. x, 243. Index. $39.95.

Lamborn, Alan C., and Stephen P. Mumme. *Statecraft, Domestic Politics, and Foreign Policy Making: The El Chamizal Dispute.* Boulder and London: Westview Press, 1988. Pp. ix, 211. Index. $29.50, paper.

Payne, Richard J. *Opportunities and Dangers of Soviet-Cuban Expansion: Toward a Pragmatic U.S. Policy.* Albany: State University of New York Press, 1988. Pp. xv, 261. Index. $34.50, cloth; $10.95, paper.

Thompson, Kenneth W. (ed.). *Papers on Presidential Disability and the Twenty-Fifth Amendment by Six Medical, Legal and Political Authorities.* Lanham, New York, London: University Press of America; Charlottesville: The Miller Center, 1988. Pp. xii, 190. $21.50, cloth; $9.75, paper.

Wormuth, Francis D., and Edwin B. Firmage, with Francis P. Butler. *To Chain the Dog of War: The War Power of Congress in History and Law.* Dallas: Southern Methodist University Press, 1986. Pp. xi, 347. Indexes. $27.50.

Arms Control & Disarmament

Fujita, Hisakazu. *International Regulation of the Use of Nuclear Weapons.* Osaka: Kansai University Press, 1988. Pp. ix, 394. Index. ¥9,500. Distributed by Maruzen Company, Ltd.

Miatello, Angelo. *L'arme nucléaire en droit international.* Bern, Frankfurt am Main, New York, Paris: Peter Lang, 1987. Pp. xxxvi, 722. Author index. $75.40.

Sims, Nicholas A. *The Diplomacy of Biological Disarmament: Vicissitudes of a Treaty in Force, 1975–85.* New York: St. Martin's Press, 1988. Pp. xv, 356. Index. $49.95, cloth.

Regional, Foreign & Comparative Law & Politics

Comparative Law Yearbook. Volume 10, 1986. Issued by The Center for International Legal Studies. Dordrecht, Boston, London: Martinus Nijhoff Publishers, 1988. Pp. vi, 219. Dfl.165; $89.50; £49.

Fleiner-Gerster, Thomas, and Silvan Hutter (eds.). *Federalism and Decentralization: Constitutional Problems of Territorial Decentralization in Federal and Centralized States.* Fribourg: Editions Universitaires; Boulder: Westview Press, 1987. Pp. 488. $48, paper.

Frenzke, Dietrich (ed.). *Das Zivilgesetzbuch und das Ehe- und Familiengesetzbuch der Russischen Sowjetrepublik (RSFSR).* Berlin: Berlin Verlag Arno Spitz, 1988. Pp. 346. DM 68.

Ioffe, Olimpiad S. *Soviet Civil Law.* Dordrecht, Boston, Lancaster: Martinus Nijhoff Publishers, 1988. Pp. ix, 382. Index. Dfl.205; $112; £62.

Lipgens, Walter (ed.). *Documents on the History of European Integration. Volume 1: Continental Plans for European Union 1939–1945 (including 250 Documents in their Original Language on 6 Microfiches).* Berlin and New York: Walter de Gruyter, 1985. Pp. xxiii, 823. Indexes. DM 296.

—— (ed.). *Documents on the History of European Integration. Volume 2: Plans for European Union in Great Britain and in Exile 1939–1945 (Including 107 Documents in their Original Languages on 3 Microfiches).* Berlin and New York: Walter de Gruyter, 1986. Pp. xxiv, 847. Indexes. DM 324.

Mahnke, Hans Heinrich (ed.), for the Forschungsinstitut der Deutschen Gesellschaft für Auswärtige Politik e. V. in collaboration with the Senate of Berlin. *Dokumente zur Berlin-Frage 1967–1986.* Munich: R. Oldenbourg Verlag, 1987. Pp. 700. Index.

Manual de integración latinoamericana. Published under the auspices of the Centro Interuniversitario de Desarrollo and the Instituto de Altos Estudios de América Latina de la Universidad Simón Bolívar. Caracas, 1987. Pp. 455.

Muñoz Valenzuela, Heraldo, and Francisco Orrego Vicuña (comps.). *La Cooperación regional en América Latina: Diagnóstico y proyecciones futuras.* Mexico: El Colegio de México, 1987 (in cooperation with the Instituto de Estudios Internacionales de la Universidad de Chile). Pp. 613.

Puig, Juan Carlos. *Integración Latinoamericana y régimen internacional / Latin American Integration and the International Regime.* Caracas: Universidad Simón Bolívar, Instituto de Altos Estudios de América Latina, 1987. Pp. 408.

Spittmann, Ilse (ed.). *Die SED in Geschichte und Gegenwart.* Cologne: Edition Deutschland Archiv, 1987. Pp. 255.

Vondracek, Th. J. *Commentary on the Czechoslovak Civil Code.* Dordrecht, Boston, Lancaster: Martinus Nijhoff Publishers, 1988. Pp. xxix, 473. Index. Dfl.235; $130; £72.95.

International Relations & Politics

Claude, Inis L., Jr. *States and the Global System: Politics, Law and Organization.* New York: St. Martin's Press, 1988. Pp. x, 205. Index. $39.95.

Jáuregui Bereciartu, Gurutz. *Las Comunidades autónomas y las relaciones internacionales.* Oñati: Instituto Vasco de Administración Pública, 1986. Pp. 177. 1,200 Ptas.

Lundestad, Geir. *East, West, North, South: Major Developments in International Politics 1945–1986.* Translated from the Norwegian by Gail Adams Kvam. Oslo: Norwegian University Press, 1986. Pp. 308. Index. $17.95. Distributed by Oxford University Press.

Mikus, Joseph A. *Beyond Deterrence: From Power Politics to World Public Order.* New York, Bern, Frankfurt am Main, Paris: Peter Lang, 1988. Pp. viii, 219. Index.

Miscellaneous

Eisenberg, Melvin Aron. *The Nature of the Common Law.* Cambridge, Mass., and London: Harvard University Press, 1988. Pp. x, 204. Index. $22.50.

Stephen, Frank H. *The Economics of the Law.* Ames: Iowa State University Press, 1988. Pp. x, 224. Index. $24.95.

INTERNATIONAL LEGAL MATERIALS*

CONTENTS

VOL. XXVII, NO. 4 (July 1988)

PAGE

TREATIES AND AGREEMENTS

Antarctic Treaty Special Consultative Meeting on Antarctic Mineral Resources: Final Act and Convention on the *Regulation of Antarctic Mineral Resource Activities*
- I.L.M. Background/Content Summary 859
- Final Act 865
- Text of Convention 868

Argentina-Brazil: Agreement on *Argentine-Brazilian Integration*
- I.L.M. Background/Content Summary 901
- Text of Agreement 905

Diplomatic Conference for the Adoption of the Draft *Unidroit Conventions on International Factoring and International Financial Leasing:* Final Act and Text of Two Conventions
- I.L.M. Background/Content Summary 922
- Final Act 927
- Text of Convention on International Financial Leasing 931
- Text of Convention on International Factoring 943

Nicaragua-Nicaraguan Resistance: Preliminary *Cease-Fire Agreement*
- I.L.M. Background/Content Summary 954
- Text of Agreement 955

Nicaraguan Verification Commission–United States: *Cooperative Assistance Agreement for the Verification Commission* through the U.S. Agency for International Development
- I.L.M. Background/Content Summary 957
- Text of Agreement 959

LEGISLATION AND REGULATIONS

Andean Group: Commission Decision 220 Replacing Decision 24, the Common *Foreign Investment and Technology Licensing* Code
- Introductory Note 974
- I.L.M. Content Summary 976
- Text of Decision 978

Brazil: Law and Implementing Decree on *Software Protection*
- I.L.M. Background/Content Summary 989
- Text of Law No. 7646 993
- Text of Decree No. 96036 1007

Lebanon: *International Arbitration* Provisions of the Code of Civil Procedure
- Introductory Note 1022
- I.L.M. Content Summary 1027
- Text of Decree No. 90/83 1028

JUDICIAL AND SIMILAR PROCEEDINGS

United Kingdom: House of Lords Judgment in Deutsche Schachtbau -und Tiefbohrgesellschaft mbH and Others *v.* Shell International Petroleum Company

* ILM subscription, $100; concessionary rate to ASIL members, $50. Address orders to ILM, 2223 Massachusetts Ave., NW, Wash., D.C. 20008. Outside U.S., please add $6.50.

Limited (*Enforcement of Arbitral Award; Execution through Debtor Payment to Third Party; Risk of Debtor Being Compelled to Pay Twice by Existing Order of Foreign Court*)
I.L.M. Content Summary 1032
Text of Judgment 1034
United States:
District Court for the Southern District of New York Decision in United States *v.* Palestine Liberation Organization (*U.S. Obligations under U.N. Headquarters Agreement; U.S. Anti-Terrorism Act*)
I.L.M. Content Summary 1055
Text of Decision 1056
Supreme Court Opinion in Volkswagenwerk Aktiengesellschaft *v.* Schlunk (*Applicability of Hague Service Convention When Domestic Subsidiary of Foreign Corporation*)
Syllabus of Reporter of Decisions 1092
Text of Opinion 1093

RECENT ACTIONS REGARDING TREATIES TO WHICH THE UNITED STATES IS A PARTY 1105
RECENT ACTIONS REGARDING TREATIES TO WHICH THE UNITED STATES IS NOT A PARTY 1107
NOTICE OF OTHER RECENT DOCUMENTS (not reproduced) 1108

Table of Cases

(*Italicized* page numbers indicate where decisions are excerpted or cases discussed at length. Abbreviations: arb., arbitration; concil., conciliation; IACommHR, Inter-American Commission of Human Rights; ICJ, International Court of Justice; PCIJ, Permanent Court of International Justice; S.Ct., Supreme Court.)

Admission of a State to the United Nations (ICJ), 737
Air Services Agreement (arb.), 253
Amerada Hess Shipping Corp. v. Argentine Republic, *126–9*, *323–30*, 585
American International Group, Inc. v. Iran (arb.), *73*
Amoco International Finance Corp. v. Islamic Republic of Iran (arb.), *358–62*
(The) Antelope, 758
Anti-Defamation League v. Kissinger, 835
Applicability of the Obligation to Arbitrate under Section 21 of the United Nations Headquarters Agreement (ICJ), 756, 801
Asakura v. City of Seattle, 773
Asociacion de Reclamantes v. United Mexican States, 132
Banco Nacional de Cuba v. Chase Manhattan Bank, *71–2*
Banco Nacional de Cuba v. Chemical Bank N.Y. Trust Co., *58–61*
Banco Nacional de Cuba v. Sabbatino, 58, 60
Bandes v. Harlow & Jones, *820–4*
Barcelona Traction (ICJ), 70–1, 73, 76, 78
Carl Marks & Co. v. Union of Soviet Socialist Republics, *129–32*
Case No. 9647 (IACommHR), *601–3*
Certain Expenses of the United Nations (ICJ), 316
Chaser Shipping Corp. v. United States, 143
Chemical Bank II. *See* Banco Nacional de Cuba v. Chemical Bank N.Y. Trust Co.
Chorzów Factory (PCIJ), 360, 362
Coalition to Preserve Integrity of American Trademarks v. United States, 143
Continental Ore Co. v. Union Carbide & Carbon Corp., 353
Corfu Channel (ICJ), *263–4*
Dames & Moore v. Regan, 594
Dayton v. Czechoslovak Socialist Republic, *585–7*
Delassus v. United States, 771
Desir v. Ilchert, *830–2*
Edwards v. Carter, *778–81*
Elettronica Sicula (ELSI) (ICJ), 558
Empresa Cubana Exportadora, Inc. v. Lamborn & Co., 60
Fellows v. Blacksmith, 773
Filartiga v. Pena-Irala, *329*
First National City Bank v. Banco Nacional de Cuba, 59
Foster v. Neilson, *766–7*, *770–1*, 772
Fourteen Diamonds v. United States, 161
Frontier Dispute (Burkina Faso/Republic of Mali) (ICJ), 556–8
Gould Marketing, Inc. v. Ministry of Defence of the Islamic Republic of Iran (arb.), 591–4
Guinée/Guinée-Bissau (arb.), 799
Gulf of Maine (ICJ), 451–2, 456, 556–8, 562, *798–800*
Hamilton v. Eaton, 764–5
Immigration and Naturalization Service v. Abudu, *580–3*
INA Corp. v. Iran (arb.), 73
In re Piracy Jure Gentium, 273, *274*
In re Request for Assistance from Ministry of Legal Affairs of Trinidad and Tobago, *824–8*
Interhandel (ICJ), 102
International Shoe Co. v. Washington, 833
International Tin Council v. Amalgamet Inc., *837–40*
Jackson v. People's Republic of China, 143
Jan Mayen (concil.), *443–58*
Japan Whaling Association v. American Cetacean Society, 579
Jean-Juste v. Duvalier, *594–6*
Judgment No. 134 B/1981 (Norwegian S.Ct., reported to UN Committee on the Elimination of Racial Discrimination), 508–9
Kelly v. S.A. Belge, 161
Lamborn case. *See* Empresa Cubana Exportadora, Inc. v. Lamborn & Co.
Land, Island and Maritime Frontier Dispute (ICJ), 557–8, *559*
Libyan Arab Foreign Bank v. Bankers Trust Co., *132–6*
Libyan Arab Jamahiriya/Malta Case concerning the Continental Shelf (ICJ), 562, 724
Lowry v. Reagan, *596–7*
Maiorano v. Baltimore & Ohio R.R., 773

Maritime International Nominees Establishment v. Republic of Guinea (arb.), *598–9*
Martin v. Republic of South Africa, *583–5*
Military and Paramilitary Activities in and against Nicaragua (ICJ), *102*, *248*, 714–5, 757, 799–80
Ministry of Defense of the Islamic Republic of Iran v. Gould, *591–4*
Mobil Oil Iran Inc. v. Islamic Republic of Iran (arb.), *136–40, 600*
New York Indians v. United States, 161
Nicaragua case. *See* Military and Paramilitary Activities in and against Nicaragua
North Sea Continental Shelf Cases (ICJ), 562, 724
Nuclear Tests (ICJ), 565
O.N.E. Shipping Ltd. v. Flota Mercante Grancolombiana, S.A., *351–3*
Owings v. Norwood's Lessee, 765, 766, 771
Rankin v. Islamic Republic of Iran (arb.), *353–7*
Reclamantes case. *See* Asociacion de Reclamantes v. United Mexican States
Remington Rand Corp. v. Business Systems, Inc., *587–91*
Republic of Panama v. Republic National Bank of New York, 568
Republic of the Philippines v. Marcos, 143
Sabbatino case. *See* Banco Nacional de Cuba v. Sabbatino
Saint Francis College v. Al-Khazraji, 509
Schmidt v. Polish People's Republic, 131
Sedco, Inc. v. National Iranian Oil Co. (arb.), 72
Shaare Tefila Congregation v. Cobb, 509
Short v. Islamic Republic of Iran (arb.), *140–3*, 357
Societe Nationale Industrielle Aerospatiale v. U.S. District Court for the Southern District of Iowa, *521–55*, 819
Starrett Housing Corp. v. Islamic Republic of Iran (arb.), 362
Strother v. Lucas, 772–3
Sullivan v. Kidd, 161
Tchacosh Co., Ltd. v. Rockwell International Corp., 824
Tehran case. *See* United States Diplomatic and Consular Staff in Tehran
Texas Trading & Milling Corp. v. Federal Republic of Nigeria, 584
Tunisia/Libyan Arab Jamahiriya Case concerning the Continental Shelf (ICJ), 562, 724
United States v. Brig Malek Adhel, *273–4*
United States v. Palestine Liberation Organization, *833–7*
United States v. Percheman, 768–9, 771
United States v. Sisal Sales Corp., 353
United States v. The Ambrose Light, *274*
United States v. The Schooner Peggy, 765
United States Diplomatic and Consular Staff in Tehran (ICJ), 102, 723, 734
Volkswagen Aktiengesellschaft v. Schlunk, *816–20*
Von Dardel v. Union of Soviet Socialist Republics, 131–2
Ware v. Hylton, 766, *769–70*
West v. Multibanco Comermex, 143
Worcester v. Georgia, 772
Yeager v. Islamic Republic of Iran (arb.), *353–7*
Zedan v. Kingdom of Saudi Arabia, *828–30*
Zernicek v. Brown & Root, Inc., 583–4, 585

INDEX

(The following abbreviations refer to sections of the *Journal*: *Ag.*, Agora; *BN*, Briefer Notices; *BR*, Book Reviews and Notes; *CD*, Current Developments; *Corr.*, Correspondence; *CP*, Contemporary Practice of the US Relating to International Law; *Ed.*, Editorial Comments; *ID*, International Decisions; *JD*, Judicial Decisions; *LA*, Leading Article; *NC*, Notes and Comments. Other abbreviations include: AJIL, *American Journal of International Law*; ASIL, American Society of International Law; FRG, Federal Republic of Germany; FSIA, US Foreign Sovereign Immunities Act; ICJ, International Court of Justice; ICSID, International Centre for Settlement of Investment Disputes; ILC, International Law Commission; IMO, International Maritime Organization; INF Treaty, Treaty on the Elimination of Intermediate-Range and Shorter-Range Missiles; INS, Immigration and Naturalization Service; LOS, law of the sea; MARPOL, International Convention for the Prevention of Pollution from Ships; PLO, Palestine Liberation Organization; UK, United Kingdom; UN, United Nations; UNGA, United Nations General Assembly; UNSC, United Nations Security Council; US, United States; USSR, Union of Soviet Socialist Republics.)

Aaland Islands, and principle of self-determination, 744, 746

Abbott, Kenneth W. *BR* of Seward, 425

ABM Treaty (1972), excerpts from Senate report on interpreting, *CD*, 151

(The) ABM Treaty Interpretation Resolution, *CD*, 151

Acevedo, Domingo E. *BR* of Bernhardt, 175

Achille Lauro, seizure of, 104, 295, 301: whether constitutes piracy, 269–70, 276, 282, 287, 289, 291

(The) Action Does Not Violate International Law, *Ag.* on ASIL divestment, 314

(The) Action Violates International Law and Policy, *Ag.* on ASIL divestment, 311

Act of state doctrine: and acts of bankruptcy trustees, 587, 588; applicability of, 838, 839; extraterritorial exception to, *ID*, 820–4; treaty exception to, 586; US courts' interpretation of, *Ed.*, 58; *JD*, 351–3

Advancing the Freedom of Religion or Belief Through the UN Declaration on the Elimination of Religious Intolerance and Discrimination, *LA*, 487

Afghanistan: Soviet intervention and concept of legitimacy, 736; whether conflict is international or noninternational, *LA*, 459

Africa, concept of individual and group in, 82–4, 100

African Charter on Human and Peoples' Rights. *See* Banjul Charter on Human and Peoples' Rights

African Commission on Human and Peoples' Rights, 100, 101

Ago, Roberto, reelection to ICJ, 369

Agora: Is the ASIL Policy on Divestment in Violation of International Law? Further Observations, 311; McDougal-Lasswell Redux, 41; The U.S. Decision Not to Ratify Protocol I to the Geneva Conventions on the Protection of War Victims (Cont'd), 784

Aircraft, Convention for the Suppression of Unlawful Seizure of (1970), 570, 807: and IMO Maritime Safety Convention, 291, 292, 294, 300–1, 303, 305; legitimacy of rules under, 722

Aircraft, Convention on Offenses and Certain Other Acts Committed on Board (1963), 570

Alaska, Convention Treaty on the Cession of (1867), 455, 456

Albania, British threat of force re Corfu Channel, 242–3, 263–4

Aldrich, George H. *BR* of Levie, 679

Algeria, and self-determination, 746–8. *See also* Algiers Accords

Algiers Accords, 69, 592, 593–4: whether self-executing, 593. *See also* Claims Settlement Declaration

Algiers Declaration. *See* Universal Declaration on the Rights of Peoples

Aliens: reopening of deportation proceedings to request asylum, *JD*, 580–3; responsibility for expulsions from Iran, *JD*, 140–3; standard for asylum under US law, *ID*, 830–2. *See also* United States, Alien Tort Claims Act

Alien Tort Claims, Sovereign Immunity and International Law in U.S. Courts, *NC*, 323

(The) Alien Tort Statute and the Founding of the Constitution, *Ed.*, 62

Almond, Harry H., Jr. Waldemar A. Solf (1913–1987), *NC*, 562

Alston, Philip, & Bruno Simma. Second Session of the UN Committee on Economic, Social and Cultural Rights, *CD*, 603

American Arbitration Association, 598, 837

American Convention on Human Rights, US ratification and juvenile punishment, 601–3

American Declaration of the Rights and Duties of Man, US execution of juveniles held to violate, *CD*, 601

American Society of International Law: contribution of William W. Bishop, Jr., 321, 322; divestment of stock portfolio, *Ag.*, 311; *Corr.*, 800; Tunkin address to, on Soviet attitudes, 788, 791, 794

Ames, Walter L. *BR* of McCreary, 433

Amin, Hafizullah, 468, 469, 470–4, 482, 485

Antitrust: blocking extraterritorial application of US jurisdiction, 549; transnational cases and act of state doctrine, 58, 61; *JD*, 351–3

Apartheid, Convention on the Suppression and Punishment of the Crime of (1973), 800

Arangio-Ruiz, Gaetano, 144

Arbitration: Chamber procedure in World Court and, 558–60; and disputes under LOS Convention, 332, 334; enforceability of contract clause, 837–9; of France-US civil aviation dispute, 253; ICSID, on good faith performance of contracts, *JD*, 598–9; whether required in US dispute with PLO, 833–4. *See also* Iran–United States Claims Tribunal

Arend, Anthony Clark (ed.). The United States and the Compulsory Jurisdiction of the International Court of Justice, *BR*, 870

Argentina: jurisdiction of US courts re destruction of neutral ship, *JD*, 126–9; *NC*, 323. *See also* Falkland Islands

Austinians, on rules of international law, 706–7, 708, 751

Austria: and drafting of IMO Maritime Safety Convention, 270, 291–2, 307; and the 1871 London Declaration, 18; lump sum agreements, 79; and 19th-century straits agreements, 7, 11, 12, 13–4

Aviation, Convention for the Suppression of Unlawful Acts Against the Safety of Civil (1971): and IMO Maritime Safety Convention, 291, 292, 294, 300–1, 303, 305; Protocol to on airport safety, *CP*, 569–71

Aviation, Protocol for the Suppression of Unlawful Acts of Violence at Airports Serving International Civil (1988), *CP*, 569–71

Baker, Wallace R. *BR* of Baptista & Durand-Barthez, 214

Baldwin, Gordon B. *BR* of Richardson, 196

Ball, Milner S. *BR* of International Law and the Grotian Heritage: A Commemorative Colloquium, 183

Bangladesh, secession of, and self-determination, 90

Banjul Charter on Human and Peoples' Rights (Banjul Charter): meaning of "people" in, *NC*, 80

Baptista, Luiz O., & Pascal Durand-Barthez. Les Associations d'Entreprises (Joint Ventures) dans le commerce international, *BR*, 214

Barboza, Julio, 150

Barrie, George N. The Action Violates International Law and Policy, *Ag.* on ASIL divestment, 311; response by Szasz, *Ag.*, 314; *Corr.* on by Richardson, 800

Bassiouni, M. Cherif (ed.). International Criminal Law, Vol. II: Procedure, & Vol. III: Enforcement, *BR*, 899; New Horizons in International Criminal Law, *BR*, 413

Bederman, David J. *BR* of Bourguignon, 854; The 1871 London Declaration, Rebus sic Stantibus and a Primitivist View of the Law of Nations, *LA*, 1

Belgium: agreement with US on missile inspections, 342, 343, 349–50; lump sum agreement, 79

Benin, 96: Constitution and minority rights, 94–5
Bernhardt, Rudolf. *BR* of Kaiser & Schwarz, 650
——— (ed.). Encyclopedia of Public International Law. Instalment 8: Human Rights and the Individual in International Law, *BR*, 175
Bernstein letter, 59, 60
Bilder, Richard B. *BR* of Merrills, 184
Bingham, Joseph W., Comment to Harvard Draft Convention on Piracy, 277–9
Bishop, Elizabeth S. Professor William W. Bishop, Jr. (1906–1987): Personal Recollections, *NC*, 323
Bishop, William W., Jr., memorials on, *NC*, 321
Bismarck, Otto von, 13, 27, 33: and change of circumstances, 19, 20
Blanchard, Margaret A. Exporting the First Amendment: The Press-Government Crusade of 1945–1952, *BR*, 913
Blishchenko, I. P. (ed.). Osvobodivshiesia strany i mezhdunarodnoe pravo (The Liberated Countries and International Law), *BR*, 887
Blocking statutes, and US discovery orders, 528–9, 532–3, 534, 547, 548–51, 552
Bocalandro, Laura. *BR* of Gutiérrez Espada & Calvo Caravaca, 853
Bonn Declaration (1978), 722–3
Book Reviews and Notes, 166, 370, 616, 841
Borgese, Elisabeth Mann. The Future of the Oceans: A Report to the Club of Rome, *BR*, 191
Bosporus and Dardanelles, 19th-century agreements on, 5–7, 8–20, 25, 33, 35
Bossuyt, Marc J. Guide to the "Travaux Préparatoires" of the International Covenant on Civil and Political Rights, *BR*, 680
Bourguignon, Henry J. Sir William Scott, Lord Stowell: Judge of the High Court of Admiralty, 1798–1828, *BR*, 854
Bourne, C. B. (ed.). The Canadian Yearbook of International Law, Vol. XXIII, 1985, *BR*, 225
Boutard-Labarde, Marie-Chantal. Nationalisations Imposées—Nationalisations Négociées, *BR*, 409
Boyd, A. C., on the 1871 London Declaration, 21
Boyle, Francis A. *BR* of Yambrusic, 650; World Politics and International Law, *BR*, 635
Brand, Joseph L. *BR* of Khadduri, 431
Breitenmoser, Stephan. Der Schutz der Privatsphäre gemäß Art. 8 EMRK, *BR*, 189
Brennan, William J., Jr., on internal law and applying Hague Service Convention, 818–20
Briggs, Herbert W. *BR* of Rosenne, 387; *BR* of Schwebel, 394; *BR* of Sinclair, 643
Broglie, J. V. A., and the 1871 London Declaration, 19, 20, 27, 33
Brosche, Hartmut, on legality of economic sanctions, 313
Brower, Charles N., 72, 358: on responsibility for expulsions from Iran, 142–3; on "voluntary" termination of contract, 140
Brownlie, Ian, 249: definition of "people," 87
Brunnow, Philip, 15: and observation of treaties, 2, 39
Buckley, James L., on ABM Treaty, 162
Bulgaria, 109: lump sum agreement, 79
Burke, Susan. *ID*, 830–2
Buthelezi, Mangosuthu, 312, 800
Butler, William E. *BR* of Meissner, 229

Calabrese, Michael R. *ID*, 820–4
Calvo Caravaca, Alfonso-Luis, & Cesáreo Gutiérrez Espada. Textos de Derecho internacional público, *BR*, 853
Canada, 261–2: agreement with US on Arctic marine environment, *CP*, 340–1; lump sum agreements, 79; maritime boundary delimitation with US, 451–2, 456–7, 558, 562, 798–800; Protocol amending Extradition Treaty with US, *CP*, 337–40
(The) Canadian Yearbook of International Law, Vol. XXIII, 1985, *BR*, 225
Cançado Trindade, Antônio Augusto. Repertório da Prática Brasileira do Direito Internacional Público, Vols. IV and V, *BR*, 891
Capotorti, Francesco, definition of minority, 92

Cappelletti, Mauro. *BR* of McWhinney, 421
Carnahan, Burrus M. *BR* of Bassiouni, Vols. II and III, 899
Caron, David D. *BR* of Rebagliati, 403
Carothers, Thomas. *BR* of Recueil des Cours de l'Académie de Droit International de La Haye, 1985, Vols. I, II, III and IV, 374
Carreau, Dominique. Droit International, *BR*, 385
Carroll, F. M. *BR* of Josephson, 419
Carter, Jimmy, 603: proposal for human rights Advocate General, *Ed.*, 319
Cassese, Antonio: on "internal" self-determination, 99–100; on peoples' rights over natural resources, 98–9
Castel, J. G., A. L. C. de Mestral & W. C. Graham. International Business Transactions and Economic Relations, *BN*, 436
Catholic Church: and "just war" concept, 720, 724–5; rituals of and legitimacy, 727, 728, 737, 740
Cerna, Christina M. *BR* of Israel Yearbook on Human Rights, Vol. 13, 1983, 675; *BR* of Vol. 14, 1984, 677
Change of circumstances, and 1871 London Declaration, *LA*, 1
Chase, Samuel, on "executory" treaty provisions, 770
Chile, human rights reporting by, 611
China, ancient: and legitimizing rituals and pedigrees, 727, 729, 730, 735–6
China, People's Republic of, 109: delivery of missiles to Iran, 707–8, 712; lump sum agreements practice, 79–80, 802; UN veto power and legitimacy, 749; withholding of admission to UN and legitimacy, 738, 739. *See also* China, ancient
Chiu, Hungdah. *BR* of Qiu & Zhang, of Zhu *et al.*, of Hu *et al.*, and of Wei *et al.*, 894; *BR* of Shen Yu & Wei, of Liu Ding, of Shen Daming, Feng & Zhao, of Liu Longheng, of Yao, of Shen Yu, and of Shen Daming & Feng, 892
Choice of law: act of state doctrine as rule of, *Ed.*, 58; for foreign government's taking of property in US, *ID*, 820–4; for internationalized contract, 138–9
Chowdhury, Subrata Roy, & Kamal Hossain (eds.). Permanent Sovereignty Over Natural Resources in International Law: Principle and Practice, *BR*, 405
Christenson, Gordon A. *BR* of Spinedi & Simma, 858
Clagett, Brice, on lump sum agreements and rule of compensation, 73–4, 76
Claims: contribution of lump sum agreements to law of, *NC*, 69; *Corr.* on, 801; liability for misappropriation of trade secrets, *JD*, 587–91; liability of branch bank in UK for Libyan, *JD*, 132–6; liability of USSR for tsarist bonds, *JD*, 129–32; measure of future lost profits, 599. *See also* Antitrust; Contracts; Expropriation; Iran–United States Claims Tribunal; United States, Alien Tort Claims Act
Claims Settlement Declaration (Iran-US), jurisdiction of Tribunal under, 141. *See also* Algiers Accords
Clark, Joe, exchange of letters re extradition of "bounty hunters," 339–40. *See also* Canada
Collected Edition of the "Travaux Préparatoires" of the European Convention on Human Rights, Vols. VI, VII and VIII, *BR*, 680
Collected Essays, 231, 693
Colombia, US extraterritorial jurisdiction and instrumentality of, *JD*, 351–3
Colson, David A. *BR* of Borgese, and of Pontecorvo, 191
Comity: balancing test and US extraterritorial jurisdiction, *JD*, 351–3; 525, 532, 539, 552; and international discovery, 524, 525–6, 529, 530–1, 539–47, 551, 553; and misappropriation of trade secrets, *JD*, 587–91; and US recognition of UK law, 838, 839–40
Communist Party of the Soviet Union: on class struggle and peaceful coexistence, 789, 790–1; on inevitability of world war, 791
Compensation: lump sum agreements and rule of, 71–8, 802; standard for expropriation, *JD*, 358–62. *See also* Expropriation
Concert of Europe, 7, 19, 22, 33, 39
Conciliation, of *Jan Mayen* dispute between Iceland and Norway, *LA*, 443
Connally reservation, and US defense in *Nicaragua* case, 102, 714–5
Contemporary Practice of the United States Relating to International Law, 103, 336, 566, 803

Continental shelf. *See* Law of the sea
Contracts: breach by foreign sovereign and US jurisdiction, *ID*, 828–30; with government entity and expropriation, 359; performance and supervening illegality, 133, 134–5; terminated, liability for claims regarding, *JD*, 136–40; corrigendum to, 600; treaties as, and self-execution, 770, 771–2. *See also* Arbitration
Cotter, William R. *BR* of Sethi, 684
Cristescu, Aureliu, definition of "people," 87, 88
Critical legal studies, 22: and change of circumstances, 3–4, 31, 34–5, 37, 38; and international law generally, 29–31, 36, 40
Cuba: expropriation cases in US, *Ed.*, 58; 71–2; lump sum agreements, 79; missile crisis and threat of force, 254–5, 257, 260, 261–2, 265
Current Developments, 144, 363, 601
Cutler, Lloyd, on disadvantages of *Gulf of Maine* adjudication, 451–2
Czechoslovakia, 258, 259: immunity in US courts for expropriation, *JD*, 585–7; lump sum agreements, 79; and missile inspections under INF Treaty, 342, 349; and self-determination, 743, 745

Daillier, Patrick, & Alain Pellet (eds.). [Nguyen Quoc Dinh,] Droit International Public (3d ed.), *BR*, 384
Damaška, Mirjan R. The Faces of Justice and State Authority: A Comparative Approach to the Legal Process, *BR*, 203
D'Amato, Anthony. The Alien Tort Statute and the Founding of the Constitution, *Ed.*, 62; *Corr.* in response to Pellet on French sources in AJIL, 564; International Law: Process and Prospect, *BR*, 370
Daoud Khan, Mohammad, 467–8
Dardanelles. *See* Bosporus
Dashwood, Alan, Richard Hacon & Robin White. A Guide to the Civil Jurisdiction and Judgments Convention, *BR*, 419
Davie, William, on treaties as supreme law of the land, 762
de la Rosa, José, & Rick Silberstein. *BR* of Pablo-Romero Gil-Delgado, 659
De Lupis, Ingrid Detter. The Concept of International Law, *BR*, 631; International Law and the Independent State (2d ed.), *BR*, 640
Delvalle, Eric Arturo, and US sanctions against Noriega government, *CP*, 566–9; 572–3, 574
de Mestral, A. L. C., J. G. Castel & W. C. Graham. International Business Transactions and Economic Relations, *BN*, 436
Denmark: continental shelf delimitation with Ireland and UK, 457; lump sum agreements, 78
Developing countries: GATT preferential system and legitimacy, 750; and lump sum agreements, 74–6; and Protocol on Ozone Layer, 121, 123, 124, 125. *See also* New International Economic Order; Third World
de Vries, Margaret Garritsen. Balance of Payments Adjustment, 1945 to 1986: The IMF Experience, *BR*, 895
de Zayas, Alfred-Maurice. *BR* of Swinarski, 416
Díaz-González, Leonardo, 151
Dinstein, Yoram, definition of people, 86–7
——— (ed.). Israel Yearbook on Human Rights, Vol. 13, 1983, *BR*, 675; Vol. 14, 1984, *BR*, 677
Diplomatic courier and bag, ILC progress on, 144
Diplomatic missions: US action against PLO Mission at UN, 67, 756, 801–2; *ID*, 833–7; US designation of Palestine Information Office as, *CP*, 103–6; US limitations on use of, *CP*, 808–10; US moratorium on honorary consular posts, *CP*, 111–2. *See also* Diplomatic privileges and immunities
Diplomatic practice, legitimizing force of, 733–4
Diplomatic privileges and immunities: legitimacy of rules on, 716–7, 718, 723, 734; legitimizing force of extension of, 732–3; and traffic offenses in US, 108, 110; US expulsion of Nicaraguan OAS representatives, *CP*, 803–6; US policy on crimes by foreign mission personnel and, *CP*, 106–11. *See also* Diplomatic missions

Discrimination. *See* Discrimination Against Women, Convention on the Elimination of All Forms of; International Convention on the Elimination of All Forms of Racial Discrimination; United Nations Declaration on the Elimination of All Forms of Intolerance and of Discrimination Based on Religion or Belief
Discrimination Against Women, Convention on the Elimination of All Forms of (1979), and Declaration on Religious Intolerance and Discrimination, 497, 498, 504, 507, 515–7
Dispute settlement: under IMO Maritime Safety Convention, 308; under LOS Convention, *Corr.*, 332; threats of force and, 246, 267. *See also* Arbitration; International Court of Justice; International Court of Justice, Statute of; Jan Mayen
Dobrynin, Anatolii, on war and social progress, 792–3
Dobson, Tracy. *BR* of Schmandt & Roderick, 200
Dolzer, Rudolf. *BR* of Boutard-Labarde, 409; on lump sum agreements and rule of compensation, 76, 77
Dorsey, Gray L. The McDougal-Lasswell Proposal to Build a World Public Order, *Ag.*, 41
(The) Dorsey Comment: A Modest Retrogression, *Ag.*, 51
Dowty, Alan. Closed Borders: The Contemporary Assault on Freedom of Movement, *BR*, 411
Dugard, John. Recognition and the United Nations, *BR*, 391
Durand-Barthez, Pascal, & Luiz O. Baptista. Les Associations d'Entreprises (Joint Ventures) dans le commerce international, *BR*, 214
Duvalier, Jean-Claude: political nature of security forces under, 831–2; US court on misappropriation of funds by, *JD*, 594–6
Duvalier, Michelle Bennett, US court on misappropriation of funds by, *JD*, 594–6
Dworkin, Ronald, on nature of legal obligation, 709, 741, 742, 748, 758–9

Eastern Europe: *perestroika* and Committee on Economic, Social and Cultural Rights, 605, 613; and self-determination, 745. *See also* Warsaw Pact
Ebert, Klaus Wolfgang. Rechtliche Beschränkungen des Technologietransfers im Außenwirtschaftsverkehr, *BR*, 657
Egypt, 96: and drafting of IMO Maritime Safety Convention, 270, 291–2; lump sum agreement, 79
(The) 1871 London Declaration, Rebus sic Stantibus and a Primitivist View of the Law of Nations, *LA*, 1
Empell, Hans-Michael. Die Kompetenzen des UN-Menschenrechtsausschusses im Staatenberichtsverfahren (Art. 40 des Internationalen Paktes über bürgerliche und politische Rechte), *BR*, 868
Encyclopedia of Public International Law. Instalment 8: Human Rights and the Individual in International Law, *BR*, 175
Entin, M. L. Mezhdunarodnye sudebnye uchrezhdenya (International Judicial Institutions), *BR*, 396
Environment, Protocol to Convention on Ozone Layer, *CP*, 120–5. *See also* Law of the sea, Fisheries; Law of the sea, Marine environment; Watercourses, international
Ermacora, Felix: on law applicable to Afghan conflict, 480–1; on minorities and self-determination, 92, 93–4
Esquípulas II Accord, 804–5
Ethiopia: conflict in Eritrea and self-determination, 89, 90–1; lump sum agreement, 80
Evensen, Jens, 147, 444
Evidence: International Discovery after Aerospatiale, *LA*, 521; new, and reopening deportation proceedings, *JD*, 580–3; of persecution, and asylum, 831; requirements for US assistance for foreign investigations, *ID*, 824–8; US-UK legal assistance treaty re Caymans, *CP*, 112–8
Exclusive economic zone. *See* Law of the sea
Expropriation: Cuban cases in US, *Ed.*, 58; 71–2; lawful vs. unlawful, *JD*, 358–62; private claims for in US courts, *JD*, 585–7; without compensation, and act of state, *ID*, 820–4. *See also* Compensation
Extradition: and ILC draft code on offenses against peace and security, 147; under IMO Maritime Safety Convention, 292–3, 294, 297, 300–1, 302–3, 305, 306; political offense

exception and Protocol amending Canada-US Treaty, 338; under Protocol on airport safety, 571; under Torture Convention, 807

Falk, Richard: on peoples' rights, 83; Reviving the World Court, *BR*, 166
Falkland Islands, war between Argentina and UK over: Argentinean destruction of neutral ship and US courts, *JD*, 126–9; *NC*, 323; postwar threats of force by parties, 247, 260–1
Farer, Tom J., 313, 314: *BR* of Zartman, 665
(The) Federalist, on treaties as law of the land, 762
Feldbrugge, F. J. M. (ed.). The Distinctiveness of Soviet Law, *BR*, 886
Feng Datong & Shen Daming. Guoji Maoyifa (International Trade Law), *BR*, 893
———, Shen Daming & Zhao Hongxun. Guoji Shangfa (International Commercial Law), 2 vols., *BR*, 892
Fenwick, Charles G.: on the 1871 London Declaration, 24; on *Santa María* seizure, 286–7
Fikentscher, Wolfgang. *BR* of Ebert, 657
Finkelstein, Lawrence S. *BR* of Henrikson, 399
Finland, lump sum agreement, 80
Fischer Williams, John, on the 1871 London Declaration, 25–6, 34
Fishing, fisheries. *See* Law of the sea
Fitzmaurice, Gerald, 333: The Law and Procedure of the International Court of Justice, Vols. I and II, *BN*, 231; on warships and piracy, 280–1
Flinterman, Cees, Barbara Kwiatkowska & Johan G. Lammers (eds.). Transboundary Air Pollution: International Legal Aspects of the Co-operation of States, *BR*, 197
Fong, Hiram L., on ABM Treaty, 161–2
Force, threats of, *LA*, 239: lawfulness of, 240–1, 242, 244, 246, 248–51, 254–68
Force, use of: conclusion of US-USSR INF Treaty, *CP*, 341–50; 796; 810–5; economic coercion as, 313; and threats of force, 239–40, 242, 247, 248, 250, 256, 258, 266. *See also* Afghanistan; United Nations Charter
Foreign government (sovereign) compulsion defense, 352, 549–50
Foreign Relations of the United States, 1952–1954, Vol. VI: Western Europe and Canada, *BR*, 670; 1952–1954, Vol. XII: East Asia and the Pacific, *BR*, 911
Fox, Donald T. Inter-American Commission on Human Rights Finds United States in Violation, *CD*, 601
France: aviation arbitration with US, 253; discovery requests in US of corporation in, 522–6, 530–1, 543–4, 546–7, 549, 550–1, 552; and the 1871 London Declaration, 19; joint management of resources with Spain, 450; and 19th-century straits agreements, 7, 10, 11, 13–4; and self-determination, 743–4, 745, 746–8; UN veto power and legitimacy, 749
Francescakis, Phocion. La Pensée des autres en droit international privé. Comptes Rendus bibliographiques (1946–1984) réunis en hommage à leur auteur, *BN*, 231
Franck, Thomas M. Judging the World Court, *BR*, 870; Legitimacy in the International System, *LA*, 705; on *Santa María* seizure, 287; Taking Treaties Seriously, *Ed.*, 67; *Corr.* on, 801
François, J. P. A., on ILC piracy draft articles, 277–8, 279–81, 285, 290
Fraser, Arvonne S. The U.N. Decade for Women: Documents and Dialogue, *BR*, 682
Frenzke, Dietrich, & Alexander Uschakow. Der Warschauer Pakt und seine bilateralen Bündnisverträge: Analyse und Texte, *BR*, 420
Frigo, Manlio. La Protezione dei beni culturali nel diritto internazionale, *BR*, 674
Fritzemeyer, Wolfgang. Die Intervention vor dem Internationalen Gerichtshof, *BR*, 186
Frowein, Jochen A. *BR* of Breitenmoser, 189
Functionalism, 32, 36, 39: and change of circumstances, 33–5
Further Thoughts on the Chambers Procedure of the International Court of Justice, *NC*, 556

Gadbaw, R. Michael, & Rosemary E. Gwynn. *BR* of Woolcock, Hart & van der Ven, 654
Gasser, Hans-Peter: on humanitarian law and Afghan conflict, 480; response by Sofaer to 1987 *Ag.* on Protocol I, *Ag.*, 784
General Agreement on Tariffs and Trade (GATT): most-favored-nation system and legitimacy, 743, 750; Soviet application for observer status in, 788, 795

Geneva Convention on the Continental Shelf (1958), underwater boundary under, 713–4
Geneva Convention on the High Seas (1958), piracy under, 270, 271–2, 276–85, 287, 290–1
Geneva Convention on the Territorial Sea and the Contiguous Zone (1958), 265
Geneva Conventions for the protection of war victims (1949): applicability to Afghan conflict, 460–5, 466, 479, 481, 482–6; common Art. 3 and Afghan conflict, 460, 462–4, 466, 479, 480, 481
Geneva Conventions for the protection of war victims, Additional Protocols to (1977): applicability of, 464–5, 466; US decision not to ratify Protocol I, *Ag.*, 784
Georges Bank, and Canada-US maritime boundary, 451–2
Gerber, David J. International Discovery after Aerospatiale: The Quest for an Analytical Framework, *LA*, 521
Germany (pre-1945): and the 1871 London Declaration, 11, 15, 19, 20, 24–5, 26, 27, 33, 39; and self-determination, 743–4; threat of force against Poland in 1939, 243
Germany, Democratic Republic of, 109, 258: lump sum agreements, 80; and missile inspections under INF Treaty, 342, 349, 350
Germany, Federal Republic of: agreement with US on missile inspections, 342, 343, 349–50; dismantling of missiles, 344; lump sum agreements, 79
Ginther, Konrad. *BR* of Wöhlcke, 668
Gladstone, William, and Russia's denunciation of Black Sea clauses, 14
Glennon, Michael J. *BR* of Zoller, 648
Goodman, Rosabel E. Everard, & J. Stewart McClendon (eds.). International Commercial Arbitration in New York, *BR*, 616
Gorbachev, Mikhail, 341: Perestroika. New Thinking for Our Country and the World, *BR*, 878; *perestroika* policy and international law, *NC*, 788
Gorchakov, A. M., denunciation of Black Sea clauses, 9–14, 19, 39
Gorman, Robert F. Coping with Africa's Refugee Burden: A Time for Solutions, *BR*, 690
Gorove, Stephen (ed.). The Teaching of Space Law Around the World, *BN*, 693
Graham, W. C., J. G. Castel & A. L. C. de Mestral. International Business Transactions and Economic Relations, *BN*, 436
Granville, George: and the 1871 London Declaration, 17–8; and Russia's denunciation of Black Sea clauses, 9, 12–4, 39
Gray, Christine D. Judicial Remedies in International Law, *BR*, 648
Great Britain, 1794 complaint for Americans' conduct in Sierra Leone, 66–7. *See also* United Kingdom
Greece, 452: lump sum agreement, 79
Green, L. C., on *Santa María* seizure, 287
Greiter, Ivo. How To Get Your Money in Foreign Countries: A Survey of Court Costs and Lawyer's Fees in 151 Countries, *BN*, 918
Grieves, Forest L. *BR* of The Canadian Yearbook of International Law, Vol. XXIII, 1985, 225
Gross, Leo. *BR* of Falk, 166
Grzybowski, Kazimierz. *BR* of Uschakow & Frenzke, 420
Guinea, Republic of, arbitration on contract with private party, *JD*, 598–9
Gulf of Mexico, US Senate understanding to MARPOL regulations regarding, 120
Gutiérrez Espada, Cesáreo, & Alfonso-Luis Calvo Caravaca. Textos de Derecho internacional público, *BR*, 853
Gwynn, Rosemary E., & R. Michael Gadbaw. *BR* of Woolcock, Hart & van der Ven, 654

Habermas, Jürgen, on legitimacy, 709
Hackworth, Green H., on ICJ Chamber procedure, 560
Hacon, Richard, Alan Dashwood & Robin White. A Guide to the Civil Jurisdiction and Judgments Convention, *BR*, 419
Hague Convention on the Service Abroad of Judicial and Extrajudicial Documents in Civil or Commercial Matters (1965), whether service of process on US subsidiary requires recourse to, *ID*, 816–20
Hague Convention on the Taking of Evidence Abroad in Civil or Commercial Matters (1970), applicability of in US courts, 522–6, 544–6, 555

Hague Conventions on Laws and Customs of War on Land (1907), and Afghan conflict, 460, 466, 481, 482
Hague law. *See* Hague Conventions on Laws and Customs of War on Land
Hahn, Peter K., & Thomas F. Marsteller. *BR* of von Münch, 909
Haiti: asylum standard for persecuted refugee from, *ID*, 830–2; US court on claims against Duvaliers, *JD*, 594–6
Halberstam, Malvina. Terrorism on the High Seas: The Achille Lauro, Piracy and the IMO Convention on Maritime Safety, *LA*, 269
Hall, William: on the 1871 London Declaration, 20–1, 24, 33; on nature of piracy, 275, 282–3, 284–5
Hamilton, Alexander, on denial of justice to aliens and federal jurisdiction, 64–5, 67
Hammarskjöld, Dag, 739
Hannum, Hurst. *BR* of Bossuyt, and of Collected Edition of the "Travaux Préparatoires" of the European Convention on Human Rights, Vols. VI, VII and VIII, 680
Haraszti, György, on the 1871 London Declaration, 29
Hart, H. L. A., on nature of rules in international system, 712, 751–2, 756–7
Hart, Jeffrey, Stephen Woolcock & Hans van der Ven. Interdependence in the Post-Multilateral Era: Trends in U.S.-European Trade Relations, *BR*, 654
Harvard Research in International Law: Draft Convention on Jurisdiction with Respect to Crime, 298, 299–300; Draft Convention on Piracy, 277–80, 282, 283–4, 285, 288, 290
Hauser, Rita E. *BR* of Fraser, 682
Hawk, Barry E. *BR* of Maxeiner, 208
Hazard, John N. *BR* of Blishchenko, 887; *BR* of Feldbrugge, 886; *BR* of Soviet Year-Book of International Law, 1985, 227; 1986, 889
Headquarters Agreement (US-UN), and US action against PLO Observer Mission, 67, 756, 802: ICJ on, 756, 801; US court on, *ID*, 833–7
Helms, Jesse, and interpreting ABM Treaty, 159–65
Helsinki Final Act (1975), 815
Henkin, Louis, 332: on act of state doctrine, 58; on treaty interpretation by President and Senate, 152–3, 161
Henrikson, Alan K. (ed.). Negotiating World Order: The Artisanship and Architecture of Global Diplomacy, *BR*, 399
Higgins, Rosalyn, on economic coercion as use of force, 313
Highet, Keith. *BR* of Mériboute, 862
High seas. *See* Law of the sea
Hill, Brian H. W., Kenneth R. Simmonds & Sigvard Jarvin (eds.). Commercial Arbitration Law in Asia and the Pacific, *BN*, 918
Hobbes, Thomas, 2, 249, 251
Holtzmann, Howard M., 73
Honnold, John O. *BR* of Szász, 429
Hossain, Kamal, & Subrata Roy Chowdhury (eds.). Permanent Sovereignty Over Natural Resources in International Law: Principle and Practice, *BR*, 405
Hostages, Convention Against the Taking of (1979), 807: and IMO Maritime Safety Convention, 291, 292, 294, 300–1, 305, 307
Hudson, Manley O., on ICJ Chamber procedure, 561
Hufbauer, Gary. *BR* of Winham, 898
Human dignity, McDougal-Lasswell concept of, 41, 48–50, 54–6
Human rights: apartheid and ASIL divestment of stock portfolio, *Ag.*, 311; *Corr.*, 800; apartheid and US sanctions against South Africa, 315–6; asylum in US because of persecution, *ID*, 828–30; Declaration on Elimination of Religious Intolerance and Discrimination, *LA*, 487; improving US image in, *Ed.*, 319; jurisdiction over deposed foreign sovereign re violations of, *JD*, 594–6; jurisdiction over foreign sovereigns re violations of, 329–30; and "peoples' rights" in Banjul Charter, *NC*, 80; submission of Torture Convention to US Senate, *CP*, 806–8; and threats of force, 250; treaties on as self-executing, 771; US measures against Noriega government and, 566–9, 576; US violations of inter-American standards on juvenile punishment, *CD*, 601; in USSR and Senate conditions to INF Treaty, 815. *See also* United Nations Committee on Economic, Social and Cultural Rights

Hungary, 109, 745: lump sum agreements, 78–9
Hunter, Martin, & Alan Redfern. Law and Practice of International Commercial Arbitration, *BR*, 616
Hu Wenzhi *et al.* Guojifa Gailun (Introduction to International Law), *BR*, 894
Hyde, C. C., on nature of piracy, 275, 282

Iceland, joint management resources agreement with Norway, *LA*, 443: special interests of Iceland, 447, 448, 450–1
Improving the Image of the United States in International Human Rights, *Ed.*, 319
INF Treaty. *See* United States, Treaty on the Elimination of Intermediate-Range and Shorter-Range Missiles
Inter-American Commission on Human Rights, on individual complaint re US execution of juveniles, *CD*, 601
Inter-American Commission on Human Rights Finds United States in Violation, *CD*, 601
Inter-American Treaty of Reciprocal Assistance (Rio Treaty), and Cuban missile crisis, 260
International Bank for Reconstruction and Development (World Bank), equality of participation in and legitimacy, 730–1
International Centre for Settlement of Investment Disputes, arbitration on good faith performance of contracts, *JD*, 598–9
International Civil Aviation Organization (ICAO), conclusion of Protocol on airport safety, *CP*, 569–71
International Committee of the Red Cross (ICRC), 462, 463, 464, 784: and Afghan conflict, 479–80; and distinction between international and internal conflicts, 465–6; Waldemar Solf's work on humanitarian law, 563
International Convention on the Elimination of All Forms of Racial Discrimination (1966), and Declaration on Religious Intolerance and Discrimination, 501–2, 503, 504, 506, 519
International Court of Justice, 316, 734: on admission of states to UN membership, 737; on bindingness of customary law, 757; on British threat of force in Corfu Channel, 263–4; Canada-US maritime boundary delimitation, 451–2, 558, 562, 798–800; and disputes involving IMO Maritime Safety Convention, 308; and disputes under LOS Convention, 332–3, 334–5; election of November 1987 to, *CD*, 369; and legitimacy of rule on continental shelf delimitation, 724–5; on lump sum agreements, 70–1, 74, 75, 76; Soviet views on, 788, 795; on UN Charter as customary law, 248–9; use of Chamber procedure, *NC*, 556; on US law closing PLO Mission, 756, 801. *See also* Dispute settlement; International Court of Justice, Statute of; Nicaragua
International Court of Justice, Statute of, 71; Chamber procedure and, *NC*, 556; *Corr.* on, 797; optional clause and *Nicaragua* case, *Corr.* on, 102; 714–5
International Covenant on Civil and Political Rights: and Declaration on Religious Intolerance and Discrimination, 492–3, 496–7, 499, 500, 507, 519; and ILC draft code on offenses against peace and security, 147; and minority rights, 87, 94
International Covenant on Economic, Social and Cultural Rights. *See* International Human Rights Covenants; United Nations Committee on Economic, Social and Cultural Rights
International Decisions, 816
International Discovery after Aerospatiale: The Quest for an Analytical Framework, *LA*, 521
International Human Rights Covenants, 495, 498: and self-determination, 81, 85, 93, 94, 98. *See also* International Covenant on Civil and Political Rights; United Nations Committee on Economic, Social and Cultural Rights
International Labour Organisation (ILO), and reporting to UN Committee on Economic, Social and Cultural Rights, 609–10, 612
International Law and the Grotian Heritage: A Commemorative Colloquium, *BR*, 183
International Law Commission, 326: deliberations on piracy articles, 277–8, 279–81, 282, 283, 290; legitimacy of rules drafted by, 726; 39th session of, *CD*, 144
International Legal Materials (Contents), 237, 439, 702, 924
International liability for lawful acts, ILC 39th session on, 144, 150–1
Internationally Protected Persons, including Diplomatic Agents, Convention on the Prevention and Punishment of Crimes Against (1973), 807: and IMO Maritime Safety Convention, 291, 292, 294, 300–1

International Maritime Organization (IMO), drafting of Convention on Maritime Safety, 270–1, 291–2, 293–4, 296, 303–4, 307: issues reserved for 1988 Diplomatic Conference, 271, 293, 294, 305–8. *See also* Pollution from Ships, International Convention for the Prevention of; Safety of Maritime Navigation, Convention for the Suppression of Unlawful Acts Against

International Monetary Fund, 312: possible Soviet participation in, 788, 795

International organizations: ILC progress on relations between states and, 144, 151; regional economic integration, and Protocol on Ozone Layer, 122, 124, 125; requirements for immunity in US, 837–8, 839, 840

International Tin Council, whether immune from suit in US, *ID*, 837–40

International trade: extraterritorial effect of US sanctions against Libya, *JD*, 132–6; good faith performance of shipping contracts, *JD*, 598–9; misappropriation of trade secrets held by foreign subsidiary, *JD*, 587–91; Protocol on Substances that Deplete the Ozone Layer, *CP*, 120–5. *See also* Antitrust; Sanctions

International Whaling Commission, quotas and Japanese research, *CP*, 577–9

Iran: hostages crisis and legitimacy, 723, 734; proposed US interception of missiles for, 707–8, 712; religious practice in, 496, 500, 516. *See also* Iran–United States Claims Tribunal

Iran–United States Claims Tribunal, 69, 78: on compensation standard for expropriation, *JD*, 358–62; enforcement of awards in US courts, *JD*, 591–4; on liability for claims regarding terminated contract, *JD*, 136–40; corrigendum to, 600; on lump sum agreements and rule of compensation, 72–3; on responsibility for expulsion of US nationals, *JD*, 140–3; *JD*, 353–7

Iredell, James, and self-execution of treaties, 761, 762, 769–70

Ireland, continental shelf delimitation with Denmark and UK, 457

Israel, 243: and *Achille Lauro* seizure, 269, 282, 301

Israel Yearbook on Human Rights, Vol. 13, 1983, *BR*, 675; Vol. 14, 1984, *BR*, 677

Italy, 113: agreement with US on missile inspections, 342, 343, 349–50; and drafting of IMO Maritime Safety Convention, 270, 291–2; and the 1871 London Declaration, 11, 15, 16, 18, 19

Jackson, John H. *BR* of Long, 653

Jacobson, Harold K. *BR* of James, 188

James, Alan. Sovereign Statehood: The Basis of International Society, *BR*, 188

Jan Mayen, joint management of continental shelf resources, *LA*, 443: recommendations of conciliation commission, 443, 444–8, 457–8

Jan Mayen in Perspective, *LA*, 443

Japan, US policy on observation of whaling quotas, *CP*, 577–9

Jaruzelski, Wojciech, 259

Jarvin, Sigvard, Kenneth R. Simmonds & Brian H. W. Hill (eds.). Commercial Arbitration Law in Asia and the Pacific, *BN*, 918

Jay, John, on treaties as law of the land, 760–1

Jennings, Robert, on UN Charter as customary law, 248

Jewish law, and Declaration on Religious Intolerance and Discrimination, 517

Jiménez de Aréchaga, Eduardo, on ICJ Chamber procedure, 559

Josephson, Harold (ed.). Biographical Dictionary of Modern Peace Leaders, *BR*, 419

Joyner, Christopher C. *BR* of Triggs, 903; on economic sanctions, 313–4

Judicial assistance: under IMO Maritime Safety Convention, 305; International Discovery after Aerospatiale, *LA*, 521; scope and applicability of Hague Service Convention, *ID*, 816–20; scope of US statute on, *ID*, 824–8; US-UK treaty re Caymans, *CP*, 112–8

Judicial Decisions, 126, 351, 580. *See also* International Decisions

Judicial review: of cases under War Powers Resolution, 597; standard for INS decisions, *JD*, 580–3

Jurisdiction: and attempted closure of PLO Mission, 833–4; over cases arising under War Powers Resolution, *JD*, 596–7; to enforce Iran-US Tribunal awards, *JD*, 591–4; extraterritorial application of US antitrust laws, *JD*, 351–3; extraterritorial discovery under US law, *LA*, 521; over offenses under airport safety Protocol, 571; over piracy, 272, 277–80, 283–4, 287–91, 299, 327; of religious courts and protection of human rights, 514, 517–8; universality principle, and terrorism, 299–302, 309, 310; and use of ICJ Chambers, 558–9. *See also* Act of state doctrine; Nicaragua; United States, Alien Tort Claims Act; United States, Foreign Sovereign Immunities Act; United States, International Organizations Immunities Act

"just war" concept, 720, 724–5

Kaiser, Karl, & Hans-Peter Schwarz (eds.). Weltpolitik: Strukturen—Akteure—Perspektiven, *BR*, 650

Kamenka, Eugene, on collective rights, 86

Kampuchea, representation of in UN and legitimacy, 739, 740

Kaplan, Abraham, work with Lasswell on world social process, 43–4, 46, 48

Kappeler, Dietrich. *BR* of Gorman, 690; *BR* of Wulff, 220

Karmal, Babrak, 468, 476, 478, 479: and Soviet presence in Afghanistan, 472–4, 481, 485

Kearse, Amalya: on compensation for expropriation, 72; on subject matter jurisdiction under FSIA, 128–9

Kelsen, Hans, 251

Kennedy, John F., and Cuban missile crisis, 254–5, 260

Kenney, William Sumner. *BR* of Bassiouni, 413

Khadduri, Majid. The Islamic Conception of Justice, *BR*, 431

Khomeini, Ruhollah, and expulsion of Americans from Iran, 142, 143, 354, 356

Khrushchev, Nikita S., threat of force after U–2 incident, 243–4

Kindleberger, Charles P. *BR* of de Vries, 895

Kirgis, Frederic L., Jr. Alien Tort Claims, Sovereign Immunity and International Law in U.S. Courts, *NC*, 323; *BR* of D'Amato, 370; Understanding the Act of State Doctrine's Effect, *Ed.*, 58

Kirkpatrick, Jeane J., 720–1: Legitimacy and Force, Vol. One: Political and Moral Dimensions; Vol. Two: National and International Dimensions, *BN*, 918

Kiwanuka, Richard N. The Meaning of "People" in the African Charter on Human and Peoples' Rights, *NC*, 80

Kly, Y. N. International Law and the Black Minority in the U.S., *BR*, 688

Koenig, Eric S. *ID*, 833–7

Kohona, Palitha Tikiri Bandara. The Regulation of International Economic Relations Through Law, *BR*, 651

Kokott, Julia B. *BR* of Empell, 868; *BR* of Fritzemeyer, 186

Krishnaswami, Arcot, study on religious intolerance and discrimination, 494, 511

Kuwait, 301: proposal on offenders under IMO Maritime Safety Convention, 305–6

Kwiatkowska, Barbara. *Corr.* on ocean panel's proposal on dispute settlement, 332

———, Cees Flinterman & Johan G. Lammers (eds.). Transboundary Air Pollution: International Legal Aspects of the Co-operation of States, *BR*, 197

Lachs, Manfred, on ICJ Chamber procedure, 797

Lammers, Johan G., Cees Flinterman & Barbara Kwiatkowska (eds.). Transboundary Air Pollution: International Legal Aspects of the Co-operation of States, *BR*, 197

Lasswell, Harold D., proposal with McDougal on world public order, *Ag.* on, 41; response by McDougal, *Ag.*, 51

Lauterpacht, E. *BR* of Arend, and of Franck, 870

Lauterpacht, Hersch, 273, 333

Law of the sea

- Continental shelf: delimitation disputes with joint development potential, 453–7; delimitation, and Jan Mayen, 443, 444–7, 458; Iceland-Norway resources agreement on Jan Mayen, *LA*, 443; legitimacy of rules on delimitation, 713–4, 724–5
- Exclusive economic zone: arrangements for Jan Mayen area, 443–4, 447–8
- Fisheries: and Canada-US maritime boundary, 451–2; and Jan Mayen area, 443–4, 450; Norwegian-Soviet agreement, 452; Trinidad and Tobago–Venezuela agreement, 454–5; US policy on Japanese whaling, *CP*, 577–9
- High seas: defining piracy, 272–85, 288, 289–91; US seabed mining policy, *CD*, 363

Marine environment: Canada-US agreement on research in Arctic, *CP*, 340–1; US approval of MARPOL regulations on garbage disposal, *CP*, 118–20; US policy on Japan's observation of whaling quotas, *CP*, 577–9
Preparatory Commission: progress of, 366–7
Territorial sea: and applicability of IMO Maritime Safety Convention, 304
UN Convention, 265, 443, 457: deep seabed mining and, *CD*, 363; dispute settlement under, *Corr.*, 332; legitimacy of rules under, 713–4, 724–5; piracy under, 270, 271–2, 276–7, 284, 290–1; on provisional arrangements pending delimitation, 453
Law of Treaties Between States and International Organizations or Between International Organizations, Convention on, 333
Law of war: contribution of Waldemar Solf, 563–4; legitimacy of, and US conduct in Persian Gulf, 707–8, 712. *See also* Afghanistan; Geneva Conventions on the protection of war victims; Geneva Conventions on the protection of war victims, Additional Protocols to; Hague Conventions on Laws and Customs of War on Land
Lawrence, T. J., 285: on the 1871 London Declaration, 21, 24, 34
League of Nations: Covenant and modification of treaties, 22–4, 26, 27; "peaceful change" and the 1871 London Declaration, 20, 22–4, 25–8, 29, 34, 38; and self-determination, 744; and terrorism, 309–10. *See also* Permanent Court of International Justice
Lebiecki, Andrzej E. Załatwianie Międzynarodowych Sporów Gospodarczych, *BR*, 428
Lecuyer-Thieffry, Christine, & Patrick Thieffry. Le Règlement des litiges civils et commerciaux avec les Etats-Unis, *BR*, 616
Legitimacy in the International System, *LA*, 705
Legitimacy of international rules, *LA*, 705: adherence to a normative hierarchy and, 712, 751–9; coherence and, 712, 735–51; determinacy and, 712, 713–25, 735–6, 738; and lack of coercive authority, 705–12, 713, 751, 759; symbolic validation, ritual and pedigree and, 705, 712, 725–41, 748
Leich, Marian Nash. Contemporary Practice of the United States Relating to International Law, 103, 336, 566, 803
Leigh, Edward M. *ID*, 828–30
Leigh, Monroe. Judicial Decisions, 126, 351, 580; retirement as AJIL Judicial Decisions Editor, 816
Less-developed countries. *See* Developing countries
Levie, Howard S. *BR* of Meron, 876
——— (ed.). The Law of Non-International Armed Conflict: Protocol II to the 1949 Geneva Conventions, *BR*, 679
Levis, Mirta Noemí (ed.). Régimen jurídico de las inversiones extranjeras en los países de la ALADI, 9 binders, *BR*, 662
Liberia, Argentinean attack on vessel of, *JD*, 126–9; *NC*, 323
Libya: diplomatic immunities and London People's Bureau, 716–7, 734; extraterritorial effect of US economic sanctions against, *JD*, 132–6
Lillich, Richard B., & Burns H. Weston. Lump Sum Agreements: Their Continuing Contribution to the Law of International Claims, *NC*, 69; *Corr.* on, 801
Limitation of Anti-Ballistic Missile Systems, Treaty between the US and USSR on. *See* ABM Treaty
Litt, David G. *BR* of Dashwood, Hacon & White, 419
Litvinov Assignment (1933), 131
Liu Ding. Guoji Jingifa (International Economic Law), *BR*, 892
Liu Longheng. Guoji Shuifa (International Tax Law), *BR*, 893
London Conference (1871), 17–9: and pacta sunt servanda, 2–3, 15
London Declaration (1871), and changed circumstances, *LA*, 1
Long, Olivier. Law and its Limitations in the GATT Multilateral Trade System, *BR*, 653
Lopez, Diane V. *BN* of Remacha, 435
Lorimer, James, on the 1871 London Declaration, 21–2, 33, 34
Lump Sum Agreements: Their Continuing Contribution to the Law of International Claims, *NC*, 69; *Corr.* on, 801

McCaffrey, Stephen C. The Thirty-ninth Session of the International Law Commission, *CD*, 144
McClendon, J. Stewart, & Rosabel E. Everard Goodman (eds.). International Commercial Arbitration in New York, *BR*, 616
McCreary, Don R. Japanese-U.S. Business Negotiations: A Cross-Cultural Study, *BR*, 433
McDougal, Myres S. The Dorsey Comment: A Modest Retrogression, *Ag.*, 51; public order study with Lasswell, *Ag.* on by Dorsey, 41
(The) McDougal-Lasswell Proposal to Build a World Public Order, *Ag.*, 41; *Ag.* in response, 51
Machiavelli, Niccolò, on coercion and observance of laws, 707, 708
McWhinney, Edward. *Corr.* on ICJ Chamber procedure, 797; Supreme Courts and Judicial Law-Making: Constitutional Tribunals and Constitutional Review, *BR*, 421
Madison, James, 761–2, 763
Maier, Harold G. *BR* of Malekian, 381
Malekian, Farhad. The System of International Law: Formation, Treaties, Responsibility, *BR*, 381
Mann, F. A. *Corr.* on *Ed.* by Franck and *NC* by Lillich & Weston, 801
Marshall, John, 758: and self-execution of treaties, 765, 766–72, 774, 775
Marsteller, Thomas F., & Peter K. Hahn. *BR* of von Münch, 909
Matson, Ruth C., & Thomas Naff (eds.). Water in the Middle East: Conflict or Cooperation?, *BN*, 230
Mauritius, lump sum agreement, 79
Maxeiner, James. Policy and Methods in German and American Antitrust Law: A Comparative Study, *BR*, 208
(The) Meaning of "People" in the African Charter on Human and Peoples' Rights, *NC*, 80
Medvedev, V. A., on peaceful coexistence, 794
Meissner, Boris. Aussenpolitik und Völkerrecht der Sowjetunion, *BR*, 229
Menegas, Dean N. *BR* of Boyle, 635
Mériboute, Zidane. La Codification de la succession d'Etats aux traités: Décolonisation, sécession, unification, *BR*, 862
Meron, Theodor: on a hierarchy of human rights, 497; Human Rights in Internal Strife: Their International Protection, *BR*, 876
Merrills, J. G. International Dispute Settlement, *BR*, 184
Merryman, John Henry. *BR* of Frigo, 674
Mexico: claims of nationals for property in pre-1845 Texas, 132; legitimizing ritual and pedigree of Aztecs, 727, 729, 730, 731
Mill, John Stuart, and observation of treaties, 19–20, 27, 28, 33
Morocco, 91: lump sum agreement, 79
Mosk, Richard M., on lump sum agreements and rule of compensation, 73
Murphy, Ewell E., Jr. *BR* of Levis, 662

Naff, Thomas, & Ruth C. Matson (eds.). Water in the Middle East: Conflict or Cooperation?, *BN*, 230
Namibia, 740: UN competence to impose sanctions in behalf of, 317
Nanda, Ved P. *BN* of Naff & Matson, 230
Nascimento e Silva, G. E. do. *BR* of Cançado Trindade, 891
Nationality: US repatriation of stateless renunciants, *CP*, 336–7; of victim, jurisdiction based on in international conventions, 296–9, 300–2, 309
Natural resources: and peoples' rights, 95–9; "shared," international watercourses as, 147–8; US policy on seabed mining, *CD*, 363. *See also* Law of the sea, Continental shelf; Law of the sea, Marine environment
Negotiation: of INF Treaty, 343–4; record of, and interpreting ABM Treaty, 153–4, 156, 160, 164. *See also* Conciliation
Netherlands, 113: agreement with US on missile inspections, 342, 343, 349–50; misappropriation of US-owned trade secrets by corporation in, *JD*, 587–91

New International Economic Order, 792: and Banjul Charter, 96–8; Soviet support for implementing, 794
Nguyen Quoc Dinh (rev. and updated by Patrick Daillier & Alain Pellet). Droit International Public (3d ed.), *BR*, 384
Nicaragua, 720–1: case against US and customary law, 757; expulsion of 8 US diplomats, 803, 805–6; ICJ jurisdiction over case against US, *Corr.* on, 102; 714–5; jurisdiction over expropriated property in US, *ID*, 820–4; US expulsion of 8 diplomats, *CP*, 803–6
Nigeria, and self-determination for Biafra, 745–6, 747–8
Non-Aligned Group, on defining terrorism, 719
Nongovernmental organizations, and human rights reporting, 608, 610, 612
Non-self-governing territories, UN trusteeship and self-determination, 744–5
Noriega, Manuel Antonio: US indictments of, 566; US sanctions against government of, *CP*, 566–9; *CP*, 571–7
Norms of international law: hierarchy of and legitimacy, 751–9; Soviet views of, 788–9, 795–6
North Atlantic Treaty Organization (NATO), 243, 255, 266, 451: "dual-track" policy on missile deployment and control, 343; and negotiating treaty on conventional stability in Europe, 813–4
Norway: Court on religious discrimination and ethnicity, 508–9; joint management resources agreement with Iceland, *LA*, 443: special responsibilities of Norway, 447, 448; joint management of resources with UK, 450; joint management of resources with USSR, 452; lump sum agreement, 78
Nuclear weapons: legality of threat to use, 250; and Soviet view of international cooperation, 790, 791, 792, 795; US Senate report on interpreting ABM Treaty, *CD*, 151; US-USSR INF Treaty and risk reduction measures, *CP*, 341–50; 813–4
Nunn, Sam, and interpreting ABM Treaty, 155–6, 159, 163, 164
Nuremberg Principles (1950), and ILC draft code of offenses against peace and security, 146
Nyon Arrangement (1937), and laws of piracy, 280–1

Oda, Shigeru, 335, 798: Further Thoughts on the Chambers Procedure of the International Court of Justice, *NC*, 556
Odio Benito, Elizabeth, study on religious intolerance and discrimination, 489, 519–20
Ogiso, Motoo, 144
Oppenheim, Lassa, on nature of piracy, 273, 280, 285, 289
Orentlicher, Diane F. *BR* of Thoolen & Verstappen, 873
Organization of African Unity (OAU), 745–6. *See also* Banjul Charter on Human and Peoples' Rights
Organization of American States (OAS), 255, 260: US expulsion of Nicaragua's ambassador to, *CP*, 803–6. *See also* Inter-American Commission on Human Rights
Osakwe, Christopher. *BR* of De Lupis, 631; *BR* of De Lupis, 640
Ottoman Empire. *See* Turkey
Oxman, Bernard H. *BR* of Smith, 193; on ocean panel's proposal on dispute settlement, 332–3
Ozone Layer, Convention for the Protection of (1985), Montreal Protocol to (1987), *CP*, 120–5

Pablo-Romero Gil-Delgado, María Concepción. La inversión directa en el régimen de las inversiones extranjeras, *BR*, 659
Pakistan, and the Afghanistan conflict, 468, 469–70, 471, 478
Palestine Liberation Organization: and Protocol I to 1949 Geneva Conventions, 785–6; US action against information office, *CP*, 103–6; US action against observer mission, 67, 756, 801–2; *ID*, 833–7; US response to UNSC resolution on Israeli raid against, 243
Panama, US economic measures against Noriega government, *CP*, 566–9; *CP*, 571–7
Panel on the Law of Ocean Uses. Deep Seabed Mining and the 1982 Convention on the Law of the Sea, *CD*, 363; *Corr.* on 1986 dispute settlement statement by, 332
Park, William W. Review Article: National Legal Systems and Private Dispute Resolution, *BR* of McClendon & Goodman, of Redfern & Hunter, and of Thieffry & Lecuyer-Thieffry, 616
Paust, Jordan J. Self-Executing Treaties, *LA*, 760

Peace and Security of Mankind, Draft Code of Offences Against, ILC 39th session on, 144–7
Pechota, Vratislav, on lump sum agreements and rule of compensation, 76–7
Pellet, Alain. *Corr.* on lack of French sources in AJIL, 331; *Corr.* in response by D'Amato, 564
———, & Patrick Daillier (eds.). [Nguyen Quoc Dinh,] Droit International Public (3d ed.), *BR*, 384
Perestroika and International Law, *NC*, 788
Pérez de Cuéllar, Javier, 740
Permanent Court of International Justice: and Chamber procedure, 556, 557, 560; on compensation for expropriation, 360; and the 1871 London Declaration, 26
Peru, lump sum agreement, 79
Peterson, M. J. *BR* of Dugard, 391; The General Assembly in World Politics, *BR*, 178
Philippines, 109
Pictet, Jean, 484: on applicability of 1949 Geneva Conventions, 461, 463–4, 482–3
Plischke, Elmer. *BR* of Foreign Relations of the United States, 1952–1954, Vol. VI: Western Europe and Canada, 670; *BR* of Vol. XII: East Asia and the Pacific, 911
Polach, Jay G. *BR* of Lebiecki, 428
Poland, 109: China's seizure of ships, and piracy, 280; German threat of force against in 1939, 243; imposition of martial law and threats of force, 258–9, 262, 266; limitations period on pre-World War II notes, 131; lump sum agreements, 79; and self-determination after World War I, 744
Pollution from Ships, International Convention for the Prevention of (MARPOL, 1973), US approval of Annex V to 1978 Protocol, *CP*, 118–20
Pontecorvo, Giulio (ed.). The New Order of the Oceans: The Advent of a Managed Environment, *BR*, 191
Portugal, *Santa María* incident and piracy, 286–7
Pouritch, B., on the 1871 London Declaration, 23
Pressler, Larry, and interpreting ABM Treaty, 159–65
Primitivist view of international law, 1–2, 36–7, 40: and change of circumstances, 4, 37, 38–9
Privileges and Immunities, Agreement Relating to (US-OAS), 805
Professor William W. Bishop, Jr. (1906–1987): A Tribute, *NC*, 321; Personal Recollections, *NC*, 323
Prussia. *See* Germany (pre-1945)

Qiu Zaiyu & Zhang Jincao. Xiandai Guojifa Jichu (Foundation of Modern International Law), *BR*, 894
Quigley, John. *Perestroika* and International Law, *NC*, 788

Racial Discrimination, Declaration on the Elimination of All Forms of. *See* United Nations General Assembly
(The) Rationale for the United States Decision, *Ag.* on nonratification of Geneva Protocol I, 784
Ratner, Steven R. *ID*, 837–40
Reagan, Ronald, 341, 803: action re Japanese whaling, 578–9; interpretation of ABM Treaty, *CD*, 151; 1981 sanctions against USSR and Poland, 259; and sanctions against Noriega government, *CP*, 571–7; on Senate condition re interpreting INF Treaty, 811–2; transmittal to Senate of INF Treaty, *CP*, 341–50; transmittal to Senate of Torture Convention, *CP*, 806–8. *See also* United States President
Reagan Doctrine, and legitimacy, 720–1
Realist view of international law, 32–3, 36, 39–40: and change of circumstances, 33, 34–5
Rebagliati, Orlando Rubén. La Plataforma Continental y su límite exterior, *BR*, 403
Recognition: access to US courts of government lacking, *JD*, 591–4; and legitimacy, 726, 736, 737–40, 758; and US measures against Noriega government, *CP*, 566–9
Recognition and Enforcement of Foreign Arbitral Awards, Convention on (1958), jurisdiction under, to enforce Iran-US Tribunal awards, *JD*, 591–4
Recueil des Cours de l'Académie de Droit International de La Haye, 1983, Vols. I, II, III, IV and V, *BR*, 841; 1985, Vols. I, II, III and IV, *BR*, 374

Redfern, Alan, & Martin Hunter. Law and Practice of International Commercial Arbitration, *BR*, 616
Reimann, Mathias. *BR* of Damaška, 203
Reisman, W. Michael, & James Silk. Which Law Applies to the Afghan Conflict?, *LA*, 459
Religious Intolerance and Discrimination, Declaration on the Elimination of All Forms of. *See* United Nations Declaration on the Elimination of All Forms of Intolerance and of Discrimination Based on Religion or Belief
Remacha, José Ramón. Derecho Internacional Codificado. Derecho de Gentes: Recopilación Sistemática de Textos y Tratados, *BN*, 435
Representation of States in Their Relations with International Organizations of a Universal Character, Convention on (1975), 151
Reservations, 125: to Hague Evidence Convention, 545–6; and other conditions to US ratification of INF Treaty, *CP*, 810–5; US, to Torture Convention, 806–8
Restatement of Foreign Relations Law of the United States (Revised). *See* Restatement (Third) of Foreign Relations Law of the United States
Restatement (Second) of Foreign Relations Law of the United States, and sovereign immunity, 583–4
Restatement (Third) of Foreign Relations Law of the United States: on customary law human rights violations, 330; on international discovery, 525–6; on self-execution of treaties, 773–5, 777–8, 779–80, 782; on a state's jurisdiction over non-nationals, 298–9
Ribeiro, Angelo d'Almeida, report on religious intolerance and discrimination, 489, 519–20
Richardson, Elliot L. Jan Mayen in Perspective, *LA*, 443
Richardson, Henry J., III: response by Barrie to *CD* on ASIL divestment, *Ag.*, 311; 315; *Corr.* in reply by Richardson, 800
Richardson, Jacques G. (ed.). Managing the Ocean: Resources, Research, Law, *BR*, 196
Riddle, Dorothy I. Service-Led Growth: The Role of the Service Sector in World Development, *BR*, 224
Rigaux, Marie-Françoise. La Théorie des limites matérielles à l'exercice de la fonction constituante, *BR*, 645
Roach, Colleen. *BR* of Blanchard, 913
Roberts, Adam, on international character of Afghan conflict, 483–4
Roderick, Hilliard, & Jurgen Schmandt (eds.). Acid Rain and Friendly Neighbors: The Policy Dispute between Canada and the United States, *BR*, 200
Romania, 109: lump sum agreement, 79; and 19th-century Russia's interests in Black Sea, 10, 16
Rosenne, Shabtai. Breach of Treaty, *BR*, 387
Roxburgh, Ronald, on the 1871 London Declaration, 23–4
Rubin, Alfred P. *BR* of Recueil des Cours de l'Académie de Droit International de La Haye, 1983, Vols. I, II, III, IV and V, 841
Russian Empire: denunciation of Black Sea clauses, 9–15, 19, 33, 39; and 19th-century straits agreements, 5–7, 8, 16–7, 18
Rutledge, John, on treaties as law paramount, 763

Sadurska, Romana. Threats of Force, *LA*, 239
Safety of Maritime Navigation, Convention for the Suppression of Unlawful Acts Against (1988), *LA* on draft, 269: extradition or prosecution under, 292–3, 294, 297, 300–1, 302–3, 305, 306, 308–9; jurisdiction under, 295–303, 308–9
Salazar, Antonio de Oliveira, 286–7
Sampson, Pedro, 803–5
Sanctions, economic, 319: ASIL divestment of stock portfolio, *Ag.*, 311; *Corr.*, 800; legality of, 253–4; as threats of force, 241, 244; US against Japan re fishing, 578–9; US against Panama's Noriega government, *CP*, 566–9; *CP*, 571–7; US against Poland and USSR in 1981, 259
Sandstrom, Mark Roy. *BR* of Kohona, 651
San Francisco Conference. *See* Washington Committee of Jurists
Santa María, whether seizure constituted piracy, 286–7, 291

São Tomé and Príncipe, Constitution and natural resources, 96
Sapoa Agreement, 804–5
Saudi Arabia: breach of contract by and immunity in US, *ID*, 828–30; proposal on IMO Maritime Safety Convention, 306
Schachter, Oscar, 322: on nature of legal obligation, 709–10, 712, 726; on "threat of force" under UN Charter Art. 2(4), 240; on use of force under Art. 2(4), 263–4
Schmandt, Jurgen, & Hilliard Roderick (eds.). Acid Rain and Friendly Neighbors: The Policy Dispute between Canada and the United States, *BR*, 200
Schuck, Peter H. *BR* of Dowty, 411
Schwarz, Hans-Peter, & Karl Kaiser (eds.). Weltpolitik: Strukturen—Akteure—Perspektiven, *BR*, 650
Schwebel, Stephen M., 147, 756: International Arbitration: Three Salient Problems, *BR*, 394; reelection to ICJ, 369; on use of Chamber procedure, 556, 557, 559, 797, 798, 799
Second Session of the UN Committee on Economic, Social and Cultural Rights, *CD*, 603
Seidl-Hohenveldern, Ignaz. *BR* of Wegen, 865
Self-defense: and economic coercion, 312–4, 315, 316; and threats of force, 250, 254, 256–7, 260, 265
Self-determination: and Banjul Charter, 81, 86–91, 92–100; and drafting instrument on terrorism, 310, 719; Protocol I to 1949 Geneva Conventions and, 464; "right" to, and legitimacy, 743–8; and threats of force, 259–60, 262
Self-Executing Treaties, *LA*, 760
Sethi, S. Prakash (ed.). The South African Quagmire: In Search of a Peaceful Path to Democratic Pluralism, *BR*, 684
Seward, Bernard L., Jr. (ed.). Technology Control, Competition and National Security: Conflict and Consensus, *BR*, 425
Shahabuddeen, M., election to ICJ, *CD*, 369
Shen Daming & Feng Datong. Guoji Maoyifa (International Trade Law), *BR*, 893
———, Feng Datong & Zhao Hongxun. Guoji Shangfa (International Commercial Law), 2 vols., *BR*, 892
Shen Yu. Guoji Huobifa Gailun (Introduction to International Monetary Law), *BR*, 893
——— & Wei Jiajui. Guojifa Xin Lingyu Jianlun (A Concise Introduction to the New Areas of International Law), *BR*, 892
Shultz, George P.: exchange of letters re extradition of "bounty hunters," 339–40; report on airport safety Protocol, *CP*, 569–71; report on INF Treaty, 342–50; report on Torture Convention, 807–8. *See also* United States Department of State
Silberstein, Rick, & José de la Rosa. *BR* of Pablo-Romero Gil-Delgado, 659
Silk, James, & W. Michael Reisman. Which Law Applies to the Afghan Conflict?, *LA*, 459
Simma, Bruno, & Philip Alston. Second Session of the UN Committee on Economic, Social and Cultural Rights, *CD*, 603
———, & Marina Spinedi (eds.). United Nations Codification of State Responsibility, *BR*, 858
Simmonds, Kenneth R., Brian H. W. Hill & Sigvard Jarvin (eds.). Commercial Arbitration Law in Asia and the Pacific, *BN*, 918
Sims, William, and interpreting ABM Treaty, 156
Sinclair, Ian. The International Law Commission, *BR*, 643
Smith, Bradford L. *ID*, 824–8
Smith, Robert W. Exclusive Economic Zone Claims: An Analysis and Primary Documents, *BR*, 193
Sobrino Heredia, José Manuel. Las Relaciones de cooperación para el desarrollo CEE–Estados ACP, *BN*, 692
Sofaer, Abraham D.: on ABM Treaty, 153–7, 164; The Rationale for the United States Decision, *Ag.* on nonratification of Geneva Protocol I, 784
"soft" law of human rights, and collective economic action, validity of, 318
Sohn, Louis B.: on collective rights, 85; Improving the Image of the United States in International Human Rights, *Ed.*, 319; on self-determination, 93
———, & Kristen Gustafson, proposal on ICJ jurisdiction and LOS Convention, 332–3
Solf, Waldemar A., memorial on, *NC*, 562

Solidarity (Polish trade union), 258, 262
Solís Palma, Manuel, 567, 573, 574
Somoza Debayle, Anastasio, US court on expropriated property of generals under, 820–3
Sondaal, Henricus Hermanus Maria. De Nederlandse Verdragspraktijk, *BR*, 389
Sornarajah, M., on lump sum agreements and rule of compensation, 74–5, 76
Sosa, Juan Bautista, and Panama-related property in US banks, 567–9
South Africa: ASIL divestment re companies investing in, *Ag.*, 311; *Corr.*, 800; jurisdiction over injury to US citizen in, *JD*, 583–5; recognition of Bantustans and legitimacy, 738; and self-determination of minorities, 89–90; UNGA's refusal to seat and legitimacy, 738–9, 740
Sovereign immunity: ILC codification and violations of international law, 326; ILC progress on codification, 144; and legitimacy, 734–5. *See also* United States, Foreign Sovereign Immunities Act; United States, International Organizations Immunities Act
Soviet Year-Book of International Law, 1985, *BR*, 227; 1986, *BR*, 889
Spain: joint management of resources with France, 450; treaty with US as self-executing, 768, 771
Spinedi, Marina, & Bruno Simma (eds.). United Nations Codification of State Responsibility, *BR*, 858
Stańczyk, Janusz. *Corr.* on 1987 Note by Glennon, 102
Statement by Expert Panel: Deep Seabed Mining and the 1982 Convention on the Law of the Sea, *CD*, 363
State responsibility, 306: for expulsion of US citizens from Iran, *JD*, 140–3; *JD*, 353–7; and ILC draft code on offenses against peace and security, 145, 146–7; ILC progress on codification, 144. *See also* Compensation
Stein, Eric. Professor William W. Bishop, Jr. (1906–1987): A Tribute, *NC*, 321
Story, Joseph: on nature of piracy, 273–4, 289; on treaties as supreme law of the land, 771–2
Straits Convention (1841), legal regime of, 6–7
Succession of states: and legitimacy, 757–8; responsibility of successor government for revolutionaries' actions, 142, 143, 356–7
Sucharitkul, Sompong, 144
Sullivan, Colleen Driscoll. *BN* of Gorove, 693
Sullivan, Donna J. Advancing the Freedom of Religion or Belief Through the UN Declaration on the Elimination of Religious Intolerance and Discrimination, *LA*, 487
Sweden: foreign submarines law as threat of force, 255–6, 257, 261, 264–6; lump sum agreement, 80
Swift, Richard N. *BR* of Peterson, 178
Swinarski, Christophe. Studies and essays on international humanitarian law and Red Cross principles in honour of Jean Pictet, *BR*, 416
Switzerland, 113: lump sum agreements, 79; and Protocol I to 1949 Geneva Conventions, 784, 786
Szász, Iván. The CMEA Uniform Law for International Sales (2d rev. ed.), *BR*, 429
Szasz, Paul C. The Action Does Not Violate International Law, *Ag.* on ASIL divestment, 314; 800
Szawlowski, Richard. *BR* of Entin, 396; *BR* of Gorbachev, 878

Taking Treaties Seriously, *Ed.*, 67; *Corr.* on, 801
Talwani, Manik, role in *Jan Mayen* settlement, 445–6
Taraki, Nur Mohammad, 468–70
Tarassov, N. K., reelection to ICJ, 369
Tate letter, 131
Territorial sea. *See* Law of the sea
Territorial sovereignty: McDougal-Lasswell theories and, 41–2, 43, 45–6, 47, 51–3, 54, 57; noninterference principle and extraterritorial discovery, 534–9, 543–4; Soviet annexation of Wakhan corridor, 478–9
Terrorism: on the high seas, *LA*, 269; jurisdiction regarding, 299–302, 309, 310, 330; legitimacy of rules on, 722–3; and political offense exception in amended Canada-US treaty, 338; Protocol on airport safety, *CP*, 569–71; and Protocol I to 1949 Geneva Conventions, 786, 787; UNGA effort to draft instrument on, 310, 719–20; US policy on, 243

Terrorism on the High Seas: The Achille Lauro, Piracy and the IMO Convention on Maritime Safety, *LA*, 269
Tesón, Fernando R. *BN* of Sobrino Heredia, 692
Thant, U, 739–40
Thiam, Doudou, 144
Thieffry, Patrick, & Christine Lecuyer-Thieffry. Le Règlement des litiges civils et commerciaux avec les Etats-Unis, *BR*, 616
Third World: concept of peoples' rights, 83; and drafting of Protocol I to 1949 Geneva Conventions, 784, 785; and seabed mining, 364, 367; Soviet "new thinking" and, 794, 795, 796; Soviet views on changes in international status of, 792, 793
(The) Thirty-ninth Session of the International Law Commission, *CD*, 144
Thoolen, Hans, & Berth Verstappen. Human Rights Missions: A study of the fact-finding practice of non-governmental organizations, *BR*, 873
Threats of Force, *LA*, 239
Thurmond, Strom, on ABM Treaty, 162
Tobin, Harold, and the 1871 London Declaration, 27, 28–9, 34
Torture and Other Cruel, Inhuman or Degrading Treatment or Punishment, Convention Against (1984), submission of to US Senate, *CP*, 806–8
Treaties: and balance of power in 19th-century Europe, 4–8, 9, 13–4; contribution of lump sum agreements, *NC*, 69; 802; list of lump sum agreements, 78–80; mutual legal assistance, US-UK re Caymans, *CP*, 112–8; non-self-executing, legal effect of, 781–2; obligations under and legitimacy, 755–7, 758–9; pacta sunt servanda and rebus sic stantibus, *LA*, 1; self-executing, *LA*, 760; US attitude toward, *Ed.*, 67; *Corr.* on, 801. *See also* Headquarters Agreement; Reservations
Treaty of Paris (1856), 7: Russia's denunciation of Black Sea clauses, 9–17, 19
Trible, Paul S., and interpreting ABM Treaty, 159–65
Triennial Elections of Five Members of the International Court of Justice, *CD*, 369
Triggs, Gillian D. (ed.). The Antarctic Treaty regime: Law, Environment and Resources, *BR*, 903
Trinidad and Tobago: joint management of resources with Venezuela, 454–5; request for US judicial assistance for criminal investigation, *ID*, 824–8
Tripartite Covenant (1856), 7, 13–5
Trooboff, Peter D. International Decisions, 816
Tunkin, G. I.: ASIL address on Soviet attitudes toward international law, 788, 791, 794, 795; on peaceful coexistence and international law, 789–90
Tunnermann, Carlos, US expulsion of, *CP*, 803–6
Turkey, 113, 452: and 19th-century straits agreements, 5–7, 8, 15–7; and Russia's denunciation of Black Sea clauses, 9–14

Understanding the Act of State Doctrine's Effect, *Ed.*, 58
Union of Soviet Socialist Republics, 109: Agreement with US on nuclear risk reduction, 347, 348; alleged violations of ABM Treaty by, 164–5; applicable law to conduct in Afghanistan, *LA*, 459; conclusion of INF Treaty with US, *CP*, 341–50; 796; *CP*, 810–5; immunity from suit re tsarist bonds, *JD*, 129–32; intervention in Afghanistan and concept of legitimacy, 736; joint management of resources with Norway, 452; joint management of resources with US, 455–6; lump sum agreement, 80; *Perestroika* and International Law, *NC*, 788; and self-determination, 747, 748; and threats of force, 243–4, 254–5, 257, 258–60, 261, 262, 265, 266; and UN Committee on Economic, Social and Cultural Rights, 604, 613–4; UN veto power and legitimacy, 749. *See also* Russian Empire
United Kingdom: agreement with US on missile inspections, 342, 343, 349–50; continental shelf delimitation with Ireland and Denmark, 457; courts on piracy, 273, 274, 289; and the 1871 London Declaration, 17–8; and ICJ Chamber procedure, 558, 560, 561; joint management of resources with Norway, 450; liability of US branch bank for Libyan claims, *JD*, 132–6; lump sum agreements practice, 79–80, 802; mutual legal assistance treaty with US re Caymans, *CP*, 112–8; and 19th-century straits agreements, 7, 9, 10, 11, 12-4; parliamentary rituals and legitimacy, 726, 727–9; parliamentary supremacy as "unifying rule of recognition," 751, 753–4; response to abuses of diplomatic privileges and immunities in, 109,

716–7, 734; and self-determination, 744, 745, 747–8; and threats of force, 242–3, 247, 260–2, 263–4; UN veto power and legitimacy, 749; US recognition of law of, and comity, 838, 839–40. *See also* Great Britain

United Nations *Ad Hoc* Committee on International Terrorism, 310

United Nations Charter, 737: Arts. 2(4) and 51 and legitimacy, 720, 721–2; and Declaration on Religious Intolerance and Discrimination, 497, 498; "threat of force" under Art. 2(4), 240, 242, 248–50, 254, 256–8, 264, 267, 268, 316; and "unifying rules of recognition," 753, 758; US withholding from budget and, 67; voting under, and legitimacy, 749

United Nations Commission on Human Rights: and measures on religious intolerance and discrimination, 489, 503, 519–20; report on Afghanistan, 480–1; work on economic rights and new committee, 608

United Nations Committee against Torture, US views on recognizing competence of, 806–7

United Nations Committee on Economic, Social and Cultural Rights, second session of, *CD*, 603

United Nations Committee on the Elimination of All Forms of Discrimination Against Women, 606–7

United Nations Convention on the Law of the Sea. *See* Law of the sea

United Nations Declaration on the Elimination of All Forms of Intolerance and of Discrimination Based on Religion or Belief, *LA*, 487: conflicts within and with other instruments, 490, 495–6, 498–9, 504, 510–8; defining religion and belief under, 491–2, 499

United Nations Economic and Social Council, 520: early reports on compliance with Covenant, 610–1; relationship with new committee, 614–5; reporting by new committee to, 605–13

United Nations Educational, Scientific and Cultural Organization (UNESCO), and reporting to UN Committee on Economic, Social and Cultural Rights, 609–10

United Nations Environment Programme, and Protocol to Ozone Layer Convention, 120, 122

United Nations General Assembly: acceptance of credentials and legitimacy, 736, 737–40, 741; and collective economic sanctions, 312–3, 316–8; Declaration on Establishment of International Peace and Security, 795; Declaration on Inadmissibility of Intervention, 312–3, 315; Declaration on Independence to Colonial Countries and Peoples, 746; Declaration on Principles concerning Friendly Relations, 312–3, 790; Declaration on Racial Discrimination, 502, 504; Declaration on Religious Intolerance and Discrimination, *LA*, 487; Declaration on Social Progress and Development, 614; Definition of Aggression, legitimacy of, 717–8; effort to draft instrument on terrorism, 310, 719–20; resolution on Permanent Sovereignty over Resources, 312, 315

United Nations Human Rights Committee, and Committee on Economic, Social and Cultural Rights, 605, 606, 607, 615

United Nations Organization: admission of members and legitimacy, 736; legitimizing force of emblems and immunities of, 731–3; Soviet views on increased role for, 794–5, 796

United Nations Security Council: as centralized enforcement mechanism, 251; and collective economic sanctions, 316–7; resolution on Israeli raid against PLO in Tunisia, 243; veto, sovereign equality of states, and legitimacy, 749

United States

Administrative Procedure Act, standard of judicial review under, 582–3

Agreement on the Establishment of Nuclear Risk Reduction Centers (1987), with USSR, 347, 348

Agreement Regarding Inspections Relating to the Treaty Between the United States of America and the Union of Soviet Socialist Republics on the Elimination of Their Intermediate-Range and Shorter-Range Missiles (Basing Country Agreement, 1987), with Belgium, the FRG, Italy, the Netherlands and the UK, 342, 343, 349–50

agreement with Canada on Arctic marine environment, *CP*, 340–1

Agricultural Trade Development and Assistance Act (1954), 575

Alien Tort Claims Act: and foreign sovereign's tortious violations of international law, *JD*, 126–9; *NC*, 323; 585; and misappropriation of public funds by deposed ruler, *JD*, 594–6; origins of, *Ed.*, 62

analyzing extraterritorial discovery disputes under US law, *LA*, 521: developing principles through appellate review, 553; US foreign relations interests and, 548, 552

Anti-Terrorism Act (1987), closure of PLO Mission under, *ID*, 833–7
Arms Control and Disarmament Act, 814
Arms Export Control Act, 575
attitude toward treaties, *Ed.*, 67; *Corr.* on, 801
Bankruptcy Code, and comity for foreign bankruptcy proceedings, *JD*, 587–91
Caribbean Basin Economic Recovery Act, 572
courts on piracy, 273, 274
and dispute settlement under LOS Convention, *Corr.*, 332
Export-Import Bank Act (1945), 575
Federal Rules of Civil Procedure, 351: resort to under requests for discovery abroad, 523–5, 554
Fishermen's Protective Act (1967), Japanese whaling and Pelly Amendment to, *CP*, 577–9
Fishery Conservation and Management Act (1976), Japanese whaling and Packwood-Magnuson Amendment to, *CP*, 577–9
Foreign Assistance Act (1961), withholding of US assistance to Panama under, 571–2, 575
Foreign Missions Act: and action against Palestine Information Office, 103–5; limitations on use of foreign missions under, *CP*, 808–10
Foreign Operations, Export Financing, and Related Programs Appropriations Act (1987), measures against Noriega government, 574–6
Foreign Relations Authorization Act, Fiscal Years 1988 and 1989, 808
Foreign Sovereign Immunities Act (1976), 837, 839: commercial activity exception, 130; *ID*, 828–30; direct effect in US under, *JD*, 583–5; *ID*, 828–30; expropriation by foreign state and instrumentality under, *JD*, 585–7; retroactive jurisdiction and, *JD*, 129–32; and tortious violations of international law, *JD*, 126–9; 325–6, 329
Foreign Trade Antitrust Improvements Act (1982), 352–3
Immigration and Nationality Act: asylum standard under, *ID*, 830–2; repatriation of stateless former nationals under, *CP*, 336–7; review of deportation proceedings under, *JD*, 580–3
Inter-American Foundation Act, 575
International Emergency Economic Powers Act, 573–4
International Organizations Immunities Act, applicability of, 837–8, 839, 840
joint management of resources with USSR, 455–6
Judiciary Act (1789), 62, 63, 65
and jurisdiction under IMO Maritime Safety Convention, 297, 301, 302
and lump sum agreements, 69–70, 71–3, 74, 79–80
maritime boundary delimitation with Canada, 451–2, 456–7, 558, 562, 798–800
National Emergencies Act, 573
policy on seabed mining, *CD*, 363
proposal for human rights Advocate General, *Ed.*, 319
proposal on ICJ Chambers, 560–2
Sherman Antitrust Act, 351
Soviet views on relations with, 793–4
and threats of force, 254–5, 257, 259, 260, 261–2, 265
Treaty Concerning the Cayman Islands Relating to Mutual Legal Assistance in Criminal Matters, with UK (1986), *CP*, 112–8
Treaty of Amity, Economic Relations and Consular Rights with Iran (1955), compensation standard for expropriation under, 359–60, 361
Treaty on Extradition with Canada (1971), Protocol amending, *CP*, 337–40
Treaty on the Elimination of Intermediate-Range and Shorter-Range Missiles, with USSR (1987), *CP*, 341–50: Senate condition on interpreting, *CP*, 810–5; and Soviet "new thinking," 796
and UN Committee on Economic, Social and Cultural Rights, 614
UN veto power and legitimacy, 749
violations of inter-American human rights standards, *CD*, 601
War Powers Resolution, justiciability of cases arising under, *JD*, 596–7
See also Iran–United States Claims Tribunal; Palestine Liberation Organization

United States Coast Guard, transit of Northwest Passage by icebreaker, 340–1

United States Commission on International Rules of Judicial Procedure, 1964 proposals of, 825–6

United States Congress: and breach of treaties, 67–8; and enforcement of War Powers Resolution, *JD*, 596–7; and immunity of foreign state instrumentalities, 586; intent re Anti-Terrorism Act and treaties, 835–6, 837; intent re changes in judicial assistance law, 825–6; intent re commercial activity exception to FSIA, 829, 830; intent re extraterritorial antitrust jurisdiction, 352–3; intent re subject matter jurisdiction under FSIA, 128–9, 326; proposal for human rights Advocate General, *Ed.*, 319; and sanctions against Noriega government, 571, 574–6; and self-execution of treaties, 760–1, 764, 766, 770, 775–81, 782; war power as *sui generis*, 778–80, 781, 782. *See also* United States House of Representatives; United States Senate

United States Constitution: Eighth Amendment and "evolving standards of decency," 603; and origins of Alien Tort Claims Act, *Ed.*, 63; self-execution of treaties under, 760, 762, 763–6, 767, 769–70, 772–5, 777, 778–81, 782–3; treaty interpretation conflicts between President and Senate and, 152–3, 157, 811–2; and treaty power, 67; as "unifying rule of recognition," 751, 753, 754

United States Department of Commerce, policy on Japan's observation of whaling quotas, *CP*, 577–9

United States Department of Defense: proposed interception of missiles in Persian Gulf, 707–8, 712; and Protocol I to 1949 Geneva Conventions, 785

United States Department of Justice: early application of Alien Tort statute, 66–7; on Anti-Terrorism Act and closing of PLO Mission, 836–7

United States Department of State: and act of state doctrine, 58, 59; on closure of PLO Mission, 834–7; defense in *Nicaragua* case, 714–5; and economic measures against Noriega government, *CP*, 566–9; on federal intervention in state sentences, 601; on legal assistance treaty with UK re Caymans, *CP*, 112–8; and limitations on use of foreign missions, 808–10; on MARPOL regulations on garbage disposal, *CP*, 118–20; moratorium on honorary consular posts, *CP*, 111–2; Nicaragua's expulsion of 8 US diplomats, 803, 805–6; policy on crimes by foreign mission personnel, *CP*, 106–11; on proposed interception of missiles in Persian Gulf, 707–8; on repatriation of stateless former nationals, *CP*, 336–7; on Soviet "new thinking," 796; statement to OAS on expulsion of Nicaraguan representatives, 804–6; statements on Palestine Information Office, *CP*, 103–6. *See also* Shultz, George P.; Sofaer, Abraham D.

United States Department of the Treasury: and Libyan claims against US, 132, 136; and measures against Noriega government, 568–9, 573–4, 576, 577

United States House of Representatives: implementing legislation on MARPOL garbage regulations, 120; and self-execution of treaties, 761–2, 763, 766, 779, 780–1. *See also* United States Congress

United States Immigration and Naturalization Service: discretion in deportation proceedings, *JD*, 580–3; and standard for asylum, 830–1

United States Internal Revenue Service, and payment of Panamanian income taxes, 569

United States President: economic sanctions against Libya, 132–3, 136; letter of transmittal of Protocol II to 1949 Geneva Conventions, 784, 787; reporting requirements under War Powers Resolution, *JD*, 596–7; and self-execution of treaties, 761–2, 764, 775–6; and treaty interpretation conflicts with Senate, 152–3, 160–1. *See also* Carter, Jimmy; Reagan, Ronald

United States Senate: approval of MARPOL regulations on garbage disposal, *CP*, 118–20; bill to subject foreign mission personnel to criminal jurisdiction, 106, 107–11; excerpts from report on interpreting ABM Treaty, *CD*, 151; resolution of ratification of INF Treaty, *CP*, 810–5; and self-execution of treaties, 761–2, 764, 775–6, 780. *See also* Reagan, Ronald; United States Congress; United States President

United States Supreme Court: on act of state doctrine, 59, 60; on extraterritorial discovery, 522–7, 530–1, 533, 543–4, 546–7, 549, 550–1, 552; interpretation of FSIA, 127–8, 129; on racial groups and civil rights, 509; on scope and applicability of Hague Service Convention, *ID*, 816–20; and self-execution of treaties, 760, 765, 766–73; on standard for reviewing deportation proceedings, *JD*, 580–3; and US policy on Japan's observation of whaling quotas, 579

Universal Declaration of Human Rights, 801, 815: and Declaration on Religious Intolerance and Discrimination, 495, 497, 499, 507; and individual participation in world social process, 42, 52, 54
Universal Declaration on the Rights of Peoples (1976), and Banjul Charter, 81, 99, 101
Uschakow, Alexander, & Dietrich Frenzke. Der Warschauer Pakt und seine bilateralen Bündnisverträge: Analyse und Texte, *BR*, 420

Vagts, Detlev. Book Reviews and Notes, 166, 370, 616, 841
van Boven, Theo. *BR* of Sondaal, 389
van der Ven, Hans, Stephen Woolcock & Jeffrey Hart. Interdependence in the Post-Multilateral Era: Trends in U.S.-European Trade Relations, *BR*, 654
Vanuatu, lump sum agreement, 80
Vasak, Karel, on "solidarity rights," 84–5
Vázquez, Carlos M. *ID*, 816–20
Venezuela, joint management of resources with Trinidad and Tobago, 454–5
Verstappen, Berth, & Hans Thoolen. Human Rights Missions: A study of the fact-finding practice of non-governmental organizations, *BR*, 873
Verzijl, Jan, on change of circumstances, 3–4
Vienna Convention on Consular Relations (1963), 109, 810
Vienna Convention on Diplomatic Relations (1961), 108, 111, 718, 810
Vienna Convention on the Law of Treaties (1969), 68, 333, 718: and change of circumstances, 28, 34; on *jus cogens*, 601–2; legitimacy of obligations under, 757; and treaty interpretation, 160, 164, 802
Vietnam, Democratic People's Republic of, 1964 UN negotiations with and legitimacy, 739–40
Vietnam War, and Protocol I to 1949 Geneva Conventions, 784
von Münch, Ingo. Internationales Seerecht, *BR*, 909

Wälde, Thomas W. *BR* of Hossain & Chowdhury, 405
Waldheim, Kurt, 719
Warsaw Pact, 243, 266, 745: possible intervention in Poland in 1980–81, 258–9
Washington, George, 760, 763
Washington Committee of Jurists, and ICJ Chamber procedure, 560–2
Watercourses, international, ILC 39th session on, 144, 147–50
Weber, Max, and legitimacy, 709, 729
Wegen, Gerhard. Vergleich und Klagerücknahme im internationalen Prozeß, *BR*, 865
Wei Jiajui & Shen Yu. Guojifa Xin Lingyu Jianlun (A Concise Introduction to the New Areas of International Law), *BR*, 892
Wei Min *et al.* Guojifa Gailun (Introduction to International Law), *BR*, 894
Weiss, Edith Brown. *BR* of Flinterman, Kwiatkowska & Lammers, 197
Western Europe, representation on ICJ Chambers, 557–8, 798–9
Western Sahara, and self-determination, 89, 91
Weston, Burns H., & Richard B. Lillich. Lump Sum Agreements: Their Continuing Contribution to the Law of International Claims, *NC*, 69; *Corr.* on, 801
Wharton, Francis, on universality principle of jurisdiction, 300
Which Law Applies to the Afghan Conflict?, *LA*, 459
White, Gillian. *BR* of Rigaux, 645
White, Robin, Alan Dashwood & Richard Hacon. A Guide to the Civil Jurisdiction and Judgments Convention, *BR*, 419
Whiteman, Marjorie M., on *Santa María* seizure, 287
Williams, Robert A., Jr. *BR* of Kly, 688
Wilson, James, on treaties as supreme law of the land, 763
Wilson, Woodrow, principle of self-determination, 743–4
Winham, Gilbert R. International Trade and the Tokyo Round Negotiation, *BR*, 898
Wöhlcke, Manfred. Ein Dritter Weg für die Dritte Welt? Nachholende Nationenbildung im Schnittpunkt entwicklungspolitischer und hegemonialer Interessen, *BR*, 668

Woolcock, Stephen, Jeffrey Hart & Hans van der Ven. Interdependence in the Post-Multilateral Era: Trends in U.S.-European Trade Relations, *BR*, 654
Woolsey, L. H., on the 1871 London Declaration, 24, 26
World public order, McDougal-Lasswell proposal on, *Ag.*, 41: culture-dependent societies and, 42–3, 47–8, 49–51, 55–6
Wulff, Otto. Entwicklungshilfe zwischen Völkerrechtsordnung und Weltwirtschaftssystem, *BR*, 220

Yambrusic, Edward Slavko. Treaty Interpretation: Theory and Reality, *BR*, 650
Yao Meizhen. Guoji Touzifa (International Investment Law), *BR*, 893
Yoffie, David B. *BR* of Riddle, 224
Yugoslavia, lump sum agreement, 79

Zaire: human rights reporting by, 611; lump sum agreement, 79
Zartman, I. William (ed.). Positive Sum: Improving North-South Negotiations, *BR*, 665
Zhang Jincao & Qiu Zaiyu. Xiandai Guojifa Jichu (Foundation of Modern International Law), *BR*, 894
Zhao Hongxun, Shen Daming & Feng Datong. Guoji Shangfa (International Commercial Law), 2 vols., *BR*, 892
Zhu Lisun *et al.* Guoji Gongfa (Public International Law), *BR*, 894

Zoller, Elisabeth. *BR* of Carreau, 385; *BR* of Gray, 648; *BR* of Nguyen Quoc Dinh (3d ed.) (rev. and updated by Patrick Daillier & Alain Pellet), 384; Enforcing International Law Through U.S. Legislation, *BR*, 648; recipient of Deák prize, 565
Zourek, Jaroslav, on warships and piracy, 280

STATEMENT OF OWNERSHIP, MANAGEMENT AND CIRCULATION

(Act of August 12, 1970; Sec. 3685, Title 39, U.S. Code)

Filed October 1988, *American Journal of International Law* (issued quarterly, January, April, July, October), Prince & Lemon Streets, Lancaster, Pennsylvania 17603. Published by American Society of International Law, 2223 Massachusetts Avenue, N.W., Washington, D.C. 20008-2864. Editor in Chief, Thomas M. Franck, New York University School of Law, New York, N.Y. 10012. Owner, American Society of International Law. *Average* number of copies per issue, last 12 months: total printed, 7,369; paid circulation, 6,215; mail subscriptions, 6,215; total paid circulation, 6,215; free distribution, 101; total distribution, 6,316; office use, left over, unaccounted, spoiled after printing, 1,053. For *single* issue nearest to filing date: total printed, 7,163; paid circulation, 6,211; mail subscriptions, 6,211; total paid circulation, 6,211; free distribution, 101; total distribution, 6,312; office use, left over, unaccounted, spoiled after printing, 851.

Be sure to check membership type on reverse side.

Name (please print) ____ Member, U.S. Bar?____ State:____ Year____

Mailing Address ____ Firm, School or Other Affiliation:____

Street, P.O. Box, etc. ____ Signature:____

City, State, Zip ____

Country ____ Phone ____

Please start my membership January 1, ____. Membership is on a calendar year basis, and includes the *Journal* and the ASIL *Newsletter.* Check below for special rate on *Proceedings* or *International Legal Materials.* Student members receive, in addition to these materials, the International Law Students Association *NEWSLETTER*.

☐ *Proceedings of the Annual Meeting,* at $15.

☐ *International Legal Materials.* Subscription at special member rate of $50 (plus $6.50 for mailing outside U.S.A.) for six issues per year.

VERIFICATION OF STUDENT STATUS. The following form may be completed by a professor or administrative officer of your school. I hereby certify that the above applicant is regularly registered in (school):

____ Completion Year____

Signed____ Title____ Date____

$____ Amount Enclosed (U.S. Dollars)(Include Contributions and Publications Order Payment).

AMERICAN SOCIETY OF INTERNATIONAL LAW

Be sure to check membership type on reverse side.

Name (please print) ____ Member, U.S. Bar?____ State:____ Year____

Mailing Address ____ Firm, School or Other Affiliation:____

Street, P.O. Box, etc. ____ Signature:____

City, State, Zip ____

Country ____ Phone ____

Please start my membership January 1, ____. Membership is on a calendar year basis, and includes the *Journal* and the ASIL *Newsletter.* Check below for special rate on *Proceedings* or *International Legal Materials.* Student members receive, in addition to these materials, the International Law Students Association *NEWSLETTER*.

☐ *Proceedings of the Annual Meeting,* at $15.

☐ *International Legal Materials.* Subscription at special member rate of $50 (plus $6.50 for mailing outside U.S.A.) for six issues per year.

VERIFICATION OF STUDENT STATUS. The following form may be completed by a professor or administrative officer of your school. I hereby certify that the above applicant is regularly registered in (school):

____ Completion Year____

Signed____ Title____ Date____

$____ Amount Enclosed (U.S. Dollars)(Include Contributions and Publications Order Payment).

AMERICAN SOCIETY OF INTERNATIONAL LAW

Be sure to check membership type on reverse side.

Name (please print) ____ Member, U.S. Bar?____ State:____ Year____

Mailing Address ____ Firm, School or Other Affiliation:____

Street, P.O. Box, etc. ____ Signature:____

City, State, Zip ____

Country ____ Phone ____

Please start my membership January 1, ____. Membership is on a calendar year basis, and includes the *Journal* and the ASIL *Newsletter.* Check below for special rate on *Proceedings* or *International Legal Materials.* Student members receive, in addition to these materials, the International Law Students Association *NEWSLETTER*.

☐ *Proceedings of the Annual Meeting,* at $15.

☐ *International Legal Materials.* Subscription at special member rate of $50 (plus $6.50 for mailing outside U.S.A.) for six issues per year.

VERIFICATION OF STUDENT STATUS. The following form may be completed by a professor or administrative officer of your school. I hereby certify that the above applicant is regularly registered in (school):

____ Completion Year____

Signed____ Title____ Date____

$____ Amount Enclosed (U.S. Dollars)(Include Contributions and Publications Order Payment).

Membership Status *(Check one)*

☐ **Regular Membership:**
$70 a year. Persons, regardless of nationality or profession, resident in a member country of the OECD (see below).

☐ **Special Members:**
$30 a year. Persons *not* resident in a member country of the OECD (see below).

☐ **Intermediate Members:**
$30 a year. Persons who are under 30 years of age at the time of application for membership may be Intermediate Members for the first three consecutive years of membership.
Date of Birth ______________________

Student Members (Mark appropriate box.)

☐ $20 a year, and certification of student status (see form on reverse). Includes free membership in International Law Students Association.

☐ $10 a year with certification of membership in International Law Students Association.

The member countries of the OECD are Australia, Austria, Belgium, Canada, Denmark, Federal Republic of Germany, Finland, France, Greece, Iceland, Ireland, Italy, Japan, Luxembourg, Netherlands, New Zealand, Norway, Portugal, Spain, Sweden, Switzerland, Turkey, United Kingdom, United States.

☐ **Contributing Members:**
$100 a year.

☐ **Supporting Members:**
$200 a year.

☐ **Annual Patron:**
$500 a year. Any individual or organization eligible for membership may become an Annual Patron for a contribution of at least $500.

☐ **Corporate Members:**
$1,500 a year. Any corporation, partnership, association, or other organization acceptable to the Executive Council is eligible for Corporate Membership.

☐ **Life Members:**
$1,000 payment (during 1988).

☐ **Patron:**
One-time contribution of $5,000.

☐ **Retired:**
$25 a year. Persons who are retired and who are 70 years of age or older.

Check Interest Groups in which you would
to participate, and enclose fee listed.

☐ $5 a year. Antarctica Law, Politics and Re
Policy (31)
☐ $5 a year. Dispute Resolution in Internati
Commercial Contracts (32)
☐ $5 a year. Indigenous Rights (33)
☐ $7.50 a year. International Economic Law
☐ $5 a year. International Environmental La
☐ $5 a year. International Human Rights (3
☐ $5 a year. International Organizations (37
☐ $5 a year. Private International Law (38)
☐ $5 a year. Law in the Pacific Region (39)
☐ $10 a year. International Space Law (40)
☐ $5 a year. Women in International Law (4
☐ $5 a year. Wildlife Law (42)

Membership Status *(Check one)*

☐ **Regular Membership:**
$70 a year. Persons, regardless of nationality or profession, resident in a member country of the OECD (see below).

☐ **Special Members:**
$30 a year. Persons *not* resident in a member country of the OECD (see below).

☐ **Intermediate Members:**
$30 a year. Persons who are under 30 years of age at the time of application for membership may be Intermediate Members for the first three consecutive years of membership.
Date of Birth ______________________

Student Members (Mark appropriate box.)

☐ $20 a year, and certification of student status (see form on reverse). Includes free membership in International Law Students Association.

☐ $10 a year with certification of membership in International Law Students Association.

The member countries of the OECD are Australia, Austria, Belgium, Canada, Denmark, Federal Republic of Germany, Finland, France, Greece, Iceland, Ireland, Italy, Japan, Luxembourg, Netherlands, New Zealand, Norway, Portugal, Spain, Sweden, Switzerland, Turkey, United Kingdom, United States.

☐ **Contributing Members:**
$100 a year.

☐ **Supporting Members:**
$200 a year.

☐ **Annual Patron:**
$500 a year. Any individual or organization eligible for membership may become an Annual Patron for a contribution of at least $500.

☐ **Corporate Members:**
$1,500 a year. Any corporation, partnership, association, or other organization acceptable to the Executive Council is eligible for Corporate Membership.

☐ **Life Members:**
$1,000 payment (during 1988).

☐ **Patron:**
One-time contribution of $5,000.

☐ **Retired:**
$25 a year. Persons who are retired and who are 70 years of age or older.

Check Interest Groups in which you woul
to participate, and enclose fee listed.

☐ $5 a year. Antarctica Law, Politics and Re
Policy (31)
☐ $5 a year. Dispute Resolution in Internat
Commercial Contracts (32)
☐ $5 a year. Indigenous Rights (33)
☐ $7.50 a year. International Economic Law
☐ $5 a year. International Environmental L
☐ $5 a year. International Human Rights (3
☐ $5 a year. International Organizations (3
☐ $5 a year. Private International Law (38)
☐ $5 a year. Law in the Pacific Region (39)
☐ $10 a year. International Space Law (40)
☐ $5 a year. Women in International Law (4
☐ $5 a year. Wildlife Law (42)

Membership Status *(Check one)*

☐ **Regular Membership:**
$70 a year. Persons, regardless of nationality or profession, resident in a member country of the OECD (see below).

☐ **Special Members:**
$30 a year. Persons *not* resident in a member country of the OECD (see below).

☐ **Intermediate Members:**
$30 a year. Persons who are under 30 years of age at the time of application for membership may be Intermediate Members for the first three consecutive years of membership.
Date of Birth ______________________

Student Members (Mark appropriate box.)

☐ $20 a year, and certification of student status (see form on reverse). Includes free membership in International Law Students Association.

☐ $10 a year with certification of membership in International Law Students Association.

The member countries of the OECD are Australia, Austria, Belgium, Canada, Denmark, Federal Republic of Germany, Finland, France, Greece, Iceland, Ireland, Italy, Japan, Luxembourg, Netherlands, New Zealand, Norway, Portugal, Spain, Sweden, Switzerland, Turkey, United Kingdom, United States.

☐ **Contributing Members:**
$100 a year.

☐ **Supporting Members:**
$200 a year.

☐ **Annual Patron:**
$500 a year. Any individual or organization eligible for membership may become an Annual Patron for a contribution of at least $500.

☐ **Corporate Members:**
$1,500 a year. Any corporation, partnership, association, or other organization acceptable to the Executive Council is eligible for Corporate Membership.

☐ **Life Members:**
$1,000 payment (during 1988).

☐ **Patron:**
One-time contribution of $5,000.

☐ **Retired:**
$25 a year. Persons who are retired and who are 70 years of age or older.

Check Interest Groups in which you w
to participate, and enclose fee listed.

☐ $5 a year. Antarctica Law, Politics and
Policy (31)
☐ $5 a year. Dispute Resolution in Inte
Commercial Contracts (32)
☐ $5 a year. Indigenous Rights (33)
☐ $7.50 a year. International Economic
☐ $5 a year. International Environment
☐ $5 a year. International Human Righ
☐ $5 a year. International Organization
☐ $5 a year. Private International Law (
☐ $5 a year. Law in the Pacific Region (
☐ $10 a year. International Space Law
☐ $5 a year. Women in International La
☐ $5 a year. Wildlife Law (42)